For the Student

ONLINE QUIZZING

Do you understand the material? You'll know after taking an Online Quiz! Try the Multiple Choice and True/False questions for each chapter. They're auto-graded with feedback and you have the option to send results directly to faculty.

WEB LINKS

This section references various Web sites including all company Web sites linked from the text.

MICROSOFT® POWERPOINT® PRESENTATIONS

View and download presentations created for each text. Great for pre-class preparation and post-class review.

INTERNET APPLICATION QUESTIONS

Go online to learn how companies use the Internet in their day-to-day activities. Answer questions based on current organization Web sites and strategies.

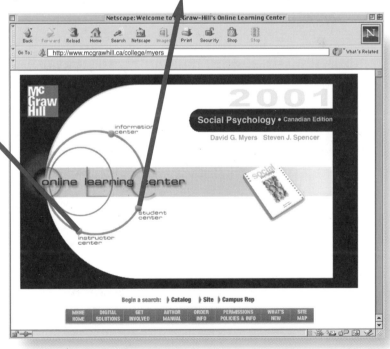

Your Internet companion to the most exciting educational tools on the Web!

The Online Learning Centre can be found at:

www.mcgraw

EDUCATIONAL CONT

social
psychology
Canadian Edition

David G. Myers
Hope College
Holland, Michigan

Steven J. Spencer
University of Waterloo
Waterloo, Ontario

McGraw-Hill
Ryerson

Toronto   Montréal   Burr Ridge, IL   Dubuque, IA   Madison, WI   New York   San Francisco
St. Louis Bangkok   Beijing   Bogotá   Caracas   Kuala Lumpur   Lisbon   London   Madrid
Mexico City   Milan   New Delhi   Santiago   Seoul   Singapore   Sydney   Taipei

McGraw-Hill
Ryerson Limited

A Subsidiary of The **McGraw-Hill** *Companies*

Social Psychology
Canadian Edition

Copyright © 2001 by McGraw-Hill Ryerson Limited, a Subsidiary of The McGraw-Hill Companies. Copyright © 1999, 1983, 1987, 1990, 1993, 1996 by The McGraw-Hill Companies, Inc. All rights reserved. No part of this publication may be reproduced or transmitted in any form or by any means, or stored in a data base or retrieval system, without the prior written permission of McGraw-Hill Ryerson Limited, or in the case of photocopying or other reprographic copying, a license from CANCOPY (the Canadian Copyright Licensing Agency), 6 Adelaide Street East, Suite 900, Toronto, Ontario, M5C 1H6.

ISBN 0–07–086500–0

1 2 3 4 5 6 7 8 9 10 TCP 0 9 8 7 6 5 4 3 2 1

Printed and bound in Canada.

Care has been taken to trace ownership of copyright material contained in this text, however, the publisher will welcome any information that enables them to rectify any reference or credit for subsequent editions.

Vice President and Editorial Director: *Pat Ferrier*
Senior Sponsoring Editor: *Veronica Visentin*
Associate Sponsoring Editor: *Marianne Minaker*
Supervising Editor: *Alissa Messner*
Copyeditor: *Dianne Broad*
Production Coordinator: *Jennifer Vassiliou*
Marketing Manager: *Ralph Courtney*
Typesetter: *GAC/Indy*
Cover Design: *Greg Devitt*
Cover Image: *Gerald Bustamante/SIS ©*
Printer: *Transcontinental Printing*

Canadian Cataloguing in Publication Data

Myers, David G.
  Social psychology

Canadian ed.
Includes bibliographical references and index
ISBN 0–07–086500–0

1. Social psychology.   I. Spencer, Steven J.   II. Title.

HM251.M94 2000   302   C00-930831-8

Brief contents

About the authors

david G. Myers is the John Dirk Werkman Professor of Psychology at Michigan's Hope College, where he has been voted "Outstanding Professor" by students. Myers' love of teaching psychology is evident in his writing for the lay public. He has written for many magazines, including *Scientific American* and *Today's Education*. His ten books include texts for Introductory and Social Psychology, and *The Pursuit of Happiness: Who Is Happy—and Why*.

Also an award-winning researcher, Dr. Myers received the Gordon Allport Prize from Division 9 of the American Psychological Association for his work on group polarization. His scientific articles have appeared in more than two dozen journals, including *Science*, *American Scientist*, *Psychological Bulletin*, and *Psychological Science*. He has served his discipline as consulting editor to the *Journal of Experimental Social Psychology* and the *Journal of Personality and Social Psychology*.

In his spare time he has chaired his city's Human Relations Commission, helped found a Community Action Center that assists poverty-level families, and spoken to numerous collegiate and religious groups. David and Carol Myers are parents of two sons and a daughter.

Steven J. Spencer is an Assistant Professor and chair of the social psychology division at the University of Waterloo. He teaches popular classes in Social Psychology and Social Cognition, and is known for his lively lectures and engaging classroom demonstrations.

Dr. Spencer also maintains an active research program that investigates self-image maintenance processes, motivated social perception, and stereotyping. In particular, he has examined how threat to the self-concept can lead people to stereotype others, and how being stereotyped by others can threaten people and undermine their performance on academic tasks. His work has been published in the *Journal of Personality and Social Psychology*, *Personality and Social Psychology Bulletin*, and the *Journal of Experimental Social Psychology*.

In his spare time he plays on an intramural basketball team organized by the graduate students in social psychology at the University of Waterloo, and enjoys spending time with his family. Steven and Shelley Spencer are parents of two children, a daughter and a son.

Table of contents

Part Two   Social Influence

Part Three   Social Relations

chapter 9
Prejudice: Disliking Others   **335**

chapter 10
Aggression: Hurting Others   **383**

chapter 11
**Attraction and Intimacy: Liking and
Loving Others**   **427**

chapter 12
Altruism: Helping Others   **473**

Modules: Social Psychology Applied

Preface for the Canadian Edition

When I was asked to write this book, I was excited, but I also knew it would be a challenge. After all, David G. Myers' *Social Psychology* has been the market leader since its first edition. It is beautifully and warmly written and yet has a thorough and scholarly presentation of the research. It is truly a classic. How was I going to enhance it for a Canadian audience? How was I going to maintain the consistent quality of the original?

As I worked on the book it became clear that the answer to the first question was that to capture the imaginations of Canadian students the book needed to have a lot more Canadian content. When talking to my students who used the American 6th edition, I found that they liked the book, but often they could not relate to the examples in the text and were put off by the emphasis on problems that were undoubtedly central to the United States, but weren't as applicable to Canada. In addition, for Canadian university students the text needed to have a stronger research focus. I think you will find that this book is the most scientifically rigorous Canadian edition available, balancing classic research in this field with significant, current Canadian research.

Changes to the Canadian Edition

In developing this edition I wrote with the outlook and experiences of Canadian students in mind. The following changes have been made with the goal of making this a more useful and involving text for students:

- Canadian statistics have been added throughout.
- Eleven "Behind the Scenes" boxes have been added to profile the research of Canadians such as Karen Dion, Ken Dion, Mark Schaller, and Don Taylor.
- A number of new studies and new figures have been added throughout to describe cutting-edge research conducted by Canadians. Some examples include: Mark Baldwin on the study of subliminal stimuli; Penelope Lockwood and Ziva Kunda on social comparisons; Victoria Esses and Mark Zanna on mood and ethnic stereotypes.
- Over fifty new examples from Canadian society have been incorporated to illustrate important points in the text. Some examples include:
  - the Quebec referendum as an example of the effect of question wording in polls
  - an analysis of the faulty group dynamics involved in the Swissair plane crash
  - prejudice in Canada, as illustrated by racial tensions at a Cole Harbour, N.S. high school
  - the Taber, Alberta school shooting as an example of aggression
  - the bicultural identity of B.C. premier Ujjal Dosanjh

In making these changes I worked hard to maintain the consistently high quality of the writing in the book. I tried to write the additions in the same friendly and personal style as the original. As a result, you will see that despite the fact that there are two authors on the title page, the first person "I" is used for the authorial voice throughout the book. Canadian students will find this style of authorial address more accessible and intimate than the alternative and aloof-sounding "we," and as a writer I found that using the first-person voice prompted very effective integration of new Canadian material with the original 6th edition content.

The Canadian edition, therefore, builds on the solid foundation of excellent writing and superb scholarship that David Myers brought to the original 6th edition, and provides a perspective that is relevant and engaging for Canadians.

Supplements

A full range of Canadian supplements is available to complement *Social Psychology*, Canadian Edition.

Teacher's Resource Manual, Martin Bolt/Steven J. Spencer: This resource contains numerous ideas and demonstrations for classroom use (ISBN 0-07-087230-9).

Student Study Guide, Martin Bolt/Steven J. Spencer: This invaluable resource for students includes chapter objectives, chapter reviews, practice tests, and ideas and resources for papers. For the Canadian edition, new conceptual level questions have been added for each chapter (ISBN 0-07-086700-3).

Test Item File, Julia Zuwerink Jacks/Catherine Borshuk: The Canadian edition of this extensive test item file includes an increased number of conceptual and application questions, as well as questions that reflect the book's Canadian content. Available in print form (ISBN 0-07-087232-5) or as Computerized Test Bank by Brownstone. Diploma software by Brownstone allows instructors to generate tests, manage students' grades, and deliver secure or practice tests over a network (ISBN 0-07-087231-7).

Online Learning Center, Adapted by Dan Hare: This Web site provides vital support for learning and teaching online. For students it includes Interactive quizzes, Web Resources, Psych Around the World, Online Experiments, Psych in the News, Internet Primer, Careers in Psychology, and a Statistics Primer. For instructors it includes a downloadable Teacher's Resource Manual, PowerPoint slides and Image Bank. Available on WebCT, Blackboard, and PageOut.

PageOut, The McGraw-Hill On-line Course Management System: With PageOut, an exclusive McGraw-Hill product, you can create a professionally designed Web site in under an hour. No knowledge of HTML coding is required. Simply fill in your course information and click on one of 16 designs. PageOut is free with an adoption of any McGraw-Hill text.

Other supplements available:

Presentation Manager: Available to faculty to help organize and custom design their lectures. This product offers a variety of supplementary materials including videos, instructor's manual materials, PowerPoint slides, and images (ISBN 0-07-290223-X).

PowerPoint Slides: (ISBN 0-07-228859-0)

McGraw-Hill Social Psychology Image Database: (ISBN 0-07-043499-9)

McGraw-Hill Overhead Transparencies for Social Psychology: Offers a comprehensive set of four-color images that have been formatted for enhanced classroom presentation (ISBN 0-07-290607-3).

McGraw-Hill Social Psychology Videotape, Martin Bolt: These 4- to 8-minute clips of classic social psychology experiments are drawn from social psychology archives and arranged to complement the text (ISBN 0-07-074617-6).

Candid Camera Social Psychology Videotape, Allen Funt: Edited from the original Candid Camera show, these 3- to 5-minute clips also follow the text organization and can stimulate class discussion (ISBN 0-07-022805-1).

Annual Editions: Social Psychology

In appreciation

I would also like to thank the many people who helped me in writing the book. The following Canadian scholars provided thoughtful and thorough reviews of past editions of this text and their suggestions greatly improved the book:

Tara Burke, Ryerson Polytechnic University

Laura Methot, St. Mary's University

Romin Tafarodi, University of Toronto

Dan Yarmey, University of Guelph

The text is significantly enhanced by its supplements, and the strong contributions of the Canadian adapters, Dan Hare, for the Online Learning Center, and Catherine Borshuk, for the test bank, are much appreciated. I also want to thank the editorial staff at McGraw-Hill Ryerson for their excellent work on the book. Veronica Visentin was instrumental in shaping the vision for the text. Marianne Minaker provided excellent editorial assistance by suggesting numerous revisions and countless editorial touches throughout the manuscript. Alissa Messner and Dianne Broad also provided excellent help in guiding the book through the final changes needed for publication. Finally, I would like to thank my wife, Shelley, and my children, Emily and Jonathan, for their patience during the many evenings I was away from home while writing this book.

Steven J. Spencer
University of Waterloo
Waterloo, Ont. N2L 3G4
Canada
Email: sspencer@watarts.uwaterloo.ca

Preface to the U.S. 6th Edition

In all of recorded history, human social behavior has been scientifically studied for just one century—our century. Considering that we have barely begun, the results are gratifying. We have amassed significnt insights into belief and illusion, love and hate, conformity and independence. Much about human behavior remains a mystery, yet social psychology can now offer partial answers to many intriguing questions: Will people act differently if we can first persuade them to adopt new attitudes? If so, how can we best persuade them? What leads people sometimes to hurt and sometimes to help one another? What kindles social conflict, and how can we transform closed fists into helping hands? Answering such questions expands our self-understanding and sensitizes us to the social forces at work upon us.

When first invited to write this book I envisioned a text that would be at once solidly scientific and warmly human, factually rigorous and intellectually provocative. It would reveal social psychology as an investigative reporter might, by providing an up-to-date summary of important social phenomena, and of how scientists uncover and explain such phenomena. It would be reasonably comprehensive, yet would also stimulate students' *thinking*—their readiness to inquire, to analyze, to relate principles to everyday happenings.

How does one select material for inclusion in a "reasonably comprehensive" introduction to the discipline? I have sought to present theories and findings that are neither too esoteric for the typical undergraduate nor better suited to other courses, such as developmental and personality psychology. I have chosen instead to emphasize material that casts social psychology in the intellectual tradition of the liberal arts. By the teaching of great literature, philosophy, and science, liberal education seeks to expand our thinking and awareness and to liberate us from the confines of the present. Social psychology can contribute to these goals. Many undergraduate social psychology students are not psychology majors; virtually all will enter other professions. By focusing on humanly significant issues, one can present the fundamental content that preprofessional psychology students need in ways that are stimulating and useful to all students.

The book opens with a single chapter that introduces our methods of inquiry. The chapter also warns students how findings can seem obvious—once you know them—and how social psychologists' own values permeate the discipline. The intent is to give students just enough to prepare them for what follows.

The book then unfolds around its definition of social psychology: the scientific study of how people *think about* (part one), *influence* (part two), and *relate* (part three) to one another.

Part One on *social thinking* examines how we view ourselves and others. It assesses the accuracy of our impressions, intuitions, and explanations.

Part Two explores *social influence*. By appreciating the cultural sources of our attitudes and by learning the nature of conformity, persuasion, and group influence, we can better recognize subtle social forces at work upon us.

Part Three considers the attitudinal and behavioral manifestations of both negative and positive *social relations*. It flows from prejudice to aggression, and from attraction to altruism, and concludes by exploring the dynamics of conflict and peacemaking.

Applications of social psychology are both interwoven throughout every chapter and highlighted in the applied chapters now clustered as modules, "Social Psychology in the Clinic" and "Social Psychology in Court."

This edition, like its predecessors, has a multicultural emphasis that can be seen in the treatment of cultural influences in chapter 6 and throughout the book in the inclusion of research from various cultural settings. The book's focus remains the fundamental principles of social thinking, social influence, and social relations as revealed by careful empirical research. But these principles are illustrated transnationally, thereby broadening our awareness of the whole human family.

This sixth edition offers thorough updating, with 550 new citations and dozens of fresh examples. Each chapter now concludes with a "personal postscript" in which I reflect on social psychology's human significance. There are also fresh and revised "Behind the Scenes" personal reflections by selected investigators worldwide. The pedagogical strategy breaks chapters into digestible modules: Typically three or four major sections begin with previews and end with section summaries that highlight the organization and key concepts.

Believing with Thoreau that "Anything living is easily and naturally expressed in popular language," I have sought, paragraph by paragraph, to craft the most engaging and effective book possible. A bright four-color design complements the text revisions and enhances the impact of the photos and figures. As before, definitions of key terms appear both in the margins and in the end-of-book Glossary.

In appreciation

Although only one person's name appears on this book's cover, the truth is that a whole community of scholars has invested itself in it. Although none of these people should be held responsible for what I have written—nor do any of them fully agree with everything said—their suggestions made this a better book than it could otherwise have been.

This new edition still retains many of the improvements contributed by consultants and reviewers on the first five editions. To the following esteemed colleagues I therefore remain indebted:

Robert Arkin, Ohio State University

Susan Beers, Sweet Briar College

George Bishop, National University of Singapore

Galen V. Bodenhausen, Michigan State University

Martin Bolt, Calvin College

Dorothea Braginsky, Fairfield University at Fredonia

David Buss, University of Texas

Russell Clark, North Texas State University

Cynthia Crown, Xavier University

Jack Croxton, State University of New York at Fredonia

Anthony Doob, University of Toronto

Philip Finney, Southeast Missouri State University

William Froming, Pacific Graduate School of Psychology

Stephen Fugita, Santa Clara University

David A. Gershaw, Arizona Western College

Mary Alice Gordon, Southern Methodist University

Ranald Hansen, Oakland University

Allen Hart, University of Iowa

Elaine Hatfield, University of Hawaii

James L. Hilton, University of Michigan

Bert Hodges, Gordon College

William Ickes, University of Texas at Arlington

Marita Inglehart, University of Michigan

Chester Insko, University of North Carolina

Edward Jones, Princeton University [deceased]

Judi Jones, Georgia Southern College

Martin Kaplan, Northern Illinois University

Janice Kelly, Purdue University

Douglas Kenrick, Arizona State University

Norbert Kerr, Michigan State University

Charles Kiesler, University of Missouri

Marjorie Krebs, Gannon University

David McMillen, Mississippi State University

Robert Millard, Vassar College

Arthur Miller, Miami University

Teru Morton, Vanderbilt University

Darren Newtson, University of Virginia

Chris O'Sullivan, Bucknell University

Paul Paulus, University of Texas at Arlington

Scott Plous, Wesleyan University

Nicholas Reuterman, Southern Illinois University of Edwardsville

Robert D. Ridge, Brigham Young University

Linda Silka, University of Lowell

Royce Singleton, Jr., College of the Holy Cross

Stephen Slane, Cleveland State University

Richard A. Smith, University of Kentucky

Mark Snyder, University of Minnesota

Sheldon Solomon, Skidmore College

Garold Stasser, Miami University

Homer Stavely, Keene State College

Elizabeth Tanke, University of Santa Clara

William Titus, Braircliff College

Tom Tyler, University of California, Berkeley

Rhoda Unger, Montclair State College

Billy Van Jones, Abilene Christian College

Mary Stewart Van Leeuwen, Calvin College

Ann L. Weber, University of North Carolina at Asheville

Daniel M. Wegner, University of Virginia

Gary Wells, Iowa State University

Bernard Whitley, Ball State University

Kipling Williams, University of New South Wales

Midge Wilson, DePaul University.

I have additionally benefited from reviews of the previous edition that helped guide the creation of this new sixth edition. My sincere thanks to the following:

Jerome M. Chertkoff, Indiana University

Donald Granberg, University of Missouri

John W. McHoskey, University of Evansville

Ellen E. Pastorino, Gainesville College

JoNell Strough, West Virginia University.

Finally, a number of teacher-scholars reviewed these new chapters, rescuing me from occasional mistakes and offering constructive suggestions (and encouragement):

Mike Aamodt, Radord University

Fred B. Bryant, Loyola University

Shawn Meghan Burn, California Polytechnic State University

Karen A. Couture, Notre Dame College

Carrie B. Fried, Indiana University, South Bend

Todd D. Nelson, California State University

Sandra Sims Patterson, Spelman College

Wesley Schultz, California State University, San Marcos

Chistine M. Smith, Grand Valley State University.

I am indebted to each of these colleagues.

Hope College, Michigan, and the University of St. Andrews, Scotland, have been wonderfully supportive of these successive editions. Both the people and the environment provided by these two institutions have helped make the gestation of *Social Psychology* a pleasure. At Hope College, poet Jack Ridl helped shape the voice you will hear in these pages, and Kathy Adamski has again contributed her good cheer and secretarial support. Phyllis and Rick Vandervelde prepared each of the successive drafts with remarkable skill and efficiency. Gretchen Rumohr-Voskuil contributed library research, proofreading, and paperwork management. She also painstakingly created the name index and page-referenced bibliography.

Were it not for the inspiration of Nelson Black of McGraw-Hill, it never would have occurred to me to write a textbook. Alison Meersschaert guided and encouraged the formative first edition. Psychology editor Mickey Cox helped envision the plan for this sixth edition and its teaching supplements. Developmental editor Jeannine Ciliotta gently nurtured this new edition, suggesting numerous revisions and offering countless ideas and editorial touches along the way. As editorial coordinator, Stephanie Cappiello has overseen the development of both the manuscript and the teaching supplements. And Marilyn Rothenberger has patiently guided the process of converting the manuscript into finished book.

To all in this supporting cast, I am indebted. Working with all these people has made the creation of this book a stimulating, gratifying experience.

David G. Myers
Hope College
Holland, MI 49422-9000
USA
e-mail: myers@hope.edu

chapter 1

Introducing Social Psychology

There once was a man whose second wife was a vain and selfish woman. This woman had two daughters who were similarly vain and selfish. The man's own daughter, however, was sweet and kind. This sweet, kind daughter, whom we all know as Cinderella, learned early on that she had best do as she was told, accept insults, and not upstage her vain stepsisters.

But then, thanks to her fairy godmother, Cinderella was able to escape her situation and go to a grand ball, where she attracted a handsome prince. When the love-struck prince later encountered a homelier Cinderella back in her degrading home, he at first failed to recognize her.

Implausible? The folk tale demands that we accept the power of the situation. In one situation, playing one role in the presence of her oppressive step-mother, the meek and unattractive Cinderella was a different person from the charming and beautiful Cinderella whom the prince met. At home, she cowered. At the ball, Cinderella felt more beautiful and walked and talked and smiled as if she were.

The French philosopher-novelist Jean-Paul Sartre (1946) would have had no problem accepting the Cinderella premise. We humans are "first of all beings in a situation," he believed. 'We cannot be distinguished from our situations, for they form us and decide our possibilities' (pp. 59–60, paraphrased). Social psychology is a science that studies the influences of our situations, with special attention to how we view and affect one another. "Our lives are connected by a thousand invisible threads," said the novelist Herman Melville. Social psychology aims to illuminate those threads. It does so by asking questions that have intrigued us all:

How Much of Our Social World Is Just in Our Heads? Social behavior varies not just with the objective situation, but with how people construe it. Happily married people will attribute their spouse's acid "Can't you ever put that where it goes?" to something external ("He must have had a frustrating day"). Unhappily married people will attribute the same remark to a mean disposition ("Is he ever hostile!") and may therefore respond with a counterattack. Moreover, expecting hostility from their spouse, they may behave resentfully, thereby eliciting the hostility they expect.

As we will see in later chapters, people who expect a doctor's child to be bright, an attractive person to be warm, or a person from another group to be uncooperative also often get what they expect. Are our own social beliefs similarly self-fulfilling? And do others ever prejudge us in ways that influence our reactions? Might someone, construing your shyness as unfriendliness, snub you—leading you to bad-mouth the person, thereby confirming her suspicion of your "antagonism"?

Did officers of the RCMP go too far in obeying orders when they used pepper spray against a crowd of demonstrators at the APEC summit in Vancouver?

Would You Be Cruel If You Were Ordered to Be? In Nazi Germany over six million Jews were slaughtered in concentration camps. These evil acts could not have occurred unless thousands of people followed orders and participated in the killing. Hitler ordered the killing, but many nameless people brought the prisoners on trains, herded them into crowded showers, and poisoned them with gas. How could these people engage in such horrific actions? Will normal people engage in such acts of barbarism?

Stanley Milgram (1974) conducted a number of studies to test this question. He set up a situation where people were ordered to administer increasingly higher levels of electric shock to another person who was having difficulty learning a series of words. People were asked to administer shocks to the point where it was clear they could be deadly. As we will see more fully in chapter 6, the results of these experiments were quite disturbing: nearly two-thirds of the participants administered a shock high enough to have killed the person they were shocking.

What caused these people to engage in such cruel acts? Would you have done the same thing if you were in the experiment? How can people resist the influence of authority figures when they make evil demands?

To Help? Or to Help Oneself?   As bags of cash tumbled from an armored truck on a fall day in 1987, $2 million was scattered along a Toronto, Ontario, street. Some motorists who stopped to help returned $100,000. Judging from what disappeared, many more stopped to help themselves. When similar incidents occurred in San Francisco, California and Columbus, Ohio, the results were the same: Passersby grabbed most of the money (Bowen, 1988).

What situations trigger people to be helpful or greedy? For that matter, what stimulates us to like or dislike someone? And why are we sometimes friendly, sometimes antagonistic toward others? Do some cultural contexts—perhaps villages and small towns—breed greater helpfulness?

A common thread runs through these questions: They all deal with how people view and affect one another. And that is what social psychology is all about. Social psychologists study attitudes and beliefs, conformity and independence, love and hate. To put it formally, **social psychology** is *the scientific study of how people think about, influence, and relate to one another.*

Social psychology is still a young science. We keep reminding people of this, partly as an excuse for our incomplete answers to some of its questions. But it's true. The first social psychology experiments were reported just a century ago (1898), and the first social psychology text was published just three-quarters of a century ago (1924). Not until the 1930s did social psychology assume its current form. And it was not until World War II, when psychologists contributed imaginative studies of persuasion and soldier morale, that it began to emerge as the vibrant field it is today. In just three decades, the number of social psychology periodicals has more than doubled.

Today the expanding field of social psychology emphasizes:

- *The power of the situation.* We are creatures of our *cultures and contexts.* Thus, evil situations sometimes overwhelm good intentions, inducing people to follow falsehoods or comply with cruelty. In the early 1990s, in a bitter conflict with Bosnian Muslims, scores of young Serbs whom we would have welcomed as neighbors became vicious rapists.

- *The power of the person.* We also are the creators of our social worlds. If a group is evil, its members contribute to (or resist) its being so. Facing the same situation, different people may react differently. Emerging from

Throughout this book, sources for information are cited parenthetically, then fully provided in the reference section that begins on page 638.

social psychology The scientific study of how people think about, influence, and relate to one another.

The power of the situation. The Rev. Desmond Tutu, chair of South Africa's Truth and Reconciliation Commission, demonstrates how some individuals respond constructively to situations that embitter others. Tutu is shown here accepting National Party leader's F. W. de Klerk acknowledgment of the suffering caused by his party's apartheid policies.

years of political imprisonment, one person exudes bitterness. Another, such as South Africa's Nelson Mandela, moves forward and works to unite his country.

- *The importance of cognition.* People react differently partly because they think differently. How we intuitively reason matters. How we react to a friend's insult depends on how we explain it—as reflecting hostility or as just a bad day. Social reality is something we subjectively construct. Our beliefs about ourselves also matter. Do we have an optimistic outlook? Do we sense that we are in control? Do we see ourselves as superior or inferior? Such thoughts (cognitions) influence our attitudes and our behaviors.

- *The applicability of social psychological principles.* As we will see, social psychologists are more and more applying their concepts and methods to current social concerns, such as emotional well-being, health, courtroom decision making, prejudice reduction, environmental design and conservation, and the quest for peace.

But how does social psychology differ from sociology and from other areas of psychology? Are social psychologists influenced by their own *values?* What are social psychology's research tactics, and how might we apply these in everyday life? In this chapter, these are our questions.

Social psychology and related disciplines

Social psychologists are keenly interested in how people think about, influence, and relate to one another. But so are sociologists and personality psychologists. How does social psychology differ?

Social psychology and sociology

People often confuse social psychology with sociology. Sociologists and social psychologists do share an interest in studying how people behave in groups.

But most sociologists study groups, from small to very large (societies and their trends), whereas most social psychologists study individuals—how one person thinks about others, is influenced by them, relates to them. This includes studies of how groups affect individual people and how an individual affects a group.

Some examples: In studying close relationships, a sociologist might study trends in marriage, divorce, and cohabitation rates; a social psychologist might examine how certain individuals become attracted to one another. Or a sociologist might investigate how the racial attitudes of middle-class people as a group differ from those of lower-income people. A social psychologist might study how racial attitudes develop within the individual.

Although sociologists and social psychologists use some of the same research methods, social psychologists rely much more heavily upon experiments in which they *manipulate* a factor, such as the presence or absence of peer pressure, to see what effect it has. The factors that sociologists study, such as socioeconomic class, are typically difficult or unethical to manipulate.

Social psychology and personality psychology

Social psychology and personality psychology are allies in their focus on the individual. Thus, the American Psychological Association includes the two subfields in the same journals (the *Journal of Personality and Social Psychology* and the *Personality and Social Psychology Bulletin*). Their difference lies in social psychology's *social* character. Personality psychologists focus on private internal functioning and on *differences* between individuals—for example, why some individuals are more aggressive than others. Social psychologists focus on our common humanity—on how people, in general, view and affect one another. They ask how social situations can lead *most* individuals to act kindly or cruelly, to conform or be independent, to feel liking or prejudice.

There are other differences: Social psychology has a shorter history. Many of personality psychology's heroes—people like Sigmund Freud, Carl Jung, Karen Horney, Abraham Maslow, and Carl Rogers—lived and worked during the first two-thirds of this century. Most of social psychology's contributors whom you will meet in this book are still alive. And social psychology has fewer famous theorists and many more unsung ones—creative researchers who contribute smaller-scale concepts. We will meet some of these people in the autobiographical "Behind the Scenes" boxes sprinkled throughout this book.

Levels of explanation

We study human beings from the different perspectives that we know as academic disciplines. These perspectives range from basic sciences, such as physics and chemistry, to integrative disciplines, such as philosophy and theology. Which perspective is relevant depends on what you want to talk about. Take love, for example. A physiologist might describe love as a state of arousal. A social psychologist might examine how various characteristics and conditions—good looks, the partners' similarity, sheer repeated exposure—enhance the feeling we call love. A poet would extol the sublime experience love can sometimes be. A theologian might describe love as the God-given goal of human relationships.

We needn't assume that any one of these levels is the *real* explanation. The physiological and emotional perspectives on love, for example, are simply two

> "You can never foretell what any man will do, but you can say with precision what an average number will be up to. Individuals may vary, but percentages remain constant."
>
> Sherlock Holmes, in Sir Arthur Conan Doyle's *A Study in Scarlet*, 1887

Different sciences offer different perspectives.

ways of looking at the same event. Likewise, an evolutionary explanation of universal incest taboos (in terms of the genetic penalty offspring pay for inbreeding) does not replace a sociological explanation (which might see incest taboos as a way of preserving the family unit) or a theological one (which might focus on moral truth). The various explanations can complement one another (Figure 1–1).

If all truth is part of one fabric, then different levels of explanation should fit together to form a whole picture. Recognizing the complementary relationship of various explanatory levels liberates us from useless argument over whether we should view human nature scientifically or subjectively: It's not an either/or matter. Sociologist Andrew Greeley (1976) explains: "Try as it might, psychology cannot explain the purpose of human existence, the meaning of human life, the ultimate destiny of the human person." Social psychology is *one* important perspective from which we can view and understand ourselves, but it is not the only one.

> "Knowledge is one. Its division into subjects is a concession to human weakness."
>
> Sir Halford John MacKinder, 1887

Summing up

Social psychology is the scientific study of how people think about, influence, and relate to one another. Sociology and psychology are social psychology's parent disciplines. Social psychology tends to be more individualistic in its content and more experimental in its method than sociology. Compared to personality psychology, social psychology focuses less on differences among individuals and more on how people, in general, view and affect one another.

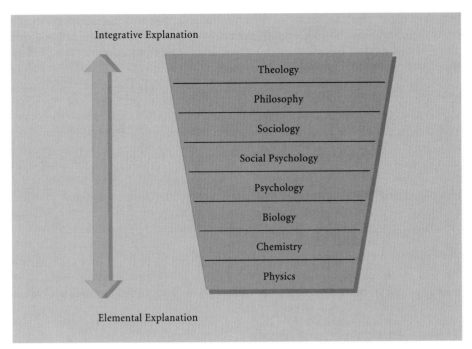

figure 1–1

Partial hierarchy of disciplines.

The disciplines range from basic sciences that study nature's building blocks up to integrative disciplines that study complex systems. A successful explanation of human functioning at one level need not contradict explanations at other levels.

Social psychology is an environmental science; it reveals how the social environment influences behavior. There are many additional perspectives on human nature, each of which asks its own set of questions and provides its own set of answers. These different perspectives are complementary, not contradictory.

Social psychology and human values

Social psychologists' values penetrate their work in ways both obvious and subtle. What are such ways?

Social psychology is less a collection of findings than a set of strategies for answering questions. In science, as in courts of law, personal opinions are inadmissible. When ideas are put on trial, evidence determines the verdict. But are social psychologists really this objective? As human beings, don't our *values*— our personal convictions about what is desirable and how people ought to behave—seep into our work? And if they do, can social psychology really be scientific?

Obvious ways in which values enter

Values enter the picture with our choice of research topics. It was no accident that the study of prejudice flourished during the 1940s as fascism raged in Europe; that the 1950s, a time of look-alike fashions and rows of identical suburban homes, gave us studies of conformity; that the 1960s saw interest in aggression increase with riots and rising crime rates; that the 1970s feminist movement helped stimulate a wave of research on gender and sexism;

that the 1980s offered a resurgence of attention to psychological aspects of the arms race; and that the 1990s are marked by heightened interest in how people respond to cultural diversity. These trends reflect the social concerns of their time. Social psychology reflects social history.

Values also influence the type of people attracted to various disciplines (Campbell, 1975; Moynihan, 1979). At your school, too, do the students attracted to the humanities, the natural sciences, and the social sciences noticeably differ? Do psychology and sociology attract people who are eager to challenge tradition, people who would rather shape the future than preserve the past?

Finally, values obviously enter the picture as the *object* of social-psychological analysis. Social psychologists investigate how values form, why they change, and how they influence attitudes and actions. None of this, however, tells us which values are "right."

Not-so-obvious ways in which values enter

> "Science does not simply describe and explain nature; it is part of the interplay between nature and ourselves; it describes nature as exposed to our method of questioning."
>
> Werner Heisenberg, *Physics and Philosophy*, 1958

We less often recognize the subtler ways in which value commitments masquerade as objective truth. Consider three not-so-obvious ways in which values enter social psychology and related areas.

The subjective aspects of science

Both scientists and philosophers now agree: Science is not purely objective. Scientists do not simply read the book of nature. Rather, they interpret nature, using their own mental categories. In our daily lives, too, we view the world through the lens of our preconceptions. Pause a moment: What do you see in Figure 1–2?

figure 1–2
What do you see?

Can you see a Dalmatian sniffing the ground at the picture's center? Without this preconception, most people are blind to the Dalmatian. Once your mind has the concept, it controls your interpretation of the picture—so much so that it becomes difficult *not* to see the dog.

This is the way our minds work. While reading these words you have been unaware that you are also looking at your nose. Your mind blocks from awareness something that is there, if only you were predisposed to perceive it. This tendency to prejudge reality based on our expectations is a basic fact about the human mind.

A 1951 university football game provided a classic demonstration of how opinions control interpretations (Hastorf & Cantril, 1954; see also Loy & Andrews, 1981). The game lived up to its billing as a grudge match; it turned out to be one of the roughest and dirtiest games in the history of either school. For example, one of the stars was gang-tackled, piled on, and finally forced out of the game with a broken nose. Fistfights erupted, and there were further injuries on both sides. It was generally agreed that the whole performance was a disgrace to everyone involved.

Not long afterwards, two psychologists, one from each school, showed films of the game to students on each campus as part of a social psychology experiment. The students played the role of scientist-observer, noting each infraction as they watched and who was responsible for it. But they could not set aside their loyalties. Students were much more likely to see players from their team as passive victims to the horribly illegal acts committed by the players from the other school. In general, students saw twice as many violations committed by members of the opposing team as committed by their own team. The moral: There *is* an objective reality out there; but, in science as in everyday life, we always view it through the lens of our beliefs and values.

Because the community of scholars at work in any given area often share a common viewpoint or come from the same **culture**, their assumptions may go unchallenged. What we take for granted—the shared beliefs that European social psychologists call our **social representations** (Augoustinos & Innes, 1990; Moscovici, 1988; Pettifor, 1996)—are our most important but often most unexamined convictions. Sometimes, however, someone from outside the camp will call attention to these assumptions. During the 1980s, feminists and Marxists exposed some of social psychology's unexamined assumptions. Feminist critics called attention to subtle biases—for example, the political conservatism of many scientists who favor a biological interpretation of gender differences in social behavior (Unger, 1985). Marxist critics called attention to competitive, individualist biases—for example, the assumption that conformity is bad and that individual rewards are good. Marxists and feminists, of course, make their own assumptions, as critics of academic "political correctness" are fond of noting. In Chapter 4 we will see more ways in which our preconceptions guide our interpretations. What's crucial for our behavior is less the situation-as-it-is than the situation-as-we-construe-it.

culture
the enduring behaviors, ideas, attitudes, and traditions shared by a large group of people and transmitted from one generation to the next

social representations
socially shared beliefs. Widely held ideas and values, including our assumptions and cultural ideologies. Our social representations help us make sense of our world.

Psychological concepts contain hidden values

Values also influence concepts. Consider psychologists' attempts to specify the good life. We refer to people as mature or immature, as well-adjusted or poorly adjusted, as mentally healthy or mentally ill. We talk as if these were statements of fact, when really they are *value judgments*. The personality psychologist

Abraham Maslow, for example, was known for his sensitive descriptions of "self-actualized" people—people who, with their needs for survival, safety, "belongingness," and self-esteem satisfied, go on to fulfill their human potential. Few readers noticed that Maslow himself, guided by his own values, selected the sample of self-actualized people he described. The resulting description of self-actualized personalities—as spontaneous, autonomous, mystical, and so forth—reflected Maslow's personal values. Had he begun with someone else's heroes—maybe Napoleon, Alexander the Great, and John D. Rockefeller—the resulting description of self-actualization would have differed (Smith, 1978).

Psychological advice also reflects the advice giver's personal values. When mental health professionals advise us how to live our lives, when child-rearing experts tell us how to handle our children, and when some psychologists encourage us to live free of concern for others' expectations, they are expressing their personal values. (In Western cultures, those values usually will be individualistic—encouraging what feels best for "me." Nonwestern cultures more often encourage what's best for "we.") Many people, unaware of this, defer to the "professional." Because value decisions concern us all, we should not feel intimidated by scientists and professionals. Science can help us discern how better to achieve our goals, once we have settled on them. But science does not and cannot answer questions of ultimate moral obligation, of purpose and direction, and of life's meaning.

Hidden values even seep into psychology's research-based concepts. Pretend you have taken a personality test and the psychologist, after scoring your answers, announces: "You scored high in self-esteem. You are low in anxiety. And you have exceptional ego-strength." "Ah," you think, "I suspected as much, but it feels good to know that." Now another psychologist gives you a

Hidden (and not-so-hidden) values seep into psychological advice. They permeate popular psychology books that offer guidance on living and loving.

similar test. For some peculiar reason this test asks some of the same questions. Afterward the psychologist informs you that you seem defensive, for you scored high in "repressiveness." "How could this be," you wonder, "the other psychologist said such nice things about me." It could be because all these labels describe the same set of responses (a tendency to say nice things about oneself and not to acknowledge problems). Shall we call it high self-esteem or defensiveness? The label reflects the researcher's value judgment about the trait.

That value judgments are often hidden within our social-psychological language is no reason to fault social psychology. This is true of everyday language, which sometimes describes the same thing with either "purr-words" or "snarl-words." Whether we label someone engaged in guerrilla warfare a "terrorist" or a "freedom fighter" depends on our view of the cause. Whether we call public assistance "welfare" or "aid to the needy" reflects our political views. When "they" exalt their country and people, it's nationalism; when "we" do it, it's patriotism. Whether someone involved in an extramarital affair is practicing "open marriage" or "adultery" depends on one's personal values. Brainwashing is social influence we do not approve of. Perversions are sex acts we do not practice. Remarks about "ambitious" men and "aggressive" women or about "cautious" boys and "timid" girls convey a hidden message.

To repeat, values lie hidden within our cultural definitions of mental health and self-esteem, our psychological advice for living, and our psychological labels. Throughout this book I will call your attention to additional examples of hidden values. The point is never that the implicit values are necessarily bad. The point is that scientific interpretation, even at the level of labeling phenomena, is a human activity. It is therefore quite natural and quite inevitable that prior beliefs and values will influence what social psychologists think and write.

There is no bridge from "is" to "ought"

A seductive error for those who work in the social sciences is sliding from a description of *what is* into a prescription of *what ought to be*. Philosophers call this the **naturalistic fallacy**. The gulf between "is" and "ought," between scientific description and ethical prescription, remains as wide today as when philosopher David Hume pointed it out 200 years ago. No survey of human behavior—say, of sexual practices—logically dictates what is "right" behavior. If most people don't do something, that does not make it wrong. If most people do it, that does not make it right. We inject our values whenever we move from objective statements of fact to prescriptive statements of what ought to be.

naturalistic fallacy
The error of defining what is good in terms of what is observable. For example: What's typical is normal; what's normal is good.

In such ways, both obvious and subtle, social psychologists' personal values influence their work. We do well to remember this and also to remember that what is true of them is true of each of us. Our values and assumptions color our view of the world. To discover how much our assumed values and social representations shape what we take for granted, we need to encounter a different cultural world—as periodically throughout this book we will do. If you assume without question that people should, above all, be true to themselves, that women are (or aren't) better suited than men for certain roles, or that romantic love should come before marriage, stay tuned.

So what do we conclude: That because science has its subjective side, we should dismiss it? Quite the contrary: The realization that human thinking always involves interpretation is precisely why we need scientific analysis. By constantly checking our beliefs against the facts, as best we know them, we check and restrain our biases. Observation and experimentation help us clean the lens through which we see reality.

Social psychology in three worlds

Psychology's roots are international as well as interdisciplinary. The pioneering experimenter Ivan Pavlov was a Russian physiologist. Child watcher Jean

Piaget was a Swiss biologist. Sigmund Freud was an Austrian physician. But it was in North America that these and other transplanted roots flourished, thanks to abundant laboratories, sophisticated equipment, and a wealth of trained personnel. Surveying the world scene, social psychologist Fathali Moggaddam (1987, 1990) describes North America as the psychological first world. He sees Canadian and U.S. social psychology as intermeshed—"indistinguishable" says Moghaddam—and he characterizes them as the superpowers of academic psychology, and especially of social psychology. Michael Bond (1988) from the Chinese University of Hong Kong concurs. He sees North America as the "professional center of gravity" where most of the research is conducted and where much of the research agenda is set.

The other industrialized nations form social psychology's second world. Great Britain, for example, shares with North America a strong tradition of scientific psychology. But because of its much smaller university system, Britain has only one twenty-fifth as many academic psychologists as North America. Likewise, the former Soviet Union has a similar population to North America but one-tenth as many psychologists (Kolominsky, 1991).

Some social psychologists in Britain, Germany, France, and the other European countries are contributing new approaches. Their methodology supplements laboratory experiments with natural observation of behavior and social discourse.

European and North American social psychologists share interests in the personal and interpersonal levels of explaining social behavior, but European scholars tend to give more attention to the intergroup and societal levels as well (Doise, 1986; Hewstone, 1988). Thus Europeans may question the U.S. focus on individualism; conflict, they say, arises not so much from the misperceptions of individuals as from a power struggle between groups. The European political agenda stimulates their interests in social issues, such as unemployment, political ideology, and relations between different linguistic and ethnic groups.

Other nations, such as Bangladesh, Cuba, and Nigeria, form social psychology's third world. Hampered by their limited resources, such countries have

behind the scenes

After being born in Iran and educated in England, I joined hundreds of thousands of Iranians returning home after the revolution of 1978. I soon found that my new Ph.D. ill-equipped me for work in a culture that was suspicious of western psychology and demanding that my teaching and research reflect Iranian concerns and values. Through my experiences there, and subsequently with the United Nations Development Programme, I became aware of the urgent need for a psychology that is appropriate to the poor and illiterate masses of third world people. Believing that internationalizing psychology will benefit psychologists in all three worlds, I am now working to bridge the gap between social psychology in North America and other parts of the world and to educate psychologists for work in the third world.

Fathali M. Moghaddam
Georgetown University

had to import their psychology from the first- and second-world nations. Yet their problems are distinctive: Pressing issues related to poverty, conflict, and traditional agricultural lifestyles demand attention. In third-world societies, social psychologists seldom have the luxury of exploring the basics of human nature, nor can illiterate people answer questionnaires.

A complete social psychology would draw upon the insights of psychologists in all three worlds in describing processes of social thinking, social influence, and social relations common to all humans. As the global village continues to shrink and as we share knowledge and viewpoints, a world-based social psychology is our goal.

Summing up

Social psychologists' values penetrate their work in obvious ways, such as their choice of research topics, and in subtler ways, such as their hidden assumptions when forming concepts, choosing labels, and giving advice. There is a growing awareness of the subjectivity of scientific interpretation, of values hidden in social psychology's concepts and labels, and of the gulf between scientific description of what is and ethical prescription of what ought to be. This penetration of values into science is not unique to social psychology. That human thinking is seldom dispassionate is precisely why we need systematic observation and experimentation if we are to check our cherished ideas against reality, and why social psychologists from the discipline's "three worlds" are eager to exchange ideas and findings.

I knew it all along: Is social psychology simply common sense?

But do social psychology's theories provide new insight into the human condition? Or do they only describe the obvious?

Many of the conclusions presented in this book will probably have already occurred to you, for social psychology is all around you. We constantly observe people thinking about, influencing, and relating to one another. Much of our thinking aims to discern and explain relationships among social events. It pays to know what that facial expression predicts, how to get someone to do something, or whether to regard another person as friend or foe. For centuries, philosophers, novelists, and poets have observed and commented upon social behavior, often with keen insight. Social psychology is everybody's business.

Might it therefore be said that social psychology is only common sense in different words? Social psychology faces two contradictory criticisms: One is that it is trivial because it documents the obvious; the second is that it is dangerous because its findings could be used to manipulate people. Is the first objection valid—does social psychology simply formalize what any amateur already knows intuitively?

Cullen Murphy (1990) thinks so: "Day after day social scientists go out into the world. Day after day they discover that people's behavior is pretty much what you'd expect." Nearly a half-century earlier, historian Arthur Schlesinger, Jr., (1949) reacted with similar scorn to social scientists' studies of World War II soldiers.

What were the findings? Another reviewer, Paul Lazarsfeld (1949), offered a sample with interpretive comments, a few of which I paraphrase:

1. Better-educated soldiers suffered more adjustment problems than did less-educated soldiers. (Intellectuals were less prepared for battle stresses than street-smart people.)
2. Soldiers from southern climents coped better with the hot South Sea Island climate than did northern soldiers. (People from southern climates are more accustomed to hot weather.)
3. Soldiers from rural backgrounds were usually in better spirits during their Army life than soldiers from city backgrounds. (After all, they are more accustomed to hardships).
4. Soldiers were more eager to return home during the fighting than they were after the German surrender. (You cannot blame people for not wanting to be killed).

One problem with common sense, however, is that we invoke it *after* we know the facts. Events are far more "obvious" and predictable in hindsight than beforehand. Experiments reveal that when people learn the outcome of an experiment, that outcome suddenly seems unsurprising—certainly less surprising than it is to people who are simply told about the experimental procedure and the possible outcomes (Slovic & Fischhoff, 1977). People overestimate their ability to have foreseen the result. This happens especially when the result seems determined and not a mere product of chance (Hawkins & Hastie, 1990).

> "A first-rate theory predicts; a second-rate theory forbids; and a third-rate theory explains after the event."
>
> Aleksander Isaakovich Kitaigorodskii

You perhaps experienced this phenomenon when reading Lazarsfeld's summary of the findings reported above. For Lazarsfeld went on to say, "Every one of these statements is the direct opposite of what was actually found." In reality, it was found that poorly educated soldiers adapted more poorly. People from southern climates were not more likely than people from northern climates to adjust to a tropical climate. Soldiers from city backgrounds were usually in better spirits than soldiers from rural backgrounds. And soldiers were actually more eager to come home after the fighting ended than while it was still ongoing. "If we had mentioned the actual results of the investigation first [as Schlesinger experienced], the reader would have labeled these 'obvious' also."

Likewise, in everyday life we often do not expect something to happen until it does. We *then* suddenly see clearly the forces that brought it about and feel unsurprised. After the Quebec sovereignty vote in 1995, commentators—forgetting they had predicted a large win for the federalists—found the close vote unsurprising. It seems we often think we knew what we actually did not. As the philosopher-theologian Soren Kierkegaard put it, "Life is lived forward, but understood backwards."

hindsight bias
The tendency to exaggerate, *after* learning an outcome, one's ability to have foreseen how something turned out. Also known as the *I-knew-it-all-along phenomenon*.

If this **hindsight bias** (also called the I-knew-it-all-along phenomenon) is pervasive, you may now be feeling that you already knew about it. Indeed, almost any conceivable result of a psychological experiment can seem like common sense—*after* you know the result.

Here's how you can demonstrate the phenomenon. Give half a group one psychological finding and the other half the opposite result. For example, tell half as follows:

© Sidney Harris

In hindsight, events seem obvious and predictable.

> Social psychologists have found that, whether choosing friends or falling in love, we are most attracted to people whose traits are different from our own. There seems to be wisdom in the old saying "Opposites attract."

Tell the other half:

> Social psychologists have found that, whether choosing friends or falling in love, we are most attracted to people whose traits are similar to our own. There seems to be wisdom in the old saying "Birds of a feather flock together."

Ask the people first to explain the result. Then ask them to say whether it is "surprising" or "not surprising." Virtually all will find whichever result they were given "not surprising."

As this example shows, we can draw upon our stockpile of proverbs to make almost any result seem to make sense. Shall we say with John Donne, "No man is an island," or with Thomas Wolfe, "Every man is an island"? If a social psychologist reports that separation intensifies romantic attraction, Joe Public responds, "You get paid for this? Everybody knows that 'absence makes the heart grow fonder.'" Should it turn out that separation weakens attraction, Judy Public may say, "My grandmother could have told you, 'Out of sight, out of mind.'" No matter what happens, there will be someone who knew it would.

Karl Teigen (1986) must have had a few chuckles when asking University of Leicester (England) students to evaluate actual proverbs and their opposites. When given the proverb "Fear is stronger than love," most rated it as true. But so did students who were given its reversed form, "Love is stronger than fear." Likewise, the genuine proverb "He that is fallen cannot help him who is down" was rated highly; but so too was "He that is fallen can help him who is down." My favorites, however, were the two highly rated proverbs: "Wise men make proverbs and fools repeat them" (authentic) and its made-up counterpart,

Perhaps best remembered for his banal discourses and frequent use of clichés was the early Greek philosopher Mediocrates.

"Fools make proverbs and wise men repeat them."

The hindsight bias creates a problem for many psychology students. Sometimes results are genuinely surprising (for example, that Olympic bronze medalists take more joy in their achievement than do silver medalists). More often, when you read the results of experiments in your textbooks, the material seems easy, even obvious. When you later take a multiple-choice test on which you must choose among several plausible conclusions, the task may become surprisingly difficult. "I don't know what happened," the befuddled student later moans. "I thought I knew the material." (A word to the wise: Beware of this phenomenon when studying for exams, lest you fool yourself into thinking that you know the material better than you do.)

The I-knew-it-all-along phenomenon not only can make social science findings seem like common sense, it also can have pernicious consequences. It is conducive to arrogance—an overestimation of our own intellectual powers. Moreover, because outcomes seem as if they should have been foreseeable, we are

focus

Competing proverbs

Cullen Murphy (1990), managing editor of *The Atlantic*, faults "sociology, psychology, and other social sciences for too often merely discerning the obvious or confirming the commonplace." His own casual survey of social science findings "turned up no ideas or conclusions that can't be found in *Bartlett's* or any other encyclopedia of quotations." So true, because for many a conceivable finding there is a quotation (Evens & Berent, 1993). As the philosopher Alfred North Whitehead (1861–1947) once remarked, "Everything important has been said before." Nevertheless, to sift the truth of competing quotations we need research. Consider . . .

Is it more true that . . .	*Or that . . .*
Too many cooks spoil the broth.	Two heads are better than one.
The pen is mightier than the sword.	Actions speak louder than words.
You can't teach an old dog new tricks.	You're never too old to learn.
Blood is thicker than water.	Many kinfolk, new friends.
He who hesitates is lost.	You should look before you leap.
Forewarned is forearmed.	You shouldn't cross the bridge until you come to it.

more likely to blame decision makers for what are in retrospect "obvious" bad choices than to praise them for good choices, which also seem "obvious." After the 1999 NATO air attack on Yugoslavia, it seemed obvious that NATO's air superiority would force Slobodan Milosevic to allow peacekeeping troops into Kosovo, though it was hardly clear to most politicians and pundits beforehand.

Likewise, we sometimes blame ourselves for "stupid mistakes"—perhaps for not having handled a person or situation better. Looking back, we see how we should have handled it. Many students have come to me at the end of the semester and said, "If only I had known I would be so busy now, I would have started my paper earlier." But sometimes we are too hard on ourselves. We forget that what is obvious to us *now* was not nearly so obvious at the time. Physicians told both a patient's symptoms and the cause of death (as determined by autopsy) sometimes wonder how an incorrect diagnosis could have been made. Other physicians, given only the symptoms, don't find the diagnosis nearly so obvious (Dawson & others, 1988). (Would juries be slower to assume malpractice if they were forced to take a foresight rather than a hindsight perspective?)

So what do we conclude—that common sense is usually wrong? Sometimes it is. Until science dethroned the commonsense view, centuries of daily experience assured people that the sun revolved around the earth. Medical experience assured doctors that bleeding was an effective treatment for typhoid fever, until someone in the middle of the last century bothered to experiment—to divide patients into two groups, one bled, the other given mere bed rest.

"Other times, conventional wisdom is right—or it falls on both sides of an issue: Does happiness come from knowing the truth, or preserving illusions? From being with others, or living in peaceful solitude? From living a virtuous life, or getting away with evil? Opinions are a dime a dozen; no matter what we find, there will be someone who foresaw it. But which of the many competing ideas best fit reality? So the point is not that common sense is predictably wrong. Rather, common sense usually is right *after the fact*. We therefore easily deceive ourselves into thinking that we know and knew more than we do and did. And this is precisely why we need science—to help us sift reality from illusion, and genuine predictions from easy hindsight.

> "It is easy to be wise after the event."
>
> Sherlock Holmes, in Arthur Conan Doyle's *"The Problem of Thor Bridge"*

Summing up

Social psychology's findings sometimes seem obvious. Experiments reveal that outcomes are more "obvious," however, after the facts are known. This hindsight bias often makes people overconfident about the validity of their judgments and predictions.

How we do social psychology

Social psychologists propose theories that organize their observations and imply testable hypotheses and practical predictions. Social psychologists also do research that predicts behavior using correlational studies, often conducted in natural settings. And they seek to explain behavior by conducting experiments that manipulate one or more factors under controlled conditions.

"Nothing has such power to broaden the mind as the ability to investigate systematically and truly all that comes under thy observation in life."

Marcus Aurelius, *Meditations*

theory
an integrated set of principles that explain and predict observed events

hypothesis
a testable proposition that describes a relationship that may exist between events

Unlike other scientific disciplines, social psychology has nearly six billion amateur practitioners. People-watching is a universal hobby—in parks, at the beach, at school. As we observe people, we form ideas about how human beings think about, influence, and relate to one another. Professional social psychologists do the same, only more systematically (by forming theories) and painstakingly (often with experiments that create miniature social dramas that pin down cause and effect).

Forming and testing

Many of us are social psychologists because we have a hard time thinking of anything more fascinating than human existence. If, as Socrates counseled, "The unexamined life is not worth living," then simply "knowing thyself" seems a worthy enough goal.

As we wrestle with human nature to pin down its secrets, we organize our ideas and findings into theories. A **theory** is *an integrated set of principles that explain and predict* observed events. Theories are a scientific shorthand.

In everyday conversation, "theory" often means "less than fact"—a middle rung on a confidence ladder from fact to theory to guess. But to any kind of scientist, facts and theories are different things, not different points on a continuum. Facts are agreed-upon statements about what we observe. Theories are *ideas* that summarize and explain facts. "Science is built up with facts, as a house is with stones," said Jules Henri Poincaré, "but a collection of facts is no more a science than a heap of stones is a house."

Theories not only summarize, they also imply testable predictions, which we call **hypotheses**. Hypotheses serve several purposes. First, they allow us to *test* the theories on which they are based. By making specific predictions, a theory puts its money where its mouth is. Second, predictions give *direction* to research. Any scientific field will mature more rapidly if its researchers have a sense of direction. Theoretical predictions suggest new areas for research; they send investigators looking for things they might never have thought of. Third, the predictive feature of good theories can also make them *practical*. What, for example, would be of greater practical value today than a theory of aggression that would predict when to expect it and how to control it? As Kurt Lewin, one of modern social psychology's founders, declared, "There is nothing so practical as a good theory."

Consider how this works. Say we observe that people sometimes explode violently when in crowds. We might therefore theorize that the presence of other people makes individuals feel anonymous and lowers their inhibitions. Let's allow our minds to play with this idea for a moment. Perhaps we could test it by constructing a laboratory experiment similar to execution by electric chair. What if we asked individuals in groups to administer punishing shocks to a hapless victim without knowing which one of the group was actually shocking the victim? Would these individuals administer stronger shocks than individuals acting alone, as our theory predicts?

We might also manipulate anonymity: Would people hiding behind masks deliver stronger shocks because they could not be identified? If the results confirm our hypothesis, they might suggest some practical applications. Perhaps police brutality could be reduced by having officers wear large name tags and drive cars identified with large numbers or by videotaping their arrests.

But how do we conclude that one theory is better than another? A good theory: (1) effectively summarizes a wide range of observations; and (2) makes clear predictions that we can use to (a) confirm or modify the theory, (b) generate new exploration, and (c) suggest practical application. When we discard theories, usually it's not because they have been proved false. Rather, like an old car, they get replaced by newer, better models.

Correlational research: Detecting natural associations

Most of what you will learn about social-psychological research methods you will absorb as you read later chapters. But let us go backstage now and take a brief look at how social psychology is done. This glimpse behind the scenes will be just enough, I trust, for you to appreciate findings discussed later and to think critically about everyday social events.

Social-psychological research varies by location. It can take place in the *laboratory* (a controlled situation) or in the **field** (everyday situations). And it varies by method—being **correlational** (asking whether two or more factors are naturally associated) or **experimental** (manipulating some factor to see its effect on another). If you want to be a critical reader of psychological research reported in newspapers and magazines, it will pay you to understand the difference between correlational and experimental research.

Using some real examples, let's first consider the advantages of **correlational research** (often involving important variables in natural settings) and the disadvantage (ambiguous interpretation of cause and effect). As we will see in Chapter 13, today's psychologists are relating personal and social factors to human health. Among the researchers are Douglas Carroll at Glasgow Caledonian University and his colleagues George Davey Smith and Paul Bennett (1994). In search of possible links between socioeconomic status and health, the researchers ventured into Glasgow's old graveyards. As a measure of health, they noted from grave markers the life spans of 843 individuals. As an indication of status, they measured the height of pillars over the grave, reasoning that height reflected cost and therefore affluence. As Figure 1–3 shows, higher markers were related to longer lives, for both men and women.

Carroll and his colleagues explain how other researchers, using contemporary data, have confirmed the status-longevity correlation. Scottish postal-code regions having the least overcrowding and unemployment also have the greatest longevity. In Canada, income correlates with longevity (poor and lower-status people are more at risk for premature death). In contemporary Britain, occupational status correlates with longevity. One study followed 17,350 British civil service workers over ten years.

field research
research done in natural, real-life settings outside the laboratory

experimental research
studies that seek clues to cause-effect relationships by manipulating one or more factors (independent variables) while controlling others (holding them constant)

correlational research
the study of the naturally occurring relationships among variables

Commemorative markers in Glasgow Cathedral graveyard.

figure 1–3

Status and longevity.
Tall grave pillars commemorated people who also tended to live longer.

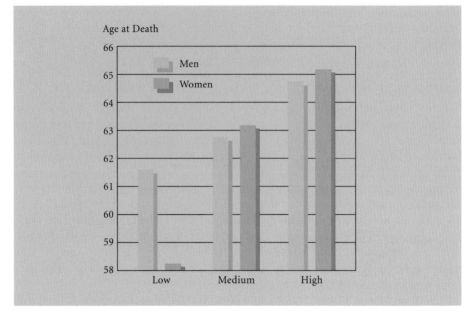

Age at Death

(Adapted from Carroll & others, 1994.)

Compared to top-grade administrators, those at the professional-executive grade were 1.6 times more likely to die. Clerical workers were 2.2 times and laborers 2.7 times more likely to have died (Adler & others, 1993, 1994). Across times and places, the status-health correlation seems reliable.

Correlation versus causation

The status-longevity question illustrates the most irresistible thinking error made by both amateur and professional social psychologists: When two factors like status and health go together, it is terribly tempting to conclude that one is causing the other. Status, we might presume, somehow protects a person from health risks. Or might it be the other way around? Maybe health promotes vigor and success. Perhaps people who live longer accumulate more wealth (enabling them to have more expensive grave markers). Correlational research allows us to *predict*, but it cannot tell us whether changing one variable (such as social status) will *cause* changes in another (such as health).

The correlation-causation confusion is behind much muddled thinking in popular psychology. Consider another very real correlation—between self-esteem and academic achievement. Children with high self-esteem tend also to have high academic achievement. (As with any correlation, we can also state this the other way around: High achievers tend to have high self-esteem.) Why do you suppose this is (Figure 1–4)?

Some people believe a "healthy self-concept" contributes to achievement. Thus, boosting a child's self-image may also boost school achievement. Others argue that high achievement produces a favorable self-image. Do well and you will feel good about yourself; goof off and fail and you will feel like a dolt. A study of 635 Norwegian schoolchildren suggests that a string of gold stars by one's name on the spelling chart and constant praise from an admiring teacher

Researchers have found a modest but positive correlation between adolescents' preference for heavy metal music and their having attitudes favorable to premarital sex, pornography, satanism, and drug and alcohol use (Landers, 1988). What are some possible explanations for this correlation?

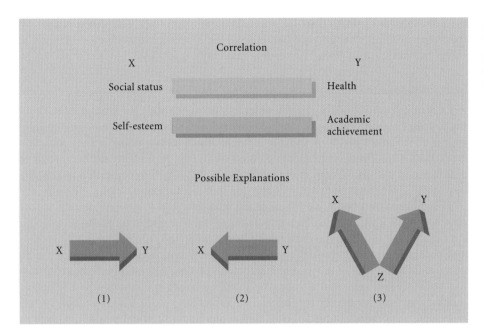

figure 1–4
When two variables correlate, any combination of three explanations is possible.

can boost a child's self-esteem (Skaalvik & Hagtvet, 1990). It's also possible that self-esteem and achievement correlate because both are linked to underlying intelligence and family social status.

That possibility was raised in two studies—one study of 1,600 young men, another of 715 teenagers (Bachman & O'Malley, 1977; Maruyama & others, 1981). When the researchers statistically removed the effect of intelligence and family status, the correlation between self-esteem and achievement evaporated. Similarly, John McCarthy and Dean Hoge (1984) dispute the idea that the correlation between low self-esteem and delinquency means that low self-esteem causes delinquency; rather, their study of 1,658 teenagers suggests that delinquent acts lower self-esteem. Breaking rules leads to condemnation, which leads to lowered self-esteem.

Advanced correlational techniques can *suggest* cause-effect relations. *Time-lagged* correlations reveal the *sequence* of events (for example, by indicating whether changed achievement more often precedes or follows changed self-esteem). Researchers can also use statistical techniques that extract the influence of "confounded" variables. Thus, the researchers just mentioned saw the correlation between self-esteem *and* achievement evaporate after extracting differences in intelligence and family status. (Among people of similar intelligence and family status, the self-esteem-achievement relationship was minimal.) The Scottish research team wondered whether the status-longevity relationship would survive their removing the effect of cigarette smoking, which is now much less common among those higher in status. It did, which suggested that some other factors, such as increased stress and decreased feelings of control, must also account for the greater mortality of the poor.

So the great strength of correlational research is that it tends to occur in real-world settings where we can examine factors like race, sex, and social status that we cannot manipulate in the laboratory. Its great disadvantage lies in the ambiguity of the results. The point is so important that, even if it fails to impress people the first 25 times they hear it, it is worth making a 26th time: Knowing that two variables change together enables us to predict one when we know the other; but correlation does not specify cause and effect.

Survey research

How do we measure such variables as status and health? One way is by surveying representative samples of people. Survey researchers obtain a representative group by taking a **random sample**—*one in which every person in the population being studied has an equal chance of inclusion.* With this procedure any subgroup of people—red-haired people, for example—will tend to be represented in the survey to the extent that they are represented in the total population.

It is an amazing fact that whether we survey people in a city or in a whole country, 1,200 randomly selected participants will enable us to be 95 percent confident of describing the entire population with an error margin of 3 percentage points or less. Imagine a huge jar filled with beans, 50 percent red and 50 percent white. Randomly sample 1,200 of these, and you will be 95 percent certain to draw out between 47 percent and 53 percent red beans—regardless of whether the jar contains 10,000 beans or 100 million beans. If we think of the red beans as supporters of one political party and the white beans as supporters of the other party, we can understand why polls taken before national elections have diverged from election results by an average of less than two percent. As a few drops of blood can speak for the whole body, so can a random sample speak for a population.

Bear in mind that polls do not literally *predict* voting; they only *describe* public opinion as of the moment they are taken. Public opinion can shift. To evaluate surveys, we must also bear in mind four potentially biasing influences: unrepresentative samples, order of questions, response options, and wording of the questions.

Unrepresentative samples.   Not only does sample size matter in a survey but also how closely the sample represents the population under study. In 1984, columnist Ann Landers accepted a letter writer's challenge to poll her readers on the question of whether women find affection more important than sex. Her question: "Would you be content to be held close and treated tenderly and forget about 'the act'?" Of the more than 100,000 women who replied, 72 percent said yes. An avalanche of worldwide publicity followed. In response to critics, Landers (1985, p. 45) granted that "the sampling may not be representative of all American women. But it does provide honest—valuable—insights from a cross section of the public. This is because my column is read by people from every walk of life, approximately 70 million of them." Still, one wonders, are the 70 million readers representative of the entire population? And are the 1 in 700 readers who participated representative of the 699 in 700 who did not?

The importance of representativeness was effectively demonstrated in 1936, when a weekly news magazine, *Literary Digest*, mailed a postcard election poll to over 10 million people. Among the more than 2 million returns, Alf Landon won by a landslide over Franklin D. Roosevelt. When the actual votes were counted a few days later, the results were the opposite—Roosevelt won in a landslide over Landon. The magazine sent the poll only to people whose names it had obtained from telephone books and automobile registrations—thus omitting all those who could afford neither (Cleghorn, 1980).

random sample
survey procedure in which every person in the population being studied has an equal chance of inclusion

Sampling bias can plague even the best survey. Simultaneous political opinion polls, each supposedly having a 3 percent error margin, commonly vary from one another by more than 3 percent. Philip Converse and Michael Traugott (1986) attribute such discrepancies partly to the fact that some 30 percent of those sampled refuse to cooperate or are unavailable, which makes the sample obtained not a perfect random sample. For instance, when voters were surveyed by phone during one election, those answering when their home was first called favored the leading candidate by a 3 percent margin. After interviewers persisted in callbacks until they reached everyone, the leading candidate's margin increased by 13 percentage points. (Apparently this candidate's supporters were home less often.)

Order of questions.   Given a representative sample, we must also contend with other sources of bias, such as the order in which we ask questions. Asked whether "the Japanese government should be allowed to set limits on how much American industry can sell in Japan," most Americans answered no (Schuman & Ludwig, 1983). Simultaneously, two-thirds of an equivalent sample were answering yes to the same question because they were first asked whether "the American government should be allowed to set limits on how much Japanese industry can sell in the United States." Most of these people said the United States has the right to limit imports. To appear consistent, they then said that Japan should have the same right.

Response options.   Consider, too, the dramatic effects of the response options. When Joop van der Plight and his co-workers (1987) asked English voters what

This state-of-the-art survey research center at the University of Michigan's Institute for Social Research has 60 interviewing carrels with monitoring stations. Staff and visitors must sign a pledge to honor the strict confidentiality of all interviews.

percentage of Britain's nuclear energy they wished came from nuclear power, the average preference was 41 percent. They asked others what percentage they wished came from (1) nuclear, (2) coal, and (3) other sources. Their average preference for nuclear power was 21 percent.

A similar effect occurred when Howard Schuman and Jacqueline Scott (1987) asked people, "What do you think is the most important problem facing this country today—the energy shortage, the quality of public schools, legalized abortion, or pollution—or if you prefer, you may name a different problem as most important." Given these choices, 32 percent felt that the quality of public schools was the biggest problem. Among others they simply asked, "What do you think is the most important problem facing this country today?" Only 1 percent named the schools. So remember: The form of the question may guide the answer.

Question wording.   The precise wording of questions may also influence answers. One poll found that people favored cutting "foreign aid" yet opposed cutting funding "to help hungry people in other nations" (Simon, 1996). Even subtle changes in the tone of a question can have large effects (Schuman & Kalton, 1985). Thus it is not surprising that politicians in Ottawa and Quebec have fought bitterly about the wording of referendum questions about Quebec sovereignty. Federalists have long charged that the Parti Québécois purposely has devised questions that are unclear and designed to elicit a "yes" vote. In the 1995 election, Quebecers voted on the question, "Do you agree that Quebec should become sovereign, after having made a formal offer to Canada for a new economic and political partnership, within the scope of the Bill respecting the future of Quebec and the agreement signed on June 12, 1995?" Did this question affect the outcome of the election? It certainly might have because even when people say they feel strongly about an issue, a question's form and wording may affect their answer (Krosnick & Schuman, 1988; Lehman & others, 1992).

Order, response, and wording effects enable political manipulators to use surveys to show public support for their views. Consultants, advertisers, and physicians can have similar disconcerting influences upon our decisions by how they "frame" our choices. No wonder the meat lobby in 1994 objected to a

Survey researchers must be sensitive to subtle—and not so subtle—biases.

DOONESBURY   by Garry Trudeau

new labeling law that requires declaring ground beef, for example, as "30 percent fat," rather than "70 percent lean, 30 percent fat."

The moral: The way choices are worded can make a big difference. A young monk was once rebuffed when asking if he could smoke while he prayed. Ask a different question, advised a friend: Ask if you can pray while you smoke (Crossen, 1993).

Experimental research: Searching for cause and effect

The near impossibility of discerning cause and effect among naturally correlated events prompts most social psychologists to create laboratory simulations of everyday processes whenever this is feasible and ethical. These simulations are roughly similar to how aeronautical engineers work. They don't begin by observing how flying objects perform in a wide variety of natural environments. The variations in both atmospheric conditions and flying objects are so complex that they would surely find it difficult to organize and use such data to design better aircraft. Instead, they construct a simulated reality that is under their control—a wind tunnel. Then they can manipulate wind conditions and ascertain the precise effect of particular wind conditions on particular wing structures.

Control: Manipulating variables

Like aeronautical engineers, social psychologists experiment by constructing social situations that simulate important features of our daily lives. By varying just one or two factors at a time—called **independent variables**—the experimenter pinpoints how changes in these one or two things affect us. As the wind tunnel helps the aeronautical engineer discover principles of aerodynamics, so the experiment enables the social psychologist to discover principles of social thinking, social influence, and social relations. The ultimate aim of wind tunnel simulations is to understand and predict the flying characteristics of complex aircraft; social psychologists experiment to understand and predict human behavior.

independent variable
the experimental factor that a researcher manipulates

Social psychologists have used the experimental method in about three-fourths of their research studies (Higbee & others, 1982), and in two out of three studies the setting has been a research laboratory (Adair & others, 1985). To illustrate the laboratory experiment, consider two experiments that typify research from upcoming chapters on prejudice and aggression. Each suggests possible cause-effect explanations of correlational findings.

The first concerns prejudice against people who are obese. People often perceive the obese as slow, lazy, and sloppy (Ryckman & others, 1989). Do such attitudes spawn discrimination? In hopes of finding out, Steven Gortmaker and his colleagues (1993) studied 370 obese 16- to 24-year-olds. When they restudied them seven years later, two-thirds of the women were still obese, and these were less likely to be married and earning high salaries than a comparison group of some 5,000 other women. Even after correcting for any differences in aptitude test scores, race, and parental income, the obese women's incomes were $7,000 a year below average.

Although correcting for certain other factors makes it look like discrimination might explain the correlation between obesity and lower status, we can't be sure. (Can you think of other possibilities?) Enter social psychologists Mark Snyder and Julie Haugen (1994, 1995). They asked 76 University of Minnesota

A billboard for the Stop the Violence, Save the Child program in New York City. Does viewing violence on TV or in other media lead to imitation, especially among children? Experiments suggest that it does.

men students to have a getting acquainted phone conversation with one of 76 women students. Each man was shown a photo *said* to picture his conversational partner. Half were shown an obese woman (not the actual partner); the other half a normal weight woman. In one part of the experiment, the men were asked to form an impression of the women's traits. Later analysis of just the women's side of the conversation revealed that when women were being evaluated they spoke less warmly and happily if they were presumed obese. Clearly, the men's beliefs induced them to behave in a way that led their supposedly obese partners to confirm the idea that such women are undesirable. Prejudice and discrimination were having an effect. Recalling the effect of the stepmother's attitudes, perhaps we should call this "The Cinderella effect."

As a second example of how an experiment can clarify causation, consider the correlation between television viewing and children's behavior. Children who watch many violent television programs tend to be more aggressive than those who watch few. This suggests that children might be learning from what they see on the screen. But, as I hope you now recognize, this is a correlational finding. Figure 1–4 reminds us that there are two other cause-effect interpretations that do not implicate television as the cause of the children's aggression. (What are they?)

Social psychologists have therefore brought television viewing into the laboratory, where they control the amount of violence the children see. By exposing children to violent and nonviolent programs, researchers can observe how the amount of violence affects behavior. Robert Liebert and Robert Baron (1972) showed young boys and girls a violent excerpt from a gangster television show or an excerpt from an exciting track race. The children who viewed the violence were subsequently most likely to press vigorously a special red button that supposedly would heat a rod, causing a burning pain to another child. This measure of behavior we call the **dependent variable**. (Actually, there was no other

dependent variable the variable being measured, so-called because it may *depend* on manipulations of the independent variable

child, so no one was harmed.) Such experiments indicate that television *can* be one cause of children's aggressive behavior.

So far we have seen that the logic of experimentation is simple: By creating and controlling a miniature reality, we can vary one factor and then another and discover how these factors, separately or in combination, affect people. Now let's go a little deeper and see how an experiment is done.

Every social-psychological experiment has two essential ingredients. One we have just considered—*control*. We manipulate one or two independent variables while trying to hold everything else constant. The other ingredient is *random assignment*.

Random assignment: The great equalizer

Recall that we were reluctant, on the basis of a correlation, to assume that obesity *caused* lower status (via discrimination) or that violence viewing *caused* aggressiveness. A survey researcher might measure and statistically extract other possibly pertinent factors and see if the correlations survive. But one can never control for all the factors that might distinguish obese from nonobese, and violence-viewers from nonviewers. Maybe violence-viewers differ in education, culture, intelligence—or in dozens of ways the researcher hasn't considered.

In one fell swoop, **random assignment** eliminates all such extraneous factors. With random assignment, each person has an equal chance of viewing the violence or the nonviolence. Thus, the people in both groups would, in every conceivable way—family status, intelligence, education, initial aggressiveness—average about the same. Highly intelligent people, for example, are equally likely to appear in both groups. Because random assignment creates equivalent groups, any later aggression difference between the two groups must have something to do with the only way they differ—whether or not they viewed violence (Figure 1–5). And thanks to random assignment of the Minnesota students to the photo conditions, the women's behavior *must* have been influenced by the men's beliefs about their obesity.

The ethics of experimentation

Our television example illustrates why some experiments are ethically sensitive. Social psychologists would not, over long time periods, expose one group of children to brutal violence. Rather, they briefly alter people's social experience and note the effects. Sometimes the experimental treatment is a harmless,

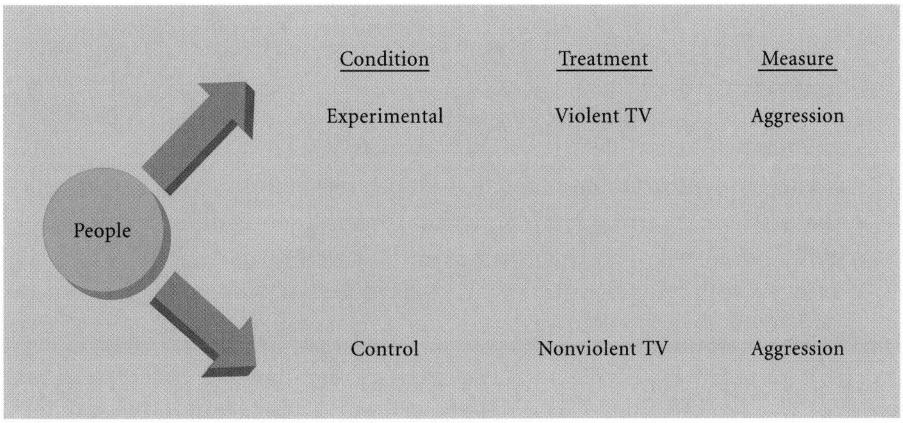

random assignment the process of assigning participants to the conditions of an experiment such that all persons have the same chance of being in a given condition. (Note the distinction between random *assignment* in experiments and random *sampling* in surveys. Random assignment helps us infer cause and effect. Random sampling helps us generalize to a population.)

figure 1–5

Randomly assigning people either to a condition that receives the experimental treatment or to a control condition that does not give the researcher confidence that any later difference is somehow caused by the treatment.

	Condition	Treatment	Measure
People	Experimental	Violent TV	Aggression
	Control	Nonviolent TV	Aggression

perhaps even enjoyable experience to which people give their knowing consent. Sometimes, however, researchers find themselves operating in that gray area between the harmless and the risky.

Social psychologists often venture into that ethical gray area when they design experiments that engage intense thoughts and emotions. Experiments need not have what Elliot Aronson, Marilynn Brewer, and Merrill Carlsmith (1985) call **mundane realism**. That is, laboratory behavior (for example, delivering electric shocks as part of an experiment on aggression) need not be literally the same as everyday behavior. For many researchers, that sort of realism is indeed mundane—not important. But the experiment *should* have **experimental realism**—it should absorb and involve the participants. Experimenters do not want their people consciously play-acting or ho-humming it; they want to engage real psychological processes. Forcing people to choose whether to give intense or mild electric shock to someone else can, for example, be a realistic measure of aggression. It functionally simulates real aggression.

Achieving experimental realism often requires deceiving people with a plausible cover story. If the person in the next room is actually not receiving the shocks, the experimenter does not want the participants to know this. That would destroy the experimental realism. Thus, about one-third of social-psychological studies (though a decreasing number) have required deception (Korn & Nicks, 1993; Vitelli, 1988).

Experimenters also seek to hide their predictions lest the participants, in their eagerness to be "good subjects," merely do what's expected—or, in an ornery mood, do the opposite. In subtle ways, the experimenter's words, tone of voice, and gestures may call forth desired responses. To minimize such **demand characteristics**—cues that seem to "demand" certain behavior—experimenters typically standardize their instructions or even use a computer to present them.

Researchers often walk a tightrope in designing experiments that will be involving yet ethical. To believe that you are hurting someone, or to be subjected to strong social pressure to see if it will change your opinion or behavior, may be temporarily uncomfortable. Such experiments raise the age-old question of whether ends justify means. Do the insights gained justify deceiving and sometimes distressing people?

University ethics committees now review social-psychological research to ensure that it will treat people humanely. Ethical principles developed by major psychological organizations and government organizations, such as Canada's tricouncil, urge investigators to:

- Tell potential participants enough about the experiment to enable their **informed consent**.
- Be truthful. Use deception only if justified by a significant purpose and if there is no alternative.
- Protect people from harm and significant discomfort.
- Treat information about the individual participants confidentially.
- Fully explain the experiment afterward, including any deception. The only exception to this rule is when the feedback would be distressing, say by making people realize they have been stupid or cruel.

The experimenter should be sufficiently informative *and* considerate that people leave feeling at least as good about themselves as when they came in.

---

mundane realism
degree to which an experiment is superficially similar to everyday situations

experimental realism
degree to which an experiment absorbs and involves its participants

demand characteristics
cues in an experiment that tell the participant what behavior is expected

informed consent
an ethical principle requiring that research participants be told enough to enable them to choose whether they wish to participate

THE FAR SIDE   By GARY LARSON

The Far Side

Better yet, the participants should be repaid by having learned something about the nature of psychological inquiry. When treated respectfully, few participants mind being deceived (Christensen, 1988; Sharpe & others, 1992). Indeed, say social psychology's defenders, we provoke far greater anxiety and distress by giving and returning course exams than we now do in our experiments.

Generalizing from laboratory to life

As the research on children, television, and violence illustrates, social psychology mixes everyday experience and laboratory analysis. Throughout this book we will do the same by drawing our data mostly from the laboratory and our illustrations mostly from life. Social psychology displays a healthy interplay between laboratory research and everyday life. Hunches gained from everyday experience often inspire laboratory research, which deepens our understanding of our experience. This interplay appears in the children's television experiment. What people saw in everyday life suggested experimental research. Network and government policymakers, those with the power to make changes, are now aware of the results.

We need to be cautious, however, in generalizing from laboratory to life. Although the laboratory uncovers basic dynamics of human existence, it is still a simplified, controlled reality. It tells us what effect to expect of variable X, all other things being equal—which in real life they never are. Moreover, as you will see, the participants in many experiments are university students. Although this may help you identify with them, university students are hardly a random

British fans at a game in Dusseldorf, Germany. What influences occasionally trigger postgame violence among European soccer fans? Social psychologists have proposed hypotheses that have been tested with groups behaving under controlled conditions.

sample of all humanity. Would we get similar results with people of different ages, educational levels, and cultures? This is always an open question.

Nevertheless, we can distinguish between the *content* of people's thinking and acting (their attitudes, for example) and the *process* by which they think and act (for example, how attitudes affect actions and vice versa). The content varies more from culture to culture than does the process. People of different cultures may hold different opinions, yet form them in similar ways. Consider:

- University students in Puerto Rico report greater loneliness than do other North American students. Yet in both cultures the ingredients of loneliness are much the same—shyness, uncertain purpose in life, low self-esteem. (Jones & others, 1985)

- Ethnic groups differ in school achievement and delinquency, but the differences are "no more than skin deep," report David Rowe and his colleagues (1994). To the extent that family structure, peer influences, and parental education predict achievement or delinquency for one ethnic group, they do so for other groups.

Our behaviors may differ, yet be influenced by the same social forces.

Summing up

Social psychologists organize their ideas and findings into theories. A good theory will distill an array of facts into a much shorter list of predictive principles. We can use these predictions to confirm or modify the theory, to generate new research, and to suggest practical application.

Most social psychological research is either correlational or experimental. Correlational studies, sometimes conducted with systematic survey methods, discern the relationship between variables, such as between amount of education and amount of income. Knowing two things are naturally related is valuable information, but it seldom indicates what is causing what.

When possible, social psychologists prefer to conduct experiments that explore cause and effect. By constructing a miniature reality that is under their control, experimenters can vary one thing and then another and discover how these things, separately or in combination, affect behavior. We randomly assign participants to an experimental condition, which receives the experimental treatment, or to a control condition, which does not. We can then attribute any resulting difference between the two conditions to the independent variable.

In creating experiments, social psychologists sometimes stage situations that engage people's emotions. In doing so, they are obliged to follow professional ethical guidelines, such as obtaining people's informed consent, protecting them from harm, and fully disclosing afterward any temporary deceptions. Laboratory experiments enable social psychologists to test ideas gleaned from life experience and then to apply the principles and findings back in the real world.

Þ Personal postscript: Why I wrote this book

I write this text gladly giving you, and hoping that you will gladly receive, social psychology's powerful, hard-wrought principles. They have, I believe, the power to expand your mind and enrich your life. If you finish this book with sharpened critical thinking skills and with a deeper understanding of how we view and affect one another—and why we sometimes like, love, and help one another and sometimes dislike, hate, and harm one another—then I will be a satisfied author and you, I trust, will be a rewarded reader.

I write with what I hope is disciplined passion, knowing that many readers are in the process of defining their life goals, identities, values, and attitudes. The novelist Chaim Potok recalls being urged by his mother to forgo writing: "Be a brain surgeon. You'll keep a lot of people from dying; you'll make a lot more money." Potok's response: "Mama, I don't want to keep people from dying; I want to show them how to live" (quoted by Peterson, 1992, p. 47).

Many of us who teach and write psychology are driven not only by a love for giving psychology away, but also by wanting to help students live better lives— wiser, more fulfilling, more compassionate lives. In this we are like teachers and writers in other fields. "Why do we write?" asks theologian Robert McAfee Brown. "I submit that beyond all rewards . . . *we write because we want to change things*. We write because we have this [conviction that we] can make a difference. The 'difference' may be a new perception of beauty, a new insight into self-understanding, a new experience of joy, or a decision to join the revolution" (quoted by Marty, 1988). Indeed, I write hoping to do my part to restrain intuition with critical thinking, judgmentalism with compassion, and illusion with understanding.

Each chapter concludes with a brief, personal reflection on social psychology's human significance.

part one

Social Thinking

This book unfolds around its definition of social psychology: the scientific study of how we *think about* (part one), *influence* (part two), and *relate to* (part three) one another.

These chapters on social thinking examine how we view ourselves and others. In varying ways, each chapter confronts an overriding question: How reasonable are our social attitudes, explanations, and beliefs? Are our impressions of ourselves and others generally accurate? How is our social thinking prone to bias and error, and how might we bring it closer to reality?

Chapter 2 explores the interplay between our sense of self and our social worlds. How do our social surroundings shape our self-identity? How does self-interest color our social judgments and motivate our social behavior?

Chapter 3 looks at the amazing and sometimes rather amusing ways in which we form beliefs about our social worlds. It also reveals a half-dozen ways in which we are prone to err.

Chapter 4 explores the links between attitudes and behaviors: Do our attitudes determine our behaviors? Do our behaviors determine our attitudes? Or does it work both ways?

chapter 2

The Self in a Social World

Put yourself in the shoes of the students showing up for a simple experiment by Jacquie Vorauer from the University of Manitoba and Dale Miller from Princeton University (1997). The experimenter explains to you and one other participant that the study explores students' experiences at the university. By a coin toss, the other participant is sent off to complete a questionnaire while you collect your thoughts before being interviewed. Fifteen minutes later, the experimenter gives you a peek at the other student's glum report:

I guess I don't really feel like I have had very many positive academic experiences. . . . I've found a lot of the material very difficult. . . . The worst moment I can think of was my French final; I went completely blank at the start. . . . I haven't made many new friends since I got to Princeton. Mostly, I have to rely on the people that I knew before.

When you then self-describe your personal experiences would you be more negative than had you just read (as other subjects did) a report of someone "doing well in my courses. . . . I have had some wonderful friendships and roommates. . . . I feel more socially accepted than I used to"? So it happened with the actual student subjects. The positivity of their self-presentations echoed those of the other student. Yet, remarkably, they did not recognize this social influence on their self-presentation. They were blind to the interplay between their social surroundings and their self-presentation.

This is but one of many examples of the subtle connections between what's happening in the world around us and what's going on in our heads. Some more examples:

• *Social surroundings affect self-awareness* As individuals in a group of a different culture, race, or sex, we notice how we differ and how others are reacting to our difference. The only woman in an executive meeting or math class is likely to be acutely aware of her gender. I have noticed this phenomenon when I volunteer at my children's school where almost all the teachers are women. In the teacher's lounge, I become quite aware that I am the only male.

• *Self-interest colors social judgment* We are not objective, dispassionate judges of events. When problems arise in a close relationship such as marriage, we usually attribute more responsibility to our partners than to ourselves. Few divorced people blame themselves. When things go *well* at home or work or play, we see ourselves as more responsible. In competing for prizes, scientists seldom under-rate their own contributions. After Canadians Frederick Banting and John Macleod received a 1923 Nobel Prize for discovering insulin, Banting claimed that Macleod, who headed the laboratory, had been more a hindrance than a help. Macleod omitted Banting's name in speeches about the discovery (Ross, 1981).

• *Self-concern motivates social behavior* Our actions are often strategic. In hopes of making a positive impression, we spend billions on cosmetics and diet programs. Like politicians, we also monitor others' behavior and expectations and adjust our behavior accordingly. As adolescents, and even as adults, concern for self-image drives much of our behavior.

As these examples suggest, the traffic between self and society runs both ways. Your ideas and feelings about yourself affect how you interpret events, how you recall them, and how you respond to others. Others, in turn, help shape your sense of self.

For these reasons, no topic in psychology is today more researched than the self. In 1996 the word "self" appeared in nearly 4453 book and article summaries in *Psychological Abstracts*—triple the number in 1970. Our sense of self organizes our thoughts, feelings, and actions. We therefore begin our tour of social psychology with a look at *self-concept* (how we come to know ourselves) and at *the self in action* (how our sense of self drives our attitudes and actions).

Self-concept: Who am I?

Whatever we do in our fourscore years on this global spaceship, whatever we infer and interpret, whatever we conceive and create, whomever we meet and greet will be filtered through our self. How, and how accurately, do we know ourselves? What determines our self-concept?

Who are you? As a unique and complex creature, you have many ways to complete the sentence "I am ___." (What five answers might you give?) Taken together, your answers define your **self-concept**. The elements of your self-concept, the specific beliefs by which you define who you are, are your **self-schemas** (Markus & Wurf, 1987). *Schemas* are mental templates by which we organize our worlds. Our *self*-schemas—our perceiving ourselves as athletic, overweight, smart, or whatever—powerfully affect how we process social information. They influence how we perceive, remember, and evaluate both other people and ourselves. If athletics is a central part of our self-concept (if being an athlete is one of our self-schemas), then we will tend to notice others' bodies and skills. We will quickly recall sports-related experiences. And we will welcome information that is consistent with our self-schema (Kihlstrom & Cantor, 1984; Conway & Howell, 1989). Thus the self-schemas that make up our self-concept serve like a mental Dewey Decimal System for cataloguing and retrieving information.

Consider how the self influences memory, a phenomenon known as the **self-reference effect:** *When information is relevant to our self-concepts, we process it quickly and remember it well* (Higgins & Bargh, 1987; Kuiper & Rogers, 1979; Symons & Johnson, 1997). If asked whether specific words, such as "outgoing" describe *us*, we later remember those words better than if asked whether they describe someone else. If asked to compare ourselves with a character in a short story, we remember that character better. Two days after a conversation with someone, our recall is best for what the person said about us (Kahan & Johnson, 1992). Thus, memories form around our primary interest: ourselves. When we think about something in relation to ourselves, we remember it better.

The self-reference effect illustrates a basic fact of life: Our sense of self is at the center of our worlds. Because we tend to see ourselves as center stage, we overestimate the extent to which others' behavior is aimed at us. We often see ourselves as responsible for events in which we played only a small part (Fenigstein, 1984). When judging someone else's performance or behavior, we often spontaneously compare it with our own (Dunning & Hayes, 1996). And if, while talking to one person, we overhear our name spoken by another in the room, our auditory radar instantly shifts our attention.

Our self-concepts include not only our self-schemas about who we currently are but also who we might become—our **possible selves**. Hazel Markus and her colleagues (Inglehart & others, 1989; Markus & Nurius, 1986) note that our possible selves include our visions of the self we dream of becoming—the rich self, the thin self, the passionately loved and loving self. They also include the self we fear becoming—the unemployed self, the sick self, the academically failed self. Such possible selves motivate us with specific goals—a vision of the life we long for.

Is **self-esteem**—our overall self-evaluation—the summation of all our self-schemas and possible selves? If we see ourselves as attractive, athletic, smart, and destined to be rich and loved, will we have high self-esteem? That's what psychologists assume when they suggest that to help people feel better about themselves, one must first make them feel more attractive, athletic, smarter, and so forth. But Jonathon Brown and Keith Dutton (1994) argue that this "bottom-up" view of self-esteem is backwards. The causal arrow, they believe, goes the other way. People who value themselves in a general way—those with high self-esteem—are more likely then to accept their looks, abilities, and so forth. They are like new parents who, loving their infant, delight in its fingers, toes,

self-concept
a person's answers to the question "Who am I?"

self-schema
beliefs about self that organize and guide the processing of self-relevant information

self-reference effect
the tendency to process efficiently and remember well information related to oneself

possible selves
images of what we dream of or dread becoming in the future

self-esteem
a person's overall self-evaluation or sense of self worth

and hair. (The parents do not first evaluate their infant's fingers or toes and then decide how much to value the whole baby.)

To test their idea that global self-esteem affects specific self-perceptions ("top down"), Brown and Dutton introduced University of Washington students to a supposed trait called "integrative ability." (They gave the students sets of three words—for example, "car," "swimming," "cue"—and challenged them to think of a word that linked the three words. Hint: The word begins with *p*.) High self-esteem people were more likely to report having this ability if told it was very important than if told there was no known use for the ability. Feeling good about oneself in a general way, it seems, casts a rosy glow over one's specific self-schemas and possible selves.

Consistent with this top-down view of self-esteem, Stephen Smith and Richard Petty (1995) have shown how high self-esteem people maintain positive emotions. Put low self-esteem people in a negative mood and they will retrieve mostly negative memories from their past and from newspaper headlines. Put high self-esteem people in a negative mood, and they will often restore their mood by retrieving *positive* memories. Likewise, if put in a negative mood, low self-esteem people will usually imagine a mood-consistent negative story in response to an ambiguous picture. If put in the same negative mood, high self-esteem people will usually spin a mood-enhancing positive story.

Development of the social self

The self has become a major social psychological focus because it helps organize our thinking and guide our social behavior. But what determines our self-concept? Twin studies point to genetic influences on personality and self-concept. But social experience also shapes self-concept. Among the influences that we will explore, here and elsewhere, are the roles we play, social comparison, success and failure experiences, other people's judgments, and culture.

figure 2–1

Social comparison and self-evaluation.

People are inspired by a role model if they can attain similar success but demoralized if they cannot. (Data from Lockwood & Kunda, 1997)

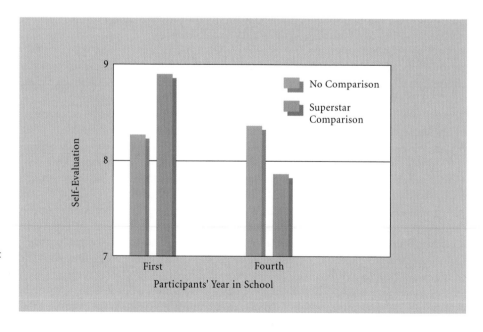

The roles we play

As we enact a new role—university student, parent, salesperson—we may initially feel self-conscious. Gradually, however, what begins as play-acting in the theater of life gets absorbed into our sense of self. For example, when playing a role we may speak in support of something we haven't really thought much about. In such cases, we strive to justify our actions. Moreover, observing ourselves can be self-revealing; we may now perceive ourselves as holding the views we expressed. Pretense becomes reality (see Chapter 4).

Social comparison

In addition to the roles we play, the role models to which we compare ourselves have a strong influence on our self-views. Take, for example, a study conducted by Penelope Lockwood from the University of Toronto and Ziva Kunda from the University of Waterloo (Lockwood & Kunda, 1997). They exposed first-year or fourth-year accounting students to an article about a star accounting student who had won numerous awards, attained a very high grade average, and landed a spectacular job. For first-year students this role model represented an achievement they could hope to attain. If all went well, they too could have such a fantastic future. For fourth-year students, however, this role model did not present such hope. They knew all too well that at this point in their studies they would never measure up to such a superstar student. As you can see in Figure 2-1, such comparisons had strong effects on these students' self-evaluations. When first- and fourth-year students did not compare to the superstar they had similar self-evaluations, but when they were exposed to the superstar, first-year students seemed inspired; their self-evaluations rose dramatically. Fourth-year students, on the other hand, seemed dejected; their self-evaluations dropped steeply. This research demonstrates the fundamental principle that our comparisons to others are a strong determinant of our self-views.

These **social comparisons** shape our identities as rich or poor, smart or dumb, tall or short: We compare ourselves with those around us and become conscious of how we differ. We then use others as a benchmark by which we can evaluate our performance and our beliefs (more on this in Chapter 7).

Social comparison helps explain why students tend to have a higher academic self-concept if they attend a school with few exceptionally capable students (Marsh & Parker, 1984). After finishing secondary school near the top of their class, many academically confident students find their academic self-esteem threatened after entering big, selective universities where many students graduated near the top of their class. Given a little pond, a fish feels bigger.

Social identity

Our self-concept—our sense of who we are—contains not just our personal identity (our sense of our personal attributes) but our social identity. The social definition of who you are—your race, religion, sex, academic major, and so forth—implies a definition of who you are not. The circle that includes "us" excludes "them."

When we're part of a small group surrounded by a larger group, we are often conscious of our social identity; when our social group is the majority, we think less about it. As a solo female in a group of men, or as a solo Canadian in a

social identity
the "we" aspect of our self-concept. The part of our answer to "Who am I?" that comes from our group memberships. Examples: "I am Australian." "I am Catholic."

social comparison
evaluating one's abilities and opinions by comparing oneself to others

group of Europeans, we are conscious of our uniqueness. To be a Black student on a mostly White campus, or a White student on a mostly Black campus, is to feel one's ethnic identity more keenly and to react accordingly. In Canada, most people identify themselves as "Canadian"—except in Quebec, where the francophones are more likely to identify themselves as "Québécois" (Kalin & Berry, 1995).

In Britain, where the English outnumber the Scots 10 to 1, Scottish identity defines itself partly by differences with the English. "To be Scottish is, to some degree, to dislike or resent the English" (Meech & Kilborn, 1992). The English, as the majority, are less conscious of being not-Scottish. In the guest book of one Scottish hotel where I checked in recently, all the English guests reported "British" nationality, and all the Scots (who are equally British) reported their nationality as "Scottish." Moreover, the more students at English universities identify themselves as British, the less they identify themselves as European (Cinnirella, 1997).

Other people's judgments

Achievements boost self-concept when we see ourselves reflected in others' appraisals. When people think well of us, it helps us think well of ourselves. Children whom others label as gifted, hard working, or helpful tend to incorporate such ideas into their self-concepts and behavior (see Chapter 3). If minority students feel threatened by negative stereotypes of their academic ability, or if women feel threatened by low expectations for their math and science performance, they may "disidentify" with these realms. Rather than fight such prejudgments, they may identify their interests elsewhere (Steele, 1997).

The *looking-glass self* is how sociologist Charles H. Cooley (1902) described our using others as a mirror for perceiving ourselves. We see our reflection in how we appear to others, said Cooley. Fellow sociologist George Herbert Mead (1934) refined this concept, noting that what matters for our self-concept is not what others actually think of us, but what we *perceive* them as thinking. Partly because most people feel freer to praise than criticize us, we sometimes overestimate their appraisal, and our self-appraisal becomes a tad inflated.

Self-inflation, as we will see, is found most strikingly in Western countries. Shinobu Kitayama (1996) reports that Japanese visitors to North America are routinely struck by the many words of praise that friends offer one another. When he and his colleagues asked people how many days ago they last complimented someone, the modal North American response was one day. In Japan, where people are socialized less to feel pride in personal achievement than shame in failing others, the modal response was four days.

Our ancestors' fate depended on what others thought of them. Their survival chances increased when protected by their group. Thus there was wisdom to their feeling shame and low self-esteem when perceiving their group's disapproval. As their heirs, having a similar deep-seated need to belong, we feel the pain of low self-esteem when facing social exclusion, note Mark Leary and his colleagues (1995). Self-esteem, they argue, is a psychological gauge by which we monitor and react to how others appraise us.

Self and culture

How did you complete the "I am ___" statement on page 39? With information about your personal traits, such as "I am honest," "I am tall," or "I am outgoing"? Or also with information about your social identity, such as "I am a Pisces," "I am a MacDonald," or "I am Canadian"?

For some people, especially those in industrialized Western cultures, **individualism** prevails. Identity is pretty much self-contained. Adolescence is a time of separating from parents, becoming self-reliant, and defining one's personal, *independent self*. Uprooted and placed in a foreign land, one's identity—as a unique individual with particular abilities, traits, values, and dreams—would remain intact. The psychology of Western cultures assumes that your life will be enriched by defining your possible selves and believing in your power of personal control. Don't conform to others' expectations. Rather, be true to yourself. Seek your own bliss. Do your own thing. To love others, first love yourself.

Western literature, from the *Iliad* to *The Adventures of Huckleberry Finn*, celebrates the self-reliant individual more than the person who fulfills others' expectations. Movie plots feature rugged heroes who buck the establishment. Songs proclaim that "I Did it My Way" and "I Gotta Be Me" and revere "The Greatest Love of All"—loving oneself (Schoeneman, 1994). Individualism flourishes when people experience affluence, mobility, urbanism, and mass media (Freeman, 1997; Marshall, 1997; Triandis, 1994).

Cultures native to Asia, Africa, and Central and South America place a greater value on **collectivism.** They nurture what Shinobu Kitayama and Hazel Markus (1995) call the *interdependent self*. Identity is defined more in relation to others. Malaysians, Indians, Japanese, and traditional Kenyans such as the Maasai, for example, are *much* more likely than Australians, Canadians, and the British to complete the "I am" statement with their group identities (Bochner, 1994; Dhawan & others, 1995; Ma & Schoeneman, 1997; Markus & Kitayama, 1991).

With an *inter*dependent self one has a greater sense of belonging. Uprooted and cut off from family, colleagues, and loyal friends, one would lose the social connections that define who one is. One has not one self but many selves: self-with-parents, self-at-work, self-with-friends (Cross & others, 1992). As Figure 2–2 and Table 2–1 suggest, the interdependent self is embedded in, and partly defined by, social memberships. Thus the goal of social life is not so much to enhance one's individual self as to harmonize with and support one's communities. Conversation is less direct and more polite (Holtgraves, 1997). Self-esteem correlates closely with "what others think of me and my group." For

individualism
the concept of giving priority to one's own goals over group goals and defining one's identity in terms of personal attributes rather than group identifications

collectivism
the concept of giving priority to the goals of one's groups (often one's extended family or work group) and defining one's identity accordingly

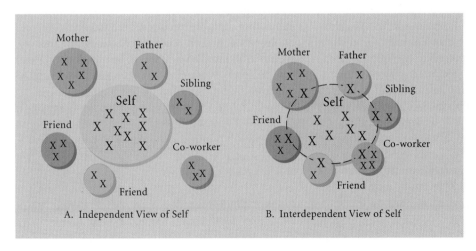

figure 2–2

Self-construal as independent or interdependent.
The independent self acknowledges relationships with others. But the interdependent self is more deeply embedded in others. (Markus & Kitayama, 1991)

table 2–1   Self-concept: Independent or interdependent

	Independent	Interdependent
Identity is	Personal, defined by individual traits and goals	Social, defined by connections with others
What matters	Me—personal achievement and fulfillment; my rights and liberties	We—group goals and solidarity; our social responsibilities and relationships
Disapproves of	Conformity	Egotism
Illustrative motto	"To thine own self be true"	"No one is an island"
Cultures that support	Individualistic Western	Collectivistic Asian and Third World

those in individualistic cultures, and especially for minorities who have learned to discount others' prejudices, these "outside" appraisals of oneself and one's group matter somewhat less (Crocker, 1994; Crocker & others, 1994; Kwan & others, 1997). Self-esteem is more personal and less relational.

In *collectivist* cultures, books and movies therefore celebrate those who, despite temptations to self-indulgence, remember who they are and do their social duty. When Kobe, Japan, was struck by the devastating 1995 earthquake, Western reporters were struck by the absence of looting and the orderly way in which people lined up for relief supplies—"as if they were waiting for a bus." Collectivism flourishes where people face shared threats such as famine, where

behind the scenes

In 1991, after nearly ten years of research and teaching at the Universities of Michigan and Oregon, I visited my Japanese alma mater, Kyoto University, and met with Japanese graduate students to plan some cross-cultural research on self-concept. When I explained the western idea of the independent self to these very bright students, they were astounded. "This oversimplified statement about self does no justice to the full complexity of social life," they insisted. I persisted in explaining this western notion of self-concept—one that my American students understood intuitively—and finally began to persuade them that, indeed, many Americans do have such a disconnected notion of self. Still, one of them, sighing deeply, said at the end, "Could this *really* be true?"

As a person who has lived and learned in both the West and the East, I have been fascinated by the surprising variability of the self in our differing cultures. As we come to understand this variability better, perhaps social psychology's horizon can expand. And, more significantly, perhaps we will better appreciate the relative strengths of our world's many cultures.

Shinobu Kitayama
Kyoto University

Collectivism in action: People resisted the temptation to loot and acted with civility following the 1995 earthquake in Kobe, a major Japanese city. Here they line up for water.

families are large, and where life requires cooperation, as when building canals or harvesting and storing food. In Australia, for example, Aboriginal people tend to value collectivism, while non-Aboriginal people value individualism (Fogarty & White, 1994). In North America, persons of color score higher on collectivism than Whites (Gaines & others, 1997).

For collectivists, social networks provide one's bearings and help define who one is. Extended families are close-knit. One's family name may even be written first to emphasize one's social identity (Hui Harry). Self-reliance means not "doing one's own thing" but "being responsible" (Triandis & others, 1994). Compared to North American magazine ads, for example, Korean magazine ads are less likely to appeal to individual interests ("She's got a style all her own") and more likely to appeal to collective interests ("We have a way of bringing people closer together") (Han & Shavitt, 1994).

So, when East meets West—as happens, for example, thanks to Western influences in urban Japan and to Japanese exchange students visiting Western countries—does the self-concept become more individualized? Does being bombarded with examples of promotions based on individual achievement rather than seniority, admonitions to "believe in one's own possibilities," and movies in which the heroic individual police officer catches the crook *despite* others' interference have an influence? It may, indeed, report Steven Heine and Darrin Lehman and their colleagues (1995; Heine & others, 1999). Personal self-esteem increased among Japanese exchange students after spending seven months at the University of British Columbia. Individual self-esteem is also higher among long-term Asian immigrants to Canada than among more recent immigrants and among those living in Asia.

Self-knowledge

"Know thyself," admonished the Greek philosopher Socrates. We certainly try. We readily form beliefs about ourselves, and we don't hesitate to explain why we feel and act as we do. But how well do we actually know ourselves?

"There is one thing, and only one in the whole universe which we know more about than we could learn from external observation," noted C. S. Lewis (1960, pp. 18–19). "That one thing is [ourselves]. We have, so to speak, inside information; we are in the know." Indeed. Yet sometimes we *think* we know, but our inside information is wrong. This is the unavoidable conclusion of some fascinating research.

Explaining our behavior

Why did you choose your university? Why did you lash out at your roommate? Why did you fall in love with that special person? Sometimes we know. Sometimes we don't know. Asked why we have felt or acted as we have, we produce plausible answers. Yet, when causes and determinants are not obvious, our self-explanations are often wrong. Factors that have big effects we sometimes report as innocuous. Factors that have little effect we sometimes perceive as influential.

Richard Nisbett and Stanley Schachter (1966) demonstrated this by asking students to take a series of electric shocks of steadily increasing intensity. Beforehand, some took a fake pill that, they were told, would produce heart palpitations, breathing irregularities, and butterflies in the stomach—the very symptoms that usually accompany being shocked. Nisbett and Schachter anticipated that people would attribute the shock symptoms to the pill and thus should tolerate more shock than people not given the pill. Indeed, the effect was enormous—people given the fake pill took four times as much shock.

When informed they had taken more shock than average, and were asked why, their answers did not mention the pill. When pressed (even after the experimenter explained the hypotheses in detail), they denied the pill's influence. They would usually say the pill probably did affect some people, but not them. A typical reply was, "I didn't even think about the pill."

Sometimes people think they *have* been affected by something that has had no effect. Nisbett and Timothy Wilson (1977) had students rate a documentary film. While some of them watched, a power saw roared just outside the room. Most people felt that this distracting noise affected their ratings. But it didn't; their ratings were similar to those of control subjects who viewed the film without distraction.

Even more thought provoking are studies in which people recorded their moods every day for two or three months (Stone & others, 1985; Weiss & Brown, 1976; Wilson & others, 1982). They also recorded factors that might affect their moods—the day of the week, the weather, the amount they slept, and so forth. At the end of each study, the people judged how much each factor had affected their moods. Remarkably (given that their attention was being drawn to their daily moods), there was little relationship between their perceptions of how important a factor was and how well the factor actually predicted their mood. These findings raise a disconcerting question: How much insight do we really have into what makes us happy or unhappy?

"You don't know your own mind."

Jonathan Swift,
Polite Conversation, 1738

"There are three things extremely hard, Steel, a Diamond, and to know one's self."

Benjamin Franklin

Predicting our behavior

People also err when predicting their behavior. Asked whether they would obey demands to deliver severe electric shocks or would hesitate to help a victim if several other people were present, people overwhelmingly deny their vulnerability to such influences. But as we will see, experiments have shown that many of us are vulnerable. Moreover, consider what Sidney Shrauger (1983) discovered when he had students predict the likelihood of their experiencing dozens of different events during the ensuing two months (becoming romantically involved, being sick, and so forth): Their self-predictions were hardly more accurate than predictions based on the average person's experience.

Dating couples predict the longevity of their relationship through rose-colored glasses. Focusing on the positives, lovers may feel sure they will always be lovers. Their friends and family often know better, report Tara MacDonald and Michael Ross (1997) from studies with University of Waterloo students. The less optimistic predictions of their parents and roommates tend to be more accurate. (Many a parent, having seen a child lunge confidently into an ill-fated relationship against all advice, nods yes.)

When predicting negative behaviors such as crying or lying, self-predictions are more accurate than predictions by one's mother and friends (Shrauger & others, 1996). Nevertheless, the surest thing we can say about your individual future is that it is sometimes hard for even you to predict. When predicting yourself, the best advice is to consider your past behavior in similar situations (Osberg & Shrauger, 1986, 1990).

Predicting our feelings

Many of life's big decisions involve predicting our future feelings. Would marrying this person lead to lifelong contentment? Would entering this profession make for satisfying work? Would going on this vacation produce a happy experience? Or would the likelier results be divorce, job burnout, and holiday disappointment?

Sometimes we know how we will feel—if we fail that exam, win that big game, or soothe our tensions with a half-hour jog. But often we don't. George Loewenstein and David Schkade (1998) offer some examples:

- People overestimate how much their well-being would be affected by such things as gaining or losing weight, a changed climate, increased television channels, or more free time. Even extreme events, such as winning a lottery or suffering a paralyzing accident, affect long-term happiness less than most people suppose.

- When people being tested for HIV predict how they will feel five weeks after getting the results, they expect to be feeling misery over bad news and elation over good news. Yet given devastating news, people cope better than they expected. And after adapting to good news, they feel not quite so elated as they anticipated.

- When male youths are shown sexually arousing photographs, then exposed to a passionate date scenario in which their date asks them to "stop," they acknowledge the possibility that they might not stop. If not first shown sexually arousing pictures, male youths more routinely deny the possibility of their being sexually aggressive. When not aroused, one easily mispredicts how one will feel and act when aroused—a phenomenon that also leads to many unintended pregnancies.

"When a feeling was there, they felt as if it would never go; when it was gone, they felt as if it had never been; when it returned, they felt as if it had never gone."

George MacDonald,
What's Mine's Mine, 1886

Predicting behavior, even one's own, is no easy matter—which may be why this visitor to Burma has turned to an astrologer for help.

- Only 1 in 7 occasional smokers (of less than a cigarette per day) predict they will be smoking in 5 years. But they underestimate the power of their drug cravings, for nearly half will be (Lynch & Bonnie, 1994).

The wisdom and delusions of self-analysis

So, to a striking extent, our intuitions are often dead wrong about what has influenced us and what we will feel and do. But let's not overstate the case. When the causes of our behavior are conspicuous and the correct explanation fits our intuition, our self-perceptions will be accurate (Gavanski & Hoffman, 1987). Peter Wright and Peter Rip (1981) found that third-year high school students *could* discern how such features of a university as its size, tuition, and distance from home influenced their reactions to it. But when the causes of behavior are not obvious to an observer, they are not obvious to the person, either.

As Chapter 3 will explain, we are unaware of much that goes on in our minds. Studies of perception and memory show that we are more aware of the *results* of our thinking than we are of the thinking *process*. Gazing across our mental sea, we behold little below its conscious surface. We experience the *results* of our mind's unconscious workings when we set a mental clock to record the passage of time and to awaken us at an appointed hour, or when we somehow achieve a spontaneous creative insight after a problem has unconsciously "incubated." Creative scientists and artists, for example, often cannot report the thought process that produced their insights.

Social psychologist Timothy Wilson (1985) offers a bold idea: the mental processes that *control* our social behavior are distinct from the mental processes through which we *explain* our behavior. Our rational explanations may therefore omit the gut-level attitudes that actually guide our behavior. In nine experiments, Wilson and his co-workers (1989) found that expressed attitudes toward things or people usually predicted later behavior reasonably well. If they first asked the participants to *analyze* their feelings, however, their attitude reports became useless. For example, dating couples' happiness with their relationship was a reasonably good predictor of whether they were still dating several months later. But if before rating their happiness they first listed all the reasons they could think of why their relationship was good or bad, then their attitude reports were useless in predicting the future of the relationship! Apparently the process of dissecting the relationship drew attention to easily verbalized factors that actually were less important than aspects of the relationship that were harder to verbalize.

In a later study, Wilson and his co-workers (1993) had people choose one of two art posters to take home. Those asked first to identify *reasons* for their choice preferred a humorous poster (whose positive features they could more easily verbalize). But a few weeks later, they were less satisfied with their choice than were those who just went by their gut feelings and generally chose the other poster. Compared to reasoned judgments of people with various facial attributes, gut-level reactions also are more consistent, report Gary Levine and colleagues (1996). First impressions can be telling.

Murray Millar and Abraham Tesser (1992) believe that Wilson overstates our ignorance of self. Their research suggests that, yes, drawing people's attention to *reasons* diminishes the usefulness of attitude reports in predicting behaviors that are driven by *feelings*. If instead of having people analyze their romantic relationships Wilson had first asked them to get more in touch with their feelings ("How do you feel when you are with and apart from your partner?"), the attitude reports might have been *more* insightful. Other behavior domains—say, choosing which school to attend based on considerations of cost, career advancement, and so forth—seem more cognitively driven. For these, an analysis of reasons rather than feelings may be most useful. Although the heart has its reasons, sometimes the mind's own reasons are decisive.

> "Self-contemplation is a curse
> That makes an old confusion worse."
>
> Theodore Roethke, *The Collected Poems of Theodore Roethke*, 1975

This research on the limits of our self-knowledge has two practical implications. The first is for psychological inquiry. Although intuitions may provide useful clues to psychological processes, *self-reports are often untrustworthy.* Errors in self-understanding limit the scientific usefulness of subjective personal reports.

The second implication is for our everyday lives. The sincerity with which people report and interpret their experiences is no guarantee of the validity of these reports. Personal

An inventor with his monocycle. Like everyone else, creative people are more aware of the results of their thinking than of the underlying cognitive processes.

testimonies are powerfully persuasive, but they may also be wrong. Keeping this potential for error in mind can help us feel less intimidated by others and be less gullible.

Summing up

Our sense of self helps organize our thoughts and actions. When we process information with reference to ourselves, we remember it well (a phenomenon called the *self-reference* effect). The elements of our self-concept are the specific *self-schemas* that guide our processing of self-relevant information and the *possible selves* that we dream of or dread. Our *self-esteem* is an overall sense of self-worth that influences how we appraise our traits and abilities.

What determines our self-concept? There are multiple influences, including the roles we play, the comparisons we make, how we perceive others appraising us, and our experiences of success and failure. Cultures shape the self, too. Some people, especially in individualistic Western cultures, assume an *independent self*. Others, often in Asian and third world cultures, assume a more *interdependent self*. As Chapter 6 will further explain, these contrasting ideas contribute to cultural differences in social behavior.

Our self-knowledge is curiously flawed. We often do not know why we behave the way we do. When powerful influences upon our behavior are not so conspicuous that any observer could spot them, we, too, can miss them.

Perceived self-control

Several concepts and lines of research point to the significance of perceived control over one's life!

So far we have considered what our self-concept is, how it develops, and how well we know ourselves. Now let's see why our self-concepts matter, by viewing the self in action. The self's action capacity has limits, note Roy Baumeister and his colleagues (1998; Muraven & others, 1998). People who exert self-control—by forcing themselves to eat radishes rather than chocolates, or by suppressing forbidden thoughts—subsequently quit faster when given unsolvable puzzles. People who try to control their emotions to an upsetting movie exhibit decreased physical stamina. Effortful self-control depletes our limited willpower reserves, it seems.

Nevertheless, our self-concept does influence our behavior (Graziano & others, 1997). Given challenging tasks, people who imagine themselves as hardworking and successful outperform those who imagine themselves as failures (Ruvolo & Markus, 1992). Envision your positive possibilities and you become more likely to plan and enact a successful strategy. Perceived self-control matters.

self-efficacy
a sense that one is competent and effective, distinguished from self-esteem, one's sense of self-worth. A bombardier might feel high self-efficacy and low self-esteem.

Self-efficacy

Albert Bandura (1997) has captured the benefits of believing one is competent and effective in his research and his theory of **self-efficacy.** The concept is a scholar's version of the wisdom behind the power of positive thinking. An optimistic belief in our own possibilities pays dividends (Gecas, 1989; Maddux, in press; Scheier & Carver, 1992). People with strong feelings of self-efficacy are more persistent, less anxious, and less depressed. They also live healthier, more focused lives and thus *are* healthier and more academically successful.

In everyday life, self-efficacy leads us to set challenging goals and persist when facing difficulties. When problems arise, a strong sense of self-efficacy leads us to keep calm and seek solutions rather than ruminate on our inadequacy. Striving plus persistence equals accomplishment. And with accomplishment, our self-confidence grows. Self-efficacy, like self-esteem, grows with hard-won achievements.

Even subtle manipulations of self-efficacy can affect behavior. Becca Levy (1996) discovered this when she subliminally exposed 90 older adults to words that "primed" (activated) either a negative or positive stereotype of aging. Some subjects viewed .066 second presentations of words like *decline, forgets,* and *senile,* or words like *sage, wise,* and *learned.* The participants consciously perceived only a flash or blur of light. Yet being given the positive words led to heightened "memory self-efficacy" (confidence in one's memory). Viewing the negative words had the opposite effect. Older adults in China, where positive images of aging prevail and memory self-efficacy may be greater, seem not to suffer the memory decline commonly observed in Western countries (Schachter & others, 1991).

Your self-efficacy is how competent you feel to do something. If you believe you can do something, will the belief make a difference? Do you have *control* over your outcomes? You may, for example, feel like an effective driver (high self-efficacy), yet feel endangered by drunken drivers (low control). You may feel like a competent student or worker; but fearing discrimination based on your age, gender, or appearance, you may think your prospects are dim.

Locus of control

"I have no social life," complained a 40-something single man to student therapist Jerry Phares. At Phares' urging, the patient went to a dance, where several women danced with him. "I was just lucky," he later reported, "it would never happen again." When Phares reported this to his mentor, Julian Rotter, it crystallized an idea he had been forming. In Rotter's experiments and in his clinical practice, some people seemed to persistently "feel that what happens to them is governed by external forces of one kind or another, while others feel that what happens to them is governed largely by their own efforts and skills" (quoted by Hunt, 1993, p. 334).

What do you think? Are people more often captains of their destinies or victims of their circumstances? The playwrights, directors, and actors of their own lives or prisoners of invisible situations? Rotter called this dimension **locus of control.** With Phares, he developed 29 paired statements to measure a person's locus of control. Imagine yourself taking their test. Which do you more strongly believe?

locus of control
the extent to which people perceive outcomes as internally controllable by their own efforts and actions or as externally controlled by chance or outside forces

In the long run people get the respect often they deserve in this world.	or	Unfortunately, people's worth passes unrecognized no matter how hard they try.
What happens to me is my own doing.	or	Sometimes I feel that I don't have enough control over the direction my life is taking.

The average person can have an influence in government decisions.   or   This world is run by the few people in power, and there is not much the little guy can do about it.

Do your answers to such questions from Rotter (1973) indicate that you believe you control your own destiny (*internal* locus of control)? Or that chance or outside forces determine your fate (*external* locus of control)? Those who see themselves as internally controlled are more likely to do well in school, successfully stop smoking, wear seat belts, practice birth control, deal with marital problems directly, make lots of money, and delay instant gratification in order to achieve long-term goals (Findley & Cooper, 1983; Lefcourt, 1982; McLean, 1997; Miller & others, 1986).

How competent and effective we feel depends on how we explain setbacks. Perhaps you have known students who view themselves as victims—who, say, blame poor grades on things beyond their control, such as their feelings of stupidity or their "poor" teachers, texts, or tests. If such students are coached to adopt a more hopeful attitude—to believe that effort, good study habits, and self-discipline can make a difference—their grades tend to go up (Noel & others, 1987; Peterson & Barrett, 1987).

Successful people are more likely to see setbacks as a fluke or to think "I need a new approach." New life insurance sales representatives who view failures as controllable ("It's difficult, but with persistence I'll get better") sell more policies. They are half as likely as their more pessimistic colleagues to quit during their first year (Seligman & Schulman, 1986). Among university swim team members, those with an optimistic "explanatory style" are more likely than pessimists to perform beyond expectations (Seligman & others, 1990). As the Roman poet Virgil said in the *Aeneid*, "They can because they think they can."

> "If my mind can conceive it and my heart can believe it, I know I can achieve it. Down with dope! Up with hope! I am somebody!"
>
> Jesse Jackson, The March on Washington, 1983

Learned helplessness versus self-determination

The benefits of feelings of control also appear in animal research. Dogs taught they cannot escape shocks while confined will learn a sense of helplessness. Later these dogs cower passively in other situations when they *could* escape punishment. Dogs that learn personal control (by escaping their first shocks successfully) adapt easily to a new situation. Researcher Martin Seligman (1975, 1991) notes similarities to this **learned helplessness** in human situations. Depressed or oppressed people, for example, become passive because they believe their efforts have no effect. Helpless dogs and depressed people both suffer paralysis of the will, passive resignation, even motionless apathy (Figure 2–3).

Here is a clue to how institutions—whether malevolent, like concentration camps, or benevolent, like hospitals—can dehumanize people. In hospitals, "good patients" don't ring bells, don't ask questions, don't try to control what's

learned helplessness the hopelessness and resignation learned when a human or animal perceives no control over repeated bad events

figure 2–3

Learned helplessness.

When animals and people experience uncontrollable bad events, they learn to feel helpless and resigned.

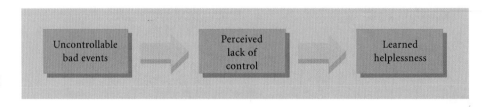

happening (Taylor, 1979). Such passivity may be good for hospital efficiency, but it is bad for people. Feelings of efficacy, of an ability to control one's life, enhance health and survival. Losing control over what you do and what others do to you can make unpleasant events profoundly stressful (Pomerleau & Rodin, 1986). Several diseases are associated with feelings of helplessness and diminished choice. So is the rapidity of decline and death in concentration camps and nursing homes. Hospital patients who are trained to believe in their ability to control stress require fewer pain relievers and sedatives and nurses see them as exhibiting less anxiety (Langer & others, 1975).

Ellen Langer and Judith Rodin (1976) showed the importance of personal control by treating elderly patients in a high-rated nursing home in one of two ways. With one group the benevolent caregivers stressed "our responsibility to make this a home you can be proud of and happy in." They gave the passive patients their normal well-intentioned, sympathetic care. Three weeks later, most were rated by themselves, by interviewers, and by nurses as further debilitated. Langer and Rodin's other treatment promoted personal control. It stressed opportunities for choice, the possibilities for influencing nursing-home policy, and the person's responsibility "to make of your life whatever you want." These patients were given small decisions to make and responsibilities to fulfill. Over the ensuing three weeks, 93 percent of this group showed improved alertness, activity, and happiness.

The experience of the first group must have been similar to that of James MacKay (1980), an 87-year-old psychologist:

> I became a nonperson last summer. My wife had an arthritic knee which put her in a walker, and I chose that moment to break my leg. We went to a nursing home. It was all nursing and no home. The doctor and the head nurse made all decisions; we were merely animate objects. Thank heavens it was only two weeks. . . . The top man of the nursing home was very well trained and very compassionate; I considered it the best home in town. But we were nonpersons from the time we entered until we left.

Studies confirm that systems of governing or managing people that promote self-efficacy will indeed promote health and happiness (Deci & Ryan, 1987).

- Prisoners given some control over their environments—by being able to move chairs, control TV sets, and switch the lights—experience less stress, exhibit fewer health problems, and commit less vandalism (Ruback & others, 1986; Wener & others, 1987).

- Workers given leeway in carrying out tasks and making decisions experience improved morale (Miller & Monge, 1986).

- Institutionalized residents allowed choice in such matters as what to eat for breakfast, when to go to a movie, whether to sleep late or get up early, may live longer and certainly are happier (Timko & Moos, 1989).

- Homeless shelter residents who perceive little choice in when to eat and sleep, and little control over their privacy, are more likely to have a passive, helpless attitude regarding finding housing and work (Burn, 1992).

Although this psychological research and comment on perceived self-control is new, the emphasis on taking charge of one's life and realizing one's potential is not. The notion that "you can do it if you try hard enough" has permeated

"Argue for your limitations, and sure enough they're yours."

Richard Bach, *Illusions: Adventures of a Reluctant Messiah,* 1977

Personal control: Inmates of Spain's modern Valencia prison can, with appropriate behavior, gain access to classes, sports facilities, and cultural opportunities. Salary earned for work is credited to an account, which they can charge for extra snacks.

© 1983, The New Yorker Magazine, Inc.

"*This gives my confidence a real boost.*"

Confidence and feelings of self-efficacy grow from successes.

our culture. When we were little children most of us were taught the story about the Little Engine That Could. The cultural lesson is clear: If you try hard enough and keep a positive attitude you can achieve whatever you dream. The same lesson we find in many self-help books and videos.

Research on self-control gives us greater confidence in traditional virtues such as perseverance and hope. Yet Bandura emphasizes that self-efficacy does not grow primarily by self-persuasion ("I think I can, I think I can") or by puffing people up like hot-air balloons ("You're terrific!"). Its chief source is the experience of success. If your initial efforts to lose weight, stop smoking, or improve your grades succeed, your self-efficacy increases.

Summing up

Several lines of research show the benefits of a sense of efficacy and feelings of control. People who believe in their own competence and effectiveness, and who have an internal locus of control, cope better and achieve more than do those who have learned a helpless, pessimistic outlook.

Self-serving bias

As we process self-relevant information, a potent bias intrudes. We readily excuse our failures, accept credit for our successes, and in many ways see ourselves as better than average. Such self-enhancing perceptions enable most people to enjoy the benefits of high self-esteem, while occasionally suffering the perils of pride.

It is widely believed that most of us suffer low self-esteem. A generation ago, humanistic psychologist Carl Rogers (1958) concluded that most people he knew "despise themselves, regard themselves as worthless and unlovable." Many popularizers of humanistic psychology concur. "All of us have inferiority complexes," contends John Powell (1989). "Those who seem not to have such a complex are only pretending." As Groucho Marx (1960) lampooned, "I don't want to belong to any club that would accept me as a member."

Actually, most of us have a good reputation with ourselves. In studies of self-esteem, even low-scoring people respond in the midrange of possible scores. (A low self-esteem person responds to such statements as "I have good ideas" with a qualifying adjective, such as "somewhat" or "sometimes.") Moreover, one of social psychology's most provocative yet firmly established conclusions concerns the potency of **self-serving bias.**

self-serving bias the tendency to perceive oneself favorably

Explanations for positive and negative events

Time and again, experimenters have found that people readily accept credit when told they have succeeded (attributing the success to their ability and effort), yet attribute failure to such external factors as bad luck or the problem's inherent "impossibility" (Whitley & Frieze, 1985). Similarly, in explaining their victories, athletes commonly credit themselves, but attribute losses to something else: bad breaks, bad referee calls, or the other team's super effort or dirty play (Grove & others, 1991; Lalonde, 1992; Mullen & Riordan, 1988). And how

Frank and Ernest

© 1997 Thaves / Newspaper distribution by NEA, Inc.

The self-serving bias.
(Reprinted from Better
Homes and Gardens
Magazine. ©Copyright
Meredith Corporation
1975. All rights reserved.)

"*I'm drawing up a list of all my good points and all my flaws,*
and so far my good points are running way, way ahead of my flaws."

much responsibility do you suppose car drivers tend to accept for their accidents? On insurance forms, drivers have described their accidents in words such as these: "An invisible car came out of nowhere, struck my car and vanished," "As I reached an intersection, a hedge sprang up, obscuring my vision and I did not see the other car," "A pedestrian hit me and went under my car" (*Toronto News*, 1977).

Situations that combine skill and chance (games, exams, job applications) are especially prone to the phenomenon: Winners can easily attribute their successes to their skill, while losers can attribute their losses to chance. When I win at Scrabble, it's because of my verbal dexterity; when I lose, it's because "Who could get anywhere with a *Q* but no *U*?" Politicians similarly tend to attribute their wins to themselves (hard work, constituent service, reputation, and strategy) and their losses to factors beyond their control (their district's party make-up, their opponent's name, political trends) (Kingdon, 1967).

Michael Ross and Fiore Sicoly (1979) observed a marital version of self-serving bias. They found that young married Canadians usually felt they took more responsibility for such activities as cleaning the house and caring for the children than their spouses credited them for. In one survey, 91 percent of wives but only 76 percent of husbands credited the wife with doing most of the food shopping (Burros, 1988). In another study, husbands estimated they did slightly more of the housework than their wives did; the wives, however, estimated their efforts were more than double their husbands' (Fiebert, 1990). Every night, my wife and I pitch our laundry at the foot of our bedroom clothes hamper. In the morning, one of us puts it in. When she suggested that I take more responsibility for this, I thought, "Huh? I already do it 75 percent of the time." So I asked her how often she thought she picked up the clothes. "Oh," she replied, "about 75 percent of the time." Small wonder that divorced people usually blame their partner for the breakup (Gray & Silver, 1990), or that managers usually blame poor performance on workers' lack of ability or effort (Imai, 1994; Rice, 1985). (Workers are more likely to blame something external—inadequate supplies, excessive workload, difficult co-workers, ambiguous assignments.) Small wonder, too, that people evaluate reward distributions such as pay raises as fairer when receiving more rather than less than most others (Diekmann & others, 1997).

Adam's excuse: "The woman whom you gave to be with me, she gave me fruit from the tree, and I ate."

Students also exhibit self-serving bias. After receiving an exam grade, those who do well tend to accept personal credit. They judge the exam to be a valid measure of their competence (Arkin & Maruyama, 1979; Briere & Vallerand, 1990; Davis & Stephan, 1980; Gilmor & Reid, 1979; Griffin & others, 1983). Those who do poorly are much more likely to criticize the exam.

Reading this research, I couldn't resist a satisfied "knew-it-all-along" feeling. But consider teachers' ways of explaining students' good and bad performances. When there is no need to feign modesty, those assigned the role of teacher tend to take credit for positive outcomes and blame failure on the student (Arkin & others, 1980; Davis, 1979). Teachers, it seems, are likely to think, "With my help, Maria graduated with honors. Despite all my help, Melinda flunked out."

Can we all be better than average?

Self-serving bias also appears when people compare themselves to others. If the sixth-century B.C. Chinese philosopher Lao-tzu was right that "at no time in the world will a man who is sane over-reach himself, over-spend himself, over-rate himself," then most of us are a little insane. For on nearly any dimension that is both *subjective* and *socially desirable,* most people see themselves as better than average. This is especially so when comparing oneself to people in general rather than to known individuals (Alicke & others, 1995). Consider:

- Most businesspeople see themselves as more ethical than the average businessperson (Baumhart, 1968; Brenner & Molander, 1977). One national survey asked, "How would you rate your own morals and values on a scale from one to 100 (100 being perfect)?" Fifty percent of people rated themselves 90 or above; only 11 percent said 74 or less (Lovett, 1997).

- Ninety percent of business managers rate their performance as superior to their average peer (French, 1968). In Australia, 86 percent of people rate their job performance as above average, 1 percent as below average (Headey & Wearing, 1987).
- In The Netherlands, most high school students rate themselves as more honest, persistent, original, friendly, and reliable than the average high school student (Hoorens, 1993, in press).
- Most drivers—even most drivers who have been hospitalized for accidents—believe themselves to be safer and more skilled than the average driver (Guerin, 1994; McKenna & Myers, 1997; Svenson, 1981).
- Most people perceive themselves as more intelligent than their average peer (Wylie, 1979), as better looking (*Public Opinion*, 1984), and as less prejudiced than others in their communities (Fields & Schuman, 1976; Lenihan, 1965; Messick & others, 1985; O'Gorman & Garry, 1976).
- Most adults believe they support their aging parents more than do their siblings (Lerner & others, 1991).
- Most people view themselves as healthier than most of their neighbors, and most university students believe they will outlive their actuarially predicted age of death by about 10 years (Larwood, 1978; C. R. Snyder, 1978).

Every community, it seems, is like Garrison Keillor's fictional Lake Wobegon, where "all the women are strong, all the men are good-looking, and all the children are above average." Perhaps one reason for this optimism is that although 12 percent of people feel old for their age, many more—66 percent—think they

Most people perceive themselves as better than average.

© 1984, The New Yorker Magazine, Inc.

"I dread to think of all the inaccuracies there would be if you wrote my biography after I'm gone."

are young for their age (*Public Opinion*, 1984). All of which calls to mind Freud's joke about the husband who told his wife, "If one of us should die, I think I would go live in Paris."

Subjective dimensions (such as "disciplined") trigger greater self-serving bias than objective behavioral dimensions (such as "punctual"). Students are more likely to rate themselves superior in "moral goodness" than in "intelligence" (Allison & others, 1989; Van Lange, 1991). And community residents overwhelmingly see themselves as *caring* more than most others about the environment, about hunger, and about other social issues, though they don't see themselves as *doing* more, such as contributing time or money to those issues (White & Plous, 1995). Education doesn't eliminate self-serving bias; even social psychologists exhibit it, by believing themselves more ethical than most social psychologists (Van Lange & others, 1997).

Subjective qualities give us leeway in constructing our own definitions of success (Dunning & others, 1989, 1991). Rating my "athletic ability," I ponder my basketball play, not the agonizing weeks I spent as a Little League baseball player hiding in right field. Assessing my "leadership ability," I conjure up an image of a great leader whose style is similar to mine. By defining ambiguous criteria in our own terms, each of us can see ourselves as relatively successful. In one survey of 829,000 high school seniors, 0 percent rated themselves below average in "ability to get along with others" (a subjective, desirable trait), 60 percent rated themselves in the top 10 percent, and 25 percent saw themselves among the top 1 percent!

We also support our self-image by assigning importance to the things we're good at. Over a semester, those who ace an introductory computer science course come to place a higher value on their identity as a computer-literate person in today's world. Those who do poorly are more likely to scorn computer geeks and to exclude computer skills as pertinent to their self-image (Hill & others, 1989).

Unrealistic optimism

Optimism predisposes a positive approach to life. "The optimist," notes H. Jackson Brown (1990, p. 79), "goes to the window every morning and says, 'Good morning, God.' The pessimist goes to the window and says, 'good god, morning.'" Many of us however, have what researcher Neil Weinstein (1980, 1982) terms "an unrealistic optimism about future life events." Students perceive themselves as far more likely than their classmates to get a good job, draw a good salary, and own a home, and as far less likely to experience negative events, such as developing a drinking problem, having a heart attack before age 40, or being fired. In Scotland, most late adolescents think they are much less likely than their peers to become infected by the AIDS virus (Abrams, 1991). After experiencing an earthquake, students did lose

WHAT LEMMINGS BELIEVE

"Views of the future are so rosy that they would make Pollyanna blush."

Shelley E. Taylor,
Positive Illusions, 1989

their optimism about being less vulnerable than their classmates to injury in a natural disaster, but within three months their illusory optimism had rebounded (Burger & Palmer, 1991).

Linda Perloff (1987) notes how illusory optimism increases our vulnerability. Believing ourselves immune to misfortune, we do not take sensible precautions. In one survey, 137 marriage license applicants accurately estimated that half of marriages end in divorce, yet most assessed their chance of divorce as zero percent (Baker & Emery, 1993). Sexually active undergraduate women who don't consistently use contraceptives perceive themselves, compared to other women at their university, as much *less* vulnerable to unwanted pregnancy (Burger & Burns, 1988). Those who cheerfully shun seat belts, deny the effects of smoking, and stumble into ill-fated relationships remind us that blind optimism, like pride, may, as the ancient proverb warns, go before a fall.

Optimism definitely beats pessimism in promoting self-efficacy, health, and well-being (Armor & Taylor, in press). Yet a dash of realism can save us from the perils of unrealistic optimism. Self-doubt can energize students, most of whom—especially those destined for low grades—exhibit excess optimism about upcoming exams (Prohaska, 1994; Sparrell & Shrauger, 1984). (Such illusory optimism often disappears as the time approaches for receiving the exam back—Shepperd & others, 1996.) Students who are overconfident tend to underprepare. Their equally able but more anxious peers, fearing that they are going to bomb on the upcoming exam, study furiously and get higher grades (Goodhart, 1986; Norem & Cantor, 1986; Showers & Ruben, 1987). The moral: Success in school and beyond requires enough optimism to sustain hope and enough pessimism to motivate concern.

> "O God, give us grace to accept with serenity the things that cannot be changed, courage to change the things which should be changed, and the wisdom to distinguish the one from the other."
>
> Reinhold Niebuhr, *"The Serenity Prayer,"* 1943

---

focus

The illusion of invulnerability

In 1943, psychologist Gordon W. Allport (1978, pp. 19–20) described the perils of unrealistic optimism:

Recently I examined two hundred life histories written by refugees from Nazi Germany. With scarcely an exception these people had found themselves blinded by their own hopes.

Not one of them would at first believe that Hitlerism could bring such a catastrophe on them.

In 1932 they hoped and therefore believed that Hitler would never come to power.

In 1933 they hoped and therefore believed that he could not put his threats into execution.

In 1934 they hoped and therefore believed that the nightmare would soon pass.

In 1938 the Austrians were certain that Hitler could never come to Austria, because they hoped that Austrians were different from Germans.

Another example comes from a study of college undergraduates who were asked to estimate their income in five years' and in ten years' time after leaving college. The results, I regret to report, are quite fantastic. Most of them picture themselves as well-to-do, quite overlooking probabilities.

If they were headed for medicine, they estimated their income within a range which only about 5 percent of the medical profession achieves. If they were to become airplane pilots, they figured a salary above that obtained by any pilot.

Hope based on ignorance may spring eternal, but it certainly spells a fall. It is more of a vice than a virtue.

Illusory optimism: Most couples marry feeling confident of long-term love. Actually, in individualistic cultures, new marriages often fail.

False consensus and uniqueness

We have a curious tendency to further enhance our self-image by overestimating or underestimating the extent to which others think and act as we do—a phenomenon called the **false consensus effect.** On matters of *opinion*, we find support for our positions by overestimating the extent to which others agree (Krueger & Clement, 1994; Marks & Miller, 1987; Mullen & Goethals, 1990). If we favor a Canadian referendum or support New Zealand's National Party, we wishfully overestimate the extent to which others agree (Babad & others, 1992; Koestner, 1993). When we behave badly or fail in a task, we reassure ourselves by thinking that such lapses are common. We guess that others think and act as we do: "I do it, but so does everyone else." If we cheat on our income taxes or smoke, we are likely to overestimate the number of other people who do likewise. If we harbor negative ideas about another racial group, we presume that many others also have negative stereotypes; thus our perceptions of others' stereotypes may reveal something of our own (Krueger, 1996).

False consensus may occur because we generalize from a limited sample, which prominently includes ourselves (Dawes, 1990). Lacking other information, why not "project" ourselves—why not use our own responses as a clue to others' likely responses?

Also, we're more likely to associate with people who share our attitudes and behaviors, and then to judge the world from the people we know. But on matters of *ability* or when we behave well or successfully, a **false uniqueness effect** more often occurs (Goethals & others, 1991). We serve our self-image by seeing our talents and moral behaviors as relatively unusual (Table 2–2). Thus those who drink heavily but use seat belts will *over*estimate (false consensus) the number of other heavy drinkers and *under*estimate (false uniqueness) the commonality of seat belt use (Suls & others, 1988). This seems a natural result of a tendency to more often ascribe positive than negative traits to themselves

Penthouse publisher Bob Guccione, responding to a national survey revealing that 83 percent of adults reported zero or one sexual partner in the past year: "Positively, outrageously stupid and unbelievable. I would say five partners a year is the average for men." (Elmer-DeWitt, 1994)

false consensus effect
the tendency to overestimate the commonality of one's opinions and one's undesirable or unsuccessful behaviors

false uniqueness effect
the tendency to underestimate the commonality of one's abilities and one's desirable or successful behaviors

Actress Pamela Lee:
"Everybody says I'm
plastic from head to toe.
Can't stand next to a
radiator or I'll melt. I had
(breast) implants, but so
has every single person
in L.A." (Talbert, 1997)

table 2–2   False uniqueness: who follows the ten commandments?

Ten Commandments	I Follow	Most Others Follow
Do Not Take the Lord's Name in Vain	64%	15%
Worship None Before God	64%	22%
Honor Your Mother and Father	95%	49%
Do Not Kill	91%	71%
Attend Services on Holy Days	86%	45%
Do Not Commit Adultery	90%	54%
Do Not Steal	88%	33%
Do Not Bear False Witness	76%	23%
Do Not Covet Your Neighbor's Spouse	84%	42%
Do Not Envy Your Neighbor's Possessions	81%	49%

Source: Rosenblatt (1993).

(Gross & Miller, 1997; Krueger, 1997; Krueger & Clement, 1997). The less common a behavior, the more people overestimate its frequency. If 20 percent of people are selfish, there is lots of room for people to *over*estimate the extent to which others (relative to themselves) are selfish. And if 80 percent of people are honest, there is more room to *under*estimate how many others are honest. Thus people may see their failings as relatively normal and their virtues as less commonplace than they are.

Other self-serving tendencies

"How little we should
enjoy life if we never
flattered ourselves!"

La Rochefoucauld,
Maxims, 1665

These tendencies toward self-serving attributions, self-congratulatory comparisons, and illusory optimism are not the only signs of favorably biased self-perceptions. Earlier we noted that most of us overestimate how desirably we would act in a given situation. Chapter 3 explains that we also display a "cognitive conceit" by overestimating the accuracy of our beliefs and judgments and by misremembering our own past in self-enhancing ways.

Additional streams of evidence converge to form a river:

- If an undesirable act cannot be misremembered or undone, then, as we will see in Chapter 4, we may justify it.
- The more favorably we perceive ourselves on some dimension (intelligence, persistence, sense of humor), the more we use that dimension as a basis for judging others (Lewicki, 1983).
- The more favorably we view ourselves, the more we think others perceive us in flattering ways (Kenny & DePaulo, 1993).
- If a test or some other source of information—even a horoscope—flatters us, then we believe it, and we evaluate positively both the test and any

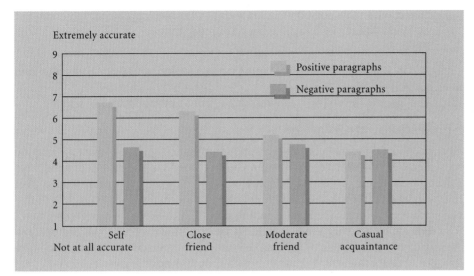

figure 2–4

"If it's positive, it sounds like me" (and my best friend). Joel Johnson and his colleagues (1985) found that subjects judged favorable descriptions (such as "finds it easy to be open and demonstrative") to be (a) not especially accurate descriptions of their casual acquaintances, (b) better descriptions of their friends, and (c) even better descriptions of themselves.

"I admit it *does* look very impressive. But you see nowadays *everyone* graduates in the top ten per cent of his class."

Can we all be better than average? (William W. Haefeli, Saturday Review, 1/20/79)

evidence suggesting that the test is valid (Ditto, 1994; Glick & others, 1989; Pyszczynski & others, 1985). (See Figure 2–4.)

- Most university students, however, think that standardized tests under-estimate their ability (Shepperd, 1993). (In fact, however, the higher scores they *think* they deserved would *less* accurately predict their obtained grades.)

- Judging from photos, we not only guess that attractive people have desirable personalities, we also guess that they have personalities more like our own than do unattractive people (Marks & others, 1981).

- We like to associate ourselves with others' success. We bask in reflected glory if some famous person attended our school. If we find ourselves linked with (say, born on the same day as) some reprehensible person, we boost ourselves by softening our view of the rascal (Finch & Cialdini, 1989).

So is pop psychology right that most people suffer from low self-esteem and insufficient self-love? Many streams of evidence suggest otherwise. To revise Elizabeth Barrett Browning, "How do I love me? Let me count the ways!"

Self-esteem motivation

Why do people perceive themselves in self-enhancing ways? One explanation sees the self-serving bias as a by-product of how we process and remember information about ourselves. Recall the study in which married people gave themselves credit for doing more housework than their spouses did. Might this not be due, as Michael Ross and Fiore Sicoly (1979) believe, to our greater recall for what we've actively done and our lesser recall for what we've not done or merely observed others doing? I can easily picture myself picking up the laundry, but I have difficulty picturing myself absentmindedly overlooking it.

But are the biased perceptions simply a perceptual error, an unemotional bent in how we process information? Or are self-serving *motives* also involved? It's now clear from research that we have multiple motives. Questing for self-knowledge, we're eager to *assess* our competence (Dunning, 1995). Questing for self-confirmation, we're eager to *verify* our self-conceptions (Sanitioso & others, 1990; Swann, 1996, 1997). Questing for self-affirmation, we're *especially* motivated to *enhance* our self-image (Sedikides, 1993).

Among sibling relationships, the threat to self-esteem is greatest for an older child with a highly capable younger brother or sister.

behind the scenes

Suppose that you have collaborated on a project with another student and that the two of you evaluated each other's contributions to the final product. You may be disappointed to discover that your partner is less impressed with the quality and extent of your contribution than you are. In the history of science, there are many examples of such disagreements; erstwhile friends and colleagues become bitter enemies as they contest each other's contributions to important discoveries. Sicoly and I suggested that individuals generally tend to accept more responsibility for a joint product than other contributors attribute to them. In many everyday activities, participants are unaware of their divergent views because they don't share their opinions with each other. After cleaning the kitchen, for example, spouses don't usually discuss how much each contributed to the cleanup. When such opinions are voiced, people are likely to be upset because they believe that the other person is not giving them sufficient credit. If the consequences are high (e.g., academic grades, job promotions, or Nobel prizes are at stake), they may well assume that their partner is deliberately downgrading their contributions to enhance his or her own achievements. In our research, Sicoly and I showed that differences in assessments of responsibility are common in many everyday contexts, and that contrasting judgments may reflect normal cognitive processes rather than deliberate deceit. Differences in judgment can result from honest evaluations of information that is differentially available to the two participants.
Michael Ross
University of Waterloo

Experiments confirm that a motivational engine powers our cognitive machinery (Kunda, 1990). Finding their favorable self-esteem threatened, people often react by putting others down, and sometimes with violence (Baumeister, 1997). Facing failure, high self-esteem people sustain their self-worth by perceiving other people as failing, too, and by exaggerating their superiority over others (Agostinelli & others, 1992; Brown & Gallagher, 1992). The more physiologically aroused people are after a failure, the more likely they are to excuse the failure with self-protective attributions (Brown & Rogers, 1991). We are not just cool information-processing machines.

Abraham Tesser (1988) reports that a "self-esteem maintenance" motive predicts a variety of interesting findings, even friction among brothers and sisters. Do you have a sibling of the same sex who is close to you in age? If so, people probably compared the two of you as you grew up. Tesser presumes that people's perceiving one of you as more capable than the other will motivate the less able one to act in ways that maintain his or her self-esteem. (Tesser thinks the threat to self-esteem is greatest for an older child with a highly capable younger sibling.) Men with a more or less able brother typically recall not getting along well with him; men with a similarly able brother are more likely to recall very little friction.

Self-esteem threats occur among friends and married partners, too. Although shared interests are healthy, *identical* career goals may produce tension or jealousy (Clark & Bennett, 1992). Similarly, people feel greater jealousy toward a romantic rival whose achievements are in the domain of their own aspirations (DeSteno & Salovey, 1996).

What underlies our motive to maintain or enhance self-esteem? Mark Leary and his colleagues (1995; Leary & Downs, 1995) believe that our self-esteem feelings are like a fuel gauge. As we noted earlier, relationships are conducive to our surviving and thriving. Thus, the self-esteem gauge alerts us to threatened social rejection, motivating us to act with greater sensitivity to others' expectations. Studies confirm that social rejection lowers our self-esteem, strengthening our eagerness for approval. Spurned or jilted, we feel unattractive or inadequate. This pain can motivate self-improvement and a search for acceptance elsewhere.

LOW SELF-ESTEEM

Reflections on self-efficacy and self-serving bias

No doubt many readers are finding all this either depressing or contrary to their own occasional feelings of inadequacy. To be sure, the most of us who exhibit the self-serving bias may still feel inferior to specific individuals, especially those who are a step or two higher on the ladder of success, attractiveness, or skill. And not everyone operates with a self-serving bias. Some people *do* suffer from low self-esteem.

Moreover, when feeling good about ourselves, we are less defensive (Epstein & Feist, 1988). We are also less thin-skinned and judgmental—less likely to inflate those who like us and berate those who don't (Baumgardner & others, 1989). In experiments, people whose self-esteem is temporarily bruised—say, by being told they did miserably on an intelligence test—are more likely to disparage others (Beauregard & Dunning, in press). Those whose ego has recently been wounded also are more prone to self-serving explanations of success or failure than are those whose ego has recently received a boost (McCarrey & others, 1982). So threats to self-esteem may provoke self-protective defensiveness. When feeling unaffirmed, people may offer self-affirming boasts, excuses, and put-downs of others. More generally, people who are down on themselves tend also to be down on others (Wills, 1981). Mockery says as much about the mocker as the one mocked.

Nevertheless, high self-esteem goes hand in hand with self-serving perceptions. Those who score highest on self-esteem tests (who say nice things about themselves) also say nice things about themselves when explaining their successes and failures (Ickes & Layden, 1978; Levine & Uleman, 1979; Rosenfeld, 1979; Schlenker & others, 1990), when evaluating their group (Brown & others, 1988), and when comparing themselves to others (Brown, 1986).

The self-serving bias as adaptive

Self-serving bias and its accompanying excuses help protect people from depression (Snyder & Higgins, 1988). Nondepressed people excuse their failures on laboratory tasks or perceive themselves as being more in control than they are. Depressed people's self-appraisals are more accurate: sadder but wiser. (More on this in Module A.)

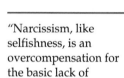

"Narcissism, like selfishness, is an overcompensation for the basic lack of self-love."

Erich Fromm, *Escape from Freedom*, 1941

And consider this: Thanks to people's reluctance to criticize, it's easy to over-estimate how others are really perceiving us (DePaulo & others, 1987; Kenny & Albright, 1987). Mildly depressed people are less prone to illusions; they gener-ally see themselves *as* other people see them—which may, at times, be under-standably depressing (Lewinsohn & others, 1980). This prompts the unsettling thought that Pascal may have been right: "I lay it down as a fact that, if all men knew what others say of them, there would not be four friends in the world."

In their "terror management theory," Jeff Greenberg, Sheldon Solomon, and Tom Pyszczynski (1997) propose another reason why positive self-esteem is adaptive—it buffers anxiety, including anxiety related to our certain death. In childhood we learn that when we meet the standards taught us by our parents, we are loved and protected; when we don't, love and protection may be with-drawn. We therefore come to associate viewing ourselves as good with feeling secure. Greenberg and colleagues argue that positive self-esteem—viewing one-self as good and secure—even protects us from feeling terror over our eventual death. Their research shows that reminding people of their mortality (say, by writing a short essay on dying) motivates them to affirm their self-worth. More-over, when facing threats, increased self-esteem leads to decreased anxiety.

As this new research on depression and anxiety suggests, there may be some practical wisdom in self-serving perceptions. It may be strategic to believe we are smarter, stronger, and more socially successful than we are. Cheaters may give a more convincing display of honesty if they believe themselves honorable. Belief in our superiority can also motivate us to achieve—creating a self-fulfilling prophecy—and can sustain a sense of hope in difficult times.

The self-serving bias as maladaptive

Although self-serving pride may help protect us from depression, it can at times be maladaptive. People who blame others for their social difficulties are often unhappier than people who can acknowledge their mistakes (C. A. Anderson & others, 1983; Newman & Langer, 1981; Peterson & others, 1981). Moreover, the most self-enhancing people often come across to others as egotistical, conde-scending, and deceitful (Colvin & others, 1995). In human history, expansive egos have marked genocidal dictators, White supremacists, and drunken spouse-abusers (Baumeister & others, 1996). When someone's inflated self-esteem is challenged by others' criticisms or taunts, the result is sometimes an abusive or murderous rage.

Research by Barry Schlenker (1976; Schlenker & Miller, 1977a, 1977b) has also shown how self-serving perceptions can poison a group. In nine experiments at the University of Florida, Schlenker had people work together on some task. He then falsely informed them that their group had done either well or poorly. In every one of these studies the members of successful groups claimed more responsibility for their group's performance than did members of groups that supposedly failed at the task. Most presented themselves as contributing more than the others in their group when the group did well; few said they con-tributed less.

Such self-deception can lead individual group members to expect greater than average rewards when their organization does well and less than average blame when it does not. If most individuals in a group believe they are underpaid and underappreciated relative to their contributions, disharmony and envy are likely. University presidents and academic deans will readily recognize the

"No one speaks of us in our presence as in our absence."

Pascal, *Pensées*, 1670

"Victory finds a hundred fathers but defeat is an orphan."

Count Galeazzo Ciano, *The Ciano Diaries*, 1938

phenomenon. Ninety percent or more of university faculty members rate themselves as superior to their average colleague (Blackburn & others, 1980; Cross, 1977). It is therefore inevitable that when merit salary raises are announced and half receive an average raise or less, many will feel themselves victims of injustice.

Self-serving biases also inflate people's judgments of their groups. When groups are comparable, most people consider their own group superior (Codol, 1976; Jourden & Heath, 1996; Taylor & Doria, 1981). Thus,

- most university sorority members perceive those in their sorority as far less likely to be conceited and snobby than those in other sororities (Biernat & others, 1996).
- 66 percent of parents give their oldest child's public schools a grade of A or B. But nearly as many—64 percent—give the public schools in general a grade of C or D (Whitman, 1996).
- 53 percent of Dutch adults rate their marriage or partnership as better than that of most others; only 1 percent rate it as worse than most (Buunk & van der Eijnden, 1997).
- most corporation presidents and production managers overpredict their own firms' productivity and growth (Kidd & Morgan, 1969; Larwood & Whittaker, 1977).

Self-serving pride in group settings can become especially dangerous.

"Then we're in agreement. There's nothing rotten here in Denmark. Something is rotten everywhere else."

© 1983, The New Yorker Magazine, Inc.

After just one brief conversation with a prospective employee, interviewers are prone to overconfidence in their intuitive judgments.

Such overoptimism sometimes goes before a fall. If those who deal in the stock market or in real estate perceive their business intuition to be superior to that of their competitors, they may be in for severe disappointment. Even the seventeenth-century economist Adam Smith, a defender of human economic rationality, foresaw that people would overestimate their chances of gain. This "absurd presumption in their own good fortune," he said, arises from "the overweening conceit which the greater part of men have of their own abilities" (Spiegel, 1971, p. 243).

That people see themselves with a favorable bias is hardly new—the tragic flaw portrayed in ancient Greek drama was *hubris*, or pride. Like the subjects of our experiments, the Greek tragic figures were not self-consciously evil; they merely thought too highly of themselves. In literature, the pitfalls of pride are portrayed again and again. In religion, pride has long been first among the "seven deadly sins."

If pride is akin to the self-serving bias, then what is humility? Is it self-contempt? Or can we be self-affirming and self-accepting without a self-serving bias? To paraphrase the English scholar-writer C. S. Lewis, humility is not handsome people trying to believe they are ugly and clever people trying to believe they are fools. False modesty can actually be a cover for pride in one's better-than-average humility. (James Friedrich [1996] reports that most students congratulate themselves on being better than average at not thinking themselves better than average!) True humility is more like self-forgetfulness than false modesty. It leaves people free to rejoice in their special talents and, with the same honesty, to recognize others.

> "Other men's sins are before our eyes; our own are behind our back."
>
> Seneca, *De Ira*, 43 A.D.

Summing up

Contrary to the presumption that most people suffer from low self-esteem or feelings of inferiority, researchers consistently find that most people exhibit a *self-serving bias*. In experiments and everyday life, we often blame failures on the situation while taking credit for successes. We typically rate ourselves as better than average on subjective, desirable traits and abilities. Believing in ourselves, we exhibit unrealistic optimism about our futures. And we overestimate the commonality of our opinions and foibles (*false consensus*) while underestimating the commonality of our abilities and virtues (*false uniqueness*). Such perceptions arise partly from a motive to maintain and enhance self-esteem, a motive that protects people from depression but contributes to misjudgment and group conflict.

Self-presentation

We humans seem motivated not only to perceive ourselves in self-enhancing ways but also to present ourselves to others in desired ways. How might our tactics of "impression management" lead to false modesty or to self-defeating behavior?

So far we have seen that the self is at the center of our social worlds, that self-esteem and self-efficacy pay dividends, and that self-serving pride biases self-evaluations. But are self-enhancing expressions always sincere? Do people privately feel as they publicly talk? Or will they put on a positive face even while living with self-doubt?

False modesty

There is indeed evidence that people sometimes present a different self than they feel. The clearest example, however, is not false pride but false modesty. Perhaps you have by now recalled times when someone was not self-praising but self-disparaging. Such put-downs can be subtly self-serving, for often they elicit reassuring "strokes." "I felt like a fool" may trigger a friend to reassure that "you did fine!" Even a remark such as "I wish I weren't so ugly" may elicit at least a "Come now. I know a couple of people who are uglier than you."

> "Humility is often but a trick whereby pride abases itself only to exalt itself later."
>
> La Rochefoucauld, *Maxims*, 1665

There is another reason people disparage themselves and praise others. Think of the coach who, before the big game, extols the opponent's strength. Is the coach utterly sincere? When coaches publicly exalt their opponents, they convey an image of modesty and good sportsmanship and set the stage for a favorable evaluation no matter what the outcome. A win becomes a praiseworthy achievement; a loss is attributable to the opponent's "great defense." Modesty, said the seventeenth-century philosopher Francis Bacon, is but one of the "arts of ostentation." Thus, Robert Gould, Paul Brounstein, and Harold Sigall (1977) found that, in a laboratory contest, their students similarly aggrandized their anticipated opponent, but only when the assessment was made publicly. Anonymously, they credited their future opponent with much less ability.

False modesty also appears in people's autobiographical accounts of their achievements. At awards ceremonies, honorees graciously thank others for their support. Upon receiving an Academy Award, Maureen Stapleton thanked "my family, my children, my friends, and everyone I have ever met in my entire life." Does such generous sharing of credit contradict the common finding that people readily attribute success to their own effort and competence?

To find out, Roy Baumeister and Stacey Ilko (1995) invited students to write a description of "an important success experience." Those whom they asked to sign their names and who anticipated reading their story to others often acknowledged the help or emotional support they had received. Those who wrote anonymously rarely made such mentions; rather, they portrayed themselves achieving their successes on their own. To Baumeister and Ilko, these results suggest "shallow gratitude"—superficial gratitude offered to *appear* humble, while "in the privacy of their own minds" the subjects credited themselves.

Self-handicapping

Sometimes people sabotage their chances for success by creating impediments that make success less likely. Far from being deliberately self-destructive, such behaviors typically have a self-protective aim (Arkin & others, 1986; Baumeister & Scher, 1988; Rhodewalt, 1987): "I'm really not a failure—I would have done well except for this problem."

Why would people handicap themselves with self-defeating behavior? Recall that we eagerly protect our self-images by attributing failures to external factors. Can you see why, *fearing failure*, people might handicap themselves by partying half the night before a job interview or playing video games instead of studying before a big exam? When self-image is tied up with performance, it can be more self-deflating to try hard and fail than to procrastinate and have a ready excuse. If we fail while working under a handicap, we can cling to a sense of competence; if we succeed under such conditions, it can only boost our self-image. Handicaps protect our self-esteem and public image by allowing us to attribute failures to something temporary or external ("I was feeling sick"; "I was out too late the night before") rather than to lack of talent or ability.

This analysis of **self-handicapping,** proposed by Steven Berglas and Edward Jones (1978), has been confirmed. One experiment was said to concern "drugs and intellectual performance." Imagine yourself in the position of their participants. You guess answers to some difficult aptitude questions and then are told, "Yours was one of the best scores seen to date!" Feeling incredibly lucky, you are then offered a choice between two drugs before answering more of these items. One drug will aid intellectual performance and the other will inhibit it. Which drug do you want? Most students wanted the drug that would supposedly disrupt their thinking and thus provide a handy excuse for anticipated poorer performance.

Researchers have documented other ways in which people self-handicap. Fearing failure, people will:

- Reduce their preparation for important individual athletic events (Rhodewalt & others, 1984)
- Give their opponent an advantage (Shepperd & Arkin, 1991)
- Report feeling depressed (Baumgardner, 1991)
- Perform poorly at the beginning of a task in order not to create unreachable expectations (Baumgardner & Brownlee, 1987)

self-handicapping protecting one's self-image with behaviors that create a handy excuse for later failure

"With no attempt there can be no failure; with no failure no humiliation."

William James, *Principles of Psychology,* 1890

After losing to some young rivals, tennis great Martina Navratilova confessed that she was "afraid to play my best. . . . I was scared to find out if they could beat me when I'm playing my best because if they can, then I am finished" (Frankel & Snyder, 1987).

self-presentation
the act of expressing oneself and behaving in ways designed to create a favorable impression or an impression that corresponds to one's ideals

self-monitoring
being attuned to the way one presents oneself in social situations and adjusting one's performance to create the desired impression

"Public opinion is always more tyrannical towards those who obviously fear it than towards those who feel indifferent to it."

Bertrand Russell,
The Conquest of Happiness,
1930

- Not try as hard as they could during a tough ego-involving task (Hormuth, 1986; Pyszczynski & Greenberg, 1983; Riggs, 1992; Turner & Pratkanis, 1993)

Impression management

Self-serving bias, false modesty, and self-handicapping reveal the depth of our concern for self-image. To varying degrees, we are continually managing the impressions we create. Whether we wish to impress, to intimidate, or to seem helpless, we are social animals, playing to an audience.

Self-presentation refers to our wanting to present a desired image both to an external audience (other people) and to an internal audience (ourselves). We work at managing the impressions we create. We excuse, justify, or apologize as necessary to shore up our self-esteem and verify our self-image (Schlenker & Weigold, 1992). In familiar situations, this happens without conscious effort. In unfamiliar situations, perhaps at a party with people we would like to impress or in conversation with someone of the other sex, we are acutely self-conscious of the impression we are creating and we are therefore less modest than when among friends who know us well (Leary & others, 1994; Tice & others, 1995). Preparing to present ourselves in a photograph, we may even try out different faces in a mirror.

No wonder, say self-presentation researchers, that people will self-handicap when failure might make them look bad (Arkin & Baumgardner, 1985). No wonder that people take health risks—tanning their skin with wrinkle- and cancer-causing radiation; becoming anorexic; failing to obtain and use condoms; yielding to peer pressures to smoke, get drunk, and do drugs (Leary & others, 1994). No wonder people express more modesty when their self-flattery is vulnerable to being debunked, perhaps by experts who will be scrutinizing their self-evaluations (Arkin & others, 1980; Riess & others, 1981; Weary & others, 1982). Professor Smith will express less confidence in the significance of her work when presenting it to professional colleagues than when presenting to students.

For some people, conscious self-presentation is a way of life. By continually monitoring their own behavior and noting how others react, they adjust their social performance when it's not having the desired effect. Those who score high on a scale of **self-monitoring** tendency (who, for example, agree that "I tend to be what people expect me to be") act like social chameleons—they adjust their behavior in response to external situations (Snyder, 1987). Having attuned their behavior to the situation, they are more likely to espouse an attitude they don't really hold (Zanna & Olson, 1982). Being conscious of others, they are less likely to act on their own attitudes. For high self-monitors, attitudes, therefore, serve a social adjustment function; they help these people adapt to new jobs, roles, and relationships (Snyder & DeBono, 1989; Snyder & Copeland, 1989).

Those who score low in self-monitoring care less about what others think. They are more internally guided and thus more likely to talk and act as they feel and believe (McCann & Hancock, 1983). Thus, when low self-monitoring British university women answered questions about their gender-related attitudes, it mattered not when the female interviewer dressed and acted in a feminine guise (Smith & others, 1997). (High self-monitoring women presented a much more feminine self to the feminine interviewer.) Most of us fall somewhere

Dance class in a Tokyo kindergarten. In Asian countries, self-presentation is restrained. Children learn to identify themselves with their groups.

between the high self-monitoring extreme of the con artist and the low self-monitoring extreme of stubborn insensitivity to others.

Presenting oneself in ways that create a desired impression is a very delicate matter. People want to be seen as able, but also as modest and honest (Carlston & Shovar, 1983). Modesty creates a good impression, and unsolicited boasting creates a bad impression (Forsyth & others, 1981; Holtgraves & Srull, 1989; Schlenker & Leary, 1982). Thus, the false modesty phenomenon: We often display *less* self-esteem than we privately feel (Miller & Schlenker, 1985). But when we have obviously done extremely well, false disclaimers ("I did well, but it's no big deal") may come across as feigned humility. To make good impressions—as modest yet competent—requires social skill.

The tendency to self-present modesty and restrained optimism is especially great in cultures that value self-restraint, such as those of China and Japan (Heine & Lehman, 1995, 1997; Lee & Seligman, 1997; Markus & Kitayama, 1991; Wu & Tseng, 1985). In China and Japan, people exhibit less self-serving bias. Children learn to share credit for success and accept responsibility for failures. In Western countries, children learn to feel pride in success while attributing failure to the situation. The result, reports Philip Zimbardo (1993), is greater modesty and shyness among the Japanese.

Despite such self-presentational concerns, people worldwide privately are self-enhancing. Self-serving bias has been noted among Dutch high school and university students, Belgian basketball players, Indian Hindus, Japanese drivers, Israeli and Singaporean schoolchildren, Australian students and workers, Chinese students, Hong Kong sports writers, and French people of all ages (Codol, 1976; de Vries & van Knippenberg, 1987; Falbo & others, 1997; Feather, 1983; Hagiwara, 1983; Hallahan & others, 1997; Jain, 1990; Liebrand & others, 1986; Lefebvre, 1979; Murphy-Berman & Sharma, 1986; and Ruzzene & Noller, 1986, respectively).

> "It is not, therefore, necessary for a prince to have all the desirability qualities . . . but it is very necessary to seem to have them."
>
> Niccolo Machiavelli, 1469–1527

> "If an American is hit on the head by a ball at the ballpark, he sues. If a Japanese person is hit on the head he says, 'It's my honor. It's my fault. I shouldn't have been standing there.'"
>
> Japanese bar-association official Koji Yanase, explaining why there are half as many lawyers in his country as in the Greater Washington area alone, *Newsweek*, February 26, 1996

Summing up

As social animals, we adjust our words and actions to suit our audiences. To varying degrees, we *self-monitor*; we note our performance and adjust it to create a desired impression. Such *impression management* tactics explain examples of false modesty, in which people put themselves down, extol future competitors, or publicly credit others when privately they credit themselves. Sometimes people will even *self-handicap* with self-defeating behaviors that protect self-esteem by providing excuses for failure.

Personal postscript: Twin truths—The perils of pride, the power of positive thinking

The truth concerning *self-efficacy* encourages us not to resign ourselves to bad situations, to persist despite initial failures, to exert effort without being overly distracted by self-doubts. High self-esteem is likewise adaptive. When we believe in our positive possibilities, we are less vulnerable to depression and we increase our chances for success.

The truth concerning illusory optimism and other forms of *self-serving bias* reminds us that self-efficacy is not the whole story of the self in a social world. If positive thinking can accomplish anything, then if we are unhappily married, poor, or depressed we have only ourselves to blame. For shame! If only we had tried harder, been more disciplined, less stupid. Failing to appreciate that difficulties sometimes reflect the oppressive power of social situations can tempt us to blame people for their problems and failures, or even to blame ourselves too harshly for our own. Life's greatest achievements, but also its greatest disappointments, are born of the highest expectations.

These twin truths remind me of what Pascal taught 300 years ago: No single truth is ever sufficient, because the world is complex. Any truth, separated from its complementary truth, is a half-truth.

chapter 3

Social Beliefs
and Judgments

d riving out the back entrance of the Ritz Hotel on that August 1997, night, Henri Paul soon was on a Paris highway alongside the River Seine. With his passengers, Princess Diana, Dodi Fayed, and their bodyguard, he sped faster and faster as he dipped into a tunnel. With the car careening out of control, he suddenly smashed head-on into a pillar, leaving their Mercedes a crumpled wreck and killing himself and his two illustrious passengers.

In the weeks that followed there were endless analyses and debates. To what should the crash be attributed? To the driver and his alcohol intake earlier that evening? To the situation, especially the paparazzi photographers buzzing the car and shooting their flash guns? "I am disgusted and nauseated," said the anchor of French television's main evening news program, comparing the paparazzi to "rats." But the popular press responded with outrage at this explanation: "The driver was totally drunk and that is the essence of the story," said one newspaper editor.

In the summer of 1972, Canada played a landmark hockey series with the former Soviet Union. The Canadian team was made up of veterans who had all played for years in the physical National Hockey League (NHL). The Soviet team played in a style that was less physical and demanded precision passing.

After the fourth game in the series the Soviet media roundly criticized the "goons" from Canada who, from their perspective, were dirty players using brute force when confronted with the superior skill of the Soviets. From this point in the series the officiating was much tighter, with most of the penalties going against Canada. The Canadian media saw the change in officiating as the Soviets' attempt to steal the series—the Soviets had picked the referees.

Was the media in each country right to attribute the players' and referees' actions to evil intent? Or was each act an understandable response to the situation? Was the Canadians' style of play shaped by years in the NHL? Were the referees simply trying to keep the contest under control?

As these cases illustrate, our judgments of what people and nations do depend on how we explain their behavior. Depending on our explanation, we may judge killing someone as murder, manslaughter, self-defense, or patriotism. Depending on our explanation, we may view a homeless person as indolent or as victimized by job and welfare cutbacks. Depending on our explanation, we may attribute friendliness toward us as reflecting affection or ingratiation.

Our explanations matter: Our conclusions about why people act as they do determine our reactions to others and our decisions regarding them.

Explaining others

People make it their business to explain other people, and social psychologists make it their business to explain people's explanations. So, how—and how accurately—do people explain others' behavior? Attribution theory suggests some answers.

The car and airplane tragedies illustrate a question we face daily. In trying to understand people, we wonder *why* they act that way. The human mind wants to make sense of its world. If worker productivity declines, do we assume the workers are getting lazier? Or has their equipment become less efficient? Does a young boy who hits his classmates have a hostile personality? Or is he responding to relentless teasing? When a salesperson says, "That outfit really looks nice on you," does this reflect genuine feeling? Or is it a sales ploy?

Attributing causality: To the person or the situation?

We endlessly analyze and discuss why things happen as they do, especially when something negative or unexpected occurs (Bohner & others, 1988; Weiner, 1985). Amy Holtzworth-Munroe and Neil Jacobson (1985, 1988) report that mar-

In 1998 Former Nova Scotia premier Gerald Regan was tried for eight sex-related charges dating back to the 1950s. The jury had to decide whether to believe his explanation of his actions over that of the woman accusing him.

ried people often analyze their partners' behaviors, especially their negative behaviors. Cold hostility is more likely than a warm hug to leave the partner wondering "why?" Spouses' answers correlate with their marriage satisfaction. Those in unhappy relationships typically offer distress-maintaining explanations for negative acts ("she was late because she doesn't care about me"). Happy couples more often externalize negative acts ("she was late because of heavy traffic"). With positive partner behavior their explanations again work to maintain distress ("he brought me flowers because he wants sex") or to enhance the relationship ("he brought me flowers to show he loves me") (Gelinas & other, 1995; Hewstone & Fincham, 1996; Weiner, 1995).

Antonia Abbey (1987, 1991) and her colleagues have repeatedly found that men are more likely than women to attribute a woman's friendliness to mild sexual interest. This misreading of warmth as a sexual come-on (called "misattribution") can lead to behavior that women regard as sexual harassment (Johnson & others, 1991; Pryor & others, 1997; Saal & others, 1989). This misreading is especially likely when men are in positions of power. The boss may misinterpret a subordinate woman's submissive or friendly behavior and, full of himself, may see women only in sexual terms (Bargh & Raymond, 1995).

Such misattributions help explain the greater sexual assertiveness exhibited by men across the world (Kenrick & Trost, 1987) and the greater tendency of men in various cultures, from Toronto to Tokyo, to justify rape by blaming the victim's behavior (Kanekar & Nazareth, 1988; Muehlenhard, 1988; Shotland, 1989). Misattributions also help explain why the 23 percent of women who say they have been forced into unwanted sexual behavior is eight times the

To what should we attribute this student's sleepiness? To lack of sleep? To boredom? Whether we make internal or external attributions depends on whether we notice him consistently sleeping in this and other classes, and on whether other students react as he does to this particular class.

3 percent of men who say they have ever forced a woman into a sexual act (Laumann & others, 1994). Sexually aggressive men are especially likely to misread women's communications (Malamuth & Brown, 1994). They "just don't get it."

attribution theory
the theory of how people explain others' behavior—for example, by attributing it either to internal dispositions (enduring traits, motives, and attitudes) or to external situations

Attribution theory analyzes how we explain people's behavior. The variations of attribution theory share some common assumptions. As Daniel Gilbert and Patrick Malone (1995) explain, each "construes the human skin as a special boundary that separates one set of 'causal forces' from another. On the sunny side of the epidermis are the external or situational forces that press inward upon the person, and on the meaty side are the internal or personal forces that exert pressure outward. Sometimes these forces press in conjunction, sometimes in opposition, and their dynamic interplay manifests itself as observable behavior."

Fritz Heider (1958), widely regarded as attribution theory's originator, analyzed the "commonsense psychology" by which people explain everyday events. Heider concluded that people tend to attribute someone's behavior to *internal* causes (for example, the person's disposition) or *external* causes (for example, something about the person's situation). A teacher may wonder whether a child's underachievement is due to lack of motivation and ability (a "dispositional attribution") or to physical and social circumstances (a "situational attribution").

This distinction between internal (dispositional) and external (situational) causes often blurs, because external situations produce internal changes (White, 1991). To say a schoolchild "is fearful" may be a short semantic leap from saying "School frightens the child." Moreover, situations act upon dispositions. So we shouldn't think that dispositional and situational influences are separate factors

"So! If it's good, it's Mister Coffee. If it's bad, it's me."

We tend to attribute someone's behavior or the outcome of an event either to internal (dispositional) or external (situational) causes.

that sum to 100 percent. Nevertheless, social psychologists have discovered that we often attribute the behavior of others *either* to their dispositions *or* to the situation. For example, one study (Sedikides & Anderson, 1991) found that when people made dispositional attributions they were unlikely to make situational attributions. The converse was true as well, when people made situational attributions they were unlikely to make dispositional attributions.

Inferring traits

Edward Jones and Keith Davis (1965) noted that we often infer that other people's intentions and dispositions *correspond* to their actions. If I observe Rick making a sarcastic comment to Linda, I infer that Rick is a hostile person. Jones and Davis's "theory of correspondent inferences" specifies the conditions under which such attributions are most likely. For example, normal or expected behavior tells us less about the person than does unusual behavior. If Rick is sarcastic in a job interview, where a person would normally be pleasant, this tells us more about Rick than if he is sarcastic about his new car just having been dented in a parking lot.

The ease with which we infer traits is remarkable. In one set of experiments James Uleman (1989) gave students statements to remember, like "The librarian carries the old woman's groceries across the street." The students would instantly, unintentionally, and unconsciously infer a trait. When later they were helped to recall the sentence, the most valuable clue word was not "books" (to cue librarian) or "bags" (to cue groceries) but "helpful"—the inferred trait that I suspect you, too, spontaneously attributed to the librarian.

figure 3–1

Harold Kelley's theory of attributions.

Three factors—consistency, distinctiveness, and consensus—influence whether we attribute someone's behavior to internal or external causes.

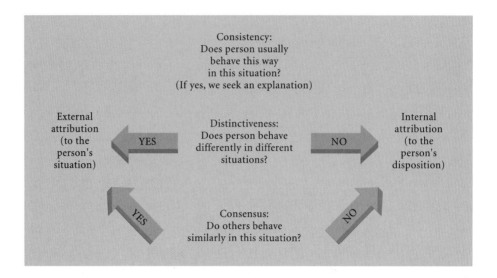

First impressions matter, for they can color later information and judgments.

Commonsense attributions

As these examples suggest, attributions often are rational. In testimony to the reasonable ways in which we explain behavior, attribution theorist Harold Kelley (1973) described how we use information about "consistency," "distinctiveness," and "consensus" (Figure 3–1). When explaining why Edgar is having trouble with his XYZ computer, most people appropriately use information concerning *consistency* (Is Edgar usually unable to get his computer to work?), *distinctiveness* (Does Edgar have trouble with other computers, or only the XYZ?), and *consensus* (Do other people have similar problems with the XYZ?). If we learn that Edgar alone consistently has trouble with this and other computers, we likely will attribute the troubles to Edgar, not to defects in the XYZ.

So our commonsense psychology often explains behavior logically. But Kelley also found that in everyday explanations, people often discount a contributing cause of behavior if other plausible causes are already known. If I can specify one or two reasons a student might have done poorly on an exam, I may ignore or discount other possibilities.

Information integration

Further evidence of the reasonableness of our social judgments comes from research on information integration. Norman Anderson (1968, 1974) and his collaborators discerned some rules by which we combine different pieces of information about a person into an overall impression. Suppose that you have an upcoming blind date with someone described as intelligent, daring, lazy, and sincere. Research on how people combine such information suggests that you would likely weight each item of information according to its importance. If you consider sincerity especially important, you will give it more weight. If you are like the participants in experiments by Solomon Asch (1946), Bert Hodges (1974), and Roos Vonk (1993), you may also give extra weight to information that comes first, and you may be more sensitive to negative information.

First impressions can color your interpretation of later information. Having been told that someone is "intelligent," you may then interpret the person's being "daring" as meaning courageous rather than reckless. Negative information, such as "she is dishonest," also has extra potency, perhaps because it is more unusual. Once you have interpreted and weighed each piece of information, you then use your mental algebra to integrate the different items. The result is your overall impression of your "blind" date.

The fundamental attribution error

As later chapters will reveal, social psychology's most important lesson concerns how much we are affected by our social environment. At any moment, our internal state, and therefore what we say and do, depends on the situation, as well as on what we bring to the situation. In experiments, a slight difference between two situations sometimes greatly affects how people respond. I have seen this when teaching classes at both 8:30 A.M. and 7:00 P.M. Silent stares would greet me at 8:30; at 7:00 I had to break up a party. In each situation some individuals were more talkative than others, but the difference between the two situations exceeded the individual differences.

Attribution researchers have found that we often fail to appreciate this important lesson. When explaining someone's behavior, we underestimate the impact of the situation and overestimate the extent to which it reflects the individual's traits and attitudes. Thus, even knowing the effect of the time of day on classroom conversation, I found it terribly tempting to assume that the people in the 7:00 P.M. class were more extraverted than the "silent types" who come at 8:30 A.M.

This discounting of the situation, dubbed by Lee Ross (1977) the **fundamental attribution error**, appears in many experiments. In the first such study, Edward Jones and Victor Harris (1967) had students read debaters' speeches supporting or attacking Cuba's leader, Fidel Castro. When the position taken was said to have been chosen by the debater, the students logically enough assumed it reflected the person's own attitude. But what happened when the students were told that the debate coach had

fundamental attribution error The tendency for observers to underestimate situational influences and overestimate dispositional influences upon others' behavior. (Also called *correspondence bias*, because we so often see behavior as corresponding to a disposition.)

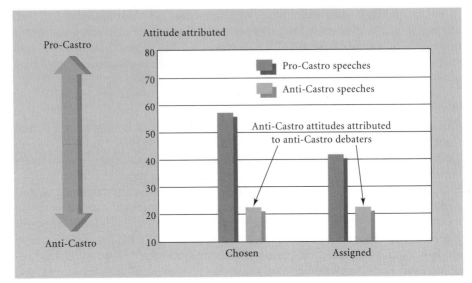

figure 3–2

The fundamental attribution error.

When people read a debate speech supporting or attacking Fidel Castro, they attributed corresponding attitudes to the speech writer, even when the debate coach assigned the writer's position.

(Data from Jones & Harris, 1967.)

assigned the position? People write stronger statements than you'd expect from those feigning a position they don't hold (Allison & others, 1993; Miller & others, 1990). Thus, even knowing that the debater had been told to take a pro-Castro position did not prevent students' inferring that the debater in fact had some pro-Castro leanings (Figure 3–2). People seemed to think, "Yeah, I know he was assigned that position, but to some extent I think he really believes it."

Peter Ditto and his colleagues (1997) replicated the phenomenon when they asked men to meet a woman who was actually working for the experimenters. The woman wrote her supposed impressions of each man, who was then to guess how much she liked him. When she wrote only negative statements, the men discounted her criticisms when told she was under orders to be negative. But when the woman wrote only positive impressions, the typical man inferred she *really* liked him—and it didn't matter whether he believed she did so freely or was under orders to be positive. The fundamental attribution error looms large when it serves our self-interest.

The error is so irresistible that even when people know they are causing someone else's behavior, they still underestimate external influences. If subjects dictate an opinion that someone else must then express, they still tend to see the person as actually holding that opinion (Gilbert & Jones, 1986). If subjects are asked to be either self-enhancing or self-deprecating during an interview, they are very aware of why they are acting so. But they are *un*aware of their effect on another person. If Juan acts modestly, his naive partner Bob is likely to exhibit modesty as well. Juan will easily understand his own behavior, but he will think that poor Bob suffers low self-esteem (Baumeister & others, 1988). In short, we tend to presume that others *are* the way they act. Observing Cinderella cowering in her oppressive home, people infer she is meek; dancing with her at the ball, the prince sees a suave and glamorous person.

We commit the fundamental attribution error when explaining *other people's* behavior. We often explain our own behavior in terms of the situation while holding others responsible for their behavior. So John might attribute his behavior to the situation ("I was angry because everything was going wrong"), while Alice might think, "John was hostile because he is an angry person." When referring to ourselves, we typically use verbs that describe our actions and reactions ("I get annoyed when . . ."). Referring to someone else, we more often describe what that person *is* ("He is nasty") (Fiedler & others, 1991; McGuire & McGuire, 1986; White & Younger, 1988).

The fundamental attribution error in everyday life

If we know the checkout cashier is programmed to say, "Thank you and have a nice day," do we nevertheless automatically conclude that the cashier is a friendly, grateful person? We certainly know how to discount behavior that we attribute to ulterior motives (Fein & others, 1990). Yet consider what happened when students talked with a supposed clinical psychology graduate student who acted either warm and friendly or aloof and critical. Researchers David Napolitan and George Goethals (1979) told half the students beforehand that her behavior would be spontaneous. They told the other half that for purposes of the experiment she had been instructed to feign friendly (or unfriendly) behavior. The effect of the information? None. If she acted friendly, they assumed she was really a friendly person; if she acted unfriendly, they assumed she was an unfriendly person. As when viewing a dummy on the ventriloquist's lap or a movie actor playing a "good-guy" or "bad-guy" role, we find it difficult to escape the illusion that the programmed behavior reflects an inner disposition. Perhaps this is why Leonard Nimoy, who played Mr. Spock on the original *Star Trek*, entitled his book *I Am Not Spock*.

The discounting of social constraints was further revealed in a thought-provoking experiment by Lee Ross and his collaborators (Ross & others, 1977). The experiment re-created Ross's firsthand experience of moving from graduate student to professor. His doctoral oral exam had proved a humbling experience as his apparently brilliant professors quizzed him on topics they specialized in. Six months later, *Dr.* Ross was himself an examiner, now able to ask penetrating questions on *his* favorite topics. Ross's hapless student later confessed to feeling exactly as Ross had a half year before—dissatisfied with his ignorance and impressed with the apparent brilliance of the examiners.

In the experiment, with Teresa Amabile and Julia Steinmetz, Ross set up a simulated quiz game. He randomly assigned some students to play the role of questioner, some to play the role of contestant, and others to observe. The researchers invited the questioners to make up difficult questions that would demonstrate their wealth of knowledge. It's fun to imagine the questions: "Where is Bainbridge Island?" "What is the seventh book in the Old Testament?" "Which has the longer coastline, Europe or Africa?" If even these

People often attribute keen intelligence to those, such as Alex Trebek of Jeopardy, *who test others' knowledge.*

figure 3–3

Both contestants and observers of a simulated quiz game assumed that a person who had been randomly assigned the role of questioner was far more knowledgeable than the contestant. Actually the assigned roles of questioner and contestant simply made the questioner seem more knowledgeable. The failure to appreciate this illustrates the fundamental attribution error. (Data from Ross, Amabile, & Steinmetz, 1977.)

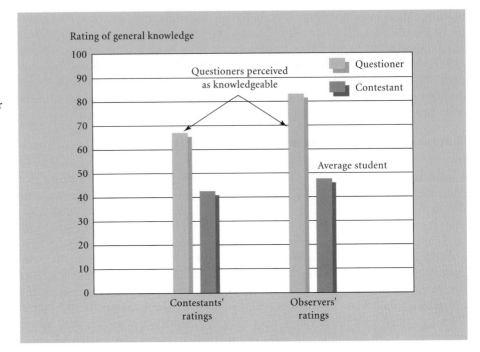

few questions have you feeling a little uninformed, then you will appreciate the results of this experiment.*

Everyone had to know that the questioner would have the advantage. Yet both contestants and observers (but not the questioners) came to the erroneous conclusion that the questioners *really were* more knowledgeable than the contestants (Figure 3–3). Follow-up research shows that these misimpressions are hardly a reflection of low social intelligence. If anything, intelligent and socially competent people are *more* likely to make the attribution error (Block & Funder, 1986).

In real life, those with social power usually initiate and control conversation, which often leads underlings to overestimate their knowledge and intelligence. Medical doctors, for example, are often presumed to be experts on all sorts of questions unrelated to medicine. Similarly, students often overestimate the brilliance of their teachers. (As in the experiment, teachers are questioners on subjects of their special expertise.) When some of these students later become teachers, they are usually amazed to discover that teachers are not so brilliant after all.

To illustrate the fundamental attribution error, most of us need look no further than our own experience. Determined to make some new friends, Bev plasters a smile on her face and anxiously plunges into a party. Everyone else seems quite relaxed and happy as they laugh and talk with one another. Bev wonders to herself, "Why is everyone always so at ease in groups like this while I'm feeling shy and tense?" Actually, everyone else is feeling nervous, too, and making

---

*Bainbridge Island is across Puget Sound from Seattle. The seventh Old Testament book is Judges. Although the African continent is more than double the area of Europe, Europe's coastline is longer. (It is more convoluted, with lots of harbors and inlets, a geographical fact that contributed to its role in the history of maritime trade.)

the same attribution error in assuming that Bev and the others *are* as they *appear*—confidently convivial.

Attributions of responsibility are at the heart of many judicial decisions (Fincham & Jaspars, 1980). When Karla Homolka was accused of the murder of her sister and two other young girls, her lawyers argued that she was an unwilling participant in these crimes, a battered wife at the mercy of her husband Paul Berndardo. The crown attorneys took this into account and agreed to a deal that only required Homolka to spend twelve years in prison. Victims' advocates have decried this decision claiming that she deserved a far greater punishment. The case exemplifies many judicial controversies: The prosecution argues, "You are to blame, for you could have done otherwise"; the defendant replies, "It wasn't my fault; I was a victim of the situation" or "Under the circumstance I did no wrong."

Why do we make the attribution error?

So far we have seen a bias in the way we explain other people's behavior: We often ignore powerful situational determinants. Why do we tend to underestimate the situational determinants of others' behavior but not of our own?

Perspective and situational awareness

An actor-observer difference. Attribution theorists point out that we have a different perspective when observing others than when acting (Jones & Nisbett, 1971; Jones, 1976). When we act, the environment commands our attention. When we watch another person act, that *person* occupies the center of our attention and the situation becomes relatively invisible. To use the perceptual analogy of figure and ground, the person is the figure that stands out from the surrounding environmental ground. So the person seems to cause whatever happens. If this theory is true, what might we expect if the perspectives were reversed? What if we could see ourselves as others see us and if we saw the world through their eyes? Shouldn't this eliminate or reverse the typical attribution error?

See if you can predict the result of a clever experiment conducted by Michael Storms (1973). Picture yourself as a subject in Storms's experiment. You are seated facing another student with whom you are to talk for a few minutes. Beside you is a TV camera that shares your view of the other student. Facing you from alongside the other student are an observer and another TV camera. Afterward, both you and the observer judge whether your behavior was caused more by your personal characteristics or by the situation.

Question: Which of you—subject or observer—will attribute the least importance to the situation? Storms found it was the observer (another demonstration of the fundamental attribution tendency). What if we reverse points of view by having you and the observer each watch the videotape recorded from the other's perspective? (You now view yourself, while the observer views what you saw.) This reverses the attributions: The observer now attributes your behavior mostly to the situation you faced, while you now attribute it to your person. *Remembering* an experience from an observer's perspective—by "seeing" oneself from the outside—has the same effect (Frank & Gilovich, 1989).

In another experiment, people viewed a videotape of a suspect confessing during a police interview. If they viewed the confession through a camera focused on the suspect, they perceived the confession as genuine. If they viewed it through a camera focused on the detective, they perceived it as more coerced

(Lassiter & Irvine, 1986). In courtrooms, most confession videotapes focus on the confessor. As we might expect, note Daniel Lassiter and Kimberly Dudley (1991), such tapes yield a nearly 100 percent conviction rate when played by prosecutors. Perhaps a more impartial videotape would show both interrogator and suspect.

Perspectives change with time. As the once-visible person recedes in their memory, observers often give more and more credit to the situation. Immediately after hearing someone argue an assigned position, people assume that's how the person really felt. A week later they are much more likely to credit the situational constraints (Burger, 1991). The day after a major election, Jerry Burger and Julie Pavelich (1994) asked voters why the election turned out the way it did. Most attributed the outcome to the candidates' personal traits and positions (the winner was likeable; the loser had poor ideas). When they asked the same voters the same question a year later, only a third attributed the verdict to the candidates. More people now credited the circumstances, such as the mood of the electorate and the nature of the economy.

Burger and Pavelich (1994) found that newspaper editorials on elections show the same increase in situational explanations with time. Right after the election, pundits focused on the campaigns and personalities of the candidates. Two years later, however, they focused on social trends, shifts in voting patterns, and political crises. It seems that at first we see people as the primary causes of an event, but in time we come to appreciate the role played by the situation.

Circumstances can also shift our perspective on ourselves. Seeing ourselves on television redirects our attention to ourselves. Seeing ourselves in a mirror, hearing our tape-recorded voices, having our pictures taken, filling out biographical questionnaires similarly focus our attention inward, making us *self-*conscious instead of *situation*-conscious.

Self-awareness. Robert Wicklund, Shelley Duval, and their collaborators have explored the effects of becoming **self-aware** (Duval & Wicklund, 1972; Wicklund, 1979, 1982). When our attention focuses upon ourselves, we attribute more responsibility to ourselves. Allan Fenigstein and Charles Carver (1978) demonstrated this by having students imagine themselves in hypothetical situations. Those who were made self-conscious by thinking they were hearing their own heartbeats while pondering the situation saw themselves as more responsible for the imaginary outcome than did those who thought they were just hearing extraneous noises.

Some people are typically quite self-conscious. In experiments, people who report themselves as privately self-conscious (who agree with statements such as "I'm generally attentive to my inner feelings") behave similarly to people whose attention has been self-focused with a mirror (Carver & Scheier, 1978). Thus, people whose attention focuses on themselves—either briefly during an experiment or because they are self-conscious persons—view themselves more as observers typically do; they attribute their behavior more to internal factors and less to the situation.

All these experiments point to a reason for the attribution error: *We find causes where we look for them.* To see this in your own experience, consider: Would you say your social psychology instructor is a quiet or a talkative person?

My guess is you inferred that he or she is fairly outgoing. But consider the situation further: Your attention focuses on your instructor while he or she

self-awareness
A self-conscious state in which attention focuses on oneself. It makes people more sensitive to their own attitudes and dispositions

behaves in a public context that demands speaking. The instructor also observes his or her own behavior in many different situations—in the classroom, in meetings, at home. "Me talkative?" your instructor might say. "Well, it all depends on the situation. When I'm in class or with good friends, I'm rather outgoing. But at conventions and in unfamiliar situations I feel and act rather shy."

If we are acutely aware of how our behavior varies with the situation, we should also see ourselves as more variable than other people. And that is precisely what studies in Canada, the United States, and Germany have found (Baxter & Goldberg, 1987; Kammer, 1982; Sande & others, 1988). Moreover, the less opportunity we have to observe people's behavior in context, the more we attribute to their personalities. Thomas Gilovich (1987) explored this by showing people a videotape of someone and then having them describe the person's actions to other people. The secondhand impressions were more extreme, partly because retellings focus attention on the person rather than on the situation (Baron & others, 1997). Similarly, people's impressions of someone they have heard about from a friend are typically more extreme than their friend's firsthand impressions (Prager & Cutler, 1990).

Culture differences

Cultures also influence the attribution error (Ickes, 1980; Watson, 1982). A Western worldview predisposes people to assume that people, not situations, cause events. Jerald Jellison and Jane Green (1981) reported that among University of Southern California students, internal explanations are more socially approved. "You can do it!" we are assured by the pop psychology of positive-thinking Western culture.

The assumption here is that, with the right disposition and attitude, anyone can surmount almost any problem: You get what you deserve and deserve what you get. Thus we often explain bad behavior by labeling the person as "sick," "lazy," or "sadistic." As children grow up in Western culture, they increasingly

behind the scenes

Once upon a time there was a boy who loved nothing more than hearing and telling stories about people. So it seemed quite natural that the boy should grow up to become a writer. By the time he was 20, he had dropped out of school and published many stories. One day he decided to take a psychology course at a local college—just to see what all the fuss was about—and within a few months he knew he would rather spend his life understanding people than inventing them.

In making the switch from writing science fiction to researching science fact, I've been puzzled about one thing. We all know that we can be cajoled and bribed and threatened and embarrassed into being polite to those we dislike, or unkind to those we adore. Our actions needn't mirror our private attitudes. Yet we seem quite willing to take *other people's* actions at face value. How can we realize something about ourselves and ignore it when understanding others? Aided by our experiments, we are seeking to explain when and why people believe that others are as they act.

Daniel T. Gilbert
University of Texas

The fundamental attribution error: People are biased to assume that people's behavior corresponds to their inner dispositions. Such assumptions are sometimes, but not always, correct. Some weekend bikers are weekday professionals.

explain behavior in terms of the other's personal characteristics (Rholes & others, 1990; Ross, 1981). As a first-grader, one of my sons brought home an example. He unscrambled the words "gate the sleeve caught Tom on his" into "The gate caught Tom on his sleeve." His teacher, applying the Western cultural assumptions of the curriculum materials, marked this wrong. The "right" answer located the cause within Tom: "Tom caught his sleeve on the gate."

Some languages promote external attributions. Instead of "I was late," Spanish idiom allows one to say, "The clock caused me to be late." In collectivist cultures, people less often perceive others in terms of personal dispositions (Lee & others, 1996; Zebrowitz-McArthur, 1988). They are less likely to spontaneously interpret a behavior as reflecting an inner trait (Newman, 1993). When told of someone's actions, people from India are less likely than U.S. students to offer dispositional explanations ("She is kind") and more likely to offer situational explanations ("Her friends were with her") (Miller, 1984).

How fundamental is the fundamental attribution error?

Like most provocative ideas, the presumption that we're all prone to a fundamental attribution error has its critics. Granted, say some, there is an attribution *bias*. But in any given instance, this may or may not produce an "error," just as parents who are biased to believe their child does not use drugs may or may not be correct (Harvey & others, 1981). We can be biased to believe what is true. Moreover, some everyday circumstances, such as being in church or on a job interview, are like the experiments we have been considering: As actors realize better than observers, the circumstances involve clear constraints. Hence the attribution error. But in other settings—in one's room, at a park—people exhibit their individuality. In such settings, people may see their own behavior as *less* constrained than do observers (Monson & Snyder, 1977; Quattrone, 1982; Robins & others, 1996). So it's an overstatement to say that at all times and in all

THATCH by Jeff Shesol

settings observers underestimate situational influences. For this reason, many social psychologists follow Edward Jones in referring to the fundamental attribution error—seeing behavior as corresponding to an inner disposition—as the *correspondence bias.*

Nevertheless, experiments reveal that the bias occurs even when we are aware of the situational forces—when we know that an assigned debate position is not a good basis for inferring someone's real attitudes (Croxton & Morrow, 1984; Croxton & Miller, 1987; Reeder & others, 1989) or that the questioners' role in the quiz game gives the questioners an advantage (Johnson & others, 1984). It is sobering to think that you and I can know about a social process that distorts our thinking and still be susceptible to it. Perhaps that's because it takes more mental effort to assess social effects on someone's behavior than merely to attribute it to a disposition (Gilbert & others, 1988, 1992; Webster, 1993). It's as if the busy person thinks, "This isn't a very good basis for making a judgment, but it's easy and all I've got time to look at."

In many ways, this is adaptive (psychologists generally assume that even our biases serve a purpose, or else nature would have rejected rather than selected those who exhibit them). Attributing behavior to dispositions rather than to situations is not only efficient, it often does little harm. For one thing, our dispositions often lead us to choose our situations. If bankers dress conservatively, note Daniel Gilbert and Patrick Malone (1995), that may reflect not only their profession's demands but also the conservative person's choice of a profession. Assume that the banker really is more conservative than the artist and you are likely right. Some situations really are of our own making. Moreover, when we experience people only in a single role—as a banker, teacher, or grandmother— we can predict their behavior equally well whether attributing it to their role or to their disposition. It's only when we experience a person in a new situation that our disposition-based predictions may go astray. And remember: Even when it is logically incorrect, assuming an internal locus of control may gain us the psychological dividends of self-efficacy noted in Chapter 2.

The attribution error is, however, *fundamental* because it colors our explanations in basic and important ways. Researchers in Britain, India, Australia, and the United States have found, for example, that people's attributions predict their attitudes toward the poor and unemployed (Feather, 1983; Furnham, 1982; Pandey & others, 1982; Wagstaff, 1983; Zucker & Weiner, 1993). Those who attribute poverty and unemployment to personal dispositions ("They're just

figure 3–4

Attributions and reactions.

How we explain someone's negative behavior determines how we feel about it.

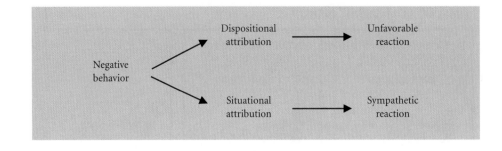

"Most poor people are not lazy. . . . They catch the early bus. . . . They raise other people's children. . . . They clean the streets. No, no, they're not lazy."

The Reverend Jesse Jackson, address to the Democratic National Convention, July 1988

lazy and undeserving") tend to adopt political positions unsympathetic to such people (Figure 3–4). Their views differ from those who make external attributions ("If you or I were to live with the same overcrowding, poor education, and discrimination, would we be any better off?"). French investigators Jean-Leon Beauvois and Nicole Dubois (1988) report that "relatively privileged" middle-class people are more likely than less advantaged people to assume that people's behaviors have internal explanations. (Those who have made it tend to assume that you get what you deserve.

After describing the toxic effects of growing up in an oppressive crime-laden neighborhoods, Jonathan Kozol (1995, p. 163) noted that some people, making dispositional attributions, think the crime problem could be solved by weeding out the relatively few bad people. If we'd incarcerate the bad apples, the many more good ones could thrive. But Kozol doubts it, because there would remain a "market of tormented people who need drugs, or think they do, to face the pain of living. . . . Where, then, would the 'weeding' process stop? how many boys—and girls too, for that matter—would we ultimately need to 'weed out' from the poisoned fields before we end up with a happy ghetto?"

Can we benefit from being aware of the attribution error? I once assisted with some interviews for a faculty position. One candidate was interviewed by six of us at once; each of us had the opportunity to ask two or three questions. I came away thinking, "What a stiff, awkward person he is." The second candidate I met privately over coffee, and we immediately discovered we had a close, mutual friend. As we talked, I became increasingly impressed by what a "warm, engaging, stimulating person she is." Only later did I remember the fundamental attribution error and reassess my analysis. I had attributed his stiffness and her warmth to their dispositions; in fact, I later realized, such behavior resulted partly from the difference in their interview situations. Had I viewed these interactions through their eyes instead of my own, I might have come to different conclusions.

Why we study attribution errors

This chapter, like the one before, explains some foibles and fallacies in our social thinking. Reading these may make it seem, as one of my students put it, that "social psychologists get their kicks out of playing tricks on people." Actually, the experiments are not designed to demonstrate "what fools these mortals be" (although some of the experiments *are* amusing); their purpose is to reveal how we think about ourselves and others.

If our capacity for illusion and self-deception is shocking, remember that our modes of thought are generally adaptive. Illusory thinking is often a by-product of our mind's strategies for simplifying complex information. It parallels our perceptual mechanisms, which generally give us a useful image of the world, but sometimes lead us astray.

A second reason for focusing on the biases that invade our thinking is that we are mostly unaware of them. My hunch is that you will find more surprises, more challenges, and more benefit in an analysis of errors and biases than you would in a string of testimonies to the human capacity for logic and intellectual achievement. This is also why world literature so often portrays pride and other human failings. Liberal education exposes us to fallacies in our thinking in the hope that we will become more rational, more in touch with reality.

The hope is not in vain: Psychology students explain behavior less simplistically than equally able natural science students (Fletcher & others, 1986). So remembering this overriding aim—*developing our capacity for critical thinking*—let us continue looking at how the new research on social thinking can enhance our social reasoning.

Summing up

Attribution researchers study how we explain people's behavior. When will we attribute someone's behavior to a person's disposition and when to the situation? By and large we make reasonable attributions. When explaining other people's behavior, however, we often commit the *fundamental attribution error* (also called *correspondence bias*). We attribute their behavior so much to their inner traits and attitudes that we discount situational constraints, even when these are obvious. If a balloon moves because it is pushed by an invisible wind, we don't assume it is internally propelled. But people are not inanimate objects; thus, when a *person* acts we more often discount the situational winds and assume internal propulsion.

We make this attribution error partly because when we watch someone act, that *person* is the focus of our attention and the situation is relatively invisible. When *we* act, our attention is usually on what we are reacting to—the situation is more visible. Thus we are more sensitive to the situational influences upon ourselves.

Constructing interpretations and memories

Striking experiments reveal the extent to which prejudgments can bias our perceptions and interpretations, and misinformation can bias our recall.

Chapter 1 noted a significant fact about the human mind—that our preconceptions guide how we perceive and interpret information. People will grant that preconceptions influence social judgments, yet fail to realize how great the effect is. Consider recent experiments. Some examine how *pre*judgments affect the way people perceive and interpret information. Others plant a judgment in people's minds *after* they have been given information to study how after-the-fact ideas bias recall. The overarching point: *We respond not to reality as it is but to reality as we construe it.*

When information is ambiguous, preconceptions matter.

Perceiving and interpreting events

The effects of prejudgments and expectations are standard fare for psychology's introductory course. Recall the Dalmatian photo in Chapter 1. Or consider this phrase:

A
BIRD
IN THE
THE HAND

Did you notice anything wrong with it? There is more to perception than meets the eye. This was tragically demonstrated in 1988 when the crew of the USS Vincennes misperceived an Iranian passenger jet as a hostile enemy and shot it down. As social psychologist Richard Nisbett (1988) noted in explaining the incident, "The effects of expectations on generating and sustaining mistaken hypotheses can be dramatic."

The same is true of social perception. Because social perceptions are very much in the eye of the beholder, even a simple stimulus may strike two people quite differently. Saying Canada's Jean Chrétien is "an okay prime minister" may sound like a put-down to one of his ardent admirers and as positively biased to someone who regards him with contempt. When social information is subject to multiple interpretations, preconceptions matter (Hilton & von Hippel, 1990).

An experiment by Robert Vallone, Lee Ross, and Mark Lepper (1985) reveals just how powerful preconceptions can be. They showed pro-Israeli and pro-Arab students six network news segments describing the 1982 killing of civilian refugees at two camps in Lebanon. As Figure 3–5 illustrates, each group perceived the networks as hostile to its side. The phenomenon is commonplace: Political candidates and their supporters nearly always view the news media as unsympathetic to their cause. Sports fans perceive referees as partial to the other side. People in conflict (married couples, labor and management, opposing racial groups) see impartial mediators as biased against them. When my two children fight, and I am called upon to settle the dispute, in more cases than not, they both think that I am unfairly favoring the other one.

Our shared assumptions about the world can even make contradictory evidence seem supportive. For example, Ross and Lepper assisted Charles Lord (1979) in asking students to evaluate the results of two supposedly new research studies. Half the students favored capital punishment and half opposed it. One study confirmed and the other disconfirmed the students' beliefs about the deterrence effect of the death penalty. The results: Both proponents and opponents of capital punishment readily accepted evidence that

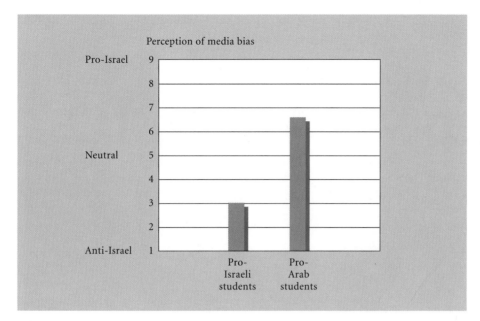

figure 3–5

Pro-Israeli and pro-Arab students who viewed network news descriptions of the "Beirut massacre" believed the coverage was biased against their point of view. (Data from Vallone, Ross, & Lepper, 1985.)

confirmed their belief but were sharply critical of disconfirming evidence. Showing the two sides an *identical* body of mixed evidence had therefore not lessened their disagreement but *increased* it. In follow-up studies people exposed to mixed information have been discomfited by the challenging evidence, provoked to think more about the issues, and motivated to refute the contrary evidence (Edwards & Smith, 1996; Kuhn & Lao, 1996; Munro & Ditto, 1997). Thus each side ends up perceiving the evidence as supporting its belief and now believes even more strongly. In general, people are less critical of information when it supports their preferred conclusions (Ditto & Lopez, 1992).

Is this why, in politics, religion, and science, ambiguous information often fuels conflict? When political debates have no clear-cut winner they mostly reinforce predebate opinions. In one study of three different series of debates, by nearly a 10 to 1 margin, those who already favored one candidate over the others perceived their candidate as having won (Kinder & Sears, 1985). Not only do people think their candidate won, but they report becoming even more supportive of them after the debate (Munro, Ditto, Lockhart, Fagerlin, Gready, & Peterson, 1997). It seems people can perceive and interpret the identical arguments quite differently. Given the same mixed information, opposing people can each assimilate it to their views and find their views strengthened.

Preconceptions sway scientists, too. In Chapter 1 we noted that beliefs and values penetrate science. Philosophers of science remind us that our observations are "theory-laden." There is an objective reality out there, but we view it through the spectacles of our beliefs, attitudes, and values. This is one reason our beliefs are so important; they shape our interpretation of everything else. Often, this is justifiable. Your preconceptions of the editorial standards of certain tabloid newspapers probably justify your disregarding headlines proclaiming, "Computers talk with the dead." So preconceptions can be useful:

"As I am, so I see."

Ralph Waldo Emerson, *Essays*

"Once you have a belief, it influences how you perceive all other relevant information. Once you see a country as hostile, you are likely to interpret ambiguous actions on their part as signifying their hostility."

Political scientist Robert Jervis (1985)

Supporters of a particular candidate or cause tend to see the media as favoring the other side.

The occasional biases they create are the price we pay for their helping us filter and organize vast amounts of information efficiently.

Experiments have manipulated preconceptions with astonishing effects upon how people interpret and recall what they observe. Myron Rothbart and Pamela Birrell (1977) had students assess the facial expression of the man shown in Figure 3–6. Those told he was a Gestapo leader responsible for barbaric medical experiments on concentration camp inmates during World War II intuitively judged his expression as cruel. (Can you see that barely suppressed sneer?) Those told he was a leader in the anti-Nazi underground movement whose courage saved thousands of Jewish lives judged his facial expression as warm and kind. (On second thought, look at those caring eyes and that almost smiling mouth.)

West German researcher Harald Wallbott (1988) controlled people's perceptions of emotion by manipulating the setting in which they see a face. Filmmakers call this the "Kulechov effect," after a Russian film director who would skillfully guide viewers' inferences by manipulating their assumptions. Kulechov demonstrated the phenomenon by creating three short films that presented the face of an actor with a neutral expression after viewers had first been shown a dead woman, a dish of soup, or a girl playing—making the actor seem sad, thoughtful, or happy. The moral: There is a reality out there, but our understanding of it is construed in our minds.

> "The error of our eye directs our mind: What error leads must err."
>
> Shakespeare, *Troilus and Cressida*, 1601–1602

> "We hear and apprehend only what we already half know."
>
> Henry David Thoreau, 1817–1862

Belief perseverance

If a false idea biases information processing, will later discrediting erase its effects? Imagine a baby-sitter who decides, during an evening with a crying infant, that bottle feeding produces colicky babies: "Come to think of it, cow's

figure 3–6
The photo of "Kurt Walden" as shown by Myron Rothbart and Pamela Birrell. Judge for yourself: Is this man cruel or kind?

milk obviously better suits calves than babies." If the infant turns out to be suffering a high fever, will the sitter nevertheless persist in believing that bottle feeding causes colic (Ross & Anderson, 1982)? To find out, Lee Ross, Craig Anderson, and their colleagues planted a falsehood in people's minds and then tried to discredit it.

Their experiments reveal that it is surprisingly difficult to demolish a falsehood, once the person conjures up a rationale for it. Each experiment first implanted a belief, either by proclaiming it was true or by inducing people to come to that conclusion after inspecting two sample cases. Then the people were asked to explain *why* it is true. Finally, the researchers totally discredited the initial information by telling the person the truth: The information was manufactured for the experiment, and half the people in the experiment had received opposite information. Nevertheless, the new belief survived about 75 percent intact, presumably because the people still retained their invented explanations for the belief. This phenomenon, named **belief perseverance**, shows that beliefs can take on a life of their own and survive discrediting of the evidence that gave them birth.

belief perseverance persistence of one's initial conceptions, as when the basis for one's belief is discredited but an explanation of why the belief might be true survives

For instance, Anderson, Lepper, and Ross (1980) asked people, after giving them two concrete cases to inspect, to decide whether people who take risks make good or bad firefighters. One group considered a risk-prone person who was a successful firefighter and a cautious person who was an unsuccessful one. The other group considered cases suggesting the opposite conclusion. After forming their theory that risk-prone people make better or worse firefighters, the individuals wrote explanations for it—for example, that risk-prone people are brave or that cautious people are careful. Once formed, each explanation could exist independently of the information that initially created the

Do people who take risks make the best firefighters? Or the worst?

"No one denies that new evidence can change people's beliefs. Children do eventually renounce their belief in Santa Claus. Our contention is simply that such changes generally occur slowly, and that more compelling evidence is often required to alter a belief than to create it."

Lee Ross & Mark Lepper (1980)

"Two-thirds of what we see is behind our eyes."

Chinese proverb

belief. When that information was discredited, the people still held their self-generated explanations and therefore continued to believe that risk-prone people really *do* make better or worse firefighters.

These experiments also show that the more we examine our theories and explain how they *might* be true, the more closed we become to information that challenges our belief. Once we consider why an accused person might be guilty, why someone of whom we have a negative first impression acts that way, or why a favored stock might rise in value, our explanations may survive challenging evidence to the contrary (Davies, 1997; Jelalian & Miller, 1984).

The evidence is compelling: Our beliefs and expectations powerfully affect how we mentally construct events. Usually we benefit from our preconceptions, just as scientists benefit from creating theories that guide them in noticing and interpreting events. But the benefits sometimes entail a cost; we become prisoners of our own thought patterns. Thus the "canals" that were so often seen on Mars turned out to be the product of intelligent life—an intelligence on earth's side of the telescope.

Is there any way we can restrain belief perseverance? There is a simple remedy: *Explain the opposite.* Charles Lord, Mark Lepper, and Elizabeth Preston (1984) repeated the capital punishment study described earlier and added two variations. First, they asked some of their subjects when evaluating the evidence to be *"as objective* and *unbiased* as possible." It was to no avail; whether for or against capital punishment, those who received this plea made evaluations as biased as those who did not.

The researchers asked a third group of subjects to consider the opposite—to ask themselves "whether you would have made the same high or low evaluations had exactly the same study produced results on the *other* side of the issue." After imagining an opposite finding, these people were much less biased in their evaluations of the evidence for and against their views. In his experiments, Craig Anderson (1982; Anderson & Sechler, 1986) consistently

focus

Perseverance in the Monty Hall Dilemma

Consider this problem, named after the TV host of *Let's Make a Deal*, which featured two-stage decisions involving options to stick with one's initial guess or switch to another option:

> Suppose you're on a game show and you're given the choice of three doors. Behind one door is a car; behind the others, goats. You pick a door, say number 1, and the host who knows what's behind the doors, opens another door, say number 3, which has a goat. He then says to you, "Do you want to switch to door number 2?" Is it to your advantage to switch your choice?

When Craig F. Whitaker of Columbia, Maryland, posed this question to *Parade* columnist Marilyn vos Savant, she answered "Yes; you should switch," triggering a storm of letters, 9 out of 10 disagreeing. One math professor (among others) wrote that "I have on my shelf more than 50 probability texts, each of which solves the problem correctly, and warns against Marilyn's error, as a result frequently obtained by unskilled mathematical amateurs."

Nevertheless, when the dust settled, it was apparent from empirical simulations of the puzzle (which any reader can conduct) as well as from further mathematical analysis that vos Savant was right. Think of it this way: The odds are 1 in 3 that you initially picked the right door, and 2 in 3 that it's one of the other two. When the host eliminates one of those two, which always happens, there still are 2 chances in 3 that the correct door is *not* the one you picked.

When social psychologist Donald Granberg (1996) walked students through simulations of the dilemma, only 9 percent switched after first committing themselves to a door (91 percent persevered). When another person made the initial selection and the participant then decided whether to stick or switch, however, 38 percent switched. To Granberg, this suggested that mistakenly sticking to one's initial guess reflects not only people's misapprehending the odds, but also their persevering in their initial beliefs and behavior. Once committed to a decision, an investment, or an opinion, cognitive inertia works to sustain it.

found that explaining why an opposite theory might be true—why a cautious rather than a risk-taking person might be a better firefighter—reduces or eliminates belief perseverance. Indeed, explaining *any* alternative outcome, not just the opposite, drives people to ponder various possibilities (Hirt & Markman, 1995).

Constructing memories

Do you agree or disagree with this statement?

> Memory can be likened to a storage chest in the brain into which we deposit material and from which we can withdraw it later if needed. Occasionally, something is lost from the "chest," and then we say we have forgotten.

About 85 percent of university students agree (Lamal, 1979). As a 1988 ad in *Psychology Today* put it, "Science has proven the accumulated experience of a lifetime is preserved perfectly in your mind."

Actually, psychological research has proved the opposite. Many memories are not copies of experiences that remain on deposit in a memory bank. Rather, we construct memories at the time of withdrawal, for memory involves

Unlike photos, memories get reconstructed when withdrawn from the memory bank.

"Memory isn't like reading a book: it's more like writing a book from fragmentary notes."

John F. Kihlstrom, 1994

backward reasoning. It infers what must have been, given what we now believe or know. Like a paleontologist inferring the appearance of a dinosaur from bone fragments, we reconstruct our distant past by combining fragments of information using our current feelings and expectations (Hirt, 1990; Ross & Buehler, 1994). Thus we can easily (though unconsciously) revise our memories to suit our current knowledge. When one of my sons complained, "The June issue of *Cricket* never came," and was then shown where it was, he delightedly responded, "Oh good, I knew I'd gotten it."

When an experimenter or a therapist manipulates people's presumptions about our past, a sizeable fraction will construct false memories. Asked to vividly imagine a childhood time when they ran, tripped, fell, and stuck their hand through a window, or a time when they knocked over a punch bowl at a wedding, about one-fourth will later recall the fictitious event as something that actually happened (Garry & others, 1996; Hyman & others, 1995, 1996; Loftus & Pickerell, 1995). In its search for truth, the mind sometimes constructs a falsehood.

Reconstructing past attitudes

Five years ago, how did you feel about nuclear power? About Lucien Bouchard or Jean Chrétien? About your parents? If your attitudes have changed, do you know the extent of the change?

Experimenters have tried to answer such questions, and the results have been unnerving. People whose attitudes have changed often insist that they have always felt much as they now feel. Daryl Bem and Keith McConnell (1970) conducted a survey to test these ideas among students at their university. Buried in it was a question concerning student control over the university curriculum. A week later the students agreed to write an essay opposing student control. After doing so, their attitudes shifted toward greater opposition to student control. When asked to recall how they had answered the question before writing the essay, they "remembered" holding the opinion that they *now* held and denied that the experiment had affected them. After observing students similarly denying their former attitudes, researchers D. R. Wixon and James Laird (1976) commented, "The speed, magnitude, and certainty" with which the students revised their own histories "was striking."

In 1973, researchers interviewed a sample of high school seniors and then reinterviewed them in 1982 (Markus, 1986). When recalling their 1973 attitudes on issues such as aid to minorities, the legalization of marijuana, and equality for women, people's reports were much closer to their 1982 attitudes than to those they actually expressed in 1973. As George Vaillant (1977, p. 197) noted after following some adults for a period of time, "It is all too common for caterpillars to become butterflies and then to maintain that in their youth they had been little butterflies. Maturation makes liars of us all."

The construction of positive memories does brighten our recollections. Terence Mitchell, Leigh Thompson, and their colleagues (1994, 1997) report that people often exhibit *rosy retrospection*—they *recall* mildly pleasant events more favorably than they experienced them. University students on a three-week bike trip, older adults on a guided tour of Austria, and undergraduates on vacation all report enjoying their experiences as they have them. But they later recall such experiences even more fondly, minimizing the unpleasant or boring aspects and remembering the high points. Thus, the pleasant times during which I have sojourned in Scotland I now (back in my office facing deadlines and interruptions) romanticize as pure bliss. With any positive experience, some of the pleasure resides in the anticipation, some in the actual experience, and some in the rosy retrospection.

Cathy McFarland and Michael Ross (1985) found that we also revise our recollections of other people as our relationships with them change. They had university students rate their steady dating partners. Two months later, they rated them again. Students who were more in love than ever had a tendency to recall love at first sight. Those who had broken up were more likely to recall having recognized the partner as somewhat selfish and bad-tempered.

Diane Holmberg and John Holmes (1994) discovered the same phenomenon among 373 newlywed couples, most of whom reported being very happy. When resurveyed two years later, those whose marriages had soured recalled that things had always been bad. The results are "frightening," say Holmberg and Holmes: "Such biases can lead to a dangerous downward spiral. The worse your current view of your partner is, the worse your memories are, which only further confirms your negative attitudes."

It's not that we are totally unaware of how we used to feel, just that when memories are hazy, current feelings guide our recall. Parents of every generation bemoan the values of the next generation, partly because they misrecall their youthful values as being closer to their current values.

Reconstructing past behavior

Memory construction enables us to revise our own histories. Michael Ross, Cathy McFarland, and Garth Fletcher (1981) exposed some University of Waterloo students to a message convincing them of the desirability of toothbrushing.

> "A man should never be ashamed to own that he has been in the wrong, which is but saying, in other words, that he is wiser today than he was yesterday."
>
> Jonathan Swift, *Thoughts on Various Subjects*, 1711

> "Travel is glamorous only in retrospect."
>
> Paul Theroux, in *The Observer*

Later, in a supposedly different experiment, these students recalled brushing their teeth more often during the preceding two weeks than did students who had not heard the message. Likewise

"Vanity plays lurid tricks with our memory."

Novelist Joseph Conrad, 1857–1924

- When you select people at random and ask them about their cigarette smoking and their reports are projected to the population as a whole, at least a third of the cigarettes sold annually are unaccounted for (Hall, 1985). Someone is smoking those cigarettes.

- In a recent survey, 61 percent of the adult population reported voting in the last election, in which only 55 percent of adults voted. Some of the people who said they voted must not have.

- Most people think their lifestyle is healthier than that of their average peer. If challenged by information about the actual frequency with which their peers drink to excess, eat greasy foods and so forth, people revise their recollections and report engaging in such behaviors even less often (Klein & Kunda, 1993).

Noting the similarity of such findings to happenings in George Orwell's *Nineteen Eighty-Four*—where it was "necessary to remember that events happened in the desired manner"—social psychologist Anthony Greenwald (1980) surmised that we all have "totalitarian egos" that revise the past to suit our present views.

Sometimes our present view is that we've improved—in which case we may misrecall our past as more *un*like the present than it actually was. This tendency resolves a puzzling pair of consistent findings: Those who participate in self-improvement programs (weight-control programs, antismoking programs, exercise programs, psychotherapy) show only modest improvement on average. Yet they often claim considerable benefit (Myers, 1998). Michael Conway and Michael Ross (1985, 1986) explain why: Having expended so much time, effort, and money on self-improvement, people may think, "I may not be perfect now, but I was worse before; this did me a lot of good."

Reconstructing our experiences

misinformation effect
incorporating "misinformation" into one's memory of the event, after witnessing an event and receiving misleading information about it

In experiments involving more than 20,000 people, Elizabeth Loftus has revealed our tendency to construct memories we recall with great confidence but sometimes little accuracy. In the typical experiment, people witness an event, receive misleading information about it (or not), and then take a memory test. The repeated finding is the **misinformation effect**. People incorporate the misinformation into their memories: They recall a yield sign as a stop sign, hammers as screwdrivers, *Vogue* magazine as *Mademoiselle*, Dr. Henderson as "Dr. Davidson," breakfast cereal as eggs, and a clean-shaven man as a fellow with a mustache (Loftus & others, 1989). Suggested misinformation may even produce false memories of supposed child sexual abuse, argues Loftus (1993).

Pause to recall a scene from a favorite past experience. . . . Do you see yourself in the scene? If so, your memory must be a reconstruction, for in reality you did not see yourself.

In one famous experiment with John Palmer, Loftus showed University of Washington students a film of a traffic accident and then asked them questions about what they had witnessed (Loftus & Palmer, 1974). People asked "How fast were the cars going when they smashed into each other?" gave higher estimates than those asked "How fast were the cars going when they hit each other?" A week later they were also asked whether they recalled seeing any broken glass. There was no broken glass. Yet people who had been asked the "smashed into" question were more than twice as likely as those asked the "hit" question to report seeing broken glass.

What is more, it's difficult for untrained observers to distinguish between unreal memories (those constructed from suggestion, as with the broken glass) and memories of actual experience (Schooler & others, 1986). As such experiments show, in constructing a memory, we unconsciously use our general knowledge and beliefs to fill in the holes, thus organizing fragments from our actual past into a convincing story.

This process affects our recall of social as well as physical events. Jack Croxton and his colleagues (1984) had students spend 15 minutes talking with someone. Those later informed that this person reported liking them recalled the person's behavior as relaxed, comfortable, and happy. Those informed that the person disliked them recalled the person as nervous, uncomfortable, and not so happy.

To understand why, it helps to have an idea of how our memories work. We can think of memories as stored in a web of associations. To retrieve a memory, we need to activate one of the strands that leads to it, a process that we earlier noted is called **priming** (Bower, 1986). Priming is what the philosopher-psychologist William James described as the "wakening of associations."

priming
activating particular associations in memory

Events may awaken or prime our associations without our realizing it. Watching a scary movie while alone at home can prime our thinking—by activating frightening memories that cause us to interpret furnace noises as an intruder. For many psychology students, reading about psychological disorders primes how they interpret their own anxieties and gloomy moods. In experiments, ideas implanted in people's minds act like preconceptions: They automatically—unintentionally, effortlessly, and without awareness—influence how people interpret and recall events (Bargh, 1989, 1994). Having recently seen words such as "adventurous" and "self-confident," people will later, in a different context, form positive impressions of an imagined mountain climber or Atlantic sailor. If, instead, their thinking is primed with such negative words as "reckless," their impressions are more negative (Higgins & others, 1977).

In Module A we will see that psychiatrists and clinical psychologists are not immune to these human tendencies. We all selectively notice, interpret, and recall events in ways that sustain our ideas. Our social judgments are a mix of observation and expectation, reason and passion.

Summing up

Our preconceptions strongly influence how we interpret and remember events. In experiments, people's prejudgments have striking effects upon how they perceive and interpret information. Other experiments have planted judgments or false ideas in people's minds *after* they have been given information. These experiments reveal that as before-the-fact judgments bias our perceptions and interpretations, so after-the-fact judgments bias our recall.

Judging others

As we have already noted, our cognitive mechanisms are efficient and adaptive, yet error-prone. Usually they serve us well, but sometimes clinicians misjudge patients, employers misjudge employees, people of one race misjudge another, and spouses misjudge their mates. The results are misdiagnoses, labor strife, prejudices, and divorces. So, how—and how well—do we make intuitive social judgments?

When historians describe social psychology's first century, they will surely record the last thirty years as the era of social cognition. By drawing upon advances in cognitive psychology—in how people perceive, represent, and remember events—social psychologists have shed welcome light on how we form impressions. Let's look at what this research reveals of the marvels and mistakes of our social judgements.

The Unconscious: Perceiving and interpreting without awareness

Can we really perceive things and even interpret them without knowing it? Just how much of our thinking goes on without our knowledge? Debate about the importance of the unconscious has waxed and waned over the years, but recently has been a hot topic. Some researchers like John Bargh (1999) see the unconscious as a "cognitive monster" controlling most behaviors. Others see the unconscious as an interesting but hardly central form of thinking. Let's examine the evidence on both sides of the debate.

The powers of the unconscious

"The heart has its reasons which reason does not know," observed seventeenth-century philosopher–mathematician Blaise Pascal. Three centuries later, scientists have proved Pascal correct. We know more than we know we know. Studies of our unconscious information processing confirm our limited access to what's going on in our minds (Bargh, 1994; Greenwald & Banaji, 1995). Our thinking is partly controlled (deliberate and conscious) and—more than most of us once supposed—partly automatic (effortless and without our awareness). Automatic thinking occurs not "on screen" but off screen; out of sight, where reason does not know. Consider the following:

- *Schemas*—mental templates—automatically, intuitively, guide our perceptions and interpretations of our experience. Whether we hear someone speaking of religious *sects* or *sex* depends not only on the word spoken but on how we automatically interpret the sound.
- *Emotional reactions* are often nearly instantaneous, before there is time for deliberate thinking. One neural shortcut takes information from the eye or ear to the brain's sensory switchboard (the thalamus) and out to its emotional control center (the amygdala) before the thinking cortex has had any chance to intervene (LeDoux, 1994, 1996).
  Simple likes, dislikes, and fears typically involve little analysis. Although our intuitive reactions sometimes defy logic, they may still be adaptive. Our ancestors who intuitively feared a sound in the bushes were usually fearing nothing, but they were more likely to survive to pass their genes down to us than their more deliberative cousins.
- Given sufficient *expertise*, people may intuitively know the answer to a problem. The situation cues information stored in their memory. Without knowing quite how we do it, we recognize a friend's voice after the first spoken word of a phone conversation. Master chess players intuitively recognize meaningful patterns that novices miss.

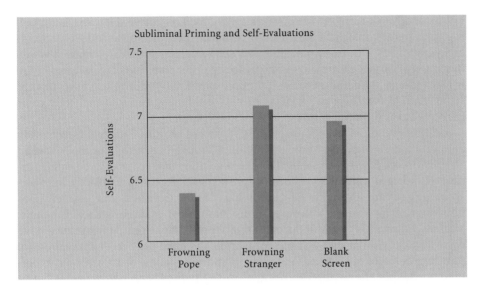

figure 3–7

Subliminal priming and self-evaluations.
Catholic students primed with a subliminal picture of the Pope frowning rated themselves lower on a number of traits. (Data from Baldwin, et al., 1989).

- Some things—facts, names, and past experiences—we remember explicitly (consciously). But other things—skills and conditioned dispositions—we remember *implicitly,* without consciously knowing and declaring that we know. It's true of us all, but most strikingly evident in brain-damaged persons who cannot form new explicit memories. Having learned how to solve a block-stacking puzzle or play golf, they will deny ever having experienced the task. Yet (surprisingly to themselves) they perform like practiced experts.

- Although below our threshold for conscious awareness, subliminal stimuli may nevertheless have intriguing effects. For example, consider the following study conducted by McGill University's Mark Baldwin and his colleagues (1989). He had Catholic women read a sexually explicit passage and then subliminally flashed either a picture of the Pope frowning, the picture of a stranger frowning, or a blank screen. He then had the women rate themselves on a number of different dimensions of their self-concept. As you can see in Figure 3-7, he found that when the women were exposed to the frowning Pope they rated themselves more negatively than when they were exposed to the frowning stranger or the blank screen. This effect was particularly pronounced for those who reported higher levels of participation in their faith. Evidently, the subliminal priming of a disapproving Pope lowered these women's ratings of themselves.

To repeat, many routine cognitive functions occur automatically, unintentionally, without awareness. Our minds function rather like big corporations. Our CEO—our controlled consciousness—attends to the most important or novel issues and assigns routine affairs to subordinates. This delegation of resources enables us to react to many situations quickly, efficiently, and intuitively, without expending limited time to reason and analyze.

The limits of unconscious

Although researchers affirm that unconscious information processing can produce flashes of intuition, they have their doubts about its brilliance. Elizabeth

Loftus and Mark Klinger (1992) speak for today's cognitive scientists in reporting "a general consensus that the unconscious may not be as smart as previously believed." For example, although subliminal stimuli can trigger a weak, fleeting response—enough to evoke a feeling if not conscious awareness—there is no evidence that commercial subliminal tapes can "reprogram your unconscious mind" for success. (A mass of new evidence indicates that they can't [Greenwald & others, 1991].)

Despite the efficiency of our thought processes, our judgments err often enough to understand why poet T. S. Eliot would describe "The hollow man . . . Headpiece filled with straw." Social psychologists have explored our error-prone hindsight judgments (our intuitive sense, after the fact, that we knew-it-all-along). Other domains of psychology have explored our capacity for illusion—perceptual misinterpretations, fantasies, and constructed beliefs. Michael Gazzaniga (1992) reports that patients whose brain hemispheres have been surgically separated will instantly fabricate—and believe—explanations of puzzling behaviors. If the patient gets up and takes a few steps after the experimenter flashes the instruction "walk" to the patient's nonverbal right hemisphere, the verbal left hemisphere will instantly invent a plausible explanation ("I felt like getting a drink").

> "People are good enough to get through life, poor enough to make predictable and consequential mistakes."
>
> Baruch Fischhoff, 1981

Illusory thinking also appears in the vast new literature on how we take in, store, and retrieve social information. As perception researchers study visual illusions for what they reveal about our normal perceptual mechanisms, social psychologists study illusory thinking for what it reveals about normal information processing. These researchers want to give us a map of everyday social thinking, with the hazards clearly marked. As we examine some of these efficient thinking patterns, remember this: Demonstrations of how people create counterfeit beliefs do not prove that all beliefs are counterfeit. Still, to recognize counterfeiting, it helps to know how it's done. So let's explore how efficient information processing can go awry, beginning with our self-knowledge.

Judgmental overconfidence

So far we have seen that our cognitive system processes a vast amount of information efficiently and automatically, resulting in those impressive *intuitive judgments*. But our adaptive efficiency has a trade-off; as we interpret our experiences and construct memories, our intuitive judgments often err. Usually, we are unaware of our flaws. The "intellectual conceit" evident in judgments of past knowledge ("I knew it all along") extends to estimates of current knowledge.

overconfidence phenomenon
the tendency to be more confident than correct—to overestimate the accuracy of one's beliefs

To explore this **overconfidence phenomenon,** Daniel Kahneman and Amos Tversky (1979) gave people factual questions and asked them to fill in the blanks, as in the following: "I feel 98 percent certain that the air distance between New Delhi and Beijing is more than ____ miles but less than ____ miles." Most subjects were overconfident: About 30 percent of the time, the correct answers lay outside the range they felt 98 percent confident about.

To find out whether overconfidence extends to social judgments, David Dunning and his associates (1990) created a little game show. They asked students to guess a stranger's answers to a series of questions, such as "Would you prepare for a difficult exam alone or with others?" and "Would you rate your lecture notes as neat or messy?" Knowing the type but not the actual questions, the subjects first interviewed their target person about background, hobbies, academic interests, aspirations, astrological sign—anything they thought might be helpful. Then, while the targets privately answered 20 of the two-choice questions, the interviewers predicted their target's answers and rated their own confidence in the predictions.

The air distance between New Delhi and Beijing is 2500 miles.

The interviewers guessed right 63 percent of the time, beating chance by 13 percent. But, on average, they *felt* 75 percent sure of their predictions. When guessing their own roommates' responses, they were 68 percent correct and 78 percent confident. Moreover, the most confident people were most likely to be *over*confident. Studies reveal a similar meagre correlation between self-confidence and accuracy in discerning whether someone is telling the truth (DePaulo & others, 1997). People also are markedly overconfident when estimating such things as the sexual history of their dating partner or the activity preferences of their roommates (Swann & Gill, 1997).

Are people better at predicting their own behavior? To find out, Robert Vallone and his colleagues (1990) had university students predict in September whether they would drop a course, declare a major, elect to live off campus next year, and so forth. Although the students felt, on average, 84 percent sure of these self-predictions, they were wrong nearly twice as often as they expected to be. Even when feeling 100 percent sure of their predictions, they erred 15 percent of the time.

In estimating their chances for success on a task, such as a major exam, people's confidence runs highest when removed in time from "the moment of truth." By exam day, the possibility of failure looms larger and confidence typically drops (Gilovich & others, 1993). Roger Buehler and his colleagues (1994) report that most students also confidently underestimate how long it will take them to complete papers and other major assignments. They are not alone:

- Planners routinely underestimate the time and expense of projects. In 1969, Montreal Mayor Jean Drapeau proudly announced that a $120 million stadium with a retractable roof would be built for the 1976 Olympics. The roof was completed in 1989 and cost $120 million by itself.

- Investment experts market their services with the confident presumption that they can beat the stock market average, forgetting that for every stockbroker or buyer saying "Sell!" at a given price there is another saying "Buy!" A stock's price is the balance point between these mutually confident judgments. Thus, incredible as it may seem, economist Burton Malkiel (1985, 1995) reports that mutual fund portfolios selected by investment analysts have not outperformed randomly selected stocks.

- Editors' assessments of manuscripts also reveal surprising error. Writer Chuck Ross (1979), using a pseudonym, mailed a typewritten copy of Jerzy Kosinski's novel *Steps* to 28 major publishers and literary agencies. All rejected it, including Random House, which had published the book in 1968 and watched it win the National Book Award and sell more than 400,000 copies. The novel came closest to being accepted by Houghton Mifflin, publisher of three other Kosinski novels: "Several of us read your untitled novel here with admiration for writing and style. Jerzy Kosinski comes to mind as a point of comparison. . . . The drawback to the manuscript, as it stands, is that it doesn't add up to a satisfactory whole."

- Overconfident decision makers can wreak havoc. It was a confident Adolf Hitler who from 1939 to 1945 waged war against the rest of

behind the scenes

As a graduate student at the University of Waterloo, I noticed something peculiar about my work-related predictions. Most evenings I would stuff my briefcase with work to complete at home and then return the following day with much of it untouched. Yet each time I packed that briefcase I was sure my plans were realistic. In my Ph.D. dissertation and subsequent research (conducted with Dale Griffin and Michael Ross) I have addressed two related questions: Why do people often underestimate how long it will take to finish tasks? Why don't people learn from past experience and adjust their estimates accordingly? The findings suggest that people's unwarranted optimism stems in part from a desire to finish projects promptly and in part from the thought processes that they naturally engage in to generate predictions. People tend to focus narrowly on their plans for completing the task at hand and consequently dismiss other valuable sources of information, such as how long similar tasks have taken in the past. These research insights have, unfortunately, had little impact on my own predictions and I'm still lugging around an overweight briefcase.

Roger Buehler
Wilfrid Laurier University

Europe. In 1812 it was a confident James Madison who led the newly formed United States into a war to take over Upper Canada. It was a confident Slobodan Milosevic who in 1999 proclaimed that he would never allow peacekeeping troops into Kosovo.

What produces overconfidence? Why does experience not lead us to a more realistic self-appraisal? There are several reasons (Klayman & Ha, 1987; Sanbomatsu & others, 1993; Skov & Sherman, 1986). For one thing, people tend not to seek information that might disprove what they believe. P. C. Wason (1960) demonstrated this, as you can, by giving people a sequence of three numbers— 2, 4, 6—that conformed to a rule he had in mind (the rule was simply *any three ascending numbers*). To enable the people to discover the rule, Wason invited each person to generate sets of three numbers. Each time Wason told the person whether or not the set conformed to his rule. When they were sure they had discovered the rule, the people were to stop and announce it.

The result? Seldom right but never in doubt: 23 of the 29 people convinced themselves of a wrong rule. They typically formed some erroneous belief about the rule (for example, counting by two's) and then searched for *confirming* evidence (for example, by testing 8, 10, 12) rather than attempting to *disconfirm* their hunches. We are eager to verify our beliefs but less inclined to seek evidence that might disprove them. We call this phenomenon the **confirmation bias.**

Our preference for confirming information helps explain why our self-images are so remarkably stable. In several experiments, William Swann and Stephen Read (1981; Swann & others, 1992a, b, 1994) discovered that students seek, elicit, and recall feedback that confirms their beliefs about themselves. People seek as friends and spouses those who bolster their own self views—even if they think poorly of themselves (Swann & others, 1991, 1992, in press). Swann and Read liken this *self-verification* to how someone with a domineering self-image might behave at a party. Upon arriving

> "When you know a thing, to hold that you know it; and when you do not know a thing, to allow that you do not know it; this is knowledge."
>
> Confucius, *Analects*

confirmation bias
a tendency to search for information that confirms one's preconceptions

the person *seeks* those guests whom she knows acknowledge her dominance. In conversation she then presents her views in ways that *elicit* the respect she expects. After the party, she has trouble recalling conversations in which her influence was minimal and more easily *recalls* her persuasiveness in the conversations that she dominated. Thus her experience at the party confirms her self-image.

Remedies for overconfidence

What lessons can we draw from research on overconfidence? One lesson is to be careful about other people's dogmatic statements. Even when people seem sure they are right, they may be wrong. Confidence and competence need not coincide.

Two techniques have successfully reduced the overconfidence bias. One is prompt feedback (Lichtenstein & Fischhoff, 1980). In everyday life, weather forecasters and those who set the odds in horse racing both receive clear, daily feedback. Experts in both groups, therefore, do quite well at estimating their probable accuracy (Fischhoff, 1982).

When people think about why an idea *might* be true it begins to seem true (Koehler, 1991). Thus, another way to reduce overconfidence is to get people to think of one good reason *why their judgments might be wrong*: force them to consider disconfirming information (Koriat & others, 1980). Managers might foster more realistic judgments by insisting that all proposals and recommendations include reasons why they might not work.

Still, we should be careful not to undermine people's self-confidence to a point where they spend too much time in self-analysis or where self-doubts begin to cripple decisiveness. In times when their wisdom is needed, those lacking self-confidence may shrink from speaking up or making tough decisions. *Over*confidence can cost us, but realistic self-confidence is adaptive.

Heuristics

With such precious little time to process so much information, our cognitive system specializes in mental shortcuts. With remarkable ease, we form impressions, make judgments, and invent explanations. In many situations, our snap generalizations—"That's dangerous!"—are adaptive. Their speed promotes our survival. The biological purpose of thinking is less to make us right than to keep us alive. In some situations, however, haste makes error.

Representativeness heuristic

A panel of psychologists interviewed a sample of 30 engineers and 70 lawyers and summarized their impressions in thumbnail descriptions. The following description has been drawn at random from the sample of 30 engineers and 70 lawyers:

> Twice divorced, Frank spends most of his free time hanging around the country club. His clubhouse bar conversations often center around his regrets at having tried to follow his esteemed father's footsteps. The long hours he had spent at academic drudgery would have been better invested in learning how to be less quarrelsome in his relations with other people.
>
> *Question:* What is the probability that Frank is a lawyer rather than an engineer?

Asked to guess Frank's occupation, more than 80 percent of students surmised he was one of the lawyers (Fischhoff & Bar-Hillel, 1984). Fair enough. But how do you suppose their estimates changed when the sample description was changed to say that 70 percent were engineers? Not in the slightest. The students took no account of the base rate of engineers and lawyers; in their minds Frank was more *representative* of lawyers, and that was all that seemed to matter.

To judge something by intuitively comparing it to our mental representation of a category is to use the **representativeness heuristic.** *Heuristics* are simple, efficient thinking strategies—implicit rules of thumb. Like most heuristics, representativeness usually is a reasonable guide to reality. But not always. Consider Linda, who is 31, single, outspoken, and very bright. She majored in philosophy in college. As a student she was deeply concerned with discrimination and other social issues, and she participated in antinuclear demonstrations. Based on this description, would you say it is more likely that

a.   Linda is a bank teller.

b.   Linda is a bank teller and active in the feminist movement.

Most people think *b* is more likely, partly because Linda better *represents* their image of feminists. Consider: Is there a better chance that Linda is *both* a bank teller *and* a feminist than that she's a bank teller (whether feminist or not)? As Amos Tversky and Daniel Kahneman (1983) remind us, the conjunction of two events can't be more likely than either event alone.

Ignoring base-rate information

As these experiments show, anecdotal information is persuasive. A research team led by Richard Nisbett (1976) explored the tendency to overuse such information. They showed students videotaped interviews of people who supposedly had participated in an experiment in which most subjects failed to assist a seizure victim. Learning how *most* subjects acted had little effect upon people's predictions of how the individual they observed acted. The apparent niceness of this individual was more vivid and compelling than the general truth about how most subjects really acted: "Ted seems so pleasant that I can't imagine him being unresponsive to another's plight."

This experiment illustrates the **base-rate fallacy:** *Focusing upon the specific individual can push into the background useful information about the population the person came from and distort our perception of what is generally true.* Our impressions of a group, for example, tend to be overly influenced by its extreme members. When a U.S. citizen murdered a Norwegian some years ago, there was talk in Norway of expelling all U.S. citizens (Triandis, 1994). As psychologist Gordon Allport put it, "Given a thimbleful of facts we rush to make generalizations as large as a tub."

People *will* use base-rate data when their relevance is obvious (Ginossar & Trope, 1987; Krosnick & others, 1990). If told that students taking a particular exam had a high failure rate, we infer the exam was difficult. This lowers our estimated likelihood of a particular student passing the exam. Moreover, argues Norbert Schwarz (1994), subjects in experiments overuse anecdotal information because they presume—following the normal rules of conversation—that "if the experimenter provides it, I should use it."

Nevertheless, the research reveals a basic principle of social thinking: People are slow to deduce particular instances from a general truth but are remarkably

representativeness heuristic
the strategy of judging the likelihood of things by how well they represent, or match, particular prototypes; may lead one to ignore other relevant information

base-rate fallacy
the tendency to ignore or underuse base-rate information (information that describes most people) and instead to be influenced by distinctive features of the case being judged

quick to infer general truth from a vivid instance. No wonder that after hearing and reading countless instances of rapes, robberies, and beatings, 9 out of 10 Canadians overestimate—usually by a considerable margin—the percentage of crimes that involve violence (Doob & Roberts, 1988).

Sometimes the vivid example is a personal experience. Before buying a new Honda, I consulted the *Consumer Reports* survey of car owners and found the repair record of the Dodge Colt, which for a time I considered, to be quite good. A short while later, I mentioned my interest in the Colt to a student. "Oh no," he moaned, "don't buy a Colt. I worked in a garage last summer and serviced two Dodge Colts that kept falling apart and being brought in for one thing after another." How did I use this information—and the glowing testimonies from two friends who were Honda owners? Did I simply add to the *Consumer Reports* surveys of Colt and Honda owners two more people each? Although I knew that, logically, that is what I should have done, it was nearly impossible to ignore my awareness of those vivid accounts. I bought the Honda.

"Most people reason dramatically, not quantitatively."

Jurist Oliver Wendell Holmes, Jr., 1809–1894

"Testimonials may be more compelling than mountains of facts and figures (as mountains of facts and figures in social psychology so compellingly demonstrate)."

Mark Snyder (1988)

If you went to the Middle East would you be more concerned about terrorist attacks or traffic accidents? Traffic accidents are actually more dangerous, but vivid media images of terrorist attacks make them seem more likely. This is an example of the availability heuristic.

When viewing scenes such as this Oloha Airlines 1988 disaster, many people exaggerate the risk of flying.

The availability heuristic

Consider: Does the letter *k* appear in print more often as the first letter of a word or as the third letter? Do more people live in Cambodia or in Tanzania?

You probably answered in terms of how readily instances of them come to mind. If examples are readily *available* in our memory—as letters beginning with *k* and as Cambodians tend to be—then we presume that the event is commonplace. Usually it is, so we are often well served by this cognitive rule of thumb, called the **availability heuristic.**

But sometimes the rule deludes us. If people hear a list of famous people of one sex (Mother Teresa, Jane Fonda, Tina Turner) intermixed with an equal size list of unfamous people of the other sex (Donald Scarr, William Wood, Mel Jasper), the famous names will later be more cognitively available. Most people will therefore recall having heard more (in this instance) women's names (McKelvie, 1995, 1997; Tversky & Kahneman, 1973). Vivid, easy-to-imagine events, such as diseases with easy-to-picture symptoms, may likewise seem more likely than harder-to-picture events (MacLeod & Campbell, 1992; Sherman & others, 1985). Even fictional happenings in novels, television, and movies leave images that later penetrate our judgments (Gerrig & Prentice, 1991).

The availability heuristic explains why powerful anecdotes are often more compelling than base-rate statistical information and why perceived risk is therefore often badly out of joint with real risks (Allison & others, 1992). Because news footage of airplane crashes is a readily available memory for most of us, we often suppose we are more at risk traveling in a commercial airplane than in a car. Actually, U.S. travelers during the 1980s were 26 times more likely to die in a car crash than on a commercial flight covering the same distance (National Safety Council, 1991). In the 27 months following March 22, 1992, major U.S. airlines had more than *16 million* flights without a single death. For most air travelers, the most dangerous part of the journey is the drive to the airport.

Easily imagined (cognitively available) events also influence our experiences of guilt, regret, frustration, and relief. If our team loses (or wins) a big game by one point, we can easily imagine how the game might have gone the other way, and thus we feel greater regret (or relief). Imagining worse alternatives helps us

availability heuristic An efficient but fallible rule-of-thumb that judges the likelihood of things in terms of their availability in memory. If instances of something come readily to mind, we presume it to be commonplace.

feel better. Imagining better alternatives, and pondering what we might do differently next time, helps us prepare to do better in the future (Boninger & others, 1994; Roese, 1994).

In Olympic competition, two cutoff points separate (a) the event-winning gold medalist from the nonwinners, and (b) the medal-winning bronze medalist from the nonmedalists. Thus, during the 1992 Olympics, bronze medalists (for whom an easily imagined alternative was finishing without a medal) exhibited more joy than silver medalists (who could more easily imagine having won the gold) (Medvec & others, 1995). Similarly, the higher a student's score within a grade category such as B+, the *worse* they feel (Medvec & Savitsky, 1997). The B+ student who misses an A− by a point feels worse than the B+ student who actually did worse and just made a B+ by a point. People's proximity to higher and lower cutoff points determines the direction of their counterfactual thinking.

Such **counterfactual thinking**—*mentally simulating what might have been*—occurs when we can easily picture an alternative outcome (Kahneman & Miller, 1986; Gavanski & Wells, 1989; Mandel & Lehman, 1996; Roese, 1997; Rose & Olson, 1993). If we barely miss a plane or bus, we imagine making it *if only* we had left at our usual time, taken our usual route, not paused to talk. If we miss our connection by a half hour or after taking our usual route, it's harder to simulate a different outcome, so we feel less frustration.

The more significant the event, the more intense the counterfactual thinking. Bereaved people who have lost a spouse or child in a vehicle accident, or a child to sudden infant death syndrome, commonly report replaying and undoing the event (Davis & others, 1995, 1996). One friend of mine, having lost his wife, daughter, and mother in a head-on collision with a drunk driver, reported that "For months I turned the events of that day over and over in my mind. I kept reliving the day, changing the order of events so that the accident wouldn't occur" (Sittser, 1994).

Most people, however, live with less regret over things done than over things they failed to do, such as "I wish I had been more serious in university" or "I should have told my father I loved him before he died" (Gilovich & Medvec, 1994; Savitsky & others, 1997). (In one survey of adults, the most common regret was not taking their education more seriously [Kinnier & Metha, 1989].) Might we therefore live with less regret if we dared more often to leave the safe harbor—to venture out, risking failure, but at least having tried? The fruit is out on the limb.

Illusory thinking

Another influence on everyday thinking is our search for order in random events, a tendency that can lead us down all sorts of wrong paths.

Illusory correlation

It's easy to see a correlation where none exists. When we expect significant relationships, we easily associate random events, perceiving an **illusory correlation**. William Ward and Herbert Jenkins (1965) showed people the results of a hypothetical 50-day cloud-seeding experiment. They told their subjects which of the 50 days the clouds had been seeded and which days it rained. This information was nothing more than a random mix of results: Sometimes it rained after seeding; sometimes it didn't. People nevertheless became convinced—in conformity with their ideas about the effects of cloud seeding—that they really had observed a relationship between cloud seeding and rain.

Answer to Question 1: *The letter* k *appears in print two to three times more often as the third letter. Yet most people judge that* k *appears more often at the beginning of a word. Words beginning with* k *are more readily available to memory, surmise Amos Tversky and Daniel Kahneman (1974), and ease of recall—availability—is our heuristic for judging the frequency of events.*

Answer to Question 2: *Tanzania's 24 million people greatly outnumber Cambodia's 7 million. Most people, having more vivid images of Cambodians, guess wrong.*

counterfactual thinking
imagining alternative scenarios and outcomes that might have happened, but didn't

illusory correlation
perception of a relationship where none exists, or perception of a stronger relationship than actually exists

Other experiments confirm that people easily misperceive random events as confirming their beliefs (Crocker, 1981; Jennings & others, 1982; Trolier & Hamilton, 1986). If we believe a correlation exists, we are more likely to notice and recall confirming instances. If we believe that premonitions correlate with events, we notice and remember the joint occurrence of the premonition and the event's later occurrence. We seldom notice or remember all the times unusual events do not coincide. If, after we think about a friend, the friend calls us, we notice and remember this coincidence. We don't notice all the times we think of a friend without any ensuing call, or receive a call from a friend about whom we've not been thinking.

People see not only what they expect, but correlations they *want* to see. In one experiment, Mariëtte Berndsen and her co-researchers (1996) showed University of Amsterdam students supposed student statements favoring or opposing a switch from Dutch to English lectures at Dutch universities, and told them that the policy would be tried at a university where surveys found the most support. They were then shown identical opinion distributions from Amsterdam and another university. For students with a vested interest, the result was an illusory correlation; students opposed to the language switch were especially likely to misperceive student statements from their own university as more opposed than those from the other university.

This intense human desire to find order, even in random events, leads us to seek reasons for unusual happenings or mystifying mood fluctuations. By attributing events to a cause, we order our worlds and make things seem more predictable and controllable. Again, this tendency is usually adaptive but occasionally leads us astray.

Illusion of control

Our tendency to perceive random events as related feeds an **illusion of control**—*the idea that chance events are subject to our influence.* This is what keeps

> "I see men ordinarily more eager to discover a reason for things than to find out whether the things are so."
>
> French essayist Montaigne, 1533–1592

illusion of control
perception of uncontrollable events as subject to one's control or as more controllable than they are

Peter Steiner

The illusion of control takes many forms.

"The next dance you will see is for partly cloudy conditions with moderating temperatures."

gamblers going and what makes the rest of us do all sorts of unlikely things. During a 1988 summer drought, for example, retired farmer Elmer Carlson arranged a rain dance by 16 Hopis. The next day it rained 1 inch. "The miracles are still here, we just have to ask for them," explained Carlson (Associated Press, 1988).

Gambling   Ellen Langer (1977) demonstrated the illusion of control with experiments on gambling. Compared to those given an assigned lottery number, people who chose their own number demanded four times as much money when asked about selling their ticket. When playing a game of chance against an awkward and nervous person, they bet significantly more than when playing against a dapper, confident opponent. In these and other ways, more than 50 experiments have consistently found people acting as if they can predict or control chance events (Presson & Benassi, 1996). Moreover, the more people *need* a random outcome (a food prize for the hungry vs. full participants in one experiment), the more illusory confidence they feel (Biner & others, 1995).

Observations of real-life gamblers confirm these experimental findings. Dice players may throw softly for low numbers and hard for high numbers (Henslin, 1967). The gambling industry thrives on gamblers' illusions. Gamblers attribute wins to their skill and foresight. Losses become "near misses" or "flukes"—perhaps (for the sports gambler) a bad call by the referee or a freakish bounce of the ball (Gilovich & Douglas, 1986).

Regression Toward the Average   Tversky and Kahneman (1974) noted another way by which an illusion of control may arise: We fail to recognize the statistical phenomenon of **regression toward the average**. Because exam scores fluctuate partly by chance, most students who get extremely high scores on an exam will get lower scores on the next exam. Because their first score is at the ceiling, their second score is more likely to fall back ("regress") toward their own average than to push the ceiling even higher. (This is why a student who does consistently good work, even if never the best, will sometimes end a course at the top of the class.) Conversely, the lowest-scoring students on the first exam are likely to improve. If those who scored lowest go for tutoring after the first exam, the tutors are likely to feel effective when the student improves, even if the tutoring had no effect.

regression toward the average
the statistical tendency for extreme scores or extreme behavior to return toward one's average

behind the scenes

Observing people's keen desire for control even in chance situations, such as choosing lottery numbers, led me to wonder about people who typically have little control over their lives. In studying hospital patients and the elderly, I discovered that enhancing their sense of control benefited their health and well-being. People suffering the stress of crowded situations or divorce also benefited from an enhanced sense of control. All this makes clear to me that perceived control is extremely important for successful functioning.

Ellen Langer
Harvard University

Regression to the average: When we are at an extremely low point, anything we try, like meditation or yoga, will usually seem effective as we return to our more usual state.

Indeed, when things reach a low point, we will try anything, and whatever we try—going to a psychotherapist, starting a new diet-exercise plan, reading a self-help book—is more likely to be followed by improvement than by further deterioration. Sometimes we recognize that events are not likely to continue at an unusually good or bad extreme. Experience has taught us that when everything is going great, something will go wrong, and that when life is dealing us terrible blows, we can usually look forward to things getting better. Often, though, we fail to recognize this regression effect. We puzzle at why baseball's rookie-of-the-year often has a more ordinary second year—did he become overconfident? self-conscious? We forget that exceptional performance tends to regress toward normality.

To simulate the consequences of using praise and punishment, Paul Schaffner (1985) invited students to train an imaginary fourth-grade boy, "Harold," to come to school by 8:30 each morning. For each school day of a three-week period, a computer displayed Harold's arrival time, which was always between 8:20 and 8:40. The subjects would then select a response to Harold, ranging from strong praise to strong reprimand. As you might expect, they usually praised Harold when he arrived before 8:30 and reprimanded him when he arrived after 8:30. Because Schaffner had programmed the computer to display a random sequence of arrival times, Harold's arrival time tended to improve (to regress toward 8:30) after being reprimanded. For example, if Harold arrived at 8:39, he was almost sure to be reprimanded, and his randomly selected next-day arrival time was likely to be earlier than 8:39. Thus, *even though their reprimands were having no effect,* most subjects ended the experiment believing that their reprimands had been effective.

This experiment demonstrates Tversky and Kahneman's provocative conclusion: Nature operates in such a way that we often feel punished for rewarding others and rewarded for punishing them. In actuality, as every student of psychology knows, positive reinforcement for doing things right is usually more effective and has fewer negative side effects.

Mood and judgment

Social judgment involves efficient, though fallible, information processing. It also involves our feelings: Our moods infuse our judgments. We are not cool computing machines, we are emotional creatures. The extent to which feeling infuses cognition appears in new studies comparing happy and sad individuals (Myers, 1993). Unhappy people—especially those bereaved or depressed—tend to be lethargic, socially withdrawn, even hostile. They also are more self-focused and brooding. Unless it overwhelms people with hopelessness, a depressed mood motivates intense thinking—a search for information that makes one's environment more understandable and controllable (Weary & Edwards, 1994).

Happy people, by contrast, are strikingly energetic, decisive, creative, and sociable. Compared to unhappy people, they are more trusting, more loving, more responsive. If made temporarily happy by receiving a small gift while mall-shopping, they will report, a few moments later on an unrelated survey, that their cars and TV sets are working beautifully—better, if you took their word for it, than those belonging to folks who didn't receive a gift.

Happy people tolerate more frustration. Whether temporarily or enduringly happy, they are more loving and forgiving and less likely to exaggerate or over-interpret slight criticism. They choose long-term rewards over immediate small pleasures. Given a chance to look at happy pictures (people laughing, playing) and sad pictures (funerals, disasters), they literally spend more time looking at the brighter side. Sad people look more at the gloomy side of life and prefer less upbeat people, stories, movies, and music.

The dramatic effect of moods pervades our thinking. To West Germans enjoying their team's World Cup soccer victory (Schwarz & others, 1987) and to Australians emerging from a heartwarming movie (Forgas & Moylan, 1987), people seem good-hearted, life seems wonderful. After (but not before) a 1990 football game between rivals Alabama and Auburn, victorious Alabama fans deemed war less likely and potentially devastating than did the gloomier Auburn fans (Schweitzer & others, 1992). In a happy mood, the world seems friendlier, decisions are easier, good news more readily comes to mind (Johnson & Tversky, 1983; Isen & Means, 1983; Stone & Glass, 1986).

Let our mood turn gloomy, and our thoughts switch onto a different track. Off come the rose-colored glasses; on come the dark glasses. Now the bad mood primes our recollections of negative events (Bower, 1987; Johnson & Magaro, 1987). Our relationships seem to sour. Our self-image takes a dive. Our hopes for the future dim. Other people's behavior seems more sinister (Brown & Taylor, 1986; Esses, 1989; Mayer & Salovey, 1987).

Imagine yourself in an experiment by Joseph Forgas and his colleagues (1984). Using hypnosis, they put you in a good or bad mood and then have you watch a videotape (made the day before) of yourself talking with someone. If made to feel happy, you feel pleased with what you see, and you are able to detect many instances of your poise, interest, and social skill. If put in a bad mood, viewing the same tape seems to reveal a quite different you—one who is frequently stiff, nervous, and inarticulate (Figure 3–8). Given how your mood colors your judgments, you feel relieved at how things brighten when the experimenter switches you to a happy mood before leaving the experiment. Curiously, note Michael Ross and Garth Fletcher (1985), we don't attribute our changing perceptions to our mood shifts. Rather, the world really seems different.

figure 3–8

A temporary good or bad mood strongly influenced people's ratings of their videotaped behavior. Those in a bad mood detected far fewer positive behaviors. (Forgas & others, 1984.)

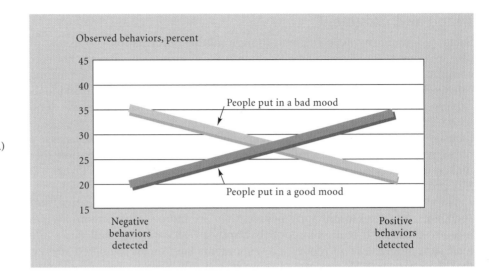

Our moods color how we see our worlds partly by bringing to mind past experiences associated with the mood. In a bad mood we have more depressing thoughts. Mood-related thoughts may distract us from complex thinking about something else. Thus, when emotionally aroused—when angry or even in a very good mood—we become more likely to make snap judgments and evaluate others based on stereotypes (Bodenhausen & others, 1994; Paulhus & Lim, 1994). (Besides, why risk a postgame great mood by thinking deeply about some novel issue, such as the likelihood of a war?)

Our moods affect simple, "automatic" thinking less than complex, "effortful" thinking (Hartlage & others, 1993). Thus, notes Forgas (1994, 1995), moods are most likely to invade thinking when we evaluate unusual rather than typical

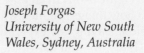

behind the scenes

We all know moody people, and I have often been struck by how their feelings seem to invade their thinking. It almost appears that their memories and judgments change with the color of their mood. For some years now, I have been trying to understand how and why this mood infusion occurs.

One day while sitting in a restaurant, I noticed an odd couple at the next table—a beautiful young woman with an unattractive elderly man. As I found myself repeatedly wondering about this relationship, it occurred to me that the more I thought about them, the more opportunity there might be for my mood to infuse my thoughts. Testing this idea in the laboratory, we found that, indeed, mood had a greater effect on complex judgments of odd couples than on snap judgments of well-matched couples. Such findings have helped us to develop a theory that predicts when moodiness will infuse judgments.

Joseph Forgas
University of New South Wales, Sydney, Australia

people, explain complex rather than simple human conflicts, and make sense of odd rather than well-matched couples. The more we think, the more our moods may infuse our thinking.

Research psychologists have for a long time explored the mind's impressive capacity for processing information. We have an enormous capacity for automatic, efficient, intuitive thinking. Our cognitive efficiency, though generally adaptive, comes at the price of occasional error. Since we are generally unaware of these errors entering our thinking, it can pay us to identify ways in which we form and sustain false beliefs—"reasons for unreason."

First, we often overestimate our judgments. This "overconfidence phenomenon" stems partly from the much greater ease with which we can imagine why we might be right than why we might be wrong. Moreover, people are much more likely to search for information that can confirm their beliefs than information that can disconfirm them.

Second, when given compelling anecdotes or even useless information, we often ignore useful base-rate information. This is partly due to the later ease of recall ("availability") of vivid information.

Third, we are often swayed by illusions of correlation and personal control. It is tempting to perceive correlations where none exist ("illusory correlation") and to think we can predict or control chance events (the "illusion of control").

Finally, moods infuse judgments. Good and bad moods trigger memories of experiences associated with those moods. Moods color our interpretation of current experiences. And by distracting us, moods can also influence how deeply or superficially we think when making judgments.

Summing up

Self-fulfilling beliefs

Having considered how we explain and judge others—efficiently, adaptively, but sometimes wrongly—we conclude by pondering the effects of our social judgments. Do our beliefs about social reality matter? Do they change reality?

Our social beliefs and judgments matter because they have effects. They influence how we feel and act, and by so doing may generate their own reality. When our ideas lead us to act in ways that produce their apparent confirmation, they have become self-fulfilling prophecies. Social perceptions therefore subtly influence social realities.

In his well-known studies of "experimenter bias," Robert Rosenthal (1985) found that research subjects sometimes live up to what is expected of them. In one study, experimenters asked subjects to judge the success of people in various photographs. The experimenters read the same instructions to all their subjects and showed them the same photos. Nevertheless, experimenters led to expect high ratings obtained higher ratings than did those who expected their subjects to see the photographed people as failures. Even more startling—and controversial—are reports that teachers' beliefs about their students similarly serve as self-fulfilling prophecies.

Teacher expectations and student performance

Teachers do have higher expectations for some students than for others. Perhaps you have detected this after having a brother or sister precede you in school, after receiving a label such as "gifted" or "learning disabled," or after being tracked with "high-ability" or "average-ability" students. Perhaps conversation in the teachers' lounge sent your reputation ahead of you, or your new teacher scrutinized your school file or discovered your family's social status. Do such teacher expectations affect student performance? It's clear that teachers' evaluations *correlate* with student achievement: Teachers think well of students who do well. That's mostly because teachers accurately perceive their students' abilities and achievements (Jussim, 1989, 1991; Jussim & others, 1996).

But are teachers' evaluations ever a *cause* as well as a consequence of student performance? One correlational study of 4,300 British schoolchildren by William Crano and Phyllis Mellon (1978) suggested yes. Not only is high performance followed by higher teacher evaluations, but the reverse is true as well.

Could we test this "teacher-expectations effect" experimentally? Pretend we gave a teacher the impression that Dana, Sally, Todd, and Manuel—four randomly selected students—are unusually capable. Will the teacher give special treatment to these four and elicit superior performance from them? In a now famous experiment, Rosenthal and Lenore Jacobson (1968) reported precisely that. Randomly selected children in an elementary school who were said (on the basis of a fictitious test) to be on the verge of a dramatic intellectual spurt did then spurt ahead in IQ score.

This dramatic result seemed to suggest that the school problems of "disadvantaged" children might reflect their teachers' low expectations. The findings were soon publicized in the media as well as in many university textbooks in psychology and education. Further analysis revealed the teacher-expectations effect to be not so powerful and reliable as this initial study had led many people to believe. Some critics questioned the IQ measure and the statistical procedures (Thorndike, 1968; Elashoff & Snow, 1971). Moreover, by Rosenthal's own count, in only 39 percent of the 448 published experiments do expectations significantly affect performance (Rosenthal, 1991). Low expectations do not doom a capable child, nor do high expectations magically transform a slow learner into a valedictorian. Human nature is not so pliable.

Still, in 4 of 10 studies, teacher expectations mattered. High expectations are especially potent with low achievers, for whom a teacher's positive attitude may be a hope-giving breath of fresh air (Madon & others, 1997). Why do expectations sometimes matter? Rosenthal and other investigators report that teachers look, smile, and nod more at "high-potential students." Teachers also may teach more to their "gifted" students, set higher goals for them, call on them more, and give them more time to answer (Cooper, 1983; Harris & Rosenthal, 1985, 1986; Jussim, 1986).

In one study, Elisha Babad, Frank Bernieri, and Rosenthal (1991) videotaped teachers talking to, or about, unseen students for whom they held high or low expectations. A random 10-second clip of either the teacher's voice or face was enough to tell viewers—both children and adults—whether this was a good or poor student and how much the teacher liked the student. (You read that right: 10 seconds.) Although teachers may think they can conceal their feelings, students are acutely sensitive to teachers' facial expressions and body movements.

Reading the experiments on teacher expectations makes me wonder about the effect of *students'* expectations upon their teachers. You no doubt begin

To judge a teacher or professor's overall warmth and enthusiasm also takes but a thin slice of behavior—mere seconds.

(Ambady & Rosenthal, 1992, 1993)

many of your courses having heard "Professor Smith is interesting" and "Professor Jones is a bore." Robert Feldman and Thomas Prohaska (1979; Feldman & Theiss, 1982) found that such expectations can affect both student and teacher. Students in a learning experiment who expected to be taught by a competent teacher perceived their teacher (who was unaware of their expectations) as more competent and interesting than did students with low expectations. Furthermore, the students actually learned more. In a follow-up experiment, Feldman and Prohaska videotaped teachers and had observers later rate their performance. Teachers were judged most capable when assigned a student who nonverbally conveyed positive expectations.

To see whether such effects might also occur in actual classrooms, a research team led by David Jamieson (1987) experimented with four Ontario high school classes taught by a newly transferred teacher. During individual interviews they told students in two of the classes that both other students and the research team rated the teacher very highly. Compared to the control classes, whose expectations they did not raise, the students given positive expectations paid better attention during class. At the end of the teaching unit, they also got better grades and rated the teacher as clearer in her teaching. The attitudes that a class has toward its teacher are as important, it seems, as the teacher's attitude toward the students.

Getting from others what we expect

So the expectations of experimenters and teachers, though usually reasonably accurate assessments, occasionally act as self-fulfilling prophecies. How general is this effect? Do we get from others what we expect of them? There are times when negative expectations of someone lead us to be extra nice to that person, which induces them to be nice in return—thus *dis*confirming our expectations. But a more common finding in studies of social interaction is that, yes, we do to some extent get what we expect (Olson & others, 1996).

In laboratory games, hostility nearly always begets hostility: People who *perceive* their opponents as noncooperative will readily induce them to *be* noncooperative (Kelley & Stahelski, 1970). Self-confirming beliefs abound when there is conflict. Each party's perception of the other as aggressive, resentful, and vindictive induces the other to display these behaviors in self-defense, thus creating a vicious self-perpetuating circle. Whether I expect my wife to be in a bad mood or in a warm, loving mood may affect how I relate to her, thereby inducing her to confirm my belief.

So do intimate relationships prosper when partners idealize one another? Are positive illusions of the other's virtues self-fulfilling? Or are they more often self-defeating, by creating expectations that can't be met and that ultimately spell doom? Among University of Waterloo dating couples followed by Sandra Murray and her associates (1996), positive ideals of one's partner were good omens. Idealization helped buffer conflict, bolster satisfaction, and turn self-perceived frogs into princes or princesses. When someone loves and admires us, it helps us become more the person he or she imagines us to be.

Several experiments conducted by Mark Snyder (1984) show how, once formed, erroneous beliefs about the social world can induce others to confirm those beliefs, a phenomenon called **behavioral confirmation**. In a now-classic study, Snyder, Elizabeth Tanke, and Ellen Berscheid (1977) had men students talk on the telephone with women they thought (from having been shown a picture) were either attractive or unattractive. Analysis of

behavioral confirmation a type of self-fulfilling prophecy whereby people's social expectations lead them to act in ways that cause others to confirm their expectations

What we believe about someone can lead us to treat the person in ways that create a self-fulfilling prophecy.

just the women's comments during the conversations revealed that the supposedly attractive women spoke more warmly than the supposedly unattractive women. The men's erroneous beliefs had become a self-fulfilling prophecy by leading them to act in a way that influenced the women to fulfill their stereotype that beautiful people are desirable people.

Expectations influence children's behavior, too. After observing the amount of litter in three classrooms, Richard Miller and his colleagues (1975) had the teacher and others repeatedly tell one class that they should be neat and tidy. This persuasion increased the amount of litter placed in wastebaskets from 15 to 45 percent, but only temporarily. Another class, which also had been placing only 15 percent of its litter in wastebaskets, was repeatedly congratulated for being so neat and tidy. After eight days of hearing this, and still two weeks later, these children were fulfilling the expectation by putting more than 80 percent of their litter in wastebaskets. Repeatedly tell children they are hard-working and kind (rather than lazy and mean), and they may live up to their label.

These experiments help us understand how social beliefs, such as stereotypes about people with disabilities or about people of a particular race or sex, may be self-confirming. We help construct our own social realities. How others treat us reflects how we and others have treated them.

As with every social phenomenon, the tendency to confirm others' expectations has its limits. Expectations often predict behavior simply because they are accurate (Jussim, 1993). Also, people who are forewarned about another's expectation may work to overcome it (Hilton & Darley, 1985; Swann, 1987). If Chuck knows Jane thinks he's an airhead, he may strive to disprove her impression. If Jane knows that Chuck expects her to be aloof, she may actively refute his expectation.

William Swann and Robin Ely (1984) report another condition under which we are unlikely to confirm others' expectations: when their expectations clash with our clear self-concept. For example, Swann and Ely found that when a strongly outgoing person was interviewed by someone who expected her to be introverted, the interviewer's perceptions changed, not the interviewee's behavior. In contrast, interviewees who were unsure of themselves more often lived up to the interviewer's expectations.

Our beliefs about ourselves can also be self-fulfilling. In several experiments, Steven Sherman (1980) found that people often fulfill predictions they make of their own behavior. When people were called and asked to volunteer three hours to a Cancer Society drive, only 4 percent agreed to do so. When a comparable group of other residents were called and asked to *predict* how they would react if they were to receive such a request, almost half predicted they would agree to help—and most of these did indeed agree to do so when they were contacted by the Cancer Society. Formulating a plan for how we would want to act in a given situation makes it more likely that we will really do it.

focus

The self-fulfilling psychology of the stock market

On the evening of January 6, 1981, Joseph Granville, a popular investment adviser, wired his clients: "Stock prices will nose-dive; sell tomorrow." Word of Granville's advice soon spread, and January 7 became the heaviest day of trading in the history of the stock market. All told, stock values lost $40 billion.

Nearly a half-century ago, John Maynard Keynes likened such stock market psychology to the popular beauty contests then conducted by London newspapers. To win, one had to pick the six faces out of a hundred that were, in turn, chosen most frequently by the other newspaper contestants. Thus, as Keynes wrote, "Each competitor has to pick not those faces which he himself finds prettiest, but those which he thinks likeliest to catch the fancy of the other competitors."

Investors likewise try to pick not the stocks that touch their fancy but the stocks that other investors will favor. The name of the game is predicting others' behavior. As one stock fund manager explained, "You may or may not agree with Granville's view—but that's usually beside the point." If you think his advice will cause others to sell, then you want to sell quickly, before prices drop more. If you expect others to buy, you buy now to beat the rush.

The self-fulfilling psychology of the stock market worked to an extreme on Monday, October 19, 1987, when the stock market crashed, causing people to lose—on paper—about 20 percent of the value of their stock investments. Part of what happens during such slides is that the media and rumor mill focus on whatever bad news is available to explain them. Once reported, the explanatory news stories further diminish people's expectations, causing declining prices to fall still lower—and vice versa by amplifying good news when stock prices are rising.

Summing up

Our beliefs sometimes take on a life of their own. Usually, our beliefs about others have a basis in reality. But studies of experimenter bias and teacher expectations show that an erroneous belief that certain people are unusually capable (or incapable) can lead teachers and researchers to give those people special treatment. This may elicit superior (or inferior) performance and, therefore, seem to confirm an assumption that is actually false. Similarly, in everyday life we often get "behavioral confirmation" of what we expect.

Conclusions

Social cognition studies reveal that our information-processing powers are impressive for their efficiency and adaptiveness ("in apprehension how like a god!" exclaimed Shakespeare's Hamlet), yet vulnerable to predictable errors and misjudgments ("headpiece filled with straw," said T. S. Eliot). What practical lessons, and what insights into human nature, can we take home from this research?

We could extend our list of reasons for unreason, but surely this has been a sufficient glimpse at how people come to believe what may be untrue. We cannot easily dismiss these experiments: Most of their participants were intelligent people, mostly students at leading universities. Moreover, these predictable distortions and biases occurred even when payment for right answers motivated people to think optimally. As one researcher concluded, the illusions "have a persistent quality not unlike that of perceptual illusions" (Slovic, 1972).

Research in cognitive social psychology thus mirrors the mixed review given humanity in literature, philosophy, and religion. Many research psychologists have spent lifetimes exploring the awesome capacities of the human mind. We are smart enough to have cracked our own genetic code, to have invented talking computers, to have sent people to the moon. Three cheers for human reason.

Well, two cheers—because the mind's premium on efficient judgment makes our intuition more vulnerable to misjudgment than we suspect. With remarkable ease, we form and sustain false beliefs. Led by our preconceptions, overconfident, persuaded by vivid anecdotes, perceiving correlations and control even where none may exist, we construct our social beliefs and then influence others to confirm them. "The naked intellect," observed novelist Madeline L'Engle, "is an extraordinarily inaccurate instrument."

"In creating these problems, we didn't set out to fool people. All our problems fooled us, too."

Amos Tversky (1985)

But have these experiments just been intellectual tricks played on hapless participants, thus making them look worse than they are? Richard Nisbett and Lee Ross (1980) contend that, if anything, laboratory procedures overestimate our intuitive powers. The experiments usually present people with clear evidence and warn them that their reasoning ability is being tested. Seldom does life say to us: "Here is some evidence. Now put on your intellectual Sunday best and answer these questions."

Often our everyday failings are inconsequential, but not always so. False impressions, interpretations, and beliefs can produce serious consequences. Even small biases can have profound social effects when we are making important social judgments: Why are so many people homeless? unhappy? homicidal? Does my friend love me or my money? Cognitive biases even creep into sophisticated scientific thinking. Apparently human nature has not changed in the 3000 years since the Psalmist noted that "no one can see his own errors."

Lest we succumb to the cynical conclusion that all beliefs are absurd, I hasten to balance the picture. The elegant analyses of the imperfections of our thinking are themselves a tribute to human wisdom. (Were one to argue that all human thought is illusory, the assertion would be self-refuting, for it, too, would be but an illusion. It would be logically equivalent to contending "all generalizations are false, including this one.")

As medical science assumes that any given body organ serves a function, so behavioral scientists find it useful to assume that our modes of thought and behavior are generally adaptive (Funder, 1987; Kruglanski & Ajzen, 1983; Swann, 1984). The rules of thought that produce false beliefs and striking deficiencies in our statistical intuition usually serve us well. Frequently, the errors are a by-product of our mental shortcuts that simplify the complex information we receive.

Nobel laureate psychologist Herbert Simon (1957) was among the modern researchers who first described the bounds of human reason. Simon contends that to cope with reality, we simplify it. Consider the complexity of a chess game: The number of possible games is greater than the number of particles in the universe. How do we cope? We adopt some simplifying rules of thumb—heuristics. These heuristics sometimes lead us to defeat. But they do enable us to make efficient snap judgments.

Illusory thinking can likewise spring from useful heuristics that aid our survival. The belief in our power to control events helps maintain hope and effort. If things are sometimes subject to control and sometimes not, we maximize our outcomes by positive thinking. Optimism pays dividends. We might even say that our beliefs are like scientific theories—sometimes in error yet useful as generalizations. As Susan Fiske (1992) says, "thinking is for doing."

As we constantly seek to improve our theories, might we not also work to reduce error in our social thinking? In school, math teachers teach, teach, teach until the mind is finally trained to process numerical information accurately and automatically. We assume that such ability does not come naturally; otherwise, why bother with the years of training? Research psychologist Robyn Dawes (1980)—who is dismayed that "study after study has shown [that] people have very limited abilities to process information on a conscious level, particularly social information"—suggests that we should also teach, teach, teach how to process social information.

Richard Nisbett and Lee Ross (1980) believe that education could indeed reduce our vulnerability to certain types of error. They propose that:

- We train people to recognize likely sources of error in their own social intuition.

- We set up statistics courses geared to everyday problems of logic and social judgment. Given such training, people do in fact reason better about everyday events (Lehman & others, 1988; Nisbett & others, 1987).

- We make such teaching more effective by richly illustrating it with concrete, vivid anecdotes and examples from everyday life.

- We teach memorable and useful slogans, such as: "It's an empirical question." Or "Which hat did you draw that sample out of?" Or "You can lie with statistics, but a well-chosen example does the job better."

"The purposes in the human mind are like deep water, but the intelligent will draw them out."

Proverbs 20:5

"The spirit of liberty is the spirit which is not too sure that it is right; the spirit of liberty is the spirit which seeks to understand the minds of other men and women; the spirit of liberty is the spirit which weighs their interests alongside its own without bias."

Learned Hand, *The Spirit of Liberty*, 1952

focus

How journalists think: cognitive bias in newsmaking

"That's the way it is," concluded anchorperson Walter Cronkite at the end of each newscast. And that's the journalistic ideal—to present reality the way it is. One major paper's reporters' manual states the ideal plainly: "A reporter must never hold inflexibly to his preconceptions, straining again and again to find proof of them where little exists, ignoring contrary evidence. . . . Events, not preconceptions, should shape all stories to the end" (Blundell, 1986, p. 25).

We might wish that it were so. But journalists are human, conclude Holly Stocking and Paget Gross in their book *How Do Journalists Think?* Like laypeople and scientists, journalists "construct reality." The cognitive biases considered in this chapter therefore color newsmaking, in at least six ways.

1. *Preconceptions may control interpretations.* Typically, reporters "go after an idea," which may then affect how they interpret information. Beginning with the idea that homelessness reflects a failure of mental health programs, a reporter may interpret ambiguous information accordingly while discounting other complicating factors.

2. *Confirmation bias may guide them toward sources and questions that will confirm their preconceptions.* Hoping to report the newsworthy story that a radiation leak is causing birth defects, a reporter might interview someone who accepts the idea and then someone else recommended by the first person. Believing that devastating disabilities can be overcome, a reporter might ask disabled people, "How did you overcome the obstacles you faced?" Assuming that a coach is disliked, a reporter may interview the coach's detractors and ask *how* the coach offends people.

3. *Belief perseverance may sustain preconceptions in the face of discrediting.* While "greedy" Ivan Boesky awaited sentencing on a 1987 insider-trading scandal, he looked for volunteer work, something "a lot of whitecollar crooks do to

impress sentencing judges," noted a contemptuous reporter. On the other hand, a politician caught lying can, if respected, be reported as "confused" or "forgetful."

4. *Compelling anecdotes may seem more informative than base-rate information.* Like their readers, journalists may be more persuaded by vivid stories of ESP and other psychic happenings than by dispassionate research. They may be more taken by someone's apparent "cure" by a new therapy than by statistics on the therapy's success rate. After an air crash, they may describe "the frightening dangers of modern air travel," without noting its actual safety record.

5. *Events may seem correlated when they are not.* A striking co-occurrence—say three minority athletes' problems with drugs—may lead reporters to infer a relationship between race and drug use in the absence of representative evidence.

6. *Hindsight makes for easy after-the-fact analysis.* The federal government's attempt to recognize the sovereignty and unique cultural heritage of Quebec in the Meech Lake Accord was "doomed from the start"; so said journalists *after* they knew it had failed. The RCMP's decision to use pepper spray against a group of protesters during the APEC meeting in Vancouver was roundly criticized *after* the negative public reaction that followed the incident. Decisions that turn out poorly have a way of seeming *obviously* dumb, after the fact.

Indeed, surmise Stocking and Gross, given all the information that reporters and editors must process quickly, how could they avoid the illusory thinking tendencies that penetrate human thinking? But on the positive side, exposing these points of bias may alert journalists to ways of reducing them—by considering opposite conclusions, by seeking sources and asking questions that might counter their ideas, by seeking statistical information first and then seeking representative anecdotes, by remembering that well-meaning people make decisions without advance knowledge of their consequences.

Summing up

Research on social beliefs and judgments reveals how we form and sustain beliefs that usually serve us well, but sometimes lead us astray. Even our misjudgments are by-products of thinking strategies (heuristics) that usually serve us well, just as visual illusions are a by-product of perceptual mechanisms that help us organize sensory information. But they are still errors, errors that can warp our perceptions of reality and prejudice our judgments of others.

PS Personal postscript: Reflecting on intuition's powers and limits

Is research on pride and error too humbling? Surely we can acknowledge the hard truth of our human limits and still sympathize with the deeper message that people are more than machines. Our subjective experiences are the stuff of our humanity—our art and our music, our enjoyment of friendship and love, our mystical and religious experiences.

> "Rob the average man of his life-illusion, and you rob him also of his happiness."
>
> Henrik Ibsen, *The Wild Duck*, 1884

The cognitive and social psychologists who explore illusory thinking are not out to remake us into logical machines. They know that intuition and feeling not only enrich human experience but also are an important source of creative ideas. They add, however, the humbling reminder that our susceptibility to error also makes clear the need for disciplined training of the mind. Norman Cousins (1978) called this "the biggest truth of all about learning: that its purpose is to unlock the human mind and to develop it into an organ capable of thought—conceptual thought, analytical thought, sequential thought."

Research on error and illusion in social judgment reminds us to "judge not"—to remember, with a dash of humility, our potential for misjudgment. It also encourages us not to feel intimidated by the arrogance of true believers—people who fail to appreciate their own potential for bias and error. We humans are wonderfully intelligent yet fallible creatures, having dignity but not deity.

Such humility and distrust of human authority is at the heart of both religion and science. No wonder many of the founders of modern science were religious people whose convictions predisposed them to be humble before nature and skeptical of human authority (Hooykaas, 1972; Merton, 1938). Science always involves an interplay between intuition and rigorous test, between creative hunch and skepticism. To sift reality from illusion requires both open-minded curiosity and hard-headed rigor. This perspective could prove to be a good attitude for approaching all of life: to be critical but not cynical, curious but not gullible, open, but not exploitable.

chapter 4

Behavior and Attitudes

each year throughout the industrialized world, the tobacco industry kills some two million of its best customers (Peto & others, 1992). Given present trends, estimates a 1994 World Health Organization report, *half a billion* people alive today will be killed by tobacco. In the United States, for example, smoking kills 420,000 people a year—surpassing the combined fatalities from homicide, suicide, AIDS, car accidents, and alcohol and drug abuse. Although quick assisted suicide may be illegal, slow-motion suicide assisted by the tobacco industry is not.

People wonder: With the tobacco industry responsible for fatalities equal to fourteen loaded and crashed jumbo jets a day (not including those in the expanding but hard to count third world market), how do tobacco company executives live with themselves? At one of the world's two largest tobacco advertisers, upper-level executives—mostly intelligent, family-oriented, community-minded people—resent being called "mass murderers."

Attitudes and actions: Many sports events, which glorify health and physical prowess, are sponsored by manufacturers of products like cigarettes, which are dangerous to health.

They were less than pleased when one government official (Koop, 1997) called them "a sleazy bunch of people who misled us, deceived us and lied to us for three decades." Moreover, they defend smokers' right to choose. "Is it an addiction issue?" asks one vice-president. "I don't believe it. People do all sorts of things to express their individuality and to protest against society. And smoking is one of them, and not the worst" (Rosenblatt, 1994).

Social psychologists wonder if such statements reflect privately held attitudes—or social pressure to say things one doesn't believe. Does this executive really think smoking is a comparatively healthy expression of individuality? If so, how are such attitudes internalized?

When people question someone's attitude, they refer to beliefs and feelings related to a person or event and the resulting behavior. Taken together, favorable or unfavorable evaluative reactions—whether exhibited in beliefs, feelings, or inclinations to act—define a person's **attitude** toward something (Olson & Zanna, 1993). Attitudes are an efficient way to size up the world. When we have to respond quickly to something, how we feel about it can guide how we react (Bassili & Roy, 1998; Breckler & Wiggins, 1989; Sanbonmatsu & Fazio, 1990). For example, a person who believes a particular ethnic group is lazy and aggressive may feel dislike for such people and therefore intend to act in a discriminatory manner. When assessing attitudes, we tap one of these three dimensions. You can remember them as the ABCs of attitudes: affect (feelings), behavior (intention), and cognition (thoughts).

The study of attitudes is close to the heart of social psychology and historically was one of its first concerns. Researchers wondered: how much do our attitudes affect our actions?

attitude
a favorable or unfavorable evaluative reaction toward something or someone, exhibited in one's beliefs, feelings, or intended behavior

behind the scenes

I began studying attitudes while I was a graduate student working with Mark Zanna at the University of Waterloo. Initially, I was most interested in the consequences of attitudes, rather than attitude formation or change. For example, Mark and I investigated the effects of attitudes on behavior (attitude-behavior consistency) and memory (selective learning). I then became interested in self-perception processes—the tendency for people to make inferences about their attitudes from their behaviors. More recently, my research has turned to issues concerning the nature and origins of attitudes, such as the functions of attitudes, the effects of attitude accessibility, the relation between attitudes and values, and the heritability of attitudes. I have been extremely fortunate to work with many outstanding graduate students at the University of Western Ontario, including Carolyn Hafer, Douglas

Hazelwood, Gregory Maio, and Neal Roese, whose thinking has helped to shape my work.

James T. Olson
University of Western Ontario

Do attitudes determine behavior?

To what extent, and under what conditions, do the attitudes of the heart drive our outward actions? Why were social psychologists at first surprised by a seemingly small connection between attitudes and actions?

Asking whether attitudes determine behavior asks a basic question about human nature: What is the relationship between what we *are* (on the inside) and what we *do* (on the outside)? Philosophers, theologians, and educators have long speculated about the connection between thought and action, character and conduct, private word and public deed. The prevailing assumption, which underlies most teaching, counseling, and child rearing, has been that our private beliefs and feelings determine our public behavior. So if we want to alter the way people act, we need to change their hearts and minds.

> "The ancestor of every action is a thought."
>
> Ralph Waldo Emerson, *Essays, First Series*, 1841

Are we all hypocrites?

In the beginning, social psychologists agreed: To know people's attitudes is to predict their actions. But in 1964, Leon Festinger—judged by some to have been social psychology's most important contributor (Gerard, 1994)—concluded the evidence did *not* show that changing attitudes changes behavior. Festinger believed the attitude-behavior relation works the other way around, with our behavior as the horse and our attitudes as the cart. As Robert Abelson (1972) put it, we are "very well trained and very good at finding reasons for what we do, but not very good at doing what we find reasons for."

A further blow to the supposed power of attitudes came in 1969, when social psychologist Allan Wicker reviewed several dozen research studies covering a wide variety of people, attitudes, and behaviors, and offered a shocking conclusion: People's expressed attitudes hardly predicted their varying behaviors. Student attitudes toward cheating bore little relation to the likelihood of their actually cheating. Attitudes toward the church were only modestly linked with church attendance on any given Sunday. Self-described racial attitudes provided little clue to behaviors in actual situations.

This was dramatically apparent during the early 1930s, when many U.S. residents expressed intense prejudice against Asians. To discern the extent of such prejudice, Richard LaPiere (1934) wrote 251 restaurants and hotels, asking, "Will you accept members of the Chinese race as guests in your establishment?" Among the 128 who replied, 92 percent said no, and only one said yes. But LaPiere and a "personable and charming" young Chinese couple had traveled the country six months previously and actually received courteous treatment at all but one of these establishments. Faced with specific people who did not fit the stereotypes, the proprietors laid aside their negative attitudes.

If people don't play the same game that they talk, it's little wonder that attempts to change behavior by changing attitudes often fail. Warnings about the dangers of smoking only minimally affect those who already smoke. Increasing public awareness of the desensitizing and brutalizing effects of a prolonged diet of television violence has stimulated many people to voice a desire for less violent programming—yet they still watch media murder as much as ever. Appeals for safe driving have had far less effect on accident rates than have lower speed limits, divided highways, and drunk driving penalties (Etzioni, 1972).

While Wicker and others were describing the weakness of attitudes, some personality psychologists found personality traits equally ineffective in predicting behavior (Mischel, 1968). If we want to know how helpful people are going to be, we usually won't learn much by giving them tests of self-esteem, anxiety, or defensiveness. In a situation with clear-cut demands, we are better off knowing how most people react. Likewise, many critics of psychotherapy began to argue that talking therapies, such as psychoanalysis, seldom "cure" problems. Instead of analyzing personality defects, the critics said, the way to change an attitude was to change the problem *behavior*.

"It may be desirable to abandon the attitude concept."

Allan Wicker, 1971

All in all, the developing picture of what controls behavior emphasized external social influences and played down internal factors, such as attitudes and personality. The emerging image was of little billiard balls that have different stripes and colors, to be sure, but are all buffeted by outside forces. In short, the original thesis that attitudes determine actions was countered during the 1960s by the antithesis that attitudes determine virtually nothing. Thesis. Antithesis. Is there a synthesis? The surprising finding that what people *say* often differs from what they *do* sent social psychologists scurrying to find out why. Surely, we reasoned, convictions and feelings *must* sometimes make a difference.

Indeed. In fact, what I am about to explain now seems so obvious that I wonder why most social psychologists (myself included) were not thinking this way before the early 1970s. I must remind myself that truth never seems obvious until it is known.

When do attitudes predict behavior?

We sometimes violate our expressed attitudes because, as Figure 4–1 suggests, our behavior and our expressed attitudes are both subject to other influences. One social psychologist counted 40 separate factors that complicate their relationship (Triandis, 1982; see also Kraus, 1995). If we could just neutralize the other influences—make all other things equal—might attitudes accurately predict behaviors? Let's see.

Minimizing social influences on expressed attitudes

Unlike a physician measuring heart rate, social psychologists never get a direct reading on attitudes. Rather, we measure *expressed* attitudes. Like other behaviors, expressions are subject to outside influences. This was vividly demonstrated when the politicians once overwhelmingly passed a salary increase for themselves in an off-the-record vote, then moments later overwhelmingly defeated the same bill on a roll-call vote. Fear of criticism had distorted the true sentiment on the roll-call vote. We sometimes say what we think others want to hear.

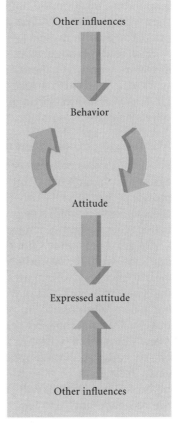

figure 4-1

Our expressed attitudes imperfectly predict our behavior, because both are subject to other influences.

Knowing that people don't wear their hearts on their sleeves, social psychologists have longed for a "pipeline to the heart." Edward Jones and Harold Sigall (1971) therefore devised a **bogus pipeline** method that fools people into exposing their real attitudes. In one experiment, conducted with Richard Page, Sigall (1971) had students hold a locked wheel that, if unlocked, could turn a pointer to the left, indicating disagreement, or to the right, indicating agreement. When electrodes were attached to their arms, the fake machine supposedly measured tiny muscular responses said to gauge their tendency to turn the wheel left (disagree) or right (agree). To demonstrate this amazing new machine, the researcher asked the students some questions. After a few moments of impressive flashing lights and whirring sounds, a meter on the machine announced the student's attitude—which was nothing more than an attitude the student had earlier expressed as part of a now-forgotten survey. The procedure convinced everyone.

Once the students were convinced, the attitude meter was hidden and they were asked questions concerning their attitudes toward Blacks and requested to guess what the meter revealed. How do you suppose these White university students responded? Compared to other students who responded through a typical questionnaire, those responding by the bogus pipeline admitted more negative belief. Unlike those responding to the paper-and-pencil scale—who rated Blacks as being more sensitive than other people—those

bogus pipeline
A procedure that fools people into disclosing their attitudes. Participants are first convinced that a machine can use their psychological responses to measure their private attitudes. Then they are asked to predict the machine's reading, thus revealing their attitudes.

responding through the bogus pipeline reversed these judgments. It was as if they were thinking, "I'd better tell the truth or the experimenter will think I'm out of touch with myself."

Such findings suggest a reason why subjects who are first persuaded that lie detectors work may then admit the truth (in which case, the lie detector *has* worked!). They also suggest one reason for a weak attitude-behavior link: Under everyday conditions, such as those faced by tobacco executives and politicians, people sometimes express attitudes they don't privately hold.

Minimizing other influences on behavior

Social influences color other behaviors as well. As Chapters 5 to 8 will illustrate again and again, social influences can be enormous—enormous enough to induce people to violate their deepest convictions. Before Jesus' crucifixion, his disciple Peter denied ever knowing him. Government aides may go along with actions they know are wrong. Prisoners of war may lie to placate their captors.

On any occasion it's not only our inner attitudes that guide us but also the situation we face. Would *averaging* many occasions enable us to detect more clearly the impact of our attitudes? Predicting people's behavior is like predicting a baseball or cricket player's hitting. The outcome of any particular time at bat is nearly impossible to predict, because it is affected not only by the batter but also by what the pitcher throws and by chance factors. When we aggregate many times at bat, we neutralize these complicating factors. Knowing the players, we can predict their approximate batting *averages*.

To use a research example, people's general attitude toward religion poorly predicts whether they will go to worship next weekend (because the weather, the preacher, how one is feeling, and so forth also influence attendance). But religious attitudes predict quite well the total quantity of religious behaviors over time (Fishbein & Ajzen, 1974; Kahle & Berman, 1979). The findings define a *principle of aggregation*: The effects of an attitude on behavior become more apparent when we look at a person's aggregate or average behavior rather than at isolated acts.

Examining attitudes specific to the behavior

Other conditions further improve the predictive accuracy of attitudes. As Icek Ajzen and Martin Fishbein (1977; Ajzen, 1982) point out, when the measured attitude is general—say, an attitude toward Asians—and the behavior is very specific—say, a decision whether to help the particular Asian couple in LaPiere's study—we should not expect a close correspondence between words and actions. Indeed, report Fishbein and Ajzen, in 26 out of 27 such research studies, attitudes did not predict behavior. But attitudes *did* predict behavior in all 26 studies they could find in which the measured attitude was directly pertinent to the situation. Thus, attitudes toward the general concept of "health fitness" poorly predict specific exercise and dietary practices. Whether people jog is more likely to depend on their opinions about the costs and benefits of *jogging*.

Further studies—more than 500 in all—confirmed that specific, relevant attitudes *do* predict behavior (Bassili, 1995; Six & Eckes, 1996; Wallace & others, 1996). For example, attitudes toward contraception strongly predict contraceptive use (Morrison, 1989). And attitudes toward recycling (but not general attitudes toward environmental issues) predict participation in recycling (Oskamp, 1991).

> "Do I contradict myself? Very well then I contradict myself. (I am large, I contain multitudes.)"
>
> Walt Whitman, *Song of Myself*, 1855

Compared to their general attitudes toward a healthy lifestyle, people's specific attitudes regarding jogging predict their jogging behavior much better.

To change health habits through persuasion, we had best alter people's attitudes toward *specific* practices (Olson & Zanna, 1981; Ajzen & Timko, 1986; Courneya, 1995).

So far we have seen two conditions under which attitudes will predict behavior: (1) When we minimize other influences upon our attitude statements and our behavior, and (2) when the attitude is specifically relevant to the observed behavior. There is a third condition: An attitude predicts behavior better when it is potent.

Making attitudes potent

When we act automatically our attitudes often lie dormant. We act out familiar scripts, without reflecting on what we're doing. We respond to people we meet in the hall with an automatic "Hi." We answer the restaurant cashier's question, "How was your meal?" by saying, "Fine," even if we found it tasteless. Such mindless reaction is adaptive. It frees our minds to work on other things. As the philosopher Alfred North Whitehead argued, "Civilization advances by extending the number of operations which we can perform without thinking about them." But when we are on automatic pilot, our attitudes are dormant.

Bringing attitudes to mind.   In novel situations our behavior is less automatic; lacking a script, we think before we act. If they are prompted to think about their attitudes before acting, will people be truer to themselves? Mark Snyder and William Swann (1976) wanted to find out. So two weeks after 120 of their students indicated their attitudes toward affirmative-action employment policies, Snyder and Swann invited them to act as jurors in a sex-discrimination court case. Only if they first induced the students to remember their attitudes—by giving them "a few minutes to organize your

"Thinking is easy, acting difficult, and to put one's thoughts into action, the most difficult thing in the world."

German poet Goethe, 1749–1832

thoughts and views on the affirmative-action issue"—did attitudes predict verdicts. Similarly, people who take a few moments to review their past behavior express attitudes that better predict their future behavior (Zanna & others, 1981). Our attitudes guide our behavior if we think about them.

Self-conscious people usually are in touch with their attitudes (Miller & Grush, 1986). This suggests another way to induce people to focus on their inner convictions: *Make* them self-conscious, perhaps by having them act in front of a mirror (Carver & Scheier, 1981). Maybe you can recall suddenly being acutely aware of yourself upon entering a room with a large mirror. Making people self-aware in this way promotes consistency between words and deeds (Gibbons, 1978; Froming & others, 1982).

Edward Diener and Mark Wallbom (1976) noted that nearly all university students *say* that cheating is morally wrong. But will they follow the advice of Shakespeare's Polonius, "To thine own self be true"? Diener and Wallbom set students to work on an anagram-solving task (said to predict IQ) and told them to stop when a bell in the room sounded. Left alone, 71 percent cheated by working past the bell. Among students made self-aware—by working in front of a mirror while hearing their tape-recorded voices—only 7 percent cheated. It makes one wonder: Would eye-level mirrors in stores make people more conscious of their attitudes about stealing?

The potency of attitudes forged through experience.   Finally, we acquire attitudes in a manner that makes them sometimes potent, sometimes not. An extensive series of experiments by Russell Fazio and Mark Zanna (1981) shows that when attitudes arise from experience, they are far more likely to endure and to guide actions. They conducted one of their studies with the unwitting help of their university. A housing shortage forced the university to assign some first-year students to several weeks on cots in dormitory lounges while others basked in the relative luxury of permanent rooms.

When questioned by Dennis Regan and Fazio (1977), students in both groups had equally negative attitudes about the housing situation and how the administration was dealing with it. Given opportunities to act upon their attitudes—to sign a petition and solicit other signatures, to join a committee to investigate the situation, to write a letter—only those whose attitudes grew from direct experience with the temporary housing acted. Moreover, compared to attitudes formed passively, those forged in the fire of experience are more thoughtful, more certain, more stable, more resistant to attack, more accessible, and more emotionally charged (Millar & Millar, 1996; Sherman & others, 1983; Watts, 1967; Wu & Shaffer, 1987). And when the emotional and belief components of an attitude are consistent, the attitude moves behavior—as strong attitudes do (Chaiken & others, 1995).

Some conclusions

To summarize, our attitudes predict our actions if

- Other influences are minimized
- The attitude is specific to the action
- The attitude is potent—because something reminds us of it, or because we gained it in a manner that makes it strong

Do these conditions seem obvious? It may be tempting to think we "knew them all along." But remember: They were not obvious to researchers in 1970.

> "Without doubt it is a delightful harmony when doing and saying go together."
>
> Montaigne, *Essays*, 1588

Nor were they obvious to German university students, when asked to guess the outcomes of published studies on attitude-behavior consistency (Six & Krahe, 1984).

So it is now plain that, depending on the circumstances, the relationship between attitude statements and behavior can range from no relationship to a strong one (Kraus, 1995). Yet we can breathe a sigh of relief that our attitudes are, after all, *one* determinant of our actions. To return to our philosophical question, there *is* a connection between what we are and what we do, even if that connection is looser than most of us would have guessed.

> "It is easier to preach virtue than to practice it."
>
> La Rochefoucauld, *Maxims*, 1665

Summing up

How do our inner attitudes relate to our external actions? Social psychologists agree that attitudes and actions feed each other. Popular wisdom stresses the impact of attitudes on action. Surprisingly, attitudes—usually assessed as feelings toward some object or person—are often poor predictors of actions. Moreover, changing people's attitudes typically fails to produce much change in their behavior. These findings sent social psychologists scurrying to find out why we so often fail to play the game we talk. The answer: Our expressions of attitudes and our behaviors are each subject to many influences.

Our attitudes *will* predict our behavior (1) if these "other influences" are minimized, (2) if the attitude corresponds very closely to the predicted behavior (as in voting studies), and (3) if the attitude is potent (because something reminds us of it, or because we acquired it by direct experience). Thus there *is* a connection between what we think and feel and what we do, but in many situations that connection is weaker than we'd like to believe.

Does behavior determine attitudes?

If social psychology has taught us anything during the last 25 years, it is that we are likely not only to think ourselves into a way of acting but also to act ourselves into a way of thinking. What lines of evidence support this assertion?

Now we turn to the more startling idea that behavior determines attitudes. It's true that we sometimes stand up for what we believe, but it's also true that we come to believe in what we stand up for (Figure 4–2). Social-psychological theories inspired much of the research that underlies this conclusion. Instead of beginning with these theories, I think it more interesting to first present the wide-ranging evidence that behavior affects attitudes. This way you can play theorist as you read. Speculate *why* actions affect attitudes, and then compare your ideas with the explanations proposed by social psychologists.

Consider the following incidents, each based on actual happenings:

> "Thought is the child of Action."
>
> Benjamin Disraeli, *Vivian Grey*, 1826

- Sarah is hypnotized and told to take off her shoes when a book drops on the floor. Fifteen minutes later a book drops, and Sarah quietly slips out of her loafers. "Sarah," asks the hypnotist, "why did you take off your shoes?" "Well . . . my feet are hot and tired," Sarah replies. "It has been a long day." The act produces the idea.

- George has electrodes temporarily implanted in the brain region that controls his head movements. When neurosurgeon José Delgado (1973) stimulates the electrode by remote control, George always turns his head.

figure 4–2
Attitudes and actions
generate one another,
like chickens and eggs.

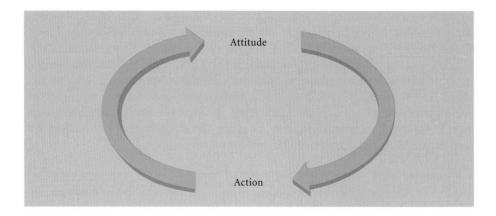

Unaware of the remote stimulation, he offers a reasonable explanation for it: "I'm looking for my slipper." "I heard a noise." "I'm restless." "I was looking under the bed."

- Carol's severe seizures were relieved by surgically separating her two brain hemispheres. Now, in an experiment, psychologist Michael Gazzaniga (1985) flashes a picture of a nude woman to the left half of Carol's field of vision and thus to her nonverbal right brain hemisphere. A sheepish smile spreads over her face, and she begins chuckling. Asked why, she invents—and apparently believes—a plausible explanation: "Oh—that funny machine." Frank, another split-brain patient, has the word "smile" flashed to his nonverbal right hemisphere. He obliges and forces a smile. Asked why, he explains, "This experiment is very funny."

The mental aftereffects of our behavior indeed appear in a rich variety of social situations: *Our attitudes follow our behavior.* The following examples will illustrate the power of self-persuasion.

Role playing

role
a set of norms that
define how people in a
given social position
ought to behave

The word **role** is borrowed from the theater and, as in the theater, refers to *actions expected of those who occupy a particular social position.* When stepping into a new social role, we must perform its actions, even if we feel phony. But our unease seldom lasts.

Think of a time when you stepped into some new role—perhaps your first days on a job, or at university, or in a sorority or fraternity. That first week on campus, for example, you may have been supersensitive to your new social situation and tried valiantly to act appropriately and root out your high school behavior. At such times we feel self-conscious. We observe our new speech and actions because they aren't natural to us. Then one day an amazing thing happens: We notice that our sorority enthusiasm or our pseudo-intellectual talk no longer feels forced. The role has begun to fit as comfortably as our old jeans and T-shirt.

"No man, for any
considerable period,
can wear one face to
himself and another to
the multitude without
finally getting
bewildered as to
which may be true."

Nathanial Hawthorne, 1850

In one study, university men volunteered to spend time in a simulated prison constructed in the psychology department by Philip Zimbardo (1971). Zimbardo, like so many others, wondered whether prison brutality is a product of evil prisoners and malicious guards or whether the institutional roles of guard and prisoner would embitter and harden even compassionate people. Do

Before long, these RCMP cadets will be internalizing attitudes appropriate to their new role.

the people make the place violent? Or does the place make the people violent?

By a flip of a coin, he designated some students as guards. He gave them uniforms, billy clubs, and whistles and instructed them to enforce the rules. The other half, the prisoners, were locked in cells and made to wear humiliating outfits. After a jovial first day of "playing" their roles, the guards and prisoners, and even the experimenters, got caught up in the situation. The guards began to disparage the prisoners, and some devised cruel and degrading routines. The prisoners broke down, rebelled, or became apathetic. There developed, reported Zimbardo (1972b), a "growing confusion between reality and illusion, between role-playing and self-identity.

Guards and prisoners in the Stanford prison simulation quickly absorbed the roles they played.

. . . This prison which we had created . . . was absorbing us as creatures of its own reality." Observing the emerging social pathology, Zimbardo was forced to call off the planned two-week simulation after only six days.

The effect of behavior on attitude appears even in the theater. Self-conscious acting may diminish as the actor becomes absorbed in the role and experiences genuine emotion. In William Golding's novel *Lord of the Flies*, a group of shipwrecked English boys become wild and exhibit brutal, uncivilized behavior. When a movie version of the book was made, the youngsters who acted in it became the creatures defined by their roles. The director, Peter Brook (1969), reported that "Many of their off-screen relationships completely paralleled the story, and one of our main problems was to encourage them to be uninhibited within the shots but disciplined in between them" (p. 163). Jonathan Winters has remarked that a hazard for stand-up comics like himself is that "You get to believing your own stuff." After several years of constructing fantastic characters, Winters underwent therapy to treat a confused personal identity (Elliott, 1986).

> "My whole personality changed during the time I was doing the part."
>
> Ian Charleson on his role as serene and devout Olympic hero Eric Liddell in *Chariots of Fire*

The deeper lesson of role-playing studies concerns how what is unreal (an artificial role) can evolve into what is real. In a new career, as teacher, soldier, or businessperson, we act a role that shapes our attitudes. Imagine playing the role of slave—not just for six days but for decades. If a few days altered the behavior of those in Zimbardo's "prison," then imagine the corrosive effects of decades of subservient behavior. The master may be even more profoundly affected, because the master's role is chosen. Frederick Douglass, a former slave, recalls his slave mistress's transformation as she absorbed her role:

> My new mistress proved to be all she appeared when I first met her at the door— a woman of the kindest heart and finest feelings. She had never had a slave under her control previously to myself, and prior to her marriage she had been dependent upon her own industry for a living. She was by trade a weaver; and by constant application to her business, she had been in a good degree preserved from the blighting and dehumanizing effects of slavery. I was utterly astonished at her goodness. I scarcely knew how to behave towards her. She was entirely unlike any other white woman I had ever seen. I could not approach her as I was accustomed to approach other white ladies. My early instruction was all out of place. The crouching servility, usually so acceptable a quality in a slave, did not answer when manifested toward her. Her favor was not gained by it; she seemed to be disturbed by it. She did not deem it impudent or unmannerly for a slave to look her in the face. The meanest slave was put fully at ease in her presence, and none left without feeling better for having seen her. Her face was made of heavenly smiles, and her voice of tranquil music.
>
> But, alas! this kind heart had but a short time to remain such. The fatal poison of irresponsible power was already in her hands, and soon commenced its infernal work. That cheerful eye, under the influence of slavery, soon became red with rage; that voice, made all of sweet accord, changed to one of harsh and horrid discord; and that angelic face gave place to that of a demon. (Douglass, 1845, pp. 57–58)

Saying becomes believing

Closely related to role playing's effect is the *saying-becomes-believing* effect. Consider, first, the human tendency to adapt what we say to please our listeners:

"Good God! He's giving the white-collar voters' speech to the blue collars."

© 1984; The New Yorker and Joseph Farris.

Impression management: In expressing our thoughts to others, we sometimes tailor our words to what we think the others will want to hear.

- We are quicker to tell people good news than bad, and we adjust our message toward our listener's position (Manis & others, 1974; Tesser & others, 1972; Tetlock, 1983).

- Faculty members writing supposedly candid letters of recommendation to graduate schools are more glowing in their comments when the students reserve their right to inspect the letters (Ceci & Peters, 1984).

- Social psychologist Philip Tetlock (1981) reports that politicians' policy statements tend to be simplistic during the political campaign ("To bring down the deficit we need major spending cuts"). After the election their statements become more complex—until the next campaign.

- The urge to shade one's views to suit one's audience seems strongest in Asian cultures. One study asked people to consider a father's best response to his daughter's introducing her fiance from another race. Although the father privately thought he "would never allow them to marry," 2 percent of people from the U.S. and 44 percent of people from Japan felt he should tell them he "was in favor of their marriage" (Iwao, 1988).

In 1785, Thomas Jefferson hypothesized that shaded messages can affect the messenger: "He who permits himself to tell a lie once finds it much easier to do it a second and third time, till at length it becomes habitual; he tells lies without attending to it, and truths without the world's believing him. This falsehood of the tongue leads to that of the heart, and in time depraves all its good dispositions." Experiments have proved Jefferson right. People induced to give spoken or written witness to something about which they have real doubts will often feel bad about their deceit. Nevertheless, they begin to believe what they are saying—*provided* they weren't bribed or coerced into doing so. When there is no compelling external explanation for one's words, saying becomes believing (Klaas, 1978).

Tory Higgins and his colleagues (Higgins & Rholes, 1978; Higgins & McCann, 1984) illustrated how saying becomes believing. They had university students read a personality description of someone and then summarize it for someone else who was believed either to like or dislike this person. The students wrote a more positive description when the recipient liked the person, and, having said positive things, then liked the person more themselves. Asked to recall what they had read, they remembered the description as being more positive than it was. In short, it seems that we are prone to adjust our messages to our listeners, and having done so, to believe the altered message.

The foot-in-the-door phenomenon

Most of us can recall times when, after agreeing to help out with a project or an organization, we ended up more involved than we ever intended, vowing that in the future we would say no to such requests. How does this happen? Experiments suggest that if you want people to do a big favor for you, one technique is to get them to do a small favor first. In the best-known demonstration of this **foot-in-the-door** principle, researchers posing as safety-drive volunteers asked people to permit the installation of a huge, poorly lettered "Drive Carefully" sign in their front yards. Only 17 percent consented. Others were first approached with a small request: Would they display a 3-inch "Be a safe driver" window sign? Nearly all readily agreed. When approached two weeks later to allow the large, ugly sign in their front yards, 76 percent consented (Freedman & Fraser, 1966). One project helper who went from house to house

foot-in-the-door phenomenon
the tendency for people who have first agreed to a small request to comply later with a larger request

focus

Acting oneself into belief— Saying is believing

Psychologist Ray Hyman (1981) described how acting the role of a palm reader convinced him that palmistry worked.

> I started reading palms when I was in my teens as a way to supplement my income from doing magic and mental shows. When I started I did not believe in palmistry. But I knew that to "sell" it I had to act as if I did.

After a few years I became a firm believer in palmistry. One day the late Stanley Jaks, who was a professional mentalist and a man I respected, tactfully suggested that it would make an interesting experiment if I deliberately gave readings opposite to what the lines indicated. I tried this out with a few clients. To my surprise and horror my readings were just as successful as ever. Ever since then I have been interested in the powerful forces that convince us, [palm] reader and client alike, that something is so when it really isn't. (p. 86)

The foot-in-the-door phenomenon.

A foot in the door. To get people to donate blood or money, it often helps to first elicit a smaller commitment to the same cause.

later recalled that, not knowing who had been previously visited, "I was simply stunned at how easy it was to convince some people and how impossible to convince others" (Ornstein, 1991).

Other researchers have confirmed the foot-in-the-door phenomenon with altruistic behaviors.

- Patricia Pliner and her collaborators (1974) found 46 percent of Toronto suburbanites willing to give to the Cancer Society when approached directly. Others, asked a day ahead to wear a lapel pin publicizing the drive (which all agreed to do), were nearly twice as likely to donate.

- Joseph Schwarzwald and his colleagues (1983) asked some Israelis to donate to a collection for the mentally impaired. Fifty-three percent gave. Two weeks earlier, other residents had been approached to sign a petition supporting a recreation center for the impaired; among these, 92 percent now gave.

"You will easily find folk to do favors if you cultivate those who have done them."

Publilius Syrus, 42 B.C.

- Anthony Greenwald and his co-researchers (1987) approached a sample of registered voters the day before an election and asked them a small question: "Do you expect that you will vote or not?" All said yes. Compared to other voters not asked their intentions, they were 41 percent more likely to vote.
- Angela Lipsitz and others (1989) report that ending blood-drive reminder calls with "We'll count on seeing you then, OK? [pause for response]" increased the show-up rate from 62 to 81 percent.

Note that in these experiments the initial compliance—signing a petition, wearing a lapel pin, stating one's intention—was voluntary. We will see again and again that when people commit themselves to public behaviors *and* perceive these acts to be their own doing, they come to believe more strongly in what they have done.

Robert Cialdini [chal-DEE-nee] and his collaborators (1978) demonstrated a variation of the foot-in-the-door phenomenon by experimenting with the **low-ball technique,** a tactic reportedly used by some car dealers. After the customer agrees to buy a new car because of its great price and begins completing the sales forms, the salesperson removes the price advantage by charging for options the customer thought were included or by checking with a boss who disallows the deal because, "We'd be losing money." Folklore has it that more customers now stick with the higher-priced purchase than would have agreed to it at the outset.

Airlines and hotels have also used the tactic by attracting inquiries with great deals available on only a few seats or rooms, then hoping the customer will agree to a higher priced option. Cialdini and his collaborators found that this technique indeed works. When they invited introductory psychology students to participate in an experiment at 7:00 A.M., only 24 percent showed up. But if the students first agreed to participate without knowing the time and only then were asked to participate at 7:00 A.M., 53 percent came.

Marketing researchers and salespeople have found that the principle works even when we are aware of a profit motive (Cialdini, 1988). A harmless initial commitment—returning a card for more information and a gift, agreeing to listen to an investment possibility—often moves us toward a larger commitment. The day after I wrote this sentence, a life insurance salesperson came to my office and offered a thorough analysis of my family's financial situation. He did

low-ball technique
A tactic for getting people to agree to something. People who agree to an initial request will often still comply when the requester ups the ante. People who receive only the costly request are less likely to comply with it.

The low-ball technique.

Born Loser reprinted by permission of USF, Inc.

behind the scenes

All my life I've been a patsy. For as long as I can recall, I've been an easy mark for the pitches of peddlers, fund-raisers, and operators of one sort or another. Being a sucker contributes to my interest in the study of compliance: Just what are the factors that cause one person to say yes to another person? To help answer this question, I conduct laboratory experiments. I also spent three years infiltrating the world of compliance professionals. By becoming a trainee in various sales, fund-raising, and advertising organizations, I discovered how they exploit the weapons of influence and how we can spot these weapons at work.

Robert B. Cialdini
Arizona State University

not ask whether I wished to buy his life insurance or even whether I wished to try his free service. His question was instead a small foot-in-the-door, one carefully calculated to elicit agreement: Did I think people should have such information about their financial situation? I could only answer yes, and before I realized what was happening, I had agreed to the analysis. But I'm learning. Just the other evening a paid fund-raiser came to my door, first soliciting a petition signature supporting environmental cleanup, then welcoming my contribution to what I had signed my support of. (I sign, but resisting manipulation, don't give.)

Salespeople may exploit the power of small commitments when trying to bind people to purchase agreements. Many places now have laws that allow customers of door-to-door salespeople a few days to think over their purchases and cancel. To combat the effect of these laws, many companies use what the sales-training program of one encyclopedia company calls "a very important psychological aid in preventing customers from backing out of their contracts" (Cialdini, 1988, p. 78). They simply have the customer, rather than the salesperson, fill out the agreement. Having written it themselves, people usually live up to their commitment.

The process of step-by-step commitment, of spiraling action and attitude, contributed to the build-up of nuclear arms during the Cold War. After making and defending difficult decisions, political and military leaders seemed blind to information incompatible with their acts. They noticed and remembered comments that harmonized with their actions, but ignored or dismissed information that undermined their assumptions. As Ralph White (1971) has noted, when actions do not match attitudes such leaders have a tendency to "align their ideas with their actions."

The foot-in-the-door phenomenon is well worth learning about. Someone trying to seduce us—financially, politically, or sexually—usually will try to create a momentum of compliance. Before agreeing to a small request, think about what may follow.

Evil acts and attitudes

The attitudes-follow-behavior principle works with more immoral acts as well. Evil sometimes results from gradually escalating commitments. A trifling evil

Cruel acts, such as the massacre of these Rwandan Tutsis, breed even crueler and more hate-filled attitudes.

act can make a less trifling evil act easier. Evil acts gnaw at the moral sensitivity of the actor. To paraphrase La Rochefoucauld's *Maxims* (1665), it is not as difficult to find a person who has never succumbed to a given temptation as to find a person who has succumbed only once.

For example, cruel acts corrode the consciences of those who perform them. Harming an innocent victim—by uttering hurtful comments or delivering electric shocks—typically leads aggressors to disparage their victims, thus helping them justify their behavior (Berscheid & others, 1968; Davis & Jones, 1960; Glass, 1964). We tend not only to hurt those we dislike but to dislike those we hurt. In studies establishing this, people would justify an action especially when coaxed, not coerced, into it. When we voluntarily agree to do a deed, we take more responsibility for it.

The phenomenon almost always appears in wartime, as soldiers denigrate their victims: World War II soldiers for the allies called their enemy "the Japs." In the 1990s the Serbs considered Croats and Muslims less than human. This is another instance of spiraling action and attitude: The more one commits atrocities, the easier it becomes. Conscience mutates.

The same holds for prejudice. If one group holds another in slavery, it is likely to perceive the slaves as having traits that justify their oppression. Actions and attitudes feed one another, sometimes to the point of moral numbness.

Good acts and attitudes

"Our self-definitions are not constructed in our heads; they are forged by our deeds."

Robert McAfee Brown,
Creative Dislocation—The Movement of Grace, 1980

If evil acts shape the self, so, thankfully, do moral acts. Character, it is said, is reflected in what we do when we think no one is looking. Researchers have tested character by giving children temptations when it seems no one is watching. Consider what happens when children resist the temptation. They internalize the conscientious act *if* the deterrent is strong enough to elicit the desired *behavior* yet mild enough to leave them with a sense of *choice*. In a dramatic experiment, Jonathan Freedman (1965) introduced elementary school children to an enticing battery-controlled robot, instructing them not to play with it while he was out of the room. Freedman used a severe threat with half the children and a mild threat with the others. Both were sufficient to deter the children.

Several weeks later a different researcher, with no apparent relation to the earlier events, left each child to play in the same room with the same toys. Of the 18 children who had been given the severe threat, 14 now freely played with the robot; but two-thirds of those who had been given the mild deterrent still resisted playing with it. Having earlier made a conscious choice *not* to play with the toy, the mildly deterred children apparently internalized their decision. This new attitude controlled their subsequent action. Thus, moral action, especially when chosen rather than coerced, affects moral thinking.

If moral action feeds moral attitudes, can laws and rules that require moral conduct lead to genuine moral beliefs? Elliot Aronson (1992) has argued that such change is possible. His argument runs like this: If we wait for the heart to change—through preaching and teaching—we will wait a long time. But if we legislate moral action, we can, under the right conditions, indirectly affect heart-felt attitudes.

The idea runs counter to the presumption that "you can't legislate morality." Yet attitude change has, in fact, followed changes in the laws. Consider some of the following:

- In the 1980s and 1990s many governments began requiring the use of seatbelts by all people riding in automobiles. Initially, these laws were seen as burdensome and were opposed by many. But over time seatbelt use has risen dramatically, and now most people in these jurisdictions favor mandatory seatbelt laws.

- In 1954 the Supreme Court of the United States ruled that schools segregated by race were inherently unfair and that such schools were required to desegregate. Since that decision the percentage of Whites in the U.S. favoring integrated schools has more than doubled and now includes nearly everyone.

- In the 1970s many National Hockey League players did not wear helmets. Older players saw this as a measure of toughness. But in the 1980s, almost all bantam and junior hockey leagues required players to wear helmets. Now all players in the NHL wear helmets and see them as an important safety measure. Having grown up with helmets, they now believe they are useful.

Do laws always lead to the adoption of consistent attitudes? Almost certainly not. There are times when it is true that "you can't legislate morality." But research in social psychology confirms that under the right conditions people's attitudes follow their behaviors even when these behaviors are required. For example, experiments demonstrate that positive behavior toward someone fosters liking for that person.

Doing a favor for an experimenter or another subject, or tutoring a student, usually increases liking of the person helped (Blanchard & Cook, 1976). It is a lesson worth remembering: If you wish to love someone more, act as if you do.

In 1793, Benjamin Franklin tested the idea that doing a favor engenders liking. As clerk of the Assembly, he was disturbed by opposition from another important legislator. So Franklin set out to win him over:

> I did not . . . aim at gaining his favour by paying any servile respect to him but, after some time, took this other method. Having heard that he had in his library a certain very scarce and curious book I wrote a note to him expressing my desire of perusing that book and requesting he would do me the favour of lending it to me for a few days. He sent it immediately and I return'd it in about a week, expressing strongly my sense of the favour. When we next met in the House he spoke to me (which he had never done before), and with great civility; and he ever after

"We do not love people so much for the good they have done us, as for the good we have done them."

Leo Tolstoy, *War and Peace*, 1867–1869

manifested a readiness to serve me on all occasions, so that we became great friends and our friendship continued to his death. (Quoted by Rosenzweig, 1972, p. 769)

Social movements

The effect of a society's behavior on its people's attitudes suggests the possibility, and the danger, of employing the same idea for political socialization on a mass scale. For many Germans during the 1930s, participation in Nazi rallies, wearing uniforms, demonstrating, and especially the public greeting "Heil Hitler" established a profound inconsistency between behavior and belief. Historian Richard Grunberger (1971) reports that for those who had their doubts about Hitler, "The 'German greeting' was a powerful conditioning device. Having once decided to intone it as an outward token of conformity, many experienced schizophrenic discomfort at the contradiction between their words and their feelings. Prevented from saying what they believed, they tried to establish their psychic equilibrium by consciously making themselves believe what they said" (p. 27).

The practice is not limited to totalitarian regimes. Political rituals—the daily flag salute by schoolchildren, singing the national anthem—use public conformity to build a private belief in patriotism. I was amazed at the strong sense of being a Canadian that my son developed in junior kindergarten. Before school he had virtually no identity as a Canadian, but after three weeks of singing *O Canada* on Mondays he was Canadian through and through. Observers noted how the civil rights marches of the 1960s strengthened the demonstrators' commitments. Their actions expressed an idea whose time had come and drove that idea more deeply into their hearts. The 1980s move toward gender-inclusive language has similarly strengthened inclusive attitudes.

Many people assume that the most social indoctrination comes through *brainwashing*, a term coined to describe what happened to prisoners of

"One does what one is; one becomes what one does."

Robert Musil, *Kleine Prosa*, 1930

Our political actions—like participating in flag day ceremonies—help shape our attitudes.

Celebrating Canada Day: Patriotic actions strengthen patriotic attitudes.

war (POWs) during the 1950s Korean war. Actually, the Chinese "thought-control" program, developed to re-educate the Chinese populace into communism, was not nearly as irresistible as this term suggests. But the results still were disconcerting. Hundreds of prisoners cooperated with their captors. Twenty-one chose to remain after being granted permission to return to America. And many of those who did return came home believing "although communism won't work in America, I think it's a good thing for Asia" (Segal, 1954).

Edgar Schein (1956) interviewed many of the POWs during their journey home and reported that the captors' methods included a gradual escalation of demands. The Chinese always started with trivial requests and gradually worked up to more significant ones. "Thus after a prisoner had once been 'trained' to speak or write out trivia, statements on more important issues were demanded." Moreover, they always expected active participation, be it just copying something or participating in group discussions, writing self-criticism, or uttering public confessions. Once a prisoner had spoken or written a statement, he felt an inner need to make his beliefs consistent with his acts. This often drove prisoners to persuade themselves of what they had done. The "start-small-and-build" tactic was an effective application of the foot-in-the-door technique, as it continues to be today in the socialization of terrorists and torturers (Chapter 6).

Let me ask you, before reading further, to play theorist. Ask yourself: Why in these studies and real-life examples did attitudes follow behavior? Why might playing a role or making a speech influence how *you* feel about something?

"You can use small commitments to manipulate a person's self-image; you can use them to turn citizens into 'public servants,' prospects into 'customers,' prisoners into 'collaborators.'"

Robert Cialdini, *Influence*, 1988

Summing up

The attitude-action relation also works in the reverse direction: We are likely not only to think ourselves into action but also to act ourselves into a way of thinking. When we act, we amplify the idea underlying what we have done, especially when we feel responsible for it.

Many streams of evidence converge on this principle. The actions prescribed by social roles mold the attitudes of the role players. Research on the foot-in-the door phenomenon reveals that committing a small act later makes people more willing to do a larger one. Actions also affect our moral attitudes: That which we have done we tend to justify as right. Similarly, our racial and political behaviors help shape our social consciousness: We not only stand up for what we believe, we also believe in what we have stood up for.

Why do actions affect attitudes?

What theories help explain the attitudes-follow-behavior phenomenon? How does the contest between these competing ideas illustrate the process of scientific explanation?

We have seen that several streams of evidence merge to form a river: the effect of actions on attitudes. Do these observations contain any clues to *why* action affects attitude? Social psychology's detectives suspect three possible sources. **Self-presentation theory** assumes that for strategic reasons we express attitudes that make us *appear* consistent. **Cognitive dissonance theory** assumes that to reduce discomfort, we *justify* our actions to ourselves. **Self-perception theory** assumes that our actions are *self-revealing* (when uncertain about our

Self-presentation theory assumes that our behavior aims to create desired impressions.

"*My not wearing a hairpiece indicates to others that I'm comfortable with myself.*"

feelings or beliefs, we look to our behavior, much as anyone else would). Let's examine each.

Self-presentation: Impression management

The first explanation began as a simple idea, which you may recall from Chapter 2. Who among us does not care what people think? We spend countless dollars on clothes, diets, cosmetics, even plastic surgery—all because we worry about what others think of us. To make a good impression is often to gain social and material rewards, to feel better about ourselves, even to become more secure in our social identities (Leary, 1994).

Indeed, no one wants to look foolishly inconsistent. To avoid seeming so, we express attitudes that match our actions. To *appear* consistent, we may pretend attitudes we don't really believe in. Even if it means displaying a little insincerity or hypocrisy, it can pay to manage the impression one is making. Or so *self-presentation theory* suggests.

We have seen that people do engage in "impression management." They will adjust what they say to please rather than offend. Sometimes it may take a bogus pipeline to cut through the pretense. Moreover, people take longer to deliver news of failure (for example, signaling wrong answers on an IQ-type test) than news of success; but this effect occurs only if the bearers of the news are identifiable and therefore concerned about making a bad impression (Bond & Anderson, 1987).

For some people, making a good impression is a way of life. By continually monitoring their own behavior and noting how others react, they adjust their social performance when it's not having the desired effect. Those who score high on a scale of **self-monitoring** tendency (who, for example, agree that "I tend to be what people expect me to be") act like social chameleons—they adjust their behavior in response to external situations (Snyder, 1987). Having attuned their behavior to the situation, they are more likely to espouse an attitude they don't really hold (Zanna & Olson, 1982). Being conscious of others, they are less likely to act on their own attitudes. By self-monitoring, such people readily adapt to new jobs, roles, and relationships (Snyder & DeBono, 1989; Snyder & Copeland, 1989).

Those who score low in self-monitoring care less about what others think. They are more internally guided and thus more likely to talk and act as they feel and believe (McCann & Hancock, 1983). Their attitudes therefore predict their behavior. Most of

self-monitoring
being attuned to the way one presents oneself in social situations and adjusting one's performance to create the desired impression

"Hmmm... what shall I wear today...?"

High self-monitoring.

us fall somewhere between the high self-monitoring extreme of the con artist and the low self-monitoring extreme of stubborn insensitivity to others.

Does our eagerness to *appear* consistent explain why expressed attitudes shift toward consistency with behavior? To some extent, yes—people exhibit a much smaller attitude change when a bogus pipeline inhibits trying to make a good impression (Paulhus, 1982; Tedeschi & others, 1987). Moreover, self-presentation involves not just impressing others but expressing our ideals and identity (Baumeister, 1982, 1985; Schlenker & others, 1996).

But there is more to the attitude changes we have reviewed than self-presentation, for people express their changed attitudes even to someone who doesn't know how they have behaved. Two other theories explain why people sometimes internalize their self-presentations as genuine attitude changes.

Self-justification: Cognitive dissonance

cognitive dissonance
Tension that arises when one is simultaneously aware of two inconsistent cognitions. For example, dissonance may occur when we realize that we have, with little justification, acted contrary to our attitudes or made a decision favoring one alternative despite reasons favoring another.

One theory is that our attitudes change because we are motivated to maintain consistency among our cognitions. This is the implication of Leon Festinger's (1957) **cognitive dissonance theory.** The theory is simple, but its range of application is enormous. It assumes *we feel tension ("dissonance") when two simultaneously accessible thoughts or beliefs ("cognitions") are psychologically inconsistent*—as when we decide to say or do something we have mixed feelings about. Festinger argued that to reduce this unpleasant arousal, we often adjust our thinking.

Dissonance theory pertains mostly to discrepancies between behavior and attitudes. We are aware of both. Thus, if we sense some inconsistency, perhaps some hypocrisy, we feel pressure for change. That helps explain why, in a British survey, half of cigarette smokers therefore disagreed with the near-consensus among nonsmokers that smoking is "really as dangerous as people say" (Eiser & others, 1979) and why the perception of risk among those who have quit declines after relapsing (Gibbons & others, 1997).

"A foolish consistency is the hobgoblin of little minds."

Ralph Waldo Emerson,
"Self-Reliance," 1841

So if we can persuade others to adopt a *new* attitude, their behavior should change accordingly; that's common sense. Or if we can induce people to behave differently, their attitude should change (that's the self-persuasion effect we have been reviewing). But cognitive dissonance theory offers several surprising predictions. See if you can anticipate them.

behind the scenes

Following a 1934 earthquake in India, there were rumors outside the disaster zone of worse disasters to follow. It occurred to me that these rumors might be "anxiety-justifying"—cognitions that would justify their lingering fears. From that germ of an idea, I developed my theory of dissonance reduction—making your view of the world fit with how you feel or what you've done.

Leon Festinger
1920–1989

Insufficient justification

Imagine you are a subject in a famous experiment staged by the creative Festinger and his student, J. Merrill Carlsmith (1959). For an hour, you are required to perform dull tasks, such as turning wooden knobs again and again. After you finish, the experimenter (Carlsmith) explains that the study concerns how expectations affect performance. The next subject, waiting outside, must be led to expect an interesting experiment. The seemingly distraught experimenter, whom Festinger had spent hours coaching until he became extremely convincing, explains that the assistant who usually creates this expectation couldn't make this session. Wringing his hands, he pleads, "Could you fill in and do this?"

It's for science and you are being paid, so you agree to tell the next subject (who is actually the experimenter's real assistant) what a delightful experience you have just had. "Really?" responds the supposed subject. "A friend of mine was in this experiment a week ago, and she said it was boring." "Oh, no," you respond, "it's really very interesting. You get good exercise while turning some knobs. I'm sure you'll enjoy it." Finally, someone else who is studying how people react to experiments has you complete a questionnaire that asks how much you actually enjoyed your knob-turning experience.

Now for the prediction: Under which condition are you most likely to believe your little lie and say the experiment was indeed interesting? When paid $1 for doing so, as some of the subjects were? Or when paid a then-generous $20, as others were? Contrary to the common notion that big rewards produce big effects, Festinger and Carlsmith made an outrageous prediction: Those paid just $1 (hardly sufficient justification for a lie) would be most likely to adjust their attitudes to their actions. Having **insufficient justification** for their action, they would experience more discomfort (dissonance) and thus be more motivated to believe in what they had done. Those paid $20 had sufficient justification for what they did and hence should have experienced less dissonance. As Figure 4–3 shows, the results fit this intriguing prediction.*

In dozens of later experiments, the attitudes-follow-behavior effect was strongest when people felt some *choice* and when their action had foreseeable *consequences*. One experiment had people read disparaging lawyer jokes into a recorder (for example, "How can you tell when a lawyer is lying? His lips are moving"). The reading produced more negative attitudes toward lawyers when it was a chosen rather than coerced activity (Hobden & Olson, 1994). Other experiments have engaged people to write an essay for a measly $1.50 or so. When the essay argues something they don't believe in—say, a tuition increase—the underpaid writers begin to feel somewhat greater sympathy with the policy. Advocating a policy favorable to another race may improve your attitudes not only toward the policy but toward the race. This is especially so if something makes you face the inconsistency or if you think important people will actually read an essay with your name on it (Leippe & Eisenstadt, 1994;

insufficient justification effect reduction of dissonance by internally justifying one's behavior when external justification is "insufficient"

---

*There is a seldom-reported final aspect of this 1950s experiment. Imagine yourself finally back with the experimenter, who is truthfully explaining the whole study. Not only do you learn that you've been duped, but the experimenter asks for the $20 back. Do you comply? Festinger and Carlsmith note that all their student subjects willingly reached into their pockets and gave back the money. This is a foretaste of some quite amazing observations on compliance and conformity discussed in Chapter 6. As we will see, when the social situation makes clear demands, people usually respond accordingly.

figure 4–3

Insufficient justification.

Dissonance theory predicts that when our actions are not fully explained by external rewards or coercion, we will experience dissonance, which we can reduce by believing what we have done.

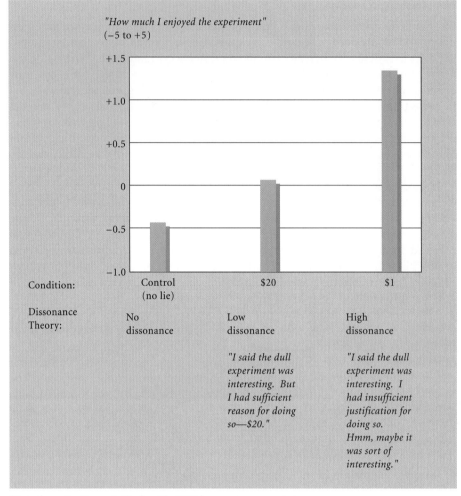

(Data from Festinger & Carlsmith, 1959.)

Leippe & Elkin, 1987). Feeling responsible for statements you have made, you will now believe them more strongly. Pretense becomes reality.

Earlier we noted how the insufficient justification principle works with punishments. Children were more likely to internalize a request not to play with an attractive toy if given a mild threat that insufficiently justified their compliance. When a parent says, "Clean up your room, Johnny, or I'll knock your block off," Johnny won't need to internally justify cleaning his room. The severe threat is justification enough.

Note that cognitive dissonance theory focuses on what *induces* a desired action, rather than the relative effectiveness of rewards and punishments administered *after* the act. It aims to have Johnny say, "I am cleaning up my room because I want a clean room," rather than, "I am cleaning up my room because my parents will kill me if I don't." The principle: We accept responsibility for our behavior if we have chosen it without obvious pressure and incentives.

These implications of dissonance theory have led some to view it as an integration of humanistic and scientific perspectives. Authoritarian management

Dissonance theory suggests that parents should aim to elicit desired behavior noncoercively, thus motivating children to internalize the appropriate attitudes.

will be effective, the theory predicts, only when the authority is present—because people are unlikely to internalize forced behavior. Bree, a formerly enslaved talking horse in C. S. Lewis's *The Horse and His Boy* (1974), observes that "One of the worst results of being a slave and being forced to do things is that when there is no one to force you any more you find you have almost lost the power of forcing yourself" (p. 193). Dissonance theory insists that encouragement and inducement should be enough to elicit the desired action. But it suggests that managers, teachers, and parents should use only enough incentive to elicit the desired behavior.

Dissonance after decisions

The emphasis on perceived choice and responsibility implies that *decisions* produce dissonance. When faced with an important decision—what university to attend, whom to date, which job to accept—we are sometimes torn between two equally attractive alternatives. Perhaps you can recall a time when, having committed yourself, you become painfully aware of dissonant cognitions—the desirable features of what you had rejected and the undesirable features of what you had chosen. If you decided to live on campus, you may have realized you were forgoing the spaciousness and freedom of an apartment in favor of cramped, noisy dorm quarters. If you elected to live off campus, you may have realized that your decision meant physical separation from campus and friends and having to cook for yourself.

After making important decisions, we usually reduce dissonance by upgrading the chosen alternative and downgrading the unchosen option. In the first published dissonance experiment (1956), Jack Brehm had women rate eight products, such as a toaster, a radio, and a hair dryer. Brehm then showed the women two objects they had rated closely and told them they could have whichever they chose. Later, when rerating the eight objects, the women increased their evaluations of the item they had chosen and decreased their evaluations of the rejected item. It seems that after we have made our choice, the grass does *not* then grow greener on the other side of the fence.

With simple decisions, this deciding-becomes-believing effect can occur very quickly. Robert Knox and James Inkster (1968) found that racetrack bettors who had just put down their money on a horse felt more optimistic about their bet than did those who were about to bet. In the few moments that intervened between standing in line and walking away from the betting window, nothing had changed—except the decisive action and the person's feelings about it. Contestants in carnival games of chance feel more confident of winning right after agreeing to play than right before. And voters indicate more esteem and confidence in a candidate just after voting than just before (Younger & others, 1977). There may sometimes be but a slight difference between the two options, as I can recall in helping make faculty tenure decisions. The competence of one faculty member who barely makes it and that of another who barely loses seem not very different—until after you make and announce the decision.

These experiments and examples suggest that, once made, decisions grow their own self-justifying legs of support. Often, these new legs are strong enough that when one leg is pulled away—perhaps the original one—the decision does not collapse. Alison decides to take a trip home if it can be done for an airfare under $400. It can, so she makes her reservation and begins to think of

"Every time you make a choice you are turning the central part of you, the part of you that chooses, into something a little different from what it was before."

C. S. Lewis, *Mere Christianity*, 1943

Big decisions can produce big dissonance when one later ponders the negative aspects of what is chosen and the positive aspects of what is not chosen.

additional reasons why she is glad she is going. When she goes to buy the tickets, however, she learns there has been a fare increase to $475. No matter, she is now determined to go. As when being low-balled by a car dealer, it never occurs to people, reports Robert Cialdini (1984, p. 103), "that those additional reasons might never have existed had the choice not been made in the first place."

Self-perception

Although dissonance theory has inspired much research, an even simpler theory explains its phenomena. Consider how we make inferences about other people's attitudes. We see how a person acts in a particular situation, and then we attribute the behavior either to the person's traits and attitudes or to environmental forces. If we see parents coercing their little Susie into saying, "I'm sorry," we attribute Susie's reluctant behavior to the situation, not to her personal regret. If we see Susie apologizing with no apparent inducement, we attribute the apology to Susie herself.

Self-perception theory (proposed by Daryl Bem, 1972) assumes that we make similar inferences when we observe our own behavior. When our attitudes are weak or ambiguous, we are in the position of someone observing us from the outside. We discern people's attitudes by looking closely at their actions when they are free to act as they please. We similarly discern our own attitudes. Hearing myself talk informs me of my attitudes; seeing my actions provides clues to how strong my beliefs are. This is especially so when I can't easily attribute my behavior to external constraints. The acts we freely commit are self-revealing.

William James proposed a similar explanation for emotion a century ago. We infer our emotions, he suggested, by observing our bodies and our behaviors. A stimulus such as a growling bear confronts a woman in the forest. She tenses, her heartbeat increases, adrenaline flows, and she runs away. Observing all this, she then experiences fear. At a university where I am to lecture, I awake before dawn and am unable to get back to sleep. Noting my wakefulness, I conclude that I must be anxious.

You may be skeptical of the self-perception effect. I was when I first heard it. Experiments on the effects of facial expressions, however, suggest a way for you to experience it. When James Laird (1974, 1984; Duclos & others, 1989) induced university students to frown while attaching electrodes to their faces—"contract these muscles," "pull your brows together"—they reported feeling angry. It's more fun to try out Laird's other finding: Those induced to make a smiling face felt happier and found cartoons more humorous.

We have all experienced this phenomenon. We're feeling crabby, but then the phone rings or someone comes to the door and elicits from us warm, polite behavior. "How's everything?" "Just fine, thanks. How are things with you?" "Oh, not bad. . . ." If our feelings are not intense, this warm behavior may change our whole attitude. It's tough to smile and feel grouchy. When Miss Universe parades her smile, she may, after all, be helping herself feel happy. As Rodgers and Hammerstein reminded us, when we are afraid it may help to "whistle a happy tune." Going through the motions can trigger the emotions.

The effect sometimes endures into later behavior. After people are induced to *act* in an outgoing, talkative manner (during an interview), their self-presentation may carry over into greater self-perceived outgoingness and more

self-perception theory
the theory that when unsure of our attitudes, we infer them much as would someone observing us—by looking at our behavior and the circumstances under which it occurs

"Self-knowledge is best learned, not by contemplation, but action."
Goethe, 1749–1832

"I can watch myself and my actions, just like an outsider."
Anne Frank, *The Diary of a Young Girl*, 1947

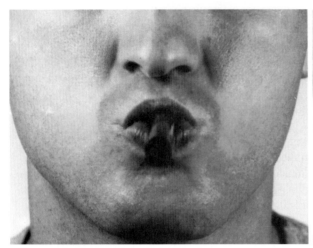 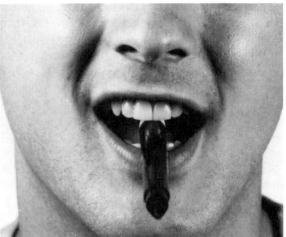

According to German psychologist Fritz Strack and colleagues (1988), people find cartoons funnier while holding a pen with their teeth using a smiling muscle) than while holding it with their lips (using muscles incompatible with smiling).

"The free expression by outward signs of emotion intensifies it. On the other hand, the repression as far as possible, of all outward signs softens our emotions."

Charles Darwin, *The Expression of the Emotions in Man and Animals*, 1897

outgoing social behavior (Schlenker & others, 1994; Tice, 1992). Act *as if* you are outgoing, and you may become more so.

Even your gait can affect how you feel. When you get up from reading this chapter, walk for a minute taking short, shuffling steps, with eyes downcast. It's a great way to feel depressed. "Sit all day in a moping posture, sigh, and reply to everything with a dismal voice, and your melancholy lingers," noted William James (1890, p. 463). Want to feel better? Walk for a minute taking long strides with your arms swinging and your eyes straight ahead. Can you, like the participants in an experiment by Sara Snodgrass (1986), feel the difference?

If our expressions influence our feelings, then would imitating others' expressions help us know what they are feeling? An experiment by Katherine Burns Vaughan and John Lanzetta (1981) suggests it would. They asked students to observe someone receiving electric shock. They told some of the observers to make a pained expression whenever the shock came on. If, as Freud and others supposed, expressing an emotion allows us to discharge it, then the pained expression should be inwardly calming (Cacioppo & others, 1991). Actually, compared to other students who did not act out the expressions, these grimacing students perspired *more* and had a faster heart rate whenever they saw the person shocked. Acting out the person's emotion apparently enabled the observers to feel more empathy. The implication: To sense how other people are feeling, let your own face mirror their expressions.

Actually, you hardly need try. Observing others' faces, postures, and voices, we naturally and unconsciously mimic their moment-to-moment reactions (Hatfield & others, 1992). We synchronize our movements, postures, and tones of voice with theirs. Doing so helps us tune in to what they're feeling. It also makes for "emotional contagion," helping explain why it's fun to be around happy people and depressing to be around depressed people (Module A).

Our facial expressions also influence our attitudes. In a clever experiment, Gary Wells and Richard Petty (1980) had University of Alberta students "test headphone sets" by making either vertical or horizontal head movements while listening to a radio editorial. Who most agreed with the editorial? Those who had been nodding their heads up and down. Why? Wells and Petty surmised that positive thoughts are compatible with vertical nodding and incompatible with horizontal motion. Try it your-self when listening to someone: Do you feel more agreeable when nod-ding rather than shaking your head?

In an even zanier experiment, John Cacioppo and his colleagues (1993) had people rate Chinese char-acters when pressing their arms upward (as when lifting food) or downward (as when pushing some-thing or someone away). Which flex condition do you suppose triggered the most positive ratings? It was the upward flex. (Try it out: Do you get a more positive feeling while lifting a table edge with upturned hands rather than pressing down? Might this motion-affects-emotion phe-nomenon predispose people to feel better at parties while holding food or drink?) In a follow-up experiment

BIZARRO © 1997 by Dan Piraro. Reprinted with permission of UNIVERSAL PRESS SYNDICATE. All rights reserved.

This assumes you are not in Bulgaria—where an abrupt vertical head nod signifies not yes, but "no."

Joseph Priester, working with Cacioppo and Richard Petty (1996), found the muscle flex effect works best for neutral stimuli. It works better for meaningless "words" such as *rapley* and *primet* than words such as *player* and *permit* (for which we may have emotional associations).

Overjustification and intrinsic motivations

Recall the insufficient justification effect—the *smallest* incentive that will get people to do something is usually the most effective in getting them to like the activity and keep on doing it. Cognitive dissonance theory offers one explana-tion for this: When external inducements are insufficient to justify our behavior, we reduce dissonance by justifying the behavior internally.

Self-perception theory offers another explanation: People explain their behavior by noting the conditions under which it occurs. Imagine hearing someone proclaim the wisdom of a tuition increase after being paid $20 to do so. Surely the statement would seem less sincere than if you thought the person was expressing those opinions for no pay. Perhaps we make similar inferences when observing ourselves.

Self-perception theory goes even a step further. Contrary to the notion that rewards always increase motivation, it suggests that unnecessary rewards sometimes have a hidden cost. Rewarding people for doing what they already enjoy may lead them to attribute their doing it to the reward, thus undermining their self-perception that they do it because they like it. Experiments by Edward Deci and Richard Ryan (1991, 1997), by Mark Lepper and David Greene (1979), and by Ann Boggiano and her colleagues (1985, 1987) confirm this **overjustifi-cation effect.** Pay people for playing with puzzles, and they will later play with the puzzles less than those who play without being paid; promise children a reward for doing what they intrinsically enjoy (for example, playing with magic markers) and you will turn their play into work (Figure 4–4).

overjustification effect
the result of bribing people to do what they already like doing; they may then see their action as externally controlled rather than intrinsically appealing

Self-perception at work.

"*I don't sing because I am happy. I am happy because I sing.*"

© 1991, The New Yorker Magazine, Inc.

A folktale illustrates the overjustification effect. An old man lived alone on a street where boys played noisily every afternoon. The din annoyed him, so one day he called the boys to his door. He told them he loved the cheerful sound of children's voices and promised them each 50 cents if they would return the next day. Next afternoon the youngsters raced back and played more lustily than ever. The old man paid them and promised another reward the next day. Again they returned, whooping it up, and the man again paid them; this time 25 cents. The following day they got only 15 cents, and the man explained that his meager resources were being exhausted. "Please, though, would you come to play for 10 cents tomorrow?" The disappointed boys told the man they would not be back. It wasn't worth the effort, they said, to play all afternoon at his house for only 10 cents.

As self-perception theory implies, an *unanticipated* reward does *not* diminish intrinsic interest, because people can still attribute their action to their own motivation (Bradley & Mannell, 1984; Tang & Hall, 1994). (It's like the heroine who, having fallen in love with the woodcutter, now learns that he's really a prince.) And if compliments for a good job make us feel more competent and

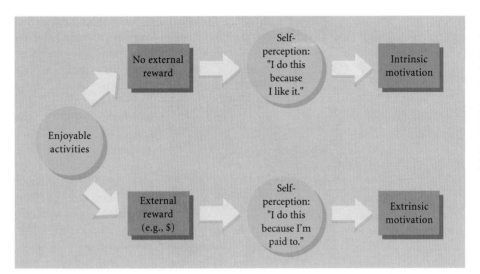

figure 4–4
When people do something they enjoy, without reward or coercion, they attribute their behavior to their love of the activity. External rewards undermine intrinsic motivation by leading people to attribute their behavior to the incentive.

successful, this can actually *increase* our intrinsic motivation. When rightly administered, rewards may also boost creativity (Eisenberger & Armeli, 1997; Eisenberger & Cameron, 1996).

The overjustification effect occurs when someone offers an unnecessary reward beforehand in an obvious effort to control behavior. What matters is what a reward implies: Rewards and praise that *inform* people of their achievements (that make them feel, "I'm very good at this") *boost* intrinsic motivation. Rewards that seek to *control* people and lead them to believe it was the reward that caused their effort ("I did it for the money") *diminish* the intrinsic appeal of an enjoyable task (Freedman & others, 1992; Rosenfeld & others, 1980; Sansone, 1986).

How then can we cultivate people's enjoyment of tasks that are not intrinsically appealing? Young Maria may find her first piano lessons frustrating. Tommy may not have an intrinsic love of fifth-grade science. Sandra may not look forward to making those first sales calls. In such cases, the parent, teacher, or manager should probably use some incentives to coax the desired behavior (Boggiano & Ruble, 1985; Workman & Williams, 1980). After the person complies, suggest an intrinsic reason for doing so: "I knew you'd share your toys because you're a generous person" (Cialdini & others, 1992).

If we provide students with *just enough* justification to perform a learning task and use rewards and labels to help them feel competent, we may enhance their enjoyment and their eagerness to pursue the subject on their own. When there is too much justification—as happens in classrooms where teachers dictate behavior and use rewards to control the children—child-driven learning may diminish (Deci & Ryan, 1985, 1991). My younger son eagerly consumed six or eight library books a week—until our library started a reading club that promised a party to those who read ten books in three months. Three weeks later he began checking out only one or two books during our weekly visit. Why? "Because you only need to read ten books, you know."

Comparing the theories

We have seen one explanation of why our actions *seem* to affect our attitudes (self-presentation theory). And we have seen two explanations of why our

Natural mimicry and emotional contagion. People in sync, like these volunteers videotaped during an Oregon State University study by Frank Bernieri and Colleagues, feel more rapport with each other.

actions *genuinely* affect our attitudes: (1) The dissonance-theory assumption that we justify our behavior to reduce our internal discomfort, and (2) the self-perception theory assumption that we observe our behavior and make reasonable inferences about our attitudes, as we do when observing other people.

The last two explanations seem to contradict one another. Which is right? It's difficult to find a definitive test. In most instances they make the same predictions, and we can bend each theory to accommodate most of the findings we have considered (Greenwald, 1975). Daryl Bem (1972), the self-perception theorist, even suggested it boils down to a matter of loyalties and esthetics. This illustrates the subjectivity of scientific theorizing (see Chapter 1). Neither dissonance theory nor self-perception theory has been handed to us by nature. Both are products of human imagination—creative attempts to simplify and explain what we've observed.

It is not unusual in science to find that a principle, such as "attitudes follow behavior," is predictable from more than one theory. Physicist Richard Feynman (1967) marveled that "one of the amazing characteristics of nature" is the "wide range of beautiful ways" in which we can describe it: "I do not understand the reason why it is that the correct laws of physics seem to be expressible in such a tremendous variety of ways" (pp. 53–55). Like different roads leading to the same place, different sets of assumptions can lead to the same principle. If any-

© 1989 North America Syndicate, Inc. All rights reserved

thing, this *strengthens* our confidence in the principle. It becomes credible not only because of the data supporting it but also because it rests on more than one theoretical pillar.

Dissonance as arousal

Can we say that one of our theories is better? On one key point, strong support has emerged for dissonance theory. Recall that dissonance is, by definition, *an aroused state of uncomfortable tension*. To reduce this tension, we supposedly change our attitudes. Self-perception theory says nothing about tension being aroused when our actions and attitudes are not in harmony. It assumes merely that when our attitudes are weak to begin with, we will use our behavior and its circumstances as a clue to those attitudes (like the person who said, "How do I know how I feel until I hear what I say?").

Are conditions that supposedly produce dissonance (for example, making decisions or acting contrary to one's attitudes) actually uncomfortably arousing? Clearly yes, considering the classic study by the University of Waterloo's Mark Zanna and Princeton University's Joel Cooper (1974). They had students write an essay banning all speakers on campus, a view with which all the students disagreed. Half the students were told that they had no choice but to write the essay, while the other half were given the illusion that they chose to write the essay. Thus far, the study is just a replication of many previous dissonance studies, but Zanna and Cooper added a simple manipulation that helped establish arousal as central to the experience of dissonance. They had all the students take a pill (actually filled with powdered milk) at the beginning of the experiment. One-third of the students were told that the pill would make them feel aroused, one third were told that it would make them feel relaxed, and one third were given no information about the effects of the pill. Zanna and Cooper reasoned that if students thought the pill would make them feel aroused, when they experienced the arousal from the cognitive dissonance they were feeling they would blame the arousal on the pill and would not change their attitude. As you can see in Figure 4-5 the results of the experiment supported this reasoning. When students thought the pill would be arousing, students who had

figure 4–5

Dissonance and the pill.

When people attributed their arousal to a pill they had taken, they did not change their attitudes, demonstrating the role of dissonance in attitude change. (Data from Zanna & Cooper, 1974.)

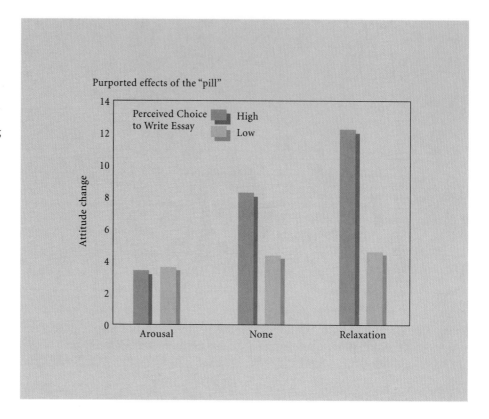

high and low choice to write the essay did not differ in their attitudes. When they were given no information about the pill students showed the typical dissonance pattern of attitude change—students who were given the illusion of choice to write the essay changed their attitudes more than students who were given no choice to write it. Finally, the students who were told the pill would be relaxing showed an especially large amount of attitude change. These results demonstrate that feeling aroused is a central part of the experience of cognitive dissonance and that people must attribute this arousal to their own actions before they engage in self-justifying attitude change.

There is a reason why "volunteering" to say or do undesirable things is arousing, suggests Claude Steele (1988). Such acts are embarrassing. They make us feel foolish. They threaten our sense of personal competence and goodness. Justifying our actions and decisions is therefore self-protective; it affirms our sense of integrity and self-worth.

So what do you suppose happens if, after committing a self-contradictory act, we offer people some other way to reaffirm their sense of self-worth, such as by doing a good deed? In several experiments Steele found that, with their self-concepts secure, people (especially those who came to the experiments with strong self-concepts) felt much less need to justify their acts (Steele & others, 1993). Therefore, say Steele and others, people are aroused by undesirable dissonant behaviors because such acts threaten their positive self-concepts. Had the Chinese in Korea used torture to gain compliance, the POWs would have had less need to justify their acts to themselves. You don't need to feel guilty about, or to justify, forced acts.

"No, Hoskins, you're not going to do it just because I'm telling you to do it. You're going to do it because you believe in it."

© 1988, The New Yorker Magazine, Inc.

People rarely internalize coerced behavior.

So dissonance conditions do indeed arouse tension, especially when they threaten positive feelings of self-worth. (In the study of relapsed smokers, it was those with high self-esteem who especially downplayed the risks.) But is this arousal necessary for the attitudes-follow-behavior effect? Steele and his colleagues (1981) believe the answer is yes. When drinking alcohol reduces dissonance-produced arousal, the attitudes-follow-behavior effect disappears. In one of their experiments, they induced students to write an essay favoring a big tuition increase. The students reduced their resulting dissonance by softening their antituition attitudes—*unless* after writing the unpleasant essay they drank alcohol, supposedly as part of a beer- or vodka-tasting experiment.

behind the scenes

I have always been fascinated by cognitive dissonance theory's portrayal of people as rationalizers. The idea seems to capture something profoundly important—our relentless interest in explaining ourselves. Yet Festinger's idea about *why* we rationalize seems incomplete. My research convinces me that the real goal of rationalization is not consistency but a sense of self-adequacy. We find that people can easily tolerate inconsistency—if they are allowed to affirm their overall worth. Thus it is the war for global self-worth, not the battle against specific inconsistencies, that causes our rationalizations.

*Claude Steele
Stanford University*

Four decades after Festinger first proposed his theory, social psychologists continue to study and debate alternative views of what causes dissonance. Some say Festinger was right to think that merely behaving *inconsistently* with one's attitudes—say, writing privately that one liked a foul-tasting drink and being simultaneously aware of the inconsistency—is enough to provoke some attitude change (Harmon-Jones & others, 1996; Johnson & others, 1995; McGregor & others, 1998). Others argue that the crucial inconsistency is between one's behavior and one's self-concept (Prislin & Pool, 1996; Stone & others, in press). Thus, Japanese people, who are less concerned with affirming their personal sense of self, don't exhibit the behavior rationalization that is so commonly found in dissonance experiments (Heine & Lehman, 1997). Although the dust has not settled, this much is clear, say Richard Petty, Duane Wegener, and Leandre Fabrigar (1997):"Dissonance theory has captivated the imagination of social psychologists as virtually no other, and it has continued to generate interesting new research."

Self-perceiving when not self-contradicting

Dissonance procedures are uncomfortably arousing, which leads to self-persuasion after acting contrary to one's attitudes. But dissonance theory cannot explain all the findings. When people argue a position that is in line with their opinion, although a step or two beyond it, procedures that usually eliminate arousal do not eliminate attitude change (Fazio & others, 1977, 1979). Dissonance theory also does not explain the overjustification effect, since being paid to do what you like to do should not arouse great tension. And what about situations where the action does not contradict any attitude—when, for example, people are induced to smile or grimace. Here, too, there should be no dissonance. For these cases, self-perception theory has a ready explanation.

In short, it appears that dissonance theory successfully explains what happens when we act contrary to clearly defined attitudes: We feel tension, so we adjust our attitudes to reduce it. Dissonance theory, then, explains attitude *change*. In situations where our attitudes are not well formed, self-perception theory explains attitude *formation*. As we act and reflect, we develop a more readily accessible attitude to guide our future behavior (Fazio, 1987; Roese & Olson, 1994).

Summing up

Three competing theories explain *why* our actions affect our attitude reports. *Self-presentation theory* assumes that people, especially those who self-monitor their behavior hoping to create a good impression, will adapt their attitude reports to *appear* consistent with their actions. The available evidence confirms that people do adjust their attitude statements out of concern for what other people will think. But it also shows that some genuine attitude change occurs.

Two theories propose that our actions trigger genuine attitude change. *Dissonance theory* explains this attitude change by assuming that we feel tension after acting contrary to our attitudes or making a difficult decision. To reduce this arousal, we internally justify our behavior. Dissonance theory further proposes that the less external justification we have for an undesirable action, the more we feel responsible for it, and thus the more dissonance arises and the more attitudes change.

Self-perception theory assumes that when our attitudes are weak, we simply observe our behavior and its circumstances and infer our attitudes. One interesting implication of self-perception theory is the "overjustification effect": Rewarding people to do what they like doing anyway can turn their pleasure into drudgery (if the reward leads them to attribute their behavior to the reward). Evidence supports predictions from both theories, suggesting that each describes what happens under certain conditions.

℞ Personal postscript: Changing ourselves through action

This chapter's attitudes-follow-behavior principle offers a powerful lesson for life: If we want to change ourselves in some important way, it's best not to wait for insight or inspiration. Sometimes we need to act—begin writing that paper, to make those phone calls, to see that person—even if we don't feel like acting. Jacques Barzun (1975) recognized the energizing power of action when he advised aspiring writers to engage in the act of writing even if contemplation had left them feeling uncertain about their ideas:

> If you are too modest about yourself or too plain indifferent about the possible reader and yet are required to write, then you have to pretend. Make believe that you want to bring somebody around to your opinion; in other words, adopt a thesis and start expounding it. . . . With a slight effort of the kind at the start—a challenge to utterance—you will find your pretense disappearing and a real concern creeping in. The subject will have taken hold of you as it does in the work of all habitual writers. (pp. 173–174)

> "If we wish to conquer undesirable emotional tendencies in ourselves we must . . . cold-bloodedly go through the outward motions of those contrary dispositions we prefer to cultivate."
>
> William James, *"What Is an Emotion?"* 1884

This attitudes-follow-behavior phenomenon is not irrational or magical. That which prompts us to act may also prompt us to think. Writing an essay or role-playing an opposing view forces us to consider arguments we otherwise might have ignored. What is more, we remember information best when we have actively explained it in our own terms. In one experiment, Gordon Bower and Mark Masling (1979) gave students a list of bizarre correlations like this one: "As the number of fire hydrants in an area decreases, the crime rate increases." Students who simply studied or were given explanations for these correlations recalled only about 40 percent of them when tested later. But students who invented their own explanations recalled 73 percent of the correlations.

The memorability of self-produced information is one reason we are most affected by information we have reformulated in our own terms (Greenwald, 1968; Petty & others, 1981). As one student wrote me, "It wasn't until I tried to verbalize my beliefs that I really understood them." As a teacher and a writer, I must therefore remind myself not always to lay out finished results. It is better to stimulate students to think through the implications of a theory, to make them active listeners and readers. Even taking notes deepens the impression. The philosopher-psychologist William James (1899) made the same point a century ago: "No reception without *reaction*, no impression without correlative expression—this is the great maxim which the teacher ought never to forget."

part two

Social Influence

Social psychology studies not only how we think about one another—our topic in the preceding chapters—but also how we influence and relate to one another. In chapters 5 through 8 we therefore probe social psychology's central concern: the powers of social influence.

What are these unseen social forces that push and pull us? How powerful are they? Research on social influence helps illuminate the invisible strings by which our social worlds move us about. This unit reveals these subtle powers, especially the cultural sources of attitudes and behavior (chapter 5), the forces of social conformity (chapter 6), the principles of persuasion (chapter 7), the consequences of participation in groups (chapter 8), and how all these influences operate together in everyday situations.

Seeing these influences, we may better understand why people feel and act as they do. And we may ourselves become less vulnerable to unwanted manipulation and more adept at pulling our own strings.

chapter 5

Genes, Culture, and Gender

approaching earth from light-years away, alien scientists assigned to study the species Homo sapiens can hardly contain their excitement. Their plan: to observe, then abduct two randomly sampled humans for a week of study. Their first subject, Peter, is a verbally combative Toronto trial lawyer who grew up in Saskatchewan but moved east seeking an "urban lifestyle." After a series of brief affairs and a divorce, Peter is enjoying a second marriage, and wishes he had more time to spend with his two children. Friends describe him as an independent thinker who is self-confident, competitive, and somewhat domineering in relationships.

Their second subject, Tomoko, lives with her husband and daughter in a rural Japanese village, a walk from the homes of both their parents. Tomoko prides herself on being a good daughter, loyal wife, and protective mother. Friends describe her as kind, gentle, respectful, sensitive, and supportive of her extended family.

From their small sample of two people of differing gender and culture, what might our alien scientists conclude about human nature? Would they wonder whether both are actually of the same species? Or would they be struck by deeper similarities beneath the surface differences?

The questions faced by our alien scientists are those faced by today's earth-bound scientists: How do we humans differ? How are we alike? These questions are central to a world where social diversity has become, as historian Arthur Schlesinger (1991) said, "the explosive problem of our times." In a world ripped apart by ethnic, cultural, and gender differences, how can we learn to accept our diversity, value our cultural identity, and recognize the extent of our human kinship? So let's step back for a look at the evolutionary and cultural perspectives, and then see how each might help us understand gender similarities and differences.

Human nature and cultural diversity

In viewing human similarities and differences, two perspectives dominate current thinking: an evolutionary perspective, emphasizing human kinship, and a cultural perspective, emphasizing human diversity. Nearly everyone agrees that we need both: Our genes design an adaptive human brain—a hard drive that receives the culture's software.

In many important ways, Peter and Tomoko are more alike than different. As members of one great family with common ancestors, they share not only a common biology but common behavior tendencies. Each perceives the world, feels thirst, and develops language through identical mechanisms. Peter and Tomoko both prefer sweet tastes to sour and divide the visual spectrum into similar colors. They and their kin across the globe all know how to read one another's frowns and smiles.

Peter and Tomoko—and humans everywhere—are intensely social creatures. They join groups, conform, and recognize distinctions of social status. They return favors, punish offenses, and grieve a child's death. As children, beginning at about eight months of age, they feared strangers, and as adults they favor members of their own groups. Confronted by those with dissimilar attitudes or attributes, they react warily or negatively. Our alien scientists could drop in anywhere and find humans feasting and dancing, laughing and crying, singing and worshipping. Everywhere, humans prefer living with others—in families and communal groups—to living alone.

"Good news, Mr. Vanderfirth. We've traced your lineage back to a woman who lived in East Africa two hundred thousand years ago."

Such commonalities define our shared human nature. In truth, Peter and Tomoko are more alike than different.

Evolution and behavior

The universal behaviors that define human nature arise from our biological similarity. Some 100,000 to 200,000 years ago, most anthropologists believe, we humans were all Africans. Feeling the urge to "be fruitful and multiply, and fill the earth," many of our ancestors moved out of Africa, displacing cousins such as Europe's Neanderthals (Simons, 1989; Stringer, 1990). In adapting to their new environments, these early humans developed differences that, measured on anthropological scales, are relatively recent and superficial. Those who went far north of the equator, for example, evolved lighter skins capable of synthesizing vitamin D in less direct sunlight. Still, historically, we all are Africans.

To explain the traits of our species, and all species, the British naturalist Charles Darwin (1859) proposed an evolutionary process. As organisms vary, nature selects those best equipped to survive and reproduce in particular environments. Genes that produced traits that increased the odds of leaving descendants became more abundant. In the snowy Arctic environment, for example, polar bear genes programming a thick coat of camouflaging white fur have won the genetic competition and now predominate. This process of **natural selection,** long an organizing principle of biology, has recently become an important principle for psychology as well.

Evolutionary psychology studies how natural selection predisposes not just adaptive physical traits, such as polar bear coats, but psychological traits and social behaviors that enhance the preservation and spread of one's genes. We humans are the way we are, say evolutionary psychologists, because among our ancestors' descendants, nature selected those who preferred nutritious, energy-providing foods rich in protein, sugar, and fat (and who disliked bitter, sour, often toxic tastes). Those who lacked such preferences were less likely to survive to contribute their genes to posterity. As mobile gene machines, we carry the legacy of our ancestors' adaptive preferences. We long for whatever helped them survive, reproduce, and nurture their offspring to survive and reproduce. Biologically speaking, one major purpose of life is to leave grandchildren.

The evolutionary perspective highlights our universal human nature. We not only maintain certain food preferences, we also share answers to social questions such as: Whom should I trust, and fear? Whom should I help? When, and with whom, should I mate? To whom should I defer, and whom may I control? Our emotional and behavioral tendencies are those that worked for our ancestors.

Because these social tasks are common to people everywhere, we inherit shared predispositions that answer these recurring questions. Thus, all evolutionary psychologists highlight the universal characteristics that have evolved through natural selection. All humans rank others by authority and status. And all have ideas about economic justice (Fiske, 1992). Cultures provide the specific rules for working out these elements of social life.

Culture and behavior

Among our universal similarities, the hallmark of our species is our capacity to learn and adapt. Evolution has prepared us to live creatively in a changing world and to adapt to environments from equatorial jungles to arctic icefields. Compared to bees, birds, and bulldogs, nature has us on a looser genetic leash. Ironically, therefore, our shared human biology enables our cultural diversity. It enables those in one **culture** to value promptness, welcome frankness, and

natural selection
the evolutionary process by which nature selects traits that best enable organisms to survive and reproduce in particular environmental niches

evolutionary psychology
the study of the evolution of behavior using principles of natural selection

"Psychology will be based on a new foundation."

Charles Darwin, *The Origin of Species*, 1859

culture
the enduring behaviors, ideas, attitudes, and traditions shared by a large group of people and transmitted from one generation to the next

accept premarital sex, while those in another culture do not. Whether we equate beauty with slimness or shapeliness depends on when and where we live. Whether we define social justice as equality (all receive the same) or as equity (those who produce more receive more) depends on whether Marxism or capitalism shapes our ideology. Whether we tend to be expressive or reserved, casual or formal, hinges partly on whether we have spent our lives in an African, a European, or an Asian culture.

Evolutionary psychology incorporates environmental influences. We humans have been selected not only for big brains and biceps but also for social competence. We come prepared to learn language and to cooperate in securing food, caring for young, and protecting ourselves. Nature therefore predisposes us to learn whatever culture we are born into (Fiske & others, 1998). The cultural perspective, while acknowledging that all behavior requires our evolved genes, highlights human adaptability.

Cultural diversity

The diversity of our languages, customs, and expressive behaviors suggests that much of our behavior is socially programmed, not hardwired. The genetic leash is indeed long. As sociologist Ian Robertson (1987) has noted:

> Americans eat oysters but not snails. The French eat snails but not locusts. The Zulus eat locusts but not fish. The Jews eat fish but not pork. The Hindus eat pork but not beef. The Russians eat beef but not snakes. The Chinese eat snakes but not people. The Jalé of New Guinea find people delicious. (p. 67)

The range of dress habits is equally great. If you were a traditional Muslim woman, you would cover your entire body, even your face, and be thought deviant if you didn't. If you were a North American woman, you would expose your face, arms, and legs, but you would cover your breasts and pelvic region, and be thought deviant if you didn't. If you were a Tasaday tribe woman in the Philippines, you would go about your daily activities naked, and be thought deviant if you didn't.

If we all lived as homogeneous ethnic groups in separate regions of the world, as some people still do, cultural diversity would be less relevant. In Japan, where there are 120 million people, of whom 119 million are Japanese, internal cultural differences are minimal compared with those found in Toronto, where dozens of ethnic groups coexist.

Increasingly, cultural diversity surrounds us. More and more we live in a global village, connected to our fellow villagers by telecommunications, jumbo jets, and international trade. Cultural diversity exists within nations, too. As Middle Easterners, Northern Islanders, and East Europeans know well, conflicts stemming from cultural differences are longstanding. Cultural conflicts have been described as "the AIDS of international politics—lying dormant for years, then flaring up to destroy countries" (*Economist*, 1991).

Migration and refugee evacuations are mixing cultures more than ever. "East is East and West is West, and never the twain shall meet," wrote the nineteenth-century British author Rudyard Kipling. But today, East and West, and North and South, meet all the time. Italy is home to many Albanians, Germany to Turks, England to Pakistanis and West Indians, and the result is both new friendship and surging hate crimes. For North Americans and Australians, too, one's country is more and more a mingling of cultures. One in six Canadians is an immigrant. In half of the 100 largest North American cities, ethnic minorities will together have become the majority by the end of this decade (Jones, 1990). As we work, play, and live with people from diverse cultural backgrounds, it helps to understand how our cultures influence us and to appreciate important ways in which cultures differ. In a world divided by wars, genuine peace requires respect for both differences and similarities.

To feel the impact of culture, we need only confront another culture. North American males may feel uncomfortable when Middle Eastern heads of state greet their head of state with a kiss on the cheek. A German student, accustomed to speaking rarely to "Herr Professor," considers it strange that at my institution most faculty office doors are open and students stop by freely. An Iranian student on her first visit to a North American McDonald's restaurant fumbles around in her paper bag looking for the eating utensils until she sees the other customers eating their french fries with, of all things, their hands. In many areas of the globe your and my best manners are a serious breach of etiquette. Foreigners visiting Japan often struggle to master the rules of the social game—when to take their shoes off, how to pour the tea, when to give and open gifts, how to act toward someone higher or lower in the social hierarchy.

As etiquette rules illustrate, all cultures have their accepted ideas about appropriate behavior. We often view these social expectations, or **norms,** as a

norms
rules for accepted and expected behavior. Norms *prescribe* "proper" behavior. (In a different sense of the word, norms also *describe* what most others do—what is *normal.*)

"*Women kiss women good night. Men kiss women good night. But men do not kiss men good night—especially in Armonk.*"

Although some norms are universal, every culture has its own norms—rules for accepted and expected social behavior.

negative force that imprisons people in a blind effort to perpetuate tradition. Norms restrain and control us so successfully and so subtly that we hardly sense their existence. Like fish in the ocean, we are so immersed in our culture that we must leap out of it to understand it. "When we see other Dutch people behaving in what foreigners would call a Dutch way," note Dutch psychologists Willem Koomen and Anton Dijker (1997), we often do not realize that the behavior is typically Dutch."

There is no better way to learn the norms of our culture than to visit another culture and see that its members do things *that* way, whereas we do them *this* way. I tell my children that yes, Europeans eat meat with the fork facing down in the left hand, but we North Americans consider it good manners to cut the meat and then transfer the fork to the right hand: "I admit it's inefficient. But it's the way *we* do it."

Such norms may seem arbitrary and confining. Just as a play moves smoothly when the actors know their lines, however, so social behavior occurs smoothly when people know what to expect. Norms grease the social machinery. In unfamiliar situations, when the norms may be unclear, we monitor others' behavior and adjust our own accordingly. In familiar situations, our words and acts come effortlessly.

Cultures also vary in their norms for expressiveness and personal space. To someone from a relatively formal northern European culture, a person whose roots are in an expressive Mediterranean culture may seem "warm, charming, inefficient, and time-wasting." To the Mediterranean person, the northern European may seem "efficient, cold, and overconcerned with time" (Triandis, 1981).

Depending partly on their culture, some people prefer more personal space than others.

"You're not one of those guys who are afraid of intimacy, are you?"

Drawing by Mankoff; © 1988 The New Yorker Magazine, Inc.

Latin American business executives who arrive late for a dinner engagement may be mystified by how obsessed their North American counterparts are with punctuality.

Personal space is a sort of portable bubble or buffer zone that we like to maintain between ourselves and others. As the situation changes, the bubble varies in size (Albas & Albas, 1989). With strangers we maintain a fairly large personal space, keeping a distance of 4 feet or more between us. On uncrowded buses, or in restrooms or libraries, we protect our space and respect others' space. We let friends come closer, often within 2 or 3 feet.

Individuals differ: Some people prefer more personal space than others (Smith, 1981; Sommer, 1969; Stockdale, 1978). Groups differ, too: Adults maintain more distance than children. Men keep more distance from one another than do women. For reasons unknown, cultures near the equator prefer less space and more touching and hugging. Thus the British and Scandinavians prefer more distance than the French and Arabs; North Americans prefer more space than Latin Americans.

To see the effect of encroaching on another's personal space, play space invader. Stand or sit a foot or so from a friend and strike up a conversation. Does the person fidget, look away, back off, show other signs of discomfort? These are some signs of arousal noted by space-invading researchers (Altman & Vinsel, 1978).

personal space
the buffer zone we like to maintain around our bodies. Its size depends on our familiarity with whoever is near us.

"Some 30 inches from my nose, the frontier of my person goes."
W. H. Auden, 1907–1973

Cultural Similarity

Thanks to human adaptability, cultures differ. Yet beneath the veneer of cultural differences, cross-cultural psychologists see "an essential universality" (Lonner, 1980). As members of one species, we are more alike than different.

Norms—rules for accepted and expected behavior—vary by culture.

Drawing by P. Steiner, © 1980 The New Yorker Magazine, Inc.

Despite the enormous cultural variation in norms, we humans do hold some norms in common.

"*Look, everyone here loves vanilla, right? So let's start there.*"

"I am confident that [if] modern psychology had developed in, let us say, India, the psychologists there would have discovered most of the principles discovered by the Westerners."

Cross-cultural psychologist John E. Williams (1993)

In *The Female Eunuch*, Germaine Greer notes how the language of affection reduces women to foods and baby animals—honey, lamb, sugar, sweetie-pie, kitten, chick.

Although norms vary by culture, humans do hold some norms in common. Best known is the taboo against incest: Parents are not to have sexual relations with their children, nor siblings with one another. Although the taboo apparently is violated more often than psychologists once believed, the norm is still universal. Every society disapproves of incest. Given the biological penalties for inbreeding, evolutionary psychologists can easily understand why people everywhere are predisposed against incest.

People everywhere also have some common norms for friendship. From studies conducted in Britain, Italy, Hong Kong, and Japan, Michael Argyle and Monika Henderson (1985) noted several cultural variations in the norms that define the role of friend (in Japan it's especially important not to embarrass a friend with public criticism). But there are also some apparently universal norms: Respect the friend's privacy, make eye contact while talking, don't divulge things said in confidence. These are among the rules of the friendship game. Break them and the game is over.

Roger Brown (1965, 1987; Kroger & Wood, 1992) noticed another universal norm. Everywhere—in 27 languages studied to date—people not only form status hierarchies, they also talk to higher-status people in the respectful way they often talk to strangers. And they talk to lower-status people in the more familiar, first name way they speak to friends. Patients call their physician "Dr. So and So"; the physician often replies using their first name. Students and professors typically address one another in a similar nonmutual way.

Most languages have two forms of the English pronoun "you": a respectful form and a familiar form (for example, *Sie* and *du* in German, *vous* and *tu* in French, *usted* and *tu* in Spanish). People typically use the familiar form with intimates and subordinates (not only with close friends and family members but also in speaking to children and dogs). A German child receives a boost when strangers begin addressing the child as "Sie" instead of "du." Nouns, too, can express assumed social inequalities. Among faculty studied by Rebecca Rubin (1981),

Stephen Reid, serving his sentence for bank robbery (left), and with his wife, author Susan Musgrave (right).

young female professors were far more likely than young male professors to have students call them by their first name. Women tennis players will empathize: Sportscasters refer to them using only their first name 53 percent of the time but refer to men players this way only 8 percent of the time (*Harper's Index*, 1991).

This first aspect of Brown's universal norm—that *forms of address communicate not only social distance but also social status*—correlates with a second aspect: *Advances in intimacy are usually suggested by the higher-status person.* In Europe, where most twosomes begin a relationship with the polite, formal "you" and may eventually progress to the more intimate "you," someone obviously has to initiate the increased intimacy. Who do you suppose does so? On some congenial occasion, the elder, or richer, or more distinguished of the two may say, "Why don't we say *du* to one another?"

This norm extends beyond language to every type of advance in intimacy. It is more acceptable to borrow a pen from or put a hand on the shoulder of one's intimates and subordinates than to behave in such a casual way with strangers or superiors. Similarly, the president of my university invites faculty to his home before they invite him to theirs. In general, then, the higher-status person is the pacesetter in the progression toward intimacy.

The force of culture appears in varying norms, and also in the roles that people play. Cultures everywhere influence people by assigning them to play certain roles. Chapter 4 illustrated a powerful phenomenon: Playing a role often leads people to internalize their behavior. Acting becomes believing. So let's consider how roles vary within and across cultures.

Social roles

All the world's a stage,
And all the men and women merely players:
They have their exits and their entrances;
And one man in his time plays many parts.
                    William Shakespeare

Role theorists assume, as did William Shakespeare, that social life is like acting on a theatrical stage, with all its scenes, masks, and scripts. Like the role of Jaques, who speaks these lines in *As You Like It*, social roles, such as parent, student, and friend, outlast those who play them. And, as Jaques says, these roles allow some freedom of interpretation to those who act them out; great performances are defined by the way the role is played. Some aspects of any role *must* be performed, however. A student must at least show up for exams, turn in papers, and maintain some minimum grade point average. Some roles (student, healer, mother, father) exist in all cultures, yet (as we will see) vary with culture.

When only a few norms are associated with a social category (for example, sidewalk pedestrians should keep to the right and not jaywalk), we do not regard the position as a social role. It takes a whole cluster of norms to define a role. I could readily generate a long list of norms prescribing my activities as a professor or as a father. Although I may acquire my particular image by violating the least important norms (valuing efficiency, I rarely arrive early for anything), violating my role's most important norms (failing to meet my classes, abusing my children) could lead to my being fired or divorced.

Roles have powerful effects. In Chapter 4, we noted that we tend to absorb our roles. On a first date or on a new job, we may act the role self-consciously. As we internalize the role, self-consciousness subsides. What felt awkward now feels genuine.

"Nowhere is social psychology further apart from public consciousness," noted Philip Brickman (1978), "than in its understanding of how things become real for people." Take the case of Stephen Reid. In the 1970s Reid was part of the notorious group of bank robbers called the "Stop Watch Gang." They robbed over 100 banks, stealing more than $15 million. Reid was eventually arrested and while in prison he wrote the highly regarded novel, *Jackrabbit Parole*. Award-winning Canadian poet Susan Musgrave edited the book and asked Reid to marry her. They were married and when he was released they raised two children. By all accounts Reid was a happy and devoted husband and father. He was fond of saying, "My criminal career ended the day I began writing."

Sadly this was not to be. In 1998, Reid began using drugs and became addicted. On June 9, 1999 he robbed a Victoria bank, shot at a police officer, and held an elderly couple hostage. If Reid had been a bank robber all along and only pretended to be a good family man, people could have more easily understood his actions. What they could not understand was that he could really be a bank robber, then really a devoted husband and father, and then really a bank robber again. Could such a thing happen to you or me?

Yes and no. As we'll see later in this chapter, our actions depend not only on the social situation but also on our dispositions. Reid may have had a predisposition to drug abuse, which probably played a role in his criminal activities. You and I might well have respond differently. Nevertheless, some social situations can move most "normal" people to behave in "abnormal" ways. This is clear from experiments that put well-intentioned people in a bad situation to see whether good or evil prevails. To a dismaying extent, evil wins. Nice guys often don't finish nice.

High- and low-status roles.   In George Orwell's *Animal Farm*, the livestock overthrow their human masters and form an egalitarian society in which "All animals are equal." As the story unfolds, the pigs—who assume the managerial role—soon evade chores and accept comforts they consider appropriate to their status. "All animals are equal," they affirm, "but some animals are more equal than others."

Lawrence Messé, Norbert Kerr, and David Sattler (1992) note that the effects of status on self-perceptions aren't limited to pigs. In many everyday and laboratory situations, people assigned a superior status come to see themselves as meriting favorable treatment or as capable of superior performance. Ronald Humphrey (1985) showed this when he set up a simulated business office. By lottery, some people became managers, others clerks. As in real offices, the managers gave orders to the clerks and did higher-level work. Afterward, both clerks and managers perceived the equally able (randomly assigned) managers as *more* intelligent, assertive, and supportive—as really being more leaderlike.

Likewise, playing a *subservient* role can have demeaning effects. Ellen Langer and Ann Benevento (1978) discovered this when they had pairs of women solve arithmetic problems. After solving the problems individually, the women solved more problems together, with one of the women designated "boss" and the other "assistant." When they then went back to working individually, the "bosses" now solved more problems than they had in the first round, and the "assistants" solved fewer. Similar effects of assigned status on performance have been found in experiments with elementary schoolchildren (Jemmott & Gonzalez, 1989; Musser & Graziano, 1991): Demeaning roles undermine self-efficacy.

Role reversal.   Role playing can also be a positive force. By intentionally playing a new role, people sometimes change themselves or empathize with people whose roles differ from their own. Psychodrama, a form of psychotherapy, uses role playing for just this purpose. In George Bernard Shaw's *Pygmalion*, Eliza Doolittle, the cockney flower vendor, discovers that if she plays the role of a lady and is viewed by others as a lady, then she in fact is a lady. What wasn't real now is.

Roles often come in pairs defined by relationships—parent and child, husband and wife, teacher and student, doctor and patient, employer and employee, police and citizen. To help each understand the other, role reversals can help. The problem with much human conversation and argument, observed La Rochefoucauld, is that people pay more attention to their own utterances than to giving exact answers to questions. "Even the most charming and clever do little more than appear attentive . . . so anxious are they to return to their own ideas" (1665, No. 139). A negotiator or group leader can therefore create better communication by having the two sides reverse roles, with each arguing the other's position. Or each side can be asked to restate the other party's point (to the other's satisfaction) before replying. The next time you get into a difficult argument with a friend or parent, try to stop it in the middle and have each of you restate the other's perceptions and feelings before going on with your own. Likely, your mutual understanding will increase.

So far in this chapter we have affirmed our biological kinship as members of one human family, we have acknowledged our cultural diversity, and we have noted how norms and roles vary within and across cultures. Remember that our primary quest in social psychology is not to catalog differences but to identify universal principles of behavior. Our aim is what cross-cultural psychologist Walter Lonner (1989) calls "a universalistic psychology—a psychology that is as valid and meaningful in Omaha and Osaka as it is in Rome and Botswana."

"It is the peculiar triumph of society—and its loss—that it is able to convince those people to whom it has given inferior status of the reality of this decree."

James Baldwin, *Notes of a Native Son*, 1955

"Great Spirit, grant that I may not criticize my neighbor until I have walked for a moon in his moccasins."

Native prayer

Attitudes and behaviors will always vary with culture, but the processes by which attitudes influence behavior vary much less. People in Nigeria and Japan define teen roles differently than do those in Europe and North America, but in all cultures role expectations guide social relations. G. K. Chesterton had the idea nearly a century ago: When someone "has discovered why men in Bond Street wear black hats he will at the same moment have discovered why men in Timbuctoo wear red feathers."

Summing up

How are we humans alike, how do we differ—and why? Evolutionary psychologists study how natural selection favors traits that promote the perpetuation of one's genes. Although part of evolution's legacy is our human capacity to learn and adapt (and therefore to differ from one another), the evolutionary perspective highlights the kinship that results from our shared human nature.

The cultural perspective highlights human diversity—the behaviors, ideas, and traditions that help define a group and which are transmitted across generations. The remarkably wide diversity of attitudes and behaviors from one culture to another indicates the extent to which we are the products of cultural norms and roles.

Yet cross-cultural psychologists also seek to identify the "essential universality" of all people. For example, despite their differences, cultures share some norms in common. One apparently universal norm concerns how people of unequal status relate to one another.

All cultures assign people to social roles. Playing a cultural role often leads people to internalize their behavior. Switching roles can therefore change our perspective.

Gender similarities and differences

Both evolutionary psychologists and psychologists working from a cultural perspective have sought to explain gender variations. Before considering their views, let's see what there is to explain: As males and females, how are we alike? How do we differ? And why?

There are many obvious dimensions of human diversity—height, weight, hair color, to name just a few. But for people's self-concepts and social relationships, the two dimensions that matter most, and that people first attune to, are race and, especially, sex (Stangor & others, 1992). For our self-concepts and identities, for selecting friends and mates, and for how others regard and treat us, height and hair may matter, but ethnicity and sex matter much more. When you were born, the first thing people wanted to know about you was "Is it a boy or a girl?" When your sex was ambiguous—say, when not cued by a pink or blue outfit—people were unsure how to react. When a hermaphrodite child is born with a combination of male and female sex organs, physicians and family feel compelled to assign the child a sex and to surgically diminish the ambiguity. The simple message: Everyone *must* be assigned a sex. Between day and night there is dusk. But between male and female there is, socially speaking, nothing.

In Chapter 9, we look closely at how race and sex affect the way others regard and treat us. For now, let's consider **gender**—*the characteristics people*

gender
in psychology, the characteristics, whether biologically or socially influenced, by which people define male and female. Because "sex" is a biological category, social psychologists sometimes refer to biologically based gender differences as "sex differences."

associate with male and female. What behaviors *are* universally characteristic and expected of males? *of* females?

"Of the 46 chromosomes in the human genome, 45 are unisex," notes Judith Rich Harris (1998). Females and males are therefore similar in many physical traits, such as age of sitting, teething, and walking. They also are alike in many psychological traits, such as overall vocabulary, creativity, intelligence, happiness, and self-esteem. So shall we conclude that men and women are essentially the same, except for a few anatomical oddities that hardly matter apart from special occasions?

Actually, there are some differences, and it is these differences, not the many similarities, that capture attention and make news. In both science and everyday life, differences excite interest. Compared to the average man, the average woman has 70 percent more fat, possesses 40 percent less muscle, and is 5 inches shorter. Men enter puberty two years later, are twenty times more likely to have color-deficient vision, and die five years sooner. Women are twice as vulnerable to anxiety disorders and depression. Women have a slightly better sense of smell. They more easily become re-aroused immediately after orgasm. Men are three times more likely to commit suicide, and five times more likely to become alcoholic. Men also are much more likely to suffer hyperactivity or speech disorders as children, to display antisocial personalities as adults, and to be able to wiggle their ears.

During the 1970s, many scholars worried that studies of such gender differences might reinforce stereotypes and that gender differences might be construed as women's deficits. Focusing attention on gender differences will provide "battle weapons against women" warned sociologist Jesse Bernard (1976, p. 13). It's true that explanations for differences usually focus on the group that's seen as different (Miller & others, 1991). In discussing wage gaps between men and women most commentators wonder why women earn less than they should. Almost no commentaries discuss why men earn more than they should. People more often wonder what causes homosexuality than what causes heterosexuality (or what determines sexual orientation). People ask why Asian Americans so often excel in math and science, not why other groups less often excel.

> Even in physical traits, individual differences among men and among women far exceed the average differences between the sexes. Don Schollander's world-record-setting 4 minutes, 12 seconds in the 400-meter freestyle swim at the 1964 Olympics would have placed him eighth against the women racing in the 1996 Olympics and 5 seconds behind winner Michelle Smith.

Girls' play is often in small groups and imitate relationships. Boys' play is more often competitive or aggressive.

In each case, people define the standard by one group and wonder why the other is "different." From "different" it is but a short leap to "deviant" or "substandard."

Since the 1980s, scholars have felt freer to explore gender diversity (Ashmore, 1990). Initially, gender difference research "furthered the cause of gender equality" by reducing overblown stereotypes (Eagly, 1986). Then, during the 1980s and 1990s, reports Alice Eagly (1995), many studies revealed gender differences—differences as large as "important" behavior differences in other areas of psychology. Although the findings confirm some stereotypes of women—as less aggressive, more nurturant, more sensitive, and so forth—those are traits that many feminists celebrate and most people prefer (Swim, 1994). Small wonder, then, that most people rate their feelings regarding "women" as more *favorable* than their feelings regarding "men" (Eagly, 1994; Haddock & Zanna, 1994).

Let's compare men's and women's social connections, dominance, aggressiveness, and sexuality. Having described these differences, we can then consider how the evolutionary and cultural perspectives might explain them. Do gender differences reflect tendencies predisposed by natural selection? Or are they culturally constructed—a reflection of the roles that men and women often play and the situations in which they act?

Independence versus connectedness

Individual men display outlooks and behavior varying from fierce competitiveness to caring nurturance. So do individual women. Without denying that, psychologists Nancy Chodorow (1978, 1989), Jean Baker Miller (1986), and Carol Gilligan and her colleagues (1982, 1990) contend that women more than men give priority to close, intimate relationships.

The difference surfaces in childhood. Boys strive for independence; they define their identity in separation from the caregiver, usually their mother. Girls welcome *inter*dependence; they define their identity through their social connections. Boys' play often involves group activity. Girls' play occurs in smaller groups, with less aggression, more sharing, more imitation of relationships, and more intimate discussion (Lever, 1978).

Adult relationships extend this gender difference. In conversation, men more often focus on tasks and connections with large groups, women on personal relationships (Tannen, 1990). In groups, men talk more to give information; women talk more to share lives, give help, or show support (Dindia & Allen, 1992; Eagly, 1987). Among first-year college students, 5 in 10 males and 7 in 10 females say it is *very* important to "help others who are in difficulty" (Sax & others, 1996). In general, report Felicia Pratto and her colleagues (1997), men disproportionately gravitate to jobs that enhance inequalities (prosecuting attorney, corporate advertising); women gravitate to jobs that reduce inequalities (public defender, advertising work for a charity). Indeed, in most caregiving professions, such as social worker, teacher, and nurse, women outnumber men. Women also seem more charitable: Among individuals leaving estates worth more than $5 million, 48 percent of women and 35 percent of men make a charitable bequest, and women's colleges have unusually supportive alumni (National Council for Research on Women, 1994).

Women's connections as mothers, daughters, sisters, and grandmothers bind families (Rossi & Rossi, 1990). Women spend more time caring for both preschoolers and aging parents (Eagly & Crowley, 1986). They buy most birth-

"There should be no qualms about the forthright study of racial and gender differences; science is in desperate need of good studies that . . . inform us of what we need to do to help underrepresented people to succeed in this society. Unlike the ostrich, we cannot afford to hide our heads for fear of socially uncomfortable discoveries."

Developmental psychologist Sandra Scarr (1988)

"In the different voice of women lies the truth of an ethic of care."

Carol Gilligan, 1982, p. 173

Sally Forth by Greg Howard, with permission of North American Syndicate

Reprinted with special permisssion of King Features Syndicate.

day gifts and greeting cards (DeStefano & Colasanto, 1990; Hallmark, 1990). Asked to provide photos that portray who they are, women include more photos of parents and of themselves with others (Clancy & Dollinger, 1993). For women, especially, a sense of mutual support is crucial to marital satisfaction (Acitelli & Antonucci, 1994).

When surveyed, women are far more likely to describe themselves as having **empathy,** as being able to feel what another feels—to rejoice with those who rejoice and weep with those who weep. Although to a lesser extent, the empathy difference extends to laboratory studies. Shown slides or told stories, girls react with more empathy (Hunt, 1990). Given upsetting experiences in the laboratory or in real life, women more than men gain empathy for others enduring similar experiences (Batson & others, 1996). Women are more likely to cry or report feeling distressed at another's distress (Eisenberg & Lennon, 1983). And this helps explain why, compared to friendships with men, both men and women report friendships with women to be more intimate, enjoyable, and nurturing (Rubin, 1985; Sapadin, 1988). When they want empathy and understanding, someone to whom they can disclose their joys and hurts, both men and women usually turn to women.

Women's greater connectedness in personal relationships also gets expressed in their smiling (Hecht & others, 1993; Kolaric & Galambos, 1995). When Marianne LaFrance (1985) analyzed 9,000 university yearbook photos and when Amy Halberstadt and Martha Saitta (1987) studied 1,100 magazine and news-

empathy
the vicarious experience of another's feelings; putting oneself in another's shoes

"Contrary to what many women believe, it's fairly easy to develop a long-term, stable, intimate, and mutually fulfilling relationship with a guy. Of course this guy has to be a Labrador retriever."

Dave Barry, *Dave Barry's Complete Guide to Guys,* 1995

Empathy is feeling what another feels, as 7-year-old Lamar Pugh seemingly does.

paper photos and 1,300 people in shopping malls, parks, and streets, they consistently found that females were more likely to smile.

One explanation for this male-female empathy difference is that women tend to outperform men at reading others' emotions. In her analysis of 125 studies of men's and women's sensitivity to nonverbal cues, Judith Hall (1984) discerned that women are generally superior at decoding others' emotional messages. For example, shown a two-second silent film clip of the face of an upset woman, women guess more accurately whether she is criticizing someone or discussing her divorce. Women's sensitivity to nonverbal cues helps explain their greater emotional responsiveness in both depressing and joyful situations (Grossman & Wood, 1993; Sprecher & Sedikides, 1993; Stoppard & Gruchy, 1993). Women's sensitivity need not reflect an innate gender difference, note Tiffany Graham and William Ickes (1997). It might instead represent each gender responding to social expectations and being motivated by their needs in a particular situation.

Women also are more skilled at *expressing* emotions nonverbally, reports Hall. This is especially so for positive emotion, report Erick Coats and Robert Feldman (1996). They had people talk about times they had been happy, sad, and angry. When shown five-second silent video clips of these reports, observers could much more accurately discern women's than men's emotions when recalling happiness. Men, however, were slightly more successful in conveying anger.

Whether considered feminine or human, traits such as gentleness, sensitivity, and warmth are a boon to close relationships. In a study of married couples in Sydney, Australia, John Antill (1983) found that when either the husband or wife had these traditionally feminine qualities—or better, when *both* did—marital satisfaction was higher. People find marriage rewarding when their spouse is nurturant and emotionally supportive.

Social dominance

Imagine two people: One is "adventurous, autocratic, coarse, dominant, forceful, independent, and strong." The other is "affectionate, dependent, dreamy, emotional, submissive, and weak." If the first person sounds more to you like a

What do you think: Should Western women become more self-reliant and more attuned to their culture's individualism? Or might women's relational approach to life help transform power-oriented Western societies (marked by high levels of child neglect, loneliness, and depression) into more caring communities?

man and the second like a woman, you are not alone, report John Williams and Deborah Best (1990a, p. 15). The world around, from Asia to Africa and Europe to Australia, people rate men as more dominant, driven, and aggressive.

These perceptions and expectations correlate with reality. In essentially every society, men *are* socially dominant. In no known societies do women dominate men (Pratto, 1996). Women are 12 percent of the world's legislators (Briscoe, 1997), 3 percent of the U.N. ambassadors, less than 1 percent of the national presidents and prime ministers, and 0 percent of the economics Nobel laureates since the prize began in 1901 (Sivard, 1995). Men more than women are concerned with social dominance and are more likely to favor conservative political candidates and programs that preserve group inequality (Pratto & others, 1997). Men are half of all jurors but 90 percent of elected jury leaders and most of the leaders of ad hoc laboratory groups (Davis & Gilbert, 1989; Kerr & others, 1982). As is typical of those in higher-status positions, men initiate most of the inviting for dates.

Men's style of communicating undergirds their social power. As leaders in situations where roles aren't rigidly scripted, men tend to be directive, women to be democratic (Eagly & Johnson, 1990). Men tend to excel as directive, task-focused leaders, women as social leaders who build team spirit (Eagly & Karau, 1991; Eagly & others, 1995; Wood & Rhodes, 1991). Men more than women place priority on winning, getting ahead, and dominating others (Sidanius & others, 1994). When leading democratically, women leaders get evaluated as favorably as men. When leading autocratically, women get evaluated less favorably than men (Eagly & others, 1992). People will accept a man's "strong, assertive" leadership more readily than a woman's "pushy, aggressive" leadership.

> When women achieve equal status with men, will they, should they, feel as free as men to initiate formal dates?

"A little further, dear."

Drawing by W. Steig; © 1989 The New Yorker Magazine, Inc.

"That was a fine report, Barbara. But since the sexes speak different languages, I probably didn't understand a word of it."

Men's conversational style reflects their concern for independence, women's for connectedness. Men are more likely to act as powerful people often do—talking assertively, interrupting, touching with the hand, staring more, smiling less (Carli, 1991; Ellyson & others, 1991; Major & others, 1990). Stating the results from a female perspective, women's influence style tends to be more indirect—less interruptive, more sensitive, more polite, less cocky.

So is it right to declare (in the words of one 1990s bestseller) that *men are from Mars, women are from Venus?* Actually, note Kay Deaux and Marianne LaFrance (1998), men's and women's conversational styles vary with the social context. Much of the style we attribute to men is typical of people (men or women) in positions of status and power. Moreover, individuals vary; some men are characteristically hesitant and deferential, some women direct and assertive. Clearly, it oversimplifies to suggest that women and men are from different planets.

Aware of the varying yet oft-reported gender communication difference, Nancy Henley (1977) has argued that women should stop feigning smiles, averting their eyes, and tolerating interruptions and should instead look people in the eye and speak assertively. Judith Hall (1984), however, values women's less autocratic communication style, noting that "Whenever it is assumed that women's nonverbal behavior is undesirable, yet another myth is perpetuated: that male behavior is normal and that it is women's behavior that is deviant and in need of explanation" (pp. 15–153).

Aggression

By **aggression,** psychologists mean *behavior intended to hurt.* Throughout the world, hunting, fighting, and warring are primarily male activities. In surveys,

aggression
physical or verbal behavior intended to hurt someone. In laboratory experiments, this might mean delivering electric shocks or saying something likely to hurt another's feelings. By this social psychological definition, one can be socially assertive without being aggressive.

men admit to more aggression than do women. In laboratory experiments, men indeed exhibit more physical aggression, for example, by administering what they believe are hurtful electric shocks (Knight & others, 1996). In Canada, the male-to-female arrest rate is 11 to 1 for murder and 8 to 1 for assault (Colombo, 1994). In the United States, it is 9 to 1 for murder and 5 to 1 for assault (FBI, 1997). Across the world, murder rates vary. Yet in all regions, men are roughly 20 times more likely to murder men than women are to murder women (Daly & Wilson, 1989).

But as with communication styles, the gender difference fluctuates with context. When there is provocation, the gender gap

"It's a guy thing."

shrinks (Bettencourt & Miller, 1996). And, within less assaultive forms of aggression—say, slapping a family member or verbally attacking someone—women are no less aggressive than men (Björkqvist, 1994; White & Kowalski, 1994).

Sexuality

There is also a gender gap in sexual attitudes and assertiveness. It's true that in their physiological and subjective responses to sexual stimuli, women and men are "more similar than different" (Griffitt, 1987). Yet consider:

- Susan Hendrick and her colleagues (1985) report that many studies, including their own, reveal that women are "moderately conservative" about casual sex and men are "moderately permissive." Women are more relational, men more recreational.

- In a survey of 2,347 Newfoundland high school students, Westera and Bennett (1994) found that boys were more accepting of premarital sex than girls were. In a survey conducted in nine different bars in Ontario men reported more experience with casual sex and women reported less enjoyment and more guilt following such encounters (Harold & Mewhinney, 1993).

- In one New Brunswick study, 292 university men and women reported how often they experienced each of 56 different kinds of sexual fantasies. The results showed that men reported both a greater frequency of sexual fantasies and a greater diversity of such fantasies than women (Renaud & Byers, 1999).

Which would you prefer: finding a great bargain on clothes or having great sex?

	Women	Men
Bargain	46%	14%
Sex	41%	76%

Yankelovich poll in *Time*, (1994)

• Data gleaned from 177 studies of 130,000 people confirm that men are much more accepting of casual sex (Oliver & Hyde, 1993).

The gender difference in sexual attitudes carries over to behavior. "With few exceptions anywhere in the world," report cross-cultural psychologist Marshall Segall and his colleagues (1990, p. 244), "males are more likely than females to initiate sexual activity." Moreover, among people of both sexual orientations "men without women have sex more often, with more different partners, than women without men" (Baumeister, 1991, p. 151; Bailey & others, 1994). Casual sex is most common among men with traditional masculine attitudes (Pleck & others, 1993). Men are also more likely to take the initiative in courtship, touching and seeking sex (Hendrick, 1988; Kenrick, 1987; Lawrance, Taylor, & Byers, 1996). Like their human counterparts, the males of most animal species, too, are more sexually assertive and less selective about their partners (Hinde, 1984).

Sexual fantasies express the gender difference (Ellis & Symons, 1990). In male-oriented erotica, women are unattached and lust driven. In romance novels, whose primary market is women, a tender male is emotionally consumed by his devoted passion for the heroine. Social scientists aren't the only ones to have noticed. "Women can be fascinated by a four-hour movie with subtitles wherein the entire plot consists of a man and a woman yearning to have, but never actually having a relationship," observes humorist Dave Barry (1995). "Men HATE that. Men can take maybe 45 seconds of yearning, and they want everybody to get naked. Followed by a car chase. A movie called 'Naked People in Car Chases' would do really well among men."

Summing up

Boys and girls, and men and women, are in many ways alike. Yet their differences attract more attention. Although individual differences among women and among men exceed their gender differences, social psychologists have explored gender differences in independence versus connectedness. Women typically do more caring, express more empathy and emotion, and define themselves more in terms of relationships. Men and women also tend to exhibit differing social dominance, aggression, and sexuality.

As detectives are more intrigued by crime than virtue, so psychological detectives are more intrigued by differences than similarities. Let us therefore remind ourselves: *Individual differences far exceed gender differences.* Females and males are hardly opposite (altogether different) sexes. Rather, they differ like two folded hands—similar but not the same, fitting together yet differing as they grasp each other.

Evolution and gender: Doing what comes naturally?

In explaining gender differences, inquiry has focused on two culprits: evolution and culture.

"What do you think is the main reason men and women have different personalities, interests, and abilities?" asked the Gallup Organization (1990) in a recent survey. "Is it mainly because of the way men and women are raised, or

"I hunt and she gathers—otherwise, we couldn't make ends meet."

are the differences part of their biological makeup?" Among the 99 percent who answered the question (apparently without questioning its assumptions), nearly equal numbers answered "upbringing" and "biology."

There are, of course, those salient biological sex differences. Men have penises; women have vaginas. Men produce sperm; women, eggs. Men have the muscle mass to hunt game; women can breast-feed. Are biological sex differences limited to these obvious distinctions in reproduction and physique? Or do men's and women's genes, hormones, and brains differ in ways that also contribute to behavior differences?

Gender and mating preferences

Noting the worldwide persistence of gender differences in aggressiveness, dominance, and sexuality, evolutionary psychologist Douglas Kenrick (1987) suggests that "we cannot change the evolutionary history of our species, and some of the differences between us are undoubtedly a function of that history." Evolutionary psychology predicts no sex differences in all those domains in which the sexes faced similar adaptive challenges (Buss, 1995b). Both sexes regulate heat with sweat, have similar taste preferences to nourish their bodies, and grow calluses where the skin meets friction. But evolutionary psychology does predict sex differences in behaviors relevant to mating and reproduction.

Consider, for example, the male's greater sexual initiative. The average male produces many trillions of sperm in his lifetime, making sperm cheap compared to eggs. Moreover, while a female brings one fetus to term and then nurses it, a male can spread his genes by fertilizing many females. Thus females invest their reproductive opportunities carefully, by looking for signs of health and resources. Males compete with other males for chances to win the genetic sweepstakes by sending their genes into the future. Men, say the evolutionists, seek to reproduce widely, women wisely.

Secretariat, the greatest racehorse of modern times, sired 400 foals.

focus

Nature's mating game

Diane Ackerman vividly illustrates a core assumption of evolutionary psychology. Critics, as we will see, find this analysis speculative and incomplete. (From *A Natural History of Love* [Random House, 1994].)

One ejaculation contains about 200 million sperm. In theory, the neighbor boy could populate his own planet. If he wants his genes to survive, he should impregnate as many girls as he can. Parents of girls sense this and are worried about his "intentions" toward their daughters. After all, a female can produce only one egg a month and not many in her entire lifetime. If she becomes pregnant, she will be weaker and more vulnerable for nine months, less able to support herself, and then will have to nurse the baby and look after it for years.

The male's investment is a bit of spunk on a romantic evening. The female's investment is many years of self-sacrifice. It's in her best interest to choose someone who will stay by her and help support her child. Biologically, it's in the male's best interest to love 'em and leave 'em.

Both desire the same goal—the perpetuation of their genes. What differs in their strategy? She wants a man who will stick around, and because that's never a surefire thing she becomes very choosy. She hopes to fall mutually in love with someone protective but nurturing, faithful and fit. She tests his sincerity, grills him about whether or not he really loves her, if he would go through fire and water for her. She uses words like "always" and "forever."

Moreover, evolutionary psychology suggests, physically dominant males gained more access to females, which over generations enhanced male aggression and dominance. If our ancestral mothers benefitted from being able to read their infants' and suitors' emotions, then natural selection may have similarly favored emotion-detecting ability in females. Underlying all these presumptions is the principle that nature selects traits that help send one's genes into the future.

"A hen is only an egg's way of making another egg."

Samuel Butler, 1835–1901

Mind you, little of this is conscious. No one stops to calculate, "How can I maximize the number of genes I leave to posterity?" Rather, say evolutionary psychologists, our natural yearnings are our genes' way of making more genes. Emotions execute evolution's dispositions. "Humans are living fossils—collections of mechanisms produced by prior selection pressures," says David Buss (1995a). And that, evolutionary psychologists believe, helps explain not only male aggression but also the differing sexual attitudes and behaviors of females and males. Although a man's interpreting a woman's smile as sexual interest usually proves wrong, occasionally being right can have reproductive payoff.

Evolutionary psychology also predicts that men will strive to offer what women will desire—external resources and physical protection—and that women will strive to offer men the youthful, healthy appearance (connoting fertility) that men will desire. And sure enough, note Buss (1994a) and Alan Feingold (1992), women's and men's mate preferences confirm these predictions. Consider:

- Studies in 37 cultures, from Australia to Zambia, reveal that men everywhere feel attracted to women whose physical features, such as youthful face and form, suggest fertility. Women everywhere feel attracted to men

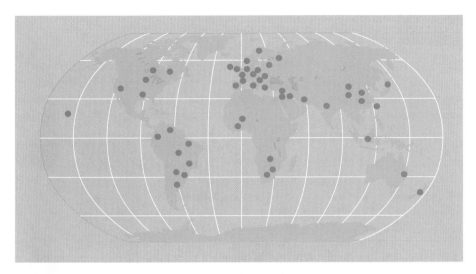

(From Buss, 1994b.)

figure 5–1

Human mating preferences.

David Buss and 50 collaborators surveyed more than 10,000 people from all races, religions, and political systems on six continents and five islands. Everywhere, men preferred attractive physical features suggesting youth and health—and reproductive fitness. Everywhere, women preferred men with resources and status.

Pierre Trudeau was 29 years older than Margaret.

CBC news anchor Peter Mansbridge is 12 years older than his third wife, Cynthia Dale.

In 1997, then Bank of Montreal chairman Matthew Barrett, 52, wed former model Anne-Marie Sten, 42, after a three-month courtship.

whose wealth, power, and ambition promise resources for protecting and nurturing offspring (Figure 5–1). Men's greater interest in physical form also makes them the consumers of most of the world's visual pornography. But there are gender similarities, too: Whether residing on an Indonesian island or in urban São Paulo, both women and men desire kindness, love, and mutual attraction.

- Men feel most jealous over their mate's having sex with someone else. Women tend to feel greater jealousy over their mate's becoming emotionally attached to someone else. Evolutionary psychologists say this gender difference reflects men's natural concern with their offspring's paternity and women's natural concern with their mate's provision of resources (Buss, 1994a).

- Men everywhere tend to marry younger women. Moreover, the older the man, the greater the age difference he prefers when selecting a mate. In their twenties, men prefer, and marry, women only slightly younger. In their sixties, men prefer, and marry, women averaging about ten years younger (Kenrick & Keefe, 1992). Women of all ages prefer men just

In life's mating game, men often desire women with beauty and youth and women desire men with wealth and power. For evolutionary psychologists, these couples illustrate men's desire for features that connote fertility and women's desire for features that connote protection and support for their offspring.

behind the scenes

When I began work in the field in 1982, no one knew whether some mating desires were universal. The dominant view was that mate preferences were arbitrarily variable across cultures, and furthermore, that men and women within cultures shared the same desires. So, I departed from traditional mainstream psychology to explore the mating behaviors predicted from evolutionary principles.

I found, somewhat to my astonishment, that men and women across the world differ in their mate preferences in precisely the ways predicted by the evolutionists. Just as our fears of snakes, heights, and spiders provide a window for viewing the survival hazards of our evolutionary ancestors, our mating desires provide a window for viewing the resources our ancestors needed for reproduction. We all carry with us today the desires of our successful forebears. Since this early study, I have been extremely gratified to witness the evolutionary psychology perspective blossoming within the social sciences.

David M. Buss
University of Texas

slightly older than themselves. Once again, say the evolutionary psychologists, we see that natural selection predisposes men to feel attracted to female features associated with fertility.

Even the masculine concern for independence and competitive achievement may reflect naturally selected gender differences, suggest some evolutionary psychologists. "Male achievement is ultimately a courtship display," says Glenn Wilson (1994), "parallel in a sense to the peacock's tail." Men, he suggests, are motivated to attain and display the sort of status and resources that women will find attractive, as illustrated in the lives of super-rich men who have relationships with a succession of beautiful women.

Gender and hormones

If genes predispose gender-related traits, they must do so by their effects on our bodies. As the results of architectural blueprints appear in physical structures, so the effects of our genetic blueprints appear in the sex hormones that differentiate males and females. In male embryos, the genes direct the formation of testes, which begin to secrete *testosterone*, the principal male sex hormone. Expose female rat, monkey, or human embryos to high levels of male sex hormones and, voila!, they, too, will exhibit masculine appearance and behavior (Berenbaum & Hines, 1992; Hines & Green, 1991). So, do biological hormone differences predispose psychological gender differences?

The gender gap in aggression does seem influenced by testosterone. In various animals, administering testosterone heightens aggressiveness. In humans, violent male criminals have higher than normal testosterone levels; so do professional football players and boisterous fraternity members (Dabbs & others, 1990, 1993, 1995). Moreover, for both humans and monkeys the gender difference in aggression appears early in life (before culture has much effect) and wanes as testosterone levels decline during adulthood. No one of these lines of evidence is conclusive. Taken together, they convince most scholars that sex hormones matter. But so, as we will see, does culture.

As people mature to middle age and beyond, a curious thing happens. Women become more assertive and self-confident, men more empathic and less domineering (Lowenthal & others, 1975; Pratt & others, 1990). Hormone changes are one possible explanation for the shrinking gender differences. Role demands are another. Some speculate that during courtship and early parenthood, social expectations lead both sexes to emphasize traits that enhance their roles. While courting, providing, and protecting, men play up their macho sides and forgo their needs for interdependence and nurturance (Gutmann, 1977). While courting and rearing young children, young women restrain their impulses to assert and be independent. As men and women graduate from these early adult roles, they supposedly express more of their restrained tendencies. Each becomes more *androgynous*—capable of both assertiveness and nurturance.

> "The finest people marry the two sexes in their own person."
> Ralph Waldo Emerson, *Journals*, 1843

Reflections on evolutionary psychology

Without disputing natural selection—nature's selecting physical and behavioral traits that enhance gene survival—critics see two problems with evolutionary explanations. First, they sometimes start with an effect (such as the male-female difference in sexual initiative) and then work backward to construct an explanation for it. This approach is reminiscent of functionalism, a dominant theory in psychology during the 1920s. "Why does that behavior occur? Because it serves such and such a function." The theorist can hardly lose at this game. It is, scorns paleontologist Stephen Jay Gould (1997), mere "speculation [and] guesswork in the cocktail-party mode."

The way to prevent the hindsight bias is to imagine things turning out otherwise. Let's try it. If human males were never known to have extramarital affairs, might we not see the evolutionary wisdom behind their fidelity? After all, argues Dorothy Einon (1994), women will mate throughout the menstrual cycle and while pregnant or lactating—which means that a man who mates at random is no more likely than a faithful married man to fertilize a woman. Moreover, because there is more to bringing offspring to maturity than merely depositing sperm, men and women both gain by jointly investing in their children. Males who are loyal to their mates and offspring are more apt to ensure that their young will survive to perpetuate their genes. (This is, in fact, an evolutionary explanation for why humans, and certain other species whose young require a heavy parental investment, tend to pair off and be monogamous. Love between man and woman is universal because of its genetic payoffs: The offspring of devoted males were less vulnerable to predators.) Or imagine that women were the stronger, more physically aggressive sex. "But of course!" someone might say, "all the better for protecting their young."

> "Sex differences in behavior may have been relevant to our ancestors gathering roots and hunting squirrels on the plains of Northern Africa, but their manifestations in modern society are less clearly 'adaptive.' Modern society is information oriented—big biceps and gushing testosterone have less direct relevance to the president of a computer firm."
> Douglas Kenrick (1987)

Evolutionary psychologists reply that such criticisms are "flat-out wrong." Hindsight plays no less a role in cultural explanations: Why do women and men differ? Because their culture *socializes* their behavior! When, as we will see, people's roles vary across time and place, "culture" *describes* those roles better than it explains them. And far from being mere hindsight conjecture, say evolutionary psychologists, their field is an empirical science that tests evolutionary predictions with data from animal behavior, cross-cultural observations, and hormonal and genetic studies. As in many scientific fields, observations inspire a theory that generates new, testable predictions (Figure 5–2). The predictions alert us to unnoticed phenomena and allow us to confirm, refute, or revise the theory.

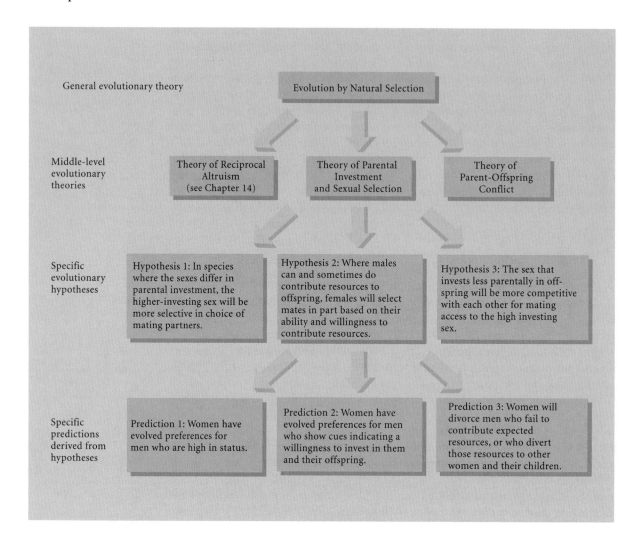

figure 5–2

Sample predictions derived from evolutionary psychology by David Buss (1995a).

Also, the evolutionary psychologist reminds us, evolutionary wisdom is *past* wisdom. It tells us what behaviors worked in the past. Whether such tendencies are still adaptive is a different question. For example, although people tend to be attracted to potential mates whose appearance and behavior fit typical masculine or feminine images, people actually report more satisfying relationships with those who are androgynous (Ickes, 1993).

Evolutionary psychology's critics acknowledge that evolution helps explain both our commonalities and our differences (a certain amount of diversity aids survival, and genetic predispositions may be triggered only in certain environmental contexts). But they contend our common evolutionary heritage does not, by itself, predict the enormous cultural variation in human marriage patterns (from one spouse to a succession of spouses to multiple wives to multiple husbands to spouse swapping). Nor does it explain cultural changes in behavior patterns over mere decades of time. The most significant trait that nature has endowed us with, it seems, is the capacity to adapt—to learn and to change. Therein lies what all agree is culture's shaping power.

Marriage patterns vary. Worldwide, monogamy is most common. But polygamy, illustrated by this Cameroon man with many wives, occurs in some cultures.

Summing up

Evolutionary psychologists theorize how evolution might have predisposed gender differences in behaviors such as aggression and sexual initiative. Nature's mating game, they suggest, favors male sexual initiative toward females—especially those with physical features suggesting fertility—and aggressive dominance in competing with other males. Females, who have a greater stake in not squandering their fewer reproductive chances, place a greater priority on selecting mates with the ability to commit resources to protecting and nurturing their young.

Culture and gender

Culture's influence is vividly illustrated by differing gender roles across place and time.

Culture, we noted earlier, is what's shared by a large group and transmitted across generations—ideas, attitudes, behaviors, and traditions. We can see the shaping power of culture in ideas about how men and women should behave. In countries everywhere, girls spend more time helping with housework and child care, while boys spend more time in unsupervised play (Edwards, 1991). Even in contemporary, dual-career, North American marriages, men do most of the household repairs and women arrange the child care (Biernat & Wortman, 1991).

Gender socialization, it has been said, gives girls "roots" and boys "wings." In Caldecott Award children's books over the last half-century, girls have four times more often than boys been shown using household objects (such as broom, sewing needle, or pots and pans), and boys have five times more often than girls been shown using production objects (such as pitchfork, plow, or

behind the scenes

When I began my career at Princeton in 1970, the first group of female undergraduates had just enrolled at this formerly all-male bastion. These pioneers were incredibly bright and very ambitious. Indeed, the majority intended to become doctors, lawyers, or professors! It was Susan Pack's intuition that, despite the great capabilities and high achievement motivation of her female peers, they still "acted dumb" when confronted with the typical attractive, though chauvinistic, Princeton male.

Susan's undergraduate honors thesis, designed to test this notion, demonstrated that Princeton females "acted dumb" or "acted smart" depending, in part, on whether they believed an attractive Princeton male held chauvinistic or liberated attitudes about women. I wonder: Would these results hold today at Princeton? At other colleges? Would males, too, act to fulfill the gender stereotypes of attractive females?

Mark Zanna
University of Waterloo

---

gun) (Crabb & Bielawski, 1994). The adult result: "Everywhere," reports the United Nations (1991), women do most household work. And "everywhere, cooking and dishwashing are the least shared household chores." Such behavior expectations for males and females define **gender roles.**

gender role
a set of behavior expectations (norms) for males or females

In an experiment with undergraduate women, Mark Zanna and Susan Pack (1975) showed the impact of gender role expectations. The women answered a questionnaire on which they described themselves to a tall, unattached, senior man they expected to meet. Those led to believe his ideal woman was home-oriented and deferential to her husband presented themselves as more traditionally feminine than did women expecting to meet a man who liked strong, ambitious women. Moreover, given a problem-solving test, those expecting to meet the nonsexist man behaved more intelligently: They solved 18 percent more problems than those expecting to meet the man with the traditional views. This adapting of themselves to fit the man's image was much less pronounced if the man was less desirable—a short, already attached freshman. In a companion experiment by Dean Morier and Cara Seroy (1994), men similarly adapted their self-presentations to meet desirable women's gender role expectations.

Do you ever present one self to members of your own sex and a different self to members of the other sex?

But does culture construct gender roles? Or do gender roles merely reflect behavior naturally appropriate for men and women? The variety of gender roles across cultures and over time shows that culture indeed constructs our gender roles.

Gender roles vary with culture

Should women do the housework? Should they be more concerned with promoting their husband's career than with their own? John Williams, Debra Best, and their collaborators (1990b) asked such questions of university students in 14 cultures. In nearly every one, women students had slightly more egalitarian views than their male peers. But the differences among the countries were far greater. Nigerian and Pakistani students, for example, had much more traditional ideas about distinct roles for men and women than did Dutch and

In western countries, gender roles are becoming more flexible. No longer is housework necessarily women's work, and mechanical work necessarily men's work.

German students. Iftikhar Hassan (1980) of Pakistan's National Institute of Psychology explains the traditional status of Pakistani women:

> She knows that parents are not happy at the birth of a girl and she should not complain about parents not sending her to school as she is not expected to take up a job. She is taught to be patient, sacrificing, obedient. . . . If something goes wrong with her marriage she is the one who is to be blamed. If any one of her children do not succeed in life, she is the main cause of their failure. And in the rare circumstance that she seeks a divorce or receives a divorce her chances of second marriage are very slim because Pakistani culture is very harsh on divorced women.

In nomadic, food-gathering societies, boys and girls receive much the same education, and men and women do much the same work. In agricultural societies, gender roles are more distinct: Women work the fields and stay with the children, while men roam more freely (Segall & others, 1990; Van Leeuwen, 1978). In industrialized societies, roles vary enormously (Figure 5–3). Women fill 2 percent of managerial positions in South Korea, 17 percent in the United States, 28 percent in Austria, and 48 percent in Switzerland (Triandis, 1994). In North America, most doctors and dentists are men; in Russia most doctors are women, as are most dentists in Denmark.

Gender roles vary over time

In the last half-century—a thin slice of our long history—gender roles have changed dramatically. In 1938, 1 in 5 approved "of a married woman earning money in business or industry if she has a husband capable of supporting her." By 1996, 4 in 5 approved (Niemi & others, 1989; NORC, 1996)—although nearly 2 in 3 still think that for children the "ideal family situation" is "father has a job

figure 5–3

Gender and education.

In North America, young adult men and women are equally likely to have completed college. In Japan, men are three times as likely as women to have done so.
(Data from American Council on Education, 1994)

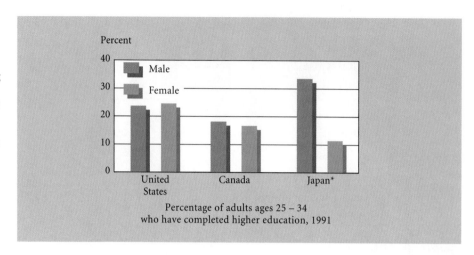

Percentage of adults ages 25 – 34 who have completed higher education, 1991

and mother stays home and cares for the children" (Gallup, 1990). In 1967, 57 percent of first-year university students agreed that "the activities of married women are best confined to the home and family." In 1996, 24 percent agreed (Astin & others, 1987; Sax & others, 1996).

Behavior changes have accompanied this attitude shift. Between 1980 and 1997, the percentage of women in the full-time workforce has steadily increased from 32 to 39 percent (Statistics Canada, 1997). A similar influx of women in the workforce has occurred in Australia, Great Britain, and the U.S. Since 1975, increasing numbers of women have been training to become lawyers, doctors and engineers—though gains in engineering have been modest (Figure 5–4). The striking variation of roles across cultures and over time signals that evolution and biology do not fix gender roles: Culture also bends the genders.

> Canadian husbands do 67 percent of the maintenance and repairs around the home, but only 27 percent of the meal preparation and clean up, and only 23 percent of the housecleaning.
>
> Statistics Canada, 1998

Peer-transmitted culture

Although roles change, cultures, like ice cream, come in many flavors. On Bay Street men mostly wear suits and women mostly wear skirts and dresses; in Scotland many men wear pleated skirts (kilts) as formal dress; in some equatorial cultures (but not others) men and women wear virtually nothing at all. How are such traditions preserved across generations?

The prevailing assumption is what Judith Rich Harris (1998) calls *The Nurture Assumption;* nurture (the way parents bring their children up) governs who their children become. On that much Freudians and behaviorists—and the person in the car ahead of you—agree. Comparing the extremes of loved and abused children suggests that parenting *does* matter. Children do absorb many of their values at home. But if children's personalities are molded by parental example and nurture, then children who grow up in the same families should be noticeably alike, yes?

That presumption is refuted by the most astonishing, agreed-upon, and dramatic recent finding of developmental psychology. In the words of behavior geneticists Robert Plomin and Denise Daniels (1987), "Two children in the same family [are on average] as different from one another as are pairs of children selected randomly from the population."

The evidence from studies of twins and biological and adoptive siblings indicates that genetic influences explain roughly 50 percent of individual variations

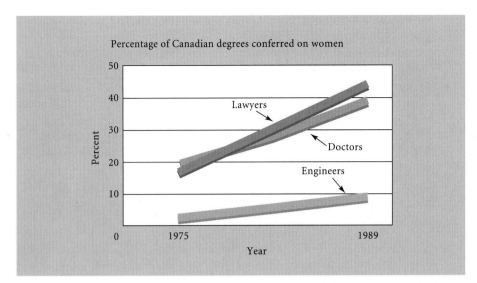

Percentage of Canadian degrees conferred on women

figure 5–4

Percentage of Canadian degrees conferred on women.

In Canada, the number of women doctors and lawyers has steadily increased, but the number of female engineers has shown more modest growth. (Data from *Report on Business Magazine,* September 1992.)

In western cultures, gender roles are changing, but not this much.

in personality traits. Shared environmental influences—including the shared home influence—account for only 0 to 10 percent of their personality differences. So what accounts for the other 40 to 50 percent? It's *peer influence,* Harris argues. What children and teens care most about is less what their parents think than what peers think. Children and youth learn their games, their musical tastes, their accents, even their dirty words mostly from peers. Consider:

- Preschoolers will often refuse to try a certain food despite parents' urgings—until they are put at a table with a group of children who like it.
- Although children of smokers have an elevated smoking rate, the effect seems largely peer mediated. Such children more often have friends who model smoking, who suggest its pleasures, and who offer cigarettes.

- Nazi youth group members 60 years ago mostly came from emotionally supportive, middle-class homes, notes David Rowe (1994). What corrupted them was not bad parenting but the "heavier weight" of cultural change around them.
- Young immigrant children whose families are transplanted into foreign cultures usually grow up preferring the language and norms of their new peer culture. They may "code-switch" when they step back into their home, but their hearts and minds are with their peer group. Likewise, deaf children of hearing parents who attend schools for the deaf usually leave their parents' culture and assimilate into deaf culture.
- By living in one neighborhood rather than another, parents can alter the odds that their children will become delinquent, quit school, use drugs, or get pregnant.

Ergo, if we left a group of children with their same schools, neighborhoods, and peers, but switched the parents around, says Harris (1996) in taking her argument to its limits, they "would develop into the same sort of adults." As it happens, the sort of adults they develop into often resemble their parents. But the cultural transmission is less from individual parent to child, she contends, than from the parental group to the children's group. The parents help define their children's schools, neighborhoods, and peers. Moreover, children often take their cues from slightly older children, who get their cues from older youth, who take theirs from young adults in the parents' generation.

And so it goes with gender roles. Some years ago, one of my feminist colleagues was startled by this conversation with her four-year-old daughter:

This Scottish wedding photo illustrates a cultural dress tradition maintained across many generations.

Sara: "I'm going to be a nurse."

Mother: "Maybe you could be a doctor."

Sara: "Oh no. Only men can be doctors."

Mother: "Could you be a dentist?"

Sara: "No. Just men are dentists."

Mother: "Could you be a professor?"

Sara: "No. Professors are men."

Mother: "Sara! I'm a professor!"

Sara: "But you're really hiding a penis."

Sara was absorbing lessons from her home environment, but already she was absorbing much else from the TV she and her friends were watching and from their peer culture.

The links of influence from parental group to child group are loose enough that the cultural transmission is never perfect. And in both human and primate cultures, change comes from the young. When one monkey discovers a better way of washing food or when a new generation develops new ideas about fashion, worship style, or gender roles, the innovation usually comes from the young and is more readily embraced by younger adults. Thus, cultural traditions continue, yet cultures change.

	Summing up
The most heavily researched of roles, gender roles, illustrate culture's impact. Gender roles vary sharply from culture to culture and from time to time. Much of this cultural influence is transmitted via peers.	

Conclusions

Biology and culture do not exist in isolation, because culture works upon what is biologically given. How, then, do biology and culture interact? And how do our individual personalities interact with our situations?

Biology *and* culture

We needn't think of evolution and culture as competitors. Cultural norms subtly but powerfully affect our attitudes and behavior. But they don't do so independent of biology. Everything social and psychological is ultimately biological. If others' expectations influence us, that is part of our biological programming. Moreover, what our biological heritage initiates, culture may accentuate. If genes and hormones predispose males to be more physically aggressive than females, culture may amplify this difference through norms that expect males to be tough and females to be the kinder, gentler sex. Natural selection and cultural selection may similarly cooperate in producing genetically advantageous traits—a process evolutionary psychologists call *coevolution*. "The present-day contributions to once-adaptive ends are both genes and culture, and the two are closely interrelated," notes John Archer (1996).

Biology and culture may also **interact**. In humans, biological traits influence how the environment reacts. People respond differently to a Sylvester Stallone than to a Woody Allen. Men, being 8 percent taller and averaging almost double the proportion of muscle mass, may likewise have different experiences than women. Or consider this: A very strong cultural norm dictates that males should be taller than their female mates. In one study, only 1 in 720 married couples violated this norm (Gillis & Avis, 1980). With hindsight, we can speculate a psychological explanation: Perhaps being taller (and older) helps men perpetuate their social power over women. But we can also speculate evolutionary wisdom that might underlie the cultural norm: If people preferred partners of the same height, tall men and short women would often be without partners. As it is, evolution dictates that men tend to be taller than women, and culture dictates the same for couples. So the height norm might well be a result of biology *and* culture.

interaction
the effect of one factor (such as biology) depends on another factor (such as environment)

Only very occasionally do couples violate the male-taller norm.

In *Sex Differences in Social Behavior,* Alice Eagly (1987, 1997) theorizes how biology and culture interact (Figure 5–5). She believes that a variety of factors, including biological influences and childhood socialization, predispose a sexual division of labor. In adult life the immediate causes of gender differences in social behavior are the *roles* that reflect this sexual division of labor. Men tend to be found in roles demanding social and physical power, and women in more nurturant roles. Each sex then tends to exhibit the behaviors expected of those who fill such roles and to have their skills and beliefs shaped accordingly. So as role assignments become more equal, Eagly predicts that gender differences "will gradually lessen."

The effects of biology and socialization may be important insofar as they influence the social roles that people play, for the roles we play influence who we become. If men are more assertive and women more nurturing, this may be an *effect* of their playing powerful versus caregiving roles. When workers (men and women) shift from talking with their supervisor to talking with a supervisee, they become more assertive (Moskowitz & others, 1994).

The great lesson of social psychology

Food for thought: If Bohr's statement is a great truth, what is its opposite?

"There are trivial truths and great truths," declared the physicist Niels Bohr. "The opposite of a trivial truth is plainly false. The opposite of a great truth is also true." Each chapter in this unit on social influence teaches a great truth: the power of the social situation. This great truth about the power of external pressures would sufficiently explain our behavior if we were passive, like tumbleweed. But unlike tumbleweed, we are not just blown here and there by the environment. We act; we react. We respond, and we get responses. We can resist the social situation and sometimes even change it. Thus each of these "social influence" chapters concludes by calling attention to the opposite of the great truth: the power of the person.

Perhaps stressing the power of culture leaves you somewhat uncomfortable. Most of us resent any suggestion that external forces determine our behavior; we see ourselves as free beings, as the originators of our actions (well, at least of

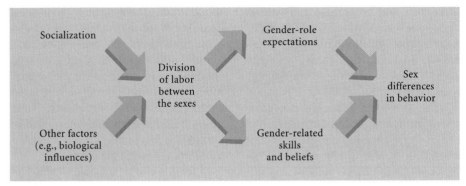

Source: Teller, 1997.

figure 5–5

A social-role theory of gender differences in social behavior. Various influences, including childhood experiences and biologic factors, bend males and females toward differing roles. It is the expectations and the skills and beli associated with these differing roles that affect men's and women's behavior. (Adapted from Eagly, 1987, and Eagly & Wood, 1991.)

our good actions). We sense that believing in social determinism can lead to what philosopher Jean-Paul Sartre called "bad faith"—evading responsibility by blaming something or someone for one's fate.

Actually, social control (the power of the situation) and personal control (the power of the person) no more compete with one another than do biological and cultural explanations. Social and personal explanations of our social behavior are both valid, for at any moment we are both the creatures and the creators of our social worlds. We may well be the products of our genes and environment. But it is also true that the future is coming, and it is our job to decide where it is going. Our choices today determine our environment tomorrow.

Social situations do profoundly influence individuals. But individuals also influence the social situation. The two *interact*. Asking whether external situations or inner dispositions (or culture or evolution) determine behavior is like asking whether length or width determines the area of a field.

The interaction occurs in at least three ways (Snyder & Ickes, 1985). First, a given social situation often *affects different people differently*. Because our minds do not see reality identically, we each respond to a situation as we construe it. And some people are more sensitive and responsive to social situations than others (M. Snyder, 1983). The Japanese, for example, are more responsive to social expectations than the British (Argyle & others, 1978).

Second, interaction between persons and situations occurs because people often *choose their situations* (Ickes & others, 1997). Given a choice, sociable people elect situations that evoke social interaction. When you chose your university, you were also choosing to expose yourself to a specific set of social influences. Ardent political liberals are unlikely to settle in rural Alberta and join the Chamber of Commerce. They are more likely to live in Toronto and join Greenpeace—in other words, to choose a social world that reinforces their inclinations.

Third, people often *create their situations*. Recall again that our preconceptions can be self-fulfilling: If we expect someone to be extraverted, hostile, feminine, or sexy, our actions toward the person may induce the very behavior we expect. What, after all, makes a social situation but the people in it? A liberal environment is created by liberals. What takes place in the sorority is created by the members. The social environment is not like the weather—something that just happens to us. It is more like our homes—something we make for ourselves.

"The words of truth are always paradoxical."

Lao-tzu, *The Simple Way*

Summing up

Biological and cultural explanations need not be contradictory. Indeed, they interact. Biological factors operate within a cultural context, and culture builds upon a biological foundation.

The great truth about the power of social influence is but half the truth if separated from its complementary truth: the power of the person. Persons and situations interact in at least three ways. First, individuals vary in how they interpret and react to a given situation. Second, people choose many of the situations that influence them. Third, people help create their social situations. Thus power resides both in persons and in situations. We create and are created by our social worlds.

PS Personal Postscript: Should we view ourselves as products or architects of our social worlds?

The reciprocal causation between situations and persons allows us to see people as either *reacting to* or *acting upon* their environment. Each perspective is correct, for we are both the products and the architects of our social worlds. Is one perspective wiser, however? In one sense, it is wise to see ourselves as the creatures of our environments (lest we become too proud of our achievements and blame ourselves too much for our problems) and to see others as free actors (lest we become paternalistic and manipulative).

Perhaps we would do well more often to assume the reverse, however—to view ourselves as free agents and to view others as influenced by their environments. We would then assume self-efficacy as we view ourselves and seek understanding and social reform as we relate to others. (If we view others as influenced by their situations, we are more likely to understand and empathize than smugly to judge unpleasant behavior as freely chosen by "immoral," "sadistic," or "lazy" persons.) Most religions encourage us to take responsibility for ourselves but to refrain from judging others. Does religion teach this because our natural inclination is to excuse our own failures while blaming others for theirs?

> "If we explain poverty, or emotional disorders, or crime and delinquency or alcoholism, or even unemployment, as resulting from personal, internal, individual defect . . . then there simply is not much we can do about prevention."
>
> George Albee, 1979

chapter 6

Conformity

i t was a long-awaited May afternoon. Three thousand family members and friends had gathered for the celebration. On cue, 400 graduating students rose to hear the long-awaited words, "I hereby confer upon each of you the degree of Bachelor of Arts, with all the rights and privileges appertaining thereto." The declaration finished, the 25 new alumni in the first row began filing forward to receive their diplomas. As they did so, the other 375 eyed one another nervously, each thinking: "Weren't we instructed to sit down now and await our turn?" But no one sat. The seconds ticked by. Half the first row now had diplomas in hand. Outwardly, the standing herd kept its cool. But inside each head, thoughts were buzzing: "We could be standing here for a half hour before it is our row's turn. . . . We're blocking the view of spectators seated behind us. . . . Why doesn't someone sit down?" Still, no one sat. Now two minutes had elapsed. The graduation marshal, whose instructions at the graduation rehearsal they were ignoring, strode up to the first standing row and subtly signaled it to sit down. No one sat. So he moved to the next row and audibly ordered it to "Sit down!" Within two seconds, 375 much-relieved people were happily relaxing in their chairs.

This scene raised three sets of questions for me. First, why, given the diversity of individuals among that large group, was their behavior so uniform? Is

"The race of men, while sheep in credulity, are wolves for conformity."

Carl Van Doren, *Why I Am an Unbeliever*

social pressure sometimes powerful enough to obliterate individual differences? Where were the rugged individualists?

Second, 25 percent of those graduates had been my students in social psychology. Although it was the furthest thing from their minds at the moment, they knew about conformity. When studying the topic, many of them had privately assured themselves that they would never be so docile as those in the famous conformity experiments. But here they were, participating in one of life's parallels. In everyday life, is courage always more easily fantasized than performed? Are we more susceptible to social influence than we realize? Does learning about social influence not liberate us from it?

Third, is conformity as bad as my description of this docile "herd" implies? Should I have been pleased at their "group solidarity" and "social sensitivity" rather than dismayed at their "mindless conformity"?

Let us take the last question first. Is conformity good or bad? This is another question that has no scientific answer. But assuming the values most of us share, we can say two things. First, conformity is at times bad (when it leads someone to drink and drive or to join in racist behavior), at times good (when it inhibits people from cutting in front of us in a theater line), and at times inconsequential (when it disposes us to wear white when playing tennis).

Second, the word "conformity" does carry a negative value judgment. How would you feel if you overheard someone describing you as a "real conformist"? I suspect you would feel hurt, because Western cultures don't prize the trait of submitting to peer pressure. Hence North American and European social psychologists, reflecting their individualistic cultures, give it negative labels (conformity, submission, compliance) rather than positive ones (communal sensitivity, responsiveness, cooperative team play).

In Japan, going along with others is a sign not of weakness but of tolerance, self-control, and maturity (Markus & Kitayama, 1994). "Everywhere in Japan," observed Lance Morrow (1983) "one senses an intricate serenity that comes to a people who know exactly what to expect from each other."

The moral: We choose labels to suit our values and judgments. When I think back to high school I viewed my friends who shunned the popular kids in school as "independent" and "inner-directed," but this didn't stop me from viewing other kids who shunned popularity as "eccentric" and "self-centered." Labels both describe and evaluate—and they are inescapable. We cannot discuss the topics of this chapter without labels. So let us be clear on the meanings of the following labels: "conformity," "compliance," "acceptance."

When, as part of a crowd, you rise to cheer a game-winning touchdown, are you conforming? When, along with millions of others, you drink milk or coffee, are you conforming? When you and everyone else agree that women look better with combable hair than with crewcuts, are you conforming? Maybe, maybe not. The key is whether your behavior and beliefs would be the same apart from the group. Would you rise to cheer the touchdown if you were the only fan in the stands? Conformity is not just acting as other people act; it is being affected by how they act. It is acting differently from the way you would act alone. Thus **conformity** is "a change in behavior or belief . . . as a result of real or imagined group pressure" (Kiesler & Kiesler, 1969, p. 2).

There are two varieties of conformity. Sometimes we conform without really believing in what we are doing. We put on the necktie or dress, though we dislike doing so. This outward conformity is **compliance.** We comply primarily to

"Whatever crushes individuality is despotism, by whatever name it may be called."

John Stuart Mill, *On Liberty,* 1859

"The social pressures community brings to bear are a mainstay of our moral values."

Amitai Etzioni, *The Spirit of Community,* 1993

conformity
a change in behavior or belief as a result of real or imagined group pressure

compliance
conformity that involves publicly acting in accord with social pressure while privately disagreeing

Compliance

reap a reward or avoid a punishment. If our compliance is to an explicit command, we call it obedience.

Sometimes we genuinely believe in what the group has convinced us to do. We may join millions of others in drinking milk because we are convinced that milk is nutritious. This sincere, inward conformity is called **acceptance**. Acceptance sometimes follows compliance. As Chapter 4 emphasized, attitudes follow behavior. Thus, unless we feel no responsibility for our behavior, we usually become sympathetic to what we have stood up for.

acceptance
conformity that involves both acting and believing in accord with social pressure

Classic studies

How have social psychologists "bottled" conformity in the laboratory? What do their results reveal about the potency of social forces and the nature of evil?

Researchers who study conformity construct miniature social worlds—laboratory microcultures that simplify and simulate important features of everyday social influence. Consider three noted sets of experiments. Each provides a method for studying conformity—and some startling findings.

Sherif's studies of norm formation

The first of the three classics provides a bridge between the focus in Chapter 5 on culture's power to create and perpetuate arbitrary norms and this chapter's focus on conformity. Muzafer Sherif (1935, 1937) wondered whether it was possible to observe the emergence of a social norm in the laboratory. Like biologists seeking to isolate a virus so they can then experiment with it, Sherif wanted to isolate and then experiment with the social phenomenon of norm formation.

Drawing by Booth; © 1977 The New Yorker Magazine, Inc.

Authorities may impose public compliance, but private acceptance is another matter.

autokinetic phenomenon
self (*auto*) motion (*kinetic*). The apparent movement of a stationary point of light in the dark. Perhaps you have experienced this when thinking you have spotted a moving satellite in the sky, only to realize later that it was merely an isolated star.

As a participant in one of Sherif's experiments, you might find yourself seated in a dark room. Fifteen feet in front of you a pinpoint of light appears. At first, nothing happens. Then for a few seconds it moves erratically and finally disappears. Now you must guess how far it moved. The dark room gives you no way to judge distance, so you offer an uncertain "six inches." The experimenter repeats the procedure. This time you say "ten inches." With further repetitions, your estimates continue to average about eight inches.

The next day you return, joined by two others who the day before had the same experience. When the light goes off for the first time, the other two people offer their best guesses from the day before. "One inch" says one. "Two inches," says the other. A bit taken aback, you nevertheless say "six inches." With successive repetitions of this group experience, both on this day and for the next two days, will your responses change? The men whom Sherif tested changed their estimates markedly. As Figure 6–1 illustrates, a group norm typically emerged. (The norm was false. Why? The light never moved! Sherif had taken advantage of an optical illusion called the **autokinetic phenomenon.**)

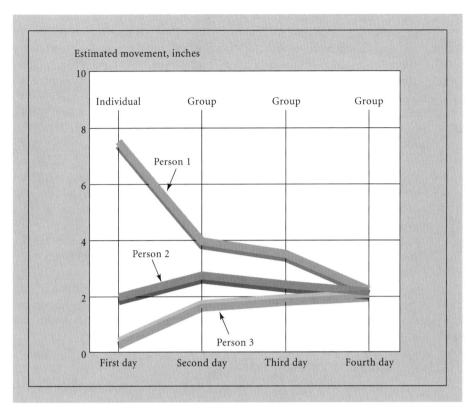

figure 6–1

A sample group from Sherif's study of norm formation.

Three individuals converge as they give repeated estimates of the apparent movement of a point of light.

Estimated movement, inches

Individual   Group   Group   Group

Person 1

Person 2

Person 3

First day   Second day   Third day   Fourth day

(Data from Sherif & Sherif, 1969, p. 209)

Sherif and others have used this technique to answer questions about people's suggestibility. When people were retested alone a year later, would their estimates again diverge or would they continue to follow the group norm? Remarkably, they continued to support the group norm (Rohrer & others, 1954). (Does this suggest compliance or acceptance?)

Struck by culture's seeming power to perpetuate false beliefs, Robert Jacobs and Donald Campbell (1961) studied the transmission of false beliefs. Using the autokinetic phenomenon, they had a **confederate** give an inflated estimate of how far the light moved. The confederate then left the experiment and was replaced by another real subject who was in turn replaced by a still newer member. The inflated illusion persisted (although less and less strongly) for five generations. These people had become "unwitting conspirators in perpetuating a cultural fraud." The lesson of these experiments: Our views of reality are not ours alone.

In everyday life the results of suggestibility are sometimes amusing. In late March 1954, one newspaper reported damage to car windshields in a city 80 miles to the north. On the morning of April 14, similar windshield damage was reported 65 miles away and later that day only 45 miles away. By nightfall, the windshield-pitting agent had reached the city where I grew up. Before the end of April 15, the police department had received complaints of damage to more than 3,000 windshields (Medalia & Larsen, 1958). That evening the mayor called on the national government for help.

I was an 11-year-old at the time. I recall searching our windshield, frightened by the explanation that an H-bomb test was raining fallout on

confederate
an accomplice of the experimenter

"Why doth one man's yawning make another yawn?"

Robert Burton, *Anatomy of Melancholy*, 1621

our city. On April 16, however, the newspapers hinted that the real culprit might be mass suggestibility. After April 17 there were no more complaints. Later analysis of the pitted windshields concluded that the cause was ordinary road damage. Why did we notice this only after April 14? Given the suggestion, we had looked carefully *at* our windshields instead of *through* them.

In real life suggestibility is not always so amusing. Hijackings, UFO sightings, and even suicides tend to come in waves. Sociologist David Phillips and his colleagues (1985, 1989) report that known suicides, as well as fatal auto accidents and private airplane crashes (which sometimes disguise suicides), increase after well-publicized suicides. For example, following Marilyn Monroe's August 6, 1962, suicide, there were 200 more August suicides than normal. Moreover, the increase happens only in areas where the suicide story is publicized. The more publicity, the greater the increase in later fatalities.

A copycat suicide phenomenon has also occurred in Germany (Jonas, 1992). In Germany, suicide rates rise slightly following fictional suicides on soap operas, and, ironically, even after serious dramas that focus on the suicide problem (Gould & Shaffer, 1986; Hafner & Schmidtke, 1989; Phillips, 1982). Phillips reports that teenagers are most susceptible, which would help explain the clusters of teen copycat suicides that occasionally occur in some communities.

Asch's studies of group pressure

Participants in the autokinetic experiments faced an ambiguous reality. Consider a less ambiguous perceptual problem faced by a young boy named Solomon Asch (1907–1996). While attending the traditional Jewish seder at Passover, recalled Asch,

> I asked my uncle, who was sitting next to me, why the door was being opened. He replied, "The prophet Elijah visits this evening every Jewish home and takes a sip of wine from the cup reserved for him."
>
> I was amazed at this news and repeated, "Does he really come? Does he really take a sip?"
>
> My uncle said, "If you watch very closely, when the door is opened you will see—you watch the cup—you will see that the wine will go down a little."
>
> And that's what happened. My eyes were riveted upon the cup of wine. I was determined to see whether there would be a change. And to me it seemed—it was tantalizing, and of course, it was hard to be absolutely sure—that indeed something was happening at the rim of the cup, and the wine did go down a little. (quoted by Aron & Aron, 1989, p. 27)

Years later, social psychologist Asch re-created his boyhood experience in his laboratory. Imagine yourself as one of Asch's volunteer subjects. You are seated sixth in a row of seven people. After explaining that you will be taking part in a study of perceptual judgments, the experimenter asks you to say which of the three lines in Figure 6–2 matches the standard line. You can easily see that it's line 2. So it's no surprise when the five people responding before you all say "line 2."

The next comparison proves as easy, and you settle in for what seems a simple test. But the third trial startles you. Although the correct answer seems just as clear-cut, the first person gives a wrong answer. When the second person gives the same wrong answer, you sit up in your chair and stare at the cards.

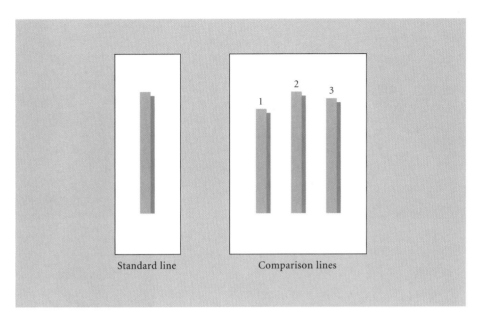

figure 6–2

Sample comparison from Solomon Asch's conformity procedure.
The participants judged which of three comparison lines matched the standard.

Standard line   Comparison lines

The third person agrees with the first two. Your jaw drops; you start to perspire. "What is this?" you ask yourself. "Are they blind? Or am I?" The fourth and fifth people agree with the others. Then the experimenter looks at you. Now you are experiencing an epistemological dilemma: "How am I to know what is true? Is it what my peers tell me or what my eyes tell me?"

Dozens of university students experienced this conflict during Asch's experiments. Those in a control condition who answered alone were correct more than 99 percent of the time. Asch wondered: If several others (confederates coached by the experimenter) gave identical wrong answers, would people declare what they would otherwise have denied? Although some people never conformed, three quarters did so at least once. All told, 37 percent of the responses were conforming (or should we say *"trusting* of others"?). Of course, that means 63 percent of the time people did not conform. Despite the independence shown by many of his subjects, Asch's (1955) feelings about the conformity were as clear as the correct answers to his questions: "That reasonably intelligent and well-meaning young people are willing to call white black is a matter of concern. It raises questions about our ways of education and about the values that guide our conduct."

Asch's procedure became the standard for hundreds of later experiments. These experiments lack what Chapter 1 called the "mundane realism" of everyday conformity, but they do have "experimental realism." People get emotionally involved in the experience. However, the procedure is expensive and difficult to control because it requires a troupe of confederates who must act with near-perfect consistency before each new participant. Richard Crutchfield (1955) fixed this by automating Asch's experiment. Five participants—each a real subject—sat in adjacent booths and viewed questions projected on the wall across the room. Each booth had a panel of lights and switches that allowed the subjects to declare their judgments and to see how others responded. After a few warm-up trials, all found themselves responding last after seeing the purported responses of the other four.

> "He who sees the truth, let him proclaim it, without asking who is for it or who is against it."
>
> Henry George, *The Irish Land Question*, 1881

> *Ethical note:*
> Professional ethics usually dictate explaining the experiment afterward (see Chapter 1). Pretend you were an experimenter who had just finished a session with a conforming participant. Could you explain the deception without making the person feel gullible and dumb?

In one of Asch's conformity experiments (top), subject number 6 experienced uneasiness and conflict after hearing five people before him give a wrong answer.

The technique lets the researcher present a variety of questions. Crutchfield tested military officers by presenting a circle and a star side by side (Figure 6–3). The area of the circle was one-third greater. But when each officer thought the others had judged the star to be larger, 46 percent of them denied the evidence of their senses and voted with the group. Tested privately, each of the officers rejected the statement, "I doubt whether I would make a good leader." Of course—these *are* leaders. Yet, when they believed all the other officers had accepted the statement, almost 40 percent agreed with it.

The Sherif, Asch, and Crutchfield results are startling because in none of them is there any open, obvious pressure to conform—there are no rewards for "team play," no punishments for individuality. If people are this compliant in response to such minimal pressure, how much more compliant will they be if they are directly coerced? Could someone force an average North American to perform cruel acts? I would have guessed not: Their humane, democratic, individualistic values would make them resist such pressure. Besides, the easy verbal pronouncements of these experiments are a giant step away from actually harming someone; you and I would never yield to coercion to hurt another. Or would we? Social psychologist Stanley Milgram wondered.

"It is too easy to go over to the majority."

Seneca, *Epistulae ad Lucilium*

Milgram's obedience experiments

Milgram's (1965, 1974) experiments on what happens when the demands of authority clash with the demands of conscience have become social psychology's most famous and controversial experiments. "Perhaps more than any

figure 6–3
Richard Crutchfield's conformity-testing procedure.
People sit in adjacent booths and answer questions presented on the wall in front of them after witnessing others' purported answers.

other empirical contributions in the history of social science," notes Lee Ross (1988), "they have become part of our society's shared intellectual legacy—that small body of historical incidents, biblical parables, and classic literature that serious thinkers feel free to draw on when they debate about human nature or contemplate human history."

Here is the scene staged by Milgram, a creative artist who wrote stories and stage plays: Two men come to the psychology laboratory to participate in a study of learning and memory. A stern experimenter in a gray technician's coat explains that this is a pioneering study of the effect of punishment on learning. The experiment requires one of them to teach a list of word pairs to the other and to punish errors by delivering shocks of increasing intensity. To assign the roles, they draw slips out of a hat. One of the men, a mild-mannered, 47-year-old accountant who is the experimenter's confederate, pretends that his slip says "learner" and is ushered into an adjacent room. The "teacher" (who has come in response to a newspaper ad) takes a mild sample shock and then looks on as the experimenter straps the learner into a chair and attaches an electrode to his wrist.

Teacher and experimenter then return to the main room where the teacher takes his place before a "shock generator" with switches ranging from 15 to 450 volts in 15-volt increments. The switches are labeled "Slight Shock," "Very Strong Shock," "Danger: Severe Shock," and so forth. Under the 435- and 450-volt switches appears "XXX." The experimenter tells the teacher to "move one level higher on the shock generator" each time the learner gives a wrong answer. With each flick of a switch, lights flash, relay switches click, and an electric buzz sounds.

If the participant complies with the experimenter's requests, he hears the learner grunt at 75, 90, and 105 volts. At 120 volts the learner shouts that the

focus

The learner's schedule of protests in Milgram's "heart disturbance" experiments

75 volts	Ugh!
90 volts	Ugh!
105 volts	Ugh! (*Louder*)
120 volts	Ugh! Hey, this really hurts.
135 volts	Ugh!!
150 volts	Ugh!!! Experimenter! That's all. Get me out of here. I told you I had heart trouble. My heart's starting to bother me now. Get me out of here, please. My heart's starting to bother me. I refuse to go on. Let me out.
165 volts	Ugh! Let me out! (*Shouting*)
180 volts	Ugh! I can't stand the pain. Let me out of here! (*Shouting*)
195 volts	Ugh! Let me out of here. Let me out of here. My heart's bothering me. Let me out of here! You have no right to keep me here! Let me out! Let me out of here! Let me out! Let me out of here! My heart's bothering me. Let me out! Let me out!
210 volts	Ugh! Experimenter! Get me out of here. I've had enough. I won't be in the experiment any more.

225 volts	Ugh!
240 volts	Ugh!
255 volts	Ugh! Get me out of here.
270 volts	(*Agonized scream*) Let me out of here. Let me out of here. Let me out of here. Let me out. Do you hear? Let me out of here.
285 volts	(*Agonized scream*)
300 volts	(*Agonized scream*) I absolutely refuse to answer any more. Get me out of here. You can't hold me here. Get me out. Get me out of here.
315 volts	(*Intensely agonized scream*) I told you I refuse to answer. I'm no longer part of this experiment.
330 volts	(*Intense and prolonged agonized scream*) Let me out of here. Let me out of here. My heart's bothering me. Let me out. I tell you. (*Hysterically*) Let me out of here. Let me out of here. You have no right to hold me here. Let me out! Let me out! Let me out! Let me out of here! Let me out! Let me out!

From *Obedience to Authority* by Stanley Milgram. New York: Harper & Row, 1974, pp. 56–57.

shocks are painful. And at 150 volts he cries out, "Experimenter, get me out of here! I won't be in the experiment anymore! I refuse to go on!" By 270 volts his protests have become screams of agony, and he continues to insist to be let out. At 300 and 315 volts he screams his refusal to answer. After 330 volts he falls silent. In answer to the "teacher's" inquiries and pleas to end the experiment, the experimenter states that the nonresponses should be treated as wrong answers. To keep the participant going, he uses four verbal prods:

Prod 1: Please continue (*or* Please go on).
Prod 2: The experiment requires that you continue.
Prod 3: It is absolutely essential that you continue.
Prod 4: You have no other choice; you *must* go on.

How far would you go? Several studies have described the experiment to psychiatrists, university students, and middle-class adults. People in all three groups guessed that they would disobey by about 135 volts, which perhaps isn't surprising. But they also said that they thought *other* people would disobey by 200 volts and virtually no one expected anyone to proceed to XXX on the shock

figure 6–4

The Milgram obedience experiment.
Percentage of subjects complying despite the learner's cries of protest and failure to respond.

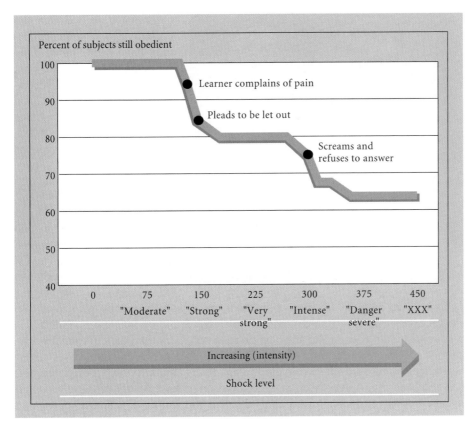

Percent of subjects still obedient

Learner complains of pain

Pleads to be let out

Screams and refuses to answer

| 0 | 75 | 150 | 225 | 300 | 375 | 450 |
| | "Moderate" | "Strong" | "Very strong" | "Intense" | "Danger severe" | "XXX" |

Increasing (intensity)

Shock level

(From Milgram, 1965)

panel (Milgram, 1963; Kaufman & Kooman, 1967). (The psychiatrists guessed about one in a thousand.)

But when Milgram conducted the experiment with 40 men—a vocational mix of 20- to 50-year-olds—25 of them (63 percent) went clear to 450 volts. In fact, all who reached 450 volts complied with a command to *continue* the procedure until, after two further trials, the experimenter called a halt.

Given this disturbing result, Milgram next made the learner's protests even more compelling. As the learner was strapped into the chair, the teacher heard him mention his "slight heart condition" and heard the experimenter's reassurance that "although the shocks may be painful, they cause no permanent tissue damage." The learner's anguished protests (see "Focus: The Learner's Schedule") were to little avail; of 40 new men in this experiment, 26 (65 percent) fully complied with the experimenter's demands (Figure 6–4).

The obedience of his subjects disturbed Milgram. The procedures he used disturbed many social psychologists (Miller, 1986; Stam & others, 1998). The "learner" in these experiments actually received no shock (he disengaged himself from the electric chair and turned on a tape recorder that delivered the protests). Nevertheless, some critics said that Milgram did to his participants what they did to their victims: He stressed them against their will. Indeed, many of the "teachers" did experience agony. They sweated, trembled, stuttered, bit their lips, groaned, or even broke into uncontrollable nervous laughter. A *New York Times* reviewer complained that the cruelty inflicted by the experiments "upon their unwitting subjects is surpassed only by the cruelty that they elicit from them" (Marcus, 1974).

An obedient subject in Milgram's "touch" condition forces the victim's hand onto the shock plate. Usually, however, "teachers" were more merciful to victims who were this close to them.

"History, despite its wrenching pain, Cannot be unlived, and if faced With courage, need not be lived again."

Maya Angelou, Presidential Inaugural Poem, January 20, 1993

Critics also argued that the participants' self-concepts may have been altered. One participant's wife told him, "You can call yourself Eichmann" (referring to Nazi death camp administrator Adolf Eichmann). CBS television depicted the results and controversy in a two-hour dramatization starring William Shatner of *Star Trek* fame as Milgram. "A world of evil so terrifying no one dares penetrate its secret. Until Now!" declared a *TV Guide* ad for the program (Elms, 1995).

In his own defense, Milgram pointed to the lessons taught by his nearly two dozen experiments with a diverse sample of more than 1,000 participants. He also reminded critics of the support he received from the participants after the deception was revealed and the experiment explained. When surveyed afterward, 84 percent said they were glad to have participated; only 1 percent regretted volunteering. A year later, a psychiatrist interviewed forty of those who had suffered most and concluded that, despite the temporary stress, none was harmed.

The ethical controversy was "terribly overblown," Milgram felt. Actually, he wrote in a letter,

> there is less consequence to subjects in this experiment from the standpoint of effects on self-esteem, than to university students who take ordinary course examinations, and who do not get the grades they want. . . . It seems that [in giving exams] we are quite prepared to accept stress, tension, and consequences for self-esteem. But in regard to the process of generating new knowledge, how little tolerance we show (quoted by Blass, 1996).

What breeds obedience?

Milgram did more than reveal the extent to which people will obey an authority; he also examined the conditions that breed obedience. In further experiments, he varied the social conditions and got compliance ranging from 0 to 93 percent fully obedient. The determining factors were these four: the victim's emotional distance, the authority's closeness and legitimacy, whether or not the authority is institutionalized, and the liberating effects of a disobedient fellow subject.

Emotional distance of the victim

Milgram's subjects acted with least compassion when the "learners" could not be seen (and could not see them). When the victim was remote and the "teachers" heard no complaints, nearly all obeyed calmly to the end. When the learner was in the same room, "only" 40 percent obeyed to 450 volts. Full compliance dropped to 30 percent when teachers were required to force the learner's hand into contact with a shock plate.

focus

Personalizing the victims

Innocent victims trigger more compassion if personalized. In a week when a soon-forgotten earthquake in Iran kills 3,000 people, a lone boy dies, trapped in a well shaft in Italy, and the whole world grieves. The projected death statistics of a nuclear war are impersonal to the point of being incomprehensible. So international law professor Roger Fisher proposed a way to personalize the victims:

It so happens that a young man, usually a navy officer, accompanies the President wherever he goes. This young man has a black attaché case which contains the codes that are needed to fire nuclear weapons.

I can see the President at a staff meeting considering nuclear war as an abstract question. He might conclude, "On SIOP Plan One, the decision is affirmative. Communicate the Alpha line XYZ." Such jargon keeps what is involved at a distance.

My suggestion, then, is quite simple. Put that needed code number in a little capsule and implant that capsule right next to the heart of a volunteer. The volunteer will carry with him a big, heavy butcher knife as he accompanies the President. If ever the President wants to fire nuclear weapons, the only way he can do so is by first, with his own hands, killing one human being.

"George," the President would say, "I'm sorry, but tens of millions must die." The President then would have to look at someone and realize what death is—what an *innocent* death is. Blood on the White House carpet: it's reality brought home.

When I suggested this to friends in the Pentagon, they said, "My God, that's terrible. Having to kill someone would distort the President's judgment. He might never push the button."

Adapted from "Preventing Nuclear War" by Roger Fisher, *Bulletin of the Atomic Scientists*, March 1981, pp. 11–17.

In everyday life, too, it is easiest to abuse someone who is distant or depersonalized. People will be unresponsive even to great tragedies. Executioners depersonalize those being executed by placing hoods over their heads. The ethics of war allow one to bomb a helpless village from 40,000 feet but not to shoot an equally helpless villager. In combat with an enemy they can see, many soldiers either do not fire or do not aim. Such disobedience is rare among those given orders to kill with the more distant artillery or aircraft weapons (Padgett, 1989).

On the positive side, people act most compassionately toward those who are personalized. This is why appeals for the unborn or the hungry are nearly always personalized with a compelling photograph or description. Perhaps even more compelling is an ultrasound picture of one's own developing fetus. When queried by John Lydon and Christine Dunkel-Schetter (1994), expectant women expressed more commitment to their pregnancy if they had earlier seen an ultrasound picture of their fetus that clearly displayed body parts.

Closeness and legitimacy of the authority

The physical presence of the experimenter also affected obedience. When Milgram gave the commands by telephone, full obedience dropped to 21 percent (although many lied and said they were obeying). Other studies confirm that when the one making the request is physically close, compliance increases. Given a light touch on the arm, people are more likely to lend a dime, sign a petition, or sample a new pizza (Kleinke, 1977; Smith & others, 1982; Willis & Hamm, 1980).

Imagine you had the power to prevent either a tidal wave that would kill 25,000 people in Pakistan, a crash that would kill 250 people at your local airport, or a car accident that would kill a close friend. Which would you prevent?

Given orders, most soldiers will torch people's homes or kill—behaviors that in other contexts they would consider immoral.

The authority, however, must be perceived as legitimate. In another twist on the basic experiment, the experimenter received a rigged telephone call that required him to leave the laboratory. He said that since the equipment recorded data automatically, the "teacher" should just go ahead. After the experimenter left, another person who had been assigned a clerical role (actually a second confederate) assumed command. The clerk "decided" that the shock should be increased one level for each wrong answer and instructed the teacher accordingly. Now 80 percent of the teachers refused to comply fully. The confederate, feigning disgust at this defiance, sat down in front of the shock generator and tried to take over the teacher's role. At this point most of the defiant participants protested. Some tried to unplug the generator. One large man lifted the zealous confederate from his chair and threw him across the room. This rebellion against an illegitimate authority contrasted sharply with the deferential politeness usually shown the experimenter.

It also contrasts with the behavior of hospital nurses who in one study were called by an unknown physician and ordered to administer an obvious overdose of a drug (Hofling & others, 1966). The researchers told one group of nurses and nursing students about the experiment and asked how they would react. Nearly all said they would not have given the medication as ordered. One explained that she would have replied, "I'm sorry, sir, but I am not authorized to give any medication without a written order, especially one so large over the usual dose and one that I'm unfamiliar with. If it were possible, I would be glad to do it, but this is against hospital policy and my own ethical standards." Nevertheless, when 22 other nurses were actually given the phoned-in overdose order, all but one obeyed without delay (until being intercepted on their way to the patient). Although not all nurses are so compliant (Krackow & Blass, 1995;

Rank & Jacobson, 1977), these nurses were following a familiar script: Doctor (a legitimate authority) orders; nurse obeys.

Compliance with legitimate authority was also apparent in the strange case of the "rectal ear ache" (Cohen & Davis, 1981, cited by Cialdini, 1988). A doctor ordered ear drops given to a patient suffering infection in the right ear. On the prescription, the doctor abbreviated "place in right ear" as "place in *R ear*." Reading the order, the compliant nurse put the required drops in the compliant patient's rectum.

Institutional authority

If the prestige of the authority is this important, then perhaps the institutional prestige of Milgram's school legitimized the commands. In postexperimental interviews, many participants volunteered that had it not been for Yale's reputation, they would not have obeyed. To see whether this was true, Milgram moved the experiment to Bridgeport, Connecticut. He set himself up in a modest commercial building as the "Research Associates of Bridgeport." When the usual "heart disturbance" experiment was run with the same personnel, what percentage of the men do you suppose fully obeyed? Though reduced, the rate remained remarkably high—48 percent.

In everyday life, too, authorities backed by institutions wield social power. Robert Ornstein (1991) tells of a psychiatrist-friend who was called to the edge of a cliff where one of his patients, Alfred, was threatening to jump. When the psychiatrist's reasoned reassurance failed to dislodge Alfred, the psychiatrist could only hope that a police crisis expert would soon arrive.

Although no expert came, another police officer, unaware of the drama, happened on to the scene, took out his power bullhorn, and yelled at the assembled cliffside group: "Who's the ass who left that Pontiac station wagon doubleparked out there in the middle of the road? I almost hit it. Move it *now*, whoever you are." Hearing the message, Alfred obediently got down at once, moved the car, and then without a word got into the policeman's car for a trip to the nearby hospital.

The liberating effects of group influence

These classic experiments give us a negative view of conformity. Can conformity be constructive? Perhaps you can recall a time you felt justifiably angry at an unfair teacher, or with someone's offensive behavior, but you hesitated to object. Then one or two others objected, and you followed their example. Milgram captured this liberating effect of conformity by placing the teacher with two confederates who were to help conduct the procedure. During the experiment, both defied the experimenter, who then ordered the real subject to continue alone. Did he? No. Ninety percent liberated themselves by conforming to the defiant confederates.

Reflections on the classic studies

The common response to Milgram's results is to note their counterparts in recent history: the "I was only following orders" defenses of Adolf Eichmann in Nazi Germany; of Lieutenant William Calley, who in 1968 directed the unprovoked slaughter of hundreds of Vietnamese in the village of My Lai; and of the

"If the commander-in-chief tells this lieutenant colonel to go stand in the corner and sit on his head, I will do so."

Oliver North, 1987

"ethnic cleansing" occurring more recently in Iraq, Rwanda, and Bosnia. A Bosnian victim explains:

> I was raped and tortured too, because they knew that I am a wife of a leader of the Muslim party. My neighbor tortured me the most, the one my husband respected as his own brother. By the end of June, Chetniks brought another neighbor of ours and with a gun pointed at him they [demanded he] rape a 14-year-old girl. He stood trembling and stuttering with fear. Then he turned to a Chetnik he believed was a leader and said: "Don't make me do it. I have known her since she was born.". . . They beat him in front of us until he died. It was an example to the other Serbs that there is no pity, that one must do what leaders order them to do. (Drakuli, 1992)

Soldiers are trained to obey superiors. In the United States, the military acknowledges that even Marines should disobey *inappropriate* orders, but the military does not train soldiers to recognize an illegal or immoral order (Staub, 1989). Thus one participant in the My Lai massacre recalled:

> [Lieutenant Calley] told me to start shooting. So I started shooting, I poured about four clips into the group. . . . They were begging and saying, "No, no." And the mothers were hugging their children and. . . . Well, we kept right on firing. They was waving their arms and begging. (Wallace, 1969)

The "safe" scientific contexts of the obedience experiments differ from the wartime contexts. The obedience experiments also differ from the other conformity experiments in the strength of the social pressure: Compliance is explicitly commanded. Without the coercion, people did not act cruelly. Yet both the Asch and Milgram experiments share certain commonalities. They show how compliance can take precedence over moral sense. They succeeded in pressuring people to go against their own conscience. They did more than teach us an academic lesson; they sensitized us to moral conflicts in our own lives. And they illustrate and affirm some familiar social psychological principles: the link between behavior and attitudes, the power of the situation, and the strength of the fundamental attribution error.

"Maybe I was too patriotic" So said ex-torturer Jeffrey Benzien, shown here demonstrating the "wet bag" technique to South Africa's Truth and Reconciliation Commission. He would place a cloth over victims' heads, bringing them to the terrifying brink of asphyxiation over and over again. Such terror by the former security police, who routinely denied such acts, were used to get an accused person to disclose, for example, where guns were hidden. "I did terrible things," Benzien admitted with apologies to his victims, though he claimed only to be following orders.

behind the scenes

While working for Solomon E. Asch, I wondered whether his conformity experiments could be made more humanly significant. First, I imagined an experiment similar to Asch's except that the group induced the person to deliver shocks to a protesting victim. But a control was needed to see how much shock a person would give in the absence of group pressure. Someone, presumably the experimenter, would have to instruct the subject to give the shocks. But now a new question arose: Just how far would a person go when ordered to administer such shocks? In my mind, the issue had shifted to the willingness of people to comply with destructive orders. It was an exciting moment for me. I realized that this simple question was both humanly important and capable of being precisely answered.

The laboratory procedure gave scientific expression to a more general concern about authority, a concern forced upon members of my generation, in particular upon Jews such as myself, by the atrocities of World War II. The impact of the Holocaust on my own psyche energized my interest in obedience and shaped the particular form in which it was examined.

Abridged from the original for this book and from Milgram, 1977, with permission of Alexandra Milgram.

Stanley Milgram
(1933–1984)
City University of New
York

Behavior and attitudes

In Chapter 4 we noted that attitudes fail to determine behavior when external influences override inner convictions. These experiments vividly illustrate this principle. When responding alone, Asch's subjects nearly always gave the correct answer. It was another matter when they stood alone against a group. In the obedience experiments, a powerful social pressure (the experimenter's commands) overcame a weaker one (the remote victim's pleas). Torn between the pleas of the victim and the orders of the experimenter, between the desire to avoid doing harm and the desire to be a good subject, a surprising number chose to obey.

Why were the participants unable to disengage themselves? How had they become trapped? Imagine yourself as the teacher in yet another version of Milgram's experiment, one he never conducted. Assume that when the learner gives the first wrong answer, the experimenter asks you to zap him with 330 volts. After flicking the switch, you hear the learner scream, complain of a heart disturbance, and plead for mercy. Do you continue?

I think not. Recall the step-by-step entrapment of the foot-in-the-door phenomenon (Chapter 4) as we compare this hypothetical experiment to what Milgram's subjects experienced. Their first commitment was mild—15 volts—and it elicited no protest. You, too, would agree to do that much. By the time they delivered 75 volts and heard the learner's first groan, they already had complied five times. On the next trial the experimenter asked them to commit an act only slightly more extreme than what they had already repeatedly committed. By the time they delivered 330 volts, after 22 acts of compliance, the subjects had reduced some of their dissonance. They were therefore in a different psychological state from that of someone beginning the experiment at that point. As we saw in Chapter 4, external behavior and internal disposition can feed one another, sometimes in an escalating spiral. Thus, reported Milgram (1974, p. 10):

> Many subjects harshly devalue the victim *as a consequence* of acting against him. Such comments as "He was so stupid and stubborn he deserved to get shocked," were common. Once having acted against the victim, these subjects found it necessary to view him as an unworthy individual, whose punishment was made inevitable by his own deficiencies of intellect and character.

"Men's actions are too strong for them. Show me a man who has acted and who has not been the victim and slave of his action."

Ralph Waldo Emerson, *Representative Men: Goethe,* 1850

During the early 1970s, the military junta then in power in Greece used this "blame-the-victim" process to train torturers (Haritos-Fatouros, 1988; Staub, 1989). In Greece, as in the training of SS officers in Nazi Germany, the military selected candidates based on their respect for and submission to authority. But such tendencies alone do not a torturer make. Thus they would first assign the trainee to guard prisoners, then to participate in arrest squads, then to hit prisoners, then to observe torture, and only then to practice it. Step by step, an obedient but otherwise decent person evolved into an agent of cruelty. Compliance bred acceptance.

From his study of human genocide across the world, Ervin Staub (1989) shows where this process can lead. Too often, criticism produces contempt, which licenses cruelty, which, when justified, leads to brutality, then killing, then systematic killing. Evolving attitudes both follow and justify actions. Staub's disturbing conclusion: "Human beings have the capacity to come to experience killing other people as nothing extraordinary" (p. 13).

But then humans also have a capacity for heroism. During the Holocaust, 3,500 French Jews and 1,500 other refugees destined for deportation to Germany were sheltered by the villagers of Le Chambon. These people were mostly Protestants, descendants of a persecuted group, and people whose own authorities, their pastors, had taught them to "resist whenever our adversaries will demand of us obedience contrary to the orders of the Gospel" (Rochat, 1993; Rochat & Modigliani, 1995). Ordered to divulge the sheltered Jews, the head pastor modeled disobedience: "I don't know of Jews, I only know of human beings." Without knowing how terrible the war would be or how much they would suffer, the resisters made an initial commitment and then—supported by their beliefs, by their own authorities, and by one another—remained defiant to the war's end. Here and elsewhere, the ultimate response to Nazi occupation usually came early. The first acts of compliance or resistance bred attitudes that influenced behavior, which strengthened attitudes. Initial helping heightened commitment, leading to more helping.

The power of the situation

The most important lesson of Chapter 5—that culture is a powerful shaper of lives—and this chapter's most important lesson—that immediate situational forces are just as powerful—reveal the strength of the social context. To feel this for yourself, imagine violating some minor norms: standing up in the middle of a class; singing out loud in a restaurant; greeting some distinguished senior professors by their first names; playing golf in a suit; munching Cracker Jacks at a piano recital; shaving half your head. In trying to break with social constraints, we suddenly realize how strong they are.

behind the scenes

After many years spent studying what makes children and adults helpful, I turned to studying what makes people unhelpful, destructive, even into perpetrators of torture and genocide. What cultural characteristics, what social conditions, what personal needs and motives, lead human beings to destroy other human beings? What can we and must we do to prevent genocidal violence? How might we help survivors of violence heal, and hostile groups to reconcile? How might we raise nonviolent, caring children and create caring societies? How might we help each other, and influence our countries, not to remain passive bystanders in the face of harmful, cruel, violent actions, whether against children at home or people in faraway lands like Bosnia and Rwanda?

I believe that my intense concern about kindness and cruelty springs from my own experience. As a young Jewish child in Budapest I survived the Holocaust, the destruction of most European Jews by Nazi Germany and its allies. My life was saved by a Christian woman who repeatedly endangered her life to help me and my family, and by Raoul Wallenberg, the Swede who came to Budapest and with courage, brilliance, and complete commitment saved the lives of tens of thousands of Jews destined for the gas chambers. These two heroes were not passive bystanders, and my work is one of the ways for me not to be one.

Ervin Staub
University of Massachusetts

Some of Milgram's own students learned this lesson when he and John Sabini (1983) asked their help in studying the effects of violating a simple social norm: asking riders on the subway system for their seats. To their surprise, 56 percent gave up their seats, even when no justification was given. The students' own reactions to making the request were as interesting: Most found it extremely difficult. Often, the words got stuck in their throat, and they had to withdraw. Once having made a request and gotten a seat, they sometimes justified their norm violation by pretending to be sick. Such is the power of the unspoken rules governing our public behavior.

The students in a recent experiment found it similarly difficult to get challenging words out of their mouths. Some students imagined themselves discussing with three others whom to select for survival on a desert island. They were asked to imagine one of the others, a man, injecting three sexist comments, such as "I think we need more women on the island to keep the men satisfied." How would they react to such sexist remarks? Only five percent predicted they would ignore each of the comments or wait to see how others react. But when Janet Swim and Lauri Hyers (1998) engaged other students in discussions where such comments were actually made by a male confederate, 56 percent (not 5 percent) said nothing. This once again demonstrates the power of normative pressures and how hard it is to predict behavior, even our own behavior.

Milgram's experiments also offer a lesson about evil. Evil sometimes results from a few bad apples. That's the image of evil symbolized by depraved killers in suspense novels and horror movies. In real life we think of Hitler's extermination of Jews, of Saddam Hussein's extermination of Kurds, of Pol Pot's

Even in an individualistic culture, few of us have the desire to rebel against society's clearest norms. The two women shown were the only participants in a topless parade in Winnipeg.

extermination of Cambodians. But evil also results from social forces—from the heat, humidity, and disease that help make a whole barrel of apples go bad. As these experiments show, situations can induce ordinary people to agree to falsehoods or to capitulate to cruelty.

This is especially true when, as happens often in complex societies, the most terrible evil evolves from a sequence of small evils. "Indeed," notes John Darley (1996),

> it may be difficult to identify the individual who perpetrates the evil; the harm [as when Ford knowingly marketed a Pinto with its vulnerable gas tank] may seem to be an organizational product, with no clear stamp of any individual actor on it. . . . When one probes behind evil actions, one normally finds, not an evil individual viciously forwarding diabolical schemes, but instead ordinary individuals who have done acts of evil because they were caught up in complex social forces.

German civil servants surprised Nazi leaders with their willingness to handle the paperwork of the Holocaust. They were not killing Jews, of course; they were merely pushing paper (Silver & Geller, 1978). When fragmented, evil becomes easier. Milgram studied this compartmentalization of evil by involving yet another 40 men more indirectly. Rather than trigger the shock, they had only to administer the learning test. Now, 37 of the 40 fully complied.

So it is in our everyday lives: The drift toward evil usually comes in small increments, without any conscious intent to do evil. Procrastination involves a similar unintended drift, toward self-harm (Sabini & Silver, 1982). A student knows the deadline for a term paper weeks ahead. Each diversion from work on the paper—a video game here, a TV program there—seems harmless enough. Yet gradually the student veers toward not doing the paper without ever consciously deciding not to do it.

The fundamental attribution error

Why do the results of these classic experiments so often startle people? Is it not because we expect people to act in accord with their dispositions? It doesn't surprise us when a surly person is nasty, but we expect those with pleasant dispositions to be kind. Bad people do bad things; good people do good things.

When you read about Milgram's experiments, what impressions did you form of the subjects? Most people attribute negative qualities to them. When told about one or two of the obedient subjects, people judge them to be aggressive, cold, and unappealing—even after learning that their behavior was typical (Miller & others, 1973). Cruelty, we presume, is inflicted by the cruel at heart.

Ghnter Bierbrauer (1979) tried to eliminate this underestimation of social forces (the fundamental attribution error). He had university students observe a vivid reenactment of the experiment or play the role of obedient teacher themselves. They still predicted that their friends would, in a repeat of Milgram's experiment, be only minimally compliant. Bierbrauer concluded that although social scientists accumulate evidence that our behavior is a product of our social history and current environment, most people continue to believe that people's inner qualities reveal themselves—that only good people do good and that only evil people do evil.

It is tempting to assume that Eichmann and the Auschwitz death camp commanders were uncivilized monsters. But after a hard day's work, the commanders would relax by listening to Beethoven and Schubert. Eichmann himself was outwardly indistinguishable from common people with ordinary jobs (Arendt, 1963). Or consider the German police battalion responsible for shooting nearly 40,000 Jews in Poland, many of them women, children, and elderly people who were shot in the back of the head, gruesomely spraying their brains. Christopher Browning (1992) portrays the "normality" of these men. Like the many, many others who ravaged Europe's Jewish ghettos, operated the deportation trains, and administered the death camps (Goldhagen, 1996), they were not Nazis, SS members, or racial fanatics. They were laborers, salesmen, clerks, and artisans—family men who were too old for military service, but who, when directly ordered to kill, were unable to refuse.

Milgram's conclusion also makes it hard to attribute the Holocaust to unique character traits in the German people: "The most fundamental lesson of our study," he noted, is that "ordinary people, simply doing their jobs, and without any particular hostility on their part, can become agents in a terrible destructive process" (Milgram, 1974, p. 6). As Mister Rogers often reminds his preschool television audience, "Good people sometimes do bad things." Perhaps then, we should be more wary of political leaders whose charming dispositions lull us into supposing they would never do evil. Under the sway of evil forces, even nice people are sometimes corrupted.

The classic conformity experiments answered some questions but raised others: (1) Sometimes people conform; sometimes they do not. When do they? (2) Why do people conform? Why don't they ignore the group and "to their own selves be true?" (3) Is there a type of person who is likely to conform? Let's take these questions one at a time.

"The assaulting quality of the Milgram experiment is really a valuable attack on the denial and indifference of all of us. Whatever upset follows facing the truth, we must eventually face up to the fact that so many of us are, in fact, available to be genociders or their assistants."

Israel W. Charny, Executive Director, International Conference on the Holocaust and Genocide, 1982

"Eichmann did not hate Jews, and that made it worse, to have no feelings. To make Eichmann appear a monster renders him less dangerous than he was. If you kill a monster you can go to bed and sleep, for there aren't many of them. But if Eichmann was normality, then this is a far more dangerous situation."

Hannah Arendt, *Eichmann in Jerusalem*, 1963

Summing up

Conformity—changing one's behavior or belief as a result of group pressure—comes in two forms. *Compliance* is outwardly going along with the group while inwardly disagreeing. *Acceptance* is believing as well as acting in accord with social pressure.

Three classic sets of experiments illustrate how researchers have studied conformity and how conforming people can be. Muzafer Sherif observed that others' judgments influenced people's estimates of the illusory movement of a point of light. Norms for "proper" answers emerged and survived both over long periods of time and through succeeding generations of subjects. This laboratory suggestibility parallels suggestibility in real life.

Solomon Asch used a task that was as clear-cut as Sherif's was ambiguous. Asch had people listen to others' judgments of which of three comparison lines was equal to a standard line and then make the same judgment themselves. When the others unanimously gave a wrong answer, the subjects conformed 37 percent of the time.

Sherif's procedure elicited acceptance; Stanley Milgram's obedience experiments, on the other hand, elicited an extreme form of compliance. Under optimum conditions—a legitimate, close-at-hand commander, a remote victim, and no one else to exemplify disobedience—65 percent of his adult male subjects fully obeyed instructions to deliver what were supposedly traumatizing electric shocks to a screaming innocent victim in an adjacent room.

These classic experiments expose the potency of social forces and the ease with which compliance breeds acceptance. Evil is not just the product of bad people in a nice world but also of powerful situations that induce people to conform to falsehoods or capitulate to cruelty.

When do people conform?

Some situations trigger much conformity, others little conformity. If you want to produce maximum conformity, what conditions would you choose?

Social psychologists wondered: If even Asch's noncoercive, unambiguous situation could elicit a 37 percent conformity rate, would other settings produce even more? Researchers soon discovered that conformity did grow if the judgments were difficult or if the subjects felt incompetent. The more insecure we are about our judgments, the more influenced we are by others.

Researchers have also found that the nature of the group has an important influence. Conformity is highest when the group has three or more people and is cohesive, unanimous, and high in status. Conformity is also highest when the response is public and made without prior commitment.

Group size

In laboratory experiments a group need not be large to have a large effect. Asch and other researchers found that three to five people will elicit much more conformity than just one or two. Increasing the number of people beyond five yields diminishing returns (Gerard & others, 1968; Rosenberg, 1961). In a field experiment, Milgram and his colleagues (1969) had 1, 2, 3, 5, 10, or 15 people pause on a busy sidewalk and look up. As Figure 6–5 shows, the

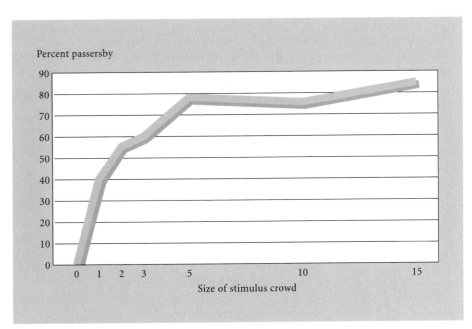

Percent passersby

Size of stimulus crowd

(Data from Milgram, Bickman, & Berkowitz, 1969)

figure 6-5

Group size and conformity.

The percentage of passers-by who imitated a group looking upward increased as group size increased to five persons.

percentage of passers-by who also looked up increased as the number looking up increased from one to five persons.

Bibb Latané (1981) accounts for the diminishing returns of increases in group size with his "social impact theory," which assumes that social influence increases with a group's immediacy and size. But there are diminishing increments with increasing numbers: The second person has less social impact than the first, and person n has less effect than person $n - 1$.

The way the group is "packaged" also makes a difference. Researcher David Wilder (1977) gave students a jury case. Before giving their own judgments, the students watched videotapes of four confederates giving their judgments. When presented as two independent groups of two people, the participants conformed more than when the four confederates presented their judgments as a single group. Similarly, two groups of three people elicited more conformity than one group of six, and three groups of two people elicited even more. Evidently, the agreement of several small groups makes a position more credible.

Unanimity

Imagine yourself in a conformity experiment where all but one of the people responding before you give the same wrong answer. Would the example of this one nonconforming confederate be as liberating as it was for the subjects in Milgram's obedience experiment? Several experiments reveal that someone who punctures a group's unanimity deflates its social power (Allen & Levine, 1969; Asch, 1955; Morris & Miller, 1975). As Figure 6–6 illustrates, subjects will nearly always voice their convictions if just one other person has also done so. The subjects in such experiments often later say they felt warm toward and close to their nonconforming ally. Yet they deny that the ally influenced them: "I would have answered just the same if he weren't there."

figure 6–6

The effect of unanimity on conformity.

When someone giving correct answers punctures the group's unanimity, subjects conform only one-fourth as often.

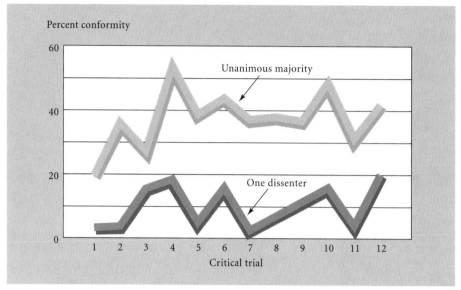

(From Asch, 1955.)

It's difficult to be a minority of one; few juries are hung because of one dissenting juror. These experiments teach the practical lesson that it is easier to stand up for something if you can find someone else to stand up with you. Many religious groups recognize this. Following the example of Jesus, who sent his disciples out in pairs, the Mormons send two missionaries into a neighborhood together. The support of the one comrade greatly increases a person's social courage.

Observing someone else's dissent—even when it is wrong—can increase our own independence. Charlan Nemeth and Cynthia Chiles (1988) discovered this after having people observe a lone individual in a group of four misjudge blue stimuli as green. Although the dissenter was wrong, observing him enabled the observers to exhibit their own form of independence. In a follow-up experiment, 76 percent of the time they correctly labeled red slides "red" even when everyone else was calling them "orange." Lacking this model of courage, others 70 percent of the time conformed to the group in calling red "orange."

> "My opinion, my conviction, gains infinitely in strength and success, the moment a second mind has adopted it."
>
> Novalis, Fragment

Cohesion

A minority opinion from someone outside the groups we identify with—from someone at another university or of a different religion—sways us less than the same minority opinion from someone within our group (Clark & Maass, 1988). A heterosexual arguing for gay rights would more effectively sway heterosexuals than would a homosexual. The more **cohesive** a group is, the more power it gains over its members. In university sororities, for example, friends tend to share binge-eating tendencies, especially as they grow closer (Crandall, 1988).

In experiments, too, group members who feel attracted to the group are more responsive to its influence (Berkowitz, 1954; Boldt, 1976; Lott & Lott, 1961; Sakurai, 1975). They do not like disagreeing with other group members. Fearing rejection by those they like, they allow them a certain power. In his *Essay Concerning Human Understanding*, the seventeenth-century philosopher John Locke

cohesiveness

a "we feeling"—the extent to which members of a group are bound together, such as by attraction for one another

It is difficult to stand alone as a minority of one. But doing so sometimes makes a hero, as was the lone dissenting jury member played by Henry Fonda in the classic movie, 12 Angry Men.

recognized the cohesiveness factor: "Nor is there one in ten thousand who is stiff and insensible enough to bear up under the constant dislike and condemnation of his own club."

Status

As you might suspect, higher-status people tend to have more impact (Driskell & Mullen, 1990). Sometimes people may actually avoid agreeing with low-status or stigmatized people. Janet Swim, Melissa Ferguson, and Lauri Hyers (1998) observed this when they placed heterosexual women students as the fifth and last person to respond in an Asch-type conformity experiment. When all were asked, "Where would you go for a romantic evening with a member of the opposite sex?" the fourth person sometimes replied, "I wouldn't go out for a romantic evening with a man because I'm a lesbian." When so identified, the actual subjects thereafter tended to avoid her answers when asked whether they thought discrimination against women was a problem or whether they considered themselves feminists. (This study also illustrates the reality of prejudice, the focus of Chapter 9.) Studies of jaywalking behavior, conducted with the unwitting aid of nearly 24,000 pedestrians, reveal that the baseline jaywalking rate of 25 percent decreases to 17 percent in the presence of a nonjaywalking confederate and increases to 44 percent in the presence of another jaywalker (Mullen & others, 1990). The nonjaywalker best discourages jaywalking when well dressed. Clothes seem to "make the person" in Australia, too. Michael Walker, Susan Harriman, and Stuart Costello (1980) found that Sydney pedestrians were more compliant when approached by a well-dressed survey taker than one who was poorly dressed.

The entire parliament fell dead silent. For the first time since anyone could remember, one of the members voted "aye."

A cohesive group.

"If you worry about missing the boat— remember the Titanic."

Anonymous

Milgram (1974) reports that in his obedience experiments people of lower status accepted the experimenter's commands more readily than people of higher status. After delivering 450 volts, one participant, a 37-year-old welder, turned to the experimenter and deferentially asked, "Where do we go from here, Professor?" (p. 46). Another participant, a divinity school professor who disobeyed at 150 volts, said: "I don't understand why the experiment is placed above this person's life," and plied the experimenter with questions about "the ethics of this thing" (p. 48).

Public response

One of the first questions researchers sought to answer was this: Would people conform more in their public responses than in their private opinions? Or would they wobble more in their private opinions but be unwilling to conform publicly, lest they appear wishy-washy? The answer is

"Dress for success." A high-status appearance can increase a person's influence.

now clear: In experiments, people conform more when they must respond publicly in front of others rather than writing their answer privately. Asch's participants, after hearing others respond, were less influenced by group pressure if they could write an answer that only the experimenter would see. It is much easier to stand up for what we believe in the privacy of the voting booth than before a group.

No prior commitment

In 1980, Genuine Risk became the second filly to win the Kentucky Derby. In her next race, the Preakness, she came off the last turn gaining on the leader, Codex, a colt. As they came out of the turn neck and neck, Codex moved sideways toward Genuine Risk, causing her to hesitate and giving him a narrow victory. Had Codex brushed Genuine Risk? Had his jockey even whipped Genuine Risk in the face? The race referees huddled. After a brief deliberation they judged that no foul had occurred and confirmed Codex as the winner. The decision caused an uproar. Televised instant replays showed that Codex had indeed brushed Genuine Risk, the sentimental favorite. A protest was filed. The officials reconsidered their decision, but they did not change it.

Did their judgment immediately after the race affect officials' openness toward reaching a different decision later? We will never know for sure. We can put people through a laboratory version of this event, however—with and without the immediate commitment—and observe whether the commitment makes a difference. Again, imagine yourself in an Asch-type experiment. The experimenter displays the lines and asks you to respond first. After you have given your judgment and then heard everyone else disagree, the experimenter offers you an opportunity to reconsider. In the face of group pressure, do you now back down?

People almost never do (Deutsch & Gerard, 1955): Once having made a public commitment, they stick to it. At most, they will change their judgments in later situations (Saltzstein & Sandberg, 1979). We may therefore expect that judges of diving or gymnastic competition, for example, will seldom change

Did Codex brush against Genuine Risk? Once race referees publicly announced their decision, no amount of evidence could budge them.

"All right! Have it your own way. It was a ball."

MANKOFF

Drawing by Mankoff; © 1980 The New Yorker Magazine, Inc.

Prior commitment: Once they commit themselves to a position, people seldom yield to social pressure. Real umpires and referees rarely reverse their initial judgments.

their ratings after seeing the other judges' ratings, although they might adjust their later performance ratings.

Prior commitments restrain persuasion, too. When simulated juries make decisions, hung verdicts are more likely in cases when jurors are polled by a show of hands rather than by secret ballot (Kerr & MacCoun, 1985). Making a public commitment makes people hesitant to back down. Smart persuaders know this. Salespeople ask questions that prompt us to make statements for, rather than against, what they are marketing. Environmentalists ask people to commit themselves to recycling, energy conservation, or bus riding—and find that behavior then changes more than when environmental appeals are heard without inviting a commitment (Katzev & Wang, 1994). Religious evangelists invite people "to get up out of your seat," knowing that people are more likely to hold to their new faith if they make a public commitment.

Public commitment may reduce conformity not only because people are more accepting after making a commitment but also because they hate to appear indecisive. Compared to people whose attitudes are stable, those whose attitudes change seem less reliable (Allgeier and others, 1979). People who "wander, waver, waffle, and wiggle," as one political candidate said contemptuously of his foe, lose respect.

"Those who never retract their opinions love themselves more than they love truth."

Joubert, *Pensées*

Summing up

Using conformity testing procedures, experimenters have explored the circumstances that produce conformity. Certain situations appear to be especially powerful. For example, conformity is affected by the characteristics of the group: People conform most when faced with the unanimous reports of three or more attractive, high-status people. People also conform most when their responses are public (in the presence of the group) and made without prior commitment.

Why conform?

"Do you see yonder cloud that's almost in the shape of a camel?" asks Shakespeare's Hamlet of Polonius. "Tis like a camel indeed," replies Polonius. "Methinks it is a weasel," says Hamlet a moment later. "It is backed like a weasel," acknowledges Polonius. "Or like a whale?" wonders Hamlet. "Very like a whale," agrees Polonius. Question: Why does Polonius so readily agree with the Prince of Denmark?

While attending a lecture at a German university, as the lecturer finished, I lifted my hands to join in the clapping. But rather than clap, the other people began rapping the tables with their knuckles. What did this mean? Did they disapprove of the speech? Surely, not everyone would be so openly rude. Nor did their faces express displeasure. No, I decided, this must be a German ovation. Whereupon, I added my knuckles to the chorus.

What prompted this conformity? There are two possibilities: A person may bow to the group to be accepted and avoid rejection or to obtain important information. Morton Deutsch and Harold Gerard (1955) named these two possibilities **normative influence** and **informational influence.**

Normative influence is "going along with the crowd" to avoid rejection, to stay in people's good graces, or to gain their approval. In the laboratory and in everyday life, groups often reject those who consistently deviate (Miller & Anderson, 1979; Schachter, 1951). Can you recall such an experience? As most of us know, social rejection is painful; when we deviate from group norms, we often pay an emotional price.

Informational influence, on the other hand, leads people to acceptance. When reality is ambiguous, as it was for subjects in the autokinetic situation, other people can be a valuable source of information. The subject may reason, "I can't tell how far the light is moving. But this guy seems to know." Others' responses may also affect how we interpret ambiguous stimuli. People who witness others agreeing that "free speech should be limited" may infer a different meaning in the statement than those who witness others disagreeing (Allen & Wilder, 1980).

So concern for social image produces normative influence. The desire to be correct produces informational influence. In day-to-day life, normative and informational influence often occur together. Normative influence can also cause people to construct reasons that justify their conformity. For example, consider the following study by University of British Columbia's Dale Griffin and Wilfrid Laurier University's Roger Buehler. Participants in their study read about a character named Robert who had to make a decision to go to medical school (a safe decision) or pursue his life's dream of attending a music conservatory (a risky decision). Initially they were ambivalent about what decision he should make, but when they were presented with the information that everyone in their group thought he should go to one school or the other, they changed their minds and went along with the group. After making the decision they also changed how risky they thought it would be for Robert to go to the music conservatory. As you can see in Figure 6–7 their reasoning clearly served to justify their decision. In subsequent research Buehler and Griffin

normative influence conformity based on a person's desire to fulfill others' expectations, often to gain acceptance

informational influence conformity that results from accepting evidence about reality provided by other people

"Do as most do and men will speak well of thee."

Thomas Fuller, *Gnomologia*

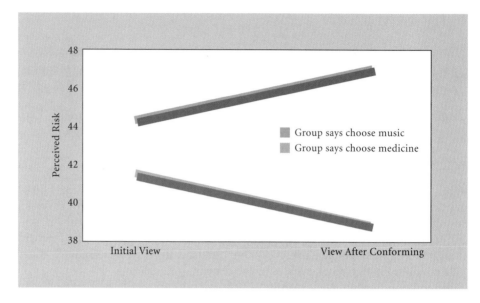

figure 6–7

Changing our beliefs after we conform.

Sometimes we change what we say is the basis of our beliefs as a result of our conformity. (Data from Buehler & Griffin, 1993.)

(1994) were able to show that this sort of justification occurred because participants had changed the meaning of the story in their mind.

Even though normative and informational influence often work together, their individual contributions can be isolated. Conformity is greater when people respond before a group; this surely reflects normative influence (because subjects receive the same information whether they respond publicly or privately). What is more, the larger the group, the greater the difference between public and private responding (Insko & others, 1985). On the other hand, conformity is greater when participants feel incompetent, when the task is difficult, and when the subjects care about being right—all signs of informational influence. Why do we conform? For two main reasons: Because we want to be liked and approved, or because we want to be right.

Summing up
Experiments reveal two reasons people conform. *Normative influence* results from a person's desire for acceptance. *Informational influence* results from others' providing evidence about reality. The tendency to conform more when responding publicly reflects normative influence. The tendency to conform more on difficult decision-making tasks reflects informational influence.

Who conforms?

Conformity varies not only with situations but also with persons. How much so? And in what social contexts do personality traits best shine through?

Are some people generally more susceptible (or, should I say, more *open*) to social influence? Among your friends, can you identify some who are "conformists" and others who are "independent"? I suspect that most of us can. Researchers are exploring several areas in their search for the conformer. Let us look briefly at three: gender, personality, and culture.

Gender

Among those tested in group-pressure situations during the last thirty years, there has been a slight tendency for women to conform more than men. Alice Eagly and Linda Carli (1981; also Becker, 1986) discerned this by statistically combining results from the dozens of available studies. Newer conformity experiments and those conducted by women, however, seldom find females more conforming. Most other gender differences in social behavior also appear uninfluenced by the sex of the investigator, reports Eagly (1987).

Is labeling this small gender effect a "conformity difference" a negative judgment on the women "conformers"? Remember, our label for the phenomenon is something we choose. Perhaps we should instead call the difference a greater "people orientation." (Recall from Chapter 5 that women are somewhat more empathic and socially sensitive.) Perhaps we should say that women are slightly more flexible, more open and responsive to their social environment, more concerned with interpersonal relations. Such language carries quite different connotations from saying that women are more conforming.

To say that women are slightly more influenceable because they are more concerned with interpersonal relations attributes the difference to personality. Eagly and Wendy Wood (1985) believe that gender differences in conformity may instead be a product of men's and women's typical social roles. Male-female differences are not just a gender difference but also (or instead) status differences. In everyday life, men tend to occupy positions of greater status and power, so we often see men exerting and women accepting influence. This explains why people *perceive* a much greater gender difference in everyday conformity than has been found in experiments that assign men and women identical roles.

> Although Milgram's 1,000 subjects (1974) were nearly all males, 40 female subjects did experience the "heart-disturbance" obedience procedure. Milgram assumed that women were generally more compliant yet also more empathic and less aggressive. What he found was no difference: 65 percent were fully compliant.

behind the scenes

I began my work on gender and social influence in the early 1970s. Like many feminist activists of the day, I initially assumed that, despite negative cultural stereotypes about women, the behavior of women and men is substantially equivalent. Over the years, my views have evolved considerably. I have found that women and men do behave somewhat differently, especially in relatively unstructured situations in which gender roles become important. Although most of these differences are gender-stereotypic, they do not necessarily reflect unfavorably on women. Women's tendencies to be more attuned to other people's concerns and to treat others more democratically are assets in many situations. In fact, my recent research (Eagly & others, 1991) on gender stereotypes shows that, if we take both negative and positive qualities into account, the stereotype of women is currently more favorable than the stereotype of men. Another feature of gender stereotypes that I am currently examining is their dynamic aspects. People assume that women and men are becoming much more similar in their characteristics and that they will continue to become more similar in the future. Most of this change is construed as women taking on characteristics that were traditionally associated with men.

Alice Eagly
Northwestern University

Personality

The history of social-psychological thinking about the relationship between personality traits and social behavior parallels the history of thinking about attitudes and behavior. During the 1950s and early 1960s psychologists studied how inner motives and dispositions influenced people's actions. For example, those who described themselves as needing social approval were more conforming (Snyder & Ickes, 1985). During the late 1960s and 1970s, efforts to link personal characteristics with social behaviors, such as conformity, found only weak connections (Mischel, 1968). In contrast to the demonstrable power of situational factors, personality scores were poor predictors of individuals' behavior. If you wanted to know how conforming or aggressive or helpful someone was going to be, it seemed you were better off knowing the details of the situation than the person's scores on a battery of psychological tests. As Milgram (1974) concluded: "I am certain that there is a complex personality basis to obedience and disobedience. But I know we have not found it" (p. 205).

Reflecting on his prison simulation and other experiments, Philip Zimbardo argued that the ultimate message

A group's unanimity versus nonunanimity affects conformity more than does individual personality.

is to say what it is we have to do to break through your egocentricism, to say you're not different, anything any human being has ever done cannot be alien to you, you can't divorce it! We must break through this "we-they" idea that our dispositional orientation promotes and understand that the situational forces operating on a person at any given moment could be so powerful as to override everything prior—values, history, biology, family, church. (Bruck, 1976)

During the 1980s, the idea that personal dispositions make little difference prompted personality researchers to pinpoint the circumstances under which traits *do* predict behavior. Their research affirms a principle that we met in Chapter 4: While internal factors (attitudes, traits) seldom precisely predict a specific action, they better predict a person's average behavior across many situations (Epstein, 1980; Rushton & others, 1983). An analogy may help: Just as your response to a single test item is hard to predict, so is your behavior in a single situation. And just as your total score across the many items of a test is more predictable, so is your total conformity (or outgoingness or aggressiveness) across many situations.

Personality also predicts behavior better when the trait is specific to a situation (such as "speech anxiety" rather than anxiety in general) and when social influences are weak. Like many other laboratory stud-

THE FAR SIDE   By GARY LARSON

Chronicle Features, 1982 Larson 11 2

"Wait! Wait! Listen to me! . . . We don't HAVE to be just sheep!"

Personality effects loom larger when we note people's differing reactions to the same situation, as when one person reacts with terror and another with delight to a roller coaster ride.

ies, Milgram's obedience experiments created "strong" situations; their clear-cut demands made it difficult for personality differences to operate. Still, Milgram's subjects differed widely in how obedient they were, and there is good reason to suspect that sometimes his subjects' hostility, respect for authority, and concern for meeting expectations affected their obedience (Blass, 1990, 1991). In the Nazi extermination camps, too, some guards displayed kindness; others used live infants as shooting targets or hurled them into the fire. Personality matters.

In "weaker" situations—as when two strangers sit in a waiting room with no cues to guide their behavior—individual personalities are even freer to shine (Ickes & others, 1982; Monson & others, 1982). If we compare two similar personalities in very different situations, the situational effect will overwhelm the personality difference. If we compare a group of Slobodan Milosevic types with a group of Mother Teresa types in a smattering of everyday situations, the personality effect will look much stronger.

Behavioral styles persist across situations. David Funder and Randall Colvin (1991) videotaped pairs of students while they got acquainted in casual conversation, then videotaped them again a few weeks later while casually chatting with a new acquaintance and while participating in a debate. Those who spoke loudly or were energetic, outgoing, or relaxed in one situation usually behaved much the same way in the other situations.

It is interesting to note how the pendulum of professional opinion swings. Without discounting the undeniable power of social forces, the pendulum is now swinging back toward an appreciation of individual personality and its genetic predispositions. Like the attitude researchers we considered earlier, personality researchers are clarifying and reaffirming the connection between who we are and what we do. Thanks to their efforts, virtually every social psychologist today would agree with pioneering theorist Kurt Lewin's (1936) dictum: "Every psychological event depends upon the state of the person and at the same time on the environment, although their relative importance is different in different cases" (p. 12).

Culture

Does cultural background help predict how conforming people will be? Indeed it does. James Whittaker and Robert Meade (1967) repeated Asch's conformity experiment in several countries and found similar conformity rates in most—31 percent in Lebanon, 32 percent in Hong Kong, 34 percent in Brazil—but 51 percent among the Bantu of Zimbabwe, a tribe with strong sanctions for nonconformity. When Milgram (1961) used a different conformity procedure to compare Norwegian and French students, he consistently found the Norwegian students to be the more conforming.

However, cultures may change. Replications of Asch's experiment with university students in Britain, Canada, and the United States sometimes trigger less conformity than Asch observed two or three decades earlier (Lalancette & Standing, 1990; Larsen, 1974, 1990; Nicholson & others, 1985; Perrin & Spencer, 1981). When researchers in Germany, Italy, South Africa, Australia, Austria, Spain, and Jordan repeated the obedience experiments, how do you think the results compared to those with American subjects? The obedience rates were similar, or even higher—85 percent in Munich (Mantell, 1971; Meeus & Raaijmakers, 1986; Milgram, 1974).

In a study of "administrative obedience" in the Netherlands, Wim Meeus and Quinten Raaijmakers (1986) ordered Dutch adults who had volunteered for an experiment to disrupt a job applicant who was taking an employment test, causing the applicant to fail the test and supposedly remain unemployed. In the guise of an experiment on the effects of stress, the subjects had to trigger 15 derogatory computer messages that caused the applicant to become progressively more upset. As the applicant's tension turned to irritation and finally to despair, the subjects found the procedure unfair and their task disagreeable. Yet by shifting responsibility to the experimenter, 90 percent fully complied.

> "I don't want to get adjusted to this world."
>
> Woody Guthrie

So conformity and obedience are universal phenomena, yet they vary by culture (Bond, 1988; Triandis & others, 1988). European and North American cultures teach individualism: You are responsible for yourself. Follow your own conscience. Be true to yourself. Define your unique gifts. Meet your own needs. Respect one another's privacy. Asian and nonwestern cultures are more likely to teach collectivism: Your family or clan is responsible for its individual members, whose actions therefore reflect shame or honor upon it. So bring honor to your group. Be true to your traditions. Show respect for elders and superiors. Cultivate harmony, and do not criticize another publicly. Be loyal to family, company, nation. Live communally, without assuming that you have a private self separate from your social context. An analysis by Rod Bond and Peter Smith (1996) of 133 studies in 17 countries confirms that these cultural values have an impact on conformity. Compared to people in individualistic countries, those in collectivist countries are more responsive to others' influence.

Summing up

The question "Who conforms?" has produced fewer definitive answers. In experiments, gender differences have varied, though females have, on the average, been slightly more conforming than males. (If this sounds negative it's because labels such as "conformity" evaluate as well as describe behavior. Call the trait "openness" or "communal sensitivity," and it takes on a more positive connotation.) Global personality scores are poor predictors of specific acts of conformity but better predict average tendencies to conformity (and other social behaviors). Trait effects are strongest in "weak" situations where social forces do not overwhelm individual differences. Although conformity and obedience are universal, culture socializes people to be more or less socially responsive.

Resisting social pressure

Will people ever actively resist social pressure? When compelled to do A will they instead do Z? What would motivate such anticonformity?

This chapter, like Chapter 5, emphasizes the power of social forces. It is therefore fitting that we conclude by again reminding ourselves of the power of the person. We are not just billiard balls; we act in response to the forces that push upon us. Knowing that someone is trying to coerce us may even prompt us to react in the *opposite* direction.

Reactance

Individuals value their sense of freedom and self-efficacy (Baer & others, 1980). So when social pressure becomes so blatant that it threatens their sense of freedom, they often rebel. Think of Romeo and Juliet, whose love was intensified by their families' opposition. Or think of children asserting their freedom and independence by doing the opposite of what their parents ask. Savvy parents therefore offer their children choices instead of commands: "It's time to clean up: Do you want a bath or a shower?"

The theory of psychological **reactance**—that people do indeed act to protect their sense of freedom—is supported by experiments showing that attempts to restrict a person's freedom often produce a "boomerang effect" (Brehm & Brehm, 1981; Nail & Van Leeuwen, 1993). Suppose someone stops you on the street and asks you to sign a petition advocating something you mildly support. While considering the petition, you are told someone else believes "people absolutely should not be allowed to distribute or sign such petitions." Reactance theory predicts that such blatant attempts to limit freedom will actually increase the likelihood of your signing. When Madeline Heilman (1976) staged this experiment, that is precisely what she found.

"To do just the opposite is also a form of imitation."

Lichtenberg, *Aphorismen*, 1764–1799

reactance
a motive to protect or restore one's sense of freedom. Reactance arises when someone threatens our freedom of action.

Reactance at work? Underage students have been found to be less often abstinent and more often drinking to excess than students over the legal drinking age.

Reactance may also contribute to underage drinking. In Canada a survey of 1,105 young adults 18–24 revealed that 76.9 percent of those who are underage, but only 68.8 percent of those who can drink legally have been drunk in the last year (Canadian Centre on Substance Abuse, 1997). Likewise, 21.5 percent of underage drinkers, but only 17 percent of legal drinkers, report that their drinking has caused personal problems in their life. They suspect this reflects a reactance against the restriction. It probably also reflects peer influence. With alcohol use, as with drugs, peers influence attitudes, provide the substance, and offer a context for its use. This helps explain why university students, living in a peer culture that often supports alcohol use, drink more alcohol than their nonuniversity peers (Atwell, 1986).

Reactance can escalate into social rebellion. Like obedience, rebellion can be produced and observed in experiments. That's what William Gamson, Bruce Fireman, and Steven Rytina (1982) learned when they posed as members of a commercial research firm. They recruited people from towns near the University of Michigan to come to a hotel conference room for "a group discussion of community standards." Once there, the people learned that the discussions were to be videotaped on behalf of a large oil company seeking to win a legal case against a local station manager who had spoken out against high gas prices.

In the first discussion, virtually everyone sided with the station manager. Hoping to convince the court that people in the local community were on its side, the "company representative" then began to tell more and more group members to defend the company. In the end, he told everyone to attack the station manager and asked them to sign an affidavit giving the company permission to edit the tapes and use them in court. By leaving the room from time to time, the experimenter gave the group members repeated opportunities to interpret and react to the injustice.

Most rebelled, objecting to and resisting the demand that they misrepresent their opinions to help the oil company. Some groups even mobilized themselves to stop the whole effort. They made plans to go to a newspaper, the Better Business Bureau, a lawyer, or the court.

By brewing small social rebellions, the researchers saw how a revolt is born. They found that successful resistance often begins very quickly; the more a group complies with unjust demands, the harder it later is to break free. And someone must be willing to seed the process by expressing the reservations the others are feeling.

These demonstrations of reactance reassure us that people are not puppets. Sociologist Peter Berger (1963) expressed the point vividly:

> We see the puppets dancing in their miniature stage, moving up and down as the strings pull them around, following the prescribed course of their various little parts. We learn to understand the logic of this theater and we find ourselves in its motions. We locate ourselves in society and thus recognize our own position as we hang from its subtle strings. For a moment we see ourselves as puppets indeed. But then we grasp a decisive difference between the puppet theater and our own drama. Unlike the puppets, we have the possibility of stopping in our movements, looking up and perceiving the machinery by which we have been moved. In this act lies the first step towards freedom. (p. 176)

Asserting uniqueness

Imagine a world of complete conformity where there were no differences among people. Would such a world be a happy place? If nonconformity can create discomfort, can sameness create comfort?

People feel uncomfortable when they appear too different from others. But, at least in Western cultures, they also feel uncomfortable when they appear exactly like everyone else. As experiments by C. R. Snyder and Howard Fromkin (1980) have shown, people feel better when they see themselves as

Asserting our uniqueness. While not wishing to be greatly deviant, most of us express our distinctiveness through our personal styles and dress.

unique. Moreover, they act in ways that will assert their individuality. In one experiment, Snyder (1980) led students to believe that their "10 most important attitudes" were either distinct from or nearly identical to the attitudes of 10,000 other students. When they then participated in a conformity experiment, those deprived of their feeling of uniqueness were most likely to assert their individuality by nonconformity. In another experiment, people who heard others express attitudes identical to their own altered their positions to maintain their sense of uniqueness.

Seeing oneself as unique also appears in people's "spontaneous self-concepts." William McGuire and his colleagues (McGuire & Padawer-Singer, 1978; McGuire & others, 1979) report that when children are invited to "tell us about yourself," they are most likely to mention their distinctive attributes. Foreign-born children are more likely than others to mention their birthplace. Redheads are more likely than black- and brown-haired children to volunteer their hair color. Light and heavy children are the most likely to refer to their body weight. Minority children are the most likely to mention their race. Likewise we become more keenly aware of our gender when we are with people of the other sex (Cota & Dion, 1986). When I recently attended a Psychological Association meeting with 10 others—all women as it happened—I immediately was aware of my gender. As we took a break at the end of the second day, I joked that the line would be short at my bathroom, triggering the woman sitting next to me to notice what hadn't crossed her mind—the group's gender make-up.

The principle, says McGuire, is that "one is conscious of oneself insofar as, and in the ways that, one is different." Thus, "If I am a Black woman in a group of White women, I tend to think of myself as a Black; if I move to a group of Black men, my blackness loses salience and I become more conscious of being a woman" (McGuire & others, 1978). This insight helps us understand why any minority group tends to be conscious of its distinctiveness and how the surrounding culture relates to it. The majority group, being less conscious of race, may see the minority group as "hypersensitive." When occasionally living in Scotland, where my accent marks me as a foreigner, I am conscious of my national identity and sensitive to how others react to it.

When the people of two cultures are nearly identical, they still will notice their differences, however small. Even trivial distinctions may provoke scorn and conflict. Jonathan Swift satirized the phenomenon in *Gulliver's Travels*—the Little-Endians war against the Big-Endians. Their difference: The Little-Endians preferred to break their eggs on the small end, the Big-Endians on the large end. On a world scale, the differences may not seem great between Scots and English, Hutus and Tutus, Serbs and Croatians, or Catholic and Protestant Northern Irelanders. But small differences can mean big conflict (Rothbart & Taylor, 1992). Rivalry is often most intense when the other group most closely resembles you.

So it seems that while we do not like being greatly deviant, we are, ironically, all alike in wanting to feel distinctive and noticing how we are distinctive. But as research on self-serving bias (Chapter 2) makes clear, it is not just any kind of distinctiveness we seek but distinctiveness in the right direction. Our quest is not merely to be different from the average, but better than average.

Finally, a comment on the experimental method used in conformity research: Conformity situations in the laboratory differ from those in everyday life. How

---

"When I'm in America, I have no doubt I'm a Jew, but I have strong doubts about whether I'm really an American. And when I get to Israel, I know I'm an American, but I have strong doubts about whether I'm a Jew."

Leslie Fiedler, *Fiedler on the Roof,* 1991

"Self-consciousness, the recognition of a creature by itself as a 'self,' [cannot] exist except in contrast with an 'other,' a something which is not the self."

C. S. Lewis, *The Problem of Pain,* 1940

"There are no exceptions to the rule that everybody likes to be an exception to the rule."

Malcolm Forbes, *Forbes Magazine*

often are we asked to judge line lengths or administer shock? As combustion is similar for a burning match and a forest fire, so we assume that psychological processes in the laboratory and in everyday life are similar (Milgram, 1974). We must be careful in generalizing from the simplicity of a burning match to the complexity of a forest fire. Yet controlled experiments on burning matches can give us insights into combustion that we cannot gain by observing forest fires. So, too, the social-psychological experiment offers insights into behavior not readily revealed in everyday life. The experimental situation is unique, but so is every social situation. By testing with a variety of unique tasks, and by repeating experiments in different times and places, researchers probe for the common principles that lie beneath the surface diversity.

Summing up

Social psychology's emphasis on the power of social pressure must be joined by a complementary emphasis on the power of the person. We are not puppets. When social coercion becomes blatant, people often experience *reactance*—a motivation to defy the coercion in order to maintain their sense of freedom. When group members experience reactance simultaneously, the result may be rebellion.

We are not comfortable being too different from a group, but neither do we want to appear the same as everyone else. Thus, we act in ways that preserve our sense of uniqueness and individuality. In a group, we are most conscious of how we differ from the others.

Personal Postscript: On being an individual within community

Do your own thing. Question authority. If it feels good, do it. Seek your own bliss. Don't conform. Think for yourself. Accept yourself. Be true to yourself. You owe it to yourself.

Such are words we hear over and again . . . if we live in an individualistic Western nation, such as those of western Europe, Australia, New Zealand, Canada, or the United States. The unchallenged assumption that individualism is good, and conformity is bad, is what Chapter 1 called a "social representation, a collectively shared idea. Our mythical cultural heroes—from Huckleberry Finn to Sherlock Holmes to Luke Skywalker to the youth of *Dead Poet's Society* standing up against institutional rules—assume the preeminence of individual rights and celebrate the one who stands against the group.

In 1831, the French writer Alexis de Tocqueville, coined the term "individualism" after traveling to North America. Individualists, he noted, owe no one "anything and hardly expect anything from anybody. They form the habit of thinking of themselves in isolation and imagine that their whole destiny is in their hands." A century and a half later, therapist Fritz Perls (1972) epitomized this radical individualism in his "Gestalt prayer":

I do my thing, and you do your thing.
I am not in this world to live up to your expectations.
And you are not in this world to live up to mine.

Psychologist Carl Rogers (1985) agreed: "The only question which matters is, 'Am I living in a way which is deeply satisfying to me, and which truly expresses me?'"

As we noted in Chapter 2, that is hardly the only question that matters to people in many other cultures, including those of Asia. Where *community* is prized, conformity is accepted. Schoolchildren often display their solidarity by wearing school uniforms. Attachments run deep. To maintain harmony, confrontation and dissent are muted. "The nail that stands out gets pounded down," say the Japanese.

Amitai Etzioni (1993), a recent president of the American Sociological Association, urges us toward a "communitarian" individualism that balances our nonconformist individualism with a spirit of community. Fellow sociologist Robert Bellah (1996) concurs. "Communitarianism is based on the value of the sacredness of the individual," he explains. But it also "affirms the central value of solidarity . . . that we become who we are through our relationships."

As Westerners in various nations, most readers of this book enjoy the benefits of nonconformist individualism, but at what communitarians believe is a cost to our communal well-being. We humans like to feel unique and in control of our lives, but we also are social creatures having a basic need to belong. Conformity is neither all bad nor all good. As individuals, we therefore need to balance our needs for independence and attachment, privacy and community, individuality and social identity.

chapter 7

Persuasion

Joseph Goebbels, Germany's minister of "popular enlightenment" and propaganda from 1933 to 1945, understood the power of persuasion. Given control of publications, radio programs, motion pictures, and the arts, he undertook to persuade Germans to accept Nazi ideology. Julius Streicher, another member of the Nazi group, published *Der Stürmer,* a weekly anti-Semitic (anti-Jewish) newspaper with a circulation of 500,000 and the only paper read cover to cover by his intimate friend, Adolf Hitler. Streicher also published anti-Semitic children's books and, with Goebbels, spoke at the mass rallies that became a part of the Nazi propaganda machine.

How effective were Goebbels, Streicher, and other Nazi propagandists? Did they, as the Allies alleged at Streicher's Nuremberg trial, "inject poison into the minds of millions and millions" (Bytwerk, 1976)? Most Germans were not persuaded to feel raging hatred for the Jews. But many were. Others became sympathetic to anti-Semitic measures. And most of the rest became either sufficiently uncertain or sufficiently intimidated to staff the huge genocidal

SEX CAN BE A REAL SCREAM.

Teenagers who go all the way don't often go very far.
THE CHILDREN'S DEFENSE FUND.

Teenage pregnancy has social consequences for both parent and child. How persuasive is this message in addressing the problem?

"Remember that to change thy mind and to follow him that sets thee right, is to be none the less a free agent."

Marcus Aurelius Antoninus, *Meditations*

"A fanatic is one who can't change his mind and won't change the subject."

Winston Churchill, 1954

program, or at least to allow it to happen. Without the complicity of millions of people, there would have been no Holocaust (Goldhagen, 1996).

Powerful persuasive forces are also at work in today's world. In the wake of publicized research on the physical and social consequences of marijuana use, adolescent attitudes have changed rapidly. From 1978 to 1991, support for marijuana's legalization among the quarter million new university students surveyed annually dropped from 50 to 21 percent (Dey & others, 1991; Sax & others, 1996). Simultaneously, high school students believing there was "great risk" to regular marijuana use more than doubled from 35 percent to 79 percent in 1991 (Johnston & others, 1996). As attitudes changed, so did behavior. In Canada, marijuana use within the prior year dropped from 29.9 percent in 1981 to 11.7 percent in 1991 (Adlaf, Smart, & Walsh, 1994). U.S. teens underwent similar attitude and marijuana-use changes. Since the early 1990s, however, drug education efforts have relaxed, median models of drug use have rebounded, and so have attitudes and behavior. By 1996 university students' support for legalization had sprung back to 33 percent, high school students perceiving "great risk" was back down to 60 percent, and their monthly marijuana use was up to 22 percent.

Thanks partly to health promotion campaigns, the Canadian Centre on Substance Abuse reports that the Canadian smoking rate has plunged to 27 percent, barely more than half the rate of 30 years ago. And the rate of Grade 13 students in Ontario that abstain from drinking beer has increased—from 8.3 percent in 1981 to 22.2 percent in 1993. More than at any time in recent decades, health- and safety-conscious educated adults are shunning cigarettes and beer.

But some persuasive efforts flop. One massive governmental experiment to persuade people to use seat belts had no discernible effect (seven carefully designed cable TV messages were broadcast 943 times during prime time to 6,400 households). Psychologist Paul Slovic (1985) thought he and his colleagues might do better. Their hunch was that only 10 percent of people use seat belts because most people perceive themselves to be invulnerable. Although it's true that only 1 trip in 100,000 produces an injury, 50,000 trips taken in an average lifetime mean that for many people the feeling of safety eventually turns out to be an "illusion of invulnerability."

Slovic and several members of his research team produced twelve television messages designed to persuade people of the risks of driving without seat belts. After pretesting with hundreds of people, several thousand people at a "screening house" evaluated six messages. The three best messages were repeatedly presented to yet another group of people. Alas, the messages had no effect on their seat-belt use. Because each safe trip reinforces nonuse of seat belts, concluded Slovic, "There seems to be no form of educational campaign or message that will persuade more than a small percentage of motorists to voluntarily wear seat belts."

Persuasion is everywhere. When we approve it, we may call it "education."

As these examples show, efforts to persuade are sometimes diabolical, sometimes salutary; sometimes effective, sometimes futile. Persuasion is neither inherently good nor bad. It is usually the content of the message that elicits judgments of good or bad. The bad we call "propaganda." The good we call "education." True, education is more factually based and less coercive than propaganda. Yet generally we call it "education" when we believe it, "propaganda" when we don't (Lumsden & others, 1980).

Our opinions have to come from somewhere. Persuasion—whether it be education or propaganda—is therefore inevitable. Indeed, persuasion is everywhere—at the heart of politics, marketing, courtship, parenting, negotiation, evangelism, and courtroom decision making. Social psychologists therefore seek to understand what makes a message effective: What factors influence us to change? And how, as persuaders, can we most effectively "educate" others?

Imagine that you are a marketing or advertising executive, one of those responsible for the nearly $300 billion spent annually worldwide on advertising (Brown & others, 1993). Or imagine that you are a preacher, trying to increase love and charity among your parishioners. Or imagine that you want to promote energy conservation, to encourage breast-feeding, or to campaign for a political candidate. What could you do to make yourself, and your message, persuasive? Or if you are wary of being manipulated by such appeals, what tactics should you be alert to?

To answer such questions, social psychologists usually study persuasion the way some geologists study erosion—by observing the effects of various factors in brief controlled experiments. The effects are small and are most potent on weak attitudes that don't touch our values (Johnson & Eagly, 1989; Petty &

"To swallow and follow, whether old doctrine or new propaganda, is a weakness still dominating the human mind."

Charlotte Perkins Gilman, *Human Work*, 1904

If you live in North America, advertisers spend about $500 annually trying to influence you.

(Brown & others, 1993.)

Krosnick, 1995). Yet they enable us to better understand how, given enough time, such factors could produce big effects.

Two routes to persuasion

What two paths lead to influence? What type of cognitive processing does each involve—and with what effects?

In choosing tactics, you must first decide if you should focus mostly on building strong *central arguments.* Or should you make your message appealing by associating it with favorable *peripheral cues,* such as sex appeal? Persuasion researchers Richard Petty and John Cacioppo (1986; Petty & Wegener, 1998) and Alice Eagly and Shelly Chaiken (1993) report that people who are able and motivated to think through an issue are best persuaded through a **central route** to persuasion—*one that marshals systematic arguments to stimulate favorable thinking.* Computer ads, for example, seldom feature Hollywood stars or great athletes; instead they offer customers information on competitive features and prices.

Some people are analytical, note Petty and Cacioppo. They like to think about issues and mentally elaborate them. Such people rely not just on the cogency of persuasive appeals but on their own cognitive responses to them as well. It's not so much the arguments that are persuasive as what they get people thinking. And when people think deeply rather than superficially, any changed attitude will more likely persist, resist attack, and influence behavior (Petty & others, 1995; Verplanken, 1991).

On issues that won't engage people's thinking, a **peripheral route**—*one that provides cues that trigger acceptance without much thinking*—works better. When people are distracted or not motivated to think, easily understood familiar statements are more persuasive than novel statements with the same meaning. Thus, for uninvolved or distracted people, "Don't put all your eggs in one basket" has more impact than "Don't risk everything on a single venture" (Howard, 1997).

Visual images can also serve as peripheral cues. Instead of providing information, cigarette ads associate the product with images of beauty and pleasure. So do soft drink ads that promote "the real thing" or "the Pepsi generation" with images of youth, vitality, and joy.

Even analytical people sometimes form tentative opinions using peripheral heuristics, such as "trust the experts" or "long messages are credible" (Chaiken & Maheswaran, 1994). Residents of my community recently voted on a complicated issue involving the legal ownership of our local hospital. I didn't have the time or interest to study this question myself (I had this book to write). But I noted that referendum supporters were all people I either liked or regarded as experts. So I used a simple heuristic—friends and experts can be trusted—and voted accordingly. We all make snap judgments using other rule-of-thumb heuristics: If a speaker is articulate and appealing, has apparently good motives, and has several arguments (or better, if the different arguments come from different sources), we usually take the easy peripheral route and accept the message without much thought (Figure 7–1).

central route persuasion
persuasion that occurs when interested people focus on the arguments and respond with favorable thoughts

"Attitude changes are stronger the more they are based on issue-relevant thinking."

Richard Petty and Duane Wegener (1998)

peripheral route persuasion
persuasion that occurs when people are influenced by incidental cues, such as a speaker's attractiveness

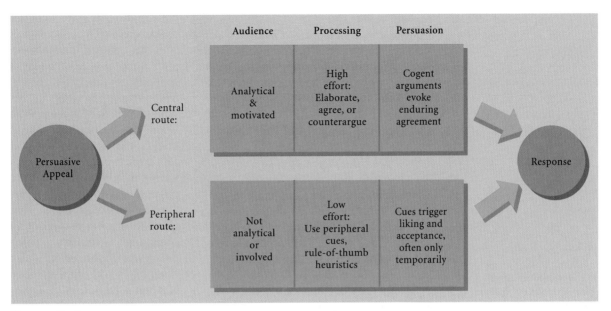

figure 7–1

The central and peripheral routes to persuasion.

Computer ads typically take the central route, by assuming their audience wants to systematically compare features and prices. Soft-drink ads usually take the peripheral route, by merely associating their product with glamor, pleasure, and good moods.

Summing up

Sometimes persuasion occurs as people focus on arguments and respond with favorable thoughts. Such systematic, or "central route," persuasion occurs when people are naturally analytical or involved in the issue. When issues don't engage systematic thinking, persuasion may occur through a faster "peripheral route" as people use heuristics or incidental cues to make snap judgments. Central route persuasion, being more thoughtful and less superficial, is more durable and more likely to influence behavior.

The elements of persuasion

Among the central and peripheral ingredients of persuasion explored by social psychologists are these four: (1) the communicator, (2) the message, (3) how the message is communicated, and (4) the audience. In other words, who *says* what *by* what means *to* whom?

Who says? The communicator

Imagine the following scene: I. M. Wright, a hockey fan who was the "goon" on his junior hockey team, is watching a sports program. One sportswriter complains about a vicious hit she saw recently and says, "This guy means to hurt

No other bottle
comes closer to breast-feeding.

*Through its written
arguments, this ad uses the
central route to persuasion.
But it also takes a peripheral
route. Note how it suggests
that mother and infant can
derive happiness from
simulating the natural
mother-infant relationship.*

people and this guy never got suspended. This is awful. This stuff should be stopped. . . . someday somebody is going to get killed." Angered, Mr. Wright mutters to his wife, "I'm sick of these people who know nothing about hockey trying to ruin it. Good hits are just part of the game." Later in the program the same sportswriter complains about Canadian fans that were booing players from an opposing country. She remarks that she felt it "was a disgrace," and that it made her feel ashamed to be Canadian. Mr. Wright chimes in and says, "Where did they find this woman? She should learn to support her country and her fellow countrymen."

Now switch the scene. Imagine Mr. Wright hearing these statements from Don Cherry on *Coach's Corner* describing a vicious hit by Swedish player Peter Forsberg on Canadian star Brendan Shanahan and describing his dismay when Canadian fans booed Canadian-born Brett Hull. Do you think Mr. Wright would react differently?

Social psychologists have found that who is saying something makes a big difference. In one experiment, when the Socialist and Liberal leaders in the Dutch parliament argued identical positions using the same words, each was most effective with members of his own party (Wiegman, 1985). It's not just the central message that matters, but a peripheral *cue*—who says it. But what makes one communicator more persuasive than another?

Credibility

Any of us would find a statement about the benefits of exercise more believable if it came from a scientific journal rather than from a tabloid newspaper. But the effects of source **credibility** (perceived expertise and trustworthiness) diminish after a month or so. If a credible person's message is persuasive, its impact may fade as its source is forgotten or dissociated from the message. The impact of a noncredible person may correspondingly *increase* over time (if people remember the message better than the reason for discounting it) (Cook & Flay, 1978; Gruder & others, 1978; Pratkanis & others, 1988). This delayed persuasion, after people forget the source or its connection with the message, is called the **sleeper effect.**

Perceived expertise.   How does one become "expert"? One way is to begin by saying things the audience agrees with, which makes you seem smart. Another is to be introduced as someone who is *knowledgeable* on the topic. A message

credibility
believability. A credible communicator is perceived as both expert and trustworthy.

sleeper effect
a delayed impact of a message that occurs when we remember the message but forget a reason for discounting it

"If I seem excited, Mr. Bolling, it's only because I know that I can make you a very rich man."

© 1987, The New Yorker Magazine, Inc.

Effective persuaders know how to convey a message effectively.

about toothbrushing from "Dr. James Rundle of the Canadian Dental Association" is much more convincing than the same message from "Jim Rundle, a local high school student who did a project with some of his classmates on dental hygiene" (Olson & Cal, 1984). After more than a decade studying high school marijuana use, researchers (Bachman & others, 1988) concluded that scare messages from unreliable sources did not affect marijuana use during the 1960s and 1970s. But from a credible source, scientific reports of the biological and psychological results of long-term marijuana use "can play an important role in reducing . . . drug use."

Another way to appear credible is to *speak confidently*. Bonnie Erickson and her collaborators (1978) had students evaluate courtroom testimony given in the straightforward manner (sometimes associated with "men's speech") or in a more hesitant manner (sometimes associated with "women's speech"). For example:

QUESTION: Approximately how long did you stay there before the ambulance arrived?

ANSWER: [*Straightforward*] Twenty minutes. Long enough to help get Mrs. David straightened out.

[*Hesitating*] Oh, it seems like it was about uh, twenty minutes. Just long enough to help my friend Mrs. David, you know, get straightened out.

The students found the straightforward witnesses much more competent and credible.

Perceived trustworthiness.   Speech style also affects a speaker's apparent trustworthiness. Gordon Hemsley and Anthony Doob (1978) found that if, while testifying, videotaped witnesses looked their questioner straight in the eye instead of gazing downward, they impressed people as more believable.

Trustworthiness is also higher if the audience believes the communicator is not trying to persuade them. In an experimental version of what later became

"Believe an expert."

Virgil, *Aeneid*

the "hidden-camera" method of television advertising, Elaine Hatfield and Leon Festinger (Walster & Festinger, 1962) had some undergraduates eavesdrop on graduate students' conversations. (What they actually heard was a tape recording.) When the conversational topic was relevant to the eavesdroppers (having to do with campus regulations), supposedly unsuspecting speakers were more influential than speakers said to be aware that someone was listening. After all, if people don't know someone's listening, why would they be less than fully honest?

People also perceive as sincere those who argue against their own self-interest. Alice Eagly, Wendy Wood, and Shelly Chaiken (1978) presented students with a speech attacking a company's pollution of a river. When they said the speech was given by a political candidate with a business background or to an audience of company supporters, it seemed unbiased and was persuasive. When the same antibusiness speech was supposedly given to environmentalists by a pro-environment politician, listeners could attribute the politician's arguments to personal bias or to the audience. Being willing to suffer for one's beliefs—which Gandhi, Martin Luther King, Jr., and other great leaders have done—also helps convince people of one's sincerity (Knight & Weiss, 1980).

These experiments all point to the importance of attribution: To what do we attribute a speaker's position—to the speaker's bias and selfish motives or to the evidence? Wood and Eagly (1981) report that when a speaker argues an *unexpected* position, we are more likely to attribute the message to compelling evidence and find it persuasive. Arguments for generous compensation in a personal-injury case are most persuasive when they come from a stingy, Scrooge-type person. Arguments for stingy compensation are most persuasive when they come from a normally warm, generous person (Wachtler & Counselman, 1981). We could therefore expect that Northern Ireland peace agreements would be most trusted by followers of both sides if negotiated by hard-line leaders.

Norman Miller and his colleagues (1976) found that trustworthiness and credibility increase when people talk fast. People who listened to tape-recorded messages on topics such as "the dangers of coffee drinking" rated fast speakers (about 190 words per minute) as more objective, intelligent, and knowledgeable than slow speakers (about 110 words per minute). They also found the more rapid speakers more persuasive.

But is it speed alone that makes rapid speakers more persuasive? Or is it something that accompanies rapid speech, like higher intensity or pitch? To find out, marketing researcher James MacLachlan (1979; MacLachlan & Siegel, 1980) electronically compressed radio and television commercials without altering the speaker's pitch, inflection, and intensity. (He deleted small segments, about a fiftieth of a second in length, from all parts of the speech.) Speed itself was a factor. When the commercials were speeded up 25 percent, the listeners comprehended as well, rated the speakers as more knowledgeable, intelligent, and sincere, and found the messages more interesting. In fact, the normal 140- to 150-word-per-minute speech rate can be almost doubled before comprehension begins to drop abruptly (Foulke & Sticht, 1969). John F. Kennedy, an exceptionally effective public speaker, sometimes spoke in bursts approaching 300 words per minute.

To North Americans (though not to Koreans) fast speech conveys power and competence (Peng & others, 1993). Although fast speech doesn't leave listeners time to elaborate favorable thoughts, it also cuts short any unfavorable thoughts (Smith & Shaffer, 1991). If an advertiser is persuading you at 70 miles per hour it's tough to counterargue at the same speed.

Some television ads are obviously constructed to make the communicator appear both expert and trustworthy. Drug companies peddle pain relievers using a white-coated speaker, who declares confidently that most doctors recommend their ingredient (the ingredient, of course, is aspirin). Given such peripheral cues, people who don't care enough to analyze the evidence may reflexively infer the product's value. Other ads seem not to use the credibility principle. Is Michael Jordan really a trustworthy expert on fast-food restaurants? And are you and I more likely to wear Nike because Tiger Woods recommends it?

Attractiveness

Most people deny that endorsements by star athletes and entertainers affect them. Everyone knows that stars are seldom knowledgeable about the products. Besides, we know the intent is to persuade us; we don't just accidentally eavesdrop on Jordan enjoying a Big Mac. Such ads are based on another characteristic of an effective communicator: attractiveness. We may think we are not influenced by attractiveness or likability, but researchers have found otherwise. Our liking may open us up to the communicator's arguments (central route persuasion) or may trigger positive associations when we later see the product (peripheral route persuasion).

Attractiveness varies in several ways. *Physical appeal* is one. Arguments, especially emotional ones, are often more influential when they come from beautiful people (Chaiken, 1979; Dion & Stein, 1978; Pallak & others, 1983). *Similarity* is another. As Chapter 11 will emphasize, we tend to like people who are like us. We also are influenced by them. For example, Theodore Dembroski, Thomas Lasater, and Albert Ramirez (1978) gave Black junior high students a taped appeal for proper dental care. When a dentist assessed the cleanliness of their teeth the next day, those who heard the appeal from a Black

attractiveness having qualities that appeal to an audience. An appealing communicator (often someone similar to the audience) is most persuasive on matters of subjective preference.

Attractive communicators, such as Jacques Villeneuve wearing a number of company logos, often trigger peripheral route persuasion. We associate their message or product with our good feeling toward the communicator, and we approve and believe.

dentist had cleaner teeth. As a general rule, people respond better to a message that comes from someone in their group (Van Knippenberg & Wilke, 1992; Wilder, 1990).

Is similarity more important than credibility? Sometimes yes, sometimes no. Timothy Brock (1965) found paint store customers more influenced by the testimony of an ordinary person who had recently bought the same amount of paint they planned to buy than by an expert who had recently purchased 20 times as much. But recall that a leading dentist (a dissimilar but expert source) was more persuasive than a student (a similar but inexpert source) when discussing dental hygiene.

Such seemingly contradictory findings bring out the detective in the scientist. They suggest that an undiscovered factor is at work—that similarity is more important given factor X and credibility is more important given not-X. Factor X, as George Goethals and Erick Nelson (1973) discovered, is whether the topic is one of *subjective preference* or *objective reality*. When the choice concerns matters of personal value, taste, or way of life, *similar* communicators have the most influence. But on judgments of *fact*—Does Sydney have less rainfall than London?—confirmation of belief by a *dissimilar* person does more to boost confidence. A dissimilar person, better yet an expert, provides a more independent judgment.

What is said? The message content

It matters not only who says a thing (a peripheral cue), but *what* that person says. If you were to help organize an appeal to get people to vote for school taxes, or to stop smoking, or to give money to world hunger relief, you might wonder how to concoct a recipe for central route persuasion. Common sense can be made to argue on either side of these questions:

- Is a carefully reasoned message most persuasive—or one that arouses emotion?
- Will you get more opinion change by advocating a position only slightly discrepant from the listeners' existing opinions? Or by advocating an extreme point of view?
- Should the message express your side only, or should it acknowledge and attempt to refute opposing views?
- If people are to present both sides—say, in successive talks at a community meeting—is there an advantage to going first or last?

Let's take these questions one at a time.

Reason versus emotion

Suppose you were campaigning in support of world hunger relief. Would it be best to itemize your arguments and cite an array of impressive statistics? Or would you be more effective presenting an emotional approach—say, the compelling story of one starving child? Of course, an argument can be both reasonable and emotional. You can marry passion and logic. Still, which is more influential—reason or emotion? Was Shakespeare's Lysander right: "The will of man is by his reason sway'd"? Or was Lord Chesterfield's advice wiser: "Address yourself generally to the senses, to the heart, and to the weaknesses of mankind, but rarely to their reason"?

"The truth is always the strongest argument."

Sophocles, *Phaedra*

"Opinion is ultimately determined by the feelings and not by the intellect."

Herbert Spencer, *Social Statics*, 1851

The answer: It depends on the audience. Well-educated or analytical people are more responsive to rational appeals than are less educated or less analytical people (Cacioppo & others, 1983, 1996; Hovland & others, 1949). Thoughtful, involved audiences travel the central route; they are most responsive to reasoned arguments. Disinterested audiences travel the peripheral route; they are more affected by how much they like the communicator (Chaiken, 1980; Petty & others, 1981).

It also depends on how people's attitudes were formed. Several studies (Edwards, 1990; Fabrigar & Petty, 1999) have shown when people's attitudes were primarily formed through emotion they are more persuaded by emotional appeals, and when their attitudes are primarily formed through reason they are more persuaded by intellectual arguments.

The effect of good feelings.   Messages also become more persuasive through association with good feelings. Irving Janis and his colleagues (1965; Dabbs & Janis, 1965) found that students were more convinced by persuasive messages if they were allowed to enjoy peanuts and Pepsi while reading them (Figure 7–2). Similarly, Mark Galizio and Clyde Hendrick (1972) found students more persuaded by folk-song lyrics accompanied by pleasant guitar music than by unaccompanied lyrics. Those who like conducting business over sumptuous lunches with soft background music can celebrate these results.

Good feelings enhance persuasion—partly by enhancing positive thinking (when people are motivated to think) and partly by linking good feelings with the message (Petty & others, 1993). As noted in Chapter 3, in a good mood, people view the world through rose-colored glasses. They also make faster, more impulsive decisions; they rely more on peripheral cues (Bodenhausen, 1993; Schwarz & others, 1991). Unhappy people ruminate more before reacting, so

> Advertising research, as in one study of the persuasiveness of 168 television commercials (Agres, 1987), reveals that the most effective ads invoke both reasons ("You'll get whiter whites with Detergent X") and emotions ("Choosy mothers choose Jif").

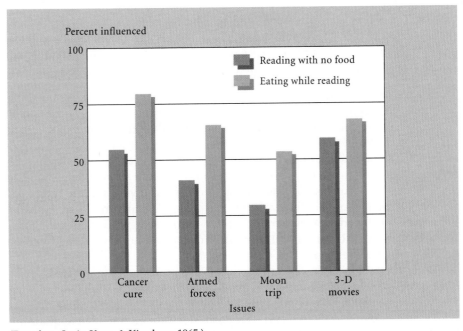

figure 7–2

People who snacked as they read were more persuaded than those who read without snacking.

(Data from Janis, Kaye, & Kirschner, 1965.)

"*If the jury had been sequestered in a nicer hotel,
this would probably never have happened.*"

*Good feelings help create
positive attitudes.*

they are less easily swayed by weak arguments. Thus, if you can't make a strong case, it's a smart idea to put your audience in a good mood and hope they'll feel good about your message without thinking too much about it.

The effect of arousing fear.   Messages also can be effective by evoking negative emotions. In trying to convince people to cut down on smoking, brush their teeth more often, get a tetanus shot, or drive carefully, a fear-arousing message can be potent (Muller & Johnson, 1990). Showing cigarette smokers the horrible things that sometimes happen to people who smoke too much adds to persuasiveness. But how much fear should you arouse? Should you evoke just a little fear, lest people become so frightened that they tune out your painful message? Or should you try to scare the daylights out of them? Experiments by Howard Leventhal (1970) and his collaborators and by Ronald Rogers and his collaborators (Robberson & Rogers, 1988) show that, often, the more frightened people are, the more they respond.

The effectiveness of fear-arousing communications is being applied in ads discouraging smoking, drinking and driving, and risky sexual behaviors. Dawn Wilson and her colleagues (1987, 1988) had doctors send a letter to their patients who smoked. Of those who received a positively framed message (explaining that by quitting they would live longer), 8 percent tried to quit smoking. Of those who received a fear-framed message (explaining that by continuing to smoke they would likely die sooner), 30 percent tried to quit. Similarly, when Claude Levy-Leboyer (1988) found that attitudes toward alcohol and drinking habits among French youth were effectively changed by fear-arousing pictures, the French government incorporated this kind of information in its TV spots.

But playing on fear won't always make a message more potent. Many people who have been made afraid of AIDS are *not* abstaining or using condoms. Many people who have been made to fear an early death from smoking continue to smoke. When the fear pertains to a pleasurable activity, notes Elliot Aronson (1997), the result often is not behavioral change but denial.

People may engage in denial because, when they aren't told how to avoid the danger, frightening messages can be overwhelming (Leventhal, 1970; Rogers & Mewborn, 1976). Fear-arousing messages are more effective if you lead people not only to fear the severity and likelihood of a threatened event but also to perceive an effective protective strategy (Maddux & Rogers, 1983). Anxiety-creating health messages about, say, the risks of high cholesterol can increase people's intentions to eat a low fat, low cholesterol diet (Millar & Millar, 1996).

Many ads aimed at reducing sexual risks aim both to arouse fear—"AIDS kills"—and to offer a protective strategy: abstain or wear a condom or save sex for a committed relationship. During the 1980s, fear of AIDS did persuade many men to alter their behavior. One study of 5,000 gay men found that as the AIDS crisis mushroomed between 1984 and 1986, the number saying they were celibate or monogamous rose from 14 to 39 percent (Fineberg, 1988).

Vividly imagined diseases seem a more likely threat than hard-to-picture diseases (Sherman & others, 1985). That little fact helps explain why health warnings like those on cigarette ads are so ineffective— "a yawnful concentration of legal jargon," say Timothy Brock and Laura Brannon (1991)—and hardly make a dent in the ad's visual impact. Making the warnings as vivid as the ad—with color photos of lung cancer surgery—makes them more effective in changing attitudes and intentions. This is especially so when the ad draws attention to a persuasive image rather than, as sexual images sometimes do, distracting the audience (Frey & Eagly, 1993). When it comes to persuasion, a pertinent, dramatic picture can indeed be worth a thousand words.

> "If those who have studied the art of writing are in accord on any one point, it is on this: the surest way to arouse and hold the attention of the reader is by being specific, definite, and concrete."
>
> William Strunk and E. B. White, *The Elements of Style*, 1979

Vivid propaganda often exploits fears. Streicher's *Der Stürmer* aroused fear with hundreds upon hundreds of unsubstantiated anecdotes about Jews who were said to have ground rats to make hash, seduced non-Jewish women, and cheated families out of their life savings. Streicher's appeals, like most Nazi propaganda, were emotional, not logical. The appeals also gave clear, specific instructions on how to combat "the danger": They listed Jewish businesses so readers would avoid them, encouraged readers to submit for publication the names of Germans who patronized Jewish shops and professionals, and directed readers to compile lists of Jews in their area (Bytwerk & Brooks, 1980). This was vivid hard-to-forget propaganda.

Then, after the Holocaust, there emerged the vivid diary of one girl, one story—"and so much impact," note Steven Sherman, Denise Beike and Kenneth Ryalls, in press). Hundreds of books have been written about the Nazi atrocities. Yet "one book by one girl has been translated into virtually every language and has sold more books than all the historical documentation of the Nazi occupation combined. More people, in fact, visit [the Anne Frank House] than any other site in Amsterdam, a city of countless museums and of much history."

Discrepancy

Picture the following scene: Wanda arrives home on spring vacation and hopes to convert her portly, middle-aged father to her new "health-fitness lifestyle." She runs five miles a day. Her father says his idea of exercise is "channel surfing." Wanda thinks, "Would I be more likely to get Dad off his duff by urging him to try a modest exercise program, say a daily walk, or by trying to get him involved in something strenuous, say a program of calisthenics and running? Maybe if I asked him to take up a rigorous exercise program he would compromise and at least take up something worthwhile. But then again maybe he'd think I'm crazy and do nothing."

Like Wanda, social psychologists can reason either way. Disagreement produces discomfort, and discomfort prompts people to change their opinions (recall from Chapter 4 the effects of dissonance). So perhaps greater disagreement will produce more change. But then again, a communicator who proclaims an uncomfortable message may get discredited. People who disagree with conclusions drawn by a newscaster rate the newscaster as more biased, inaccurate, and untrustworthy. People are more open to conclusions within their range of acceptability (Liberman & Chaiken, 1992; Zanna, 1993). So perhaps greater disagreement will produce *less* change.

Given these considerations, Elliot Aronson, Judith Turner, and Merrill Carlsmith (1963) reasoned that a *credible source*—one hard to discount—would elicit considerable opinion change when advocating a position *greatly discrepant* from the recipient's. Sure enough, when credible T. S. Eliot was said to have highly praised a disliked poem, people changed their opinion more than when he gave it faint praise. But when Agnes Stearns, a lowly university student, evaluated a disliked poem, faint praise was as persuasive as high praise. Thus, as Figure 7–3 shows, discrepancy and credibility *interact:* The effect of a large versus small discrepancy depends on whether the communicator is credible.

figure 7–3

Discrepancy interacts with communicator credibility.

Only a highly credible communicator maintains effectiveness when arguing an extreme position.

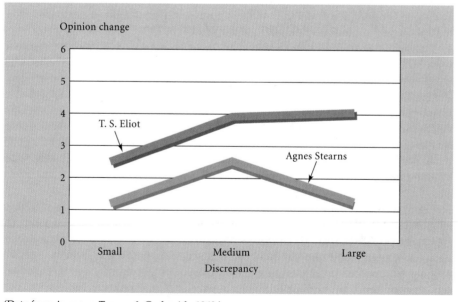

(Data from Aronson, Turner, & Carlsmith, 1963.)

So the answer to Wanda's question—"Should I argue an extreme position?"—is "It depends." Is Wanda in her adoring father's eyes a highly prestigious, authoritative source? If so, Wanda should push for a complete fitness program. If not, Wanda would be wise to make a more modest appeal.

The answer also depends on how involved her father is in the issue. Deeply involved people tend to accept only a narrow range of views. To them, a moderately discrepant message may seem foolishly radical, especially if the message argues an opposing view rather than being a more extreme version of a view they already agree with (Maio & others, 1996; Pallak & others, 1972; Petty & Cacioppo, 1979; Rhine & Severance, 1970). If Wanda's father has not yet thought or cared much about exercise, she can probably take a more extreme position than if he is strongly committed to not exercising. So *if you are a credible authority and your audience isn't much concerned with your issue, go for it:* Advocate a discrepant view.

One-sided versus two-sided appeals

Persuaders face another practical issue: how to deal with opposing arguments. Once again, common sense offers no clear answer. Acknowledging the opposing arguments might confuse the audience and weaken the case. On the other hand, a message might seem fairer, more disarming, if it recognizes the opposition's arguments.

After Germany's defeat in World War II, the Allies did not want soldiers to relax and think that the still ongoing war with Japan now would be easy. So social psychologist Carl Hovland and his colleagues (1949) designed two radio broadcasts arguing that the war in the Pacific would last at least two more years. One broadcast was one-sided; it did not acknowledge the existence of contradictory arguments, such as the advantage of fighting only one enemy instead of two. The other broadcast was two-sided; it mentioned and responded to the opposing arguments. As Figure 7–4 illustrates, the effectiveness of the message depended on the listener. A one-sided appeal was most effective with those who already

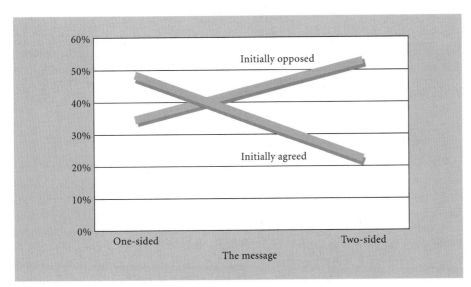

figure 7–4

The interaction of initial opinion with one- versus two-sidedness.

After Germany's defeat in World War II, Allied soldiers skeptical of a message suggesting Japan's strength were more persuaded by a two-sided communication. Soldiers initially agreeing with the message were strengthened more by a one-sided message.

(Data from Hovland, Lumsdaine, & Sheffield, 1949.)

"Opponents fancy they refute us when they repeat their own opinion and pay no attention to ours."

Goethe, *Maxims and Reflections,* early nineteenth century

agreed. An appeal that acknowledged opposing arguments worked better with those who disagreed.

Later experiments revealed that if people are (or will be) aware of opposing arguments, a two-sided presentation is more persuasive and enduring (Jones & Brehm, 1970; Lumsdaine & Janis, 1953). In simulated trials, a defense case becomes more credible when the defense brings up damaging evidence before the prosecution does (Williams & others, 1993). Apparently, a one-sided message stimulates an informed audience to think of counterarguments and to view the communicator as biased. Thus, a political candidate speaking to a politically informed group would indeed be wise to respond to the opposition. So *if your audience includes or will be exposed to opposing views, offer a two-sided appeal.*

This interaction effect typifies persuasion research. We might wish that persuasion variables had simple effects. (It would make this an easier chapter to study.) Alas, most variables, note Richard Petty and Duane Wegener (1998), "have complex effects—increasing persuasion in some situations and decreasing it in others." As students and scientists we cherish "Occam's razor"—seeking the simplest possible principles. But if human reality is complex, well, our principles will need to have some complexity as well.

Primacy versus recency

Imagine yourself a consultant to a prominent politician who must soon debate another prominent politician regarding a proposed arms limitation treaty. Three weeks before the vote, each politician is to appear on the nightly news and present a prepared statement. By the flip of a coin, your side receives the choice of whether to speak first or last. Knowing that you are a former social psychology student, everyone looks to you for advice.

You mentally scan your old books and lecture notes. Would first be best? People's preconceptions control their interpretations. Moreover, a belief, once formed, is difficult to discredit. So going first could give people ideas that would favorably bias how they would perceive and interpret the second speech. Besides, people may pay most attention to what comes first. But then again, people remember recent things best. Might it really be more effective to speak last?

Your first line of reasoning predicts what is most common, a **primacy effect:** Information presented early is most persuasive. First impressions *are* important. For example, can you sense a difference between these two descriptions?

primacy effect
other things being equal, information presented first usually has the most influence

- John is intelligent, industrious, impulsive, critical, stubborn, and envious.
- John is envious, stubborn, critical, impulsive, industrious, and intelligent.

When Solomon Asch (1946) gave these sentences to university students, those who read the adjectives in the intelligent-to-envious order rated the person more positively than did those given the envious-to-intelligent order. The earlier information seemed to color their interpretation of the later information, producing the primacy effect. A similar effect occurs in experiments where people succeed on a guessing task 50 percent of the time. Those whose successes come early seem more able than those whose successes come mostly after early failures (Jones & others, 1968; Langer & Roth, 1975; McAndrew, 1981).

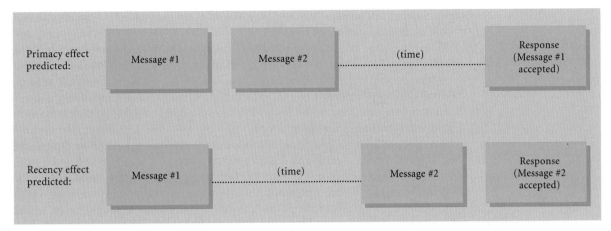

figure 7–5

Primacy effect versus recency effect.

When two persuasive messages are back to back and the audience then responds at some later time, the first message has the advantage (primacy effect). When the two messages are separated in time and the audience responds soon after the second message, the second message has the advantage (recency effect).

Is primacy the rule in persuasion as well as judgment? Norman Miller and Donald Campbell (1959) gave university students a condensed transcript from an actual civil trial. They placed the plaintiff's testimony and arguments in one block, those for the defense in another. The students read both blocks. When they returned a week later to declare their opinions, most sided with the information they had read first. Using the transcript of an actual criminal case, Gary Wells and his colleagues (1985) found a similar primacy effect when they varied the timing of a defense attorney's opening statement. The statement was more effective if presented *before* the prosecution's presentation of the evidence.

What about the opposite possibility? We have all experienced what the book of Proverbs observed: "The one who first states a case seems right, until the other comes and cross-examines." So will our better memory for recent information ever create a **recency effect**? We know from our experience (as well as from memory experiments) that today's events can temporarily outweigh significant past events. To test this, Miller and Campbell gave another group of students one block of testimony to read. A week later the researchers had them read the second block and then immediately state their opinions. Now the results were just the reverse—a recency effect. Apparently the first block of arguments, being a week old, had largely faded from memory.

Forgetting creates the recency effect (1) when enough time separates the two messages *and* (2) when the audience commits itself soon after the second message. When the two messages are back to back, followed by a time gap, a primacy effect usually occurs (Figure 7–5). This is especially so when the first message stimulates thinking (Haugtvedt & Wegener, 1994). So what advice would you now give to the political debater?

How is it said? The channel of communication

Active experience or passive reception?

In Chapter 4 we noted that our actions shape who we are. When we act, we amplify the idea behind what we've done, especially when we feel responsible. We also noted that attitudes rooted in our own experience—rather than learned secondhand—are more likely to endure and to affect our behavior. Compared to

recency effect information presented last sometimes has the most influence. Recency effects are less common than primacy effects.

channel of communication the way the message is delivered—whether face to face, in writing, on film, or in some other way

attitudes formed passively, experience-based attitudes are more confident, more stable, and less vulnerable to attack.

Commonsense psychology nevertheless places faith in the power of written words. How do we try to get people out to a campus event? We post notices. How do we get drivers to slow down and keep their eyes on the road? We put "Drive Carefully" messages on billboards. How do we discourage students from dropping garbage on campus? We litter campus bulletin boards and mailboxes with antilitter messages.

Are people so easily persuaded? Consider two well-intentioned efforts. At one university a weeklong anti-litter campaign urged students by using slogans such as, "Let's clean up our trash." Posters using such slogans were displayed in prominent places across campus, and flyers using the slogans were placed in students' mailboxes each morning. The day before the campaign began, social psychologist Raymond Paloutzian (1979) placed litter near a trash can along a well-traveled sidewalk. Then he stepped back to record the behavior of 180 passers-by. No one picked up anything. On the last day of the campaign he repeated the test with 180 more passers-by. Did the pedestrians now race one another in their zeal to comply with the appeals? Hardly. Only 2 of the 180 picked up the trash.

Are spoken appeals more persuasive? Not necessarily. Those of us who do public speaking, as teachers or persuaders, become so easily enamored of our spoken words that we are tempted to overestimate their power. Ask university students what aspect of their school experience has been most valuable or what they remember from their first year, and few, I am sad to say, recall the brilliant lectures that we faculty remember giving.

Thomas Crawford (1974) and his associates tested the impact of the spoken word by going to the homes of people from twelve churches shortly before and after they heard sermons opposing racial bigotry and injustice. When asked during the second interview whether they had heard or read anything about racial prejudice or discrimination since the previous interview, only 10 percent spontaneously recalled the sermons. When the remaining 90 percent were asked directly whether their priest had "talked about prejudice or discrimination in the last couple of weeks," more than 30 percent denied hearing such a sermon. It is therefore hardly surprising that the sermons left racial attitudes unaffected.

When you stop to think about it, the preacher has so many hurdles to surmount, it's a wonder that preaching affects as many people as it does. As Figure 7–6 shows, persuasive speakers must deliver a message that not only gets attention but also is understandable, convincing, memorable, and compelling. A carefully thought-out appeal must consider each of these steps in the persuasion process.

Passively received appeals, however, are not always futile. My drugstore sells two brands of aspirin, one heavily advertised and one unadvertised. Apart from slight differences in how fast each tablet crumbles in your mouth, any pharmacist will tell you the two brands are identical. Aspirin is aspirin. Our bodies cannot tell the difference. But our pocketbooks can. The advertised brand sells for three times the price of the unadvertised brand. And sell it does, to millions of people.

Cigarettes also sell, thanks partly to effective advertising. The tobacco industry has claimed that its ads only aim to persuade smokers to switch, not to lure

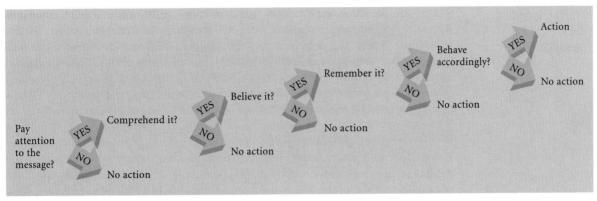

(Adapted from McGuire, 1978.)

figure 7–6
To elicit action, a persuasive message must clear several hurdles. What is crucial is not so much remembering the message itself as remembering one's own thoughts in response.

new smokers. But its ads have also helped expand the total customer base. Since the 1880s, each of four tobacco advertising drives has been associated with increased 14- to 17-year-old smoking rates—among the sex that the advertising targeted (Pierce & others, 1994, 1995).

With such power, can the media help a wealthy political candidate buy an election? Joseph Grush (1980) analyzed candidate expenditures in a number of elections in 1976 and found that those who spent the most in any election usually got the most votes. As Grush noted, the effect of this exposure was often to make an unfamiliar candidate into a familiar one. (This parallels laboratory experiments in which mere exposure to unfamiliar stimuli breeds liking—see Chapter 11.) Their message, too, may gain with repetition: Mere repetition can make things believable. People rate trivial statements like "Mercury has a higher boiling point than copper" as more truthful if they read and rated them a week before. Researcher Hal Arkes (1990) views such findings as "scary." As political manipulators know, believable lies can displace hard truths. Repeated clichés can cover complex realities.

Would the media be as effective with familiar candidates and important issues? Probably not. Researchers have time and again found little effect of political advertising on voters' attitudes in larger-scale elections (although, of course, even a small effect could swing a close election) (Kinder & Sears, 1985; McGuire, 1986).

In study after study, most people agree that mass media influence attitudes—other people's attitudes, but not their own.

(Duck & others, 1995).

Cigarette advertising companies have correlated with smoking increases. This photo shows models practicing the "correct" pucker and blow technique for a 1950s TV ad.

Because passively received appeals are sometimes effective and sometimes not, can we specify in advance the topics on which a persuasive appeal will be successful? There is a simple rule: Persuasion *decreases* as the significance and familiarity of the issue *increase*. On minor issues, such as which brand of aspirin to buy, it's easy to demonstrate the media's power. On more familiar and important issues, such as racial attitudes in racially tense cities, persuading people is like trying to push a piano uphill. It is not impossible, but one shove won't do it.

Personal versus media influence

Persuasion studies demonstrate that the major influence upon us is not the media but our contact with people. Two field experiments illustrate the strength of personal influence. Some years ago, Samuel Eldersveld and Richard Dodge (1954) studied political persuasion in a local election. They divided citizens intending not to vote for a revision of the city charter into three groups. Of those exposed only to what they saw and heard in the mass media, 19 percent voted for the revision on election day. Of a second group, who received four mailings in support of the revision, 45 percent voted for it. People in a third group were visited personally and given the appeal face to face, and 75 percent of these people cast their votes for it.

In another field experiment, a research team led by John Farquhar and Nathan Maccoby (1977; Maccoby & Alexander, 1980; Maccoby, 1980) tried to reduce the frequency of heart disease among middle-aged adults in three small California cities. To check the relative effectiveness of personal and media influence, they interviewed and medically examined some 1,200 people before the project began and at the end of each of the following three years. Residents of Tracy, California, received no persuasive appeals other than those occurring in their regular media. In Gilroy, California, a two-year multimedia campaign used TV, radio, newspapers, and direct mail to teach people about coronary risk and what they could do to reduce it. In Watsonville, California, this media campaign was supplemented by personal contacts with two thirds of those whose blood pressure, weight, and age put them in a high-risk group. Using behavior-modification principles, the researchers helped people set specific goals and reinforced their successes.

As Figure 7–7 shows, after one, two, and three years the high-risk people in Tracy (the control town) were about as much at risk as before. High-risk people in Gilroy, which was deluged with media appeals, improved their health habits and were now somewhat less at risk. Those in Watsonville, who also received the personal contacts, changed most.

Do you recognize the potency of personal influence in your own experience? In retrospect, most university students say they have learned more from their friends and other students than from contact with books or professors. Educational researchers have confirmed the students' intuition: Out-of-class personal relationships powerfully influence how students mature during university (Astin, 1972; Wilson & others, 1975).

Although face-to-face influence is usually greater than media influence, we should not underestimate the media's power. Those who personally influence our opinions must get their ideas somewhere, and often their sources are the media. Elihu Katz (1957) observed that much of the media's effects operate in a **two-step flow of communication**—from media to opinion leaders to the rank

two-step flow of communication
the process by which media influence often occurs through opinion leaders, who in turn influence others

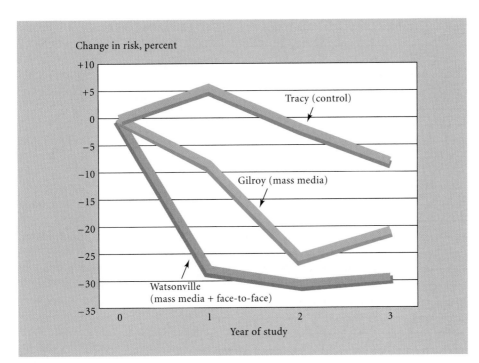

figure 7–7

Percentage change from baseline (0) in coronary risk after one, two, or three years of health education.

(Data from Maccoby, 1980.)

and file. If I want to evaluate computer equipment, I defer to the opinions of my son, who gets many of his ideas from the printed page.

The two-step flow model oversimplifies. The media also communicate directly with mass audiences. But the model does remind us that media influences penetrate the culture in subtle ways. Even if the media had little direct effect upon people's attitudes, they could still have a big indirect effect. Those rare children who grow up without watching television do not grow up beyond television's influence. Unless they live as hermits, they will join in TV-imitative play on the school ground. They will ask their parents for the TV-related toys their friends have. They will beg or demand to watch their friend's favorite programs. Parents can just say no, but they cannot switch off television's influence.

Lumping together all media, from mass mailings to television, also oversimplifies. Studies comparing different media find that the more lifelike the medium, the more persuasive its message. Thus the order of persuasiveness seems to be: live, videotaped, audiotaped, and written. But to add to the complexity, messages are best *comprehended* and *recalled* when written. Comprehension is one of the first steps in the persuasion process (recall Figure 7–6). So Shelly Chaiken and Alice Eagly (1978) reasoned that if a message is difficult to comprehend, persuasion should be greatest when the message is written. They gave students easy or difficult messages in writing, on audiotape, or videotape. Figure 7–8 displays their results: Difficult messages were indeed most persuasive when written, easy messages when videotaped. By drawing attention to the communicator and away from the message itself, the TV medium also draws attention to peripheral cues, such as the communicator's attractiveness (Chaiken & Eagly, 1983).

figure 7–8

Easy-to-understand messages are most persuasive when videotaped. Difficult messages are most persuasive when written. Thus the difficulty of the message interacts with the medium to determine persuasiveness.

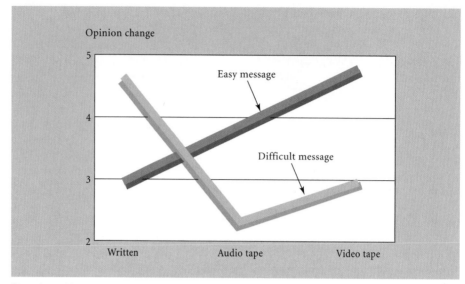

(Data from Chaiken & Eagly, 1978.)

To whom is it said? The audience

As we saw in Chapter 6, people's traits often don't predict their response to social influence. A particular trait may enhance one step in the persuasion process (Figure 7–6) but work against another. Take self-esteem. People with low self-esteem are often slow to comprehend a message and therefore hard to persuade. Those with high self-esteem may comprehend yet remain confident of their own opinions; thus self-esteem alone won't directly predict persuadability.

behind the scenes

My interest in studying persuasion was spurred when my graduate advisor, Alice Eagly, pointed me to William McGuire's analysis of media effects. McGuire reasoned that different factors might affect someone's *comprehending* a persuasive argument and their *yielding* to it. This took me back to my preteen experience watching John F. Kennedy demolish (or so I thought) Richard Nixon during their presidential debates. Yet, I later learned, the perception that Kennedy "won" may have been stronger among people who *viewed* the debates than among people who only *heard* them or *read* them. Had my verdict been influenced more than I'd imagined by my hero's attractive appearance and bearing?

My master's thesis research (Figure 7–8) confirmed that the medium of communication indeed matters. Moreover, this led to the idea that people sometimes process messages *heuristically,* basing judgments on extrinsic factors such as the communicator's likability or attractiveness. I like to take credit for this idea, but it's high time I thanked Alice Eagly, Bill McGuire, and President Kennedy for their input.

Shelly Chaiken
New York University

The conclusion: People with moderate self-esteem are the easiest to influence (Rhodes & Wood, 1992).

Let's also consider two other characteristics of those who receive a message: their age and their thoughtfulness.

How old are they?

People today tend to have different social and political attitudes depending on their age. There are two explanations for the difference. One is a *life cycle explanation:* Attitudes change (for example, become more conservative) as people grow older. The other is a *generational explanation:* The attitudes older people adopted when they were young persist largely unchanged; because these attitudes are different from those now being adopted by young people today, a generation gap develops.

The evidence mostly supports the generational explanation. In surveying and resurveying groups of younger and older people over several years, the attitudes of older people usually change less than do those of young people. As David Sears (1979, 1986) puts it, researchers have "almost invariably found generational rather than life cycle effects."

The point is not that older adults are inflexible; most people in their fifties and sixties have more liberal sexual and racial attitudes than they had in their thirties and forties (Glenn, 1980, 1981). Few of us are utterly uninfluenced by changing cultural norms. The point is that the teens and early twenties are important formative years (Krosnick & Alwin, 1989), and the attitudes formed then tend to be stable thereafter. Young people might therefore be advised to choose their social influences—the groups they join, the media they imbibe, the roles they adopt—carefully.

A striking example: During the late 1930s and early 1940s, students at one small prestigious school—women from privileged, conservative families—encountered a free-spirited environment led by a left-leaning young faculty. One of those faculty, social psychologist Theodore Newcomb, later denied the faculty was trying to make "good little liberals" out of its students. Nevertheless, they succeeded. The students became much more liberal than was typical of those from their social backgrounds. Moreover, attitudes formed at the school endured. A half-century later, the women, now seventyish, voted Democratic by a 3 to 1 margin in the 1984 presidential election, while other seventyish university-educated women were voting Republican by a 3 to 1 margin (Alwin & others, 1991). The views embraced at an impressionable time had survived a lifetime of wider experience.

Experiences during adolescence and early adulthood are formative partly because they make deep and lasting impressions. When Howard Schuman and Jacqueline Scott (1989) asked people to name the one or two most important world events over the last half century, most recalled events from their teens or early twenties. For those who experienced the Great Depression or World War II as 16- to 24-year-olds, those events overshadowed the civil rights movement and the Kennedy assassination of the early sixties, the Vietnam war and moon landing of the late sixties, and the women's movement of the seventies—all of which were imprinted on the minds of those who experienced them as 16- to 24-year-olds. We may therefore expect that for today's young adults the memorable turning points in world history will be a phenomenon such as the explosion of e-mail and the Web.

What are they thinking?

In central route persuasion, what's crucial is not the message itself but what responses it evokes in a person's mind. Our minds are not sponges that soak up whatever pours over them. If the message summons favorable thoughts, it persuades us. If it provokes us to think of contrary arguments, we remain unpersuaded.

Forewarned is forearmed—If you care enough to counterargue.   What circumstances breed counterarguing? One is a *warning* that someone is going to try to persuade you. If you had to tell your family that you wanted to drop out of school, you would likely anticipate their pleading with you to stay. So you might develop a list of arguments to counter every conceivable argument they might make. Jonathan Freedman and David Sears (1965) demonstrated the difficulty of their trying to persuade you under such circumstances. They warned one group of high schoolers that they were going to hear a talk: "Why Teenagers Should Not Be Allowed to Drive." Those forewarned did not budge. Others, not forewarned, did.

Sneak attacks on attitudes are especially useful with involved people. Given several minutes' forewarning, such people will prepare defenses (Chen & others, 1992; Petty & Cacioppo, 1977, 1979). But when people regard an issue as trivial, even blatant propaganda can be effective. Would you bother to construct counterarguments for two brands of toothpaste? Similarly, when someone slips a premise into a casual conversation—"Why was Sue hostile to Mark?"—people often accept the premise (that Sue was, in fact, hostile) (Swann, Giuliano, & Wegner, 1982).

Distraction disarms counterarguing.   Verbal persuasion is also enhanced by distracting people with something that attracts their attention just enough to inhibit counterarguing (Festinger & Maccoby, 1964; Keating & Brock, 1974; Osterhouse & Brock, 1970). Political ads often use this technique. The words promote the candidate, and the visual images keep us occupied so we don't analyze the words. Distraction is especially effective when the message is simple (Harkins & Petty, 1981; Regan & Cheng, 1973).

This research on how persuasion increases as counterarguing decreases makes me wonder: Are fast talkers more persuasive partly because they leave us less time to counterargue? Are easy messages less persuasive when written because readers can stop to counterargue? And does television shape important attitudes more through its subtle messages (for example, concerning gender roles) than through its explicit persuasive appeals? After all, if we don't notice a message, we cannot counterargue against it.

Uninvolved audiences use peripheral cues.   Recall again the two routes to persuasion—the central route of systematic thinking and the peripheral route of heuristic cues. Like the road through town, the central route has starts and stops as the mind analyzes arguments and formulates responses. Like the highway around town, the peripheral route zips people to their destination. Analytical people—those with a high *need for cognition*—prefer central routes (Cacioppo & others, 1996). Image-conscious people, who care less about whether they're right or wrong than about what sort of impression they are making, are quicker to respond to such peripheral cues as the communicator's attractiveness and the pleasantness of the surroundings (Snyder, 1989).

> "To be forewarned and therefore forearmed . . . is eminently rational if our belief is true; but if our belief is a delusion, this same forewarning and forearming would obviously be the method whereby the delusion rendered itself incurable."
>
> C. S. Lewis, *Screwtape Proposes a Toast*, 1965

figure 7–9

Attitude accessibility and persuasion.

When people's attitudes are accessible they process information through the central route, but when their attitudes are less accessible they process information through the peripheral route. (Data from Fabrigar, et al., 1998.)

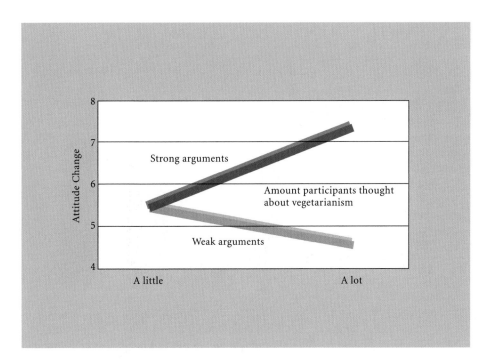

But the issue matters, too. All of us struggle actively with issues that involve us while making snap judgments about things that matter little (Johnson & Eagly, 1990; Maio & Olson, 1990). The more we think about an issue the more we take the central route. Consider the following study conducted by Queen's University's Leandre Fabrigar and his colleagues (1998). They made some students think a lot about their attitudes toward vegetarianism by asking them a lot of questions about it, others were only asked about their views once. As you can see in Figure 7-9 those who had thought a lot about their views were persuaded by strong arguments about vegetarianism but were uninfluenced by weak arguments. But for people who had not thought much about the topic, the strength of the arguments did not matter.

This basically simple theory—that what we think in response to a message is crucial, especially if we are motivated and able to think about it—helps us understand several findings. For example, we more readily believe expert communicators, because when we trust the source we think favorable thoughts and are less likely to counterargue. When we mistrust the source, we are more likely to defend our preconceptions by refuting the disagreeable message.

The theory has also generated many predictions, most of which have been confirmed by Petty, Cacioppo, and others (Axsom & others, 1987; Hafer & others; Harkins & Petty, 1987; Leippe & Elkin, 1987). Many experiments have explored ways to stimulate people's thinking—by using *rhetorical questions,* by presenting *multiple speakers* (for example, having three speakers each give one argument instead of one speaker giving three), by making people *feel responsible* for evaluating or passing along the message, by using *relaxed* rather than standing postures, by *repeating* the message, and by getting people's *undistracted*

behind the scenes

We spent many hours during graduate school trying to convince each other of our personal views. After these marathon debates, it seemed that the vulnerability of our attitudes depended on the merits of our arguments. We therefore were surprised what happened when, for a class project, we gained admittance to an introductory "cult" meeting. The cult leaders achieved success less by relying on arguments than by using peripheral cues such as source attractiveness, social approval, and the trappings of credibility. We left the meeting convinced that there were multiple routes by which attitudes change. Some people, in some situations, respond more to a central (argument-based) route; others, in other situations, respond more to peripheral cues. That basic idea is the core of our theory of persuasion, and the individual differences we observed gave birth to our research on need for cognition.

Richard Petty and John Cacioppo
Ohio State University

attention. Their consistent finding with each of these techniques: *Stimulating thinking makes strong messages more persuasive and* (because of counterarguing) *weak messages less persuasive.*

The theory also has practical implications. Effective communicators care not only about their images and their messages but also about how their audience is likely to react. How they will react depends not only on their interest in the issue but also on their dispositions—their analytical inclinations, their tolerance for uncertainty, their need to be true to themselves (Cacioppo & others, 1996; Kruglanski & others, 1993; Snyder & DeBono, 1987; Sorrentino & others, 1988).

So are people likely to think and remember thoughts that favor the persuader's point of view? If the answer is yes, quality arguments will be persuasive. One important byproduct of processing information through the central route is that such processing makes us remember the material better. The best instructors tend to get students to think actively. They ask rhetorical questions, provide intriguing examples, challenge students with difficult problems, etc. All these techniques are likely to foster processing information through the central route to persuasion. In classes where the instruction is less engaging you can provide your own central processing. If you think about the material and elaborate on the arguments you are likely to do better in the course.

Summing up

What makes persuasion effective? Researchers have explored four factors: the communicator, the message, the channel, and the audience.

Credible communicators are perceived as trustworthy experts. People who speak unhesitatingly, who talk fast, and who look listeners straight in the eye seem more credible. So are people who argue against their own self-interest. An attractive communicator also is effective on matters of taste and personal values.

Associating a message with good feelings makes it more convincing. People often make snappier, less reflective judgments while in good moods. Some messages that arouse fear can also be effective, perhaps because they are vivid and memorable.

How discrepant a message should be from an audience's existing opinions depends on the communicator's credibility. And whether a message is most persuasive when it presents only one position or when it introduces the opposing side as well depends on the listener's sophistication, agreement, and likelihood of encountering opposing arguments. When the audience already agrees with the message, is unaware of opposing arguments, and is unlikely later to consider the opposition, a one-sided appeal is most effective. With more sophisticated audiences or with those not already in agreement, two-sided messages are most successful.

When two sides of an issue are included, do the arguments presented first or second have the advantage? The common finding is a primacy effect. If a time gap separates the presentations, the effect of the early information diminishes; if a decision is made right after hearing the second side, which is therefore still fresh in the mind, the result will likely be a recency effect.

Another important consideration is *how* the message is communicated. The mass media can be effective when the issue is minor (such as which brand of aspirin to buy) or unfamiliar (such as deciding between two otherwise unknown political candidates).

Finally, it matters *who* receives the message. What does the audience think while receiving a message? Do they think agreeing thoughts? Do they counterargue? The age of the audience also makes a difference. Researchers who have resurveyed people over time find that young people's attitudes are less stable.

Case studies in persuasion: Cult indoctrination

What persuasion and group influence principles are harnessed by New Religious movements ("cults")?

On March 22, 1997, Marshall Herff Applewhite and 37 of his disciples decided the time had come to shed their bodies—mere "containers"—and be whisked up to a UFO trailing Haley-Bopp Comet, en route to heaven's gate. So they put themselves to sleep by mixing phenobarbital into pudding or applesauce, washing it down with vodka, and then fixing plastic bags over their heads so they would suffocate in their slumber. On that same day, a cottage in the French Canadian village of St. Casimir exploded in an inferno, consuming five people—the latest of 74 members of the Order of the Solar Temple to have committed suicide in Canada, Switzerland, and France. All were hoping to be transported to the star Sirius, nine light-years away. With a new millennium nearly upon us as this book is being written, predictions abound of more cult mythology and mass suicides to come. Fringe religion meets the *X-Files*.

The question on many minds: What persuades people to leave behind their former beliefs and join these mental chain gangs? Shall we attribute their strange behaviors to strange personalities? Or do their experiences illustrate the common dynamics of social influence and persuasion?

Bear two things in mind: First, this is hindsight analysis. It uses persuasion principles as categories for explaining, after the fact, a fascinating social phenomenon. Second, explaining *why* people believe something says nothing about the *truth* of their beliefs. That is a logically separate issue. A psychology of religion might tell us *why* a theist believes in God and an atheist disbelieves, but it cannot tell us who is right. Explaining either belief does not explain it away. So if someone tries to discount your beliefs by saying, "You just believe that because . . . ," you might recall Archbishop William Temple's reply to a questioner who opened the discussion after the archbishop's address with this challenge: "Well, of course, Archbishop, the point is that you believe what you believe because of the way you were brought up." To which the Archbishop replied: "That is as it may be. But the fact remains that you believe I believe what I believe because of the way I was brought up, because of the way you were brought up."

In recent decades, several **cults**—which social scientists often call New Religious movements—have gained much publicity: Sun Myung Moon's Unification Church, Jim Jones's People's Temple, David Koresh's Branch Davidians, and Marshall Applewhite's Heaven's Gate. The Reverend Moon's mixture of Christianity, anticommunism, and glorification of Moon himself as a new messiah attracted a worldwide following. In response to Moon's declaration, "What I wish must be your wish," many committed themselves and their incomes to the Unification Church. How were they persuaded to do so?

In 1978 in Guyana, 914 followers of the Reverend Jones, who had followed him there from San Francisco, shocked the world when they died by following his order to down a strawberry drink laced with tranquilizers, painkillers, and a lethal dose of cyanide.

cult (also called New Religious movement)
a group typically characterized by (1) the distinctive ritual of its devotion to a god or a person, (2) isolation from the surrounding "evil" culture, and (3) a charismatic leader. (A *sect*, by contrast, is a spinoff from a major religion.)

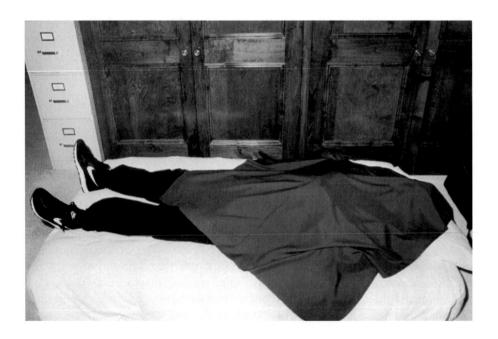

One of 37 suicide victims seeking heaven's gate.

In 1993, high-school dropout David Koresh used his talent for memorizing Scripture and mesmerizing people to seize control of a faction of a sect called the Branch Davidians. Over time, members were gradually relieved of their bank accounts and possessions. Koresh also persuaded the men to live celibately while he slept with their wives and daughters, and he convinced his 19 "wives" that they should bear his children. Under siege after a shootout that killed six members and four federal agents, Koresh told his followers they would soon die and go with him straight to heaven. When the federal agents rammed the compound with tanks, hoping to inject tear gas, cult members set it afire, consuming 86 people in the flames.

Marshall Applewhite was not similarly tempted to command sexual favors. Having been fired from two music teaching jobs for homosexual affairs with students, he sought sexless devotion by castration, as had 7 of the other 17 Heaven's Gate men who died with him (Chua-Eoan, 1997; Gardner, 1997). While in a psychiatric hospital in 1971, Applewhite had linked up with nurse and astrology dabbler Bonnie Lu Nettles, who gave the intense and charismatic Applewhite a cosmological vision of a route to "the next level." Preaching with passion, he persuaded his followers to renounce families, sex, drugs, and personal money with promises of a spaceship voyage to salvation.

How could such things happen? What persuaded these people to give such total allegiance? Shall we make disposition explanations—by blaming the victims? Shall we dismiss them as gullible kooks or dumb weirdos? Or can familiar principles of conformity, compliance, dissonance, persuasion, and group influence explain their behavior—putting them on common ground with the rest of us who in our own ways are shaped by such forces?

Attitudes follow behavior

Compliance breeds acceptance

As Chapter 4 showed over and again, people usually internalize commitments made voluntarily, publicly, and repeatedly. Cult leaders seem to know this. New converts soon learn that membership is no trivial matter. They are quickly made active members of the team. Rituals within the cult community, and public canvassing and fund-raising, strengthen the initiates' identities as members. As those in social-psychological experiments come to believe in what they bear witness to (Aronson & Mills, 1959; Gerard & Mathewson, 1966), so cult initiates become committed advocates. The greater the personal commitment, the more the need to justify it.

The foot-in-the-door phenomenon

How are we induced to make commitments? Seldom by an abrupt, conscious decision. One does not just decide, "I'm through with mainstream religion. I'm gonna find a cult." Nor do cult recruiters approach people on the street with, "Hi. I'm a Moonie. Care to join us?" Rather, the recruitment strategy exploits the foot-in-the-door principle. Unification Church recruiters would invite people to a dinner and then to a weekend of warm fellowship and discussions of philosophies of life. At the weekend retreat, they encouraged the attenders to join them in songs, activities, and discussion. Potential converts were then urged to sign up for longer training retreats. Eventually the activities became more arduous—soliciting contributions and attempting to convert others.

© 1982, The New Yorker Magazine, Inc.

"You go on home without me, Irene. I'm going to join this man's cult."

Hundreds of thousands of people in recent years have been recruited by members of some 2500 religious cults, but seldom through an abrupt decision.

Jim Jones also used this foot-in-the-door technique. Psychologist Robert Ornstein (1991) recalls Jones explaining his recruitment successes to the San Francisco mayor and himself. Unlike other street solicitors on behalf of the poor, Jones's operators would ask passers-by merely to "Help for just five minutes at work by folding and mailing a few envelopes." Having done so, Jones explained, "they came back for more. You know, once I get somebody, I can get them to do anything."

Once into the cult, monetary offerings were voluntary. He next inaugurated a required 10-percent-of-income contribution, which soon increased to 25 percent. Finally, he ordered members to turn over to him everything they owned. Workloads also became progressively more demanding. Former cult member Grace Stoen recalls the gradual progress:

> Nothing was ever done drastically. That's how Jim Jones got away with so much. You slowly gave up things and slowly had to put up with more, but it was always done very gradually. It was amazing, because you would sit up sometimes and say, wow, I really have given up a lot. I really am putting up with a lot. But he did it so slowly that you figured, I've made it this far, what the hell is the difference? (Conway & Siegelman, 1979, p. 236)

Persuasive elements

We can also analyze cult persuasion using the factors discussed in this chapter (and summarized in Figure 7–10): *Who* (the communicator) said *what* (the message) to *whom* (the audience)?

The communicator

Successful cults have a charismatic leader—someone who attracts and directs the members. As in experiments on persuasion, a credible communicator is someone the audience perceives as expert and trustworthy—for example, as "Father" Moon.

Jim Jones used "psychic readings" to establish his credibility. Newcomers were asked to identify themselves as they entered the church before services. Then one of his aides would call the person's home and say, "Hi. We're doing a survey, and we'd like to ask you some questions." During the service, one ex-member recalled, Jones would call out the person's name and say

> Have you ever seen me before? Well, you live in such and such a place, your phone number is such and such, and in your living room you've got this, that, and the other, and on your sofa you've got such and such a pillow. . . . Now do you remember me ever being in your house? (Conway & Siegelman, 1979, p. 234)

THE FAR SIDE   By GARY LARSON

© 1987 Universal Press Syndicate   1-17

"Listen—just take one of our brochures and see what we're all about. . . . In the meantime, you may wish to ask yourself, 'Am I a happy cow?'"

Some persuasive techniques are particularly difficult to resist.

Trust is another aspect of credibility. Cult researcher Margaret Singer (1979) noted that middle-class Caucasian youths are more vulnerable because they are more trusting. They lack the "street smarts" of lower-class youths (who know how to resist a hustle) and the wariness of upper-class youths (who have been warned of kidnappers since childhood). Many cult members have been recruited by friends or relatives, people they trust (Stark & Bainbridge, 1980).

The message

To lonely or depressed people, the vivid, emotional messages and the warmth and acceptance with which the group showers them can be strikingly appealing: Trust the master, join the family; we have the answer, the "one way." The

figure 7–10

Variables known to affect the impact of persuasive communications.

In real life, these variables may interact; the effect of one may depend on the level of another.

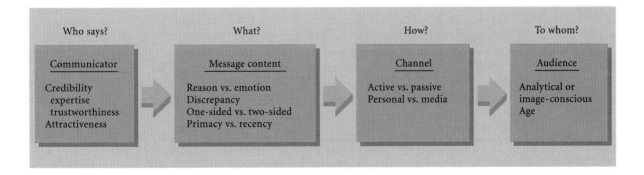

Who says?	What?	How?	To whom?

Communicator
Credibility
  expertise
  trustworthiness
Attractiveness
	Message content
	Reason vs. emotion
	Discrepancy
	One-sided vs. two-sided
	Primacy vs. recency
		Channel
		Active vs. passive
		Personal vs. media
			Audience
			Analytical or
			image-conscious
			Age

message echoes through channels as varied as lectures, small-group discussions, and direct social pressure.

The audience

Recruits are often young—people under 25 and still at that comparatively open age before attitudes and values stabilize. Some, such as the followers of Jim Jones, are less educated people who like the simplicity of the message and find it difficult to counterargue. But most are educated, middle-class people who, taken by the ideals, overlook the contradictions in those who profess selflessness and practice greed, who pretend concern and behave indifferently.

Potential converts often are at a turning point in their lives, facing a personal crisis, or vacationing or living away from home. They have needs; the cult offers them an answer (Singer, 1979; Lofland & Stark, 1965). Gail Maeder had joined Heaven's Gate after her T-shirt shop had failed. David Moore joined when he was 19, just out of high school, and searching for direction. Times of social and economic upheaval are especially conducive to an ayatollah or a "father" who can make apparent simple sense out of the confusion (O'Dea, 1968; Sales, 1972).

Group effects

Cults also illustrate the next chapter's theme: the power of a group to shape members' views and behavior. The cult typically separates members from their previous social support systems and isolates them with other cultists. There may then occur what Rodney Stark and William Bainbridge (1980) call a "social implosion": External ties weaken until the group socially collapses inward, each person engaging only with other group members. Cut off from families and former friends, they lose access to counterarguments. The group now offers identity and defines reality. Because the cult frowns on or punishes disagreements, the apparent consensus helps eliminate any lingering doubts.

Marshall Applewhite and Bonnie Nettles (who died of cancer in 1985) at first formed their own group of two, reinforcing each other's aberrant thinking—a phenomenon that psychiatrists call *folie à deux* (French for "insanity of two"). As others joined them, the group's social isolation facilitated more peculiar thinking. As conspiracy theory internet discussion groups illustrate (Heaven's Gate was skilled in internet recruiting), virtual groups can likewise foster paranoia.

Contrary to the idea that cults turn hapless people into mindless robots, these techniques—increasing behavioral commitments, persuasion, and group isolation—do not have unlimited power. The Unification Church has successfully recruited fewer than 1 in 10 people who attend its workshops (Ennis & Verrilli, 1989). Most who joined Heaven's Gate had left before that fateful day. David Koresh ruled with a mix of persuasion, intimidation, and violence. As Jim Jones made his demands more extreme, he, too, increasingly had to control people with intimidation. He used threats of harm to those who fled the community, beatings for noncompliance, and drugs to neutralize disagreeable members. By the end, he was as much an arm twister as a mind bender.

Moreover, cult influence techniques are in some ways similar to techniques used by groups more familiar to us. Fraternity and sorority members have reported that the initial "love bombing" of potential cult recruits is not unlike their own "rush" period. Members lavish prospective pledges with attention and make them feel special. During the pledge period, new members are somewhat isolated, cut off from old friends who did not pledge. They spend time

Military training in El Salvador: Terrorist and commando organizations create cohesion and commitment through some of the same tactics used by cult leaders.

studying the history and rules of their new group. They suffer and commit time on its behalf. They are expected to comply with all its demands. Not surprisingly, the result is usually a committed new member.

Much the same is true of some therapeutic communities for recovering drug and alcohol abusers. Zealous self-help groups form a cohesive "social cocoon," have intense beliefs, and exert a profound influence on members' behavior (Galanter, 1989, 1990).

Another constructive use of persuasion is in counseling and psychotherapy, which social-counseling psychologist Stanley Strong views "as a branch of applied social psychology" (1978, p. 101). Like Strong, psychiatrist Jerome Frank (1974, 1982) recognized years ago that it takes persuasion to change self-defeating attitudes and behaviors. Frank noted that the psychotherapy setting, like cults and zealous self-help groups, provides (1) a supportive, confiding social relationship, (2) an offer of expertise and hope, (3) a special rationale or myth that explains one's difficulties and offers a new perspective, and (4) a set of rituals and learning experiences that promises a new sense of peace and happiness.

I chose the examples of fraternities, sororities, self-help groups, and psychotherapy not to disparage them but to illustrate two concluding observations. First, if we attribute New Religious movements to the leader's mystical force or to the followers' peculiar weaknesses, we may delude ourselves into thinking we are immune to social control techniques. In truth, our own groups—and countless salespeople, political leaders, and other persuaders—successfully use many of these tactics on us. Between education and indoctrination, enlightenment and propaganda, conversion and coercion, therapy and mind control, there is but a blurry line.

Second, that Jim Jones abused the power of persuasion does not mean persuasion is intrinsically bad. Nuclear power enables us to light up homes or wipe out cities. Sexual power enables us to express and celebrate committed love or exploit people for selfish gratification. Persuasive power enables us to enlighten or deceive. That these powers can be harnessed for evil purposes should alert us to guard against their immoral use. But the powers themselves are neither inherently evil nor inherently good; how we use them determines whether their effect is destructive or constructive. Condemning persuasion because of deceit is like condemning eating because of gluttony.

Summing up

The successes of religious cults provide an opportunity to see powerful persuasion processes at work. It appears that their success has resulted by their eliciting behavior commitments (as described in Chapter 4), applying principles of effective persuasion (this chapter), and isolating members in like-minded groups (to be discussed in Chapter 8).

Resisting persuasion: Attitude inoculation

Having perused the "weapons of influence," we consider, finally, some tactics for resisting influence. How might we prepare people to resist unwanted persuasion?

This consideration of persuasive influences has perhaps made you wonder if it is possible to *resist* unwanted persuasion. As Daniel Gilbert and his colleagues (1990, 1993) report, 'tis easier to accept persuasive messages than to doubt them. To *understand* an assertion (say, that lead pencils are a health hazard) is to *believe* it—at least temporarily, until one actively undoes the initial, automatic acceptance. If a distracting event prevents the undoing, the acceptance lingers.

Still, blessed with logic, information, and motivation, we do resist falsehoods. If, because of an aura of credibility, the repair person's uniform and doctor's title have intimidated us into unquestioning agreement, we can rethink our habitual responses to authority. We can seek more information before committing time or money. We can question what we don't understand.

Strengthening personal commitment

Chapter 6 presented another way to resist: Before encountering others' judgments, make a public commitment to your position. Having stood up for your convictions, you will become less susceptible (or should we say less "open"?) to what others have to say. In mock civil trials, straw polls of jurors can foster a hardening of expressed positions, leading to more deadlocks (Davis & others, 1993).

Challenging beliefs

How might we stimulate people to commit themselves? From his experiments, Charles Kiesler (1971) offers one possible way: Mildly attack their position. Kiesler found that when committed people were attacked strongly enough to cause them to react, but not so strongly as to overwhelm them, they became even more committed. Kiesler explains:

> When you attack a committed person and your attack is of inadequate strength, you drive him to even more extreme behaviors in defense of his previous commitment. His commitment escalates, in a sense, because the number of acts consistent with his belief increases. (p. 88)

Perhaps you can recall a time when this happened in an argument, as those involved escalated their rhetoric, committing themselves to increasingly extreme positions.

Developing counterarguments

There is a second reason a mild attack might build resistance. When someone attacks one of our cherished attitudes, we typically feel some irritation and contemplate counterarguments (Zuwerink & Devine, 1996). Like inoculations against disease, even weak arguments will prompt counterarguments, which are then available for a stronger attack. William McGuire (1964) documented this in a series of experiments. McGuire wondered: Could we inoculate people against persuasion much as we inoculate them against a virus? Is there such a thing as **attitude inoculation**? Could we take people raised in a "germ-free ideological environment"—people who hold some unquestioned belief—and stimulate their mental defenses? And would subjecting them to a small dose of belief-threatening material inoculate them against later persuasion?

That is what McGuire did. First, he found some cultural truisms, such as, "It's a good idea to brush your teeth after every meal if at all possible." He then showed that people were vulnerable to a massive, credible assault upon these truisms (for example, prestigious authorities were said to have discovered that too much toothbrushing can damage one's gums). If, however, before having their belief attacked, they were "immunized" by first receiving a small challenge to their belief, *and* if they read or wrote an essay in refutation of this mild attack, then they were better able to resist the powerful attack.

attitude inoculation exposing people to weak attacks upon their attitudes so that when stronger attacks come, they will have refutations available

Case studies: Large-scale inoculation programs

Inoculating children against peer pressure to smoke

In a clear demonstration of how laboratory research findings can lead to practical application, a research team led by Alfred McAlister (1980) had high school students "inoculate" grade seven students against peer pressures to smoke. The grade seven students were taught to respond to advertisements implying that liberated women smoke by saying, "She's not really liberated if she is hooked on tobacco." They also acted in role plays; after being called "chicken" for not taking a cigarette, they answered with statements like, "I'd be a real chicken if I smoked just to impress you." After several such sessions during grades seven and eight, the inoculated students were half as likely to begin smoking as uninoculated students at another junior high school that had an identical parental smoking rate (Figure 7–11).

Other research teams have confirmed that such inoculation procedures, sometimes supplemented by other life skill training, reduce teen smoking (Botvin & others, 1995; Evans & others, 1984; Flay & others, 1985). Most newer efforts emphasize strategies for resisting social pressure. One study exposed students in grades six to eight to antismoking films or to information about smoking, together with role plays of student-generated ways of refusing a cigarette (Hirschman & Leventhal, 1989). A year and a half later 31 percent of those who watched the antismoking films had taken up smoking. Among those who role-played refusing, only 19 percent had done so. Another study involved the entire seventh-grade class in a diverse sample of 30 junior high schools. It warned students about pressures to smoke and use drugs and offered them strategies for

"The SLA . . . read me news items they clipped from the newspapers almost every day. Some of their stories were indisputable, sometimes I did not know what to believe. It was all very confusing. I realized that my life prior to my kidnapping had indeed been very sheltered; I had taken little or no interest in foreign affairs, politics, or economics."

Patricia Campbell Hearst, *Every Secret Thing*, 1982

behind the scenes

I confess to having felt like Mr. Clean when doing this immunization work because I was studying how to help people resist being manipulated. Then, after our research was published, an advertising executive called and said, "Very interesting, Professor: I was delighted to read about it." Somewhat righteously, I replied, "Very nice of you to say that Mr. Executive, but I'm really on the other side. You're trying to persuade people, and I'm trying to make them more resistant." "Oh, don't underrate yourself, Professor," he said. "We can use what you're doing to diminish the effect of our competitors' ads." And sure enough, it has become almost standard for advertisers to mention other brands and deflate their claims.

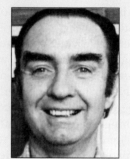

William McGuire
Yale University

resisting (Ellickson & Bell, 1990). Among nonusers of marijuana, the training curbed initiation by a third; among users, it reduced usage by half.

Antismoking and drug education programs apply other persuasion principles, too. They use attractive peers to communicate information. They trigger the students' own cognitive processing ("Here's something you might want to think about"). They get the students to make a public commitment (by making a rational decision about smoking and then announcing it, along with their rea-

figure 7–11

The percentage of cigarette smokers at an "inoculated" junior high school was much less than at a matched control school using a more typical smoking education program.

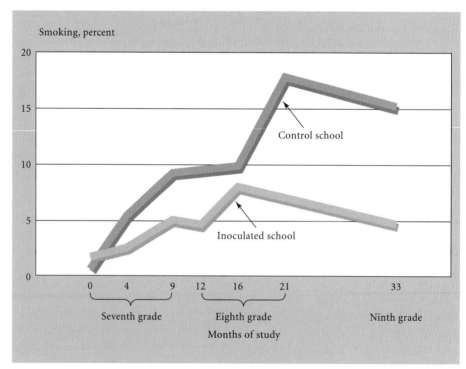

(Data from McAlister & others, 1980; Telch & others, 1981.)

soning, to their classmates). Some of these smoking-prevention programs require only two to six one-hour class sessions, using prepared printed materials or videotapes. Today any school district or teacher wishing to use the social-psychological approach to smoking prevention can do so easily, inexpensively, and with the hope of significant reductions in future smoking rates and associated health costs.

Inoculating children against the influence of advertising

Researchers have also studied how to immunize young children so they can more effectively analyze and evaluate television commercials. This research was prompted partly by studies showing that children, especially those under eight years, (1) have trouble distinguishing commercials from programs and fail to grasp their persuasive intent, (2) trust television advertising rather indiscriminately, and (3) desire and badger their parents for advertised products (Adler & others, 1980; Feshbach, 1980; Palmer & Dorr, 1980). Children, it seems, are an advertiser's dream: gullible, vulnerable, an easy sell. Moreover, half the 20,000 ads the typical child sees in a year are for low-nutrition, often sugary foods.

Armed with such data, citizens' groups have given the advertisers of such products a chewing out (Moody, 1980): "When a sophisticated advertiser spends millions to sell unsophisticated, trusting children an unhealthy product, this can only be called exploitation. No wonder the consumption of dairy products has declined since the start of television, while soft-drink consumption has almost doubled." On the other side are the commercial interests, who claim that such ads allow parents to teach their children consumer skills and, more

> A debated question: What is the cumulative effect on children's materialism of watching some 350,000 commercials during their growing-up years?

Children are the advertiser's dream. Researchers have therefore studied ways to inoculate children against the 20,000 or so ads they see each year, many as they are glued to a TV set.

important, finance children's television programs. Government agencies that oversee the media are often stuck in the middle, pushed by research findings and political pressures while trying to decide whether to place new constraints on TV ads aimed at young children.

Meanwhile, researchers have wondered whether children can be taught to resist deceptive ads. In one such effort, a team of investigators led by Norma Feshbach (1980; Cohen, 1980) gave small groups of elementary schoolchildren three half-hour lessons in analyzing commercials. The children were inoculated by viewing ads and discussing them. For example, after viewing a toy ad, they were immediately given the toy and challenged to make it do what they had just seen in the commercial. Such experiences helped breed a more realistic understanding of commercials.

Implications

Inoculation research also has some provocative implications. The best way to build resistance to brainwashing isn't to reinforce one's current beliefs. If parents are worried that their children could become members of a cult they would be better served by teaching their children about the various cults and their errors, rather than emphasizing the soundness of their own views.

For the same reason, religious educators should be wary of creating a "germ-free ideological environment" in their churches and schools. An attack, if refuted, is more likely to solidify one's position than to undermine it, particularly if the threatening material can be examined with like-minded others. Cults apply this principle by forewarning members of how families and friends will attack the cult's beliefs. When the expected challenge comes, the member is armed with counterarguments.

Another implication is that, for the persuader, an ineffective appeal can be worse than none. Can you see why? Those who reject an appeal are inoculated against further appeals. Consider an experiment in which Susan Darley and Joel Cooper (1972) invited students to write essays advocating a strict dress code. Because this was against the students' own positions and the essays were to be published, all chose *not* to write the essay—even those offered money to do so. After turning down the money, they became even more extreme and confident in their anti-dress-code opinions. Having made an overt decision against the dress code, they became even more resistant to it. Those who have rejected initial appeals to quit smoking may likewise become immune to further appeals. Ineffective persuasion, by stimulating the listener's defenses, may be counterproductive. It may "harden the heart" against later appeals.

Summing up

How do people resist persuasion? A prior public commitment to one's own position, stimulated perhaps by a mild attack on the position, breeds resistance to later persuasion. A mild attack can also serve as an inoculation, stimulating one to develop counterarguments that will then be available if and when a strong attack comes. This implies, paradoxically, that one way to strengthen existing attitudes is to challenge them, though the challenge must not be so strong as to overwhelm them.

Personal Postscript: Being open but not naive

As recipients of persuasion, our human task is to live in the land between gullibility and cynicism. Some people say that being persuadable is a weakness. "Think for yourself," we are urged. But is being closed to informational influence a virtue, or is it the mark of a fanatic? How can we live with humility and openness to others, and yet be critical consumers of persuasive appeals?

To be open, we can assume that every person we meet is, in some ways, our superior. Each person I encounter has some expertise that exceeds my own, and thus has something to teach me. As we connect, I hope to learn from this person, and perhaps to be able to reciprocate by sharing my knowledge.

To be critical thinkers, we might take a cue from inoculation research. Do you want to build your resistance to persuasion without becoming closed to valid messages? Be an active listener and a critical thinker. Force yourself to counter-argue. After hearing a political speech, discuss it with others. In other words, don't just listen; react. If the message cannot withstand careful analysis, so much the worse for it. If it can, its effect on you will be the more enduring.

chapter 8

Group Influence

Our world contains not only 5.9 billion individuals but also 200 nation-states, four million local communities, 20 million economic organizations, and hundreds of millions of other formal and informal groups—couples on dates, families, churches, housemates in bull sessions. How do these groups influence individuals?

Some groups involve others' mere presence. Tawna is nearing the end of her daily jog. Her mind prods her to keep going; her body begs her to walk it in. She compromises and slogs home. The next day conditions are identical, except that two friends run with her. Tawna runs her route two minutes faster. She wonders, "Did I run better merely because Gail and Rachel went along?"

Interacting groups often have more dramatic effects. Intellectual university students hang out with other intellectuals, accentuating one another's intellectual interests. Deviant youth hang out with other deviant youth, amplifying one another's antisocial tendencies. But *how* do groups affect attitudes? And what influences lead groups to smart and dumb decisions?

Finally, individuals influence their groups. As the 1957 movie *12 Angry Men* opens, 12 wary murder trial jurors file into the jury room. It is a hot day. The tired jurors are close to agreement and eager for a quick verdict convicting a teenage boy of knifing his father. But one maverick, played by Henry Fonda, refuses to vote guilty. As the heated deliberation proceeds, the jurors one by one change their verdicts until consensus is reached: "Not guilty." In real trials, a lone individual seldom sways the entire group. Yet, history is made by minorities that sway majorities. What helps make a minority—or an effective leader—persuasive?

We will examine these intriguing phenomena of group influence one at a time. But first things first: What is a group and why do groups exist?

What is a group?

The answer to the question seems self-evident—until several people compare their definitions. Are jogging partners a group? Are airplane passengers a group? Is a group a set of people who identify with one another, who sense they belong together? Is a group those who share common goals and rely on one another? Does a group form when individuals become organized? When their relationships with one another continue over time? These are among the social psychological definitions of a group (McGrath, 1984).

group
two or more people who, for longer than a few moments, interact with and influence one another and perceive one another as "us"

Group dynamics expert Marvin Shaw (1981) argues that all groups have one thing in common: Their members interact. He therefore defines a **group** as two or more people who interact and influence one another. Moreover, notes Australian National University social psychologist John Turner (1987), groups perceive themselves as "us" in contrast to "them." So jogging companions are indeed a group. Groups may exist for a number of reasons—to meet a need to belong, to provide information, to supply rewards, to accomplish goals.

By Shaw's definition, the passengers on a routine airplane flight would *not* be a group. Although physically together, they are more à collection of individuals than an interacting group. But the distinction between simple collective behavior among unrelated individuals on a plane and the more influential group behavior among interacting individuals sometimes blurs. People who are merely in one another's presence do sometimes influence one another. Moreover, they may perceive themselves as, say, "us" fans in contrast with "them" who root for the other team.

In this chapter we consider three examples of such collective influence: *social facilitation, social loafing,* and *deindividuation.* These three phenomena can occur with minimal interaction (in what we call "minimal group situations"), but they also influence people's behavior while interacting. Then we will consider three examples of social influence in interacting groups: *group polarization, groupthink,* and *minority influence.*

Social facilitation

coactors
a group of people working simultaneously and individually on a noncompetitive task

*Let's begin with social psychology's most elementary question: Are we affected by the mere presence of another person? "Mere presence" means people are not competing, do not reward or punish, and in fact do nothing except be present as a passive audience or as **coactors**. Would the mere presence of others affect a person's jogging, eating, typing, or exam performance? The search for the answer is a scientific mystery story.*

The presence of others

A century ago, Norman Triplett (1898), a psychologist interested in bicycle racing, noticed that cyclists' times were faster when racing together than when racing alone against the clock. Before he peddled his hunch (that the presence of others boosts performance), Triplett conducted one of social psychology's early laboratory experiments. Children told to wind string on a fishing reel as rapidly as possible wound faster when they worked with coactors than when they worked alone.

Subsequent experiments in the early decades of this century found that the presence of others also improves the speed with which people do simple multiplication problems and cross out designated letters. And it improves the accuracy with which people perform simple motor tasks, such as keeping a metal stick in contact with a dime-sized disk on a moving turntable (F. W. Allport, 1920; Dashiell, 1930; Travis, 1925). This **social-facilitation** effect, as it came to be called, also occurs with animals. In the presence of others of their species, ants excavate more sand and chickens eat more grain (Bayer, 1929; Chen, 1937). In the presence of other sexually active rat pairs, mating rats exhibit heightened sexual activity (Larsson, 1956).

Other studies conducted about the same time revealed that on other tasks the presence of others hinders performance. In the presence of others, cockroaches, parakeets, and green finches learn mazes more slowly (Allee & Masure, 1936; Gates & Allee, 1933; Klopfer, 1958). This disruptive effect also occurs with people. The presence of others diminishes efficiency at learning nonsense syllables, completing a maze, and performing complex multiplication problems (Dashiell, 1930; Pessin, 1933; Pessin & Husband, 1933).

Saying that the presence of others sometimes facilitates performance and sometimes hinders it is about as satisfying as a weather forecast predicting that

social facilitation
(1) original meaning—the tendency of people to perform simple or well-learned tasks better when others are present.
(2) current meaning—the strengthening of dominant (prevalent, likely) responses owing to the presence of others

Social facilitation: The motivating presence of a co-actor or audience strengthens well-learned responses.

it might be sunny but then again it might rain. By 1940, research activity in this area had ground to a halt. It lay dormant for 25 years until awakened by the touch of a new idea.

Social psychologist Robert Zajonc (pronounced *Zy-ence*, rhymes with *science*) wondered whether these seemingly contradictory findings could be reconciled. As often happens at creative moments in science, Zajonc (1965) used one field of research to illuminate another. In this case the illumination came from a well-established principle in experimental psychology: Arousal enhances whatever response tendency is dominant. Increased arousal enhances performance on easy tasks for which the most likely—"dominant"—response is the correct one. People solve easy anagrams, such as *akec*, fastest when they are anxious. On complex tasks, for which the correct answer is not dominant, increased arousal promotes *incorrect* responding. On harder anagrams people do worse when anxious.

Could this principle solve the mystery of social facilitation? It seemed reasonable to assume what evidence now confirms—that others' presence will arouse or energize people (Mullen & others, 1997). (Most of us can recall feeling more tense or excited before an audience.) If social arousal facilitates dominant responses, it should boost performance on easy tasks and hurt performance on difficult tasks. Now the confusing results made sense. Winding fishing reels, doing simple multiplication problems, and eating were all easy tasks for which the responses were well learned or naturally dominant. And sure enough, having others around boosted performance. Learning new material, doing a maze, and solving complex math problems were more difficult tasks for which the correct responses were initially less probable. And sure enough, the presence of others increased the number of *incorrect* responses on these tasks. The same general rule—*arousal facilitates dominant responses*—worked in both cases. Suddenly, what had looked like contradictory results no longer seemed contradictory.

Zajonc's solution, so simple and elegant, left other social psychologists thinking what Thomas H. Huxley thought after first reading Darwin's *Origin of the Species:* "How extremely stupid not to have thought of that!" It seemed obvious—once Zajonc had pointed it out. Perhaps, however, the pieces appeared to merge so neatly only because we viewed them through the spectacles of hindsight. Would the solution survive direct experimental tests?

After almost 300 studies conducted with the help of more than 25,000 volunteer subjects, it has survived (Bond & Titus, 1983; Guerin, 1993). Several experiments in which Zajonc and his associates manufactured an arbitrary dominant response confirmed that an audience enhanced this response. In one, Zajonc and Stephen Sales (1966) asked people to pronounce various nonsense words between 1 and 16 times. Then they told the people that the same words would appear on a screen, one at a time. Each time, they were to guess which had appeared. When the people were actually shown only random black lines for a hundredth of a second, they "saw" mostly the words they had pronounced most frequently. These words had become the dominant responses. People who took the same test in the presence of two others were even more likely to guess the dominant words (Figure 8–1).

In various ways, later experiments confirmed that social arousal facilitates dominant responses, whether right or wrong. Peter Hunt and Joseph Hillery (1973) found that in the presence of others, students took less time to learn a simple maze and more time to learn a complex one (just as the

> "Mere social contact begets . . . a stimulation of the animal spirits that heightens the efficiency of each individual workman."
>
> Karl Marx, *Das Kapital*, 1867

> "Discovery consists of seeing what everybody has seen and thinking what nobody has thought."
>
> Albert Axent-Gyorgyi, *The Scientist Speculates*

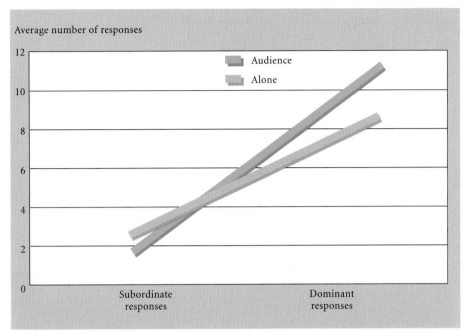

figure 8–1
Social facilitation of dominant responses.
People responded with dominant words (practiced 16 times) more frequently, and subordinate words (practiced but once) less frequently, when observers were present.

(Data from Zajonc & Sales, 1966.)

cockroaches do). And James Michaels and his collaborators (1982) found that good pool players (who had made 71 percent of their shots while being unobtrusively observed) did even better (80 percent) when four observers came up to watch them play. Poor shooters (who had previously averaged 36 percent) did even worse (25 percent) when closely observed.

Athletes perform well-practiced skills, which helps explain why they often perform best when energized by the responses of a supportive crowd. Studies of more than 80,000 university and professional athletic events in Canada, the United States, and England reveal that home teams win about 6 in 10 games (somewhat fewer for baseball and football, somewhat more for basketball and soccer—see Table 8–1). The home advantage may, however, also stem from the players' familiarity with their home environment, less travel fatigue, feelings of dominance derived from territorial control, or increased team identity when cheered by fans (Zillmann & Paulus, 1993).

Crowding: The presence of many others

So people do respond to the presence of others. But does the presence of observers really arouse people? In times of stress, a comrade can be comforting. Nevertheless, researchers have found that with others present, people perspire more, breathe faster, tense their muscles more, and have higher blood pressure and a faster heart rate (Geen & Gange, 1983; Moore & Baron, 1983).

The effect of other people increases with their number (Jackson & Latané, 1981; Knowles, 1983). Sometimes the arousal and self-conscious attention created by a large audience interferes even with well-learned, automatic behaviors, such as speaking. Given extreme pressure, we're vulnerable to choking. Stutterers tend to stutter more in front of larger audiences than when speaking to just

table 8–1 **Home advantage in major team sports**

Sport	Games Studied	Winning Percentage
baseball	135,665	54.3%
football	2,592	57.3
ice hockey	4,322	61.1
basketball	13,596	64.4
soccer	37,202	69.0

Data from Courneya & Carron (1992), except for major league baseball, 1900 to 1992, from Schlenker & others (1995).

In every sport studied, a supportive home crowd, such as the fans at the Montreal Forum, helps create a home advantage.

one or two people (Mullen, 1986). University basketball players become slightly *less* accurate in their free-throw shooting when highly aroused by a packed rather than near-empty fieldhouse (Sokoll & Mynatt, 1984).

Being *in* a crowd also intensifies positive or negative reactions. When they sit close together, friendly people are liked even more, and *un*friendly people are *dis*-liked even more (Schiffenbauer & Schiavo, 1976; Storms & Thomas, 1977). In experiments with Columbia University students and with Ontario Science Centre visitors, Jonathan Freedman and his co-workers (1979, 1980) had an accomplice listen to a humorous tape or watch a movie with other subjects. When all sat close together, the accomplice could more readily induce them to laugh and clap. As theater directors and sports fans know, and as researchers have confirmed (Agnew & Carron, 1994; Aiello & others, 1983; Worchel & Brown, 1984), a "good house" is a full house.

Perhaps you've noticed that a class of 35 students feels more warm and lively in a room that seats just 35 than when spread around a room that seats 100. This occurs partly because when others are close by, we are more likely to notice and join in their laughter or clapping. But crowding also enhances arousal, as Gary Evans (1979) found. He tested 10-person groups, either in a room 20 by 30 feet or in one 8 by 12 feet. Compared to those in the large room, those densely packed had higher pulse rates and blood pressure (indicating arousal). Though their performance on simple tasks did not suffer, on difficult tasks they made more errors. In a study of university students in India, Dinesh Nagar and Janak Pandey (1987) similarly found that crowding hampered performance only on complex tasks, such as solving difficult anagrams. So, crowding enhances arousal, which facilitates dominant responses.

Why are we aroused in the presence of others?

To this point we have seen that what you do well, you will be energized to do best in front of others (unless you become hyperaroused and self-conscious). What you find difficult may seem impossible in the same circumstances. What is it about other people that causes arousal? Is it their mere presence? There is evidence to support three possible factors.

Heightened arousal in crowded homes also tends to increase stress. Crowding produces less distress in homes divided into many spaces, however, enabling people to withdraw in privacy.

(Evans & others, 1996).

Evaluation apprehension

Nickolas Cottrell surmised that observers make us apprehensive because we wonder how they are evaluating us. To test whether **evaluation apprehension** exists, Cottrell and his associates (1968) repeated Zajonc and Sales' nonsense-syllable study and added a third condition. In this "mere presence" condition they blindfolded observers, supposedly in preparation for a perception experiment. In contrast to the effect of the watching audience, the mere presence of these blindfolded people did *not* boost well-practiced responses.

evaluation apprehension concern for how others are evaluating us

Other experiments confirmed Cottrell's conclusion: The enhancement of dominant responses is strongest when people think they are being evaluated. In one experiment, joggers on a jogging path sped up as they came upon a woman seated on the grass—*if* she was facing them rather than sitting with her back turned (Worringham & Messick, 1983).

Evaluation apprehension also helps explain:

- Why people perform best when their coactor is slightly superior (Seta, 1982)
- Why arousal lessens when a high-status group is diluted by adding people whose opinions don't matter to us (Seta & Seta, 1992)
- Why people who worry most about others' evaluations are the ones most affected by their presence (Gastorf & others, 1980; Geen & Gange, 1983)
- Why social-facilitation effects are greatest when the others are unfamiliar and hard to keep an eye on (Guerin & Innes, 1982)

The self-consciousness we feel when being evaluated can also interfere with behaviors that we perform best automatically (Mullen & Baumeister, 1987). If self-conscious basketball players analyze their body movements while shooting critical free throws, they are more likely to miss.

Driven by distraction

Glenn Sanders, Robert Baron, and Danny Moore (1978; Baron, 1986) carried evaluation apprehension a step further. They theorized that when people wonder how coactors are doing or how an audience is reacting, they get distracted. This *conflict* between paying attention to others and paying attention to the task overloads the cognitive system, causing arousal. Evidence that people are indeed "driven by distraction" comes from experiments that produce social facilitation not just by the presence of another person but even by a nonhuman distraction, such as bursts of light (Sanders, 1981a, 1981b).

Mere presence

Zajonc, however, believes that the mere presence of others produces some arousal even without evaluation apprehension or arousing distraction. For example, people's color preferences are stronger when they make judgments with others present (Goldman, 1967). On such a task, there is no "good" or "right" answer for others to evaluate and thus no reason to be concerned with their reactions.

Recall that facilitation effects also occur with nonhuman animals. This hints at an innate social arousal mechanism common to much of the zoological world. (Animals probably are not consciously worrying about how other animals are evaluating them.) At the human level, most joggers feel energized when jogging with someone else, even one who neither competes nor evaluates.

This is a good time to remind ourselves of the purpose of a theory. As we noted in Chapter 1, a good theory is a scientific shorthand: It simplifies and summarizes a variety of observations. Social-facilitation theory does this well. It is a simple summary of many research findings. A good theory also offers clear predictions that (1) help confirm or modify the theory, (2) guide new exploration, and (3) suggest practical application. Social-facilitation theory has definitely generated the first two types of prediction: (1) The basics of the theory (that the presence of others is arousing and that this social arousal enhances dominant responses) have been confirmed, and (2) the theory has brought new life to a long dormant field of research. Does it also suggest (3) some practical applications?

Application is properly the last research phase. In their study of social facilitation, researchers have not yet worked much on this. But we can make some educated guesses about possible applications. As Figure 8–2 shows, many new office buildings have replaced private offices with large, open areas divided by low partitions. Might the resulting awareness of others' presence help boost the performance of well-learned tasks, but disrupt creative thinking on complex tasks? Can you think of other possible applications?

Summing up

Social psychology's most elementary issue concerns the mere presence of others. Some early experiments on this question found that performance improved with observers or coactors present. Others found that the presence of others can hurt performance. Robert Zajonc reconciled these findings by applying a well-known principle from experimental psychology: Arousal facilitates dominant responses. Because the presence of others is arousing, the presence of observers or coactors boosts performance on easy tasks (for which the correct response is dominant) and

figure 8–2
In the "open-office plan"
people work in the
presence of others. How
might this affect worker
efficiency?

(Photo courtesy of Herman Miller Inc.)

hinders performance on difficult tasks (for which incorrect responses are dominant).

But why are we aroused by others' presence? Experiments suggest that the arousal stems partly from "evaluation apprehension" and partly from a conflict between paying attention to others and concentrating on the task. Other experiments, including some with animals, suggest that the presence of others can be arousing even when we are not evaluated or distracted.

Social loafing

In a team tug-of-war, will eight people on a side exert as much force as the sum of their best efforts in individual tugs of war? If not, why not? And what level of individual effort can we expect from members of work groups?

Social facilitation usually occurs when people work toward individual goals and when their efforts, whether winding fishing reels or solving math problems, can be individually evaluated. These situations parallel some everyday work situations, but not those where people cooperatively pool their efforts toward a *common* goal and where individuals are *not* accountable for their efforts. A team tug-of-war provides one such example. Organizational fundraising—pooling candy sale proceeds to pay for the class trip—provides another. So does a class project where all get the same grade. On such "additive tasks"—tasks where the group's achievement depends on the sum of the individual efforts—will team spirit boost productivity? Will bricklayers lay bricks faster when working as a team than when working alone? One way to attack such questions is with laboratory simulations.

figure 8–3

The rope-pulling apparatus.

People in the first position pulled less hard when they thought people behind them were also pulling.

(Data from Ingham, Levinger, Graves, & Peckham, 1974. Photo by Alan G. Ingham.)

Many hands make light work

Nearly a century ago, French engineer Max Ringelmann (reported by Kravitz & Martin, 1986) found that the collective effort of such teams was but half the sum of the individual efforts. This suggests, contrary to the common notion "in unity there is strength," that group members may actually be *less* motivated when performing additive tasks. Maybe, though, poor performance stemmed from poor coordination—people pulling a rope in slightly different directions at slightly different times. A group of researchers led by Alan Ingham (1974) cleverly eliminated this problem by making individuals think others were pulling with them, when in fact they were pulling alone. Blindfolded participants assigned the first position in the apparatus shown in Figure 8–3 and told to "pull as hard as you can" pulled 18 percent harder when they knew they were pulling alone than when they believed that behind them two to five people were also pulling.

Researchers Bibb Latané, Kipling Williams, and Stephen Harkins (1979; Harkins & others, 1980) kept their ears open for other ways to investigate this phenomenon, which they labeled **social loafing**. They observed that the noise produced by six people shouting or clapping "as loud as you can" was less than three times that produced by one person alone. Like the tug-of-war task, however, noisemaking is vulnerable to group inefficiency. So Latané and his associates followed Ingham's example by leading their participants to believe others were shouting or clapping with them, when in fact they were doing so alone.

Their method was to blindfold six people, seat them in a semicircle, and have them put on headphones, over which they were blasted with the sound of people shouting or clapping. People could not hear their own shouting or clapping, much less that of others. On various trials they were instructed to shout or clap either alone or along with the group. People who were told about this experi-

social loafing

the tendency for people to exert less effort when they pool their efforts toward a common goal than when they are individually accountable

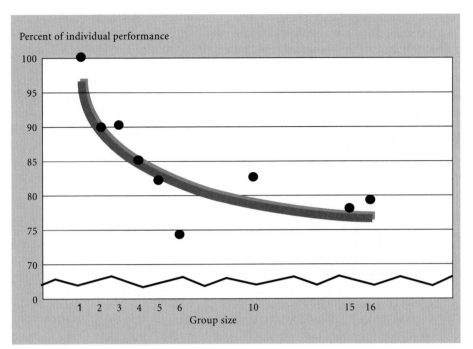

Percent of individual performance

(From Williams & others, 1992.)

figure 8–4
A statistical digest of 49 studies, involving more than 4,000 participants, revealed that effort decreases (loafing increases) as the size of the group increases. Each dot represents the aggregate data from one of these studies.

ment guessed the subjects would shout louder when with others, because they would be less inhibited (Harkins, 1981). The actual result? Social loafing: When the participants believed five others were also either shouting or clapping, they produced one-third less noise than when they thought themselves alone. Social loafing occurred even when the subjects were high school cheerleaders who believed themselves to be cheering together or alone (Hardy & Latané, 1986).

Curiously, those who clapped both alone and in groups did not view themselves as loafing; they perceived themselves as clapping equally in both situations. This parallels what happens when students work on group projects for a shared grade. Williams reports that all agree loafing occurs—but no one admits to doing the loafing. John Sweeney (1973), a political scientist interested in the policy implications of social loafing, obtained similar results. Students pumped exercise bicycles more energetically (as measured by electrical output) when they knew they were being individually monitored than when they thought their output was being pooled with that of other riders. In the group condition, people were tempted to **free-ride** on the group effort.

In this and some 160 other studies (Karau & Williams, 1993, and Figure 8–4), we see a twist on one of the psychological forces that makes for social facilitation: evaluation apprehension. In the social loafing experiments, individuals believe they are evaluated only when they act alone. The group situation (rope pulling, shouting, and so forth) *decreases* evaluation apprehension. When people are not accountable and cannot evaluate their own efforts, responsibility is diffused across all group members (Harkins & Jackson, 1985; Kerr & Bruun, 1981). By contrast, the social-facilitation experiments *increased* exposure to evaluation. When made the center of attention, people self-consciously monitor their behavior (Mullen & Baumeister, 1987). So the principle is the same: When being

free riders
people who benefit from the group but give little in return

observed *increases* evaluation concerns, social facilitation occurs; when being lost in a crowd *decreases* evaluation concerns, social loafing occurs.

To motivate group members, one strategy is to make individual performance identifiable. Some football coaches do this by individually filming and evaluating each player. Williams and his colleagues (1981) had group members wear individual microphones while engaged in group shouting. Whether in a group or not, people exert more effort when their outputs are individually identifiable: University swim team members swim faster in intrasquad relay races when someone monitors and announces their individual times (Williams & others, 1989). Even without pay consequences, actual assembly-line workers in one small experiment produced 16 percent more product when their individual output was identified (Faulkner & Williams, 1996).

Social loafing in everyday life

How widespread is social loafing? In the laboratory, the phenomenon occurs not only among people who are pulling ropes, cycling, shouting, and clapping but also among those who are pumping water or air, evaluating poems or editorials, producing ideas, typing, and detecting signals. Do these results generalize to everyday worker productivity?

On their collective farms under communism, Russian peasants worked one field one day, another field the next, with little direct responsibility for any given plot. For their own use, they were given small private plots. In one analysis, the private plots occupied 1 percent of the agricultural land, yet produced 27 percent of the Soviet farm output (H. Smith, 1976). In Hungary, private plots accounted for only 13 percent of the farmland but produced one-third of the output (Spivak, 1979). When China began allowing farmers to sell food grown in excess of that owed to the state, food production jumped 8 percent per year— 2.5 times the annual increase in the preceding 26 years (Church, 1986).

In North America, workers who do not pay dues or volunteer time to their union or professional association nevertheless are usually happy to accept its benefits. So, too, are public television viewers who don't respond to their station's fund drives. This hints at another possible explanation of social loafing. When rewards are divided equally, regardless of how much one contributes to the group, any individual gets more reward per unit of effort by free-riding on the group. So people may be motivated to slack off when their efforts are not individually monitored and rewarded.

In a pickle factory, for example, the key job is picking the right-size dill-pickle halves off the conveyor belt and stuffing them in jars. Unfortunately, workers are tempted to stuff any size pickle in, because their output is not identifiable (the jars go into a common hopper before reaching the quality-control section). Williams, Harkins, and Latané (1981) note that research on social loafing suggests "making individual production identifiable, and raises the question: 'How many pickles could a pickle packer pack if pickle packers were only paid for properly packed pickles?'"

But surely collective effort does not always lead to slacking off. Sometimes the goal is so compelling and maximum output from everyone is so essential that team spirit maintains or intensifies effort. In an Olympic crew race, will the individual rowers in an eight-person crew pull their oars with less effort than those in a one- or two-person crew?

The evidence assures us they will not. People in groups loaf less when the task is *challenging, appealing,* or *involving* (Karau & Williams, 1993). On challenging tasks, people may perceive their efforts as indispensable (Harkins & Petty, 1982; Kerr, 1983; Kerr & Bruun, 1983). When people see others in their group as unreliable or as unable to contribute much, they work harder (Vancouver & others, 1991; Williams & Karau, 1991). Adding incentives or challenging a group to strive for certain standards also promotes collective effort (Harkins & Szymanski, 1989; Shepperd & Wright, 1989). So does intergroup competition (Erev & others, 1993).

Groups also loaf less when their members are *friends* rather than strangers (Davis & Greenlees, 1992). Latané notes that Israel's communal kibbutz farms have actually outproduced Israel's noncollective farms (Leon, 1969). Cohesiveness intensifies effort. So will there be no social loafing in group-centered cultures? To find out, Latané and his co-researchers (Gabrenya & others, 1985) headed for Asia, where they repeated their sound production experiments in Japan, Thailand, Taiwan, India, and Malaysia. Their findings? Social loafing was evident in all these countries, too.

Sixteen later studies in Asia reveal that people in collectivist cultures exhibit less social loafing than do people in individualist cultures (Karau & Williams, 1993). As we noted in Chapter 2, loyalty to family and work groups runs strong in collectivist cultures. Likewise, women exhibit less social loafing than do men (who, as Chapter 5 also explained, tend to be more individualistic).

Some of these findings parallel those from studies of everyday work groups. When groups are given challenging objectives, when they are rewarded for group success, and when there is a spirit of commitment to the "team," group members work hard (Hackman, 1986). Keeping work groups small and forming them with equally competent people can also help members feel their contributions are indispensable (Comer, 1995). So while social loafing is a common occurrence when group members work collectively and without individual accountability, many hands need not always make light work.

Teamwork at the World Rowing Championships in St. Catharines. Social loafing occurs when people work in groups but without individual accountability— except if the task is challenging, appealing, or involving and the group members are friends.

Summing up

Social-facilitation researchers study people's performance on tasks where they can be individually evaluated. In many work situations people pool their efforts, however, and work toward a common goal without individual accountability. Studies show that group members often work less hard when performing such "additive tasks." This finding parallels everyday situations where diffused responsibility tempts individual group members to free-ride on the group's effort.

Deindividuation

In the spring of 1993, soldiers from the Canadian Airborne Regiment, were stationed in the remote town of Belet Huen Somalia. On March 4 some soldiers shot two young Somalis for stealing supplies and killed one of the young men with a point-blank shot to the head. A few days later they captured, tortured, and killed a 16-year-old Somali named Shidane Arone. Pictures of the torture eventually made their way back to Canada, shocking the nation into a prolonged discussion of the state of the military and group violence. People wondered: Where was the soldiers' humanity? What had happened to standards of military conduct? What could cause such behavior?

Doing together what we would not do alone

Social facilitation experiments show that groups can arouse people. Social loafing experiments show that groups can diffuse responsibility. When arousal and diffused responsibility combine and normal inhibitions diminish, the results may be startling. Acts may range from a mild lessening of restraint (throwing food in the dining hall, snarling at a referee, screaming during a rock concert) to impulsive self-gratification (group vandalism, orgies, thefts) to destructive social explosions (police brutality, riots, lynchings). In a 1967 incident, 200 university students gathered to watch a disturbed fellow student threatening to jump from a tower. They began to chant "Jump. Jump. . . ." The student jumped to his death (UPI, 1967).

The beating of 16-year-old Shidane Arone by Canadian soldiers in Somalia made people wonder: How do group situations release people from normal restraints?

These unrestrained behaviors have something in common: They are some-how provoked by the power of a group. Groups can generate a sense of excite-ment, of being caught up in something bigger than one's self. It is hard to imagine a single rock fan screaming deliriously at a private rock concert, a sin-gle Oklahoma student trying to coax someone to suicide, or even a single police officer beating a defenseless motorist. In certain kinds of group situations peo-ple are more likely to abandon normal restraints, to lose their sense of individ-ual responsibility, to become what Leon Festinger, Albert Pepitone, and Theodore Newcomb (1952) labeled **deindividuated.** What circumstances elicit this psychological state?

Group size

A group has the power not only to arouse its members but also to render them unidentifiable. The snarling crowd hides the snarling basketball fan. A lynch mob enables its members to believe they will not be prosecuted; they perceive the action as the *group's*. Rioters, made faceless by the mob, are freed to loot. In an analysis of 21 instances in which crowds were present as someone threat-ened to jump from a building or bridge, Leon Mann (1981) found that when the crowd was small and exposed by daylight, people usually did not try to bait the person. But when a large crowd or the cover of night gave people anonymity, the crowd usually baited and jeered. Brian Mullen (1986) reports a similar effect of lynch mobs: The bigger the mob, the more its members lose self-awareness and become willing to commit atrocities, such as burning, lacerating, or dis-membering the victim. In each of these examples, from sports crowds to lynch mobs, evaluation apprehension plummets. And because "everyone is doing it," all can attribute their behavior to the situation rather than to their own choices.

Philip Zimbardo (1970) speculated that the mere immensity of crowded cities produces anonymity and thus norms that permit vandalism. He purchased two 10-year-old cars and left them with the hoods up and license plates removed, one on a street near the old Bronx campus of New York University and one near the Stanford University campus in Palo Alto, a much smaller city. In New York the first auto strippers arrived within 10 minutes; they took the battery and radiator. After three days and 23 incidents of theft and vandalism (by neatly dressed White people), the car was reduced to a battered, useless hulk of metal. By contrast, the only person observed to touch the Palo Alto car in over a week was a passer-by who lowered the hood when it began to rain.

Physical anonymity

How can we be sure that the crucial difference between the Bronx and Palo Alto is greater anonymity in the Bronx? We can't. But we can experiment with anonymity to see if it actually lessens inhibitions. In one creative experiment, Zimbardo (1970) dressed women in identical white coats and hoods, rather like Ku Klux Klan members (Figure 8–5). Asked to deliver electric shocks to a woman, they pressed the shock button twice as long as did women who were visible and wearing large name tags.

Testing the phenomenon on the streets, Patricia Ellison, John Govern, and their colleagues (1995) had a confederate driver stop at a red light and wait for 12 seconds whenever she was followed by a convertible or 4x4 vehicle. While enduring the wait she recorded any horn-honking (a mild aggressive act) by the car behind. Compared to drivers of convertibles and 4x4s with the top down,

deindividuation
loss of self-awareness and evaluation apprehension; occurs in group situations that foster anonymity and draw attention away from the individual

"A mob is a society of bodies voluntarily bereaving themselves of reason."

Ralph Waldo Emerson, "Compensation," *Essays, First Series*, 1841

figure 8–5

Anonymous women
delivered more shock to
helpless victims than did
identifiable women.

those who were relatively anonymous (with the top up) honked one-third sooner, twice as often, and for nearly twice as long.

A research team led by Ed Diener (1976) cleverly demonstrated the effect both of being in a group *and* being physically anonymous. At Halloween, they observed 1,352 children trick-or-treating. As the children, either alone or in groups, approached 1 of 27 homes scattered throughout the city, an experimenter greeted them warmly, invited them to "take *one* of the candies," and then left the room. Hidden observers noted that, compared to solo children, those in groups were more than twice as likely to take extra candy. Also, compared to children who had been asked their names and where they lived, those left anonymous were also more than twice as likely to transgress. As Figure 8–6 shows, the transgression rate thus varied dramatically with the situation. When deindividuated by group immersion combined with anonymity, most children stole extra candy.

These experiments make me wonder about the effect of wearing uniforms. Preparing for battle, warriors in some tribal cultures (like rabid fans of some sports teams) depersonalize themselves with body and face paints or special masks. After the battle, some cultures kill, torture, or mutilate any remaining enemies; other cultures take prisoners alive. Robert Watson (1973) scrutinized anthropological files and discovered that the cultures with depersonalized warriors were also the cultures that brutalized the enemy. The uniformed Canadian soldiers who tortured and killed Shidane Arone were angered and aroused by their frustrating mission and the brutal desert heat, and enjoying one another's camaraderie they were unaware that outsiders would view their actions. Thus, forgetting their normal standards, they were swept away by the situation.

Does becoming physically anonymous *always* unleash our worst impulses? Fortunately, no. For one thing, the situations in which some of these experiments took place had clear antisocial cues. Robert Johnson and Leslie Downing (1979) point out that the Klan-like outfits worn by Zimbardo's subjects may have encouraged hostility. In an experiment, they had women put on nurses' uniforms before deciding how much shock someone should receive. When those wearing the nurses' uniforms were made anonymous,

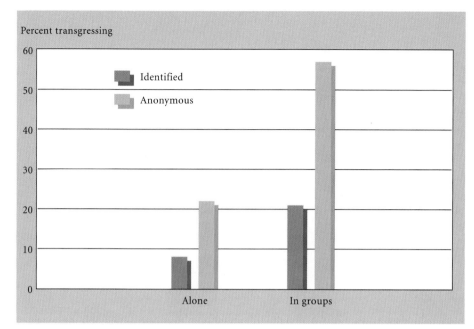

Percent transgressing

■ Identified

■ Anonymous

Alone   In groups

(Data from Diener & others, 1976.)

figure 8–6
Children were more
likely to transgress by
taking extra Halloween
candy when in a group,
when anonymous, and,
especially, when
deindividuated by the
combination of group
immersion and
anonymity.

they became *less* aggressive in administering shocks than when their names and personal identities were stressed. Evidently, being anonymous makes one less self-conscious and more responsive to cues present in the situation, whether negative (Klan uniforms) or positive (nurses' uniforms). Given altruistic cues, deindividuated people even give more money (Spivey & Prentice-Dunn, 1990).

This helps explain why wearing black uniforms—which are traditionally associated with evil and death and worn by medieval executioners, Darth Vader, and Ninja warriors—have an effect opposite to that of wearing a nurse's uniform. Mark Frank and Thomas Gilovich (1988) report that, led by the Los Angeles Raiders and the Philadelphia Flyers, black-uniformed teams consistently ranked near the top of the National Football and Hockey Leagues in penalties assessed between 1970 and 1986. Follow-up laboratory research suggests that just putting on a black jersey can trigger wearers to behave more aggressively.

Arousing and distracting activities

Aggressive outbursts by large groups are often preceded by minor actions that arouse and divert people's attention. Group shouting, chanting, clapping, or dancing serve both to hype people up and to reduce self-consciousness. One Moonie observer recalls how the "choo-choo" chant helped deindividuate:

> All the brothers and sisters joined hands and chanted with increasing intensity, choo-choo-choo, Choo-choo-choo, CHOO-CHOO-CHOO! YEA! YEA! POWW!!! The act made us a group, as though in some strange way we had all experienced something important together. The power of the choo-choo frightened me, but it made me feel more comfortable and there was something very relaxing about building up the energy and releasing it. (Zimbardo & others, 1977, p. 186)

"The use of self-control is like the use of brakes on a train. It is useful when you find yourself going in the wrong direction, but merely harmful when the direction is right."

Bertrand Russell, *Marriage and Morals*

Deindividuated English soccer fans after a 1985 riot that killed 39 people. The soccer hooligans are often likeable as individuals, reported one journalist who ran with them for eight years, but in a crowd they become demonic (Buford, 1992).

Ed Diener's experiments (1976, 1979) have shown that such activities as throwing rocks and group singing can set the stage for more disinhibited behavior. There is a self-reinforcing pleasure in doing an impulsive act while observing others doing it also. When we see others act as we are acting, we think they feel as we do, which reinforces our own feelings (Orive, 1984). Moreover, impulsive group action absorbs our attention. When we yell at the referee, we are not thinking about our values; we are reacting to the immediate situation. Later, when we stop to think about what we have done or said, we sometimes feel chagrined. Sometimes. At other times we seek deindividuating group experiences—dances, worship experiences, group encounters—where we can enjoy intense positive feelings and feel close to others.

Diminished self-awareness

Group experiences that diminish self-consciousness tend to disconnect behavior from attitudes. Experiments by Ed Diener (1980) and Steven Prentice-Dunn and Ronald Rogers (1980, 1989) reveal that unself-conscious, deindividuated people are less restrained, less self-regulated, more likely to act without thinking about their own values, more responsive to the situation. These findings complement and reinforce the experiments on *self-awareness* considered in Chapter 3.

"Attending a service in the Gothic cathedral, we have the sensation of being enclosed and steeped in an integral universe, and of losing a prickly sense of self in the community of worshippers."

Yi-Fu Tuan, 1982

Self-awareness is the opposite of deindividuation. Those made self-aware, say by acting in front of a mirror or TV camera, exhibit *increased* self-control, and their actions more clearly reflect their attitudes. In front of a mirror, people taste-testing cream cheese varieties eat less of the high-fat alternative (Sentyrz & Bushman, 1997). People made self-aware are also less likely to cheat (Beaman & others, 1979; Diener & Wallbom, 1976). So are those who generally have a strong sense of themselves as distinct and independent (Nadler & others, 1982). People who are self-conscious, or who are temporarily made so, exhibit greater consistency between their words outside a situation and their deeds in it. They also become more thoughtful and therefore less vulnerable to appeals that run counter to their values (Hutton & Baumeister, 1992).

Circumstances that decrease self-awareness, as alcohol consumption does, therefore increase deindividuation (Hull & others, 1983). And deindividuation decreases in circumstances that increase self-awareness: mirrors and cameras, small towns, bright lights, large name tags, undistracted quiet, individual clothes and houses (Ickes & others, 1978). When a teenager leaves for a party, a parent's parting advice could well be this: "Have fun, and remember who you are." In other words, enjoy being with the group, but be self-aware; don't become deindividuated.

Summing up

When high levels of social arousal combine with diffused responsibility, people may abandon their normal restraints and lose their sense of individuality. Such "deindividuation" is especially likely when, after being aroused and distracted, people feel anonymity while in a large group or wearing concealing clothing or costumes. The result is diminished self-awareness and self-restraint and increased responsiveness to the immediate situation, be it negative or positive.

Group polarization

Many conflicts grow as people on both sides talk mostly with like-minded others. Does such interaction amplify preexisting attitudes? If so, why?

Which effects—good or bad—does group interaction more often have? Police brutality and mob violence demonstrate its destructive potential. Yet support-group leaders, management consultants, and educational theorists proclaim its benefits. And social and religious movements urge their members to strengthen their identities by fellowship with like-minded others.

Research helps clarify our understanding of such effects. From studies of people in small groups, a principle emerges that helps explain both destructive and constructive outcomes: Group discussion often strengthens members' initial inclinations (good or bad). The unfolding of this research on "group polarization" illustrates the process of inquiry—how an interesting discovery often leads researchers to hasty and erroneous conclusions, which ultimately get replaced with more accurate conclusions. This is one scientific mystery I can discuss firsthand, having been one of the detectives.

The case of the "risky shift"

A research literature of more than 300 studies began with a surprising finding by James Stoner (1961). For his master's thesis in industrial management, Stoner compared risk taking by individuals and groups. To test the commonly held belief that groups are more cautious than individuals, Stoner posed decision dilemmas faced by fictional characters. The participant's task was to advise the imagined character how much risk to take. Put yourself in the participant's shoes: What advice would you give the character in this situation?

Helen is a writer who is said to have considerable creative talent but who so far has been earning a comfortable living by writing cheap westerns. Recently she has come up with an idea for a potentially significant novel. If it could be written and accepted, it might have considerable literary impact and be a big boost to her career. On the other hand, if she cannot work out her idea or if the novel is a flop, she will have expended considerable time and energy without remuneration.

Imagine that you are advising Helen. Please check the *lowest* probability that you would consider acceptable for Helen to attempt to write the novel.

Helen should attempt to write the novel if the chances that the novel will be a success are at least

_____ 1 in 10
_____ 2 in 10
_____ 3 in 10
_____ 4 in 10
_____ 5 in 10
_____ 6 in 10
_____ 7 in 10
_____ 8 in 10
_____ 9 in 10
_____ 10 in 10 (Place a check here if you think Helen should attempt the novel only if it is certain that the novel will be a success.)

After making your decision, guess what this book's average reader would advise.

Having marked their advice on a dozen such items, five or so individuals would then discuss and reach agreement on each item. How do you think the group decisions compared to the average decision before the discussions? Would the groups be likely to take greater risks? be more cautious? stay the same?

To everyone's amazement, the group decisions were usually riskier. Dubbed the "risky shift phenomenon," this finding set off a wave of investigation into group risk taking. The studies revealed that this effect occurs not only when a group decides by consensus; after a brief discussion, individuals, too, will alter their decisions. What is more, researchers successfully repeated Stoner's finding with people of varying ages and occupations in a dozen different nations.

During discussion, opinions converged. Curiously, however, the point toward which they converged was usually a lower (riskier) number than their initial average. Here was a delightful puzzle. The small risky shift effect was reliable, unexpected, and without any immediately obvious explanation. What group influences produce such an effect? And how widespread is it? Do discussions in juries, business committees, and military organizations also promote risk taking?

After several years of study and speculation about group risk taking, we became aware that the risky shift was not universal. We could write decision dilemmas on which people became more *cautious* after discussion. One of these featured "Roger," a young married man with two school-age children and a secure but low-paying job. Roger can afford life's necessities but few of its luxuries. He hears that the stock of a relatively unknown company may soon triple in value if its new product is favorably received or decline considerably if it does not sell. Roger has no savings. To invest in the company, he is considering selling his life insurance policy.

Can you see a general principle that predicts both the tendency to give riskier advice after discussing Helen's situation and more cautious advice after discussing Roger's?

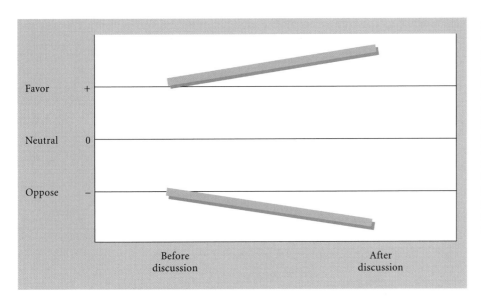

figure 8–7
The group-polarization hypothesis predicts that discussion will strengthen an attitude shared by group members. If people initially tend to favor something (say, risk on a life dilemma question), they tend to favor it even more after discussion. If they tend to oppose something, they tend to oppose it even more after discussion.

If you are like most people, you would advise Helen to take greater risk than Roger, even before talking with others. It turns out there is a strong tendency for discussion to accentuate these initial leanings.

We therefore began to realize that this group phenomenon was not, as originally assumed, a consistent shift to risk, but rather a tendency for group discussion to *enhance* the individuals' initial leanings. This idea led investigators to propose what Serge Moscovici and Marisa Zavalloni (1969) called a **group polarization** phenomenon: *Discussion typically strengthens the average inclination of group members.*

group polarization
group-produced enhancement of members' preexisting tendencies; a strengthening of the members' *average* tendency, not a split within the group

Do groups intensify opinions?

Group polarization experiments

This new view of the changes induced by group discussion prompted experimenters to have people discuss statements that most of them favored or most of them opposed. Would talking in groups enhance their initial inclinations as it did with the decision dilemmas? That's what the group polarization hypothesis predicts (Figure 8–7).

Dozens of studies confirm group polarization. Moscovici and Zavalloni (1969) observed that discussion enhanced French students' initially positive attitude toward their premier and negative attitude toward Americans. Mititoshi Isozaki (1984) found that Japanese university students gave more pronounced judgments of "guilty" after discussing a traffic case. And Glen Whyte (1993) reports that groups exacerbate the "too much invested to quit" phenomenon that has cost many businesses huge sums of money. Canadian business students imagined themselves having to decide whether to invest more money in the hope of preventing losses in various failing projects (for example, whether to make a high-risk loan to protect an earlier investment). They exhibited the typical effect: Seventy-two percent reinvested money they would seldom have invested if they were considering it as a new investment on its own merits. When making the same decision in groups, 94 percent opted for reinvestment.

figure 8–8

Discussion increased polarization between homogeneous groups of high- and low-prejudice high school students. Talking over racial issues increased prejudice in a high-prejudice group and decreased it in a low-prejudice group.

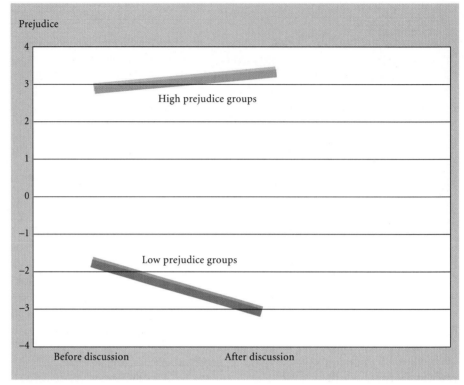

(Data from Myers & Bishop, 1970.)

Another research strategy has been to pick issues on which opinions are divided and then isolate people who hold the same view. Does discussion with like-minded people strengthen shared views? Does it magnify the attitude gap that separates the two sides?

George Bishop and I wondered. So we set up groups of relatively prejudiced and unprejudiced high school students and asked them to respond—before and after discussion—to issues involving racial attitudes, such as property rights versus open housing (Myers & Bishop, 1970). We found that the discussions among like-minded students did indeed increase the initial gap between the two groups (Figure 8–8).

Naturally occurring group polarization

In everyday life people associate mostly with others whose attitudes are similar to their own (Chapter 11). (Look at your own circle of friends.) So, does everyday group interaction with like-minded friends intensify shared attitudes? In natural situations it's hard to disentangle cause and effect. But the laboratory phenomenon does have real-life parallels.

One such parallel is what education researchers have called the "accentuation phenomenon": Over time, initial differences among university-student groups become accentuated. If the students at university X are initially more intellectual than the students at university Y, that gap is likely to grow during their time at university. Likewise, compared to fraternity and sorority members, independents tend to have more liberal political attitudes, a difference that grows with time in university (Pascarella & Terenzini, 1991). Researchers believe this results partly from group members reinforcing shared inclinations (Chickering & McCormick, 1973; Feldman & Newcomb, 1969; Wilson & others, 1975).

Polarization also occurs in communities. During community conflicts, like-minded people increasingly associate with one another. This amplifies their shared tendencies. Gang delinquency emerges from a process of mutual reinforcement within neighborhood gangs, whose members have a common socioeconomic and ethnic background (Cartwright, 1975). From their analysis of terrorist organizations around the world, Clark McCauley and Mary Segal (1987) note that terrorism does not erupt suddenly. Rather, it arises among people whose shared grievances bring them together. As they interact in isolation from moderating influences, they become progressively more extreme. The social amplifier brings the signal in stronger. The result is violent acts that the individuals, apart from the group, would never have committed.

Explaining polarization

Why do groups adopt stances that are more exaggerated than the average opinions of their individual members? Researchers hoped that solving the mystery of group polarization might provide some insights. Solving small puzzles sometimes provides clues for solving larger ones.

Among several proposed theories of group polarization, two survived scientific scrutiny. One deals with the arguments presented during a discussion, the other with how members of a group view themselves vis-à-vis the other members. The first idea is an example of what Chapter 6 called *informational influence* (influence that results from accepting evidence about reality). The second is an example of *normative influence* (influence based on a person's desire to be accepted or admired by others).

Informational influence

According to the best-supported explanation, group discussion elicits a pooling of ideas, most of which favor the dominant viewpoint. Ideas that were common knowledge to group members will often be brought up in discussion or, even if unmentioned, will jointly influence their discussion (Gigone & Hastie, 1993; Larson & others, 1994; Stasser, 1991). Other ideas may include persuasive arguments

> In two trials, South African courts reduced sentences after learning how social-psychological phenomena, including deindividuation and group polarization, led crowd members to commit murderous acts (Colman, 1991). Would you agree that courts should consider social-psychological phenomena as possible extenuating circumstances?

focus

Group polarization

Shakespeare portrayed the polarizing power of the like-minded group in this dialogue of Julius Caesar's followers:

ANTONY: Kind souls, what weep you when you but behold Our Caesar's vesture wounded? Look you here. Here is himself, marr'd, as you see, with traitors.

FIRST CITIZEN: O piteous spectacle!
SECOND CITIZEN: O noble Caesar!
THIRD CITIZEN: O woeful day!
FOURTH CITIZEN: O traitors, villains!
FIRST CITIZEN: O most bloody sight!
SECOND CITIZEN: We will be revenged!
ALL: Revenge! About! Seek! Burn! Fire! Kill! Slay! Let not a traitor live!

From Julius Caesar *by William Shakespeare, Act III, Scene ii, lines 199–209.*

Group polarization: an anticrime rally. Group interaction among like-minded people tends to strengthen their shared attitudes.

that some group members had not previously considered. When discussing Helen the writer, someone may say, "Helen should go for it, because she has little to lose. If her novel flops, she can always go back to writing cheap westerns." Such statements often entangle information about the person's *arguments* with cues concerning the person's *position* on the issue. But when people hear relevant arguments without learning the specific stands other people assume, they still shift their positions (Burnstein & Vinokur, 1977; Hinsz & others, 1997). *Arguments*, in and of themselves, matter.

But there's more to attitude change than merely hearing someone else's arguments. *Active participation* in discussion produces more attitude change than does passive listening. Participants and observers hear the same ideas, but when participants put them into their own words, the verbal commitment magnifies the impact. The more group members repeat one another's ideas, the more they rehearse and validate them (Brauer & others, 1995).

This illustrates a point made in Chapter 7: People's minds are not just blank tablets for persuaders to write on. In central route persuasion, what people *think* in response to a message is crucial. Indeed, just thinking about an issue for a couple of minutes can strengthen opinions (Tesser & others, 1995). (Perhaps you can recall your feelings becoming polarized as you merely ruminated about someone you disliked, or liked.) Even just *expecting* to discuss an issue with an equally expert person holding an opposing view can motivate people to marshal their arguments and thus to adopt a more extreme position (Fitzpatrick & Eagly, 1981).

Normative influence

social comparison
evaluating one's opinions and abilities by comparing oneself to others

A second explanation of polarization involves comparison with others. As Leon Festinger (1954) argued in his influential theory of **social comparison**, it is human nature to want to evaluate our opinions and abilities, something we can do by comparing our views with others'. We are most persuaded by people in our "reference groups"—groups we identify with (Abrams & others, 1990; Hogg & others, 1990). Moreover, wanting people to like us, we may express stronger opinions after discovering that others share our views.

Robert Baron and his colleagues (1996) explored the polarizing effect of having one's views socially corroborated. In one experiment, they asked dental clinic patients whether they considered the dental chair "comfortable" or "uncomfortable." Then the patients rated the chair on a +50 to -50 scale. Before making this rating, some subjects heard the experimenter ask: "By the way, Dr. X, what did the last patient say?" The dentist always echoed whatever response the patient had just made. Compared to subjects who did not hear their opinion corroborated, those who did gave decidedly more extreme ratings.

Perhaps you have been in the situation where you have wanted to go out with someone, but you were afraid to make the first move. You wait and watch, but the other person doesn't seem to be expressing any interest in you, so you think that he or she would probably reject you. But have you ever stopped to think that the other person might be doing the same thing you are. University of Manitoba researchers Jacquie Vorauer and Rebecca Ratner (1996) have shown that such reactions make it difficult for people to start up relationships.

Dale Miller and Cathy McFarland (1987) bottled a similar phenomenon in a laboratory experiment. They asked people to read an incomprehensible article and to seek help if they ran into "any really serious problems in understanding the paper." Although none of the subjects sought help, they presumed *other* subjects would not be similarly restrained by fear of embarrassment. They wrongly inferred that people who didn't seek help didn't need any. To overcome such **pluralistic ignorance**, someone must break the ice and enable others to reveal and reinforce their shared reactions.

pluralistic ignorance a false impression of how other people are thinking, feeling, or responding

When we ask people (as I asked you earlier) to predict how others would respond to items such as the "Helen" dilemma, they typically exhibit pluralistic ignorance: They don't realize how much others support the socially preferred tendency (in this case, writing the novel). A typical person will advise writing the novel even if its chance of success is only 4 in 10, but estimate that most other people would require 5 or 6 in 10. When the discussion begins, most people discover they are not outshining the others as they had supposed. In fact, some others are ahead of them, having taken an even stronger position for writing the novel. No longer restrained by a misperceived group norm, they are liberated to voice their preferences more strongly.

This social comparison theory prompted experiments that exposed people to others' positions but not to their arguments. This is roughly the experience we have when reading the results of an opinion poll. When people learn others' positions—without discussion—will they adjust their responses to maintain a socially favorable position? When people have made no prior commitment to a particular response, seeing others' responses *does* stimulate a small polarization (Goethals & Zanna, 1979; Sanders & Baron, 1977). (See Figure 8–9 for an example.) This polarization from mere social comparison is usually less than that produced by a lively discussion. Still, it's surprising that, instead of simply conforming to the group average, people often go it one better. Are people "one-upping" the observed norm to differentiate themselves from the group? Is this another example of our need to feel unique (Chapter 6)?

This finding is reminiscent of the self-serving bias (Chapter 2): People tend to view themselves as better-than-average embodiments of socially desirable traits and attitudes.

Group polarization research illustrates the complexity of social-psychological inquiry. As much as we like our explanations of a phenomenon to be simple, one explanation seldom accounts for all the data. Because people are complex, more than one factor frequently influences an outcome. In group discussions, persuasive arguments predominate on issues that have a factual element ("Is she

figure 8–9

On "risky" dilemma items (such as the case of Helen), mere exposure to others' judgments enhanced individuals' risk-prone tendencies. On "cautious" dilemma items (such as the case of Roger), exposure to others' judgments enhanced their cautiousness.

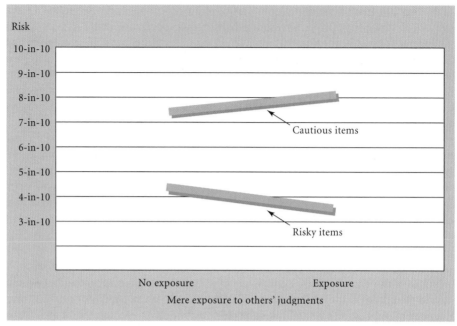

(Data from Myers, 1978.)

guilty of the crime?"). Social comparison sways responses on value-laden judgments ("How long a sentence should she serve?") (Kaplan, 1989). On the many issues that have both factual and value-laden aspects, the two factors work together. Discovering that others share one's feelings (social comparison) unleashes arguments (informational influence) supporting what everyone secretly favors.

Summing up

Potentially positive and negative results arise from group discussion. While trying to understand the curious finding that group discussion enhanced risk taking, investigators discovered that discussion actually tends to strengthen whatever is the initially dominant point of view, whether risky or cautious. In everyday situations, too, group interaction tends to intensify opinions.

The group polarization phenomenon provided a window through which researchers could observe group influence. Experiments confirmed two group influences: informational and normative. The information gleaned from a discussion mostly favors the initially preferred alternative, thus reinforcing support for it. Moreover, people may go further out on the limb when, after comparing positions, they discover surprising support for their initial inclinations.

Groupthink

When do group influences hinder smart decisions? When do groups promote good decisions, and how can we lead groups to make optimal decisions?

Do the social psychological phenomena we have been considering in these first eight chapters occur in sophisticated groups like corporate boards where people are professionals and know each other well? Is there likely to be self-justification? Self-serving bias? A cohesive "we feeling" provoking conformity and rejection of dissent? Public commitment producing resistance to change? Group polarization? Social psychologist Irving Janis (1971, 1982) wondered whether such phenomena might help explain good and bad decisions made by a number of leaders and their advisors. In particular he analyzed the decision making procedures that led to several major fiascoes. Although Janis did not analyze it, the sinking of the *Titanic*—the worst seafaring accident in history—provides a compelling example of the type of disasters Janis analyzed.

I will try to give an accurate account of this tragedy, but the particulars of the disaster will probably always be a bit of a mystery. Most of you have probably seen the movie *Titanic* written and directed by Canadian James Cameron, as it was the most widely seen movie of all-time, but there are many accounts and it is often hard to sort out the truth. The playwright George Bernard Shaw and mystery writer Sir Arthur Conan Doyle, creator of the Sherlock Holmes character, fought bitterly back and forth about many of the details in the years after the shipwreck. Sherlock himself might not have been able to completely solve all the mysteries of this disaster. Nevertheless, here are some of the basic facts that are not in dispute.

On April 10, 1912 the *Titanic* left Southampton, England on her maiden voyage across the Atlantic Ocean. At the time the *Titanic* was the largest and most fabulous ship in the world. It was as tall as an eleven-story building, as long as 8 football fields, and weighed 1000 tons more than any other ship. It had a double hull system that made many believe the ship was unsinkable. It was the pride of the White Star line of ships that owned it. The ship was cruising briskly across the Atlantic when on Sunday April 12th they received several messages that a group of icebergs was ahead. At least four of these messages reached the captain and at least one of these messages reached the president of the cruise line, who was aboard the ship. Despite these warnings the ship did not slow down. At about 11:40 p.m. one of the lookouts saw an iceberg straight ahead and sounded the warning. The first officer, who was at the helm, swung the ship to the port but only fast enough to avoid hitting the iceberg head on. The ice tore a huge gash in the side of the ship. It took the crew some time, but not a great deal of time, to know the extent of the damage—by 12:15 a.m. they knew the ship was going to sink. Lifeboats were lowered and filled, or sadly only partially filled, with passengers, and distress calls were sent out to other ships. One sad fact was that the *Titanic* had only 20 lifeboats, which was not even enough for half of the passengers. The ship finally went under at 2:20 a.m. Only 705 people survived the shipwreck; at least twice those many died. The exact number is one of those facts that is in dispute. The estimates range between 1490 and 1635.

Janis believed that such tragedies could be traced to the tendency of decision-making groups to suppress dissent in the interests of group harmony, a phenomenon he called **groupthink**. In work groups, camaraderie boosts productivity (Mullen & Cooper, 1994). Moreover, teamspirit is good for morale. But when making decisions, close-knit groups may pay a price. Janis believed that the soil from which groupthink sprouts includes an amiable, cohesive group, relative isolation of the group from dissenting viewpoints, and a directive leader who signals what decision he or she favors. When deciding what to do

groupthink
"The mode of thinking that persons engage in when concurrence-seeking becomes so dominant in a cohesive in-group that it tends to override realistic appraisal of alternative courses of action."
Irving Janis (1971)

with the threat of the icebergs ahead there is little doubt that Captain Edward J. Smith, the senior captain of the cruise line who had served for 38 years, was a strong and directive leader and he and his crew enjoyed a strong *esprit de corps*. As one source (Lord, 1955) put it Smith was "worshipped by crew and passenger alike. . . They loved everything about him." It is also clear that in the middle of the Atlantic they were isolated from other points of view. It is quite possible that groupthink may have influenced their decision-making. Let's see if they displayed the symptoms of groupthink.

Symptoms of Groupthink

From historical records and the memoirs of participants and observers, Janis identified eight groupthink symptoms. These symptoms are a collective form of dissonance reduction that surface as group members try to maintain the positive group feeling when facing a threat (Tuner & others, 1992, 1994).

The first two groupthink symptoms lead group members to *overestimate their group's might and right*:

- **An illusion of invulnerability:** There is little question that Capt. Smith and his crew had developed an illusion that nothing bad could happen to them or their ship. Five years before the crash it was clear that Capt. Smith believed a disaster with loss of life could not happen to one of his ships, saying, "I cannot conceive of any vital disaster happening . . . Modern shipbuilding has gone beyond that." (Marshall, 1912) As the ship departed from Southampton, one of the crew members expressed a view that seemed to be widespread. When asked if the *Titanic* was really unsinkable, he replied, "God Himself could not sink this ship." (Lord, 1955)
- **Unquestioned belief in the group's morality:** Group members assume the inherent morality of their group and ignore ethical and moral issues. Looking back on the tragedy of the *Titanic* it is clear that they should have had more lifeboats aboard the vessel, and sadly this would not have been difficult. But the builders of the ship and especially the president of the cruise line decided they were not needed.

Group members also become *closed-minded:*

- **Rationalization:** The group discounts challenges by collectively justifying their decisions. The officers on the Titanic knew they were in the vicinity of icebergs, but went on at full speed. In one critical conversion at 9:00 p.m. the second officer and Capt. Smith discussed how they should handle the ship. Both knew that they were in the vicinity of icebergs, but Capt. Smith remarked that it was an exceptionally clear night and therefore they did not need to slow down (Davie, 1986).
- **Stereotyped view of opponent:** One of the most controversial stories surrounding the *Titanic* is whether the ship was trying to break a speed record in crossing the Atlantic. You may recall that the movie *Titanic* portrayed the president of the cruise line as pressuring the Captain to break a speed record. This story has been suggested several times and believed by many—even though the president of the cruise line, who survived, vehemently denied it. One reason the story is believable to some is that the shipping business was intensely competitive in the early 1900s and cruise lines had very derogatory views of others. These stereotyped views of their opponents might well have led Capt. Smith and his crew to ignore the warnings from other ships.

Self-censorship contributes to an illusion of unanimity.

Finally, the group suffers from *pressures toward uniformity:*

- **Conformity pressure:** Group members rebuff those who raised doubts about the group's assumptions and plans, at times not by argument but by ridicule. When Fredrick Fleet—the lookout who eventually saw the iceberg—complained that the crew did not have binoculars he was chided by his colleagues for not being able to use his naked eye.

- **Self-censorship:** Since disagreements are often uncomfortable and the groups seem in consensus, members often withhold or discount their misgivings. Despite Fleet's belief that he needed a pair of binoculars for his task as a lookout, he did not suggest that they pick up a new pair at the next port. He was at a loss to describe his failure to do so. He maintained until his dying day that if he would have had a pair of binoculars he would have seen the iceberg soon enough to avoid hitting it.

- **Illusion of unanimity:** Self-censorship and pressure not to puncture the consensus create an illusion of unanimity. What is more, the apparent consensus confirms the group's decision. Did none of the experienced crew on the *Titanic* think they should slow down? It seems likely that the apparent unanimity about the decision to go full speed ahead was merely an illusion. This sort of illusion has been seen in other groups as well. Albert Speer (1971), an adviser to Hitler, described the atmosphere around Hitler as one where pressure to conform suppressed all deviance. The absence of dissent created the illusion of unanimity:

> People "are never so likely to settle a question rightly as when they discuss it freely."
>
> John Stuart Mill *On Liberty*, 1859

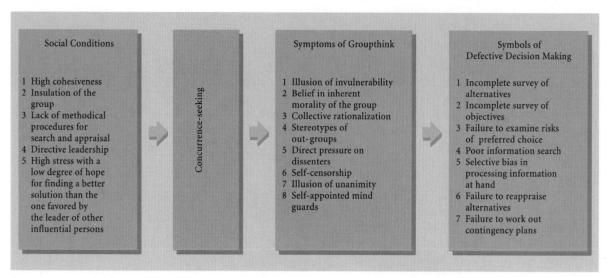

(Data from Janis & Mann, 1977, p. 132.)

figure 8–10

Theoretical analysis of groupthink.

In normal circumstances people who turn their backs on reality are soon set straight by the mockery and criticism of those around them, which makes them aware that they have lost credibility. In the Third Reich there were no such correctives, especially for those who belonged to the upper stratum. On the contrary, every self-deception was multiplied as in a hall of distorting mirrors, becoming a repeatedly confirmed picture of a fantastical dream world which no longer bore any relationship to the grim outside world. In those mirrors I could see nothing but my own face reproduced many times over. No external factors disturbed the uniformity of hundreds of unchanging faces, all mine. (p.379)

- **Mindguards:** Some members protect the group from information that would call into question the effectiveness or the morality of its decisions. The telegraph operator on the *Titanic* provided a compelling example of this symptom. After receiving several warning messages about icebergs, he failed to take down the final and most complete message about the iceberg that was struck and he failed to pass this message to the Captain. Thus the operator deprived Capt. Smith of the latest information that would challenge his decision to go full steam ahead.

Groupthink symptoms can produce a failure to seek and discuss contrary information and alternative possibilities (Figure 8–10). When a leader promotes an idea and when a group insulates itself from dissenting views, groupthink may produce defective decisions (McCauley, 1989).

Critiquing groupthink

Although Janis's ideas and observations have received enormous attention, some researchers are skeptical (Fuller & Aldag, 1998; t'Hart, 1998). The evidence was retrospective, so Janis could pick supporting cases. Follow-up experiments suggested that directive leadership is indeed associated with poorer decisions (McCauley, 1998), but that cohesiveness need not breed groupthink (Esser, 1998; Hodson & Sorrentine, 1997; Mullen & others, 1994). When members look to a group for acceptance, approval, and social identity, they may suppress

focus

The doomed flight of the *Challenger*

Groupthink was tragically evident in the decision process by which NASA decided to launch the space shuttle *Challenger* in January 1986 (Esser & Lindoerfer, 1989). Engineers at Morton Thiokol, which makes the shuttle's rocket boosters, and at Rockwell International, which manufactures the orbiter, opposed the launch because of dangers posed to equipment by the subfreezing temperatures. The Thiokol engineers feared the cold would make the rubber seals between the rocket's four segments too brittle to contain the superhot gases. Several months before the doomed mission, the company's top expert had warned in a memo that it was a "jump ball" whether the seal would hold and that if it failed, "the result would be a catastrophe of the highest order" (Magnuson, 1986).

In a telephone discussion the night before the launch, the engineers argued their case with their uncertain managers and with officials, who were eager to proceed with the already delayed launch. One Thiokol official later testified: "We got ourselves into the thought process that we were trying to find some way to prove to them [the booster] wouldn't work. We couldn't prove absolutely that it wouldn't work." The result was an *illusion of invulnerability*.

Conformity pressures also operated. One official complained, "My God, Thiokol, when do you want me to launch, next April?" The top Thiokol executive declared, "We have to make a management decision," and then asked his engineering vice-president to "take off his engineering hat and put on his management hat."

To create an *illusion of unanimity*, this executive then proceeded to poll only the management officials and ignore the engineers. The go-ahead decision now made, one of the engineers belatedly pleaded with a NASA official to reconsider: "If anything happened to this launch," he said prophetically, "I sure wouldn't want to be the person that had to stand in front of a board of inquiry to explain why I launched."

Thanks, finally, to *mindguarding*, the top executive who made the final decision never learned about the engineers' concerns, nor about the reservations of the Rockwell officials. Protected from disagreeable information, he confidently gave the go-ahead to launch the *Challenger* on its tragic flight.

disagreeable thoughts (Turner & Pratkanis, 1997). But secure, highly cohesive groups (say, a married couple) can provide members with freedom to disagree. In a free-spirited atmosphere, cohesion can enhance effective teamwork.

Moreover, when Philip Tetlock and his colleagues (1992) looked at a broader sample of historical episodes, it became clear that even good group procedures sometimes yield ill-fated decisions. As Jimmy Carter and his advisers plotted their humiliating attempt to rescue hostages in Iran in 1980, they welcomed different views and realistically considered the perils. But for a helicopter problem the rescue might have succeeded. (Carter later reflected that had he sent in one more helicopter he believed they would have suceeded.) To reword Mister Rogers, sometimes good groups do bad things.

Reflecting on the critiques of groupthink, Paul Paulus (1998) reminds us of Leon Festinger's (1987) observation that only an untestable theory is unchanging. "If a theory is at all testable, it will not remain unchanged. It has to change. All theories are wrong." Thus, said Festinger, we shouldn't ask whether a theory is right or wrong, but rather "how much of the empirical realm can it handle and how must it be modified." Irving Janis, having tested and modified his own theory before his death in 1990, would surely have welcomed others

"Truth springs from argument amongst friends."

Philosopher David Hume, 1711–1776

"There was a serious flaw in the decision-making process."

Report of the Presidential Commission on the Space Shuttle *Challenger* Accident, 1986

Groupthink in action: the space shuttle Challenger explosion, January 28, 1986.

continuing to reshape it. For in science that is how we grope our way towards truth, by testing our ideas against reality, revising them, and then testing them some more.

Preventing groupthink

Flawed group dynamics help explain many failed decisions; sometimes too many cooks always spoil the broth. But given open leadership, a cohesive team spirit can improve decisions. Sometimes two or more heads are better than one.

In search of conditions that breed good decisions, Janis also analyzed two seemingly successful ventures: the formulation of the Marshall Plan for getting Europe back on its feet after World War II and the handling of the former U.S.S.R.'s attempts to install missile bases in Cuba in 1962. Janis's (1982) recommendations for preventing groupthink incorporate many of the effective group procedures used in both cases:

- Be impartial—do not endorse any position
- Encourage critical evaluation; assign a "devil's advocate"
- Occasionally subdivide the group, then reunite to air differences
- Welcome critiques from outside experts and associates
- Before implementing, call a "second-chance" meeting to air any lingering doubts

Ineffective group dynamics may have contributed to the crash of Swissair flight 111 off Peggy's Cove, Nova Scotia. The pilot and co-pilot reportedly disagreed over how to respond to a fire in the cockpit, and were unable to take action in time. Recognizing the importance of cockpit group dynamics, ailrines now provide crew management training and seek pilots who are capable of functioning as team members.

Some of these practical principles for improved group dynamics are now being taught to airline flight crews. Training programs, called crew resource management, developed from the realization that flight crew mistakes contribute to more than two thirds of plane accidents. Having two or three people in the cockpit should increase the odds that someone will notice a problem or see its solution—if the information gets shared. Sometimes, however, groupthink pressures lead to conformity or self-censorship.

On the night of September 2, 1998 Swiss Air flight 111 crashed just off of Peggy's Cove, Nova Scotia, killing all 229 people on board. The crash appears to have occurred because faulty wiring led to a fire in the cockpit. Several stories in the media reported that the two pilots were at odds in how to respond to the fire. These reports suggested that the co-pilot wanted to forget about procedure and land the plane immediately. The pilot, on the other hand, was allegedly firm in his insistence that they follow the standard procedure, and was so busy with a checklist that he was not able to discuss a plan of action with the co-pilot. Could these faulty group dynamics have played a role in the crash? Currently, the Canadian Transportation Safety Board has not released their final report on the crash, so we do not even know if the media reports are accurate, but faulty group dynamics have been linked to other crashes (Helmrich, 1997).

But not always. In 1989, a three-person crew facing a similar problem responded as a model team to imminent disaster. The crew, which had been trained in crew resource management, faced the disintegration of the center engine, severing lines to the rudder and ailerons needed to maneuver the plane. In the 34 minutes before crash landing just short of the airport runway, the crew had to devise a strategy for bringing the plane under control, assessing damage, choosing a landing site, and preparing the crew and passengers for the crash. Minute-by-minute analysis of the cockpit conversation revealed intense interaction—31 communications per minute (one per second at its peak). In these minutes the crew members recruited a fourth pilot who was flying as a passenger, prioritized their work, and kept one another aware of unfolding events and decisions. Junior crew members freely suggested alternatives and the captain responded with appropriate commands. Bursts of social conversation provided emotional support, enabling the crew to cope with the extreme stress, and to save the lives of 185 of the 296 people on board.

Groupthink and group influence

The symptoms of groupthink illustrate self-justification, self-serving bias, and conformity. Ivan Steiner (1982) noted how the hypothesized groupthink processes also coincide with previous research on group influence. For example, researchers have observed that problem-solving groups have a strong tendency to converge on a single solution. Convergence (which Janis calls "concurrence seeking") appears in the group polarization experiments: A group's average position may polarize, but its members also converge. Groups "strain toward uniformity" (Nemeth & Staw, 1989).

Experiments on group problem-solving document self-censorship and biased discussion. Group conversation often focuses on what everyone already knows, leaving other valuable information unshared (Schittekatte, 1996; Stasser, 1992). Once a margin of support for one alternative develops, better ideas therefore have little chance of acceptance. Likewise, reports Steiner, accounts of mob lynchings reveal that once a lynching was suggested, misgivings, if not immediately expressed, got drowned out. In group polarization experiments, arguments that surface in group discussion are more one-sided than those volunteered by individuals privately. This one-sidedness helps group discussion accentuate natural tendencies toward overconfidence (Dunning & Ross, 1988).

Experiments confirm groupthink research by showing that under some conditions two heads *are* better than one. Patrick Laughlin and John Adamopoulos (1980, 1996) have shown this with various intellectual tasks. Consider one of their analogy problems:

> *Assertion* is to *disproved* as *action* is to
> a. *hindered*
> b. *opposed*
> c. *illegal*
> d. *precipitate*
> e. *thwarted*

Most university students miss this question when answering alone, but answer correctly (thwarted) after discussion. Moreover, Laughlin finds that if but two

"Two forecasters will come up with a forecast that is more accurate than either would have come up with working alone."

Joel N. Myers
President, AccuWeather,
1997

behind the scenes

The idea of *groupthink* hit me while reading Arthur Schlesinger's account of how the Kennedy administration decided to invade the Bay of Pigs. At first, I was puzzled: How could bright, shrewd people like John F. Kennedy and his advisers be taken in by the CIA's stupid, patchwork plan? I began to wonder whether some kind of psychological contagion had interfered, such as social conformity or the concurrence-seeking that I had observed in cohesive small groups. Further study (initially aided by my daughter Charlotte's work on a high school term paper) convinced me that subtle group processes had hampered their carefully appraising the risks and debating the issues. When I then analyzed other U.S. foreign policy fiascos and the Watergate cover-up, I found the same detrimental group processes at work.

Irving Janis (1918–1990)

members of a six-person group are initially correct, two thirds of the time they convince all the others. If but one person is correct, this "minority of one" almost three fourths of the time fails to convince the group. Dell Warnick and Glenn Sanders (1980) and Verlin Hinsz (1990) confirmed that several heads can be better than one when they studied the accuracy of eyewitness reports of a videotaped crime or job interview. Groups of eyewitnesses gave accounts that were much more accurate than those provided by the average isolated individual. Several heads critiquing each other can also allow the group to avoid some forms of cognitive bias and produce some higher-quality ideas (McGlynn & others, 1995; Wright & others, 1990).

But contrary to the popular idea that brainstorming in small groups generates more creative ideas than the same people working alone, researchers agree it isn't so (Paulus & others, 1995, 1997, 1998; Stroebe & Diehl, 1994). People *feel* more productive when generating ideas in groups (partly because people disproportionately credit themselves for the ideas that come out), but they don't generate more ideas. The one exception to this trend is when people brainstorm electronically on computers. Here they do not block each other from presenting ideas, and more creative ideas come forward (Gallupe, R. B., Cooper, W H., Grise, M. L., & Bastianutti, L. M., 1994). But in general, as John Watson and Francis Crick demonstrated in discovering DNA, challenging two-person conversations can more effectively engage creative thinking.

Summing up

Analysis of the decisions that led to several international fiascos indicates that group desire for harmony can override realistic appraisal of contrary views. This is especially true when group members strongly desire unity, when they are isolated from opposing ideas, and when the leader signals what he or she wants from the group.

Symptomatic of this overriding concern for harmony, labeled "groupthink," are (1) an illusion of invulnerability, (2) rationalization, (3) unquestioned belief in the group's morality, (4) stereotyped views of the opposition, (5) pressure to conform, (6) self-censorship of misgivings, (7) an illusion of unanimity, and (8) "mindguards" who protect the group from unpleasant information. Critics have noted that some aspects of Janis's groupthink model (such as directive leadership) seem more implicated in flawed decisions than others (such as cohesiveness).

Both in experiments and in actual history, however, groups sometimes decide wisely. These cases suggest remedies for groupthink. By seeking information from all sides and improving the evaluation of possible alternatives, a group can benefit from its members' combined insights.

Minority influence

Groups influence individuals, but when—and how—do individuals influence their groups? And what defines effective leadership?

Each chapter in this social influence unit concludes with a reminder of our power as individuals. We have seen that

- cultural situations mold us, but we also help create and choose these situations;
- pressures to conform sometimes overwhelm our better judgment, but blatant pressure can motivate us to assert our individuality and freedom;
- persuasive forces are indeed powerful, but we can resist persuasion by making public commitments and by anticipating persuasive appeals.

This chapter has emphasized group influences on the individual, so we conclude by seeing how individuals can influence their groups.

At the beginning of most social movements, a small minority will sometimes sway, and then even become, the majority. "All history," wrote Ralph Waldo Emerson, "is a record of the power of minorities, and of minorities of one." For good or bad minorities of one often have a huge impact. Think of Copernicus, Hitler, Galileo, and Pol Pot. In Canadian history, the Meech Lake Accord might well have been ratified as part of the constitution if not for the efforts of Elijah Harper, a member of the Manitoba legislature. Technological history is also made by innovative minorities. As Robert Fulton developed his steamboat—"Fulton's Folly"—he endured constant derision: "Never did a single encouraging remark, a bright hope, a warm wish, cross my path" (Cantril & Bumstead, 1960).

"Minority influence" refers to minority opinions, not to ethnic minorities.

What makes a minority persuasive? What might the crew of the *Titanic* have done to convince Captain Smith that the ship needed to slow down? Experiments initiated by Serge Moscovici in Paris have identified several determinants of minority influence: consistency, self-confidence, defection.

Consistency

More influential than a minority that wavers is a minority that sticks to its position. Moscovici and his associates (1969, 1985) have found that if a minority consistently judges blue slides as green, members of the majority will occasionally agree. But if the minority wavers, saying "blue" to one third of the blue slides and "green" to the rest, virtually no one in the majority will ever agree with "green."

Still debated is the nature of this influence (Clark & Maass, 1990; Levine & Russo, 1987). Moscovici believes that a minority's following the majority usually reflects just public compliance, but a majority's following a minority usually reflects genuine acceptance—really recalling the blue slide as greenish. In public, people may wish not to align themselves with a deviant minority view (Wood & others, 1994, 1996). A majority can also give us a rule of thumb for deciding truth ("All those smart cookies can't be wrong"), whereas a minority influences us by making us think more deeply (Burnstein & Kitayama, 1989; Mackie, 1987). Minority influence is therefore more likely to take the thought-filled central route to persuasion (see Chapter 7).

Experiments show—and experience confirms—that nonconformity, especially persistent nonconformity, is often painful (Levine, 1989). If you set out to be Emerson's minority of one, prepare yourself for ridicule—especially when you argue an issue that's personally relevant to the majority and when the group wants to settle an issue by reaching consensus (Kameda & Sugimori, 1993; Kruglanski & Webster, 1991; Trost & others, 1992). People may attribute your dissent to psychological peculiarities (Papastamou & Mugny, 1990). When Charlan Nemeth (1979) planted a minority of two within a simulated jury and had them oppose the majority's opinions, the duo was inevitably disliked. Nevertheless, the majority acknowledged that the persistence of the two did more than anything else to make them rethink their positions.

In so doing, a minority may stimulate creative thinking (Martin, 1996; Mucchi-Faina & others, 1991; Peterson & Nemeth, 1996). With dissent from within one's own group, people take in more information, think about it in new ways, and often make better decisions. Believing that one need not win friends to influence people, Nemeth quotes Oscar Wilde: "We dislike arguments of any kind; they are always vulgar, and often convincing."

A persistent minority is influential, even if not popular, partly because it soon becomes the focus of debate (Schachter, 1951). Being the center of conversation allows one to contribute a disproportionate number of arguments. And Nemeth reports that in experiments on minority influence, as in the studies dealing with group polarization, the position supported by the most arguments usually wins. Talkative group members are usually influential (Mullen & others, 1989).

Self-confidence

Consistency and persistence convey self-confidence. Furthermore, Nemeth and Joel Wachtler (1974) reported that any behavior by a minority that conveys self-confidence—for example, taking the head seat at the table—tends to raise self-doubts among the majority. By being firm and forceful, the minority's apparent self-assurance may prompt the majority to reconsider its position. This is especially so on matters of opinion rather than fact. In her research at Italy's University of Padova, Anne Maass and her colleagues (1996) report that minorities are less persuasive regarding fact ("from which country does Italy import most of its raw oil?") than regarding attitude ("from which country should Italy import most of its raw oil?").

Defections from the majority

A persistent minority punctures any illusion of unanimity. When a minority consistently doubts the majority wisdom, majority members become freer to express their own doubts and may even switch to the minority position. John Levine (1989) found that a minority person who had defected from the majority was more persuasive than a consistent minority voice. In her jury-simulation

"If the single man plant himself indomitably on his instincts, and there abide, the huge world will come round to him."

Ralph Waldo Emerson, *Nature, Address,* and *Lectures: The American Scholar,* 1849

behind the scenes

My heroes always stood up and told the truth as they saw it. Often they were vilified, though history would come to treat them more kindly. In 1968 at the University of Chicago, I saw colleagues tell the truth as they saw it and end up bloodied. In the midst of this conflict over ideas and values, I experienced one of the most intellectually and morally invigorating periods of my life. The next year, while a visiting professor in England and France, I had the good fortune of working with Henri Tajfel and Serge Moscovici. The three of us were "outsiders"— I an American Roman Catholic female in Europe, they having survived World War II as Eastern European Jews. Sensitivity to the value and the struggles of the minority perspective came to dominate our work. While studying jury deliberations, I discovered that, even when wrong, minority views can stimulate productive thinking. This helped me see why Senator William Fulbright was wise to say that we should "welcome and not fear the voices of dissent."

Charlan Jeanne Nemeth
University of California,
Berkeley

experiments, Nemeth found that once defections begin, others often soon follow, initiating a snowball effect.

Are these factors that strengthen minority influence unique to minorities? Sharon Wolf and Bibb Latané (1985; Wolf, 1987) and Russell Clark (1995) believe not. They argue that the same social forces work for both majorities and minorities. Informational and normative influence fuels both group polarization and minority influence. And if consistency, self-confidence, and defections from the other side strengthen the minority, such variables also strengthen a majority. The social impact of any position depends on the strength, immediacy, and number of those who support it. Minorities have less influence than majorities simply because they are smaller.

Anne Maass and Russell Clark (1984, 1986) agree with Moscovici, however, that minorities are more likely to convert people to *accepting* their views. And from their analyses of how groups evolve over time, John Levine and Richard Moreland (1985) conclude that new recruits to a group exert a different type of minority influence than do longtime members. Newcomers exert influence through the attention they receive and the group awareness they trigger in the old-timers. Established members feel freer to dissent and to exert leadership.

There is a delightful irony in this new emphasis on how individuals can influence the group. Until recently, the idea that the minority could sway the majority was itself a minority view in social psychology. Nevertheless, by arguing consistently and forcefully, Moscovici, Nemeth, and others have convinced the majority of group influence researchers that minority influence is a phenomenon worthy of study.

leadership
the process by which certain group members motivate and guide the group

Is leadership minority influence?

One example of the power of individuals is **leadership**, the process by which certain individuals mobilize and guide groups. Leadership matters, note Robert Hogan and associates (1994). In 1910, the Norwegians and English engaged in an epic race to the South Pole. The Norwegians, effectively led by Roald

Amundsen, made it. The English, ineptly led by Robert Falcon Scott, did not; Scott and three team members died. Some coaches move from team to team, transforming losers into winners each time. For example, Scotty Bowman has led three different teams to Stanley Cup championship.

Some leaders are formally appointed or elected; others emerge informally as the group interacts. What makes for good leadership often depends on the situation—the best person to lead the engineering team may not make the best leader of the sales force. Some people excel at *task leadership*—at organizing work, setting standards, and focusing on goal attainment. Others excel at *social leadership*—at building teamwork, mediating conflicts, and being supportive.

Task leaders often have a directive style—one that can work well if the leader is bright enough to give good orders (Fiedler, 1987). Being goal oriented, such leaders also keep the group's attention and effort focused on its mission. Experiments show that the combination of specific, challenging goals and periodic progress reports helps motivate high achievement (Locke & Latham, 1990).

Social leaders often have a democratic style—one that delegates authority, welcomes input from team members, and, as we have seen, helps prevent groupthink. Many experiments reveal that such leadership is good for morale. Group members usually feel more satisfied when they participate in making decisions (Spector, 1986; Vanderslice & others, 1987). Given control over their tasks, workers also become more motivated to achieve (Burger, 1987). People who value good group feeling and take pride in achievement therefore thrive under democratic leadership (Lortie–Lussier & others, 1989).

Women more often than men have a democratic leadership style

(Eagly & Johnson, 1990)

Democratic leadership can be seen in the move by many businesses toward participative management, a management style common in Sweden and Japan (Naylor, 1990; Sundstrom & others, 1990). Ironically, a major influence on this "Japanese-style" management was social psychologist Kurt Lewin. In laboratory and factory experiments, Lewin and his students demonstrated the

Participative management, illustrated in this "Quality Circle," requires democratic rather than autocratic leaders.

benefits of inviting workers to participate in decision making. Shortly before World War II, Lewin visited Japan and explained his findings to industrial and academic leaders (Nisbett & Ross, 1991). Japan's collectivist culture provided a receptive audience for Lewin's ideas about teamwork. Eventually, his influence circled back to North America.

The once-popular "great person" theory of leadership—that all great leaders share certain traits—has fallen into disrepute. Effective leadership styles, we now know, vary with the situations. People who know what they are doing may resent task leadership, while those who don't may welcome it. Recently, however, social psychologists have again wondered if there might be qualities that mark a good leader in many situations (Hogan & others, 1994). British social psychologists Peter Smith and Monir Tayeb (1989) report that studies done in India, Taiwan, and Iran have found that the most effective supervisors in coal mines, banks, and government offices score high on tests of *both* task and social leadership. They are actively concerned with how work is progressing *and* sensitive to the needs of their subordinates.

Studies also reveal that many effective leaders of laboratory groups, work teams, and large corporations exhibit the behaviors that help make a minority view persuasive. Such leaders engender trust by *consistently* sticking to their goals. And they often exude a *self-confident* charisma that kindles the allegiance of their followers (Bennis, 1984; House & Singh, 1987). Charismatic leaders typically have a compelling *vision* of some desired state of affairs, an ability to *communicate* this to others in clear and simple language, and enough optimism and faith in their group to *inspire* others to follow. Not surprisingly, then, personality tests reveal that effective leaders tend to be outgoing, energetic, conscientious, agreeable, emotionally stable, and self-confident (Hogan & others, 1994).

To be sure, groups also influence their leaders. Sometimes those at the front of the herd have simply sensed where it is already heading. Political candidates know how to read the opinion polls. A leader who deviates too radically from the group's standards may be rejected. Smart leaders usually remain with the majority and spend their influence prudently. Nevertheless, effective individual leaders can sometimes exhibit a type of minority influence by mobilizing and guiding their group's energy.

In rare circumstances, the right traits matched with the right situation yield history-making greatness, notes Dean Keith Simonton (1994). To have a Winston Churchill or a Margaret Thatcher, a Pierre Trudeau or a Karl Marx, a Napoleon or an Adolph Hitler, a Wilfrid Laurier or a Martin Luther King, Jr., takes the right person in the right place at the right time. When an apt combination of intelligence, skill, determination, self-confidence, and social charisma meets a rare opportunity, the result is sometimes a championship, a Nobel Prize, or a social revolution.

Summing up

If minority viewpoints never prevailed, history would be static and nothing would ever change. In experiments, a minority is most influential when consistent and persistent in its views, when its actions convey self-confidence, and after it begins to elicit some defections from the majority. Even if such factors do not persuade the majority to adopt the minority's views, they will increase the majority's self-doubts and prompt it to consider other alternatives, often leading to better, more creative decisions.

Through their task and social leadership, formal and informal group leaders exert disproportionate influence. Those who consistently press toward their goals and exude a self-confident charisma often engender trust and inspire others to follow.

Personal Postscript: Are groups bad for us?

A selective reading of this chapter could, I must admit, leave readers with the impression that, on balance, groups are bad. In groups we become more aroused, more stressed, more tense, more error-prone on complex tasks. Submerged in a group that gives us anonymity, we have a tendency to loaf or have our worst impulses unleashed by deindividuation. Police brutality, lynchings, gang destruction, and terrorism are all group phenomena. Discussion in groups often polarizes our views, enhancing mutual racism or hostility. It may also suppress dissent, creating a homogenized groupthink that produces disastrous decisions. No wonder we celebrate those individuals—minorities of one—who, alone against a group, have stood up for truth and justice. Groups, it seems, are baaad.

All this is true, but it's only half the truth. The other half is that, as social animals, we are group dwelling creatures. Like our distant ancestors, we depend on one another for sustenance, support, and security. Moreover, when our individual tendencies are positive, group interaction accentuates our best. In groups, runners run faster, audiences laugh louder, and givers become more generous. In self-help groups, people strengthen their resolve to stop drinking, lose weight, and study harder. In kindred-spirited groups, people expand their spiritual consciousness. "A devout communing on spiritual things sometimes greatly helps the health of the soul," observed fifteenth century cleric Thomas a Kempis, especially when people of faith "meet and speak and commune together." The moral: Depending on which tendency a group is magnifying or disinhibiting, groups can be very, very bad or very, very good. We had, therefore, best choose our group influences wisely and intentionally.

part three

Social Relations

Having explored how we think about (part one) and influence (part two) one another, we come to social psychology's third facet—how we relate to one another. Our feelings and actions toward people are sometimes negative, sometimes positive. Chapter 9, "Prejudice," and 10, "Aggression," examine the unpleasant aspects of human relations: Why do we dislike, even despise, one another? Why and when do we hurt one another? Then in Chapters 11, "Attraction and Intimacy," and 12, "Altruism," we explore the more pleasant aspects: Why do we like or love particular people? When will we offer help to friends or strangers? Lastly in Chapter 13, "Conflict and Peacemaking," we consider how social conflicts develop and how they can often be justly and amicably resolved.

chapter 9

Prejudice: Disliking Others

Prejudices come in many forms—against "city slickers" or "rural hicks"; against Arab "terrorists" or Christian "fundamentalists"; against people who are short, or fat, or homely. Consider a few actual occurrences:

On January 4, 1998, in the parking lot of a Vancouver Sikh temple, the temple's sixty-five-year-old caretaker Nirmal Singh Gill was beaten to death by five young White men, described as "skinheads." In the words of the judge who sentenced the men, the caretaker "died simply because he was Indo-Canadian. He was attacked because he was different from the accused. It is that simple."

Prejudice against girls and women is sometimes subtle, sometimes devastating. Nowhere in the modern world are female infants left on a hillside to die of exposure, as was the occasional practice in ancient Greece. Yet in many developing countries, death rates for girls exceed those for boys.

When men seek roles traditionally associated with women, discrimination can run in the other direction. Elizabeth Turner and Anthony Pratkanis (1994) sent identical job-inquiry letters from a community college student in a child-care program to 56 child-care centers and preschools in seven cities. When the letter was signed "Mary E. Johnson," nearly half the centers returned a stamped postcard, checking "we would be interested in discussing a position."When the letter was signed "David E. Johnson," only 1 in 10 replied with similar encouragement.

A group of homosexual students at one university announced that the motto for one spring day would be, "If you are gay, wear blue jeans today." When the day dawned, many students who usually wore jeans woke up with an urge to dress up in a skirt or slacks. The gay group had made its point—that attitudes toward homosexuals are such that many would rather give up their usual clothes lest anyone suspect (*RCAgenda*, 1979).

The nature and power of prejudice

How is "prejudice" distinct from "stereotyping," "discrimination," "racism," and "sexism"? Are stereotypes necessarily false or malicious? Over time, how much have racial and gender attitudes changed? What forms does prejudice assume today?

What is prejudice?

prejudice
a negative prejudgment of a group and its individual members

Prejudice, stereotyping, discrimination, racism, sexism: The terms often overlap. Before seeking to understand prejudice, let's clarify the terms. Each of the situations just described involved a negative evaluation of some group. And that is the essence of **prejudice:** *a negative prejudgment of a group and its individual members.* Prejudice biases us against a person based solely on our identifying the person with a particular group.

Prejudice is an attitude. As we saw in Chapter 4, an attitude is a distinct combination of feelings, inclinations to act, and beliefs. This combination is the ABC of attitudes: *a*ffect (feelings), *b*ehavior tendency (inclination to act), and *c*ognition (beliefs). A prejudiced person might *dislike* those different from self and *behave* in a discriminatory manner, *believing* them ignorant and dangerous. Like many attitudes, prejudice is complex, and may include a component of patronizing affection that serves to keep the target disadvantaged.

stereotype
a belief about the personal attributes of a group of people. Stereotypes can be overgeneralized, inaccurate, and resistant to new information

The negative evaluations that mark prejudice can stem from emotional associations, from the need to justify behavior, or from negative beliefs, called **stereotypes.** To stereotype is to generalize. To simplify the world, we generalize all the time: The British are reserved; Italians are outgoing. Professors are absentminded; Serbs are cruel. Here are some widely shared stereotypes uncovered in recent research:

- Women who assume the title of "Ms." are seen as more assertive and ambitious than those who call themselves "Miss" or "Mrs." (Dion, 1987; Dion & Cota, 1991; Dion & Schuller, 1991).

- In 19 nations, older adults are seen as likeable but less strong and active than younger adults (Williams, 1993).

- Public opinion surveys reveal that Europeans have definite ideas about other Europeans. They see Germans as relatively hard-working, the French as pleasure-loving, the British as cool and unexcitable, Italians as amorous, and the Dutch as reliable. (Coming from Willem Koomen and Michiel Bähler, 1996, at the University of Amsterdam, these findings one expects to be reliable.)

- Europeans also view southern Europeans as more emotional and less efficient than northern Europeans (Linssen & Hagendoorn, 1994). The stereotype of the southerner as more expressive even holds within countries: James Pennebaker and his colleagues (1996) report that across 20 Northern Hemisphere countries (but not in six Southern Hemisphere countries), southerners within a country are perceived as more expressive than northerners.

Such generalizations can have a germ of truth. Old people are less active. Southern countries in the Northern Hemisphere do have higher rates of violence. People living in the south in these countries do report being more expressive than those in the northern regions of their country. "Stereotypes," note Lee Jussim, Clark McCauley, and Yueh-Ting Lee (1995), "may be positive or negative, accurate or inaccurate." An accurate stereotype may even be desirable. We call it "sensitivity to diversity" or "cultural awareness in a multicultural world." To stereotype the British as more concerned about punctuality than are Mexicans is to understand what to expect and how to act with minimal friction in each culture.

A problem with stereotypes arises when they are *overgeneralized* or just plain wrong. To presume that most First Nations people need treatment for alcoholism is to overgeneralize, because it just isn't so. Another problem arises when people attribute negatively evaluated differences to biology, ignoring toxic social forces. People may see that women are less likely than men to become engineers or chief executive officers, but they often do not see the underlying causes that prevent women from succeeding in these fields. People are quick to judge that women do not have the math or leadership ability to succeed in these fields, but the evidence suggests otherwise (Eagly & Karau, & Makhijani, 1995; Hyde, Fenema, & Lamon, 1990; Kimball, 1989). The barriers that actually prevent women's success, such as unfair evaluations and self-fulfilling prophecies, are much harder for people to recognize.

Prejudice is a negative *attitude;* **discrimination** is negative *behavior.* Discriminatory behavior often, but not always, has its source in prejudicial attitudes (Dovidio & others, 1996). How distant we want to be from certain people stems more directly from our feelings than our beliefs about them, note Charles Stangor and his colleagues (1991).

As Chapter 4 emphasized, however, attitudes and behavior are often loosely linked, partly because our behavior reflects more than our inner convictions. Prejudiced attitudes need not breed hostile acts, nor does all oppression spring from prejudice. **Racism** and **sexism** are institutional practices that discriminate, even when there is no prejudicial intent.

If word-of-mouth hiring practices in an all-male business have the effect of excluding potential female employees, the practice could be called sexist—even if an employer intended no discrimination. This chapter explores the roots and fruits of prejudiced attitudes. Mindful that racist and sexist policies need not spring from prejudiced attitudes (though in time they often feed such), I leave it to sociologists and political scientists to explore racism and sexism in their institutional forms.

Familiar stereotypes: "Heaven is a place with an American house, Chinese food, British police, a German car, and French art. Hell is a place with a Japanese house, Chinese police, British food, German art, and a French car."

Anonymous, as reported by Yueh-Ting Lee (1996)

discrimination
unjustifiable negative behavior toward a group or its members

racism
(1) an individual's prejudicial attitudes and discriminatory behavior toward people of a given race, or (2) institutional practices (even if not motivated by prejudice) that subordinate people of a given race

sexism
(1) an individual's prejudicial attitudes and discriminatory behavior toward people of a given sex, or (2) institutional practices (even if not motivated by prejudice) that subordinate people of a given sex

behind the scenes

I grew up in Toronto and watched it evolve from a very homogeneous city to one of the most ethnically diverse cities in the world. This planted the seed for my later interest in studying intergroup attitudes. I began to study intergroup attitudes as a postdoctoral fellow at the University of Waterloo in the late 1980s, conducting research on the effects of mood on the expression of ethnic stereotypes, and the role of values, stereotypes, and emotions in determining intergroup attitudes. Since then, my interest in this topic has moved in several different directions. One important direction is the investigation of attitudes toward immigrants and immigration, which again came out of my experiences in Toronto. It struck me that immigrants seemed to be the target of considerable prejudice and discrimination, even among people who were themselves immigrants only a generation or two ago. In addition, it seemed that people justified their negative attitudes and behavior toward immigrants on the basis of competition for resources, such as jobs. This led to my current research on the role of group competition in determining prejudice and discrimination toward immigrants. I feel fortunate to be able to work in an area in which I can apply theory and research in social psychology to important social issuses.

Victoria Esses
University of Western Ontario

How pervasive is prejudice?

Is prejudice inevitable? Let's look at the most heavily studied examples—racial and gender prejudice.

Racial prejudice

In the context of the world, every race is a minority. Non-Hispanic Whites, for example, are but one-fifth of the world's people and will be but one-eighth within another half-century. Thanks to mobility and migration during the past two centuries, the world's races now intermingle, in relations that are sometimes hostile, sometimes amiable.

In Canada we sometimes think that racial prejudice is largely a problem to be found in the United States. Yet when we look closely, racial conflict, stereotyping of visible minorities, and resentment of immigrants are evident north of the border.

For example, the Cole Harbour District High School located on the outskirts of Halifax provides a vivid example of racial tension. In 1989 the school gained notoriety when a simple snowball fight erupted into a bloody brawl between Black and White students. Unfortunately, this was just the first of many such violent outbursts that were to occur at the school. The most recent series of skirmishes in 1997 led to numerous incidents of physical and verbal abuse. In the end, charges were laid against 17 people and administrators were forced to shut down the school for a week.

While such incidents of outright violence are uncommon, it is not hard to find evidence of stereotyping against visible minorities. Consider the following study conducted by Victoria Esses and Mark Zanna (1995). They had University of Waterloo students listen to one of three pieces of music that put them in a good mood, a neutral mood, or a bad mood. Then, in what students believed was a separate pilot study, they listed all the traits they could think of that they believed were typical of each of six different ethnic groups. They then rated how positive or negative they thought each trait was and how many people in the group they believed possessed the trait. For example, they would be given the label of Pakistanis and were asked to generate all the traits that they felt were typical of this group. They then rated each trait in terms of how positive or negative it was and how many Pakistanis they believed possessed the trait. Esses and Zanna then combined these trait ratings and weighted them by their positivity and their prevalence as a measure of stereotyping.

The results of the study were striking: when English-Canadian students were in a bad mood they rated the visible minorities much more negatively. In particular (see Figure 9-1), students rated Pakistanis, Arabs, and Native Indians much more negatively when they were in a bad mood. It seems that people's bad moods cued their negative thoughts and feelings about these groups. Further research by Esses and Zanna suggests that the very meaning that people ascribe to the traits describing these groups changes when they are in a bad

> Psychologists capitalize Black and White to emphasize that these are socially applied race labels, not literal color labels for persons of African and European ancestry.

> Many Europeans, too, harbor resentment of immigrants (Turks in West Germany, North Africans in France, South Asians in Britain)
>
> (Jackson & others, 1993).

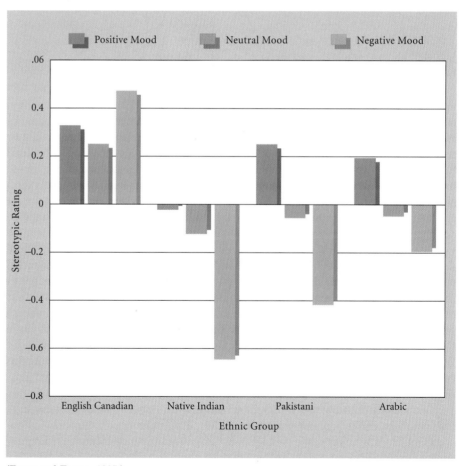

figure 9–1

Mood and ethnic stereotypes.

When University of Waterloo students listened to music that put them in a bad mood, they rated ethnic groups more stereotypically.

(Esses and Zanna, 1995.)

Although prejudice dies last in socially intimate contacts, interracial marriage has increased in most countries.

mood. What was once a positive trait becomes a negative trait. One's religious beliefs, which were once seen as admirable, are now seen as fanaticism. These effects are not limited to perceptions of visible minorities either. Miendl and Lerner (1984) found that when English-speaking Canadians experience a threat to their self-esteem they evaluate French-speaking Canadians more harshly, and Maio and Esses (1998) have found that people evaluate even a fictitious immigrant group more negatively if they believe it might be a target of affirmative action.

Despite these results there is some evidence that the acceptance of ethnic diversity and members of ethnic groups has increased in recent decades (Berry & Kalin, 1995). National surveys suggest that outright prejudice is much less common now than just 30 years ago. Berry and Kalin note that despite the prejudice toward members of ethnic groups, people in Canada are genuinely motivated to develop a truly multicultural society. So there is hope for the future.

One area where surveys still detect prejudice is concerning intimate interracial contacts. Many people who welcome diverse people as co-workers or classmates still socialize, date, and marry within their own race.

This phenomenon of *greatest prejudice in the most intimate social realms* seems universal. In India, people who accept the caste system will typically allow someone from a lower caste into their home but would not consider marrying such a person (Sharma, 1981). In a national survey of Americans, 75 percent said they would "shop at a store owned by a homosexual" but only 39 percent would "see a homosexual doctor" (Henry, 1994).

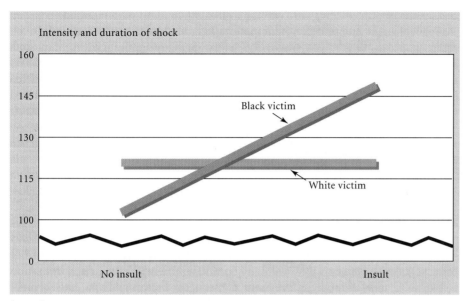

Intensity and duration of shock

Black victim

White victim

No insult   Insult

(Data from Rogers & Prentice-Dunn, 1981.)

figure 9–2

Does anger trigger latent prejudice?

When White students administered electric shock, supposedly as part of a "behavior-modification experiment," they behaved less aggressively toward an agreeable Black victim than toward a White victim. But when the victim insulted the subjects, they responded with more aggression if the victim was Black.

Subtle forms of prejudice.   Recall from Chapter 4 that when White students indicate racial attitudes while hooked up to a supposed lie detector, they admit to prejudice. Other researchers have invited people to evaluate someone's behavior, that someone being either White or Black. Birt Duncan (1976) had White students observe a videotape of one man lightly shoving another during a brief argument. When a White shoved a Black man, only 13 percent of the observers rated the act as "violent behavior." They interpreted the shove as "playing around" or "dramatizing." Not so when a Black shoved a White man: Then, 73 percent said the act was "violent."

Many experiments have assessed people's *behavior* toward Blacks and Whites. As we will see in Chapter 13, Whites are equally helpful to any person in need—except when the needy person is remote (say, a wrong-number caller with a Black accent who needs a message relayed). Likewise, when asked to use electric shocks to "teach" a task, White people give no more (if anything less) shock to a Black than to a White person—except when they are angered or when the recipient can't retaliate or know who did it (Crosby & others, 1980; Rogers & Prentice-Dunn, 1981) (Figure 9–2). Thus, discriminatory behavior surfaces when a prejudiced behavior can hide behind the screen of some other motive. In France, Britain, Germany, Australia and even the tolerant Netherlands, subtle prejudice (exaggerating ethnic differences, feeling less admiration and affection for minorities, rejecting minorities for supposedly nonracial reasons) is replacing blatant prejudice (Meertens & Pettigrew, 1997; Pedersen & Walker, 1997). Some researchers therefore call such subtle prejudice "modern racism."

Our neighbors across the street are Black and they have a 15-year-old daughter who we regularly use as a baby-sitter and who we think does an excellent job. When I asked another neighbor why they never ask her to baby-sit they said it was because she was too young. When I questioned whether it could have anything to do with her race, they replied, "Definitely not!" They seem to

Race sensitivity leads to exaggerated reactions to isolated minority persons— both overpraising their accomplishments and overcriticizing their mistakes

(Fiske, 1989; Hart & Morry, 1997; Hass & others, 1991).

"Let's just forget for a moment that you're black."

Prejudice, as this loan officer fails to realize, sometimes operates automatically and unconsciously.

hire other baby-sitters who are this young, so I still think race might be influencing their decision. But this much seems clear: Modern prejudice is seldom consciously intended. (Virtually no one will answer such a question with "Yes, I'd have hired her if she'd been White like me.") Rather, prejudice appears more subtly, such as through our preferences for what is familiar, similar, and comfortable (Dovidio & others, 1992; Esses & others, 1993a).

Prejudice may also linger where we least expect it. Mary Inman and Robert Baron (1996) report that people readily perceive prejudice and discrimination where they expect it: White against Black, male against female, young against old. In such cases, our suspicions are readily aroused. Sometimes they produce "false alarms"—perceptions of prejudicial motives where none exist. People are slower to detect prejudice when the identical bias occurs in the reverse direction, or within a group (say, a female discriminating against a female). Thus, prejudice among Blacks, Hispanics, and Koreans may go unnoticed until it erupts into violence.

As blatant prejudice subsides, automatic emotional reactions linger. Patricia Devine and her colleagues (1989, 1995) report that those low and high in prejudice are aware of the same stereotypes and often have similar automatic reactions. They differ because the low-prejudice person consciously tries to suppress prejudicial thoughts and feelings. It's like breaking a bad habit, says Devine. Try as we might to suppress unwanted thoughts—thoughts about food, thoughts about romance with a friend's partner, judgmental thoughts about another group—they sometimes refuse to go away (Macrae & others, 1994; Wegner & Erber, 1992). Unwanted thoughts and feelings often persist.

A raft of new experiments (Bargh & others, 1996; Blair & Banaji, 1996; Fazio & others, 1995; Kunda & Sinclair, 1999; Sinclair & Kunda, 1999; Spencer & others, 1998; and Wittenbrink & others, 1997) by researchers from throughout North America have confirmed the phenomenon of automatic stereotyping and prejudice. These studies briefly flash words or faces that "prime" (automatically activate) stereotypes of some racial, gender, or age group. Without their awareness, the subjects' activated stereotypes may then bias their behavior. Having been primed with images associated with Blacks, for example, they may then react with more hostility to an experimenter's annoying request. The subjects, mind you, are often people who express little or no prejudice. Rather, their prejudice operates largely as an unconscious, unintended response.

In real life, encountering a minority person may similarly trigger a knee-jerk stereotype. Those with accepting and those with disapproving attitudes toward homosexuals may both feel uncomfortable sitting with a gay male on a bus seat

"Many [people] have confessed to me . . . that even though in their minds they no longer feel prejudice toward Blacks, they still feel squeamish when they shake hands with a Black. These feelings are left over from what they learned in their families as children."

Thomas Pettigrew (1987, p. 20)

behind the scenes

"Are you Catholic?" Although initially puzzled by the question, it so reliably followed the disclosure that I have seven siblings that it became clear to me that many people relate number of children to religious affiliation. Similarly, while moving around a lot as a child, I observed that knowing others' ethnic group, cued by their last names, triggered unwarranted stereotypes about their personalities, interests, and behaviors. Such inferences were so quickly and easily supplied that they seemed automatic—even for those who believed that stereotypes and prejudice are wrong.

Why would such negative thoughts persist, even when people embrace nonprejudiced values? Could such unintentional stereotyping be overcome? In working through such issues I came to see that overcoming prejudice is like breaking a habit. As in breaking any habit, it's not easy. It requires a great deal of effort, practice, and relearning.

Patricia Devine
University of Wisconsin

(Monteith, 1993). Encountering an unfamiliar Black male, people—even those who pride themselves on not being prejudiced—may respond warily. In one experiment by E. J. Vanman and colleagues (1990), White people viewed slides of White and Black people, imagined themselves interacting with them, and rated their probable liking of the person. Although the participants saw themselves liking the Black more than the White persons, their facial muscles told a different story. Instruments revealed that when a Black face appeared, there tended to be more activity in frowning than smiling muscles. Aware of the gap between how they *should* feel and how they *do* feel, people may then feel guilty and try to inhibit their prejudicial response (Bodenhausen & Macrae, 1998; Zuwerink & others, 1996). This is especially so in circumstances that make people self-conscious, and therefore more likely to monitor how they are thinking and acting (Macrae & others, 1998).

The moral: Overcoming what Devine calls "the prejudice habit" isn't easy. If you find yourself reacting with knee-jerk presumptions or feelings, don't despair; that's not unusual. It's what you do with that awareness that matters. Do you let those feelings hijack your behavior? Or do you compensate by monitoring and correcting your behavior in future situations?

Even the very social scientists who study prejudice seem vulnerable to it, note Anthony Greenwald and Eric Schuh (1994). They analyzed biases in authors' citations of social science articles by people with selected non-Jewish names (Erickson, McBride, and so forth) and Jewish names (Goldstein, Siegel, and so forth). After analyzing nearly 30,000 citations, including 17,000 citations of prejudice research, they had a remarkable finding: Compared to Jewish authors, non-Jewish authors had 40 percent higher odds of citing non-Jewish names. (Greenwald and Schuh could not determine whether Jewish authors were overciting their Jewish colleagues, non-Jewish authors were overciting their non-Jewish colleagues, or both.)

figure 9–3

Which one of these people would you guess is the group's strongest contributor? Shown this picture, college students usually guessed one of the two men, although those shown photos of same-sex groups most commonly guessed the person at the head of the table.

Gender prejudice

How pervasive is prejudice against women? In Chapter 5, we examined gender-role norms—people's ideas about how women and men *ought* to behave. Here we consider gender *stereotypes*—people's beliefs about how women and men *do* behave.

Gender stereotypes.　From research on stereotypes, two conclusions are indisputable: Strong gender stereotypes exist, and, as often happens, members of the stereotyped group accept the stereotypes. Men and women agree that you *can* judge the book by its sexual cover. Analyzing responses from one survey, Mary Jackman and Mary Senter (1981) found that gender stereotypes were much stronger than racial stereotypes. For example, only 22 percent of men thought the two sexes equally "emotional." Of the remaining 78 percent, those who believed females were more emotional outnumbered those who thought males were by 15 to 1. And what did the women believe? To within 1 percentage point, their responses were identical.

Consider, too, a study by Natalie Porter, Florence Geis, and Joyce Jennings Walstedt (1983). They showed students pictures of "a group of graduate students working as a team on a research project" (Figure 9–3). Then they gave them a test of "first impressions," asking them to guess who contributed most to the group. When the group was either all male or all female, the students overwhelmingly chose the person at the head of the table. When the group was mixed sex, a man occupying that position was again overwhelmingly chosen. But a woman occupying that position was usually ignored. Each of the men in Figure 9–3 received more of the leadership choices than all three women combined! This stereotype of men as leaders was true not only of women as well as men but also of feminists as well as nonfeminists. How pervasive are gender stereotypes? Very.

> "All the pursuits of men are the pursuits of women also, and in all of them a woman is only a lesser man."
>
> Plato, *Republic*

Remember that stereotypes are generalizations about a group of people and may be true, false, or overgeneralized from a kernel of truth. In Chapter 5 we noted that the average man and woman do differ somewhat in social connectedness, empathy, social power, aggressiveness, and sexual initiative (though not in intelligence). Do we then conclude that gender stereotypes are accurate? Often they are, observed Janet Swim (1994). She found that Pennsylvania State University students' stereotypes of men's and women's restlessness, nonverbal sensitivity, aggressiveness, and so forth were reasonable approximations of actual gender differences. Moreover, such stereotypes have persisted across time, leading some evolutionary psychologists to believe they reflect innate, stable reality (Lueptow & others, 1995).

But sometimes gender stereotypes exaggerate small differences, as Carol Lynn Martin (1987) concluded after surveying visitors to the University of British Columbia. She asked them to check which of several traits described them and to estimate what percentage of North American males and females had each trait. Males were indeed slightly more likely than females to describe themselves as assertive and dominant and were slightly less likely to describe themselves as tender and compassionate. But stereotypes of these differences were exaggerated: The people perceived North American males as almost twice as likely as females to be assertive and dominant and roughly half as likely to be tender and compassionate.

Stereotypes (beliefs) are not prejudices (attitudes). Stereotypes may support prejudice. But then again one might believe, without prejudice, that men and women are "different yet equal." Let us therefore see how researchers probe for gender prejudice.

Gender attitudes.   Judging from what people tell survey researchers, attitudes toward women have changed as rapidly as racial attitudes. People are increasingly less likely to see women's place as in the home, and are becoming more accepting of women who seek positions of power and prestige. For example, in 1967, 56 percent of first-year university students agreed that "The activities of married women are best confined to the home and family"; by 1996, only 24 percent agreed (Astin & others, 1987; Sax & others, 1996).

Alice Eagly and her associates (1991) and Geoffrey Haddock and Mark Zanna (1994) also report that people don't respond to women with gut-level negative emotions as they do to certain other groups. Most people like "women" more than "men." They perceive women as more understanding, kind, and helpful. Thus, a *favorable* stereotype—which Eagly (1994) dubs the *women-are-wonderful effect*—results in a favorable attitude.

But gender attitudes often are ambivalent, report Peter Glick and Susan Fiske (1996). They frequently mix a "benevolent sexism" ("Women have a superior moral sensibility") with "hostile sexism" ("Once a man commits, she puts him on a tight leash"). Also, affection does not always include admiration. We can like grandmothers and day-care workers (or women in general) without admiring them. Many men express more respect than liking of feminists, report Tara MacDonald and Zanna (1998). Likewise, some people admire the achievements of Jews, Germans, or Japanese, note Susan Fiske and Janet Ruscher (1993), without liking them.

There is more good news for those who are upset by sex bias. One heavily publicized finding of prejudice against women came from a 1968 study in which

"Women are wonderful primarily because they are [perceived as] so nice. [Men are] perceived as superior to women in agentic [competitive, dominant] attributes that are viewed as equipping people for success in paid work, especially in male-dominated occupations."

Alice Eagly (1994)

behind the scenes

We were on a mission to get mainstream social psychology to broaden its individualistic emphasis and recognize intergroup relations as a central topic. Systemic discrimination was a key preoccupation for us and being the "white male" I would often ask female and visible minority students to describe their experiences with discrimination. I began to notice a theme to their responses, which took the form—"Well, I personally have never faced discrimination, but my group is unfairly treated in the following ways."

We were embarking on a large field study involving visible minority immigrants to Canada from all walks of life, and wanted to gauge the extent to which they felt discriminated against. We decided to ask participants to rate, in two separate questions, the extent to which their group, and they personally as a member of their group, had been discriminated against.

The personal/group discrimination discrepancy was born. Respondents consistently rated discrimination directed at their group to be higher than discrimination directed at themselves personally, as a member of that group.

The methodological implications were immediate and obvious. Any attempt to gauge societal prejudice and discrimination would produce very different conclusions depending on the focus of the question, personal or group. A group-based question would portray society as relatively prejudiced, whereas a question about personal discrimination would give the impression that society was relatively free from bigotry.

The bigger challenge, of course, is to explain the personal/group discrimination discrepancy. Perhaps one of you will take it up.
Don Taylor
McGill University

Philip Goldberg gave women students at Connecticut College several short articles and asked them to judge the value of each. Sometimes a given article was attributed to a male author (for example, John T. McKay) and sometimes to a female author (for example, Joan T. McKay). In general, the articles received lower ratings when attributed to a female. The historic mark of oppression—self-deprecation—surfaced clearly: Women were prejudiced against women.

Eager to demonstrate the subtle reality of gender prejudice, I obtained Goldberg's materials and repeated the experiment for my own students' benefit. They showed no such tendency to deprecate women's work. So Janet Swim, Eugene Borgida, Geoffrey Maruyama, and I (1989) searched the literature and corresponded with investigators to learn all we could about studies of gender bias in the evaluation of men's and women's work. To our surprise, the biases that occasionally surfaced were as often against men as women. But the most common result across 104 studies involving almost 20,000 people was *no difference.* On most comparisons, judgments of someone's work were unaffected by whether the work was attributed to a female or a male. Summarizing other studies of people's evaluations of women and men as leaders, professors, and so forth, Alice Eagly (1994) says that "experiments have *not* demonstrated any *overall* tendency to devalue women's work."

The attention given highly publicized studies of prejudice against women's work illustrates a familiar point: Social scientists' values often seep into their conclusions. The researchers who conducted the publicized studies did as they should in reporting their findings. My colleagues and I, however, more readily accepted and reported findings supporting our preconceived biases than those opposing them.

So is gender bias fast becoming extinct in Western countries? Has the women's movement nearly completed its work? Blatant gender prejudice is dying, but subtle bias lives. The bogus-pipeline method, for example, exposes bias. As we noted in Chapter 4, men who believe an experimenter can read their true attitudes with a sensitive lie detector express less sympathy toward women's rights. Even on paper-and-pencil questionnaires, Janet Swim and her co-researchers (1995, 1997) have found a subtle ("modern") sexism that parallels subtle ("modern") racism. Both appear in denials of discrimination and in antagonism toward efforts to promote equality.

We can also detect bias in behavior. That's what a research team led by Ian Ayres (1991) did while visiting 90 Chicago-area car dealers and using a uniform strategy to negotiate the lowest price on a new car that cost the dealer about $11,000. White males were given a final price that averaged $11,362; White females were given an average price of $11,504; Black males were given an average price of $11,783; and Black females were given an average price of $12,237.

Most women know that gender bias exists. They believe that sex discrimination affects most working women, as shown by the lower salaries for women and especially for jobs, such as child care, that are filled mostly by women. Garbage haulers (mostly men) make more than preschool teachers (mostly women). Curiously, however, Faye Crosby and her colleagues (1989) have repeatedly found that most women deny feeling personally discriminated against. Discrimination, they believe, is something *other* women face. Their employer is not villainous. They are doing better than the average woman. Hearing no complaints, managers—even in discriminatory organizations—can persuade themselves that justice prevails.

Similar denials of *personal* disadvantage, while perceiving discrimination against one's *group*, occur among unemployed people, out-of-the-closet lesbians, and Canadian minorities (Dion & Kawakami, 1996; Taylor & others, 1990). This *personal/group discrimination discrepancy*, as Donald Taylor and his colleagues (1990, Ruggiero & Taylor, 1997) label the phenomenon, enables individuals to maintain a perception of control over their performance and relationships (see Figure 9–4). (Curiously, however, personal/group discrepancy extends to nondiscriminatory events. People also see others as more likely than themselves to be affected by, say, an economic recession, rising health costs, and better physical fitness facilities—Moghaddam & others, 1997).

In the world beyond democratic Western countries, gender discrimination looms even larger:

- Two-thirds of the world's unschooled children are girls (United Nations, 1991).
- In Saudi Arabia, women are forbidden to drive (Beyer, 1990).
- In some Asian countries, parents drastically act on their preference for a boy. In South Korea, male births exceed female births by 14 percent, in China by 18 percent. Sex-selective abortions and infanticide in China and India have led to 76,000,000—let's say that slowly . . . *seventy-six million*— "missing women" (Klasen, 1994; Kristof, 1993).

To conclude, overt prejudice against people of color and against women is far less common today than it was four decades ago. The same is true of prejudice against homosexual people. Nevertheless, techniques that are sensitive to subtle prejudice still detect widespread bias. And in parts of the world, gender

Question: "Misogyny" is the hatred of women. What is the corresponding word for the hatred of men? Answer: In most dictionaries, no such word exists.

figure 9–4

The personal/group discrimination discrepancy.

People report experiencing very little discrimination personally, but they do perceive discrimination against their group.

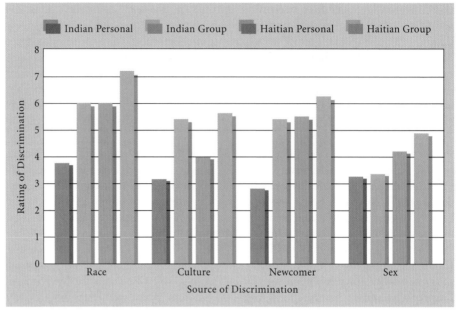

(Taylor & others, 1990.)

prejudice is literally deadly. We therefore need to look carefully and closely at the problem of prejudice and its causes.

Summing up   *Stereotypes* are *beliefs* about another group, beliefs that may be accurate, inaccurate, or overgeneralized but based on a kernel of truth. *Prejudice* is a prejudgmental negative *attitude.* Discrimination is unjustifiable negative *behavior. Racism* and *sexism* may refer to individuals' prejudicial attitudes or discriminatory behavior, or to oppressive institutional practices (even if not intentionally prejudicial).

Stereotypical beliefs, prejudicial attitudes, and discriminatory behavior have long poisoned human existence. Judging by what people have told survey researchers during the last four decades, their prejudice against Blacks and women has plunged. Nevertheless, subtle survey questions, and indirect methods for assessing people's attitudes and behavior, still reveal strong gender stereotypes and a fair amount of disguised racial and gender bias. Though less obvious, prejudice yet lurks.

Social sources of prejudice

What social conditions breed prejudice? How does society maintain prejudice?

Prejudice springs from several sources because it serves several functions (Herek, 1986, 1987). Prejudice may express our sense of who we are and gain us social acceptance. It may defend our sense of self against anxiety that arises from insecurity or inner conflict. And it may promote our self-interest by supporting what brings us pleasure and opposing what doesn't. Consider first how prejudice can function to defend self-esteem and social position.

Drawing by Vietor; © 1981 The New Yorker Magazine, Inc.

"And just why do we always call my income the second income?"

Gender prejudice gets expressed subtly.

Social inequalities

Unequal status and prejudice

A principle to remember: *Unequal status breeds prejudice.* Masters view slaves as lazy, irresponsible, lacking ambition—as having just those traits that justify the slavery. Historians debate the forces that create unequal status. But once these inequalities exist, prejudice helps justify the economic and social superiority of those who have wealth and power. You tell me the economic relationship between two groups and I'll predict the intergroup attitudes. Stereotypes rationalize unequal status (Yzerbyt & others, 1997).

Examples abound. Until recently, prejudice was greatest in regions where slavery was practiced. Nineteenth-century European politicians and writers justified imperial expansion by describing exploited colonized people as "inferior," "requiring protection," and a "burden" to be borne (G. W. Allport, 1958, pp. 204–205). Four decades ago, sociologist Helen Mayer Hacker (1951) noted how stereotypes of Blacks and women helped rationalize the inferior status of each: Many people thought both groups were mentally slow, emotional and primitive, and "contented" with their subordinate role. Blacks were "inferior"; women were "weak." Blacks were all right in their place; women's place was in the home.

In times of conflict, attitudes easily adjust to behavior. People often view enemies as subhuman and depersonalize them with a label. During World War II, the Japanese people became "the Japs." After the war was over, they became "the intelligent, hardworking Japanese." Attitudes are amazingly adaptable. As we have noted in previous chapters, cruel acts breed cruel attitudes.

Gender stereotypes, too, help rationalize gender roles. After studying these stereotypes worldwide, John Williams and Deborah Best (1990) noted that if women provide most of the care to young children, it is reassuring to think women are naturally nurturant. And if males run the businesses, hunt, and fight wars, it is comforting to suppose that men are aggressive, independent, and

> "Prejudice is never easy unless it can pass itself off for reason."
>
> William Hazlitt, 1778–1830, "On Prejudice"

> "It is human nature to hate those whom we have injured."
>
> Tacitus, *Agricola*

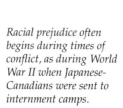

Racial prejudice often begins during times of conflict, as during World War II when Japanese-Canadians were sent to internment camps.

adventurous. In experiments, people perceive members of unknown groups as having traits that suit their roles (Hoffman & Hurst, 1990).

Religion and prejudice

Those who benefit from social inequalities while avowing that "all are created equal" need to justify keeping things the way they are. And what more powerful justification than to believe God has ordained the existing social order? For all sorts of cruel deeds, noted William James, "Piety is the mask" (1902, p. 264).

In almost every country, leaders invoke religion to sanctify the present order. The use of religion to support injustice helps explain a consistent pair of findings concerning Christianity, North America's dominant religion: (1) Church members express more racial prejudice than nonmembers, and (2) those professing traditional or fundamentalist Christian beliefs express more prejudice than those professing less traditional beliefs (Altemeyer & Hunsberger, 1992; Batson & others, 1993; Gorsuch, 1988).

Knowing the correlation between two variables—religion and prejudice—tells us nothing about their causal connection. There might be no connection at all. Perhaps people with less education are both more fundamentalist and more prejudiced. Perhaps prejudice causes religion, by leading people to create religious ideas to support their prejudices. Or perhaps religion causes prejudice, by leading people to believe that because all individuals possess free will, impoverished minorities have no one but themselves to blame for any perceived lack of virtue or achievement.

If indeed religion causes prejudice, then more religious church members should also be more prejudiced. But three other findings consistently indicate that this is not so.

- Among church members, faithful church attenders were, in 24 out of 26 comparisons, *less* prejudiced than occasional attenders (Batson & Ventis, 1982).

- Gordon Allport and Michael Ross (1967) found that those for whom religion is an end in itself (those who agree, for example, with the statement, "My religious beliefs are what really lie behind my whole approach to life") express *less* prejudice than those for whom religion is more a means to other ends (who agree, "A primary reason for my interest in religion is that my church is a congenial social activity"). And those who score highest on Gallup's "spiritual commitment" index are more welcoming of a person of another race moving in next door (Gallup & Jones, 1992).

- Protestant ministers and Roman Catholic priests gave more support to the civil rights movement than did lay people (Fichter, 1968; Hadden, 1969). In Germany, 45 percent of clergy in 1934 had aligned themselves with the Confessing Church, organized to oppose the Nazi regime (Reed, 1989).

What, then, is the relationship between religion and prejudice? The answer we get depends on *how* we ask the question. If we define religiousness as church membership or willingness to agree at least superficially with traditional beliefs, then the more religious are the more racially prejudiced—bigots often justify their prejudice with religion. If we assess depth of religious commitment in any of several other ways, however, then the very devout are less prejudiced; hence the deep religious convictions of many that have fought racism, such as Gandhi and Martin Luther King Jr. As Gordon Allport concluded, "The role of religion is paradoxical. It makes prejudice and it unmakes prejudice" (1958, p. 413).

Discrimination's impact: The self-fulfilling prophecy

Attitudes may coincide with the social hierarchy not only as a rationalization for it but also because discrimination affects its victims. "One's reputation," wrote Gordon Allport, "cannot be hammered, hammered, hammered into one's head without doing something to one's character" (1958, p. 139). If we could snap our fingers and end all discrimination, it would be naive then to say, "The tough times are all over, folks! You can now put on suits or dresses and be attache-carrying executives and professionals." When the oppression ends, its effects linger, like a societal hangover.

In his classic book *The Nature of Prejudice*, Allport cataloged 15 possible effects of victimization. Allport believed these reactions were reducible to two basic types—those that involve blaming oneself (withdrawal, self-hate, aggression against one's own group) and those that involve blaming external causes (fighting back, suspiciousness, increased group pride). If the net results are negative—say, higher rates of crime—people can use them to justify the discrimination that helps maintain them: "If we let those people in our nice neighborhood, property values will plummet."

Does discrimination affect its victims in this way? We must be careful not to overstate the point. The soul and style of Black culture is for many a proud heritage, not just a response to victimization (Jones, 1983). Thus while White youth are learning to deemphasize ethnic differences and avoid stereotypes, Black youth "are increasingly taking pride in their ethnicity and positively valuing ethnic differences," report Charles Judd and his co-researchers (1995). Cultural differences need not imply social deficits.

Nevertheless, social beliefs *can* be self-confirming, as demonstrated in a clever pair of experiments by Carl Word, Mark Zanna, and Joel Cooper (1974). In the first experiment, White men interviewed White and Black job applicants. When the applicant was Black, the interviewers sat farther away, ended the interview 25 percent sooner, and made 50 percent more speech errors than when the applicant was White. Imagine being interviewed by someone who sat at a distance, stammered, and ended the interview rather quickly. Would it affect your performance or your feelings about the interviewer?

To find out, the researchers conducted a second experiment in which trained interviewers treated students as the interviewers in the first experiment had treated either the White or Black applicants. When videotapes of the interviews were later rated, those who were treated like the Blacks in the first experiment seemed more nervous and less effective. Moreover, the interviewees could themselves sense a difference; those treated as were the Blacks judged their

"We have just enough religion to make us hate, but not enough to make us love one another."

Jonathan Swift, *Thoughts on Various Subjects*

"It is understandable that the suppressed people should develop an intense hostility towards a culture whose existence they make possible by their work, but in whose wealth they have too small a share."

Sigmund Freud, *The Future of an Illusion*, 1927

"If we foresee evil in
our fellow man, we
tend to provoke it; if
good, we elicit it."

Gordon Allport, *The Nature
of Prejudice,* 1958

stereotype threat
a concern, that one will
be evaluated based on a
negative stereotype
about one's group

"Math is hard!"

Talking Barbie Doll (later
removed from the market)

interviewers as less adequate and less friendly. The experimenters concluded part of "the 'problem' of Black performance resides . . . within the interaction setting itself."

Recall, too (from chapter 3), that social beliefs can be self-fulfilling. Prejudice affects its targets (Swim & Stangor, 1998). Placed in a situation where others expect you to perform poorly, your anxiety may cause you to confirm the belief. As a professor, I know students often think I am absent-minded, and when I am looking for a student's paper in my cluttered office, this concern seems to make it that much harder for me to find it. Claude Steele and I and our colleagues call this phenomenon **stereotype threat**—*a self-confirming apprehension that one will be evaluated based on a negative stereotype about one's group.*

In several experiments, Claude Steele, Diane Quinn, and I (Spencer, Steele, & Quinn, 1999) gave a very difficult math test to men and women who had similar math backgrounds. When we told them that there were no gender differences on the test, and they could not be evaluated based on the stereotype about their group, the women's performance consistently equaled the men's. However, when we told them that there *were* gender differences on the test, the women dramatically confirmed the stereotype (Figure 9-5).

Might racial stereotypes be similarly self-fulfilling? Steele and Joshua Aronson (1995) confirmed this when giving difficult verbal abilities tests to Whites and Blacks. Blacks underperformed Whites only when taking the tests under conditions high in stereotype threat. If you tell students they are at risk of failure (as often suggested by minority support programs), the stereotype may erode their performance, says Steele (1997), and cause them to "disidentify" with school and seek self-esteem elsewhere. Indeed, as African American students move from eighth to tenth grade, there is a weakening connection between their school performance and self-esteem (Osborne, 1995). Better, therefore, to challenge students to believe in their potential, observes Steele.

figure 9–5

**Stereotype
vulnerability and
women's math
performance.**

Steven Spencer, Diane
Quinn, and Claude
Steele (1999) gave
equally capable men and
women a difficult math
test. When subjects were
led to expect inferior
performance by women,
women fulfilled the
stereotype by scoring
lower.

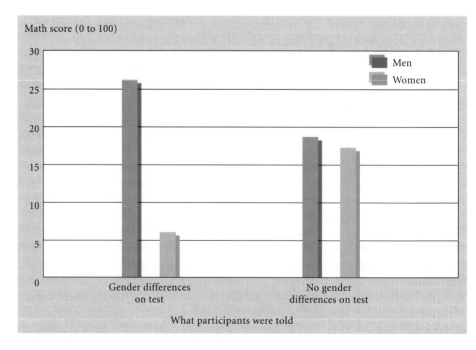

Social identity

We humans are a group-bound species. Our ancestral history prepares us to feed and protect ourselves—to live—in groups. Humans cheer on their groups, kill for their groups, die for their groups. We define ourselves by our groups, note Australian social psychologists John Turner (1981, 1987, 1991) and Michael Hogg (1992, 1996). Our self-concept—our sense of who we are—contains not just our personal identity (our sense of our personal attributes and attitudes) but our social identity. Fiona identifies herself as a woman, an Aussie, a labourite, a Melbourne University student, a member of the MacDonald family. We carry such **social identities** like playing cards, playing them as appropriate. David Berreby (1997) illustrates with an old joke that has the Lone Ranger and Tonto out of ammunition and facing a band of Native American warriors:

> "Looks like we're done for, Tonto."
> "What mean 'we,' White man?"

Working with the late British social psychologist Henri Tajfel, Turner proposed *social identity theory*. Turner and Tajfel [pronounced TOSH-fel] assumed that

- *we categorize:* We find it useful to put people, ourselves included, into categories. To label someone as a Hindu, a Scot, or a bus driver is a shorthand way of saying some other things about the person.
- *we identify:* We associate ourselves with certain groups (our **ingroups**).
- *we compare:* We contrast our groups with other groups (**outgroups**), with a favorable bias toward our own group.

We evaluate ourselves partly by our group memberships. Having a sense of "we-ness" strengthens our self-concept. It *feels* good. We seek not only *respect* for ourselves but *pride* in our groups (Smith & Tyler, 1997). Moreover, seeing our groups as superior helps us feel even better.

Lacking a positive personal identity, people often seek self-esteem by identifying with a group. Thus, many youths find pride, power, and identity in gang affiliations. Many superpatriots define themselves by their national identities (Staub, 1997). And some people feeling at loose ends find identity in their associations with new religious movements, self-help groups, or fraternal clubs.

Ingroup bias

The group definition of who you are—your race, religion, sex, academic major—implies a definition of who you are not. The circle that includes "us" (the ingroup) excludes "them" (the outgroup). Thus, the mere experience of being formed into groups may promote **ingroup bias.** Ask children, "Which are better, the children in your school or the children at [another school nearby]?" Virtually all will say their own school has the better children. Merely sharing a birthday with someone creates enough of a bond to evoke heightened cooperation in a laboratory experiment (Miller & others, in press).

So group-conscious are we that given any excuse to think of ourselves as a group we will do so—and will then exhibit ingroup bias. Cluster people into groups defined by nothing more than their social insurance number's last digit, and they'll feel a certain kinship with their number mates. In a series of experiments, Tajfel and Michael Billig (1974; Tajfel, 1970, 1981, 1982) discovered how

social identity
the "we" aspect of our self-concept. The part of our answer to "Who am I?" that comes from our group memberships. Examples: "I am Australian." "I am Catholic."

ingroup
"us"—a group of people who share a sense of belonging, a feeling of common identity

outgroup
"them"—a group that people perceive as distinctively different from or apart from their ingroup

"There is a tendency to define one's own group positively in order to evaluate oneself positively."

John C. Turner (1984)

ingroup bias
the tendency to favor one's own group

In Rwanda, ingroup bias lay behind the murder of half the minority Tutsi population and led to a huge refugee exodus when the majority Hutus were defeated.

little it takes to provoke favoritism toward *us* and unfairness toward *them*. In one study Tajfel and Billig had British teenagers evaluate modern abstract paintings and then told them that they and some others had favored the art of Paul Klee over that of Wassily Kandinsky. Finally, without ever meeting the other members of their group, the teens divided some money among members of both groups.

In experiment after experiment, defining groups even in this trivial way produced favoritism. David Wilder (1981) summarized the typical result: "When given the opportunity to divide 15 points [worth money], subjects generally award 9 or 10 points to their own group and 5 or 6 points to the other group." This bias occurs with both sexes and with people of all ages and nationalities, though especially with people from individualist cultures (Gudykunst, 1989). (People in communal cultures identify more with all their peers and so treat everyone more the same.)

We also are more prone to ingroup bias when our group is small and lower in status relative to the outgroup (Ellemers & others, 1997; Mullen & others, 1992). When we're part of a small group surrounded by a larger group, we are also more conscious of our group membership; when our ingroup is the majority, we think less about it. To be a foreign student, to be gay or lesbian, or to be of a minority race at some social gathering is to feel one's social identity more keenly and to react accordingly.

Even forming conspicuous groups on *no* logical basis—say, merely by composing groups X and Y with the flip of a coin—will produce some ingroup bias (Billig & Tajfel, 1973; Brewer & Silver, 1978; Locksley & others, 1980). In Kurt Vonnegut's novel *Slapstick*, computers gave everyone a new middle name; all "Daffodil-11's" then felt unity with one another and distance from "Raspberry-13's." The self-serving bias (Chapter 2) rides again, enabling people to achieve a more positive social identity: "We" are better than "they," even when "we" and "they" are alike. To maximize self-esteem, people evaluate their ingroups more highly than outgroups, and themselves more highly than their ingroup (Lindeman, 1997).

Because of our social identifications, we conform to our group norms. We sacrifice ourselves for team, family, nation. We dislike outgroups. The more important our social identity and the more strongly attached we feel to a group, the more we react prejudicially to threats from another group (Crocker & Luhtanen, 1990; Hinkle & others, 1992). Names such as Serbian, Tamil, Kurd, and Estonian represent ingroup identities for which people are prepared to die. Israeli historian and former Jerusalem deputy mayor Meron Benvenisti (1988) reports that among Jerusalem's Jews and Arabs, social identity is so central to self-concept that it constantly reminds them of who they are not. Thus, on the integrated street where he lives, his own children—to his dismay—"have not acquired a single Arab friend."

When our group has actually been successful, we can also make ourselves feel better by identifying more strongly with it. When queried after their football team's victory, college students frequently report *"we* won." When questioned after their team's defeat, students are more likely to say *"they* lost." Basking in the reflected glory of a successful ingroup is strongest among those who have just experienced an ego blow, such as learning they did poorly on a "creativity test" (Cialdini & others, 1976). We can also bask in the reflected glory

Drawing by Ed Fisher; © 1987 The New Yorker Magazine, Inc.

"Uh-oh! They seem to have loved it!"

Something favored by an "outgroup" may be cast in a negative light.

of a friend's achievement—except when the friend outperforms us on something pertinent to our identity (Tesser & others, 1988). If you think of yourself as an outstanding psychology student, you will likely take more pleasure in a friend's excelling in mathematics.

Ingroup bias is the favoring of one's group. Such favoritism could reflect (1) liking for the ingroup, (2) dislike for the outgroup, or (3) both. If both, loyalty to one's group should produce a devaluing of other groups. Is that true? Does ethnic pride cause prejudice? Does a strong feminist identity lead women to dislike men? Does loyalty to a particular fraternity or sorority lead its members to deprecate independents and members of other fraternities and sororities?

Experiments support both explanations. Outgroup stereotypes prosper when people feel keenly their ingroup identity, as when with other ingroup members (Wilder & Shapiro, 1991). At a club meeting, we sense most strongly our differences from those in another club. When anticipating bias against our group, we more strongly disparage the outgroup (Vivian & Berkowitz, 1993).

Yet ingroup bias results as much or more from perceiving that one's own group is good (Brewer, 1979) as from a sense that other groups are bad (Rosenbaum & Holtz, 1985). So it seems that positive feelings for our own groups need not be mirrored by equally strong negative feelings for outgroups. Devotion to one's own race, religion, and social group sometimes does predispose a person to devalue other races, religions, and social groups. But the sequence is not automatic.

> Father, Mother, and Me, sister and Auntie say
> All the people like us are We, and every one else is They.
> And They live over the sea, While We live over the way.
> But—would you believe it?—they look upon We
> As only a sort of They!
>
> Rudyard Kipling, 1926 (quoted by Mullen, 1991)

Conformity

Once established, prejudice is maintained largely by inertia. If prejudice is socially accepted, many people will follow the path of least resistance and conform to the fashion. They will act not so much out of a need to hate as out of a need to be liked and accepted.

Thomas Pettigrew's (1958) studies of Whites in South Africa and the American south revealed that during the 1950s those who conformed most to other social norms were also most prejudiced; those who were less conforming mirrored less of the surrounding prejudice. Pettigrew found that in South Africa many Whites were privately appalled by the system of apartheid that the government had implemented. Yet they kept these views to themselves, because they felt that their community would ostracize them if they did otherwise. Similar attitudes could be seen among Indiana steel workers and West Virginia miners in the 1950s. In the mills and mines, the workers accepted integration. In the neighborhood, the norm was rigid segregation (Minard, 1952; Reitzes, 1953). The setting determined the norm, and the norm determined behavior. Prejudice was clearly *not* a manifestation of "sick" personalities but simply of the social norms. Nearly a half-century later, the racial attitudes of parents and peers are still major predictors of prejudice (Agnew & others, 1994).

Conformity also maintains gender prejudice. "If we have come to think that the nursery and the kitchen are the natural sphere of a woman," wrote George Bernard Shaw in an 1891 essay, "we have done so exactly as English children come to think that a cage is the natural sphere of a parrot—because they have never seen one anywhere else." Children who *have* seen women elsewhere—children of employed women—have less stereotyped views of men and women (Hoffman, 1977).

behind the scenes

One's best ideas in social psychology often evolve from direct experience. As a White southerner, I realized when reading *The Authoritarian Personality* as an undergraduate that the book did not explain most of what I thought I knew about anti-Black prejudice in the south. I knew many people who were racially prejudiced but did not appear to be authoritarian personalities. To explain the discrepancy, I needed only to recall the times I had been expelled from the public schools of Richmond, Virginia, for opposing the traditional racial norms. These ideas led directly to my research on how societal pressures to conform shape individual attitudes and behavior.

Thomas Pettigrew
University of California,
Santa Cruz

In all this, there is a message of hope. If prejudice is not deeply ingrained in personality, then as fashions change and new norms evolve, prejudice can diminish. And so it has.

Institutional supports

Segregation is one way that social institutions (schools, government, the media) bolster widespread prejudice. Politics is another. Political leaders may both reflect and reinforce prevailing attitudes. The local government in Cole Harbour, Nova Scotia had enforced laws that implemented segregation through the 1950s. Could these laws have contributed to the violence at the high school?

Schools, too, reinforce dominant cultural attitudes. One analysis of stories in 134 children's readers written before 1970 found that male characters outnumbered female characters 3 to 1 (Women on Words and Images, 1972). Who was portrayed as showing initiative, bravery, and competence? Note the answer in this excerpt from the classic "Dick and Jane" children's reader: Jane, sprawled out on the sidewalk, her roller skates beside her, listens as Mark explains to his mother;

> "She cannot skate," said Mark.
> "I can help her.
> I want to help her.
> Look at her, mother.
> Just look at her.
> She's just like a girl.
> She gives up."

Not until the 1970s, when changing ideas about males and females brought new perceptions of such portrayals, was this blatant (to us) stereotyping widely noticed and changed.

Institutional supports for prejudice often go unnoticed. Usually, they are not deliberate attempts to oppress a group. More often, they simply reflect cultural assumptions, as when the one "flesh"-colored crayon in the Crayola box was pinkish white.

An exception to face-ism: a rare instance in which an ad focuses on a male's entire body.

What contemporary examples of institutionalized biases still go unnoticed? Here is one most of us failed to notice, although it was right before our eyes: By examining 1,750 photographs of people in magazines and newspapers, Dane Archer and his associates (1983) discovered that about two-thirds of the average male photo, but less than half of the average female photo, was devoted to the face. As Archer widened his search, he discovered that such "face-ism" is common. He found it in the periodicals of 11 countries, in 920 portraits gathered from the artwork of six centuries, and in the amateur drawings of students at his own university. Georgia Nigro and her colleagues (1988) confirmed the face-ism phenomenon in more magazines, including magazines with a predominantly female audience, such as *Ms.*

The researchers suspect that the visual prominence given men's faces and women's bodies both reflects and perpetuates sex bias. In research in Germany, Norbert Schwarz and Eva Kurz (1989) confirmed that people whose faces are prominent in photos seem more intelligent and ambitious. But better a whole-body depiction than none at all. Women continue to be stereotyped and underrepresented in the media. Men outnumber women by 2 to 1 in music videos, by 3 to 1 in prime-time television, and by 9 to 1 as authoritative narrators of television commercials (Bretl & Cantor, 1988; Gerbner & others, 1986; Lovdal, 1989; Sommers-Flanagan & others, 1993). Racial minorities are also underrepresented in many forms of the media. For example, in 1989 Ruth Thibodeau examined the previous 42 years of *New Yorker* cartoons and could only find one single cartoon where a Black appeared in a cartoon unrelated to race.

Film and television programs also embody and reinforce prevailing cultural stereotypes. The muddle-headed wide-eyed Black butlers and maids in 1930s movies helped perpetuate the stereotypes they reflected. Today most of us would find such images offensive, yet even a modern TV skit of a crime-prone

Black man can make another Black man who is accused of assault seem more guilty (Ford, 1997). Moreover, sometimes we fail to notice the stereotyping in portrayals of "savage" Native Indians (Trimble, 1988), fanatical Arabs (Shaheen, 1990) or bird-brained women.

Summing up

The social situation breeds and maintains prejudice in several ways. A group that enjoys social and economic superiority will often justify its standing with prejudicial beliefs. Moreover, prejudice can lead people to treat others in ways that trigger expected behavior, thus seeming to confirm the prejudice. Our social identity can also breed prejudice: Experiments reveal that an ingroup bias often arises from the mere fact that people are divided into groups. Once established, prejudice continues partly through the inertia of conformity and partly through institutional supports, such as the mass media.

Emotional sources of prejudice

Although prejudice is bred by social situations, emotional factors often add fuel to the fire: Frustration can feed prejudice, as can personality factors like status needs and authoritarian tendencies.

Frustration and aggression: The scapegoat theory

As we will see in Chapter 10, pain and frustration (the blocking of a goal) often evoke hostility. When the cause of our frustration is intimidating or vague, we often redirect our hostility. This phenomenon of "displaced aggression" may have contributed to the lynchings of African Americans in the south after the Civil War. Between 1882 and 1930, there were more lynchings in years when cotton prices were low and economic frustration was therefore presumably high (Hepworth & West, 1988; Hovland & Sears, 1940). Ethnic peace is easier to maintain during prosperous times.

Targets for this displaced aggression vary. Following their defeat in World War I and their country's subsequent economic chaos, many Germans saw Jews as villains. Long before Hitler came to power, one German leader explained: "The Jew is just convenient. . . . If there were no Jews, the anti-Semites would have to invent them" (quoted by G. W. Allport, 1958, p. 325). In earlier centuries people vented their fear and hostility on witches, whom they sometimes burned or drowned in public.

A famous experiment by Neal Miller and Richard Bugelski (1948) confirmed the scapegoat theory. They asked college-age men working at a summer camp to state their attitudes toward Japanese and Mexicans. Some did so before, and then after, being forced to stay in camp to take tests rather than attend a long-awaited free evening at a local theater. Compared to a control group that did not undergo this frustration, the deprived group afterward displayed increased prejudice. As new studies confirm, people put in unhappy moods often think

> "Whoever is dissatisfied with himself is continually ready for revenge."
>
> Nietzsche, *The Gay Science*, 1882–1887

Drawing by Maslin; © 1985 The New Yorker Magazine, Inc.

Scapegoats provide an outlet for frustrations and hostilities.

"*And now at this point in the meeting I'd like to shift the blame away from me and onto someone else.*"

and act more negatively toward outgroups (Esses & Zanna, 1995; Forgas & Fiedler, in press). Passions provoke prejudice.

One source of frustration is competition. When two groups compete for jobs, housing, or social prestige, one group's goal fulfillment can become the other group's frustration. Thus the **realistic group conflict theory** suggests that *prejudice arises when groups compete for scarce resources.* A corresponding ecological principle, Gause's law, states that maximum competition will exist between species with identical needs. In western Europe, for example, some people agree that "over the last five years people like yourself have been economically worse off than most [name of country's minority group]." These frustrated people express relatively high levels of blatant prejudice (Pettigrew & Meertens, 1995). In Canada, opposition to immigration since 1975 has gone up and down with the unemployment rate (Palmer, 1996). In America, the strongest anti-Black prejudice occurs among Whites who are closest to Blacks on the socioeconomic ladder (Greeley & Sheatsley, 1971; Pettigrew, 1978; Tumin, 1958). When interests clash, prejudice pays, for some people.

realistic group conflict theory
the theory that prejudice arises from competition between groups for scarce resources

Personality dynamics

Any two people, with equal reason to feel frustrated or threatened, will often not be equally prejudiced. This suggests that prejudice serves other functions besides advancing competitive self-interest.

Need for status and belonging

"By exciting emulation and comparisons of superiority, you lay the foundation of lasting mischief; you make brothers and sisters hate each other."

Samuel Johnson, quoted in James Boswell's *Life of Samuel Johnson*

Status is relative: To perceive ourselves as having status, we need people below us. Thus one psychological benefit of prejudice, or of any status system, is a feeling of superiority. Most of us can recall a time when we took secret satisfaction in another's failure—perhaps seeing a brother or sister punished or a classmate failing a test. In Europe and North America, prejudice is often greater among those low or slipping on the socioeconomic ladder and among those whose positive self-image is being threatened (Lemyre & Smith, 1985; Pettigrew & others,

Scapegoating: In difficult times, when budgets are slashed and taxes are high, homeless women with small children are often targets of hostility because they are perceived as responsible for their situation and as a drain on scarce social resources.

1997; Thompson & Crocker, 1985). In one study at Northwestern University, members of lower-status sororities were more disparaging of other sororities than were members of higher-status sororities (Crocker & others, 1987). Perhaps people whose status is secure have less need to feel superior.

But other factors associated with low status could also account for prejudice. Imagine yourself as one of the Arizona State University students who took part in an experiment by Robert Cialdini and Kenneth Richardson (1980). You are walking alone across campus. Someone approaches you and asks your help with a five-minute survey. You agree. After the researcher gives you a brief "creativity test," he deflates you with the news that "you have scored relatively low on the test." The researcher then completes the survey by asking you some evaluative questions about either your school or its traditional rival, the University of Arizona. Would your feelings of failure affect your ratings of either school? Compared with those in a control group whose self-esteem was not threatened, the students who experienced failure gave higher ratings to their own school and lower ratings to their rival. Apparently, asserting one's social identity by boasting about one's own group and denigrating outgroups can boost one's ego.

James Meindl and Melvin Lerner (1984) found that a humiliating experience—accidentally knocking over a stack of someone's important computer cards—provoked English-speaking Canadian students to express increased hostility toward French-speaking Canadians. And Teresa Amabile and Ann Glazebrook (1982) found that Dartmouth College men who were made to feel insecure judged others' work more harshly. Thinking about your own mortality—by writing a short essay on dying and the emotions aroused by thinking about death—also provokes enough insecurity to intensify ingroup favoritism and outgroup prejudice (Greenberg & others, 1990, 1994; Harmon-Jones & others, 1996).

All this suggests that a man who doubts his own strength and independence might, by proclaiming women to be pitifully weak and dependent, boost his masculine image. Indeed, when Joel Grube, Randy Kleinhesselink, and Kathleen Kearney (1982) had Washington State University men view young women's videotaped job interviews, men with low self-acceptance disliked strong, nontraditional women. Men with high self-acceptance preferred them. Experiments confirm the connection between self-image and prejudice: Affirm people and they will evaluate an outgroup more positively; threaten their self-esteem and they will restore it by denigrating an outgroup (Fein & Spencer, 1997).

A despised outgroup serves yet another need: the need to belong to an ingroup. As we will see in Chapter 13, the perception of a common enemy unites a group. School spirit is seldom so strong as when the game is with the arch-rival. The sense of comradeship among workers is often highest when they all feel a common antagonism toward management. To solidify the Nazi hold over Germany, Hitler used the "Jewish menace." Despised outgroups can strengthen the ingroup.

The authoritarian personality

ethnocentrism
a belief in the superiority of one's own ethnic and cultural group, and a corresponding disdain for all other groups

The emotional needs that contribute to prejudice are said to predominate in the "authoritarian personality." In the 1940s, University of California–Berkeley researchers—two of whom had fled Nazi Germany—set out on an urgent research mission: to uncover the psychological roots of an anti-Semitism so poisonous that it caused the slaughter of millions of Jews and turned many millions of Europeans into indifferent spectators. In studies of American adults, Theodor Adorno and his colleagues (1950) discovered that hostility toward Jews often coexisted with hostility toward other minorities. Prejudice appeared to be less an attitude specific to one group than a way of thinking about those who are different. Moreover, these judgmental, **ethnocentric** people shared authoritarian tendencies—an intolerance for weakness, a punitive attitude, and

Authoritarian tendencies feed on social upheaval.

a submissive respect for their ingroup's authorities, as reflected in their agreement with such statements as "Obedience and respect for authority are the most important virtues children should learn."

As children, authoritarian people often were harshly disciplined. This supposedly led them to repress their hostilities and impulses and to "project" them onto outgroups. The insecurity of authoritarian children seemed to predispose them toward an excessive concern with power and status and an inflexible right-wrong way of thinking that made ambiguity difficult to tolerate. Such people therefore tended to be submissive to those with power over them and aggressive or punitive toward those beneath them.

Scholars criticized the research for focusing on right-wing authoritarianism and overlooking dogmatic authoritarianism of the left. Still, its main conclusion has survived: Authoritarian tendencies, sometimes reflected in ethnic tensions, surge during threatening times of economic recession and social upheaval (Doty & others, 1991; Sales, 1973). In contemporary Russia, individuals scoring high in authoritarianism have tended to support a return to Marxist-Leninist ideology and to oppose democratic reform (McFarland & others, 1992, 1996).

Moreover, contemporary studies of right-wing authoritarians by University of Manitoba psychologist Bob Altemeyer (1988, 1992) confirm that there *are* individuals whose fears and hostilities surface as prejudice. Feelings of moral superiority may go hand in hand with brutality toward perceived inferiors.

Different forms of prejudice—toward Blacks, gays and lesbians, women, old people, fat people, AIDS victims, the homeless—*do* tend to coexist in the same individuals (Bierly, 1985; Crandall, 1994; Peterson & others, 1993; Snyder & Ickes, 1985). As Altemeyer concludes, right-wing authoritarians tend to be "equal opportunity bigots." The same is true of those with a "social dominance orientation"—who view people in terms of hierarchies of merit or goodness. By contrast, those with a more communal or universal orientation—who attend to people's similarities and presume "universal human rights" enjoyed by "all God's children"—are more welcoming of affirmative action and accepting of those who differ (Phillips & Ziller, 1997; Pratto & others, 1994; Sidanius & others, 1996; Whitley & Lee, 1997).

		Summing up
Prejudice has emotional roots, too. Frustration breeds hostility, which people sometimes vent on scapegoats and sometimes express more directly against competing groups perceived as responsible for one's frustration.	By providing a feeling of social superiority, prejudice may also help cover feelings of inferiority. Different types of prejudice are often found together in those who have an "authoritarian" attitude.	

Cognitive sources of prejudice

To understand stereotyping and prejudice, it also helps to remember how our minds work. How do the ways in which we think about the world, and simplify it, influence our stereotypes? And how do our stereotypes affect our judgments?

Much of the explanation of prejudice so far could have been written in the 1960s—but not what follows. This new look at prejudice, fueled by 1,500 research articles on stereotyping in the last 10 years (Dovidio & others, 1996), applies the new research on social thinking. The basic point is this: Stereotyped beliefs and prejudiced attitudes exist not only because of social conditioning and because they enable people to displace hostilities, but also as by-products of normal thinking processes. Many stereotypes spring less from malice than from how we simplify our complex worlds. They are like perceptual illusions, a by-product of our knack for interpreting the world.

Categorization

One way we simplify our environment is to "categorize"—to organize the world by clustering objects into groups. A biologist classifies plants and animals. A human classifies people. Having done so, we think about them more easily. If persons in a group are similar, knowing their group can provide useful information with minimal effort (Macrae & others, 1994). Customs inspectors and airplane antihijack personnel are therefore given "profiles" of suspicious individuals (Kraut & Poe, 1980).

We find it especially easy and efficient to rely on stereotypes when

- pressed for time (Kaplan & others, 1993),
- preoccupied (Gilbert & Hixon, 1991),
- tired (Bodenhausen, 1990),
- emotionally aroused (Esses & others, 1993b; Stroessner & Mackie, 1993), and
- too young to appreciate diversity (Biernat, 1991).

Ethnicity and sex are, in our current world, powerful ways of categorizing people. Imagine Tom, a 45-year-old, African American real estate agent in New Orleans. I suspect that your image of "Black male" predominates over the categories "middle-aged," "businessperson," and "southerner."

Experiments expose our spontaneous categorization of people by race. Much as we organize what is actually a color continuum into what we perceive as distinct colors, so we cannot resist categorizing people into groups. We label people of widely varying ancestry as simply "Black" or "White," as if such categories were black and white. When subjects view different people making statements, they often forget who said what, yet remember the race of the person who made each statement (Hewstone & others, 1991; Stroessner & others, 1990; Taylor & others, 1978). By itself, such categorization is not prejudice, but it does provide a foundation for prejudice.

In fact, it's necessary for prejudice. Social identity theory implies that those who feel their social identity keenly will concern themselves with correctly categorizing people as *us* or *them*. To test this prediction, Jim Blascovich, Natalie Wyer, Laura Swart, and Jeffrey Kibler (1997) compared racially prejudiced people (who feel their racial identity keenly) with nonprejudiced people—who proved equally speedy at classifying white, black, and gray ovals. But how much time did each group take to categorize *people* by race? Especially when shown faces whose race was somewhat ambiguous (Figure 9–6), prejudiced people took longer, with more apparent concern for classifying people as us (one's own race) or them (another race). Prejudice requires racial categorization.

figure 9–6
Racial categorization.
Quickly: What race is this person? Less prejudiced people respond more quickly, with less apparent concern with possibly misclassifying someone (as if thinking, who cares?).

Perceived similarities and differences

Picture the following objects: apples, chairs, pencils.

There is a strong tendency to see objects within a group as being more uniform than they really are. Were your apples all red? your chairs all straight-backed? your pencils all yellow? Once we classify two days in the same month, they seem more alike, temperature-wise, than the same interval across months. People guess the eight-day average temperature difference between, say, November 15th and 23rd to be less than the eight-day difference between November 30th and December 8th (Krueger & Clement, 1994).

It's the same with people. Once we assign people to groups—athletes, drama majors, math professors—we are likely to exaggerate the similarities within groups and the differences between them (S. E. Taylor, 1981; Wilder, 1978). Mere division into groups can create an **outgroup homogeneity effect**—a sense that *they* are "all alike" and different from "us" and "our" group (Ostrom & Sedikides, 1992). Because we generally like people we think are similar to us and dislike those we perceive as different, the natural result is ingroup bias (Byrne & Wong, 1962; Rokeach & Mezei, 1966; Stein & others, 1965).

Bad or good moods can amplify the outgroup stereotyping. Feeling bad, we perceive people and events in a more negative light. But even positive emotions can interfere with complex thinking, leading us to perceive folks in another group as more alike than they are (Mackie & others, 1996). Happy people, feeling contented, seem to commit less effort to wrestling with differences. Moreover, suggest Galen Bodenhausen and his colleagues (1994), feeling really good may prime feelings of relative superiority.

outgroup homogeneity effect perception of outgroup members as more similar to one another than are ingroup members. Thus "they are alike; we are diverse."

The mere fact of a group decision can also lead outsiders to overestimate a group's unanimity. If a conservative wins a national election by a slim majority, observers infer "the people have turned conservative." If a liberal won by a similarly slim margin, voter attitudes would hardly have differed, but observers would now attribute a "liberal mood" to the country. Whether a decision is made by majority rule or by a designated group executive, people usually presume that it reflects the entire group's attitudes, observe Scott Allison and his co-workers (1985 to 1996). When the Onex coporation tried to take over Air Canada, Buzz Hargrove, the president of the Canadian Auto Workers (CAW), sided with Onex. The media reported that the CAW was behind Onex, even though it was clear that many union members felt otherwise.

When the group is our own, we are more likely to see diversity:

- Many non-Europeans see the Swiss as a fairly homogeneous people. But to the people of Switzerland, the Swiss are diverse, encompassing French-, German-, and Italian-speaking groups.

- Those in a minority tend to feel more shared identity than those in the majority (Haslam & Oakes, 1995; Ryan, 1996). Nevertheless, those in the minority are especially likely to see important differences between their own subgroup and other subgroups, while those in the majority tend to lump all minority group members together (Huddy & Virtanen, 1995).

- Sorority sisters perceive the members of any other sorority as less diverse than the mix in their own (Park & Rothbart, 1982). And business majors and engineering majors overestimate the uniformity of the other group's traits and attitudes (Judd & others, 1991).

In general, the greater our familiarity with a social group, the more we see its diversity (Brown & Wootton-Millward, 1993; Linville & others, 1989). The less our familiarity, the more we stereotype. Also, the smaller and less powerful the group, the more we stereotype (Fiske, 1993; Mullen & Hu, 1989). To those in power, we pay attention.

Perhaps you have noticed: *They*—the members of any racial group other than your own—even *look* alike. Many of us can recall embarrassing ourselves by confusing two people of another racial group, prompting the person we've misnamed to say, "You think we all look alike." Experiments by John Brigham, June Chance, Alvin Goldstein, and Roy Malpass in the United States and by Hayden Ellis in Scotland reveal that people of other races do in fact *seem* to look more alike than do people of one's own race (Brigham & Williamson, 1979; Chance & Goldstein, 1981; Ellis, 1981). When White students are shown faces of a few White and a few Black individuals and then asked to pick these individuals out of a photographic lineup, they more accurately recognize the White faces than the Black.

I am White. When I first read this research I thought, of course: White people *are* more physically diverse than Blacks. But my reaction was apparently just an illustration of the phenomenon. For if my reaction were correct, Black people, too, would better recognize a White face among a lineup of Whites than a Black face in a lineup of Blacks. But in fact, as Figure 9–7 illustrates, Blacks more easily recognize another Black than they do a White (Bothwell & others, 1989). And Hispanics more readily recognize another Hispanic whom they saw a couple of hours earlier than they do an Anglo (Platz & Hosch, 1988).

"Women are more like each other than men [are]."

Lord (not Lady) Chesterfield

The term "own-race bias" is a misnomer in the case of Anglo and Hispanic identifications. Most Hispanic people are classified as Caucasians.

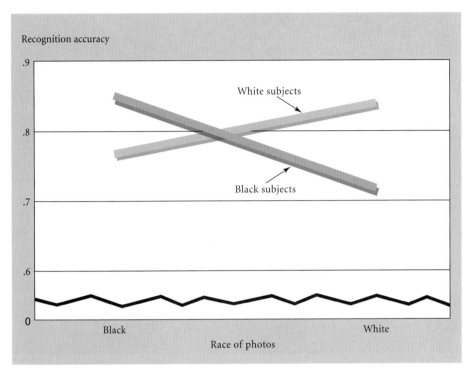

Recognition accuracy

figure 9–7

The own-race bias.
White subjects more accurately recognize the faces of Whites than of Blacks; Black subjects more accurately recognize the faces of Blacks than of Whites.

(From Devine & Malpass, 1985.)

Distinctive stimuli

Other ways we perceive our worlds also breed stereotypes. Distinctive people and vivid or extreme occurrences often capture attention and distort judgments.

Distinctive people

Have you ever found yourself in a situation where you were the only person present of your sex, race, or nationality? If so, your difference from the others probably made you more noticeable and the object of more attention. A Black in an otherwise White group, a man in an otherwise female group, or a woman in an otherwise male group seems more prominent and influential and to have exaggerated good and bad qualities (Crocker & McGraw, 1984; S. E. Taylor & others, 1979). This occurs because when someone in a group is made salient (conspicuous), we tend to see that person as causing whatever happens (Taylor & Fiske, 1978). If we are positioned to look at Joe, an average group member, Joe will seem to have a greater than average influence upon the group. People who capture our attention seem more responsible for what happens.

Have you noticed that people also define you by your most distinctive traits and behaviors? Tell people about someone who is a sky diver and a tennis player, report Lori Nelson and Dale Miller (1997), and they will think of the person as a sky diver. Asked to choose a gift book for the person, they will pick a skydiving book over a tennis book. A person who has both a pet snake and a pet dog is seen more as a snake owner than a dog owner. People also take note of those who violate expectations (Bettencourt & others, 1997). "Like a flower blooming in winter, intellect is more readily noticed where it is not expected," reflected Stephen Carter (1993, p. 54) on his experience as a Black

Distinctive people—like this tourist visiting a Saturday market in Menghum, China—draw attention. Their salience may cause exaggerated perceptions of their good and bad qualities.

intellectual. Such perceived distinctiveness makes it easier for highly capable job applicants from low-status groups to get noticed, though they also must work harder to prove their abilities are genuine (Biernat & Kobrynowicz, 1997).

Ellen Langer and Lois Imber (1980) cleverly demonstrated the attention paid distinctive people. They asked Harvard students to watch a video of a man reading. The students paid closer attention when they were led to think he was out of the ordinary—a cancer patient, a homosexual, or a millionaire. They detected characteristics that other viewers ignored, and their evaluation of him was more extreme. Those who thought the man a cancer patient noticed distinctive facial characteristics and bodily movements and thus perceived him as much more "different from most people" than did the other viewers. The extra attention we pay to distinctive people creates an illusion that they differ more from others than they really do. If people thought you had the IQ of a genius, they would probably notice things about you that otherwise would pass unnoticed.

When surrounded by Whites, Blacks sometimes detect people reacting to their distinctiveness. Many report being stared or glared at, being subject to insensitive comments, and receiving bad service (Swim & others, 1998). Sometimes we perceive others as reacting to our distinctiveness, however, when actually they aren't. At Dartmouth College, researchers Robert Kleck and Angelo Strenta (1980) discovered this when they led college women to feel disfigured. The women thought the purpose of the experiment was to assess how someone would react to a facial scar created with theatrical makeup; the scar was on the right cheek, running from the ear to the mouth. Actually, the purpose was to see how the women themselves, when made to feel deviant, would perceive others' behavior toward them. After applying the makeup, the experimenter gave each subject a small hand mirror so she could see the authentic-looking scar. When she put the mirror down, he then applied some "moisturizer" to "keep the makeup from cracking." What the "moisturizer" really did was remove the scar.

The scene that followed was poignant. A young woman, feeling terribly self-conscious about her supposedly disfigured face, talked with another woman who sees no such disfigurement and knows nothing of what has gone on before. If you have ever felt similarly self-conscious—perhaps about a physical handicap, acne, even just a bad hair day—then perhaps you can sympathize with the self-conscious woman. Compared to women led to believe their conversational partner merely thought they had an allergy, the "disfigured" women became acutely sensitive to how their partners were looking at them. They rated their partners as more tense, distant, and patronizing. But in fact, observers who later analyzed videotapes of how the partners treated "disfigured" persons could find no such differences in treatment. Self-conscious about being different, the "disfigured" women misinterpreted mannerisms and comments they would otherwise not notice.

Self-conscious interactions between a majority and minority person can therefore feel tense even when both are well-intentioned (Devine & others, 1996). Tom, who is known to be gay, meets Bill, who is straight. Tolerant Bill wants to respond without prejudice. But feeling unsure of himself, he holds back a bit. Tom, expecting negative attitudes from most people, misreads Bill's hesitancy as hostility and responds with a seeming chip on his shoulder.

> The self-consciousness created by being a token minority—say, a man in a group of women or a woman in a group of men—can also disrupt one's normal thinking and memory processes, thereby making the token person seem inept
>
> (Lord & Saenz, 1985).

Vivid cases

Our minds also use distinctive cases as a shortcut to judging groups. Are Blacks good athletes? "Well, there's Barry Sanders and Sheryl Swoopes and Michael Jordan. Yeah, I'd say so." Note the thought processes at work here: Given limited experience with a particular social group, we recall examples of it and generalize from those (Sherman, 1996). Moreover, encountering examplars of

Self-consciousness about being different affects how we interpret others' behavior.

negative stereotypes (a hostile Black person in one recent experiment) can prime such stereotypes, leading people to minimize contact with the group (Hendersen-King & Nisbett, 1996). Such generalizing from single cases can cause problems. Vivid instances, though more available in memory, are seldom representative of the larger group. Exceptional athletes, though distinctive and memorable, are not the best basis for judging the distribution of athletic talent among an entire group.

Those in a numerical minority, being more conspicuous, also may be numerically overestimated by the majority. What proportion of your country's population would you say is Muslim? What percentage is Black? People in countries where these groups are minorities often overestimate their proportion in the population. (In Canada, less than 1 percent have declared themselves Muslim, and about 2 percent have indicated they were Black in census data.) In one survey in the U.S. (Gates, 1993) people estimated that 32 percent of the population was Black while census data puts the figure at 12 percent.

Myron Rothbart and his colleagues (1978) showed how distinctive cases also fuel stereotypes. They had University of Oregon students view 50 slides, each of which stated the man's height. For one group of students, 10 of the men were slightly over 6 feet (up to 6 feet, 4 inches). For other students, these 10 men were well over 6 feet (up to 6 feet, 11 inches). When asked later how many of the men were over 6 feet, those given the moderately tall examples recalled 5 percent too many. Those given the extremely tall examples recalled 50 percent too many. In a follow-up experiment, students read descriptions of the actions of 50 men, 10 of whom had committed either nonviolent crimes, such as forgery, or violent crimes, such as rape. Of those shown the list with the violent crimes, most overestimated the number of criminal acts.

The attention-getting power of distinctive, extreme cases helps explain why middle-class people so greatly exaggerate the dissimilarities between themselves and the underclass. Contrary to stereotypes of "welfare queens" driving Cadillacs, people living in poverty generally share the aspirations of the middle class and would rather provide for themselves than accept public assistance (Cook & Curtin, 1987). Moreover, the less we know about a group, the more we are influenced by a few vivid cases (Quattrone & Jones, 1980).

Distinctive events

Stereotypes assume a correlation between group membership and individuals' characteristics ("Italians are emotional," "Jews are shrewd," "Accountants are perfectionists"). Even under the best of conditions, our attentiveness to unusual occurrences can create **illusory correlations.** Because we are sensitive to distinctive events, the co-occurrence of two such events is especially noticeable—more noticeable than each of the times the unusual events do not occur together. Thus Rupert Brown and Amanda Smith (1989) found that British faculty members overestimated the number of (relatively rare, though noticeable) female senior faculty at their university.

David Hamilton and Robert Gifford (1976) demonstrated illusory correlation in a clever experiment. They showed students slides on which various people, members of "Group A" or "Group B," were said to have done something desirable or undesirable. For example, "John, a member of Group A, visited a sick friend in the hospital." Twice as many statements described members of Group A as Group B, but both groups did nine desirable acts for every four

illusory correlation
a false impression that two variables correlate; see Chapter 3

undesirable behaviors. Since both Group B and the undesirable acts were less frequent, their co-occurrence—for example, "Allen, a member of Group B, dented the fender of a parked car and didn't leave his name"—was an unusual combination that caught people's attention. The students therefore overestimated the frequency with which the "minority" group (B) acted undesirably and judged Group B more harshly.

Remember, Group B members actually committed undesirable acts in the same proportion as Group A members. Moreover, the students had no preexisting biases for or against Group B, and they received the information more systematically than daily experience ever offers it. Although researchers debate why it happens, they agree that illusory correlation occurs and provides yet another source for the formation of racial stereotypes (Hamilton & Sherman, 1994).

The mass media reflect and feed this phenomenon. When a self-described homosexual murders someone, homosexuality often gets mentioned. When a heterosexual murders someone, the person's sexual orientation is seldom mentioned. Likewise, when ex-mental patients commit crimes, such as Mark Chapman (who shot John Lennon), the person's mental history commands attention. Assassins and mental hospitalization are both relatively infrequent, making the combination especially newsworthy. Such reporting adds to the illusion of a large correlation between (1) violent tendencies and (2) homosexuality or mental hospitalization.

Unlike those who judged groups A and B, we often have preexisting biases. David Hamilton's further research with Terrence Rose (1980) reveals that our preexisting stereotypes can lead us to "see" correlations that aren't there. They had University of California–Santa Barbara students read sentences in which various adjectives described the members of different occupational groups ("Doug, an accountant, is timid and thoughtful"). In actuality, each occupation was described equally often by each adjective; accountants, doctors, and salespeople were equally often timid, wealthy, and talkative. The students, however, *thought* they had more often read descriptions of timid accountants, wealthy doctors, and talkative salespeople. Their stereotyping led them to perceive correlations that weren't there, thus helping to perpetuate the stereotypes. To believe is to see.

Attribution: Is it a just world?

In explaining others' actions, we frequently commit the **fundamental attribution error.** We attribute their behavior so much to their inner dispositions that we discount important situational forces. The error occurs partly because our attention focuses on the persons, not on the situation. A person's race or sex is vivid and attention-getting; the situational forces working upon that person are usually less visible. Slavery was often overlooked as an explanation for slave behavior; the behavior was instead attributed to the slaves' own nature. Until recently, the same was true of how we explained the perceived differences between women and men. Because gender-role constraints were hard to see, we attributed men's and women's behavior solely to their innate dispositions.

fundamental
attribution error
see Chapter 3

Group-serving bias

Thomas Pettigrew (1979, 1980) argues that attribution errors can bias people's explanations of group members' behaviors. We grant members of our own group the benefit of the doubt: "She donated because she has a good heart; he refused because he had to under the circumstances." When explaining acts by members of other groups, we more often assume the worst: "He donated to gain favor; she refused because she's selfish." Hence, as we noted earlier in this chapter, the shove that Whites perceive as mere "horsing around" when done by another White becomes a "violent gesture" when done by a Black.

Positive behavior by outgroup members is more often dismissed. It may be seen as a "special case" ("He is certainly bright and hardworking—not at all like other Hispanics"), as owing to luck or some special advantage ("She probably got admitted just because her med school had to fill its quota for women applicants"), as demanded by the situation ("Under the circumstances, what could the cheap Scot do but pay the whole check?"), or as attributable to extra effort ("Jewish students get better grades because they're so compulsive"). Disadvantaged groups and groups that stress modesty (such as the Chinese) exhibit less of this **group-serving bias** (Fletcher & Ward, 1989; Hewstone & Ward, 1985; Jackson & others, 1993).

group-serving bias explaining away outgroup members' positive behaviors; also attributing negative behaviors to their dispositions (while excusing such behavior by one's own group)

The group-serving bias can subtly color our language. A team of University of Padova (Italy) researchers led by Anne Maass (1995, 1996) has found that positive behaviors by another ingroup member often get described as general dispositions (for example, "Lucy is helpful"). When performed by an outgroup member, the same behavior often gets described as a specific, isolated act ("Lucy held the door open for somebody"). Maass calls this group-serving bias the *linguistic intergroup bias.*

Earlier we noted that blaming the victim can justify the blamer's own superior status. Blaming occurs as people attribute an outgroup's failures to its members' flawed dispositions, notes Miles Hewstone (1990): "They fail because they're stupid; we fail because we didn't try." If women, Blacks, or Jews have been abused, they must somehow have brought it on themselves. When the British marched a group of German civilians around the Bergen-Belsen concentration camp at the close of World War II, one German responded: "What terrible criminals these prisoners must have been to receive such treatment."

The just-world phenomenon

In a series of experiments conducted at the Universities of Waterloo and Kentucky, Melvin Lerner and his colleagues (Lerner & Miller, 1978; Lerner, 1980)

behind the scenes

I still remember that day in 1979 when, as an Oxford graduate student, I was told by one of my advisors after a trip to the United States that "attribution theory was finished." Having hoped to integrate North American attribution theory with European theory about intergroup relations and prejudice, I was dismayed. Fortunately, my second advisor supported my exploring how people attribute motives to those in other groups. This research illustrates how the international field of social psychology benefits from both the North American and European perspectives. It also reminds me that, when rebuffed, students should seek a second opinion. If you glimpse an important phenomenon that begs to be studied, don't be easily deterred by current research fads and fashions.

Michael Hewstone
University of Wales

discovered that merely *observing* another person being innocently victimized is enough to make the victim seem less worthy. Imagine that you along with some others are participating in one of Lerner's studies—supposedly on the perception of emotional cues (Lerner & Simmons, 1966). One of the participants, a confederate, is selected by lottery to perform a memory task. This person receives painful shocks whenever she gives a wrong answer. You and the others note her emotional responses.

After watching the victim receive these apparently painful shocks, the experimenter asks you to evaluate her. How would you respond? With compassionate sympathy? We might expect so. As Ralph Waldo Emerson wrote, "The martyr cannot be dishonored." On the contrary, the experiments revealed that martyrs *can* be dishonored. When observers were powerless to alter the victim's fate, they often rejected and devalued the victim. Juvenal, the Roman satirist, anticipated these results: "The Roman mob follows after Fortune . . . and hates those who have been condemned."

Linda Carli and her colleagues (1989, 1990) report that this **just-world phenomenon** colors our impressions of rape victims. Carli had people read detailed descriptions of interactions between a man and a woman. For example, a woman and her boss meet for dinner, go to his home and each have a glass of wine. Some read a scenario that has a happy ending: "Then he led me to the couch. He held my hand and asked me to marry him." In hindsight, people find the ending unsurprising and admire the man's and woman's character traits. Others read the same scenario with a different ending: "But then he became very rough and pushed me onto the couch. He held me down on the couch and raped me." Given this ending, people see it as more inevitable and blame the woman for behavior that seems faultless when it has a happier outcome.

Lerner (1980) believes such disparaging of hapless victims results from our need to believe that "I am a just person living in a just world, a world where people get what they deserve." From early childhood, he argues, we are taught that good is rewarded and evil punished. Hard work and virtue pay dividends; laziness and immorality do not. From this it is but a short leap to assuming that those who flourish must be good and those who suffer must

just-world phenomenon
the tendency of people to believe the world is just and that people therefore get what they deserve and deserve what they get

The just-world phenomenon.

deserve their fate. The classic illustration is the Old Testament story of Job, a good person who suffers terrible misfortune. Job's friends surmise that, this being a just world, Job must have done something wicked to elicit such terrible suffering.

This suggests that people are indifferent to social injustice not because they have no concern for justice but because they *see* no injustice. Those who assume a just world believe that rape victims must have behaved seductively (Borgida & Brekke, 1985), that battered spouses must have provoked their beatings (Summers & Feldman, 1984), that poor people don't deserve better (Furnham & Gunter, 1984), and that sick people are responsible for their illness (Gruman & Sloan, 1983). Such beliefs enable successful people to reassure themselves that they, too, deserve what they have. The wealthy and healthy can see their own good fortune, and others' misfortune, as justly deserved. Linking good fortune with virtue and misfortune with moral failure enables the fortunate to feel pride and to avoid responsibility for the unfortunate. Small wonder that belief in a just world predicts more skepticism about the purpose and efficiency of charitable giving (Furnham, 1995).

People loathe a loser even when the loser's misfortune quite obviously stems from mere bad luck. People *know* that gambling outcomes are just good or bad luck and should not affect their evaluations of the gambler. Still, they can't resist playing Monday-morning quarterback—judging people by their results. Ignoring the fact that reasonable decisions can bring bad results, they judge losers as less competent (Baron & Hershey, 1988). Lawyers and stock market speculators may similarly judge themselves by their outcomes, becoming smug after successes and self-reproachful after failures. Talent and initiative are not unrelated to success. But the just-world assumption discounts the uncontrollable factors that can derail one's best efforts.

focus

Is it a just world? Blaming the rape victim

The 21-year-old divorced mother had been drinking and socializing in Big Dan's Bar. But had she invited her fate? Egged on by one another, several male patrons seized her, tore off most of her clothes, and gang-raped her on the barroom floor and then on the pool table while others in the bar applauded and cheered. In this and several other such incidents, dramatized in the 1988 movie *The Accused*, many people condemned the victims as having "deserved it." "She had no business being in a bar," said one elderly woman. "She should have been home with her kids instead of destroying men's lives!"

This case, in both its actual and dramatized versions, illustrates our human readiness not only to credit people for their successes but to blame them for their misfortunes. In one national survey, 33 percent of British people agreed that women who have been raped are usually to blame for it (Wagstaff, 1982). In experiments, those given a description of a woman's friendly behavior with a man judge her actions as appropriate. Others, also told she gets raped by the man, judge the same behavior as inappropriate—as having invited the rape (Janoff-Bulman & others, 1985). If it's a just world, then victims can be blamed for their fates. But is the world always just?

Cognitive consequences of stereotypes

Are stereotypes self-perpetuating?

Prejudice is prejudgment. Prejudgments are inevitable: None of us is a dispassionate bookkeeper of social happenings, tallying evidence for and against our biases. Rather, our prejudgments guide our attention, our interpretations, and our memories.

Whenever a member of a group behaves as expected, we duly note the fact; our prior belief is confirmed. When a member of a group behaves inconsistently with our expectation, we may explain away the behavior as due to special circumstances (Crocker & others, 1983). Or we may misinterpret it, leaving the prior belief intact. Stereotypes therefore influence how we construe someone's behavior (Kunda & Sherman-Williams, 1993), how we explain it (Sanbonmatsu & others, 1994), and how well we remember it (Stangor & McMillan, 1992).

Perhaps you, too, can recall a time when, try as you might, you could not overcome someone's opinion of you, a time when no matter what you did you were misinterpreted. Misinterpretations are likely when someone *expects* an unpleasant encounter with you (Wilder & Shapiro, 1989). William Ickes and his colleagues (1982) demonstrated this in an experiment with pairs of university-age men. Upon arrival, the experimenters falsely forewarned one member of each pair that the other subject was "one of the unfriendliest people I've talked to lately." The two were then introduced and left alone together for five minutes. Students in another condition were led to think the other subject was exceptionally friendly.

Both groups were friendly to the new acquaintance. In fact, those who expected him to be *un*friendly went out of their way to be friendly, and their smiles and other friendly behaviors elicited a warm response. But unlike the positively biased students, those expecting an unfriendly person attributed this reciprocal friendliness to their own "kid-gloves" treatment of him. They afterward expressed more mistrust and dislike for the person and rated his behavior as less friendly. Despite their partner's actual friendliness, the negative bias induced these students to "see" hostilities lurking beneath his "forced smiles." As researcher David Hamilton (1981) quipped, "I wouldn't have seen it if I hadn't believed it!"

> "Labels act like shrieking sirens, deafening us to all finer discriminations that we might otherwise perceive."
>
> Gordon Allport,
> *The Nature of Prejudice,*
> 1954

When people violate our stereotypes, we salvage the stereotype by splitting off a new subgroup stereotype, such as "senior Olympians."

It would be an overstatement to say that we are absolutely blind to discon-firming facts. Still, negative ideas about a person or a group are often hard to dislodge. For one thing, a positive image—that one is gentle, sincere, or dependable—is easily reversed by just a few contrary behaviors. An unfavor-able image—that one is deceitful, hostile, or unethical—is not so easily changed (Rothbart & John, 1985; Rothbart & Park, 1986). If suspicious, we can easily mis-interpret someone's genuine friendliness as superficial smoothness.

The resistance of negative stereotypes to disconfirming facts is sometimes alarming. Consider the following conversation quoted by Allport (1954): "Mr. X: 'The trouble with Jews is that they only take care of their own group.' Mr. Y: 'But the record of the Community Chest campaign shows that they give more gener-ously, . . . than do non-Jews.' Mr. X: 'That shows they are always trying to buy favor and intrude into Christian affairs. They think of nothing but money. . .' "

We do notice information that is strikingly inconsistent with a stereotype. Still, when the "exceptions" seem concentrated in a few atypical people, we can salvage the stereotype by splitting off a new category (Brewer, 1988; Hewstone, 1994; Kunda & Oleson, 1995, 1997). Homeowners who have desirable Black neighbors can form a new stereotype of "professional, middle-class" Blacks. This **subtyping**—forming a subgroup stereotype—helps maintain the larger stereotype that *most* Blacks make irresponsible neighbors (Figure 9–8). The pos-itive image British schoolchildren form of their friendly school police officers—whom they perceive as in a special category—doesn't improve their image of police officers in general (Hewstone & others, 1992). One who believes that women are basically passive and dependent can split off a new subtype of "aggressive feminist" to handle women who don't fit the basic stereotype (S. E. Taylor, 1981).

Do stereotypes bias judgments of individuals?

There is an upbeat note on which we can conclude this chapter: *People often eval-uate individuals more positively than the groups they compose* (Miller & Felicio, 1990). Anne Locksley, Eugene Borgida, and Nancy Brekke have found that once someone knows a person, "Stereotypes may have minimal, if any, impact on judgments about that person" (Borgida & others, 1981; Locksley & others, 1980, 1982). They discovered this by giving university students anecdotal information about recent incidents in the life of "Nancy." In a supposed transcript of a tele-phone conversation, Nancy told a friend how she responded to three different situations (for example, being harassed by a seedy character while shopping). Some of the students read transcripts portraying Nancy responding assertively (telling the seedy character to leave); others read a report of passive responses (simply ignoring the character until he finally drifts away). Still other students received the same information, except that the person was named "Paul" instead of Nancy. A day later the students predicted how Nancy (or Paul) would respond to other situations.

Did knowing the person's sex have any effect on these predictions? None at all. Expectations of the person's assertiveness were influenced solely by what the students had learned about that individual the day before. Even their judg-ments of masculinity and femininity were unaffected by knowing the person's sex. Gender stereotypes had been left on the shelf; the students evaluated Nancy and Paul as individuals.

The explanation for this finding is implied by an important principle dis-cussed in Chapter 3. Given (1) general (base-rate) information about a group

subtyping
accommodating individuals who deviate from one's stereotype by splitting off a subgroup stereotype (such as "middle class Blacks" or "feminist women"). Subtyping protects stereotypes.

"There are no good women climbers. Women climbers either aren't good climbers or they aren't real women."

Anonymous climber (cited by Rothbart & Lewis, 1988)

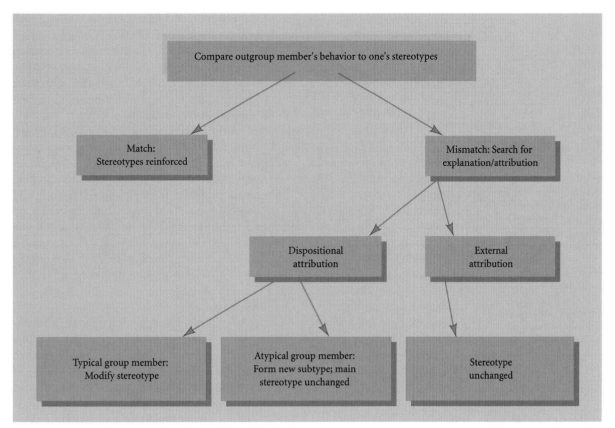

(After Hewstone, 1989 and Wilder & others, 1996)

figure 9–8

Attribution and stereotype change.

When someone's behavior doesn't fit our stereotype, we can change the stereotype, split off a subtype, or attribute the behavior to the peculiar situation.

and (2) trivial but vivid information about a particular group member, the vivid information usually overwhelms the effect of the general information. This is especially so when the person doesn't fit our image of the typical group member (Fein & Hilton, 1992; Lord & others, 1991). For example, imagine yourself being told how *most* people in an experiment actually behaved and then viewing a brief interview with one of the supposed subjects. Would you react like the typical viewer—by guessing the person's behavior from the interview, ignoring the base-rate information on how most people actually behaved?

People often believe such stereotypes, yet ignore them when given vivid, anecdotal information. Thus, many people believe "politicians are crooks" but "our MP Mr. Jones has integrity." (No wonder people have such a low opinion of politicians yet usually reelect their own representatives.)

These findings resolve a puzzling set of findings considered early in this chapter. We know that gender stereotypes (1) are strong yet (2) have little effect on people's judgments of work attributed to a man or a woman. Now we see why. People may have strong gender stereotypes yet ignore them when judging a particular individual.

Strong stereotypes do, however, color our judgments of individuals as well as groups. When Thomas Nelson, Monica Biernat, and Melvin Manis (1990) had students estimate the heights of individually pictured men and women, they judged the individual men as taller—even when their heights were equal, even when they were told that in this sample sex didn't predict height, and even when they were offered cash rewards for accuracy.

In a follow-up study, Nelson, Michele Acker, and Manis (1996) showed university students photos of other students from the university's engineering and nursing schools, along with descriptions of each student's interests. Even when informed that the sample contained an equal number of males and females from each school, the same description was judged more likely to come from a nursing student when attached to a female face. Thus, even when a strong gender stereotype is known to be irrelevant, it has an irresistible force.

Stereotypes also color how we interpret events, note David Dunning and David Sherman (1997). If told, "some felt the politician's statements were untrue," people will infer the politician was lying. If told, "some felt the physicist's statements were untrue," they infer only that the physicist was mistaken. When told two people had an altercation, people perceive it as a fist fight if told it involved two lumberjacks, but as a verbal spat if told it involved two marriage counselors. A person concerned about her physical condition seems vain if she is a model but health conscious if a triathelete. Indeed, subjects will often later "recognize" false descriptions of an event that fit their stereotype-influenced interpretations. As a prison guides and constrains its inmates, conclude Dunning and Sherman, the "cognitive prison" of our stereotypes guides and constrains our impressions.

Sometimes we make judgments, or begin interacting with someone, with little to go on but our stereotype. In such cases stereotypes can strongly bias our interpretations and memories of people. For example, Charles Bond and his colleagues (1988) found that, after getting to know their patients, White psychiatric nurses equally often put Black and White patients in physical restraints. But they restrained *incoming* Black patients more often than their White counterparts. With little else to go on, stereotypes mattered.

Such bias can also operate more subtly. In an experiment by John Darley and Paget Gross (1983), students viewed a videotape of a fourth-grade girl, Hannah. The tape depicted her either in a depressed urban neighborhood, supposedly the child of lower-class parents, or in an affluent suburban setting, the child of professional parents. Asked to guess Hannah's ability level in various subjects, both groups of viewers refused to use Hannah's class background to prejudge her ability level; each group rated her ability level at her grade level. Other students also viewed a second videotape, show-

figure 9–9

Harsher evaluation of a stereotyped target.

When University of Waterloo students received positve feedback from a "manager", his race did not matter, but when they received negative feedback, they saw a Black manager as less competent than a White manager. (Data from Sinclair & Kunda 1999.)

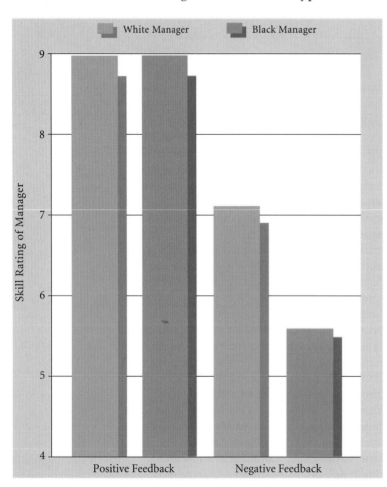

ing Hannah taking an oral achievement test in which she got some questions right and some wrong.

Those who had previously been introduced to upper-class Hannah judged her answers as showing high ability and later recalled her getting most questions right; those who had met lower-class Hannah judged her ability as below grade level and recalled her missing almost half the questions. But remember: The second videotape was *identical* for both groups. So we see that when stereotypes are strong and the information about someone is ambiguous (unlike the cases of Nancy and Paul), stereotypes can *subtly* bias our judgments of individuals.

Finally, we evaluate people more extremely when their behavior violates our stereotypes (Bettencourt & others, 1997). A woman who rebukes someone cutting in front of her in a movie line ("Shouldn't you go to the end of the line?") may seem more assertive than a man who reacts similarly (Manis & others, 1988). Are your ratings of your professors affected by such processes? A series of studies (Kunda & Sinclair, 1999; Sinclair & Kunda, 1999; Sinclair & Kunda, in press) by University of Winnipeg professor Lisa Sinclair and University of Waterloo professor Ziva Kunda suggests that they might very well be. They analyzed students' evaluations of their professors and found that when students get good grades they tend to like their professor, and this is true whether their professors are men or women. When students get bad grades, however, they are especially harsh on female professors.

Kunda and Sinclair have found similar findings in a series of laboratory studies. After completing a test of leadership ability while be watched by a "manager" in an adjacent room, participants were praised or criticized on their performance by the manager. When they were praised the participants liked both the male and the female manager, but when they were criticized they evaluated the female manager much more negatively. In another study, they found similar results with White and Black male managers (see Figure 9-9).

behind the scenes

I have long been interested in how people's motives and desires color their judgment. My earlier work suggested that people attempt to be rational, and draw their desired conclusions only if they can justify them. However, they often do not realize that their justifications can be biased by their motives—when constructing justifications, people search selectively for those beliefs that lend support to their desired conclusion. If they can successfully recruit such beliefs, they draw their desired conclusion, not realizing that they may also possess other beliefs that argue against it. It occurred to Lisa Sinclair and me that a negative group stereotype may sometimes provide a handy justification for disparaging a group member whom

one is motivated to discredit. People may be motivated to discredit anyone who has criticized them, but may be better able to justify disparaging a woman or a member or a visible minority than disparaging a White man. As a result, people may view a woman or a Black man who criticizes them more negatively than they view a White man who delivers the same criticism.

Ziva Kunda
University of Waterloo

Summing up

A fresh look at prejudice in recent research shows how the stereotyping that underlies prejudice is a by-product of our thinking—our ways of simplifying the world. First, clustering people into categories exaggerates the uniformity within a group and the differences between groups. Second, a distinctive individual, such as a lone minority person, has a compelling quality. Such persons make us aware of differences that would otherwise go unnoticed. The occurrence of two distinctive events—say, a minority person committing an unusual crime—helps create an illusory correlation between people and behavior. Third, attributing others' behavior to their dispositions can lead to the group-serving bias: assigning outgroup members' negative behavior to their natural character while explaining away their positive behaviors. Blaming the victim also results from the common presumption that because this is a just world, people get what they deserve.

Stereotypes have cognitive consequences and cognitive sources. By directing interpretations and memory, they lead us to "find" supportive evidence, even when none exists. Stereotypes are therefore resistant to change. Stereotypes are more potent when strong, when judging unknown individuals, and when deciding policies regarding whole groups. Stereotypes can also subtly color our assessments of individuals' behavior, though we tend to discard group stereotypes in interpreting the behavior of people we know.

Personal Postscript: Can we reduce prejudice?

Social psychologists have been more successful in explaining prejudice than in alleviating it. Because prejudice results from many interrelated factors, there is no simple remedy. Nevertheless, we can now anticipate techniques for reducing prejudice (discussed further in chapters to come): If unequal status breeds prejudice, then we can seek to create cooperative, equal-status relationships. If prejudice often rationalizes discriminatory behavior, then we can mandate nondiscrimination. If social institutions support prejudice, then we can pull out those supports (for example, have the media model interracial harmony). If outgroups seem more unlike one's own group than they really are, then we can make efforts to personalize their members.

Since the end of World War II in 1945, a number of these antidotes have been applied, and racial and gender prejudices have indeed diminished. It now remains to be seen whether, during the next century, progress will continue . . . or whether, as could easily happen in a time of increasing population and diminishing resources, antagonisms will again erupt into open hostility.

chapter 10

Aggression: Hurting Others

Our behavior toward one another seems increasingly destructive. Although Woody Allen's prediction that "by 1990 kidnapping will be the dominant mode of social interaction" has not been fulfilled, images of 1990s violence have horrified people across the world.

- The British, shocked by the beating death of 2-year-old James Bulger at the hands of two 10-year-old boys and by an 84 percent violent crime rate increase from 1985 to 1995, debated reasons for rising brutality in their once-genteel culture (ABC, 1995).

- Germans, appalled by neo-Nazis murdering and harassing Turkish immigrants, decried the decline of humane values.

- In Rwanda, some 500,000 people—including half the Tutsi population—were slaughtered in the genocidal summer of 1994.

- In a Canadian government survey of 12,300 women, 29 percent reported being physically or sexually assaulted by their partner (Rodgers, 1994).

- Despite a general decrease in violent crime in the '90s in Canada and the United States, senseless, brutal killings at schools have left many people stunned and horrified. In the U.S., four separate schools have had fatal shootings, including Littleton, Colorado, where 15 people were killed. In Canada non-fatal school shootings in Toronto—and a shooting in Taber, Alberta, where one student was killed—although less deadly, have been just as shocking. People are eager for answers about why these events occur and how they can be prevented in the future.

- Worldwide, we humans spend on arms and armies $2 billion per day— $2 billion that could feed, educate, and protect the environment of the world's impoverished millions. During the century now drawing to a close, 250 wars have killed 110 million people—enough to populate a "nation of the dead" with more than the combined population of France, Belgium, the Netherlands, Denmark, Finland, Norway, and Sweden (Sivard, 1996).

Why this propensity to hurt others? Is it because we, like the mythical Minotaur, are half human, half beast? What circumstances prompt hostile outbursts? Can we control aggression? In this chapter, these are our questions. First, however, we need to clarify this term "aggression."

What is aggression?

Clearly, the original Thugs, members of a criminal fraternity in northern India, were aggressing when between 1550 and 1850 they strangled more than two million people, and claimed to do so in the service of a goddess. But "aggressive" can also describe a dynamic salesperson. Social psychologists debate how to define aggression, but they agree on this much: We should sharpen our vocabulary by distinguishing self-assured, energetic, go-getting behavior from behavior that hurts, harms, or destroys. The former is assertiveness, the latter aggression.

aggression
physical or verbal behavior intended to hurt someone

Chapter 5 defines **aggression** as *physical or verbal behavior intended to hurt someone*. This excludes auto accidents, dental treatments, and sidewalk collisions. It includes slaps, direct insults, even gossipy "digs." Researchers typically measure aggression by having people decide how much to hurt someone, such as how much electric shock to impose.

This definition covers two distinct types of aggression. Animals exhibit *social* aggression, characterized by displays of rage, and *silent* aggression, as when a predator stalks its prey. Social and silent aggression involve separate brain regions. In humans, psychologists label the two types "hostile" and "instrumental" aggression. **Hostile aggression** springs from anger, its goal is to injure. **Instrumental aggression** aims to hurt only as a means to some other end. Hockey players often argue that their hard checks and even occasional fights are actually used as means to protect their star players. Hostile aggression is "hot"; instrumental aggression is "cool." Distinguishing between the two is sometimes difficult. What begins as a cool, calculating act can ignite hostility. Still, social psychologists find the distinction useful. Most murders, for example, are hostile. They are impulsive, emotional outbursts—which explains why data from 110 nations show that enforcing the death penalty has not resulted in fewer homicides (Costanzo, 1998; Wilkes, 1987). But some murders are instrumental. Most of Chicago's 1,000+ mob murders since 1919 have been cool and calculated.

hostile aggression
aggression driven by anger and performed as an end in itself

instrumental aggression
aggression that is a means to some other end

Theories of aggression

In analyzing causes of hostile and instrumental aggression, social psychologists have focused on three big ideas: (1) There is an inborn *aggressive drive. (2) Aggression is a natural response to* frustration. *(3) Aggressive behavior is* learned.

Is aggression inborn?

Philosophers have long debated whether our human nature is fundamentally that of a benign, contented "noble savage" or that of a potentially explosive brute. The first view, argued by the eighteenth-century French philosopher Jean-Jacques Rousseau, blames society, not human nature, for social evils. The second, associated with the English philosopher Thomas Hobbes (1588–1679), sees society's laws as necessary to restrain and control the human brute. In this century, the "brutish" view—that aggressive drive is inborn and thus inevitable—was argued by Sigmund Freud in Vienna and Konrad Lorenz in Germany.

Instinct theory

Freud speculated that human aggression springs from our redirecting toward others the energy of a primitive death urge (which, loosely speaking, he called the "death instinct"). Lorenz, who studied animal behavior, saw aggression as adaptive rather than self-destructive. But both agreed that aggressive energy is instinctual. If not discharged, it supposedly builds up until it explodes or until an appropriate stimulus "releases" it, like a mouse releasing a mousetrap. Although Lorenz (1976) also argued that we have innate mechanisms for inhibiting aggression (such as making ourselves defenseless), he feared the implications of arming our "fighting instinct" without arming our inhibitions. The imbalanced focus on releasing aggressive tendencies helps explain why more people have been killed in war during this century than in all of prior human history (Sivard, 1991).

The idea that aggression is an instinct collapsed as the list of supposed human instincts grew to include nearly every conceivable human behavior. Nearly 6,000 supposed instincts were enumerated in one 1924 survey of social science books (Barash, 1979). What the social scientists had tried to do was *explain* social behavior by *naming* it. It's tempting to play this explaining-by-naming game: "Why do sheep stay together?" "Because of their herd instinct." "How do you know they have a herd instinct?" "Just look at them: They're always together!"

Instinct theory also fails to account for the variation in aggressiveness, from person to person and culture to culture. How would a shared human instinct for aggression explain the difference between the peaceful Iroquois before White invaders came and the hostile Iroquois after the invasion (Hornstein, 1976)? In today's world, cultures range from nonviolent Norway, where murder is rare, to the South American Yanomamo, nearly half of whose surviving adult males have been involved in a killing (Chagnon, 1988). Although the human propensity to aggress may not qualify as instinctive behavior, aggression *is* biologically influenced.

"Our behavior toward each other is the strangest, most unpredictable, and most unaccountable of all the phenomena with which we are obliged to live. In all of nature, there is nothing so threatening to humanity as humanity itself."

Lewis Thomas (1981)

instinctive behavior an innate, unlearned behavior pattern exhibited by all members of a species

A nineteenth-century engraving of Spanish warriors conquering Montezuma's Indian empire.

Although aggressive tendencies vary, our distant ancestors did find aggression sometimes adaptive, note evolutionary psychologists David Buss and Todd Shackelford (1997). Aggressive behavior was a strategy for gaining resources, defending against attack, intimidating or eliminating male rivals for females, and deterring mates from sexual infidelity. The adaptive value of aggression, Buss and Schackelford note, helps explain the relatively high levels of male-male aggression across human history. "This does not imply . . . that men have an 'aggression instinct' in the sense of some pent-up energy that must be released. Rather, men have inherited from their successful ancestors psychological mechanisms" that improve their odds of contributing their genes to future generations.

Neural influences

Because aggression is a complex behavior, no one spot in the brain controls it. But in both animals and humans, researchers have found neural systems that facilitate aggression. When they activate these areas in the brain, hostility increases; when they deactivate them, hostility decreases. Docile animals can thus be provoked into rage, and raging animals into submission.

In one experiment, researchers placed an electrode in an aggression-inhibiting area of a domineering monkey's brain. Given a button that activated the electrode, one small monkey learned to push it every time the tyrant monkey become intimidating. Brain activation works with humans, too. After receiving painless electrical stimulation in her amygdala (a part of the brain core), one woman became enraged and smashed her guitar against the wall, barely missing her psychiatrist's head (Moyer, 1976, 1983).

Genetic influences

Heredity influences the neural system's sensitivity to aggressive cues. It has long been known that animals of many species can be bred for aggressiveness. Sometimes this is done for practical purposes (the breeding of fighting cocks). Sometimes, breeding is done for research. Finnish psychologist Kirsti Lagerspetz (1979) took normal albino mice and bred the most aggressive ones together and the least aggressive ones. After repeating the procedure for 26 generations, she had one set of fierce mice and one set of placid mice.

Aggressiveness similarly varies among primates and humans (Asher, 1987; Olweus, 1979). Our temperament—how intense and reactive we are—is partly something we bring with us into the world, influenced by our sympathetic nervous system's reactivity (Kagan, 1989). Identical twins, when asked separately, are more likely than fraternal twins to agree on whether they have "a

"Of course, we'll never actually _use_ it against a potential enemy,
but it will allow us to negotiate from a position of strength."

John Ruge

*Humanity has armed its
capacity for destruction
without comparably arming
its capacity for the
inhibition of aggression.*

violent temper" (Rushton & others, 1986). Half of identical twins of convicted
criminals (but only 1 in 5 fraternal twins) also have criminal records (Raine,
1993). A person's temperament, observed in infancy, usually endures (Larsen &
Diener, 1987; Wilson & Matheny, 1986). Thus, a fearless, impulsive, temper-
prone child is at risk for violent behavior in adolescence (American Psychological Association, 1993). With age, genetic influences on aggressiveness increase
and family influence diminishes (Miles & Carey, 1997).

Biochemical influences

Blood chemistry also influences neural sensitivity to aggressive stimulation.
Both laboratory experiments and police data indicate that when people are provoked, alcohol unleashes aggression (Bushman & Cooper, 1990; Bushman, 1993;
Taylor & Chermack, 1993). Violent people are more likely (1) to drink, and (2) to
become aggressive when intoxicated (White & others, 1993).

   In experiments, intoxicated people administer stronger shocks or higher pain
buttons. In the real world, people who have been drinking commit about half of
rapes and other violent crimes (Abbey & others, 1993, 1996; Seto & Barbaree,
1995). In 65 percent of homicides, the murderer and/or the victim had been
drinking (American Psychological Association, 1993). If spouse-battering alcoholics cease their problem drinking after treatment, their violent behavior typically ceases as well (Murphy & O'Farrell, 1996). Alcohol enhances
aggressiveness by reducing people's self-awareness, and by reducing their ability to consider consequences (Hull & Bond, 1986; Ito & others, 1996; Steele &
Southwick, 1985). Alcohol deindividuates, and it disinhibits.

Genes predispose the pit bull's aggressiveness.

Question: Some violent sex offenders, wishing to free themselves of persistent, damaging impulses and to reduce their prison terms, have requested castration, an operation that is less invasive than a hysterectomy. Should their requests be granted? If so, and if they are deemed no longer at risk of sexual violence, should their prison terms be reduced or eliminated?

Aggressiveness also correlates with the male sex hormone, testosterone. Although hormonal influences appear much stronger in lower animals than in humans, drugs that diminish testosterone levels in violent human males will subdue their aggressive tendencies. When beeped with electronic pagers, very high testosterone individuals report feeling slightly more restless and tense (Dabbs & others, 1998).

After people reach age 25, their testosterone and rates of violent crime decrease together. Among prisoners convicted of unprovoked violent crimes, testosterone levels tend to be higher than among those imprisoned for nonviolent crimes (Dabbs, 1992; Dabbs & others, 1995, 1998). And among the normal range of teen boys and adult men, those with high testosterone levels are more prone to delinquency, hard drug use, and aggressive responses to provocation (Archer, 1991; Dabbs & Morris, 1990; Olweus & others, 1988). Injecting a man with testosterone won't make him aggressive, yet men with low testosterone are somewhat less likely to react aggressively when provoked (Geen, 1998). Testosterone is roughly like battery power. Supercharging a portable tape player's batteries won't make it play faster, yet low batteries will make for slow play.

Another culprit often found at the scene of violence is low levels of the neurotransmitter serotonin—the chemical messenger that also tends to be in short supply in depressed people. In both primates and humans, low serotonin is often found among violence-prone children and adults (Bernhardt, 1997; Mehlman, 1994; Wright, 1995). Moreover, lowering people's serotonin levels in the laboratory increases their response to aversive events and willingness to deliver supposed electric shocks.

It is important to remember that the traffic between testosterone, serotonin, and behavior is two-way. Testosterone, for example, may facilitate dominance and aggressiveness, but dominating or defeating behavior also boosts testosterone levels (Gladue & others, 1989). People shunted low on the socioeconomic ladder tend to have low serotonin. Evolutionary psychologists have suggested that may be nature's way of preparing them to take risks (Wright, 1995).

So there exist important neural, genetic, and biochemical influences on aggression. Biological influences predispose some people more than others to react aggressively to conflict and provocation. But is aggression so much a part of human nature that it makes peace unattainable? The International Council of Psychologists has joined other organizations in unanimously endorsing a statement on violence developed by scientists from a dozen nations (Adams, 1991): "It is scientifically incorrect [to say that] war or any other violent behavior is

Frustrating situations can help to fuel aggressive reactions. These protestors for low-income housing confronted about 100 RCMP officers on Parliament Hill.

genetically programmed into our human nature [or that] war is caused by 'instinct' or any single motivation." Thus there are, as we will see, ways to reduce human aggression.

Is aggression a response to frustration?

It is a warm evening. Tired and thirsty after two hours of studying, you borrow some change from a friend and head for the nearest soft-drink machine. As the machine devours the change, you can almost taste the cold, refreshing cola. But when you push the button, nothing happens. You push it again. Then you flip the coin return button. Still nothing. Again, you hit the buttons. You slam them. And finally you shake and whack the machine. You stomp back to your studies, empty-handed and short-changed. Should your roommate beware? Are you now more likely to say or do something hurtful?

One of the first psychological theories of aggression, the popular frustration-aggression theory, answers yes. "Frustration always leads to some form of aggression," said John Dollard and his colleagues (1939, p. 1). **Frustration** is anything (such as the malfunctioning vending machine) that *blocks our attaining a goal*. Frustration grows when our motivation to achieve a goal is very strong, when we expected gratification, and when the blocking is complete.

frustration
the blocking of goal-directed behavior

As Figure 10–1 suggests, the aggressive energy need not explode directly against its source. We learn to inhibit direct retaliation, especially when others might disapprove or punish; instead we *displace* our hostilities to safer targets. **Displacement** occurs in the old anecdote about a man who, humiliated by his boss, berates his wife, who yells at their son, who kicks the dog, which bites the mail carrier.

displacement
the redirection of aggression to a target other than the source of the frustration. Generally, the new target is a safer or more socially acceptable target.

Frustration-aggression theory revised

Laboratory tests of the frustration-aggression theory produced mixed results: Sometimes frustration increased aggressiveness, sometimes not. For example, if

figure 10–1

The classic frustration-aggression theory.

Frustration creates a motive to aggress. Fear of punishment or disapproval for aggressing against the source of frustration may cause the aggressive drive to be displaced against some other target or even redirected against oneself.

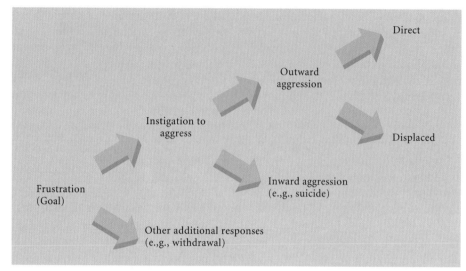

(Based on Dollard & others, 1939, and Miller, 1941.)

Note that frustration-aggression theory is designed to explain hostile aggression, not instrumental aggression.

the frustration was understandable—if, as in one experiment by Eugene Burnstein and Philip Worchel (1962), a confederate disrupted a group's problem solving because his hearing aid malfunctioned (rather than just because he paid no attention)—then frustration led to irritation, not aggression. A justifiable frustration is still frustrating, but it triggers less aggression than a frustration we perceive as unjustified (Dill & Anderson, 1995).

Leonard Berkowitz (1978, 1989) realized that the original theory overstated the frustration-aggression connection, so he revised it. Berkowitz theorized that frustration produces *anger,* an emotional readiness to aggress. Anger arises when someone who frustrates us could have chosen to act otherwise (Averill, 1983; Weiner, 1981). A frustrated person is especially likely to lash out when aggressive cues pull the cork, releasing bottled-up anger. Sometimes the cork will blow without such cues. But cues associated with aggression amplify aggression (Carlson & others, 1990).

Berkowitz (1968, 1981, 1995) and others have found that the sight of a weapon is such a cue, especially when perceived as an instrument of violence rather than recreation. In one experiment, children who had just played with toy guns became more willing to knock down another child's blocks. In another, angered male university students gave more electric shocks to their tormenter when a rifle and a revolver (supposedly left over from a previous experiment) were nearby than when badminton racquets had been left behind (Berkowitz & LePage, 1967). Guns prime hostile thoughts (Anderson & others, 1996). Thus, Berkowitz is also not surprised that half of all U.S. murders are committed with handguns and that handguns in homes are far more likely to kill household members than intruders. "Guns not only permit violence," he reported, "they can stimulate it as well. The finger pulls the trigger, but the trigger may also be pulling the finger."

Berkowitz is also not surprised that countries that ban handguns have lower murder rates. Compared to the United States, Britain has one-fourth as many people and one-sixteenth as many murders. The United States has 10,000 handgun homicides a year; Britain has about 10. Vancouver, British Columbia, and

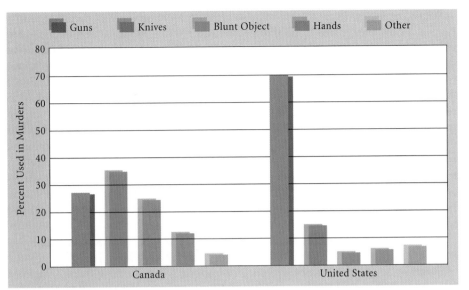

figure 10–2
A comparison of weapons used to commit murder in Canada and the United States in 1996.

(Data from Statistics Canada Uniform Crime Report and U.S. Federal Bureau of Investigation Uniform Crime Report.)

Seattle, Washington, have similar populations, climates, economies, and rates of criminal activity and assault—except that Vancouver, which carefully restricts handgun ownership, has had one-fifth as many handgun murders as Seattle and thus a 40 percent lower overall murder rate (Sloan & others, 1988). Not only does Canada have a much lower murder rate than the U.S., the difference in the percentage of murders that occur by the use of a gun is striking. As you can see in Figure 10-2, Americans are more than twice as likely as Canadians to use guns when they commit murder.

Changes in gun laws do seem to effect murder rates. For example, when one large city adopted a law restricting handgun possession, the numbers of gun-related murders dropped about 25 percent. No changes occurred in other methods of murder, nor did adjacent areas outside the reach of this law experience any such declines (Loftin & others, 1991).

Is frustration the same as deprivation?

Picture someone feeling extremely frustrated—economically, sexually, or politically.

My hunch is that you are imagining someone economically, sexually, or politically *deprived*. And with good reason: When communities experience small increases in job layoffs, violence rates rise (Catalano & others, 1997). As American unemployment declined sharply during the mid-1990s, so did violent crime.

But frustration may be unrelated to deprivation. The most sexually frustrated people are probably not celibate. The most economically frustrated people are probably not the impoverished residents of Jamaican shantytowns. When economic misery was everywhere during the 1930s depression, violent crime was not notably high.

It seems that frustration is in the eye of the beholder. Objective reality may have little to do with people's experience of frustration, but even irrational frustration can lead to devastating violence.

"I would say a person is deprived if he lacks a goal object people generally regard as attractive or desirable, but is frustrated only when he had been anticipating the pleasure to be gotten from this object and then cannot fulfill this expectation."

Leonard Berkowitz (1972)

Marc Lepine was a young man who wanted to be an engineer from the time he was a boy, but he was unable to get into a program to study engineering. He blamed his frustration on women and feminists in particular, who he felt were denying him his life-long dream. On December 6, 1989, his frustration broke out into horrifying aggression. He took a semi-automatic rifle and went to the École Polytechnique de Montreal, the engineering school that he had always wanted to attend. He entered one classroom and ordered the women to all line up on one side. He opened fire, shooting them all at close range. He entered another classroom and did the same. He prowled the hallways killing any women he could find. In the end, he killed 14 women before turning the gun on himself. A full understanding of Marc Lepine's actions may never be possible, but it seems clear that his attainments in life fell far short of his expectations. And it seems plausible that this gap between his achievements and his aspirations may have fueled his frustration and contributed to this awful tragedy.

This sort of frustration can explain revolutions as well. The political scientist-social psychologist team of Ivo and Rosaline Feierabend (1968, 1972) applied the frustration-aggression theory in a study of political instability within 84 nations. When people in rapidly modernizing nations become urbanized and literacy improves, they become more aware of material improvements. Since affluence usually diffuses slowly, however, the increasing gap between aspirations and achievements intensifies frustration. Even as deprivation diminishes, frustration and political aggression may therefore escalate. Expectation outstrips reality.

The point is not that actual deprivation and social injustice are irrelevant to social unrest; injustice can be a root cause, even if not the immediate psychological cause. The point is this: *Frustration arises from the gap between expectations and attainments.*

> "Evils which are patiently endured when they seem inevitable become intolerable when once the idea of escape from them is suggested."
>
> Alexis de Tocqueville, 1856

Does money alleviate frustration?

The principle "frustration equals expectations minus attainments" helps us understand why economic satisfaction and frustration fluctuate. Consider the following rather bewildering set of facts:

- *Fact 1:* Although people deny that "money buys happiness," they will usually grant that a little more money would make them a *little* happier (Myers, 1993). Among entering collegians in 1996, "being very well off financially" was therefore the top-rated of 19 listed objectives, outranking "raising a family" and "helping others in difficulty" (Sax & others 1996).

- *Fact 2:* During the recent decades of economic growth, people in the Western world have gained a little more money—many times over. The average American, for example, enjoys *double* the real income of the mid-1950s and has half as many children to spend it on. Doubled incomes have meant doubled purchases, including twice as many cars per person, as well as the color TVs, VCRs, microwave ovens, home computers, air conditioning, and more than doubled frequency of eating out.

- *Fact 3:* Although they have obtained more of the much desired money and possessions, people today are no happier. For example, people in recent years have been no more likely than those of the 1950s to report feeling happy and satisfied with their lives. In 1957, 35 percent reported themselves "very happy." In 1996, 30 percent said the same. By some measures, such as the rapidly rising rates of depression and teen suicide, modern affluence has been accompanied by greater despair. This trend—

increasing wealth without increasing well-being—has been seen in many nations throughout the world (Cross-National Collaborative Group, 1992; Easterlin, 1995). William Cowper's 1782 observation has proved correct: "Happiness depends, as nature shows, less on exterior things than most suppose."

Could Lucy ever experience enough "ups"? Not according to the adaptation-level phenomenon.

Why are we not happier and less frustrated given our improving affluence? And how have yesterday's luxuries—color television, air conditioning, CD sound systems—become today's necessities?

The adaptation-level phenomenon.   Two principles developed by research psychologists help explain rising expectations and therefore continuing frustrations. The **adaptation-level phenomenon** implies that feelings of success and failure, satisfaction and dissatisfaction, are relative to prior achievements. If our current achievements fall below what we previously accomplished, we feel dissatisfied, frustrated; if they rise above that level, we feel successful, satisfied.

If we continue to achieve, however, we soon adapt to success. What formerly felt good registers as neutral, and what formerly felt neutral now feels like deprivation. This helps explain why, despite the rapid increase in real income during the past several decades, the average person is no happier.

Most of us have experienced the adaptation-level phenomenon. More consumer goods, academic achievement, or social prestige provide an initial surge of pleasure. Yet all too soon the feeling wanes. Now, we need an even higher level to give us another surge of pleasure. "Even as we contemplate our satisfaction with a given accomplishment, the satisfaction fades," noted Philip Brickman and Donald Campbell (1971), "to be replaced finally by a new indifference and a new level of striving."

A study of lottery winners illustrates. Brickman and his colleagues, Dan Coates and Ronnie Janoff-Bulman (1978), found that at first the winners typically felt elated: "Winning the lottery was one of the best things that ever happened to me." Yet their self-reported overall happiness did not increase. In fact, ordinary activities they had previously enjoyed, such as reading or eating a good breakfast, became less pleasurable. Winning the lottery was apparently such an emotional high that, by comparison, their ordinary pleasures paled.

Relative deprivation.   The dissatisfaction that comes with adapting to new highs is often compounded when we compare ourselves to others. Workers' feelings of well-being depend on whether their compensation is equitable compared to others in their line of work (Yuchtman, 1976). A salary raise for a city's police officers, while temporarily lifting their morale, may deflate that of the fire fighters.

Much of life revolves around social comparisons. We feel handsome when others seem homely, smart when others seem dull, caring when others seem callous. When we witness a peer's performance, we cannot resist comparing

adaptation-level phenomenon
the tendency to adapt to a given level of stimulation and thus to notice and react to changes from that level

Parkinson's second law: Expenditures rise to meet income.

"People are never happy for a thousand days."

Chinese Proverb

behind the scenes

For the last 25+ years, I have been exploring the psychology of perceived prejudice and discrimination from the "victim" or target's perspective. When I began this work in the early 1970s, little systematic or definitive research on the topic existed. Most research on prejudice concerned the bigot and ignored the target of the bigot's negative attitudes and behavior. I felt, then as now, that there was an equally important story to be told about how people who experience prejudicce and discrimmination from others respond to these experiences.

I began with the assumption that perceived discrimination was vital for understanding the psychology of oppressed groups. My research has indicated that perceived discrimination is a social stressor and produces negative affect, but it also prompts perceivers to identify more closely with the positive aspects of their membership groups (as a likely response to stress). Perceived discrimination also has complex effects on self-esteem.

My more recent studies document the stressfulness of perceived discrimination by oppressed group members in the real social world rather that the artificial laboratory, and to explore conditions under which they will take corrective action in response. This research shows that collective deprivation consistently predicts militancy better than "egotistic" or personal deprivation.

Ken Dion
University of Toronto

"A house may be large or small; as long as the surrounding houses are equally small, it satisfies all social demands for a dwelling. But let a palace arise beside the little house, and it shrinks from a little house into a hut."

Karl Marx

relative deprivation
the perception that one is less well off than others to whom one compares oneself

"Women's discontent increases in exact proportion to her development."

Elizabeth Cady Stanton, 1815–1902, American suffragette

ourselves (Gilbert & others, 1995). We may, therefore, privately take some pleasure in a peer's failure—though especially in the failure or misfortune of an envied person (Smith & others, 1996). Our spontaneous social comparisons color our emotions more by our relative than our absolute standing. William Klein (1997) found this by having people imagine they had either a 30 or 60 percent lifetime chance of some bad event (causing a car accident, developing pancreatic disease). Those said to have a 60 percent chance when told the average was 80 percent felt like safer drivers and were less disturbed about their diagnosis than those said to have a 30 percent chance when the average was 10 percent.

Much misery springs from comparing ourselves to others. When people experience an increase in affluence, status, or achievement, they raise the standards by which they evaluate their own attainments. When feeling good and climbing the ladder of success, people look up, not down (Gruder, 1977; Suls & Tesch, 1978; Wheeler & others, 1982). Especially in people with shaky self-esteem, this "upward comparison" can cause feelings of **relative deprivation** (Collins, 1996; Wood, 1989).

Such feelings predict the reactions to perceived inequities by minority groups in Canada (Dion, 1985). Relative deprivation explains why women who make less than men working in the same occupations feel underpaid only if they compare themselves with male rather than female colleagues (Bylsma & Major, 1994; Zanna & others, 1987). And it explains why East Germans revolted against their communist regime: they had a higher standard of living than some western European countries, but a frustratingly lower one than their West German neighbors (Baron & others, 1992).

The term *relative deprivation* was coined by researchers studying the satisfaction felt by soldiers in World War II (Merton & Kitt, 1950; Stouffer & others, 1949). Ironically, those in the Air Corps felt *more* frustrated about their own rate of promotion than those in the Military Police, for whom promotions were slower and more unpredictable. The Air Corps' promotion rate was rapid, and most Air Corps personnel probably perceived themselves as better than the average Air Corps member (the self-serving bias). Thus, their aspirations soared higher than their achievements. The result? Frustration. And where there is frustration, aggression often follows.

One possible source of such frustration today is the affluence depicted in television programs and commercials. In cultures where television is a universal appliance, it helps turn absolute deprivation (lacking what others have) into relative deprivation (feeling deprived). Karen Hennigan and her co-workers (1982) analyzed crime rates in several cities around the time television was introduced. In 34 cities where television ownership became widespread in 1951, the 1951 larceny theft rate (for crimes such as shoplifting and bicycle stealing) took an observable jump. In 34 other cities, where a government freeze had delayed the introduction of television until 1955, a similar jump in the theft rate occurred—in 1955.

Some conclusions.   The principles of adaptation-level and relative deprivation have a thought-provoking implication: Seeking satisfaction through material achievement requires continually expanding affluence merely to maintain satisfaction. "Poverty," said Plato, "consists not in the decrease of one's possessions, but in the increase of one's greed."

Fortunately, adaptation also can enable us to adjust downward, should we choose or be forced to simplify our lives. If our buying power shrinks, we initially feel some pain. But eventually we adapt to the new reality. In the aftermath of the 1970s gas price hikes, North Americans managed to substantially reduce their "need" for large, gas-slurping cars. Even paraplegics, the blind, and other people with severe handicaps usually show remarkable resilience. They adapt to their disability and achieve a normal or near-normal level of life satisfaction (Brickman & others, 1978; Chwalisz & others, 1988; Schulz & Decker, 1985). Victims of traumatic incidents surely must envy those who are not paralyzed, as many of us envy those who have won a state lottery. Yet, after a period of adjustment, the astonishing fact is that none of these three groups differs appreciably from the others in moment-to-moment happiness. Human beings have an enormous capacity to adapt.

Finally, experiences that lower our comparison standards can renew our contentment. A research team led by Marshall Dermer (1979) put women through some imaginative exercises in deprivation. After viewing depictions of how grim life was in 1900, or after imagining and then writing about being burned and disfigured, the women expressed greater satisfaction with their own lives. In another experiment, Jennifer Crocker and Lisa Gallo (1985) found that those who five times completed the sentence "I'm glad I'm not a . . ." afterward felt less depressed and more satisfied with life than did those who had completed sentences beginning "I wish I were a . . ." For this reason, people facing personal threat often search for a silver lining and boost their self-esteem by comparing downward (Gibbons & Gerrard, 1989; Reis & others, 1993; Taylor, 1989). Realizing that others have it worse helps people feel better about themselves.

"All our wants, beyond those which a very moderate income will supply, are purely imaginary."

Henry St. John, *Letter to Swift,* 1719

"However great the discrepancies between men's lots, there is always a certain balance of joy and sorrow which equalizes all."

La Rochefoucauld, *Maxims,* 1665

Is aggression learned social behavior?

Theories of aggression based on instinct and frustration assume that hostile urges erupt from inner emotions, which naturally "push" aggression from within. Social psychologists contend that learning also "pulls" aggression out of us.

The rewards of aggression

By experience and by observing others, we learn that aggression often pays. Experiments have transformed animals from docile creatures into ferocious fighters. Severe defeats, on the other hand, create submissiveness (Ginsburg & Allee, 1942; Kahn, 1951; Scott & Marston, 1953).

People, too, can learn the rewards of aggression. A child whose aggressive acts successfully intimidate other children will likely become increasingly aggressive (Patterson & others, 1967). Aggressive hockey players—the ones sent most often to the penalty box for rough play—score more goals than nonaggressive players (McCarthy & Kelly, 1978a, 1978b). Canadian teenage hockey players whose fathers applaud physically aggressive play show the most aggressive attitudes and style of play (Ennis & Zanna, 1991). In these cases, aggression is instrumental in achieving certain rewards.

Collective violence can also pay. Activists throughout the world have learned that sometimes violence is rewarded with changes in policies and laws. In other instances, violence can serve as a means to prevent actions that people find objectionable. Recent demonstrations (that at times have turned violent) at meetings of the World Trade Organization have made it difficult for this organization to do its business. After the 1985 riots in South Africa became severe, the government repealed laws forbidding mixed marriages, offered to restore Black "citizenship rights" (not including the right

Aggression can be perceived as instrumental, as it is for this Palestinian terrorist, shown on videotape with Israeli soldier Nachson Waxman, who was later killed.

to vote), and eliminated the hated pass laws controlling the movement of Blacks. The point is not that people consciously plan riots for their instrumental value but that aggression sometimes has payoffs. If nothing more, it gets attention.

The same is true of terrorist acts, which enable powerless people to garner widespread attention. "Kill one, frighten ten thousand," asserts an ancient Chinese proverb. In this age of global communications, killing only a few can frighten tens of millions—as happened when the terrorist-caused deaths of 25 people in several incidents during 1985 struck more fear into the hearts of travelers than the car-accident deaths of 46,000. Such can be the effect of terrorism on those exposed to its graphic accounts in the media. Deprived of what Margaret Thatcher called "the oxygen of publicity," terrorism would surely diminish, concluded Jeffrey Rubin (1986). It's like the 1970s incidents of naked spectators "streaking" onto football fields for a few seconds of television exposure. Once the networks decided to ignore the incidents, the phenomenon ended.

Observational learning

Albert Bandura (1997) proposed a **social learning theory** of aggression. He believes that we learn aggression not only by experiencing its payoffs but also by observing others. As with most social behaviors, we acquire aggression by watching others act and noting the consequences.

Picture this scene from one of Bandura's experiments (Bandura & others, 1961). A Stanford nursery school child is put to work on an interesting art activity. An adult is in another part of the room, where there are Tinker Toys, a mallet, and a big, inflated doll. After a minute of working with the Tinker Toys, the adult gets up and for almost 10 minutes attacks the inflated doll. She pounds it with the mallet, kicks it, and throws it, all the while yelling, "Sock him in the nose. . . . Knock him down. . . . Kick him."

After observing this outburst, the child goes to a different room with many very attractive toys. But after two minutes the experimenter interrupts, saying these are her best toys and she must "save them for the other children." The frustrated child now goes into another room with various toys for aggressive and nonaggressive play, two of which are a Bobo doll and a mallet.

Seldom did children not exposed to the aggressive adult model display any aggressive play or talk. Although frustrated, they nevertheless played calmly. Those who had observed the aggressive adult were many times more likely to pick up the mallet and lash out at the doll. Watching the adult's aggressive behavior lowered their inhibitions. Moreover, the children often reproduced the model's acts and said her words. Observing aggressive behavior had both lowered their inhibitions and taught them ways to aggress.

Bandura (1979) believes that everyday life exposes us to aggressive models in the family, the subculture, and the mass media.

The family.   Children of physically punitive parents tend to use aggression when relating to others. Their parents often disciplined them by screaming, slapping, and beating—modeling aggression as a method of dealing with problems (Patterson & others, 1982). These parents often themselves had parents who were physically punitive (Bandura & Walters, 1959; Straus & Gelles, 1980). Although most abused children do not become criminals or abusive parents, 30 percent do later abuse their own children—four times the national rate (Kaufman & Zigler, 1987; Widom, 1989). Within families, violence often leads to violence.

social learning theory
the theory that we learn social behavior by observing and imitating and by being rewarded and punished

Family influence also appears in higher violence rates in cultures and families where the father plays a minimal role (Triandis, 1994). One large study reports that 70 percent of juveniles in detention did not grow up with two parents (Beck & others, 1988). Two-parent families differ not only in increased care and positive discipline by fathers but also in lesser poverty and greater educational achievement. The correlation between parental absence (usually father absence) and violence holds across races, income levels, education, and locations (Staub, 1996; Zill, 1988).

The correlation also appears over time. In the Canada of 1960, less than 7 percent of children did not live with two parents and only 3,653 juveniles were arrested for violent crime. In 1996, 19 percent of children did not live with two parents, and a similar-sized juvenile population produced more than 22,500 arrests for violent crime. The point is not that children from father-absent homes are likely to become delinquent or violent (nurtured by a caring mother and extended family, most such children do not act out). But the risk is increased. The situation, it seems, matters.

The subculture.   The social environment outside the home also provides models. In communities where "macho" images are admired, aggression is readily transmitted to new generations (Cartwright, 1975; Short, 1969). The violent subculture of teenage gangs, for instance, provides its junior members with aggressive models. At sporting events such as soccer games, player violence precedes most incidents of fan violence (Goldstein, 1982).

Richard Nisbett from the University of Michigan (1990, 1993) and Dov Cohen, from the University of Waterloo (1996) have explored the subculture effect. Within the United States, they report, the sober, cooperative White folk who settled New England and the Middle Atlantic region produced a different culture than the swashbuckling, honor-preserving White folk (many of them my Scots-Irish ancestral cousins) who settled much of the South. The former were genteel farmer-artisans, the latter aggressive hunters and herders. To the present, cities and areas that were populated by Southerners have much higher White homicide rates than those populated by Northerners. For example, the Texas panhandle (whose settlers came from the Upper South) has White homicide rates four times that of Nebraska (whose settlers came from the East, Midwest, and Europe). In the Texas panhandle even towns with low poverty rates have much higher homicide rates than Nebraska towns with high poverty rates.

It's not violence in general that Southerners are more likely to advocate, but violence that protects one's property and honor, and violence that punishes (Nisbett & Cohen, 1996). "A man has a right to kill to defend his home," agree 18 percent of White non-Southern men and 36 percent of White Southern men. White Southern men are twice as likely as rural Midwestern White men to report having guns for protection. Southerners also more strongly support wars and favor spanking (thus modeling violence in social relations).

So people learn aggressive responses both by experience and by observing aggressive models. But when will aggressive responses actually occur? Bandura (1979) contends that aggressive acts are motivated by a variety of aversive experiences—frustration, pain, insults (Figure 10–3). Such experiences arouse us emotionally. But whether we act aggressively depends upon the consequences we anticipate. Aggression is most likely when we are aroused *and* it seems safe and rewarding to aggress.

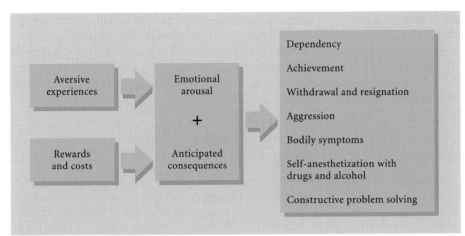

figure 10–3

The social learning view of aggression.
The emotional arousal stemming from an aversive experience motivates aggression. Whether aggression or some other response actually occurs depends on what consequences we have learned to expect.

(Based on Bandura, 1979, 1997.)

Aggression manifests itself in two forms: *hostile aggression,* which springs from emotions such as anger and intends to injure, and *instrumental aggression,* which is a means to some other end.

There are three broad theories of aggression. The *instinct* view, most commonly associated with Sigmund Freud and Konrad Lorenz, contended that aggressive energy will accumulate from within, like water accumulating behind a dam. Although the available evidence offers little support for this view, aggression *is* bio-logically influenced by heredity, blood chemistry, and the brain.

According to the second view, *frustration* causes anger and hostility. Given aggressive cues, this anger may provoke aggression. Frustration stems not from deprivation itself but from the gap between expectations and achievements.

The *social learning* view presents aggression as learned behavior. By experience and by observing others' success, we sometimes learn that aggression pays.

Summing up

Influences on aggression

Under what conditions do we aggress? The factors tugging at our trigger include aversive incidents, arousal, the media, and the group context.

Aversive incidents

The recipe for aggression often includes not only frustration but some type of aversive experience: pain, uncomfortable heat, an attack, or overcrowding.

Pain

Researcher Nathan Azrin wanted to know if switching off foot shocks would reinforce two rats' positive interactions with each other. Azrin planned to turn on the shock and then, once the rats approached each other, cut off the pain. To his great surprise, the experiment proved impossible. As soon as the rats felt pain, they attacked each other, before the experimenter could switch off the shock. The greater the shock (and pain) the more violent the attack.

Is this true of rats alone? The researchers found that with a wide variety of species, the cruelty the animals imposed upon each other matched zap for zap the cruelty imposed upon them. As Azrin (1967) explained, the pain-attack response occurred

Today's ethical guidelines restrict researchers' use of painful stimuli.

in many different strains of rats. Then we found that shock produced attack when pairs of the following species were caged together: some kinds of mice, hamsters, opossums, raccoons, marmosets, foxes, nutria, cats, snapping turtles, squirrel monkeys, ferrets, red squirrels, bantam roosters, alligators, crayfish, amphiuma (an amphibian), and several species of snakes including the boa constrictor, rattlesnake, brown rat-snake, cottonmouth, copperhead, and black snake. The shock-attack reaction was clearly present in many very different kinds of creatures. In all the species in which shock produced attack it was fast and consistent, in the same "push-button" manner as with the rats.

The animals were not choosy about their targets. They would attack animals of their own species and also those of a different species, or stuffed dolls, or even tennis balls.

The pain-attack reaction: Upon receiving a shock or other painful effect, many animals will automatically attack whatever animal is within reach.

The researchers also varied the source of pain. They found that not just shocks induce attack; intense heat and "psychological pain"— for example, suddenly not rewarding hungry pigeons that have been trained to expect a grain reward after pecking at a disk—brought the same reaction as shocks. "Psychological pain" is, of course, what we call frustration.

Marty McSorley fights with Donald Brashear. Angered by the fight, and frustrated at losing the game McSorley later slashed Brashear with his stick across the side of the head, knocking him unconscious.

Pain heightens aggressiveness in humans, also. Many of us can recall such a reaction after stubbing a toe or suffering a headache. Leonard Berkowitz and his associates demonstrated this by having students hold one hand in lukewarm water or painfully cold water. Those whose hands were submerged in the cold water reported feeling more irritable and more annoyed, and they were more willing to blast another person with unpleasant noise. In view of such results, Berkowitz (1983, 1989) now believes that aversive stimulation rather than frustration is the basic trigger of hostile aggression. Frustration is certainly one important type of unpleasantness. But any aversive event, whether a dashed expectation, a personal insult, or physical pain, can incite an emotional outburst. Even the torment of a depressed state increases the likelihood of hostile aggressive behavior.

Heat

People have theorized for centuries about the effect of climate on human action. Hippocrates (ca. 460–377 B.C.), comparing the civilized Greece of his day to the savagery in what we now know as Germany and Switzerland, believed the cause to be northern Europe's harsh climate. Later, the English attributed their "superior" culture to *England's* ideal climate. French thinkers proclaimed the same for France. Because climate remains steady while cultural traits change, the climate theory of culture obviously has limited validity.

Temporary climate variations, however, can affect behavior. Offensive odors, cigarette smoke, and air pollution have all been linked with aggressive behavior (Rotton & Frey, 1985). But the most-studied environmental irritant is heat. William Griffitt (1970; Griffitt & Veitch, 1971) found that compared to students who answered questionnaires in a room with a normal temperature, those who did so in an uncomfortably hot room (over 90°F.) reported feeling more tired and aggressive and expressed more hostility toward a stranger. Follow-up experiments revealed that heat also triggers retaliative actions (Bell, 1980; Rule & others, 1987).

Does uncomfortable heat increase aggression in the real world as well as in the laboratory? Consider:

- Riots occurring in 79 cities between 1967 and 1971 were more likely on hot than on cool days.
- When the weather is hot, violent crimes are more likely. As reported by Craig Anderson (1989), this has been found true around the world in
  - England and Wales (Leffingwell, 1892),
  - Korea (Chang, 1972),
  - Puerto Rico (Michael & Zumpe, 1983),
  - Germany (Aschaffenburg, 1903/1913),
  - South America (Lombroso (1899/1911), and
  - The United States (Cohen, 1941).
- Not only do hotter days have more violent crimes, so do hotter seasons of the year, hotter summers, hotter years, hotter cities, and hotter regions of western Europe (Anderson & Anderson, 1996; Anderson & Anderson, in press). Assuming that predicted global warming occurs, Craig Anderson, Brad Bushman, and Ralph Groom (1997) project by the mid 21st century the United States alone will annually see at least 115,000 more serious assaults.
- In hot weather, drivers without air conditioning are more likely to honk at a stalled car (Kenrick & MacFarlane, 1986).
- During the 1986 to 1988 major league baseball seasons, the number of batters hit by a pitch was two-thirds greater for games played in the 90s than for games played below 80° (Reifman & others, 1991). Pitchers weren't wilder on hot days—they had no more walks and wild pitches. They just clobbered more batters.

Do these real-world findings show that heat discomfort directly fuels aggressiveness? Although the conclusion appears plausible, these *correlations* between temperature and aggression don't prove it. People certainly could be

"I pray thee, good Mercutio, let's retire; The day is hot, the Capulets abroad, And, if we meet, we shall not 'scape a brawl, For now, these hot days, is the mad blood stirring."

Shakespeare, *Romeo and Juliet*

The number of batters hit by stray pitches increases in baseball games played in hot weather.

more irritable in hot, sticky weather. And in the laboratory, hot temperatures do increase arousal and hostile thoughts and feelings (Anderson & others, 1995). There may be other contributing factors, however. Maybe hot summer evenings drive people into the streets. There, other group influence factors may well take over. Judging from experiments on aversive stimulation and on group aggression, my hunch is that such behavior is stimulated by *both* the heat and the group.

Attacks

Being attacked or insulted by another is especially conducive to aggression. Experiments in several labs around the globe by Stuart Taylor (Taylor & Pisano, 1971), Harold Dengerink (Dengerink & Myers, 1977), and Kennichi Ohbuchi and Toshihiro Kambara (1985) confirm that intentional attacks breed retaliatory attacks. In most of these experiments one person competes with another in a reaction-time contest. After each test trial, the winner chooses how much shock to give the loser. Actually, each subject is playing a programmed opponent, who steadily escalates the amount of shock. Do the real subjects respond charitably? Hardly. Extracting "an eye for an eye" is the more likely response.

Crowding

Crowding—the subjective feeling of not having enough space—is stressful. Crammed in the back of a bus, trapped in slow-moving highway traffic, or living three to a small room in a university dorm diminishes one's sense of control (Baron & others, 1976; McNeel, 1980). Might such experiences also heighten aggression?

crowding
a subjective feeling of
not enough space per
person

The stress experienced by animals allowed to overpopulate a confined environment does heighten aggressiveness (Calhoun, 1962; Christian & others, 1960). But it is a rather large leap from rats in an enclosure or deer on an island to humans in a city. Nevertheless, it's true that dense urban areas do experience higher rates of crime and emotional distress (Fleming & others, 1987; Kirmeyer, 1978). Even when they don't suffer higher crime rates, residents of crowded cities may *feel* more fearful. Toronto's crime rate has been four times higher than Hong Kong's. Yet compared to Toronto people, people from Hong Kong—which is four times more densely populated—have reported feeling more fearful on their city's streets (Gifford & Peacock, 1979).

Arousal

So far we have seen that various aversive stimulations can arouse anger. Do other types of arousal, such as those that accompany exercise or sexual excitement, have a similar effect? Imagine that Tawna, having just finished a stimulating short run, comes home to discover that her date for the evening has called and left word that he has made other plans. Will Tawna more likely explode in fury after her run than if she discovered the same message after awakening from a nap? Or, having just exercised, will her aggressive tendencies be exorcised? To discover an answer, let's examine some intriguing research on how we interpret and label our bodily states.

In a famous experiment, Stanley Schachter and Jerome Singer (1962) found we can experience an aroused bodily state in different ways. They aroused men by injecting adrenaline. The drug produced body flushing, heart palpitation, and more rapid breathing. When forewarned that the drug would produce these effects, the men felt little emotion, even when waiting with either a hostile or a euphoric person. Of course, they could readily attribute their bodily sensations to the drug. Schachter and Singer led another group of men to believe the drug produced no such side effects. Then they, too, were placed in the company of a hostile or euphoric person. How did they feel and act? Angered when with the hostile person; amused when with the person who was euphoric. The seeming principle: *A given state of bodily arousal feeds one emotion or another, depending on how the person interprets and labels the arousal.*

Other experiments indicate that arousal is not as emotionally undifferentiated as Schachter believed. Yet being physically stirred up does intensify just about any emotion (Reisenzein, 1983). For example, Paul Biner (1991) reports that people find radio static unpleasant, *especially* when they are aroused by bright lighting. And Dolf Zillmann (1988), Jennings Bryant, and their collaborators found that people who have just pumped an exercise bike or watched a film of a Beatles rock concert find it easy to misattribute their arousal to a provocation. They then retaliate with heightened aggression. Although common sense might lead us to assume that Tawna's run would have drained her aggressive tensions, enabling her to accept bad news calmly, these studies show that arousal feeds emotions.

Sexual arousal and other forms of arousal, such as anger, can therefore amplify one another (Zillmann, 1989). Love is never so passionate as after a fight or a fright. In the laboratory, erotic stimuli are more arousing to people who have just been frightened. The arousal of a roller-coaster ride may similarly spill over into romantic feeling for one's partner.

A frustrating, hot, crowded, or insulting situation heightens arousal. When it does, the arousal, combined with hostile thoughts and feelings, may form a recipe for aggressive behavior (Figure 10–4). On February 21, 2000, the Boston Bruins' Marty McSorley, angered by an earlier fight in a hockey game, viciously slashed the Vancouver Canucks' Donald Brashear on the side of his head, rendering him unconscious.

figure 10–4

Elements of hostile aggression.

An aversive situation can trigger aggression by provoking hostile cognitions, hostile feelings, and arousal. These reactions make us more likely to perceive harmful intent and to react aggressively.

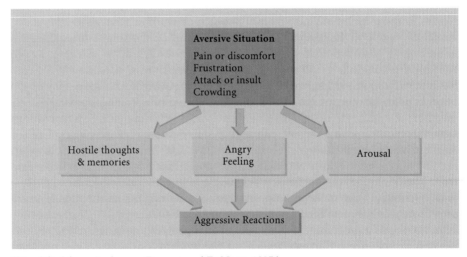

(Simplified from Anderson, Deuser, and DeNeve, 1995.)

Media influences: Pornography and sexual violence

The increase in reported violent crime, especially among juveniles, prompts us to wonder: Why the change? What social forces have caused the mushrooming violence?

Alcohol contributes to aggression, but alcohol use has not appreciably changed since 1960 (McAneny, 1994). Might the surging violence instead be fueled by the growth in individualism and materialism? by the growing gap between the powerful rich and the powerless poor? by the decline in two-parent families and the increase in father absence? by the media's increasing modeling of violence and unrestrained sexuality? The last question arises because increased rates of violence and sexual coercion have coincided with increases in media mayhem and sexual suggestion. Is the historical correlation a coincidence? What are the social consequences of pornography (which *Webster's* defines as erotic depictions intended to excite sexual arousal)? And what are the effects of modeling violence in movies and on television? Social-psychological research on pornography has focused mostly on depictions of sexual violence. A typical sexually violent episode finds a man forcing himself upon a woman. She at first resists and tries to fight off her attacker. Gradually she becomes sexually aroused, and her resistance melts. By the end she is in ecstasy, pleading for more. We have all viewed or read nonpornographic versions of this sequence: She resists, he persists. Dashing man grabs and forcibly kisses protesting woman. Within moments, the arms that were pushing him away are clutching him tight, her resistance overwhelmed by her unleashed passion. In *Gone with the Wind*, Scarlett O'Hara is carried to bed protesting and kicking, and wakes up singing.

Social psychologists report that viewing such fictional scenes of a man overpowering and arousing a woman can (1) distort one's perceptions of how women actually respond to sexual coercion and (2) increase men's aggression against women, at least in laboratory settings.

Is violent crime rising? Perceptions of increased crime can trigger gun purchases, but these guns are more likely to be used against a household member than as intended—against an intruder or attacker. Countries with fewer guns have lower murder rates.

Repeated exposure to erotic films featuring quick, uncommitted sex also tends to

- decrease attraction for one's partner
- increase acceptance of extramarital sex and of women's sexual submission to men (Zillmann, 1989)
- increase men's perceiving women in sexual terms

(Frable & others, 1994; Hansen & Hansen, 1988; 1990)

Distorted perceptions of sexual reality

Does viewing sexual violence reinforce the myth that some women would welcome sexual assault—that " 'no' doesn't really mean no"? To find out, Neil Malamuth and James Check (1981) showed University of Manitoba men either two nonsexual movies or two movies depicting a man sexually overcoming a woman. A week later, when surveyed by a different experimenter, those who saw the films with mild sexual violence were more accepting of violence against women. Note that the sexual message (that many women enjoy being "taken") was subtle and unlikely to elicit counterarguing. (Recall from Chapter 7 that more persuasion occurs when a disagreeable message slips in without provoking people to counterargue.)

Viewing slasher movies has much the same effect. Men shown films such as the *Texas Chainsaw Massacre* become desensitized to brutality and more likely to view rape victims unsympathetically (Linz & others, 1988, 1989). While spending three evenings watching sexually violent movies, male viewers in an experiment by Charles Mullin and Daniel Linz (1995) became progressively less bothered by the raping and slashing. Compared to others who were not exposed to the films, they also, three days later, expressed less sympathy for domestic violence victims and they rated the victims' injuries as less severe. In fact, said researchers Edward Donnerstein, Daniel Linz, and Steven Penrod (1987), what better way for an evil character to get people to react calmly to the torture and mutilation of women than to show a gradually escalating series of such films?

Aggression against women

Evidence also accumulates that pornography may contribute to men's actual aggression toward women. Correlational studies raise that possibility. John Court (1985) noted that across the world, as pornography became more widely available during the 1960s and 1970s, the rate of reported rapes sharply increased—except in countries and areas where pornography was controlled. (The examples that counter this trend—such as Japan, where violent pornography is available but the rape rate is low—remind us that other factors are also important.) In Hawaii, the number of reported rapes rose ninefold between 1960 and 1974, dropped when restraints on pornography were temporarily imposed, and rose again when the restraints were lifted.

In another correlational study, Larry Baron and Murray Straus (1984) discovered that the sales of sexually explicit magazines (such as *Hustler* and *Playboy*) correlated with rape rates. After controlling for a number of factors, such as the percentage of young males in each area, a positive relationship was still observed. The areas that sold the most magazines had the most rapes, and those that sold the fewest magazines had the fewest rapes.

When interviewed, Canadian sexual offenders commonly acknowledge pornography use. For example, William Marshall (1989) reported that Ontario rapists and child molesters used pornography much more than men who were not sexual offenders. Another study also reports considerable exposure to pornography among serial killers, and among most child sex abusers (Bennett, 1991; Ressler & others, 1988). Of course, this *correlation* cannot prove that pornography is a contributing *cause* of rape. Maybe the offenders' use of pornography is merely a symptom and not a cause of their basic deviance. Moreover, the evidence is mixed: Some studies find prior pornography use (including childhood exposure to pornography) uncorrelated with sexual aggression (Bauserman, 1996).

Although limited to the sorts of short-term behaviors that can be studied in the laboratory, controlled experiments reveal cause and effect. A consensus statement by 21 leading social scientists sums up the results: "Exposure to violent pornography increases punitive behavior toward women" (Koop, 1987).

"Pornography that portrays sexual aggression as pleasurable for the victim increases the acceptance of the use of coercion in sexual relations."

Social science consensus at Surgeon General's Workshop on Pornography and Public Health (Koop, 1987)

"Pornography is the theory and rape the practice."

Robin Morgan (1980, p. 139)

Was the use of pornography by Paul Bernardo (a.k.a. Paul Teale, in whose house police found pornographic tapes) merely a symptom of his derangement or a cause? Could the viewing of pornography actually have pushed him over the edge and led him to begin raping and murdering young girls? Notorious serial killer Ted Bundy saw such a role for pornography in his own life. On the eve of his execution he argued, "The most damaging kinds of pornography [involve] sexual violence. Like an addiction, you keep craving something that is harder, harder, something which, which gives you a greater sense of excitement. Until you reach a point where the pornography only goes so far, you reach that jumping off point where you begin to wonder if maybe actually doing it would give you that which is beyond just reading it or looking at it."

One of these social scientists, Edward Donnerstein (1980), had shown 120 men a neutral, an erotic, or an aggressive-erotic (rape) film. Then, the men, supposedly as part of another experiment, "taught" a male or female confederate some nonsense syllables by choosing how much shock to administer for incorrect answers. Especially when angered, the men who had watched the rape film administered markedly stronger shocks—but only to female victims (Figure 10–5).

If the ethics of conducting such experiments trouble you, rest assured that these researchers appreciate the controversial and powerful experience they are giving participants. Only after giving their knowing consent do people participate. Moreover, after the experiment researchers debunk any myths the film communicated. One hopes that such debriefing sufficiently offsets the vivid image of a supposedly euphoric rape victim. Judging from studies with University of Manitoba and Winnipeg students by James Check and Neil Malamuth (1984; Malamuth & Check, 1984), it does. Those who read erotic rape stories and were then fully debriefed became *less* accepting of the "women-enjoy-rape" myth than students who had not seen the film. Other studies confirm the effectiveness of debriefing (Allen & others, 1996). For example, Donnerstein and Berkowitz (1981) found that students who viewed pornography *and* were then thoroughly debriefed were later *less* likely than other students to agree that "being roughed up is sexually stimulating to many women."

figure 10–5

figure 10–5

After viewing an aggressive-erotic film, college men delivered stronger shocks than before, especially to a woman.

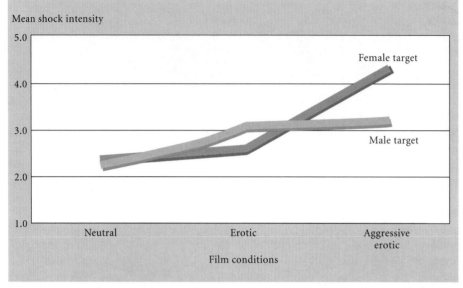

(Data from Donnerstein, 1980.)

Most, having been overcome on a date or by an acquaintance, didn't label it as such. Women's "scripts" for rape usually involve violence by a stranger.

(Kahn & others, 1994.)

Justification for this experimentation is not only scientific but also humanitarian. In one careful survey, 22 percent of women reported having been forced by a man to do something sexually (Laumann & others, 1994). In surveys of 6,200 university students and 2,200 working women, Mary Koss and her colleagues (1988, 1990, 1993) found that 28 percent of the women reported an experience that met the legal definition of rape or attempted rape. Surveys in other industrialized countries produce similar results (Table 10–1). Three in four stranger rapes and nearly all acquaintance rapes went unreported to police. Thus the known rape rate *greatly* underestimates the actual rape rate. Moreover, many more women—half in one survey of university women (Sandberg & others, 1985)—report having suffered some form of sexual assault while on a date, and even more have experienced verbal sexual coercion or harassment (Craig, 1990; Pryor, 1987).

Eight different surveys have asked university males whether there was any chance they would rape a woman "if you could be assured that no one would know and that you could in no way be punished" (Stille & others, 1987). A disturbing proportion—about one third—admit to at least a slim possibility of doing so. Compared to men who indicate no possibility of raping, these men are more like convicted rapists in their belief in rape myths, their being sexually aroused by rape depictions, and their behaving aggressively toward women—in both laboratory and dating situations. Aggression is greatest among those who have formed the sort of rape-supportive attitudes that pornography cultivates (Figure 10–6). Men who behave in sexually coercive, aggressive ways typically desire dominance, exhibit hostility toward women, and are sexually promiscuous (Anderson & others, 1997; Malamuth & others, 1995).

Malamuth, Donnerstein, and Zillmann are among those alarmed by women's increasing risk of being sexually harassed or raped. They caution against oversimplifying the complex causes of rape—which is no more attributable to any one cause than is cancer. Yet they conclude that viewing violence,

"Society doesn't expect Jews to stop anti-Semitism, or Blacks to stop racism, or children to end child abuse."

Katha Pollitt, "Georgie Porgie is a Bully," 1990

table 10–1   **Reported rape experiences in five countries**

Country	Sample of Women	Completed & Attempted Rape
Canada	national sample at 95 colleges and universities	23% rape or sexual assault
New Zealand	convenience sample of psychology students	25%
United Kingdom	convenience sample at 22 universities	19%
United States	representative sample at 32 colleges and universities	28%
Seoul, Korea	adult women	22%

Source: Studies reported by Koss, Heise, and Russo (1994)

especially sexual violence, can have antisocial effects. Just as most Germans quietly tolerated the degrading anti-Semitic images that fed the Holocaust, so most people today tolerate media images of women that feed what some call the growing "female holocaust" of sexual harassment, abuse, and rape.

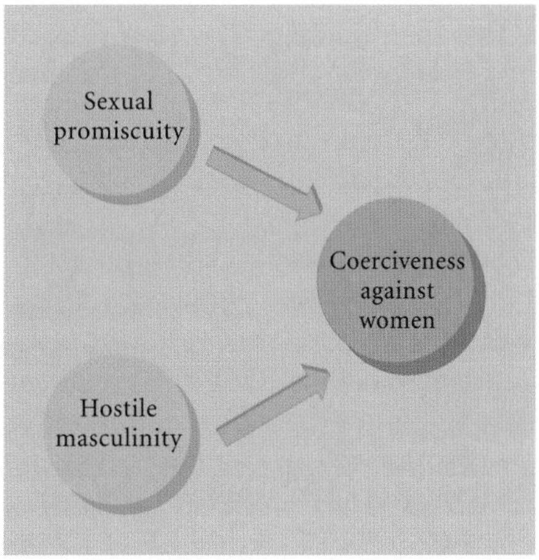

Media awareness education

In the contest of individual versus collective rights, people in most Western nations side with individual rights. So as an alternative to censorship, many psychologists favor "media awareness training." Recall that pornography

figure 10–6

Sexually aggressive men.

Men who sexually coerce women often combine a history of impersonal sex with hostile masculinity, reports Neil Malamuth (1996).

researchers have successfully resensitized and educated participants to women's actual responses to sexual violence. Could educators similarly promote critical viewing skills? By sensitizing people to the view of women that predominates in pornography and to issues of sexual harassment and violence, it should be possible to counter the myth that women enjoy being coerced. "Our utopian and perhaps naive hope," say Edward Donnerstein, Daniel Linz, and Steven Penrod (1987, p. 196), "is that in the end the truth revealed through good science will prevail and the public will be convinced that these images not only demean those portrayed but also those who view them."

Is such a hope naive? Consider: Without banning cigarettes, the number of Canadian smokers dropped from 48 percent in 1972 to 27 percent in 1994. Without censoring racism, once-common media images of Blacks as childlike, superstitious buffoons have nearly disappeared. As public consciousness changed, script writers, producers, and media executives decided that exploitative images of minorities were not good. More recently they have decided that drugs are not glamorous, as many films and songs from

focus

Is rape on the increase?

Across the world, people are alarmed and angry about increasing violent crime. Canada is no different. There is therefore now a booming business in home security systems, self-defense courses, and bodyguards. But is Canada a more dangerous place than it was a quarter of a century ago? In particular, is the incidence of crimes of rape and sexual assault increasing?

By one measure—the counting of violent crimes by local police and sheriffs, as reported in the Statistics Canada *Uniform Crime Report*—rapes and sexual assaults in Canada more than tripled between 1975 and 1993.

But the story isn't so simple. If you look at the left graph in Figure 10-7, you will see that between 1975 and 1982 the reported number of rapes and sexual assaults were relatively low. If you look at the right graph, however, you will see that in each of these years the police judged that over 30 percent of the reported rapes were unfounded accusations. You should also know that for all of the other serious crimes, police did not find that even 15 percent of their reports were unfounded.

You will also notice that there is a big change in the data after 1982. After this year there was an amendment to the law that led to a change in the categories of sexual assault. (This is also why there is no data available for 1983 and 1984.) Gone was the term rape. Instead, there were three levels of sexual assault: aggravated sexual assault; sexual assault with a weapon; and third-degree sexual assault. After this change the number of serious sexual assaults that were judged as unfounded accusations by the police plummeted. It was also after this change that the number of rapes and sexual assaults reported to the police skyrocketed.

What we have here is a correlation between the number of rapes judged to be unfounded accusations by the police, and the number of rapes and sexual assaults that are reported to the police. One compelling explanation for this pattern of data is that when the police began to be more accepting of women's accounts of their rape, women began to report the crime more often. Of course this pattern of data is just a correlation and we do not know whether the change in police judgements had any causal effect on the number of rapes that were reported. It might well be the case that the actual number of rapes and sexual assaults was dramatically increasing. Other interpretations of the data are possible as well.

You might have noted one additional feature of this data. When the shift in the law led to the redefining of the categories of sexual assault, it appears that the number of serious assaults decreased. Before 1982 the number of rapes that were reported was consistently above eight per 100,000 people in the population. After 1982, the number of serious sexual assaults (first-and second-degree) averaged about five per 100,000 people. Taken at face value, this would suggest that the most serious forms of sexual assault decreased after 1982. But again another explanation is possible: after 1982, could the police have begun to classify some of the serious assaults as only third degree sexual assaults? Indeed all of the dramatic increase in sexual assaults after 1982 is only among third degree sexual assaults.

The moral: Truth is elusive. As so often happens, simple questions—Is rape increasing?—are not simply answered. We can follow the trends and note the changes, but it is still difficult to determine the causes of these changes.

the 1960s and 1970s implied, but dangerous—and high school seniors' marijuana use during the previous month has dropped from 37 percent in 1979 to 11 percent in 1992, before rebounding to 22 percent in 1996 as the cultural antidrug voice softened and drug use became reglamorized in some music and

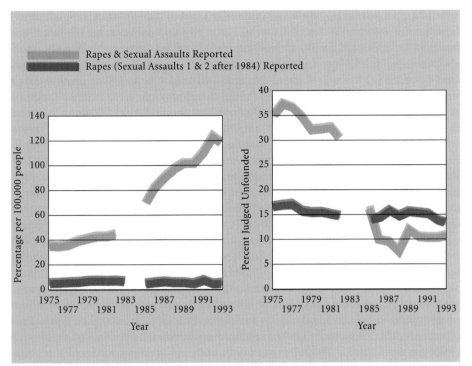

Rapes & Sexual Assaults Reported
Rapes (Sexual Assaults 1 & 2 after 1984) Reported

figure 10–7

Disparity in rape statistics.

Before 1983, a large number of rapes in Canada were judged to be unfounded accusations. When the law changed and fewer rapes were judged as unfounded, there was a large increase in the number of rapes and sexual assaults that were reported to the police. Did the change in the law make it easier for women to report such attacks?

films (Johnston, 1996). Will we one day look back with embarrassment on the time when movies entertained people with scenes of exploitation, mutilation, and sexual coercion?

Media influences: Television

We have seen that watching an aggressive model can unleash children's aggressive urges and teach them new ways to aggress. And we have seen that after viewing sexual violence, many angry men will act more violently toward women. Does television have any similar effects?

Consider these few facts about watching television. In 1945, the Gallup poll asked, "Do you know what television is?" (Gallup, 1972, p. 551). Today, in much of the industrialized world, 98 percent of households have a TV set, more than have bathtubs or telephones. Two-thirds of homes have three or more sets, which helps explain why parents' reports of what their children watch minimally correlate with children's reports of what they watch (Donnerstein, 1998). With CNN spanning the globe, and *Baywatch* having a billion viewers in 142 countries, television is creating a global pop culture (McDougal, 1994).

In the average home, the set is on seven hours a day, with individual household members averaging three hours. Women watch more than men, non-Whites more than Whites, preschoolers and retired people more than those in school or working, and the less educated more than the highly educated . For the most part, these facts are true for most industrialized countries (Murray & Kippax, 1979).

"The problem with television is that people must sit and keep their eyes glued on a screen: the average American family hasn't time for it. Therefore, the showmen are convinced that . . . television will never be a serious competitor of [radio] broadcasting."

New York Times, March 19, 1939

During all those hours, what social behaviors are modeled? Since 1967, George Gerbner and other TV watchers (1993, 1994) have sampled major network prime-time and Saturday morning entertainment programs. Several studies (National Television Violence Study, 1997; Williams, Zabrack, & Joy, 1982) have analyzed some 10,000 programs from the major networks and cable channels. Their findings? Six in ten programs contain violence ("physically compelling action that threatens to hurt or kill, or actual hurting or killing"). What does it add up to? By the end of elementary school, the average child views some 8,000 TV murders and 100,000 other violent acts (Huston & others, 1992). Reflecting on his twenty-two years of cruelty counting, Gerbner (1994) lamented: "Humankind has had more bloodthirsty eras but none as filled with *images* of violence as the present. We are awash in a tide of violent representations the world has never seen . . . drenching every home with graphic scenes of expertly choreographed brutality."

Does it matter? Does prime-time crime stimulate the behavior it depicts? Or, as viewers vicariously participate in aggressive acts, do the shows drain off aggressive energy?

The latter idea, a variation on the **catharsis** hypothesis, maintains that watching violent drama enables people to release their pent-up hostilities. Defenders of the media cite this theory frequently and remind us that violence predates television. In an imaginary debate with one of television's critics, the medium's defender might argue, "Television played no role in the genocides of Jews and Native Americans. Television just reflects and caters to our tastes." "Agreed," responds the critic, "but it's also true that during America's TV age, reported violent crime has increased several times faster than the population rate. Surely you don't mean the popular arts are mere passive reflections, without any power to influence public consciousness." The defender replies: "The violence epidemic results from many factors. TV may even reduce aggression by keeping people off the streets and by offering them a harmless opportunity to vent their aggression."

Studies of television viewing and aggression aim to identify effects more subtle and pervasive than the occasional "copy-cat" murders that capture public attention. They ask: How does television affect viewers' *behavior?* viewers' *thinking?*

Television's effects on behavior

Do viewers imitate violent models? Examples abound of people reenacting television crimes. In one survey of 208 prison convicts, 9 of 10 admitted that they learned new criminal tricks by watching crime programs. And 4 out of 10 said they had attempted specific crimes seen on television (*TV Guide*, 1977).

Correlating TV viewing and behavior.   Crime stories are not scientific evidence. Researchers therefore use correlational and experimental studies to examine the effects of viewing violence. One technique, commonly used with school-children, asks whether their TV watching predicts their aggressiveness. To some extent it does. The more violent the content of the child's TV viewing, the more aggressive the child (Eron, 1987; Turner & others, 1986). The relationship is modest but consistently found across the world.

So can we conclude that a diet of violent TV fuels aggression? Perhaps you are already thinking that because this is a correlational study, the cause-effect relation could also work in the opposite direction. Maybe aggressive children

catharsis
emotional release. The catharsis view of aggression is that aggressive drive is reduced when one "releases" aggressive energy, either by acting aggressively or by fantasizing aggression.

"One of television's great contributions is that it brought murder back into the home where it belongs. Seeing a murder on television can be good therapy. It can help work off one's antagonisms."

Alfred Hitchcock

"Watching action shows cannot only be cathartic, but can encourage play."

Margaret Loesch, President, Fox Children's Network (quoted by Kaplan, 1995)

" I TOLD YOU THE KIDS WERE WATCHING TOO MUCH TELEVISION. "

prefer aggressive programs. Or maybe some underlying third factor, such as lower intelligence, predisposes some children both to prefer aggressive programs and to act aggressively.

Researchers have developed two ways to test these alternative explanations. They test the "hidden third factor" explanation by statistically pulling out the influence of some of these possible factors. For example, British researcher William Belson (1978; Muson, 1978) studied 1,565 London boys. Compared to those who watched little violence, those who watched a great deal (especially realistic rather than cartoon violence) admitted to 50 percent more violent acts during the preceding six months (for example, "I busted the telephone in a telephone box"). Belson also examined 22 likely third factors, such as family size. The heavy and light viewers still differed after equating them with respect to potential third factors. So Belson surmised that the heavy viewers were indeed more violent *because* of their TV exposure.

Similarly, Leonard Eron and Rowell Huesmann (1980, 1985) found that violence viewing among 875 eight-year-olds correlated with aggressiveness even after statistically pulling out several obvious possible third factors. Moreover, when they restudied these individuals as 19-year-olds, they discovered that viewing violence at age eight modestly predicted aggressiveness at age 19, but that aggressiveness at age eight did *not* predict viewing violence at age 19. Aggression followed viewing, not the reverse. They confirmed these findings in follow-up studies of 758 Chicago-area and 220 Finnish youngsters (Huesmann & others, 1984). What is more, when Eron and Huesmann (1984) examined the later criminal conviction records of their initial sample of eight-year-olds, they found that at age 30, those men who as children had watched a great deal of violent television were more likely to have been convicted of a serious crime (Figure 10–8).

Even murder rates increase when and where television comes. In Canada the homicide rate doubled between 1957 and 1974 as violent television spread. In census regions where television came later, the homicide rate jumped later,

"I rarely turn down an invitation to speak to a PTA meeting or other civic groups in order to warn parents and other caretakers that they must control their children's viewing habits."

Leonard Eron (1985)

figure 10–8

Children's television viewing and later criminal activity.

Violence viewing at age eight was a predictor of a serious criminal offense by age 30.

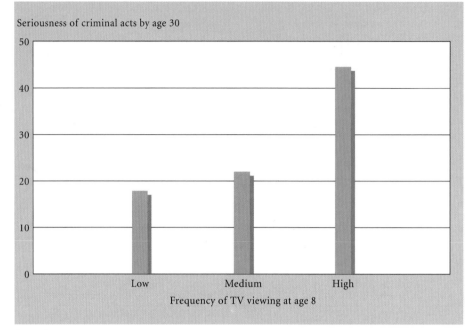

Seriousness of criminal acts by age 30

Frequency of TV viewing at age 8

(Data from Eron & Huesmann, 1984.)

too. In White South Africa, where television was not introduced until 1975, a similar near doubling of the homicide rate did not begin until after 1975 (Centerwall, 1989). And in a closely studied rural Canadian town where television came late, playground aggression doubled soon after (Williams, 1986).

Notice that these studies illustrate how researchers are now using correlational findings to *suggest* cause and effect. Yet an infinite number of possible third factors could be creating a merely coincidental relation between viewing violence and aggression. Fortunately, however, the experimental method can control these extraneous factors. If we randomly assign some children to watch a violent film and others a nonviolent film, any later aggression difference between the two groups will be due to the only factor that distinguishes them: what they watched.

TV viewing experiments. The pioneering experiments by Albert Bandura and Richard Walters (1963) sometimes had young children view the adult pounding the inflated doll on film instead of observing it live—with much the same effect. Then Leonard Berkowitz and Russell Geen (1966) found that angered university students who viewed a violent film acted more aggressively than did similarly angered students who viewed nonaggressive films. These laboratory experiments, coupled with growing public concern, were sufficient to prompt the researchers to conduct over fifty new research studies during the early 1970s. By and large, these studies confirmed that viewing violence amplifies aggression.

In a later series of experiments, research teams led by Ross Parke (1977) and Jacques Leyens (1975) showed institutionalized delinquent boys a series of either aggressive or nonaggressive commercial films. Their consistent finding:

"Then shall we simply allow our children to listen to any story anyone happens to make up, and so receive into their minds ideas often the very opposite of those we shall think they ought to have when they are grown up?"

Plato, *The Republic*

"Exposure to movie violence . . . led to an increase in viewer aggression." Compared to the week preceding the film series, physical attacks increased sharply in cottages where boys were viewing violent films.

Chris Boyatzis and his colleagues (1995) observed a similar effect when they showed some elementary schoolchildren, but not others, an episode of television's most popular—and violent—children's program, *Power Rangers.* Immediately after viewing the episode, the viewers committed seven times as many

aggressive acts per two-minute interval as the nonviewers. As in Bandura's pioneering Bobo doll studies, the boy viewers often precisely imitated the characters' acts, such as their flying karate kicks. In Norway in 1994 a five-year-old girl was stoned, kicked, and left to freeze in the snow by playmates reportedly imitating acts seen on the show—triggering the show's banning by three Scandinavian countries (Blucher, 1994).

After viewing TV's Power Rangers, *children have imitated many of the aggressive behaviors that are characteristic of the program.*

Television research has involved a variety of methods and participants. Researchers Susan Hearold (1986) and Wendy Wood and colleagues (1991) assembled the results of correlational and experimental studies. Their conclusion: Viewing antisocial portrayals is indeed associated with antisocial behavior. The effect is not overwhelming and is, in fact, at times so modest that some critics doubt it exists (Freedman, 1988; McGuire, 1986). Moreover, the aggression provoked in these experiments is not assault and battery; it's more on the scale of a shove in the lunch line, a cruel comment, a threatening gesture.

Nevertheless, the convergence of evidence is striking. "The irrefutable conclusion," said one commission of psychologists on youth violence, is "that viewing violence increases violence." This is especially so among people with aggressive tendencies (Bushman, 1995). The violence viewing effect also is strongest when an attractive person commits justified, realistic violence that goes unpunished and that shows no pain or harm (Donnerstein, 1998). Violent entertainment often creates these conditions for antisocial effects, but not always. By depicting unjustified violence by unattractive perpetrators on suffering Holocaust victims, *Schindler's List* is unlikely to have encouraged violent acts.

Experimental studies point most clearly to cause and effect, but they are sometimes remote from real life (for example, pushing a hurt button). Moreover, the experiments can but hint at the cumulative effects of witnessing more than 100,000 violent episodes and some 20,000 murders, as the average child does before becoming the average teenager in the industrialized world (Murray & Lonnborg, 1989). Uncontrolled influences complicate the correlational studies, but such studies do tap the cumulative effects of real-life viewing.

"There is absolutely no doubt that higher levels of viewing violence on television are correlated with increased acceptance of aggressive attitudes and increased aggressive behavior."

American Psychological Association Commission on Violence and Youth, 1993

behind the scenes

At the University of Louvain when I studied for my Ph.D. there was no social psychologist. But at a summer school organized by the newly founded European Association of Experimental Social Psychology, and later during two years of postdoctoral research on aggression with Leonard Berkowitz and Ross Parke at the University of Wisconsin, I learned what experimental social psychology really was about.

After returning to Belgium, I conducted the experiment on viewing violent or nonviolent movies with 12- to 18-year-old boys who were at an institution in a small village on the Belgian-French border. The boys liked this study, because their access to TV had been restricted to news, sports, and cultural programs they didn't care about. Although the data showed that viewing violence increased everyday aggression, the boys, the counselors, and the management were undisturbed by the results. When I presented the results to a NATO conference, the French newspaper, *Le Monde,* reported the story. Then a tabloid newspaper called, hoping for a story about a child who knifed his roommate after watching *The Dirty Dozen.* Although the results of one experiment are never so dramatic, experiments can alert us to corrosive forces that, over time, may indeed impact society.

*Jacques-Philippe Leyens
Universite catholique de
Louvain, Louvain-la-Neuve*

Why does TV viewing affect behavior? The conclusion drawn by these researchers is *not* that television and pornography are primary causes of social violence, any more than cyclamates are a primary cause of cancer. Rather they say television is *a* cause. Even if it is just one ingredient in a complex recipe for violence, it is one that, like cyclamates, is potentially controllable. Given the convergence of correlational and experimental evidence, researchers have explored *why* viewing violence has this effect.

Consider three possibilities (Geen & Thomas, 1986). One is that it's not the violent content itself that causes social violence but the *arousal* it produces (Mueller & others, 1983; Zillmann, 1989). As we noted earlier, arousal tends to spill over: One type of arousal energizes other behaviors.

Other research shows that viewing violence *disinhibits*. In Bandura's experiment, the adult's punching the Bobo doll seemed to legitimate such outbursts and to lower the children's inhibitions. Viewing violence primes the viewer for aggressive behavior by activating violence-related thoughts (Berkowitz, 1984; Bushman & Geen, 1990; Josephson, 1987). Listening to music with sexually violent lyrics seems to have a similar effect, predisposing younger males to behave more aggressively (Barongan & Hall, 1995; Johnson & others, 1995).

Media portrayals also evoke *imitation*. The children in Bandura's experiments reenacted the specific behaviors they had witnessed. The commercial television industry is hard-pressed to dispute that television leads viewers to imitate what they have seen: Its advertisers model consumption. Television's critics agree—and are troubled that on TV programs acts of assault outnumber affectionate acts 4 to 1 and that, in other ways as well, television models an unreal world (Table 10–2). They love to recount seeming examples of imitation, as when two men three times viewed the movie *Magnum Force,* in which the

Question: Might there be a similar effect of repeated playing of violent video games such as Mortal Kombat (in which women are attacked and dismembered)? Might such play teach youth "scripts"—mental tapes for how to act when facing conflict? (In one recent study, children's frequency of hitting and kicking more than doubled during a free play period following the playing of such a game, compared to aggression after playing Tetris [Mauro & Best, 1996].)

table 10–2 **America's television world versus the real world**
How closely does prime-time network television drama mirror the world around us? Compare the percentages of people and behaviors on TV dramas with those in the real world. Television may reflect culture's mythology, but it distorts the reality.

Item Viewed	Seen on Television (%)	In the Real World (%)
female	33	51
married	10	61
blue collar	25	67
having a religious affiliation	6	88
implied intercourse: partners unmarried	85	unknown
beverages consumed: percentage alcoholic	45	16

From an analysis of nearly 35,000 television characters since 1969 by George Gerbner (1993; Gerbner & others, 1986). TV sex data from Fernandez-Collado & others (1978). TV religion data from Skill & others (1994); actual religion data from Saad & McAneny (1994)—percent for whom religion is fairly or very important. Alcohol data from NCTV (1988). Percentage of sex acts that occur among unmarried partners is surely a fraction of that depicted on TV, given that most adults are married, that frequency of intercourse is higher among the married than among singles, and that extramarital sex is rarer than commonly believed (Greeley, 1991; Laumann & others, 1994).

caustic cleaner liquid Drano is used to kill a woman. Later that month, the men reenacted the scene, murdering three people by forcing them to drink Drano (Bushman, 1996).

If the ways of relating and problem solving modeled on television do trigger imitation, especially among young viewers, then modeling **prosocial behavior** should be socially beneficial. Chapter 12 contains good news: Television's subtle influence can indeed teach children positive lessons in behavior.

prosocial behavior
positive, constructive, helpful social behavior; the opposite of antisocial behavior

Television's effects on thinking

We have focused on television's effect on behavior. Researchers have also examined the cognitive effects of viewing violence: Does prolonged viewing desensitize us to cruelty? Does it distort perceptions of reality?

Take some emotion-arousing stimulus, like an obscene word, and repeat it over and over. What happens? From introductory psychology you may recall that the emotional response will "extinguish." After witnessing thousands of acts of cruelty, there is good reason to expect a similar emotional numbing. The most common response might well become, "Doesn't bother me at all." Such a response is precisely what Victor Cline and his colleagues (1973) observed when they measured the physiological arousal of 121 boys who watched a brutal boxing match. Compared to boys who watched little television, the responses of those who watched habitually were more a shrug than a concern.

Of course, these boys might differ in ways other than television viewing. But in experiments on the effects of viewing sexual violence, similar desensitiza-

"All television is educational. The question is, what is it teaching?"

Nicholas Johnson, Former Commissioner, Federal Communications Commission, 1978

THIS MODERN WORLD by TOM TOMORROW

IN *ANCIENT TIMES*, OUR *PRIMITIVE ANCESTORS* HUDDLED AROUND THE CAMPFIRE IN *FEARFUL IGNORANCE* OF THE WORLD AROUND THEM! IN *THIS MODERN WORLD*, HOWEVER, THE *LIGHT OF REASON* SHINES *BRIGHTLY* AS FAMILIES GATHER AROUND THE *WARM GLOW* OF THEIR *TELEVISION SETS!*

COMING UP NEXT ON THE NEWS: TERRIFYING INEXPLICABLE EVENTS OCCURRING IN FAR-AWAY PLACES, PRESENTED WITHOUT HISTORICAL OR SOCIOLOGICAL CONTEXT!

GEEZ! IT LOOKS PRETTY BAD OUT THERE!

I'M CERTAINLY GLAD *WE'RE* SAFE HERE AT HOME!

(Dan Perkins/THIS MODERN WORLD)

People who watch many hours of television see the world as a dangerous place.

"Those of us who have been active over more than 15 years in studying [television] cannot fail to be impressed with the significance of this medium for the emerging consciousness of the developing child."

Jerome Singer and Dorothy Singer (1988)

tion—a sort of psychic numbness—occurs among young men who view slasher films. Moreover, experiments by Ronald Drabman and Margaret Thomas (1974, 1975, 1976) confirmed that such viewing breeds a more blasé reaction when later viewing the film of a brawl or when actually observing two children fighting.

Does television's fictional world also mold our conceptions of the real world? George Gerbner and his associates (1979, 1994) suspect this is television's most potent effect. Their surveys of both adolescents and adults show that heavy viewers (four hours a day or more) are more likely than light viewers (two hours or fewer) to exaggerate the frequency of violence in the world around them and to fear being personally assaulted. Similar feelings of vulnerability have been expressed by South African women after viewing violence against women (Reid & Finchilescu, 1995).

One survey of 7- to 11-year-old children found that heavy viewers were more likely than light viewers to admit fears "that somebody bad might get into your house" or that "when you go outside, somebody might hurt you" (Peterson & Zill, 1981). Adults better distinguish television crime from the neighborhoods events. Those who watch crime dramas (more than those who don't) see New York as a dangerous place. They even believe that their own city could be dangerous. But they are not more afraid of their own neighborhood (Heath & Petraitis, 1987; Tyler & Cook, 1984).

Perhaps, though, television's biggest effect occurs indirectly, as it each year replaces in people's lives a thousand or more hours of other activities. If, like most others, you have spent a thousand-plus hours per year watching TV, think how you might have used that time if there were no television. What difference would that have made in who you are today?

Group influences

We have considered what provokes *individuals* to aggress. If frustrations, insults, and aggressive models heighten the aggressive tendencies of isolated people, then such factors are likely to prompt the same reaction in groups. As a riot begins, aggressive acts often spread rapidly after the "trigger" example of one antagonistic person. Seeing looters freely helping themselves to TV sets, normally law-abiding bystanders may drop their moral inhibitions and imitate.

Groups can amplify aggressive reactions partly by diffusing responsibility. Decisions to attack in war typically are made by strategists remote from the front lines. They give orders, but others carry them out. Does such distancing make it easier to recommend aggression?

Jacquelin Gaebelein and Anthony Mander (1978) simulated this situation in the laboratory. They asked their students to *shock* someone or to *advise* someone how much shock to administer. When the shock recipient provoked the front-line subjects, they and the advisers independently favored approximately the same amount of shock. But when the recipient was innocent of any provocation, as are most victims of mass aggression, the front-line subjects gave less shock than recommended by the advisers, who felt less directly responsible for any hurt.

Diffusion of responsibility increases not only with distance but with numbers. (Recall from Chapter 8 the phenomenon of deindividuation.) When Brian Mullen (1986) analyzed information from 60 lynchings that occurred between 1899 and 1946, he made an interesting discovery: The greater the number of people in a lynch mob, the more vicious the murder and mutilation.

Such situations also involve group interaction. Through social "contagion," groups magnify aggressive tendencies, much as they polarize other tendencies. As group identity develops, conformity pressures and deindividuation increase (Staub, 1996). Self-identity diminishes as members give themselves over to the group, often feeling a satisfying oneness with the others. Examples are youth gangs, soccer fans, rapacious soldiers, urban rioters, and what Scandinavians call "mobbing"—schoolchildren in groups repeatedly harassing or attacking an insecure, weak schoolmate (Lagerspetz & others, 1982).

Experiments in Israel by Yoram Jaffe and Yoel Yinon (1983) confirm that groups can polarize aggressive tendencies. In one, university men angered by a supposed fellow subject retaliated with decisions to give much stronger shocks when in groups than when alone. In another experiment (Jaffe & others, 1981), people decided, either alone or in groups, how much punishing shock to give someone for incorrect answers on an ESP task. As Figure 10–9 shows, individuals gave progressively more of the assumed shock as the experiment proceeded, and group decision making magnified this individual tendency. So, when circumstances provoke an individual's aggressive reaction, the addition of group interaction will often amplify it.

A research team led by Joseph Mikolic (1997) found that groups accentuate natural aggressive behavior, too. They had a confederate frustrate subjects by hoarding supplies that everyone needed to build some models for money. Compared to subjects working individually, those working in groups more rapidly escalated their responses to the annoying confederate and verbalized a doubled rate of demanding, complaining, or angry statements.

Studies of aggression provide an apt opportunity to ask how well social psychology's laboratory findings generalize to everyday life. Do the circumstances that trigger someone's delivering electric shock really tell us anything about the circumstances that trigger verbal abuse or a punch in the face? Craig Anderson and Brad Bushman (1997; Bushman & Anderson, in press) note that social psychologists have studied aggression in both the laboratory and everyday worlds, and the findings are strikingly consistent. In both contexts, increased aggression is predicted by

- male actors,
- aggressive or Type A personalities,
- alcohol use,
- violence viewing,

"The worst barbarity of war is that it forces men collectively to commit acts against which individually they would revolt with their whole being."

Ellen Key, *War, Peace, and the Future*, 1916

figure 10–9

Group-enhanced aggression.

When individuals chose how much shock to administer as punishment for wrong answers, they escalated the shock level as the experiment proceeded. Group decision-making further polarized this tendency.

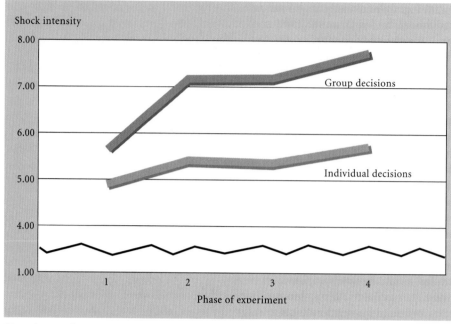

(Data from Jaffe & others, 1981.)

- anonymity,
- provocation,
- the presence of weapons, and
- group interaction.

The laboratory allows us to test and revise theories under controlled conditions. Real-world events inspire ideas and provide the venue for applying our theories. Aggression research illustrates that an interplay between studies in the controlled lab and the complex real world advances psychology's contribution to human welfare. Hunches gained from everyday experience inspire theories, which stimulate laboratory research, which then deepens our understanding and our ability to apply psychology to real problems.

Summing up

Aversive experiences include not only frustrations but also discomfort, pain, and personal attacks, both physical and verbal. Arousal from almost any source, even physical exercise or sexual stimulation, can be transformed into anger by the environment.

Television portrays considerable violence. Correlational and experimental studies converge on the conclusion that viewing violence (1) breeds a modest increase in aggressive behavior and (2) desensitizes viewers to aggression and alters their perceptions of reality. These two findings parallel the results of research on the effects of viewing violent pornography, which can increase men's aggression against women and distort their perceptions of women's responses to sexual coercion.

Much aggression is committed by groups. Circumstances that provoke individuals may also provoke groups. By diffusing responsibility and polarizing actions, group situations amplify aggressive reactions.

Reducing aggression

We have examined instinct, frustration-aggression, and social learning theories of aggression, and we have scrutinized influences on aggression. How, then, can we reduce aggression? Do theory and research suggest ways to control aggression?

Catharsis?

"Youngsters should be taught to vent their anger." So advised Ann Landers (1969). If a person "bottles up his rage, we have to find an outlet. We have to give him an opportunity of letting off steam." So asserted the prominent psychiatrist Fritz Perls (1973). Both statements assume the "hydraulic model"—accumulated aggressive energy that, like dammed-up water, needs a release.

The concept of catharsis is usually credited to Aristotle. Although Aristotle actually said nothing about aggression, he did argue that we can purge emotions by experiencing them and that viewing the classic tragedies therefore enabled a catharsis ("purgation") of pity and fear. To have an emotion excited, he believed, is to have that emotion released (Butcher, 1951). The catharsis hypothesis has been extended to include the emotional release supposedly obtained not only by observing drama but also through recalling and reliving past events, through expressing emotions, and through various actions.

Assuming that aggressive action or fantasy drains pent-up aggression, some therapists and group leaders encourage people to ventilate suppressed aggression by acting it out—by whopping one another with foam bats or beating a bed with a tennis racket while screaming. Some psychologists advise parents to encourage children's release of emotional tension through aggressive play. Many people have bought the idea, as reflected in their nearly 2 to 1 agreement with the statement, "Sexual materials provide an outlet for bottled-up impulses" (Niemi & others, 1989). But then other surveys reveal that most people also agree, "Sexual materials lead people to commit rape." So is the catharsis approach valid or not?

If viewing erotica provides an outlet for sexual impulses, then people should afterward experience diminished sexual desire and men should be less likely to view and treat women as sexual objects. But experiments show the opposite is true (Kelley & others, 1989; McKenzie-Mohr & Zanna, 1990). The near consensus among social psychologists is that catharsis does not occur as Freud, Lorenz, and their followers supposed (Geen & Quanty, 1977). For example, Robert Arms and his associates report that Canadian and American spectators of football, wrestling, and hockey games exhibit *more* hostility after viewing the event than before (Arms & others, 1979; Goldstein & Arms, 1971; Russell, 1983). Not even war seems to purge aggressive feelings. After a war, a nation's murder rate tends to jump (Archer & Gartner, 1976).

In laboratory tests of the catharsis hypothesis, Jack Hokanson and his colleagues (1961, 1962a,b, 1966) found that when students were allowed to counterattack someone who had provoked them, their arousal (as measured by their blood pressures) did more quickly return to normal. But this calming effect of retaliation occurs only in specific circumstances—when the target is the actual tormentor, not a substitute. Moreover, the retaliation must be

"It is time to put a bullet, once and for all, through the heart of the catharsis hypothesis. The belief that observing violence (or 'ventilating it') gets rid of hostilities has virtually never been supported by research."

Carol Tavris (1988, p. 194)

justifiable and the target nonintimidating, so the person does not afterward feel guilty or anxious.

Does such aggressing reduce later aggression? In some experiments, aggressing has led to heightened aggression. Ebbe Ebbesen and his co-researchers (1975) interviewed 100 engineers and technicians shortly after they were angered by layoff notices. Some were asked questions that gave them an opportunity to express hostility against their employer or supervisor—for example, "What instances can you think of where the company has not been fair with you?" Afterward, they answered a questionnaire assessing attitudes toward the company and the supervisor. Did the previous opportunity to "vent" or "drain off" their hostility reduce it? To the contrary, their hostility increased. Expressing hostility bred more hostility.

Sound familiar? Recall from Chapter 4 that cruel acts beget cruel attitudes. Furthermore, as we noted in analyzing Stanley Milgram's obedience experiments, little aggressive acts can breed their own justification. People derogate their victims, rationalizing further aggression. Even if retaliation sometimes (in the short run) reduces tension, in the long run it reduces inhibitions.

Should we therefore bottle up anger and aggressive urges? Silent sulking is hardly more effective, because it allows us to continue reciting our grievances as we conduct conversations in our head. Fortunately, there are nonaggressive ways to express our feelings and to inform others how their behavior affects us. Across cultures, those who reframe accusatory "you" messages as "I" messages— "I'm angry," or "When you talk like that I feel irritated"—communicate their feelings in a way that better enables the other person to make a positive response (Kubany & others, 1995). We can be assertive without being aggressive.

> "He who gives way to violent gestures will increase his rage."
>
> Charles Darwin, *The Expression of Emotion in Man and Animals*, 1872

focus

A clinical researcher looks at catharsis

John Bradshaw, in his best-seller *Homecoming: Reclaiming and Championing Your Inner Child*, details several of his imaginative techniques: asking forgiveness of your inner child, divorcing your parent and finding a new one, like Jesus, stroking your inner child, writing your childhood history. These techniques go by the name *catharsis*, that is, emotional engagement in past trauma-laden events. Catharsis is magnificent to experience and impressive to behold. Weeping, raging at parents long dead, hugging the wounded little boy who was once you are all stirring. You have to be made of stone not to be moved to tears. For hours afterward, you may feel cleansed and at peace—perhaps for the first time in years. Awakening, beginning again, and new departures all beckon.

Catharsis, as a therapeutic technique, has been around for more than a hundred years. It used to be a mainstay of psychoanalytic treatment, but no longer. Its main appeal is its afterglow. Its main drawback is that there is no evidence that it works. When you measure how much people like doing it, you hear high praise. When you measure whether anything changes, catharsis fares badly.

From Martin E. P. Seligman, *What You Can Change and What You Can't: The Complete Guide to Successful Self-improvement*. New York: Knopf, 1994, pp. 238–239.

A social learning approach

If aggressive behavior is learned, then there is hope for its control. Let us briefly review factors that influence aggression and speculate how to counteract them.

Aversive experiences such as frustrated expectations and personal attacks predispose hostile aggression. So it is wise to refrain from planting false, unreachable expectations in people's minds. Anticipated rewards and costs influence instrumental aggression. This suggests that we should reward cooperative, nonaggressive behavior. In experiments, children become less aggressive when caregivers ignore their aggressive behavior and reinforce their nonaggressive behavior (Hamblin & others, 1969). Punishing the aggressor is less consistently effective. Threatened punishment deters aggression only under ideal conditions—when the punishment is strong, prompt, and sure; when it is combined with reward for the desired behavior; and when the recipient is not angry (R. A. Baron, 1977). Lacking such deterence, aggression may erupt. This was evident in 1969 when the Montreal police force went on a 16-hour strike, and in 1992 when helicopter TV coverage of the Los Angeles riot showed areas abandoned by police. In both cases, looting and destruction erupted—until the police returned.

But there are limits to punishment's effectiveness. Most mortal aggression is impulsive, hot aggression—the result of an argument, an insult, or an attack. Thus, we must *prevent* aggression before it happens. We must teach nonaggressive conflict-resolution strategies. If only mortal aggression were cool and instrumental, we could hope that waiting till it happens and severely punishing the criminal afterward would deter such acts. In that world, states that impose the death penalty might have a lower murder rate than states without the death penalty. But in our world of hot homicide, that is not so (Costanzo, 1998).

Physical punishment can also have negative side effects. Punishment is aversive stimulation; it models the behavior it seeks to prevent. And it is coercive (recall that we seldom internalize actions coerced with strong external justifications). These are reasons violent teenagers and child-abusing parents so often come from homes where discipline took the form of harsh physical punishment.

To foster a gentler world we could model and reward sensitivity and cooperation from an early age, perhaps by training parents how to discipline without violence. Training programs encourage parents to reinforce desirable behaviors and to frame statements positively ("When you finish cleaning your room you can go play," rather than "If you don't clean your room, you're grounded.") One "aggression-replacement program" has reduced re-arrest rates of juvenile offenders and gang members by teaching the youths and their parents communication skills, training them to control anger, and raising their level of moral reasoning (Goldstein & Glick, 1994).

If observing aggressive models lowers inhibitions and elicits imitation, then we might also reduce brutal, dehumanizing portrayals in films and on television—steps comparable to those already taken to reduce racist and sexist portrayals. We can also inoculate children against the effects of media violence. Despairing that the TV networks would ever "face the facts and change their programming," Eron and Huesmann (1984) taught 170 children that television portrays the world unrealistically, that aggression is less common and effective than TV suggests, and that aggressive behavior is undesirable. (Drawing upon attitude research, Eron and Huesmann encouraged children to draw these inferences themselves and to attribute their expressed criticisms of television to their own convictions.) When restudied two years later, these children were less influenced by TV violence than were untrained children.

Aggressive stimuli also trigger aggression. This suggests reducing the availability of weapons such as handguns. Jamaica in 1974 implemented a sweeping anticrime program that included strict gun control and censorship of gun scenes from television and movies (Diener & Crandall, 1979). In the following year, robberies dropped 25 percent, nonfatal shootings 37 percent. In Sweden, the toy industry has discontinued the sale of war toys. The Swedish Information Service (1980) states the national attitude: "Playing at war means learning to settle disputes by violent means."

Suggestions such as these can help us minimize aggression. But given the complexity of aggression's causes and the difficulty of controlling them, who can feel the optimism expressed by Andrew Carnegie's forecast that in the twentieth century, "To kill a man will be considered as disgusting as we in this day consider it disgusting to eat one." Since Carnegie uttered those words in 1900, some 200 million human beings have been killed. It is a sad irony that although today we understand human aggression better than ever before, humanity's inhumanity is hardly diminished.

Summing up   How can we minimize aggression? Contrary to the catharsis hypothesis, expressing aggression more often breeds than reduces further aggression. The social learning approach suggests controlling aggression by counteracting the factors that provoke it—by reducing aversive stimulation, by rewarding and modeling nonaggression, and by eliciting reactions incompatible with aggression.

℞ Personal Postscript: Reforming a violent culture

Living near Toronto, I am often shocked when I watch the news.

Within the last month, I have seen stories on a shooting in one local high school; the details of a gruesome murder in which a father cut his six-year-old daughter into pieces; the dangers of a serial rapist who attacks women at a public park; and the senseless stabbing of a man in an upscale neighborhood because he would not give three young robbers his wallet.

All this violence is in stark contrast to my experience growing up in a quiet small town with very little crime. My parents did not even having working locks on their doors. I often wonder: "What will be the effect of all this crime and violence on my children?" Will they be less shocked by violence than I am? The research covered in this chapter suggests they probably will be. Will they be more likely to commit violent crimes? I certainly hope not, but again they might. Will they be more scared of being a victim of crime? It seems likely.

As we are exposed to more and more crime, it seems that people become more and more concerned with personal safety. In my neighborhood, the trend is to install home security systems—so far my small town roots have helped me resist. People are so eager to protect themselves that they are ready to implement strong measures to stop crime, including:

- Building more prisons
- Imposing long and harsh sentences to deter crimes
- Make sure that juveniles are tried for crimes and sentenced as adults

But these strategies are likely to have only limited effects. What matters more than a punishment's severity is its certainty. As one review of the evidence on causes of violent crime (National Research Council, 1993) reports a 50 percent increase in the probability of apprehension and incarceration reduces subsequent crime twice as much as does doubling incarceration duration. Even so, one high-level law enforcement officer (Freeh, 1993) is skeptical that tougher or swifter punishment is the ultimate answer: "The frightening level of lawlessness which has come upon us like a plague is more than a law enforcement problem. The crime and disorder which flow from hopeless poverty, unloved children, and drug abuse, can't be solved merely by bottomless prisons, mandatory sentencing, and more police." Reacting to crime after it happens is the social equivalent of band-aids on cancer.

An alternative approach is suggested by a story about the rescue of a drowning person from a rushing river. Having successfully administered first aid, the rescuer spots another struggling person and pulls her out, too. After a half dozen repetitions, the rescuer suddenly turns and starts running away while the river sweeps yet another floundering person into view. "Aren't you going to rescue that fellow?" asks a bystander. "Heck no," the rescuer shouts. "I'm going upstream to find out what's pushing all these people in."

To be sure, we need police, prisons, and social workers, all of whom help us deal with the social pathologies that plague us. It's fine to swat the mosquitoes, but better if we can drain the swamps. Social psychology suggests that we can begin to address these problems by creating new situations and a new environment for people to live in by revisioning our culture, challenging the social toxins that corrupt youth, and renewing the moral roots of character.

chapter 11

Attraction and Intimacy: Liking and Loving Others

need to belong
a motivation to bond with others in relationships that provide ongoing, positive interactions

O ur lifelong dependence on one another puts relationships at the core of our existence. In the beginning there was attraction—the attraction between a particular man and a particular woman to which we each owe our existence. As what Aristotle called "the social animal," we from birth have an intense **need to belong**—to connect with others in enduring, close relationships.

Social psychologists Roy Baumeister and Mark Leary (1995) illustrate the power of social attractions bred by our need to belong.

- For our ancestors, mutual attachments enabled group survival. When hunting game or erecting shelter, ten hands were better than two.

- For a woman and a man, the bonds of love lead to children, whose survival chances are boosted by the nurturing of two bonded parents who support one another.
- For children and their caregivers, social attachments enhance survival. Unexplainably separated from one another, parent and toddler may each panic, until reunited in tight embrace.
- For people everywhere, actual and hoped-for close relationships preoccupy thinking and color emotions. Finding a supportive soul mate in whom we can confide, we feel accepted and prized as we are. Falling in love, we feel irrepressible joy. Longing for acceptance and love, we spend billions on cosmetics, clothes, and diets.
- For the jilted, the widowed, and the sojourner in a strange place, the loss of social bonds triggers pain, anger, or withdrawal. Reared under extreme neglect or in institutions without belonging to anybody, children become pathetic, anxious creatures. Losing a soul-mate relationship, adults feel jealous, lonely, distraught, or bereaved. Exiled, imprisoned, or in solitary confinement, people ache for their own people and places. We are, indeed, social animals. We need to belong. And as Module A confirms, when we do belong—when we feel supported by close, intimate relationships—we tend to be healthier and happier.

Friendships

What factors nurture liking and loving? Let's start with those that help initiate attraction: proximity, physical attractiveness, similarity, and feeling liked.

The architecture of friendship. People who live in close proximity, as do these college students, are more likely to become good friends.

What predisposes one person to like, or to love, another? Few questions about human nature arouse greater interest. The ways affections flourish and fade form the stuff and fluff of soap operas, popular music, novels, and much of our everyday conversation. Long before I knew there was such a field as social psychology, I had memorized Dale Carnegie's recipe for *How to Win Friends and Influence People.*

So much has been written about liking and loving that almost every conceivable explanation—and its opposite—has been already proposed. For most people—for you—what factors nurture liking and loving? Does absence make the heart grow fonder? Or is someone who is out of sight also out of mind? Is it likes that attract? Or opposites? How much do good looks matter? What has fostered your close relationships? Let's start with those factors that help a friendship begin and then consider those that sustain and deepen a relationship.

> "I cannot tell how my ankles bend, nor whence the cause of my faintest wish, Nor the cause of the friendship I emit, nor the cause of the friendship I take again."
>
> Walt Whitman, *Song of Myself,* 1855

Proximity

One of the most powerful predictors of whether any two people are friends is sheer **proximity**. Proximity can also breed hostility; most assaults and murders involve people living close together. But far more often, proximity kindles liking. Though it may seem trivial to those pondering the mysterious origins of romantic love, sociologists have found that most people marry someone who lives in the same neighborhood, or works at the same company or job, or sits in the same class (Bossard, 1932; Burr, 1973; Clarke, 1952; Katz & Hill, 1958). Look around. If you marry, it will likely be to someone who has lived or worked or studied within walking distance.

proximity
geographical nearness. Proximity (more precisely, "functional distance") powerfully predicts liking.

Close relationships with friends and family contribute to health and happiness.

Interaction

Actually, it is not geographical distance that is critical but "functional distance"—how often people's paths cross. We frequently become friends with those who use the same entrances, parking lots, and recreation areas. Randomly assigned university roommates, who of course can hardly avoid frequent interaction, are far more likely to become good friends than enemies (Newcomb, 1961). Such interaction enables people to explore their similarities, to sense one another's liking, and to perceive themselves as a social unit (Arkin & Burger, 1980).

At the university where I teach, the men and women once lived on opposite sides of the campus. They understandably bemoaned the lack of cross-sex friendships. Now that they occupy different areas of the same dormitories and share common sidewalks, lounges, and laundry facilities, cross-sex friendships are far more frequent. So if you're new in town and want to make friends, try to get an apartment near the mailboxes, an office desk near the coffee pot, a parking spot near the main buildings. Such is the architecture of friendship.

The chance nature of such contacts helps explain a surprising finding. Consider: If you had an identical twin who became engaged to someone, wouldn't you (being in so many ways similar to your twin) expect to share your twin's attraction to this person? But no, report researchers David Lykken and Auke Tellegen (1993); only half of identical twins recall really liking their twin's selection, and only 5 percent said "I could have fallen for my twin's fiancée." Romantic love is often rather like ducklings' imprinting, surmised Lykken and Tellegen. With repeated exposure to someone, our infatuation may fix upon almost anyone who has roughly similar characteristics and who reciprocates our affection.

But why does proximity breed liking? One factor is availability; obviously there are fewer opportunities to get to know someone who attends a different school or lives in another town. But there is more to it than that. Most people like their roommates, or those one door away, better than those two doors away. Those just a few doors away, or even a floor below, hardly live at an inconvenient distance. Moreover, those close by are potential enemies as well as friends. So why does proximity encourage affection more often than animosity?

"When I'm not near the one I love, I love the one I'm near."

E. Y. Harburg, *Finian's Rainbow,* London: Chappell Music, 1947

Anticipation of interaction

Already we have noted one answer: Proximity enables people to discover commonalities and exchange rewards. What is more, merely *anticipating* interaction boosts liking. John Darley and Ellen Berscheid (1967) discovered this when they gave women ambiguous information about two other women, one of whom they expected to talk with intimately. Asked how much they liked each one, the women preferred the person they expected to meet. Expecting to date someone similarly boosts liking (Berscheid & others, 1976).

The phenomenon is adaptive. Anticipatory liking—expecting that someone will be pleasant and compatible—increases the chance of a rewarding relationship (Knight & Vallacher, 1981; Klein & Kunda, 1992; Miller & Marks, 1982). And how good that we are biased to like those we often see. Our lives are filled with relationships with people whom we may not have chosen but with whom we need to have continuing interactions—roommates, grandparents, teachers, classmates, co-workers. Liking such people is surely conducive to better relationships with them, which in turn makes for happier, more productive living.

Mere exposure

Proximity leads to liking for yet another reason: More than 200 experiments reveal that, contrary to the old proverb, familiarity does not breed contempt. Rather it breeds fondness (Bornstein, 1989). **Mere exposure** to all sorts of novel stimuli—nonsense syllables, Chinese characters, musical selections, faces— boosts people's ratings of them. Do the supposed Turkish words *nansoma, saricik,* and *afworbu* mean something better or something worse than the words *iktitaf, biwojni,* and *kadirga*? Students tested by Robert Zajonc (1968, 1970) preferred whichever of these words they had seen most frequently. The more times they had seen a meaningless word or a Chinese ideograph, the more likely they were to say it meant something good (Figure 11–1). This, I have found, makes a nifty class demonstration. Periodically flash certain nonsense words on a screen. By the end of the semester students will rate those "words" more positively than other nonsense words they have never before seen.

Or consider this: What are your favorite letters of the alphabet? People of differing nationalities, languages, and ages prefer the letters appearing in their own name and those that frequently appear in their own language (Hoorens & others, 1990, 1993; Kitayama & Karasawa, 1997; Nuttin, 1987). French students rate capital *W*, the least frequent letter in French, as their least favorite letter. Japanese students not only prefer letters from their name, but numbers corresponding to their birthdate.

The mere-exposure effect violates the commonsense prediction of *decreased* interest in repeatedly heard music or tasted foods (Kahneman & Snell, 1992). But unless the repetitions are incessant ("Even the best song becomes tiresome if heard too often," says a Korean proverb), liking usually increases. When completed in 1889, the Eiffel Tower in Paris was mocked as grotesque (Harrison, 1977). Today it is the beloved symbol of Paris. Such changes make one wonder about initial reactions to new things. Do visitors to the Louvre in Paris really adore the *Mona Lisa*, or are they simply delighted to find a familiar face? It might be both: To know her is to like her.

Zajonc and his co-workers, William Kunst-Wilson and Richard Moreland, reported that exposure leads to liking even when people don't know that they have been exposed (Kunst-Wilson & Zajonc, 1980; Moreland & Zajonc, 1977; Wilson, 1979). In fact, mere exposure has an even stronger effect when people perceive stimuli without awareness (Bornstein & D'Agostino, 1992). In one experiment, women students using head phones listened in one ear to a prose passage. They also repeated the words out loud and compared them to a written version to check for errors. Meanwhile, brief, novel melodies played in the other ear. This procedure focused attention on the verbal material and away from the tunes. Later, when the women heard the tunes interspersed among similar ones not previously played, they did not recognize them. Nevertheless, they *liked best* the tunes they had previously heard. In another experiment, people were shown a series of geometric figures, one at a time, each for a millisecond—long enough to perceive only a flash of light. Although later they were unable to recognize the figures they had been shown (they had no explicit memory of them), they nevertheless *liked* them best (indicating a nonconscious implicit memory).

Note that in both experiments conscious judgments about the stimuli were a far less reliable clue to what people had heard or seen than were instant feelings. You can probably recall immediately liking or disliking something or

mere-exposure effect
the tendency for novel stimuli to be liked more or rated more positively after the rater has been repeatedly exposed to them

" 'Tis strange—but true; for truth is always strange— Stranger than fiction."

Lord Byron, *Don Juan*

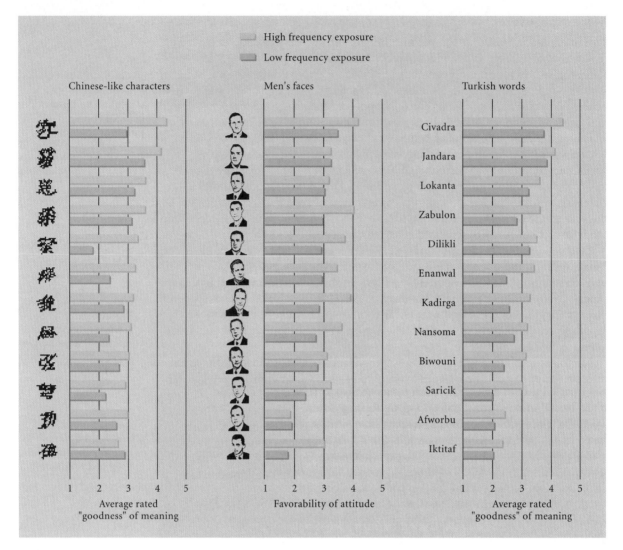

figure 11–1

The mere-exposure effect.

Students rated stimuli more positively after being shown them repeatedly. (From Zajonc, 1968.)

someone without consciously knowing why. Zajonc (1980) argues that emotions are often more instantaneous, more primitive than thinking. Fearful or prejudicial feelings are not always expressions of stereotyped beliefs; sometimes the beliefs arise later as justifications for intuitive feelings. The mere exposure effect has "enormous adaptive significance," notes Zajonc (1998). It is a "hard-wired" phenomenon that predisposes our attractions and our attachments, and that helped our ancestors categorize things and people as either familiar and safe, or unfamiliar and possibly dangerous. Of course, the phenomenon's darker side is our wariness of the unfamiliar—which may explain the primitive, automatic prejudice people often feel when confronting those who are different.

The mere-exposure effect colors our evaluations of others: Familiar people we like more (Swap, 1977). We even like ourselves better when we are the way we're used to seeing ourselves. In a delightful experiment, Theodore Mita, Marshall Dermer, and Jeffrey Knight (1977) photographed women

The mere exposure effect. If he is like most of us, Canadian Prime Minister Jean Chrétien may prefer his familiar mirror-image (left), which he sees each morning while brushing his teeth, to his actual image (right).

students and later showed each one her actual picture along with a mirror image of it. Asked which picture they liked better, most preferred the mirror image—the image they were used to seeing. (No wonder our photographs never look quite right.) When close friends of the subjects were shown the same two pictures, they preferred the true picture—the image *they* were used to seeing.

Advertisers and politicians exploit this phenomenon. When people have no strong feelings about a product or a candidate, repetition alone can increase sales or votes (McCullough & Ostrom, 1974; Winter, 1973). After endless repetition of a commercial, shoppers often have an unthinking, automatic, favorable response to the product. If candidates are relatively unknown, those with the most media exposure usually win (Patterson, 1980; Schaffner & others, 1981). Political strategists who understand the mere-exposure effect have replaced reasoned argument with brief ads that hammer home a candidate's name and sound-bite message.

The respected Washington state Supreme Court Chief Justice Keith Callow learned this lesson in 1990 when he lost an election to a nominal opponent, Charles Johnson. Johnson, an unknown attorney who handled minor criminal cases and divorces, filed for the seat on the principle that judges "need to be challenged." Neither man campaigned, and the media ignored the race. On election day the two candidates' names appeared without any identification— just one name next to the other. The result: a 53 percent to 47 percent Johnson victory. "There are a lot more Johnsons out there than Callows," offered the ousted judge afterward to a stunned legal community. Indeed, one local newspaper counted 27 Charlie Johnsons in the phonebook. There was Charles Johnson, a county judge, and in a neighboring city there was a television anchorman Charles Johnson, whose broadcasts were seen throughout the area. Forced to choose between two unknown names, many voters preferred the comfortable, familiar name of Charlie Johnson.

Physical attractiveness

"We should look to
the mind, and not
to the outward
appearances."

Aesop, *Fables*

What do (or did) you look for in a potential date? Sincerity? Good looks? Character? Conversational ability? Sophisticated, intelligent people are unconcerned with such superficial qualities as good looks; they know "beauty is only skin deep" and "you can't judge a book by its cover." At least they know that's how they *ought* to feel. As Cicero counseled, "resist appearance."

The belief that looks matter little may be another instance of our denying real influences upon us, for there is now a file cabinet full of research studies showing that appearance *does* matter. The consistency and pervasiveness of this effect is disconcerting. Good looks are a great asset.

Attractiveness and dating

"Personal beauty
is a greater
recommendation
than any letter of
introduction."

Aristotle, *Diogenes Laertius*

Like it or not, a young woman's physical attractiveness is a moderately good predictor of how frequently she dates. A young man's attractiveness is slightly less a predictor of how frequently he dates (Berscheid & others, 1971; Krebs & Adinolfi, 1975; Reis & others, 1980, 1982; Walster & others, 1966). Does this imply, as many have surmised, that women are better at following Cicero's advice? Or does it merely reflect the fact that men more often do the inviting? If women were to indicate their preferences among various men, would looks be as important to them as to men? Philosopher Bertrand Russell (1930, p. 139) thought not: "On the whole women tend to love men for their character while men tend to love women for their appearance."

To see whether indeed men are more influenced by looks, researchers have provided male and female students with various pieces of information about someone of the other sex, including a picture of the person. Or they have briefly introduced a man and a woman and later asked each about

Attractiveness and dating. For video dating customers, looks are part of what is offered and sought.

their interest in dating the other. In such experiments, men do put somewhat more value on opposite-sex physical attractiveness (Feingold, 1990, 1991; Sprecher & others, 1994). Perhaps sensing this, women worry more about their appearance and constitute nearly 90 percent of cosmetic surgery patients (Crowley, 1996; Dion & others, 1990). But women, too, respond to a man's looks.

In one ambitious study, Elaine Hatfield and her co-workers (1966) matched 752 first-year students for a "Welcome Week" computer dance. The researchers gave each student personality and aptitude tests but then matched the couples randomly. On the night of the dance, the couples danced and talked for two and one-half hours and then took a brief intermission to evaluate their dates. How well did the personality and aptitude tests predict attraction? Did people like someone better who was high in self-esteem, or low in anxiety, or different from themselves in outgoingness? The researchers examined a long list of possibilities. But so far as they could determine, only one thing mattered: how physically attractive the person was. The more attractive a woman was, the more he liked her and wanted to date her again. And the more attractive the man was, the more she liked him and wanted to date him again. Pretty pleases.

The matching phenomenon

Not everyone can end up paired with someone stunningly attractive. So how do people pair off? Judging from research by Bernard Murstein (1986) and others, they pair off with people who are about as attractive as they are. Several studies have found a strong correspondence between the attractiveness of husbands and wives, of dating partners, and even of those within particular fraternities (Feingold, 1988). People tend to select as friends and especially to marry those who are a "good match" not only to their level of intelligence but also to their level of attractiveness.

Experiments confirm this **matching phenomenon**. When choosing whom to approach, knowing the other is free to say yes or no, people usually approach someone whose attractiveness roughly matches their own (Berscheid & others, 1971; Huston, 1973; Stroebe & others, 1971). Good physical matches may also be conducive to good relationships, as Gregory White (1980) found in a study of dating couples. Those who were most similar in physical attractiveness were most likely, nine months later, to have fallen more deeply in love.

So who might we expect to be most closely matched for attractiveness—married couples or couples casually dating? White found, as have other researchers, that married couples are better matched.

Perhaps this research prompts you to think of happy couples who are not equally attractive. In such cases, the less attractive person often has compensating qualities. Each partner brings assets to the social marketplace, and the value of the respective assets creates an equitable match. Personal advertisements exhibit this exchange of assets (Cicerello & Sheehan, 1995; Koestner & Wheeler, 1988; Rajecki & others, 1991). Men typically offer wealth or status and seek youth and attractiveness; women more often do the reverse: "Attractive, bright woman, 26, slender, seeks warm, professional male." Moreover, men who advertise their income and education, and women who advertise their youth and looks, receive more responses to their ads (Baize & Schroeder, 1995). The

"If you would marry wisely, marry your equal."

Ovid, 43 B.C.–17 A.D.

matching phenomenon
the tendency for men and women to choose as partners those who are a "good match" in attractiveness and other traits

"Love is often nothing but a favorable exchange between two people who get the most of what they can expect, considering their value on the personality market."

Erich Fromm, *The Sane Society*, 1955

asset-matching process helps explain why beautiful young women often marry older men of higher social status (Elder, 1969).

The physical-attractiveness stereotype

Does the attractiveness effect spring entirely from sexual attractiveness? Clearly not, as Vicky Houston and Ray Bull (1994) discovered when they used a make-up artist to give an accomplice an apparently scarred, bruised, or birth-marked face. When riding on a Glasgow commuter rail line, people of *both* sexes avoided sitting next to the accomplice when she appeared facially disfigured. Moreover, much as adults are biased toward attractive adults, young children are biased toward attractive children (Dion, 1973; Dion & Berscheid, 1974; Langlois & Stephan, 1981). To judge from how long they gaze at someone, even babies prefer attractive faces (Langlois & others, 1987).

Adults show a similar bias when judging children. Margaret Clifford and Elaine Hatfield (Clifford & Walster, 1973) gave fifth-grade teachers identical information about a boy or girl but with the photograph of an attractive or unattractive child attached. The teachers perceived the attractive child as more intelligent and successful in school. Think of yourself as a playground supervisor having to discipline an unruly child. Might you, like the women studied by Karen Dion (1972), show less warmth and tact to an unattractive child? The sad truth is that most of us assume what we might call a "Bart Simpson effect"— that homely children are less able and socially competent than their beautiful peers.

What is more, we assume that beautiful people possess certain desirable traits. Other things being equal, we guess beautiful people are happier, sexually warmer, and more outgoing, intelligent, and successful, though not more honest or concerned for others (Eagly & others, 1991; Feingold, 1992b; Jackson & others, 1995). In collectivist Korea, where concern for others and integrity are valued above assertiveness, those are traits people associate with attractiveness (Wheeler & Kim, 1997). Added together, the findings define a **physical-attractiveness stereotype:** *What is beautiful is good.* Children learn the stereotype quite early. Snow White and Cinderella are beautiful—and kind. The witch and the stepsisters are ugly—and wicked. As one kindergarten girl put it when asked what it means to be pretty, "It's like to be a princess. Everybody loves you" (Dion, 1979). Think Princess Diana.

If physical attractiveness is this important, then permanently changing people's attractiveness should change the way others react to them. But is it ethical to alter someone's looks? Such manipulations are performed millions of times a year by plastic surgeons and orthodontists. With teeth and nose straightened, hair replaced and dyed, face lifted, fat liposuctioned, and (for more than one million American women) breasts enlarged, can a self-dissatisfied person now find happiness?

To examine the effect of such alterations, Michael Kalick (1977) had students rate their impressions of eight women based on profile photographs taken before or after cosmetic surgery. Not only did they judge the women as more physically attractive after the surgery but also as kinder, more sensitive, more sexually warm and responsive, more likeable, and so on. Ellen Berscheid (1981) noted that although such cosmetic improvements can boost self-image, they can also be temporarily disturbing:

physical-attractiveness stereotype
the presumption that physically attractive people possess other socially desirable traits as well: what is beautiful is good

Most of us—at least those of us who have *not* experienced swift alterations of our physical appearance—can continue to believe that our physical attractiveness level plays a minor role in how we are treated by others. It is harder, however, for those who have actually experienced swift changes in appearance to continue to deny and to minimize the influence of physical attractiveness in their own lives—and the fact of it may be disturbing, even when the changes are for the better.

> "Even virtue is fairer in a fair body."
>
> Virgil, *Aeneid*

To say that attractiveness is important, other things being equal, is not to say that physical appearance always outranks other qualities. Attractiveness probably most affects first impressions. But first impressions are important—and are becoming more so as societies become increasingly mobile and urbanized and as contacts with people become more fleeting (Berscheid, 1981).

Though interviewers may deny it, attractiveness and grooming affect first impressions in job interviews (Cash & Janda, 1984; Mack & Rainey, 1990; Marvelle & Green, 1980). This helps explain why attractive people have more prestigious jobs and make more money (Umberson & Hughes, 1987). Patricia Roszell and her colleagues (1990) looked at the attractiveness of a national sample of Canadians whom interviewers had rated on a 1 (homely) to 5 (strikingly attractive) scale. They found that for each additional scale unit of rated attractiveness, people earned, on average, an additional $1,988 annually. Irene Hanson Frieze and her associates (1991) did the same analysis with 737 MBA graduates after rating them on a similar 1 to 5 scale using student picture book photos. For each additional scale unit of rated attractiveness, men earned an added $2,600 and women earned an added $2,150.

Do beautiful people indeed have desirable traits? Or was Leo Tolstoy correct when he wrote that it's "a strange illusion . . . to suppose that beauty is goodness"? There is some truth to the stereotype. Attractive children and young adults are somewhat more relaxed and socially polished (Feingold, 1992b). William Goldman and Philip Lewis (1977) demonstrated this by having 60 men call and talk for five minutes with each of three women students. Afterward the men and women rated their unseen telephone partners who happened to be most attractive as somewhat more socially skillful and likeable. Physically attractive individuals tend also to be more popular, more outgoing, and more gender-typed (more traditionally masculine if male, more feminine if female) (Langlois & others, 1996).

These small average differences between attractive and unattractive people probably result from self-fulfilling prophecies. Attractive people are valued and favored, and so many develop more social self-confidence. (Recall from Chapter 2 an experiment in which men evoked a warm response from unseen women they *thought* were attractive.) By this analysis, what's crucial to your social skill is not how you look but how people treat you and how you feel about yourself—whether you accept yourself, like yourself, feel comfortable with yourself.

Despite all the advantages of being beautiful, attraction researchers Elaine Hatfield and Susan Sprecher (1986) report there is also an ugly truth about beauty. Exceptionally attractive people may suffer unwelcome sexual advances and resentment from those of their own sex. They may be unsure whether others are responding to their performance inner qualities or just to their looks, which in time will fade (Satterfield & Muehlenhard, 1997). Moreover, if they can

behind the scenes

I vividly remember the afternoon I began to appreciate the far-reaching implications of physical attractiveness. Graduate student Karen Dion (now a professor at the University of Toronto) learned that some researchers at our Institute of Child Development had collected popularity ratings from nursery school children and taken a photo of each child. Although teachers and caregivers of children had persuaded us that "all children are beautiful" and no physical-attractiveness discriminations could be made, Dion suggested we instruct some people to rate each child's looks and correlate these with popularity. After doing so, we realized our long shot had hit home: Attractive children were popular children. Indeed, the effect was far more potent than we and others had assumed, with a host of implications that investigators are still tracing.

Ellen Berscheid
University of Minnesota

coast on their looks, they may be less motivated to develop themselves in other ways. Ellen Berscheid wonders whether we might still be lighting our houses with candles if Charles Steinmetz, the homely and exceptionally short genius of electricity, had instead been subjected to the social enticements experienced by a Tom Cruise.

Who is attractive?

I have described attractiveness as if it were an objective quality like height, which some people have more of, some less. Strictly speaking, attractiveness is whatever the people of any given place and time find attractive. This, of course, varies. The beauty standards by which Miss Universe is judged hardly apply to the whole planet. Even in a given place and time, people (fortunately) disagree about who's attractive (Morse & Gruzen, 1976).

What makes for an attractive face depends somewhat on the person's sex. Consistent with men historically having greater social power, people judge women more attractive if they have "baby-faced" features, such as large eyes, that suggest nondominance (Cunningham, 1986; Keating, 1985). Men seem more attractive when their faces—and their behaviors—suggest maturity and dominance (Sadalla & others, 1987). Curiously, among homosexuals these preferences tend to reverse: Many gay males prefer baby-faced males, and many lesbians seem not to prefer baby-faced females. With this exception, report Michael Cunningham and colleagues (1995), people across the world show remarkable agreement about the features of an ideal male face and female face when judging any ethnic group.

For example, "attractive" facial and bodily features do not deviate too drastically from average (Beck & others, 1976; Graziano & others, 1978; Symons, 1981). People perceive noses, legs, or statures that are not unusually large or small as relatively attractive. Judith Langlois and Lori Roggman (1990, 1994) showed this by digitizing the faces of up to 32 university students and using a computer to average them. Students judged the composite faces as more appealing than 96 percent of the individual faces (Figure 11–2). Computer aver-

aged faces tend also to be perfectly symmetrical—another characteristic of strikingly attractive people (Gangestad & Thornhill, 1997; Grammer & Thornhill, 1994; Shackelford & Larsen, 1997). So in some respects, perfectly average is quite attractive.

Yet perfectly average isn't maximally attractive. Before I explain, make a quick gut-level judgment: Which of the faces in Figure 11–3 is most attractive?

Most people perceive the face at left—a computer composite of 60 Caucasian females created by David Perrett, K. A. May, and S. Yoshikawa (1994)—as attractive. But they perceive the middle face—a composite of the 15 females rated most attractive—as even better looking. And they perceive the face on the right, which exaggerates by 50 percent the subtle differences between the first two faces, as still more attractive. When the researchers replicated the procedure with computer composites of the faces of 326 Japanese high school girls, they got the same result: Most people (whether in Japan or Britain) judged the average of attractive faces as more attractive than the average of the larger sample though less attractive than a face that exaggerated the attractive features. Perfectly average is quite attractive, but even more attractive is a modest caricature of attractive features.

Evolution and attraction.   Psychologists working from the evolutionary perspective explain these gender differences in terms of reproductive strategy (Chapter 5). They assume that beauty signals biologically important information: health, youth, and fertility. Over time, men who preferred fertile-looking women outreproduced those who were as happy to mate with prepubescent or postmenopausal females. And they assume evolution predisposes women to favor male traits that signify an ability to provide and protect resources. That, David Buss (1989) believes, explains why the males he studied in 37 cultures— from Australia to Zambia—did indeed prefer female characteristics that signify reproductive capacity. And it explains why physically attractive females tend to marry high-status males and why men compete with such determination to achieve fame and fortune.

figure 11–2

Is beauty merely in the eye of the beholder?

Which of these faces is most attractive? People everywhere agree that the symmetrical face on the right (a composite of 32 male faces) is better looking, note Judith Langlois and her collaborators (1996). To evolutionary psychologists, such agreement suggests some universal standards of beauty rooted in our ancestral history.

  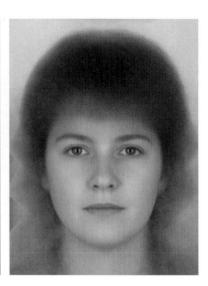

figure 11–3

Which of these computer-generated faces is most attractive?

Evolutionary psychologists have also explored men's and women's response to other cues to reproductive success:

- Judging from yesterday's Stone Age figurines to today's centerfolds and beauty pageant winners, men everywhere have felt most attracted to women whose waists are 30 percent narrower than their hips—a shape associated with peak sexual fertility (Singh, 1993, 1995a; Singh & Young, 1995). Circumstances that reduce a woman's fertility—malnutrition, pregnancy, menopause—also change her shape.

- When judging males as potential marriage partners, women, too, prefer a waist-to-hip ratio suggesting health and vigor. This makes evolutionary sense, notes Jared Diamond (1996): A muscular hunk was more likely than a scrawny fellow to gather food, build houses, and defeat rivals. But today's women prefer even more those with high incomes (Singh, 1995b).

- Men are especially prone to sexual jealousy, which motivates their enforcing their mate's faithfulness and enhancing the likelihood that the children they invest in are their own. This, David Buss (1996) believes, helps explain why feminists rightly discern that men everywhere are concerned with controlling women's sexuality and terribly upset with their sexual infidelity, while women are often more upset with their mate's *emotional* infidelity:

  > We come from a long and unbroken line of ancestral fathers who succeeded in obtaining mates, preventing their infidelity, and providing enough benefits (or inflicting enough deterrent costs) to keep them from leaving. We also come from a long line of ancestral mothers who successfully secured investing mates, acted to prevent the siphoning of a mate's resources to other women, and granted sexual access to men who provided beneficial resources. (p. 309)

- Men and women worldwide seek and display the qualities that our ancestral history promises will bring the best reproductive results. Thus, women predominate in plastic surgeons' waiting rooms and around cosmetic counters, and men tend to be more preoccupied with accumulating and exhibiting resources (Schmitt & Buss, 1996).

So in every culture the beauty business is big business that shows no signs of abating. We are, evolutionary psychologists suggest, driven by primal attractions. Like eating and breathing, attraction and mating are too important to leave to the whims of culture.

The contrast effect.   Although our mating psychology has biological wisdom, attraction is not all hard-wired. What's attractive to you also depends on your comparison standards. Douglas Kenrick and Sara Gutierres (1980) had male confederates interrupt men in their dormitory rooms and explain, "We have a friend coming to town this week and we want to fix him up with a date, but we can't decide whether to fix him up with her or not, so we decided to conduct a survey. . . . We want you to give us your vote on how attractive you think she is . . . on a scale of 1 to 7." Shown a picture of an average young woman, those who had just been watching three beautiful women on television's *Charlie's Angels* rated her less attractive than those who hadn't.

Laboratory experiments confirm this "contrast effect." To men who have recently been gazing at centerfolds, average women—or even their own wives—seem less attractive (Kenrick & others, 1989). Viewing pornographic films simulating passionate sex similarly decreases satisfaction with one's own partner (Zillmann, 1989). Being sexually aroused may *temporarily* make a person of the other sex seem more attractive. But the lingering effect of exposure to perfect "10s," or of unrealistic sexual depictions, is to make one's own partner seem less appealing—more like a "6" than an "8." It works the same way with our self-perceptions. After viewing a superattractive person of the same sex, people *feel* less attractive than after viewing a homely person (Brown & others, 1992; Thornton & Moore, 1993).

The attractiveness of those we love.   Let's conclude our discussion of attractiveness on an upbeat note. First, a 17-year-old girl's facial attractiveness is a surprisingly weak predictor of her attractiveness at ages 30 and 50. Sometimes an average-looking adolescent becomes a quite attractive middle-aged adult (Zebrowitz & others, 1993).

Second, not only do we perceive attractive people as likeable, we also perceive likeable people as attractive. Perhaps you can recall

> "Love is only a dirty trick played on us to achieve a continuation of the species."
>
> Novelist W. Somerset Maugham, 1874–1965

"I'LL TELL YOU WHY WE'RE BECOMING EXTINCT. BECAUSE WE'RE SOLITARY CREATURES, EVEN DURING THE MATING SEASON — THAT'S WHY WE'RE BECOMING EXTINCT."

Standards of beauty differ from culture to culture. Yet some people, especially those with youthful features that suggest health and fertility, are considered attractive throughout most of the world.

"Do I love you because you are beautiful, or are you beautiful because I love you?"

Prince Charming, in Rogers & Hammerstein's *Cinderella*

"Love to faults is always blind, Always is to joy inclined."

Poet William Blake, 1791

"Can two walk together except they be agreed?"

Amos 3:3

individuals who, as you grew to like them, became more attractive. Their physical imperfections were no longer so noticeable. Alan Gross and Christine Crofton (1977) had students view someone's photograph after reading a favorable or unfavorable description of the person's personality. When portrayed as warm, helpful, and considerate, people *looked* more attractive. Discovering someone's similarities to us also makes the person seem more attractive (Beaman & Klentz, 1983; Klentz & others, 1987).

Moreover, love sees loveliness: The more in love a woman is with a man, the more physically attractive she finds him (Price & others, 1974). And the more in love people are, the *less* attractive they find all others of the opposite sex (Johnson & Rusbult, 1989; Simpson & others, 1990). John Lydon and his colleagues (1999) found this is especially true for people who are committed to their relationships. They recruited McGill University students and alumni who varied in their level of commitment to their relationships. They then asked them to evaluate an attractive member of the opposite sex who was picked randomly (a moderate threat to their relationship) or the same attractive other who had picked them as somebody that he or she wanted to meet (a serious threat to their relationship). As you can see in Figure 11-4, when people were threatened at the same level as they were committed they saw the competition as less attractive. It seems that people can change how attractive they find others as a way to maintain their close relationships.

Similarity versus complementarity

From our discussion so far, one might surmise Leo Tolstoy was entirely correct: "Love depends . . . on frequent meetings, and on the style in which the hair is done up, and on the color and cut of the dress." As people get to know one another, however, other factors influence whether acquaintance develops into friendship.

Do birds of a feather flock together?

Of this much we may be sure: Birds that flock together are of a feather. Friends, engaged couples, and spouses are far more likely than people randomly paired to share common attitudes, beliefs, and values. Furthermore, the greater the

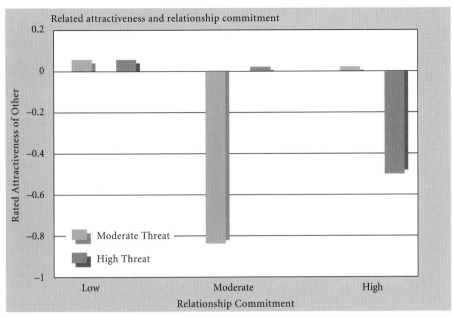

figure 11–4

Related attractiveness and relationship commitment. When people's relationships are threatened by an attractive member of the opposite sex, they rate this person as less attractive if the threat posed by the person matches their level of commitment.

(Data fom Lydon & others, 1999.)

similarity between husband and wife, the happier they are and the less likely they are to divorce (Byrne, 1971; Caspi & Herbener, 1990). Such correlational findings are intriguing. But cause and effect remain an enigma. Does similarity lead to liking? Or does liking lead to similarity?

Likeness begets liking.   To discern cause and effect, we experiment. Imagine that at a campus party Laura gets involved in a long discussion of politics, religion, and personal likes and dislikes with Les and Larry. She and Les discover they agree on almost everything, she and Larry on few things. Afterward, she reflects: "Les is really intelligent . . . and so likeable . . . hope we meet again." In experiments, Donn Byrne (1971) and his colleagues captured the essence of Laura's experience. Over and over again they found that the more similar someone's attitudes are to your own, the more likeable you will find the person. Likeness produces liking not only for college students but also for children and the elderly, for people of various occupations, and for those in various cultures.

The likeness-leads-to-liking effect has been tested in real-life situations by noting who comes to like whom.

- William Griffitt and Russell Veitch (1974) compressed the getting-to-know-you process by confining 13 unacquainted men in a fallout shelter. (The men were paid volunteers.) Knowing the men's opinions on various issues, the researchers could predict with better-than-chance accuracy those each man would most like and most dislike.

- When Susan Sprecher and Steve Duck (1994) put 83 student couples together on blind get-acquainted dates, the 16 percent who saw each other again were especially likely to see themselves as similar.

- At two of Hong Kong's universities, Royce Lee and Michael Bond (1996) found that roommate friendships flourished over a six-month period when roommates shared values and personality traits, but more so when they *perceived* their roommates as similar. As so often happens, reality matters, but perception matters more.

"And they are friends who have come to regard the same things as good and the same things as evil, they who are friends of the same people, and they who are the enemies of the same people. . . . We like those who resemble us, and are engaged in the same pursuits."

Aristotle, Rhetoric

"Actually, Lou, I think it was more than just my being in the right place at the right time. I think it was my being the right race, the right religion, the right sex, the right socioeconomic group, having the right accent, the right clothes, going to the right schools . . ."

Drawing by Miller; © 1992 The New Yorker Magazine, Inc.

So similarity breeds content. Birds of a feather *do* flock together. Surely you have noticed this upon discovering a special someone who shares your ideas, values, and desires, a soul mate who likes the same music, the same activities, even the same foods you do.

Dissimilarity breeds dislike.   We have a bias—the false consensus bias—toward assuming that others share our attitudes. When we discover that someone does not, we may dislike the person. When people do not share our attitudes, values, and beliefs we are slow to appreciate their point of view, and we are quick to evaluate them negatively. Although people believe that voters most prefer a consistent politician, people actually like more a politician who shares their views (McCaul & others, 1995).

The extent to which people perceive those of another race as similar or dissimilar therefore helps determine racial attitudes. Wherever one group of people regards another as "other"—as creatures who speak differently, live differently, think differently—the potential for oppression is high. In fact, except for intimate relationships such as dating, the perception of like minds seems more important for attraction than like skins. Most Whites express more liking for, and willingness to work with, a like-minded Black than a dissimilarly minded White (Insko & others, 1983; Rokeach, 1968). The more that Whites presume that Blacks support their values, the more positive their racial attitudes (Biernat & others, 1996). Likewise, the more Montreal residents perceive a Canadian ethnic group as similar to themselves, the more willing they are to associate with its members (Osbeck & others, 1996).

"Cultural racism" persists, argues James Jones (1988), because cultural differences are a fact of life. Black culture tends to be present-oriented, expressive, spiritual, and emotionally driven. White culture tends to be more future-

behind the scenes

As a Yale graduate student I was invited to write a book on prejudice. Wanting to take readers past the individual blame aspect of prejudice, I entitled the volume *Prejudice and Racism*, and explained how race problems are embedded in society. Prejudice is ultimately not a race problem but a culture problem. European- and African-heritage cultures differ, and their differences are the soil from which springs cultural racism—the intolerance of those whose culture differs. In today's world of ethnic mixing, we must learn to accept our cultural diversity even as we seek unifying ideals.

James Jones
University of Delaware

oriented, individualistic, materialistic, and achievement-driven. Rather than trying to eliminate such differences, says Jones, we might better appreciate what they "contribute to the cultural fabric of a multicultural society." There are situations in which expressiveness is advantageous and situations in which future orientation is advantageous. Each culture has much to learn from the other. In countries such as Canada, Britain, and the United States, where migration and different birthrates make for growing diversity, educating people to respect and enjoy those who differ is a major challenge. Given increasing cultural diversity, highlighted by multicultural awareness, and given our natural wariness of differences, this may in fact be the major social challenge of our time.

Do opposites attract?

But are we not also attracted to people who are in some ways *different* from ourselves, in ways that complement our own characteristics? Researchers have explored this question by comparing not only friends' and spouses' attitudes and beliefs but also their age, religion, race, smoking behavior, economic level, education, height, intelligence, and appearance. In all these ways and more, similarity still prevails (Buss, 1985; Kandel, 1978). Smart birds flock together. So do rich birds, Protestant birds, tall birds, pretty birds.

Still we resist: Are we not attracted to people whose needs and personalities complement our own? Would a sadist and a masochist find true love? Even *Reader's Digest* has told us that "opposites attract. . . . Socializers pair with loners, novelty-lovers with those who dislike change, free spenders with scrimpers, risk-takers with the very cautious" (Jacoby, 1986). Sociologist Robert Winch (1958) reasoned that the needs of someone who is outgoing and domineering would naturally complement those of someone who is shy and submissive. The logic seems compelling, and most of us can think of couples who view their differences as complementary: "My husband and I are perfect for each other. I'm Aquarius—a decisive person. He's Libra—can't make decisions. But he's always happy to go along with arrangements I make."

Given the idea's persuasiveness, the inability of researchers to confirm it is astonishing. For example, most people feel attracted to expressive, outgoing people (Friedman & others, 1988). Would this be especially so when one is down in the dumps? Do depressed people seek those whose gaiety will cheer

Dissimilarity breeds dislike: Like ethnic minorities elsewhere, Muslims living in France have encountered hostility.

complementarity
the popularly supposed tendency, in a relationship between two people, for each to complete what is missing in the other. The questionable complementarity hypothesis proposes that people attract those whose needs are different, in ways that complement their own.

them up? To the contrary, it is *non*depressed people who most prefer the company of happy people (Locke & Horowitz, 1990; Rosenblatt & Greenberg, 1988, 1991; Wenzlaff & Prohaska, 1989). When you're feeling blue, another's bubbly personality can be aggravating. The contrast effect that makes average people feel homely in the company of beautiful people also makes sad people more conscious of their misery in the company of cheerful people.

Some **complementarity** may evolve as a relationship progresses (even a relationship between two identical twins). Yet people seem slightly more prone to like and to marry those whose needs and personalities are *similar* (Botwin & others, 1997; Buss, 1984; Fishbein & Thelen, 1981a, 1981b; Nias, 1979). Perhaps we shall yet discover some ways (other than heterosexuality) in which differences commonly breed liking. Dominance/submissiveness may be one such way (Dryer & Horowitz, 1997). But researcher David Buss (1985) doubts it: "The tendency of opposites to marry, or mate . . . has never been reliably demonstrated, with the single exception of sex." So it seems that the "opposites-attract" rule, if it's ever true, is of hardly any importance compared to the powerful tendency of likes to attract.

Liking those who like us

Proximity and attractiveness influence our initial attraction to someone, and similarity influences longer-term attraction as well. If we have a deep need to belong and to feel liked and accepted, would we not also take a liking to those who like us? Are the best friendships mutual admiration societies? Indeed, one person's liking for another does predict the other's liking in return (Kenny & Nasby, 1980). Liking is usually mutual.

But does one person's liking another *cause* the other to return the appreciation? People's reports of how they fell in love suggest yes (Aron & others, 1989). Discovering that an appealing someone really likes you seems to awaken romantic feelings. Experiments confirm it: Those told that certain others like or admire them usually feel a reciprocal affection (Berscheid & Walster, 1978).

And consider this finding by Ellen Berscheid and her colleagues (1969): People like even better another student who says eight positive things about them than one

"Well—and I'm not just saying this because you're my husband—it stinks."

who says seven positive things and one negative thing. We are sensitive to the slightest hint of criticism. Writer Larry L. King speaks for many in noting, "I have discovered over the years that good reviews strangely fail to make the author feel as good as bad reviews make him feel bad." Whether we are judging ourselves or others, negative information carries more weight because, being less usual, it grabs more attention (Yzerbyt & Leyens, 1991). People's votes are more influenced by their impressions of candidates' weaknesses than by their impressions of strengths (Klein, 1991), a phenomenon that has not been lost on those who design negative campaigns.

That we like those we perceive as liking us was recognized long ago. Observers from the ancient philosopher Hecato ("If you wish to be loved, love") to Ralph Waldo Emerson ("The only way to have a friend is to be one") to Dale Carnegie ("Dole out praise lavishly") anticipated the findings. What they did not anticipate was the precise conditions under which the principle works.

Attribution

As we've seen, flattery *will* get you somewhere. But not everywhere. If praise clearly violates what we know is true—if someone says, "Your hair looks great," when we haven't washed it in days—we may lose respect for the flatterer and wonder whether the compliment springs from ulterior motives (Shrauger, 1975). Thus we often perceive criticism to be more sincere than praise (Coleman & others, 1987).

Laboratory experiments reveal something we've noted in previous chapters: Our reactions depend on our attributions. Do we attribute the flattery to **ingratiation**—to a self-serving strategy? Is the person trying to get us to buy something, to acquiesce sexually, to do a favor? If so, both the flatterer and the praise lose appeal (Gordon, 1996; Jones, 1964). But if there is no apparent ulterior motive, then we warmly receive both flattery and flatterer.

How we explain our own actions also matters. Clive Seligman, Russell Fazio, and Mark Zanna (1980) paid undergraduate dating couples to indicate "why

> "The average man is more interested in a woman who is interested in him than he is in a woman with beautiful legs."
>
> Actress Marlene Dietrich (1901–1992)

ingratiation
the use of strategies, such as flattery, by which people seek to gain another's favor

you go out with your girl friend/boy friend." They asked some to rank seven intrinsic reasons, such as "I go with ____ because we always have a good time together" and "because we share the same interests and concerns." Others ranked possible extrinsic reasons: "because my friends think more highly of me since I began seeing her/him" and "because she/he knows a lot of important people." Asked later to respond to a "Love Scale," those whose attention had been drawn to possible extrinsic reasons for their relationship expressed less love for their partner and saw marriage as a less likely possibility than did those made aware of possible intrinsic reasons. (Sensitive to ethical concerns, the researchers debriefed all the participants afterward and confirmed that the experiment had no long-term effects on the participants' relationships.)

Self-esteem and attraction

Elaine Hatfield (Walster, 1965) wondered if another's approval is especially rewarding after we have been deprived of approval, much as eating is most powerfully rewarding after fasting. To test this idea, she gave some women either very favorable or very unfavorable analyses of their personalities, affirming some and wounding others. Then she asked them to evaluate several people, including an attractive male confederate who just before the experiment had struck up a warm conversation with each woman and had asked each for a date. (Not one turned him down.) Which women do you suppose most liked the man?—those whose self-esteem had been temporarily shattered and who were presumably hungry for social approval. This helps explain why people sometimes fall passionately in love on the rebound, after an ego-bruising rejection.

After this experiment Dr. Hatfield spent almost an hour explaining the experiment and talking with each woman. She reports that in the end, none remained disturbed by the temporary ego blow or the broken date.

Gaining another's esteem

If approval after disapproval is powerfully rewarding, then would we most like someone who liked us after initially disliking us *or* someone who liked us from the start? Dick is in a small discussion class with his roommate's cousin, Jan. After the first week of classes, Dick learns via his "pipeline" that Jan thinks him rather shallow. As the semester progresses, however, he learns that Jan's opinion of him is steadily rising; gradually she comes to view him as bright, thoughtful, and charming. Would Dick like Jan more if she had thought well of him from the beginning? If Dick is simply counting the number of approving comments he receives, then the answer will be yes: He would like Jan better had she consistently praised him. But if after her initial disapproval, Jan's rewards become more potent, Dick then might like her better than if she had been consistently affirming.

To see which is most often true, Elliot Aronson and Darwyn Linder (1965) captured the essence of Dick's experience in a clever experiment. They "allowed" 80 women to overhear a sequence of evaluations of themselves by another woman. Some women heard consistently positive things about themselves, some consistently negative. Others heard evaluations that changed either from negative to positive (like Jan's evaluations of Dick) or from positive to negative. In this and other experiments, the target person was well liked when the subject experienced a *gain* in the other's esteem, especially when the gain occurred gradually and reversed the earlier criticism (Aronson & Mettee, 1974; Clore & others, 1975). Perhaps Jan's nice words have more credibility coming after her not-so-nice words. Or perhaps after being withheld, they are especially gratifying.

"Hatred which is entirely conquered by love passes into love, and love on that account is greater than if it had not been preceded by hatred."

Benedict Spinoza, *Ethics*

Aronson speculated that constant approval can lose value. When a husband says for the five-hundredth time, "Gee, honey, you look great," the words carry far less impact than were he now to say, "Gee, honey, you don't look good in that dress." A loved one you've doted upon is hard to reward but easy to hurt. This suggests that an open, honest relationship—one where people enjoy one another's esteem and acceptance yet are honest—is more likely to offer continuing rewards than one dulled by the suppression of unpleasant emotions, one in which people try only, as Dale Carnegie advised, to "lavish praise." Aronson (1988) put it this way:

> As a relationship ripens toward greater intimacy, what becomes increasingly important is authenticity—our ability to give up trying to make a good impression and begin to reveal things about ourselves that are honest even if unsavory. . . . If two people are genuinely fond of each other, they will have a more satisfying and exciting relationship over a longer period of time if they are able to express both positive and negative feelings than if they are completely "nice" to each other at all times. (p. 323)

In most social interactions, we self-censor our negative feelings. Thus, note William Swann and his colleagues (1991), some people receive no corrective feedback. Living in a world of pleasant illusion, they continue to act in ways that alienate their would-be friends. A true friend is one who can let us in on bad news.

Yet someone who really loves us will also tend to see us through rose-colored glasses. When Sandra Murray and her colleagues (1996) studied 60 dating and married couples from the University of Waterloo, they found that the happiest were those who idealized one another; they even saw their partners more positively than their partners saw themselves. When we're in love, we're biased to find those we love not only physically attractive, but socially attractive as well. Moreover, these relationship illusions were not only correlated with relationship satisfaction—they predicted it as well. Those who had illusions, but were unsatisfied, became satisfied over time (Murray & Holmes, 1997).

Relationship rewards

Asked why they are friends with someone or why they were attracted to their partner, most people can readily answer. "I like Carol because she's warm, witty, and well-read." What such explanations leave out—and what social psychologists believe is most important—is ourselves. Attraction involves the one who is attracted as well as the attractor. Thus a more psychologically accurate answer might be "I like Carol because of how I feel when I'm with her." We are attracted to those *we* find it satisfying and gratifying to be with. Attraction is in the eye (and brain) of the beholder.

The point can be expressed as a simple **reward theory of attraction:** *Those who reward us, or whom we associate with rewards, we like.* If a relationship gives us more rewards than costs, we will like it and will wish it to continue. This will be especially true if the relationship is more profitable than alternative relationships (Burgess & Huston, 1979; Kelley, 1979; Rusbult, 1980). In his 1665 book of *Maxims*, La Rochefoucauld conjectured that "Friendship is a scheme for the mutual exchange of personal advantages and favors whereby self-esteem may profit."

We not only like people who are rewarding to be with; we also, according to the second version of the reward principle, like those we *associate* with good

> "It takes your enemy and your friend, working together, to hurt you to the heart; the enemy to slander you and the friend to get the news to you."
>
> Mark Twain,
> *Pudd'nhead Wilson's New Calender,* 1897

reward theory of attraction
the theory that we like those whose behavior is rewarding to us or whom we associate with rewarding events

© Mell Lazarus. By permission of Mell Lazarus and Creators Syndicate.

Our liking and disliking of people is influenced by the events with which they are associated.

feelings. According to theorists Donn Byrne and Gerald Clore (1970), and to Albert Lott and Bernice Lott (1974), social conditioning creates positive feelings toward those linked to rewarding events. When, after a strenuous week, we relax in front of a fire, enjoying good food, drink, and music, we will likely feel a special warmth toward those around us. We are less likely to take a liking to someone we meet while suffering a splitting headache.

Pawel Lewicki (1985) tested this liking-by-association principle. In one experiment, University of Warsaw students were virtually 50-50 in choosing which of two pictured women (A or B in Figure 11–5) looked friendlier. Other students, having interacted with a warm, friendly experimenter who resembled woman A, chose woman A, by a 6 to 1 margin. In a follow-up study, the experimenter acted *un*friendly toward half the subjects. When these subjects later had to turn in their data to one of two women, they nearly always *avoided* the one who resembled the experimenter. (Perhaps you can recall a time when you reacted positively or negatively to someone who reminded you of someone else.)

Other experiments confirm this phenomenon of liking—and disliking—by association. In one, university students who evaluated strangers in a pleasant room liked them better than those who evaluated them in an uncomfortably hot room (Griffitt, 1970). In another, people evaluated photographs of other people while in either an elegant, sumptuously furnished, softly lit room or in a shabby,

figure 11–5

Liking by association.

After interacting with a friendly experimenter, people preferred someone who looked like her (Person A) to one who didn't (Person B). After interacting with an unfriendly experimenter, people avoided the woman who resembled her (Lewicki, 1985).

Experimenter

Person A

Person B

dirty, stark room (Maslow & Mintz, 1956). Again, the warm feelings evoked by the elegant surroundings transferred to the people being rated. Elaine Hatfield and William Walster (1978) found a practical tip in these research studies: "Romantic dinners, trips to the theatre, evenings at home together, and vacations never stop being important. . . . If your relationship is to survive, it's important that you *both* continue to associate your relationship with good things."

This simple theory of attraction—we like those who reward us and those we associate with rewards—helps us understand some of the influences on attraction:

- *Proximity* is rewarding. It costs less time and effort to receive friendship's benefits with someone who lives or works close by.

- We like *attractive* people because we perceive that they offer other desirable traits and because we benefit by associating with them.

- If others have *similar* opinions, we feel rewarded because we presume that they like us in return. Moreover, those who share our views help validate them. We especially like people if we have successfully converted them to our way of thinking (Lombardo & others, 1972; Riordan, 1980; Sigall, 1970).

- We like to be liked and love to be loved. Thus, liking is usually mutual. We like those who like us.

Summing up

We have examined four powerful influences upon liking and friendship. The best predictor of whether any two people are friends is their sheer *proximity* to one another. Proximity is conducive to repeated exposure and interaction, which enables us to discover similarities and to feel one another's liking.

A second determinant of initial attraction is *physical attractiveness*. Both in laboratory studies and in field experiments involving blind dates, university students tend to prefer attractive people. In everyday life, however, people tend actually to choose and marry someone whose attractiveness roughly matches their own (or someone who, if less attractive, has other compensating qualities). Positive attributions about attractive people define a physical-attractiveness stereotype—an assumption that what is beautiful is good.

Liking for another is greatly aided by *similarity* of attitudes, beliefs, and values. Likeness leads to liking; opposites rarely attract. We are also likely to develop friendships with people who *like us*.

A simple principle helps explain these influences upon our attractions to one another: We like people whose behavior we find rewarding or whom we have associated with rewarding events.

Love

What is this thing called "love"? Can love in its passionate form endure? If not, what can replace it?

Loving is more complex than liking and thus more difficult to measure, more perplexing to study. People yearn for it, live for it, die for it. Yet only in the last few years has loving become a serious topic in social psychology.

Most attraction researchers have studied what is most easily studied—responses during brief encounters between strangers. The influences on our initial liking of another—proximity, attractiveness, similarity, being liked—also influence our long-term, close relationships. The impressions that dating couples quickly form of each other therefore provide a clue to their long-term future (Berg, 1984; Berg & McQuinn, 1986). Indeed, if North American romances flourished *randomly*, without regard to proximity and similarity, then most Catholics (being a minority) would marry Protestants, most Blacks would marry Whites, and college graduates would be as apt to marry high school dropouts as fellow graduates.

So first impressions are important. Nevertheless, long-term loving is not merely an intensification of initial liking. Social psychologists have therefore shifted their attention from the mild attraction experienced during first encounters to the study of enduring, close relationships.

Passionate love

The first step in scientifically studying romantic love, as in studying any variable, is to decide how to define and measure it. We have ways to measure aggression, altruism, prejudice, and liking—but how do we measure love?

Elizabeth Barrett Browning asked a similar question: "How do I love thee? Let me count the ways." Social scientists have counted various ways. Psychologist Robert Sternberg (1988) views love as a triangle, whose three sides (of varying lengths) are passion, intimacy, and commitment (Figure 11–6). Drawing from ancient philosophy and literature, sociologist John Alan Lee (1988) and psychologists Clyde Hendrick and Susan Hendrick (1993) identify three primary love styles—*eros* (self-disclosing passion), *ludus* (uncommitted game playing), and *storge* (friendship)—which, like the primary colors, combine to form secondary love styles. Some love

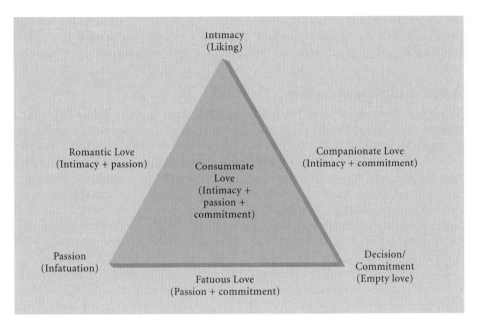

figure 11–6
Robert Sternberg's (1988) conception of kinds of loving as combinations of three basic components of love.

styles, notably eros, predict high relationship satisfaction; others, such as ludus, predict low satisfaction (Hendrick & Hendrick, 1997).

Pioneering love researcher Zick Rubin (1970, 1973) discerned somewhat different factors. To tap each, he wrote questionnaire items:

1. *Attachment* (for example, "If I were lonely, my first thought would be to seek _____ out.")
2. *Caring* (for example, "If _____ were feeling bad, my first duty would be to cheer him [her] up.")
3. *Intimacy* (for example, "I feel that I can confide in _____ about virtually everything.")

Some elements are common to all loving relationships: mutual understanding, giving and receiving support, enjoying the loved one's company. Some elements are distinctive. If we experience passionate love, we express it physically, we expect the relationship to be exclusive, and we are intensely fascinated with our partner. You can see it in our eyes. Rubin confirmed this. He administered his Love Scale to hundreds of dating couples. Later, from behind a one-way mirror in a laboratory waiting room, he clocked eye-contact among "weak-love" and "strong-love" couples. His result will not surprise you: The strong-love couples gave themselves away by gazing long into one another's eyes.

Passionate love is emotional, exciting, intense. Hatfield (1988) defines it as "*a state of intense longing for union with another*" (p. 193). If reciprocated, one feels fulfilled and joyous; if not, one feels empty or despairing. Like other forms of emotional excitement, passionate love involves a mix of elation and gloom, tingling exhilaration and dejected misery.

Passionate love is what you feel when you not only love someone, you are "in love" with him or her. As Sarah Meyers and Ellen Berscheid (1997) note,

passionate love
a state of intense longing for union with another. Passionate lovers are absorbed in one another, feel ecstatic at attaining their partner's love, and are disconsolate on losing it.

we understand that someone who says "I love you, but I'm not in love with you" means to say, "I like you. I care about you. I think you're marvellous. But I don't feel sexually attracted to you." I feel *storge* (friendship love) but not *eros* (passion).

A theory of passionate love

To explain passionate love, Hatfield notes that a given state of arousal can be steered into any of several emotions, depending on how we attribute the arousal. An emotion involves both body and mind—both arousal and how we interpret and label the arousal. Imagine yourself with pounding heart and trembling hands: Are you experiencing fear, anxiety, joy? Physiologically, one emotion is quite similar to another. You may therefore experience the arousal as joy if you are in a euphoric situation, anger if your environment is hostile, and passionate love if the situation is romantic. In this view, passionate love is the psychological experience of being biologically aroused by someone we find attractive.

If indeed passion is a revved-up state that's labeled "love," then whatever revs one up should intensify feelings of love. In several experiments, college men aroused sexually by reading or viewing erotic materials had a heightened response to a woman (for example, by scoring much higher on Rubin's Love Scale when describing their girlfriend) (Carducci & others, 1978; Dermer & Pyszczynski, 1978; Stephan & others, 1971). Proponents of the **two-factor theory of emotion** argue that when the revved-up men responded to a woman, they easily misattributed some of their arousal to her.

According to this theory, being aroused by *any* source should intensify passionate feelings—providing the mind is free to attribute some of the arousal to a romantic stimulus. Donald Dutton and Arthur Aron (1974, 1989) invited University of British Columbia men to participate in a learning experiment. After meeting their attractive female partner, some were frightened with the news that they would be suffering some "quite painful" electric shocks. Before the experiment was to begin, the researcher gave a brief questionnaire "to get some information on your present feelings and reactions, since these often influence performance on the learning task." Asked how much they would like to date and kiss their female partner, the aroused (frightened) men expressed more intense attraction toward the woman.

Does this phenomenon occur outside the laboratory? Dutton and Aron (1974) had an attractive young woman approach

two-factor theory of emotion
arousal × label = emotion

"When in doubt, Sis, you've got to listen to your heart. If it's going thump, thump, thump, slow and steady, you've got the wrong guy."

individual young men as they crossed a narrow, wobbly 450-foot-long suspension walkway hanging 230 feet above British Columbia's rocky Capilano River. The woman asked each man to help her fill out a class questionnaire. When he had finished, she scribbled her name and phone number and invited him to call if he wanted to hear more about the project. Most accepted the phone number, and half who did so called. By contrast, men approached by the woman on a low, solid bridge, and men approached on the high bridge by a *male* interviewer, rarely called. Once again, physical arousal accentuated romantic responses. Scary movies, roller-coaster rides, and physical exercise have the same effect (Cohen & others, 1989; White & Kight, 1984). Adrenaline makes the heart grow fonder.

> "The 'adrenaline' associated with a wide variety of highs can spill over and make passion more passionate. (Sort of a 'Better loving through chemistry' phenomenon.)"
>
> Elaine Hatfield and Richard Rapson (1987)

Variations in love

Time and culture.   There is always a temptation to assume that most others share our feelings and ideas. We assume, for example, that love is a precondition for marriage. But this assumption is not shared in cultures that practice arranged marriages. Moreover, until recently in North America, marital choices, especially those by women, were strongly influenced by considerations of economic security, family background, and professional status. This is still true to varying degrees in collectivist countries such as Pakistan, India, and Thailand (Levine & others, 1995). But by the mid-1980s, almost 9 in 10 North American young adults surveyed indicated that love was essential for marriage (Simpson & others, 1986).

Cultures vary in the importance they place upon romantic love. Most cultures—89 percent in one analysis of 166 cultures—have a concept of romantic love, as reflected in flirtation or couples running off together (Jankowiak & Fischer, 1992). But not all cultures build marriage on romance. In Western, individualistic cultures today, love generally precedes marriage; in others, it more often follows.

Self-monitoring.   Within any given place and time, individuals also vary in their approach to heterosexual relationships. Some seek a succession of short involvements; others value the intimacy of an exclusive and enduring relationship. In a series of studies, Mark Snyder and his colleagues (1985, 1988; Snyder & Simpson, 1985) identified a personality difference linked with these two approaches to romance. In Chapter 4 we noted that some people—those high in *self-monitoring*—skillfully monitor their own behavior to create the desired effect in any given situation. Others—those low in self-monitoring—are more internally guided, more likely to report that they act the same way regardless of the situation.

Which type of person—someone high or low in self-monitoring—would you guess to more affected by a prospect's physical appearance? to be more willing to end a relationship in favor of a new partner and therefore to date more people for shorter periods of time? to be more sexually promiscuous?

Snyder and Simpson report that in each case the answer is the person high in self-monitoring. Such people are skilled in managing first impressions but tend to be less committed to deep and enduring relationships. Low self-monitors, being less externally focused, are more committed and display more concern for people's inner qualities. When reading folders with information on potential dates or employees, they place a higher premium on personal attributes than on appearance. Given a choice between someone who shares their attitudes or

behind the scenes

For a number of years, I have been studying the social/developmental psychology of physical attractiveness. There is now considerable evidence that attractiveness affects judgments and evaluations of others. More recently, I've been interested in whether cultural values are related to the occurrence and/or strength of stereotyping based on attractiveness. Are there culture-related differences in the impact of physical attractiveness on evaluations of others?

This question reflects my more general research interest in the cultural context of attraction and interpersonal relationships. Increasingly, the importance of cultural perspectives is being acknowledged by social psychologists, as well as researchers in other areas of psychology—a promising trend within the field.

Karen Dion
University of Toronto

their preferred activities, low self-monitors (unlike high self-monitors) feel drawn to those with kindred attitudes (Jamieson & others, 1987).

Gender.   Do males and females differ in how they experience passionate love? Studies of men and women falling in and out of love reveal some surprises. Most people, including the writer of the following letter to a newspaper advice columnist, suppose that women fall in love more readily:

> Dear Dr. Brothers:
> Do you think it's effeminate for a 19-year-old guy to fall in love so hard it's like the whole world's turned around? I think I'm really crazy because this has happened several times now and love just seems to hit me on the head from nowhere. . . . My father says this is the way girls fall in love and that it doesn't happen this way with guys—at least it's not supposed to. I can't change how I am in this way but it kind of worries me.—P.T. (quoted by Dion & Dion, 1985)

P.T. would be reassured by the repeated finding that it is actually *men* who tend to fall more readily in love (Dion & Dion, 1985; Peplau & Gordon, 1985). Men also seem to fall out of love more slowly and are less likely than women to break up a premarital romance. Women in love, however, are typically as emotionally involved as their partners, or more so. They are more likely to report feeling euphoric and "giddy and carefree," as if they were "floating on a cloud." Women are also somewhat more likely than men to focus on the intimacy of the friendship and on their concern for their partner. Men are more likely than women to think about the playful and physical aspects of the relationship (Hendrick & Hendrick, 1995).

Companionate love

Although passionate love burns hot, it inevitably simmers down. The longer a relationship endures, the fewer its emotional ups and downs (Berscheid & others, 1989). The high of romance may be sustained for a few months, even a couple of years. But as we noted in the discussion of adaptation (chapter 10), no high lasts forever. The intense absorption in the other, the thrill of the

"When two people are under the influence of the most violent, most insane, most delusive, and most transient of passions, they are required to swear that they will remain in that excited, abnormal, and exhausting condition continuously until death do them part."

George Bernard Shaw

Unlike passionate love, companionate love can last a lifetime.

romance, the giddy "floating on a cloud" feeling, fades. After two years of marriage, spouses express affection about half as often as when they were newlyweds (Huston & Chorost, 1994). About four years after marriage the divorce rate peaks in cultures worldwide (Fisher, 1994). If a close relationship is to endure, it will settle to a steadier but still warm afterglow that Hatfield calls **companionate love.**

Unlike the wild emotions of passionate love, companionate love is lower key; it's a deep, affectionate attachment. And it is just as real. Nisa, a !Kung San woman of the African Kalahari Desert, explains: "When two people are first together, their hearts are on fire and their passion is very great. After a while, the fire cools and that's how it stays. They continue to love each other, but it's in a different way—warm and dependable" (Shostak, 1981).

It won't surprise those who know the rock song "Addicted to Love" to find out that the flow and ebb of romantic love follows the pattern of addictions to coffee, alcohol, and other drugs. At first, a drug gives a big kick, perhaps a high. With repetition, opponent emotions gain strength and tolerance develops. An amount that once was highly stimulating no longer gives a thrill. Stopping the substance, however, does not return you to where you started. Rather, it triggers withdrawal symptoms—malaise, depression, the blahs. The same often happens in love. The passionate high is fated to become lukewarm. The no-longer-romantic relationship becomes taken for granted—until it ends. Then the jilted lover, the widower, the divorcee, are surprised at how empty life now seems without the person they long ago stopped feeling passionately attached to. Having focused on what was not working, they stopped noticing what was (Carlson & Hatfield, 1992).

The cooling of passionate love over time and the growing importance of other factors, such as shared values, can be seen in the feelings of those who enter arranged versus love-based marriages in India. Usha Gupta and Pushpa Singh (1982) asked 50 couples in Jaipur, India, to complete Zick

companionate love
the affection we feel for those with whom our lives are deeply intertwined

Other studies provide a mixed picture of arranged marriages—confirming Gupta and Singh's finding of successful arranged marriages in India, but observing that Chinese and Japanese women were happier if they chose their mates

Blood, 1967; Xu & Whyte, 1990; Yelsma & Athappily, 1988).

figure 11–7

Romantic love between partners in arranged or love marriages in Jaipur, India.

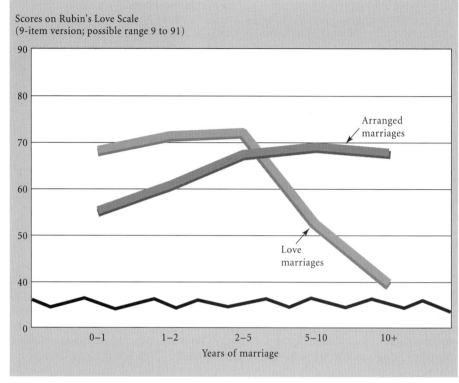

figure 11–7

Romantic love between partners in arranged or love marriages in Jaipur, India.

Scores on Rubin's Love Scale
(9-item version; possible range 9 to 91)

Arranged marriages

Love marriages

Years of marriage

(Data from Gupta & Singh, 1982.)

> "To marry a woman you love and who loves you is to lay a wager with her as to who will stop loving the other first."
>
> Alfred Capus,
> *Notes et Pensées*, 1926

Rubin's Love Scale. They found that those who married for love reported diminishing feelings of love if they had been married more than five years. By contrast, those in arranged marriages reported *more* love if they were not newlyweds (Figure 11–7).

The cooling of intense romantic love often triggers a period of disillusion, especially among those who regard such love as essential both for a marriage and for its continuation. Jeffry Simpson, Bruce Campbell, and Ellen Berscheid (1986) suspect "the sharp rise in the divorce rate in the past two decades is linked, at least in part, to the growing importance of intense positive emotional experiences (e.g., romantic love) in people's lives, experiences that may be particularly difficult to sustain over time." Compared to North Americans, Asians tend to focus less on personal feelings and more on the practical aspects of social attachments (Dion & Dion, 1988; Sprecher & others, 1994). Thus, they are less vulnerable to disillusion. Asians are also less prone to the self-focused individualism that in the long run can undermine a relationship and lead to divorce (Dion & Dion, 1991, 1996; Triandis & others, 1988).

The decline in intense mutual fascination may be natural and adaptive for species survival. The result of passionate love frequently is children, whose survival is aided by the parents' waning obsession with one another (Kenrick & Trost, 1987). Nevertheless, for those married more than twenty years, some of the lost romantic feeling is often renewed as the family nest empties and the parents are once again free to focus their attention on each other (Hatfield &

focus

Love—East and West

After four years studying in North America, a college graduate returns home to Asia—and writes back to one of her professors:

I am very happy to be at home again. I stay with my parents again and I will try to get a job. I know that in the western part of the world living with parents is the last thing young people would choose. But despite my education, I am still very much an eastern woman and so are my parents. We consider that it is the best for me to stay home with my family or my relatives.

I do not know whether I am going to get married soon. It just happened that in my last year overseas I met a person I really like. A brother of my best friend. I would like very much to marry him but in our society marriage is not only about love.

If my family (especially my mother) does not like the idea of me getting married to this guy, I have nothing to say but to obey. That is only if I want to be a good Muslim woman. If this happens, I do not know what I will do next. But whatever happens, I know I would never date like many people do. My family whom can be my cousins, uncles, and aunts would introduce me to the son of someone they know. I would only see him and talk to him once or twice or maybe more but not very often and if I like the guy I would only need to say *yes*. If I do not like the guy or I do not feel comfortable with him, I still can say *no*. I do believe if a person has a good heart, love will grow easily and beautifully around him or her.

Sprecher, 1986). "No man or woman really knows what love is until they have been married a quarter of a century," said Mark Twain. If the relationship has been intimate and mutually rewarding, companionate love rooted in a rich history of shared experiences deepens.

Summing up

Occasionally, acquaintance develops not just into friendship but into *passionate love*. Such love is often a bewildering confusion of ecstasy and anxiety, elation and pain. The two-factor theory of emotion suggests that in a romantic context arousal from any source, even painful experiences, can be steered into passion. In the best of relationships, the initial romantic high settles to a steadier, more affectionate relationship called *companionate love*.

Maintaining close relationships

What factors influence the ups and downs of our close relationships? We consider several: attachment styles, intimacy, equity, and commitment.

Attachment

Love is less an experience of choice than of biological imperative. We are, in our roots, social creatures, destined to bond with others. Cooperation promoted our species' survival. In solo combat, our ancestors were not the toughest predators. But as hunter-gatherers, and in fending off predators, they gained strength from

behind the scenes

My interest in adult attachment stems from an obvious, but perplexing, observation. On the one hand, people are highly motivated to form satisfying intimate relationships. And yet, despite this motivation, the goal of finding and maintaining the perfect (or at least good enough) intimate relationship all too often proves elusive. I have looked to attachment theory as a theoretical framework for understanding the range of difficulties people experience in their intimate relationships. My research has focused on how adult attachment orientations, as assessed through semi-structured interviews, may impact upon functioning in close relationships. During the course of a longitudinal study of attachment processes in young established couples, I became acutely aware of the high levels of abuse in some relationships and the surprisingly high stability of most of these relationships. Through this work and through an association with Donald Dutton, a family violence researcher at U.B.C., my

students and I became interested in violent relationships. Working with both clinical and community samples, we have applied an attachment perspective to understanding the dynamics of abusive relationships and the difficulty many individuals experience leaving abusive relationships. We have observed that individuals who lack confidence in the acceptance and responsiveness of their partners are prone to experience high levels of attachment anxiety, leading them (in some cases) to act in aggressive, seemingly counterproductive, ways in an attempt to gain proximity to their partners. In our most recent line of research, we are investigating attachment, childhood socialization, and partner abuse in gay men.

Kim Bartholomew
Simon Fraser University

numbers. Because group dwellers survived and reproduced, we today carry genes that predispose such bonds.

Our infant dependency strengthens our human bonds. Soon after birth we exhibit various social responses—love, fear, anger. But the first and greatest of these is love. As babies, we almost immediately prefer familiar faces and voices. We coo and smile when our parents give us attention. By eight months, we crawl after mother or father and typically let out a wail when separated from them. Reunited, we cling. By keeping infants close to their caregivers, social attachment serves as a powerful survival impulse.

Deprived of familiar attachments, sometimes under conditions of extreme neglect, children may become withdrawn, frightened, silent. After studying the mental health of homeless children for the World Health Organization, psychiatrist John Bowlby (1980, p. 442) reflected that "intimate attachments to other human beings are the hub around which a person's life revolves, not only when he is an infant or a toddler or a schoolchild but throughout his adolescence and his years of maturity as well, and on into old age. From these intimate attachments a person draws his strength and enjoyment of life. . . ."

Researchers have compared the nature of attachment and love in various close relationships—between parents and children, same-sex friends, and spouses or lovers (Davis, 1985; Maxwell, 1985; Sternberg & Grajek, 1984). Some elements are common to all loving attachments: mutual understanding, giving and receiving support, valuing and enjoying being with the loved one. Passionate love is, however, spiced with some added features: physical affection, an expectation of exclusiveness, and an intense fascination with the loved one.

Passionate love is not just for lovers. Phillip Shaver and his co-workers (1988) note that year-old infants display a passionate attachment to their parents. Much like young adult lovers, they welcome physical affection, feel distress when separated, express intense affection when reunited, and take great pleasure in the significant other's attention and approval. Knowing that infants vary in their styles of relating to caregivers, Shaver and Cindy Hazan (1993, 1994) wondered whether infant attachment styles might carry over to adult relationships.

Attachment styles

About 7 in 10 infants, and nearly that many adults, exhibit *secure attachment* (Baldwin & others, 1996; Jones & Cunningham, 1996; Mickelson & others, 1997). When placed as infants in a strange situation (usually a laboratory playroom), they play comfortably in their mother's presence, happily exploring this strange environment. If she leaves, they get distressed; when she returns, they run to her, hold her, then relax and return to exploring and playing (Ainsworth, 1973, 1989). This attachment style, many researchers believe, forms a working model of intimacy—a blueprint for one's adult intimate relationships. Secure adults find it easy to get close to others and don't fret about getting too dependent or being abandoned. As lovers, they enjoy sexuality within the context of a continuing relationship. And their relationships tend to be satisfying and enduring (Feeney, 1996; Feeney & Noller, 1990; Simpson & others, 1992; Keelan, Dion & Dion, 1998).

About 2 in 10 infants and adults exhibit *avoidant attachment*. Although internally aroused, avoidant infants reveal little distress during separation or clinging upon reunion. Avoiding closeness, these adults tend to be less invested in relationships and more likely to leave them. They also are more likely to engage in one-night stands of sex without love. Kim Bartholomew and her colleagues (1991; Bartholomew, 1994; Griffin & Bartholomew, 1994) note that avoidance individuals may be either *fearful* ("I am uncomfortable getting close to others") or *dismissing* ("It is very important to me to feel independent and self-sufficient").

Some 1 in 10 infants and adults exhibit the anxiousness and ambivalence that mark *insecure attachment*. In the strange situation, they are more likely to cling anxiously to their mother. If she leaves, they cry; when she returns, they may be indifferent or hostile. As adults, anxious-ambivalent individuals are less trusting, and therefore more possessive and jealous. They may break up repeatedly with the same person. When discussing conflicts, they get emotional and often angry (Simpson & others, 1996).

Some researchers attribute these varying attachment styles to parental responsiveness. Sensitive, responsive mothers—mothers who engender a sense of basic trust in the world's reliability—typically have securely attached infants, observed Mary Ainsworth (1979) and Erik Erikson (1963). Other researchers believe attachment styles may reflect inherited temperament (Harris, 1998). Regardless, early attachment styles do seem to lay a foundation for future relationships.

Equity

If both partners in a relationship pursue their personal desires willy-nilly, the friendship will die. Therefore, our society teaches us to exchange rewards by what Elaine Hatfield, William Walster, and Ellen Berscheid (1978) have called an **equity** principle of attraction: What you and your partner get out of a relationship should be proportional to what you each put into it. If two people receive equal outcomes, they should contribute equally; otherwise one or the other will

equity
a condition in which the outcomes people receive from a relationship are proportional to what they contribute to it. Note: Equitable outcomes needn't always be equal outcomes.

"Love is the most
subtle kind of self-
interest."

Holbrook Johnson

feel it is unfair. If both feel their outcomes correspond to the assets and efforts each contributes, then both perceive equity.

Strangers and casual acquaintances maintain equity by exchanging benefits: You lend me your class notes; later, I'll lend you mine. I invite you to my party; you invite me to yours. Those in an enduring relationship, including roommates and those in love, do not feel bound to trade similar benefits—notes for notes, parties for parties (Berg, 1984). They feel freer to maintain equity by exchanging a variety of benefits ("When you drop by to lend me your notes, why don't you stay for dinner?") and eventually to stop keeping track of who owes whom.

Long-term equity

Is it crass to suppose that friendship and love are rooted in an equitable exchange of rewards? Don't we sometimes give in response to a loved one's need, without expecting any sort of return? Indeed, those involved in an equitable long-term relationship are unconcerned with short-term equity. Margaret Clark and Judson Mills (1979, 1993; Clark, 1984, 1986) argue that people even take pains to *avoid* calculating any exchange benefits. When we help a good friend, we do not want instant repayment. If someone has us for dinner, we wait before reciprocating, lest the person attribute the motive for our return invitation to be merely paying off a social debt. True friends tune into one another's needs even when reciprocation is impossible (Clark & others, 1986, 1989). One clue that an acquaintance is becoming such a friend is the person's sharing when sharing is unexpected (Miller & others, 1989). Happily married people tend *not* to keep score of how much they are giving and getting (Buunk & Van Yperen, 1991).

In a series of experiments Clark and Mills confirmed that *not* being calculating is a mark of friendship. Tit-for-tat exchanges boosted people's liking when

Perceived inequity—thinking one contributes more to a relationship and receives less than one's spouse—predicts marital distress and dissatisfaction.

the relationship was relatively formal but *diminished* liking when the two sought friendship. Clark and Mills surmise that marriage contracts in which each partner specifies what is expected from the other are more likely to undermine than enhance love. Only when the other's positive behavior is voluntary can we attribute it to love.

Still, the long-term equity principle explains why people usually bring equal assets to romantic relationships. Recall that often they are matched for attractiveness, status, and so forth. If they are mismatched in one area, such as attractiveness, they tend to be mismatched in some other area, such as status. But in total assets, they are an equitable match. No one says, and few even think, "I'll trade you my good looks for your big income." But especially in relationships that last, equity is the rule.

Perceived equity and satisfaction

Those in an equitable relationship are more content (Fletcher & others, 1987; Hatfield & others, 1985; Van Yperen & Buunk, 1990). Those who perceive their relationship as *in*equitable feel discomfort: The one who has the better deal may feel guilty and the one who senses a raw deal may feel strong irritation. (Given the self-serving bias, the person who is "overbenefited" is less sensitive to the inequity.)

Robert Schafer and Patricia Keith (1980) surveyed several hundred married couples of all ages, noting those who felt their marriage was somewhat unfair because one spouse contributed too little to the cooking, housekeeping, parenting, or providing. Inequity took its toll: Those who perceived inequity also felt more distressed and depressed. During the child-rearing years, when wives often feel underbenefitted and husbands overbenefitted, marital satisfaction tends to dip. During the honeymoon and empty-nest stages, spouses are more likely to perceive equity and to feel satisfaction with their marriage (Feeney & others, 1994). When both partners freely give and receive, and make decisions together, the odds of sustained, satisfying love are good.

Self-disclosure

Deep, companionate relationships are intimate. They enable us to be known as we truly are and feel accepted. We discover this delicious experience in a good marriage or a close friendship—a relationship where trust displaces anxiety and where we are therefore free to open ourselves without fear of losing the other's affection (Holmes & Rempel, 1989). Such relationships are characterized by what the late Sidney Jourard called **self-disclosure** (Derlega & others, 1993). As a relationship grows, self-disclosing partners reveal more and more of themselves to one another; their knowledge of one another penetrates to deeper and deeper levels until it reaches an appropriate depth.

Research studies find that most of us enjoy such intimacy. We feel pleased when a normally reserved person says that something about us "made me feel like opening up" and share confidential information (Archer & Cook, 1986; D. Taylor & others, 1981). It's gratifying to be singled out for another's disclosure. Not only do we like those who disclose, we disclose to those whom we like. And after disclosing to them we like them more (Collins & Miller, 1994). Lacking opportunities for intimacy, we experience the pain of loneliness (Berg & Peplau, 1982; Solano & others, 1982).

self-disclosure
revealing intimate aspects of oneself to others

"*My preference is for someone who's afraid of closeness, like me.*"

Experiments have probed both the *causes* and the *effects* of self-disclosure. When are people most willing to disclose intimate information concerning "what you like and don't like about yourself" or "what you're most ashamed and most proud of"? And what effects do such revelations have upon those who reveal and receive them?

We disclose more when distressed—when angry or anxious (Stiles & others, 1992). We disclose more to those with whom we anticipate further interaction (Shaffer & others, 1996). And we disclose more if we have a secure attachment style (Keelan & others, in press). But the most reliable finding is the **disclosure reciprocity** effect: Disclosure begets disclosure (Berg, 1987; Miller, 1990; Reis & Shaver, 1988). We reveal more to those who have been open with us. But intimacy is seldom instant. (If it is, the person may seem indiscreet and unstable.) Appropriate intimacy progresses like a dance: I reveal a little, you reveal a little—but not too much. You then reveal more, and I reciprocate.

Some people—most of them women—are especially skilled "openers"—they easily elicit intimate disclosures from others, even from those who normally don't reveal very much of themselves (Miller & others, 1983; Pegalis & others, 1994; Shaffer & others, 1996). Such people tend to be good listeners. During conversation they maintain attentive facial expressions and appear to be comfortably enjoying themselves (Purvis & others, 1984). They may also express interest by uttering supportive phrases while their conversational partner is speaking. They are what psychologist Carl Rogers (1980) called "growth-promoting" listeners—people who are *genuine* in revealing their own feelings, who are *accepting* of others' feelings, and who are *empathic*, sensitive, reflective listeners.

disclosure reciprocity
the tendency for one person's intimacy of self-disclosure to match that of a conversational partner

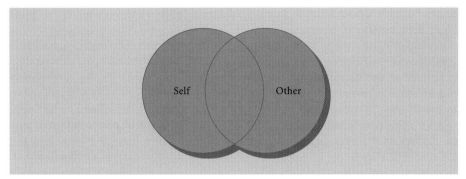

figure 11–8
Love: An overlapping of selves—you become part of me, I part of you.

(From Aron & Aron, 1994.)

What are the effects of such self-disclosure? Jourard (1964) argued that dropping our masks, letting ourselves be known as we are, nurtures love. He presumed that it is gratifying to open up to another and then to receive the trust another implies by being open with us. For example, having an intimate friend with whom we can discuss threats to our self-image seems to help us survive such stresses (Swann & Predmore, 1985). A true friendship is a special relationship that helps us cope with our other relationships. "When I am with my friend," reflected the Roman playwright Seneca, "methinks I am alone, and as much at liberty to speak anything as to think it." At its best, marriage is such a friendship, sealed by commitment.

Intimate self-disclosure is one of companionate love's delights. Dating and married couples who most reveal themselves to one another express more satisfaction with their relationship and are more likely to endure in it (Berg & McQuinn, 1986; Hendrick & others, 1988; Sprecher, 1987). John Harvey and Julia Omarzu (1997) argue that in order for couples to maintain a close and mutually satisfying relationship, they need to engage in a never-ending pattern of self-disclosure that they term "minding." This pattern requires not only mutual self-disclosure, but also careful listening to the partner and judgements about the partner that portray him or her in a positive light.

Researchers have also found that women are often more willing to disclose their fears and weaknesses than are men (Cunningham, 1981). As Kate Millett (1975) put it, "Women express, men repress." Nevertheless, men today, particularly men with egalitarian gender-role attitudes, seem increasingly willing to reveal intimate feelings and to enjoy the satisfactions that accompany a relationship of mutual trust and self-disclosure. And that, say Arthur Aron and Elaine Aron (1994), is the essence of love—two selves connecting, disclosing, and identifying with one another; two selves, each retaining their individuality, yet sharing activities, delighting in similarities, and mutually supporting (figure 11–8).

That being so, might we cultivate closeness by experiences that mirror the escalating closeness of budding friendships? The Arons and their collaborators (1997) wondered. So they paired volunteer students for 45 minutes with another student whom they didn't know. For the first 15 minutes they shared thoughts on a list of personal, but low-intimacy topics such as "When did you last sing to yourself?" The next 15 minutes were spent on more intimate topics such as "What is your most treasured memory?" The last 15 minutes invited even more self-disclosure, with questions such as: "Complete this sentence: 'I wish I had

"What is a Friend? I will tell you. It is a person with whom you dare to be yourself."

Frank Crane, *A Definition of Friendship*

someone with whom I could share . . .' " and "When did you last cry in front of another person? By yourself?"

Compared to control participants who spent the 45 minutes in small talk ("What was your high school like?" "What is your favorite holiday"?), those who experienced the escalating self-disclosure ended the hour feeling remarkably close to their conversation partner—in fact, "closer than the closest relationship in the lives of 30 percent of similar students," reported the researchers. These relationships surely were not yet marked by the loyalty and commitment of true friendship. Nevertheless, the experiment provides a striking demonstration of how readily a sense of closeness to others can grow, given open self-disclosure.

Summing up

From infancy to old age, attachments are central to human life. Secure attachments, as in an enduring marriage, mark happy lives.

One reward of companionate love is the opportunity for intimate self-disclosure, a state achieved gradually as each partner reciprocates the other's increasing openness. Companionate love is most likely to endure when both partners feel it to be equitable, with both perceiving themselves receiving from the relationship in proportion to what they contribute to it.

Ending relationships

Often love dies. What factors predict marital dissolution? How do couples typically detach or renew their relationships?

In 1971, a man wrote a love poem to his bride, slipped it into a bottle, and dropped it into the Pacific Ocean. A decade later, a jogger found it on a Guam beach:

> If, by the time this letter reaches you, I am old and gray, I know that our love will be as fresh as it is today.
> It may take a week or it may take years for this note to find you. . . . If this should never reach you, it will still be written in my heart that I will go to extreme means to prove my love for you. Your husband, Bob.

The woman to whom the love note was addressed was reached by phone. The note was read to her. She burst out laughing. And the more she heard, the harder she laughed. "We're divorced," she finally said, and slammed down the phone.

So it often goes. Comparing their unsatisfying relationship with the support and affection they imagine is available elsewhere, people are divorcing more often—at double the 1960 rate. Roughly 40 percent of Canadian marriages now end in divorce. Enduring relationships are rooted in enduring love and satisfaction, but also in inattention to possible alternative partners, fear of the costs of termination, and a sense of moral obligation (Adams & Jones, 1997; Miller, 1997). As economic and social barriers to divorce weakened during the 1960s and 1970s, thanks partly to women's increasing employment, divorce rates rose. "We are living longer, but loving more briefly," quips Os Guiness (1993, p. 309).

Sociologist Norval Glenn (1991) studied not only divorce rates, but also the marital happiness of thousands of couples between 1972 to 1988. He followed the course of marriages that began in the early 1970s, and found that by the late 1980s the divorce rates, although high, did not tell the whole story about marital happiness. In addition to the large number of people getting divorced, there were a large number of people living in less than happy marriages. This pattern is consistent with other findings (Colasanto & Shriver, 1989) that a surprisingly high number of marriages, perhaps as many as two-thirds, have divorced, separated, or seriously considered separation. These studies point to how difficult marriage can be. Contrary to the fairy tale notion of "living happily ever after," it seems that many people do not live together "happily," and many people get divorced and do not live together "ever after."

Britain's royal House of Windsor knows well the hazards of modern marriage. The fairy tale marriages of Princess Margaret, Princess Anne, Prince Charles, and Prince Andrew all crumbled, smiles replaced with stony stares. Shortly after her 1986 marriage to Prince Andrew, Sarah Ferguson gushed, "I love his wit, his charm, his looks. I worship him." Andrew reciprocated her euphoria: "She is the best thing in my life." Six years later, Andrew, having decided her friends were "philistines," and Sarah, having derided Andrew's boorish behavior as "terribly gauche," called it quits (*Time*, 1992).

Who divorces?

Divorce rates vary widely by country, ranging from .01 percent of the population annually in Bolivia, the Philippines, and Spain to 4.7 percent in the world's most divorce-prone country, the United States. To predict a culture's divorce

"Don't you understand? I love you! I need you! I want to spend the rest of my vacation with you!"

rates, it helps to know its values (Triandis, 1994). Individualistic cultures (where love is a feeling and people ask, "What does my heart say?") have more divorce than do communal cultures (where love entails obligation and people ask, "What will other people say?"). Individualists marry "for as long as we both shall love," collectivists more often for life. Individualists expect more passion and personal fulfillment in a marriage, which puts the relationship under greater pressure (Dion & Dion, 1993). "Keeping romance alive" was rated as important to a good marriage by 78 percent of U.S. women surveyed and 29 percent of Japanese women (*American Enterprise*, 1992).

Risk of divorce also depends on who marries whom (Fergusson & others, 1984; Myers, 1996; Tzeng, 1992). People usually stay married if they

- Married after age 20
- Both grew up in stable, two-parent homes
- Dated for a long while before marriage
- Are well and similarly educated
- Enjoy a stable income from a good job
- Live in a small town or on a farm
- Did not cohabit or become pregnant before marriage
- Are religiously committed
- Are of similar age, faith, and education

None of these predictors, by itself, is essential to a stable marriage. But if none of these things is true for someone, marital breakdown is an almost sure bet. If all are true, they are *very* likely to stay together until death. The English perhaps had it right, several centuries ago, when presuming that the temporary intoxication of passionate love was a foolish basis for permanent marital decisions. Better, they felt, to choose a mate based on stable friendship and compatible backgrounds, interests, habits, and values (Stone, 1977).

> "Passionate love is in many ways an altered state of consciousness. . . . In many states today, there are laws that a person must not be in an intoxicated condition when marrying. . . . But passionate love is a kind of intoxication."
>
> Roy Baumeister, *Meanings of Life*, 1991

The detachment process

Severing bonds produces a predictable sequence of agitated preoccupation with the lost partner, followed by deep sadness and, eventually, the beginnings of emotional detachment and a return to normal living (Hazan & Shaver, 1994). Even newly separated couples who have long ago ceased feeling affection are often surprised at their desire to be near the former partner. Deep and longstanding attachments seldom break quickly; detaching is a process, not an event.

Among dating couples, the closer and longer the relationship and the fewer the available alternatives, the more painful the breakup (Simpson, 1987). Surprisingly, Roy Baumeister and Sara Wotman (1992) report that months or years later people recall more pain over spurning someone's love than over having been spurned. Their distress arises from guilt over hurting someone, from upset over the heartbroken lover's persistence, or from uncertainty over how to respond. Among married couples, breakup has additional costs: shocked parents and friends, guilt over broken vows, possibly restricted parental rights. Still, each year millions of couples are willing to pay such costs to extricate themselves from what they perceive as the greater costs of continuing a painful, unrewarding relationship. Such costs include, in one study of 328 married couples, a tenfold increase in depression symptoms when a marriage is marked by discord rather than satisfaction (O'Leary & others, 1994).

When relationships suffer, there are alternatives to divorce. Caryl Rusbult and her colleagues (1986, 1987) have explored three other ways of coping with a failing relationship. Some people exhibit *loyalty*—by waiting for conditions to improve. The problems are too painful to speak of and the risks of separation are too great, so the loyal partner perseveres, hoping the good old days will return. Others (especially men) exhibit *neglect*; they ignore the partner and allow the relationship to deteriorate. When painful dissatisfactions are ignored, an insidious emotional uncoupling ensues as the partners talk less and begin redefining their lives without each other. Still others will *voice* their concerns and take active steps to improve the relationship by discussing problems, seeking advice, and attempting to change.

Study after study—in fact, 115 studies of 45,000 couples—reveal that unhappy couples disagree, command, criticize, and put down. Happy couples more often agree, approve, assent, and laugh (Karney & Bradbury, 1995; Noller & Fitzpatrick, 1990). After observing 2,000 couples, John Gottman (1994) noted that healthy marriages were not necessarily devoid of conflict. Rather, they were marked by an ability to reconcile differences and to overbalance criticism with affection. In successful marriages, positive interactions (smiling, touching, complimenting, laughing) outnumbered negative interactions (sarcasm, disapproval, insults) by at least a 5 to 1 ratio.

Successful couples have learned, sometimes aided by communication training, to restrain the cancerous putdowns and gut-level fire-with-fire reactions, to fight fair (by stating feelings without insulting), and to depersonalize conflict with comments like "I know it's not your fault" (Markman & others, 1988; Notarius & Markman, 1993; Yovetich & Rusbult, 1994). Would unhappy relationships get better if the partners agreed to *act* more as happy couples do—by complaining and criticizing less? by affirming and agreeing more? by setting times aside to voice their concerns? by having fun together daily? As attitudes trail behaviors, do affections trail actions?

Joan Kellerman, James Lewis, and James Laird (1989) wondered. They knew that among couples passionately in love, eye gazing is typically prolonged and mutual (Rubin, 1973). Would intimate eye gazing similarly stir feelings between those not in love (much as 45 minutes of escalating self-disclosure evoked feelings of closeness among those unacquainted students)? To find out, they asked unacquainted male-female pairs to gaze intently for two minutes either at one another's hands or in one another's eyes. When they separated, the eye gazers reported a tingle of attraction and affection toward each other. Simulating love had begun to stir it.

By enacting and expressing love, researcher Robert Sternberg (1988) believes the passion of initial romance can evolve into enduring love:

> "Living happily ever after" need not be a myth, but if it is to be a reality, the happiness must be based upon different configurations of mutual feelings at various times in a relationship. Couples who expect their passion to last forever, or their intimacy to remain unchallenged, are in for disappointment. . . . We must constantly work at understanding, building, and rebuilding our loving relationships. Relationships are constructions, and they decay over time if they are not maintained and improved. We cannot expect a relationship simply to take care of itself, any more than we can expect that of a building. Rather, we must take responsibility for making our relationships the best they can be.

Often love does not endure. As divorce rates rose, researchers discerned predictors of marital dissolution. These include an individualistic culture that values feelings over commitment and predictors such as the couple's age, education, values, and similarity. Researchers are also identifying the process through which couples either detach or rebuild their relationship and qualities of healthy marriages.

Summing up

From infancy to old age, attachments are central to human life. Secure attachments, as in an enduring marriage, mark happy lives. They do so thanks partly to the rewards offered by a supportive relationship: We like other people whose behavior we find rewarding or whom we have associated with rewarding events.

One reward of companionate love is the opportunity for intimate self-disclosure, a state achieved gradually as each partner reciprocates the other's increasing openness. Companionate love is most likely to endure when both partners feel it to be equitable, with both perceiving themselves receiving from the relationship in proportion to what they contribute to it.

Often, however, love does not endure. As divorce rates rose, researchers discerned predictors of marital dissolution and the process through which couples either detach or rebuild their relationship.

℞ Personal Postscript: Making love

Two facts of contemporary life seem beyond dispute:

- Close, enduring relationships are hallmarks of a happy life. In national surveys conducted in Canada, the United States, and several countries in Europe, people who are married are about twice as likely to declare their lives as being "very happy" than are single, divorced, or separated people (Inglehart, 1990; National Opinion Research Center, 1997).
- Close, enduring relationships are in decline. Compared to several decades ago, people today more often move, live alone, divorce, and have a succession of relationships.

Given the psychological ingredients of marital happiness—kindred minds, social and sexual intimacy, equitable giving and receiving of emotional and material resources—it does, however, become possible to contest the French saying "Love makes the time pass and time makes love pass." But it takes effort to stem love's decay. It takes effort to carve out time each day to talk over the day's happenings. It takes effort to forgo nagging and bickering and instead to disclose and hear one another's hurts, concerns, and dreams. It takes effort to make a relationship into "a classless utopia of social equality" (Sarnoff & Sarnoff, 1989), in which both partners freely give and receive, share decision making, and enjoy life together.

By "minding" our close relationships in such ways, sustained satisfaction is possible, note John Harvey and Julia Omarzu (1997). Australian relationships researcher Patricia Noller (1996) concurs: "Mature love . . . love that sustains marriage and family as it creates an environment in which individual family members can grow . . . is sustained by beliefs that love involves acknowledging and accepting differences and weaknesses; that love involves an internal decision to love another person and a long-term commitment to maintain that love; and finally that love is controllable and needs to be nurtured and nourished by the lovers."

For those who commit themselves to creating an equitable, intimate, mutually supportive relationship there may come the security, and the joy, of enduring, companionate love. When someone "loves you for a long, long time," explained the wise, old Skin Horse to the Velveteen Rabbit,

"not just to play with, but REALLY loves you, then you become Real."

"Does it hurt?" asked the Rabbit.

"Sometimes," said the Skin Horse, for he was always truthful. "When you are Real you don't mind being hurt."

"Does it happen all at once, like being wound up," he asked, "or bit by bit?"

"It doesn't happen all at once," said the Skin Horse. "You become. It takes a long time. That's why it doesn't often happen to people who break easily, or have sharp edges, or who have to be carefully kept. Generally, by the time you are Real, most of your hair has been loved off, and your eyes drop out and you get loose in the joints and very shabby. But these things don't matter at all, because once you are Real you can't be ugly, except to people who don't understand."

chapter 12

Altruism: Helping Others

helping comes in many forms, most strikingly in heroic, caring acts:

- Hearing the rumble of an approaching subway train, Everett Sanderson leapt down onto the tracks and raced toward the approaching headlights to rescue Michelle De Jesus, a four-year-old who had fallen from the platform. Three seconds before the train would have run her over, Sanderson flung Michelle into the crowd above. As the train roared in, he himself failed in his first effort to jump back to the platform. At the last instant, bystanders pulled him to safety (Young, 1977).

- On November 12, 1999, Rohan Wilson saw smoke and flames spewing out of an Edmonton, Alberta, apartment building. He quickly called 911 and then climbed up the outside of the building to a balcony where three children were stranded. He brought them down to safety and then climbed to another balcony and saved a pregnant woman. When asked if he was a hero, he said, "Someone needed help, I hope someone would do the same for me if I was in that position."

- On a hillside in Jerusalem, 800 trees form a simple line, the Avenue of the Righteous. Beneath each tree is a plaque with the name of a European Christian who gave refuge to one or more Jews during the Nazi Holocaust. These "righteous Gentiles" knew that if the refugees were discovered, Nazi policy dictated that both host and refugee would suffer a common fate. Many did (Hellman, 1980; Wiesel, 1985).

Less dramatic acts of comforting, caring, and helping abound: Without asking anything in return, people offer directions, donate money, give blood, volunteer time. Why, and when, will people perform altruistic acts? And what can be done to lessen indifference and increase altruism? These are this chapter's primary questions.

altruism
a motive to increase another's welfare without conscious regard for one's self-interests

Altruism is selfishness in reverse. An altruistic person is concerned and helpful even when no benefits are offered or expected in return. Jesus' parable of the Good Samaritan provides the classic illustration:

> A man was going down from Jerusalem to Jericho, and fell into the hands of robbers, who stripped him, beat him, and went away, leaving him half dead. Now by chance a priest was going down that road; and when he saw him, he passed by on the other side. So likewise a Levite, when he came to the place and saw him, passed by on the other side. But a Samaritan while traveling came near him; and when he saw him, he was moved with pity. He went to him and bandaged his wounds, having poured oil and wine on them. Then he put him on his own animal, brought him to an inn, and took care of him. The next day he took out two denarii, gave them to the innkeeper, and said, "Take care of him; and when I come back, I will repay you whatever more you spend." (Luke 10:30–35)

The Samaritan illustrates pure altruism. Filled with compassion, he gives a total stranger time, energy, and money while expecting neither repayment nor appreciation.

Why do we help?

To study altruistic acts, social psychologists examine the conditions under which people perform such deeds. Before looking at what the experiments reveal, let's consider what motivates altruism. Three complementary theories offer some answers.

Social exchange

social-exchange theory
the theory that human interactions are transactions that aim to maximize one's rewards and minimize one's costs

One explanation for altruism comes from **social-exchange theory:** Human interactions are guided by a "social economics." We exchange not only material goods and money but also *social* goods—love, services, information, status (Foa & Foa, 1975). In doing so, we use a "minimax" strategy—minimize costs, maximize rewards. Social-exchange theory does not contend that we consciously monitor costs and rewards, only that such considerations predict our behavior.

Suppose your campus is having a blood drive and someone asks you to participate. Might you not weigh the *costs* of donating (needle prick, time, fatigue) versus those of not donating (guilt, disapproval)? Might you not also weigh the *benefits* of donating (feeling good about helping someone, free refreshments) versus those of not donating (saving the time, discomfort, and anxiety)? According to social-exchange theory—and to studies of blood donors by Jane Allyn Piliavin, Dorcas Evans, and Peter Callero (1982)—such subtle calculations precede decisions to help or not. As if needing an excuse for their compassion people will donate more money to a charity when offered a product, such as candy or candles. Even when they don't want (and would never go buy) the product, it defines a social exchange (Holmes & others, 1997).

"Men do not value a good deed unless it brings a reward."

Ovid, *Epistulae ex Ponto*

Helping as disguised self-interest

Rewards that motivate helping may be external or internal. When businesses donate money to improve their corporate images or when someone offers another a ride hoping to receive appreciation or friendship, the reward is external. We give to get. Thus we are most eager to help someone attractive to us, someone whose approval we desire (Krebs, 1970; Unger, 1979).

The benefits of helping also include internal self-rewards. Near someone in distress, we typically respond with empathy. A woman's scream outside your window arouses and distresses you. If you cannot reduce your arousal by interpreting the scream as a playful shriek, then you may investigate or give aid, thereby reducing your distress (Piliavin & Piliavin, 1973). Indeed, Dennis Krebs (1975) found that men whose physiological responses and self-reports revealed the most distress in response to another's distress also gave the most help to the person. As Everett Sanderson remarked after saving the child who fell from the subway platform, "If I hadn't tried to save that little girl, if I had just stood there like the others, I would have died inside. I would have been no good to myself from then on."

Altruistic acts also increase our sense of self-worth. Nearly all blood donors in Jane Piliavin's research agreed that giving blood "makes you feel good about yourself" and "gives you a feeling of self-satisfaction."

From their analyses of why people volunteer, as when befriending AIDS patients, Mark Snyder, Allen Omoto, and Gil Clary (Clary & Snyder, 1993, 1995; Clary & others, 1998) have discerned six motivations:

- Values: to act on humanitarian values and concern for others
- Understanding: to learn about people or learn skills
- Social: to be part of a group and gain approval
- Career: to enhance job prospects with experience and contacts
- Ego protection: to reduce guilt or escape personal problems
- Esteem enhancement: to boost self-worth and confidence

This cost-benefit analysis can seem demeaning. In defense of the theory, however, is it not a credit to humanity that we can derive pleasure from helping others? that much of our behavior is not antisocial but "prosocial"? that we can find fulfillment in the giving of love? How much worse if we gained pleasure only by serving ourselves.

behind the scenes

At age 14, I was traumatized when my family moved from Vancouver, B.C. to California. I fell from President of my junior high school to an object of social ridicule because of my clothes, accent, and behavior. The skills I had acquired boxing soon generated a quite different reputation from the one I enjoyed in Canada. I sank lower and lower until, after several bouts with the law and several visits to juvenile detention homes, I was arrested for driving under the influence of drugs. I escaped from jail, hitchhiked to a logging camp in Oregon, and eventually made my way back to British Columbia. I was admitted to university on probation, graduated at the top of my class, won a Woodrow Wilson Fellowship, and was accepted at Harvard.

Concerned about my record in California, I turned myself in and suffered through the ensuing publicity. I was pardoned, in large part because of the tremendous support I received from many people. I attended Harvard, where,

after three years, I was hired as an Assistant Professor. Eventually, I returned to British Columbia to chair the Psychology Department at Simon Fraser University. Though it makes me somewhat uncomfortable, I disclose this history as a way of encouraging people with two strikes against them to remain in the game. A great deal of the energy I have invested in understanding morality has stemmed from a need to understand why I went wrong, and my interest in altruism has been fueled by the generosity of those who helped me overcome my past. I'm now working on a theory of self-deception.

Dennis Krebs
Simon Fraser University

"True," some readers may reply. "Still, doesn't social-exchange theory imply that a helpful act is never truly altruistic—that we merely *call* it 'altruistic' when its rewards are inconspicuous? If we help the screaming woman so we can gain social approval, relieve our distress, or boost our self image, is it really altruistic?" This is reminiscent of B. F. Skinner's (1971) analysis of altruism. We credit people for their good deeds, said Skinner, only when we can't explain them. We attribute their behavior to their inner dispositions only when we lack external explanations. When the external causes are obvious, we credit the causes, not the person.

There is, however, a weakness in social-exchange theory: It easily degenerates into explaining-by-naming. If someone volunteers for the Big Sister tutor program, it is tempting to "explain" her compassionate action by the satisfaction it brings her. But such after-the-fact naming of rewards creates a circular explanation: "Why did she volunteer?" "Because of the inner rewards." "How do you know there are inner rewards?" "Why else would she have volunteered?" Because of this flaw, **egoism**—the idea that self-interest motivates all behavior—has fallen into disrepute.

egoism
a motive (supposedly underlying all behavior) to increase one's own welfare. The opposite of *altruism*, which aims to increase another's welfare

To escape the circularity, we must define the rewards and costs independently of the altruistic behavior. If social approval motivates helping, then in experiments we should find that when approval follows helping, helping increases. And it does (Staub, 1978). Moreover, the cost-benefit analysis says something else. It suggests that passive bystanders to a crime or accident may not be apathetic. They may actually be greatly distressed, yet paralyzed by their awareness of the potential costs of intervening.

Empathy as a source of genuine altruism

Are life-saving heroes, everyday blood donors, and relief workers *ever* motivated by an ultimate goal of selfless concern for another? Or is their ultimate goal always some form of self-benefit, such as relief from distress or avoidance of guilt?

Philosophers have debated this question for centuries. Consider the case of Rohan Wilson that was described at the beginning of the chapter. He risked his life to save three young children and a pregnant woman. But do we really know that this was a self-less act of concern? Perhaps he only helped because he would not have been able to live with himself if he did not. Or maybe he helped because he expected the praise and accolades he received. The skeptic can always see a hidden motive of self-interest in even the most heroic acts. We can all be skeptical of some acts of helping. Take as an example corporate donations to charity. John Cleghorn (2000), the Chairman and CEO of Royal Bank noted that in 1999 his bank gave over $25 million to charity. Yet even he had to admit that, "In some cases the line between marketing and philanthropic activities has become increasingly blurred." So do people help so they just won't feel bad, and do companies give to charities only to increase their bottom lines? Until recently, psychologists have generally argued that self-interest is behind most instances of helping.

Psychologist Daniel Batson (1991, 1995), however, theorizes that our willingness to help is influenced by both self-serving *and* selfless considerations

We never know what benefits may come from helping someone in distress.

"Are you all right, Mister? Is there anything I can do?"

"Young man, you're the only one who bothered to stop! I'm a millionaire and I'm going to give you five thousand dollars!"

Drawing by Tobey; © 1972 The New Yorker Magazine, Inc.

(Figure 12–1). Distress over someone's suffering motivates us to relieve our upset, either by escaping the distressing situation (like the priest and Levite) or by helping (like the Samaritan). But especially when we feel attached to someone, report Batson and his colleagues, we also feel *empathy.* Loving parents suffer when their children suffer and rejoice over their children's joys—an empathy lacking in child abusers and other perpetrators of cruelty (Miller & Eisenberg, 1988). We also feel empathy for those we identify with. In September 1997, millions of people who never came within fifty miles of Princess Diana (but who felt like they knew her after hundreds of tabloid stories and 44 *People* magazine cover articles) wept for her and her motherless sons (after shedding no tears for the nearly one million faceless Rwandans murdered or dead in squalid refugee camps since 1994).

When feeling empathy we focus not so much on our own distress as on the sufferer. Genuine sympathy and compassion motivate us to help the person for his or her own sake. Such empathy comes naturally. Even day-old infants cry more when they hear another infant cry (Hoffman, 1981). In hospital nurseries, one baby's crying sometimes evokes a chorus of crying. We come, it seems, hard-wired for empathy.

Often distress and empathy together motivate responses to a crisis (Gordon & Mentzel, 1990). In 1983, people watched on television as an Australian bushfire wiped out hundreds of homes near Melbourne. Afterward, Paul Amato (1986) studied donations of money and goods. He found that those who felt angry or indifferent gave less than those who felt either distressed (shocked and sickened) or empathic (sympathetic and worried for the victims). Children's generosity, too, varies with their capacity for distress and empathy. George Knight and his Arizona State University co-researchers (1994) found that some 6- to 9-year-olds more than others reported feeling sorry when others were sad or being picked on. After watching a video of a burned girl, these sympathetic children were also the most generous when given a chance to contribute some of their research earnings to a children's burn unit.

To separate egoistic distress reduction from altruistic empathy, Batson's research group conducted studies that aroused feelings of empathy. Then the researchers noted whether the aroused people would reduce their own distress by escaping the situation or whether they would go out of their way to aid the person. The results were consistent: Their empathy aroused, they usually helped.

figure 12–1

Egoistic and altruistic routes to helping.

Viewing another's distress can evoke a mixture of self-focused distress and other-focused empathy. Researchers agree that distress triggers egoistic motives. But they debate whether empathy can trigger a pure altruistic motive.

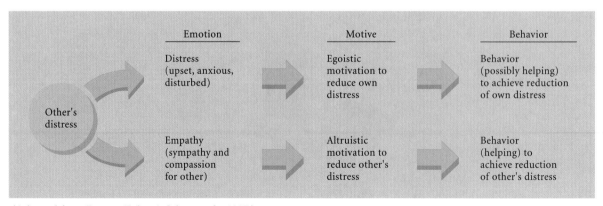

(Adapted from Batson, Fultz, & Schoenrade, 1987.)

In one of these experiments, Batson and his associates (1981) had women observe a young woman suffering while she supposedly received electric shocks. During a pause in the experiment, the obviously upset victim explained to the experimenter that a childhood fall against an electric fence left her acutely sensitive to shocks. In sympathy, the experimenter suggested that perhaps the observer (the actual subject in this experiment) might trade places and take the remaining shocks for her. Previously, half of these actual subjects had been led to believe the suffering person was a kindred spirit on matters of values and interests (thus arousing their empathy). Some also were led to believe that their part in the experiment was completed, so that in any

Might genuine empathy motivate a Humanitarian Aid worker to travel from British Columbia to Honduras to help in a medical clinic? Daniel Batson believes yes.

case they were done observing the woman's suffering. Nevertheless, their empathy aroused, virtually all these student observers willingly offered to substitute for the victim.

Is this pure altruism? Mark Schaller and Robert Cialdini (1988) doubted it. Feeling empathy for a sufferer makes one sad, they noted. In one of their experiments they led people to believe that their sadness was going to be relieved by a different sort of mood-boosting experience—listening to a comedy tape. Under such conditions, people who felt empathy were not especially helpful. Schaller and Cialdini concluded that if we feel empathy but know that something else will make us feel better, we aren't so likely to help. Also, remembering that our self-identity is collective as well as personal, Cialdini and his colleagues (1997) found that we are good to others when we are so bonded with them that we see something of ourselves in them.

Other findings suggest that genuine altruism may exist:

- Empathy produces helping even toward members of rival groups (Batson & others, 1997), but only when people believe the other will receive the needed help (Dovidio & others, 1990).
- With their empathy aroused, people will help even when they believe no one will know about their helping. Their concern continues until someone *has* helped (Fultz & others, 1986). If their efforts to help are unsuccessful, they feel bad even if the failure is not their fault (Batson & Weeks, 1996).

"How selfish soever man may be supposed, there are evidently some principles in his nature, which interest him in the fortune of others, and render their happiness necessary to him, though he derives nothing from it except the pleasure of seeing it."

Adam Smith, *The Theory of Moral Sentiments*, 1759

behind the scenes

The reasons why people do things aren't always what they seem. For instance, the things I'll tell you shortly may imply that my motive for going to graduate school was to study interesting questions about helping behavior. It's more likely, though, that I went to graduate school because I didn't fancy having to find a job in the real world. Before going to graduate school, I heard about research suggesting that the emotional experience of empathy leads to a truly altruistic motive to help others. I didn't buy it. Neither did Bob Cialdini, and so I chose to go work with him.

We conducted several studies supporting the hypothesis that the alleged altruistic motive to help is actually a mood-management motive in disguise. So even when people feel empathic toward someone else, they may help that person for selfish, not selfless, motives. Of course, these motives may not account fully for the effects of empathy on helping behavior. Recently I've been thinking that some of the effects on helping may be so automated that they may not be driven by motives and goals at all, even though they appear to be. After all, the reasons why people do things aren't always what they seem.

Mark Schaller
University of British
Columbia

- People will sometimes persist in wanting to help a suffering person even when they believe their distressed mood has been temporarily frozen by a "mood-fixing" drug (Schroeder & others, 1988).
- With their empathy for someone aroused, people will violate their own standards of fairness and justice by giving the person favored treatment (Batson & others, 1997).

So everyone agrees that some helpful acts are either obviously egoistic (done to gain rewards or avoid punishment) or subtly egoistic (done to relieve inner distress). Is there a third type of helpfulness—an altruism that aims simply to increase another's welfare (producing happiness for oneself merely as a by-product)? Is empathy-based helping a source of such altruism? Cialdini (1991) and his colleagues Mark Schaller and Jim Fultz still doubt it. They note that no experiment rules out all possible egoistic explanations for helpfulness. But after some 25 experiments testing egoism versus empathy, Batson (1991, 1995) and others (Dovidio, 1991; Staub, 1991; Wallach & Wallach, 1983) believe that sometimes people *do* focus on others' welfare, not on their own.

Out of the horrors of war, sometimes we see the most courageous acts of helping. One veteran reported this story of stray mortar rounds exploding in a village orphanage, leaving its missionary caregivers dead and an 8-year-old girl bleeding profusely (Mansur, 1987). When a doctor and nurse arrived it was immediately apparent that the girl needed a life-saving transfusion, which neither of them had the blood match to provide. Not being able to speak the native language very well they explained, as best they could, the girl's desperate need to the other children and asked if anyone would be willing to give blood.

After long moments, a small hand slowly went up, and a boy was laid on a pallet, swabbed with alcohol, and given the needle. As his blood started to flow, he shuddered, sobbed, and covered his face with his free hand. "Is it hurting?" the doctor asked. The boy shook his head and with eyes tightly shut tried to stifle his crying.

At this point a nurse who knew that native language arrived and talked with the boy, whereupon a look of great relief spread over his face. "He misunderstood you," she explained quietly to the doctor. "He thought you had asked him to give all his blood, and his life, so the little girl could live."

"But why would he be willing to do that?" asked the first nurse. The second nurse repeated the question to the boy, who answered, "She's my friend."

This story, told by one soldier to another as fact, cannot be verified. But we do know that during times of war many soldiers have used their bodies to shield their fellow soldiers from exploding devices. Most come from close-knit combat groups. Unlike other altruists, such as the 50,000 Gentiles now believed to have rescued 200,000 Jews from the Nazis, these soldiers had no time to reflect upon the shame of cowardice or the eternal rewards of self-sacrifice. Yet something drove them to act. With energy and creativity, today's social psychologists explore and debate what that something is.

Social norms

Often we help others not because we have consciously calculated that such behavior is in our self-interest but simply because something tells us we *ought* to. We ought to help a new neighbor move in. We ought to turn off a parked car's lights. We ought to return the wallet we found. We ought to protect our combat buddies from harm. Norms (as you may recall from Chapter 5) are social expectations. They *prescribe* proper behavior, the *oughts* of our lives. Researchers studying helping behavior have identified two social norms that motivate altruism.

The reciprocity norm

Sociologist Alvin Gouldner (1960) contended that one universal moral code is a **norm of reciprocity:** *To those who help us, we should return help, not harm.* Gouldner believed this norm is as universal as the incest taboo. We "invest" in others and expect dividends. Mail surveys and solicitations sometimes include a little gift of money or individualized address labels, assuming some people will reciprocate the favor. Politicians know that the one who gives a favor can later expect a favor in return. The reciprocity norm even applies with marriage. Sometimes one may give more than one receives. But in the long run, the exchange should balance out. In all such interactions, to receive without giving in return violates the reciprocity norm.

reciprocity norm
an expectation that people will help, not hurt, those who have helped them

The norm applies most strongly to interactions with equals. Those who do not see themselves as inferior or as dependent especially feel the need to reciprocate. Thus, compared to low self-esteem people, those with high self-esteem are more reluctant to seek help (Nadler & Fisher, 1986). If they cannot reciprocate, they may feel threatened and demeaned by accepting aid. Receiving unsolicited help can take one's self-esteem down a notch (Schneider & others, 1996; Shell & Eisenberg, 1992). Studies show this can happen to beneficiaries of affirmative action, especially if it fails to affirm the person's competence and chances for future success (Pratkanis & Turner, 1996).

"There is no duty more indispensable than that of returning a kindness."
Cicero

The social-responsibility norm

The reciprocity norm reminds us to balance giving and receiving in social relations. If the only norm was reciprocity, however, the Samaritan would not have been the Good Samaritan. In the parable, Jesus obviously had something more humanitarian in mind, something explicit in another of his teachings: "If you love those who love you [the reciprocity norm], what right have you to claim any credit? . . . I say to you, Love your enemies" (Matthew 5:46, 44).

With people who clearly are dependent and unable to reciprocate—children, the severely impoverished and disabled, and others perceived as unable to return as much as they receive—another social norm motivates our helping. The belief that people should help those who need help, without regard to future exchanges, is the **norm of social responsibility** (Berkowitz, 1972b; Schwartz, 1975). The norm motivates people to retrieve a dropped book for a person on crutches. In India, a relatively collectivist culture, people support the social-responsibility norm more strongly than in the individualist West (Miller & others, 1990). They voice an obligation to help even when the need is not life-threatening or the needy person is outside their family circle.

Experiments show that even when helpers remain anonymous and have no expectation of any reward, they often help needy people (Harrel, 1994; Shotland & Stebbins, 1983). However, they usually apply the social-responsibility norm selectively to those whose need appears not to be due to their own negligence. Especially among political conservatives (Skitka & Tetlock, 1993), the norm seems to be: Give people what they deserve. If they are victims of circumstance, like natural disaster, then by all means be generous. If they seem to have created their own problems, by laziness, immorality, or lack of foresight, then they should get what they deserve. Responses are thus closely tied to *attributions*. If we attribute the need to an uncontrollable predicament, we help. If we attribute the need to the person's choices, fairness does not require us to help; we say it's the person's own fault (Weiner, 1980).

Imagine yourself as one of the students in a study by Richard Barnes, William Ickes, and Robert Kidd (1979). You receive a call from a "Tony Freeman" who explains that he is in your introductory psychology class. He says that he needs help for the upcoming exam and that he has gotten your

"A language's syntax and vocabulary are not determined by our biological nature (otherwise, there could not be a multitude of tongues), but are products of human culture. Likewise, moral norms are not determined by biological processes, but by cultural traditions and principles that are products of human history."

Francisco Ayala, *The Difference of Being Human,* 1995

social-responsibility norm
an expectation that people will help those dependent upon them

When Norbert Reinhart's employee was taken hostage by leftist rebels in Columbia, he volunteered to change places. Here, he arrives home after 94 days in captivity.

name from the class roster. "I don't know. I just don't seem to take good notes in there," Tony explains. "I know I can, but sometimes I just don't feel like it, so most of the notes I have aren't very good to study with." How sympathetic would you feel toward Tony? How much of a sacrifice would you make to lend him your notes? If you are like the students in this experiment, you would probably be much less inclined to help than if Tony had just explained that his troubles were beyond his control.

Evolutionary psychology

The third explanation of altruism comes from evolutionary theory. As you may recall from Chapters 5 and 11, evolutionary psychology contends that the essence of life is gene survival. Our genes drive us in ways that have maximized their chance of survival. When our ancestors died, their genes lived on, predisposing us to behave in ways that will spread them into the future.

As suggested by the title of Richard Dawkins' (1976) popular book *The Selfish Gene*, evolutionary psychology offers a humbling human image—one that psychologist Donald Campbell (1975a,b) called a biological reaffirmation of a deep, self-serving "original sin." Genes that predispose individuals to selflessly promote strangers' welfare would not survive in the evolutionary competition. Genetic selfishness should, however, predispose us toward two specific types of selfless or even self-sacrificial altruism: kin protection and reciprocity.

Kin protection

Our genes dispose us to care for relatives in whom they reside. Thus one form of self-sacrifice that *would* increase gene survival is devotion to one's children. Parents who put their children's welfare ahead of their own are more likely to pass their genes on than parents who neglect their children. As evolutionary psychologist David Barash (1979, p. 153) has said, "Genes help themselves by being nice to themselves, even if they are enclosed in different bodies." Although evolution favors altruism toward one's children, children have less at stake in the survival of their parents' genes. Thus, parents are generally more devoted to their children than their children are to them.

Other relatives share genes in proportion to their biological closeness. You share one-half your genes with your brothers and sisters, one-eighth with your cousins. **Kin selection**—favoritism toward those who share our genes—led the evolutionary biologist J. B. S. Haldane to jest that while he would not give up his life for his brother, he would sacrifice himself for *three* brothers—or for nine cousins. Haldane would not have been surprised that, compared to fraternal twins, genetically identical twins are noticeably more mutually supportive (Segal, 1984).

The point is not that we calculate genetic relatedness before helping but that nature programs us to care about close relatives. Medals given for heroism are seldom awarded for saving an immediate family member. That we expect. What we do not expect (and therefore honor) is the altruism of those who, like our subway hero Everett Sanderson, risk themselves to save a stranger.

We also share common genes with many others. Blue-eyed people share particular genes with other blue-eyed people. But how do we detect the people in which copies of our genes occur most abundantly? As the blue-eyes example suggests, one clue lies in physical similarities (Rushton & others, 1984). Also, in

> "Fallen heroes do not have children. If self-sacrifice results in fewer descendants, the genes that allow heroes to be created can be expected to disappear gradually from the population."
>
> E. O. Wilson
> *On Human Nature,* 1978

kin selection
the idea that evolution has selected altruism toward one's close relatives to enhance the survival of mutually shared genes

"Morality governs our actions toward others in much the same way that gravity governs the motions of the planets: its strength is in inverse proportion to the square of the distance between them."

James Q. Wilson, *The Universal Aspiration,*" 1993

evolutionary history genes were shared more with neighbors than with foreigners. Are we therefore biologically biased to act more altruistically toward those similar to us and those who live near us? In the aftermath of natural disasters and other life-and-death situations, the order of who gets helped would not surprise an evolutionary psychologist: the young before the old, family members before friends, neighbors before strangers (Burnstein & others, 1994; Form & Nosow, 1958).

Some evolutionary psychologists say we can also expect ethnic ingroup favoritism—the root of countless historical and contemporary conflicts (Rushton, 1991). E. O. Wilson (1978) noted that kin selection is "the enemy of civilization. If human beings are to a large extent guided . . . to favor their own relatives and tribe, only a limited amount of global harmony is possible" (p. 167).

Reciprocity

Genetic self-interest also predicts reciprocity. An organism helps another, biologist Robert Trivers argues, because it expects help in return (Binham, 1980). The giver expects later to be the getter, whereas failure to reciprocate gets punished: The cheat, the turncoat, and the traitor are universally despised.

Reciprocity works best in small, isolated groups, groups in which one will often see the people for whom one does favors. If a vampire bat has gone a day or two without food—it can't go much more than 60 hours without starving to death—it asks a well-fed nestmate to regurgitate food for a meal (Wilkinson, 1990). The donor bat does so willingly, losing fewer hours till starvation than the recipient gains. But such favors occur only among familiar nestmates who share in the give and take. Those who always take and never give, and those who have no relationship with the donor bat, go hungry.

For similar reasons, reciprocity is stronger in the remote Cook Islands of the South Pacific than in New York City (Barash, 1979, p. 160). Small schools, towns, churches, work teams, and dorms are all conducive to a community spirit in which people care for each other. Compared to people in small-town or rural environments, those in big cities are less willing to relay a phone message, less likely to mail "lost" letters, less cooperative with survey interviewers, less helpful to a lost child, and less willing to do small favors (Hedge & Yousif, 1992; Steblay, 1987).

If individual self-interest inevitably wins in genetic competition, then why does nonreciprocal altruism toward strangers occur? What caused Mother Teresa to act as she did? What causes soldiers to throw themselves on grenades?

Donald Campbell's (1975) answer is that human societies evolved ethical and religious rules that serve as brakes on the biological bias toward self-interest. Commandments such as "Love your neighbor" admonish us to balance self-concern with concern for the group, and so contribute to the survival of the group. Richard Dawkins (1976) offered a similar conclusion: "Let us try to *teach* generosity and altruism, because we are born selfish. Let us understand what our selfish genes are up to, because we may then at least have the chance to upset their designs, something no other species has ever aspired to" (p. 3).

Comparing and evaluating theories of altruism

By now you have perhaps noticed similarities among the social-exchange, social norm, and evolutionary views of altruism. The parallels are indeed striking. As

table 12–1   Comparing theories of altruism

| | | How Is Altruism Explained? | |
| | | Mutual | |
Theory	Level of Explanation	"Altruism"	Intrinsic Altruism
social norms	sociological	reciprocity norm	social responsibility norm
social exchange	psychological	external rewards for helping	distress→inner rewards for helping
evolutionary	biological	reciprocity	kin selection

Table 12–1 shows, each proposes two types of prosocial behavior: a tit-for-tat reciprocal exchange and a more unconditional helpfulness. They do so at three complementary levels of explanation. If the evolutionary view is correct, then our genetic predispositions *should* manifest themselves in psychological and sociological phenomena.

Each theory appeals to logic. Yet each is vulnerable to charges of being speculative and after the fact. When we start with a known effect (the give and take of everyday life) and explain it by conjecturing a social-exchange process, a "reciprocity norm," or an evolutionary origin, we might be merely explaining-by-naming. The argument that a behavior occurs because of its survival function is hard to disprove. With hindsight, it's easy to think it had to be that way. If we can explain *any* conceivable behavior after the fact as the result of a social exchange, a norm, or natural selection, then we cannot disprove the theories. Each theory's task is therefore to generate predictions that enable us to test it.

An effective theory also provides a coherent scheme for summarizing a variety of observations. On this criterion, the three altruism theories get higher marks. Each offers us a broad perspective from which we can understand both enduring commitments and spontaneous help.

Summing up

Three theories explain altruistic behavior. The *social-exchange theory* assumes that helping, like other social behaviors, is motivated by a desire to minimize costs and maximize rewards. Other psychologists believe that a genuine altruistic concern for another's welfare also motivates people.

Social norms also mandate helping. The *reciprocity norm* stimulates us to return help, not harm, to those who have helped us. The *social-responsibil-ity norm* beckons us to help needy people, even if they cannot reciprocate, so long as they are deserving.

Evolutionary psychology assumes two types of altruism: devotion to kin and reciprocity. Most evolutionary psychologists, however, believe that the genes of selfish individuals are more likely to survive than the genes of self-sacrificing individuals and that society must therefore teach altruism.

When will we help?

What circumstances prompt people to help, or not to help? How and why is helping influenced by the number and behavior of other bystanders? by mood states? by traits and values?

On March 13, 1964, bar manager Kitty Genovese is set upon by a knife-wielding rapist as she returns to her apartment house at 3:00 A.M. Her screams of terror and pleas for help—"Oh my God, he stabbed me! Please help me! Please help me!"—arouse 38 of her neighbors. Many come to their windows and watch while for 35 minutes she struggles to escape her attacker. Not until her attacker departs does anyone so much as call the police. Soon after, she dies.

Why had Genovese's neighbors not come to her aid? Were they callous? indifferent? apathetic? If so, there are many such people. Consider:

- Andrew Mormille is knifed in the stomach as he rides the subway home. After his attackers leave the car, 11 other riders watch the young man bleed to death.

- An 18-year-old switchboard operator, working alone, is sexually assaulted. She momentarily escapes and runs naked and bleeding to the street and screams for help. Forty pedestrians watch as the rapist tries to drag her back inside. Fortunately, two police officers happen by and arrest the assailant.

- Eleanor Bradley trips and breaks her leg while shopping. Dazed and in pain, she pleads for help. For 40 minutes the stream of shoppers simply parts and flows around her. Finally, a cab driver helps her to a doctor (Darley & Latané, 1968).

What is shocking is not that in these cases some people failed to help but that in each of these groups (of 38, 11, 40, and 100s) almost 100 percent of those involved failed to respond. Why? In the same or similar situations, would you or I react as they did?

Social psychologists were curious and concerned about bystanders' lack of involvement during such events as the Kitty Genovese rape-murder. So they undertook experiments to identify when people will help in an emergency.

More recently, researchers have broadened the question: Who is likely to help in nonemergencies—by such deeds as giving money, donating blood, or contributing time? Let's examine these experiments by looking first at the *circumstances* that enhance helpfulness and then at the characteristics of the *people* who help.

Situational influences: Number of bystanders

Bystander passivity during emergencies has prompted social commentators to lament people's "alienation," "apathy," "indifference," and "unconscious sadistic impulses." By attributing the nonintervention to the bystanders' dispositions, we can reassure ourselves that as caring people, we *would* have helped. But were the bystanders such inhuman characters?

Social psychologists Bibb Latané and John Darley (1970) were unconvinced. So they staged ingenious emergencies and found that a single situational fac-

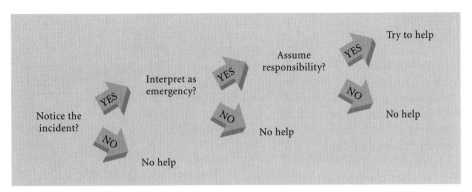

figure 12–2
Latané and Darley's decision tree.
Only one path up the tree leads to helping. At each fork of the path, the presence of other bystanders may divert a person down a branch toward not helping.

(Adapted from Darley & Latané, 1968.)

tor—the presence of other bystanders—greatly decreased intervention. By 1980 some four dozen experiments had compared help given by bystanders who perceived themselves to be either alone or with others. In about 90 percent of these comparisons, involving nearly 6,000 people, lone bystanders were more likely to help (Latané & Nida, 1981).

Sometimes, the victim was actually less likely to get help when many people were around. When Latané, James Dabbs (1975), and 145 collaborators "accidentally" dropped coins or pencils during 1,497 elevator rides, they were helped 40 percent of the time when one other person was on the elevator and less than 20 percent of the time when there were six passengers. Why? Latané and Darley surmised that as the number of bystanders increases, any given bystander is less likely to *notice* the incident, less likely to *interpret* the incident as a problem or emergency, and less likely to *assume responsibility* for taking action (Figure 12–2).

Noticing

Twenty minutes after Eleanor Bradley has fallen and broken her leg on a crowded city sidewalk, you come along. Your eyes are on the backs of the pedestrians in front of you (it is bad manners to stare at those you pass) and your private thoughts are on the day's events. Would you therefore be less likely to notice the injured woman than if the sidewalk were virtually deserted?

To find out Latané and Darley (1968) had men fill out a questionnaire in a room, either by themselves or with two strangers. While they were working (and being observed through a one-way mirror), there was a staged emergency: Smoke poured into the room through a wall vent. Solitary students, who often glanced idly about the room while working, noticed the smoke almost immediately—usually in less than five seconds. Those in groups kept their eyes on their work. It typically took them about 20 seconds to *notice* the smoke.

Interpreting

Once we notice an ambiguous event, we must interpret it. Put yourself in the room filling with smoke. Though worried, you don't want to embarrass yourself by getting flustered. You glance at the others. They look calm, indifferent. Assuming everything must be okay, you shrug it off and go back to work. Then one of the others notices the smoke and, noting your apparent unconcern, reacts

behind the scenes

Shocked by the Kitty Genovese murder, Bibb Latané and I met over dinner and began to analyze the bystanders' reactions. Being social psychologists, we thought not about the personality flaws of the "apathetic" individuals, but rather about how anyone in that situation might react as did these people. By the time we finished our dinner, we had formulated several factors that together could lead to the surprising result: no one helping. Then we set about conducting experiments that isolated each factor and demonstrated its importance in an emergency situation.

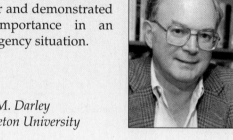

John M. Darley
Princeton University

similarly. This is yet another example of informational influence (chapter 6). Each person uses others' behavior as clues to reality.

The misinterpretations are fed by what Thomas Gilovich, Kenneth Savitsky, and Victoria Husted Medvec (1997) call an *illusion of transparency*—a tendency to overestimate others' ability to "read" our internal states. More than we usually suppose, our disgust, our deceit, and our alarm is opaque. Keenly aware of our emotions, we presume they leak out and that others see right through us. Sometimes others do. But often we keep our cool quite effectively. The result is what Chapter 8 called "pluralistic ignorance"—ignorance that others are thinking and feeling what we are. Thus, in emergencies, each person may think "I'm very concerned," but perceive others as looking not alarmed—"so maybe it's not an emergency."

So it happened in the actual experiment. When those working alone noticed the smoke, they usually hesitated a moment, then got up, walked over to the vent, felt, sniffed, and waved at the smoke, hesitated again, and then went to report it. In dramatic contrast, those in groups of three did not move. Among the 24 men in 8 groups, only one person reported the smoke within the first four minutes (Figure 12–3). By the end of the six-minute experiment, the smoke was so thick it was obscuring the men's vision and they were rubbing their eyes and coughing. Still, in only three of the eight groups did even a single person leave to report the problem.

Equally interesting, the group's passivity affected its members' interpretations. What caused the smoke? "A leak in the air conditioning," "Chemistry labs in the building," "Steam pipes," "Truth gas." They offered many explanations. Not one said, "Fire." The group members, in serving as nonresponsive models, influenced each other's interpretation.

This experimental dilemma parallels dilemmas each of us face. Are the shrieks outside merely playful antics or the desperate screams of someone being assaulted? Is the boys' scuffling a friendly tussle or a vicious fight? Is the person slumped in the doorway sleeping, high on drugs, or seriously ill, perhaps in a diabetic coma? That surely was the question confronting those who passed by Sidney Brookins (Goleman, 1993). Brookins, who had suffered a concussion when beaten, died after lying near the door to a apartment house for two days.

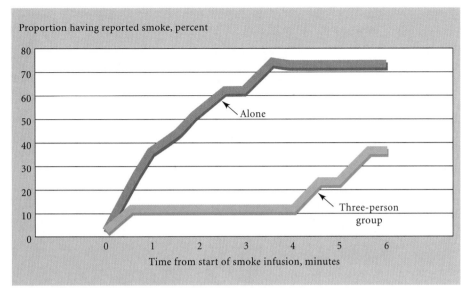

Proportion having reported smoke, percent

Alone

Three-person group

Time from start of smoke infusion, minutes

(Data from Latané & Darley, 1968.)

figure 12–3

The smoke-filled room experiment.
Smoke pouring into the testing room was much more likely to be reported by individuals working alone than by three-person groups.

Unlike the smoke-filled-room experiment, however, each of these everyday situations involves danger to passersby. To see if the same **bystander effect** occurs in such situations, Latané and Judith Rodin (1969) staged an experiment around a woman in distress. A female researcher set men to work on a questionnaire and then left through a curtained doorway to work in an adjacent office. Four minutes later she could be heard (from a tape recorder) climbing on a chair to reach some papers. This was followed by a scream and a loud crash as the chair collapsed and she fell to the floor. "Oh, my God, my foot . . . I . . . I . . . can't move it," she sobbed. "Oh . . . my ankle . . . I . . . can't get this . . . thing . . . off me." Only after two minutes of moaning did she manage to make it out her office door.

Seventy percent of those alone when they overheard the "accident" came into the room or called out to offer help. Among pairs of strangers confronting the emergency, only 40 percent of the time did either person offer help. Those who did nothing apparently interpreted the situation as a nonemergency. "A mild sprain," said some. "I didn't want to embarrass her," explained others. This again demonstrates the bystander effect: As the number of people known to be aware of an emergency increases, any given person becomes *less* likely to help. For the victim, there is therefore no safety in numbers.

People's interpretations also affect their reactions to street crimes. In staging physical fights between a man and a woman, Lance Shotland and Margaret Straw (1976) found that bystanders intervened 65 percent of the time when the woman shouted, "Get away from me; I don't know you," but only 19 percent of the time when she shouted, "Get away from me; I don't know why I ever married you." Spouse abuse, it seems, just doesn't trigger as much concern as stranger abuse.

Harold Takooshian and Herzel Bodinger (1982) suspected that interpretations could also affect bystanders' reactions to burglaries. When they staged hundreds of car burglaries in 18 cities (using a coat hanger to gain access to a valuable object, such as a TV set or fur coat), they were astonished. Fewer than

bystander effect
the finding that a person is less likely to provide help when there are other bystanders

Interpretations matter. Is this man locked out of his car or is he a burglar? Our answer affects how we respond.

1 in 10 passers-by so much as questioned their activity. Many people noticed and even stopped to stare, snicker, or offer help. Some apparently interpreted the "burglar" as the car's owner.

Assuming responsibility

Misinterpretation is not the bystander effect's only cause. Even when a shabby 14-year-old was the "burglar," when someone simultaneously broke into two adjacent cars, or when onlookers saw a different person breaking into the car than had just gotten out of it, Takooshian and Bodinger report there still was virtually no intervention. And what about those times when an emergency is obvious? Those who saw and heard Kitty Genovese's pleas for help correctly interpreted what was happening. But the lights and silhouetted figures in neighboring windows told them that others were also watching. This diffused the responsibility for action.

Few of us have observed a murder. But all of us have at times been slower to react to a need when others were present. Passing a stranded motorist on a highway, we are less likely to offer help than on a country road. To explore bystander inaction in clear emergencies, Darley and Latané (1968) simulated the Genovese drama. They placed people in separate rooms from which the participants would hear a victim crying for help. To create this situation, Darley and Latané asked some students to discuss their problems with university life over a laboratory intercom. They told the students that to guarantee their anonymity, no one would be visible, nor would the experimenter eavesdrop. During the ensuing discussion, the participants heard one person, when the experimenter turned his microphone on, lapse into an epileptic seizure. With increasing intensity and speech difficulty, he pleaded for someone to help.

Of those led to believe they were the only listener, 85 percent left their room to seek help. Of those who believed four others also overheard the victim, only 31 percent went for help. Were those who didn't respond apathetic and indifferent? When the experimenter came in to end the experiment, she did not find

Responsibility diffusion. The nine paparazzi photographers on the scene immediately after the Princess Diana car accident all had cell phones. With one exception, none called for help. Their almost unanimous explanation was that they assumed "someone else" had already called (Sancton, 1997).

this response. Most immediately expressed concern. Many had trembling hands and sweating palms. They believed an emergency had occurred but were undecided whether to act.

After the smoke-filled room, the woman-in-distress, and the seizure experiments, Latané and Darley asked the participants whether the presence of others had influenced them. We know the others had a dramatic effect. Yet the participants almost invariably denied the influence. The typical reply? "I was aware of the others, but I would have reacted just the same if they weren't there." This response reinforces a familiar point: We often do not know why we do what we do. That is why experiments such as these are revealing. A survey of uninvolved bystanders following a real emergency would have left the bystander effect hidden.

Further experiments revealed situations in which others' presence sometimes does *not* inhibit people from offering help. Irving Piliavin and his colleagues (1969) staged an emergency in a laboratory on wheels, the unwitting subjects being 4,450 riders of the subway. On each of 103 occasions, a confederate entered a subway car and stood in the center next to a pole. After the train pulled out of the station, he staggered, then collapsed. When the victim carried a cane, one or more bystanders almost always promptly offered help. Even when the victim carried a bottle and smelled of liquor, he was often promptly offered aid—aid that was especially prompt when several male bystanders were close by. Why? Did the presence of other passengers provide a sense of security to those who helped? Was it because the situation was unambiguous? (The passengers couldn't help noticing and realizing what was happening.)

To test this latter possibility, Linda Solomon, Henry Solomon, and Ronald Stone (1978) conducted experiments in which people either saw and heard someone's distress, as in the subway experiment, or only heard it, as in the woman-in-distress experiment (leaving the situation more open to interpretation). When the emergencies were very clear, those in groups were only

Compassion fatigue helps explain why those seeking help receive fewer responses from city people than from country people.

slightly less likely to help than were those alone. When the emergencies were somewhat ambiguous, however, the subjects in groups were far less likely to help than were solitary bystanders.

Most people who live in large cities are seldom alone in public places, which helps account for why city people often are less helpful than country people. "Compassion fatigue" and "sensory overload" from encountering so many people in need further restrain helping in large cities across the world (Yousif & Korte, 1995). This explains what happened when Robert LeVine and colleagues (1994) approached several thousand people in 36 cities, dropping an unnoticed pen, asking for change, simulating a blind person needing help at a corner, and so forth. The bigger and more densely populated the city, the less likely people were to help. Nations, too, have often been bystanders to catastrophes, even to genocide. "With many potential actors, each feels less responsible," notes Ervin Staub (1997). "It's not our responsibility," say the leaders of unaffected nations.

In the subway experiment, the passengers sat face-to-face, allowing them to see the alarm on one another's faces. To explore the effect of facial communication, Darley, Allan Teger, and Lawrence Lewis (1973) had people working either face-to-face or back-to-back when they heard a crash in the adjacent room as several metal screens fell on a workman. Unlike those working alone, who almost always offered help, pairs working back-to-back seldom offered help. A person working face-to-face with a partner could notice the other's facial expression and know that the person had also observed the event. Apparently, this led both people to interpret the situation as an emergency and to feel some responsibility to act, for these pairs were virtually as likely to give aid as were those working alone.

Finally, all the experiments we have considered involved groups of strangers. Imagine yourself facing any of these emergencies with a group of friends. Would your acquaintance with the other bystanders make a difference? Experiments conducted in several cities and across the world reveal that the answer is yes (Rutkowski & others, 1983; Yinon & others, 1982). Cohesive groups are *less* inhibited about helping than are solitary individuals. To summarize: The presence of other bystanders inhibits helping *if* the emergency is *ambiguous* and the other bystanders are *strangers* who *cannot easily read one another's reactions.*

These experiments raise again the issue of research ethics. Is it right to force hundreds of subway riders to witness someone's apparent collapse? Were the researchers in the seizure experiment ethical when they forced people to decide whether to abort the discussion to report the problem? Would you object to being in such a study? Note that it would have been impossible to get your "informed consent"; doing so would have destroyed the cover for the experiment.

In defense of the researchers, they were always careful to debrief the laboratory participants. After explaining the seizure experiment, probably the most stressful, the experimenter gave the participants a questionnaire. One hundred percent said the deception was justified and that they would be willing to take part in similar experiments in the future. None of the participants reported feeling angry at the experimenter. Other researchers similarly report that the overwhelming majority of participants in such experiments say afterward that their participation was both instructive and ethically justified (Schwartz & Gottlieb, 1981). In field experiments, such as the one in the subway car, an accomplice assisted the victim if no one else did, thus reassuring bystanders that the problem was being dealt with.

Remember that the social psychologist has a twofold ethical obligation: to protect the participants and to enhance human welfare by discovering influences upon human behavior. Such discoveries can alert us to unwanted influences and show us how we might exert positive influences. The ethical principle seems to be thus: After protecting participants' welfare, social psychologists fulfill their responsibility to society by doing such research.

Situational influences: Helping when someone else does

If aggressive models can heighten aggression (Chapter 10) and if unresponsive models can heighten nonresponding, then will helpful models promote helping? Imagine hearing a crash followed by sobs and moans. If another bystander said: "Uh oh. This is an emergency! We've got to do something," would this stimulate others to help?

The evidence is clear: Prosocial models do promote altruism. Some examples:

- James Bryan and Mary Ann Test (1967) found that in one field study drivers were more likely to offer help to a female driver with a flat tire if a quarter mile earlier they witnessed someone helping another woman change a tire.

- In another experiment, Bryan and Test observed that Christmas shoppers were more likely to drop money in a Salvation Army kettle if they had just seen someone else do the same.

- Philippe Rushton and Anne Campbell (1977) found British adults more willing to donate blood if they were approached after observing a confederate consent to donating.

Models sometimes contradict in practice what they preach. Parents may tell their children, "Do as I say, not as I do." Experiments show that children learn moral judgments both from what they hear preached and what they see practiced (Rice & Grusec, 1975; Rushton, 1975). When exposed to hypocrites, they imitate: They do what the model does and say what the model says.

Situational influences: Time pressures

Darley and Batson (1973) discerned another determinant of helping in the Good Samaritan parable. The priest and the Levite were both busy, important people, probably hurrying to their duties. The lowly Samaritan surely was less pressed for time. To see whether people in a hurry would behave as the priest and Levite did, Darley and Batson cleverly staged the situation described in the parable.

After collecting their thoughts prior to recording a brief extemporaneous talk (which, for half the participants, was on the Good Samaritan parable), theological seminary students were directed to a recording studio in an adjacent building. En route, they passed a man sitting slumped in a doorway, head down, coughing and groaning. Some of the students had been sent off nonchalantly: "It will be a few minutes before they're ready for you, but you might as well head on over." Of these, almost two-thirds stopped to offer help. Others were told, "Oh, you're late. They were expecting you a few minutes ago . . . so you'd better hurry." Of these, only 10 percent offered help.

Reflecting on these findings, Darley and Batson remarked:

> A person not in a hurry may stop and offer help to a person in distress. A person in a hurry is likely to keep going. Ironically, he is likely to keep going even if he is hurrying to speak on the parable of the Good Samaritan, thus inadvertently confirming the point of the parable. (Indeed, on several occasions, a seminary student going to give his talk on the parable of the Good Samaritan literally stepped over the victim as he hurried on his way!)

Are we being unfair to the seminary students, who were, after all, hurrying to *help* the experimenter? Perhaps they keenly felt the social-responsibility norm but found it pulling them two ways—toward the experimenter and toward the victim. In another enactment of the Good Samaritan situation, Batson and his associates (1978) directed 40 university students to an experiment in another building. Half were told they were late; half knew they had plenty of time. Half thought their participation was vitally important to the experimenter; half thought it was not essential. The results: Those on their way to an unimportant appointment usually stopped to help. But people seldom stopped to help if, like the White Rabbit in *Alice's Adventures in Wonderland*, they were late for a very important date.

Can we conclude that those who were rushed were callous? Did the seminarians notice the victim's distress and then consciously choose to ignore it? No. In their hurry, they never fully grasped the situation. Harried, preoccupied, rushing to meet a deadline, they simply did not take time to tune in to the person in need.

"We are, in truth, more than half what we are by imitation. The great point is, to choose good models and to study them with care."

Lord Chesterfield, *Letters*, January 18, 1750

Personal influences: Feelings

We have considered external influences on the decision to help—number of bystanders, modeling, hurrying, and characteristics of the person in need. We also need to consider internal factors, such as the helper's emotional state or personal traits.

Guilt

Throughout recorded history, guilt has been a painful emotion, so painful that cultures have institutionalized ways to relieve it: animal and human sacrifices, offerings of grain and money, penitent behavior, confession, denial. In ancient Israel, the sins of the people were periodically laid on a "scapegoat" animal that was then led into the wilderness to carry away the people's guilt (de Vaux, 1965).

To examine the consequences of guilt, social psychologists have induced people to transgress: to lie, to deliver shock, to knock over a table loaded with alphabetized cards, to break a machine, to cheat. Afterward, the guilt-laden participants may be offered a way to relieve their guilt: by confessing, by disparaging the one harmed, or by doing a good deed to offset the bad one. The results are remarkably consistent: People will do whatever can be done to expunge the guilt and restore their self-image.

Picture yourself as a participant in one such experiment conducted with university students by David McMillen and James Austin (1971). You and another student, each seeking to earn credit toward a course requirement, arrive for the experiment. Soon after, a confederate enters, portraying himself as a previous subject looking for a lost book. He strikes up a conversation in which he mentions that the experiment involves taking a multiple-choice test, for which most of the correct answers are "B." After the accomplice departs, the experimenter arrives, explains the experiment and then asks, "Have either of you been in this experiment before or heard anything about it?"

Would you lie? The behavior of those who have gone before you in this experiment—100 percent of whom told the little lie—suggests that you would. After you have taken the test (without receiving any feedback on it), the experimenter says: "You are free to leave. However, if you have some spare time, I could use your help in scoring some questionnaires." Assuming you have told the lie, do you think you would now be more willing to volunteer some time? Judging from the results, the answer again is yes. On average, those who had not been induced to lie volunteered only two minutes of time. Those who had lied were apparently eager to redeem their self-image; on average they offered a whopping 63 minutes. One moral of this experiment was well expressed by a seven-year-old girl, who, in one of our own experiments, wrote: "Don't Lie or youl Live with gilt" (and you will feel a need to relieve it).

Our eagerness to do good after doing bad reflects both our need to reduce *private* guilt and restore our shaken self-image and our desire to reclaim a positive *public* image. We are more likely to redeem ourselves with helpful behavior when other people know about our misdeeds (Carlsmith & Gross, 1969). But even when our guilt is private, we act to reduce it. Dennis Regan and his associates (1972) demonstrated this in a shopping center. They led women to think they had broken a camera. A few moments later a confederate, carrying a shopping bag with candy spilling out, crossed paths with each woman. Compared to women not put on the guilt trip—only 15 percent of whom bothered to alert the confederate to the spillage—nearly four times as many of the guilt-laden women did so. The guilt-laden women had no need to redeem themselves in the confederate's eyes. Their helpfulness offered relief from their private guilt feelings. It redeemed their self-image. Other ways of relieving guilt—as by confession—reduce guilt-induced helping (Carlsmith & others, 1968).

"Open confession is good for the soul."

Old Scottish proverb

All in all, guilt leads to much good. By motivating people to confess, apologize, help, and avoid repeated harm, it boosts sensitivity and sustains close relationships.

Negative mood

If guilt increases helping, do other negative feelings do the same? If, while depressed over a bad grade, you saw someone spill papers on the sidewalk, would you be more likely than usual to help? Or less likely?

At first glance, the results are confusing. Putting people in a negative mood (by having them read or think about something sad) sometimes increases altruism, sometimes decreases it. But if we look closely, we find order amid the confusion. First, the studies in which negative mood decreased helping usually involved children (Isen & others, 1973; Kenrick & others, 1979; Moore & others, 1973); those that found increased helping usually involved adults (Aderman & Berkowitz, 1970; Apsler, 1975; Cialdini & others, 1973; Cialdini & Kenrick, 1976). Why do you suppose a negative mood affects children and adults differently?

Robert Cialdini, Douglas Kenrick, and Donald Baumann (1981; Baumann & others, 1981) surmise that for adults, altruism is self-gratifying. It carries its own inner rewards. Blood donors feel better about themselves for having donated. Students who've helped pick up dropped materials feel better about themselves after helping (Williamson & Clark, 1989). Thus, when an adult is in a guilty, a sad, or an otherwise negative mood, a helpful deed (or any other mood-improving experience) helps neutralize the bad feelings.

Schoolchildren packing toy donations for the needy. As children mature, they usually come to take pleasure in being helpful to others.

Why doesn't this work with children? Cialdini, Kenrick, and Baumann argue that altruism is not similarly rewarding for children. When reading stories, young children view unhelpful characters as happier than helpful ones; as children grow older, their views reverse (Perry & others, 1986). Although young children exhibit empathy, they do not take much pleasure in being helpful; such behavior results from *socialization*.

To test their belief, Cialdini and his colleagues had children in early elementary school, late elementary school, and high school reminisce about sad or neutral experiences prior to a chance to donate prize coupons privately to other children (Cialdini & Kenrick, 1976). When sad, the youngest children donated slightly less, the middle groups donated slightly more, and the teenage group donated significantly more. Only the teenagers seemed to find generosity a self-gratifying technique for cheering themselves up.

As the researchers note, these results are consistent with the view that we are born selfish. But such results are also consistent with the view that altruism naturally grows with age as children come to see things from another person's point of view (Bar-Tal, 1982; Rushton, 1976; Underwood & Moore, 1982).

Exceptions to the feel bad–do good scenario

Among well-socialized adults, should we always expect to find the "feel bad–do good" phenomenon? No. In a previous chapter, we saw that one negative mood, anger, produces anything but compassion. Another exception is depression, which is characterized by brooding self-concern (Carlson & Miller, 1987; Wood & others, 1990). Yet another exception is profound grief. People who suffer the loss of a spouse or a child, whether through death or separation, often undergo a period of intense self-preoccupation, a state that makes it difficult to be giving (Aderman & Berkowitz, 1983; Gibbons & Wicklund, 1982).

In a powerfully involving laboratory simulation of self-focused grief, William Thompson, Claudia Cowan, and David Rosenhan (1980) had Stanford University students privately listen to a taped description of a person (whom they were to imagine was their best friend of the other sex) dying of cancer. The experiment focused some subjects' attention on their own worry and grief:

> He (she) could die and you would lose him, never be able to talk to him again. Or worse, he could die slowly. You would know every minute could be your last time together. For months you would have to be cheerful for him while you were sad. You would have to watch him die in pieces, until the last piece finally went, and you would be alone.

For others, it focused their attention on the friend:

> He spends his time lying in bed, waiting those interminable hours, just waiting and hoping for something to happen. Anything. He tells you that it's not knowing that is the hardest.

The researchers report that regardless of which tape the participants heard, they were profoundly moved and sobered by the experience, yet not the least regretful of participating (although some participants who listened to a boring control condition tape were regretful). Did their mood affect their helpfulness? When immediately thereafter they were given a chance to anonymously help a graduate student with her research, 25 percent of those whose attention had been self-focused helped. Of those whose attention was other-focused, 83 percent helped. The two groups were equally touched. But only the other-focused participants found helping someone especially rewarding. In short, the feel bad–do good effect occurs with people whose attention is on others, people for whom altruism is therefore rewarding (Barnett & others, 1980; McMillen & others, 1977). If not self-preoccupied by depression or grief, sad people are sensitive, helpful people.

Feel good, do good

Are happy people unhelpful? Quite the contrary. There are few more consistent findings in the entire literature of psychology: Happy people are helpful people. This effect occurs with both children and adults, regardless of whether the good mood comes from a success, from thinking happy thoughts, or from any of several other positive experiences (Salovey & others, 1991). One woman recalled her experience after falling in love:

> At the office, I could hardly keep from shouting out how deliriously happy I felt. The work was easy; things that had annoyed me on previous occasions were taken in stride. And I had strong impulses to help others; I wanted to share my joy. When Mary's typewriter broke down, I virtually sprang to my feet to assist. Mary! My former "enemy"! (Tennov, 1979, p. 22)

In experiments the one helped may be someone seeking a donation, an experimenter seeking help with paperwork, a woman who drops papers. Two examples:

- In Opole, Poland, Dariusz Dolinski and Richard Nawrat (1998) found that a positive mood of relief can dramatically boost helping. Imagine yourself as one of their unwitting subjects. After illegally parking your car for a few moments, you return to discover what looks like a ticket under your windshield wiper (where parking tickets are placed) Groaning inwardly, you pick up the apparent ticket, and then are much relieved to discover it is only an ad (or a blood drive appeal). Moments later, a university student approaches you and asks you to spend 15 minutes answering questions—to "help me complete my MA thesis." Would your positive, relieved mood make you more likely to help? Indeed, 62 percent of people whose fear had just turned to relief willingly agreed. This was nearly double the number who did so when no ticket-like paper was left or when it was left on the car door (a location not associated with a ticket.)
- Alice Isen, Margaret Clark, and Mark Schwartz (1976) had a confederate, who had supposedly spent her last dime on a wrong number, call people who had received a free sample of stationery 0 to 20 minutes earlier. As Figure 12–4 shows, their willingness to relay the phone message rose during the five minutes afterward. Then, as the good mood wore off, helpfulness dropped.

If sad people are sometimes extra helpful, how can it be that happy people are also helpful? Experiments reveal several factors are at work (Schaller & Cialdini, 1990; Carlson & others, 1988). Helping softens a bad mood and sustains a good mood. A positive mood is, in turn, conducive to positive thoughts and positive self-esteem, which predispose us to positive behavior (Berkowitz, 1987; Cunningham & others, 1990; Isen & others, 1978). In a good mood—after being given a gift or while feeling the warm glow of success—people are more likely to have positive thoughts and to have positive associations with being helpful. Positive thinkers are likely to be positive actors.

Personal influences: Personality traits

We have seen that mood and guilt dramatically affect altruism. Are there similar dramatic effects from enduring personality traits? Surely some traits must distinguish the Mother Teresa types.

"It's curious how, when you're in love, you yearn to go about doing acts of kindness to everybody."

P. G. Wodehouse, *The Mating Season*, 1949

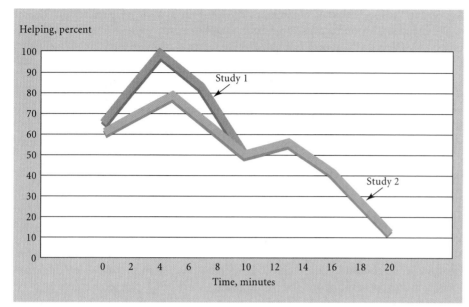

Helping, percent

Time, minutes

(Data from Isen & others, 1976.)

figure 12–4

Percentage of those willing to relay a phone message 0 to 20 minutes after receiving a free sample.

Of control subjects who did not receive a gift, only 10 percent helped.

For many years social psychologists were unable to discover a single personality trait that predicted altruistic behavior with anything close to the predictive power of the situation, guilt, and mood factors. Modest relationships were found between helping and certain personality variables, such as need for social approval. But by and large, the personality tests were unable to identify the helpers. Studies of rescuers of Jews in Nazi Europe reveal a similar conclusion: Although the social context clearly influenced willingness to help, there was no definable set of altruistic personality traits (Darley, 1995).

If that has a familiar ring, it could be from a similar conclusion by conformity researchers (Chapter 6): Conformity, too, seemed more influenced by the situation than by measurable personality traits. Perhaps, though, you recall from Chapter 2 that who we are does affect what we do. Attitude and trait measures seldom predict a *specific* act, which is what most experiments on altruism measure, in contrast to the lifelong altruism of a Mother Teresa. But they better predict average behavior across many situations.

Personality researchers have responded to the challenge. First, they have found individual differences in helpfulness and shown that these differences persist over time and are noticed by one's peers (Hampson, 1984; Rushton & others, 1981). Second, they are gathering clues to the network of traits that predispose a person to helpfulness. Those high in emotionality, empathy, and self-efficacy are most likely to be concerned and helpful (Bierhoff & others, 1991; Eisenberg & others, 1991; Tice & Baumeister, 1985). Third, personality influences how particular people react to particular situations (Carlo & others, 1991; Romer & others, 1986; Wilson & Petruska, 1984). High self-monitoring people, being attuned to other people's expectations, are especially helpful *if* they think helpfulness will be socially rewarded (White & Gerstein, 1987). Others' opinions matter less to internally guided, low self-monitoring people.

This interaction of person and situation also appears in the 172 studies that have compared the helpfulness of nearly 50,000 male and female subjects. After

"There are . . . reasons why personality should be rather unimportant in determining people's reactions to the emergency. For one thing, the situational forces affecting a person's decision are so strong."

Bibb Latané and John Darley (1970, p. 115)

analyzing these results, Alice Eagly and Maureen Crowley (1986) reported that when faced with potentially dangerous situations in which strangers need help (such as with a flat tire or a fall in a subway), men more often help. (Eagly and Crowley also report that among 6,767 individuals who have received the Carnegie medal for heroism in saving human life, 90 percent have been men.) But in safer situations, such as volunteering to help with an experiment or spend time with children with developmental disabilities, women are slightly more likely to help. Thus, the gender difference interacts with (depends on) the situation. And Eagly and Crowley guessed that if researchers were to study caring behavior in long-term, close relationships, rather than in short-term encounters with strangers, they would discover that women are significantly more helpful.

Personal influences: Religiosity

With Nazi submarines sinking ships faster than the Allied forces could replace them, the troop ship SS *Dorchester* steamed out of the harbor with 902 men headed for Greenland (Elliott, 1989; Parachin, 1992). Among those leaving anxious families behind were four chaplains, Methodist preacher George Fox, Rabbi Alexander Goode, Catholic priest John Washington, and Reformed Church minister Clark Poling. Some 150 miles from their destination, submarine *U-456* caught the *Dorchester* in its cross hairs. Within moments of the torpedo's impact, stunned men were pouring out from their bunks as the ship began listing. With power cut off, the escort vessels, unaware of the unfolding tragedy, pushed on in the darkness. On board, chaos reigned as panicky men came up from the hold without life jackets and leapt into overcrowded lifeboats.

For at least some people religion seems to be an important motivation to help people. It seems to have played such a role for Mother Teresa whose life was a model of selflessness and devotion to charitable works.

As the four chaplains arrived on the steeply sloping deck they began guiding the men to their boat stations. They opened a storage locker, distributed life jackets, and coaxed the men over the side. When Petty Officer John Mahoney turned back to retrieve his gloves, Rabbi Goode responded, "Never mind. I have two pairs." Only later did Mahoney realize that the Rabbi was not conveniently carrying an extra pair; he was giving up his own.

In the icy, oil-smeared water, Pvt. William Bednar heard the chaplains preaching courage and found the strength to swim out from under the ship until he reached a life raft. Still on board, Grady Clark watched in awe as the chaplains handed out the last life jacket and then, with ultimate selflessness, gave away their own. As Clark slipped into the waters he looked back at an unforgettable sight: the four chaplains standing—their arms linked—praying, in Latin, Hebrew, and English. Other men, now serene, joined them in a huddle as the *Dorchester* slid beneath the sea. "It was the finest thing I have ever seen or hope to see this side of heaven," said John Ladd, another of the 230 survivors.

Does the chaplains' heroic example rightly imply that faith promotes courage and caring? Most studies of altruism explore spontaneous helping acts. Confronted with a minor emergency, intrinsically religious people are only slightly more responsive (Trimble, 1993). Researchers are also now exploring planned helping—the sort of sustained helping provided by AIDS volunteers, Big Brother and Big Sister helpers, and supporters of campus service organizations (Amato, 1990; Clary & Snyder, 1991, 1993; Omoto & others, 1993). It is when making intentional choices about long-term helping that religiosity better predicts altruism.

In studies of university students, those religiously committed have reported volunteering more hours as tutors, relief workers, and campaigners for social justice than have religiously uncommitted students (Benson, 1980; Hansen & others, 1995). Among the 12 percent of people who were (George Gallup 1984) classified as "highly spiritually committed," 46 percent said they were presently working among the poor, the infirm, or the elderly—many more than the 22 percent among those "highly uncommitted" (figure 12–5). In a follow-up survey (Colasanto, 1989), charitable and social service volunteering was reported by 28 percent of those who rated religion "not very important" in their lives and by 50 percent of those who rated it "very important." In another survey, 37 percent of those attending church yearly or less, and 76 percent of those attending weekly, reported thinking at least a "fair amount" about "your responsibility to the poor" (Wuthnow, 1994).

Moreover, Sam Levenson's jest—"When it comes to giving, some people stop at nothing"—is seldom true of church and synagogue members. In a 1987 survey, people who said they never attended church or synagogue reported giving away 1.1 percent of their incomes (Hodgkinson & others, 1990). Weekly attenders were two and a half times as generous. This 24 percent of the population gave 48 percent of all charitable contributions. The other three-quarters give the remaining half. But religion may not always increase helping; in some instances it may even deter it. Lynn Jackson from Wilfrid Laurier University and Victoria Esses from the University of Western Ontario (1997) found that committed religious fundamentalists were less likely to help unemployed gays and lesbians and single mothers. As these groups threatened the beliefs of the religious fundamentalists, the groups were blamed for their problems, and the religious fundamentalists were unwilling to offer help.

> "Religion is the mother of philanthropy."
>
> Frank Emerson Andrews,
> *Attitudes toward Giving*,
> 1953

figure 12–5

Religion and long-term altruism.

Those whom George Gallup (1984) classifies as "highly spiritually committed" are more likely to report working among the needy.

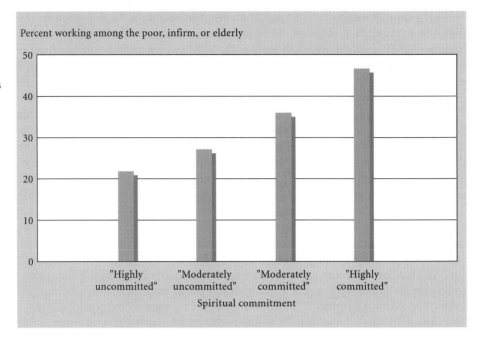

Percent working among the poor, infirm, or elderly

Spiritual commitment

Summing up

Several situational influences work to inhibit or to encourage altruism. As the number of bystanders at an emergency increases, any given bystander is (1) less likely to notice the incident, (2) less likely to interpret it as an emergency, and (3) less likely to assume responsibility.

When are people most likely to help? (1) After observing someone else helping and (2) when not hurried. Personal influences such as moods also matter. After transgressing, people often become more willing to offer help, apparently hoping to relieve guilt or to restore self-image. Sad people also tend to be helpful. This feel bad–do good effect is not found in young children, however, thus suggesting that the inner rewards of helping are a product of later socialization. Finally, there is a striking feel good–do good effect: Happy people are helpful people.

In contrast to altruism's potent situational and mood determinants, personality test scores have served as only modest predictors of helping. However, new evidence indicates that some people are consistently more helpful than others and that the effect of personality or gender may depend on the situation. Religiosity predicts long-term altruism, as reflected in volunteerism and charitable contributions.

Whom do we help?

Whom do we feel most compelled to help? Does gender matter? Does race? Type of need?

When considering the social-responsibility norm, we noted the tendency to help those most in need, those most deserving. In the subway experiment, the "victim" was helped more promptly when carrying a cane than when carrying a liquor bottle. Grocery store shoppers are more willing to give change to a woman who wants to buy milk than to one who wants to buy cookie dough (Bickman & Kamzan, 1973).

Gender

If, indeed, perception of another's need strongly determines one's willingness to help, will women, if perceived as less competent and more dependent, *receive* more help than men? It seems that this is indeed the case. Alice Eagly and Maureen Crowley (1986) located 35 studies that compared help received by male or female victims. (Virtually all the studies involved short-term encounters with strangers in need—the very situations in which people expect males to be chivalrous, note Eagly and Crowley.)

Men offered more help when the persons in need were females. Women offered help equally to males and females. Several experiments have found that women with disabled cars (for example, with a flat tire) get many more offers of help than do men (Penner & others, 1973; Pomazal & Clore, 1973; West & others, 1975). Similarly, solo female hitchhikers receive far more offers of help than do solo males or couples (Pomazal & Clore, 1973; M. Snyder & others, 1974). Of course, men's chivalry toward lone women may be motivated by something other than altruism. So it won't come as a great surprise to learn that men more frequently help attractive women (Mims & others, 1975; Stroufe & others, 1977; West & Brown, 1975).

Women not only receive more offers of help in certain situations, they also seek more help. They are twice as likely to seek medical and psychiatric help. They are the majority of callers to radio counseling programs and clients of college counseling centers. They more often welcome help from friends. Arie Nadler (1991), a Tel Aviv University expert on help seeking, attributes this to gender differences in independence versus interdependence (Chapter 5).

When the Titanic *sank, 70 percent of the females and 20 percent of the males survived. The chances of survival were 2.5 times better for a first- than a third-class passenger. Yet, thanks to gender norms for altruism, the survival odds were better for third-class passengers who were women (47 percent) than for first-class passengers who were men (31 percent).*

Similarity

Because similarity is conducive to liking (chapter 11) and liking is conducive to helping, we are also biased toward those *similar* to us. The similarity bias applies to both dress and beliefs. Tim Emswiller and his fellow researchers (1971) had confederates, dressed either conservatively or in counterculture garb, approach "straight" and "hip" university students seeking a dime for a phone call. Fewer than half the students did the favor for those dressed differently from themselves. Two-thirds did so for those dressed similarly. Likewise, Scottish shoppers were less willing to make change for someone if the person wore a T-shirt with a pro-gay slogan (Gray & others, 1991).

Does the similarity bias extend to race? During the 1970s, researchers explored this question with confusing results: Some studies found a same-race bias (Benson & others, 1976; Clark, 1974; Franklin, 1974; Gaertner, 1973; Gaertner & Bickman, 1971; Sissons, 1981; Sheldon, 1979). Others found no bias (Gaertner, 1975; Lerner & Frank, 1974; Wilson & Donnerstein, 1979; Wispe & Freshley, 1971). And still others—especially those involving face-to-face situations—found a bias toward helping those of a different race (Dutton, 1971, 1973; Dutton & Lake, 1973; Katz & others, 1975). Is there a general rule that resolves these seemingly contradictory findings?

Few people want to appear prejudiced. Thus one possibility is that people favor their own race but keep this bias secret to preserve a positive image. If so, the same-race bias should appear only when people can attribute failure to help someone of another race to factors other than race. This is what happened in experiments by Samuel Gaertner and John Dovidio (1977, 1986). For example, White women were less willing to help a Black than a White "woman in distress" *if* their responsibility could be diffused among the bystanders ("I didn't help the Black woman because there were others who could"). When there were no other bystanders, the women were equally helpful to the Black and the White women. The rule seems to be: When norms for appropriate behavior are well defined, Whites don't discriminate; when norms are ambiguous or conflicting, racial similarity may bias responses.

For me, the laboratory came to life recently as I walked from a dinner meeting to my hotel. On a deserted sidewalk, a well-dressed, distraught-seeming man about my age approached me and begged for a dollar. He explained that he had just come from London and after visiting a museum had accidentally left his wallet in a taxi. So here he was stranded, now needing a $24 taxi fare to a friend's home in the suburbs.

"So how's one dollar going to get you there?" I asked.

"I asked people for more, but no one would help me," he nearly sobbed, "so I thought maybe if I asked for less I could collect taxi fare."

"But why not take the Metro?" I challenged.

"It stops about five miles from where I need to go," he explained. "Oh my, how am I ever going to get there? If you could help me out, I will mail you back the money on Monday."

Here I was, as if a subject in an on-the-street altruism experiment. Having grown up in a city, and as a frequent visitor to large cities, I am accustomed to panhandling and have never rewarded it. But I also consider myself a caring person. Moreover, this fellow was unlike any panhandler I had ever met. He was sharply dressed. He was intelligent. He had a convincing story. And he looked like me! If he's lying, he's a slimeball, I said to myself, and giving him money would be stupid, naive, and rewarding slimeballism. If he's a truth-teller and I turn my back on him, I'm a slimeball.

He had asked for $1. I gave him $30, along with my name and address, which he gratefully took, and quickly disappeared into the night.

As I walked on, I began to realize—correctly as it turned out—that I had been a patsy. Having lived in Britain, why had I not tested his knowledge of England? Why had I not taken him to a phone booth to call his friend? Why had I at least not offered to pay a taxi driver and send him on his way, rather than give him the money? And why after a lifetime of resisting scams, had I succumbed to this one?

Sheepishly, because I like to think myself not influenced by ethnic stereotypes, I had to admit that it was not only his socially skilled, personal approach but also the mere fact of his similarity to me.

In crisis or short-term needs situations, women receive more offers of help than men, especially from men. Women also seek more help. We are most likely to help those judged to both need and deserve it and those similar to us.

Summing up

How can we increase helping?

To increase helping, we can reverse the factors that inhibit helping. Or we can teach altruistic norms and socialize people to see themselves as helpful.

As social scientists, our goal is to understand human behavior, thus also suggesting ways to improve it. We therefore wonder how we might apply insights from research to increase altruism.

Undoing the restraints on helping

One way to promote altruism is to reverse those factors that inhibit it. Given that hurried, preoccupied people are less likely to help, can we think of ways to encourage them to slow down and turn their attention outward? If the presence of others diminishes each bystander's sense of responsibility, how can we enhance responsibility?

Reduce ambiguity, increase responsibility

If Latané and Darley's decision tree (figure 12–2) describes the dilemmas bystanders face, then assisting people to interpret an incident correctly and to assume responsibility should increase their involvement. Leonard Bickman and his colleagues (1975, 1977, 1979) tested this presumption in a series of experiments on crime reporting. In each, supermarket or bookstore shoppers witnessed a shoplifting. Some witnesses had seen signs that attempted to sensitize them to shoplifting and to inform them how to report it. But the signs had little effect. Other witnesses heard a bystander interpret the incident: "Say, look at her. She's shoplifting. She put that into her purse." (The bystander then left to look for a lost child.) Still others heard this person add, "We saw it. We should report it. It's our responsibility." Both face-to-face comments substantially boosted reporting of the crime.

The potency of personal influence is no longer in doubt. Robert Foss (1978) surveyed several hundred blood donors and found that neophyte donors, unlike veterans, were usually there at someone's personal invitation. Leonard Jason and his collaborators (1984) confirmed that personal appeals for blood donation are much more effective than posters and media announcements—*if* the personal appeals come from friends. Nonverbal appeals can also be effective when they are personalized. Mark Snyder and his co-workers (1974) found that hitchhikers doubled the number of ride offers by looking drivers straight in the eye. A personal approach, as my panhandler knew, makes one feel less anonymous, more responsible.

Henry Solomon and Linda Solomon (1978; Solomon & others, 1981) explored ways to reduce anonymity. They found that bystanders who had identified themselves to one another—by name, age, and so forth—were more likely to offer aid to a sick person than were anonymous bystanders. Similarly, when a female experimenter caught the eye of another shopper and gave her a warm smile prior to stepping on an elevator, that shopper was far more likely than other shoppers to offer help when the experimenter later said, "Damn. I've left my glasses. Can anyone tell me what floor the umbrellas are on?" Even a trivial momentary conversation with someone ("Excuse me, aren't you Suzie Spear's sister?" "No, I'm not") dramatically increased the person's later helpfulness.

Helpfulness also increases when one expects to meet the victim and other witnesses again. Using a laboratory intercom system, Jody Gottlieb and Charles Carver (1980) led students to believe they were discussing problems of university living with other students. (Actually, the other discussants were tape-recorded.) When one of the supposed fellow discussants had a choking fit and cried out for help, she was helped most quickly by subjects who believed they would soon be meeting the discussants face-to-face. In short, anything that personalizes bystanders—a personal request, eye contact, stating one's name, anticipation of interaction—increases willingness to help.

Personal treatment makes bystanders more self-aware and therefore more attuned to their own altruistic ideals. Recall from earlier chapters that people made self-aware by acting in front of a mirror or TV camera exhibit increased consistency between attitudes and actions. By contrast, "deindividuated" people are less responsible. Thus, circumstances that promote self-awareness—name tags, being watched and evaluated, undistracted quiet—should also increase helping. Shelley Duval, Virginia Duval, and Robert Neely (1979) confirmed this. They showed some women their own image on a TV screen or had them complete a biographical questionnaire just before giving them a chance to contribute time and money to people in need. Those made self-aware contributed more. Similarly, pedestrians who have just had their picture taken by someone became more likely to help another pedestrian pick up dropped envelopes (Hoover & others, 1983). Self-aware people more often put their ideals into practice.

Guilt and concern for self-image

Earlier we noted that people who feel guilty will act to reduce guilt and restore their self-worth. Can heightening people's awareness of their transgressions therefore increase desire to help? A research team led by Richard Katzev (1978) wondered. So when visitors to an art museum disobeyed a "Please do not touch" sign, experimenters reprimanded some of them: "Please don't touch the objects. If everyone touches them, they will deteriorate." Likewise, when visitors to a zoo fed unauthorized food to the bears, some of them were admonished with, "Hey, don't feed unauthorized food to the animals. Don't you know it could hurt them?" In both cases, 58 percent of the now guilt-laden subjects shortly thereafter offered help to another experimenter who had "accidentally" dropped something. Of those not reprimanded, only one-third helped.

People also care about their public image. When Robert Cialdini and his colleagues (1975) asked some of their university students to chaperone delinquent children on a zoo trip, only 32 percent agreed to do so. With other students the questioner first made a very large request—that the students commit two years as volunteer counselors to delinquent children. After getting the **door-in-the-face** in response to this request (all refused), the questioner then counteroffered with the chaperoning request, saying, in effect, "OK, if you won't do that, would you do just this much?" With this technique, nearly twice as many—56 percent—agreed to help.

Cialdini and David Schroeder (1976) offer another practical way to trigger concern for self-image: Ask for a contribution so small that it's hard to say no without feeling like a Scrooge. Cialdini (1995) discovered this when a United Way canvasser came to his door. As she solicited his contribution, he was mentally preparing his refusal—until she said magic words that demolished his financial excuse: "Even a penny will help." "I had been neatly finessed into compliance," recalled Cialdini. "And there was another interesting feature of our exchange as well. When I stopped coughing (I really had choked on my attempted rejection), I gave her *not* the penny she had mentioned but the amount I usually allot to legitimate charity solicitors. At that, she thanked me, smiled innocently, and moved on."

Was Cialdini's response atypical? To find out, he and Schroeder had a solicitor approach suburbanites. When the solicitor said they were collecting money for the cancer society," 29 percent contributed an average of $1.44 each. When the solicitor added, "Even a penny will help," 50 percent contributed, an average of $1.54 each. When James Weyant (1984) repeated this experiment, he found similar results: The "even a penny will help" boosted the number contributing from 39 to 57 percent. And when 6,000 people were solicited by mail for the Cancer Society, those asked for small amounts were more

door-in-the-face technique
a strategy for gaining a concession. After someone first turns down a large request (the door-in-the-face), the same requester counteroffers with a more reasonable request.

likely to give—and gave no less on average—than those asked for larger amounts (Weyant & Smith, 1987). When approaching previous donors, bigger requests (within reason) do elicit bigger donations (Doob & McLaughlin, 1989). But with door-to-door solicitation, there is more success with requests for small contributions, which are difficult to turn down and still allow the person to maintain an altruistic self-image.

Labeling people as helpful can also strengthen a helpful self-image. After they had made a charitable contribution, Robert Kraut (1973) told women, "you are a generous person." Two weeks later, these women were more willing than those not so labeled to contribute to a different charity. Likewise, Angelo Strenta and William DeJong (1981) told some students a personality test revealed that "you are a kind, thoughtful person." These students were later more likely than others to be kind and thoughtful toward a confederate who dropped a stack of computer cards.

Socializing altruism

If we can learn altruism, then how might we teach it? Here are three ways.

Teaching moral inclusion

Rescuers of Jews in Nazi Europe, relief workers in foreign countries and volunteers at homeless shelters share at least one thing in common: They include people who differ from them within the human circle to which their moral values and rules of justice apply. These people are *morally inclusive*, as illustrated by one rescuer who faked a pregnancy on behalf of a pregnant hidden Jew—thus including the soon-to-be-born child within the circle of her own children's identities (Fogelman, 1994).

Moral exclusion—omitting certain people from one's circle of moral concern—has the opposite effect. It justifies all sorts of harm, from discrimination to genocide (Opotow, 1990; Staub, 1990; Tyler & Lind, 1990). Exploitation or cruelty becomes acceptable, even appropriate, toward those we regard as undeserving or as nonpersons. The Nazis excluded Jews from their moral community; so does anyone who participates in enslavement, death squads, or torture. To a lesser extent, moral exclusion describes any of us who concentrate our concerns, favors, and financial inheritance upon "our people" (for example, our children) to the exclusion of others.

A first step toward socializing altruism is therefore to counter the natural ingroup bias favoring kin and tribe by broadening the range of people whose well-being concerns us. Daniel Batson (1983) notes how religious teachings do this. They extend the reach of kin-linked altruism by urging "brotherly and sisterly" love toward all "children of God" in the whole human "family." If everyone is part of our family, then everyone has a moral claim on us. The boundaries between "we" and "they" fade. Nurturing children to have a secure sense of self also helps, by enabling them to accept social diversity without feeling threatened (Deutsch, 1990).

Modeling altruism

Earlier we learned that when we see unresponsive bystanders, we, too, are unlikely to help. If we see someone helping, we are more likely to offer assistance. A similar modeling effect occurred within the families of European Christians who risked their lives to rescue Jews in the 1930s and 1940s and of the civil

moral exclusion the perception of certain individuals or groups as outside the boundary within which one applies moral values and rules of fairness. Moral *inclusion* is regarding others as within one's circle of moral concern.

"We consider humankind our family."

Parliament of the World Religions, *Towards a Global Ethic*, 1993

rights activists of the late 1950s. In both cases these exceptional altruists had warm and close relationships with at least one parent who was, similarly, a strong "moralist" or committed to humanitarian causes (London, 1970; Oliner & Oliner, 1988; Rosenhan, 1970). Their family—and often their friends and church—had taught them the norm of helping and caring for others. This "prosocial value orientation" led them to include people from other groups in their circle of moral concern and to feel responsible for others' welfare (Staub, 1989, 1991, 1992). People reared by extremely punitive parents, as were many delinquents, chronic criminals, and Nazi mass murderers, show much less of the empathy and principled caring that typify altruistic rescuers.

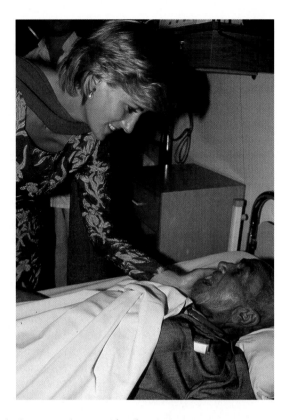

Princess Diana earned the admiration of millions by modeling moral inclusiveness—reaching out to lepers, hugging AIDS patients, visiting sick children.

Modeling also helps increase blood donations, as Irwin Sarason and his colleagues (1991) discovered after soliciting nearly 10,000 students at 66 high schools across North America. The researchers compared students who experienced the procedure that blood centers believed most effective in recruiting students with students who viewed a slide show that included 38 photos of high school blood drive scenes. Those exposed to the modeling were 17 percent more likely to donate.

Do television's positive models promote helping, much as its aggressive portrayals promote aggression? Prosocial TV models have actually had even greater effects than antisocial models. Susan Hearold (1986) statistically combined 108 comparisons of prosocial programs with neutral programs or no program. She found that, on average, "If the viewer watched prosocial programs instead of neutral programs, he would [at least temporarily] be elevated from the 50th to the 74th percentile in prosocial behavior—typically altruism."

In one such study, researchers Lynette Friedrich and Aletha Stein (1973; Stein & Friedrich, 1972) showed preschool children *Mister Rogers' Neighborhood* episodes each day for four weeks as part of their nursery school program. (*Mister Rogers* aims to enhance young children's social and emotional development.) During this viewing period, children from less educated homes became more cooperative, helpful, and likely to state their feelings. In a follow-up study, kindergartners who viewed four *Mister Rogers* programs were able to state its prosocial content, both on a test and in puppet play (Friedrich & Stein, 1975; also Coates & others, 1976).

Attributing helpful behavior to altruistic motives

overjustification
effect
see Chapter 4

Another clue to socializing altruism comes from research on the **overjustification effect:** When the justification for an act is more than sufficient, the person may attribute the act to the extrinsic justification rather than to an inner motive. Rewarding people for doing what they would do anyway therefore undermines intrinsic motivation. We can state the principle positively: By providing people with just enough justification to prompt a good deed (weaning them from bribes and threats when possible), we may increase their pleasure in doing such deeds on their own.

Daniel Batson and his associates (1978, 1979) put the overjustification phenomenon to work. In several experiments they found that university students felt most altruistic after they agreed to help someone without payment or implied social pressure. When pay had been offered or social pressures were present, people felt less altruistic after helping. In another experiment, the researchers led students to attribute a helpful act to compliance ("I guess we really don't have a choice") or to compassion ("The guy really needs help"). Later, when the students were asked to volunteer their time to a local service agency, 25 percent of those who had been led to perceive their previous helpfulness as mere compliance now volunteered; of those led to see themselves as compassionate, 60 percent volunteered. The moral? Simple: When people wonder, "Why am I helping?" it's best if the circumstances enable them to answer, "Because help was needed, and I am a caring, giving, helpful person."

As you may recall from Chapter 4, rewards undermine intrinsic motivation when they function as controlling bribes. An unanticipated compliment, however, can make people feel competent and worthy. When Joe is coerced with, "If you quit being chicken and give blood, we'll win the fraternity prize for most donations," he isn't likely to attribute his donation to altruism. When Jocelyn is rewarded with, "That's terrific that you'd choose to take an hour out of such a busy week to give blood," she's more likely to walk away with an altruistic self-image—and thus to contribute again (Piliavin & others, 1982; Thomas & Batson, 1981; Thomas & others, 1981).

Learning about altruism

Researchers have found another way to boost altruism, one that provides a happy conclusion to this chapter. Some social psychologists worry that as people become more aware of social psychology's findings, their behavior may change, thus invalidating the findings (Gergen, 1982). Will learning about the factors that inhibit altruism reduce their influence? Sometimes, such "enlightenment" is not our problem but one of our goals.

Experiments with university students by Arthur Beaman and his colleagues (1978) revealed that once people understand why the presence of bystanders inhibits helping, they become more likely to help in group situations. The researchers used a lecture to inform some students how bystander inaction can affect the interpretation of an emergency and feelings of responsibility. Other students heard either a different lecture or no lecture at all. Two weeks later, as part of a different experiment in a different location, the participants found themselves walking (with an unresponsive confederate) past someone slumped over or past a person sprawled beneath a bicycle. Of those who had not heard the helping lecture, a fourth paused to offer help; twice as many of those "enlightened" did so. Having read this chapter, you, too, have perhaps changed. As you come to understand what influences people's responses, will your attitudes and your behavior be the same?

focus

Behavior and attitudes among rescuers of Jews

Munich, 1948: Oskar Schindler with some of the Jews he saved from the Nazis during World War II.

Goodness, like evil, often evolves in small steps. The Gentiles who saved Jews often began with a small commitment—to hide someone for a day or two. Having taken that step, they began to see themselves differently, as people who help. Then they became more intensely involved. Given control of a confiscated Jewish-owned factory, Oskar Schindler began by doing small favors for his Jewish workers, who were earning him handsome profits. Gradually, he took greater and greater risks to protect them. He got permission to set up workers' housing next to the factory. He rescued individuals separated from their families and reunited loved ones. Finally, as the Russians advanced, he saved some 1200 Jews by setting up a fake factory in his home town, and taking along his entire group of "skilled workers" to staff it (Rappoport & Kren, 1993).

Others, like Raoul Wallenberg, began by agreeing to a personal request for help, and ended up repeatedly risking their lives. Wallenberg became Swedish ambassador to Hungary, where he saved tens of thousands of Hungarian Jews from extermination at Auschwitz. One of those given protective identity papers was six-year-old Ervin Staub (1993), now a University of Massachusetts social psychologist whose experience set him on a lifelong mission to understand why some people perpetrate evil, some stand by, and some heroically help.

Coincidentally, shortly before I wrote the last paragraph, a former student, now living in a large city, stopped by. She mentioned that she recently found herself part of a stream of pedestrians striding past a man lying unconscious on the sidewalk. "It took my mind back to our social psych class and the accounts of why people fail to help in such situations. Then I thought, well, if I just walk by, too, who's going to help him?" So she made a call to an emergency help number and waited with the victim—and other bystanders who now joined her—until help arrived.

Another student, happening upon a drunk man beating up a street person near midnight in a Vienna subway station, flowed by with the crowd.

Finally, I was convinced enough of the truth we learned in social psychology to go back and pull the drunk off the street person. Suddenly he was very mad at me and chased me through the subway until police came, arrested him, and got an ambulance for the victim. It was pretty exciting and made me feel good. But the coolest part was how a little insight into social-psychological aspects of our own behavior can help us overcome the power of the situation and change our predicted actions.

Summing up

Research suggests that we can enhance helpfulness in two ways. First, reverse those factors that inhibit helping. We can take steps to reduce the ambiguity of an emergency situation or to increase feelings of responsibility. We can even use reprimands or the door-in-the-face technique to evoke guilt feelings or a concern for self-image. Second, we can teach altruism. Research into television's portrayals of prosocial models shows the medium's power to teach positive behavior. Children who view helpful behavior tend to act helpfully.

If we want to coax altruistic behavior from people, we should remember the overjustification effect: When we coerce good deeds, intrinsic love of the activity often diminishes. If we provide people with enough justification for them to decide to do good, but not much more, they will attribute their behavior to their own altruistic motivation and henceforth be more willing to help.

Personal Postscript: Wealth, well-being, and generosity

In Chapter 10, I noted that three-fourths of today's entering university students consider it "very important" or "essential" that they become "very well off financially." In today's materialistic cultures, money matters. "Whoever said money can't buy happiness isn't spending it right," proclaimed a Lexus ad.

As it happens, however, the correlation between wealth and well-being is "surprisingly weak," as Ronald Inglehart (1990) noted from one 16-nation survey of 170,000 people. Even lottery winners and the mega-wealthy, after adapting to their abundance, have been found not to be much happier than average middle-class people. Moreover, economic growth in the industrialized nations during the past four decades has *not* been accompanied by improved morale. Absolute poverty can breed misery. But gaining great wealth and its accompanying pleasures buys less happiness than one might suppose from watching *Lifestyles of the Rich and Famous.*

We know it, sort of. Sociologist Robert Wuthnow (1994) reports that 89 percent of people say "our society is much too materialistic." *Other* people are too materialistic, that is. For 84 percent also wished they had more money, and 78 percent said it was "very or fairly important" to have "a beautiful home, a new car and other nice things."

But one has to wonder, what's the point? A recent magazine story on Ted Turner's billion dollar gift to the United Nations reported that "eighty percent of all estates of more than $1 million leave *nothing* to charity." That statistic misleads, because some of those folks gave away significant assets while still alive. Still, what's the point of leaving significant inherited wealth to one's heirs, as if it could buy them happiness? And what's the point of our accumulating stacks of unplayed CDs, closets full of seldom worn clothes, garages with luxury cars—all purchased in a vain quest for an elusive joy—when our excess income could do so much good in a hurting world?

chapter 13

Conflict and Peacemaking

there is a speech that has been spoken in many languages by the leaders of many countries. It goes like this: "The intentions of our country are entirely peaceful. Yet, we are also aware that other nations, with their new weapons, threaten us. Thus we must defend ourselves against attack. By so doing, we shall protect our way of life and preserve the peace" (Richardson, 1960). Almost every nation claims concern only for peace but, mistrusting other nations, arms itself in self-defense. The result: a world that has seen 110 million war-related deaths this century, a world still with a nuclear weapons stockpile equal to 700 times the explosive power used in World War II and the Korean and Vietnam Wars combined, a world that spends $1.4 million per minute on arms and armies (Sivard, 1996).

The elements of such **conflict** (a perceived incompatibility of actions or goals) are similar at all levels, from nations in an arms race, to Bosnian Serbs warring against Muslims, to corporate executives and workers disputing salaries, to a feuding married couple. Whether their perceptions are accurate or

conflict
a perceived incompatibility of actions or goals

Although workers and management often cooperate in their work, they also can experience conflict, which is most evident during a strike.

inaccurate, people in conflict sense that one side's gain is the other's loss. "We want peace and security." "So do we, but you threaten us." "We want more pay." "We can't give it to you." "I'd like the music off." "I'd like it on."

A relationship or an organization without conflict is probably apathetic. Conflict signifies involvement, commitment, and caring. If understood, if recognized, it can stimulate renewed and improved human relations. Without conflict, people seldom face and resolve their problems.

Peace, in its most positive sense, is more than the suppression of open conflict, more than a tense, fragile, surface calmness. Peace is the outcome of a creatively managed conflict, one in which the parties reconcile their perceived differences and reach genuine accord. "We got our increased pay. You got your increased profit. Now we're helping each other achieve our aspirations."

Conflict

What kindles conflict? Social-psychological studies have identified several ingredients. What's striking (and what simplifies our task) is that these ingredients are common to all levels of social conflict, whether interpersonal, intergroup, or international.

Social dilemmas

Several of the problems that most threaten our human future—nuclear arms, global warming, overpopulation, natural resource depletion—arise as various parties pursue their self-interest, ironically, to their collective detriment. Anyone can think, "It would cost me lots to buy expensive pollution controls. Besides, by itself my pollution is trivial." Many others reason similarly, and the result is unclean air and water.

In some societies individuals benefit by having many children who, they assume, can assist with the family tasks and provide security in the parents' old age. But when most families have many children, the result is the collective devastation of overpopulation. Choices that are individually rewarding become collectively punishing. We therefore have an urgent dilemma: How can we

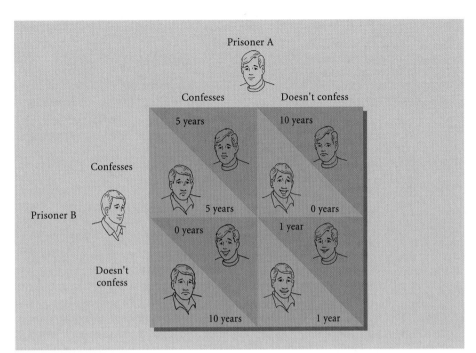

figure 13–1

The Prisoners' Dilemma.

In each box, the number above the diagonal is prisoner A's outcome. Thus, if both prisoners confess, both get five years. If neither confesses, each gets a year. If one confesses, that prisoner is set free in exchange for evidence used to convict the other of a crime bringing a 10-year sentence. If you were one of the prisoners, would you confess?

reconcile individuals' well-being, including their right to pursue their personal interests, with communal well-being?

To isolate and illustrate this dilemma, social psychologists have used laboratory games that expose the heart of many real social conflicts. By showing us how well-meaning people become trapped in mutually destructive behavior, they illuminate some fascinating, yet troubling, paradoxes of human existence. Consider two examples: the Prisoners' Dilemma and the Tragedy of the Commons.

The Prisoners' Dilemma

One dilemma derives from an anecdote concerning two suspects questioned separately by the Crown attorney (Rapoport, 1960). They are jointly guilty; however, the Crown has only enough evidence to convict them of a lesser offense. So the Crown creates an incentive for each to confess privately: If one confesses and the other doesn't, the Crown will grant the confessor immunity (and will use the confession to convict the other of a maximum offense). If both confess, each will receive a moderate sentence. If neither confesses, each will receive a light sentence. The matrix of Figure 13–1 summarizes the choices. Faced with such a dilemma, would you confess?

To minimize their own sentence, many would, despite the fact that mutual confession elicits more severe sentences than mutual nonconfession. Note from the matrix that no matter what the other prisoner decides, each is better off confessing. If the other confesses, one then gets a moderate sentence instead of a severe one. If the other does not confess, one goes free. Of course, each prisoner reasons the same way. Hence, the social trap.

In some 2,000 studies (Dawes, 1991), university students have faced variations of the Prisoners' Dilemma with the outcomes being not prison terms but

figure 13–2

Laboratory version of the Prisoners' Dilemma.

The numbers represent some reward, such as money. In each box, the number above the diagonal lines is the outcome for person A.

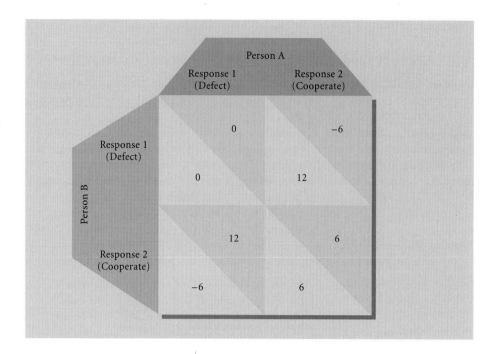

chips, money, or course points. As Figure 13–2 illustrates, on any given decision, a person is better off defecting (because such behavior exploits the other's cooperation or protects against the other's exploitation). However—and here's the rub—by not cooperating, both parties end up far worse off than if they had trusted each other and thus had gained a joint profit. This dilemma often traps each one in a maddening predicament in which both realize they *could* mutually profit but, mistrusting one another, become "locked in" to not cooperating.

In such dilemmas, the unbridled pursuit of self-interest can be detrimental to all. This can be the case in some labor management relations. In 1872, Prime Minister John A. MacDonald's government introduced the Trade Union Act. This law gave workers the right to strike. During a strike if workers remain off the job and management makes concessions, then the workers will likely gain greater rewards. On the other hand, if management refuses to settle and the union gives in, then management is likely to gain greater rewards. If both sides cooperate and make fair concessions, everyone is better off because the workers will not face lost wages and the company will not face decreased production. If both sides engage in unbridled pursuit of self-interest, however, both sides can face massive losses.

An arms race between two or more hostile countries can also function as a prisoner's dilemma. It may occasionally be true that maintaining a balance of terror helps prevent war that might occur if one nation could easily exploit another's weaknesses. But neither the historical record nor the psychological evidence we will consider supports the idea that threatening an enemy with big sticks, such as nuclear weapons, deters war (Lebow & Stein, 1987). More wars were fought during the heavily armed 1980s than in any previous decade in history (Sivard, 1991). Moreover, the people of all nations would surely be more secure if there were no weapons threat and if military spending were available for productive purposes. And consider the irony of countries where ordinary people demand

"When multiplied by 2, a national policy of Peace Through Strength leads inevitably to an arms race."

George Levinger (1987)

the right to own guns for personal security—and end up collectively less secure than those in countries where ordinary people are not armed.

It's easy to say all this, but the dilemma faced by national leaders—and by university students in laboratory simulations of the arms race dilemma—is that one-sided disarmament makes one vulnerable to attack or blackmail. In the laboratory, those who adopt an unconditionally cooperative strategy often get exploited (Oskamp, 1971; Reychler, 1979; Shure & others, 1965). So, alas, the arms spending continues.

The tragedy of the commons

Many social dilemmas involve more than two parties. The greenhouse effect stems from widespread deforestation and from the carbon dioxide emitted by the world's cars, oil burners, and coal-fired power plants. Each gas-guzzling car contributes infinitesimally to the problem, and the harm each does is diffused over many people. To model such social predicaments, researchers have developed laboratory dilemmas that involve multiple people.

A metaphor for the insidious nature of social dilemmas is what ecologist Garrett Hardin (1968) called the "tragedy of the commons." He derived the name from the centrally located pasture area in old English towns, but the "commons" can be air, water, whales, cookies, or any shared and limited resource. If all use the resource in moderation, it may replenish itself as rapidly as it's harvested. The grass will grow, the whales will reproduce, and the cookie jar gets restocked. If not, there occurs a tragedy of the commons.

Imagine 100 farmers surrounding a commons capable of sustaining 100 cows. When each grazes one cow, the common feeding ground is optimally used. But then someone reasons, "If I put a second cow in the pasture, I'll double my output, minus the mere 1 percent overgrazing." So this farmer adds a second cow. So do each of the other farmers. The inevitable result? The Tragedy of the Commons—a grassless mud field.

Many real predicaments parallel this story. Internet congestion occurs as unregulated individuals, seeking to maximize their own gain, surf the Web,

behind the scenes

I am brash enough to believe that laboratory studies of conflict can illumine our understanding of the dynamics of war, peace, and social justice. From small groups to nations, the social processes appear similar. Thus social psychologists who study conflict are in much the same position as the astronomers. We cannot conduct true experiments with large-scale social events. But we can identify the conceptual similarities between the large scale and the small, as the astronomers have between the planets and Newton's apple. By experimenting with small-scale social situations, we may thus be able to understand, predict, and influence large-scale social processes. That is why the games people play as subjects in our laboratory may advance our understanding of war, peace, and social justice.

Morton Deutsch
Columbia University

filling its pipelines with graphical information (Huberman & Lukose, 1997). Likewise, environmental pollution is the sum of many minor pollutions, each of which benefits the individual polluters much more than they could benefit themselves (and the environment) if they stopped polluting. We litter public places—dorm lounges, parks, zoos—while keeping our personal spaces clean. And we deplete our natural resources because the immediate personal benefits of, say, taking a long, hot shower outweigh the seemingly inconsequential costs. Whalers knew others would exploit the whales if they didn't and that taking a few whales would hardly diminish the species. Therein lay the tragedy. Everybody's business (conservation) became nobody's business.

The elements of the commons dilemma have been isolated in laboratory games. Put yourself in the place of students playing Julian Edney's Nuts Game (1979). You and several others sit around a shallow bowl that initially has 10 metal nuts. The experimenter explains that your goal is to accumulate as many nuts as possible. Each of you at any time may take as many as you want, and every 10 seconds the number of nuts remaining in the bowl will be doubled. Would you leave the nuts in the bowl to regenerate, thus producing a greater harvest for all?

Likely not. Unless they were given time to devise and agree upon a conservation strategy, 65 percent of Edney's groups never reached the first 10-second replenishment. Often the people knocked the bowl on the floor grabbing for their share.

Is such individualism uniquely American? Kaori Sato (1987) gave students in a more collective culture, Japan, opportunities to harvest—for actual money—trees from a simulated forest. When the students shared equally the costs of planting the forest, the result was like those in Western cultures. More than half the trees were harvested before they had grown to the most profitable size.

Edney's nut bowl and Sato's forest remind me of the cookie jar in our home. What we *should* have done is conserve cookies during the interval between weekly restockings, so that each day we could each munch two or three. Lacking regulation and fearing that other family members would soon deplete the resource, what we actually did was maximize our individual cookie consumption by downing one after the other. The result: Within 24 hours the cookie glut would often end, the jar sitting empty.

One solution might have been to announce how many cookies went into the jar, implying each family member's share number. When resources are not partitioned, people often consume more than they realize (Herlocker & others, 1997). As a bowl of mashed potatoes starts passing around a table of ten, people are more likely to scoop out more than a 10 percent helping than when a platter of ten chicken drumsticks starts passing.

The Prisoners' Dilemma and the Tragedy of the Commons games have several similar features. First, both tempt people to explain their own behavior situationally ("I had to protect myself against exploitation by my opponent") and to explain their partners' behavior dispositionally ("she was greedy," "he was untrustworthy"). Most never realize that their counterparts are viewing them with the same fundamental attribution error (Hine & Gifford, 1996).

Second, motives often change. At first, people are eager to make some easy money, then to minimize their losses, and finally to save face and avoid defeat (Brockner & others, 1982; Teger, 1980). These shifting motives can make it harder to negotiate a solution. Early on, mediators can focus on proposing reso-lutions that maximize the benefits to both sides. As time progresses, however, solutions must increasingly address not only the substantive issues, but they must let all parties enter an agreement with the sense that they have prevented important losses and avoided defeat.

Third, most real-life conflicts, like the Prisoners' Dilemma and Commons Dilemma, are **non-zero-sum games.** The two sides' profits and losses need not add up to zero. Both can win; both can lose. Each game pits the immediate interests of individuals against the well-being of the group. Each is a diabolical social trap that shows how, even when individuals behave "rationally," harm can result. No malicious person planned for Los Angeles to be smothered in smog, nor for the horrendous destruction of the Bosnian conflict, nor for the earth's atmosphere to be warmed by a blanket of carbon dioxide.

Not all self-serving behavior leads to collective doom. In a plentiful com-mons—as in the world of the eighteenth-century capitalist economist Adam Smith (1776, p. 18)—individuals who seek to maximize their own profit may also give the community what it needs: "It is not from the benevolence of the butcher, the brewer, or the baker, that we expect our dinner," he observed, "but from their regard to their own interest."

non-zero-sum games games in which outcomes need not sum to zero. With cooperation, both can win; with competition, both can lose. (Also called *mixed-motive situations.*)

Resolving social dilemmas

In those situations that are indeed social traps, how can we induce people to cooperate for their mutual betterment? Research with the laboratory dilemmas reveals several ways (Gifford & Hine, 1997).

Regulation.   Reflecting on the Tragedy of the Commons, Garrett Hardin (1968) wrote, "Ruin is the destination to which all men rush, each pursuing his own best interest in a society that believes in the freedom of the commons. Freedom in a commons brings ruin to all." Consider this: If taxes were entirely

When after eight years of war, more than a million casualties, and ruined economies, Iran and Iraq finally laid down their arms, the border over which they had fought was exactly the same as when they started.

voluntary, how many would pay their full share? Surely, many would not, which is why modern societies do not depend on charity to pay for social and military security.

We also develop laws and regulations for our common good. An International Whaling Commission sets an agreed-upon "harvest" that enables whales to regenerate. Countries with nuclear weapons mutually commit themselves to an Atmospheric Test Ban Treaty that reduces radiation in our common air. When enforced, environmental regulations equalize the burden for all; no steel company need fear that other companies will gain a competitive advantage by disregarding their environmental responsibilities.

Similarly, participants in laboratory games often seek ways to regulate their behavior for what they know to be their common good. Players of the Nuts Game may agree to take but 1 or 2 nuts every 10 seconds, leaving the rest to regenerate, or they may elect a leader to decide each person's share (Messick & others, 1983; Samuelson & others, 1984).

But in everyday life, regulation has costs—costs of administering and enforcing the regulations, costs of diminished personal freedom. A volatile political question thus arises: At what point does a regulation's cost exceed its benefits?

Small Is Beautiful.   There is another way to resolve social dilemmas: Make the group small. In small commons, each person feels more responsible and effective (Kerr, 1989). As a group grows larger, people more often think "I couldn't have made a difference anyway"—a common excuse for noncooperation (Kerr & Kaufman-Gilliland, 1997). In small groups, people also feel more identified with a group's success. Anything else that enhances group identity will also increase cooperation. Even just a few minutes of discussion or just believing that one shares similarities with others in the group can increase "we feeling," and cooperation (Brewer, 1987; Orbell & others, 1988).

In small rather than large groups, individuals are also more likely to take no more than their equal share of available resources (Allison & others, 1992). On the Puget Sound island where I grew up, our small neighborhood shared a communal water supply. On hot summer days when the reservoir ran low, a light came on, signaling our fifteen families to conserve. Recognizing our responsibility to one another, and feeling like our conservation really mattered, each of us conserved. Never did the reservoir run dry.

"For that which is common to the greatest number has the least care bestowed upon it."

Aristotle

In a much larger commons—say, a city—voluntary conservation is less successful. Because the harm one does diffuses across many others, each individual can rationalize away personal accountability. Some political theorists and social psychologists therefore argue that, where feasible, the commons should be divided into smaller territories (Edney, 1980). In his 1902 *Mutual Aid*, the Russian revolutionary Pyotr Kropotkin set down a vision of small communities rather than central government making consensus decisions for the benefit of all (Gould, 1988).

Communication.   To escape a social trap, people must communicate. In the laboratory, group communication sometimes degenerates into threats and name calling (Deutsch & Krauss, 1960). More often, communication enables groups to cooperate more—much more (Bornstein & others, 1988, 1989; Jorgenson & Papciak, 1981). Discussing the dilemma forges a group identity, which enhances concern for the group's welfare. It devises group norms and consensus expectations and puts pressure on members to follow them. And it enables people to

Distrust fuels conflict. Believing gas wells near their farm were poisoning the family and their livestock and that the oil company and the government did not care, Alberta farmer Wiebo Ludwig and members of his well-armed family had several tense confrontations with the police and allegedly committed several acts of oilfield vandalism.

commit themselves to cooperation (Bouas & Komorita, 1996; Kerr & others, 1994, 1997; Pruitt, 1998).

A clever experiment by Robyn Dawes (1980, 1994) illustrates. Imagine that an experimenter offered you and six strangers each a choice: You could each have $6. Or you could give it to the others, knowing that the experimenter would double your gift and allocate $2 to each of the strangers. No one will be told whether you chose to give or keep. So if all seven cooperate and give, everyone pockets $12. If you alone keep the $6 and the others give, you pocket $18. If you give and the others keep, you pocket nothing. Clearly, cooperation is mutually advantageous, but it requires sacrifice and risk. Dawes found that, without discussion, about 30 percent of people gave; with discussion, about 80 percent gave.

Open, clear, forthright communication also reduces mistrust. Without communication, those who expect others not to cooperate will usually refuse to cooperate themselves (Messé & Sivacek, 1979; Pruitt & Kimmel, 1977). One who mistrusts almost has to be uncooperative (to protect against exploitation). Noncooperation, in turn, feeds further mistrust ("What else could I do? It's a dog-eat-dog world"). In experiments, communication reduces mistrust, enabling people to reach agreements that lead to their common betterment.

Changing the payoffs.   Cooperation rises when experimenters change the payoff matrix to make cooperation more rewarding, exploitation less rewarding (Komorita & Barth, 1985; Pruitt & Rubin, 1986). Changing payoffs also helps resolve actual dilemmas. In some cities, freeways clog and skies smog because people prefer the convenience of driving themselves directly to work. Each knows that one more car does not add noticeably to the congestion and pollution. To alter the personal cost-benefit calculations, many cities now give carpoolers incentives, such as designated freeway lanes or reduced tolls.

To change behavior, many cities have changed the payoff matrix. Fast carpool-only lanes increase the benefits of carpooling and the costs of driving alone.

Appeals to altruistic norms.   In Chapter 12, we saw how increasing people's feelings of responsibility for others boosts altruism. Can we therefore assume that appeals to altruistic motives will prompt people to act for the common good?

The evidence is mixed. On the one hand, it seems that just *knowing* the dire consequences of noncooperation has little effect. In laboratory games, people realize that their self-serving choices are mutually destructive, yet they continue to make them. Outside the laboratory, warnings of doom and appeals to conserve have brought little response. Pleas to carpool, conserve water, even to refrain from littering, often go unheeded. In the summer of 1999 the town of Guelph, which is near my home, had a ban on lawn sprinkling, yet driving through town I would estimate that eighty percent of the lawns remained green. *Knowing* the good does not necessarily lead to *doing* the good.

Still, most people do adhere to norms of social responsibility, reciprocity, equity, and keeping one's commitments (Kerr, 1992). The problem is how to tap such feelings. One such way is by defining situations in ways that imply cooperative norms. Lee Ross and Andrew Ward (1996) invited Stanford dormitory advisors to nominate male students who they thought especially likely to cooperate and to defect while playing a prisoner's dilemma game. In reality the two groups of students were equally likely to cooperate. What dramatically affected cooperation was whether the researchers labeled the simulation the "Wall Street Game" (in which case one-third of the participants cooperated) or the "Community Game" (with two-thirds cooperating).

Communication can also tap altruistic norms. When permitted to communicate, participants in laboratory games frequently appeal to the social-responsibility norm: "If you defect on the rest of us, you're going to have to live with it for the rest of your life" (Dawes & others, 1977). Noting this, researcher Robyn Dawes (1980) and his associates gave people a short sermon about group benefits, exploitation, and ethics. Then the people played a dilemma game. The appeal worked: People were convinced to forgo immediate personal gain for the common good. (Recall, too, from Chapter 12, the disproportionate volunteerism and charitable contributions by people who regularly hear sermons in churches and synagogues.)

Could such appeals work in large-scale dilemmas? Jeffery Scott Mio and his colleagues (1993) found that, after reading about the commons dilemma (as you have), theatre patrons littered less than patrons who read about voting. Moreover, when cooperation obviously serves the public good, one can usefully appeal to the social-responsibility norm (Lynn & Oldenquist, 1986). When, for example, people believe public transportation can save time, they will be more likely to use it if they also believe it reduces pollution (Van Vugt & others, 1996). In the struggle for civil rights, many marchers willingly agreed, for the sake of the larger group, to suffer harassment, beatings, and jail. In wartime, people make great personal sacrifices for the good of their group. As Winston Churchill said of the Battle of Britain, the actions of the Royal Air Force pilots were genuinely altruistic: A great many people owed a great deal to those who flew into battle knowing there was a high probability they would not return.

To summarize, we can minimize destructive entrapment in social dilemmas by establishing rules that regulate self-serving behavior, by keeping groups small, by enabling people to communicate, by changing payoffs to make cooperation more rewarding, and by invoking altruistic norms.

> "Never in the field of human conflict was so much owed by so many to so few."
>
> Sir Winston Churchill, House of Commons, August 20, 1940

Competition

Hostilities often arise when groups compete for jobs and housing; when interests clash, conflict erupts—a phenomen described by "realistic group conflict theory" (Chapter 9). This was powerfully evident in the Shantung compound, a World War II internment camp into which the invading Japanese military herded foreigners residing in China. According to one of those interned, Langdon Gilkey (1966), the need to distribute the barely adequate food and floor space provoked frequent conflicts among the doctors, missionaries, lawyers, professors, businesspeople, junkies, and prostitutes. The effects of competition for space, jobs, and political power have helped fuel the conflict in Northern Ireland, where since 1969 hostilities between the ruling Protestant majority and the Catholic minority have claimed more than 3,200 lives. (A comparable population proportion would number close to 40,000 in Canada, and 27,000 in Australia.)

But does competition by itself provoke hostile conflict? To find out, we could experiment. Craig Anderson and Melissa Morrow (1995) did so by having people alternate with someone else playing Nintendo's Super Mario Brothers. Half played as competition (comparing points), half as cooperation (combining points). Given the competitive mindset, people unnecessarily killed (by stomping or fireballing) 61 percent more of the game creatures. Competition primed aggression.

Will competition also trigger destructive behavior under more realistic circumstances? To experiment, we could randomly divide people into two groups, have the groups compete for a scarce resource, and note what happens. This is precisely what Muzafer Sherif (1966) and his colleagues did in a dramatic series of experiments with typical 11- and 12-year-old boys. The inspiration for these experiments dated back to Sherif's witnessing, as a teenager, Greek troops invading his Turkish province in 1919.

> They started killing people right and left. [That] made a great impression on me. There and then I became interested in understanding why these things were happening among human beings. . . . I wanted to learn whatever science or specialization was needed to understand this intergroup savagery. (quoted by Aron & Aron, 1989, p. 131)

After studying the social roots of savagery, Sherif introduced the seeming essentials into several three-week summer camping experiences. In one such study, he divided 22 unacquainted Oklahoma City boys into two groups, took them to a Boy Scout camp in separate buses, and settled them in bunkhouses about a half-mile apart. For most of the first week, they were unaware of the other group's existence. By cooperating in various activities—preparing meals, camping out, fixing up a swimming hole, building a rope bridge—each group soon became close-knit. They gave themselves names: "Rattlers" and "Eagles." Typifying the good feeling, a sign appeared in one cabin: "Home Sweet Home."

Group identity thus established, the stage was set for the conflict. Toward the end of the first week, the Rattlers "discovered the Eagles on 'our' baseball field." When the camp staff then proposed a tournament of competitive activities between the two groups (baseball games, tugs-of-war, cabin inspections, treasure hunts, and so forth), both groups responded enthusiastically. This was win-lose competition. The spoils (medals, knives) would all go to the tournament victor.

The result? The camp gradually degenerated into open warfare. It was like a scene from William Golding's novel *Lord of the Flies*, which depicts the social disintegration of boys marooned on an island. In Sherif's study, the conflict began with each side calling the other names during the competitive activities. Soon it escalated to dining hall "garbage wars," flag burnings, cabin ransackings, even fistfights. Asked to describe the other group, the boys said "they" were "sneaky," "smart alecks," "stinkers," while referring to their own group as "brave," "tough," "friendly."

The win-lose competition had produced intense conflict, negative images of the outgroup, and strong ingroup cohesiveness and pride. All this occurred

Competition kindles conflict. Here, in the Sherif experiment, one group of boys raids the bunkhouse of another.

without any cultural, physical, or economic differences between the two groups and with boys who were their communities' "cream of the crop." Sherif noted that had we visited the camp at this point, we would have concluded these "were wicked, disturbed, and vicious bunches of youngsters" (1966, p. 85). Actually, their evil behavior was triggered by an evil situation. Fortunately, as we will see, Sherif not only made strangers into enemies; he then made the enemies into friends.

Perceived injustice

"That's unfair!" "What a ripoff!" "We deserve better!" Such comments typify conflicts bred by perceived injustice. But what is "justice"? According to some social-psychological theorists, people perceive justice as *equity*—the distribution of rewards in proportion to individuals' contributions (Walster & others, 1978). If you and I have a relationship (employer-employee, teacher-student, husband-wife, colleague-colleague), it is equitable if

$$\frac{\text{My outcomes}}{\text{My inputs}} = \frac{\text{Your outcomes}}{\text{Your inputs}}$$

If you contribute more and benefit less than I do, you will feel exploited and irritated; I may feel exploitative and guilty. Chances are, though, that you more than I will be sensitive to the inequity (Greenberg, 1986; Messick & Sentis, 1979). In experiments, people often don't demand a distribution that favors themselves or their group. But they do accept and readily rationalize a big piece of the pie (Diekmann & others, 1997). Latisha and George might not demand an above-average bonus for their work group, yet may easily justify such when someone else decides in their favor.

We may agree with the equity principle's definition of justice yet disagree on whether our relationship is equitable. If two people are colleagues, what will each consider a relevant input? The one who is older may favor basing pay on seniority, the other on current productivity. Given such a disagreement, whose definition is likely to prevail? More often than not, those with social power convince themselves and others that they deserve what they're getting (Mikula, 1984). This has been called a "golden" rule: Whoever has the gold makes the rules.

As this suggests, the exploiter can relieve guilt by valuing or devaluing inputs to justify the existing outcomes. Men may perceive the lower pay of women as equitable, given women's "less important" inputs. As we noted in Chapter 9, those who inflict harm may blame the victim and thus maintain their belief in a just world.

And how do those who are exploited react? Elaine Hatfield, William Walster, and Ellen Berscheid (1978) detected three possibilities. They can accept and justify their inferior position ("We're poor; it's what we deserve, but we're happy"). They can demand compensation, perhaps by harassing, embarrassing, even cheating their exploiter. If all else fails, they may try to restore equity by retaliating.

An interesting implication of equity theory—an implication that has been confirmed experimentally—is that the more competent and worthy people feel (the more they value their inputs), the more they will feel underbenefitted and thus eager to retaliate (Ross & others, 1971). Intense social protests generally come from those who believe themselves worthy of more than they are receiving.

"Do unto others 20% better than you would expect them to do unto you, to correct for subjective error."

Linus Pauling (1962)

table 13–1 **Gallup polls reveal increased perceptions of gender inequality**

All things considered, who has a better life in this country—men or women?

	1972	1993
Men	29%	60%
Women	35	21
Same	30	15
No opinion	6	5

Source: Roper Center for Public Opinion Research, 1997

"Awards should be 'according to merit'; for all people agree that what is just in distribution must be according to merit in some sense, though they do not all specify the same sort of merit."

Aristotle

"Solutions to the distribution problem are nontrivial. Children fight, colleagues complain, group members resign, tempers flare, and nations battle over issues of fairness. As parents, employers, teachers, and presidents know, the most frequent response to an allocation decision is 'not fair.' "

Arnold Kahn & William Gaeddert (1985)

Since 1970, professional opportunities for women have significantly increased. Ironically, though understandably to an equity theorist, so have people's feelings that women's status is *in*equitable (Table 13–1). So long as women compared their opportunities and earnings with other women, they felt generally satisfied—as they still do with their disproportionate share of family labor (Jackson, 1989; Major, 1989, 1993). Now that women are more likely to see themselves as men's equals, their sense of relative deprivation has grown. If secretarial work and truck driving have "comparable worth" (for the skills required), then they deserve comparable pay; that's equity, say advocates of gender equality (Lowe & Wittig, 1989).

Critics argue that equity is not the only conceivable definition of justice. (Pause a moment: Can you imagine any other?) Edward Sampson (1975) says equity theorists wrongly assume that the economic principles that guide Western, capitalist nations are universal. Some noncapitalist cultures define justice not as equity but as equality or even fulfillment of need: "From each according to his abilities, to each according to his needs" (Karl Marx). When rewards are distributed to those within one's group, people socialized under the influence of collectivist cultures, such as China and India, likewise favor need or equality more than do individualistic Westerners (Hui & others, 1991; Leung & Bond, 1984; Murphy-Berman & others, 1984).

In collectivist, age-respecting Japan, pay is less often based on productivity, more often on seniority (Kitayama & Markus, in press). Even within individualistic cultures, criteria other than equity sometimes define justice (Deutsch, 1985). In Spain only 26 percent of people favor basing pay on performance; in Britain 32 percent do; and in the U.S. 53 percent do. And should government reduce income differences or guarantee incomes? Yes, say 39 percent of Americans, 48 percent of Canadians, and 65 percent of Britishers (Brown, 1995). Different criteria are also applied in different situations. In a family or an altruistic institution, the criterion may be need. In a friendship, it may be equality. In a competitive relationship, the winner may take all.

How universal, then, is the tendency to define justice as equity? And on what basis *should* rewards be distributed? Need? Equality? Merit? Some combination of these? Political philosopher John Rawls (1971) invites us to consider a future in which our own place on the economic ladder was unknown. Which standard of justice would we prefer? Gregory Mitchell and his colleagues (1993) report that university students want enough priority placed on equality to

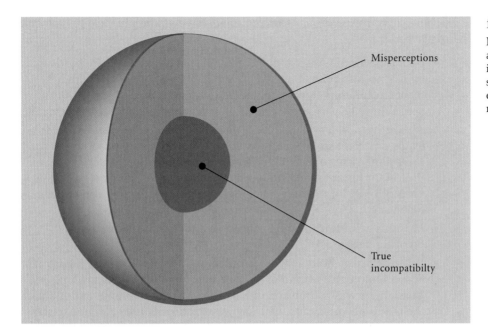

figure 13–3
Many conflicts contain a core of truly incompatible goals surrounded by a larger exterior of misperceptions.

meet their own needs, should they find themselves at the bottom, but also some reward for productivity.

Misperception

Recall that conflict is a *perceived* incompatibility of actions or goals. Many conflicts contain but a small core of truly incompatible goals; the bigger problem is the misperceptions of the other's motives and goals. The Eagles and the Rattlers did indeed have some genuinely incompatible aims. But their perceptions subjectively magnified their differences (Figure 13–3).

In earlier chapters we considered the seeds of such misperception. The *self-serving bias* leads individuals and groups to accept credit for their good deeds and shuck responsibility for bad deeds, without according others the same benefit of the doubt. A tendency to *self-justify* further inclines people to deny the wrong of their evil acts that cannot be shucked off. Thanks to the *fundamental attribution error,* each side sees the other's hostility as reflecting an evil disposition. One then filters the information and interprets it to fit one's *preconceptions.* Groups frequently *polarize* these self-serving, self-justifying, biasing tendencies. One symptom of *groupthink* is the tendency to perceive one's own group as moral and strong, the opposition as evil and weak. Terrorist acts that are despicable brutality to most people are "holy war" to others. Indeed, the mere fact of being in a group triggers an *ingroup bias.* And negative *stereotypes,* once formed, are often resistant to contradictory evidence.

So it should not surprise us, though it should sober us, to discover that people in conflict form distorted images of one another. Even the types of misperception are intriguingly predictable.

Mirror-image perceptions

To a striking degree, the misperceptions of those in conflict are mutual. People in conflict attribute similar virtues to themselves and vices to the other.

Such negative mirror-image perceptions have been an obstacle to peace in many places:

- Both sides of the Arab-Israeli conflict insisted that "we" are motivated by our need to protect our security and our territory, while "they" want to obliterate us and gobble up our land (Heradstveit, 1979; R.K. White, 1977). Given such intense mistrust, negotiation is difficult.
- At Northern Ireland's University of Ulster, J.A. Hunter and his colleagues (1991) showed Catholic and Protestant students videos of a Protestant attack at a Catholic funeral and a Catholic attack at a Protestant funeral. Most students attributed the other side's attack to "bloodthirsty" motives but its own side's attack to retaliation or self-defense.
- Muslims and Hindus in Bangladesh exhibit the same ingroup-favoring perceptions (Islam & Hewstone, 1993).
- When U.S. psychologist Urie Bronfenbrenner (1961) visited the former Soviet Union in 1960 and conversed with many ordinary citizens in Russian, he was astonished to hear them saying the same things about the U.S. that Americans were saying about the Russians. The Russians said that the U.S. government was militarily aggressive; that it exploited and deluded the American people; that in diplomacy it was not to be trusted—"Slowly and painfully, it forced itself upon one that the Russians' distorted picture of us was curiously similar to our view of them—a mirror image."

table 13–2   **Mirror image perceptions that fed the arms race**

Assumption	Sample Statement by the U.S. President	Sample Statement by the Soviet General Secretary
1: "We prefer mutual disarmament."	"We want more than anything else to join with them in reducing the number of weapons." (*New York Times*, 6/15/84)	"We do not strive . . . for military superiority over them; we want termination, not continuation of the arms race." (*New York Times*, 3/12/85)
2: "We must avoid disarming while the other side arms."	"We refuse to become weaker while potential adversaries remain committed to their imperialist adventures." (*New York Times*, 6/18/82)	"Our country does not seek [nuclear] superiority, but it also will not allow superiority to be gained over it." (*Pravda*, 4/9/84)
3: "Unlike us, the other side aims for military superiority."	"For the [former] Soviet leaders peace is not the real issue; rather, the issue is the attempt to spread their dominance using military power." (*New York Times*, 6/28/84)	"The main obstacle—and the entire course of the Geneva talks is persuasive evidence of this—is the attempts by the U.S. and its allies to achieve military superiority." (*Pravda*, 1/3/84)

Adapted from Plous (1985, 1993)

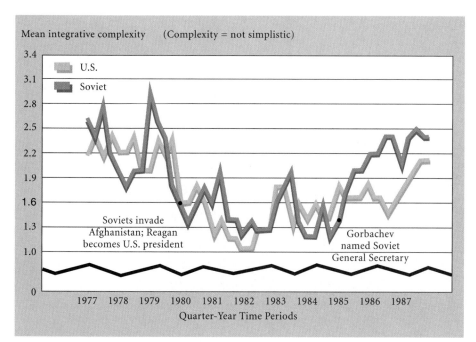

figure 13–4

Complexity of official U.S. and Soviet policy statements, 1977–1986.

(From Tetlock, 1988.)

In 1992, Richard Tobin and Monroe Eagles tested whether distorted perceptions of Russia persisted into the 1990s. They asked 77 American and 137 French Canadian students to evaluate a number of actions taken by the U.S. and Russia. Perhaps not surprisingly, the U.S. students showed a double standard, evaluating the Russian actions more harshly than the U.S. actions. But the Canadians did the same thing although to a lesser extent. It appears that distorted perceptions of Russia persisted into the 1990s in both the U.S. and Canada.

Mirror-image perceptions also fueled the arms race. Political statements revealed that people in both the U.S. and Russia (1) preferred mutual disarmament to all other outcomes, (2) wanted above all not to disarm while the other side armed, but (3) perceived the other side as preferring to achieve military superiority (Plous, 1985, 1993; Table 13–2). Thus, though both nations claimed to prefer disarmament, both felt compelled to arm themselves.

When the two sides have such clashing perceptions, at least one of the two is misperceiving the other. And when such misperceptions exist, noted Bronfenbrenner, "It is a psychological phenomenon without parallel in the gravity of its consequences. . .for it is characteristic of such images that they are self-confirming.:" If A expects B to be hostile, A may treat B in such a way that B fulfills A's expectations, thus beginning a vicious circle. Morton Deutsch (1986) explains:

> You hear the false rumor that a friend is saying nasty things about you; you snub him; he then badmouths you, confirming your expectation. Similarly, if the policymakers of East and West believe that war is likely and either attempts to increase its military security vis-a-vis the other, the other's response will justify the initial move.

Destructive mirror-image perceptions also operate in conflicts between small groups and between individuals. As we saw in the dilemma games, both parties may say, "We want to cooperate. But their refusal to cooperate forces us to react

Self-confirming, mirror-image perceptions are a hallmark of intense conflict, as in the former Yugoslavia.

mirror-image perceptions
reciprocal views of one another often held by parties in conflict; for example, each may view itself as moral and peace-loving and the other as evil and aggressive

defensively." In a study of executives, Kenneth Thomas and Louis Pondy (1977) uncovered such attributions. Asked to describe a significant recent conflict, only 12 percent felt the other party was cooperative; 74 percent perceived themselves as cooperative. The executives explained that they had "suggested," "informed," and "recommended," while their antagonist had "demanded," "disagreed with everything I said," and "refused." Likewise, Dutch negotiators and government officials tend to see their own tactics as "collaborating," "listening," "being well-prepared," and their opponents as more often "threatening," "bluffing," or "avoiding the issue" (De Dreu & others, 1995).

When tension rises—as happens during an international crisis—rational thinking becomes more difficult (Janis, 1989). Views of the enemy become more simplistic and stereotyped, and seat-of-the-pants judgments become more likely. Social psychologist Philip Tetlock (1988) observed this phenomenon when he analyzed the complexity of Russian and American rhetoric since 1945. During the Berlin blockade, the Korean War, and the Russian invasion of Afghanistan, political statements became simplified into stark, good-versus-bad terms. At other times—notably after Mikhail Gorbachev became the Soviet general secretary (Figure 13–4)—political statements acknowledged that each country's motives were complex.

Such shifts away from simplistic we-are-good—they-are-bad rhetoric typically preceded new agreements, reports Tetlock. His optimism was confirmed in 1988 when the intermediate-range nuclear force (INF) treaty was signed in Moscow, and a few weeks later Gorbachev visited New York and told the United Nations that he would remove 500,000 Soviet troops from eastern Europe:

> I would like to believe that our hopes will be matched by our joint effort to put an end to an era of wars, confrontation and regional conflicts, to aggressions against nature, to the terror of hunger and poverty as well as to political terrorism. This is our common goal and we can only reach it together.

Group conflicts are often fueled by an illusion that the enemy's top leaders are evil but their people, though controlled and manipulated, are pro-us. This evil leader–good people perception was clearly evident in the NATO allies' perceptions of Yugoslavia during the air campaign to liberate Kosovo. Slobodan Milosovic was seen as a kin to Hitler and despite reports that the people of Yugoslavia were vehemently opposed to the bombing, NATO leaders held out hope that these people would overthrow Milosevic.

Another type of mirror-image perception is each side's exaggeration of the other's position. People with opposing views on issues such as abortion, capital punishment, and government budget cuts often differ less than they suppose. Each side overestimates the extremity of the other's views, especially those of the group seeking change. And each presumes that "our" beliefs follow from the facts while "their" ideology dictates their interpretation of facts (Keltner & Robinson, 1996; Robinson & others, 1995). From such exaggerated perceptions arise culture wars. Ralph White (1996) reports that the Serbs started the war in Bosnia partly out of an exaggerated fear of the relatively secularized Bosnian Muslims, whose beliefs they wrongly associated with Middle Eastern Islamic fundamentalism and fanatical terrorism.

Shifting perceptions

If misperceptions accompany conflict, then they should appear and disappear as conflicts wax and wane. And they do, with startling ease. The same processes that create the enemy's image can reverse that image when the enemy becomes an ally. Thus the "bloodthirsty, cruel, treacherous, buck-toothed little Japs" of World War II (who were deemed so dangerous that even Canadian citizens of Japanese descent were sent to internment camps) soon became our "intelligent, hardworking, self-disciplined, resourceful allies." Our World War II allies, the Russians, then became the "warlike, treacherous" ones.

The Germans, who after two world wars were hated, then admired, and then again hated, were once again admired—apparently no longer plagued by what earlier was presumed to be cruelty in their national character. So long as Iraq was attacking Iran, even while using chemical weapons and massacring its own Kurds, many nations supported it. Our enemy's enemy is our friend. When Iraq ended its war with Iran and invaded oil-rich Kuwait, Iraq's behavior suddenly became "barbaric." Clearly, images of our enemies not only justify our actions but also change with amazing ease.

The extent of misperceptions during conflict provides a chilling reminder that people need not be insane or abnormally evil to form these distorted images of their antagonists. When in conflict with another nation, another group, or simply a roommate or parent, we readily develop misperceptions that allow us to perceive our own motives and actions as wholly good and the other's as totally evil. Our antagonists usually form a mirror-image perception of us.

So, trapped in a social dilemma, competing for scarce resources, or perceiving injustice, the conflict continues until something enables both parties to peel away their misperceptions and work at reconciling their actual differences. Good advice, then, is when in conflict do not assume that the other fails to share your values and morality. Rather, compare perceptions, assuming that the other is likely perceiving the situation differently.

Shifting perceptions. Germany and Canada, enemies during World War II, now enjoy friendly relations.

Summing up

Whenever two people, two groups, or two nations interact, their perceived needs and goals may conflict. Many social problems arise as people pursue individual self-interest, to their collective detriment. Two laboratory games, the Prisoner's Dilemma and the Tragedy of the Commons, capture this clash of individual versus communal well-being. In real life, as in laboratory experiments, we can avoid such traps by establishing rules that regulate self-serving behavior; by keeping social groups small so people feel responsibility for one another; by enabling communication, thus reducing mistrust; by changing payoffs to make cooperation more rewarding; and by invoking altruistic norms.

When people compete for scarce resources, human relations often sink into prejudice and hostility. In his famous experiments, Muzafer Sherif found that win-lose competition quickly made strangers into enemies, triggering outright warfare even among normally upstanding boys.

Conflicts also arise when people feel unjustly treated. According to equity theory, people define justice as the distribution of rewards in proportion to one's contributions. Conflicts occur when people disagree on the extent of their contributions and thus on the equity of their outcomes.

Conflicts frequently contain a small core of truly incompatible goals, surrounded by a thick layer of misperceptions of the adversary's motives and goals. Often, conflicting parties have *mirror-image perceptions*. When both sides believe "we are peace-loving—they are hostile," each may treat the other in ways that provoke confirmation of its expectations. International conflicts are sometimes also fed by an evil leader–good people illusion.

Peacemaking

Although toxic forces can breed destructive conflict, we can harness other forces to bring conflict to a constructive resolution. What are these ingredients of peace and harmony?

We have seen how conflicts are ignited: by social traps, competition, perceived injustices, and misperceptions. Although grim, the picture is not hopeless. Sometimes closed fists become open arms as hostilities evolve into friendship. Social psychologists have focused on four strategies for helping enemies become comrades. We can remember these as the four Cs of peacemaking: contact, cooperation, communication, conciliation.

Contact

Might putting two conflicting individuals or groups into close contact enable them to know and like each other? Or might it cause them to act on prejudices, escalating the conflict? There are reasons to think that either reaction could occur. In Chapter 11, we saw that proximity—and the accompanying interaction, anticipation of interaction, and mere exposure—boosts liking. On the other hand, we saw in Chapter 3 how negative expectations can color people's judgments and can even create self-fulfilling prophecies, leading people to evaluate others negatively and bring out their worst. Such competing predictions are just the sort of puzzle that excites the scientist's detective spirit.

The original hypothesis, labeled the contact hypothesis by Gordon Allport (1954), was that contact between members of groups in conflict would lead to friendlier relations and a reduction in prejudiced attitudes. This hypothesis has been examined in hundreds of studies and the results of these investigations have enabled researchers to tell an interesting detective story.

Does contact improve intergroup relations?

A bird's eye view of the studies suggests that contact improves intergroup relations. In a comprehensive review of the studies that have investigated the contact hypothesis, Thomas Pettigrew (1999) has concluded that there is clear evidence that contact does promote harmony between groups.

Studies in numerous countries including Canada, Germany, Pakistan, the United States, France, England, and Holland have found that increased contact between members of ethnic groups tends to be associated with better relations between groups (Brown, Vivian, & Hewstone, 1999; Hamberger & Hewstone, 1997; Kalin & Berry, 1982; Pettigrew, 1997; Wagner, Hewstone, & Machleit, 1989). Likewise, anti-gay feelings are lower among people who know gays personally (Herek, 1993). Additional studies of attitudes toward the elderly, the mentally ill, AIDS patients, and those with disabilities confirm that contact often predicts positive attitudes (Pettigrew, 1998).

We must be careful interpreting these studies, however. The reported relationship between contact and positive intergroup evaluations is a correlation. Maybe when groups begin to evaluate each other positively they engage in more contact rather than the other way around. Maybe some other variable, like community norms, promotes intergroup contact and positve intergroup evaluations. To determine whether contact actually causes harmony between groups, experiments need to be conducted. Results of such experiments generally support the contact hypothesis (Pettigrew, 1999). But not all experiments support it.

For example, Walter Stephan (1986), in his review of research on school integration in the U.S., concluded that such contact has had little effect on racial attitudes. Many student exchange programs have likewise had less-than-hoped-for positive effects on student attitudes toward their host countries. For example, when eager Canadian students study in France, often living with other Canadians as they do so, their stereotypes of the French tend not to improve (Stroebe & others, 1988).

So sometimes intergroup contact improves group relations; sometimes it doesn't. What explains the difference? So far, we've been lumping all kinds of contact together. Actual contact occurs in many ways and under vastly different conditions.

When does contact improve intergroup relations?

As social psychologists have unraveled the effects of contact on intergroup relations they have discovered that some types of contact work better than others in promoting positive group interactions. From the beginning researchers expected this to be the case. They expected poor results when contacts were competitive, unsupported by authorities, and unequal, and the research supports the contention that these factors make contact less effective (Pettigrew, 1988, 1999; Stephan, 1987).

Recently researchers have added to the story by uncovering a number of factors that make contact more effective. One factor that seems particularly important is cross-group friendships. When contact promotes friendships across group lines improved intergroup relations usually follow. For example, surveys of nearly 4,000 Europeans reveal that friendship is a key to successful contact: If you have a minority-group friend, you become much more likely to express sympathy and support for the friend's group, and even somewhat more support for immigration by that group (Hamberger & Hewstone, 1997; Pettigrew, 1997). Stephen Wright and his colleagues (1997, 1999) have confirmed the importance of friendship in experiments as well. In their studies, forming a friendship with a member of the outgroup leads to development of positive attitudes toward the outgroup.

Another important factor is developing a sense of common group identity between the members of the conflicting groups. If they can come to see themselves as members of a larger, more inclusive group, then positive group relations usually follow. Samuel Gaertner, John Dovidio and their colleagues (1994, 1996) have conducted a number of experiments and surveys demonstrating that when people's perceptions are transformed from "Us" versus "Them" into "We," intergroup harmony is promoted. For example, when feuding groups at a high school define themselves as all members of the same school, positive intergroup relations are likely to follow. They also suggest that one reason competitive, unequal contacts often fail to improve intergroup relations is that such contacts make it hard for a common group identity to form.

Intergroup contact is also more effective if it shows that people are members of many different groups (Brewer, 1996). We are all members of lots of different social groups; we attend a particular university, we come from a certain family, we are one of the genders, etc. When contact highlights that the people are not just members of the outgroup but members of other groups as well, including some of which we belong to then contact is more effective.

In addition to these factors it is also important that people do not come to believe that the outgroup members with which they come into contact are different from all other outgroup members. Such beliefs can prevent positive intergroup relations from spreading to people's opinions about the outgroup. If they come to like the people they know, but hate the groups that those people belong to, then clearly contact is not as effective as one would hope. Miles Hewstone and his colleagues (1999) have shown that in order to prevent such perceptions it is important for people to see the outgroup members they come into contact with as typical members of the outgroup.

Thus, for intergroup contact to be most effective, unequal, competitive contacts that are not supported by the authorities should be avoided. As well, contacts that promote friendships, a common group identity, and expose multiple group memberships while maintaining that members of the conflicting groups are typical members of their groups should be encouraged.

equal-status contact contact made on an equal basis. Just as a relationship between people of unequal status breeds attitudes consistent with their relationship, so do relationships between those of equal status. Thus, to reduce prejudice, interracial contact should be between persons equal in status.

Cooperation

Although equal-status contact can help, it is sometimes not enough. It didn't help when Muzafer Sherif stopped the Eagles versus Rattlers competition and brought the groups together for noncompetitive activities, such as watching movies, shooting off fireworks, and eating. By this time, their hostility was so strong that what contact provided was the opportunity for taunts and attacks. When an Eagle was bumped by a Rattler, his fellow Eagles urged him to "brush off the dirt." Obviously, desegregating the two groups had hardly promoted their social integration.

Given entrenched hostility, what can a peacemaker do? Sherif brought the Eagles and the Rattlers together by having them cooperate on a number of activities in which both groups wanted to achieve a goal, but needed the other group's help to achieve it. Together, they were fighting for a common cause, striving toward a shared goal.

Contrast this interdependence with the competitive situation in the typical classroom, desegregated or not. Is the following scene familiar (Aronson, 1980)? Students compete for good grades, teacher approval, and various honors and privileges. The teacher asks a question. Several students' hands shoot up; other students sit, eyes downcast, trying to look invisible. When the teacher calls on one of the eager faces, the others hope for a wrong answer, giving them a chance to display their knowledge. The losers in this academic sport often resent the "nerds" or "geeks" who succeed. The situation abounds with both competition and painfully obvious status inequalities; we could hardly design it better to create divisions among the children.

Does this suggest a second factor that predicts whether the effect of desegregation will be favorable? Does competitive contact divide and *cooperative* contact unite? Consider what happens to people who together face a common predicament.

Common external threats

Together with others, have you ever been victimized by the weather; harassed as part of your initiation into a group; punished by a teacher; or persecuted and ridiculed because of your social, racial, or religious identity? If so, you may

Shared predicaments are a powerful trigger for cooperation. Montreal residents pitch in to clean up after the ice storm and Manitobans help others to evacuate during a flood.

recall feeling close to those with whom you shared the predicament. Perhaps previous social barriers were dropped as you helped one another dig out of the snow or struggled to cope with a common enemy.

Such friendliness is common among those who experience a shared threat. John Lanzetta (1955) observed this when he put four-man groups of students to work on problem-solving tasks and then began informing them over a loudspeaker that their answers were wrong, their productivity inexcusably low, their thinking stupid. Other groups did not receive this harassment. Lanzetta observed that the group members under duress became friendlier to one another, more cooperative, less argumentative, less competitive. They were in it together. And the result was a cohesive spirit.

Having a common enemy unified the groups of competing boys in Sherif's camping experiments—and in many subsequent experiments (Dion, 1979). Think back to the last Olympics. National unity is rarely as strong as when we can cheer for our fellow citizens as they compete against people from other countries. Soldiers who together face combat often maintain lifelong ties with their comrades (Elder & Clipp, 1988). Few things so unite a people as having a common hatred.

Times of interracial strife may therefore be times of heightened group pride. For Chinese university students in Toronto, facing discrimination heightens a sense of kinship with other Chinese (Pak & others, 1991). Just being reminded of an outgroup (say, a rival school) heightens people's responsiveness to their own group (Wilder & Shapiro, 1984). When keenly conscious of who "they" are, we also know who "we" are.

Leaders may even *create* a threatening external enemy as a technique for building group cohesiveness. George Orwell's novel *Nineteen Eighty-Four* illustrates the tactic: The leader of the protagonist nation uses border conflicts with the other two major powers to lessen internal strife. From time to time the enemy shifts, but there is always an enemy. Indeed, the nation seems to *need* an enemy. For the world, for a nation, for a group, having a common enemy is powerfully unifying.

superordinate goal
a shared goal that necessitates cooperative effort; a goal that overrides people's differences from one another

Superordinate goals

Closely related to the unifying power of an external threat is the unifying power of **superordinate goals,** goals compelling for all in a group and requiring cooperative effort. To promote harmony among his warring campers, Sherif introduced such goals. He created a problem with the camp water supply, necessitating their cooperation to restore the water. Given an opportunity to rent a movie, one expensive enough to require the joint resources of both groups, they again cooperated. When a truck "broke down" on a camping trip, a staff member casually left the tug-of-war rope nearby, prompting one boy to suggest that they all pull the truck to get it started. When it started, a backslapping celebration ensued over their victorious "tug-of-war against the truck."

After working together to achieve such superordinate goals, the boys ate together and enjoyed themselves around a campfire. Friendships sprouted across group lines. Hostilities plummeted (Figure 13–5). On the last day, the boys decided to travel home together on one bus. During the trip they no longer sat by groups. As the bus approached Oklahoma City and home, they, as one, spontaneously sang "Oklahoma" and then bade their friends farewell. With isolation and competition, Sherif made strangers into bitter enemies. With superordinate goals, he made enemies into friends.

Are Sherif's experiments mere child's play? Or can pulling together to achieve superordinate goals be similarly beneficial with adults in conflict? Robert Blake and Jane Mouton (1979) wondered. So in a series of two-week experiments involving more than 1,000 executives in 150 different groups, they re-created the essential features of the situation experienced by the Rattlers and Eagles. Each group first engaged in activities by itself, then competed with another group, and then cooperated with the other group in working toward jointly chosen superordinate goals. Their results provided "unequivocal evidence that adult reactions parallel those of Sherif's younger subjects."

Extending these findings, Samuel Gaertner, John Dovidio, and their collaborators (1993, 1998) report that working cooperatively has especially favorable

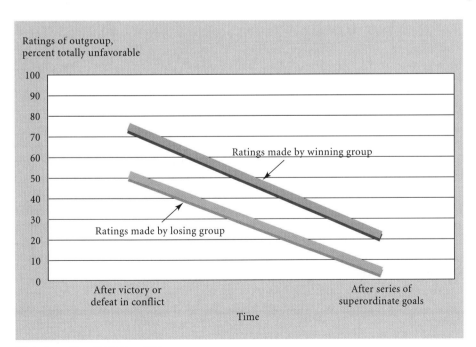

figure 13–5

After competition, the Eagles and Rattlers rated each other unfavorably. After they worked cooperatively to achieve superordinate goals, hostility dropped sharply.

Ratings of outgroup, percent totally unfavorable

Ratings made by winning group

Ratings made by losing group

After victory or defeat in conflict

After series of superordinate goals

Time

(Data from Sherif, 1966, p. 84.)

Promoting "common identity." The common European practice of school uniforms—used in many Canadian Schools as well— aim to change "us" and "them" to "we."

effects under conditions that lead people to define a new, inclusive group that dissolves their former subgroups. Old feelings of bias against another group diminish when members of the two groups sit alternately around a table (rather than on opposite sides), give their new group a single name, and then work together under conditions that foster a good mood. "Us" and "them" become "we." To combat Germany, Italy, and Japan during World War II, Canada, France, the United States, and England, along with other nations, formed one united group named the Allies. So long as the superordinate goal of defeating a common enemy lasted, so did supportive ties between these countries.

The cooperative efforts by Rattlers and Eagles ended in success. Would the same harmony have emerged if the water had remained off, the movie unaffordable, the truck still stalled? Likely not. In experiments with University of Virginia students, Stephen Worchel and his associates (1977, 1978, 1980) confirmed that *successful* cooperation between two groups boosts their attraction for one another. If previously conflicting groups *fail* in a cooperative effort, however, *and* if conditions allow them to attribute their failure to each other, the conflict may worsen. Sherif's groups were already feeling hostile to one another. Thus, failure to raise sufficient funds for the movie might have been attributed to the one group's "stinginess" and "selfishness." This would have exacerbated rather than alleviated their conflict.

Cooperative learning

So far we have noted that contact between conflicting groups when it is unequal does not improve intergroup relations, but cooperative contacts between members of rival groups has dramatic social benefits. Could promoting cooperative contacts serve as an antidote to the unequal contacts between rival groups that are seen in some situations? Several independent research teams speculated yes. Each wondered whether, without affecting academic achievement, we could promote interracial friendships by replacing competitive learning situations with cooperative ones. Given the diversity of their methods—all involving students on integrated study teams, sometimes in competition with other teams— the results are striking and very heartening.

Are students who participate in existing cooperative activities, such as interracial athletic teams and class projects, less prejudiced? Robert Slavin and Nancy Madden (1979) analyzed survey data from 2,400 students in 71 high schools and found encouraging results. Those of different races who play and work together are more likely to report having friends of another race and to express positive racial attitudes. Charles Green and his colleagues (1988) confirmed this in a study of 3,200 Florida middle school students. Compared to students at traditional, competitive schools, those at schools with interracial learning "teams" had more positive racial attitudes.

From this correlational finding, can we conclude that cooperative interracial activity improves racial attitudes? Again, the way to find out is to experiment. Randomly designate some students, but not others, to work together in racially mixed groups. Slavin (1985) and his colleagues divided classes into interracial teams, each composed of four or five students from all achievement levels. Team members sat together, studied a variety of subjects together, and at the end of each week competed with the other teams in a class tournament. All members contributed to the team score by doing well, sometimes by competing with other students whose recent achievements were similar to their own, sometimes by competing with their own previous scores. Everyone had a chance to succeed. Moreover, team members were motivated to help one another prepare for the weekly tournament—by drilling each other on fractions, spelling, or historical events—whatever was the next event. Rather than isolating students from one another, team competition brought them into closer contact and drew out mutual support.

Another research team, led by Elliot Aronson (1978, 1979; Aronson & Gonzalez, 1988), elicited similar group cooperation with a "jigsaw" technique. In experiments in elementary schools, the researchers assigned children to racially and academically diverse six-member groups. The subject was then divided into six parts, with each student becoming the expert on his or her part. In a unit on Chile, one student might be the expert on Chile's history, another on its geography, another on its culture. First, the various "historians," "geographers," and so forth got together to master their material. Then each returned to the home group to teach it to their classmates. Each group

Interracial cooperation—on athletic teams, in class projects and extracurricular activities—melts differences and improves racial attitudes.

focus

Branch Rickey, Jackie Robinson, and the integration of baseball

On April 10, 1947, 19 words that forever changed the face of baseball would also put social psychological principles to the test. In the sixth inning of a Brooklyn Dodgers exhibition game with their top minor league club, the Montreal Royals, radio announcer Red Barber read a statement from Dodger president Branch Rickey: "The Brooklyn Dodgers today purchased the contract of Jackie Roosevelt Robinson from the Montreal Royals. He will report immediately." Five days later, Robinson became the first Black

since 1887 to play major league baseball. In the fall, Dodger fans realized their dreams of going to the World Series. Robinson, after enduring racial taunts, beanballs, and spikes, was voted *Sporting News* rookie of the year. It was clear that Jackie Robinson had now gained a measure of respect and that baseball's color barrier was forever broken.

Motivated by both his Methodist morality and a drive for baseball success, Rickey had been planning the move for some time, report social psychologists Anthony Pratkanis and Marlene Turner (1994a,b). Three years earlier, Rickey had been approached by the sociologist-chair of the Mayor's Committee on Unity and asked to desegregate his team. His response was to ask for time, so the hiring would not be attributed to pressure—and for advice on how best to do it. In 1945, Rickey cast the lone vote in a 15 to 1 owners' vote against bringing Blacks into baseball. In 1947 he made his move using principles identified by Pratkanis and Turner, including these:

- *Create a perception that change is inevitable.* Leave little possibility that protest or resistance can turn back the clock. The announcer Red Barber, a traditional South-

member held, so to speak, a piece of the jigsaw. The self-confident students therefore had to listen to and learn from the reticent students, who in turn soon realized they had something important to offer their peers. Other research teams—led by David Johnson and Roger Johnson (1987, 1994), Elizabeth Cohen (1980), Shlomo Sharan and Yael Sharan (1976), and Stuart Cook (1985)—have devised additional methods for cooperative learning that are also highly effective.

From all this research—818 studies by one count (Druckman & Bjork, 1994)—what can we conclude? With cooperative learning, students learn not only the material but other lessons as well. Cooperative learning is an effective means of promoting intergroup harmony and of helping children succeed academically (Slavin, 1990). Aronson reported that "children in the interdependent, jigsaw classrooms grow to like each other better, develop a greater liking for school, and develop greater self-esteem than children in traditional classrooms" (1980, p. 232).

Cross-group friendships also begin to blossom, which the contact literature suggests is crucial for promoting intergroup harmony. Perhaps this is why after

erner, recalled that in 1945 Rickey took him to lunch and explained very slowly and strongly that his scouts were searching for "the first Black player I can put on the White Dodgers. I don't know who he is or where he is, but, he is coming." An angered Barber at first intended to quit, but in time decided to accept the inevitable and keep the world's "best sports announcing job." Rickey was equally matter of fact with the players in 1947, offering to trade any player who didn't want to play with Robinson.

- *Establish equal status contact with a superordinate goal.* As one sociologist explained to Rickey, when relationships focus on an overarching goal, such as winning the pennant, "the people involved would adjust appropriately." One of the players initially opposed to Robinson later helped him with his hitting, explaining, "When you're on a team, you got to pull together to win."
- *Puncture the norm of prejudice.* Rickey led the way, but others helped. Team leader, shortstop Pee Wee Reese, a Southerner, set a pattern of sitting and eating with Robinson. One day in Cincinnati, as the crowd was hurling slurs—"get the nigger off the field"—Reese left his shortstop position,

walked over to Robinson at first base, smiled and spoke to him, and then—with a hushed crowd watching—put his arm around Robinson's shoulder.

- *Cut short the spiral of violence by practicing nonviolence.* Rickey, wanting "a ballplayer with guts enough not to fight back," role-played for Robinson the kind of insults and dirty play he would experience, and gained Robinson's commitment not to return violence with violence. When Robinson was taunted and spiked, he left the responses to his teammates. Team cohesion was thereby increased.
- *Individuate the new group member.* Treat the person as an individual—in this case, as Jackie Robinson and not as "the Negro ballplayer." Rickey engaged his media friends in introducing Robinson as an accomplished individual in sports, academics, and the military.

Robinson and Bob Feller later became the first players in baseball history elected to the Hall of Fame in their first year of eligibility. As he received the award, Robinson asked three persons to stand beside him: his mother, Mallie, his wife, Rachel, and his friend, Branch Rickey.

the experiments are over, many teachers continue using cooperative learning (D.W. Johnson & others, 1981; Slavin, 1990). These techniques seem to be effective in helping students to learn and in helping them to get along with one another.

Donna Desforges and her colleagues (1991) found that even university students can be dramatically affected by a cooperative learning experience. When they had undergraduates engage in a cooperative learning task with a confederate they believed was a former mental patient, even the students who were most prejudiced about mental patients came to view both their partner and mental patients in general more positively. It seems that cooperative learning reduced these students' prejudice. Generally, it seems that cooperative learning is a strategy that provides a compelling way to implement intergroup contact in the classroom.

So, cooperative, equal-status contacts exert a positive influence on boy campers, industrial executives, university students, and schoolchildren. Does the principle extend to all levels of human relations? Are families unified by pulling together to farm the land, restore an old house, or sail a sloop? Are communal

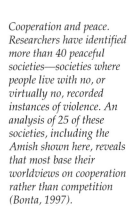

Cooperation and peace. Researchers have identified more than 40 peaceful societies—societies where people live with no, or virtually no, recorded instances of violence. An analysis of 25 of these societies, including the Amish shown here, reveals that most base their worldviews on cooperation rather than competition (Bonta, 1997).

identities forged by barn raisings, group singing, or cheering on the football team? Is international understanding bred by international collaboration in science and space, by joint efforts to feed the world and conserve resources, by friendly personal contacts between people of different nations? Indications are that the answer to all these questions is yes (Brewer & Miller, 1988; Desforges & others, 1991, 1997; Deutsch, 1985, 1994). Thus an important challenge facing our divided world is to identify and agree on our superordinate goals and to structure cooperative efforts to achieve them.

Generalizing positive attitudes

Given cooperative, equal status contacts with those from another group, will we generalize? If we come to like people in another group, will we generalize this positive attitude to the whole outgroup? As Northern Ireland's Catholic and Protestant farmers cooperate in agricultural pursuits, can we expect them to become more accepting of all Protestants (or Catholics)? The answer appears to be yes if

- we see others in our group modeling friendships with outgroup members (Wright & others, 1997),
- we perceive the others as representative of their group rather than atypical (Desforges & others, 1997), and
- we think of them not just as individuals but as having a different group identity than our own (Vivian & others, 1997; Pettigrew, 1998).

Initially, we will be most likely to interact with people if their outgroup identity is minimized—if we see them as essentially like us rather than feeling threatened by their being different. But if our liking is to generalize, their group identity must at some point become salient. An effective sequence was neatly illustrated by one experiment in which highly prejudiced White participants operated an imaginary railway system over 40 sessions with two supposed other participants, one Black, one White (Cook, 1984). As they shared successes and failures and won bonus money, the White participants came to like their new friends. To enhance generalization, the Black confederate, once rapport was established, told of a personal experience with racial discrimination, which the other White confederate lamented. By the end of the lengthy experiment, the subjects not only genuinely liked their Black partner, they expressed more positive racial attitudes than did control subjects not given the experience. So, generalizing from positive interracial experiences may be enhanced by initially minimizing group diversity, then acknowledging it, then transcending it.

Group and superordinate identities

In everyday life, we often reconcile dual identities (Gaertner & others, 1998; Hewstone, 1996; Huo & others, 1996). We acknowledge our subgroup identity (as parent or child) and then transcend it (sensing our superordinate identity as a family). Blended families and corporate mergers leave us mindful of who we were, and who we are. Pride in our ethnic heritage need not displace our larger communal or national identity. Subgroup identity and social cohesion can co-exist.

For many in our society they see themselves as Canadians and a member of another culture. This sense of identifying with both the ethnic culture and the larger culture is what researcher Jean Phinney (1990) calls a "bicultural" identity. Ujjal Dosanjh, British Columbia's and Canada's first Indo-Canadian premier is an excellent example of someone who seems to have such an identity, and it seems to have played a crucial role in his political career. He grew up in a highly political family. His grandfather was jailed and his uncle was killed in India's fight for independence. His father was a member of Mahatma Gandhi's Congress party. So it comes as little surprise that he pursued a career in politics, but he sees his Indian heritage as playing a critical role in his politics. "All around me has been politics and activism," Dosanjh says. "I have been a political animal most of my life. There's no question the fact that I am an Indo-Canadian has led me to do certain things in life that others might not have done."

Forging such a bicultural identity is not always easy. Many people feel a tension between the two identities, and not all people identify with both their culture of origin and the larger culture. Ethnically conscious Asians living in England may or may not also feel strongly British (Hutnik, 1985). French Canadians who identify with their ethnic roots may or may not also feel strongly Canadian (Driedger, 1975). Hispanic Americans who retain a strong sense of their "Cubanness" (or of their Mexican or Puerto Rican heritage) may or may not feel strongly American (Roger & others, 1991). When people find the larger culture as uninviting and unfriendly they are more likely to remain solely identified with their culture of origin.

Nevertheless, with time, identification with a new culture often grows. Second-generation Chinese immigrants to Australia feel their Chinese identity somewhat less keenly, and their new national identity more strongly than do immigrants who were born in China (Rosenthal & Feldman, 1992). Often,

A Difficult Balancing Act These ethnically conscious French Canadians— supporting Bill 101 "live French in Quebec"—may or not also feel strongly Canadian. As countries become more ethnically diverse, people debate how we can build societies that are both plural and unified.

however, the *grand*children of immigrants feel more comfortable identifying with their ethnicity (Triandis, 1994).

Researchers have wondered whether pride in one's group competes with identification with the larger culture. As we noted in Chapter 9, we evaluate ourselves partly in terms of our group memberships. Seeing our own group (our school, our employer, our family, our race, our nation) as good helps us feel good about ourselves. A positive ethnic identity can therefore contribute to positive self-esteem. So can a positive social identity among those who have assimilated into the mainstream culture. "Marginal" people, who have neither an ethnic nor a mainstream identity (Table 13–3), often have low self-esteem. Bicultural people, who affirm both identities, typically have a strongly positive self-concept (Phinney, 1990). Often, they alternate between their two cultures, adapting their language and behavior to whichever group they are with (LaFromboise & others, 1993).

Taken to an extreme, group pride becomes destructive tribalism. Preoccupation with diversity may counter the "universalism" that is basic to a nonviolent conflict resolution strategies (Mayton & others, 1996). By seeking to understand, appreciate, and protect all people, universalists such as Gandhi, Martin Luther King, Jr., and Nelson Mandela advocate peaceful routes to justice.

By forging national identities with unifying ideals, immigrant countries such as Canada and Australia have avoided ethnic wars. In these countries, Irish and Italians, Swedes and Scots, Asians and Africans seldom kill in defense of their ethnic identities. Nevertheless, even the immigrant nations struggle between separation and wholeness, between people's pride in their distinct heritage and unity as one nation, between acknowledging the reality of diversity and questing for shared values. These tensions pose a very real and urgent challenge for our society as we try to develop and foster a truly multicultural society.

"We rededicate ourselves to the very idea of America. . . . An idea ennobled by the faith that our nation can summon from its myriad diversity the deepest measure of unity."

President Bill Clinton
Inaugural Address,
January 20, 1993

Communication

Conflicting parties have other ways to resolve their differences. When husband and wife, or labor and management, or nation X and nation Y disagree, they can **bargain** with one another directly. They can ask a third party to **mediate** by

table 13–3   **Ethnic and cultural identity**

Identification With Majority Group	Identification With Ethnic Group	
	Strong	**Weak**
strong	bicultural	assimilated
weak	separated	marginal

making suggestions and facilitating their negotiations. Or they can **arbitrate** by submitting their disagreement to someone who will study the issues and impose a settlement.

Bargaining

If you or I want to buy or sell a new car, are we better off adopting a tough bargaining stance—opening with an extreme offer so that splitting the difference will yield a favorable result? Or are we better off beginning with a sincere "good-faith" offer?

Experiments suggest no simple answer. On the one hand, those who demand more will often get more. Robert Cialdini, Leonard Bickman, and John Cacioppo (1979) provide a typical result: In a control condition, they approached various Chevrolet dealers and asked the price of a new Monte Carlo sports coupe with designated options. In an experimental condition, they approached other dealers and first struck a tougher bargaining stance, asking for and rejecting a price on a *different* car ("I need a lower price than that. That's a lot"). When they then asked the price of the Monte Carlo, exactly as in the control condition, they received offers that averaged some $200 lower.

Tough bargaining may lower the other party's expectations, making the other side willing to settle for less (Yukl, 1974). But toughness can sometimes backfire. Many a conflict is not over a pie of fixed size but over a pie that shrinks if the conflict continues. Yet often negotiators fail to realize their common interests, and about 20 percent of the time negotiate "lose-lose" agreements that are mutually costly (Thompson & Hrebec, 1996).

Delayed agreements can also be costly. When a strike is prolonged, both labor and management lose. Being tough can also diminish the chances of actually reaching an agreement. If the other party responds with an equally extreme stance, both may be locked into positions from which neither can back down without losing face. The nurse's strike in Quebec in the summer of 1999 had some of these features. Premier Lucien Bouchard had announced before the strike that he would not give a raise greater than 5 percent over three years, and the nurses announced they would not accept such a deal. After such statements it is difficult for either side to compromise and reach an agreement.

Mediation

A third-party mediator may offer suggestions that enable conflicting parties to make concessions and still save face (Pruitt, 1998). If my concession can be attributed to a mediator, who is gaining an equal concession from my antagonist, then neither of us will be viewed as caving in to the other's demands.

bargaining
seeking an agreement through direct negotiation between parties to a conflict

mediation
an attempt by a neutral third party to resolve a conflict by facilitating communication and offering suggestions

arbitration
resolution of a conflict by a neutral third party who studies both sides and imposes a settlement

Turning win-lose into win-win.　　Mediators also help resolve conflicts by facilitating constructive communication. Their first task is to help the parties rethink the conflict and gain information about other's interests (Thompson, 1998). Typically, people on both sides have a competitive "win-lose" orientation: They are successful if their opponent is unhappy with the result, and unsuccessful if their opponent is pleased (Thompson & others, 1995). The mediator aims to replace this win-lose orientation with a cooperative "win-win" orientation, by prodding them to set aside their conflicting demands and instead to think about each other's underlying needs, interests, and goals. In experiments, Leigh Thompson (1990) found that, with experience, negotiators become better able to make mutually beneficial tradeoffs and thus to achieve win-win resolutions.

A classic story of such a resolution concerns the two sisters who quarreled over an orange (Follett, 1940). Finally they compromised and split the orange in half, whereupon one sister squeezed her half for juice while the other used the peel to make a cake. In a series of compelling experiments, Dean Pruitt and his associates induced bargainers to search for **integrative agreements.** If the sisters had agreed to split the orange, giving one sister all the juice and the other all the peel, they would have hit on such an agreement, one that integrates both parties' interests (Kimmel & others, 1980; Pruitt & Lewis, 1975, 1977). Compared to compromises, in which each party sacrifices something important, integrative agreements are more enduring. Because they are mutually rewarding, they also lead to better ongoing relationships (Pruitt, 1986).

integrative agreements
win-win agreements that reconcile both parties' interests to their mutual benefit

Unraveling misperceptions with controlled communications.　　Communication often helps reduce self-fulfilling misperceptions. Perhaps you can recall experiences similar to that of this university student:

> Often, after a prolonged period of little communication, I perceive Martha's silence as a sign of her dislike for me. She, in turn, thinks that my quietness is a result of my being mad at her. My silence induces her silence, which makes me even more silent . . . until this snowballing effect is broken by some occurrence that makes it necessary for us to interact. And the communication then unravels all the misinterpretations we had made about one another.

The outcome of such conflicts often depends on *how* people communicate their feelings to one another. Roger Knudson and his colleagues (1980) invited married couples to come to the psychology laboratory and relive, through role playing, one of their past conflicts. Before, during, and after their conversation (which often generated as much emotion as the actual previous conflict), the couples were closely observed and questioned. Couples who evaded the issue—by failing to make their positions clear or failing to acknowledge their spouse's position—left with the illusion that they were more in harmony and agreement than they really were. Often, they came to believe they now agreed more when actually they agreed less. In contrast, those who engaged the issue—by making their positions clear and by taking one another's views into account—achieved more actual agreement and gained more accurate information about one another's perceptions. That helps explain why couples who communicate their concerns directly and openly are usually happily married (Grush & Glidden, 1987).

Such findings have triggered new programs that train couples and children how to manage conflicts constructively (Horowitz and Boardman, 1994). Chil-

focus

How to fight constructively

With every close relationship comes conflict. If managed constructively, conflict provides opportunities for reconciliation and a more genuine harmony. Psychologists Ian Gotlib and Catherine Colby (1988) offer advice on how to avoid destructive quarrels and to have good quarrels.

DO NOT

1. Apologize prematurely.
2. Evade the argument, give the silent treatment, or walk out on it.
3. Use your intimate knowledge of the other person to hit below the belt and humiliate.
4. Bring in unrelated issues.
5. Feign agreement while harboring resentment.
6. Tell the other party how she or he are feeling.
7. Attack indirectly by criticizing someone or something the other person values.
8. Undermine the other by intensifying his or her insecurity or threatening disaster.

DO

1. Fight privately, away from children.
2. Clearly define the issue and repeat the other's arguments in your own words.
3. Divulge your positive and negative feelings.
4. Welcome feedback about your behavior.
5. Clarify where you agree and disagree and what matters most to each of you.
6. Ask questions that help the other find words to express the concern.
7. Wait for spontaneous explosions to subside, without retaliating.
8. Offer positive suggestions for mutual improvement.

---

dren, for example, learn that conflict is normal, that people can learn to get along with those who are different, that most disputes can be resolved with two winners, and that nonviolent communication strategies are an alternative to a world of bullies and victims. This "violence prevention curriculum . . . is not about passivity," notes Deborah Prothrow-Stith (1991, p. 183). "It is about using anger not to hurt oneself or one's peers, but to change the world."

David Johnson and Roger Johnson (1995) put grade one through nine children through about a dozen hours of conflict resolution training in six schools, with very heartening results. Before the training, most students were involved in daily conflicts—put-downs and teasing, playground turn-taking conflicts, conflicts over possessions—conflicts that nearly also resulted in a winner and a loser. After training, the children more often found win-win solutions, better mediated friends' conflicts, and retained and applied their new skills in and out of school throughout the school year. When implemented with a whole student body, the result is a more peaceful student community and increased academic achievement.

Conflict researchers report that a key factor is *trust* (Ross & Ward, 1995). If you believe the other person is well intentioned, you are then more likely to divulge your needs and concerns. Lacking such trust, you may fear that being open will give the other party information that might be used against you.

When the two parties mistrust each other and communicate unproductively, a third-party mediator—a marriage counselor, a labor mediator, a diplomat—

"[There is] a psychological barrier between us, a barrier of suspicion, a barrier of rejection; a barrier of fear, of deception, a barrier of hallucination. . . ."

President Anwar al-Sadat, to the Israeli Knesset, 1977

Communication facilitators work to break down barriers, as in this diversity training exercise for teenagers.

sometimes helps. After coaxing the conflicting parties to rethink their perceived win-lose conflict, the mediator often has each party identify and rank its goals. When goals are compatible, the ranking procedure makes it easier for each to concede on less important goals so that both achieve their chief goals (Erickson & others, 1974; Schulz & Pruitt, 1978).

Once labor and management both believe that management's goal of higher productivity and profit is compatible with labor's goal of better wages and working conditions, they can begin to work for an integrative win-win solution. If workers will forgo benefits that are moderately beneficial to them but very costly to management (perhaps company-provided dental care), and if management will forgo moderately valuable arrangements that workers very much resent (perhaps inflexibility of working hours), then both sides may gain (Ross & Ward, 1995). Rather than seeing itself as making a concession, each side can see the negotiation as an effort to exchange bargaining chips for things more valued.

When the parties then convene to communicate directly, they are usually *not* set loose in the hope that, eyeball to eyeball, the conflict will resolve itself. In the midst of a threatening, stressful conflict, emotions often disrupt the ability to understand the other party's point of view. Communication may become most difficult just when it is most needed (Tetlock, 1985). The mediator will therefore often structure the encounter to help each party understand and feel understood by the other. The mediator may ask the conflicting parties to restrict their arguments to statements of fact, including statements of how they feel and how they respond when the other acts in a given way: "I enjoy having music on. When you play it loud, I find it hard to concentrate. That makes me crabby." Also, the mediator may ask people to reverse roles and argue the other's position, or to restate one another's positions before replying with their own: "My turning up the stereo bugs you."

Neutral third parties may also suggest mutually agreeable proposals that would be dismissed—"reactively devalued"—if offered by either side. The very same proposal that is seen as a cheap trick when presented by the opposition is often seen as an interesting suggestion when presented by the mediator. Even good proposals are greeted with suspicion when presented by the opposition. Likewise, people will often reactively devalue a concession offered by an adversary ("they must not value it"); the same concession may seem less like a token gesture when suggested by a third party.

These peacemaking principles, based partly on laboratory experiments, partly on practical experience, have helped mediate both international and industrial conflicts (Blake & Mouton, 1962, 1979; Fisher, 1994; Wehr, 1979). One small team of Arab and Jewish Americans, led by social psychologist Herbert Kelman (1997), has conducted workshops bringing together influential Arabs and Israelis, and Pakistanis and Indians. Using methods such as those we've considered, Kelman and colleagues counter misperceptions and have participants creatively seek solutions for their common good. Isolated, the participants are free to speak directly to their adversaries without fear of their constituents' second-guessing what they are saying. The result? Those from both sides typically come to understand the other's perspective and how the other side responds to their own group's actions.

When direct communication is impossible, a third party can meet with one party, then the other. Henry Kissinger's "shuttle diplomacy" in the two years after the Arab-Israeli war of 1973 produced three disengagement agreements between Israel and its Arab neighbors. Kissinger's strategy gave him control over the communications and enabled both sides to concede to him without appearing to capitulate to one another (Pruitt, 1981).

Negotiation sometimes receives a boost from smaller mediating efforts. In 1976, Kelman drove Egyptian social scientist Boutros Boutros-Ghali (who in 1991 became the UN secretary general) to the Boston airport. En route, they formulated plans for an Egyptian conference on misperceptions in Arab-Israeli relations. The conference later took place, and Kelman conveyed its promising results to influential Israelis. A year later, Boutros-Ghali became Egypt's acting foreign minister and Egyptian President Anwar Sadat made his historic trip to Israel, opening a road to peace. Afterward, Boutros-Ghali said happily to Kelman, "You see the process that we started at the Boston airport last year" (Armstrong, 1981).

A year later, mediator Jimmy Carter secluded Sadat and Israeli Prime Minister Menachem Begin. Rather than begin by having each side state its demands, Carter had them identify their underlying interests and goals—security for Israel, authority over its historic territory for Egypt. Thirteen days later, the trio emerged with "A Framework for Peace in the Middle East," granting each what they desired—security in exchange for territory (Rubin, 1989). Six months later, after further mediation by Carter during visits to both countries, Begin and Sadat signed a treaty ending a state of war that had existed since 1948.

Arbitration

Some conflicts are so intractable, the underlying interests so divergent, that a mutually satisfactory resolution is unattainable. Bosnian Serbs and Muslims could not both have jurisdiction over the same homelands. In a divorce dispute

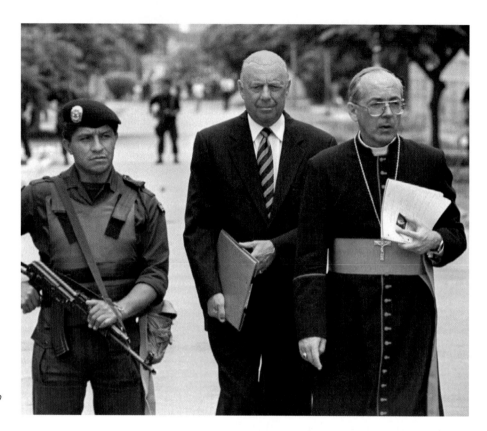

Canada's ambassador Anthony Vincent and Archbishop Juan Luis Cipriani negotiated with Tupac Amaru rebels in Peru in the hopes of mediating a peaceful end to a hostage crisis.

> "In the research on the effects of mediation one finding stands out: The worse the state of the parties' relationship is with one another, the dimmer the prospects that mediation will be successful."
>
> Kenneth Kressel & Dean Pruitt (1985)

over custody of a child, both parents cannot enjoy full custody. In these and many other cases (disputes over tenants' repair bills, athletes' wages, and national territories), a third-party mediator may—or may not—help resolve the conflict.

If not, the parties may turn to *arbitration* by having the mediator or another third party *impose* a settlement. Disputants usually prefer to settle their differences without arbitration, so they retain control over the outcome. Neil McGillicuddy and others (1987) observed this preference in an experiment involving disputants coming to one arbitration center. When people knew they would face an arbitrated settlement if mediation failed, they tried harder to resolve the problem, exhibited less hostility, and thus were more likely to reach agreement.

In cases where differences seem large and irreconcilable, the prospect of arbitration may have an opposite effect (Pruitt, 1986). The disputants may freeze their positions, hoping to gain an advantage when the arbitrator chooses a compromise. To combat this tendency, some disputes, such as those involving salaries of individual baseball players, are settled with "final-offer arbitration" in which the third party chooses one of the two final offers. Final-offer arbitration motivates each party to make a reasonable proposal.

Typically, however, the final offer is not so reasonable as it would be if each party, free of self-serving bias, saw its own proposal through others' eyes. Negotiation researchers report that most disputants are made stubborn by "optimistic overconfidence" (Kahneman & Tversky, 1995). Successful mediation is hindered when, as often happens, both parties believe they have a two-thirds chance of winning a final-offer arbitration (Bazerman, 1986, 1990).

Conciliation

Sometimes tension and suspicion run so high that communication, much less resolution, becomes all but impossible. Each party may threaten, coerce, or retaliate against the other. Unfortunately, such acts tend to be reciprocated, thus escalating the conflict. So, would a strategy of appeasing the other party by being unconditionally cooperative produce a satisfying result? Often not. In laboratory games, those who are 100 percent cooperative often get exploited. Politically, a one-sided pacifism is out of the question anyway.

GRIT

Social psychologist Charles Osgood (1962, 1980) advocated a third alternative—one that is conciliatory, rather than retaliatory, yet strong enough to discourage exploitation. Osgood called it "graduated and reciprocated initiatives in tension reduction," nicknamed **GRIT,** a label that suggests the determination it requires. GRIT aims to reverse the "conflict spiral" by triggering reciprocal deescalation. To do so, it draws upon social-psychological concepts, such as the norm of reciprocity and the attribution of motives.

GRIT requires one side to initiate a few small deescalatory actions, after *announcing a conciliatory intent.* The initiator states its desire to reduce tension, declares each conciliatory act prior to making it, and invites the adversary to reciprocate. Such announcements create a framework that helps the adversary correctly interpret what otherwise might be seen as weak or tricky actions. They also bring public pressure on the adversary to follow the reciprocity norm.

GRIT
acronym for "graduated and reciprocated initiatives in tension reduction"—a strategy designed to deescalate international tensions

"Don't worry, dear—it's just a *peace* offensive."

People perceive that they respond more favorably to conciliation, but that others might be responsive to coercion.

"Perhaps the best policy in the nuclear age is to speak softly and carry a small- to medium-sized stick."

Richard Ned Lebow and Janice Stein (1987)

Next, the initiator establishes credibility and genuineness by carrying out, exactly as announced, several verifiable *conciliatory acts.* This intensifies the pressure to reciprocate. Making conciliatory acts diverse—perhaps offering medical information, closing a military base, and lifting a trade ban—keeps the initiator from making a significant sacrifice in any one area and leaves the adversary freer to choose its own means of reciprocation. If the adversary reciprocates voluntarily, its own conciliatory behavior may soften its attitudes.

GRIT *is* conciliatory. But it is not "surrender on the installment plan." The remaining aspects of the plan protect each side's self-interest by *maintaining retaliatory capability.* The initial conciliatory steps entail some small risk but do not jeopardize either one's security; rather, they are calculated to begin edging both sides down the tension ladder. If one side takes an aggressive action, the other side reciprocates in kind, making it clear it will not tolerate exploitation. Yet the reciprocal act is not an overresponse that would reescalate the conflict. If the adversary offers its own conciliatory acts, these, too, are matched or even slightly exceeded. Conflict expert Morton Deutsch (1993) captures the spirit of GRIT in advising negotiators to be " 'firm, fair, and friendly': *firm* in resisting intimidation, exploitation, and dirty tricks; *fair* in holding to one's moral principles and not reciprocating the other's immoral behavior despite his or her provocations; and *friendly* in the sense that one is willing to initiate and reciprocate cooperation."

Does GRIT really work? In laboratory dilemma games a successful strategy has proved to be simple "tit-for-tat," which begins with a cooperative opening play and thereafter matches the other party's last response (Axelrod & Dion, 1988; Komorita & others, 1992; Smith, 1987). Cooperate-unless-you've-just-been-exploited is another successful strategy that tries to cooperate and is forgiving, yet does not tolerate exploitation (Nowak & Sigmund, 1993). In a lengthy series of experiments at Ohio University, Svenn Lindskold and his associates (1976 to 1988) have tested other aspects of the GRIT strategy. Lindskold (1978) reports that his own and others' studies provide "strong support for the various steps in the GRIT proposal." In laboratory games, announcing cooperative intent *does* boost cooperation. Repeated conciliatory acts *do* breed greater trust (although self-serving biases often make one's own acts seem more conciliatory and less hostile than those of the adversary). Maintaining an equality of power *does* protect against exploitation.

Lindskold is not contending that the world of the laboratory experiment mirrors the more complex world of everyday life. Rather, experiments enable us to formulate and verify powerful theoretical principles, such as the reciprocity norm and the self-serving bias. Notes Lindskold (1981), "It is the theories, not the individual experiments, that are used to interpret the world."

Applications in the real world

GRIT-like strategies have occasionally been tried outside the laboratory, with promising results. One of the best examples of such a strategy was Lester B. Pearson's handling of the Suez Canal crisis. In the summer of 1956 Egyptian president Gamal Abdal Nasser declared that the Egyptian government was taking control of the Suez Canal. He hoped to raise money from tolls charged to ships going through the canal to finance the Aswan High Dam on the Nile River. A company controlled by British and French interests had previously controlled the canal. England and France were taken aback by the announcement

"I am not suggesting that principles of individual behavior can be applied to the behavior of nations in any direct, simpleminded fashion. What I am trying to suggest is that such principles may provide us with hunches about internation behavior that can be tested against experience in the larger arena."

Charles E. Osgood (1966)

and were worried that Egyptian control of the canal might eventually restrict the flow of goods (particularly oil) to Western Europe. In October 1956, these worries led England, France, and their ally Israel to invade the canal zone. They gained control of the area but were roundly criticized in international circles, precipitating a major international crisis. Would the Soviet Union come to Egypt's aid? Would the world powers stumble into another war? International outrage forced Britain, France, and Israel to withdraw from the canal zone, and Anthony Eden, the British Foreign Minister, to resign.

Into this pressure cooker of a situation stepped Lester B. Pearson, then the Foreign Minister of Canada. He formulated a plan where concessions were made to both Egypt and Britain, as well as France, and Israel. In exchange, United Nations peacekeeping troops were sent into the canal zone to ensure that the plan would be implemented. Egypt was allowed to collect tolls on ships going through the canal to finance the building of the Aswan High Dam. Britain and France were assured that the canal would remain open and trade would not be restricted to Western Europe. Israel was given shipping rights that they had not previously enjoyed.

Lester B. Pearson received international acclaim (and the Nobel Peace Prize in 1957) for his role in handling the crisis. He, of course, went on to become Prime Minister of Canada.

Might conciliatory efforts also help reduce tension between individuals? There is every reason to expect so. When a relationship is strained and communication nonexistent, it sometimes takes only a conciliatory gesture—a soft answer, a warm smile, a gentle touch—for both parties to begin easing down the tension ladder, to a rung where contact, cooperation, and communication again become possible.

Summing up

Although conflicts are readily kindled and fueled by social dilemmas, competition, and misperceptions, some equally powerful forces, such as contact, cooperation, communication, and conciliation, can transform hostility into harmony.

Might putting people into close contact reduce their hostilities? Despite some encouraging early studies, other studies show that in schools mere desegregation has little effect upon racial attitudes. But when interracial contact is prolonged and intimate, and when it is structured to convey *equal status*, hostilities often lessen.

Contacts are especially beneficial when people work together to overcome a common threat or to achieve a superordinate goal. Taking their cue from experiments on cooperative contact, several research teams have replaced competitive classroom learning situations with opportunities for cooperative learning, with heartening results.

Conflicting parties can also seek to resolve their differences by bargaining either directly or through a third-party mediator. Third-party mediators can help by prodding the antagonists to replace their competitive win-lose view of their conflict with a more cooperative win-win orientation. Mediators can also structure communications that will peel away misperceptions and increase mutual understanding and trust. When a negotiated settlement is not reached, the conflicting parties may defer the outcome to an arbitrator, who either dictates a settlement or selects one of the two final offers.

Sometimes tensions run so high that genuine communication is impossible. In such cases, small conciliatory gestures by one party may elicit reciprocal conciliatory acts by the other party. One such conciliatory strategy, GRIT (graduated and reciprocated initiatives in tension reduction), aims to alleviate tense international situations.

Those who mediate tense labor-management and international conflicts sometimes use another peacemaking strategy. They instruct the participants, as this chapter instructed you, in the dynamics of conflict and peacemaking in the hope that understanding can help us establish and enjoy peaceful, rewarding relationships.

Personal Postscript: Communitarianism

Many social conflicts are a contest between individual and collective rights. One person's right to own handguns conflicts with a neighborhood's right to safe streets. One person's right to smoke conflicts with others' rights to a smoke-free environment. One industrialist's right to do unregulated business conflicts with a community's right to clean air.

Hoping to blend the best of individualist and collectivist values, some social scientists are now exploring a communitarian synthesis that aims to balance individual rights with the collective right to communal well-being. Communitarians welcome incentives for individual initiative and appreciate why Marxist economies have crumbled. "If I were, let's say, in Albania at this moment," said communitarian sociologist Amitai Etzioni (1991), "I probably would argue that there's too much community and not enough individual rights." But communitarians also question the other extreme—the rugged individualism and self-indulgence of the 1960s ("Do your own thing"), the 1970s (the "Me decade"), and the 1980s ("Greed is good"). Unrestrained personal freedom, they say, destroys a culture's social fabric; unrestrained commercial freedom, they add, plunders our shared environment. Echoing the French Revolutionists, their motto might well be "liberty, equality, *and* fraternity."

During the last half-century, Western individualism has intensified. Parents have become more likely to prize independence and self-reliance in their children, and less concerned with obedience (Alwin, 1990; Remley, 1988). Clothing and grooming styles have become more diverse, personal freedoms have increased, and common values have waned (Schlesinger, 1991). Accompanying this growing individualism has been not only increased depression but other indicators of social recession. For example, in Canada since 1960:

"There is no society. There are only individuals and their families."

Prime Minister Margaret Thatcher, after her third election

- The divorce rate has doubled.
- The teen suicide rate has tripled.
- The reported sexual assault rate has quadrupled.
- Juvenile violent crime and reports of child abuse and neglect have tripled.
- The proportion of children born to single parents has increased threefold.

Some words of caution: Such trends have multiple causes. The mere correlation over time between increased individualism and social decay does not prove cause and effect. Also, communitarians are not advocating a nostalgia trip—a return, for example, to the more restrictive and unequal gender roles of the 1950s. Rather, they propose a middle ground between the individualism of the West and the collectivism of the East, between the macho independence traditionally associated with males and the caregiving connectedness traditionally associated with females, between concerns for individual rights and for communal well-being, between liberty and fraternity, between me-thinking and we-thinking.

As with luggage searches at airports, smoking bans on planes, and sobriety checkpoints and speeding limits on highways, societies are accepting some adjustments to individual rights in order to protect the public good. Environmental restraints on individual freedoms (to pollute, to whale, to deforest) similarly exchange certain short-term liberties for long-term communal gain. Some individualists warn that such constraints on individual liberties may plunge us down a slippery slope leading to the loss of more important liberties. If today we let them search our luggage, tomorrow they'll be knocking down the doors of our houses. If today we censor cigarette ads or pornography on television, tomorrow they'll be removing books from our libraries. If today we ban handguns, tomorrow they'll take our hunting rifles. In protecting the interests of the majority do we risk suppressing the basic rights of minorities? Communitarians reply that if we don't balance concern for individual rights with concern for our collective well-being, we risk worse civic disorder, which in turn *will* fuel cries for an autocratic crackdown.

This much is sure: As the conflict between individual and collective rights continues, cross-cultural and gender scholarship can illuminate alternative cultural values and make visible our own assumed values.

m modules

Social Psychology Applied

Throughout this book, I have aimed to link laboratory and life by relating social psychology's principles and findings to everyday happenings. We now conclude by recollecting a number of these big ideas and applying them in two practical contexts. Module A, "Social Psychology in the Clinic," applies social psychology to evaluating and promoting mental and physical health. Module B, "Social Psychology in Court," explores social thinking and social influences as individual jurors, as well as groups, make judgments.

module a

Social Psychology in the Clinic

If you are a typical university student, you may occasionally feel mildly depressed—dissatisfied with your life, discouraged about the future, sad, lacking appetite and energy, unable to concentrate, perhaps even wondering if life is worth it. Maybe you think disappointing grades have jeopardized your career goals. Perhaps the breakup of a relationship has left you in despair. At such times your self-focused brooding only worsens your feelings. For some 10 percent of men and nearly twice that many women, life's down times are not just temporary blue moods but one or more major depressive episodes that last for weeks without any obvious cause.

Among the many thriving areas of applied social psychology is one that relates social psychology's concepts to depression and to other problems such as loneliness, anxiety, and physical illness. This bridge-building research between social psychology and **clinical psychology** seeks answers to four important questions: (1) As laypeople or as professional psychologists, how can we improve our judgments and predictions about others? (2) How can the ways

clinical psychology
the study, assessment, and treatment of people with psychological difficulties

in which we think about self and others feed such problems as depression, loneliness, anxiety, and ill health? (3) How might these maladaptive thought patterns be reversed? (4) What part do close, supportive relationships play in health and happiness? In this chapter we explore some answers by examining social psychology's contributions to improving the process of clinical judgment and prediction and to the understanding and treatment of disorders such as depression.

Making clinical judgments

Do the influences on our social judgment discussed in chapters 2 to 4 also affect clinicians' judgments of clients? If so, what biases should clinicians (and their clients) be wary of?

"To free a man of error is to give, not to take away. Knowledge that a thing is false is a truth."

Arthur Schopenhauer, 1788–1860

Is Susan suicidal? Should John be committed to a mental hospital? If released, will Tom be a homicide risk? Facing such questions, clinical psychologists struggle to make accurate judgments, recommendations, and predictions.

Such clinical judgments are also *social* judgments, and thus vulnerable to illusory correlations, overconfidence bred by hindsight, and self-confirming diagnoses (Maddux, 1993). Let's see why alerting mental health workers to how people form impressions (and *mis*impressions) might help avert serious misjudgments.

Illusory correlations

Consider the following court transcript in which a seemingly confident psychologist (PSY) is being questioned by an attorney (ATT):

ATT: You asked the defendant to draw a human figure?

PSY: Yes.

ATT: And this is the figure he drew for you? What does it indicate to you about his personality?

PSY: You will note this is a rear view of a male. This is very rare, statistically. It indicates hiding guilt feelings, or turning away from reality.

ATT: And this drawing of a female figure, does it indicate anything to you; and, if so, what?

PSY: It indicates hostility toward women on the part of the subject. The pose, the hands on the hips, the hard-looking face, the stern expression.

ATT: Anything else?

PSY: The size of the ears indicates a paranoid outlook, or hallucinations. Also, the absence of feet indicates feelings of insecurity. (Jeffery, 1964)

The assumption here, as in so many clinical judgments, is that test results reveal something important. Do they? There is a simple way to find out. Have one clinician administer and interpret the test. Have another clinician assess the same person's symptoms. Repeat this process with many people. The proof is in the pudding: Are test outcomes in fact correlated with reported symptoms? Some tests are indeed predictive. Others, such as the Draw-a-Person test above, have correlations far weaker than their users suppose. Why, then, do clinicians continue to express confidence in uninformative or ambiguous tests?

Pioneering experiments by Loren Chapman and Jean Chapman (1969, 1971) help us see why. They invited both university students and professional clinicians to study some test performances and diagnoses. If the students or clinicians *expected* a particular association they generally *perceived* it, regardless of whether the data were supportive. For example, clinicians who believed that suspicious people draw peculiar eyes on the Draw-a-Person test perceived such a relationship—even when shown cases in which suspicious people drew peculiar eyes *less* often than nonsuspicious people. Believing that a relationship existed between two things, they were more likely to notice confirming instances. To believe is to see.

In fairness to clinicians, illusory thinking also occurs among political analysts, historians, sportscasters, personnel directors, stockbrokers, and many other professionals, including the research psychologists who point them out. As a researcher I have often been blind to the shortcomings of my theoretical analyses. I so eagerly presume that my idea of truth is *the* truth that, no matter how hard I try, I cannot see my own error. This is evident in the editorial review process that precedes any research publication. During the last thirty years I have read dozens of reviews of my own manuscripts and have been a reviewer for dozens of others. My experience is that it is far easier to spot someone else's sloppy thinking than to perceive one's own.

> "No one can see his own errors."
> Psalms 19:12

Hindsight and overconfidence

If someone we know commits suicide, how do we react? One common reaction is to think that we, or those close to the person, should have been able to predict and therefore to prevent the suicide: "We should have known." In hindsight, we can see the suicidal signs and the pleas for help. One experiment gave people a description of a depressed person who later committed suicide. Compared to those not informed of the suicide, those told the person committed suicide were more likely to say they "would have expected" it (Goggin & Range, 1985). Moreover, if they were told of the suicide, their reactions to the victim's family were more negative. After a tragedy, an I-should-have-known-it-all-along phenomenon can leave family, friends, and therapists feeling guilty.

David Rosenhan (1973) and seven associates provided a striking example of potential error in after-the-fact explanations. To test mental health workers' clinical insights, they each made an appointment with a different mental

> "Undergraduate psychology can, and I believe should, seek to liberate the student from ignorance, but also from the arrogance of believing we know more about ourselves and others than we really do."
> David L. Cole (1982)

Kurt Cobain, member of the Nirvana rock group, whose songs often expressed depressed, suicidal thinking. Should others have used such signs to predict or prevent his suicide?

hospital admissions office and complained of "hearing voices." Apart from giving false names and vocations, they reported their life histories and emotional states honestly and exhibited no further symptoms. Most got diagnosed as schizophrenic and remained hospitalized for two to three weeks. Hospital clinicians then searched for early incidents in the pseudo-patients' life histories and hospital behavior that "confirmed" and "explained" the diagnosis. Rosenhan tells of one pseudo-patient who truthfully explained to the interviewer that he

> had a close relationship with his mother but was rather remote from his father during his early childhood. During adolescence and beyond, however, his father became a close friend, while his relationship with his mother cooled. His present relationship with his wife was characteristically close and warm. Apart from occasional angry exchanges, friction was minimal. The children had rarely been spanked.

The interviewer, "knowing" the person suffered from schizophrenia, explained the problem this way:

> This white 39-year-old male . . . manifests a long history of considerable ambivalence in close relationships, which begins in early childhood. A warm relationship with his mother cools during his adolescence. A distant relationship to his father is described as becoming very intense. Affective stability is absent. His attempts to control emotionality with his wife and children are punctuated by angry outbursts and, in the case of the children, spankings. And while he says that he has several good friends, one senses considerable ambivalence embedded in those relationships also.

Rosenhan later told some staff members (who had heard about his controversial experiment but doubted such mistakes could occur in their hospital) that during the next three months one or more pseudo-patients would seek admission to their hospital. After the three months, he asked the staff to guess which of the 193 patients admitted during that time were really pseudo-patients. Of the 193 new patients, 41 were accused by at least one staff member of being pseudo-patients. Actually, there were none.

Self-confirming diagnoses

So far we've seen that mental health workers sometimes perceive illusory correlations and that hindsight explanations are often questionable. A third problem with clinical judgment is that people may also supply information that fulfills clinicians' expectations. In a clever series of experiments, Mark Snyder (1984), in collaboration with William Swann and others, gave interviewers some hypotheses to test concerning individuals' traits. To get a feel for their experiments, imagine yourself on a blind date with someone who has been told that you are an uninhibited, outgoing person. To see whether this is true, your date slips questions into the conversation, such as "Have you ever done anything crazy in front of other people?" As you answer such questions, will your date meet a different "you" than if you were probed for instances when you were shy and retiring?

Snyder and Swann found that people often test for a trait by looking for information that confirms it. If they are trying to find out if someone is an extravert, they often solicit instances of extraversion ("What would you do if you wanted to liven things up at a party?"). Testing for introversion, they are more likely to ask, "What factors make it hard for you to really open up to people?" Such questions feel more empathic than would questions that don't match the person's presumed traits (Leyens & others, in press). But they also lead those being tested for extraversion to behave more sociably and those being tested for introversion to appear more shy and reserved. *Our* behavior sometimes creates the kind of people we expect to see.

Fazio and his colleagues (1981) reproduced this finding and also discovered that those asked the "extraverted questions" later perceived themselves as actually more outgoing than those asked the introverted questions. Moreover, they really became noticeably more outgoing when their behavior was later observed. An accomplice of the experimenter later met each participant in a waiting room and 70 percent of the time correctly guessed from the person's behavior which condition the person had come from. Likewise, the framing of questions asked of an alleged rape victim—"Did you dance with Peter?" vs. "Did Peter dance with you?"—can subtly influence who gets perceived as responsible (Semin & De Poot, 1997).

When given the structured list of questions to choose from, even experienced psychotherapists prefer the extraverted questions when testing for extraversion and thus unwittingly trigger extraverted behavior among their interviewees (Dallas & Baron, 1985; Copeland & Snyder, in press; Snyder & Thomsen, 1988). Even when making up their own questions, interviewers' expectations may influence their questioning *if* they have definite preexisting ideas (Devine & others, 1990; Hodgins & Zuckerman, 1993; Swann & Giuliano, 1987). Strong beliefs may generate their own confirmation.

Confirmation bias also appears when people evaluate themselves. Consider for a moment: Are you happy with your social life? Ziva Kunda and colleagues (1993) put this question to students at the University of Waterloo and elsewhere. The students searched their memories for confirming instances and thus ended up feeling happier than students asked, "Are you unhappy with your social life?" Seek and you shall find.

In other experiments, Snyder and his colleagues (1982) tried to get people to search for behaviors that would *disconfirm* the trait they were testing. In one experiment, they told the interviewers, "It is relevant and informative to find out ways in which the person . . . may not be like the stereotype." In another experiment Snyder (1981a) offered "$25 to the person who develops the set of questions that tell the most about . . . the interviewee." Still, confirmation bias persisted: People resisted choosing "introverted" questions when testing for extraversion.

Based on Snyder's experiments, can you see why the behaviors of people undergoing psychotherapy come to fit the theories of their therapists (Whitman & others, 1963)? When Harold Renaud and Floyd Estess (1961) conducted life-history interviews of 100 healthy, successful adult men, they were startled to discover that their subjects' childhood experiences were loaded with "traumatic events," tense relations with certain people, and bad decisions by their parents—the very factors usually used to explain psychiatric problems. When Freudian therapists go fishing for traumas in early childhood experiences, they often find their hunches confirmed. Thus, surmises Snyder (1981a):

> The psychiatrist who believes (erroneously) that adult gay males had bad childhood relationships with their mothers may meticulously probe for recalled (or fabricated) signs of tension between their gay clients and their mothers, but neglect to so carefully interrogate their heterosexual clients about their maternal relationships. No doubt, any individual could recall some friction with his or her mother, however minor or isolated the incidents.

"As is your sort of mind,
So is your sort of search:
You'll find
What you desire."

Robert Browning,
1812–1889

Skeptics argue that therapists' search for hunch-confirming information explains many "recovered memories." Books such as Ellen Bass and Laura Davis' (1988) *The Courage to Heal* suggest that survivors of child sex abuse are likely to experience feelings of depression, shame, unworthiness, perfectionism, and powerlessness. When patients present such symptoms (which may actually result from many causes), some therapists will actively search for evidence that confirms their suspicions of sex abuse (Harris, 1994; Loftus & Ketcham, 1994; Poole & others, 1995). The therapist may explain that "people who've been abused often have your symptoms, so you probably were abused." If the patient cannot remember any abuse, the therapist may use hypnosis, guided imagery, or dream interpretation in hopes of recovering confirming information. Such confirmation-seeking tactics have led some clients to create memories for events that never happened.

Clinical versus statistical prediction

Given these hindsight- and diagnosis-confirming tendencies, it will come as no surprise that most clinicians and interviewers express more confidence in their intuitive assessments than in statistical data. Yet when researchers pit statistical prediction (as when predicting graduate school success using a formula that includes grades and aptitude scores) against intuitive prediction, the statistics usually win. Statistical predictions are indeed unreliable, but human intuition—even expert intuition—is even more unreliable (Dawes & others, 1989; Faust & Ziskin, 1988; Meehl, 1954).

Three decades after demonstrating the superiority of statistical over intuitive prediction, Paul Meehl (1986) found the evidence stronger than ever:

> There is no controversy in social science which shows [so many] studies coming out so uniformly in the same direction as this one. . . . When you are pushing 90 investigations, predicting everything from the outcome of football games to the diagnosis of liver disease and when you can hardly come up with a half dozen studies showing even a weak tendency in favor of the clinician, it is time to draw a practical conclusion. . . .

In *House of Cards: Psychology and Psychotherapy Built on Myth*, Robyn Dawes (1994) explodes the pretensions of clinical intuition. For example, during the 1970s one medical school admitted 150 students annually based on interviewers' ratings of their 800 most qualified candidates. When the legislature suddenly required them to admit 50 more students, they admitted the only ones still available—those to whom the interviewers had given low ratings. So what was the difference in performance between the two groups? Nil. The top-rated 150 and bottom 50 each had 82 percent of their group receive the M.D. and similar proportions receive honors. Even after the first year of residency, both groups were doing equally well. The unavoidable conclusion: Some people just interview better than others, but this did not predict medical school success.

Ah, but what if we combined statistical prediction with clinical intuition? What if we gave professional clinicians the statistical prediction of someone's future academic performance or risk of parole violation or suicide, and asked them to refine or improve on the prediction? Alas, in the few studies where this has been done, prediction was better if the "improvements" were ignored (Dawes, 1994).

Psychiatrists and psychologists often testify in criminal cases, as Stanley Semrau depicted in this artist's sketch did in a Surrey, B.C. case; they would do best to consider statistical predictors of risk rather than their own impressions.

So, why do so many clinicians continue to interpret Rorschach inkblot tests and offer intuitive predictions about parolees, suicide risks, and likelihood of child abuse? Partly out of sheer ignorance, says Meehl, but also partly out of "mistaken conceptions of ethics":

> If I try to forecast something important about a college student, or a criminal, or a depressed patient by inefficient rather than efficient means, meanwhile charging this person or the taxpayer 10 times as much money as I would need to achieve greater predictive accuracy, that is not a sound ethical practice. That it feels better, warmer, and cuddlier to me as predictor is a shabby excuse indeed.

Such words are shocking. Do Meehl and the other researchers underestimate our intuition? To see why their findings are apparently true, consider the assessment of human potential by graduate admissions interviewers. Dawes (1976) explained why statistical prediction is so often superior to an interviewer's intuition when predicting certain outcomes such as graduate school success:

> What makes us think that we can do a better job of selection by interviewing (students) for a half hour, than we can by adding together relevant (standardized) variables, such as undergraduate GPA, GRE score, and perhaps ratings of letters of recommendation. The most reasonable explanation to me lies in our overevaluation of our cognitive capacity. And it is really cognitive conceit. Consider, for example, what goes into a GPA. Because for most graduate applicants it is based on at least $3^1/_2$ years of undergraduate study, it is a composite measure arising from a minimum of 28 courses and possibly, with the popularity of the quarter system, as many as 50. . . . Yet you and I, looking at a folder or interviewing someone for a half hour, are supposed to be able to form a better impression than one based on $3^1/_2$ years of the cumulative evaluations of 20–40 different professors. . . . Finally, if we do wish to ignore GPA, it appears that the only reason for doing so is believing that the candidate is particularly brilliant even though his or her record may not show it. What better evidence for such brilliance can we have than a score on a carefully devised aptitude test? Do we really think we are better equipped to assess such aptitude than is the Educational Testing Service, whatever its faults?

Implications

Professional clinicians are "vulnerable to insidious errors and biases," concludes James Maddux (1993). They

- are frequently the victims of illusory correlation,
- are too readily convinced of their own after-the-fact analyses,
- often fail to appreciate that erroneous diagnoses can be self-confirming, and
- often overestimate the predictive powers of their clinical intuition.

The implications for mental health workers are more easily stated than practiced: Be mindful that clients' verbal agreement with what you say does not prove its validity. Beware of the tendency to see relationships that you expect to see or that are supported by striking examples readily available in your memory. Rely on your notes more than your memory. Recognize that hindsight is seductive: It can lead you to feel overconfident and sometimes to judge yourself too harshly for not having foreseen outcomes. Guard against the tendency to ask questions that assume your preconceptions are correct; consider opposing ideas and test them, too (Garb, 1994).

Research on illusory thinking has implications not only for mental health workers but for all psychologists. What Lewis Thomas (1978) said of biology may as justly be said of psychology:

> The solidest piece of scientific truth I know of, the one thing about which I feel totally confident, is that we are profoundly ignorant about nature. Indeed, I regard this as the major discovery of the past 100 years of biology. . . . It is this sudden confrontation with the depth and scope of ignorance that represents the most significant contribution of 20th century science to the human intellect. We are, at last, facing up to it. In earlier times, we either pretended to understand how things worked or ignored the problem, or simply made up stories to fill the gaps.

"One thing I have learned in a long life: that all our science, measured against reality, is primitive and childlike—and yet it is the most precious thing we have."

Albert Einstein, in
B. Hoffman & H. Dukes,
*Albert Einstein: Creator
and Rebel,* 1973

When analyzing clients, mental health workers, like all of us, are vulnerable to cognitive illusions.

focus

A physician looks at social psychology

Reading this book helps me understand the human behaviors I observe in my work as a cancer specialist and as medical director of a large staff of physicians. A few examples:

Reviews of medical records illustrate the "I-knew-it-all-along phenomenon." Physician reviewers who assess the medical records of their colleagues often believe, in hindsight, that problems such as cancer or appendicitis should clearly have been recognized and treated much more quickly. Once you know the correct diagnosis, it's easy to look back and interpret the early symptoms accordingly.

For many physicians I have known, the intrinsic motives behind their entering the profession—to help people, to be scientifically stimulated—soon become "overjustified" by the high pay. Before long, the joy is lost. The extrinsic rewards become the reason to practice, and the physician, having lost the altruistic motives, works to increase "success," measured in income.

"Self-serving bias" is ever present. We physicians gladly accept personal credit when things go well. When they don't—when the patient is misdiagnosed or doesn't get well or dies—we attribute the failure elsewhere. We were given inadequate information or the case was ill-fated from the beginning.

I also observe many examples of "belief perseverance." Even when presented with the documented facts about, say, how AIDS is transmitted, people will strangely persist in wrongly believing that it is just a "gay" disease or that they should fear catching it from mosquito bites. It makes me wonder: How can I more effectively persuade people of what they need to know and act upon?

Indeed, as I observe medical attitudes and decision making I feel myself submerged in a giant practical laboratory of social psychology. To understand the goings-on around me, I find social psychological insights invaluable and would strongly advise premed students to study the field. (Burton F. VanderLaan, Chicago, Illinois)

Psychology has crept only a little way across the edge of insight into our human condition. Ignorant of their ignorance, some psychologists invent theories to fill gaps in their understanding. Intuitive observation seems to support these theories, even if they are mutually contradictory. Research on illusory thinking therefore leads us to a new humility: It reminds research psychologists why they must test their preconceptions before presenting them as truth. To seek the hard facts, even if they threaten cherished illusions, is the goal of every science.

I am *not* arguing that the scientific method can answer all human questions. There are questions that it cannot address and ways of knowing that it cannot capture. But science *is* one means for examining claims about nature, human nature included. Propositions that imply observable results are best evaluated by systematic observation and experiment—which is the whole point of social psychology. We also need inventive genius, or we may test only trivialities. But whatever unique and enduring insights psychology can offer will be hammered out by research psychologists sorting through competing claims. Science always involves an interplay between intuition and rigorous test, between creative hunch and skepticism.

> "Science is the great antidote to the poison of enthusiasm and superstition."
>
> Adam Smith, *Wealth of Nations*, 1776

Summing up As psychiatrists and clinical psychologists diagnose and treat their clients, they may perceive illusory correlations. Hindsight explanations of people's difficulties are sometimes too easy. Indeed, after-the-fact explaining can breed overconfidence in clinical judgment. When interacting with clients, erroneous diagnoses are sometimes self-confirming, because interviewers tend to seek and recall information that verifies what they are looking for.

Research on the errors that so easily creep into intuitive judgments illustrates the need for rigorous testing of intuitive conclusions. The scientific method cannot answer all questions and is itself vulnerable to bias. Thankfully, however, it can help us sift truth from falsehood.

Social cognition in problem behaviors

One of psychology's most intriguing research frontiers concerns the cognitive processes that accompany psychological disorders. What are the memories, attributions, and expectations of depressed, lonely, shy, or illness-prone people?

Social cognition and depression

As we all know from experience, depressed people are negative thinkers. They view life through dark-colored glasses. With seriously depressed people—those who are feeling worthless, lethargic, uninterested in friends and family, and unable to sleep or eat normally—the negative thinking becomes self-defeating. Their intensely pessimistic outlook leads them to magnify bad experiences and minimize good ones. A depressed young woman illustrates, "The real me is worthless and inadequate. I can't move forward with my work because I become frozen with doubt" (Burns, 1980, p. 29).

Distortion or realism?

Are all depressed people unrealistically negative? To find out, Lauren Alloy and Lyn Abramson (1979) studied university students who were either mildly depressed or not depressed. They had the students observe whether their pressing a button was linked with a light coming on. Surprisingly, the depressed students were quite accurate in estimating their degree of control. It was the *non*depressives whose judgments were distorted, who exaggerated the extent of their control.

depressive realism
the tendency of mildly depressed people to make accurate rather than self-serving judgments, attributions, and predictions

This surprising phenomenon of **depressive realism,** nicknamed the "sadder-but-wiser effect," shows up in various judgments of one's control or skill (Ackermann & DeRubeis, 1991; Alloy & others, 1990). Shelley Taylor (1989, p. 214) explains:

Normal people exaggerate how competent and well liked they are. Depressed people do not. Normal people remember their past behavior with a rosy glow. Depressed people [unless severely depressed] are more evenhanded in recalling their successes and failures. Normal people describe themselves primarily positively. Depressed people describe both their positive and negative qualities. Normal people take credit for successful outcomes and tend to deny responsibility

Stresses challenge some people and defeat others. Researchers have sought to understand the "explanatory style" that makes some people more vulnerable to depression than others.

for failure. Depressed people accept responsibility for both success and failure. Normal people exaggerate the control they have over what goes on around them. Depressed people are less vulnerable to the illusion of control. Normal people believe to an unrealistic degree that the future holds a bounty of good things and few bad things. Depressed people are more realistic in their perceptions of the future. In fact, on virtually every point on which normal people show enhanced self-regard, illusions of control, and unrealistic visions of the future, depressed people fail to show the same biases. "Sadder but wiser" does indeed appear to apply to depression.

> "Life is the art of being well deceived."
> William Hazlitt, 1778–1830

Underlying the thinking of depressed people are their attributions of responsibility. Consider: If you fail an exam and blame yourself, you may conclude that you are stupid or lazy, and feel depressed. If you attribute the failure to an unfair exam or to other circumstances beyond your control, you are more likely to feel angry. In over 100 studies involving 15,000 subjects (Sweeney & others, 1986), depressed people have been more likely than nondepressed people to exhibit a negative **explanatory style** (Figure A–1). They are more likely to attribute failure and setbacks to causes that are *stable* ("It's going to last forever"), *global* ("It's going to affect everything I do"), and *internal* ("It's all my fault"). The result of this pessimistic, overgeneralized, self-blaming thinking, say Abramson and her colleagues (1989), is a depressing sense of hopelessness.

explanatory style one's habitual way of explaining life events. A negative pessimistic, depressive explanatory style attributes failures to stable, global, and internal causes.

Is negative thinking a cause or a result of depression?

The cognitive accompaniments of depression raise a chicken-and-egg question: Do depressed moods cause negative thinking, or does negative thinking cause depression?

Depressed moods cause negative thinking.   As we saw in Chapter 3, our moods definitely color our thinking. When we *feel* happy, we *think* happy. We see and recall a good world. But let our mood turn gloomy, and our thoughts switch on to a different track. Off come the rose-colored glasses; on come the dark glasses. Now the bad mood primes our recollections of negative events (Bower, 1987; Johnson & Magaro, 1987). Our relationships seem to sour, our self-image takes a dive, our hopes for the future dim, people's behavior seems more sinister

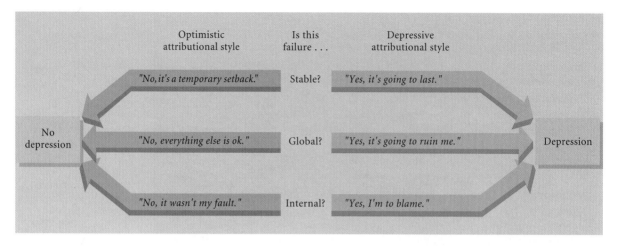

figure A–1

Depressive explanatory style.
Depression is linked with a negative, pessimistic way of explaining and interpreting failures.

(Brown & Taylor, 1986; Mayer & Salovey, 1987). As depression increases, memories and expectations plummet; when depression lifts, thinking brightens (Barnett & Gotlib, 1988; Kuiper & Higgins, 1985). Thus, *currently* depressed people recall their parents as having been rejecting and punitive. But *formerly* depressed people recall their parents in the same positive terms as do never-depressed people (Lewinsohn & Rosenbaum, 1987).

As Edward Hirt and his colleagues (1992) demonstrated in a study of rabid basketball fans from one university, a bad mood induced by rejection or defeat can darken our thinking. After the fans were either depressed by watching their team lose or elated by a victory, the researchers asked them to predict the team's future performance, and their own. After a loss, people offered bleaker assessments not only of the team's future but also of their own likely performance at throwing darts, solving anagrams, and getting a date. When things aren't going our way, it may seem as though they never will.

A depressed mood also affects behavior. The person who is withdrawn, glum, and complaining does not elicit joy and warmth in others. Stephen Strack and James Coyne (1983) found that depressed people were realistic in thinking that others didn't appreciate their behavior. Their pessimism and bad moods trigger social rejection (Carver & others, 1994). Depressed behavior can also trigger reciprocal depression in others. University students who have depressed roommates tend to become a little depressed themselves (Burchill & Stiles, 1988; Joiner, 1994; Sanislow & others, 1989). Depressed people are therefore at risk for being divorced, fired, or shunned, thus magnifying their depression (Coyne & others, 1991; Gotlib & Lee, 1989; Sacco & Dunn, 1990). They may also seek out those whose unfavorable views of them verify, and further magnify, their low self-image (Lineham, 1997; Swann & others, 1991). One experiment gave people a choice between reading a favorable assessment of their personality by one graduate student or an unfavorable assessment by another student. Twenty-five percent of high self-esteem people and 82 percent of depressed people elected to see the unfavorable feedback (Giesler & others, 1996).

So being depressed has cognitive and behavioral effects. Does it also have cognitive origins?

behind the scenes

Some years ago, I was conducting interviews with people who had cancer for a study on adjustment to intensely stressful events. I was surprised to learn that, for some people, the cancer experience actually seemed to have brought benefits, as well as the expected liabilities. Many people told me that they thought they were better people for the experience, they felt they were better adjusted to cancer than other people, they believed that they could exert control over their cancer in the future, and they believed their futures would be cancer-free, even when we knew from their medical histories that their cancers were likely to recur.

As a result, I became fascinated by how people can construe even the worst of situations as good, and I've studied these "positive illusions" ever since. Through our research, we learned quickly that you don't have to experi-

ence a trauma to demonstrate positive illusions. Most people, including the majority of university students, think of themselves as somewhat better than average, as more in control of the circumstances around them than may actually be true, and as likely to experience more positive future outcomes in life than may be realistic. These illusions are not a sign of maladjustment, quite the contrary. Good mental health may depend on the ability to see things as somewhat better than they are and to find benefits even when things seem most bleak.

Shelley Taylor, UCLA

Negative thinking causes depressed moods.   Many people feel depressed when experiencing severe stress—losing a job, getting divorced or rejected, suffering physical trauma—anything that disrupts their sense of who they are and why they are a worthy human being (Hamilton & others, 1993; Kendler & others, 1993). Such brooding can be adaptive; insights gained during times of depressed inactivity may later result in better strategies for interacting with the world. But depression-prone people respond to bad events in an especially self-focused, self-blaming way (Pyszczynski & others, 1991; Wood & others, 1990a,b). Their self-esteem fluctuates more rapidly up with boosts and down with threats (Butler & others, 1994).

Why are some people so affected by *minor* stresses? Evidence suggests that a negative explanatory style contributes to depressive reactions. Colin Sacks and Daphne Bugental (1987) asked some young women to get acquainted with a stranger who sometimes acted cold and unfriendly, creating an awkward social situation. Unlike optimistic women, those with a pessimistic explanatory style—who characteristically offer stable, global, and internal attributions for bad events—reacted to the social failure by feeling depressed. Moreover, they then behaved more antagonistically toward the next person they met. Their negative thinking led to a negative mood response, which then led to negative behavior.

Outside the laboratory, studies of children, teenagers, and adults confirm that those with the pessimistic explanatory style are more likely to become depressed when bad things happen (Alloy & Clements, 1992; Brown & Siegel, 1988; Nolen-Hoeksema & others, 1986). "A recipe for severe depression is

figure A–2

The vicious cycle of depression.

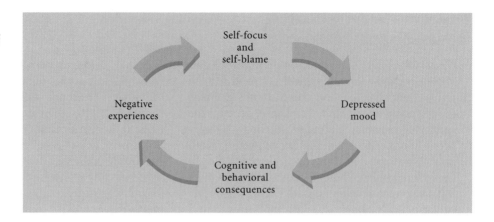

preexisting pessimism encountering failure," notes Martin Seligman (1991, p. 78). Moreover, patients who end therapy no longer feeling depressed but still with a negative explanatory style tend to relapse as bad events occur (Seligman, 1992). If those with a more optimistic explanatory style relapse, they often recover quickly (Metalsky & others, 1993; Needles & Abramson, 1990).

Researcher Peter Lewinsohn and his colleagues (1985) have assembled these findings into a coherent psychological understanding of depression. In their view, the negative self-image, attributions, and expectations of a depressed person are an essential link in a vicious cycle that is triggered by negative experience—perhaps academic or vocational failure, or family conflict, or social rejection (Figure A–2). In those vulnerable to depression, such stresses trigger brooding, self-focused, self-blaming thoughts (Pyszczynski & others, 1991; Wood & others, 1990a,b). Such ruminations create a depressed mood that drastically alters the way a person thinks and acts, which then fuels further negative experiences, self-blame, and depressed mood. In experiments, mildly depressed people's moods brighten when a task diverts their attention to something external (Nix & others, 1995). (Happiness seems best pursued by focusing not on oneself but beyond oneself.) Depression is therefore *both* a cause and a consequence of negative cognitions.

Martin Seligman (1991) believes that self-focus and self-blame help explain the near-epidemic levels of depression in the Western world today. In North America, for example, young adults today are three times as likely as their grandparents to have suffered depression—despite their grandparents' greater years at risk (Cross-National Collaborative Group, 1992). Seligman believes that the decline of religion and family, plus the growth of individualism, breeds hopelessness and self-blame when things don't go well. Failed courses, careers, and marriages produce despair when we stand alone, with nothing and no one to fall back on. If, as a macho *Fortune* ad declared, you can "make it on your own," on "your own drive, your own guts, your own energy, your own ambition," then whose fault is it if you *don't* make it? In nonwestern cultures, where close-knit relationships and cooperation are the norm, major depression is less common and less tied to guilt and self-blame over perceived failure. In Japan, for example, depressed people instead tend to report feeling shame over letting down their family or co-workers (Draguns, 1990).

These insights into the thinking style linked with depression have prompted social psychologists to study thinking patterns associated with other problems.

How do those who are plagued with excessive loneliness, shyness, or substance abuse view themselves? How well do they recall their successes and their failures? To what do they attribute their ups and downs? Where is their attention focused—on themselves or on others?

Social cognition and loneliness

If depression is the common cold of psychological disorders, then loneliness is the headache. Loneliness, whether chronic or temporary, is a painful awareness that our social relationships are less numerous or meaningful than we desire. Jenny de Jong-Gierveld (1987) observed in her study of Dutch adults that unmarried and unattached people are more likely to feel lonely. This prompted her to speculate that the modern emphasis on individual fulfillment and the depreciation of marriage and family life may be "loneliness-provoking" (as well as depression-provoking). Job-related mobility also makes for fewer long-term family and social ties and increased loneliness (Dill & Anderson, 1998).

But loneliness need not coincide with aloneness. One can feel lonely in the middle of a party. And one can be utterly alone—as I am while writing these words in the solitude of an isolated turret office at a British university 5,000 miles from home—without feeling lonely. To feel lonely is to feel excluded from a group, unloved by those around you, unable to share your private concerns, or different and alienated from those in your surroundings (Beck & Young, 1978; Davis & Franzoi, 1986).

Adolescents experience such feelings more commonly than do adults. When beeped by an electronic pager at various times during a week and asked to record what they were doing and how they felt, adolescents more often than adults reported feeling lonely when alone (Larsen & others, 1982). Males and females feel lonely under somewhat different circumstances—males when isolated from group interaction, females when deprived of close one-to-one relationships (Berg & McQuinn, 1988; Stokes & Levin, 1986). As many recently

behind the scenes

My dual background in social and personality psychology often leads me to topics at the intersection of the two fields; for example, how do personality impressions develop in social contexts? Several speculations about the topic arose from the inclusion of discussion groups in some of my undergraduate courses. When students met several times to work on a task, one thing became clear: First impressions don't always rule. For certain personality types, the first impression they make on other group members does not necessarily match the group's final impression of them. So my graduate students and I designed a series of studies to follow one type of individual whose bad first impression improves over type, namely, the shy person. We also studied another type of individual whose good shiny first impression gradually darkens, namely, the self-enhancer. The moral of this scientific story: Social perceptions are a constantly shifting product of the context, the time frame, and the target's actual personality.

Del Paulhus
University of British Columbia

figure A–3

The interplay of chronic shyness, loneliness, and depression.

Solid arrows indicate primary cause-effect direction, as summarized by Jody Dill and Craig Anderson (1998).

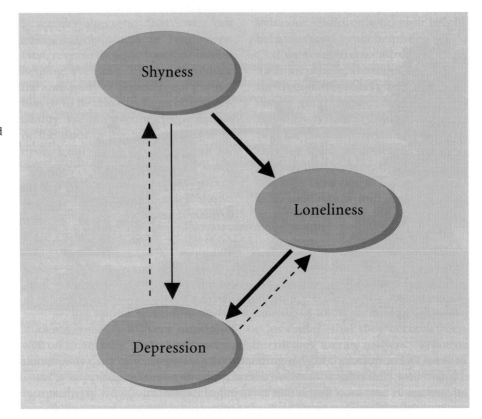

widowed people know, the loss of a person with whom one has been attached can produce unavoidable feelings of loneliness (Stroebe & others, 1996).

Like depressed people, chronically lonely people seem caught in a vicious cycle of self-defeating social cognitions and social behaviors. They have some of the negative explanatory style of the depressed; they blame themselves for their poor social relationships and see most things as beyond their control (Anderson & others, 1994; Snodgrass, 1987). Moreover, they perceive others in negative ways. When paired with a stranger of the same sex or with a first-year university roommate, lonely students are more likely to perceive the other person negatively (Jones & others, 1981; Wittenberg & Reis, 1986; Rotenber, K.J. 1997). As Figure A–3 illustrates, loneliness, depression, and shyness sometimes feed one another.

These negative views may both reflect and color the lonely person's experience. Believing in their social unworthiness and feeling pessimistic about others inhibit lonely people from acting to reduce their loneliness. Lonely people often do find it hard to introduce themselves, make phone calls, and participate in groups (Rook, 1984; Spitzberg & Hurt, 1987; Nurmi & others, 1996, 1997). They tend to be self-conscious and low in self-esteem (Check & Melchior, 1990; Vaux, 1988). When talking with a stranger, they spend more time talking about themselves and take less interest in their conversational partners than do nonlonely people (Jones & others, 1982). After such conversations, the new acquaintances often come away with more negative impressions of the lonely people (Jones & others, 1983).

Social cognition and anxiety

Being interviewed for a much-wanted job, dating someone for the first time, stepping into a roomful of strangers, performing before an important audience, or (the most common phobia) giving a speech can make almost anyone feel anxious. Some people, especially those who are shy or easily embarrassed, feel anxious in almost any situation in which they might be evaluated. For these people, anxiety is more a trait than a temporary state.

What causes us to feel anxious in social situations? Why are some people shackled in the prison of their own shyness? Barry Schlenker and Mark Leary (1982b, 1985; Leary & Kowalski, 1995) answer these questions by applying self-presentation theory. As you may recall from Chapters 2 and 4, self-presentation theory assumes that we are eager to present ourselves in ways that make a good impression. The implications for social anxiety are straightforward: *We feel anxious when we are motivated to impress others but doubt our ability to do so.* This simple principle helps explain a variety of research findings, each of which may ring true in your own experience. We feel most anxious when

- dealing with powerful, high-status people—people whose impressions of us matter,
- in an evaluative context, as when making a first impression on the parents of one's fiancé,
- we are self-conscious (as shy people often are) and our attention is focused on ourselves and how we are coming across,
- the interaction focuses on something central to our self-image, as when a university professor presents ideas before peers at a professional convention,
- we are in novel or unstructured situations, such as a first school dance or first formal dinner, where we are unsure of the social rules.

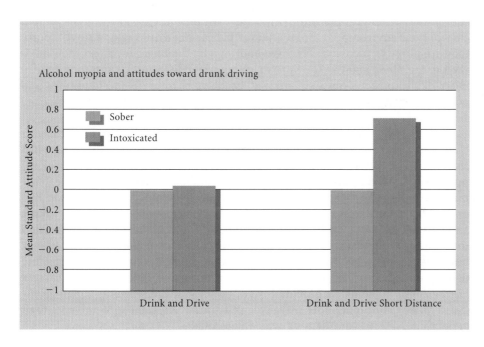

figure A–4

When people are intoxicated, they can only focus on a very limited amount of information, an effect called alcohol myopia. If people focus on cues that lower their inhibition, such as the short distance home, then they may be more likely to drink and drive.
MacDonald, Fong, & Zanna, 1995

The natural tendency in all such situations is to be cautiously self-protective: to talk less; to avoid topics that reveal one's ignorance; to be guarded about oneself; to be unassertive, agreeable, and smiling. Ironically, such anxious concern with making a good impression often makes a first bad impression (Broome & Wegner, 1994; Meleshko & Alden, 1993). With time, however, shy people often become better liked than their self-enhancing peers. Consider a series of interesting studies conducted by Del Paulhus (Paulhus, 1998; Paulhus & Morgan, 1997) at the University of British Columbia. Unlike in other studies, he examined how people perceive each other over time. In the short run they found results consistent with previous research—self-enhancing people were evaluated positively and shy people were evaluated negatively. After seven meetings, however, this pattern reversed—the egotistical self-enhancers got on people's nerves, but the modesty, sensitivity, and discretion of shy people eventually led people to like them.

But shy people may have trouble appreciating such evaluations. Shyness is a form of social anxiety characterized by self-consciousness and worry about what others think (Anderson & Harvey, 1988; Asendorpf, 1987; Carver & Scheier, 1986). Shown someone they think is interviewing them live (actually a videotaped interviewer), they perceive the interviewer as less accepting and interested in them (Pozo & others, 1991). If their hair won't comb right or they have a facial blemish, they assume everyone else notices and judges them accordingly.

To reduce social anxiety, some people turn to alcohol. Alcohol lowers anxiety as it reduces self-consciousness (Hull & Young, 1983). Thus, chronically self-conscious people are especially likely to drink following a failure. If they become alcoholics, they are more likely than those low in self-consciousness to relapse from treatment when they again experience stress or failure.

Alcohol can also reduce anxiety by restricting people's ability to think about their internal states. Claude Steele and Robert Josephs (1990) have called this effect of alcohol "alcohol myopia." In their research Steele and Josephs have shown that when people are drunk they can only focus on the most salient cues in their environment. So, if anxious people are drinking at a rowdy party they are likely to focus on the party and thus be unable to focus on their anxiety. On the other hand, if they are drinking alone in a quiet room they will be more likely to focus on their anxiety (as there is little else to focus on) and become more anxious. This may be one reason that people often drink in social situations.

Alcohol myopia can also lead to serious health consequences, as Queen's University professor Tara McDonald and University of Waterloo professors Mark Zanna and Geoff Fong (1995) have shown. They had students at a local pub answer a survey about drinking and driving either when they came to the pub (i.e., when they were sober) or at the end of the night after they had had quite a bit to drink. They either asked people their attitudes about drinking and driving or about drinking and driving only a short distance. They found that the way they asked the question made no difference for sober students, but the students who were intoxicated were less negative about drinking and driving only a short distance than about drinking and driving in general (see Figure A–4). It seems that alcohol myopia made these students focus on the cue that it was only a short distance, and they were unable to retrieve their belief that drinking and driving was dangerous.

Social cognition and illness

In the industrialized world, at least half of all deaths are linked with behavior—with consuming cigarettes, alcohol, drugs, and harmful foods; with reactions to stress; with lack of exercise and not following a doctor's orders. Efforts to study and change these behavioral contributions to illness helped create a new inter-disciplinary field called **behavioral medicine.** Psychology's contribution to this interdisciplinary science is its new subfield, **health psychology.** Its numbers include many of the estimated 3,500 psychologists now working in Canadian and U.S. medical schools (Michaelson, 1993). Health psychologists study how people respond to illness symptoms and how emotions and explanations influence health.

behavioral medicine
an interdisciplinary field that integrates and applies behavioral and medical knowledge about health and disease

Reactions to illness

How do people decide whether they are ill? How do they explain their symptoms? What influences their willingness to seek and follow treatment?

health psychology
a subfield of psychology that provides psychology's contribution to behavioral medicine

Noticing symptoms.   Chances are you have recently experienced at least one of these physical complaints: headache, stomachache, nasal congestion, sore muscles, ringing in the ears, excess perspiration, cold hands, racing heart, dizziness, stiff joints, and diarrhea or constipation (Pennebaker, 1982). Such symptoms require interpretation. Are they meaningless? Or are you coming down with something? Hardly a week goes by without our playing doctor by self-diagnosing the significance of some symptom.

Noticing and interpreting our body's signals is like noticing and interpreting how our car is running. Unless the signals are loud and clear, we often miss them. Most of us cannot tell whether a car needs an oil change merely by listening to its engine. Similarly, most of us are not astute judges of our heart rate, blood-sugar level, or blood pressure. People guess their blood pressure based on how they feel, which often is unrelated to their actual blood pressure (Baumann & Leventhal, 1985). Furthermore, the early signs of many illnesses, including cancer and heart disease, are subtle and easy to miss. Half or more of heart attack victims die before seeking and receiving medical help (Friedman & DiMatteo, 1989).

Explainings symptoms: Am I sick?   With more serious aches and pains, the questions become more specific—and more critical. Does the small cyst match our idea of a malignant lump? Is the stomachache bad enough to be appendicitis? Is the pain in the chest area merely—as many heart attack victims suppose—a muscle spasm? What factors influence how we explain symptoms?

Once we notice symptoms, we tend to interpret them according to familiar disease schemas (Bishop, 1991). In medical schools, this can have amusing results. As part of their training, medical students learn the symptoms associated with various diseases. Because they also experience various symptoms, they sometimes attribute their symptoms to recently learned disease schemas. ("Maybe this wheeze is the beginning of pneumonia.") As you may have discovered, psychology students are prone to this same effect as they read about psychological disorders.

The commonness and ambiguity of mild symptoms opens the door to social suggestion. On April 13, 1989, some 2,000 spectators assembled to enjoy music performances by 600 secondary school students. Shortly after the program began, the nervous students began complaining to one another of headaches, dizziness, stomachaches, and nausea. Eventually 247 became ill, forcing evacuation of the auditorium. A fire department treatment operation was set up on the lawn outside. Later investigation revealed nothing—no diagnosable illnesses and no environmental problems. The symptoms subsided quickly and were not shared by the audience. The instant epidemic, it seemed, was socially constructed (Small & others, 1991).

Socially constructed disorders.   Might people also socially construct an everyday ailment? Might people form the idea that their everyday symptoms match those of an ailment they've heard about, and then use it to explain such symptoms? That, researchers Pamela Kato and Diane Ruble (1992) maintain, helps explain why many women believe they are more depressed, tense, and irritable during the two or three days before menstruation. As we saw in Chapter 4, illusory correlations occur when people notice and remember instances that confirm their beliefs and do not notice instances that contradict them. Thus, a woman who feels tense the day before her period is due may attribute the tension to the so-called premenstrual syndrome (PMS). But if the woman feels similarly tense a week later or does not feel tense the day her next period is about to start, she may be less likely to notice and remember these disconfirming instances.

Many researchers now believe that some women do indeed experience not only menstrual discomfort but also premenstrual tension (Hurt & others, 1992; Richardson, 1990). Thus, the American Psychiatric Association included a severe form of PMS (called *premenstrual dysphoric disorder*) in DSM-IV. They did so despite objections and evidence from several researchers and from the Psychiatric Association's Committee on Women, which maintain that women's menstrual cycle problems should not be pathologized as a psychiatric disorder (DeAngelis, 1993).

Several studies have engaged Canadian and Australian women in keeping daily mood diaries (Hardie, 1997; and see Figure A–5). Although many women *recall* feeling out of sorts just before their last period, their own day-to-day self-reports often reveal little emotional fluctuation across the menstrual cycle. Moreover, women who *say* they suffer PMS don't differ in mood fluctuations from those who don't. In one study, those who reported severe premenstrual symptoms differed only slightly from other women in actual day-to-day reports throughout their menstrual cycles (Gallant & others, 1992). And contrary to the presumptions of some employers, women's physical and mental skills do not fluctuate noticeably with their menstrual cycles. Leta Hollingworth discovered this in her 1914 doctoral dissertation (using women's daily reports rather than their recollections). Many others since then have confirmed her finding (Rosenberg, 1984; Sommer, 1992).

Moreover, PMS complaints vary with culture but not with any known biological differences among women. All this is just what one would expect from a socially constructed disorder, say critics (Richardson, 1993; Rodin, 1992; Usher, 1992). With so many everyday symptoms on PMS checklists—lethargy, sadness, irritability, headaches, insomnia (or sleepiness), disinterest in sex (or heightened interest in sex)—"who wouldn't have 'PMS'?" asks Carol Tavris (1992).

Do I need treatment?   Once people notice a symptom and interpret it as possibly serious, several factors influence their decision to seek medical care. People

"When a man can't explain a woman's actions, the first thing he thinks about is the condition of her uterus."

Clare Boothe Luce
Slam the Door Softly, 1970

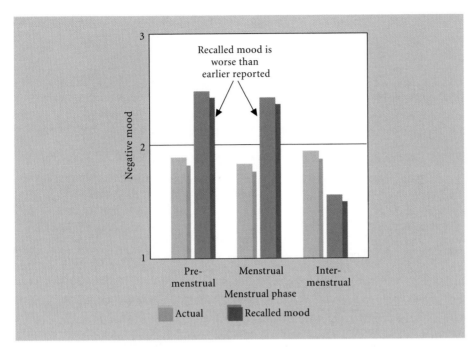

figure A–5

Menstruation, actual mood, and recalled mood.

Cathy McFarland and her colleagues (1989) found that Ontario women's daily mood reports did not vary across their menstrual cycle. Yet they *recalled* that their moods were generally worse just before and during menstruation and better at other times of the cycle.

more often seek treatment if they believe their symptoms have a physical rather than a psychological cause (Bishop, 1987). They may delay seeking help, however, if they feel embarrassed, if they think the likely benefits of medical attention won't justify the cost and inconvenience, or if they want to avoid a possibly devastating diagnosis.

Numerous studies have found a gender difference in decisions to seek medical treatment: Women report more symptoms, use more prescription and nonprescription drugs, and visit physicians 40 percent more often. Women also visit psychotherapists 50 percent more often (Olfson & Pincus, 1994). Are women more often sick? Apparently not. In fact, men may be more disease-prone. Among other problems, men have higher rates of hypertension, ulcers, and cancer, as well as shorter life expectancies. So why are women more likely to see a doctor? Perhaps women are more attentive to their internal states. Perhaps they are less reluctant to admit "weakness" and seek help (Bishop, 1984). Or perhaps women not employed full-time simply feel freer to make time for a doctor's appointment (Marcus & Siegel, 1982).

Patients are more willing to follow treatment instructions when they have a warm relationship with their doctor, when they help plan their treatment, and when options are framed attractively. People are more likely to elect an operation when given "a 40 percent chance of surviving" than when given "a 60 percent chance of not surviving" (Rothman & Salovey, 1997; Wilson & others, 1987).

Emotions and illness

Do our emotions predict our susceptibility to heart disease, stroke, cancer, and other ailments (Figure A–6)? Consider.

Heart disease has been linked with a competitive, impatient, and—the aspect that matters—*anger-prone* personality (Matthews, 1988; Williams, 1993). Under

figure A–6

Stress-caused negative emotions may have various effects on health. This is especially so for depressed or anger-prone people.

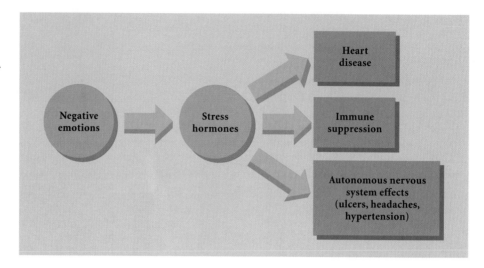

stress, reactive, anger-prone "Type A" people secrete more of the stress hormones believed to accelerate the buildup of plaque on the walls of the heart's arteries.

Depression also increases the risk of various ailments. Mildly depressed people are more vulnerable to heart disease, even after controlling for differences in smoking and other disease-related factors (Anda & others, 1993). The year after a heart attack, depressed people have a doubled risk of further heart problems (Frasure-Smith & others, 1995). The toxicity of negative emotions contributes to the high rate of depression and anxiety among chronically ill people (Cohen & Rodriguez, 1995).

When George Valliant (1997) followed a group of male university graduates from mid-life into old age he witnessed the effect of distress and negative emotion. Of those whom at age 52 he classified as "squares" (having never abused alcohol, used tranquilizers, or seen a psychiatrist), only 5 percent had died by age 75. Of those classified as "distressed" (who had abused alcohol and either used tranquilizers or seen a psychiatrist), 38 percent had died.

Optimism and health.   Stories abound of people who take a sudden turn for the worse when something makes them lose hope, or who suddenly improve when hope is renewed. As cancer attacks the liver of nine-year-old Jeff, his doctors fear the worst. But Jeff remains optimistic. He is determined to grow up to be a cancer research scientist. One day Jeff is elated. A specialist who has taken a long-distance interest in his case is planning to stop off while on a cross-country trip. There is so much Jeff wants to tell the doctor and to show him from the diary he has kept since he got sick. On the anticipated day, fog blankets his city. The doctor's plane is diverted to another city, from which the doctor flies on to his final destination. Hearing the news, Jeff cries quietly. The next morning, pneumonia and fever have developed, and Jeff lies listless. By evening he is in a coma. The next afternoon he dies (Visintainer & Seligman, 1983).

Understanding the links between attitudes and disease requires more than dramatic true stories. If hopelessness coincides with cancer we are left to wonder: Does cancer breed hopelessness, or does hopelessness also hinder resistance to cancer? To resolve this chicken-and-egg riddle, researchers have

(1) experimentally created hopelessness by subjecting organisms to uncontrollable stresses and (2) correlated the hopeless explanatory style with future illnesses.

Stress and illness

The clearest indication of the effects of hopelessness—what Chapter 2 labels *learned helplessness*—comes from experiments that subject animals to mild but uncontrollable electric shocks, loud noises, or crowding. Such experiences do not *cause* diseases such as cancer, but they do lower the body's resistance. Rats injected with live cancer cells more often develop and die of tumors if they also receive inescapable shocks than if they receive escapable shocks or no shocks. Moreover, compared to juvenile rats given controllable shocks, those given uncontrollable shocks are twice as likely in adulthood to develop tumors if given cancer cells and another round of shocks (Visintainer & Seligman, 1985). Animals that have learned helplessness react more passively, and blood tests reveal a weakened immune response.

It's a big leap from rats to humans. But a growing body of evidence reveals that people who undergo highly stressful experiences become more vulnerable to disease. Sustained stress suppresses the immune system, leaving us more vulnerable to infections and malignancy (Cohen & others, 1991, 1993; Institute of Medicine, 1989). The death of a spouse, the stress of a space flight landing, even the strain of an exam week have all been associated with depressed immune defenses (Jemmott & Locke, 1984).

Consider:

- In one experiment, a temporary stress magnified the severity of symptoms experienced by volunteers who were knowingly infected with a cold virus (Dixon, 1986).

- In another experiment, newlywed couples who became angry while discussing problems suffered more immune system suppression the next day (Kiecolt-Glaser & others, 1993).

- A large Swedish study found that, compared with unstressed workers, those with a history of workplace stress had 5.5 times greater risk of colon cancer (Courtney & others, 1993). The cancer difference was not attributable to differences in age, smoking, drinking, or physical traits.

- Compared to nonprocrastinating students, carefree procrastinators reported lower stress and illness early in a semester but higher stress and illness late in the term. Overall, the self-defeating procrastinators also were sicker and got lower grades (Tice & Baumeister, 1997).

Explanatory style and illness

If uncontrollable stress affects health by diverting energy and, thus depressing immune functioning and generating a passive, hopeless resignation, then will people who exhibit such pessimism be more vulnerable to illness? Several studies have confirmed that a pessimistic style of explaining bad events (saying, "It's my responsibility, it's going to last, and it's going to undermine everything") makes illness more likely. Christopher Peterson and Martin Seligman (1987) studied the press quotations of 94 members of baseball's Hall of Fame and gauged how often they offered pessimistic (stable, global, internal) explanations for bad events, such as losing big games. Those who routinely did so tended to

The Delaney sisters, both over 100, attribute their longevity to a positive outlook on life.

die at somewhat younger ages. Optimists—who offered stable, global, and internal explanations for *good* events—usually outlived the pessimists.

Peterson, Seligman, and George Valliant (1988) offer other findings: university graduates who expressed the most optimism when interviewed in 1946 were healthiest when restudied in 1980. Introductory psychology students who offered optimistic explanations for bad events suffered fewer colds, sore throats, and flus a year later. Other researchers (Sheier & Carver, 1991, 1992; Long & Sangster, 1993) similarly report that optimists (who agree, for example, that "I usually expect the best") are less often bothered by various illnesses and recover faster from coronary bypass surgery.

Even cancer patients appear more likely to survive if their attitude is hopeful and determined (Levy & others, 1988; Pettingale & others, 1985). One study of 86 women undergoing breast cancer therapy reported a finding that stunned the researchers: Those who participated in morale-boosting weekly support group sessions survived an average of 37 months, double the 19-month average survival time among the nonparticipants (Spiegel & others, 1989). (At least a half-dozen research teams are now attempting to replicate this finding.) Blood tests suggest a possible reason, by linking the pessimistic explanatory style with weaker immune defenses (Kamen & others, 1988). Compared to cancer patients in a control group, those who participated in support groups became more upbeat, with an associated increase in immune cells (Cousins, 1989). Beliefs, it seems, can boost biology.

From their own studies, researchers Howard Tennen and Glenn Affleck (1987) agree that a positive, hopeful explanatory style is generally good medicine. But they also remind us that every silver lining has a cloud. Optimists may see themselves as invulnerable and thus fail to take sensible precautions. (Those who smoke hazardous high-tar cigarettes optimistically underestimate the risks involved—Segerstrom & others, 1993.) And when things go wrong in a big way—when the optimist encounters a devastating illness—adversity can be shattering. Optimism *is* good for health. But remember: Even optimists have a mortality rate of 100 percent.

"You are dust, and to dust you shall return."

Genesis 3:19

Social psychologists are actively exploring the attributions and expectations of depressed, lonely, socially anxious, and physically ill people. Depressed people have a negative explanatory style. Compared to non-depressed people, they engage in more self-blame, they interpret and recall events in a more negative light, and they are less hopeful about the future. Despite their more negative judgments, mildly depressed people in laboratory tests tend to be surprisingly realistic.

Depressed thinking has consequences for the depressed person's behavior, which in turn helps maintain a self-defeating cycle. Much the same can be said of those who suffer chronic loneliness and states of social anxiety, such as extreme shyness.

The mushrooming field of health psychology is exploring how people decide they are ill, how they explain their symptoms, and when they seek and follow treatment. It also is exploring the effects of negative emotions and the links among illness, stress, and a pessimistic explanatory style.

Summing up

Social-psychological approaches to treatment

We have considered patterns of social thinking that are linked with problems in living, ranging from serious depression to everyday shyness to physical illness. Do these maladaptive thought patterns suggest any treatments?

There is no social-psychological therapy. But therapy is a social encounter, and social psychologists are now suggesting how their principles might be integrated into existing treatment techniques (Forsyth & Leary, 1997; Strong & others, 1992). Consider three examples.

Inducing internal change through external behavior

In Chapter 4, we reviewed a broad range of evidence for a simple but powerful principle: Our actions affect our attitudes. The roles we play, the things we say and do, and the decisions we make influence who we are.

Consistent with this attitudes-follow-behavior principle, several psychotherapy techniques prescribe action. Behavior therapists try to shape behavior and assume that inner dispositions will tag along after the behavior changes. Assertiveness training employs the foot-in-the-door procedure. The individual first role-plays assertiveness in a supportive context, then gradually becomes assertive in everyday life. Rational-emotive therapy assumes that we generate our own emotions; clients receive "homework" assignments to talk and act in new ways that will generate new emotions: Challenge that overbearing relative. Stop telling yourself you're an unattractive person and ask someone out. Self-help groups subtly induce participants to behave in new ways in front of the group—to express anger, cry, act with high self-esteem, express positive feelings. All these techniques share a common assumption: If we cannot directly control our feelings by sheer willpower, we can influence them indirectly through our behavior.

Experiments confirm that what we say about ourselves can affect how we feel. In one experiment, students were induced to write self-laudatory essays (Mirels & McPeek, 1977). These students, more than others who wrote essays about a current social issue, later expressed higher self-esteem when privately rating themselves for a different experimenter. In several more experiments, Edward Jones and his associates (1981; Rhodewalt & Agustsdottir, 1986) influenced students to present themselves to an interviewer in either self-enhancing or self-deprecating ways. Again, the public displays—whether upbeat or downbeat — carried over to later private responses on a test of actual self-esteem. Saying is believing, even when we talk about ourselves. This was especially true when the students were made to feel responsible for how they presented themselves.

The importance of perceived choice was apparent in an experiment by Pamela Mendonca and Sharon Brehm (1983). They invited one group of over-weight children who were about to begin a weight-loss program to choose the treatment they preferred. Then they periodically reminded them that they had chosen their treatment. Compared to no-choice children who simultaneously experienced the same eight-week program, those who felt responsible for their treatment had lost more weight when reweighed at the end of the eight weeks and three months later.

When a sense of choice and personal responsibility is yoked with a high level of effort, the impact is even greater, report Danny Axom and Joel Cooper (1985; Axom, 1989). They put women who wanted to lose weight through some sup-posedly (but not actually) therapeutic tasks, such as making perceptual judg-ments. Those who committed the most effort to the tasks lost the most weight. This result is especially evident when the commitment is freely chosen. So, the most therapeutic commitments are both uncoerced and effortful.

Breaking vicious cycles

If depression, loneliness, and social anxiety maintain themselves through a vicious cycle of negative experiences, negative thinking, and self-defeating behavior, it should be possible to break the cycle at any of several points—by changing the environment, by training the person to behave more construc-tively, by reversing negative thinking. And it is. Several different therapy meth-ods help free people from depression's vicious cycle.

Social skills training

Depression, loneliness, and shyness are not just problems in someone's mind. To be around a depressed person for any length of time can be irritating and depressing. As lonely and shy people suspect, they may indeed come across poorly in social situations. In these cases, social skills training may help. By observing and then practicing new behaviors in safe situations, the person may develop the confidence to behave more effectively in other situations.

As the person begins to enjoy the rewards of behaving more skillfully, a more positive self-perception develops. Frances Haemmerlie and Robert Mont-gomery (1982, 1984, 1986) demonstrated this in several heartwarming studies with shy, anxious university students. Those who are inexperienced and nerv-ous around those of the other sex may say to themselves: "I don't date much, so I must be socially inadequate, so I shouldn't try reaching out to anyone." To reverse this negative sequence, Haemmerlie and Montgomery enticed such stu-dents into pleasant interactions with people of the other sex.

Social skills training: When shy, anxious people observe, then rehearse, then try out more assertive behaviors in real situations, their social skills often improve.

In one experiment, men completed social anxiety questionnaires and then came to the laboratory on two different days. Each day they enjoyed 12-minute conversations with each of six young women. The men thought the women were also subjects. Actually, the women had been asked to carry on a natural, positive, friendly conversation with each of the men.

The effect of these two and a half hours of conversation was remarkable. As one subject wrote afterward, "I had never met so many girls that I could have a good conversation with. After a few girls, my confidence grew to the point where I didn't notice being nervous like I once did." Such comments were supported by a variety of measures. Unlike men in a control condition, those who experienced the conversations reported considerably less female-related anxiety when retested one week and six months later. Placed alone in a room with an attractive female stranger, they also became much more likely to start a conversation. Outside the laboratory they actually began occasional dating.

Haemmerlie and Montgomery note that not only did all this occur without any counseling but it may very well have occurred *because* there was no counseling. Having behaved successfully on their own, the men could now perceive themselves as socially competent. Although seven months later the researchers did debrief the participants, by that time the men had presumably enjoyed enough social success to maintain their internal attributions for success. "Nothing succeeds like success," concluded Haemmerlie (1987)—"as long as there are no external factors present that the client can use as an excuse for that success!"

Explanatory style therapy

The vicious cycles that maintain depression, loneliness, and shyness can be broken by social skills training, by positive experiences that alter self-perceptions, *and* by changing negative thought patterns. Some people have social skills, but their experiences with hypercritical friends and family have convinced them they do not. For such people it may be enough to help them reverse their negative beliefs about themselves and their futures. Among the cognitive therapies with this aim is an *explanatory style therapy* proposed by social psychologists (Abramson, 1988; Försterling, 1986; Greenberg & others, 1992).

One such program taught depressed university students to change their typical attributions. Mary Anne Layden (1982) first explained the advantages of making attributions more like those of the typical nondepressed person (by accepting credit for successes and seeing how circumstances can make things go wrong). After assigning a variety of tasks, she helped the students see how they typically interpreted success and failure. Then came the treatment phase: Layden instructed each person to keep a diary of daily successes and failures, noting how they contributed to their own successes and noting external reasons for their failures. When retested after a month of this attributional retraining and compared with an untreated control group, their self-esteem had risen and their attributional style had become more positive. And the more their explanatory style improved, the more their depression lifted. By changing their attributions, they had changed their emotions.

Maintaining change through internal attributions for success

Two of the principles considered so far—that internal change may follow behavior change and that changed self-perceptions and self-attributions can help break a vicious cycle—converge on a corollary principle: Once achieved, improvements endure best if people attribute them to factors under their own control rather than to a treatment program.

As a rule, coercive techniques trigger the most drastic and immediate behavior changes (Brehm & Smith, 1986). By making the unwanted behavior extremely costly or embarrassing and the healthier behavior extremely rewarding, a therapist may achieve quick and dramatic results. The problem, as 30 years of social-psychological research reminds us, is that coerced behavior changes soon wane.

To appreciate why, consider the experience of Martha, who is concerned with her mild obesity and frustrated with her inability to do anything about it. Martha is considering several different commercial weight-control programs. Each claims it achieves the best results. She chooses one and is ordered onto a strict 1,200-calorie-a-day diet. Moreover, she is required to record and report her calorie intake each day and to come in once a week and be weighed so she and her instructor can know precisely how she is doing. Confident of the program's value and not wanting to embarrass herself, Martha adheres to the program and is delighted to find the unwanted pounds gradually disappearing. "This unique program really does work!" Martha tells herself as she reaches her target weight.

Sadly, however, after graduating from the program, Martha's experience repeats that of most weight-control graduates (Wing & Jeffrey, 1979): She regains the lost weight. On the street, she sees her instructor approaching. Embarrassed, she moves to the other side of the sidewalk and looks away. Alas, she is recognized by the instructor, who warmly invites her back into "the program." Admitting that the program achieved good results for her the first time, Martha grants her need of it and agrees to return, beginning a second round of yo-yo dieting.

Martha's experience typifies that of the participants in several weight-control experiments, including one by Janet Sonne and Dean Janoff (1979). Half the participants were led, like Martha, to attribute their changed eating behavior to the program. The others were led to credit their own efforts. Both groups lost weight during the program. But when reweighed 11 weeks later, those in the self-control condition had maintained the weight loss best. These people, like those in the shy-man-meets-women study described earlier, illustrate the benefits of self-efficacy. Having learned to cope successfully and believing that *they did it*, they now felt more confident and were more effective.

Having emphasized what changed behavior and thought patterns can accomplish, we do well to remind ourselves of their limits. Social skills training and positive thinking cannot transform us into consistent winners who are loved and admired by everyone. Furthermore, temporary depression, loneliness, and shyness are perfectly appropriate responses to profoundly sad events. It is when such feelings exist chronically and without any discernible cause that there is reason for concern and a need to change the self-defeating thoughts and behaviors.

By the 1990s, psychologists more and more accepted the idea that social influence—one person affecting another—is at the heart of therapy. Stanly Strong (1991) offers a prototypical example: A thirtyish woman comes to a therapist complaining of depression. The therapist gently probes her feelings and her situation. She explains her helplessness and her husband's demands. Although admiring her devotion, the therapist helps her see how she takes responsibility for his problems. She protests. But the therapist persists. In time, she grants that her husband may not be as fragile as she presumed. She begins to see how she can respect both her husband and herself. With the therapist, she plans strategies for each new week. At the end of a long stream of reciprocal influences between therapist and client, she emerges no longer depressed and with new ways of behaving.

Early analyses of psychotherapeutic influence focused on how therapists establish credible expertise and trustworthiness and how their credibility enhances their influence (Strong, 1968). More recent analyses have focused less on the therapist than on how the interaction affects the client's thinking (Cacioppo & others, 1991; McNeill & Stoltenberg, 1988; Neimeyer & others, 1991). Peripheral cues, such as therapist credibility, may open the door for ideas that the therapist can now get the client to think about. But the thoughtful central route to persuasion provides the most enduring attitude and behavior change. Therapists should therefore aim not to elicit a client's superficial agreement with their expert judgment but to change the client's own thinking.

Fortunately, most clients entering therapy are motivated to take the central route, to think deeply about their problems under the therapist's guidance. The therapist's task is to offer arguments and raise questions calculated to elicit favorable thoughts. The therapist's insights matter less than the thoughts they evoke in the client. The therapist needs to put things in ways that a client can hear and understand, ways that will prompt agreement rather than counterargument, and that will allow time and space for the client to reflect. Questions such as "How do you respond to what I just said?" can stimulate the client's thinking.

Martin Heesacker (1989) illustrates with the case of Dave, a 35-year-old male graduate student. Having seen what Dave denied—an underlying substance abuse problem—the counselor drew on his knowledge of Dave, an intellectual person who liked hard evidence, in persuading him to accept the diagnosis and join a treatment-support group. The counselor said, "OK, if my diagnosis is wrong, I'll be glad to change it. But let's go through a list of the characteristics of a substance abuser to check out my accuracy." The counselor then went through each criterion slowly, giving Dave time to think about each point. As he finished, Dave sat back and exclaimed, "I don't believe it: I'm a damned alcoholic."

In an experiment, John Ernst and Heesacker (1993) showed the effectiveness of escorting participants in an assertion training workshop through the central route to persuasion. Some participants experienced the typical assertiveness workshop by learning and rehearsing concepts of assertiveness. Others learned the same concepts but also volunteered a time when they hurt themselves by being unassertive. Then they heard arguments that Ernst and Heesacker knew were likely to trigger favorable thoughts (for example, "By failing to assert yourself, you train others to mistreat you"). At the workshop's end, Ernst and Heesacker asked the people to stop and reflect on how they now felt about all they had learned. Compared to those in the first group, those who went through the thought-evoking workshop left the experience with more favorable attitudes and intentions regarding assertiveness. Moreover, their roommates noticed greater assertiveness during the ensuing two weeks.

In his 1620 *Pensées*, the philosopher Pascal foresaw this principle: "People are usually more convinced by reasons they discover themselves than by those found by others." It's a principle worth remembering in our own lives.

Summing up

Among the social-psychological principles that may be usefully applied in treatment are these three: (1) Changes in external behavior can trigger internal change. (2) A self-defeating cycle of negative attitudes and behaviors can be broken by training more skillful behavior, by positive experiences that alter self-perceptions, and by changing negative thought patterns. (3) Improved states are best maintained after treatment if people attribute their improvement to internal factors under their continued control rather than to the treatment program itself.

Mental health workers also are recognizing that changing clients' attitudes and behaviors requires persuasion. Therapists, aided by their image as expert, trustworthy communicators, aim to stimulate healthier thinking by offering cogent arguments and raising questions.

Social support and well-being

There is one other major topic in the social psychology of mental and physical well-being. Supportive close relationships—feeling liked, affirmed, and encouraged by intimate friends and family—predict both health and happiness.

Our relationships are fraught with stress. "Hell is others," wrote Jean-Paul Sartre. When Peter Warr and Roy Payne (1982) asked a representative sample of British adults what, if anything, had emotionally strained them the day before, "family" was their most frequent answer. And stress, as we have seen, aggravates health problems such as coronary heart disease, hypertension, and suppression of our disease-fighting immune system.

Still, on balance, close relationships contribute less to illness than to health and happiness. Asked what prompted yesterday's times of pleasure, the same British sample, by an even larger margin, again answered "family." Close relationships provide our greatest heartaches, but also our greatest joys.

Close relationships and health

Six massive investigations, each interviewing thousands of people across several years, have reached a common conclusion: Close relationships promote health (Cohen, 1988; House & others, 1988). Compared to those with few social ties, those who have close relationships with friends, kin, or other members of close-knit religious or community organizations are less likely to die prematurely. And losing such ties heightens the risk of disease. A Finnish study of 96,000 widowed people found their risk of death doubled in the week following their partner's death (Kaprio & others, 1987). Another large scale study reveals that those recently widowed become more vulnerable to disease and death (Dohrenwend & others, 1982). Among the elderly, those having long-term close relationships with less than three people were, in one recent study, much more likely to die in the next three years (Cerhan & Wallace, 1997).

So there is a link between social support and health. But why? Perhaps those who enjoy close relationships eat better, exercise more, and smoke and drink less. Perhaps friends and family help bolster our self-esteem. Perhaps a supportive network helps us evaluate and overcome stressful events (Taylor & others, 1997). In more than 80 studies, social support has been linked with better functioning cardiovascular and immune systems (Uchino & others, 1996). Thus, when we are wounded by someone's dislike or the loss of a job, a friend's advice, help, and reassurance may indeed be good medicine (Cutrona, 1986; Rook, 1987). Even when the problem isn't mentioned, friends provide us with distraction and a sense that, come what may, we're accepted, liked, and respected. "Friendship is a sovereign antidote against all calamities," said Seneca.

With someone we consider a close friend, we may confide painful feelings. In one study, James Pennebaker and Robin O'Heeron (1984) contacted the surviving spouses of suicide or car accident victims. Those who bore their grief alone had more health problems than those who expressed it openly. When Pennebaker (1990) surveyed more than 700 university women, he found 1 in 12 reported a traumatic sexual experience in childhood. Compared with women who had experienced nonsexual traumas, such as parental death or divorce, the sexually abused women reported more headaches, stomach ailments, and other health problems, *especially if they had kept their secret to themselves.*

To isolate the confiding, confessional side of close relationships, Pennebaker asked the bereaved spouses to share what upsetting events had been preying on their minds. Those they first asked to describe a trivial event were physically tense. They stayed tense until they confided their troubles. They then relaxed. Writing about personal traumas in a diary also seems to help. When volunteers in another experiment did so, they had fewer health problems during the next six months. One participant explained, "Although I have not talked with anyone about what I wrote, I was finally able to deal with it, work through the pain instead of trying to block it out. Now it doesn't hurt to think about it." Even if it's only "talking to my diary," it helps to be able to confide.

Close relationships and happiness

Confiding painful feelings is good not only for the body but for the soul as well. That's the conclusion of studies showing that people are happier when supported by a network of friends and family.

Some studies, summarized in Chapter 2, compare people in a competitive, individualistic culture, such as that of Canada, Australia, and United States, with those in collectivist cultures, such as those of Japan and many developing countries. Individualistic cultures offer independence, privacy, and pride in personal achievements. The tighter social bonds of collectivist cultures offer protection from loneliness, alienation, divorce, and stress-related diseases. Even within an individualistic country, those who have a relatively group-centered approach to life report greater life satisfaction than do individualists (Bettencourt & Dorr, 1997).

> "Woe to him who is alone when he falls and has not another to lift him up."
>
> Ecclesiastes 4:10b

Friendships and happiness

Other studies compare individuals with few or many close relationships. Being attached to friends with whom we can share intimate thoughts has two effects, observed the seventeenth-century philosopher Francis Bacon. "It redoubleth joys, and cutteth griefs in half." So it seems from answers to a question asked in one large scale survey (Burt, 1986): "Looking over the last six months, who are the people with whom you discussed matters important to you?" Compared to those who could not name a single person with whom they had such interactions those who named five or more such friends were 60 percent more likely to feel "very happy."

Other findings confirm the importance of social networks. Across the lifespan, friendships foster self-esteem and well-being (Hartup & Stevens, 1997). For example,

- The happiest university students are those who feel satisfied with their love life (Emmons & others, 1983).
- Those who enjoy close relationships cope better with various stresses, including bereavement, rape, job loss, and illness (Abbey & Andrews, 1985; Perlman & Rook, 1987).
- Compared to army soldiers in large units with changing memberships, those on stable, cohesive, 12-person A-teams experience greater social support, better physical and mental health, and more career satisfaction (Manning & Fullerton, 1988).
- People report greater well-being if their friends and families support their goals, by frequently expressing interest and offering help and encouragement (Israel & Antonucci, 1987; Ruehlman & Wolchik, 1988).
- Among 800 alumni of one university surveyed by Wesley Perkins, those with "Yuppie values"—those who preferred a high income and occupational success and prestige to having very close friends and a close marriage—were twice as likely as their former classmates to describe themselves as "fairly" or "very" unhappy (Perkins, 1991).
- Asked, "What is necessary for your happiness?" or "What is it that makes your life meaningful?" most people mention—before anything else—satisfying close relationships with family, friends, or romantic partners (Berscheid, 1985; Berscheid & Peplau, 1983). As C. S. Lewis

(1949) said, "The sun looks down on nothing half so good as a household laughing together over a meal." Happiness hits close to home.

Marital attachment and happiness

For more than 9 in 10 people worldwide, one eventual example of a close relationship is marriage. So, does marriage correlate positively with happiness? Or is there more happiness in the pleasure-seeking single life than in the "bondage," "chains," and "yoke" of marriage?

A mountain of data reveal that most people are happier attached than unattached. Survey after survey of many tens of thousands of people from around the world have produced a consistent result: Compared to those single or widowed, and especially compared to those divorced or separated, married people report being happier and more satisfied with life (Inglehart, 1990; Gove & others, 1990). In Canada, married people are more satisfied with their lives than people who have never been married, who are more satisfied than people who have been widowed or divorced (Tepperman & Curtis, 1995). This marriage-happiness link occurs across ethnic groups (Parker & others, 1995). Moreover, satisfaction with marriage predicts overall happiness much better than does satisfaction with job, finances, or community (Lane, 1998). And among the non-married, rates of suicide and depression run higher (Stack, 1992; and see Figure A–7). Indeed, there are few stronger predictors of happiness than a close, nurturing, equitable, intimate, lifelong companionship with one's best friend.

Is marriage, as is so often supposed, more strongly associated with men's happiness than women's? Given women's greater contribution to household work and to supportive nurturing, we might expect so. The married vs. never-married happiness gap, however, is only slightly greater among men than women. Moreover, in European surveys, and in a statistical digest of 93 other studies, this happiness gap is virtually identical for men and women (Inglehart, 1990; Wood &

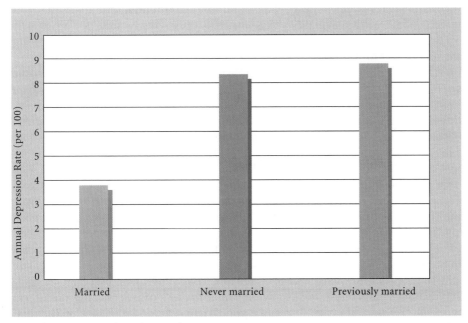

figure A–7

Marital status and depression.

A Statistics Canada survey of treatment for depression found depression rates more than two times greater among adults not married.

(Data from Statistics Canada, 1996.)

others, 1989). Although a bad marriage is often more depressing to a woman than to a man, the myth that single women are happier than married women can be laid to rest. Throughout the Western world, married people of both sexes report more happiness than those never married, divorced, or separated.

More important than being married, however, is the marriage's quality. People who say their marriage is satisfying—who find themselves still in love with their partner—rarely report being unhappy, discontented with life, or depressed. Fortunately, most married people *do* declare their marriages happy ones. In one large survey, almost two-thirds say their marriage is "very happy." Three out of four say their spouse is their best friend. Four out of five people say they would marry the same person again. The consequence? Most such people feel quite happy with life as a whole.

But why are married people generally happier? Does marriage promote happiness? Or is it the other way around—does happiness promote marriage? Are happy people more appealing as marriage partners? Do grouchy or depressed people more often stay single or suffer divorce? Certainly, happy people are more fun to be with. They are also more outgoing, trusting, compassionate, and focused on others (Myers, 1993). Unhappy people, as we have noted, are more often socially rejected. Depression often triggers marital stress, which deepens the depression (Davila & others, 1997). So, positive, happy people more readily form happy relationships.

But "the prevailing opinion of researchers," reports University of Oslo sociologist Arne Mastekaasa (1995), is that the marriage-happiness connection is "mainly due" to the beneficial effects of marriage. Consider: If the happiest people marry sooner and more often, then as people age (and progressively less happy people move into marriage), the average happiness of both married and never-married people should decline. (The older, less happy newlyweds would pull down the average happiness of married people, and the unmarried group would be increasing a concentration of unhappy people.) But the data do not support this prediction. This suggests that marital intimacy does—for most people—pay emotional dividends. One team that followed 1,380 adults over 15 years concurs (Horwitz & others, 1997). The tendency for married people to be less depressed occurs even after controlling for premarital happiness.

Marriage enhances happiness for at least two reasons. First, married people are more likely to enjoy an enduring, supportive, intimate relationship, and are less likely to suffer loneliness. No wonder male medical students in a study by Robert Coombs survived medical school with less stress and anxiety if married (Coombs, 1991). A good marriage gives each partner a dependable companion, a lover, a friend.

There is a second, more prosaic, reason why marriage promotes happiness, or at least buffers us from misery. Marriage offers the roles of spouse and parent, which can provide additional sources of self-esteem (Crosby, 1987). True, multiple roles can multiply stress. Our circuits can and do overload. Yet each also provides rewards, status, avenues to enrichment, escape from stress faced in other parts of one's life. A self with many identities is like a mansion with many rooms. When fire struck one wing of Windsor Castle most of the castle still remained for royals and tourists to enjoy. When our personal identity stands on several legs, it, too, holds up under the loss of any one. If I mess up at work, well, I can tell myself I'm still a good husband and father, and in the final analysis, these parts of me are what matter most.

Summing up

Health and happiness are influenced not only by social cognition but also by social relations. People who enjoy close, supportive relationships are at less risk for illness and premature death. Such relationships assist people's coping with stress, especially when they enable people to confide their intimate emotions.

Close relationships also foster happiness. People who have intimate, long-term attachments with friends and family members cope better with loss and report greater happiness. Compared to unmarried adults, those married, for example, are much more likely to report being very happy, and are less at risk for depression. This appears due both to the greater social success of happy people and to the well-being engendered by a supportive life companion.

Personal postscript: Enhancing happiness

Several years ago I wrote a book, *The Pursuit of Happiness*, that reported key findings from new research studies of happiness. When the editors wanted to subtitle the book *What Makes People Happy?*, I cautioned them: That's not a question this or any book can answer. What we have learned is simply what correlates with—and therefore predicts—happiness. Thus, the book's revised subtitle: *Who is Happy—and Why?*

Nevertheless, in 250 subsequent media interviews concerning happiness, the most frequent question has been "what can people do to be happy?" So without claiming any easy formula for health and happiness, I assembled nine research-based points to ponder:

1. **Realize that enduring happiness doesn't come from making it.** People adapt to changing circumstances—even to wealth or a disability. Thus wealth is like health: Its utter absence breeds misery, but having it (or any circumstance we long for) doesn't guarantee happiness.
2. **Savor the moment.** Happiness, said Benjamin Franklin, "is produced not so much by great pieces of good fortune that seldom happen as by little advantages that occur every day." Pause to take delight in the day's magic moments.
3. **Take control of your time.** Happy people feel in control of their lives, often aided by mastering their use of time—setting goals, breaking them into daily aims. Although we often overestimate how much we will accomplish in any given day (leaving us frustrated), we generally *under-*estimate how much we can accomplish in a year, given just a little progress every day.
4. **Act happy.** We can act ourselves into at least a temporary frame of mind. Manipulated into a smiling expression, people feel better; when they scowl, the whole world seems to scowl back. So . . . put on a happy face. Talk *as if* you feel positive self-esteem, optimistic, and outgoing. Going through the motions can trigger the emotions.
5. **Seek work and leisure that engages your skills.** Happy people often are in a zone called "flow"—absorbed in a task that challenges them without overwhelming them. The most expensive forms of leisure (sitting on a yacht) often provide less flow experience than gardening, socializing, or craft work. Off your duffs, couch potatoes.

6. **Join the movement movement.** An avalanche of recent studies reveals that aerobic exercise not only promotes health and energy, it also is an antidote for mild depression and anxiety. Sound minds reside in sound bodies.

7. **Sleep.** Happy people live active, vigorous lives, yet reserve time for renewing sleep and solitude. Students, especially, suffer from the effects of sleep debt, with resulting fatigue, diminished alertness, and gloomy moods.

8. **Give priority to close relationships.** There are few better remedies for unhappiness than an intimate friendship with someone who cares deeply about you. Confiding is good for soul and body. If married, resolve to nurture your relationship, to *not* take your partner for granted, to display to your spouse the sort of kindness that you display to others, to affirm your partner, to play together and share together. To rejuvenate your affections, resolve in such ways to *act* lovingly.

9. **Take care of the soul.** In many studies, actively religious people have reported themselves happier. For many people, faith provides a support community, a sense of life's meaning, feelings of ultimate acceptance, a reason to focus beyond self, and a timeless perspective on life's woes.

module b

Social Psychology in Court

On January 31, 1969, Gail Miller set out in −42 degree weather for her job as a nursing assistant at the Saskatoon City Hospital. She never made it. She was found later that day lying face down in a snow bank, lifeless. She had been brutally beaten, raped, and stabbed. A trail of evidence (blood, a knife handle, a boot, and a wallet) led to a building not far away. There, visiting an acquaintance with two of his traveling companions, was a sixteen-year-old drifter named David Milgaard.

Milgaard was questioned and denied any involvement in the murder. His companions, when questioned, backed his alibi, but after extensive questioning (and deprivation from the drugs they were addicted to) changed their story. One companion said he could not account for Milgaard's whereabouts and the other said that she saw Milgaard commit the murder. The police felt they had their man. Milgaard was tried, convicted, and sentenced to life in prison.

Unbeknownst to the police, another man, Larry Fisher, was living in the same building where David Milgaard had stayed that fateful night. As he confessed in 1970, he had committed a series of rapes in Saskatoon that winter, and as DNA testing later demonstrated, he was the man that killed Gail Miller. David Milgaard spent 23 years in prison for a crime he did not commit. How could the criminal justice system fail him in such a fundamental way? The case raised other questions as well; all examined in social psychological experiments:

- There were no true eyewitnesses to this crime. But, how influential was the eyewitness testimony? What makes a credible witness?
- Milgaard was a drifter and seen as a hippie. Can jurors ignore, as they should, their prejudices and the defendant's appearance and social status?
- How well do jurors comprehend important information, such as statistical probabilities involved in DNA blood tests?
- In cases such as this, a 12-member jury deliberates before delivering a verdict. During deliberations, how do jurors influence one another? Can a minority win over the majority? Do 12-member juries reach the same decisions as 6-member juries?

Such questions fascinate lawyers, judges, and defendants. And they are questions to which social psychology can suggest answers, as most law schools have recognized when they hire professors of "law and social science."

We can think of a courtroom as a miniature social world, one that magnifies everyday social processes with major consequences for those involved. Here, as elsewhere, people think about and influence one another. There is, then, a long list of topics pertinent to both social psychology and law (Ellsworth & Mauro, 1998). For example,

- How do a culture's norms and traditions influence its legal decisions? How, say, do cultural ideas about women's and men's roles in child rearing influence whether judges in divorce cases award child custody to the mother or father?
- What legal procedures strike people as fair? How important are perceptions of the judge's or mediator's neutrality and honesty? (Quite important reports Tom Tyler, 1988, 1989.) Most English-speaking countries have an adversarial justice system in which attorneys "zealously" represent their side. Most other countries have a nonadversarial system in which the court takes a more active role.
- Which procedure do people in English-speaking and non-English-speaking coutries regard as fairer? (In both North America and

"What are you—some kind of justice freak?"

Cultural norms governing men's and women's roles were debated in a recent child custody case in which Steven Smith obtained custody of his daughter because the mother worked and left the daughter in day care.

Europe, most people regard the adversarial system as fairer, report Allan Lind & others, 1976, 1978).

- In cases of civil liability, why do clients and their attorneys spend such enormous sums on legal fees before reaching settlements? Is it partly because cognitive bias leads defendants to overestimate their own case and therefore to reject reasonable settlement offers? (Jeffrey Rachlinski's 1990 analysis of civil cases reveals the answer is yes.)

- How do we, and should we, attribute responsibility? When will judges or jurors allow a defense of insanity or a more specific "syndrome" (battered women syndrome, abused child syndrome, war stress syndrome)?

In criminal cases, psychological factors may influence decisions involving arrest, interrogation, prosecution, plea bargaining, sentencing, and parole. Of criminal cases disposed of in Canadian courts, three in four never come to trial (Statistics Canada, 1996). Much of the trial lawyer's work therefore "is not persuasion in the courtroom but bargaining in the conference room" (Saks & Hastie, 1978, pp. 119–120). Even in the conference room, decisions are made based on speculation about what a jury or judge might do.

So, whether a case reaches a jury verdict or not, the social dynamics of the courtroom matter. Let's therefore consider two sets of factors that have been heavily researched: (1) features of the courtroom drama that can influence jurors' judgments of a defendant and (2) characteristics of both the jurors and their deliberations.

Eyewitness testimony

As the courtroom drama unfolds, jurors hear testimony, form impressions of the defendant, listen to instructions from the judge, and render a verdict. Let's take these steps one at a time, starting with eyewitness testimony.

How persuasive is eyewitness testimony?

In Chapter 3 we noted that anecdotes and personal testimonies, being vivid and concrete, can be powerfully persuasive, often more so than information that is logically compelling but abstract. There's no better way to end an argument than to say, "I saw it with my own eyes!" Seeing is believing.

Elizabeth Loftus (1974, 1979) found that those who had "seen" were indeed believed, even when their testimony was shown to be useless. When students were presented with a hypothetical robbery-murder case with circumstantial evidence but no eyewitness testimony, only 18 percent voted for conviction. Other students received the same information but with the addition of a single eyewitness. Now, knowing that someone had declared, "That's the one!" 72 percent voted for conviction. For a third group, the defense attorney discredited this testimony (the witness had 20/400 vision and was not wearing glasses). Did this discrediting reduce the effect of the testimony? In this case, not much: Sixty-eight percent still voted for conviction.

Follow-up experiments reveal discrediting often does reduce the number of guilty votes (Whitley, 1987). Unless contradicted by another eyewitness (Leippe, 1985), a vivid eyewitness account is difficult to erase from jurors' minds. That helps explain why, compared to criminal cases lacking eyewitness testimony, those that have eyewitness testimony are more likely to produce convictions (Visher, 1987).

Ah, but can't jurors spot erroneous testimony? To find out, Gary Wells, R. C. L. Lindsay, and their colleagues staged hundreds of eyewitnessed thefts of a University of Alberta calculator. Afterward, they asked each eyewitness to identify the culprit from a photo lineup. Other people, acting as jurors, observed the eyewitnesses being questioned and then evaluated their testimony. Are incorrect eyewitnesses believed less often than those who are accurate? As it happened, both correct and incorrect eyewitnesses were believed 80 percent of the time (Wells & others, 1979). This led the researchers to speculate that "human observers have absolutely no ability to discern eyewitnesses who have mistakenly identified an innocent person" (Wells & others, 1980).

In a follow-up experiment, Lindsay, Wells, and Carolyn Rumpel (1981) staged the theft under conditions that sometimes allowed witnesses a good, long look at the thief and sometimes didn't. The jurors believed the witnesses more when conditions were good. But even when conditions were so poor that two-thirds of the witnesses had actually misidentified an innocent person, 62 percent of the jurors still usually believed the witnesses.

Wells and Michael Leippe (1981) also have found that jurors are more skeptical of eyewitnesses whose memory for trivial details is poor—though these tend to be the most *accurate* witnesses. Jurors think a witness who can remember that there were three pictures hanging in the room must have "really been paying attention" (Bell & Loftus, 1988, 1989). Actually, those who pay attention to details are *less* likely to pay attention to the culprit's face.

Eyewitness recall of detail is sometimes impressive. When John Yuille and Judith Cutshall (1986) studied accounts of a midafternoon murder on a busy Burnaby, British Columbia, street, they found that eyewitnesses' recall for detail was 80 percent accurate.

How accurate are eyewitnesses?

David Milgaard is not the only person who has been falsely accused of a crime. Stories abound of innocent people who have wasted years in prison because of the testimony of eyewitnesses who were sincerely wrong (Brandon & Davies, 1973). Yet there are tens of thousands of cases each year that depend on eyewit-

"As it turned out, my battery of lawyers was no match for their battery of eyewitnesses."

© 1984, The New Yorker Magazine, Inc.

ness testimony, so even dozens of such cases would not prove that eyewitness accounts are unreliable. To assess the accuracy of eyewitness recollections, we need to learn their overall rates of "hits" and "misses." One way to gather such information is to stage crimes comparable to those in everyday life and then solicit eyewitness reports.

This has now been done many times, sometimes with disconcerting results. For example, in one study, 141 students witnessed an "assault" on a professor. Seven weeks later, when Robert Buckhout (1974) asked them to identify the assailant from a group of six photographs, 60 percent chose an innocent person. No wonder eyewitnesses to actual crimes sometimes disagree about what they saw.

Of course, some witnesses are more confident than others. And Wells and his colleagues report that it's the confident witnesses jurors find most believable. So it is disconcerting that unless conditions are very favorable, as when the culprit is very distinctive-looking, the certainty of witnesses bears only a modest relation to their accuracy (Luus & Wells, 1994; Sporer & others, 1995). Intuitive confidence does correlate somewhat with accuracy, especially among people who make positive identifications. Yet some people—whether right or wrong—chronically express themselves more assertively. And that, says Michael Leippe (1994), explains why mistaken eyewitnesses are so often persuasive.

This finding would surely come as a surprise to many judges. In most cases the law is such that judges are supposed to take a witness' certainty of their testimony into account. One panel of judges even declared that among the factors to be considered in determining accuracy is "the level of certainty demonstrated by the witness" (Wells & Murray, 1983). If judges and juries take this to heart they will often be swayed by certain but wrong testimony.

Errors sneak into our perceptions and our memories because our minds are not videotape machines. Rather, we construct our memories, based partly on what we perceived at the time and partly on our expectations, beliefs, and current knowledge (Figures B–1 and B–2).

"Certitude is not the test of certainty."

Oliver Wendell Holmes,
Collected Legal Papers

figure B–1

Sometimes believing is seeing.

Cultural expectations affect perceiving, remembering, and reporting. In a 1947 experiment on rumor transmission, Gordon Allport and Leo Postman showed people this picture of a White man holding a razor blade and then had them tell a second person about it, who then told a third person, and so on. After six tellings, the razor blade in the White man's hand usually shifted to the Black man's.

(Allport, G. W. and L. Postman (1947, 1975). Figure from *The Psychology of Rumor* by Gordon W. Allport and Leo Postman, copyright © 1947 and renewed 1975 by Holt, Rinehart and Winston, reproduced by permission of the publisher.)

figure B–2

Expectations affect perception.

Is the drawing on the far right a face or figure?

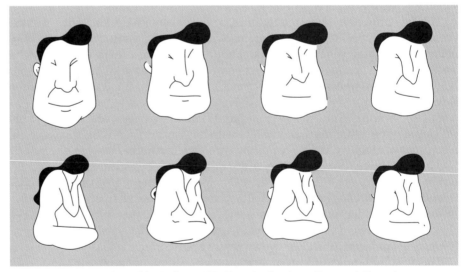

(From Fisher, 1968, adapted by Loftus, 1979. Drawing by Anne Canevari Green.)

The misinformation effect

Elizabeth Loftus and her associates (1978) provided a dramatic demonstration of memory construction. They showed students 30 slides depicting successive stages of an automobile-pedestrian accident. One critical slide showed a red Datsun stopped at a stop sign or a yield sign. Afterward they asked half the

behind the scenes

The legal system has always struck me as relying heavily on doctrine and precedent in making assumptions. What attracted me to social psychology was the possibility of scientifically testing many of these assumptions. Consider the assumption that eyewitnesses to crimes can report reliably on events they have observed. Using staged crimes, I have shown that eyewitnesses can be highly inaccurate and yet sincerely confident. This reserch reveals that people's confidence in the accuracy of their memories reflects social and personality factors rather than the quality of their memories. One

exciting development from this research is that I have been able to devise ways to improve eyewitness accuracy. This shows that social psychologists can do more than identify problems, we can also develop solutions.

Gary L. Wells
Iowa State University

students, among other questions, "Did another car pass the red Datsun while it was stopped at the stop sign?" They asked the other half the same question but with the words "stop sign" replaced by "yield sign." Later, all viewed both slides in Figure B–3 and recalled which one they had previously seen. Those earlier asked the question consistent with what they had seen were 75 percent correct. Those previously asked the misleading question were only 41 percent correct; more often than not, they *denied* seeing what they had actually seen and instead "remembered" the picture they had never seen!

In other studies of this **misinformation effect** (remembering wrong information), Loftus (1979a, b) found that after suggestive questions witnesses may believe that a red light was actually green or that a robber had a mustache when he didn't. When questioning eyewitnesses, police and attorneys commonly ask questions framed by their own understanding of what happened. So it is troubling to discover how easily witnesses incorporate misleading information into their memories, especially when they believe the questioner is well informed and when suggetive questions are repeated (Smith & Ellsworth, 1987; Zaragoza & Mitchell, 1996).

It also is troubling to realize that false memories feel and look like real memories. Thus, they can be as persuasive as real memories—convincingly sincere, yet sincerely wrong. This is true of young children (who are especially susceptible to misinformation) as well as adults. Stephen Ceci and Maggie Bruck (1993a,b) demonstrated children's suggestibility by asking children, once a week for 10 weeks, to "Think real hard, and tell me if this ever happened to you." For example, "Can you remember going to the hospital with the mousetrap on your finger." Remarkably, when then interviewed by a new adult who asked the same question, 58 percent of preschoolers produced false and often detailed stories about the fictitious event. One boy explained that his brother had pushed him into a basement woodpile, where his finger got stuck in the trap. "And then we went to the hospital, and my mommy, daddy, and Colin drove me there, to the hospital in our van, because it was far away. And the doctor put a bandage on this finger."

misinformation effect
witnessing an event, receiving misleading information about it, and then incorporating the "misinformation" into one's memory of the event

figure B–3

The misinformation effect.

When shown one of these two pictures and then asked a question suggesting the sign from the other photo, most people later "remembered" seeing the sign they had never actually seen.

(From Loftus, Miller, & Burns, 1978. Photos courtesy of Elizabeth Loftus.)

Given such vivid stories, professional psychologists were often fooled. They could not reliably separate real from false memories—nor could the children. Told the incident never actually happened, some protested. "But it really did happen. I remember it!" For Ceci (1993), such findings raise the possibility of false accusations, as in alleged child sex abuse cases where children's memories may have been contaminated by repeated suggestive questioning and where there is no corroborating evidence.

Retelling

Retelling events commits people to their recollections, accurate or not. An accurate retelling helps them later resist misleading suggestions (Bregman &

focus

Mistaken identity

Fifty years ago, law professor Edwin Borchard (1932) documented 65 convictions of people whose innocence was ultimately established beyond a doubt. Most resulted from mistaken identifications of the culprit by eyewitnesses. Borchard observed that in several of the cases the convicted prisoner, later proved innocent, was saved from hanging or electrocution by a hairbreadth. Only by rare good fortune were some of the sentences of hanging and electrocution commuted to life imprisonment, so the error could still be corrected.

How many wrongfully convicted persons have actually been executed it is impossible to say. But a 1995 analysis estimated that 0.5 percent of 1.5 million criminal convictions each year are in error, and that perhaps 4,500 of these 7,500 errors are based on mistaken iden-

tifications (Cutler & Penrod, 1995). When the National Institute of Justice examined 28 cases of people released from long prison terms (thanks to definitive DNA evidence) they found 24 had been misidentified by eyewitnesses (Connors & others, 1996).

Eyewitness misidentification put Randall Ayers, shown here with his sisters on his first day of freedom in eight years, behind bars for a rape he didn't commit. The actual culprit—who strikingly resembles Ayers—confessed to the rape when arrested for the murders of two women. Jurors later admitted being bothered by the absence of supporting evidence and by Ayers being an inch shorter than the victim, although the attacker was supposedly an inch or two taller. Nevertheless, the eyewitnesses' repeated and confident identification of Ayers was persuasive.

McAllister, 1982). Other times, the more we retell a story, the more we convince ourselves of a falsehood. Wells, Ferguson, and Lindsay (1981) demonstrated this by having eyewitnesses to a staged theft rehearse their answers to questions before taking the witness stand. Doing so increased the confidence of those who were wrong, and thus made jurors who heard their false testimony more likely to convict the innocent person.

In Chapter 4 we noted that we often adjust what we say to please our listeners and, having done so, come to believe the altered message. Imagine witnessing an argument that erupts into a fight in which one person injures the other. Afterward, the injured party sues. Before the trial a smooth lawyer for one of the two parties interviews you. Might you slightly adjust your testimony, giving a version of the fight that supports this lawyer's client? If you did so, might your later recollections in court be similarly slanted?

Blair Sheppard and Neil Vidmar (1980) report that the answer to both questions is yes. At the University of Western Ontario, they had some students serve as witnesses to a fight and others as lawyers and judges. When interviewed by lawyers for the defendant, the witnesses later gave the judge testimony that was more favorable to the defendant. In a follow-up experiment, Vidmar and Nancy Laird (1983) noted that witnesses did not omit important facts from their testimony; they just changed their tone of voice and choice of words depending on whether they thought they were a witness for the defendant or for the plaintiff. Even this was enough to bias the impressions of those who heard the testimony. So it's not only suggestive questions that can distort eyewitness recollections but also their own retellings, which may be subtly adjusted to suit their audience.

Feedback to witnesses

Eyewitness to a crime on viewing a lineup: "Oh, my God . . . I don't know . . . It's one of those two . . . but I don't know . . . Oh, man . . . the guy a little bit taller than number two . . . It's one of those two, but I don't know . . . "

Months later at trial: "You were positive it was number two? It wasn't a maybe?"

Eyewitness's answer: "There was no maybe about it . . . I was absolutely positive." (*Missouri vs. Hutching,* 1994, reported by Wells & Bradfield, 1998).

What explains witnesses misrecalling their original uncertainty? Gary Wells and Amy Bradfield (1998) wondered. Past research has shown that one's confidence gains a boost from learning that another witness has fingered the same person, from being asked the same question repeatedly, and from preparing for cross-examination (Luus & Wells, 1994; Shaw, 1996; Wells & others, 1981). Might the lineup interviewer's feedback also influence not just confidence but—the I-knew-it-all-along phenomenon rides again—recollections of earlier confidence?

To find out, Wells and Bradfield conducted two experiments in which 352 Iowa State University students viewed a grainy security camera video of a man entering a store. Moments later, off camera, he murders a security guard. They then viewed the photo spread from the actual criminal case, minus the gunman's photo, and were asked to identify the gunman. All 352 students made a false identification, following which the experimenter gave confirming feedback ("Good. You identified the actual suspect"), disconfirming feedback ("Actually, the suspect was number ____"), or no feedback. Finally, all were later asked, "At the time that you identified the person in the photo spread, how certain were you that the person you identified from the photos was the gunman that you saw in the video?" (from 1, not at all certain, to 7, totally certain).

The experiment produced two striking results: First, the effect of the experimenter's casual comment was huge. In the confirming feedback condition, 58 percent of the eyewitnesses rated their certainty as 6 or 7 when making their initial judgment—four times the 14 percent who said the same in the no-feedback condition and eleven times the 5 percent in the disconfirming condition. We shouldn't be surprised that witnesses' post-feedback confidence would be raised by confirming feedback, but these were ratings of their remembered *pre*-feedback confidence.

It wasn't obvious to the subjects that those judgments would be affected. For the second rather amazing finding is that when asked if the feedback had

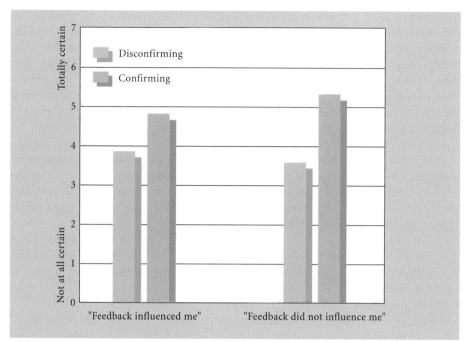

figure B–4

Recalled certainty of eyewitnesses after receiving confirming or disconfirming feedback (Experiment 2).

Note that participants who said feedback did *not* influence them were influenced no less.

(Data from Wells & Bradfield, 1998.)

influenced their answer, 58 percent said no. Moreover, as a group those who felt uninfluenced were no less so than those who said they were (Figure B–4).

The lesson here runs deeper than jury research. Once again we see why we need social psychological research. As social psychologists have so often found—recall Milgram's obedience experiments—simply asking people how they would act, or asking what explains their actions, sometimes gives us wrong answers. Benjamin Franklin was right: "There are three things extremely hard, Steel, a Diamond, and to know one's self." And that is why we need to do not only surveys that ask people to explain themselves, but experiments in which we see what they actually do.

Reducing error

Given these error-prone tendencies, what constructive steps can be taken to increase the accuracy of eyewitnesses and jurors? Experts have several ideas.

Train police interviewers

When Ronald Fisher and his co-workers (1987) examined tape-recorded interviews of eyewitnesses conducted by experienced Florida police detectives, they found a typical pattern. Following an open-ended beginning ("Tell me what you recall"), the detectives would occasionally interrupt with follow-up questions, including questions eliciting terse answers ("How tall was he?"). Fisher and Edward Geiselman (1996) say interviews should begin by allowing eyewitnesses to offer their own unprompted recollections.

The recollections will be most complete if the interviewer jogs the memory by first guiding people to reconstruct the setting. Have them visualize the scene and what they were thinking and feeling at the time. Even showing pictures of the setting—of, say, the store checkout lane with a clerk standing where she was robbed—can promote accurate recall (Cutler & Penrod, 1988). After giving witnesses ample, uninterrupted time to report everything that comes to mind, the interviewer then jogs their memory with evocative questions ("Was there anything unusual about the voice? Was there anything unusual about the person's appearance or clothing?"). When Fisher and his colleagues (1989, 1994) trained detectives to question in this way, the information they elicited from eyewitnesses increased 50 percent without increasing the false memory rate. In response to such results, most police agencies in North America and Britain have adopted this "cognitive interview" procedure (Geiselman, 1996). Many agencies now include the procedure in their training program, including the witness interviewing manual distributed to all police officers in England and Wales (Bower, 1997). (The procedure also shows promise for enhancing information gathered in oral histories and medical surveys.)

Interviewers on memory reconnaissance missions must be careful to keep their questions free of hidden assumptions. Loftus and Guido Zanni (1975) found that questions such as "Did you see the broken headlight?" triggered twice as many "memories" of nonexistent events as did questions without the hidden assumption: "Did you see a broken headlight?"

Flooding eyewitnesses with an array of mugshots also reduces accuracy in later identifying the culprit (Brigham & Cairns, 1988). Errors are especially likely when the witness has to stop, think, and analytically compare faces. Accurate identifications tend to be automatic and effortless. The right face just pops out (Dunning & Stern, 1994).

Minimize false lineup identifications

The case of Ron Shatford illustrates how the composition of a police lineup can promote misidentification (Doob & Kirshenbaum, 1973). After a suburban Toronto department store robbery, the cashier involved could only recall that the culprit was not wearing a tie and was "very neatly dressed and rather good looking." When police put the good-looking Shatford in a lineup with 11 unattractive men, all of whom wore ties, the cashier readily identified him as the culprit. Only after he had served 15 months of a long sentence did another person confess, allowing Shatford to be retried and found not guilty.

Gary Wells (1984, 1993) reports that one way to reduce misidentifications is to give eyewitnesses a "blank" lineup that contains no suspects and screen out those who make false identifications. Those who do not make such errors turn out to be more accurate when they later face the actual lineup. Mistakes can also be reduced by having witnesses simply make individual yes or no judgments in response to a *sequence* of people (Cutler & Penrod, 1988; Lindsay & Wells, 1985). Witnesses viewing just one suspect (in a "show-up") are more likely to say "not there" than those viewing a lineup (Gonzalez & others, 1993). If witnesses view a group of photos or people simultaneously, they are more likely to choose whoever most resembles the culprit.

Police can also minimize false identifications by including instructions acknowledging that the offender may not be in the lineup (Malpaas & Devine, 1984). Compared to lineups of several suspects, a lineup composed of one suspect and several people known to be innocent further reduces misidentifications (Wells, 1993). Lineups containing innocent people enable police to disregard eyewitnesses who make errors; with all-suspect lineups, there is no opportunity to weed out those who are guessing.

> "While the rules of evidence and other safeguards provide protection in the courtroom, they are absent in the backroom of the precinct station."
>
> Ernest Hilgard & Elizabeth Loftus (1979)

These no-cost procedures make police lineups more like good experiments. They contain a *control group* (a no-suspect lineup or a lineup in which mock witnesses try to guess the suspect based merely on a general description). They have an experimenter who is *blind* to the hypotheses (an officer who doesn't know which person is the suspect). Questions are *scripted and neutral*, so they don't subtly demand a particular response (the procedure doesn't imply the culprit *is* in the lineup). And they prohibit confidence-inflating post-line-up comments ("you got him") prior to trial testimony.

Such procedures greatly reduce the natural human confirmation bias (having an idea and seeking confirming evidence). Using these social-psychological insights, Canada's Law Reform Commission recommended new eyewitness identification procedures to reduce the likelihood of future Ron Shatfords (Wells & Luus, 1990).

THE FAR SIDE   By GARY LARSON

"*That's* him! *That's* the one! ... I'd recognize that silly little hat *anywhere*!"

The Far Side Copyright 1985 Universal Press Syndicate. All rights reserved.

Lineup fairness? From the suspect's perspective a lineup is fair, note John Brigham, David Ready, and Stacy Spier (1990), when "the other lineup members are reasonably similar in general appearance to the suspect."

Educate jurors

Do jurors evaluate eyewitness testimony critically? Do they intuitively understand how the circumstances of a lineup determine its reliability? Do they know whether to take an eyewitness's self-confidence into account? Do they realize how memory can be influenced by earlier misleading questions, by stress at the time of the incident, by the interval between the event and the questioning, by whether the suspect is the same or a different race, by whether recall of other details is sharp or hazy? Studies in Canada, Great Britain, and the United States reveal that jurors discount most of these factors, all of which are known to influence eyewitness testimony (Cutler & others, 1988; Noon & Hollin, 1987; Wells & Turtle, 1987).

To educate jurors, experts are now frequently asked (usually by defense attorneys) to testify about eyewitness testimony. Their aim is to offer jurors the sort of information you have been reading, to help them evaluate the testimony of both prosecution and defense witnesses. Table B–1, drawn from a survey of 63 experts on eyewitness testimony, lists the most agreed-upon phenomena. These experts therefore explain that

- Eyewitnesses often perceive events selectively.
- Discussions of the events can alter or add to their memories.
- Research using staged crimes has shown that witnesses often choose a wrong person from a lineup, especially when the alternative people differ sharply from the witness's basic description of the perpetrator.

table B–1 **Influences upon eyewitness testimony**

Phenomenon	Eyewitness Experts Agreeing*
1. *Question wording.* An eyewitness's testimony about an event can be affected by how the questions put to that eyewitness are worded.	97%
2. *Lineup instructions.* Police instructions can affect an eyewitness's willingness to make an identification and/or the likelihood that he or she will identify a particular person.	95%
3. *Postevent information.* Eyewitness testimony about an event often reflects not only what they actually saw but information they obtained later on.	87%
4. *Accuracy versus confidence.* An eyewitness's confidence is not a good predictor of his or her identification accuracy.	87%
5. *Attitudes and expectations.* An eyewitness's perception and memory or an event may be affected by his or her attitudes and expectations.	85%

*"This phenomenon is reliable enough for psychologists to present it in courtroom testimony."

Source: From S. M. Kassin, P. C. Ellsworth, & V. L. Smith (1989).

- Eyewitnesses are especially prone to error when trying to identify someone of another race (Chapter 9).
- Jurors should disregard the confidence with which an eyewitness offers testimony.

Taught the conditions under which eyewitness accounts *are* trustworthy, jurors become more likely to trust such testimony (Cutler & others, 1989; Wells, 1986). Moreover, attorneys and judges are recognizing the importance of some of these factors when deciding when to ask for or permit suppression of lineup evidence (Stinson & others, 1996, 1997).

Summing up

Courtroom procedures have been on trial in hundreds of recent experiments, because social psychologists believe that the courtroom offers a natural context for studying how people form judgments and that social psychology's principles and methods can shed new light on important judicial issues.

Experiments reveal that both witnesses and jurors readily succumb to an illusion that a given witness's mental-recording equipment functions free of significant error. But as witnesses construct and rehearse memories of what they have observed, errors creep in. Research suggests ways to lessen such error, both in eyewitness reports and in jurors' use of such reports.

Other influences on judgments

Are the defendant's attractiveness and similarity to jurors likely to bias them? How faithfully do jurors follow judges' instructions?

The defendant's characteristics

According to the famed trial lawyer Clarence Darrow (1933), jurors seldom convict a person they like or acquit one they dislike. He argued that the main job of the trial lawyer is to make a jury like the defendant. Was he right? And is it true, as Darrow also said, that "facts regarding the crime are relatively unimportant"?

Darrow overstated the case. One study of more than 3,500 criminal cases and some 4,000 civil cases found that 4 times in 5 the judge agreed with the jury's decision (Kalven & Zeisel, 1966). Although both may have been wrong, the evidence usually is clear enough that jurors can set aside their biases, focus on the facts, and agree on a verdict (Saks & Hastie, 1978; Visher, 1987). Darrow was too cynical; facts do matter.

Nevertheless, when jurors are asked to make social judgments—would *this* defendant commit *this* offense? intentionally?—facts are not all that matter. As we noted in Chapter 7, communicators are more persuasive if they seem credible and attractive. Jurors cannot help forming impressions of the defendant. Can they put these impressions aside and decide the case based on the facts alone? To judge from the more lenient treatment often received by high-status defendants (McGillis, 1979), it seems that some cultural bias lingers. But actual cases vary in so many ways—in the type of crime, in the status, age, sex, and race of the defendant—that it's hard to isolate the factors that influence jurors. So experimenters have controlled such factors by giving mock jurors the same basic facts of a case while varying, say, the defendant's attractiveness or similarity to the jurors.

Physical attractiveness

In Chapter 11, we noted a physical attractiveness stereotype: Beautiful people seem like good people. Michael Efran (1974) wondered whether this stereotype would bias students' judgments of someone accused of cheating. He asked some of his University of Toronto students whether attractiveness should affect presumption of guilt. Their answer: "No, it shouldn't." But did it? Yes. When Efran gave other students a description of the case with a photograph of either an attractive or an unattractive defendant, they judged the most attractive as least guilty and recommended that person for the least punishment.

Other experimenters have confirmed that when the evidence is meager or ambiguous, justice is not blind to a defendant's looks (Mazzela & Feingold, 1994). Diane Berry and Leslie Zebrowitz-McArthur (1988) discovered this when they asked people to judge the guilt of baby-faced and mature-faced defendants. Baby-faced adults (people with large, round eyes and small chins) seemed more naive and were found guilty more often of crimes of negligence and less often of intentional criminal acts. If convicted, unattractive people also strike people as more dangerous, especially if they are sexual offenders (Esses & Webster, 1988). And these judgements are likely to result in unattractive people receiving stiffer sentences.

THE FAR SIDE   By GARY LARSON

And so I ask the jury . . . is that the face of a mass murderer?

Other things being equal, people often judge physically appealing defendants more leniently.

To see if these findings extend to the real world, Chris Downs and Phillip Lyons (1991) asked police escorts to rate the physical attractiveness of 1,742 defendants appearing before 40 judges in misdemeanor cases. Whether the misdemeanor was serious (such as forgery), moderate (such as harassment), or minor (such as public intoxication), the judges set greater bails and fines for less attractive defendants (Figure B–5). What explains this dramatic effect? Are unattractive people also lower in status? Are they indeed more likely to flee or to commit crime, as the judges perhaps suppose? Or are judges simply ignoring the Roman statesman Cicero's advice: "The final good and the supreme duty of the wise man is to resist appearance."

supreme duty of the wise man is to resist appearance."

Similarity to the jurors

If Clarence Darrow was even partly right in his declaration that liking or disliking a defendant colors judgments, then other factors that influence liking should also matter. Among such influences is the principle, noted in Chapter 7, that likeness (similarity) leads to liking. When people pretend they are jurors, they are indeed more sympathetic to a defendant who shares their attitudes, religion, race, or (in cases of sexual assault) gender (Selby & others, 1977; Towson & Zanna, 1983; Ugwuegbu, 1979).

Some examples:

- When Paul Amato (1979) had Australian students read evidence concerning a left- or right-wing person accused of a politically motivated burglary, they judged the defendant less guilty if his or her political views were similar to their own.

- When Cookie Stephan and Walter Stephan (1986) had English-speaking people judge someone accused of assault, they were more likely to think the person not guilty if the defendant's testimony was in English, rather than translated from Spanish or Thai.

- In the U.S., for "White crimes," such as embezzlement and fraud, (mostly White) mock jurors punish White defendants more severely (Mazzella & Feingold, 1994). For violent crimes, mock jurors punish Black defendants more severely (Sweeney & Haney, 1992). One analysis found that U.S. federal judges sentenced Blacks to 10 percent longer sentences than Whites when comparing cases with the same seriousness and criminal

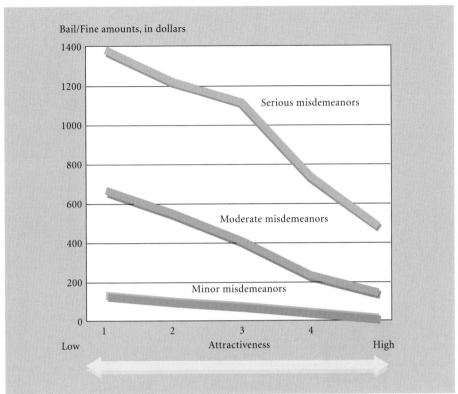

figure B–5

Attractiveness and legal judgments.
Texas Gulf Coast judges set higher bails and fines for less attractive defendants.

(Data from Downs & Lyons, 1991.)

history (Associated Press, 1995). In Canada, modern racism also seems to effect jurors' assignments of punishment. Neil Rector and Michael Bagby (1995) found that when legal instruction provided an excuse, White mock jurors assigned more severe sentences for interracial rape cases, but when these instructions were omitted they assigned more severe sentences for intraracial rape cases.

It seems we are more sympathetic toward a defendant with whom we can identify. If we think *we* wouldn't have committed that criminal act, we may assume that someone like us is also unlikely to have done it. That helps explain why, in acquaintance rape trials, men more often than women judge the defendant not guilty (Fischer, 1997). In the David Milgaard trial were the staid middle-age jurors influenced by his "hippie" appearance? Might they have found it easier to convict him because he was different? Would they have been more likely to question the testimony of the questionable eyewitnesses if the accused had been an upstanding middle-aged citizen? We will never know the answers to these questions, but it seems plausible that the jurors did not give Milgaard the benefit of the doubt because he was seen as different, and in seeing him as different they were ready to think he could have committed the crime.

Ideally, jurors would leave their biases outside the courtroom and begin a trial with open minds. These biases jeopardize the very purpose of the court: to

"Surely not guilty. Next case."

© 1988, The New Yorker Magazine, Inc.

administer justice with impartiality. In its concern for objectivity, the judicial system is similar to science: Both scientists and jurors are supposed to sift and weigh the evidence. Both the courts and science have rules about what evidence is relevant. Both keep careful records and assume that others given the same evidence would decide similarly.

When the evidence is clear and jurors focus on it (as when they reread and debate the meaning of testimony), their biases are indeed minimal (Kaplan & Schersching, 1980). The quality of the evidence matters more than the prejudices of the jurors.

The judge's instructions

In the courtroom, judges instruct jurors to ignore biasing information. All of us can recall courtroom dramas in which an attorney exclaimed, "Your honor, I object!" whereupon the judge sustained the objection and ordered the jury to ignore the other attorney's suggestive question or the witness's remark. In 1983 Canada passed the "rape shield" law, and although it has changed in recent years it still serves to prohibit or limit testimony concerning the victim's prior sexual activity. Such testimony, though irrelevant to the case at hand, tends to make jurors more sympathetic to the accused rapist's claim that the woman consented to sexual relations (Borgida, 1981; Cann & others, 1979).

If such reliable, illegal, or prejudicial testimony is nevertheless slipped in by the defense or blurted out by a witness, will jurors follow a judge's instruction to ignore it? And is it enough for the judge to remind jurors that "the issue is not whether you like or dislike the defendant but whether the defendant committed the offense"?

Very possibly not. Several experimenters report that it is hard for jurors to ignore inadmissible evidence, such as the defendant's previous convictions. In one study, Stanley Sue, Ronald Smith, and Cathy Caldwell (1973) gave students a description of a grocery store robbery-murder and a summary of the prosecution's case and the defense's case. When the crown's case was weak, no one judged the defendant guilty. When a tape recording of an incriminating phone call made by the defendant was added to the weak case, about one-third judged the person guilty. The judge's instructing jurors that the tape was not legal evidence and they should ignore it did nothing to erase the effect of the damaging testimony.

Indeed, Sharon Wolf and David Montgomery (1977) found that a judge's order to ignore testimony—"It must play no role in your consideration of the case. You have no choice but to disregard it"—can even boomerang, adding to the testimony's impact. Perhaps such statements create **reactance** in the jurors. Or perhaps they sensitize jurors to the inadmissible testimony, as what happens when I warn you *not* to look at your nose as you finish this sentence. Judges can more easily strike inadmissible testimony from the court records than from the jurors' minds. As trial lawyers sometimes say, "You can't unring a bell." This is especially so with emotional information (Edwards & Bryan, 1997). When jurors are told vividly about a defendant's past record ("hacking up a woman"), a judge's instructions to ignore are more likely to boomerang than when the inadmissible information is less emotional ("assault with a deadly weapon").

reactance
the desire to assert one's sense of freedom

David Milgaard was released from prison after DNA evidence implicated another man in the killing of Gail Miller.

It is not easy for jurors to erase inadmissible testimony from memory.

"*The jury will disregard the witness's last remarks.*"

Pretrial publicity is also hard for jurors to ignore, as Geoffrey Kramer and his colleagues (1990) confirmed. In a massive experiment, they exposed nearly 800 mock jurors (most from actual jury rolls) to incriminating news reports about the past convictions of a man accused of robbing a supermarket. After the jurors viewed a videotaped re-enactment of the trial, they either did or did not hear the judge's instructions to disregard the pretrial publicity. The effect of the judicial admonition was nil. Moreover, people whose opinions are biased by such publicity typically deny its effect on them, and this denial makes it hard to eliminate biased jurors (Moran & Cutler, 1991). In experiments, even getting mock jurors to pledge their impartiality and their willingness to disregard prior information has not eliminated the pretrial publicity effect (Dexter & others, 1992). In the U.S. they have not yet devised a way to counteract these negative effects. In Canada, however, the problems of pretrial publicity are usually dealt with by banning publication of any information that could affect the trial's outcome.

To minimize the effects of inadmissible testimony, judges can *forewarn* jurors that certain types of evidence, such as a rape victim's sexual history, are irrelevant. Once jurors form impressions based on such evidence, a judge's admonitions have much less effect (Borgida & White, 1980; Kassin & Wrightsman, 1979). Thus, reports Vicki Smith (1991), a pretrial training session pays dividends. Teaching jurors legal procedures and standards of proof improves their understanding of the trial procedure and their willingness to withhold judgment until after they have heard all the trial information.

Better yet, judges could cut inadmissible testimony before the jurors hear it—by videotaping testimonies and removing the inadmissible parts. Live and videotaped testimony have much the same impact as do live and videotaped lineups (Cutler & others, 1989; Miller & Fontes, 1979). Perhaps, then, courtrooms of the future will have life-size television monitors.

behind the scenes

While I was a new University of Illinois graduate student, my advisor, James Davis, began studying how a group's size affects its decisions. Coincidentally, the Supreme Court had just guessed that jury size wouldn't much matter. So Jim, with my help, decided to experiment with jury size. As I eavesdropped on the mock juries I became fascinated by the jurors' insightful arguments, their mix of amazing recollections and memory fabrications, their prejudices, their attempts to persuade or coerce, and their occasional courage in standing alone. Here brought to life before me were so many of the psychological processes I had been studying!

Although our student jurors understood they were only simulating a real trial, they really cared about reaching a fair verdict. Ever since listening in on those first jury deliberations, I've been hooked on studying juror behavior.

Norbert Kerr
Michigan State University

Critics object that the procedure prevents jurors from observing how the defendant and others react to the witness. Proponents argue that videotaping not only enables the judge to edit out inadmissible testimony but also speeds up the trial and allows witnesses to talk about crucial events before memories fade.

Other issues

We have considered three courtroom factors—eyewitness testimony, the defendant's characteristics, and the judge's instructions. Researchers are also studying the influence of other factors. For example, Norbert Kerr and his colleagues (1978, 1981, 1982) have studied these issues: Does a severe potential punishment make jurors less willing to convict—and would it therefore be strategic in some cases for the crown to seek a lighter sentence? Do experienced jurors' judgments differ from those of novice jurors? Are defendants judged more harshly when the *victim* is attractive or has suffered greatly? Kerr's research suggests that the answer to all three questions is yes.

Experiments by Mark Alicke and Teresa Davis (1989), and by Michael Enzle and Wendy Hawkins (1992), show that the victim's characteristics can affect jurors' judgments of blame and punishment even when the defendant was unaware of them. Consider the 1984 case of the "subway vigilante" Bernard Goetz. When four teens approached Goetz for $5 on a subway, the frightened Goetz pulled out a loaded gun and shot each of them, leaving one partly paralyzed. When Goetz was charged with attempted homicide, there was an outcry of public support for him based partly on the disclosure that the youths had extensive criminal records and that three of them were carrying concealed, sharpened screwdrivers. Although Goetz didn't know any of this, he was acquitted of the attempted homicide charge and convicted only of illegal firearm possession.

Summing up   The facts of a case are usually compelling enough that jurors can lay aside their biases and render a fair judgment. When the evidence is ambiguous, jurors are more likely to interpret it with their preconceived biases and to feel sympathetic to a defendant who is attractive or similar to themselves.

When jurors are exposed to damaging pretrial publicity or to inadmissible evidence, will they follow a judge's instruction to ignore it? In simulated trials, the judge's orders were sometimes followed, but often, especially when the judge's admonition came *after* an impression was made, they were not.

The jurors as individuals

Verdicts depend on what happens in the courtroom—the eyewitness testimonies, the defendant's characteristics, the judge's instructions. But verdicts also depend on how the individual jurors process information.

Courtroom influences on "the average juror" are worth pondering. But no juror is the average juror; each carries into the courthouse individual attitudes and personalities. And when deliberating, jurors influence one another. So two key questions are: How are their verdicts influenced by their individual dispositions? And by their group deliberation?

Juror comprehension

To gain insight into juror comprehension, Nancy Pennington and Reid Hastie (1993) have studied the thought processes of mock jurors, sampled from courthouse jury pools, while viewing reenactments of actual trials. In making their decisions, jurors first construct a story that makes sense of all the evidence. After observing one murder trial, some jurors concluded that a quarrel made the defendant angry, triggering him to get a knife, search for the decedent, and stab him to death. Others surmised that the frightened defendant picked up a knife that he used to defend himself when he later encountered the decedent. When the jurors begin deliberating, they are often surprised to discover that others have constructed different stories. This implies—and research confirms—that jurors are persuaded when attorneys present evidence like a narrative story. In felony cases—where the conviction rate can be as high as 80 percent—the crown case follows a story structure more often than the defense case.

Next the jurors must grasp the judge's instructions concerning the available verdict categories. For these instructions to be effective, jurors must first understand them. Study after study has found that many people do not understand the standard legalese of judicial instructions. Depending on the type of case, a jury may be told that the standard of proof is a "preponderance of the evidence," "clear and convincing evidence," or "beyond a reasonable doubt." Such statements may have one meaning for the legal community and different meanings in the minds of jurors (Kagehiro, 1990). In one study of criminal instructions, viewers of videotaped instructions could answer only 15 percent of 89 questions posed to them about what they had heard (Elwork & others, 1982).

After observing actual cases and later interviewing the jurors, Stephen Adler (1994) found "lots of sincere, serious people who—for a variety of reasons—were missing key points, focusing on irrelevant issues, succumbing to barely recognized prejudices, failing to see through the cheapest appeals to sympathy or hate, and generally botching the job."

In the trial of Imelda Marcos, who was charged with transferring hundreds of millions of dollars of Philippine money into banks for her own use, lawyers eliminated anyone who was aware of her role in her husband's dictatorship. Ill-equipped to follow the complex money transactions, the uninformed people who made it onto the jury fell back on sympathy for Imelda, whom they would see dressed in black, clutching her rosaries, and wiping away tears (Adler, 1994).

Faced with an incomprehensibly complex accounting of Imelda Marcos's alleged thefts of public money, jurors fell back on their intuitive assessments of the seemingly devout and sincere woman and found her not guilty.

Jurors may be further confused if the criteria change as proceedings move from the trial phase that determines guilt or innocence into the penalty phase (Luginbuhl, 1992). In some cases, for example, jurors are to convict only if there is "proof beyond a reasonable doubt." But a "preponderance of the evidence" is sufficient when judging whether mitigating circumstances, such as an abusive childhood, should lighten the sentence.

Finally, jurors must compare their explanation with the verdict categories. When using the judge's definition of, say, justifiable self-defense, jurors must decide whether "pinned against a wall" matches their understanding of the required circumstance "unable to escape." Often a judge's abstract, jargon-filled definition of verdict categories loses in the competition with the jurors' own mental images of these crimes. Vicki Smith (1991) reports that, regardless of the judge's definition, if a defendant's actions match jurors' images of "vandalism," "assault," or "robbery," they will find the person guilty.

People also have a hard time comprehending statistics and scientific information when it is presented as evidence. When Larry Fisher was finally tried for Gail Miller's murder in 1999, the jury was presented with evidence that there was only one chance in 950 trillion that the DNA from the sperm found on Gail Miller's clothes belonged to anyone other than Larry Fisher. This evidence by all rational accounts should have ruled David Milgaard out as a suspect in the case. These sorts of statistics, however, are difficult to comprehend and jurors often have trouble figuring out exactly what they mean. Perhaps aware of jurors' fragile understanding of such statistical principles, Fisher's lawyer tried to argue that despite the DNA evidence there was still a good chance that David Milgaard was the person who really raped and murdered Gail Miller. In this instance the jury was able to see through the lawyer's erroneous argument. Unfortunately, juries are not always able to do so. The more typical finding is that juries do not pay enough attention to statistical evidence.

Gary Wells (1992) reports that even when people (including experienced trial judges) understand naked statistical probabilities, they may be unpersuaded. The numbers, it seems, must be supported by a convincing story. Thus, reports Wells, one Toronto mother lost a paternity suit seeking child support from her child's alleged father despite a blood test showing a 99.8 percent probability that the man was her child's father. She lost after the man took the stand and persuasively denied the allegation.

Understanding how jurors misconstrue judicial instructions and statistical information is a first step toward better decisions. A next step might be giving jurors access to transcripts rather than forcing them to rely on their memories in processing complex information (Bourgeois & others, 1993). A further step is devising and testing clearer, more effective ways to present information—a task on which several social psychologists are currently at work. For example, when a judge quantifies the required standard of proof (as, say, 51, 71, or 91 percent certainty) jurors understand and respond appropriately (Kagehiro, 1990).

And surely there must be a simpler way to tell jurors, as required in Illinois death penalty cases, not to impose the death sentence in murder cases when there are justifying circumstances: "If you do not unanimously find from your consideration of all the evidence that there are no mitigating factors sufficient to preclude imposition of a death sentence, then you should sign the verdict requiring the court to impose a sentence other than death" (Diamond, 1993). Given jury instructions rewritten into simple language, jurors are less susceptible to the judge's biases (Halverson & others, 1997).

Phoebe Ellsworth and Robert Mauro (1998) sum up the dismal conclusions of jury researchers: "Legal instructions are typically delivered in a manner likely to frustrate the most conscientious attempts at understanding. . . . The language is technical and . . . no attempt is made either to assess jurors' mistaken preconceptions about the law or to provide any kind of useful education."

Characteristics of Jurors

Given that jurors come to a trial with different attitudes, beliefs, values, and personalities, can psychologists use their knowledge of these constructs to predict the verdict that a juror is likely to make? Surprisingly, the answer to this question is that to a large extent psychologists have been unable to make such predictions. Individual differences that predict verdicts mostly consist of reactions to specific features of a case. Racial prejudice becomes relevant in racially charged cases; gender seems linked with verdicts only in rape and battered woman cases; belief in personal responsibility vs. corporate responsibility relates to personal injury awards in suits against businesses. (Ellsworth & Mauro, 1998).

Experiments reveal that attitudes and personal characteristics don't always predict verdicts. There are "no magic questions to be asked of prospective jurors, not even a guarantee that a particular survey will detect useful attitude-behavior or personality-behavior relationships," caution Steven Penrod and Brian Cutler (1987). Researchers Michael Saks and Reid Hastie (1978) agree: "The studies are unanimous in showing that evidence is a substantially more potent determinant of jurors' verdicts than the individual characteristics of jurors" (p. 68). In courtrooms, jurors' public pledge of fairness and the judge's instruction to "be fair" strongly commits most jurors to the norm of fairness.

Variations in the situation, especially in the evidence, are what matter most. Saks and Hastie believe that "what this implies about human behavior, on juries or off, is that while we are unique individuals, our differences are vastly overshadowed by our similarities. Morever, the range of situations we are likely to encounter is far more varied than the range of human beings who will encounter them" (p. 69).

Despite these findings lawyers believe that they can have a big influence on a trial by influencing who is on the jury. As one lawyer boldly proclaimed, "Trial attorneys are acutely attuned to the nuances of human behavior, which enables them to detect the minutest traces of bias or inability to reach an appropriate decision" (Bigam, 1977).

Mindful that people's assessments of others are error-prone, social psychologists doubt that lawyers come equipped with fine-tuned social Geiger counters. Nevertheless, lawyers remain convinced they can spot a sympathetic juror. Even here in Canada where lawyers are not allowed to exclude jurors without cause and they are not allowed to ask jurors probing quesions, lawyers believe they can influence the outcome of the trial by seeking to eliminate jurors based on gender, social-economic status, and appearance (Tait, Hawrish, & Clark, 1974).

In the U.S. a whole industry has developed that seeks to use their less restricitve jury-selection procedures to affect the outcome of a trial. The utility of these jury-selection procedures is largely unknown, but there is some evidence that certain questions can predict jurors' leanings in some cases. For example, if the judge allows an attorney to check prospective juror's attitudes toward drugs, the attorney can often guess their verdicts in a drug-trafficking case (Moran & others, 1990). Likewise, people who acknowledge they "don't put much faith in the testimony of psychiatrists" are less likely to accept an insanity defense (Cutler & others, 1992).

In addition, it's when the evidnece is ambiguous that jurors' personalities and general attitudes have an effect. And only a small number of personality characteristics and general attitudes have been shown to affect verdicts. One such attitude is people's belief in the use of the death penalty. In criminal cases, people who do not oppose the death penalty are more prone to favor the prosecution, to feel that courts coddle criminals, and to oppose protecting the rights of defendants (Bersoff, 1987). Simply put, those who favor the death penalty are more concerned with crime control and less concerned with due process of law. One reason that people who support the death penalty may be more prone to convict is that they also tend to be more authoritarian—more rigid, punitive, closed to mitigating circumstances, and contemptuous of those of lower status (Gerbasi & others, 1977; Luginbuhl & Middendorf, 1988; Moran & Comfort, 1982, 1986; Werner & others, 1982).

This is not to say that all people who support the death penalty do so because they are closed-minded, rigid thinkers. For example, Neil Vidmar (1974) found that some University of Western Ontario students support capital punishment because they believe that it is the only just punishment for someone who has killed another person. Despite this finding he confirmed that supporters of the death penalty tend to be authoritarian, and he also found that some people support the death penalty because they believe it deters crime. But does the death penalty benefit society? Does it have a positive or negative effect on jury deliberation? Does is really deter murder?

Johnathan Freedman (1990) took advantage of a unique opportunity to examine the effect of capital punishment on jury deliberation. He was allowed to survey 151 jurors who served on 32 first-degree murder trials in the Toronto area. He asked them if they would have been more or less likely to vote for a guilty verdict if the case had been a death penalty case. Fifty-five jurors indicated they would have been less likely to vote for a guilty verdict and only 6 indicated they would have been more likely to vote for a guilty verdict. Freedman concluded that the death penalty may make it harder to obtain a guilty verdict in a murder case.

The social science answer to the question of whether capital punishment is a deterrent is clear, note social psychologists Mark Costanzo (1997) and Craig Haney and Deana Logan (1994). Capital punishment is not a deterrent. Consider the following evidence. In the U.S., states with the death penalty do not have lower homicide rates. Homicide rates have not dropped when states have initiated the death penalty. And they have not risen when states have abandoned it. When committing a crime of passion, people don't pause to calculate the consequences (which include life in prison without parole as another potent deterrent). Nevertheless, people in support of the death penalty, including the U.S. Supreme Court, have determined that "the death penalty undoubtedly is a significant deterrent."

Humanitarian considerations aside, say the appalled social scientists, what is the rationale for clinging to cherished assumptions and intuitions in the face of contradictory evidence? Why not put our cultural ideas to the test? If they find support, so much the better for them. If they crash against a wall of contradictory evidence, so much the worse for them. Such are the ideals of critical thinking that fuel both psychological science and civil democracy.

Summing up

What matters is what happens not only in the courtroom but also within and among the jurors themselves.

In forming their judgments, individual jurors (1) construct a story that explains the evidence, (2) consider the judge's instructions, and (3) compare their understandings with the possible verdicts. In a close case, the jurors' own characteristics can influence their verdicts. Jurors who favor capital punishment or who are highly authoritarian appear more likely to convict certain types of defendants. Nevertheless, what matters most is not the jurors' personalities and general attitudes but rather the situation they must react to.

The jury as a group

What influences how individual jurors' prejudgments coalesce into a group decision?

Imagine a jury that, having finished a trial, has entered the jury room to begin its deliberations. Researchers Harry Kalven and Hans Zeisel (1966) reported that chances are about 2 in 3 that the jurors will initially *not* agree on a verdict.

Yet, after discussion, 95 percent emerge with a consensus. Obviously, group influence has occurred.

Thousands of times a year small groups sampled from the people called for jury duty convene to seek a group decision (Kagehiro, 1990). Are they subject to the social influences that mold other decision groups—to patterns of majority and minority influence, to group polarization, to groupthink? Let's start with a simple question: If we knew the jurors' initial leanings, could we predict their verdict?

The law prohibits observation of actual juries. So researchers simulate the jury process by presenting a case to mock juries and having them deliberate as a real jury would. In a series of such studies James Davis, Robert Holt, Norbert Kerr, and Garold Stasser tested various mathematical schemes for predicting group decisions, including decisions by mock juries (Davis & others, 1975, 1977, 1989; Kerr & others, 1976). Will some mathematical combination of initial decisions predict the final group decision? Davis and his colleagues found that the scheme that predicts best varies according to the nature of the case. But in several experiments, a "two-thirds-majority" scheme fared best: The group verdict was usually the alternative favored by at least two-thirds of the jurors at the outset. Without such a majority, a hung jury was likely.

Likewise, in Kalven and Zeisel's survey of juries, 9 in 10 reached the verdict favored by the majority on the first ballot. Although you or I might fantasize about someday being the courageous lone juror who sways the majority, the fact is it seldom happens.

Minority influence

Seldom, yet sometimes, what was initially a minority prevails. A typical 12-person jury is like a typical small university class: The three quietest people rarely talk and the three most vocal people contribute more than half the talking (Hastie & others, 1983). If jurors who favored a particular verdict are vocal and persist in their views, they are more likely to eventually prevail. From the research on minority influence we know that jurors in the minority will be most persuasive when they are consistent, persistent, and self-confident, especially if they can begin to trigger some defections from the majority.

The personal characteristics of the jurors also matter. For example, high-status male jurors tend to be most influential (Gerber & others, 1977).

Group polarization

Jury deliberation shifts people's opinions in other intriguing ways as well. In experiments, deliberation often magnifies initial sentiments. For example, Robert Bray and Audrey Noble (1978) had University of Kentucky students listen to a 30-minute tape of a murder trial. Then, assuming the defendant was found guilty, they recommended a prison sentence. Groups of high authoritarians initially recommended strong punishments (56 years) and after deliberation were even more punitive (68 years). The low-authoritarian groups were initially more lenient (38 years) and after deliberation became more so (29 years).

Confirmation that group polarization can occur in juries comes from an ambitious study in which Reid Hastie, Steven Penrod, and Nancy Pennington (1983) put together 69 twelve-person juries from Massachusetts citizens on jury duty. Each jury was shown a reenactment of an actual murder case, with roles played by an experienced judge and actual attorneys. Then they were given unlimited time to deliberate the case in a jury room. As Figure B–6 shows, the evidence was incriminating: Four out of five jurors voted guilty before deliberation, but felt unsure enough that a weak verdict of manslaughter was their most popular preference. After deliberation, nearly all agreed the accused was guilty, and most now preferred a stronger verdict—second-degree murder. Through deliberation, their initial leanings had grown stronger.

Leniency

In many experiments, one other curious effect of deliberation has surfaced: Especially when the evidence is not highly incriminating, as it was in the experiment just described, deliberating jurors often become more lenient (MacCoun & Kerr, 1988). This qualifies the "two-thirds-majority-rules" finding, for if even a bare majority initially favors *acquittal*, it usually will prevail (Stasser & others, 1981). Moreover, a minority that favors acquittal stands a better chance of prevailing than one that favors conviction (Tindale & others, 1990).

Once again, a survey of actual juries confirms the laboratory results. Kalven and Zeisel (1966) report that in those cases where the majority does not prevail, it usually shifts to acquittal. When a judge disagrees with the jury's decision, it is usually because the jury acquits someone the judge would have convicted.

Might "informational influence" (stemming from others' persuasive arguments) account for the increased leniency? The "innocent-unless-proved-guilty" and "proof-beyond-a-reasonable-doubt" rules put the burden of proof on those who favor conviction. Perhaps this makes evidence of the defendant's innocence more persuasive. Or perhaps "normative influence" creates the leniency effect, as jurors who view themselves as fair-minded confront other jurors who are even more concerned with protecting a possibly innocent defendant.

> "It is better that ten guilty persons escape than one innocent suffer."
>
> William Blackstone, 1769

Are 12 heads better than 1?

In Chapter 8 we saw that on thought problems where there is an objective right answer, group judgments surpass those by most individuals. Does the same hold true in juries? When deliberating, jurors exert normative pressure by trying to shift others' judgments by the sheer weight of their own. But they also share information, thus enlarging one another's knowledge of the case. So does informational influence produce superior collective judgment?

The evidence, though meager, is encouraging. Groups recall information from a trial better than do their individual members (Vollrath & others, 1989). Moreover, some of the biases that contaminate individual judgments have much less effect after the jurors deliberate (Kaplan & Schersching, 1980). Deliberation not only cancels out certain biases but also draws jurors' attention away from their own prejudgments and to the evidence. Moreover, it restrains jurors' use of inadmissable evidence (Kerwin & Shaffer, 1994). Twelve heads are, it seems, better than one.

Are 6 heads as good as 12?

In keeping with their British heritage, juries in Canada, Australia, and the United States have traditionally been composed of 12 people whose task is to reach con-

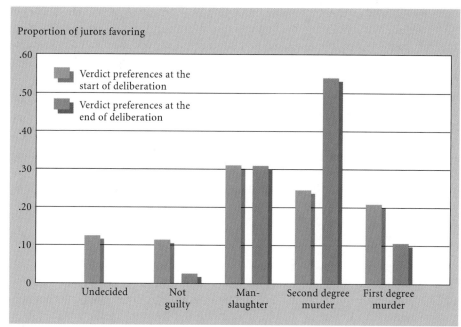

figure B–6

Group polarization in juries.

In highly realistic simulations of a murder trial, 828 Massachusetts jurors stated their initial verdict preferences, then deliberated the case for periods ranging from three hours to five days. Deliberation strengthened initial tendencies, which favored the prosecution.

(From Hastie & others, 1983.)

sensus—a unanimous verdict. However, in several cases appealed during the early 1970s, the U.S. Supreme Court declared that in civil cases and state criminal cases, courts could use 6-person juries. Moreover, they affirmed a state's right to allow less than unanimous verdicts, even upholding one conviction based on a 9 to 3 vote (Tanke & Tanke, 1979). There is no reason to suppose, they argued; that smaller juries, or juries not required to reach consensus, will deliberate or decide differently from the traditional jury.

These assumptions triggered an avalanche of criticism from both legal scholars and social psychologists (Saks, 1974). Some criticisms were matters of simple statistics. For example, if 10 percent of a community's total jury pool is Black, then 72 percent of 12–member juries but only 47 percent of 6–member juries may be expected to have at least one Black person. So smaller juries are less likely to reflect a community's diversity. And if, in a given case, one-sixth of the jurors initially favor acquittal, that would be a single individual in a 6-member jury and 2 people in a 12-member jury. But, psychologically, are the two situations identical? You may recall from our discussion of conformity, resisting group pressure is far more difficult for a minority of one than for a minority of two. Psychologically speaking, a jury split 10 to 2 is not equivalent to a jury split 5 to 1. Not surprisingly, then, 12-person juries are twice as likely as 6-person juries to have hung verdicts (Ellsworth & Mauro, 1998).

Other criticisms were based on experiments by James Davis and others (1975), Charlan Nemeth (1977), and Michael Saks (1977). In these mock jury experiments, the overall distribution of verdicts from small or nonunanimous juries did not differ much from the verdicts pronounced by unanimous 12-member juries (although verdicts from the smaller juries were slightly more unpredictable). There are, however, greater effects on deliberation. A smaller jury has the advantage of greater and more evenly balanced participation per juror but the disadvantage of eliciting less total deliberation. Moreover, once they realize that the necessary majority has been achieved, juries not required to reach consensus seem to discuss minority views rather superficially (Davis & others, 1975; Foss, 1981; Hastie & others, 1983; Kerr & others, 1976).

From lab to life: Simulated and real juries

Perhaps while reading this chapter, you have wondered what some critics (Tapp, 1980; Vidmar, 1979) have wondered: Isn't there an enormous gulf between college students discussing a hypothetical case and real jurors deliberating a real person's fate? Indeed there is. It is one thing to ponder a pretend decision given minimal information and quite another to agonize over the complexities and profound consequences of an actual case. So Reid Hastie, Martin Kaplan, James Davis, Eugene Borgida, and others have asked their participants, who sometimes are drawn from actual juror pools, to view enactments of actual trials. The enactments are so realistic that sometimes participants forget the trial they are watching on television is staged (Thompson & others, 1981).

Researchers also defend the laboratory simulations, by noting that the laboratory offers a practical, inexpensive method for studying important issues under controlled conditions (Bray & Kerr, 1982; Dillehay & Nietzel, 1980). What is more, as researchers have begun testing them in more realistic situations, findings from the laboratory studies have often held up quite well. No one contends that the simplified world of the jury experiment mirrors the complex world of the real courtroom. Rather, the experiments help us formulate theories with which we interpret the complex world.

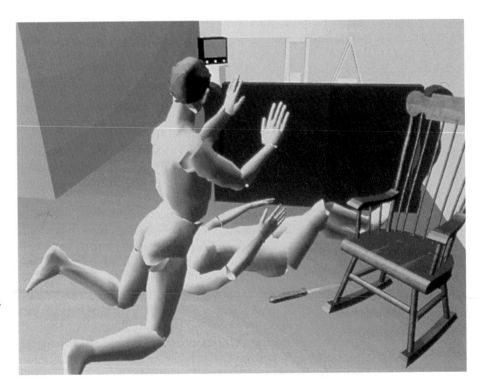

Lawyers are using new technology to present crime stories in ways jurors can easily grasp, as in this computer simulation of a homicide generated on the basis of forensic evidence.

Come to think of it, are these jury simulations any different from social psychology's other experiments, all of which create simplified versions of complex realities? By varying just one or two factors at a time in this simulated reality, the experimenter pinpoints how changes in one or two aspects can affect us. And that is the essence of social psychology's experimental method.

Summing up

Juries are groups, and are swayed by the same influences that bear upon other types of groups—patterns of majority and minority influence, group polarization, information exchange. Researchers have also shown that permitting smaller juries and juries that do not make unanimous decisions can lead to increased group pressure and decreased discussion of the case.

Simulated juries are not real juries, so we must be cautious in generalizing research findings to actual courtrooms. Yet, like all experiments in social psychology, laboratory jury experiments help us formulate theories and principles that we can use to interpret the more complex world of everyday life.

Personal postscript: A final word

If you have read this entire book, your introduction to social psychology is complete. In the preface I offered my hope that this book "would be at once solidly scientific and warmly human, factually rigorous and intellectually provocative." You, not I, are the judge of whether that goal has been achieved. But I can tell you that giving away the discipline has been a joy for me as your author. If your receiving my gift has brought you any measure of pleasure, stimulation, and enrichment, then my joy is compounded.

A knowledge of social psychology, I do believe, has the power to restrain intuition with critical thinking, illusion with understanding, and judgmentalism with compassion. In these 15 chapters and modules, we have assembled social psychology's insights into belief and persuasion, love and hate, conformity and independence. We have glimpsed incomplete answers to intriguing questions: How do our attitudes feed and get fed by our actions? What leads people sometimes to hurt and sometimes to help one another? What kindles social conflict, and how can we transform closed fists into helping hands? Answering such questions expands our minds. And, "once expanded to the dimensions of a larger idea," noted Oliver Wendell Holmes, the mind "never returns to its original size." Such has been my experience, and perhaps yours as you, through this and other courses, become an educated person.

Best Wishes,

Dave Myers

As Canadians, we live in a distinct and multi-faceted culture. I hope that this Canadian edition of *Social Psychology* has challenged you, engaged you, and provided you with a better understanding of issues confronting our society. As you have seen the discipline of social psychology is scientifically rigorous and seeks to develop sound theories, but as Kurt Lewin (1936), one of the founders of social psychology, has said, "There is nothing quite so practical as a good theory." I have tried throughout the book not only to help you understand the theories of social psychology, but also their practical applications. I hope that you will take this knowledge and apply it as you live, work, and relate to others.

Best wishes,

Steven J. Spencer

glossary

A

acceptance conformity that involves both acting and believing in accord with social pressure.

adaptation-level phenomenon the tendency to adapt to a given level of stimulation and thus to notice and react to changes from that level.

aggression physical or verbal behavior intended to hurt someone. In laboratory experiments, this might mean delivering electric shocks or saying something likely to hurt another's feelings. By this social psychological definition, one can be socially assertive without being aggressive.

altruism a motive to increase another's welfare without conscious regard for one's self-interests.

arbitration resolution of a conflict by a neutral third party who studies both sides and imposes a settlement.

attitude a favorable or unfavorable evaluate reaction toward something or someone, exhibited in one's beliefs, feelings, or intended behavior.

attitude inoculation exposing people to weak attacks upon their attitudes so that when stronger attacks come, they will have refutations available.

attractiveness having qualities that appeal to an audience. An appealing communicator (often someone similar to the audience) is most persuasive on matters of subjective preference.

attribution theory the theory of how people explain others' behavior—for example, by attributing it either to internal *dispositions* (enduring traits, motives, and attitudes) or to external *situations*.

autokinetic phenomenon self (*auto*) motion (*kinetic*). The apparent movement of a stationary point of light in the dark. Perhaps you have experienced this when thinking you have spotted a moving satellite in the sky, only to realize later that it was merely an isolated star.

availability heuristic an efficient but fallible rule-of-thumb that judges the likelihood of things in terms of their availability in memory. If instances of something come readily to mind, we presume it to be commonplace.

B

bargaining seeking an agreement through direct negotiation between parties to a conflict.

base-rate fallacy the tendency to ignore or underuse base-rate information (information that describes most people) and instead to be influenced by distinctive features of the case being judged.

behavioral confirmation a type of self-fulfilling prophecy whereby people's social expectations lead them to act in ways that cause others to confirm their expectations.

behavioral medicine an interdisciplinary field that integrates and applies behavioral and medical knowledge about health and disease.

belief perserverance persistence of one's initial conceptions, as when the basis for one's belief is discredited but an explanation of why the belief might be true survives.

bogus pipeline a procedure that fools people into disclosing their attitudes. Participants are first convinced that a machine can use their psychological responses to measure their private attitudes. Then they are asked to predict the machine's reading, thus revealing their attitudes.

bystander effect the finding that a person is less likely to provide help when there are other bystanders.

C

catharsis emotional release. The catharsis view of aggression is that aggressive drive is reduced when one "releases" aggressive energy, either by acting aggressively or by fantasizing aggression.

central route persuasion persuasion that occurs when interested people focus on the arguments and respond with favorable thoughts.

channel of communication the way the message is delivered—whether face to face, in writing, on film, or in some other way.

clinical psychology the study, assessment, and treatment of people with psychological difficulties.

coactors a group of people working simultaneously and individually on a noncompetitive task.

cognitive dissonance tension that arises when one is simultaneously aware of two inconsistent cognitions. For example, dissonance may occur when we realize that we have, with little justification, acted contrary to our attitudes or made a decision favoring one alternative despite reasons favoring another.

cohesiveness a "we feeling"—the extent to which members of a group are bound together, such as by attraction for one another.

collectivism the concept of giving priority to the goals of one's groups (often one's extended family or work group) and defining one's identity accordingly.

companionate love the affection we feel for those with whom our lives are deeply intertwined.

complementarity the popularly supposed tendency, in a relationship between two people, for each to complete what is missing in the other. The questionable complementarity hypothesis proposes that people attract those whose needs are different, in ways that complement their own.

compliance conformity that involves publicly acting in accord with social pressure while privately disagreeing.

confederate an accomplice of the experimenter.

confirmation bias a tendency to search for information that confirms one's preconceptions.

conflict a perceived incompatibility of actions or goals.

conformity a change in behavior or belief as a result of real or imagined group pressure.

correlational research the study of the naturally occurring relationships among variables.

counterfactual thinking imagining alternative scenarios and outcomes that might have happened, but didn't.

credibility believability. A credible communicator is perceived as both expert and trustworthy.

crowding a subjective feeling of not enough space per person.

cult (also called New Religious movement) a group typical characterized by (1) the distinctive ritual of its devotion to a god or a person, (2) isolation from the surrounding "evil" culture, and (3) a charismatic leader. (A *sect*, by contrast, is a spinoff from a major religion.

culture the enduring behaviors, ideas, attitudes, and traditions shared by a large group of people and transmitted from one generation to the next.

D

deindividuation loss of self-awareness and evaluation apprehension; occurs in group situations that foster anonymity and draw attention away from the individual.

demand characteristics cues in an experiment that tell the participant what behavior is expected.

dependent variable the variable being measured, so-called because it may *depend* on manipulations of the independent variable.

depressive realism the tendency of mildly depressed people to make accurate rather than self-serving judgments, attributions, and predictions.

disclosure reciprocity the tendency for one person's intimacy of self-disclosure to match that of a conversational partner.

discrimination unjustifiable negative behavior toward a group or its members.

displacement the redirection of aggression to a target other than the source of the frustration. Generally, the new target is a safer or more socially acceptable target.

door-in-the-face technique a strategy for gaining a concession. After someone first turns down a large request (the door-in-the-face), the same requester counteroffers with a more reasonable request.

E

egoism a motive (supposedly underlying all behavior) to increase one's own welfare. The opposite of *altruism*, which aims to increase another's welfare.

empathy   the vicarious experience of another's feeling; putting oneself in another's shoes.

equal-status contact   contact made on an equal basis. Just as a relationship between people of unequal status breeds attitudes consistent with their relationship, so do relationships between those of equal status. Thus, to reduce prejudice, interracial contact should be between persons equal in status.

equity   a condition in which the outcomes people receive from a relationship are proportional to what they contribute to it. Note: Equitable outcomes needn't always be equal outcomes.

ethnocentrism   a belief in the superiority of one's own ethnic and cultural group, and a corresponding disdain for all other groups.

evaluation apprehension   concern for how others are evaluating us.

evolutionary psychology   the study of the evolution of behavior using principles of natural selection.

experimental realism   degree to which an experiment absorbs and involves its participants.

experimental research   studies that seek clues to cause-effect relationships by manipulating one or more factors (independent variables) while controlling others (holding them constant).

explanatory style   one's habitual way of explaining life events. A negative pessimistic, depressive explanatory style attributes failures to stable, global, and internal causes.

F

false consensus effect   the tendency to overestimate the commonality of one's opinions and one's undesirable or unsuccessful behaviors.

false uniqueness effect   the tendency to underestimate the commonality of one's abilities and one's desirable or successful behaviors.

field research   research done in natural, real-life settings outside the laboratory.

foot-in-the-door phenomenon   the tendency for people who have first agreed to a small request to comply later with a larger request.

frustration   the blocking of goal-directed behavior.

fundamental attribution error   the tendency for observers to underestimate situational influences and overestimate dispositional influences upon others' behavior. (Also called *correspondence bias,* because we so often see behavior as corresponding to a disposition.)

G

gender   in psychology, the characteristics, whether biologically or socially influenced, by which people derive male and female. Because "sex" is a biological category, social psychologists sometimes refer to biologically based gender differences as "sex differences."

gender role   a set of behavior expectations (norms) for males or females.

GRIT   acronym for "graduated and reciprocated initiatives in tension reduction"—a strategy designed to deescalate international tensions.

group   two or more people who, for longer than a few moments, interact with and influence one another and perceive one another as "us."

group polarization   group-produced enhancement of members' preexisting tendencies; a strengthening of the members' *average* tendency, not a split within the group.

group-serving bias   explaining away outgroup members' positive behaviors; also attributing negative behaviors to their dispositions (while excusing such behavior by one's own group).

H

health psychology   a subfield of psychology that provides psychology's contribution to behavioral medicine.

hindsight bias   the tendency to exaggerate, *after* learning an outcome, one's ability to have foreseen how something turned out. Also known as the *I-knew-it-all-along phenomenon.*

hostile aggression   aggression driven by anger and performed as an end in itself.

hypothesis   a testable proposition that describes a relationship that may exist between events.

illusion of control   perception of uncontrollable events as subject to one's control or as more controllable than they are.

illusory correlation   (1) Perception of a relationship where none exists, or perception of a stronger relationship than actually exists. (2) A false impression that two variables correlate.

independent variable   the experimental factor that a researcher manipulates.

individualism   the concept of giving priority to one's goals over group goals and defining one's identity in terms of personal attributes rather than group identifications.

informational influence   conformity that results from accepting evidence about reality provided by other people.

informed consent   an ethical principle requiring that research participants be told enough to enable them to choose whether they wish to participate.

ingratiation   the use of strategies such a flattery, by which people seek to gain another's favor.

ingroup   "us"—a group of people who share a sense of belonging, a feeling of common identity.

ingroup bias   the tendency to favor one's own group.

instinctive behavior   an innate, unlearned behavior pattern exhibited by all members of a species.

instrumental aggression   aggression that is a means to some other end.

insufficient justification effect   reduction of dissonance by internally justifying one's behavior when external justification is "insufficient."

integrative agreements   win-win agreements that reconcile both parties' interests to their mutual benefit.

interaction   the effect of one factor (such as biology) depends on another factor (such as environment).

J

just-world phenomenon   the tendency of people to believe the world is just and that people therefore get what they deserve and deserve what they get.

K

kin selection   the idea that evolution has selected altruism toward one's close relatives to enhance the survival of mutually shared genes.

L

leadership   the process by which certain group members motivate and guide the group.

learned helplessness   the hopelessness and resignation learned when a human or animal perceives no control over repeated bad events.

locus of control   the extent to which people perceive outcomes as internally controllable by their own efforts and actions or as externally controlled by chance or outside forces.

low-ball technique   a tactic for getting people to agree to something. People who agree to an initial request will often still comply when the requester ups the ante. People who receive only the costly request are less likely to comply with it.

M

matching phenomenon   the tendency for men and women to choose as partners those who are a "good match" in attractiveness and other traits.

mediation   an attempt by a neutral third party to resolve a conflict by facilitating communication and offering suggestions.

mere-exposure effect   the tendency for novel stimuli to be liked more or rated more positively after the rater has been repeatedly exposed to them.

mirror-image perceptions   reciprocal views of one another often held by parties in conflict; for example, each may view itself as moral and peace-loving and the other as evil and aggressive.

misinformation effect   (1) incorporating "misinformation" into one's memory of the event, after witnessing an event and receiving misleading information about it. (2) Witnessing an event, receiving misleading information about it, and then incorporating the "misinformation" into one's memory of the event.

moral exclusion   the perception of certain individuals or groups as outside the boundary within which one applies moral values and rules of fairness. Moral *inclusion* is regarding others as within one's circle of moral concern.

mundane realism   degree to which an experiment is superficially similar to everyday situations.

N

natural selection   the evolutionary process by which nature selects traits that best enable organisms to survive and reproduce in particular environmental niches.

naturalistic fallacy   the error of defining what is good in terms of what is observable. For example: What's typical is normal; what's normal is good.

need to belong   a motivation to bond with others in relationships that provide ongoing, positive interactions.

non-zero sum games   games in which outcomes need not sum to zero. With cooperation, both can win; with competition, both can lose. (Also called *mixed-motive situations*.)

normative influence   conformity based on a person's desire to fulfill others' expectations often to gain acceptance.

norms   rules for accepted and expected behavior. Norms *prescribe* "proper" behavior. (In a different sense of the word, norms also *describe* what most others do—what is *normal*.)

O

outgroup   "them"—a group that people perceive as distinctively different from or apart from their ingroup.

outgroup homogeneity effect   perception of outgroup members as more similar to one another than are ingroup members. Thus "they are alike; we are diverse."

overconfidence phenomenon   the tendency to be more confident than correct—to overestimate the accuracy of one's beliefs.

overjustification effect   the result of bribing people to do what they already like doing; they may then see their action as externally controlled rather than intrinsically appealing.

P

passionate love   a state of intense longing for union with another. Passionate lovers are absorbed in one another, feel ecstatic at attaining their partner's love, and are disconsolate on losing it.

peripheral route persuasion   persuasion that occurs when people are influenced by incidental cues, such as a speaker's attractiveness.

personal space   the buffer zone we like to maintain around our bodies. Its size depends on our familiarity with whoever is near us.

physical-attractiveness stereotype   the presumption that physically attractive people possess other socially desirable traits as well: What is beautiful is good.

pluralistic ignorance   a false impression of how other people are thinking, feeling, or responding.

possible selves   images of what we dream of or dread becoming in the future.

prejudice   a negative prejudgment of a group and its individual members.

primacy effect   other things being equal, information presented first usually has the most influence.

priming   activating particular associations in memory.

prosocial behavior   positive, constructive, helpful social behavior; the opposite of antisocial behavior.

proximity   geographical nearness. Proximity (more precisely, "functional distance") powerfully predicts liking.

R

racism   (1) an individual's prejudicial attitudes and discriminatory behavior toward people of a given race, or (2) institutional practices (even if not motivated by prejudice) that subordinate people of a given race.

random assignment   the process of assigning participants to the conditions of an experiment such that all persons have the same chance of being in a given condition. (Note the distinction between random *assignment* in experiments and random *sampling* in surveys. Random assignment helps us infer cause and effect. Random sampling helps us generalize to a population.)

random sample   survey procedure in which every person in the population being studied has an equal chance of inclusion.

reactance   (1) a motive to protect or restore one's sense of freedom. Reactance arises when someone threatens our freedom of action. (2) The desire to assert one's sense of freedom.

recency effect information presented last sometimes has the most influence. Recency effects are less common than primacy effects.

reciprocity norm an expectation that people will help, not hurt, those who have helped them.

regression toward the average the statistical tendency for extreme scores or extreme behavior to return toward one's average.

relative deprivation the perception that one is less well off then others to whom one compares oneself.

representativeness heuristic the strategy of judging the likelihood of things by how well they represent, or match , particular prototypes; may lead one to ignore other relevant information.

reward theory of attraction the theory that we like those whose behavior is rewarding to us or whom we associate with rewarding events.

role a set of norms that define how people in a given social position ought to behave.

S

self-awareness a self-conscious state in which attention focuses on oneself. It makes people more sensitive to their own attitudes and dispositions.

self-concept a person's answers to the question "Who am I?"

self-disclosure revealing intimate aspects of oneself to others.

self-efficacy a sense that one is competent and effective. Distinguished from self-esteem, one's sense of self-worth. A bombardier might feel high self-efficacy and low self-esteem.

self-esteem a person's overall self-evaluation or sense of self worth.

self-handicapping protecting one's self-image with behaviors that create a handy excuse for later failure.

self-monitoring being attuned to the way one presents oneself in social situations and adjusting one's performance to create the desired impression.

self-perception theory the theory that when unsure of our attitudes, we infer them much as would someone observing us—by looking at our behavior and the circumstances under which it occurs.

self-presentation the act of expressing oneself and behaving in ways designed to create a favorable impression or an impression that corresponds to one's ideals.

self-reference effect the tendency to process efficiently and remember well information related to oneself.

self-schema beliefs about the self that organize and guide the processing of self-relevant information.

self-serving bias the tendency to perceive oneself favorably.

sexism (1) an individual's prejudicial attitudes and discriminatory behavior toward people of a given sex, or (2) institutional practices (even if not motivated by prejudice) that subordinate people of a given sex.

sleeper effect a delayed impact of a message; occurs when we remember the message but forget a reason for discounting it.

social comparison evaluating one's abilities and opinions by comparing oneself to others.

social-exchange theory the theory that human interactions are transactions that aim to maximize one's rewards and minimize one's costs.

social facilitation (1) Original meaning—the tendency of people to perform simple or well-learned tasks better when others are present. (2) Current meaning—the strengthening of dominant (prevalent, likely) responses owing to the presence of others.

social identity the "we" aspect of our self-concept. The part of our answer to "Who am I?" that comes from our group memberships. Examples: "I am Australian." "I am Catholic."

social learning theory the theory that we learn social behavior by observing and imitating and by being rewarded and punished.

social loafing the tendency for people to exert less effort when they pool their efforts toward a common goal than when they are individually accountable.

social psychology the scientific study of how people think about, influence, and relate to one another.

social representations socially shared beliefs. Widely held ideas and values, including our assumptions and cultural ideologies. Our social representations help us make sense of our world.

social-responsibility norm an expectation that people will help those dependent upon them.

stereotype a belief about the personal attributes of a group of people. Stereotypes can be overgeneralized, inaccurate, and resistant to new information.

stereotype threat a concern, that one will be evaluated based on a negative stereotype about one's group.

subtyping accommodating individuals who deviate from one's stereotype by splitting off a subgroup stereotype (such as "middle class Blacks" or "feminist women"). Subtyping protects stereotypes.

superordinate goal a shared goal that necessitates cooperative effort; a goal that overrides people's differences from one another.

T

theory an integrated set of principles that explain and predict observed events.

two-factor theory of emotion arousal $\times$ label = emotion.

two-step flow of communication the process by which media influence often occurs through opinion leaders, who in turn influence others.

references

Abbey, A. (1987). Misperceptions of friendly behavior as sexual interest: A survey of naturally occurring incidents. *Psychology of Women Quarterly,* **11,** 173–194. (p. 795)

Abbey, A. (1991). Misperception as an antecedent of acquaintance rape: A consequence of ambiguity in communication between women and men. In A. Parrot (Ed.), *Acquaintance rape.* New York: John Wiley. (p. 79)

Abbey, A., & Andrews, F. M. (1985). Modeling the psychological determinants of life quality. *Social Indicators Research,* **16,** 1–34. (p. 592)

Abbey, A., Ross, L. T., & McDuffie, D. (1993). Alcohol's role in sexual assault. In R. R. Watson (Ed.), *Drug and alcohol abuse reviews, vol 5: Addictive behaviors in women.* Totowa, NJ: Humana Press. (p. 387)

Abbey, A., Ross, L. T., McDuffie, D., & McAuslan, P. (1996). Alcohol and dating risk factors for sexual assault among college women. *Psychology of Women Quarterly,* **20,** 147–169. (p. 387)

ABC News (1995, April 9). U.K. violent crime rate report. (p. 383)

Abelson, R. (1972). Are attitudes necessary? In B. T. King & E. McGinnies (Eds.), *Attitudes, conflict and social change.* New York: Academic Press. (p. 131)

Abelson, R. P., Kinder, D. R., Peters, M. D., & Fiske, S. T. (1982). Affective and semantic components in political person perception. *Journal of Personality and Social Psychology,* **42,** 619–630. (p. 261)

Abrams, D. (1991). AIDS: What young people believe and what they do. Paper presented at the British Association for the Advancement of Science conference. (p. 59)

Abrams, D., Wetherell, M., Cochrane, S., Hogg, M. A., & Turner, J. C. (1990). Knowing what to think by knowing who you are: Self-categorization and the nature of norm formation, conformity and group polarization. *British Journal of Social Psychology,* **29,** 97–119. (p. 314)

Abramson, L. Y. (Ed.) (1988). *Social cognition and clinical psychology: A synthesis.* New York: Guilford. (p. 587)

Abramson, L. Y., Metalsky, G. I., & Alloy, L. B. (1989). Hopelessness depression: A theory-based subtype. *Psychological Review,* **96,** 358–372. (p. 571)

Acitelli, L. K., & Antonucci, T. C. (1994). Gender differences in the link between marital support and satisfaction in older couples. *Journal of Personality and Social Psychology,* **67,** 688–698. (p. 185)

Ackermann, R., & DeRubeis, R. J. (1991). Is depressive realism real? *Clinical Psychology Review,* **11,** 565–584. (p. 570)

Adair, J. G., Dushenko, T. W., & Lindsay, R. C. L. (1985). Ethical regulations and their impact on research practice. *American Psychologist,* **40,** 59–72. (p. 27)

Adams, D. (Ed.) (1991). *The Seville statement on violence: Preparing the ground for the constructing of peace.* UNESCO. (p. 388)

Adams, J. M., & Jones, W. H. (1997). The conceptualization of marital commitment: An integrative analysis. *Journal of Personality and Social Psychology,* **72,** 1177–1196. (p. 466)

Aderman, D., & Berkowitz, L. (1970). Observational set, empathy, and helping. *Journal of Personality and Social Psychology,* **14,** 141–148. (p. 496)

Aderman, D., & Berkowitz, L. (1983). Self-concern and the unwillingness to be helpful. *Social Psychology Quarterly,* **46,** 293–301. (p. 497)

Adlaf, E. M., Smart, R. G., & Walsh, G. W. (1994). *The Ontario Student Drug Use Survey.* Toronto: Addiction Research Foundation of Ontario. (p. 252)

Adler, N. E., Boyce, T., Chesney, M. A., Cohen, S., Folkman, S., Kahn, R. L., & Syme, S. L. (1994). Socioeconomic status and health: The challenge of the gradient. *American Psychologist,* **49,** 15–24. (p. 22)

Adler, N. E., Boyce, T., Chesney, M. A., Cohen, S., Folkman, S., Kahn, R. L., & Syme, S. L. (1993). Socioeconomic inequalities in health: No easy solution. *Journal of the American Medical Association,* **269,** 3140–3145. (p. 22)

Adler, R. P., Lesser, G. S., Meringoff, L. K., Robertson, T. S., & Ward, S. (1980). *The effects of television advertising on children.* Lexington, Mass.: Lexington Books. (p 287)

Adler, S. J. (1994). *The jury.* New York: Times Books. (p. 621)

Adorno, T., Frenkel-Brunswik, E., Levinson, D. J., & Sanford, R. N. (1950). *The authoritarian personality,* New York: Harper. (p. 362)

Agnew, C. R., Currey, D. P., & Thompson, V. D. (1994). Will racism theories with significant empirical support please stand up? Paper presented at the American Psychological Association convention. (p. 356)

Agnew, G. A., & Carron, A. V. (1994). Crowd effects and the home advantage. *International Journal of Sport Psychology,* **25,** 53-62. (p. 296)

Agostinelli, G., Sherman, S. J., Presson, C. C., & Chassin, L. (1992). Self-protection and self-enhancement biases in estimates of population prevalence. *Personality and Social Psychology Bulletin,* **18,** 631–642. (p. 65)

Agres, S. J. (1987). Rational, emotional and mixed appeals in advertising: Impact on recall and persuasion. Paper presented at the American Psychological Association convention. (Available from Lowe Marschalk, Inc., 1345 Avenue of the Americas, New York, N.Y., 10105.) (p. 261)

Aiello, J. R., Thompson, D. E., & Brodzinsky, D. M. (1983). How funny is crowding anyway? Effects of room size, group size, and the introduction of humor. *Basic and Applied Social Psychology,* **4,** 193–207. (p. 296)

Ainsworth, M. D. S. (1973). The development of infant-mother attachment. In B. Caldwell & H. Ricciuti (Eds.), *Review of child development research* (Vol. 3). Chicago: University of Chicago Press. (p. 461)

Ainsworth, M. D. S. (1979). Infant-mother attachment. *American Psychologist,* **34,** 932–937. (p. 461)

Ajzen, I. (1982). On behaving in accordance with one's attitudes. In M. P. Zanna, E. T. Higgins, & C. P. Herman (Eds.). *Consistency in social behavior: The Ontario Symposium,* vol. 2. Hillside, N.J.: Erlbaum. (p. 134)

Ajzen, I., & Fishbein, M. (1977). Attitude-behavior relations: A theoretical analysis and review of empirical research. *Psychological Bulletin,* **84,** 888–918. (p. 134)

Ajzen, I., & Timko, C. (1986). Correspondence between health attitudes and behavior. *Basic and Applied Social Psychology,* **7,** 259–276. (p. 135)

Albas, D. C., & Albas, C. A. (1989). Meaning in context: The impact of eye contact and perception of threat on proximity. *Journal of Social Psychology,* **129,** 525-531. (p. 177)

Albee, G. (1979, June 19). Politics, power, prevention, and social change. Keynote address to Vermont Conference on Primary Prevention of Psychopathology. (p. 206)

Alicke, M. D., & Davis, T. L. (1989). The role of *a posteriori* victim information in judgments of blame and sanction. *Journal of Experimental Social Psychology,* **25,** 362–377. (p. 619)

Alicke, M. D., Klotz, M. L., Breitenbecher, D. L., Yurak, T. J., & Vredenburg, D. S. (1995). Personal contact, individuation and the better than average effect. *Journal of Personality and Social Psychology*, **68**, 804–825. (p. 57)

Allee, W. C., & Masure, R. M. (1936). A comparison of maze behavior in paired and isolated shell-parakeets (*Melopsittacus undulatus Shaw*) in a two-alley problem box. *Journal of Comparative Psychology*, **22**, 131–155. (p. 293)

Allen, M., D'Alessio, D., Emmers, T. M., & Gebhardt, L. (1996). The role of educational briefings in mitigating effects of experimental exposure to violent sexually explicit material: A meta-analysis. *Journal of Sex Research*, **33**, 133–141. (p. 407)

Allen, V. L., & Levine, J. M. (1969). Consensus and conformity. *Journal of Experimental Social Psychology*, **5**, 389–399. (p. 231)

Allen, V. L., & Wilder, D. A. (1980). Impact of group consensus and social support on stimulus meaning: Mediation of conformity by cognitive restructuring. *Journal of Personality and Social Psychology*, **39**, 1116–1124. (p. 237)

Allgeier, A. R., Byrne, D., Brooks, B., & Revnes, D. (1979). The waffle phenomenon: Negative evaluations of those who shift attitudinally. *Journal of Applied Social Psychology*, **9**, 170–182. (p. 236)

Allison, S. T., Beggan, J. K., McDonald, R. A., & Rettew, M. L. (1995). The belief in majority determination of group decision outcomes. *Basic and Applied Social Psychology*, **16**, 367–382. (p. 366)

Allison, S. T., Jordan, M. R., & Yeatts, C. E. (1992). A cluster-analytic approach toward identifying the structure and content of human decision making. *Human Relations*, **45**, 49–72. (p. 366)

Allison, S. T., Mackie, D. M., & Messick, D. M. (1996). Outcome biases in social perception: Implications for dispositional inference, attitude change, stereotyping, and social behavior. *Advances in Experimental Social Psychology*, **28**, 53–93. (p. 366)

Allison, S. T., Mackie, D. M., Muller, M. M., & Worth, L. T. (1993). Sequential correspondence biases and perceptions of change: The Castro studies revisited. *Personality and Social Psychology Bulletin*, **19**, 151–157. (pp. 84, 366)

Allison, S. T., McQueen, L. R., & Schaerfl, L. M. (1992). Social decision making processes and the equal partitioning of shared resources. *Journal of Experimental Social Psychology*, **28**, 23–42. (pp. 112, 366, 522)

Allison, S. T., & Messick, D. M. (1985). The group attribution error. *Journal of Experimental Social Psychology*, **21**, 563–579. (p. 366)

Allison, S. T., & Messick, D. M. (1987). From individual inputs to group outputs, and back again: Group processes and inferences about members. In C. Hendrick (Ed.), *Group processes: Review of personality and social psychology*, Vol. 8. Newbury Park, Ca.: Sage. (p. 366)

Allison, S. T., Messick, D. M., & Goethals, G. R. (1989). On being better but not smarter than others: The Muhammad Ali effect. *Social Cognition*, **7**, 275–296. (pp. 59, 366)

Allison, S. T., Worth, L. T., & King, M. W. C. (1990). Group decisions as social inference heuristics. *Journal of Personality and Social Psychology*, **58**, 801–811. (p. 366)

Alloy, L. B., & Abramson, L. Y. (1979). Judgment of contingency in depressed and nondepressed students: Sadder but wiser? *Journal of Experimental Psychology: General*, **108**, 441–485. (p. 570)

Alloy, L. B., Albright, J. S., Abramson, L. Y., & Dykman, B. M. (1990). Depressive realism and nondepressive optimistic illusions: The role of the self. In R. E. Ingram (Ed.), *Contemporary psychological approaches to depression: Theory, research and treatment*. New York: Plenum. (p. 570)

Alloy, L. B., & Clements, C. M. (1992). Illusion of control: Invulnerability to negative affect and depressive symptoms after laboratory and natural stressors. *Journal of Abnormal Psychology*, **101**, 234–245. (p. 573)

Allport, F. H. (1920). The influence of the group upon association and thought. *Journal of Experimental Psychology*, **3**, 159–182. (p. 293)

Allport, G. (1954). *The nature of prejudice*. Cambridge, Mass.: Addison-Wesley. (p. 543)

Allport, G. W. (1958). *The nature of prejudice* (abridged). Garden City, NY: Anchor Books. (pp. 349, 351, 352, 359)

Allport, G. W. (1978). *Waiting for the Lord: 33 Meditations on God and Man* (Edited by P. A. Bertocci). New York: Macmillan. (p. 60)

Allport, G. W., & Ross, J. M. (1967). Personal religious orientation and prejudice. *Journal of Personality and Social Psychology*, **5**, 432–443. (p. 350)

Altemeyer, B. (1988). *Enemies of freedom: Understanding right-wing authoritarianism*. San Francisco: Jossey-Bass. (p. 363)

Altemeyer, B. (1992). Six studies of right-wing authoritarianism among American state legislators. Unpublished manuscript, University of Manitoba. (p. 363)

Altermeyer, B., & Hunsberger, B. (1992). Authoritarianism, religious fundamentalism, quest, and prejudice. *International Journal for the Psychology of Religion*, **2**, 113–133. (p. 350)

Altman, I., & Vinsel, A. M. (1978). Personal space: An analysis of E. T. Hall's proxemics framework. In I. Altman & J. Wohlwill (Eds.), *Human behavior and the environment*. New York: Plenum Press. (p. 177)

Alwin, D. F. (1990). Historical changes in parental orientations to children. In N. Mandell (Ed.), *Sociological studies of child development*, Vol. 3. Greenwich, Ct.: JAI Press. (p. 556)

Alwin, D. F., Cohen, R. L., & Newcomb, T. M. (1991). *Political attitudes over the life span: The Bennington women after fifty years*. Madison, WI: University of Wisconsin Press. (p. 273)

Amabile, T. M., & Glazebrook, A. H. (1982). A negativity bias in interpersonal evaluation. *Journal of Experimental Social Psychology*, **18**, 1–22. (p. 361)

Amato, P. R. (1979). Juror-defendant similarity and the assessment of guilt in politically motivated crimes. *Australian Journal of Psychology*, **31**, 79–88. (p. 614)

Amato, P. R. (1986). Emotional arousal and helping behavior in a real-life emergency. *Journal of Applied Social Psychology*, **16**, 633–641. (p. 478)

Amato, P. R. (1990). Personality and social network involvement as predictors of helping behavior in everyday life. *Social Psychology Quarterly*, **53**, 31–43. (p. 501)

Ambady, N., & Rosenthal, R. (1992). Thin slices of expressive behavior as predictors of interpersonal consequences: A meta-analysis. *Psychological Bulletin*, **111**, 256–274. (p. 121)

Ambady, N., & Rosenthal, R. (1993). Half a minute: Predicting teacher evaluations from thin slices of nonverbal behavior and physical attractiveness. *Journal of Personality and Social Psychology*, **64**, 431–441. (p. 121)

American Enterprise (1992, January/February). Women, men, marriages & ministers. P. 106. (p. 468)

American Psychological Association (1981). Ethical principles of psychologists. *American Psychologist*, **36**, 633–638. (p. 30)

American Psychological Association (1992). Ethical principles of psychologists and code of conduct. Washington, D.C.: American Psychological Association, **47**, 1597–1611. (p. 30)

American Psychological Association (1993). *Violence and youth: Psychology's response. Vol I: Summary report of the American Psychological Association Commission on Violence and Youth*. Washington DC: Public Interest Directorate, American Psychological Association. (pp. 387, 415)

Anda, R., Williamson, D., Jones, D., Macera, C., Eaker, E., Glassman, A., & Marks, J. (1993). Depressed affect, hopelessness, and the risk of ischemic heart disease in a cohort of U.S. adults. *Epidemiology*, **4**, 285–294. (p. 582)

Anderson, C. A. (1982). Inoculation and counter-explanation: Debiasing techniques in the perseverance of social theories. *Social Cognition*, **1**, 126–139. (p. 98)

Anderson, C. A. (1989). Temperature and aggression: Ubiquitous effects of heat on occurrence of human violence. *Psychological Bulletin*, **106**, 74–96. (p. 402)

Anderson, C. A., & Anderson, K. B. (1996). Violent crime rate studies in philosophical context: A destructive testing approach to heat and southern culture of violence effects. *Journal of Personality and Social Psychology*, **70**, 740–756. (p. 402)

Anderson, C. A., & Anderson, K. B. (in press). Temperature and aggression: Paradox, controversy, and a (fairly) clear picture. In R. Geen & E. Donnerstein (eds.), *Human aggression: Theories, research and implications for policy*. (p. 402)

Anderson, C. A., Anderson, K. B., & Deuser, W. E. (1996). Examining an affective aggression framework: Weapon and temperature effects on aggressive thoughts, affect, and attitudes. *Personality and Social Psychology Bulletin*, **22**, 366–376. (p. 390)

Anderson, C. A., & Bushman, B. J. (1997). External validity of "trivial" experiments: The case of laboratory aggression. *Review of General Psychology*, **1**, 19–41. (p. 419)

Anderson, C. A., Bushman, B. J., & Groom, R. W. (1997). Hot years and serious and deadly assault: Empirical tests of the heat hypothesis. *Journal of Personality and Social Psychology*, **73**, 1213–1223. (p. 402)

Anderson, C. A., Deuser, W. E., & DeNeve, K. M. (1995). Hot temperatures, hostile affect, hostile cognition, and arousal: Tests of a general model of affective aggression. *Personality and Social Psychology Bulletin*, **21**, 434–448. (pp. 403, 404)

Anderson, C. A., & Harvey, R. J. (1988). Discriminating between problems in living: An examination of measures of depression, loneliness, shyness, and social anxiety. *Journal of Social and Clinical Psychology*, **6**, 482–491. (p. 578)

Anderson, C. A., Horowitz, L. M., & French, R. D. (1983). Attributional style of lonely and depressed people. *Journal of Personality and Social Psychology*, **45**, 127–136. (p. 67)

Anderson, C. A., Lepper, M. R., & Ross, L. (1980). Perseverance of social theories: The role of explanation in the persistence of discredited information. *Journal of Personality and Social Psychology*, **39**, 1037–1049. (p. 97)

Anderson, C. A., Miller, R. S., Riger, A. L., Dill, J. C., & Sedikides, C. (1994). Behavioral and characterological attributional styles as predictors of depression and loneliness: Review, refinement, and test. *Journal of Personality and Social Psychology*, **66**, 549–558. (p. 576)

Anderson, C. A., & Morrow, M. (1995). Competitive aggression without interaction: Effects of competitive versus cooperative instructions on aggressive behavior in video games. *Personality and Social Psychology Bulletin*, in press. (p. 525)

Anderson, C. A., & Sechler, E. S. (1986). Effects of explanation and counter-explanation on the development and use of social theories. *Journal of Personality and Social Psychology*, **50**, 24–34. (p. 98)

Anderson, K. B., Cooper, H., & Okamura, L. (1997). Individual differences and attitudes toward rape: A meta-analytic review. *Personality and Social Psychology Review*, **23**, 295–315. (p. 408)

Anderson, N. H. (1968). A simple model of information integration. In R. B. Abelson, E. Aronson, W. J. McGuire, T. M. Newcomb, M. J. Rosenberg, & P. H. Tannenbaum (Eds.), *Theories of cognitive consistency: A sourcebook*. Chicago: Rand McNally. (p. 83)

Anderson, N. H. (1974). Cognitive algebra: Integration theory applied to social attribution. In L. Berkowitz (Ed.), *Advances in experimental social psychology*, Vol. 7. New York: Academic Press. (p. 83)

Antill, J. K. (1983). Sex role complementarity versus similarity in married couples. *Journal of Personality and Social Psychology*, **45**, 145–155. (p. 186)

Apsler, R. (1975). Effects of embarrassment on behavior toward others. *Journal of Personality and Social Psychology*, **32**, 145–153. (p. 496)

Archer, D., & Gartner, R. (1976). Violent acts and violent times: A comparative approach to postwar homicide rates. *American Sociological Review*, **41**, 937–963. (p. 421)

Archer, D., Iritani, B., Kimes, D. B., & Barrios, M. (1983). Face-ism: Five studies of sex differences in facial prominence. *Journal of Personality and Social Psychology*, **45**, 725–735. (p. 358)

Archer, J. (1991). The influence of testosterone on human aggression. *British Journal of Psychology*, **82**, 1–28. (p. 388)

Archer, J. (1996). Sex differences in social behavior: Are the social role and evolutionary explanations compatible? *American Psychologist*, **51**, 909–917. (p. 203)

Archer, R. L., & Cook, C. E. (1986). Personalistic self-disclosure and attraction: Basis for relationship or scarce resource. *Social Psychology Quarterly*, **49**, 268–272. (p. 463)

Arendt, H. (1963). *Eichmann in Jerusalem: A report on the banality of evil*. New York: Viking Press. (p. 229)

Argyle, M., & Henderson M. (1985). *The anatomy of relationships*. London: Heinemann. (p. 178)

Argyle, M., Shimoda, K., & Little, B. (1978). Variance due to persons and situations in England and Japan. *British Journal of Social and Clinical Psychology*, **17**, 335–337. (p. 205)

Arkes, H. R. (1990). Some practical judgment/decision making research. Paper presented at the American Psychological Association convention. (p. 269)

Arkin, R. M., Appleman, A., & Burger, J. M. (1980). Social anxiety, self-presentation, and the self-serving bias in causal attribution. *Journal of Personality and Social Psychology*, **38**, 23–35. (p. 72)

Arkin, R. M., & Baumgardner, A. H. (1985). Self-handicapping. In J. H. Harvey & C. Weary (Eds.), *Attribution: Basic issues and applications*. New York: Academic Press. (p. 72)

Arkin, R. M., & Burger, J. M. (1980). Effects of unit relation tendencies on interpersonal attraction. *Social Psychology Quarterly*, **43**, 380–391. (p. 430)

Arkin, R. M., Cooper, H., & Kolditz, T. (1980). A statistical review of the literature concerning the self-serving attribution bias in interpersonal influence situations. *Journal of Personality*, **48**, 435–448. (p. 57)

Arkin, R. M., Lake, E. A., & Baumgardner, A. H. (1986). Shyness and self-presentation. In W. H. Jones, J. M. Cheek, & S. R. Briggs (Eds.), *Shyness: Perspectives on research and treatment*. New York: Plenum. (p. 71)

Arkin, R. M., & Maruyama, G. M. (1979). Attribution, affect, and college exam performance. *Journal of Educational Psychology*, **71**, 85–93. (p. 57)

Armor, D. A., & Taylor, S. E. (in press). Situated optimism: Specific outcome expectancies and self-regulation. In M. P. Zanna (ed.), *Advances in experimental social psychology*, vol. 30. San Diego: Academic Press. (p. 60)

Arms, R. L., Russell, G. W., & Sandilands, M. L. (1979). Effects on the hostility of spectators of viewing aggressive sports. *Social Psychology Quarterly*, **42**, 275–279. (p. 424)

Armstrong, B. (1981). An interview with Herbert Kelman. *APA Monitor*, January, pp. 4–5, 55. (p. 551)

Aron, A., & Aron, E. (1989). *The heart of social psychology*, 2nd ed. Lexington, MA: Lexington Books. (pp. 214, 526)

Aron, A., & Aron, E. N. (1994). Love. In A. L. Weber & J. H. Harvey (eds.), *Perspective on close relationships*. Boston: Allyn & Bacon. (p. 465)

Aron, A., Dutton, D. G., Aron, E. N., & Iverson, A. (1989). Experiences of falling in love. *Journal of Social and Personal Relationships*, **6**, 243–257. (p. 447)

Aron, A., Melinat, E., Aron, E. N., Vallone, R. D., & Bator, R. J. (1997). The experimental generation of interpersonal

closeness: A procedure and some preliminary findings. *Personality and Social
Psychology Bulletin*, **23**, 363–377. (p. 465)

Aronson, E. (1980). *The social animal.* New
York: Freeman. (pp. 537, 542)

Aronson, E. (1988). *The social animal.* New
York: Freeman. (p. 449)

Aronson E. (1992). Stateways can change
folkways. In R.M. Baird & S.E.
Rosenbaum (Eds.), *Bigotry, prejudice, and
hatred: Definitions, causes and solutions*, pp.
185-201. (p. 147)

Aronson, E. (1997). Bring the family
address to American Psychological
Society annual convention, reported in
APS Observer, July/August, pp. 17, 34, 35.
(p. 263)

Aronson, E., Blaney, N., Stephan, C.,
Sikes, J., & Snapp, M. (1978). *The jigsaw
classroom.* Beverly Hills, Calif.: Sage
Publications. (p. 541)

Aronson, E., Brewer, M., & Carlsmith,
J. M. (1985). Experimentation in social
psychology. In G. Lindzey & E. Aronson
(Eds.), *Handbook of social psychology*, vol.
1. Hillsdale, N.J.: Erlbaum. (p. 30)

Aronson, E., & Bridgeman, D. (1979).
Jigsaw groups and the desegregated
classroom: In pursuit of common goals.
Personality and Social Psychology Bulletin,
5, 438–446. (p. 541)

Aronson, E., & Gonzalez, A. (1988).
Desegregation, jigsaw, and the Mexican-
American experience. In P. A. Katz & D.
Taylor (Eds.), *Towards the elimination of
racism: Profiles in controversy.* New York:
Plenum. (p. 541)

Aronson, E., & Linder, D. (1965). Gain and
loss of esteem as determinants of
interpersonal attractiveness. *Journal of
Experimental Social Psychology*, **1**, 156–171.
(p. 448)

Aronson, E., & Mettee, D. R. (1974). Af-
fective reactions to appraisal from others.
Foundations of interpersonal attraction.
New York: Academic Press. (p. 448)

Aronson, E., & Mills, J. (1959). The effect
of severity of initiation on liking for a
group. *Journal of Abnormal and Social
Psychology*, **59**, 177–181. (p. 279)

Aronson, E., Turner, J. A., & Carlsmith,
J. M. (1963). Communicator credibility
and communicator discrepancy as
determinants of opinion change. *Journal
of Abnormal and Social Psychology*, **67**,
31–36. (p. 264)

Asch, S. E. (1946). Forming impressions of
personality. *Journal of Abnormal and Social
Psychology*, **41**, 258–290. (pp. 83, 266)

Asch, S. E. (1955, November). Opinions
and social pressure. *Scientific American*,
pp. 31–35. (pp. 214, 231)

Aschaffenburg, G. (1903/1913). *Crime and
its repression.* Boston: Little, Brown.
(p. 402)

Asendorpf, J. B. (1987). Videotape reconstruction of emotions and cognitions

related to shyness. *Journal of Personality
and Social Psychology*, **53**, 541–549.
(p. 578)

Asher, J. (1987, April). Born to be shy?
Psychology Today, pp. 56–64. (p. 386)

Ashmore, R. D. (1990). Sex, gender, and
the individual. In L. A. Pervin (Ed.),
*Handbook of personality: Theory and re-
search.* New York: Guilford Press.
(p. 184)

Associated Press (1988, July 10). Rain in
Iowa. *Grand Rapids Press*, p. A6. (p. 115)

Associated Press (1995, September 25).
Blacks are given tougher sentences,
analysis shows. *Grand Rapids Press*, p. A3.
(p. 615)

Astin, A. W. (1972). *Four critical years.* San
Francisco: Jossey-Bass. (p. 270)

Astin, A. W., Green, K. C., Korn, W. S., &
Schalit, M. (1987). *The American freshman:
National norms for Fall 1987.* Los Angeles:
Higher Education Research Institute,
UCLA. *(b)* (pp. 200, 345)

Atwell, R. H. (1986, July 28). Drugs on
campus: A perspective. *Higher Education
& National Affairs*, p. 5. (p. 244)

Augoustinos, M., & Innes, J. M. (1990).
Towards an integration of social
representations and social schema theory.
British Journal of Social Psychology, **29**,
213–231. (p. 11)

Averill, J. R. (1983). Studies on anger and
aggression: Implications for theories of
emotion. *American Psychologist*, **38**,
1145–1160. (p. 390)

Axelrod, R., & Dion, D. (1988). The further
evolution of cooperation. *Science*, **242**,
1385–1390. (p. 554)

Axom, D. (1989). Cognitive dissonance and
behavior change in psychotherapy.
Journal of Experimental Social Psychology,
25, 234–252. (p. 586)

Axom, D., & Cooper, J. (1985). Cognitive
dissonance and psychotherapy: The role
of effort justification in inducing weight
loss. *Journal of Experimental Social
Psychology*, **21**, 149–160. (p. 586)

Axsom, D., Yates, S., & Chaiken, S. (1987).
Audience response as a heuristic cue in
persuasion. *Journal of Personality and
Social Psychology*, **53**, 30–40. (p. 275)

Ayres, I. (1991). Fair driving: Gender and
race discrimination in retail car
negotiations. *Harvard Law Review*, **104**,
817–872. (p. 347)

Azrin, N. H. (1967, May). Pain and aggression. *Psychology Today*, pp. 27–33. (p. 400)

Babad, E., Bernieri, F., & Rosenthal, R.
(1991). Students as judges of teachers'
verbal and nonverbal behavior. *American
Educational Research Journal*, **28**, 211–234.
(p. 121)

Babad, E., Hills, M., & O'Driscoll, M.
(1992). Factors influencing wishful
thinking and predictions of election
outcomes. *Basic and Applied Social
Psychology*, **13**, 461–476. (p. 61)

Bachman, J. G., Johnston, L. D., O'Malley,
P. M., & Humphrey, R. N. (1988).
Explaining the recent decline in
marijuana use: Differentiating the effects
of perceived risks, disapproval, and
general lifestyle factors. *Journal of Health
and Social Behavior*, **29**, 92–112. (p. 257)

Bachman, J. G., & O'Malley, P. M. (1977).
Self-esteem in young men: A longitudinal
analysis of the impact of educational and
occupational attainment. *Journal of
Personality and Social Psychology*, **35**,
365–380. (p. 23)

Baer, R., Hinkle, S., Smith, K., & Fenton,
M. (1980). Reactance as a function of
actual versus projected autonomy. *Journal
of Personality and Social Psychology*, **38**,
416–422. (p. 243)

Bailey, J. M., Gaulin, S., Agyei, Y., &
Gladue, B. A. (1994). Effects of gender
and sexual orientation on evolutionary
relevant aspects of human mating psychology. *Journal of Personality and Social
Psychology*, **66**, 1081–1093. (p. 190)

Baize, H. R., Jr., & Schroeder, J. E. (1995).
Personality and mate selection in
personal ads: Evolutionary preferences in
a public mate selection process. *Journal of
Social Behavior and Personality*, **10**,
517–536. (p. 435)

Baker, L. A., & Emery, R. E. (1993). When
every relationship is above average:
Perceptions and expectations of divorce
at the time of marriage. *Law and Human
Behavior*, **17**, 439–450. (p. 60)

Baldwin, M.W., & Carrell, S.E., & Lopez,
D.F. (1989). Priming relationship
schemas: My advisor and the Pope are
watching me from the back of my head.
Journal of Experimental Social Psychology,
26, 435-454. (p. 106)

Baldwin, M. W., Keelan, J. P. R., Fehr, B.,
Enns, V., Koh-Rangarajoo, E. (1996).
Social-cognitive conceptualization of
attachment working models: Availability
and accessibility effects. *Journal of
Personality and Social Psychology*, **71**,
94–109. (p. 461)

Bandura, A. (1979). The social learning
perspective: Mechanisms of aggression.
In H. Toch (Ed.), *Psychology of crime and
criminal justice.* New York: Holt, Rinehart
& Winston. (pp. 397, 398, 399)

Bandura, A. (1997). *Self-efficacy: The exercise
of control.* New York: Freeman. (pp. 50,
397, 399)

Bandura, A., Ross, D., & Ross, S. A.
(1961). Transmission of aggression
through imitation of aggressive models.
Journal of Abnormal and Social Psychology,
63, 575–582. (p. 397)

Bandura, A., & Walters, R. H. (1959).
Adolescent aggression. New York: Ronald
Press. (p. 397)

Bandura, A., & Walters, R. H. (1963). *Social
learning and personality development.* New
York: Holt, Rinehart and Winston. (p. 414)

Barash, D. (1979). *The whisperings within.* New York: Harper & Row. (pp. 385, 483, 484)

Bargh, J. A. (1989). Conditional automaticity: Varieties of automatic influence in social perception and cognition. In J. S. Uleman & J. A. Bargh (Eds.), *Unintended thought: Causes and consequences for judgment, emotion, and behavior.* New York: Guilford. (p. 103)

Bargh, J. A. (1994). The four horsemen of automaticity: Awareness, intention, efficiency, and control in social cognition. In R. S. Wyer & T. K. Srull (Eds.), *Handbook of social cognition,* 2nd ed. (Vol. 1). Hillsdale, NJ: Erlbaum. (pp. 103, 104)

Bargh, J. A. (1999). The cognitive monster: The case against the controllability of automatic stereotype effects. In Chaiken, S., & Trope, Y. (Eds.) *Dual-process theories in social psychology.* (pp. 361-382). New York, NY, USA: The Guilford Press. (p. 103)

Bargh, J. A., Chen, M., & Burrows, L. (1996). Automaticity of social behavior: Direct effects of trait construct and stereotype activation on action. *Journal of Personality and Social Psychology,* **71,** 230–244. (p. 342)

Bargh, J. A., & Raymond, P. (1995). The naive misuse of power: Nonconscious sources of sexual harassment. *Journal of Social Issues,* **51,** 85–96. (p. 79)

Barnes, R. D., Ickes, W., & Kidd, R. F. (1979). Effects of the perceived intentionality and stability of another's dependency on helping behavior. *Personality and Social Psychology Bulletin,* **5,** 367–372. (p. 482)

Barnett, M. A., King, L. M., Howard, J. A., & Melton, E. M. (1980). Experiencing negative affect about self or other: Effects on helping behavior in children and adults. Paper presented at the Midwestern Psychological Association convention. (p. 497)

Barnett, P. A., & Gotlib, I. H. (1988). Psychosocial functioning and depression: Distinguishing among antecedents, concomitants, and consequences. *Psychological Bulletin,* **104,** 97–126. (p. 572)

Baron J., & Hershey, J. C. (1988). Outcome bias in decision evaluation. *Journal of Personality and Social Psychology,* **54,** 569–579. (p. 374)

Baron, L., & Straus, M. A. (1984). Sexual stratification, pornography, and rape in the United States. In N. M. Malamuth & E. Donnerstein (Eds.), *Pornography and sexual aggression.* New York: Academic Press. (p. 406)

Baron, R. A. (1977). *Human aggression.* New York: Plenum Press. (p. 423)

Baron, R. M., Mandel, D. R., Adams, C. A., & Griffen, L. M. (1976). Effects of social density in university residential environments. *Journal of Personality and Social Psychology,* **34,** 434–446. (p. 493)

Baron, R. S. (1986). Distraction-conflict theory: Progress and problems. In L. Berkowitz (Ed.), *Advances in experimental social psychology,* Orlando, Fla.: Academic Press. (p. 298)

Baron, R. S., David, J. P., Inman, M., & Brunsman, B. M. (1997). Why listeners hear less than they are told: Attentional load and the teller-listener extremity effect. *Journal of Personality and Social Psychology,* **72,** 826–838. (p. 89)

Baron, R. S., Hoppe, S. I., Kao, C. F., Brunsman, B., Linneweh, B., & Rogers, D. (1996). Social corroboration and opinion extremity. *Journal of Experimental Social Psychology,* **32,** 537–560. (p. 315)

Baron, R. S., Kerr, N. L., & Miller, N. (1992). *Group process, group decision, group action.* Pacific Grove, CA: Brooks/Cole. (p. 394)

Barongan, C., & Hall, G. C. N. (1995). The influence of misogynous rap music on sexual aggression against women. *Psychology of Women Quarterly,* **19,** 195–207. (p. 416)

Barry, D. (1995, January). Bored Stiff. *Funny Times,* p. 5. (p. 190)

Bar-Tal, D. (1982). Sequential development of helping behavior: A cognitive-learning approach. *Development Review,* **2**(2), 101–124. (p. 497)

Bartholomew, K. (1994). Assessment of individual differences in adult attachment. *Psychological Inquiry,* **5,** 23-27. (p. 461)

Bartholomew, K., & Horowitz, L. (1991). Attachment styles among young adults: A test of a four-category model. *Journal of Personality and Social Psychology,* **61,** 226–244. (p. 461)

Barzun, J. (1975). *Simple and direct.* New York: Harper & Row, pp. 173–174. (p. 167)

Bass, E., & Davis, L. (1988). *The courage to heal.* New York: Harper & Row. (p. 566)

Bassili, J. N. (1995). Response latency and the accessibility of voting intentions: What contributes to accessibility and how it affects vote choice. *Personality and Social Psychology Bulletin,* **21,** 686-695. (p. 134)

Bassili, J. N., & Roy, J. P. (1998). On the representation of strong and weak attitudes about policy in memory. *Political Psychology,* **19,** 669-681. (p. 130)

Batson, C. D. (1983). Sociobiology and the role of religion in promoting prosocial behavior: An alternative view. *Journal of Personality and Social Psychology,* **45,** 1380–1385. (p. 508)

Batson, C. D. (1991). *The altruism question: Toward a social-psychological answer.* Hillsdale, NJ: Erlbaum. (pp. 477, 480)

Batson, C. D. (1995). Prosocial motivation: Why do we help others? In A. Tesser (ed.), *Advanced social psychology.* New York: McGraw-Hill. (pp. 477, 480)

Batson, C. D., Bolen, M. H., Cross, J. A., & Neuringer-Benefiel, H. E. (1986). Where is the altruism in the altruistic personality? *Journal of Personality and Social Psychology,* **50,** 212–220. (p. 477)

Batson, C. D., Cochran, P. J., Biederman, M. F., Blosser, J. L., Ryan, M. J., & Vogt, B. (1978). Failure to help when in a hurry: Callousness or conflict? *Personality and Social Psychology Bulletin,* **4,** 97–101. (p. 494)

Batson, C. D., Coke, J. S., Jasnoski, M. L., & Hanson, M. (1978). Buying kindness: Effect of an extrinsic incentive for helping on perceived altruism. *Personality and Social Psychology Bulletin,* **4,** 86–91. (pp. 494, 510)

Batson, C. D., Duncan, B. D., Ackerman, P., Buckley, T., & Birch, K. (1981). Is empathic emotion a source of altruistic motivation? *Journal of Personality and Social Psychology,* **40,** 290–302. (p. 479)

Batson, C. D., Harris, A. C., McCaul, K. D., Davis, M., & Schmidt, T. (1979). Compassion or compliance: Alternative dispositional attributions for one's helping behavior. *Social Psychology Quarterly,* **42,** 405–409. (p. 510)

Batson, C. D., Klein, T. R., Highberger, L., & Shaw, L. L. (1997). Immorality from empathy-induced altruism: When compassion and justice conflict. *Journal of Personality and Social Psychology,* **68,** 1042–1058. (p. 480)

Batson, C. D., Sager, K., Garst, E., Kang, M., Rubchinsky, K., & Dawson, K. (1997). Is empathy-induced helping due to self-other merging? *Journal of Personality and Social Psychology,* **73,** 495–509. (p. 479)

Batson, C. D., Schoenrade, P., & Ventis, W. L. (1993). *Religion and the individual: A social-psychological perspective.* New York: Oxford University Press. (p. 350)

Batson, C. D., & Ventis, W. L. (1982). *The religious experience: A social psychological perspective.* New York: Oxford University Press. (p. 350)

Batson, C. D., & Weeks, J. L. (1996). Mood effects of unsuccessful helping: Another test of the empathy-altruism hypothesis. *Personality and Social Psychology Bulletin,* **22,** 148–157. (p. 479)

Baumann, D. J., Cialdini, R. B., & Kenrick, D. T. (1981). Altruism as hedonism: Helping and self-gratification as equivalent responses. *Journal of Personality and Social Psychology,* **40,** 1039–1046. (p. 496)

Baumann, L. J., & Leventhal, H. (1985). "I can tell when my blood pressure is up, can't I?" *Health Psychology,* **4,** 203–218. (p. 579)

Baumeister, R. F. (1982). A self-presentational view of social phenomena. *Psychological Bulletin*, **91**, 3–26. (p. 152)

Baumeister, R. F. (1985). Four selves and two motives: Outline of self-presentation theory. Paper presented to the Midwestern Psychological Association convention. (p. 152)

Baumeister, R. F. (1991). *Meanings of life.* New York: Guilford. (p. 190)

Baumeister, R. F. (1997). Esteem threat, self-regulatory breakdown, and emotional distress as factors in self-defeating behavior. *Review of General Psychology*, **1**, 145–174. (p. 65)

Baumeister, R. F., Bratslavsky, E., Muraven, M., & Tice, D. M. (1998). Ego depletion: Is the active self a limited resource? *Journal of Personality and Social Psychology*, in press. (p. 50)

Baumeister, R. F., Chesner, S. P., Senders, P. S., & Tice, D. M. (1988). Who's in charge here? Group leaders do lend help in emergencies. *Personality and Social Psychology Bulletin*, **14**, 17–22. (p. 84)

Baumeister, R. F., & Ilko, S. A. (1995). Shallow gratitude: Public and private acknowledgement of external help in accounts of success. *Basic and Applied Social Psychology*, **16**, 191–209. (p. 71)

Baumeister, R. F., & Leary, M. R. (1995). The need to belong: Desire for interpersonal attachment as a fundamental human motivation. *Psychological Bulletin*, **117**, 497–529. (p. 427)

Baumeister, R. F., & Scher, S. J. (1988). Self-defeating behavior patterns among normal individuals: Review and analysis of common self-destructive tendencies. *Psychological Bulletin*, **104**, 3–22. (p. 71)

Baumeister, R. F., Smart, L., & Boden, J. (1996). The dark side of high self-esteem. *Psychological Review*. (p. 67)

Baumeister, R. F., & Wotman, S. R. (1992). *Breaking hearts: The two sides of unrequited love.* New York: Guilford. (p. 469)

Baumgardner, A. H. (1991). Claiming depressive symptoms as a self-handicap: A protective self-presentation strategy. *Basic and Applied Social Psychology*, **12**, 97–113. (p. 71)

Baumgardner, A. H., & Brownlee, E. A. (1987). Strategic failure in social interaction: Evidence for expectancy disconfirmation process. *Journal of Personality and Social Psychology*, **52**, 525–535. (p. 71)

Baumgardner, A. H., Kaufman, C. M., & Levy, P. E. (1989). Regulating affect interpersonally: When low esteem leads to greater enhancement. *Journal of Personality and Social Psychology*, **56**, 907–921. (p. 66)

Baumhart, R. (1968). *An honest profit.* New York: Holt, Rinehart & Winston. (p. 57)

Bauserman, R. (1996). Sexual aggression and pornography: A review of correlational research. *Basic and Applied Social Psychology*, **18**, 405–427. (p. 406)

Baxter, T. L., & Goldberg, L. R. (1987). Perceived behavioral consistency underlying trait attributions to oneself and another: An extension of the actor-observer effect. *Personality and Social Psychology Bulletin*, **13**, 437–447. (p. 89)

Bayer, E. (1929). Beitrage zur zeikomp-onenten theorie des hungers. *Zeitschrift fur Psychologie*, **112**, 1–54. (p. 293)

Bazerman, M. H. (1986, June). Why negotiations go wrong. *Psychology Today*, pp. 54–58. (p. 553)

Bazerman, M. H. (1990). *Judgment in managerial decision making*, 2nd ed. New York: Wiley. (p. 553)

Beaman, A. L., Barnes, P. J., Klentz, B., & McQuirk, B. (1978). Increasing helping rates through information dissemination: Teaching pays. *Personality and Social Psychology Bulletin*, **4**, 406–411. (p. 510)

Beaman, A. L., & Klentz, B. (1983). The supposed physical attractiveness bias against supporters of the women's movement: A meta-analysis. *Personality and Social Psychology Bulletin*, **9**, 544–550. (p. 442)

Beaman, A. L., Klentz, B., Diener, E., & Svanum, S. (1979). Self-awareness and transgression in children: Two field studies. *Journal of Personality and Social Psychology*, **37**, 1835–1846. (p. 308)

Beauregard, K. S., & Dunning, D. (in press). Turning up the contrast: Self-enhancement motives prompt egocentric contrast effects in social judgments. *Journal of Personality and Social Psychology*. (p. 66)

Beauvois, J. L., & Dubois, N. (1988). The norm of internality in the explanation of psychological events. *European Journal of Social Psychology*, **18**, 299–316. (p. 92)

Beck, A. J., Kline, S. A., & Greenfeld, L. A. (1988). Survey of youth in custody, 1987. U.S. Department of Justice, Bureau of Justice Statistics Special Report. (p. 398)

Beck, A. T., & Young, J. E. (1978, September). College blues. *Psychology Today*, pp. 80–92. (p. 575)

Beck, S. B., Ward-Hull, C. I., & McLear, P. M. (1976). Variables related to women's somatic preferences of the male and female body. *Journal of Personality and Social Psychology*, **34**, 1200–1210. (p. 438)

Becker, B. J. (1986). Influence again: Another look at studies of gender differences in social influence. In J. S. Hyde & M. Linn (Eds.), *The psychology of gender: Advances through meta-analysis.* Baltimore: Johns Hopkins University Press. (p. 239)

Bell, B. E., & Loftus, E. F. (1988). Degree of detail of eyewitness testimony and mock juror judgments. *Journal of Applied Social Psychology*, **18**, 1171–1192. (p. 602)

Bell, B. E., & Loftus, E. F. (1989). Trivial persuasion in the courtroom: The power of (a few) minor details. *Journal of Personality and Social Psychology*, **56**, 669–679. (p. 602)

Bell, P. A. (1980). Effects of heat, noise, and provocation on retaliatory evaluative behavior. *Journal of Social Psychology*, **110**, 97–100. (p. 401)

Bellah, R. N. (1995/1996, Winter). Community properly understood: A defense of 'democratic communitarianism.' *The Responsive Community*, pp. 49–54. (p. 248)

Belson, W. A. (1978). *Television violence and the adolescent boy.* Westmead, England: Saxon House, Teakfield Ltd. (p. 413)

Bem, D. J. (1972). Self-perception theory. In L. Berkowitz (Ed.), *Advances in experimental social psychology.* Vol. 6. New York: Academic Press. (pp. 157, 162)

Bem, D. J., & McConnell, H. K. (1970). Testing the self-perception explanation of dissonance phenomena: On the salience of premanipulation attitudes. *Journal of Personality and Social Psychology*, **14**, 23–31. (p. 100)

Bennett, R. (1991, February). Pornography and extrafamilial child sexual abuse: Examining the relationship. Unpublished manuscript, Los Angeles Police Department Sexually Exploited Child Unit. (p. 406)

Bennis, W. (1984). Transformative power and leadership. In T. J. Sergiovani & J. E. Corbally (Eds.), *Leadership and organizational culture.* Urbana: University of Illinois Press. (p. 330)

Benson, P. L., Dehority, J., Garman, L., Hanson, E., Hochschwender, M., Lebold, C., Rohr, R., & Sullivan, J. (1980). Intrapersonal correlates of nonspontaneous helping behavior. *Journal of Social Psychology*, **110**, 87–95. (p. 501)

Benson, P. L., Karabenick, S. A., & Lerner, R. M. (1976). Pretty pleases: The effects of physical attractiveness, race, and sex on receiving help. *Journal of Experimental Social Psychology*, **12**, 409–415. (p. 504)

Benvenisti, M. (1988, October 16). Growing up in Jerusalem. *New York Times Magazine*, pp. 34–37. (p. 355)

Berenbaum, S. A., & Hines, M. (1992). Early androgens are related to childhood sex-typed toy preferences. *Psychological Science*, **3**, 203–206. (p. 194)

Berg, J. H. (1984). Development of friendship between roommates. *Journal of Personality and Social Psychology*, **46**, 346–356. (pp. 452, 462)

Berg, J. H. (1987). Responsiveness and self-disclosure. In V. J. Derlega & J. H. Berg (Eds.), *Self-disclosure: Theory, research, and therapy.* New York: Plenum. (p. 464)

Berg, J. H., & McQuinn, R. D. (1986). Attraction and exchange in continuing and noncontinuing dating relationships. *Journal of Personality and Social Psychology*, **50**, 942–952. (pp. 452, 465)

Berg, J. H., & McQuinn, R. D. (1988). Loneliness and aspects of social support networks. Unpublished manuscript, University of Mississippi. (p. 575)

Berg, J. H., & Peplau, L. A. (1982). Loneliness: The relationship of self-disclosure and androgyny. *Personality and Social Psychology Bulletin*, **8**, 624–630. (p. 463)

Berger, P. (1963). *Invitation to sociology: A humanistic perspective.* Garden City, N.Y.: Doubleday Anchor Books. (p. 245)

Berglas, S., & Jones, E. E. (1978). Drug choice as a self-handicapping strategy in response to noncontingent success. *Journal of Personality and Social Psychology*, **36**, 405–417. (p. 71)

Berkowitz, L. (1954). Group standards, cohesiveness, and productivity. *Human Relations*, **7**, 509–519. (p. 232)

Berkowitz, L. (1968, September). Impulse, aggression and the gun. *Psychology Today*, pp. 18–22. (p. 390)

Berkowitz, L. (1972). Frustrations, comparisons, and other sources of emotional arousal as contributors to social unrest. *Journal of Social Issues*, **28**, 77–91. *(a)* (p. 391)

Berkowitz, L. (1972). Social norms, feelings, and other factors affecting helping and altruism. In L. Berkowitz (Ed.), *Advances in experimental social psychology* (Vol. 6). New York: Academic Press. *(b)* (p. 482)

Berkowitz, L. (1978). Whatever happened to the frustration-aggression hypothesis? *American Behavioral Scientists*, **21**, 691–708. (p. 390)

Berkowitz, L. (1981, June). How guns control us. *Psychology Today*, pp. 11–12. (p. 390)

Berkowitz, L. (1983). Aversively stimulated aggression: Some parallels and differences in research with animals and humans. *American Psychologist*, **38**, 1135–1144. (p. 401)

Berkowitz, L. (1984). Some effects of thoughts on anti- and prosocial influences of media events: A cognitive-neoassociation analysis, *Psychological Bulletin*, **95**, 410–427. (p. 416)

Berkowitz, L. (1987). Mood, self-awareness, and willingness to help. *Journal of Personality and Social Psychology*, **52**, 721–729. (p. 498)

Berkowitz, L. (1989). Frustration-aggression hypothesis: Examination and reformulation. *Psychological Bulletin*, **106**, 59–73. (pp. 390, 401)

Berkowitz, L. (1995). A career on aggression. In G. G. Brannigan & M. R. Merrens (eds.), *The social psychologists: Research adventures.* New York: McGraw-Hill. (p. 390)

Berkowitz, L., & Geen, R. G. (1966). Film violence and the cue properties of

available targets. *Journal of Personality and Social Psychology*, **3**, 525–530. (p. 414)

Berkowitz, L., & LePage, A. (1967). Weapons as aggression-eliciting stimuli. *Journal of Personality and Social Psychology*, **7**, 202–207. (p. 390)

Bernard, J. (1976). *Sex differences: An overview.* New York: MSS Modular Publications. (p. 183)

Berndsen, M., Spears, R., & Van der Plight, J. (1996). Illusory correlation and attitude-based vested interest. *European Journal of Social Psychology*, **26**, 247–264. (p. 114)

Bernhardt, P. C. (1997). Influences of serotonin and testosterone in aggression and dominance: Convergence with social psychology. *Current Directions in Psychology*, **6**, 44–48. (p. 388)

Berreby, D. (1997, March/April). Primary colors. *The Sciences*, pp. 38–43. (p. 353)

Berry, D. S., & Zebrowitz-McArthur, L. (1988). What's in a face: Facial maturity and the attribution of legal responsibility. *Personality and Social Psychology Bulletin*, **14**, 23–33. (p. 613)

Berry, J. W., & Kalin, R. (1995). Multicultural and ethnic attitudes in Canada: An overview of the 1991 national survey. *Canadian Journal of Behavioural Science*, **27**, 301–320. (p. 338)

Berscheid, E. (1981). An overview of the psychological effects of physical attractiveness and some comments upon the psychological effects of knowledge of the effects of physical attractiveness. In W. Lucker, K. Ribbens, & J. A. McNamera (Eds.), *Logical aspects of facial form (craniofacial growth series).* Ann Arbor: University of Michigan Press. (pp. 436, 437)

Berscheid, E. (1985). Interpersonal attraction. In G. Lindzey & E. Aronson (Eds.), *The handbook of social psychology.* New York: Random House. (p. 592)

Berscheid, E., Boye, D., & Walster (Hatfield), E. (1968). Retaliation as a means of restoring equity. *Journal of Personality and Social Psychology*, **10**, 370–376. (p. 146)

Berscheid, E., Dion, K., Walster (Hatfield), E., & Walster, G. W. (1971). Physical attractiveness and dating choice: A test of the matching hypothesis. *Journal of Experimental Social Psychology*, **7**, 173–189. (pp. 434, 435)

Berscheid, E., Graziano, W., Monson, T., & Dermer, M. (1976). Outcome dependency: Attention, attribution, and attraction. *Journal of Personality and Social Psychology*, **34**, 978–989. (pp. 430, 435)

Berscheid, E., & Peplau, L. A. (1983). The emerging science of relationships. In Kelley, H. H., Berscheid, E., Christensen, A., Harvey, J. H., Huston, T. L., Levinger, G., McClintock, E., Peplau, L. A. & Peterson, D. R. (Eds.), *Close relationships.* New York: Freeman. (p. 592)

Berscheid, E., Snyder, M., & Omoto, A. M. (1989). Issues in studying close relationships: Conceptualizing and measuring closeness. In C. Hendrick (Ed.), *Review of personality and social psychology*, Vol. 10. Newbury Park, Ca.: Sage. (p. 456)

Berscheid, E., & Walster (Hatfield), E. (1978). *Interpersonal attraction.* Reading, Mass.: Addison-Wesley. (p. 447)

Berscheid, E., Walster, G. W., & Hatfield (was Walster), E. (1969). Effects of accuracy and positivity of evaluation on liking for the evaluator. Unpublished manuscript. Summarized by E. Berscheid and E. Walster (Hatfield) (1978), *Interpersonal attraction.* Reading, Mass.: Addison-Wesley. (p. 447)

Bersoff, D. N. (1987). Social science data and the Supreme Court: Lockhart as a case in point. *American Psychologist*, **42**, 52–58. (p. 623)

Bettencourt, A., & Dorr, N. (1997). Collective self-esteem as a mediator of the relationship between allocentrism and subjective well-being. *Personality and Social Psychology Bulletin*, **23**, 955-965. (p. 592)

Bettencourt, B. A., Dill, K. E., Greathouse, S. A., Charlton, K., & Mulholland, A. (1997). Evaluations of ingroup and outgroup members: The role of category-based expectancy violation. *Journal of Experimental Social Psychology*, **33**, 244–275. (pp. 369, 379)

Bettencourt, B. A., & Miller, N. (1996). Gender differences in aggression as a function of provocation: A meta-analysis. *Psychological Bulletin*, **119**, 422–447. (p. 189)

Beyer, L. (1990, Fall issue on women). Life behind the veil. *Time*, p. 37. (p. 347)

Bickman, L. (1975). Bystander intervention in a crime: The effect of a mass-media campaign. *Journal of Applied Social Psychology*, **5**, 296–302. (p. 505)

Bickman, L. (1979). Interpersonal influence and the reporting of a crime. *Personality and Social Psychology Bulletin*, **5**, 32–35. (p. 505)

Bickman, L., & Green, S. K. (1977). Situational cues and crime reporting: Do signs make a difference? *Journal of Applied Social Psychology*, **7**, 1–18. 505)

Bickman, L., & Kamzan, M. (1973). The effect of race and need on helping behavior. *Journal of Social Psychology*, **89**, 73–77. (p. 503)

Bierbrauer, G. (1979). Why did he do it? Attribution of obedience and the phenomenon of dispositional bias. *European Journal of Social Psychology* **9**, 67–84. (p. 229)

Bierhoff, H. W., Klein, R., & Kramp, P. (1991). Evidence for the altruistic personality from data on accident research. *Journal of Personality*, **59**, 263–280. (p. 499)

Bierly, M. M. (1985). Prejudice toward contemporary outgroups as a generalized attitude. *Journal of Applied Social Psychology*, **15**, 189–199. (p. 363)

Biernat, M. (1991). Gender stereotypes and the relationship between masculinity and femininity: A developmental analysis. *Journal of Personality and Social Psychology*, **61**, 351–365. (p. 364)

Biernat, M., & Kobrynowicz, D. (1997). Gender- and race-based standards of competence: Lower minimum standards but higher ability standards for devalued groups. *Journal of Personality and Social Psychology*, **72**, 544–557. (p. 368)

Biernat, M., Vescio, T. K., & Green, M. L. (1996). Selective self-stereotyping. *Journal of Personality and Social Psychology*, **71**, 1194–1209. (p. 68)

Biernat, M., Vescio, T. K., & Theno, S. A. (1996). Violating American values: A "Value congruence" approach to understanding outgroup attitudes. *Journal of Experimental Social Psychology*, **32**, 387–410. (p. 444)

Biernat, M., & Wortman, C. B. (1991). Sharing of home responsibilities between professionally employed women and their husbands. *Journal of Personality and Social Psychology*, **60**, 844–860. (p. 197)

Bigam, R. G. (1977, March). Voir dire: The attorney's job. *Trial 13*, p. 3. Cited by G. Bermant & J. Shepard in "The voir dire examination, juror challenges, and adversary advocacy." In B. D. Sales (Ed.), *Perspectives in law and psychology (Vol. II): The trial process.* New York: Plenum Press, 1981. (p. 622)

Billig, M., & Tajfel, H. (1973). Social categorization and similarity in intergroup behaviour. *European Journal of Social Psychology*, **3**, 27–52. (p. 354)

Biner, P. M. (1991). Effects of lighting-induced arousal on the magnitude of goal valence. *Personality and Social Psychology Bulletin*, **17**, 219–226. (p. 404)

Biner, P. M., Angle, S. T., Park, J. H., Mellinger, A. E., & Barber, B. C. (1995). Need state and the illusion of control. *Personality and Social Psychology Bulletin*, **21**, 899–907. (p. 115)

Binham, R. (1980, March-April). Trivers in Jamaica. *Science 80*, pp. 57–67. (p. 484)

Birt, C. M., & Dion, K. L. (1987). Relative deprivation theory and responses to discrimination in a gay male and lesbian sample. *British Journal of Social Psychology*, **26**, 139-145. (p. 394)

Bishop, G. D. (1984). Gender, role, and illness behavior in a military population. *Health Psychology*, **3**, 519–534. (p. 581)

Bishop, G. D. (1987). Lay conceptions of physical symptoms. *Journal of Applied Social Psychology*, **17**, 127–146. (p. 581)

Bishop, G. D. (1991). Understanding the understanding of illness: Lay disease representations. In J. A. Skelton & R. T. Croyle (Eds.), *Mental representation in health and illness.* New York: Springer-Verlag. (p. 579)

Björkqvist, K. (1994). Sex differences in physical, verbal, and indirect aggression: A review of recent research. *Sex Roles*, **30**, 177–188. (p. 189)

Blackburn, R. T., Pellino, G. R., Boberg, A., & O'Connell, C. (1980). Are instructional improvement programs off target? *Current Issues in Higher Education*, **1**, 31–48. (p. 68)

Blair, I. V., & Banaji, M. R. (1996). Automatic and controlled processes in stereotype priming. *Journal of Personality and Social Psychology*, **70**, 1142–1163. (p. 342)

Blair, S. L., & Lichter, D. T. (1991). Measuring the division of household labor: Gender segregation of housework among American couples. *Journal of Family Issues*, **12**, 91–113. (p. 200)

Blake, R. R., & Mouton, J. S. (1962). The intergroup dynamics of win-lose conflict and problem-solving collaboration in union-management relations. In M. Sherif (Ed.), *Intergroup relations and leadership.* New York: Wiley. (p. 551)

Blake, R. R., & Mouton, J. S. (1979). Intergroup problem solving in organizations: From theory to practice. In W. G. Austin and S. Worchel (Eds.), *The social psychology of intergroup relations.* Monterey, Calif.: Brooks/Cole. (pp. 539, 551)

Blanchard, F. A., & Cook, S. W. (1976). Effects of helping a less competent member of a cooperating interracial group on the development of interpersonal attraction. *Journal of Personality and Social Psychology*, **34**, 1245–1255. (p. 147)

Blascovich, J., Wyer, N. A., Swart, L. A., & Kibler, J. L. (1997). Racism and racial categorization. *Journal of Personality and Social Psychology*, **72**, 1364–1372. (p. 364)

Blass, T. (1990). Psychological approaches to the Holocaust: Review and evaluation. Paper presented to the American Psychological Association convention. (p. 241)

Blass, T. (1991). Understanding behavior in the Milgram obedience experiment: The role of personality, situations, and their interactions. *Journal of Personality and Social Psychology*, **60**, 398–413. (p. 241)

Blass, T. (1996). Stanley Milgram: A life of inventiveness and controversy. In G. A. Kimble, C. A. Boneau, & M. Wertheimer (eds.). *Portraits of pioneers in psychology*, Vol. II. Washington, D.C.: American Psychological Association. (p. 220)

Block J., & Funder, D. C. (1986). Social roles and social perception: Individual differences in attribution and error. *Journal of Personality and Social Psychology*, **51**, 1200–1207. (p. 86)

Blood, R. O., Jr. (1967). *Love match and arranged marriage.* New York: Free Press. (p. 457)

Blucher, J. (1994, October 27). Tuning in to violence: Are "Power Rangers" and other TV shows making children more aggressive? *Anchorage Daily News*, pp. E1–E2. (p. 415)

Blundell, W. E. (1986). *Storyteller step by step: A guide to better feature writing.* New York: Dow Jones. Cited by S. H. Stocking & P. H. Gross (1989), *How do journalists think? A proposal for the study of cognitive bias in newsmaking.* Bloomington, IN: ERIC Clearinghouse on Reading and Communication Skills, Smith Research Center, Indiana University. (p. 126)

Bochner, S. (1994). Cross-cultural differences in the self-concept: A test of hofstede's individualism/collectivism distinction. *Journal of Cross-Cultural Psychology*, **25**, 273–283. (p. 43)

Bodenhausen, G. V. (1990). Stereotypes as judgmental heuristics: Evidence of circadian variations in discrimination. *Psychological Science*, **1**, 319–322. (p. 364)

Bodenhausen, G. V. (1993). Emotions, arousal, and stereotypic judgments: A heuristic model of affect and stereotyping. In D. M. Mackie & D. L. Hamilton (eds.), *Affect, cognition, and stereotyping: Interactive processes in group perception.* San Diego, CA: Academic Press. (p. 261)

Bodenhausen, G. V., Kramer, G. P., & Susser, K. (1994). Happiness and stereotypic thinking in social judgment. *Journal of Personality and Social Psychology*, **66**, 621–632. (p. 365)

Bodenhausen, G. V., & Macrae, C. N. (1998). Stereotype activation and inhibition. In R. S. Wyer, Jr., *Stereotype activation and inhibition: Advances in social cognition*, vol. 11. Mahwah, NJ: Erlbaum. (p. 343)

Bodenhausen, G. V., Sheppard, L. A., & Kramer, G. F. (1994). Negative affect and social judgment: The differential impact of anger and sadness. *European Journal of Social Psychology*, **24**, 45–62. (p. 118)

Boggiano, A. K., Barrett, M., Weiher, A. W., McClelland, G. H., & Lusk, C. M. (1987). Use of the maximal-operant principle to motivate children's intrinsic interest. *Journal of Personality and Social Psychology*, **53**, 866–879. (p. 159)

Boggiano, A. K., Harackiewicz, J. M., Bessette, J. M., & Main, D. S. (1985). Increasing children's interest through performance-contingent reward. *Social Cognition*, **3**, 400–411. (p. 159)

Boggiano, A. K., & Ruble, D. N. (1985). Children's responses to evaluative feedback. In R. Schwarzer (Ed.), *Self-related cognitions in anxiety and motivation.* Hillsdale, N.J.: Erlbaum. (p. 161)

Bohner, G., Bless, H., Schwarz, N., & Strack, F. (1988). What triggers causal attributions? The impact of valence and subjective probability. *European Journal of Social Psychology, 18*, 335–345. (p. 78)

Boldt, E. D. (1976). Acquiescence and conventionality in a communal society. *Journal of Cross Cultural Psychology, 7*, 21–36. (p. 232)

Bond, C. F., Jr., & Anderson, E. L. (1987). The reluctance to transmit bad news: Private discomfort or public display? *Journal of Experimental Social Psychology, 23*, 176–187. (p. 151)

Bond, C. F., Jr., DiCandia, C. G., & MacKinnon, J. R. (1988). Responses to violence in a psychiatric setting: The role of patient's race. *Personality and Social Psychology Bulletin, 14*, 448–458. (p. 378)

Bond, C. F., Jr., & Titus, L. J. (1983). Social facilitation: A meta-analysis of 241 studies. *Psychological Bulletin, 94*, 265–292. (p. 294)

Bond, M. H. (1988). Finding universal dimensions of individual variation in multi-cultural studies of values: The Rokeach and Chinese Value Surveys. *Journal of Personality and Social Psychology, 55*, 1009–1015. (p. 14)

Bond, R., & Smith, P. B. (1996). Culture and conformity: A meta-analysis of studies using Asch's (1952b, 1956) line judgment task. *Psychological Bulletin, 119*, 111–137. (p. 242)

Boninger, D. S., Gleicher, F., & Strathman, A. (1994). Counterfactual thinking: From what might have been to what may be. *Journal of Personality and Social Psychology, 67*, 297–307. (p. 113)

Bonta, B. D. (1997). Cooperation and competition in peaceful societies. *Psychological Bulletin, 121*, 299–320. (p. 544)

Borchard, E. M. (1932). *Convicting the innocent: Errors of criminal justice.* New Haven: Yale University Press. Cited by E. R. Hilgard & E. F. Loftus (1979) "Effective interrogation of the eyewitness." *International Journal of Clinical and Experimental Hypnosis, 17*, 342–359. (p. 607)

Borgida, E. (1981). Legal reform of rape laws. In L. Bickman (Ed.), *Applied social psychology annual.* Vol. 2. Beverly Hills, Calif.: Sage Publications, pp. 211–241. (p. 616)

Borgida, E., & Brekke, N. (1985). Psycholegal research on rape trials. In A. W. Burgess (Ed.), *Rape and sexual assault: A research handbook.* New York: Garland. (p. 374)

Borgida, E., Locksley, A., & Brekke, N. (1981). Social stereotypes and social judgment. In N. Cantor & J. Kihlstrom (Eds.), *Cognition, social interaction, and personality.* Hillsdale, N.J.: Lawrence Erlbaum. (p. 376)

Borgida, E., & White, P. (1980). Judgmental bias and legal reform. Unpublished manuscript, University of Minnesota. (p. 618)

Bornstein, G., & Rapoport, A. (1988). Intergroup competition for the provision of step-level public goods: Effects of preplay communication. *European Journal of Social Psychology, 18*, 125–142. (p. 522)

Bornstein, G., Rapoport, A., Kerpel, L., & Katz, T. (1989). Within- and between-group communication in intergroup competition for public goods. *Journal of Experimental Social Psychology, 25*, 422–436. (p. 522)

Bornstein, R. F. (1989). Exposure and affect: Overview and meta-analysis of research, 1968–1987. *Psychological Bulletin, 106*, 265–289. (p. 431)

Bornstein, R. F., & D'Agostino, P. R. (1992). Stimulus recognition and the mere exposure effect. *Journal of Personality and Social Psychology, 63*, 545–552. (p. 431)

Bossard, J. H. S. (1932). Residential propinquity as a factor in marriage selection. *American Journal of Sociology, 38*, 219–224. (p. 429)

Bothwell, R. K., Brigham, J. C., & Malpass, R. S. (1989). Cross-racial identification. *Personality and Social Psychology Bulletin, 15*, 19–25. (p. 366)

Botvin, G. J., Schinke, S., & Orlandi, M. A. (1995). School-based health promotion: Substance abuse and sexual behavior. *Applied & Preventive Psychology, 4*, 167–184. (p. 285)

Botwin, M. D., Buss, D. M., & Shackelford, T. K. (1997). Personality and mate preferences: Five factors in mate selection and marital satisfaction. *Journal of Personality, 65*, 107–136. (p. 446)

Bouas, K. S., & Komorita, S. S. (1996). Group discussion and cooperation in social dilemmas. *Personality and Social Psychology Bulletin, 22*, 1144–1150. (p. 523)

Bourgeois, M. J., Horowitz, I. A., & Lee, L. F. (1993). Effects of technicality and access to trial transcripts on verdicts and information processing in a civil trial. *Personality and Social Psychology Bulletin, 19*, 219–226. (p. 622)

Bowen, E. (1988, April 4). What ever became of Honest Abe? *Time.* (p. 5)

Bower, B. (1997). Thanks for the memories: Scientists evaluate interviewing tactics for boosting eyewitness recall. *Science, 151*, 246–247. (p. 610)

Bower, G. H. (1986). Prime time in cognitive psychology. In P. Eelen (Ed.), *Cognitive research and behavior therapy: Beyond the conditioning paradigm.* Amsterdam: North Holland Publishers. (p. 103)

Bower, G. H. (1987). Commentary on mood and memory. *Behavioral Research and Therapy, 25*, 443–455. (pp. 117, 571)

Bower, G. H., & Masling, M. (1979). Causal explanations as mediators for re-membering correlations. Unpublished manuscript, Stanford University. (p. 167)

Bowlby, J. (1980). *Loss, sadness and depression. Vol. III of Attachment and loss.* London: Basic Books. (p. 460)

Boyatzis, C. J., Matillo, G. M., & Nesbitt, K. M. (1995). Effects of the "Mighty Morphin Power Rangers" on children's aggression with peers. *Child Study Journal, 25*, 45–55. (p. 415)

Bradley, W., & Mannell, R. C. (1984). Sensitivity of intrinsic motivation to reward procedure instructions. *Personality and Social Psychology Bulletin, 10*, 426–431. (p. 160)

Brandon, R., & Davies, C. (1973). *Wrongful imprisonment: Mistaken convictions and their consequences.* Hamden, Conn.: Archon Books. (p. 602)

Brauer, M., Judd, C. M., & Gliner, M. D. (1995). The effects of repeated expressions on attitude polarization during group discussions. *Journal of Personality and Social Psychology, 68*, 1014–1029. (p. 314)

Bray, R. M., & Kerr, N. L. (1982). Methodological considerations in the study of the psychology of the courtroom. In N. L. Kerr & R. M. Bray (Eds.), *The psychology of the courtroom.* Orlando, Fla.: Academic Press. (p. 629)

Bray, R. M., & Noble, A. M. (1978). Authoritarianism and decisions of mock juries: Evidence of jury bias and group polarization. *Journal of Personality and Social Psychology, 36*, 1424–1430. (p. 626)

Breckler, S. J., & Wiggins, E. C. (1989). Affect versus evaluation in the structure of attitudes. *Journal of Experimental Social Psychology, 25*, 253–271. (p. 130)

Bregman, N. J., & McAllister, H. A. (1982). Eyewitness testimony: The role of commitment in increasing reliability. *Social Psychology Quarterly, 45*, 181–184. (pp. 606–607)

Brehm, J. W. (1956). Post-decision changes in desirability of alternatives. *Journal of Abnormal Social Psychology, 52*, 384–389. (p. 155)

Brehm, S., & Brehm, J. W. (1981). *Psychological reactance: A theory of freedom and control.* New York: Academic Press. (p. 243)

Brehm, S. S., & Smith, T. W. (1986). Social psychological approaches to psychotherapy and behavior change. In S. L. Garfield & A. E. Bergin (Eds.), *Handbook of psychotherapy and behavior change*, 3rd ed. New York: Wiley. (p. 588)

Brenner, S. N., & Molander, E. A. (1977). Is the ethics of business changing? *Harvard Business Review*, January-February, pp. 57–71. (p. 57)

Bretl, D. J., & Cantor, J. (1988). The portrayal of men and women in U.S. television commercials: A recent content analysis and trends over 15 years. *Sex Roles, 18*, 595–609. (p. 359)

Brewer, M. B. (1979). In-group bias in the minimal intergroup situation: A cognitive-motivational analysis. *Psychological Bulletin, 86*, 307–324. (p. 356)

Brewer, M. B. (1987). Collective decisions. *Social Science, 72*, 140–143. (p. 522)

Brewer, M. B. (1988). A dual process model of impression formation. In T. Srull & R. Wyer (Eds.), *Advances in social cognition*, Vol. 1. Hillsdale, N.J.: Erlbaum. (p. 376)

Brewer, M. B. (1996). When contact is not enough: Social identity and intergroup cooperation. *International Journal of Intercultural Relations, 20*, 291-303. (p. 535)

Brewer, M. B., & Miller, N. (1988). Contact and cooperation: When do they work? In P. A. Katz & D. Taylor (Eds.), *Towards the elimination of racism: Profiles in controversy.* New York: Plenum. (p. 544)

Brewer, M. B., & Silver, M. (1978). In-group bias as a function of task characteristics. *European Journal of Social Psychology, 8*, 393–400. (p. 354)

Brickman, P. (1978). Is it real? In J. Harvey, W. Ickes, & R. Kidd (Eds.), *New directions in attribution research.* Vol. 2. Hillsdale, N.J.: Erlbaum. (p. 180)

Brickman, P., & Campbell, D. T. (1971). Hedonic relativism and planning the good society. In M. H. Appley (Ed.), *Adaptation-level theory.* New York: Academic Press. (p. 393)

Brickman, P., Coates, D., & Janoff-Bulman, R. J. (1978). Lottery winners and accident victims: Is happiness relative? *Journal of Personality and Social Psychology, 36*, 917–927. (pp. 394, 395)

Briere, N. M. & Vallerand, R. J. (1990). Effect of private self-consciousness and success outcome on causal dimensions. *Journal of Social Psychology, 130*, 325-332. (p. 57)

Brigham, J. C., & Cairns, D. L. (1988). The effect of mugshot inspections on eyewitness identification accuracy. *Journal of Applied Social Psychology, 18*, 1394–1410. (p. 610)

Brigham, J. C., Ready, D. J., & Spier, S. A. (1990). Standards for evaluating the fairness of photograph lineups. *Basic and Applied Social Psychology, 11*, 149-163. (p. 611)

Brigham, J. C., & Williamson, N. L. (1979). Cross-racial recognition and age: When you're over 60, do they still all look alike? *Personality and Social Psychology Bulletin, 5*, 218–222. (p. 366)

Briscoe, D. (1997, February 16). Women lawmakers still not in charge. Associated Press (*Grand Rapids Press*, p. A23). (p. 187)

British Psychological Society (1991). *Code of conduct ethical principles & guidelines.* Leicester. (p. 30)

Brock, T. C. (1965). Communicator-recipient similarity and decision change. *Journal of Personality and Social Psychology, 1*, 650–654. (p. 260)

Brock, T. C., & Brannon, L. A. (1991, April 4). Tobacco ad warning should be shocking (letter). *Wall Street Journal.* (p. 263)

Brockner, J., Rubin, J. Z., Fine, J., Hamilton, T. P., Thomas, B., & Turetsky, B. (1982). Factors affecting entrapment in escalating conflicts: The importance of timing. *Journal of Research in Personality, 16*, 247–266. (p. 520)

Bronfenbrenner, U. (1961). The mirror image in Soviet-American relations. *Journal of Social Issues, 17*(3), 45–56. (p. 530)

Brook, P. (1969). Filming a masterpiece. *Observer Weekend Review*, July 26, 1964. Cited by L. Tiger in *Men in groups.* New York: Random House, p. 163. (p. 140)

Broome, A., & Wegner, D. M. (1994). Some positive effects of releasing socially anxious people from the need to please. Paper presented to the American Psychological Society convention. (p. 578)

Brown, H. J., Jr. (1990). *P.S. I love you.* Nashville, TN: Rutledge Hill. (p. 59)

Brown, J. D. (1986). Evaluations of self and others: Self-enhancement biases in social judgments. *Social Cognition, 4*, 353–376. (p. 66)

Brown, J. D. (1991). Accuracy and bias in self-knowledge: Can knowing the truth be hazardous to your health? In C. R. Snyder & D. F. Forsyth (Eds.), *Handbook of social and clinical psychology: The health perspective.* New York: Pergamon Press. (p. 42)

Brown, J. D., Collins, R. L., & Schmidt, G. W. (1988). Self-esteem and direct versus indirect forms of self-enhancement. *Journal of Personality and Social Psychology, 55*, 445–453. (p. 66)

Brown, J. D., & Dutton, K. A. (1994). From the top down: Self-esteem and self-evaluation. Unpublished manuscript, University of Washington. (p. 39)

Brown, J. D., & Gallagher, F. M. (1992). Coming to terms with failure: Private self-enhancement and public self-effacement. *Journal of Experimental Social Psychology, 28*, 3–22. (p. 65)

Brown, J. D., Novick, N. J., Lord, K. A., & Richards, J. M. (1992). When Gulliver travels: Social context, psychological closeness, and self-appraisals. *Journal of Personality and Social Psychology, 62*, 717–727. (p. 441)

Brown, J. D., & Siegel, J. M. (1988). Attributions for negative life events and depression: The role of perceived control. *Journal of Personality and Social Psychology, 54*, 316–322. (p. 573)

Brown, J. D., & Taylor, S. E. (1986). Affect and the processing of personal information: Evidence for mood-activated self-schemata. *Journal of Experimental Social Psychology, 22*, 436–452. (pp. 117, 572)

Brown, L. R., Hane, H., & Ayres, E. (Eds.) (1993). *Vital signs 1993: The trends that are shaping our future.* New York: Norton. (p. 253)

Brown, P. A. (1995, April 9). Survey shows Americans are different (reporting on Roper Center for Public Opinion Research study). Scripps Howard News Service, *Grand Rapids Press*, p. A10. (p. 528)

Brown, R. (1965). *Social psychology.* New York: Free Press. (p. 178)

Brown, R. (1987). Theory of politeness: An exemplary case. Paper presented to the Society of Experimental Social Psychology meeting. Cited by R. O. Kroker & L. A. Wood, 1992, Are the rules of address universal? IV: Comparison of Chinese, Korean, Greek, and German usage. *Journal of Cross-Cultural Psychology, 23*, 148–162. (p. 178)

Brown, R., & Smith, A. (1989). Perceptions of and by minority groups: The case of women in academia. *European Journal of Social Psychology, 19*, 61–75. (p. 370)

Brown, R., Vivian, J., & Hewstone, M. (1999). Changing attitudes through intergroup contact: The effects of group membership salience. *European Journal of Social Psychology, 29*, 741-764. (p. 535)

Brown, R., & Wootton-Millward, L. (1993). Perceptions of group homogeneity during group formation and change. *Social Cognition, 11*, 126–149. (p. 366)

Browning, C. (1992). *Ordinary men: Reserve police battalion 101 and the final solution in Poland.* New York: HarperCollins. (p. 229)

Bruck, C. (1976, April). Zimbardo: Solving the maze. *Human Behavior*, pp. 25–31. (p. 240)

Bryan, J. H., & Test, M. A. (1967). Models and helping: Naturalistic studies in aiding behavior. *Journal of Personality and Social Psychology, 6*, 400–407. (p. 493)

Buckhout, R. (1974, December). Eyewitness testimony. *Scientific American*, pp. 23–31. (p. 603)

Buehler, R., & Griffin, D. (1994). Change of meaning effects in conformity and dissent: Observing construal processes over time. *Journal of Personality and Social Psychology, 67*, 984–996. (p. 237)

Buehler, R., Griffin, D., & Ross, M. (1994). Exploring the "planning fallacy": When people underestimate their task completion times. *Journal of Personality and Social Psychology, 67*, 366–381. (p. 107)

Buford, B. (1992). *Among the thugs.* New York: Norton. (p. 308)

Burchill, S. A. L., & Stiles, W. B. (1988). Interactions of depressed college students with their roommates: Not necessarily negative. *Journal of Personality and Social Psychology, 55*, 410–419. (p. 572)

Burger, J. M. (1987). Increased performance with increased personal control: A self-presentation interpretation. *Journal of Experimental Social Psychology*, **23**, 350–360. (p. 329)

Burger, J. M. (1991). Changes in attributions over time: The ephemeral fundamental attribution error. *Social Cognition*, **9**, 182–193. (p. 88)

Burger, J. M., & Burns, L. (1988). The illusion of unique invulnerability and the use of effective contraception. *Personality and Social Psychology Bulletin*, **14**, 264–270. (p. 60)

Burger, J. M., & Palmer, M. L. (1991). Changes in and generalization of unrealistic optimism following experiences with stressful events: Reactions to the 1989 California earthquake. *Personality and Social Psychology Bulletin*, **18**, 39–43. (p. 60)

Burger, J. M., & Pavelich, J. L. (1994). Attributions for presidential elections: The situational shift over time. *Basic and Applied Social Psychology*, **15**, 359–371. (p. 88)

Burgess, R. L., & Huston, T. L. (Eds.) (1979). *Social exchange in developing relationships*. New York: Academic Press. (p. 449)

Burn, S. M. (1992). Locus of control, attributions, and helplessness in the homeless. *Journal of Applied Social psychology*, **22**, 1161–1174. (p. 53)

Burns, D. D. (1980). *Feeling good: The new mood therapy*. New York: Signet. (p. 570)

Burnstein, E., Crandall, R., & Kitayama, S. (1994). Some neo-Darwinian decision rules for altruism: Weighing cues for inclusive fitness as a function of the biological importance of the decision. *Journal of Personality and Social Psychology*, **67**, 773–789. (p. 484)

Burnstein, E., & Kitayama, S. (1989). Persuasion in groups. In T. C. Brock & S. Shavitt (Eds.), *The psychology of persuasion*. San Francisco: Freeman. (p. 326)

Burnstein, E., & Vinokur, A. (1977). Persuasive argumentation and social comparison as determinants of attitude polarization. *Journal of Experimental Social Psychology*, **13**, 315–332. (p. 314)

Burnstein, E., & Worchel, P. (1962). Arbitrariness of frustration and its consequences for aggression in a social situation. *Journal of Personality*, **30**, 528–540. (p. 390)

Burr, W. R. (1973). *Theory construction and the sociology of the family*. New York: Wiley. (p. 429)

Burros, M. (1988, February 24). Women: Out of the house but not out of the kitchen. *New York Times*. (p. 57)

Burt, R. S. (1986). Strangers, friends and happiness. *GSS Technical Report No. 72*. Chicago: National Opinion Research Center, University of Chicago. (p. 592)

Bushman, B. J. (1993). Human aggression while under the influence of alcohol and other drugs: An integrative research review. *Current Directions in Psychological Science*, **2**, 148–152. (p. 387)

Bushman, B. J. (1995). Moderating role of trait aggressiveness in the effects of violent media on aggression. *Journal of Personality and Social Psychology*, **69**, 950–960. (p. 415)

Bushman, B. J. (1996). Individual differences in the extent and development of aggressive cognitive-associative networks. *Personality and Social Psychology Bulletin*, **22**, 811–819. (p. 417)

Bushman, B. J., & Anderson, C. A. (in press). Methodology in the study of aggression: Integrating experimental and nonexperimental findings. In R. Geen & E. Donnerstein (eds.), *Human aggression: Theories, research and implications for policy*. San Diego: Academic Press (p. 419)

Bushman, B. J., & Cooper, H. M. (1990). Effects of alcohol on human aggression: An integrative research review. *Psychological Bulletin*, **107**, 341–354. (p. 387)

Bushman, B. J., & Geen, R. G. (1990). Role of cognitive-emotional mediators and individual differences in the effects of media violence on aggression. *Journal of Personality and Social Psychology*, **58**, 156–163. (p. 416)

Buss, D. M. (1984). Toward a psychology of person-environment (PE) correlation: The role of spouse selection. *Journal of Personality and Social Psychology*, **47**, 361–377. (p. 446)

Buss, D. M. (1985). Human mate selection. *American Scientist*, **73**, 47–51. (pp. 445, 446)

Buss, D. M. (1989). Sex differences in human mate preferences: Evolutionary hypotheses tested in 37 cultures. *Behavioral and Brain Sciences*, **12**, 1–49. (p. 439)

Buss, D. M. (1994a). *The evolution of desire: Strategies of human mating*. New York: Basic Books. (pp. 192, 193)

Buss, D. M. (1994b). The strategies of human mating. *American Scientist*, **82**, 238–249. (p. 193)

Buss, D. M. (1995a). Evolutionary psychology: A new paradigm for psychological science. *Psychological Inquiry*, **6**, 1–30. (pp. 192, 196)

Buss, D. M. (1995b). Psychological sex differences: Origins through sexual selection. *American Psychologist*, **50**, 164–168. (p. 191)

Buss, D. M. (1996). Sexual conflict: Evolutionary insights into feminism and the "Battle of the Sexes." In D. M. Buss & N. M. Malamuth (eds.), *Sex, power, conflict: Evolutionary and feminist perspectives*. New York: Oxford University Press. (p. 440)

Buss, D. M., & Shackelford, T. K. (1997). Human aggression in evolutionary psychological perspective. *Clinical Psychology Review*, **17**, 605–619. (p. 386)

Butcher, S. H. (1951). *Aristotle's theory of poetry and fine art*. New York: Dover Publications. (p. 421)

Butler, A. C., Hokanson, J. E., & Flynn, H. A. (1994). A comparison of self-esteem lability and low trait self-esteem as vulnerability factors for depression. *Journal of Personality and Social Psychology*, **66**, 166–177. (p. 573)

Buunk, B. P., & van der Eijnden, R. J. J. M. (1997). Perceived prevalence, perceived superiority, and relationship satisfaction: Most relationships are good, but ours is the best. *Personality and Social Psychology Bulletin*, **23**, 219–228. (p. 68)

Buunk, B. P., & Van Yperen, N. W. (1991). Referential comparisons, relational comparisons, and exchange orientation: Their relation to marital satisfaction. *Personality and Social Psychology Bulletin*, **17**, 709–717. p. 462)

Bylsma, W. H., & Major, B. (1994). Social comparisons and contentment. *Psychology of Women Quarterly*, **18**, 241–249. (p. 394)

Byrne, D. (1971). *The attraction paradigm*. New York: Academic Press. (pp. 442, 443)

Byrne, D., & Clore, G. L. (1970). A reinforcement model of evaluative responses. *Personality: An International Journal*, **1**, 103–128. (p. 450)

Byrne, D., & Wong, T. J. (1962). Racial prejudice, interpersonal attraction, and assumed dissimilarity of attitudes. *Journal of Abnormal and Social Psychology*, **65**, 246–253. (p. 365)

Bytwerk, R. L. (1976). Julius Streicher and the impact of *Der Stürmer*. *Wiener Library Bulletin*, **29**, 41–46. (p. 251)

Bytwerk, R. L., & Brooks, R. D. (1980). Julius Streicher and the rhetorical foundations of the holocaust. Paper presented to the Central States Speech Association convention. (p. 263)

Cacioppo, J. T., Claiborn, C. D., Petty, R. E., & Heesacker, M. (1991). General framework for the study of attitude change in psychotherapy. In C. R. Snyder & D. R. Forsyth (Eds.), *Handbook of social and clinical psychology*. New York: Pergamon. (p. 589)

Cacioppo, J. T., Petty, R. E., Feinstein, J. A., & Jarvis, W. B. G. (1996). Dispositional differences in cognitive motivation: The life and times of individuals varying in need for cognition. *Psychological Bulletin*, **119**, 197–253. (pp. 261, 274, 276)

Cacioppo, J. T., Petty, R. E., & Morris, K. J. (1983). Effects of need for cognition on message evaluation, recall, and persuasion. *Journal of Personality and Social Psychology*, **45**, 805–818. (p. 261)

Cacioppo, J. T., Priester, J. R., & Bernston, G. G. (1993). Rudimentary determinants of attitudes. II: Arm flexion and extension have differential effects on attitudes. *Journal of Personality and Social Psychology,* **65**, 5–17. (p. 159)

Cacioppo, J. T., Uchino, B. N., Crites, S. L., Snydersmith, M. A., Smith, G., Berntson, G. G., & Lang, P. J. (1991). Relationship between facial expressiveness and sympathetic activation in emotion: A critical review, with emphasis on modeling underlying mechanisms and individual differences. *Journal of Personality and Social Psychology,* **62**, 110–128. (p. 158)

Calhoun, J. B. (1962, February). Population density and social pathology. *Scientific American,* pp. 139–148. (p. 403)

Campbell, D. T. (1975). On the conflicts between biological and social evolution and between psychology and oral tradition. *American Psychologist,* **30**, 1103–1126. *(b)* (pp. 10, 483, 484)

Campbell, D. T. (1975). The conflict between social and biological evolution and the concept of original sin. *Zygon,* **10**, 234–249. *(a)* (pp. 483, 484)

Canadian Centre on Substance Abuse (1997). *Canadian Profile: Alcohol, Tobacco, & Other Drugs.* Ottawa: Canadian Centre on Substance Abuse. (p. 244)

Cann, A., Calhoun, L. G., & Selby, J. W. (1979). Attributing responsibility to the victim of rape: Influence of information regarding past sexual experience. *Human Relations,* **32**, 57–67. (p. 616)

Cantril, H., & Bumstead, C. H. (1960). *Reflections on the human venture.* New York: New York University Press. (p. 326)

Carducci, B. J., Cosby, P. C., & Ward, D. D. (1978). Sexual arousal and interpersonal evaluations. *Journal of Experimental Social Psychology,* **14**, 449–457. (p. 454)

Carli, L. L. (1991). Gender, status, and influence. In E. J. Lawler & B. Markovsky (Ed.), *Advances in group processes: Theory and research,* vol. 8. Greenwich, CT: JAI Press. (p. 188)

Carli, L. L., Columbo, J., Dowling, S., Kulis, M., & Minalga, C. (1990). Victim derogation as a function of hindsight and cognitive bolstering. Paper presented at the American Psychological Association convention. (p. 373)

Carli, L. L., & Leonard, J. B. (1989). The effect of hindsight on victim derogation. *Journal of Social and Clinical Psychology,* **8**, 331–343. (p. 373)

Carlo, G., Eisenberg, N., Troyer, D., Switzer, G., & Speer, A. L. (1991). The altruistic personality: In what contexts is it apparent? *Journal of Personality and Social Psychology,* **61**, 450–458. (p. 499)

Carlsmith, J. M., Ellsworth, P., & Whiteside, J. (1968). Guilt, confession and compliance. Unpublished manuscript, Stanford University. Cited by J. L. Freeman, D. O. Sears, & J. M. Carlsmith in *Social psychology.*

Englewood Cliffs, N.J.: Prentice-Hall, 1970, pp. 275–276. (p. 496)

Carlsmith, J. M., & Gross, A. E. (1969). Some effects of guilt on compliance. *Journal of Personality and Social Psychology,* **11**, 232–239. (p. 495)

Carlson, J., & Hatfield, E. (1992). *The psychology of emotion.* Fort Worth, TX: Holt, Rinehart & Winston. (p. 457)

Carlson, J., & Miller, N. (1987). Explanation of the relation between negative mood and helping. *Psychological Bulletin,* **102**, 91–108.(p. 497)

Carlson, M., Charlin, V., & Miller, N. (1988). Positive mood and helping behavior: A test of six hypotheses. *Journal of Personality and Social Psychology,* **55**, 211–229. (p. 498)

Carlson, M., Marcus-Newhall, A., & Miller, N. (1990). Effects of situational aggression cues: A quantitative review. *Journal of Personality and Social Psychology,* **58**, 622–633. (p. 390)

Carlston, D. E., & Shovar, N. (1983). Effects of performance attributions on others' perceptions of the attributor. *Journal of Personality and Social Psychology,* **44**, 515–525. (p. 73)

Carroll, D., Davey Smith, G., & Bennett, P. (1994, March). Health and socioeconomic status. *The Psychologist,* pp. 122–125. (pp. 21, 22)

Carter, S. L. (1993). *Reflections of an affirmative action baby.* New York: Basic Books. (p. 367)

Cartwright, D. S. (1975). The nature of gangs. In D. S. Cartwright, B. Tomson, & H. Schwartz (Eds.), *Gang delinquency.* Monterey, Calif.: Brooks/Cole. (pp. 313, 398)

Carver, C. S., Kus, L. A., & Scheier, M. F. (1994). Effect of good versus bad mood and optimistic versus pessimistic outlook on social acceptance versus rejection. *Journal of Social and Clinical Psychology,* **13**, 138–151. (p. 572)

Carver, C. S., & Scheier, M. F. (1978). Self-focusing effects of dispositional self-consciousness, mirror presence, and audience presence. *Journal of Personality and Social Psychology,* **36**, 324–332. (p. 88)

Carver, C. S., & Scheier, M. F. (1981). *Attention and self-regulation.* New York: Springer-Verlag. (p. 136)

Carver, C. S., & Scheier, M. F. (1986). Analyzing shyness: A specific application of broader self-regulatory principles. In W. H. Jones, J. M. Cheek, & S. R. Briggs (Eds.), *Shyness: Perspectives on research and treatment.* New York: Plenum. (p. 578)

Cash, T. F., & Janda, L. H. (1984, December). The eye of the beholder. *Psychology Today,* pp. 46–52. (p. 437)

Caspi, A., & Herbener, E. S. (1990). Continuity and change: Assortative marriage and the consistency of personality in adulthood. *Journal of*

Personality and Social Psychology, **58**, 250–258. (p. 442)

Catalano, R., Novaco, R., & McConnell, W. (1997). A model of the net effect of job loss on violence. *Journal of Personality and Social Psychology,* **72**, 1440–1447. (p. 391)

Ceci, S. J., & Bruck, M. (1993). Child witnesses: Translating research into policy. *Social Policy Report* (Society for Research in Child Development), **7**(3), 1–30. (pp. 605, 606)

Ceci, S. J., & Bruck, M. (1993). Suggestibility of the child witness: A historical review and synthesis. *Psychological Bulletin,* **113**, 403–439. (pp. 605, 606)

Ceci, S. J., & Peters, D. (1984). Letters of reference: A naturalistic study of the effects of confidentiality. *American Psychologist,* **39**, 29–31. (p. 141)

Centerwall, B. S. (1989). Exposure to television as a risk factor for violence. *American Journal of Epidemiology,* **129**, 643–652. (p. 414)

Cerhan, J. R., & Wallace, R. B. (1997). Change in social ties and subsequent mortality in rural elders. *Epidemiology,* **8**, 475–481. (p. 591)

Chagnon, N. A. (1988). Life histories, blood revenge, and warfare in a tribal population. *Science,* **239**, 985–991. (p. 385)

Chaiken, S. (1979). Communicator physical attractiveness and persuasion. *Journal of Personality and Social Psychology,* **37**, 1387–1397. (p. 259)

Chaiken, S. (1980). Heuristic versus systematic information processing and the use of source versus message cues in persuasion. *Journal of Personality and Social Psychology,* **39**, 752–766. (p. 261)

Chaiken, S., & Eagly, A. H. (1978). Communication modality as a determinant of message persuasiveness and message comprehensibility. *Journal of Personality and Social Psychology,* **34**, 605–614. (pp. 271, 272)

Chaiken, S., & Eagly, A. H. (1983). Communication modality as a determinant of persuasion: The role of communicator salience. *Journal of Personality and Social Psychology,* **45**, 241–256. (p. 271)

Chaiken, S., & Maheswaran, D. (1994). Neuristic processing can bias systematic processing: Effects of source credibility, argument ambiguity, and task importance on attitude judgment. *Journal of Personality and Social Psychology,* **66**, 460–473. (p. 254)

Chaiken, S., Pomerantz, E. M., & Giner-Sorolla, R. (1995). Structural consistency and attitude strength. In R. E. Petty and J. A. Krosnick (eds.), *Attitude strength: antecedents and consequences.* Hillsdale, NJ: Erlbaum. (p. 136)

Chance, J. E., & Goldstein, A. G. (1981). Depth of processing in response to own and other-race faces. *Personality and Social Psychology Bulletin, 7,* 475–480. (p. 366)

Chang, D. H. (1972). Environmental influences on criminal activity in Korea. *Criminology, 10,* 338-352. (p. 402)

Chapman, L. J., & Chapman, J. P. (1969). Genesis of popular but erroneous psychodiagnostic observations. *Journal of Abnormal Psychology, 74,* 272–280. (p. 563)

Chapman, L. J., & Chapman, J. P. (1971, November). Test results are what you think they are. *Psychology Today,* pp. 18–22, 106–107. (p. 563)

Check, J. M., & Melchior, L. A. (1990). Shyness, self-esteem, and self-consciousness. In H. Leitenberg (Ed.), *Handbook of social and evaluation anxiety.* New York: Plenum. (p. 576)

Check, J., & Malamuth, N. (1984). Can there be positive effects of participation in pornography experiments? *Journal of Sex Research, 20,* 14–31. (p. 407)

Chen, H. C., Reardon, R., & Rea, C. (1992). Forewarning of content and involvement: Consequences for persuasion and resistance to persuasion. *Journal of Experimental Social Psychology, 28,* 523–541. (p. 274)

Chen, S. C. (1937). Social modification of the activity of ants in nest-building. *Physiological Zoology, 10,* 420–436. (p. 293)

Chickering, A. W., & McCormick, J. (1973). Personality development and the college experience. *Research in Higher Education,* No. 1, 62–64. (p. 313)

Chodorow, N. J. (1978). *The reproduction of mother: Psychoanalysis and the sociology of gender.* Berkeley, CA: University of California Press. (p. 184)

Chodorow, N. J. (1989). *Feminism and psychoanalytic theory.* New Haven, CT: Yale University Press. (p. 184)

Christensen, L. (1988). Deception in psychological research: When is its use justified? *Personality and Social Psychology Bulletin, 14,* 664–675. (p. 31)

Christian, J. J., Flyger, V., & Davis, D. E. (1960). Factors in the mass mortality of a herd of sika deer, *Cervus Nippon. Chesapeake Science, 1,* 79–95. (p. 403)

Chua-Eoan, H. (1997, April 7). Imprisoned by his own passions. *Time,* pp. 40–42. (p. 279)

Church, G. J. (1986, January 6). China. *Time,* pp. 6–19. (p. 302)

Chwalisz, K., Diener, E., & Gallagher, D. (1988). Autonomic arousal feedback and emotional experience: Evidence from the spinal cord injured. *Journal of Personality and Social Psychology, 54,* 820–828. (p. 395)

Cialdini, R. B. (1984). *Influence: How and why people agree to things.* New York: William Morrow. (p. 157)

Cialdini, R. B. (1988). *Influence: Science and practice.* Glenview, Il.: Scott, Foresman/Little, Brown. (pp. 144, 145, 149, 223)

Cialdini, R. B. (1991). Altruism or egoism? That is (still) the question. *Psychological Inquiry, 2,* 124–126. (p. 480)

Cialdini, R. B. (1995). A full-cycle approach to social psychology. In G. G. Brannigan & M. R. Merrens (eds.), *The social psychologists: Research adventures.* New York: McGraw-Hill. (p. 507)

Cialdini, R. B., Bickman, L., & Cacioppo, J. T. (1979). An example of consumeristic social psychology: Bargaining tough in the new car showroom. *Journal of Applied Social Psychology, 9,* 115–126. (p. 547)

Cialdini, R. B., Borden, R. J., Thorne, A., Walker, M. R., Freeman, S., & Sloan, L. R. (1976). Basking in reflected glory: Three (football) field studies. *Journal of Personality and Social Psychology, 39,* 406–415. (p. 355)

Cialdini, R. B., Brown, S. L., Lewis, B. P., Luce, C., & Neuberg, S. L. (1997). Reinterpreting the empathy-altruism relationship: When one into one equals oneness. *Journal of Personality and Social Psychology, 73,* 481–494. (p. 479)

Cialdini, R. B., Cacioppo, J. T., Bassett, R., & Miller, J. A. (1978). Lowball procedure for producing compliance: Commitment then cost. *Journal of Personality and Social Psychology, 36,* 463–476. (p. 144)

Cialdini, R. B., Darby, B. L., & Vincent, J. E. (1973). Transgression and altruism: A case for hedonism. *Journal of Experimental Social Psychology, 9,* 502–516. (p. 496)

Cialdini, R. B., Green, B. L., & Rusch, A. J. (1992). When tactical pronouncements of change become real change: The case of reciprocal persuasion. *Journal of Personality and Social Psychology, 63,* 30–40. (p. 161)

Cialdini, R. B., & Kenrick, D. T. (1976). Altruism as hedonism: A social development perspective on the relationship of negative mood state and helping. *Journal of Personality and Social Psychology, 34,* 907–914. (pp. 496, 497)

Cialdini, R. B., Kenrick, D. T., & Baumann, D. J. (1981). Effects of mood on prosocial behavior in children and adults. In N. Eisenberg-Berg (Ed.), *The development of prosocial behavior.* New York: Academic Press. (p. 496)

Cialdini, R. B., & Richardson, K. D. (1980). Two indirect tactics of image management: Basking and blasting. *Journal of Personality and Social Psychology, 39,* 406–415. (p. 361)

Cialdini, R. B., & Schroeder, D. A. (1976). Increasing compliance by legitimizing paltry contributions: When even a penny helps. *Journal of Personality and Social Psychology, 34,* 599–604. (p. 507)

Cialdini, R. B., Vincent, J. E., Lewis, S. K., Catalan, J., Wheeler, D., & Danby, B. L. (1975). Reciprocal concessions procedure for inducing compliance: The door-in-the-face technique. *Journal of Person-ality and Social Psychology, 31,* 206–215. (p. 507)

Cicerello, A., & Sheehan, E. P. (1995). Personal advertisements: A content analysis. *Journal of Social Behavior and Personality, 10,* 751–756. (p. 435)

Cinnirella, M. (1997). Towards a European identity? Interactions between the national and European social identities manifested by university students in Britain and Italy. *British Journal of Social Psychology, 36,* 19–31. (p. 41)

Clancy, S. M., & Dollinger, S. J. (1993). Photographic depictions of the self: Gender and age differences in social connectedness. *Sex Roles, 29,* 477–495. (p. 185)

Clark, M. S. (1984). Record keeping in two types of relationships. *Journal of Personality and Social Psychology, 47,* 549–557. (p. 462)

Clark, M. S. (1986). Evidence for the effectiveness of manipulations of desire for communal versus exchange relationships. *Personality and Social Psychology Bulletin, 12,* 414–425. (p. 462)

Clark, M. S., & Bennett, M. E. (1992). Research on relationships: Implications for mental health. In D. Ruble, P. Costanzo (ed.), *The social psychology of mental health.* New York: Guilford. (p. 65)

Clark, M. S., & Mills, J. (1979). Interpersonal attraction in exchange and communal relationships. *Journal of Personality and Social Psychology, 37,* 12–24. (p. 462)

Clark, M. S., & Mills, J. (1993). The difference between communal and exchange relationships: What it is and is not. *Personality and Social Psychology Bulletin, 19,* 684–691. (p. 462)

Clark, M. S., Mills, J., & Corcoran, D. (1989). Keeping track of needs and inputs of friends and strangers. *Personality and Social Psychology Bulletin, 15,* 533–542. (p. 462)

Clark, M. S., Mills, J., & Powell, M. C. (1986). Keeping track of needs in communal and exchange relationships. *Journal of Personality and Social Psychology, 51,* 333–338. (p. 462)

Clark, R. D., III (1974). Effects of sex and race on helping behavior in a nonreactive setting. *Representative Research in Social Psychology, 5,* 1–6. (p. 504)

Clark, R. D., III (1995). A few parallels between group polarization and minority influence. In S. Moscovici, H. Mucchi-Faina, & A. Maass (eds.), *Minority influence.* Chicago: Nelson-Hall. (p. 327)

Clark, R. D., III, & Maass, A. (1990). The effects of majority size on minority influence. *European Journal of Social Psychology, 20,* 99–117. (p. 326)

Clark, R. D., III, & Maass, S. A. (1988). The role of social categorization and perceived source credibility in minority influence. *European Journal of Social Psychology, 18,* 381–394. (p. 232)

Clarke, A. C. (1952). An examination of the operation of residual propinquity as a factor in mate selection. *American Sociological Review, 27,* 17–22. (p. 429)

Clary, E. G., & Snyder, M. (1991). A functional analysis of altruism and prosocial behavior: The case of volunteerism. In M. Clark (Ed.), *Prosocial behavior.* Newbury Park, CA: Sage. (p. 501)

Clary, E. G., & Snyder, M. (1993). Persuasive communications strategies for recruiting volunteers. In D. R. Young, R. M. Hollister, & V. A. Hodgkinson (eds.), *Governing, leading, and managing nonprofit organizations.* San Francisco: Jossey-Bass. (pp. 475, 501)

Clary, E. G., & Snyder, M. (1995). Motivations for volunteering and giving: A functional approach. In C. H. Hamilton & W. E. Ilchman (eds.), *Cultures of giving II: How heritage, gender, wealth, and values influence philanthropy.* Bloomington, IN: Indiana University Center on Philanthropy. (p. 475)

Clary, E. G., Snyder, M., Ridge, R. D., Copeland, J., Stukas, A. A., Haugen, J., & Miene, P. (1998). Understanding and assessing the motivations of volunteers: A functional approach. *Journal of Personality and Social Psychology,* in press. (p. 475)

Cleghorn, J. (2000). Beyond the bottom line: Redefining philanthropy in the 21st Century. *Ketchum Leaders in Philanthropy Series.* Canadian Centre for Philanthropy: Toronto. (p. 477)

Cleghorn, R. (1980, October 31). ABC News, meet the Literary Digest. *Detroit Free Press.* (p. 24)

Clifford, M. M., & Walster, E. H. (1973). The effect of physical attractiveness on teacher expectation. *Sociology of Education, 46,* 248–258. (p. 436)

Cline, V. B., Croft, R. G., & Courrier, S. (1973). Desensitization of children to television violence. *Journal of Personality and Social Psychology, 27,* 360–365. (p. 417)

Clore, G. L., Wiggins, N. H., & Itkin, G. (1975). Gain and loss in attraction: Attributions from nonverbal behavior. *Journal of Personality and Social Psychology, 31,* 706–712. (p. 448)

Coates, B., Pusser, H. E., & Goodman, I. (1976). The influence of "Sesame Street" and "Mister Rogers' Neighborhood" on children's social behavior in the preschool. *Child Development, 47,* 138–144. (p. 509)

Coats, E. J., & Feldman, R. S. (1996). Gender differences in nonverbal correlates of social status. *Personality and Social Psychology Bulletin, 22,* 1014–1022. (p. 186)

Codol, J.-P. (1976). On the so-called superior conformity of the self behavior: Twenty experimental investigations. *European Journal of Social Psychology, 5,* 457–501. (pp. 68, 73)

Cohen, B., Waugh, G., & Place, K. (1989). At the movies: An unobtrusive study of arousal attraction. *Journal of Social Psychology, 129,* 691–693. (p. 455)

Cohen, D. (1996). Law, social policy, and violence: The impact of regional cultures. *Journal of Personality and Social Psychology, 70,* 961–978. (p. 398)

Cohen, D., Nisbett, R. E., Bowdle, B. F., & Schwarz, N. (1996). Insult, aggression, and the southern culture of honor: An "Experimental Ethnography." *Journal of Personality and Social Psychology, 70,* 945–960. (p. 398)

Cohen, J. (1941). The geography of crime. *Annals of the American Academy of Political and Social Science, 217,* 29-37. (p. 402)

Cohen, M., & Davis, N. (1981). *Medication errors: Causes and prevention.* Philadelphia: G. F. Stickley Co. Cited by R. B. Cialdini (1989). Agents of influence: Bunglers, smugglers, and sleuths. Paper presented at the American Psychological Association convention. (p. 223)

Cohen, S. (1980). Training to understand TV advertising: Effects and some policy implications. Paper presented at the American Psychological Association convention. (p. 288)

Cohen, S. (1988). Psychosocial models of the role of social support in the etiology of physical disease. *Health Psychology, 7,* 269–297. (p. 591)

Cohen, S., & Rodriguez, M. S. (1995). Pathways linking affective disturbances and physical disorders. *Health Psychology, 14,* 374–380. (p. 582)

Cohen, S., & Williamson, G. M. (1991). Stress and infectious disease in humans. *Psychological Bulletin, 109,* 5–24. (p. 583)

Colasanto, D. (1989, November). Americans show commitment to helping those in need. *Gallup Report,* No. 290, pp. 17–24. (p. 501)

Colasanto, D., & Shriver, J. (1989, May). Mirror of America: Middle-aged face marital crisis. *Gallup Report* No. 284, pp. 34–38. (p. 467)

Cole, D. L. (1982). Psychology as a liberating art. *Teaching of Psychology, 9,* 23-26. (p. 563)

Coleman, L. M., Jussim, L., & Abraham, J. (1987). Students' reactions to teachers' evaluations: The unique impact of negative feedback. *Journal of Applied Social Psychology, 17,* 1051–1070. (p. 447)

Collins, N. L., & Miller, L. C. (1994). Self-disclosure and liking: A meta-analytic review. *Psychological Bulletin, 116,* 457–475. (p. 463)

Collins, R. L. (1996). For better or worse: The impact of upward social comparison on self-evaluations. *Psychological Bulletin, 119,* 51–69. (p. 394)

Colman, A. M. (1991). Crowd psychology in South African murder trials. *American Psychologist, 46,* 1071–1079. See also, A. M. Colman (1991), Psychological evidence in South African murder trials. *The Psychologist, 14,* 482–486. (p. 313)

Colombo, J. R. (Ed.) (1994). *The 1994 Canadian global almanac.* Toronto: Macmillan Canada. (p. 189)

Colvin, C. R., Block, J., & Funder, D. C. (1995). Overly-positive self evaluations and personality: Negative implications for mental health. *Journal of Personality and Social Psychology, 68,* 1152–1162. (p. 67)

Comer, D. R. (1995). A model of social loafing in real work group. *Human Relations, 48,* 647–667. (p. 303)

Converse, P. E., & Traugott, M. W. (1986). Assessing the accuracy of polls and surveys. *Science, 234,* 1094–1098. (p. 25)

Conway, F., & Siegelman, J. (1979). *Snapping: America's epidemic of sudden personality change.* New York: Delta Books. (pp. 280, 281)

Conway, M. & Howell, A. (1989). Ego-involvement leads to positive self-schema activation and to a positivity bias in information processing. *Motivation and Emotion, 13,* 159-177. (p. 39)

Conway, M., & Ross, M. (1985). Remembering one's own past: The construction of personal histories. In R. Sorrentino & E. T. Higgins (Eds.), *Handbook of motivation and cognition.* New York: Guilford. (p. 102)

Conway, M., & Ross, M. (1986). Remembering one's own past: The construction of personal histories. In R. Sorrentino & E. T. Higgins (Eds.), *Handbook of motivation and cognition.* New York: Guilford. (p. 102)

Cook, S. W. (1984). Cooperative interaction in multiethnic contexts. In N. Miller & M. B. Brewer (eds.), *Groups in contact: The psychology of desegregation.* Orlando, FL: Academic Press. (p. 545)

Cook, S. W. (1985). Experimenting on social issues: The case of school desegregation. *American Psychologist, 40,* 452–460. (p. 542)

Cook, T. D., & Curtin, T. R. (1987). The mainstream and the underclass: Why are the differences so salient and the similarities so unobtrusive? In J. C. Masters & W. P. Smith (Eds.), *Social comparison, social justice, and relative deprivation: Theoretical, empirical, and policy perspectives.* Hillsdale, N.J.: Erlbaum. (p. 370)

Cook, T. D., & Flay, B. R. (1978). The persistence of experimentally induced attitude change. In L. Berkowitz (Ed.), *Advances in experimental social psychology.* Vol. 11. New York: Academic Press. (p. 256)

Cooley, C. H. (1902). *Human nature and the social order.* New York: Schocken Books. (p. 42)

Coombs, R. H. (1991, January). Marital status and personal well-being: A literature review. *Family Relations, 40,* 97–102. (p. 594)

Cooper, H. (1983). Teacher expectation effects. In L. Bickman (Ed.), *Applied social psychology annual,* Vol. 4. Beverly Hills, Ca.: Sage. (p. 121)

Copeland, J., & Snyder, M. (in press). When counselors confirm: A functional analysis. *Personality and Social Psychology Bulletin.* (p. 565)

Costanzo, M. (1997). *Just revenge: Costs and consequences of the death penalty.* New York: St. Martin's. (p. 624)

Costanzo, M. (1998). *Just revenge.* New York: St. Martins. (pp. 384, 423)

Cota, A. A., & Dion, K. L. (1986). Salience of gender and sex composition of ad hoc groups: An experimental test of distinctiveness theory. *Journal of Personality and Social Psychology, 50,* 770–776. (p. 246)

Cottrell, N. B., Wack, D. L., Sekerak, G. J., & Rittle, R. M. (1968). Social facilitation of dominant responses by the presence of an audience and the mere presence of others. *Journal of Personality and Social Psychology, 9,* 245–250. (p. 297)

Courneya, K. S. (1995). Understanding readiness for regular physical activity in older individuals: An application of the theory of planned behavior. *Health Psychology, 14,* 80-87. (p. 135)

Courneya, K. S., & Carron, A. V. (1992). The home advantage in sport competitions: A literature review. *Journal of Sport and Exercise Psychology, 14,* 13–27. (p. 296)

Court, J. H. (1985). Sex and violence: A ripple effect. In N. M. Malamuth & E. Donnerstein (Eds.), *Pornography and sexual aggression.* New York: Academic Press. (p. 406)

Courtney, J. G., Longnecker, M. P., Theorell, T., & de Verdier, M. G. (1993). Stressful life events and the risk of colorectal cancer. *Epidemiology, 4,* 407–414. (p. 583)

Cousins, N. (1989). *Head first: the biology of hope.* New York: Dutton. (p. 584)

Cousins, N. (1978, September 16). The taxpayers revolt: Act two. *Saturday Review,* p. 56. (p. 127)

Coyne, J. C., Burchill, S. A. L., & Stiles, W. B. (1991). In C. R. Snyder & D. O. Forsyth (Eds.), *Handbook of social and clinical psychology: The health perspective.* New York: Pergamon. (p. 572)

Crabb, P. B., & Bielawski, D. (1994). The social representation of material culture and gender in children's books. *Sex Roles, 30,* 6979. (p. 198)

Craig, M. E. (1990). Coercive sexuality in dating relationships: A situational model. *Clinical Psychology Review, 10,* 395–423. (p. 408)

Crandall, C. S. (1988). Social contagion of binge eating. *Journal of Personality and Social Psychology, 55,* 588–598. (p. 232)

Crandall, C. S. (1994). Prejudice against fat people: Ideology and self-interest. *Journal of Personality and Social Psychology, 66,* 882–894. (p. 363)

Crano, W. D., & Mellon, P. M. (1978). Causal influence of teachers' expectations on children's academic performance: A cross-legged panel analysis. *Journal of Educational Psychology, 70,* 39–49. (p. 120)

Crawford, T. J. (1974). Sermons on racial tolerance and the parish neighborhood context. *Journal of Applied Social Psychology, 4,* 1–23. (p. 268)

Crocker, J. (1981). Judgment of covariation by social perceivers. *Psychological Bulletin, 90,* 272–292. (p. 114)

Crocker, J. (1994, October 14). Who cares what they think? Reflected and deflected appraisal. Presentation to the Society of Experimental Social Psychology meeting. (p. 44)

Crocker, J., & Gallo, L. (1985). The self-enhancing effect of downward comparison. Paper presented at the American Psychological Association convention. (p. 395)

Crocker, J., Hannah, D. B., & Weber, R. (1983). Personal memory and causal attributions. *Journal of Personality and Social Psychology, 44,* 55–56. (p. 375)

Crocker, J., & Luhtanen, R. (1990). Collective self-esteem and ingroup bias. *Journal of Personality and Social Psychology, 58,* 60–67. (p. 355)

Crocker, J., Luhtanen, R., Blaine, B., & Broadnax, S. (1994). Collective self-esteem and psychological well-being among White, Black, and Asian college students. *Personality and Social Psychology Bulletin, 20,* 503–513. (p. 44)

Crocker, J., & McGraw, K. M. (1984). What's good for the goose is not good for the gander: Solo status as an obstacle to occupational achievement for males and females. *American Behavioral Scientist, 27,* 357–370. (p. 367)

Crocker, J., Thompson, L. L., McGraw, K. M., & Ingerman, C. (1987). Downward comparison, prejudice, and evaluations of others: Effects of self-esteem and threat. *Journal of Personality and Social Psychology, 52,* 907–916. (p. 361)

Crosby, F., Bromley, S., & Saxe, L. (1980). Recent unobtrusive studies of black and white discrimination and prejudice: A literature review. *Psychological Bulletin, 87,* 546–563. (p. 341)

Crosby, F. J. (Ed.) (1987). *Spouse, parent, worker: On gender and multiple roles.* New Haven, CT: Yale University Press. (p. 594)

Crosby, F., Pufall, A., Snyder, R. C., O'Connell, M., & Whalen, P. (1989). The denial of personal disadvantage among

you, me, and all the other ostriches. In M. Crawford & M. Gentry (Eds.), *Gender and thought.* New York: Springer-Verlag. (p. 347)

Cross, P. (1977). Not *can* but *will* college teaching be improved? *New Directions for Higher Education,* Spring, No. 17, pp. 1–15. (p. 68)

Cross, S. E., Liao, M-H., & Josephs, R. (1992). A cross-cultural test of the self-evaluation maintenance model. Paper presented at the American Psychological Association convention. (p. 43)

Cross-National Collaborative Group (1992). The changing rate of major depression. *Journal of the American Medical Association, 268,* 3098–3105. (pp. 393, 574)

Crossen, C. (1993). *Tainted truth: The manipulation of face in America.* New York: Simon & Schuster. (p. 27)

Crowley, G. (1996, June 3). The biology of beauty. *Newsweek,* pp. 61-69. (p. 435)

Croxton, J. S., Eddy, T., & Morrow, N. (1984). Memory biases in the reconstruction of interpersonal encounters. *Journal of Social and Clinical Psychology, 2,* 348–354. (p. 103)

Croxton, J. S., & Miller, A. G. (1987). Behavioral disconfirmation and the observer bias. *Journal of Social Behavior and Personality, 2,* 145-152. (p. 91)

Croxton, J. S., & Morrow, N. (1984). What does it take to reduce observer bias? *Psychological Reports, 55,* 135–138. (p. 91)

Crutchfield, R. A. (1955). Conformity and character. *American Psychologist, 10,* 191–198. (p. 214)

Cunningham, J. D. (1981). Self-disclosure intimacy: Sex, sex-of-target, cross-national, and generational differences. *Personality and Social Psychology Bulletin, 7,* 314–319. (p. 465)

Cunningham, M. R. (1986). Measuring the physical in physical attractiveness: Quasi-experiments on the sociobiology of female facial beauty. *Journal of Personality and Social Psychology, 50,* 925–935. (p. 438)

Cunningham, M. R., Roberts, A. R., Barbee, A. P., Druen, P. B., & Wu, C-H. (1995). "Their ideas of beauty are, on the whole, the same as ours": Consistency and variability in the cross-cultural perception of female physical attractivness. *Journal of Personality and Social Psychology, 68,* 261–279. (p. 438)

Cunningham, M. R., Shaffer, D. R., Barbee, A. P., Wolff, P. L., & Kelley, D. J. (1990). Separate processes in the relation of elation and depression to helping: Social versus personal concerns. *Journal of Experimental Social Psychology, 26,* 13–33. (p. 498)

Cutler, B. L., Moran, G., & Narvy, D. J. (1992). Jury selection in insanity defense cases. *Journal of Research in Personality, 26,* 165–182. (p. 623)

Cutler, B. L., & Penrod, S. D. (1988). Context reinstatement and eyewitness identification. In G. M. Davies & D. M. Thomson (Eds.), *Context reinstatement and eyewitness identification.* New York: Wiley. *(a)* (p. 610)

Cutler, B. L., & Penrod, S. D. (1988). Improving the reliability of eyewitness identification: Lineup construction and presentation. *Journal of Applied Psychology, 73,* 281–290. *(b)* (p. 610)

Cutler, B. L., & Penrod, S. D. (1995). Mistaken identification: The eyewitness, psychology, and the law. New York: Cambridge University Press. (p. 607)

Cutler, B. L., Penrod, S. D., & Dexter, H. R. (1989). The eyewitness, the expert psychologist and the jury. *Law and Human Behavior, 13,* 311–332. (pp. 612, 618)

Cutler, B. L., Penrod, S. D., & Stuve, T. E. (1988). Juror decision making in eyewitness identification cases. *Law and Human Behavior, 12,* 41–55. (p. 611)

Cutrona, C. E. (1986). Behavioral manifestations of social support: A microanalytic investigation. *Journal of Personality and Social Psychology, 51,* 201–208. (p. 591)

Dabbs, J. M., & Janis, I. L. (1965). Why does eating while reading facilitate opinion change? An experimental inquiry. *Journal of Experimental Social Psychology, 1,* 133–144. (p. 261)

Dabbs, J. M., Jr. (1992). Testosterone measurements in social and clinical psychology. *Journal of Social and Clinical Psychology, 11,* 302–321. (p. 388)

Dabbs, J. M., Jr., Carr, T. S., Frady, R. L., & Riad, J. K. (1995). Testosterone, crime, and misbehavior among 692 male prison inmates. *Personality and Individual Differences, 18,* 627–633. (pp. 194, 388)

Dabbs, J. M., Jr., de La Rue, D., & Williams, P. M. (1990). Testosterone and occupational choice: Actors, ministers, and other men. *Journal of Personality and Social Psychology, 59,* 1261–1265. (p. 194)

Dabbs, J. M., Jr., & Hargrove, M. F. (1998). Age, testosterone, and behavior among female prison inmates. *Psychosomatic Medicine,* in press. (p. 388)

Dabbs, J. M., Jr., Hargrove, M. F., & Heusel, C. (1993). Testosterone differences among college fraternities: Well-behaved vs. rambunctious. Unpublished manuscript, Georgia State University. (p. 194)

Dabbs, J. M., Jr., & Morris, R. (1990). Testosterone, social class, and antisocial behavior in a sample of 4,462 men. *Psychological Science, 1,* 209–211. (p. 388)

Dabbs, J. M., Jr., Strong, R., & Milun, R. (1998). Exploring the mind of testosterone: A beeper study. Journal of Research in Personality, in press. (p. 388)

Dallas, M. E. W., & Baron, R. S. (1985). Do psychotherapists use a confirmatory strategy during interviewing? *Journal of Social and Clinical Psychology, 3,* 106–122. (p. 565)

Daly, M., & Wilson, M. (1989). Killing the competition: Female/female and male/male homicide. *Human Nature, 1,* 81–107. (p. 189)

Damon, W. (1995). *Greater Expectations: Overcoming the Culture of Indulgence in America's Homes and Schools.* New York: Free Press. (p. 42)

Darley, J. (1996). How organizations socialize individuals into evil-doing. In D. Messick and Ann Tenbrunsel (eds.), *Codes of conduct: Behavioral research into business ethics.* New York: Russell Sage. (p. 228)

Darley, J. M. (1995). Book review essay. *Political Psychology,* in press. (p. 499)

Darley, J. M., & Batson, C. D. (1973). From Jerusalem to Jericho: A study of situational and dispositional variables in helping behavior. *Journal of Personality and Social Psychology, 27,* 100–108. (p. 494)

Darley, J. M., & Berscheid, E. (1967). Increased liking as a result of the anticipation of personal contact. *Human Relations, 20,* 29–40. (p. 430)

Darley, J. M., & Gross, P. H. (1983). A hypothesis-confirming bias in labelling effects. *Journal of Personality and Social Psychology, 44,* 20–33. (p. 378)

Darley, J. M., & Latané, B. (1968). Bystander intervention in emergencies: Diffusion of responsibility. *Journal of Personality and Social Psychology, 8,* 377–383. (pp. 486, 487, 490)

Darley, J. M., Teger, A. I., & Lewis, L. D. (1973). Do groups always inhibit individuals' response to potential emergencies? *Journal of Personality and Social Psychology, 26,* 395–399. (p. 492)

Darley, S., & Cooper, J. (1972). Cognitive consequences of forced noncompliance. *Journal of Personality and Social Psychology, 24,* 321–326. (p. 288)

Darrow, C. (1933), cited by E. H. Sutherland & D. R. Cressy, *Principles of criminology.* Philadelphia: Lippincott, 1966, p. 442. (p. 613)

Darwin, C. (1859/1988). *The origin of species.* Vol. 15 of *The Works of Charles Darwin,* edited by P. H. Barrett & R. B. Freeman. New York: New York University Press. (p. 173)

Dashiell, J. F. (1930). An experimental analysis of some group effects. *Journal of Abnormal and Social Psychology, 25,* 190–199. (p. 293)

Davie, M. (1987). *The Titanic: The Full Story of a Tragedy.* London: Collins.(p. 319)

Davies, M. F. (1997). Belief persistence after evidential discrediting: The impact of generated versus provided explanations on the likelihood of

discredited outcomes. *Journal of Experimental Social Psychology, 33,* 561–578. (p. 98)

Davila, J., Bradbury, T. N., Cohan, C. L., & Tochluk, S. (1997). Marital functioning and depressive symptoms: Evidence for a stress generation model. *Journal of Personality and Social Psychology, 73,* 849–861. (p. 594)

Davis, B. M., & Gilbert, L. A. (1989). Effect of dispositional and situational influences on women's dominance expression in mixed-sex dyads. *Journal of Personality and Social Psychology, 57,* 294–300. (p. 187)

Davis, C. G., Lehman, D. R., Silver, R. C., Wortman, C. B., & Ellard, J. H. (1996). Self-blame following a traumatic event: The role of perceived avoidability. *Personality and Social Psychology Bulletin, 22,* 557–567. (p. 113)

Davis, C. G., Lehman, D. R., Wortman, C. B., Silver, R. C., & Thompson, S. C. (1995). The undoing of traumatic life events. *Personality and Social Psychology Bulletin, 21,* 109–124. (p. 113)

Davis, J. H., Kameda, T., Parks, C., Stasson, M., & Zimmerman, S. (1989). Some social mechanics of group decision making: The distribution of opinion, polling sequence, and implications for consensus. *Journal of Personality and Social Psychology, 57,* 1000–1012. (p. 625)

Davis, J. H., Kerr, N. L., Atkin, R. S., Holt, R., & Meek, D. (1975). The decision processes of 6- and 12-person mock juries assigned unanimous and two-thirds majority rules. *Journal of Personality and Social Psychology, 32,* 1–14. (pp. 625, 628)

Davis, J. H., Kerr, N. L., Strasser, G., Meek, D., & Holt, R. (1977). Victim consequences, sentence severity, and decision process in mock juries. *Organizational Behavior and Human Performance, 18,* 346–365. (p. 625)

Davis, J. H., Stasson, M. F., Parks, C. D., Hulbert, L., Kameda, T., Zimmerman, S. K., & Ono, K. (1993). Quantitative decisions by groups and individuals: Voting procedures and monetary awards by mock civil juries. *Journal of Experimental Social Psychology, 29,* 326–346. (p. 284)

Davis, K. E. (1985, February). Near and dear: Friendship and love compared. *Psychology Today,* pp. 22–30. (p. 460)

Davis, K. E., & Jones, E. E. (1960). Changes in interpersonal perception as a means of reducing cognitive dissonance. *Journal of Abnormal and Social Psychology, 61,* 402–410. (p. 146)

Davis, L., & Greenlees, C. (1992). Social loafing revisited: Factors that mitigate—and reverse—performance loss. Paper presented at the Southwestern Psychological Association convention. (p. 303)

Davis, M. H. (1979). The case for attributional egotism. Paper presented at the American Psychological Association convention. (p. 57)

Davis, M. H., & Franzoi, S. L. (1986). Adolescent loneliness, self-disclosure, and private self-consciousness: A longitudinal investigation. *Journal of Personality and Social Psychology*, **51**, 595–608. (p. 575)

Davis, M. H., & Stephan, W. G. (1980). Attributions for exam performance. *Journal of Applied Social Psychology*, **10**, 235–248. (p. 57)

Dawes, R. M. (1976). Shallow psychology. In J. S. Carroll & J. W. Payne (Eds.), *Cognition and social behavior*. Hillsdale, N.J.: Lawrence Erlbaum. (p. 567)

Dawes, R. M. (1980). Social dilemmas. *Annual Review of Psychology*, **31**, 169–193. (p. 523)

Dawes, R. M. (1980). You can't systematize human judgment: Dyslexia. In R. A. Shweder (Ed.), *New directions for methodology of social and behavioral science: Fallible judgment in behavioral research*. San Francisco: Jossey-Bass. (pp. 125, 525)

Dawes, R. M. (1989, January). Resignation letter to the American Psychological Association. *APS Observer*, pp. 14–15. (p. 567)

Dawes, R. M. (1990). The potential non-falsity of the false consensus effect. In R. M. Hogarth (Ed.), *Insights in decision making: A tribute to Hillel J. Einhorn*. Chicago: University of Chicago Press. (p. 61)

Dawes, R. M. (1991). Social dilemmas, economic self-interest, and evolutionary theory. In D. R. Brown & J. E. Keith Smith (Eds.), *Frontiers of mathematical psychology: Essays in honor of Clyde Coombs*. New York: Springer-Verlag. (p. 517)

Dawes, R. M. (1994). *House of cards: Psychology and psychotherapy built on myth*. New York: Free Press. (pp. 42, 523, 566)

Dawes, R. M., Faust, D., & Meehl, P. E. (1989). Clinical versus actuarial judgment. *Science*, **243**, 1668–1674. (p. 566)

Dawes, R. M., McTavish, J., & Shaklee, H. (1977). Behavior, communication, and assumptions about other people's behavior in a commons dilemma situation. *Journal of Personality and Social Psychology*, **35**, 1–11. (p. 525)

Dawkins, R. (1976). *The selfish gene*. New York: Oxford University Press. (pp. 483, 484)

Dawson, N. V., Arkes, H. R., Siciliano, C., Blinkhorn, R., Lakshmanan, M., & Petrelli, M. (1988). Hindsight bias: An impediment to accurate probability estimation in clinicopathologic conferences. *Medical Decision Making*, **8**, 259–264. (p. 19)

DeAngelis, T. (1993, September). Controversial diagnosis is voted into latest DSM. *Monitor*, pp. 32–33. (p. 580)

Deaux, K., & LaFrance, M. (1998). Gender. In D. Gilbert, S. Fiske, and G. Lindzey (eds.), *The handbook of social psychology*, 4th edition. Hillsdale, NJ: Erlbaum. (p. 188)

Deci, E. L., & Ryan, R. M. (1985). *Intrinsic motivation and self-determination in human behavior*. New York: Plenum. (p. 161)

Deci, E. L., & Ryan, R. M. (1987). The support of autonomy and the control of behavior. *Journal of Personality and Social Psychology*, **53**, 1024–1037. (p. 53)

Deci, E. L., & Ryan, R. M. (1991). A motivational approach to self: Integration in personality. In R. Dienstbier (Ed.) Vol. 38. Perspectives on motivation (pp. 237–288), Lincoln, NE: University of Nebraska Press. *Nebraska Symposium on Motivation*. (pp. 159, 161)

Deci, E. L., & Ryan, R. M. (1997). Behaviorists in search of the null: Revisiting the undermining of intrinsic motivation by extrinsic rewards. Unpublished manuscript, University of Rochester. (p. 159)

De Dreu, C. K. W., Nauta, A., & Van de Vliert, E. (1995). Self-serving evaluations of conflict behavior and escalation of the dispute. *Journal of Applied Social Psychology*, **25**, 2049–2066. (p. 532)

de Jong-Gierveld, J. (1987). Developing and testing a model of loneliness. *Journal of Personality and Social Psychology*, **53**, 119–128. (p. 575)

Dekeseredy, W. S., Schwartz, M. D., & Tait, K. (1993). Sexual assault and stranger aggression on a Canadian university campus. *Sex Roles*, **28**, 263–277. (p. 408)

Delgado, J. (1973). In M. Pines, *The brain changers*. New York: Harcourt Brace Jovanovich. (p. 137)

Dengerink, H. A., & Myers, J. D. (1977). Three effects of failure and depression on subsequent aggression. *Journal of Personality and Social Psychology*, **35**, 88–96. (p. 403)

DePaulo, B. M., Charlton, K., Cooper, H., Lindsay, J. J., & Muhlenbruck, L. (1997). The accuracy-confidence correlation in the detection of deception. *Personality and Social Psychology Review*, **1**, 346–357. (p. 107)

DePaulo, B. M., Kenny, D. A., Hoover, C. W., Webb, W., & Oliver, P. V. (1987). Accuracy of person perception: Do people know what kinds of impressions they convey? *Journal of Personality and Social Psychology*, **52**, 303–315. (p. 66)

Derlega, V., Metts, S., Petronio, S., & Margulis, S. T. (1993). *Self-disclosure*. Newbury Park, CA: Sage. (p. 463)

Dermer, M., Cohen, S. J., Jacobsen, E., & Anderson, E. A. (1979). Evaluative judgments of aspects of life as a function of vicarious exposure to hedonic extremes. *Journal of Personality and Social Psychology*, **37**, 247–260. (p. 395)

Dermer, M., & Pyszczynski, T. A. (1978). Effects of erotica upon men's loving and liking responses for women they love. *Journal of Personality and Social Psychology*, **36**, 1302–1309. (p. 454)

Desforges, D. M., Lord, C. G., Ramsey, S. L., Mason, J. A., Van Leeuwen, M. D., West, S. C. & Lepper, M. R. (1991). Effects of structured cooperative contact on changing negative attitudes toward stigmatized social groups. *Journal of Personality and Social Psychology*, 60, 531-544. (p. 542)

Desforges, D. M., Lord, C. G., Pugh, M. A., Sia, T. L., Scarberry, N. C., & Ratcliff, C. D. (1997). Role of group representativeness in the generalization part of the contact hypothesis. *Basic and Applied Social Psychology*, **19**, 183–204. (p. 544)

Desforges, D. M., Lord, C. G., Ramsey, S. L., Mason, J. A., Van Leeuwen, M. D., West, S. C., & Lepper, M. R. (1991). Effects of structured cooperative contact on changing negative attitudes toward stigmatized social groups. *Journal of Personality and Social Psychology*, **60**, 531–544. (p. 544)

DeStefano, L., & Colasanto, D. (1990, February). Unlike 1975, today most Americans think men have it better. *Gallup Poll Monthly*, No. 293, 25–36. (p. 185)

DeSteno, D. A., & Salovey, P. (1996). Jealousy and the characteristics of one's rival: A self-evaluation maintenance perspective. *Personality and Social Psychology Bulletin*, **22**, 920–932. (p. 65)

Deutsch, M. (1985). *Distributive justice: A social psychological perspective*. New Haven: Yale University Press. (pp. 528, 544)

Deutsch, M. (1986). Folie à deux: A psychological perspective on Soviet-American relations. In M. P. Kearns (Ed.), *Persistent patterns and emergent structures in a waving century*. New York: Praeger. (p. 531)

Deutsch, M. (1990). Psychological roots of moral exclusion. *Journal of Social Issues*, **46**, 21–25. (p. 508)

Deutsch, M. (1993). Educating for a peaceful world. *American Psychologist*, **48**, 510–517. (p. 554)

Deutsch, M. (1994). Constructive conflict resolution: Principles, training, and research. *Journal of Social Issues*, **50**, 13–32. (p. 544)

Deutsch, M., & Gerard, H. B. (1955). A study of normative and informational social influence upon individual judgment. *Journal of Abnormal and Social Psychology*, **51**, 629–636. (pp. 235, 237)

Deutsch, M., & Krauss, R. M. (1960). The effect of threat upon interpersonal bargaining. *Journal of Abnormal and Social Psychology*, **61**, 181–189. (p. 522)

deVaux, R. (1965). *Ancient Israel (Vol. 2): Religious institutions*. New York: McGraw-Hill. (p. 495)

Devine, P. G. (1989). Stereotypes and prejudice: Their automatic and controlled components. *Journal of Personality and Social Psychology*, **56**, 5–18. (p. 342)

Devine, P. G. (1995). Prejudice and outgroup perception. In A. Tesser (ed.), *Advanced social psychology*. New York: McGraw-Hill. (p. 342)

Devine, P. G., Evett, S. R., & Vasquez-Suson, K. A. (1996). Exploring the interpersonal dynamics of intergroup contact. In R. Sorrentino & E. T. Higgins (eds.), *Handbook of motivation and cognition: The interpersonal content*, vol. 3. New York: Guilford. (p. 369)

Devine, P. G., Evett, S. R., & Vasquez-Suson, K. A. (in press). Exploring the interpersonal dynamics of intergroup contact. In R. Sorrentino & E. T. Higgins (eds.), *Handbook of motivation and cognition: The interpersonal content*, vol. 3. New York: Guilford. (p. 342)

Devine, P. G., Hirt, E. R., & Gehrke, E. M. (1990). Diagnostic and confirmation strategies in trait hypothesis testing. *Journal of Personality and Social Psychology*, **58**, 952–963. (p. 565)

Devine, P. G., & Malpass, R. S. (1985). Orienting strategies in differential face recognition. *Personality and Social Psychology Bulletin*, **11**, 33–40. (p. 367)

de Vries, N. K., & Van Knippenberg, A. (1987). Biased and unbiased self-evaluations of ability: The effects of further testing. *British Journal of Social Psychology*, **26**, 9–15. (p. 73)

Dexter, H. R., Cutler, B. L., & Moran, G. (1992). A test of voir dire as a remedy for the prejudicial effects of pretrial publicity. *Journal of Applied Social Psychology*, **22**, 819–832. (p. 618)

Dhawan, M., Roseman, I. J., Naidu, R. K., Thapa, K., & Rettek, S. I. (1995). Self-concepts across two cultures: India and the United States. *Journal of Cross-Cultural Psychology*, **26**, 606–621. (p. 43)

Diamond, J. (1996, December). The best ways to sell sex. *Discover*, pp. 78–86. (p. 440)

Diamond, S. S. (1993). Instructing on death: Psychologists, juries, and judges. *American Psychologist*, **48**, 423–434. (p. 622)

Diekmann, K. A., Samuels, S. M., Ross, L., & Bazerman, M. H. (1997). Self-interest and fairness in problems of resource allocation: Allocators versus recipients. *Journal of Personality and Social Psychology*, **72**, 1061–1074. (pp. 57, 527)

Diener, E. (1976). Effects of prior destructive behavior, anonymity, and group presence on deindividuation and aggression. *Journal of Personality and Social Psychology*, **33**, 497–507. (pp. 306, 308)

Diener, E. (1979). Deindividuation, self-awareness, and disinhibition. *Journal of Personality and Social Psychology*, **37**, 1160–1171. (p. 308)

Diener, E. (1980). Deindividuation: The absence of self-awareness and self-regulation in group members. In P. Paulus (Ed.), *The psychology of group influence*. Hillsdale, N.J.: Erlbaum. (p. 308)

Diener, E., & Crandall, R. (1979). An evaluation of the Jamaican anticrime program. *Journal of Applied Social Psychology*, **9**, 135–146. (p. 424)

Diener, E., Fraser, S. C., Beaman, A. L., & Kelem, R. T. (1976). Effects of deindividuation variables on stealing among Halloween trick-or-treaters. *Journal of Personality and Social Psychology*, **33**, 178–183. (p. 307)

Diener, E., & Wallbom, M. (1976). Effects of self-awareness on antinormative behavior. *Journal of Research in Personality*, **10**, 107–111. (pp. 136, 308)

Dill, J. C., & Anderson, C. A. (1995). Effects of frustration justification on hostile aggression. *Aggressive Behavior*, **21**, 359–369. (p. 390)

Dill, J. C., & Anderson, C. A. (1998). Loneliness, shyness, and depression: The etiology and interrelationships of everyday problems in living. In T. Joiner & J. C. Coyne (eds.), *Recent advances in interpersonal approaches to depression*. Washington, D.C.: American Psychological Association. (pp. 575, 576)

Dillehay, R. C., & Nietzel, M. T. (1980). Constructing a science of jury behavior. In L. Wheeler (Ed.), *Review of personality and social psychology* (Vol. 1). Beverly Hills, Calif.: Sage Publications. (p. 629)

Dindia, K., & Allen, M. (1992). Sex differences in self-disclosure: A meta-analysis. *Psychological Bulletin*, **112**, 106–124. (p. 184)

Dion, K. K. (1972). Physical attractiveness and evaluations of children's transgressions. *Journal of Personality and Social Psychology*, **24**, 207–213. (p. 436)

Dion, K. K. (1973). Young children's stereotyping of facial attractiveness. *Developmental Psychology*, **9**, 183–188. (p. 436)

Dion, K. K. (1979). Physical attractiveness and interpersonal attraction. In M. Cook & G. Wilson (Eds.), *Love and attraction*. New York: Pergamon Press. (p. 436)

Dion, K. K., & Berscheid, E. (1974). Physical attractiveness and peer perception among children. *Sociometry*, **37**, 1–12. (p. 436)

Dion, K. K., & Dion, K. L. (1985). Personality, gender, and the phenomenology of romantic love. In P. R. Shaver (Ed.), *Review of personality and social psychology*, vol. 6. Beverly Hills, Ca.: Sage. (p. 456)

Dion, K. K., & Dion, K. L. (1991). Psychological individualism and romantic love. *Journal of Social Behavior and Personality*, **6**, 17–33. (p. 458)

Dion, K. K., & Dion, K. L. (1993). Individualistic and collectivistic perspectives on gender and the cultural context of love and intimacy. *Journal of Social Issues*, **49**, 53–69. (p. 468)

Dion, K. K., & Dion, K. L. (1996). Cultural perspectives on romantic love. *Personal Relationships*, **3**, 5–17. (p. 458)

Dion, K. K., & Stein, S. (1978). Physical attractiveness and interpersonal influence. *Journal of Experimental Social Psychology*, **14**, 97–109. (p. 258)

Dion, K. L. (1979). Intergroup conflict and intragroup cohesiveness. In W. G. Austin, & S. Worchel (Eds.), *The social psychology of intergroup relations*. Monterey, Calif.: Brooks/Cole. (p. 538)

Dion, K. L. (1985). Responses to perceived discrimination and relative deprivation. In J. M. Olson, C. P. Herman, & M. P. Zanna (Eds.), *Relative deprivation and social comparison: The Ontario symposium*, vol. 4. Hillsdale, N.J.: Erlbaum. (p. 394)

Dion, K. L. (1987). What's in a title? The Ms. stereotype and images of women's titles of address. *Psychology of Women Quarterly*, **11**, 21–36. (p. 336)

Dion, K. L., & Cota, A. A. (1991). The Ms. stereotype: Its domain and the role of explicitness in title preference. *Psychology of Women Quarterly*, **15**, 403–410. (p. 336)

Dion, K. L., & Dion, K. K. (1988). Romantic love: Individual and cultural perspectives. In R. J. Sternberg & M. L. Barnes (Eds.), *The psychology of love*. New Haven, Conn.: Yale University Press. (p. 458)

Dion, K. L., Dion, K. K., & Keelan, J. P. (1990). Appearance anxiety as a dimension of social-evaluative anxiety: Exploring the ugly duckling syndrome. *Contemporary Social Psychology*, **14**(4), 220–224. (p. 435)

Dion, K. L., & Kawakami, K. (1996). *Canadian Journal of Behavioural Science*, **28**, 203–213. (p. 347)

Dion, K. L., & Schuller, R. A. (1991). The Ms. stereotype: Its generality and its relation to managerial and marital status stereotypes. *Canadian Journal of Behavioural Science*, **23**, 25–40. (p. 336)

Ditto, P. H. (1994). Walking the line between passion and reason: Motivated judgment in an adaptive context. Paper presented to the American Psychological Society convention. (p. 63)

Ditto, P. H., & Lopez, D. F. (1992). Motivated skepticism: Use of differential decision criteria for preferred and nonpreferred conclusions. *Journal of Personality and Social Psychology*, **63**, 568–584. (p. 95)

Ditto, P. H., Scepansky, J. A., Munro, G. D., Apanovitch, A. M., & Lockhart, L. K. (1997). Motivated sensitivity to preference-inconsistent information.

Unpublished manuscript, Kent State University. (p. 84)

Dixon, B. (1986, April). Dangerous thoughts: How we think and feel can make us sick. *Science 86*, pp. 63–66. (p. 583)

Dohrenwend, B., Pearlin, L., Clayton, P., Hamburg, B., Dohrenwend, B. P., Riley, M., & Rose, R. (1982). Report on stress and life events. In G. R. Elliott & C. Eisdorfer (Eds.), *Stress and human health: Analysis and implications of research* (A study by the Institute of Medicine/National Academy of Sciences). New York: Springer. (p. 591)

Doise, W. (1986). *Levels of explanation in social psychology.* Cambridge: Cambridge University Press. (p. 14)

Dolinski, D., & Nawrat, R. (1998). "Fear-then-relief" procedure for producing compliance: Beware when the danger is over. *Journal of Experimental Social Psychology, 34,* 27–50. (p. 498)

Dollard, J., Doob, L., Miller, N., Mowrer, O. H., & Sears, R. R. (1939). *Frustration and aggression.* New Haven, Conn.: Yale University Press. (pp. 389, 390)

Donnerstein, E. (1980). Aggressive erotica and violence against women. *Journal of Personality and Social Psychology, 39,* 269–277. (pp. 407, 408)

Donnerstein, E. (1998). Why do we have those new ratings on television. Invited address to the National Institute on the Teaching of Psychology. (pp. 411, 415)

Donnerstein, E., & Berkowitz, L. (1981). Victim reactions in aggressive erotic films as a factor in violence against women. *Journal of Personality and Social Psychology, 41,* 710–724. (p. 407)

Donnerstein, E., Linz, D., & Penrod, S. (1987). *The question of pornography.* London: Free Press. (pp. 406, 409)

Doob, A. N., & Kirshenbaum, H. M. (1973). Bias in police lineups—partial remembering. *Journal of Police Science and Administration, 1,* 287–293. (p. 610)

Doob, A. N., & McLaughlin, D. S. (1989). Ask and you shall be given: Request size and donations to a good cause. *Journal of Applied Social Psychology, 19,* 1049–1056. (p. 508)

Doob, A. N., & Roberts, J. (1988). Public attitudes toward sentencing in Canada. In N. Walker & M. Hough (Eds.), *Sentencing and the public.* London: Gower. (p. 111)

Doty, R. M., Peterson, B. E., & Winter, D. G. (1991). Threat and authoritarianism in the United States, 1978–1987. *Journal of Personality and Social Psychology, 61,* 629–640. (p. 363)

Douglass, F. (1845/1960). *Narrative of the life of Frederick Douglass, an American slave: Written by himself.* (B. Quarles, Ed.). Cambridge, Mass.: Harvard University Press. (p. 140)

Dovidio, J. F. (1991). The empathy-altruism hypothesis: Paradigm and promise. *Psychological Inquiry, 2,* 126–128. (p. 480)

Dovidio, J. F., Allen, J. L., & Schroeder, D. A. (1990). Specificity of empathy-induced helping: Evidence for altruistic motivation. *Journal of Personality and Social Psychology, 59,* 249–260. (p. 479)

Dovidio, J. F., Gaertner, S. L., Anastasio, P. A., & Sanitioso, R. (1992). Cognitive and motivational bases of bias: Implications of aversive racism for attitudes toward Hispanics. In S. Knouse, P. Rosenfeld, & A. Culbertson (Eds.), *Hispanics in the workplace.* Newbury Park, CA: Sage. (p. 342)

Dovidio, J. R., Brigham, J. C., Johnson, B. T., & Gaertner, S. L. (1996). Stereotyping, prejudice, and discrimination: Another look. In N. Macrae, M. Hewstone, & C. Stangor (eds.), *Stereotypes and stereotyping.* New York: Guilford. (pp. 337, 364)

Downs, A. C., & Lyons, P. M. (1991). Natural observations of the links between attractiveness and initial legal judgments. *Personality and Social Psychology Bulletin, 17,* 541–547. (pp. 614, 615)

Drabman, R. S., & Thomas, M. H. (1974). Does media violence increase children's toleration of real-life aggression? *Developmental Psychology, 10,* 418–421. (p. 418)

Drabman, R. S., & Thomas, M. H. (1975). Does TV violence breed indifference? *Journal of Communications, 25*(4), 86–89. (p. 418)

Drabman, R. S., & Thomas, M. H. (1976). Does watching violence on television cause apathy? *Pediatrics, 57,* 329–331. (p. 418)

Draguns, J. G. (1990). Normal and abnormal behavior in cross-cultural perspective: Specifying the nature of their relationship. *Nebraska Symposium on Motivation 1989, 37,* 235–277. (p. 574)

Driedger, L. (1975). In search of cultural identity factors: A comparison of ethnic students. *Canadian Review of Sociology and Anthropology, 12,* 150–161. (p. 545)

Driskell, J. E., & Mullen, B. (1990). Status, expectations, and behavior: A meta-analytic review and test of the theory. *Personality and Social Psychology Bulletin, 16,* 541–553. (p. 233)

Druckman, D., & Bjork, R. A. (eds.). (1994). Cooperative learning. Chapter 5 in *Learning, remembering, believing: Enhancing human performance.* Washington, DC: National Academy Press. (p. 542)

Dryer, D. C., & Horowitz, L. M. (1997). When do opposites attract? Interpersonal complementarity versus similarity. *Journal of Personality and Social Psychology, 72,* 592–603. (p. 446)

Duck, J. M., Hogg, M. A., & Terry, D. J. (1995). Me, us and them: political identification and the third-person effect in the 1993 Australian federal election. *European Journal of Social Psychology, 25,* 195–215. (p. 269)

Duclos, S. E., Laird, J. D., Schneider, E., Sexter, M., Stern, L., & Van Lighten, O. (1989). Emotion-specific effects of facial expressions and postures on emotional experience. *Journal of Personality and Social Psychology, 57,* 100–108. (p. 157)

Duncan, B. L. (1976). Differential social perception and attribution of intergroup violence: Testing the lower limits of stereotyping of blacks. *Journal of Personality and Social Psychology, 34,* 590–598. (p. 341)

Dunning, D. (1995). Trait importance and modifiability as factors influencing self-assessment and self-enhancement motives. *Personality and Social Psychology Bulletin, 21,* 1297–1306. (p. 64)

Dunning, D., Griffin, D. W., Milojkovic, J. D., & Ross, L. (1990). The overconfidence effect in social prediction. *Journal of Personality and Social Psychology, 58,* 568–581. (p. 106)

Dunning, D., & Hayes, A. F. (1996). Evidence for egocentric comparison in social judgment. *Journal of Personality and Social Psychology, 71,* 213–229. (p. 39)

Dunning, D., Meyerowitz, J. A., & Holzberg, A. D. (1989). Ambiguity and self-evaluation. *Journal of Personality and Social Psychology, 57,* 1082–1090. (p. 59)

Dunning, D., Perie, M., & Story, A. L. (1991). Self-serving prototypes of social categories. *Journal of Personality and Social Psychology, 61,* 957–968. (p. 59)

Dunning, D., & Ross, L. (1988). Overconfidence in individual and group prediction: Is the collective any wiser? Unpublished manuscript, Cornell University. (p. 324)

Dunning, D., & Sherman, D. A. (1997). Stereotypes and tacit inference. *Journal of Personality and Social Psychology, 73,* 459–471. (p. 378)

Dunning, D., & Stern, L. B. (1994). Distinguishing accurate from inaccurate eyewitness identifications via inquiries about decision processes. *Journal of Personality and Social Psychology, 67,* 818–835. (p. 610)

Dutton, D. G. (1971). Reactions of restauranteurs to blacks and whites violating restaurant dress regulations. *Canadian Journal of Behavioural Science, 3,* 298–302. (p. 504)

Dutton, D. G. (1973). Reverse discrimination: The relationship of amount of perceived discrimination toward a minority group and the behavior of majority group members. *Canadian Journal of Behavioural Science, 5,* 34–45. (p. 504)

Dutton, D. G., & Aron, A. (1989). Romantic attraction and generalized liking for others who are sources of conflict-based arousal. *Canadian Journal of Behavioural Science, 21,* 246–257. (p. 454)

Dutton, D. G., & Aron, A. P. (1974). Some evidence for heightened sexual attraction under conditions of high anxiety. *Journal of Personality and Social Psychology, 30,* 510–517. (p. 454)

Dutton, D. G., & Lake, R. A. (1973). Threat of own prejudice and reverse discrimination in interracial situations. *Journal of Personality and Social Psychology, 28,* 94–100. (p. 504)

Duval, S., Duval, V. H., & Neely, R. (1979). Self-focus, felt responsibility, and helping behavior. *Journal of Personality and Social Psychology, 37,* 1769–1778. (p. 506)

Duval, S., & Wicklund, R. A. (1972). *A theory of objective self-awareness.* New York: Academic Press. (p. 88)

Eagly, A. (1994). Are people prejudiced against women? Donald Campbell Award invited address, American Psychological Association convention. (pp. 184, 345, 346)

Eagly, A. H. (1986). Some meta-analytic approaches to examining the validity of gender-difference research. In J. S. Hyde & M. C. Linn (Eds.), *The psychology of gender: Advances through meta-analysis.* Baltimore: Johns Hopkins University Press. (p. 184)

Eagly, A. H. (1987). Sex differences in social behavior: A social-role interpretation. Hillsdale, N.J.: Erlbaum. (pp. 184, 204, 239)

Eagly, A. H. (1995). The science and politics of comparing women and men. *American Psychologist, 50,* 145–158. (p. 184)

Eagly, A. H. (1997). Sex differences in social behavior: Social psychology meets evolutionary psychology. Midwestern Psychological Association invited address. (p. 204)

Eagly, A. H., Ashmore, R. D., Makhijani, M. G., & Longo, L. C. (1991). What is beautiful is good, but . . .: A meta-analytic review of research on the physical attractiveness stereotype. *Psychological Bulletin, 110,* 109–128. (p. 436)

Eagly, A. H., & Carli, L. L. (1981). Sex of researcher and sex-typed communications as determinants of sex differences in influenceability: A metaanalysis of social influence studies. *Psychological Bulletin, 90,* 1–20. (p. 239)

Eagly, A. H., & Chaiken, S. (1993). *The psychology of attitudes.* San Diego: Harcourt Brace Jovanovich. (p. 254)

Eagly, A. H., & Crowley, M. (1986). Gender and helping behavior: A meta-analytic review of the social psychological literature. *Psychological Bulletin, 100,* 283–308. (pp. 184, 500, 503)

Eagly, A. H., & Johnson, B. T. (1990). Gender and leadership style: A meta-analysis. *Psychological Bulletin, 108,* 233–256. (pp. 187, 329)

Eagly, A. H., & Karau, S. J. (1991). Gender and the emergence of leaders: A meta-analysis. *Journal of Personality and Social Psychology, 60,* 685–710. (p. 187)

Eagly, A. H., Karau, S. J., & Makhijani, M. G. (1995). Gender and the effectiveness of leaders: A meta-analysis. *Psychological Bulletin, 117,* 125–145. (p. 187)

Eagly, A. H., Makhijani, M. G., & Klonsky, B. G. (1992). Gender and the evaluation of leaders: A meta-analysis. *Psychological Bulletin, 111,* 3–22. (p. 187)

Eagly, A. H., Mladinic, A., & Otto, S. (1991). Are women evaluated more favorably than men? *Psychology of Women Quarterly, 15,* 203–216. (pp. 239, 345)

Eagly, A. H., & Wood, W. (1985). Gender and influenceability: Stereotype versus behavior. In V. E. O'Leary, R. K. Unger, & B. S. Wallston (Eds.), *Women, gender, and social psychology.* Hillsdale, N.J.: Erlbaum. (p. 239)

Eagly, A. H., Wood, W., & Chaiken, S. (1978). Casual inferences about communicators and their effect on opinion change. *Journal of Personality and Social Psychology, 36,* 424–435. (p. 258)

Easterlin, R. (1995). Will raising the incomes of all increase the happiness of all? *Journal of Economic Behavior and Organization, 27,* 35–47. (p. 393)

Ebbesen, E. B., Duncan, B., & Konecni, V. J. (1975). Effects of content of verbal aggression on future verbal aggression: A field experiment. *Journal of Experimental Social Psychology, 11,* 192–204. (p. 422)

Economist (1991, July 6). War in Europe. P. 11. (p. 174)

Edney, J. J. (1979). The nuts game: A concise commons dilemma analog. *Environmental Psychology and Nonverbal Behavior, 3,* 252–254. (p. 520)

Edney, J. J. (1980). The commons problem: Alternative perspectives. *American Psychologist, 35,* 131–150. (p. 522)

Edwards, C. P. (1991). Behavioral sex differences in children of diverse cultures: The case of nurturance to infants. In M. Pereira & L. Fairbanks (Eds.), *Juveniles: Comparative socioecology.* Oxford: Oxford University Press. (p. 197)

Edwards, E., & Smith, E. E. (1996). A disconfirmation bias in the evaluation of arguments. *Journal of Personality and Social Psychology, 71,* 5–24. (p. 95)

Edwards, K. (1990). The interplay of affect and cognition in attitude formation and change. *Journal of Personality and Social Psychology, 59,* 202–216. (p. 261)

Edwards, K., & Bryan, T. S. (1997). Judgmental biases produced by instructions to disregard: The (paradoxical) case of emotional information. *Personality and Social Psychology Bulletin, 23,* 849–864. (p. 617)

Efran, M. G. (1974). The effect of physical appearance on the judgment of guilt, interpersonal attraction, and severity of recommended punishment in a simulated jury task. *Journal of Research in Personality, 8,* 45–54. (p. 613)

Einon, D. (1994). Are men more promiscuous than women? *Ethology and Sociobiology, 15,* 131–143. (p. 195)

Eisenberg, N., Fabes, R. A., Schaller, M., Miller, P., Carlo, G., Poulin, R., Shea, C., & Shell, R. (1991). Personality and socialization correlates of vicarious emotional responding. *Journal of Personality and Social Psychology, 61,* 459–470. (p. 499)

Eisenberg, N., & Lennon, R. (1983). Sex differences in empathy and related capacities. *Psychological Bulletin, 94,* 100–131. (p. 185)

Eisenberger, R., & Armeli, S. (1997). Can salient reward increase creative performance without reducing intrinsic creative interest? *Journal of Personality and Social Psychology, 72,* 652–660. (p. 161)

Eisenberger, R., & Cameron, J. (1996). Detrimental effects of reward: Reality or myth? *American Psychologist, 51,* 1153–1166. (p. 161)

Eiser, J. R., Sutton, S. R., & Wober, M. (1979). Smoking, seat-belts, and beliefs about health. *Addictive Behaviors, 4,* 331–338. (p. 152)

Elashoff, J. R., & Snow, R. E. (1971). *Pygmalion reconsidered.* Worthington, Ohio: Charles A. Jones. (p. 121)

Elder, G. H., Jr. (1969). Appearance and education in marriage mobility. *American Sociological Review, 34,* 519–533. (p. 436)

Elder, G. H., Jr., & Clipp, E. C. (1988). Wartime losses and social bonding: Influences across 40 years in men's lives. *Psychiatry, 51,* 177–197. (p. 538)

Eldersveld, S. J., & Dodge, R. W. (1954). Personal contact or mail propaganda? An experiment in voting turnout and attitude change. In D. Katz, D. Cartwright, S. Eldersveld, & A. M. Lee (Eds.), *Public opinion and propaganda.* New York: Dryden Press. (p. 270)

Ellemers, N., Van Rijswijk, W., Roefs, M., & Simons, C. (1997). Bias in intergroup perceptions: Balancing group identity with social reality. *Personality and Social Psychology Bulletin, 23,* 186–198. (p. 354)

Ellickson, P. L., & Bell, R. M. (1990). Drug prevention in junior high: A multi-site longitudinal test. *Science, 247,* 1299–1305. (p. 286)

Elliott, G. C. (1986). Self-esteem and self-consistency: A theoretical and empirical link between two primary motivations. *Social Psychological Quarterly, 49,* 207–218. (p. 140)

Elliott, L. (1989, June). Legend of the four chaplains. *Reader's Digest,* pp. 66–70. (p. 500)

Ellis, B. J., & Symons, D. (1990). Sex difference in sexual fantasy: An evolutionary psychological approach. *Journal of Sex Research, 27,* 490–521. (p. 190)

Ellis, H. D. (1981). Theoretical aspects of face recognition. In G. H. Davies, H. D. Ellis, & J. Shepherd (Eds.), *Perceiving and remembering faces.* London: Academic Press. (p. 366)

Ellison, P. A., Govern, J. M., Petri, H. L., & Figler, M. H. (1995). Anonymity and aggressive driving behavior: A field study. *Journal of Social Behavior and Personality, 10,* 265–272. (p. 305)

Ellsworth, P. (1985, July). Juries on trial. *Psychology Today,* pp. 44–46. (p. 624)

Ellsworth, P. C., & Mauro, R. (1998). Psychology and law. In D. Gilbert, S. T. Fiske, & G. Lindzey (eds.), *Handbook of social psychology,* 4th ed. New York: McGraw-Hill. (pp. 600, 622, 623, 628)

Ellyson, S. L., Dovidio, J. F., & Brown, C. E. (1991). The look of power: Gender differences and similarities in visual dominance behavior. In C. Ridgeway (Ed.), *Gender and interaction: The role of microstructures in inequality.* New York: Springer-Verlag. (p. 188)

Elmer-DeWitt, P. (1995, July 3). Cyberporn. *Time,* pp. 38-45. (p. 61)

Elms, A. C. (1995). Obedience in retrospect. *Journal of Social Issues, 51,* 21–31. (p. 220)

Elwork, A., Sales, B. D., & Alfini, J. J. (1982). *Making jury instructions understandable.* Charlottesville, Va.: The Michie Co. (p. 620)

Emerging Trends (1997, January). Attitudes towards acceptance of homosexual clergy are changing slowly. P. 5. (p. 348)

Emmons, R. A., Larsen, R. J., Levine, S., & Diener, E. (1983). Factors predicting satisfaction judgments: A comparative examination. Paper presented at the Midwestern Psychological Association. (p. 592)

Emswiller, T., Deaux, K., & Willits, J. E. (1971). Similarity, sex, and requests for small favors. *Journal of Applied Social Psychology, 1,* 284–291. (p. 504)

Ennis, B. J., & Verrilli, D. B., Jr. (1989). Motion for leave to file brief amicus curiae and brief of Society for the Scientific Study of Religion, American Sociological Association, and others. U.S. Supreme Court Case No. 88–1600, Holy Spirit Association for the Unification of World Christianity, *et al.,* v. David Molko and Tracy Leal. On petition for write of certiorari to the Supreme Court of California. Washington, DC: Jenner & Block, 21 Dupont Circle NW. (p. 282)

Ennis, R., & Zanna, M. P. (1991). Hockey assault: Constitutive versus normative violations. Paper presented at the Canadian Psychological Association convention. (p. 396)

Enzle, M. E., & Hawkins, W. L. (1992). A priori actor negligence mediates a posteriori outcome. *Journal of Experimental Social Psychology, 28*(2), 169–185. (p. 619)

Epstein, S. (1980). The stability of behavior: II. Implications for psychological research. *American Psychologist, 35,* 790–806. (p. 240)

Epstein, S., & Feist, G. J. (1988). Relation between self- and other-acceptance and its moderation by identification. *Journal of Personality and Social Psychology, 54,* 309–315. (p. 66)

Erev, I., Bornstein, G., & Gallili, R. (1993). Constructive intergroup competition as a solution to the free rider problem: A field experiment. *Journal of Experimental Social Psychology, 29,* 463–478. (p. 305)

Erickson, B., Holmes, J. G., Frey, R., Walker, L., & Thibaut, J. (1974). Functions of a third party in the resolution of conflict: The role of a judge in pretrial conferences. *Journal of Personality and Social Psychology, 30,* 296–306. (p. 550)

Erickson, B., Lind, E. A. Johnson, B. C., & O'Barr, W. M. (1978). Speech style and impression formation in a court setting: The effects of powerful and powerless speech. *Journal of Experimental Social Psychology, 14,* 266–279. (p. 257)

Erikson, E. H. (1963). *Childhood and society.* New York: Norton. (p. 461)

Ernst, J. M., & Heesacker, M. (1993). Application of the elaboration likelihood model of attitude change to assertion training. *Journal of Counseling Psychology, 40,* 37–45. (p. 590)

Eron, L. D. (1985). The social responsibility of the researchers. In J. H. Goldstein (Ed.), *Reporting science: The case of aggression.* Hillsdale, N.J.: Erlbaum. (p. 413)

Eron, L. D. (1987). The development of aggressive behavior from the perspective of a developing behaviorism. *American Psychologist, 42,* 425–442. (p. 412)

Eron, L. D., & Huesmann, L. R. (1980). Adolescent aggression and television. *Annals of the New York Academy of Sciences, 347,* 319–331. (p. 413)

Eron, L. D., & Huesmann, L. R. (1984). The control of aggressive behavior by changes in attitudes, values, and the conditions of learning. In R. J. Blanchard & C. Blanchard (Eds.), *Advances in the study of aggression,* vol. 1. Orlando, Fla.: Academic Press. (pp. 413, 414, 423)

Eron, L. D., & Huesmann, L. R. (1985). The role of television in the development of prosocial and antisocial behavior. In D. Olweus, M. Radke-Yarrow, and J. Block (Eds.), *Development of antisocial and prosocial behavior.* Orlando, Fla.: Academic Press. (p. 413)

Esser, J. K. (1998). Alive and well after 25 years. A review of groupthink research.

Organizational Behavior and Human Decision Processes, in press. (p. 320)

Esser, J. K., & Lindoerfer, J. S. (1989). Groupthink and the space shuttle Challenger accident: Toward a quantitative case analysis. *Journal of Behavioral Decision Making, 2,* 167–177. (p. 321)

Esses, V. M. (1989). Mood as a moderator of acceptance of interpersonal feedback. *Journal of Personality and Social Psychology, 57,* 769-781. (p. 117)

Esses, V. M., Haddock, G., & Zanna, M. P. (1993a). Values, stereotypes, and emotions as determinants of intergroup attitudes. In D. Mackie & D. Hamilton (Eds.), *Affect, cognition and stereotyping: Interactive processes in intergroup perception.* San Diego, CA: Academic Press. (p. 342)

Esses, V. M., Haddock, G., & Zanna, M. P. (1993b). The role of mood in the expression of intergroup stereotypes. In M. P. Zanna & J. M. Olson (eds.), *The psychology of prejudice: The Ontario symposium,* vol. 7. Hillsdale, NJ: Erlbaum. (p. 364)

Esses, V. M., & Webster, C. D. (1988). Physical attractiveness, dangerousness, and the Canadian criminal code. *Journal of Applied Social Psychology, 18,* 1017–1031. (p. 613)

Esses, V. M., & Zanna, M. P. (1995). Mood and the expression of ethnic stereotypes. *Journal of Personality and Social Psychology, 69,* 1052–1068. (p. 368)

Etzioni, A. (1972, June 3). Human beings are not very easy to change after all. *Saturday Review,* 45–47. (p. 132)

Etzioni, A. (1991, May–June). The community in an age of individualism (interview). *The Futurist,* pp. 35–39. (p. 556)

Etzioni, A. (1993). *The spirit of community.* New York: Crown. (p. 248)

Evans, G. W. (1979). Behavioral and physiological consequences of crowding in humans. *Journal of Applied Social Psychology, 9,* 27–46. (p. 297)

Evans, G. W., Lepore, S. J., & Schroeder, A. (1996). The role of interior design elements in human responses to crowding. *Journal of Personality and Social Psychology, 70,* 41–46. (p. 297)

Evans, R., & Berent, I. (1993). *Getting your words' worth.* New York: Warner Books. (p. 18)

Evans, R. I., Smith, C. K., & Raines, B. E. (1984). Deterring cigarette smoking in adolescents: A psycho-social-behavioral analysis of an intervention strategy. In A. Baum, J. Singer, & S. Taylor (Eds.), *Handbook of psychology and health: Social psychological aspects of health,* vol. 4, Hillsdale, N.J.: Erlbaum. (p. 285)

Fabrigar, L. R., & Petty, R. E. (1999). The role of the affective and cognitive bases of attitudes in susceptibility to affectively and cognitively based persuasion. *Personality and Social Psychology Bulletin, 25,* 363-381. (p. 261)

Fabrigar, L. R., Priester, J. R., Petty, R. E., & Wegener, D. T. (1998). The impact of attitude accessibility on elaboration of persuasive messages. *Personality and Social Psychology Bulletin, 24,* 339-352. (p. 275)

Fairchild, H. H., & Cowan, G. (1997). The O. J. Simpson trial: Challenges to science and society. *Journal of Social Issues, 53,* 583–591. (p. 615)

Falbo, T., Poston, D. L., Jr., Triscari, R. S., & Zhang, X. (1997). Self-enhancing illusions among Chinese schoolchildren. *Journal of Cross-Cultural Psychology, 28,* 172–191. (p. 730)

Farquhar, J. W., Maccoby, N., Wood, P. D., Alexander, J. K., Breitrose, H., Brown, B. W., Jr., Haskell, W. L., McAlister, A. L., Meyer, A. J., Nash, J. D., & Stern, M. P. (1977, June 4). Community education for cardiovascular health. *Lancet,* 1192–1195. (p. 270)

Faulkner, S. L., & Williams, K. D. (1996). A study of social loafing in industry. Paper presented to the Midwestern Psychological Association convention. (p. 302)

Faust, D., & Ziskin, J. (1988). The expert witness in psychology and psychiatry. *Science, 241,* 31–35. (p. 566)

Fazio, R. (1987). Self-perception theory: A current perspective. In M. P. Zanna, J. M. Olson, & C. P. Herman (Eds.), *Social influence: The Ontario symposium,* vol. 5. Hillsdale, N.J.: Erlbaum. (p. 166)

Fazio, R. H., Effrein, E. A., & Falender, V. J. (1981). Self-perceptions following social interaction. *Journal of Personality and Social Psychology, 41,* 232-242. (p. 565)

Fazio, R. H., Jackson, J. R., Dunton, B. C., & Williams, C. J. (1995). Variability in automatic activation as an unobtrusive measure of racial attitudes: A bona fide pipeline? *Journal of Personality and Social Psychology, 69,* 1013–1027. (p. 342)

Fazio, R. H., & Zanna, M. P. (1981). Direct experience and attitude-behavior consistency. In L. Berkowitz (Ed.), *Advances in experimental social psychology,* Vol. 14. New York: Academic Press. (p. 136)

Fazio, R. H., Zanna, M. P., & Cooper, J. (1977). Dissonance versus self-perception: An integrative view of each theory's proper domain of application. *Journal of Experimental Social Psychology, 13,* 464–479. (p. 166)

Fazio, R. H., Zanna, M. P., & Cooper, J. (1979). On the relationship of data to theory: A reply to Ronis and Greenwald. *Journal of Experimental Social Psychology, 15,* 70–76. (p. 166)

FBI (1997). *Uniform crime reports for the United States.* Washington, DC: Federal Bureau of Investigation. (pp. 189, 391)

Feather, N. T. (1983). Causal attributions and beliefs about work and unemployment among adolescents in state and independent secondary schools. *Australian Journal of Psychology, 35,* 211–232. *(a)* (p. 91)

Feather, N. T. (1983). Causal attributions for good and bad outcomes in achievement and affiliation situations. *Australian Journal of Psychology, 35,* 37–48. *(b)* (pp. 73, 91)

Feeney, J. A. (1996). Attachment, caregiving, and marital satisfaction. *Personal Relationships, 3,* 401–416. (p. 461)

Feeney, J. A., & Noller, P. (1990). Attachment style as a predictor of adult romantic relationships. *Journal of Personality and Social Psychology, 58,* 281–291. (p. 461)

Feeney, J., Peterson, C., & Noller, P. (1994). Equity and marital satisfaction over the family life cycle. *Personality Relationships, 1,* 83–99. (p. 463)

Feierabend, I., & Feierabend, R. (1968, May). Conflict, crisis, and collision: A study of international stability. *Psychology Today,* pp. 26–32, 69–70. (p. 392)

Feierabend, I., & Feierabend, R. (1972). Systemic conditions of political aggression: An application of frustration-aggression theory. In I. K. Feierabend, R. L. Feierabend, & T. R. Gurr (Eds.), *Anger, violence, and politics: Theories and research.* Englewood Cliffs, N.J.: Prentice Hall. (p. 392)

Fein, S., & Hilton, J. L. (1992). Attitudes toward groups and behavioral intentions toward individual group members: The impact of nondiagnostic information. *Journal of Experimental Social Psychology, 28,* 101–124. (p. 377)

Fein, S., Hilton, J. L., & Miller, D. T. (1990). Suspicion of ulterior motivation and the correspondence bias. *Journal of Personality and Social Psychology, 58,* 753–764. (p. 85)

Fein, S., & Spencer, S. J. (1997). Prejudice as self-image maintenance: Affirming the self through derogating others. *Journal of Personality and Social Psychology, 73,* 31–44. (p. 362)

Feingold, A. (1988). Matching for attractiveness in romantic partners and same-sex friends: A meta-analysis and theoretical critique. *Psychological Bulletin, 104,* 226–235. (p. 435)

Feingold, A. (1990). Gender differences in effects of physical attractiveness on romantic attraction: A comparison across five research paradigms. *Journal of Personality and Social Psychology, 59,* 981–993. (p. 435)

Feingold, A. (1991). Sex differences in the effects of similarity and physical attractiveness on opposite-sex attraction. *Basic and Applied Social Psychology, 12,* 357–367. (p. 435)

Feingold, A. (1992). Gender differences in mate selection preferences: A test of the parental investment model. *Psychological Bulletin, 112,* 125–139. (p. 192)

Feingold, A. (1992). Good-looking people are not what we think. *Psychological Bulletin, 111,* 304–341. (pp. 436, 437)

Feldman, K. A., & Newcomb, T. M. (1969). *The impact of college on students.* San Francisco: Jossey-Bass. (p. 313)

Feldman, R. S., & Prohaska, T. (1979). The student as Pygmalion: Effect of student expectation on the teacher. *Journal of Educational Psychology, 71,* 485–493. (p. 121)

Feldman, R. S., & Theiss, A. J. (1982). The teacher and student as Pygmalions: Joint effects of teacher and student expectations. *Journal of Educational Psychology, 74,* 217–223. (p. 121)

Fenigstein, A. (1984). Self-consciousness and the overperception of self as a target. *Journal of Personality and Social Psychology, 47,* 860–870. (pp. 39, 578)

Fenigstein, A., & Carver, C. S. (1978). Self-focusing effects of heartbeat feedback. *Journal of Personality and Social Psychology, 36,* 1241–1250. (p. 88)

Fenigstein, A., & Vanable, P. A. (1992). Paranoia and self-consciousness. *Journal of Personality and Social Psychology, 62,* 129–138. (p. 578)

Fergusson, D. M., Horwood, L. J., & Shannon, F. T. (1984). A proportional hazards model of family breakdown. *Journal of Marriage and the Family, 46,* 539–549. (p. 468)

Fernandez-Collado, C., & Greenberg, B. S., with Korzenny, F., & Atkin, C. K. (1978). Sexual intimacy and drug use in TV series. *Journal of Communication, 28*(3), 30–37. (p. 417)

Feshbach, N. D. (1980). The child as "psychologist" and "economist": Two curricula. Paper presented at the American Psychological Association convention. (p. 288)

Feshbach, S. (1980). Television advertising and children: Policy issues and alternatives. Paper presented at the American Psychological Association convention. (p. 287)

Festinger, L. (1954). A theory of social comparison processes. *Human Relations, 7,* 117–140. (p. 314)

Festinger, L. (1957). *A theory of cognitive dissonance.* Stanford: Stanford University Press. (p. 152)

Festinger, L. (1987). Reflections on cognitive dissonance theory: 30 years later. Paper presented at the American Psychological Association convention. (p. 320)

Festinger, L., & Carlsmith, J. M. (1959). Cognitive consequences of forced compliance. *Journal of Abnormal and Social Psychology, 58,* 203–210. (p. 153)

Festinger, L., & Maccoby, N. (1964). On resistance to persuasive communications. *Journal of Abnormal and Social Psychology, 68,* 359–366. (p. 275)

Festinger, L., Pepitone, A., & Newcomb, T. (1952). Some consequences of deindividuation in a group. *Journal of Abnormal and Social Psychology*, **47**, 382–389. (p. 305)

Feynman, R. (1967). *The character of physical law*. Cambridge, Mass.: MIT Press. (p. 162)

Fichter, J. (1968). *America's forgotten priests: What are they saying?* New York: Harper. (p. 350)

Fiebert, M. S. (1990). Men, women and housework: The Roshomon effect. *Men's Studies Review*, **8**, 6. (p. 57)

Fiedler, F. E. (1987, September). When to lead, when to stand back. *Psychology Today*, pp. 26–27. (p. 328)

Fiedler, K., Semin, G. R., & Koppetsch, C. (1991). Language use and attributional biases in close personal relationships. *Personality and Social Psychology Bulletin*, **17**, 147–155. (p. 85)

Fields, J. M., & Schuman, H. (1976). Public beliefs about the beliefs of the public. *Public Opinion Quarterly*, **40**, 427–448. (p. 58)

Finch, J. F., & Cialdini, R. B. (1989). Another indirect tactic of (self-) image management: Boosting. *Personality and Social Psychology Bulletin*, **15**, 222–232. (p. 64)

Fincham, F. D., & Jaspars, J. M. (1980). Attribution of responsibility: From man the scientist to man as lawyer. In L. Berkowitz (Ed.), *Advances in experimental social psychology* (Vol. 13). New York: Academic Press. (p. 87)

Findley, M. J., & Cooper, H. M. (1983). Locus of control and academic achievement: A literature review. *Journal of Personality and Social Psychology*, **44**, 419–427. (p. 52)

Fineberg, H. V. (1988). Education to prevent AIDS: Prospects and obstacles. *Science*, **239**, 592–596. (p. 263)

Fischer, G. J. (1997). Gender effects on individual verdicts and on mock jury verdicts in a simulated acquaintance rape trial. *Sex Roles*, **36**, 491–501. (p. 615)

Fischhoff, B. (1982). Debiasing. In D. Kahneman, P. Slovic, & A. Tversky (Eds.), *Judgment under uncertainty: Heuristics and biases*. New York: Cambridge University Press. (p. 109)

Fischhoff, B., & Bar-Hillel, M. (1984). Diagnosticity and the base rate effect. *Memory and Cognition*, **12**, 402–410. (p. 110)

Fishbein, D., & Thelen, M. H. (1981). Husband-wife similarity and marital satisfaction: A different approach. Paper presented at the Midwestern Psychological Association convention. *(a)* (p. 446)

Fishbein, D., & Thelen, M. H. (1981). Psychological factors in mate selection and marital satisfaction: A review (Ms. 2374). *Catalog of Selected Documents in Psychology*, **11**, 84. *(b)* (p. 446)

Fishbein, M., & Ajzen, I. (1974). Attitudes toward objects as predictive of single and multiple behavioral criteria. *Psychological Review*, **81**, 59–74. (p. 134)

Fisher, G. H. (1968). Ambiguity of form: Old and new. *Perception and Psychophysics*, **4**, 189–192. (p. 604)

Fisher, H. (1994, April). The nature of romantic love. *Journal of NIH Research*, pp. 59–64. (p. 457)

Fisher, R. J. (1994). Generic principles for resolving intergroup conflict. *Journal of Social Issues*, **50**, 47–66. (p. 551)

Fisher, R. P., Geiselman, R. E., & Amador, M. (1989). Field test of the cognitive interview: Enhancing the recollection of actual victims and witnesses of crime. *Journal of Applied Psychology*, **74**, 722–727. (p. 610)

Fisher, R. P., Geiselman, R. E., & Raymond, D. S. (1987). Critical analysis of police interview techniques. *Journal of Police Science and Administration*, **15**, 177–185. (p. 609)

Fisher, R. P., McCauley, M. R., & Geiselman, R. E. (1994). Improving eyewitness testimony with the Cognitive Interview. In D. F. Ross, J. D. Read, & M. P. Toglia (eds.), *Adult eyewitness testimony: Current trends and developments*. Cambridge, England: Cambridge University Press. (p. 610)

Fiske, A. P., Kitayama, S., Markus, H. R., & Nisbett, R. E. (1998). The cultural matrix of social psychology. In D. Gilbert, S. Fiske, and G. Lindzey (eds.), *The handbook of social psychology*, 4th edition. Hillsdale, NJ: Erlbaum. (p. 176)

Fiske, S. T. (1989). Interdependence and stereotyping: From the laboratory to the Supreme Court (and back). Invited address, American Psychological Association convention. (p. 341)

Fiske, S. T. (1992). Thinking is for doing: Portraits of social cognition from Daguerrotype to Laserphoto. *Journal of Personality and Social Psychology*, **63**, 877–889. (pp. 125, 173)

Fiske, S. T. (1993). Controlling other people: The impact of power on stereotyping. *American Psychologist*, **48**, 621–628. (p. 366)

Fiske, S. T., & Ruscher, J. B. (1993). Negative interdependence and prejudice: Whence the affect? In D. Mackie & D. Hamilton (Eds.), *Affect, cognition and stereotyping: Interactive processes in intergroup perception*. San Diego, CA: Academic Press. (p. 345)

Fitzpatrick, A. R., & Eagly, A. H. (1981). Anticipatory belief polarization as a function of the expertise of a discussion partner. *Personality and Social Psychology Bulletin*, **1**, 636–642. (p. 314)

Flay, B. R., Ryan, K. B., Best, J. A., Brown, K. S., Kersell, M. W., d'Avernas, J. R., & Zanna, M. P. (1985). Are social-psychological smoking prevention programs effective? The Waterloo study. *Journal of Behavioral Medicine*, **8**, 37–59. (p. 285)

Fleming, I., Baum, A., & Weiss, L. (1987). Social density and perceived control as mediators of crowding stress in high-density residential neighborhoods. *Journal of Personality and Social Psychology*, **52**, 899–906. (p. 403)

Fletcher, G. J. O., Danilovics, P., Fernandez, G., Peterson, D., & Reeder, G. D. (1986). Attributional complexity: An individual differences measure. *Journal of Personality and Social Psychology*, **51**, 875–884. (p. 93)

Fletcher, G. J. O., Fincham, F. D., Cramer, L., & Heron, N. (1987). The role of attributions in the development of dating relationships. *Journal of Personality and Social Psychology*, **53**, 481–489. (p. 463)

Fletcher, G. J. O., & Ward, C. (1989). Attribution theory and processes: A cross-cultural perspective. In M. H. Bond (Ed.), *The cross-cultural challenge to social psychology*. Newbury Park, Ca.: Sage. (p. 372)

Foa, U. G., & Foa, E. B. (1975). *Resource theory of social exchange*. Morristown, N.J.: General Learning Press. (p. 474)

Fogarty, G. J., & White, C. (1994). Differences between values of Australian Aboriginal and non-Aboriginal students. *Journal of Cross-Cultural Psychology*, **25**, 394–408. (p. 45)

Fogelman, E. (1994). *Conscience and courage: Rescuers of Jews during the Holocaust*. New York: Doubleday Anchor. (p. 508)

Follett, M. P. (1940). Constructive conflict. In H. C. Metcalf & L. Urwick (Eds.), *Dynamic administration: The collected papers of Mary Parker Follett*. New York: Harper. (p. 548)

Ford, T. E. (1997). Effects of stereotypical television portrayals of African-Americans on person perception. *Social Psychology Quarterly*, **60**, 266–278. (p. 358)

Forgas, J. P. (1994). The role of emotion in social judgments: An introductory review and an Affect Infusion Model (AIM). *European Journal of Social Psychology*, **24**, 1–24. (p. 118)

Forgas, J. P. (1995). Mood and judgment: The affect infusion model (AIM). *Psychological Bulletin*, **117**, 39–66. (p. 118)

Forgas, J. P., Bower, G. H., & Krantz, S. E. (1984). The influence of mood on perceptions of social interactions. *Journal of Experimental Social Psychology*, **20**, 497–513. (pp. 117, 118)

Forgas, J. P., & Fiedler, K. (in press). Mood effects on intergroup discrimination: The role of affect in reward allocation decisions. *Journal of Personality and Social Psychology*. (p. 360)

Forgas, J. P., & Moylan, S. (1987). After the movies: Transient mood and social judgments. *Personality and Social Psychology Bulletin*, **13**, 467–477. (p. 117)

Form, W. H., & Nosow, S. (1958). *Community in disaster*. New York: Harper. (p. 484)

Försterling, F. (1986). Attributional conceptions in clinical psychology. *American Psychologist*, **41**, 275–285. (p. 587)

Forsyth, D. R., Berger, R. E., & Mitchell, T. (1981). The effects of self-serving vs. other-serving claims of responsibility on attraction and attribution in groups. *Social Psychology Quarterly*, **44**, 59–64. (p. 73)

Forsyth, D. R., & Leary, M. R. (1997). Achieving the goals of the scientist-practitioner model: The seven interfaces of social and counseling psychology. *The Counseling Psychologist*, **25**, 180–200. (p. 585)

Foss, R. D. (1978). The role of social influence in blood donation. Paper presented at the American Psychological Association convention. (p. 506)

Foss, R. D. (1981). Structural effects in simulated jury decision making. *Journal of Personality and Social Psychology*, **40**, 1053–1062. (p. 628)

Foulke, E., & Sticht, T. G. (1969). Review of research on the intelligibility and comprehension of accelerated speech. *Psychological Bulletin*, **72**, 50–62. (p. 258)

Frable, D. E. S., Johnson, A., & Kellman, H. (1994). Seeing masculine men, sexy women and gender differences: Exposure to pornography and cognitive constructions of gender. Paper presented at the American Psychological Association convention. (p. 405)

Frank, J. (1974). *Persuasion and healing: A comparative study of psychotherapy*. New York: Schocken. (p. 283)

Frank, M. G., & Gilovich, T. (1988). The dark side of self and social perception: Black uniforms and aggression in professional sports. *Journal of Personality and Social Psychology*, **54**, 74–85. (p. 307)

Frank, M. G., & Gilovich, T. (1989). Effect of memory perspective on retrospective causal attributions. *Journal of Personality and Social Psychology*, **57**, 399–403. (p. 87)

Frankel, A., & Snyder, M. L. (1987). Egotism among the depressed: When self-protection becomes self-handicapping. Paper presented at the American Psychological Association convention. (p. 72)

Franklin, B. J. (1974). Victim characteristics and helping behavior in a rural southern setting. *Journal of Social Psychology*, **93**, 93–100. (p. 504)

Frasure-Smith, N., Lesperance, F., & Talajic, M. (1995). The impact of negative emotions on prognosis following myocardial infarction: Is it more than depression? *Health Psychology*, **14**, 388–398. (p. 582)

Freedman, J. L. (1988). Television violence and aggression: What the evidence shows. In S. Oskamp (Ed.), *Television as a social issue. Applied social psychology annual*, Vol. 8. Newbury Park, Ca.: Sage. (p. 415)

Freedman J. L. (1990). The effect of capital punishment on jurors' willingness to convict. *Journal of Applied Social Psychology*, **20**, 465–477. (p. 624)

Freedman, J. L., Birsky, J., & Cavoukian, A. (1980). Environmental determinants of behavioral contagion: Density and number. *Basic and Applied Social Psychology*, **1**, 155–161. (p. 296)

Freedman, J. L., Cunningham, J. A., & Krismer, K. (1992). Inferred values and the reverse-incentive effect in induced compliance. *Journal of Personality and Social Psychology*, **62**, 357-368. (p. 165)

Freedman, J. L., & Fraser, S. C. (1966). Compliance without pressure: The foot-in-the-door technique. *Journal of Personality and Social Psychology*, **4**, 195–202. (p. 142)

Freedman, J. L., & Perlick, D. (1979). Crowding, contagion, and laughter. *Journal of Experimental Social Psychology*, **15**, 295–303. (p. 296)

Freedman, J. L., & Sears, D. O. (1965). Warning, distraction, and resistance to influence. *Journal of Personality and Social Psychology*, **1**, 262–266. (p. 274)

Freedman, J. S. (1965). Long-term behavioral effects of cognitive dissonance. *Journal of Experimental Social Psychology*, **1**, 145–155. (p. 146)

Freeh, L. (1993, September 1). Inaugural address as FBI Director. (p. 425)

Freeman, M. A. (1997). Demographic correlates of individualism and collectivism: A study of social values in Sri Lanka. *Journal of Cross-Cultural Psychology*, **28**, 321–341. (p. 32)

French, J. R. P. (1968). The conceptualization and the measurement of mental health in terms of self-identity theory. In S. B. Sells (Ed.), The definition and measurement of mental health. Washington, D.C.: Department of Health, Education, and Welfare. (Cited by M. Rosenberg, 1979, *Conceiving the self*. New York: Basic Books.) (p. 58)

Frey, K. P., & Eagly, A. H. (1993). Vividness can undermine the persuasiveness of messages. *Journal of Personality and Social Psychology*, **65**, 32–44. (p. 263)

Friedman, H. S., & DiMatteo, M. R. (1989). *Health psychology*. Englewood Cliffs, NJ: Prentice-Hall. (p. 579)

Friedman, H. S., Riggio, R. E., & Casella, D. F. (1988). Nonverbal skill, personal charisma, and initial attraction. *Personality and Social Psychology Bulletin*, **14**, 203–211. (p. 445)

Friedrich, J. (1996). On seeing oneself as less self-serving than others: The ultimate self-serving bias? *Teaching of Psychology*. (p. 69)

Friedrich, J. (1996). On seeing oneself as less self-serving than others: The ultimate self-serving bias? *Teaching of Psychology*, **23**, 107–109. (p. 69)

Friedrich, L. K., & Stein, A. H. (1973). Aggressive and prosocial television programs and the natural behavior of preschool children. *Monographs of the Society of Research in Child Development*, **38** (4, Serial No. 151). (p. 509)

Friedrich, L. K., & Stein, A. H. (1975). Prosocial television and young children: The effects of verbal labeling and role playing on learning and behavior. *Child Development*, **46**, 27–38. (p. 509)

Frieze, I. H., Olson, J. E., & Russell, J. (1991). Attractiveness and income for men and women in management. *Journal of Applied Social Psychology*, **21**, 1039–1057. (p. 437)

Froming, W. J., Walker, G. R., & Lopyan, K. J. (1982). Public and private self-awareness: When personal attitudes conflict with societal expectations. *Journal of Experimental Social Psychology*, **18**, 476–487. (p. 136)

Fuller, S. R., & Aldag, R. J. (1998). Organizational Tonypandy: Lessons from a quarter century of the groupthink phenomenon. *Organizational Behavior and Human Decision Processes*, in press. (p. 320)

Fultz, J., Batson, C. D., Fortenbach, V. A., McCarthy, P. M., & Varney, L. L. (1986). Social evaluation and the empathy-altruism hypothesis. *Journal of Personality and Social Psychology*, **50**, 761–769. (p. 479)

Funder, D. C. (1987). Errors and mistakes: Evaluating the accuracy of social judgment. *Psychological Bulletin*, **101**, 75–90. (p. 125)

Funder, D. C., & Colvin, C. R. (1991). Explorations in behavioral consistency: Properties of persons, situations, and behaviors. *Journal of Personality and Social Psychology*, **60**, 773–794. (p. 241)

Furnham, A. (1982). Explanations for unemployment in Britain. *European Journal of Social Psychology*, **12**, 335–352. (p. 91)

Furnham, A. (1995). The just world, charitable giving and attitudes to disability. *Personality and Individual Differences*, **19**, 577–583. (p. 374)

Furnham, A., & Gunter, B. (1984). Just world beliefs and attitudes towards the poor. *British Journal of Social Psychology*, **23**, 265–269. (p. 374)

Gabrenya, W. K., Jr., Wang, Y.-E., & Latané, B. (1985). Social loafing on an optimizing task: Cross-cultural differences among Chinese and Americans. *Journal of Cross-Cultural Psychology*, **16**, 223–242. (p. 303)

Gaebelein, J. W., & Mander, A. (1978). Consequences for targets of aggression as a function of aggressor and instigator roles: Three experiments. *Personality and Social Psychology Bulletin*, **4**, 465–468. (p. 419)

Gaertner, S. L. (1973). Helping behavior and racial discrimination among liberals and conservatives. *Journal of Personality and Social Psychology*, **25**, 335–341. (p. 504)

Gaertner, S. L. (1975). The role of racial attitudes in helping behavior. *Journal of Social Psychology*, 97, 95–101. (p. 504)

Gaertner, S. L., & Bickman, L. (1971). Effects of race on the elicitation of helping behavior. *Journal of Personality and Social Psychology*, 20, 218–222. (p. 504)

Gaertner, S. L., & Dovidio, J. F. (1977). The subtlety of white racism, arousal, and helping behavior. *Journal of Personality and Social Psychology*, 35, 691–707. (p. 504)

Gaertner, S. L., & Dovidio, J. F. (1986). The aversive form of racism. In J. F. Dovidio & S. L. Gaertner (Eds.), *Prejudice, discrimination, and racism*. Orlando, Fl.: Academic Press. (p. 504)

Gaertner, S. L., Dovidio, J. F., Anastasio, P. A., Bachman, B. A., & Rust, M. C. (1993). The Common Ingroup Identity Model: Recategorization and the reduction of intergroup bias. In W. Stroebe & M. Hewstone (eds.), *European Review of Social Psychology*, vol. 4. London: Wiley. (p. 539)

Gaertner, S. L., Dovidio, J. F., Bachman, B. A. (1996). Revisiting the contact hypothesis: The induction of a common ingroup identity. *International Journal of Intercultural Relations*, 20, 271–290. (p. 535)

Gaertner, S. L., Dovidio, J. F., Nier, J. A., Ward, C. M., & Banker, B. S. (1998). Across cultural divides: The value of superordinate identity. In D. Prentice & D. Miller (eds.), *Cultural divides: The social psychology of intergroup contact*. New York: Russell Sage Foundation. (pp. 539, 545)

Gaertner, S. L., Rust, M. C., Dovidio, J. F., & Bachman, B. A. (1994). The contact hypothesis: The role of a common ingroup identity on reducing intergroup bias. *Small Group Research*, 25, 224–249. (p. 535)

Gaines, S. O., Jr., & 15 others (1997). Links between race/ethnicity and cultural values as mediated by racial/ethnic identity and moderated by gender. *Journal of Personality and Social Psychology*, 72, 1460–1476. (p. 45)

Galanter, M. (1989). *Cults: Faith, healing, and coercion*. New York: Oxford University Press. (p. 283)

Galanter, M. (1990). Cults and zealous self-help movements: A psychiatric perspective. *American Journal of Psychiatry*, 147, 543–551. (p. 283)

Galizio, M., & Hendrick, C. (1972). Effect of musical accompaniment on attitude: The guitar as a prop for persuasion. *Journal of Applied Social Psychology*, 2, 350–359. (p. 261)

Gallant, S. J., Popiel, D. A., Hoffman, D. M., Chakraborty, P. K., and Hamilton, J. A. (1992). Using daily ratings to confirm premenstrual syndrome/late luteal phase disorder. Part I. Effects of demand characteristics and expectations. *Psychosomatic Medicine*, 54, 149–166. (p. 580)

Gallup, G., Jr. (1984, March). Religion in America. *The Gallup Report*, Report No. 222. (pp. 370, 501, 502)

Gallup, G. H., Jr., & Jones, T. (1992). *The saints among us*. Harrisburg, PA: Morehouse. (p. 350)

Gallup Organization (1990). April 19–22 survey reported in *American Enterprise*, September/October, 1990, p. 92. (pp. 190, 200)

Gallupe, R. B., Cooper, W. H., Grise, M. L., & Bastianutti, L. M. (1994). Blocking electronic brainstorms. *Journal of Applied Psychology*, 79, 77-86. (p. 324)

Gamson, W. A., Fireman, B., & Rytina, S. (1982). *Encounters with unjust authority*. Homewood, Ill.: Dorsey Press. (p. 244)

Gangestad, S. W., & Thornhill, R. (1997). Human sexual selection and developmental stability. In J. A. Simpson & D. T. Kenrick (eds.), *Evolutionary social psychology*. Mahway, NJ: Erlbaum. (p. 439)

Garb, H. N. (1994). Judgment research: Implications for clinical practice and testimony in court. *Applied and Preventive Psychology*, 3, 173–183. (p. 568)

Gardner, M. (1997, July/August). Heaven's Gate: The UFO cult of Bo and Peep. *Skeptical Inquirer*, pp. 15–17. (p. 279)

Garry, M., Manning, C. G., Loftus, E. F., & Sherman, S. J. (1996). Imagination inflation: Imagining a childhood event inflates confidence that it occurred. *Psychonomic Bulletin & Review*, 3, 208–214. (p. 100)

Gastorf, J. W., Suls, J., & Sanders, G. S. (1980). Type A coronary-prone behavior pattern and social facilitation. *Journal of Personality and Social Psychology*, 8, 773–780. (p. 297)

Gates, D. (1993, March 29). White male paranoia. *Newsweek*, pp. 48–53. (p. 370)

Gates, M. F., & Allee, W. C. (1933). Conditioned behavior of isolated and grouped cockroaches on a simple maze. *Journal of Comparative Psychology*, 15, 331–358. (p. 293)

Gavanski, I., & Hoffman, C. (1987). Awareness of influences on one's own judgments: The roles of covariation detection and attention to the judgment process. *Journal of Personality and Social Psychology*, 52, 453–463. (p. 48)

Gavanski, I., & Wells, G. L. (1989). Counterfactual processing of normal and exceptional events. *Journal of Experimental Social Psychology*, 35, 314–325. (p. 113)

Gazzaniga, M. (1985). *The social brain: Discovering the networks of the mind*. New York: Basic Books. (p. 138)

Gazzaniga, M. S. (1992). *Nature's mind: The biological roots of thinking, emotions, sexuality, language, and intelligence*. New York: Basic Books. (p. 106)

Gecas, V. (1989). The social psychology of self-efficacy. *Annual Review of Sociology*, 15, 291–316. (p. 50)

Geen, R. G. (1998). Aggression and antisocial behavior. In D. Gilbert, S. Fiske, & G. Lindzey (eds.), *Handbook of social psychology*, 4th ed. New York: McGraw-Hill. (p. 388)

Geen, R. G., & Gange, J. J. (1983). Social facilitation: Drive theory and beyond. In H. H. Blumberg, A. P. Hare, V. Kent, & M. Davies (Eds.), *Small groups and social interaction*, Vol. 1. London: Wiley. (pp. 295, 297)

Geen, R. G., & Quanty, M. B. (1977). The catharsis of aggression: An evaluation of a hypothesis. In L. Berkowitz (Ed.), *Advances in experimental social psychology* (Vol. 10). New York: Academic Press. (p. 421)

Geen, R. G., & Thomas, S. L. (1986). The immediate effects of media violence on behavior. *Journal of Social Issues*, 42(3), 7–28. (p. 416)

Geiselman, R. E. (1996, May 14). On the use and efficacy of the cognitive interview: Commentary on Memon & Stevenage on witness memory. *Psycoloquy.96.7.11.witnessmemory.2.geiselman* (from psyc@-phoenix. princeton.edu/ukacr1.bitnet). (pp. 609, 610)

Gelinas, C., Lussier, Y., & Sabourin, S. (1995). Marital adjustment: The role of attribution and psychological distress. *Canadian Journal of Behavioural Science*, 27, 21-35. (p. 79)

Gerard, H. B. (1994). A retrospective review of Festinger's *A theory of cognitive dissonance*. *Contemporary Psychology*, 39, 1013–1017. (p. 131)

Gerard, H. B., & Mathewson, G. C. (1966). The effects of severity of initiation on liking for a group: A replication. *Journal of Experimental Social Psychology*, 2, 278–287. (p. 279)

Gerard, H. B., Wilhelmy, R. A., & Conolley, E. S. (1968). Conformity and group size. *Journal of Personality and Social Psychology*, 8, 79–82. (p. 230)

Gerbasi, K. C., Zuckerman, M., & Reis, H. T. (1977). Justice needs a new blindfold: A review of mock jury research. *Psychological Bulletin*, 84, 323–345. (pp. 624, 626)

Gerbner, G. (1993, June). Women and minorities on television: A study in casting and fate. A report to the Screen Actors Guild and the American Federation of Radio and Television Artists. (pp. 412, 417)

Gerbner, G. (1994). The politics of media violence: Some reflections. In C. Hamelink & O. Linne (eds.), *Mass communication research: On problems and policies*. Norwood, NJ: Ablex. (pp. 412, 418)

Gerbner, G., Gross, L., Morgan, M., & Signorielli, N. (1986). Living with television: The dynamics of the cultivation process. In J. Bryant & D. Zillman (Eds.), *Perspectives on media effects*. Hillsdale, N.J.: Erlbaum. (pp. 359, 417)

Gerbner, G., Gross, L., Signorielli, N., Morgan, M., & Jackson-Beeck, M. (1979). The demonstration of power: Violence profile No. 10. *Journal of Communication, 29,* 177–196. (p. 418)

Gergen, K. E. (1982). *Toward transformation in social knowledge.* New York: Springer-Verlag. (p. 510)

Gibbons, F. X. (1978). Sexual standards and reactions to pornography: Enhancing behavioral consistency through self-focused attention. *Journal of Personality and Social Psychology, 36,* 976–987. (p. 136)

Gibbons, F. X., Eggleston, T. J., & Benthin, A. C. (1997). Cognitive reactions to smoking relapse: The reciprocal relation between dissonance and self-esteem. *Journal of Personality and Social Psychology, 72,* 184–195. (p. 152)

Gibbons, F. X., & Gerrard, M. (1989). Effects of upward and downward social comparison on mood states. *Journal of Social and Clinical Psychology, 8,* 14–31. (p. 395)

Gibbons, F. X., & Wicklund, R. A. (1982). Self-focused attention and helping behavior. *Journal of Personality and Social Psychology, 43,* 462–474. (p. 497)

Giesler, R. B., Josephs, R. A., & Swann, W. B., Jr. (1996). Self-verification in clinical depression: The desire for negative evaluation. *Journal of Abnormal Psychology, 105,* 358–368. (p. 572)

Gifford, R., & Hine, D. W. (1997). Toward cooperation in commons dilemmas. *Canadian Journal of Behavioural Science, 29,* 167–179. (p. 521)

Gifford, R., & Peacock, J. (1979). Crowding: More fearsome than crime-provoking? Comparison of an Asian city and a North American city. *Psychologia, 22,* 79–83. (p. 403)

Gigone, D., & Hastie, R. (1993). The common knowledge effect: Information sharing and group judgment. *Journal of Personality and Social Psychology, 65,* 959–974. (p. 313)

Gilbert, D. T., Giesler, R. B., & Morris, K. A. (1995). When comparisons arise. *Journal of Personality and Social Psychology, 69,* 227–236. (p. 394)

Gilbert, D. T., & Hixon, J. G. (1991). The trouble of thinking: Activation and application of stereotypic beliefs. *Journal of Personality and Social Psychology, 60,* 509–517. (p. 364)

Gilbert, D. T., & Jones, E. E. (1986). Perceiver-induced constraint: Interpretations of self-generated reality. *Journal of Personality and Social Psychology, 50,* 269–280. (p. 84)

Gilbert, D. T., Krull, D. S., & Malone, P. S. (1990). Unbelieving the unbelievable: Some problems in the rejection of false information. *Journal of Personality and Social Psychology, 59,* 601–613. (p. 284)

Gilbert, D. T., & Malone, P. S. (1995). The correspondence bias. *Psychological Bulletin, 117,* 21–38. (pp. 80, 91)

Gilbert, D. T., McNulty, S. E., Giuliano, T. A., & Benson, J. E. (1992). Blurry words and fuzzy deeds: The attribution of obscure behavior. *Journal of Personality and Social Psychology, 62,* 18–25. (p. 91)

Gilbert, D. T., Pelham, B. W., & Krull, D. S. (1988). On cognitive busyness: When person perceivers meet persons perceived. *Journal of Personality and Social Psychology, 54,* 733–740. (p. 91)

Gilbert, D. T., Tafarodi, R. W., & Malone, P. S. (1993). You can't not believe everything you read. *Journal of Personality and Social Psychology, 65,* 221–233. (p. 284)

Gilkey, L. (1966). *Shantung compound.* New York: Harper & Row. (p. 525)

Gilligan, C. (1982). *In a different voice: Psychological theory and women's development.* Cambridge, Mass.: Harvard University Press. (p. 184)

Gilligan, C., Lyons, N. P., & Hanmer, T. J. (Eds.) (1990). *Making connections: The relational worlds of adolescent girls at Emma Willard School.* Cambridge, MA: Harvard University Press. (p. 184)

Gillis, J. S., & Avis, W. E. (1980). The male-taller norm in mate selection. *Personality and Social Psychology Bulletin, 6,* 396–401. (p. 203)

Gilmor, T. M., & Reid, D. W. (1979). Locus of control and causal attribution for positive and negative outcomes on university examinations. *Journal of Research in Personality, 13,* 154–160. (p. 57)

Gilovich, T. (1987). Secondhand information and social judgment. *Journal of Experimental Social Psychology, 23,* 59–74. (p. 89)

Gilovich, T., & Douglas, C. (1986). Biased evaluations of randomly determined gambling outcomes. *Journal of Experimental Social Psychology, 22,* 228–241. (p. 115)

Gilovich, T., Kerr, M., & Medvec, V. H. (1993). Effect of temporal perspective on subjective confidence. *Journal of Personality and Social Psychology, 64,* 552–560. (p. 107)

Gilovich, T., & Medvec, V. H. (1994). The experience of regret: What, when, and why. Unpublished manuscript, Cornell University. (p. 113)

Gilovich, T., & Medvec, V. H. (1994). The temporal pattern to the experience of regret. *Journal of Personality and Social Psychology, 67,* 357–365. (p. 113)

Gilovich, T., Savitsky, K., & Medvec, V. H. (1997). The illusion of transparency: Biased assessments of others' ability to read our emotional states. Unpublished manuscript, Cornell University. (p. 488)

Ginossar, Z., & Trope, Y. (1987). Problem solving in judgment under uncertainty. *Journal of Personality and Social Psychology, 52,* 464–474. (p. 110)

Ginsburg, B., & Allee, W. C. (1942). Some effects of conditioning on social dominance and subordination in inbred strains of mice. *Physiological Zoology, 15,* 485–506. (p. 396)

Gladue, B. A., Boechler, M., & McCaul, K. D. (1989). Hormonal response to competition in human males. *Aggressive Behavior, 15,* 409–422. (p. 388)

Glass, D. C. (1964). Changes in liking as a means of reducing cognitive discrepancies between self-esteem and aggression. *Journal of Personality, 32,* 531–549. (p. 146)

Glenn, N. D. (1980). Aging and attitudinal stability. In O. G. Brim, Jr., & J. Kagan (Eds.), *Constancy and change in human development.* Cambridge, Mass.: Harvard University Press. (p. 273)

Glenn, N. D. (1981). Personal communication. (p. 273)

Glenn, N. D. (1991). The recent trend in marital success in the United States. *Journal of Marriage and the Family, 53,* 261–270. (p. 467)

Glick, D., Gottesman, D., & Jolton, J. (1989). The fault is not in the stars: Susceptibility of skeptics and believers in astrology to the Barnum effect. *Personality and Social Psychology Bulletin, 15,* 572–583. (p. 63)

Glick, P., & Fiske, S. T. (1996). The ambivalent sexism inventory: Differentiating hostile and benevolent sexism. *Journal of Personality and Social Psychology, 70,* 491–512. (p. 345)

Goethals, G. R., Messick, D. M., & Allison, S. T. (1991). The uniqueness bias: Studies of constructive social comparison. In J. Suls & T. A. Wills (Eds.), *Social comparison: Contemporary theory and research.* Hillsdale, NJ: Erlbaum. (p. 61)

Goethals, G. R., & Nelson, E. R. (1973). Similarity in the influence process: The belief-value distinction. *Journal of Personality and Social Psychology, 25,* 117–122. (p. 260)

Goethals, G. R., & Zanna, M. P. (1979). The role of social comparison in choice shifts. *Journal of Personality and Social Psychology, 37,* 1469–1476. (p. 315)

Goggin, W. C., & Range, L. M. (1985). The disadvantages of hindsight in the perception of suicide. *Journal of Social and Clinical Psychology, 3,* 232–237. (p. 563)

Goldberg, P. (1968, April). Are women prejudiced against women? *Transaction,* pp. 28–30. (pp. 345–346)

Goldhagen, D. J. (1996). *Hitler's willing executioners.* New York: Knopf. (pp. 229, 252)

Goldman, W., & Lewis, P. (1977). Beautiful is good: Evidence that the physically attractive are more socially skillful. *Journal of Experimental Social Psychology, 13,* 125–130. (p. 437)

Goldstein, A. P., & Glick, B. (1994). Aggression replacement training:

Curriculum and evaluation. *Simulation and Gaming*, **25**, 9–26. (p. 423)

Goldstein, J. H. (1982). Sports violence. *National Forum*, **62**(1), 9–11. (p. 398)

Goldstein, J. H., & Arms, R. L. (1971). Effects of observing athletic contests on hostility. *Sociometry*, **34**, 83–90. (p. 421)

Gonzalez, R., Ellsworth, P. C., & Pembroke, M. (1993). Response biases in lineups and showups. *Journal of Personality and Social Psychology*, **64**, 525–537. (p. 610)

Goodhart, D. E. (1986). The effects of positive and negative thinking on performance in an achievement situation. *Journal of Personality and Social Psychology*, **51**, 117–124. (p. 60)

Gordon, R. A. (1996). Impact of ingratiation on judgments and evaluations: A meta-analytic investigation. *Journal of Personality and Social Psychology*, **71**, 54–70. (p. 447)

Gordon, R., & Mentzel, R. K. (1990). Sympathy and altruism in response to disasters. *Journal of Social Psychology*, **130**, 309-316. (p. 478)

Gorsuch, R. L. (1988). Psychology of religion. *Annual Review of Psychology*, **39**, 201–222. (p. 350)

Gortmaker, S. L., Must, A., Perrin, J. M., Sobol, A. M., & Dietz, W. H. (1993). Social and economic consequences of overweight in adolescence and young adulthood. *New England Journal of Medicine*, **329**, 1008–1012. (p. 27)

Gotlib, I. H., & Colby, C. A. (1988). How to have a good quarrel. In P. Marsh (Ed.), *Eye to eye: How people interact*. Topsfield, MA: Salem House. (p. 549)

Gotlib, I. H., & Lee, C. M. (1989). The social functioning of depressed patients: A longitudinal assessment. *Journal of Social and Clinical Psychology*, **8**, 223–237. (p. 572)

Gottlieb, J., & Carver, C. S. (1980). Anticipation of future interaction and the bystander effect. *Journal of Experimental Social Psychology*, **16**, 253–260. (p. 506)

Gottman, J. (with N. Silver) (1994). *Why marriages succeed or fail*. New York: Simon & Schuster. (p. 469)

Gough, H. G., & Thorne, A. (1986). Positive, negative, and balanced shyness. In W. H. Jones, J. M. Cheek, & S. R. Briggs (eds.), *Shyness: Perspectives on Research and Treatment*. New York: Plenum. (p. 578)

Gould, M. S., & Shaffer, D. (1986). The impact of suicide in television movies: Evidence of imitation. *New England Journal of Medicine*, **315**, 690–694. (p. 214)

Gould, R., Brounstein, P. J., & Sigall, H. (1977). Attributing ability to an opponent: Public aggrandizement and private denigration. *Sociometry*, **40**, 254–261. (p. 70)

Gould, S. J. (1988, July). Kropotkin was no crackpot. *Natural History*, pp. 12–21. (p. 522)

Gould, S. J. (1997, October 20). Quoted by J. M. Nash, Evolutionary pop star. *Time*, p. 92. (p. 195)

Gouldner, A. W. (1960). The norm of reciprocity: A preliminary statement. *American Sociological Review*, **25**, 161–178. (p. 481)

Gove, W. R., Style, C. B., & Hughes, M. (1990). The effect of marriage on the well-being of adults: A theoretical analysis. *Journal of Family Issues*, **11**, 4–35. (p. 593)

Graham, T., & Ickes, W. (1997). When women's intuition isn't greater than men's. In W. Ickes (ed.), *Empathic accuracy*. New York: Guilford. (p. 186)

Grammer, K., & Thornhill, R. (1994). Human facial attractiveness and sexual selection: The role of symmetry and averageness. *Journal of Comparative Psychology*, **108**, 233–242. (p. 439)

Granberg, D. (1996). The Monty Hall Dilemma: To switch or not to switch. Appendix to M. vos Savant, *The power of logical thinking*. New York: St. Martin's Press. (p. 99)

Gray, C., Russell, P., & Blockley, S. (1991). The effects upon helping behaviour of wearing pro-gay identification. *British Journal of Social Psychology*, **30**, 171–178. (p. 504)

Gray, J. D., & Silver, R. C. (1990). Opposite sides of the same coin: Former spouses' divergent perspectives in coping with their divorce. *Journal of Personality and Social Psychology*, **59**, 1180–1191. (p. 57)

Graziano, W., Brothen, T., & Berscheid, E. (1978). Height and attraction: Do men and women see eye-to-eye? *Journal of Personality*, **46**, 128–145. (p. 438)

Graziano, W. G., Jensen-Campbell, L. A., & Finch, J. F. (1997). The self as a mediator between personality and adjustment. *Journal of Personality and Social Psychology*, **73**, 392–404. (p. 50)

Greeley, A. M. (1976). Pop psychology and the Gospel. *Theology Today*, **23**. (p. 8)

Green, C. W., Adams, A. M., & Turner, C. W. (1988). Development and validation of the school interracial climate scale. *American Journal of Community Psychology*, **16**, 241–259. (p. 541)

Greenberg, J. (1986). Differential intolerance for inequity from organizational and individual agents. *Journal of Applied Social Psychology*, **16**, 191–196. (p. 527)

Greenberg, J., Pyszczynski, T., Burling, J., & Tibbs, K. (1992). Depression, self-focused attention, and the self-serving attributional bias. *Personality and Individual Differences*, **13**, 959–965. (p. 587)

Greenberg, J., Pyszczynski, T., Solomon, S., Rosenblatt, A., Veeder, M., Kirkland, S., & Lyon, D. (1990). Evidence for terror management theory II: The effects of mortality salience on reactions to those who threaten or bolster the cultural worldview. *Journal of Personality and Social Psychology*, **58**, 308–318. (p. 361)

Greenberg, J., Pyszczynski, T., Solomon, S., Simon, L., & Breus, M. (1994). Role of consciousness and accessibility of death-related thoughts in mortality salience effects. *Journal of Personality and Social Psychology*, **67**, 627–637. (p. 361)

Greenberg, J., Solomon, S., & Pyszczynski, T. (1997). Terror management theory of self-esteem and cultural worldviews: Empirical assessments and conceptual refinements. *Advances in Experimental Social Psychology*, **29**, in press. (p. 66)

Greenwald, A. G. (1968). Cognitive learning, cognitive response to persuasion, and attitude change. In A. G. Greenwald, T. C. Brock, & T. M. Ostrom (Eds.), *Psychological foundations of attitudes*. New York: Academic Press. (p. 167)

Greenwald, A. G. (1975). On the inconclusiveness of crucial cognitive tests of dissonance versus self-perception theories. *Journal of Experimental Social Psychology*, **11**, 490–499. (p. 162)

Greenwald, A. G. (1980). The totalitarian ego: Fabrication and revision of personal history. *American Psychologist*, **35**, 603–618. (p. 102)

Greenwald, A. G., & Banaji, M. R. (1995). Implicit social cognition: Attitudes, self-esteem, and stereotypes. *Psychological Review*, **102**, 4–27. (p. 104)

Greenwald, A. G., Carnot, C. G., Beach, R., & Young, B. (1987). Increasing voting behavior by asking people if they expect to vote. *Journal of Applied Psychology*, **72**, 315–318. (p. 144)

Greenwald, A. G., & Schuh, E. S. (1994). An ethnic bias in scientific citations. *European Journal of Social Psychology*, **24**, 623–639. (p. 343)

Greenwald, A. G., Spangenberg, E. R., Pratkanis, A. R., & Eskenazi, J. (1991). Double-blind tests of subliminal self-help audiotapes. *Psychological Science*, **2**, 119–122. (p. 106)

Griffin, B. Q., Combs, A. L., Land, M. L., & Combs, N. N. (1983). Attribution of success and failure in college performance. *Journal of Psychology*, **114**, 259–266. (p. 57)

Griffin D. W., & Bartholomew, K. (1994). Models of the self and other: Fundamental dimensions underlying measures of adult attachment. *Journal of Personality and Social Psychology*, **67**, 430-445. (p. 461)

Griffin, D., & Buehler, R. (1993). Role of construal process in conformity and dissent. *Journal of Personality and Social Psychology*, **65**, 657-669. (p. 237)

Griffitt, W. (1970). Environmental effects on interpersonal affective behavior.

Ambient effective temperature and attraction. *Journal of Personality and Social Psychology*, **15**, 240–244. (pp. 401, 450)

Griffitt, W. (1987). Females, males, and sexual responses. In K. Kelley (Ed.), *Females, males, and sexuality: Theories and research*. Albany: State University of New York Press. (p. 189)

Griffitt, W., & Veitch, R. (1971). Hot and crowded: Influences of population density and temperature on interpersonal affective behavior. *Journal of Personality and Social Psychology*, **17**, 92–98. (p. 401)

Griffitt, W., & Veitch, R. (1974). Preacquaintance attitude similarity and attraction revisited: Ten days in a fallout shelter. *Sociometry*, **37**, 163–173. (p. 443)

Grofman, B. (1980). The slippery slope: Jury size and jury verdict requirements—legal and social science approaches. In B. H. Raven (Ed.), *Policy studies review annual* (Vol. 4). Beverly Hills, Calif.: Sage Publications. (p. 628)

Gross, A. E., & Crofton, C. (1977). What is good is beautiful. *Sociometry*, **40**, 85–90. (p. 442)

Gross, S. R., & Miller, N. (1997). The "Golden Section" and bias in perceptions of social consensus. *Personality and Social Psychology Review*, **1**, 241–271. (p. 62)

Grossman, M., & Wood, W. (1993). Sex differences in intensity of emotional experience: A social role interpretation. *Journal of Personality and Social Psychology*, **65**, 1010–1022. (p. 186)

Grove, J. R., Hanrahan, S. J., & McInman, A. (1991). Success/failure bias in attributions across involvement categories in sport. *Personality and Social Psychology Bulletin*, **17**, 93–97. (p. 55)

Grube, J. W., Kleinhesselink, R. R., & Kearney, K. A. (1982). Male self-acceptance and attraction toward women. *Personality and Social Psychology Bulletin*, **8**, 107–112. (p. 362)

Gruder, C. L. (1977). Choice of comparison persons in evaluating oneself. In J. M. Suls & R. L. Miller (Eds.), *Social comparison processes*. Washington: Hemisphere Publishing. (p. 394)

Gruder, C. L., Cook, T. D., Hennigan, K. M., Flay, B., Alessis, C., & Kalamaj, J. (1978). Empirical tests of the absolute sleeper effect predicted from the discounting cue hypothesis. *Journal of Personality and Social Psychology*, **36**, 1061–1074. (p. 256)

Gruman, J. C., & Sloan, R. P. (1983). Disease as justice: Perceptions of the victims of physical illness. *Basic and Applied Social Psychology*, **4**, 39–46. (p. 374)

Grunberger, R. (1971). *The 12-year-Reich: A social history of Nazi Germany 1933–1945*. New York: Holt, Rinehart & Winston. (p. 148)

Grush, J. E. (1980). Impact of candidate expenditures, regionality, and prior outcomes on the 1976 Democratic presidential primaries. *Journal of Personality and Social Psychology*, **38**, 337–347. (p. 269)

Grush, J. E., & Glidden, M. V. (1987). Power and satisfaction among distressed and nondistressed couples. Paper presented at the Midwestern Psychological Association convention. (p. 548)

Gudykunst, W. B. (1989). Culture and intergroup processes. In M. H. Bond (Ed.), *The cross-cultural challenge to social psychology*. Newbury Park, Ca.: Sage. (p. 354)

Guerin, B. (1993). *Social facilitation*. Paris: Cambridge University Press. (p. 294)

Guerin, B. (1994). What do people think about the risks of driving? Implications for traffic safety interventions. *Journal of Applied Social Psychology*, **24**, 994–1021. (p. 58)

Guerin, B., & Innes, J. M. (1982). Social facilitation and social monitoring: A new look at Zajonc's mere presence hypothesis. *British Journal of Social Psychology*, **21**, 7–18. (p. 297)

Guiness, O. (1993). *The American hour: A time of reckoning and the once and future role of faith*. New York: Free Press. (p. 466)

Gupta, U., & Singh, P. (1982). Exploratory study of love and liking and type of marriages. *Indian Journal of Applied Psychology*, **19**, 92–97. (pp. 457, 458)

Gutmann, D. (1977). The cross-cultural perspective: Notes toward a comparative psychology of aging. In J. E. Birren & K. Warner Schaie (Eds.), *Handbook of the psychology of aging*. New York: Van Nostrand Reinhold. (p. 195)

Hacker, H. M. (1951). Women as a minority group. *Social Forces*, **30**, 60–69. (p. 349)

Hackman, J. R. (1986). The design of work teams. In J. Lorsch (Ed.), *Handbook of organizational behavior*. Englewood Cliffs, N.J.: Prentice-Hall. (p. 303)

Hadden, J. K. (1969). *The gathering storm in the churches*. Garden City, N.Y.: Doubleday. (p. 350)

Haddock, G., & Zanna, M. P. (1994). Preferring "housewives" to "feminists." *Psychology of Women Quarterly*, **18**, 25–52. (pp. 184, 345)

Haemmerlie, F. M. (1987). Creating adaptive illusions in counseling and therapy using a self-perception theory perspective. Paper presented at the Midwestern Psychological Association, Chicago. (p. 587)

Haemmerlie, F. M., & Montgomery, R. L. (1982). Self-perception theory and unobtrusively biased interactions: A treatment for heterosocial anxiety. *Journal of Counseling Psychology*, **29**, 362–370. (p. 586)

Haemmerlie, F. M., & Montgomery, R. L. (1984). Purposefully biased interventions: Reducing heterosocial anxiety through self-perception theory. *Journal of Personality and Social Psychology*, **47**, 900–908. (p. 586)

Haemmerlie, F. M., & Montgomery, R. L. (1986). Self-perception theory and the treatment of shyness. In W. H. Jones, J. M. Cheek, & S. R. Briggs (Eds.), *A sourcebook on shyness: Research and treatment*. New York: Plenum. (p. 586)

Hafer, C. L., Reynolds, K. L., & Obertynski, M. A. Message comprehensibility and persuasion: Effects of complex language in counterattitudinal appeals of laypeople. *Social Cognition*, **14**, 317-337. (p. 275)

Hafner, H., & Schmidtke, A. (1989). Do televised fictional suicide models produce suicides? In D. R. Pfeffer (Ed.), *Suicide among youth: Perspectives on risk and prevention*. Washington, DC: American Psychiatric Press. (p. 214)

Hagiwara, S. (1983). Role of self-based and sample-based consensus estimates as mediators of responsibility judgments for automobile accidents. *Japanese Psychological Research*, **25**, 16–28. (p. 73)

Halberstadt, A. G., & Saitta, M. B. (1987). Gender, nonverbal behavior, and perceived dominance: A test of the theory. *Journal of Personality and Social Psychology*, **53**, 257–272. (p. 185)

Hall, J. A. (1984). *Nonverbal sex differences: Communication accuracy and expressive style*. Baltimore: Johns Hopkins University Press. (pp. 186, 188)

Hall, T. (1985, June 25). The unconverted: Smoking of cigarettes seems to be becoming a lower-class habit. *Wall Street Journal*, pp. 1, 25. (p. 102)

Hallahan, M., Lee, F., & Herzog, T. (1997). It's not just whether you win or lose, it's also where you play the game: A naturalistic, cross-cultural examination of the positivity bias. *Journal of Cross-Cultural Psychology*, **28**, 768–778. (p. 73)

Hallmark Cards (1990). Cited in *Time*, Fall special issue on women. (p. 185)

Halverson, A. M., Hallahan, M., Hart, A. J., & Rosenthal, R. (1997). Reducing the biasing effects of judges' nonverbal behavior with simplified jury instruction. *Journal of Applied Psychology*, **82**, 590–598. (p. 622)

Hamberger, J., & Hewstone, M. (1997). Inter-ethnic contact as a predictor of blatant and subtle prejudice: Tests of a model in four West European nations. *British Journal of Social Psychology*, **36**, 173–190. (p. 536)

Hamblin, R. L., Buckholdt, D., Bushell, D., Ellis, D., & Feritor, D. (1969). Changing the game from get the teacher to learn. *Transaction*, January, pp. 20–25, 28–31. (p. 423)

Hamilton, D. L. (1981). Illusory correlation as a basis for stereotyping. In D. L. Hamilton (Ed.), *Cognitive processes in stereotyping and intergroup behavior.* Hillsdale, N.J.: Erlbaum. (p. 375)

Hamilton, D. L., & Gifford, R. K. (1976). Illusory correlation in interpersonal perception: A cognitive basis of stereotypic judgments. *Journal of Experimental Social Psychology,* **12,** 392–407. (p. 370)

Hamilton, D. L., & Rose, T. L. (1980). Illusory correlation and the maintenance of stereotypic beliefs. *Journal of Personality and Social Psychology,* **39,** 832–845. (p. 371)

Hamilton, D. L., & Sherman, J. W. (1994). Stereotypes. In R. S. Wyer, Jr., & T. K. Srull (eds.), *Handbook of social cognition,* 2nd ed. Hillsdale, NJ: Erlbaum. (p. 371)

Hampson, R. B. (1984). Adolescent prosocial behavior: Peer-group and situational factors associated with helping. *Journal of Personality and Social Psychology,* **46,** 153–162. (p. 499)

Han, S-P., & Shavitt, S. (1994). Persuasion and culture: Advertising appeals in individualistic and collectivistic societies. *Journal of Experimental Social Psychology,* **30,** 326–350. (p. 45)

Haney, C. (1993). Psychology and legal change. *Law and Human Behavior,* **17,** 371–398. (p. 624)

Haney, C., & Logan, D. D. (1994). Broken promise: The Supreme Court's response to social science research on capital punishment. *Journal of Social Issues,* **50,** 75–101. (p. 624)

Hansen, C. H., & Hansen, R. D. (1988). Priming stereotypic appraisal of social interactions: How rock music videos can change what's seen when boy meets girl. *Sex Roles,* **19,** 287–316. (p. 405)

Hansen, C. H., & Hansen, R. D. (1990). Rock music videos and antisocial behavior. *Basic and Applied Social Psychology,* **11,** 357–369. (p. 405)

Hansen, D. E., Vandenberg, B., & Patterson, M. L. (1995). The effects of religious orientation on spontaneous and nonspontaneous helping behaviors. *Personality and Individual Differences,* **19,** 101–104. (p. 501)

Hardie, E. A. (1997). Prevalence and predictors of cyclic and noncyclic affective change. *Psychology of Women Quarterly,* **21,** 299–314. (p. 580)

Hardin, G. (1968). The tragedy of the commons. *Science,* **162,** 1243–1248. (pp. 519, 521)

Hardy, C., & Latané, B. (1986). Social loafing on a cheering task. *Social Science,* **71,** 165–172. (p. 301)

Haritos-Fatouros, M. (1988). The official torturer: A learning model for obedience to the authority of violence. *Journal of Applied Social Psychology,* **18,** 1107–1120. (p. 226)

Harkins, S. G. (1981). Effects of task difficulty and task responsibility on social loafing. Presentation to the First International Conference on Social Processes in Small Groups, Kill Devil Hills, North Carolina. (p. 301)

Harkins, S. G., & Jackson, J. M. (1985). The role of evaluation in eliminating social loafing. *Personality and Social Psychology Bulletin,* **11,** 457–465. (p. 301)

Harkins, S. G., & Petty, R. E. (1981). Effects of source magnification of cognitive effort on attitudes: An information-processing view. *Journal of Personality and Social Psychology,* **40,** 401–413. (p. 274)

Harkins, S. G., & Petty, R. E. (1982). Effects of task difficulty and task uniqueness on social loafing. *Journal of Personality and Social Psychology,* **43,** 1214–1229. (p. 303)

Harkins, S. G., & Petty, R. E. (1987). Information utility and the multiple source effect. *Journal of Personality and Social Psychology,* **52,** 260–268. (p. 275)

Harkins, S. G., & Szymanski, K. (1989). Social loafing and group evaluation. *Journal of Personality and Social Psychology,* **56,** 934–941. (p. 303)

Harmon-Jones, E., Brehm, J. W., Greenberg, J., Simon, L., & Nelson, D. E. (1996). Evidence that the production of aversive conse-quences is not necessary to create cognitive dissonance. *Journal of Personality and Social Psychology,* **70,** 5–16. (p. 166)

Harmon-Jones, E., Greenberg, J., Solomon, S., & Simon, L. (1996). The effects of mortality salience on intergroup bias between minimal groups. *European Journal of Social Psychology,* **26,** 677–681. (p. 361)

Harper's Index (1991, September). *Harper's Magazine,* p. 15. Data from Amateur Athletic Foundation of Los Angeles. (p. 179)

Harrel, W. A. (1994). Effects of blind pedestrians on motorists. *Journal of Social Psychology,* **134,** 529-539. (p. 482)

Harris, J. R. (1996). Quoted from an article by Jerome Burne for the *Manchester Observer* (via Harris: 72073.1211@CompuServe.com).

Harris, J. R. (1998). *The nurture assumption.* New York: Free Press. (pp. 183, 200, 202, 461)

Harris, M. J. (1994). Self-fulfilling prophecies in the clinical context: Review and implications for clinical practice. *Applied & Preventive Psychology,* **3,** 145–158. (p. 566)

Harris, M. J., & Rosenthal, R. (1985). Mediation of interpersonal expectancy effects: 31 meta-analyses. *Psychological Bulletin,* **97,** 363–386. (p. 121)

Harris, M. J., & Rosenthal, R. (1986). Four factors in the mediation of teacher expectancy effects. In R. S. Feldman (Ed.), *The social psychology of education.* New York: Cambridge University Press. (p. 121)

Harrison, A. A. (1977). Mere exposure. In L. Berkowitz (Ed.), *Advances in experimen-tal social psychology* (Vol. 10). New York: Academic Press, pp. 39–83. (p. 431)

Hart, A. J., & Morry, M. M. (1997). Trait inferences based on racial and behavioral cues. *Basic and Applied Social Psychology,* **19,** 33–48. (p. 341)

Hartlage, S., Alloy, A. B., Vazquez, C., & Dykman, B. (1993). Automatic and effortful processing in depression. *Psychological Bulletin,* **113,** 247–278. (p. 118)

Hartup, W. W., & Stevens, N. (1997). Friendships and adaptation in the life course. *Psychological Bulletin,* **121,** 355–370. (p. 592)

Harvey, J. H., & Omarzu, J. (1997). Minding the close relationship. *Personality and Social Psychology Review,* **1,** 224–240. (p. 470)

Harvey, J. H., Town, J. P., & Yarkin, K. L. (1981). How fundamental is the fundamental attribution error? *Journal of Personality and Social Psychology,* **40,** 346–349. (p. 90)

Haslam, S. A., & Oakes, P. J. (1995). How context-independent is the group homogeneity effect? A response to Bartsch and Judd. *European Journal of Social Psychology,* **25,** 469–475. (p. 366)

Hass, R. G., Katz, I., Rizzo, N., Bailey, J., & Eisenstadt, D. (1991). Cross-racial appraisal as related to attitude ambivalence and cognitive complexity. *Personality and Social Psychology Bulletin,* **17,** 83–92. (p. 341)

Hassan I. N. (1980). Role and status of women in Pakistan: An empirical research review. *Pakistan Journal of Psychology,* **13,** 36–56. (p. 199)

Hastie, R., Penrod, S. D., & Pennington, N. (1983). *Inside the jury.* Cambridge, Mass.: Harvard University Press. (pp. 625–628)

Hastorf, A., & Cantril, H. (1954). They saw a game: A case study. *Journal of Abnormal and Social Psychology,* **49,** 129–134. (p. 11)

Hatfield, E. (1988). Passionate and compassionate love. In R. J. Sternberg & M. L. Barnes (Eds.), *The psychology of love.* New Haven, Conn.: Yale University Press. (p. 453)

Hatfield (Walster), E., Aronson, V., Abrahams, D., & Rottman, L. (1966). Importance of physical attractiveness in dating behavior. *Journal of Personality and Social Psychology,* **4,** 508–516. (p. 435)

Hatfield, E., Cacioppo, J. T., & Rapson, R. (1992). The logic of emotion: Emotional contagion. In M. S. Clark (Ed.), *Review of Personality and Social Psychology.* Newbury Park, CA: Sage. (p. 158)

Hatfield, E., & Rapson, R. L. (1987). Passionate love: New directions in research. In W. H. Jones & D. Perlman (Eds.), *Advances in personal relationships,* Vol. 1. Greenwich, Ct.: JAI Press. (p. 455)

Hatfield, E., & Sprecher, S. (1986). *Mirror, mirror: The importance of looks in everyday life*. Albany, N.Y.: SUNY Press. (pp. 437, 458–459)

Hatfield, E., Traupmann, J., Sprecher, S., Utne, M., & Hay, J. (1985). Equity and intimate relations: Recent research. In W. Ickes (Ed.), *Compatible and incompatible relationships*. New York: Springer-Verlag. (p. 463)

Hatfield (was Walster), E., Walster, G. W., & Berscheid, E. (1978). *Equity: Theory and research*. Boston: Allyn and Bacon. (pp. 451, 461)

Haugtvedt, C. P., & Wegener, D. T. (1994). Message order effects in persuasion: An attitude strength perspective. *Journal of Consumer Research, 21*, 205–218. (p. 267)

Hazan, C., & Shaver, P. R. (1994). Attachment as an organizational framework for research on close relationships. *Psychological Inquiry, 5*, 1–22. (p. 468)

Headey, B., & Wearing, A. (1987). The sense of relative superiority—central to well-being. *Social Indicators Research, 20*, 497–516. (p. 58)

Hearold, S. (1986). A synthesis of 1043 effects of television on social behavior. In G. Comstock (Ed.), *Public communication and behavior*, Vol. 1. Orlando, Fl.: Academic Press. (pp. 415, 509)

Heath, L., & Petraitis, J. (1987). Television viewing and fear of crime: Where is the mean world? *Basic and Applied Social Psychology, 8*, 97–123. (p. 418)

Hecht, M. A., LaFrance, M., & Haertl, J. C. (1993). Gender differences in smiling: A meta-analysis of archival data. Paper presented at the American Psychological Association convention. (p. 185)

Hedge, A., & Yousif, Y. H. (1992). Effects of urban size, urgency, and cost on helpfulness: A cross-cultural comparison between the United Kingdom and the Sudan. *Journal of Cross-Cultural Psychology, 23*, 107–115. (p. 484)

Heesacker, M. (1989). Counseling and the elaboration likelihood model of attitude change. In J. F. Cruz, R. A. Goncalves, & P. P. Machado (Eds.), *Psychology and education: Investigations and interventions.* (Proceedings of the International Conference on Interventions in Psychology and Education, Porto, Portugal, July, 1987.) Porto, Portugal: Portugese Psychological Association. (p. 589)

Heider, F. (1958). *The psychology of interpersonal relations*. New York: Wiley. (p. 80)

Heilman, M. E. (1976). Oppositional behavior as a function of influence attempt intensity and retaliation threat. *Journal of Personality and Social Psychology, 33*, 574–578. (p. 243)

Heine, S. J., & Lehman, D. R. (1995). Cultural variation in unrealistic optimism: Does the West feel more invulnerable than the East? *Journal of*

Personality and Social Psychology, 68, 595–607. (p. 73)

Heine, S. J., & Lehman, D. R. (1995). When the twain meet: Self-assessments and exposure to Western culture. Unpublished manuscript, University of British Columbia. (p. 45)

Heine, S. J., & Lehman, D. R. (1997). Culture, dissonance, and self-affirmation. *Personality and Social Psychology Bulletin, 23*, 389–400. (p. 166)

Heine, S. J., & Lehman, D. R. (1997). The cultural construction of self-enhancement: An examination of group-serving biases. *Journal of Personality and Social Psychology, 72*, 1268–1283. (p. 73)

Heine, S. J., Lehman, D. R., Markus, H. R., & Kitayama, S. (1999). Is There a Universal Need for Positive Self-Regard? *Psychological Review, 106*, 766–794. (p. 45)

Hellman, P. (1980). *Avenue of the righteous of nations*. New York: Atheneum. (p. 474)

Helmrich, R. L. (1997, May). Managing human error in aviation. *Scientific American*, pp. 62–67. (p. 322)

Hemsley, G. D., & Doob, A. N. (1978). The effect of looking behavior on perceptions of a communicator's credibility. *Journal of Applied Social Psychology, 8*, 136–144. (p. 257)

Henderson-King, E. I., & Nisbett, R. E. (1996). Anti-black prejudice as a function of exposure to the negative behavior of a single black person. *Journal of Personality and Social Psychology, 71*, 654–664. (p. 370)

Hendrick, C. (1988). Roles and gender in relationships. In S. Duck (Ed.), *Handbook of personal relationships*. Chichester, England: Wiley. (p. 190)

Hendrick, C., & Hendrick, S. (1993). *Romantic love*. Newbury Park, CA: Sage. (p. 452)

Hendrick, S. S., & Hendrick, C. (1995). Gender differences and similarities in sex and love. *Personal Relationships, 2*, 55–65. (p. 456)

Hendrick, S. S., & Hendrick, C. (1997). Love and satisfaction. In R. J. Sternberg & M. Hojjat (eds.), *Satisfaction in close relationships*. New York: Guilford Publications. (p. 453)

Hendrick, S. S., Hendrick, C., & Adler, N. L. (1988). Romantic relationships: Love, satisfaction, and staying together. *Journal of Personality and Social Psychology, 54*, 980–988. (p. 465)

Hendrick, S. S., Hendrick, C., Slapion-Foote, J., & Foote, F. H. (1985). Gender differences in sexual attitudes. *Journal of Personality and Social Psychology, 48*, 1630–1642. (p. 189)

Henley, N. (1977). *Body politics: Power, sex, and nonverbal communication*. Englewood Cliffs, N.J.: Prentice-Hall. (p. 188)

Hennigan, K. M., Del Rosario, M. L., Health, L., Cook, T. D., Wharton, J. D., & Calder, B. J. (1982). Impact of the introduction of television on crime in the United States: Empirical findings and theoretical implications. *Journal of Personality and Social Psychology, 42*, 461–477. (p. 395)

Henry, W. A. III (1994, June 27). Pride and prejudice. *Time*, pp. 54–59. (p. 340)

Henslin, M. (1967). Craps and magic. *American Journal of Sociology, 73*, 316–330. (p. 115)

Hepworth, J. T., & West, S. G. (1988). Lynchings and the economy: A time-series reanalysis of Hovland and Sears (1940). *Journal of Personality and Social Psychology, 55*, 239–247. (p. 359)

Heradstveit, D. (1979). *The Arab-Israeli conflict: Psychological obstacles to peace* (Vol. 28). Oslo, Norway: Universitetsforlaget. Distributed by Columbia University Press. Reviewed by R. K. White, *Contemporary Psychology*, 1980, *25*, 11–12. (p. 532)

Herek, G. (1993). Interpersonal contact and heterosexuals' attitudes toward gay men: Results from a national survey. *Journal of Sex Research, 30*, 239–244. (p. 536)

Herek, G. M. (1986). The instrumentality of attitudes: Toward a neofunctional theory. *Journal of Social Issues, 42*, 99–114. (p. 348)

Herek, G. M. (1987). Can functions be measured? A new perspective on the functional approach to attitudes. *Social Psychology Quarterly, 50*, 285–303. (p. 348)

Herlocker, C. E., Allison, S. T., Foubert, J. D., & Beggan, J. K. (1997). Intended and unintended overconsumption of physical, spatial, and temporal resources. *Journal of Personality and Social Psychology, 73*, 992–1004. (p. 520)

Herold, E. S., & Mewhinney, D. M. K. (1993). Gender differences in casual sex and AIDS prevention: A survey of dating bars. *Journal of Sex Research, 30*, 36-42. (p. 189)

Hewstone, M. (1988). Causal attribution: From cognitive processes to collective beliefs. *The Psychologist, 8*, 323–327. (p. 14)

Hewstone, M. (1989). *Causal attribution: From cognitive processes to collective beliefs*. Oxford: Basil Blackwell. (p. 377)

Hewstone, M. (1990). The 'ultimate attribution error'? A review of the literature on intergroup causal attribution. *European Journal of Social Psychology, 20*, 311–335. (p. 372)

Hewstone, M. (1994). Revision and change of stereotypic beliefs: In search of the elusive subtyping model. In S. Stroebe & M. Hewstone (eds.), *European review of social psychology*, vol. 5. Chichester, England: Wiley. (p. 376)

Hewstone, M. (1996). Contact and categorization: Social psychological interventions to change intergroup relations. In N. Macrae, C. Stangor, & M. Hewstone (eds.), *Foundations of stereotypes and stereotyping.* New York: Guilford. (p. 545)

Hewstone, M., Cairns, E., Crisp, R. J., & Voci, A. (1999, October). Cross-Community contact in Northern Ireland: The role of intergroup anxiety. Presentation at the Society of Experimental Social Psychology Convention. (p. 537)

Hewstone, M., & Fincham, F. (1996). Attribution theory and research: Basic issues and applications. In M. Hewstone, W. Stroebe, and G. M. Stephenson (eds.), *Introduction to social psychology: A European perspective.* Oxford, UK: Blackwell. (p. 79)

Hewstone, M., Hantzi, A., & Johnston, L. (1991). Social categorisation and person memory: The pervasiveness of race as an organizing principle. *European Journal of Social Psychology, 21,* 517–528. (p. 364)

Hewstone, M., Hopkins, N., & Routh, D. A. (1992). Cognitive models of stereotype change: Generalization and subtyping in young people's views of the police. *European Journal of Social Psychology, 22,* 219–234. (p. 376)

Hewstone, M., & Ward, C. (1985). Ethnocentrism and causal attribution in southeast Asia. *Journal of Personality and Social Psychology, 48,* 614–623. (p. 372)

Higbee, K. L., Millard, R. J., & Folkman, J. R. (1982). Social psychology research during the 1970s: Predominance of experimentation and college students. *Personality and Social Psychology Bulletin, 8,* 180–183. (p. 27)

Higgins, E. T., & Bargh, J. A. (1987). Social cognition and social perception. *Annual Review of Psychology, 38,* 369–425. (p. 39)

Higgins, E. T., & McCann, C. D. (1984). Social encoding and subsequent attitudes, impressions and memory: "Context-driven" and motivational aspects of processing. *Journal of Personality and Social Psychology, 47,* 26–39. (p. 142)

Higgins, E. T., & Rholes, W. S. (1978). Saying is believing: Effects of message modification on memory and liking for the person described. *Journal of Experimental Social Psychology, 14,* 363–378. (p. 142)

Higgins, E. T., Rholes, W. S., & Jones, C. R. (1977). Category accessibility and impression formation. *Journal of Experimental Social Psychology, 13,* 141–154. (p. 103)

Hilgard, E. R., & Loftus, E. F. (1979). Effective interrogation of the eyewitness. *International Journal of Clinical and Experimental Hypnosis, 27,* 342–357. (p. 610)

Hill, T., Smith, N. D., & Lewicki, P. (1989). The development of self-image bias: A real-world demonstration. *Personality and Social Psychology Bulletin, 15,* 205–211. (p. 59)

Hilton, J. L., & von Hippel, W. (1990). The role of consistency in the judgment of stereotype-relevant behaviors. *Personality and Social Psychology Bulletin, 16,* 430–448. (p. 94)

Hinde, R. A. (1984). Why do the sexes behave differently in close relationships? *Journal of Social and Personal Relationships, 1,* 471–501. (p. 190)

Hine, D. W., & Gifford, R. (1996). Attributions about self and others in commons dilemmas. *European Journal of Social Psychology, 26,* 429–445. (p. 520)

Hines, M., & Green, R. (1991). Human hormonal and neural correlates of sex-typed behaviors. *Review of Psychiatry, 10,* 536–555. (p. 194)

Hinkle, S., Brown, R., & Ely, P. G. (1992). Social identity theory processes: Some limitations and limiting conditions. *Revista de Psicologia Social,* 99–111. (p. 355)

Hinsz, V. B. (1990). Cognitive and consensus processes in group recognition memory performance. *Journal of Personality and Social Psychology, 59,* 705–718. (p. 324)

Hinsz, V. B., Tindale, R. S., & Vollrath, D. A. (1997). The emerging conceptualization of groups as information processors. *Psychological Bulletin, 121,* 43–64. (p. 314)

Hirschman, R. S., & Leventhal, H. (1989). Preventing smoking behavior in school children: An initial test of a cognitive-development program. *Journal of Applied Social Psychology, 19,* 559–583. (p. 285)

Hirt, E. R. (1990). Do I see only what I expect? Evidence for an expectancy-guided retrieval model. *Journal of Personality and Social Psychology, 58,* 937–951. (p. 100)

Hirt, E. R., & Markman, K. D. (1995). Multiple explanation: A consider-an-alternative strategy for debiasing judgments. *Journal of Personality and Social Psychology, 69,* 1069–1088. (p. 99)

Hirt, E. R., Zillmann, D., Erickson, G. A., & Kennedy, C. (1992). Costs and benefits of allegiance: Changes in fans' self-ascribed competencies after team victory versus defeat. *Journal of Personality and Social Psychology, 63,* 724–738. (p. 572)

Hobden, K. L., & Olson, J. M. (1994). From jest to antipathy: Disparagement humor as a source of dissonance-motivated attitude change. *Basic and Applied Social psychology, 15,* 239–249. (p. 153)

Hodges, B. H. (1974). Effect of valence on relative weighting in impression formation. *Journal of Personality and Social Psychology, 30,* 378–381. (p. 83)

Hodgins, H. S., & Zuckerman, M. (1993). Beyond selecting information: Biases in spontaneous questions and resultant conclusions. *Journal of Experimental Social Psychology, 29,* 387–407. (p. 565)

Hodgkinson, V. A., Weitzman, M. S., & Kirsch, A. D. (1990). From commitment to action: How religious involvement affects giving and volunteering. In R. Wuthnow, V. A. Hodgkinson & Associates (Eds.), *Faith and philanthropy in America: Exploring the role of religion in America's voluntary sector.* San Francisco: Jossey-Bass. (p. 501)

Hodson, G., & Sorrentino, R. M. (1997). Groupthink and uncertainty orientation: Personality differences in reactivity to the group situation. *Group Dynamics, 1,* 144-155. (p. 320)

Hoffman, C., & Hurst, N. (1990). Gender stereotypes: Perception or rationalization? *Journal of Personality and Social Psychology, 58,* 197–208. (p. 350)

Hoffman, L. W. (1977). Changes in family roles, socialization, and sex differences. *American Psychologist, 32,* 644–657. (p. 356)

Hoffman, M. L. (1981). Is altruism part of human nature? *Journal of Personality and Social Psychology, 40,* 121–137. (p. 478)

Hofling, C. K., Brotzman, E., Dairymple, S., Graves, N., & Pierce, C. M. (1966). An experimental study in nurse-physician relationships. *Journal of Nervous and Mental Disease, 143,* 171–180. (p. 222)

Hogan, R., Curphy, G. J., & Hogan, J. (1994). What we know about leadership: Effectiveness and personality. *American Psychologist, 49,* 493–504. (pp. 328, 329, 330)

Hogg, M. A. (1992). *The social psychology of group cohesiveness: From attraction to social identity.* London: Harvester Wheatsheaf. (p. 353)

Hogg, M. A. (1996). Intragroup processes, group structure and social identity. In W. P. Robinson (ed.), *Social groups and identies: Developing the legacy of Henri Tajfel.* Oxford: Butterworth Heinemann. (p. 353)

Hogg, M. A., Turner, J. C., & Davidson, B. (1990). Polarized norms and social frames of reference: A test of the self-categorization theory of group polarization. *Basic and Applied Social Psychology, 11,* 77–100. (p. 314)

Hokanson, J. E., & Burgess, M. (1962). The effects of three types of aggression on vascular processes. *Journal of Abnormal and Social Psychology, 64,* 446–449. (b) (p. 421)

Hokanson, J. E., & Burgess, M. (1962). The effects of frustration and anxiety on overt aggression. *Journal of Abnormal and Social Psychology, 65,* 232–237. (a) (p. 421)

Hokanson, J. E., & Edelman, R. (1966). Effects of three social responses on vascular processes. *Journal of Personality and Social Psychology, 3,* 442–447. (p. 421)

Hokanson, J. E., & Shetler, S. (1961). The effect of overt aggression on physiological arousal. *Journal of Abnormal and Social Psychology, 63,* 446–448. (p. 421)

Hollander, E. P. (1958). Conformity, status, and idiosyncrasy credit. *Psychological Review, 65,* 117–127. (p. 237)

Holmberg, D., & Holmes, J. G. (1994). Reconstruction of relationship memories: A mental models approach. In N. Schwarz & S. Sudman (Eds.), *Autobiographical memory and the validity of retrospective reports.* New York: Springer-Verlag. (p. 101

Holmes, J. G., Miller, D. T., & Lerner, M. J. (1997). Committing altruism under the cloak of self-interest: The exchange fiction. Unpublished manuscript, University of Waterloo. (p. 475)

Holmes, J. G., & Rempel, J. K. (1989). Trust in close relationships. In C. Hendrick (Ed.), *Review of personality and social psychology,* Vol. 10. Newbury Park, Ca.: Sage. (p. 463)

Holtgraves, T. (1997). Styles of language use: Individual and cultural variability in conversational indirectness. *Journal of Personality and Social Psychology, 73,* 624–637. (p. 43)

Holtgraves, T., & Srull, T. K. (1989). The effects of positive self-descriptions on impressions: General principles and individual differences. *Personality and Social Psychology Bulletin, 15,* 452–462. (p. 73)

Holtzworth, A., & Jacobson, N. S. (1988). An attributional approach to marital dysfunction and therapy. In J. E. Maddux, C. D. Stoltenberg, & R. Rosenwein (Eds.), *Social processes in clinical and counseling psychology.* New York: Springer-Verlag. (p. 78)

Holtzworth-Munroe, A., & Jacobson, N. S. (1985). Causal attributions of married couples: When do they search for causes? What do they conclude when they do? *Journal of Personality and Social Psychology, 48,* 1398–1412. (p. 78)

Hoorens, V. (1993). Self-enhancement and superiority biases in social comparison. In W. Stroebe & M. Hewstone (Eds.), *European review of social psychology,* vol. 4. Chichester: Wiley. (p. 58)

Hoorens, V. (in press). Self-favoring biases, self-presentation and the self-other asymmetry in social comparison. *Journal of Personality.* (p. 58)

Hoorens, V., & Nuttin, J. M. (1993). Overvaluation of own attributes: Mere ownership or subjective frequency? *Social Cognition, 11,* 177–200. (p. 431)

Hoorens, V., Nuttin, J. M., Herman, I. E., & Pavakanun, U. (1990). Mastery pleasure versus mere ownership: A quasi-experimental cross-cultural and cross-alphabetical test of the name letter effect. *European Journal of Social Psychology, 20,* 181–205. (p. 431)

Hoover, C. W., Wood, E. E., & Knowles, E. S. (1983). Forms of social awareness and helping. *Journal of Experimental Social Psychology, 19,* 577–590. (p. 506)

Hooykaas, R. (1972). *Religion and the rise of modern science.* Grand Rapids, MI: Eerdmans. (p. 127)

Hormuth, S. E. (1986). Lack of effort as a result of self-focused attention: An attributional ambiguity analysis.

European Journal of Social Psychology, 16, 181–192. (p. 72)

Hornstein, H. (1976). *Cruelty and kindness.* Englewood Cliffs, N.J.: Prentice-Hall. (p. 385)

Horowitz, S. V., & Boardman, S. K. (1994). Managing conflict: Policy and research implications. *Journal of Social Issues, 50,* 197–211. (p. 548)

Horwitz, A. V., White, H. R., Howell-White, S. (1997). Becoming married and mental health: A longitudinal study of a cohort of young adults. *Journal of Marriage and the Family, 58,* 895–907. (p. 594)

House, J. S., Landis, K. R., & Umberson, D. (1988). Social relationships and health. *Science, 241,* 540–545. (p. 591)

House, R. J., & Singh, J. V. (1987). Organizational behavior: Some new directions for I/O psychology. *Annual Review of Psychology, 38,* 669–718. (p. 330)

Houston, V., & Bull, R. (1994). Do people avoid sitting next to someone who is facially disfigured? *European Journal of Social Psychology, 24,* 279–284. (p. 436)

Hovland, C. I., Lumsdaine, A. A., & Sheffield, F. D. (1949). *Experiments on mass communication. Studies in social psychology in World War II* (Vol. III). Princeton, N.J.: Princeton University Press. (pp. 261, 265)

Hovland, C. I., & Sears, R. (1940). Minor studies of aggression: Correlation of lynchings with economic indices. *Journal of Psychology, 9,* 301–310. (p. 359)

Howard, D. J. (1997). Familiar phrases as peripheral persuasion cues. *Journal of Experimental Social Psychology, 33,* 231–243. (p. 254)

Huberman, B., & Lukose, R. (1997). Social dilemmas and internet congestion. *Science, 277,* 535–537. (p. 520)

Huddy, L., & Virtanen, S. (1995). Subgroup differentiation and subgroup bias among Latinos as a function of familiarity and positive distinctiveness. *Journal of Personality and Social Psychology, 68,* 97–108. (p. 366)

Huesmann, L. R., Lagerspetz, K., & Eron, L. D. (1984). Intervening variables in the TV violence-aggression relation: Evidence from two countries. *Developmental Psychology, 20,* 746–775. (p. 413)

Hugick, L., & McAneny, L. (1992, September). A gloomy America sees a nation in decline, no easy solutions ahead. *Gallup Poll Monthly,* p. 4. (p. 410)

Hui, C. H., Triandis, H. C., & Yee, C. (1991). Cultural differences in reward allocation: Is collectivism the explanation? *British Journal of Social Psychology, 30,* 145–157. (p. 528)

Hull, J. G., & Bond, C. F., Jr. (1986). Social and behavioral consequences of alcohol consumption and expectancy: A meta-analysis. *Psychological Bulletin, 99,* 347–360. (p. 387441)

Hull, J. G., Levenson, R. W., Young, R. D., & Sher, K. J. (1983). Self-awareness-reducing effects of alcohol consumption. *Journal of Personality and Social Psychology, 44,* 461–473. (p. 309331)

Hull, J. G., & Young, R. D. (1983). The self-awareness-reducing effects of alcohol consumption: Evidence and implications. In J. Suls & A. G. Greenwald (Eds.), *Psychological perspectives on the self,* Vol. 2. Hillsdale, N.J.: Erlbaum. (p. 578)

Humphrey, R. (1985). How work roles influence perception: Structural-cognitive processes and organizational behavior. *American Sociological Review, 50,* 242–252. (p. 181)

Hunt, M. (1993). *The story of psychology.* New York: Doubleday. (p. 51)

Hunt, P. J., & Hillery, J. M. (1973). Social facilitation in a location setting: An examination of the effects over learning trials. *Journal of Experimental Social Psychology, 9,* 563–571. (p. 294)

Hunter, J. A., Stringer, M., & Watson, R. P. (1991). Intergroup violence and intergroup attributions. *British Journal of Social Psychology, 30,* 261–266. (p. 532)

Huo, Y. J., Smith, H. J., Tyler, T. R., & Lind, E. A. (1996). Superordinate identification, subgroup identification, and justice concerns: Is separatism the problem; is assimilation the answer? *Psychological Science, 7,* 40–45. (p. 545)

Hurt, S. W., Schnurr, P. P., Severino, S. K., Freeman, E. W., Gise, L. H., Rivera-Tovar, A., & Steege, J. F. (1992). Late luteal phase dysphoric disorder in 670 women evaluated for premenstrual complaints. *American Journal of Psychiatry, 149,* 525–530. (p. 580)

Huston, A. C., Donnerstein, E., Fairchild, H., Feshbach, N. D., Katz, P. A., & Murray, J. P. (1992). *Big world, small screen: The role of television in American society.* Lincoln, NE: University of Nebraska Press. (p. 412)

Huston, T. L. (1973). Ambiguity of acceptance, social desirability, and dating choice. *Journal of Experimental Social Psychology, 9,* 32–42. (p. 435)

Huston, T. L., & Chorost, A. F. (1994). Behavioral buffers on the effect of negativity on marital satisfaction: A longitudinal study. *Personal Relationships, 1,* 223–239. (p. 457)

Hutnik, N. (1985). Aspects of identity in a multi-ethnic society. *New Community, 12,* 298–309. (p. 545)

Hutton, D. G., & Baumeister, R. F. (1992). Self-awareness and attitude change: Seeing oneself on the central route to persuasion. *Personality and Social Psychology Bulletin, 18,* 68–75. (p. 308)

Hyde, J. S., Fennema, E. H., & Lamon, S. J. (1990). Gender differences in mathematics performance: A meta-analysis. *Psychological Bulletin, 107.* (p. 337)

Hyman, I. E., Jr., Husband, T. H., & Billings, F. J. (1995). False memories of childhood experiences. *Applied Cognitive Psychology*, **9**, 181–197. (p. 100)

Hyman, I. E., Jr., & Pentland, J. (1996). The role of mental imagery in the creation of false childhood memories. *Journal of Memory and Language*, **35**, 101–117. (p. 100)

Hyman, R. (1981). Cold reading: How to convince strangers that you know all about them. In K. Frazier (Ed.), *Paranormal borderlands of science*. Buffalo, N.Y.: Prometheus Books. (p. 142)

Ickes, W. (1993). Traditional gender roles: Do they make, and then break, our relationships? *Journal of Social Issues*, **49**, 7185. (p. 196)

Ickes, W., & Layden, M. A. (1978). Attributional styles. In J. H. Harvey, W. Ickes, & R. F. Kidd (Eds.), *New directions in attribution research* (Vol. 2). Hillsdale, N.J.: Lawrence Erlbaum. (p. 66)

Ickes, W., Layden, M. A., & Barnes, R. D. (1978). Objective self-awareness and individuation: An empirical link. *Journal of Personality*, **46**, 146–161. (p. 309)

Ickes, W., Patterson, M. L., Rajecki, D. W., & Tanford, S. (1982). Behavioral and cognitive consequences of reciprocal versus compensatory responses to preinteraction expectancies. *Social Cognition*, **1**, 160–190. (pp. 241, 375)

Ickes, W., Snyder, M., & Garcia, S. (1997). Personality influences on the choice of situations. In R. Hogan, J. Johnson, & S. Briggs (eds.), *Handbook of Personality Psychology*. San Diego: Academic Press. (p. 205)

Imai, Y. (1994). Effects of influencing attempts on the perceptions of powerholders and the powerless. *Journal of Social Behavior and Personality*, **9**, 455–468. (p. 57)

Ingham, A. G., Levinger, G., Graves, J., & Peckham, V. (1974). The Ringelmann effect: Studies of group size and group performance. *Journal of Experimental Social Psychology*, **10**, 371–384. (p. 300)

Inglehart, M. R., Markus, H., & Brown, D. R. (1989). The effects of possible selves on academic achievement—a panel study. In J. P. Forgas & J. M. Innes (Eds.), *Recent advances in social psychology: An international perspective*. North-Holland: Elsevier Science Publishers. (p. 39)

Inglehart, R. (1990). *Culture shift in advanced industrial society*. Princeton, NJ: Princeton University Press. (pp. 470, 512, 593)

Inman, M. L., & Baron, R. S. (1996). The influence of prototypes on perceptions of prejudice. *Journal of Personality and Social Psychology*, in press. (p. 342)

Inman, M. L., & Baron, R. S. (1996). The influence of prototypes on perceptions of prejudice. *Journal of Personality and Social Psychology*, **70**, 727–739. (p. 342)

Insko, C. A., Nacoste, R. W., & Moe, J. L. (1983). Belief congruence and racial discrimination: Review of the evidence and critical evaluation. *European Journal of Social Psychology*, **13**, 153–174. (p. 444)

Insko, C. A., Smith, R. H., Alicke, M. D., Wade, J., & Taylor, S. (1985). Conformity and group size: The concern with being right and the concern with being liked. *Journal of Personality and Social Psychology*, **11**, 41–50. (p. 238)

Institute of Medicine (1989). *Behavioral influences on the endocrine and immune systems*. Washington, DC: National Academy Press. (p. 583)

Isen, A. M., Clark, M., & Schwartz, M. F. (1976). Duration of the effect of good mood on helping: Footprints on the sands of time. *Journal of Personality and Social Psychology*, **34**, 385–393. (pp. 498, 499)

Isen, A. M., Horn, N., & Rosenhan, D. L. (1973). Effects of success and failure on children's generosity. *Journal of Personality and Social Psychology*, **27**, 239–247. (p. 496)

Isen, A. M., & Means, B. (1983). The influence of positive affect on decision-making strategy. *Social Cognition*, **2**, 28–31. (p. 117)

Isen, A. M., Shalker, T. E., Clark, M., & Karp, L. (1978). Affect, accessibility of material in memory, and behavior: A cognitive loop. *Journal of Personality and Social Psychology*, **36**, 1–12. (p. 498)

Islam, M. R., & Hewstone, M. (1993). Dimensions of contact as predictors of intergroup anxiety, perceived out-group variability, and out-group attitude: An integrative model. *Personality and Social Psychology Bulletin*, **19**, 700–710. (p. 532)

Isozaki, M. (1984). The effect of discussion on polarization of judgments. *Japanese Psychological Research*, **26**, 187–193. (p. 311)

Israel, B. A., & Antonucci, T. C. (1987). Social network characteristics and psychological well-being: A replication and extension. *Health Education Quarterly*, **14**, 461–481. (p. 592)

Ito, T. A., Miller, N., & Pollock, V. E. (1996). Alcohol and aggression: A meta-analysis on the moderating effects of inhibitory cues, triggering events, and self-focused attention. *Psychological Bulletin*, **120**, 60–82. (p. 387)

Iwao, S. (1988). Social psychology's models of man: Isn't it time for East to meet West? Invited address to the International Congress of Scientific Psychology, Sydney, Australia. Cited by H. C. Triandis (1989). The self and social behavior in differing cultural contexts. *Psychological Review*, **96**, 506–520. (p. 141)

Iyer, P. (1993, Fall). The global village finally arrives. *Time*, pp. 86–87. (p. 174)

Jackman, M. R., & Senter, M. S. (1981). Beliefs about race, gender, and social class different, therefore unequal: Beliefs about trait differences between groups of unequal status. In D. J. Treiman & R. V. Robinson (Eds.), *Research in stratification and mobility* (Vol. 2). Greenwich, Conn.: JAI Press. (pp. 339, 344)

Jackson, J. M., & Latané, B. (1981). All alone in front of all those people: Stage fright as a function of number and type of co-performers and audience. *Journal of Personality and Social Psychology*, **40**, 73–85. (p. 295)

Jackson, J. S., Kirby, D., Barnes, L, & Shepard, L. (1993). Institutional racism and pluralistic ignorance: A cross-national comparison. In M. Wievorka (ed.), *Racisme et modernite*. Paris: Editions la Découverte. (p. 339)

Jackson, L. A. (1989). Relative deprivation and the gender wage gap. *Journal of Social Issues*, **45**(4), 117–133. (p. 528)

Jackson, L. A., Hunter, J. E., & Hodge, C. N. (1995). Physical attractiveness and intellectual competence: A meta-analytic review. *Social Psychology Quarterly*, in press. (p. 436)

Jackson, L. A., Sullivan, L. A., & Hodge, C. N. (1993). Stereotype effects on attributions, predictions, and evaluations: No two social judgments are quite alike. *Journal of Personality and Social Psychology*, **65**, 69–84. (pp. 339, 372)

Jackson, L. M., & Esses, V. M. (1997). Of scripture and ascription: The relation between religious fundamentalism and intergroup helping. *Personality and Social Bulletin*, **23**, 893-906. (p. 501)

Jacobs, R. C., & Campbell, D. T. (1961). The perpetuation of an arbitrary tradition through several generations of a laboratory microculture. *Journal of Abnormal and Social Psychology*, **62**, 649–658. (p. 213)

Jacoby, S. (1986, December). When opposites attract. *Reader's Digest*, pp. 95–98. (p. 445)

Jaffe, Y., Shapir, N., & Yinon, Y. (1981). Aggression and its escalation. *Journal of Cross-Cultural Psychology*, **12**, 21–36. (pp. 419, 420)

Jain, U. (1990). Social perspectives on causal attribution. In G. Misra (Ed.), *Applied social psychology in India*. New Delhi: Sage. (p. 73)

James, W. (1890, reprinted 1950). *The principles of psychology*, vol. 2. New York: Dover Publications. (p. 158)

James, W. (1902, reprinted 1958). *The varieties of religious experience*. New York: Mentor Books. (p. 350)

James, W. (1976). *Talks to teachers on psychology: And to students on some of life's ideals*. New York: Holt, 1922, p. 33. (Originally published, 1899). Cited by W. J. McKeachie, Psychology in

America's bicentennial year. *American Psychologist*, **31**, 819–833. (p. 167)

Jamieson, D. W., Lydon, J. E., Stewart, G., & Zanna, M. P. (1987). Pygmalion revisited: New evidence for student expectancy effects in the classroom. *Journal of Educational Psychology*, **79**, 461–466. (p. 121)

Jamieson, D. W., Lydon, J. E., & Zanna, M. P. (1987). Attitude and activity preference similarity: Differential bases of interpersonal attraction for low and high self-monitors. *Journal of Personality and Social Psychology*, **53**, 1052–1060. (p. 456)

Janis, I. (1989). Crucial decisions: Leadership in policymaking and crisis management. New York: Free Press. (p. 530)

Janis, I. L. (1971, November). Groupthink. *Psychology Today*, pp. 43–46. (p. 317)

Janis, I. L. (1982). Counteracting the adverse effects of concurrence-seeking in policy-planning groups: Theory and research perspectives. In H. Brandstatter, J. H. Davis, & G. Stocker-Kreichgauer (Eds.), *Group decision making*. New York: Academic Press. (pp. 317, 321)

Janis, I. L., Kaye, D., & Kirschner, P. (1965). Facilitating effects of eating while reading on responsiveness to persuasive communications. *Journal of Personality and Social Psychology*, **1**, 181–186. (p. 261)

Janis, I. L., & Mann, L. (1977). *Decision-making: A psychological analysis of conflict, choice and commitment*. New York: Free Press. (p. 320)

Jankowiak, W. R., & Fischer, E. F. (1992). A cross-cultural perspective on romantic love. *Ethnology*, **31**, 149–155. (p. 455)

Janoff-Bulman, R., Timko, C., & Carli, L. L. (1985). Cognitive biases in blaming the victim. *Journal of Experimental Social Psychology*, **21**, 161–177. (p. 374)

Jason, L. A., Rose, T., Ferrari, J. R., & Barone, R. (1984). Personal versus impersonal methods for recruiting blood donations. *Journal of Social Psychology*, **123**, 139–140. (p. 506)

Jeffery, R. (1964). The psychologist as an expert witness on the issue of insanity. *American Psychologist*, **19**, 838–843. (p. 562)

Jelalian, E., & Miller, A. G. (1984). The perseverance of beliefs: Conceptual perspectives and research developments. *Journal of Social and Clinical Psychology*, **2**, 25–56. (p. 98)

Jellison, J. M., & Green, J. (1981). A self-presentation approach to the fundamental attribution error: The norm of internality. *Journal of Personality and Social Psychology*, **40**, 643–649. (p. 89)

Jemmott, J. B., III, & Gonzalez, E. (1989). Social status, the status distribution, and performance in small groups. *Journal of Applied Social Psychology*, **19**, 584–598. (p. 181)

Jemmott, J. B., III., & Locke, S. E. (1984). Psychosocial factors, immunologic mediation, and human susceptibility to infectious diseases: How much do we know? *Psychological Bulletin*, **95**, 78–108. (p. 583)

Jennings, D. L., Amabile, T. M., & Ross, L. (1982). Informal covariation assessment: Data-based vs theory-based judgments. In D. Kahneman, P. Slovic, & A. Tversky (Eds.), *Judgment under uncertainty: Heuristics and biases*. New York: Cambridge University Press. (p. 114)

Johnson, B. T., & Eagly, A. H. (1989). Effects of involvement on persuasion: A meta-analysis. *Psychological Bulletin*, **106**, 290–314. (p. 253)

Johnson, B. T., & Eagly, A. H. (1990). Involvement and persuasion: Types, traditions, and the evidence. *Psychological Bulletin*, **107**, 375–384. (p. 275)

Johnson, C. B., Stockdale, M. S., & Saal, F. E. (1991). Persistence of men's misperceptions of friendly cues across a variety of interpersonal encounters. *Psychology of Women Quarterly*, **15**, 463–475. (p. 79)

Johnson, D. J., & Rusbult, C. E. (1989). Resisting temptation: Devaluation of alternative partners as a means of maintaining commitment in close relationships. *Journal of Personality and Social Psychology*, **57**, 967–980. (p. 442)

Johnson, D. W., & Johnson, R. T. (1987). *Learning together and alone: Cooperative, competitive, and individualistic learning*, 2nd ed. Englewood Cliffs, N.J.: Prentice-Hall. (p. 542)

Johnson, D. W., & Johnson, R. T. (1994). Constructive conflict in the schools. *Journal of Social Issues*, **50**, 117–137. (p. 542)

Johnson, D. W., & Johnson, R. T. (1995). Teaching students to be peacemakers: Results of five years of research. *Peace and Conflict: Journal of Peace Psychology*, **1**, 417–438. (p. 549)

Johnson, D. W., Maruyama, G., Johnson, R., Nelson, D., & Skon, L. (1981). Effects of cooperative, competitive, and individualistic goal structures on achievement: A meta-analysis. *Psychological Bulletin*, **89**, 47–62. (p. 543)

Johnson, E. J., & Tversky, A. (1983). Affect, generalization, and the perception of risk. *Journal of Personality and Social Psychology*, **45**, 20–31. (p. 117)

Johnson, J. D., Jackson, L. A., & Gatto, L. (1995). Violent Attitudes and Deferred Academic Aspirations: Deleterious Effects of Exposure to Rap Music. *Basic and Applied Social Psychology*, **16**, 27–41. (p. 416)

Johnson, J. T., Gain, L. M., Falke, T. L., Hayman, J., & Perillo, E. (1985). The Barnum effect revisited: Cognitive and motivational factors in the acceptance of personality descriptions. *Journal of Personality and Social Psychology*, **49**, 1378–1391. (p. 63)

Johnson, J. T., Jemmott, J. B., III, & Pettigrew, T. F. (1984). Causal attribution and dispositional inference: Evidence of inconsistent judgments. *Journal of Experimental Social Psychology*, **20**, 567–585. (p. 91)

Johnson, M. H., & Magaro, P. A. (1987). Effects of mood and severity on memory processes in depression and mania. *Psychological Bulletin*, **101**, 28–40. (pp. 117, 571)

Johnson, R. D., & Downing, L. J. (1979). Deindividuation and valence of cues: Effects of prosocial and antisocial behavior. *Journal of Personality and Social Psychology*, **37**, 1532–1538. (p. 306)

Johnson, R. W., Kelly, R. J., & LeBlanc, B. A. (1995). Motivational basis of dissonance: Aversive consequences or inconsistency. *Personality and Social Psychology Bulletin*, **21**, 850–855. (p. 166)

Johnston, L. D. (1996, December 19). Monitoring the future study of drug use. News and Information Services, University of Michigan. (p. 252)

Joiner, T. E., Jr. (1994). Contagious depression: Existence, specificity to depressed symptoms, and the role of reassurance seeking. *Journal of Personality and Social Psychology*, **67**, 287–296. (p. 572)

Jonas, K. (1992). Modelling and suicide: A test of the Werther effect. *British Journal of Social Psychology*, **31**, 295–306. (p. 214)

Jones, E. E. (1964). *Ingratiation*. New York: Appleton-Century-Crofts. (p. 447)

Jones, E. E. (1976). How do people perceive the causes of behavior? *American Scientist*, **64**, 300–305. (p. 87)

Jones, E. E., & Davis, K. E. (1965). From acts to dispositions: The attribution process in person perception. In L. Berkowitz (Ed.), *Advances in experimental social psychology* (Vol. 2). New York: Academic Press. (p. 81)

Jones, E. E., & Harris, V. A. (1967). The attribution of attitudes. *Journal of Experimental Social Psychology*, **3**, 2–24. (pp. 83, 84)

Jones, E. E., & Nisbett, R. E. (1971). *The actor and the observer: Divergent perceptions of the cases of behavior*. Morristown, N.J.: General Learning Press. (p. 87)

Jones, E. E., Rhodewalt, F., Berglas, S., & Skelton, J. A. (1981). Effects of strategic self-presentation on subsequent self-esteem. *Journal of Personality and Social Psychology*, **41**, 407–421. (p. 586)

Jones, E. E., Rock, L., Shaver, K. G., Goethals, G. R., & Ward, L. M. (1968). Pattern of performance and ability attribution: An unexpected primacy effect. *Journal of Personality and Social Psychology*, **10**, 317–340. (p. 266)

Jones, E. E., & Sigall, H. (1971). The bogus pipeline: A new paradigm for measuring affect and attitude. *Psychological Bulletin*, **76**, 349–364. (p. 133)

Jones, J. M. (1983). The concept of race in social psychology: From color to culture. In L. Wheeler & P. Shaver (Eds.), *Review of personality and social psychology*, Vol. 4. Beverly Hills, Ca.: Sage. (p. 351)

Jones, J. M. (1988). Piercing the veil: Bicultural strategies for coping with prejudice and racism. Invited address at the national conference, "Opening Doors: An Appraisal of Race Relations in America," University of Alabama, June 11. (p. 444)

Jones, J. M. (1990). Promoting diversity in an individualistic society. Keynote address, Great Lakes College Association conference, "Multiculturalism transforming the 21st century." (p. 175)

Jones, J. T., & Cunningham, J. D. (1996). Attachment styles and other predictors of relationship satisfaction in dating couples. *Personal Relationships, 3*, 387–399. (p. 461)

Jones, R. A., & Brehm, J. W. (1970). Persuasiveness of one- and two-sided communications as a function of awareness there are two sides. *Journal of Experimental Social Psychology, 6*, 47–56. (p. 266)

Jones, W. H., Carpenter, B. N., & Quintana, D. (1985). Personality and interpersonal predictors of loneliness in two cultures. *Journal of Personality and Social Psychology, 48*, 1503–1511. (p. 32)

Jones, W. H., Freemon, J. E., & Goswick, R. A. (1981). The persistence of loneliness: Self and other determinants. *Journal of Personality, 49*, 27–48. (p. 576)

Jones, W. H., Hobbs, S. A., & Hockenbury, D. (1982). Loneliness and social skill deficits. *Journal of Personality and Social Psychology, 42*, 682–689. (p. 576)

Jones, W. H., Sansone, C., & Helm, B. (1983). Loneliness and interpersonal judgments. *Personality and Social Psychology Bulletin, 9*, 437–441. (p. 576)

Jorgenson, D. O., & Papciak, A. S. (1981). The effects of communication, resource feedback, and identifiability on behavior in a simulated commons. *Journal of Experimental Social Psychology, 17*, 373–385. (p. 522)

Josephson, W. L. (1987). Television violence and children's aggression: Testing the priming, social script, and disinhibition predictions. *Journal of Personality and Social Psychology, 53*, 882–890. (p. 416)

Jourard, S. M. (1964), *The transparent self.* Princeton, N.J.: Van Nostrand. (p. 465)

Jourden, F. J., & Heath, C. (1996). The evaluation gap in performance perceptions: Illusory perceptions of groups and individuals. *Journal of Applied Psychology, 81*, 369–379. (p. 68)

Judd, C. M., Park, B., Ryan, C. S., Brauer, M., & Kraus, S. (1995). Stereotypes and ethnocentrism: Diverging interethnic perceptions of African American and White American youth. *Journal of Personality and Social Psychology, 69*, 460–481. (p. 351)

Judd, C. M., Ryan, C. S., & Park, B. (1991). Accuracy in the judgment of in-group and out-group variability. *Journal of Personality and Social Psychology, 61*, 366–379. (p. 366)

Jussim, L. (1986). Self-fulfilling prophecies: A theoretical and integrative review. *Psychological Review, 93*, 429–445. (p. 121)

Jussim, L. (1989). Teacher expectations: Self-fulfilling prophecies, perceptual biases, and accuracy. *Journal of Personality and Social Psychology, 57*, 469–480. (p. 120)

Jussim, L. (1991). Social perception and social reality: A reflection-construction model. *Psychological Review, 98*, 54–73. (p. 120)

Jussim, L. (1993). Accuracy in interpersonal expectations: A reflection-construction analysis of current and classic research. *Journal of Personality, 61*, 637–668. (p. 123)

Jussim, L., Eccles, J., & Madon, S. (1996). Social perception, social stereotypes, and teacher expectations: Accuracy and the quest for the powerful self-fulfilling prophecy. *Advances in Experimental Social Psychology.* (p. 120)

Jussim, L., McCauley, C. R., & Lee, Y-T. (1995). Introduction: Why study stereotype accuracy and innaccuracy? In Y. T. Lee, L. Jussim, & C. R. McCauley (eds.), *Stereotypes accuracy: Toward appreciating group differences.* Washington, DC: American Psychological Association. (p. 337)

Kagan, J. (1989). Temperamental contributions to social behavior. *American Psychologist, 44*, 668–674. (p. 386)

Kagehiro, D. K. (1990). Defining the standard of proof in jury instructions. *Psychological Science, 1*, 194–200. (pp. 620, 622, 625)

Kahan, T. L., & Johnson, M. K. (1992). Self effects in memory for person information. *Social Cognition, 10*, 30–50. (p. 39)

Kahle, L. R., & Berman, J. (1979). Attitudes cause behaviors: A cross-lagged panel analysis. *Journal of Personality and Social Psychology, 37*, 315–321. (p. 134)

Kahn, A. S., & Gaeddert, W. P. (1985). From theories of equity to theories of justice. In V. W. O'Leary, R. K. Unger, & B. S. Wallston (Eds.), *Women, gender, and social psychology.* Hillsdale, N.J.: Erlbaum. (p. 528)

Kahn, A. S., Mathie, V. A., & Torgler, C. (1994). Rape scripts and rape acknowledgment. *Psychology of Women Quarterly, 18*, 53–66. (p. 408)

Kahn, M. W. (1951). The effect of severe defeat at various age levels on the aggressive behavior of mice. *Journal of Genetic Psychology, 79*, 117–130. (p. 396)

Kahneman, D., & Miller, D. T. (1986). Norm theory: Comparing reality to its alternatives. *Psychological Review, 93*, 75–88. (p. 113)

Kahneman, D., & Snell, J. (1992). Predicting a changing taste: Do people know what they will like? *Journal of Behavioral Decision Making, 5*, 187–200. (p. 431)

Kahneman, D., & Tversky, A. (1979). Intuitive prediction: Biases and corrective procedures. *Management Science, 12*, 313–327. (p. 106)

Kahneman, D., & Tversky, A. (1995). Conflict resolution: A cognitive perspective. In K. Arrow, R. Mnookin, L. Ross, A. Tversky, & R. Wilson (eds.), *Barriers to the negotiated resolution of conflict.* New York: Norton. (p. 552)

Kalick, S. M. (1977). *Plastic surgery, physical appearance, and person perception.* Unpublished doctoral dissertation, Harvard University. Cited by E. Berscheid in, An overview of the psychological effects of physical attractiveness and some comments upon the psychological effects of knowledge of the effects of physical attractiveness. In W. Lucker, K. Ribbens, & J. A. McNamera (Eds.), *Logical aspects of facial form* (craniofacial growth series). Ann Arbor: University of Michigan Press, 1981. (p. 436)

Kalin R., & Berry, J. W., (1982). The social ecology of ethnic attitudes in Canada. *Canadian Journal of Behavioural Science, 14*, 97-109. (p. 535)

Kalin, R., & Berry, J. W. (1995). Ethnic and civic self-identity in Canada: Analyses of 1974 and 1991 national surveys. *Canadian Ethnic Studies, 27*, 1–15. (p. 41)

Kalven, H., Jr., & Zeisel, H. (1966). *The American jury.* Chicago: University of Chicago Press. (pp. 613, 625, 626)

Kameda, T., & Sugimori, S. (1993). Psychological entrapment in group decision making: An assigned decision rule and a groupthink phenomenon. *Journal of Personality and Social Psychology, 65*, 282–292. (p. 326)

Kamen, L. P., Seligman, M. E. P., Dwyer, J., & Rodin, J. (1988). Pessimism and cell-mediated immunity. Unpublished manuscript, University of Pennsylvania. (p. 584)

Kammer, D. (1982). Differences in trait ascriptions to self and friend: Unconfounding intensity from variability. *Psychological Reports, 51*, 99–102. (p. 89)

Kandel, D. B. (1978). Similarity in real-life adolescent friendship pairs. *Journal of Personality and Social Psychology, 36*, 306–312. (p. 445)

Kanekar, S., & Nazareth, A. (1988). Attributed rape victim's fault as a function of her attractiveness, physical hurt, and emotional disturbance. *Social Behaviour, 3*, 37–40. (p. 79)

Kaplan, J. (1995, March 4–10). Why kids need heroes. *TV Guide*, pp. 25–30. (p. 412)

Kaplan, M. F. (1989). Task, situational, and personal determinants of influence processes in group decision making. In E. J. Lawler (Ed.), *Advances in group processes* (vol. 6). Greenwich, CT: JAI Press. (p. 316)

Kaplan, M. F., & Schersching, C. (1980). Reducing juror bias: An experimental approach. In P. D. Lipsitt & B. D. Sales (Eds.), *New directions in psycholegal research*. New York: Van Nostrand Reinhold, pp. 149–170. (pp. 616, 627)

Kaplan, M. F., Wanshula, L. T., & Zanna, M. P. (1993). Time pressure and information integration in social judgment: The effect of need for structure. In O. Svenson & J. Maule (Eds.), *Time pressure and stress in human judgment and decision making*. Cambridge: Cambridge University Press. (p. 364)

Kaprio, J., Koskenvuo, M., & Rita, H. (1987). Mortality after bereavement: A propsective study of 95,647 widowed persons. *American Journal of Public Health, 77*, 283–287. (p. 591)

Karau, S. J., & Williams, K. D. (1993). Social loafing: A meta-analytic review and theoretical integration. *Journal of Personality and Social Psychology, 65*, 681–706. (pp. 301, 302, 303)

Karney, B. R., & Bradbury, T. N. (1995). The longitudinal course of marital quality and stability: A review of theory, method, and research. *Psychological Bulletin, 118*, 3–34. (p. 469)

Kassin, S. M., Ellsworth, P. C., & Smith, V. L. (1989). The "general acceptance" of psychological research on eyewitness testimony: A survey of the experts. *American Psychologist, 44*, 1089–1098. (p. 612)

Kassin, S. M., & Wrightsman, L. S. (1979). On the requirements of proof: The timing of judicial instruction and mock juror verdicts. *Journal of Personality and Social Psychology, 37*, 1877–1887. (p. 618)

Kato, P. S., & Ruble, D. N. (1992). Toward an understanding of women's experience of menstrual cycle symptoms. In V. Adesso, D. Reddy, & R. Fleming (Eds.), *Psychological perspectives on women's health*. Washington, DC: Hemisphere. (p. 580)

Katz, A. M., & Hill, R. (1958). Residential propinquity and marital selection: A review of theory, method, and fact. *Marriage and Family Living, 20*, 237–335. (p. 429)

Katz, E. (1957). The two-step flow of communication: An up-to-date report on a hypothesis. *Public Opinion Quarterly, 21*, 61–78. (p. 270)

Katz, I., Cohen, S., & Glass, D. (1975). Some determinants of cross-racial helping behavior. *Journal of Personality and Social Psychology, 32*, 964–970. (p. 504)

Katzev, R., Edelsack, L., Steinmetz, G., & Walker, T. (1978). The effect of reprimanding transgressions on subsequent helping behavior: Two field experiments. *Personality and Social Psychology Bulletin, 4*, 126–129. (p. 506)

Katzev, R., & Wang, T. (1994). Can commitment change behavior? A case study of environmental actions. *Journal of Social Behavior and Personality, 9*, 13–26. (p. 236)

Kaufman, J., & Zigler, E. (1987). Do abused children become abusive parents? *American Journal of Orthopsychiatry, 57*, 186–192. (p. 397)

Kaufmann, H., & Kooman, A. (1967). Predicted compliance in obedience situations as a function of implied instructional variables. *Psychonomic Science, 7*, 205-206. (p. 218)

Kawakami, K., & Dion, K. L. (1993). The impact of salient self-identities on relative deprivation and action intentions. *European Journal of Social Psychology, 23*, 525-540. (p. 394)

Kawakami, K., & Dion, K. L. (1995). Social identity and affect as determinants of collective action: Toward an integration of relative deprivation and social identity theories. *Theory and Psychology, 5*, 551-577. (p. 394)

Keating, C. F. (1985). Gender and the physiognomy of dominance and attractiveness. *Social Psychology Quarterly, 48*, 61–70. (p. 438)

Keating, J. P., & Brock, T. C. (1974). Acceptance of persuasion and the inhibition of counterargumentation under various distraction tasks. *Journal of Experimental Social Psychology, 10*, 301–309. (p. 274)

Keelan, J. P. R., Dion, K. K., & Dion, K. L. (in press). Attachment style and relationship satisfaction: Test of a self-disclosure explanation. *Canadian Journal of Behavioural Science*. (p. 464)

Keelan, J. P. , Dion, K. K., & Dion, K. L. (1998). Attachment style and relationship satisfaction: Test of a self-disclosure explanation. *Canadian Journal of Behavioural Science, 30*, 24-35. (p. 461)

Kellerman, J., Lewis, J., & Laird, J. D. (1989). Looking and loving: The effects of mutual gaze on feelings of romantic love. *Journal of Research in Personality, 23*, 145–161. (p. 469)

Kelley, H. H. (1973). The process of causal attribution. *American Psychologist, 28*, 107–128. (p. 82)

Kelley, H. H. (1979). *Personal relationships: Their structures and processes*. Hillsdale, N.J.: Lawrence Erlbaum. (p. 449)

Kelley, H. H., & Stahelski, A. J. (1970). The social interaction basis of cooperators' and competitors' beliefs about others. *Journal of Personality and Social Psychology, 16*, 66–91. (p. 121)

Kelley, K., Dawson, L., & Musialowski, D. M. (1989). Three faces of sexual explicitness: The good, the bad, and the useful. In D. Zillmann & J. Bryant (Eds.), *Pornography: Reesearch advances and policy considerations*. Hillsdale, NJ: Erlbaum. (p. 421)

Kelman, H. C. (1997). Group processes in the resolution of international conflicts: Experiences from the Israeli-Palestinian case. *American Psychologist, 52*, 212–220. (p. 551)

Keltner, D., & Robinson, R. J. (1996). Extremism, power, and the imagined basis of social conflict. *Current Directions in Psychological Science, 5*, 101–105. (p. 533)

Kennedy, J. F. (1956). *Profiles in courage*. New York: Harper. (p. 237)

Kenny, D. A., & Albright, L. (1987). Accuracy in interpersonal perception: A social relations analysis. *Psychology Bulletin, 102*, 390–402. (p. 66)

Kenny, D. A., & DePaulo, B. M. (1993). Do people know how others view them? An empirical and theoretical account. *Psychological Bulletin, 114*, 145–161. (p. 62)

Kenny, D. A., & Nasby, W. (1980). Splitting the reciprocity correlation. *Journal of Personality and Social Psychology, 38*, 249–256. (p. 447)

Kenrick, D. T. (1987). Gender, genes, and the social environment: A biosocial interactionist perspective. In P. Shaver & C. Hendrick (Eds.), *Sex and gender: Review of personality and social psychology*, vol. 7. Beverly Hills, Ca.: Sage. (pp. 190, 191) 209)

Kenrick, D. T., Baumann, D. J., & Cialdini, R. B. (1979). A step in the socialization of altruism as hedonism: Effects of negative mood on children's generosity under public and private conditions. *Journal of Personality and Social Psychology, 37*, 747–755. (p. 496)

Kenrick, D. T., & Gutierres, S. E. (1980). Contrast effects and judgments of physical attractiveness: When beauty becomes a social problem. *Journal of Personality and Social Psychology, 38*, 131–140. (p. 441)

Kenrick, D. T., Gutierres, S. E., & Goldberg, L. L. (1989). Influence of popular erotica on judgments of strangers and mates. *Journal of Experimental Social Psychology, 25*, 159–167. (p. 441)

Kenrick, D. T., & Keefe, R. C. (1992). Age preferences in mates reflect sex differences in reproductive strategies. *Behavioral and Brain Sciences, 15*, 75–133. (p. 193)

Kenrick, D. T., & MacFarlane, S. W. (1986). Ambient temperature and horn-honking: A field study of the heat/ aggression relationship. *Environment and Behavior, 18*, 179–191. (p. 402)

Kenrick, D. T., & Trost, M. R. (1987). A biosocial theory of heterosexual relationships. In K. Kelly (Ed.), *Females, males, and sexuality.* Albany: State University of New York Press. (pp. 79, 458)

Kerr, N. L. (1978). Beautiful and blameless: Effects of victim attractiveness and responsibility on mock jurors' verdicts. *Journal of Personality and Social Psychology,* **4,** 479–482. *(a)* (p. 619)

Kerr, N. L. (1978). Severity of prescribed penalty and mock jurors' verdicts. *Journal of Personality and Social Psychology,* **36,** 1431–1442. *(b)* (p. 619)

Kerr, N. L. (1981). Effects of prior juror experience on juror behavior. *Basic and Applied Social Psychology,* **2,** 175–193. (p. 619)

Kerr, N. L. (1983). Motivation losses in small groups: A social dilemma analysis. *Journal of Personality and Social Psychology,* **45,** 819–828. (p. 303)

Kerr, N. L. (1989). Illusions of efficacy: The effects of group size on perceived efficacy in social dilemmas. *Journal of Experimental Social Psychology,* **25,** 287–313. (p. 522)

Kerr, N. L. (1992). Norms in social dilemmas. In D. Schroeder (Ed.), *Social dilemmas: Psychological perspectives.* New York: Praeger. (p. 524)

Kerr, N. L., Atkin, R. S., Stasser, G., Meek, D., Holt, R. W., & Davis, J. H. (1976). Guilt beyond a reasonable doubt: Effects of concept definition and assigned decision rule on the judgments of mock jurors. *Journal of Personality and Social Psychology,* **34,** 282–294. (pp. 625, 628)

Kerr, N. L., & Bruun, S. E. (1981). Ringelmann revisted: Alternative explanations for the social loafing effect. *Personality and Social Psychology Bulletin,* **7,** 224–231. (p. 301)

Kerr, N. L., & Bruun, S. E. (1983). Dispensibility of member effort and group motivation losses: Free-rider effects. *Journal of Personality and Social Psychology,* **44,** 78–94. (p. 303)

Kerr, N. L., Garst, J., Lewandowski, D. A., & Harris, S. E. (1997). That still, small voice: Commitment to cooperate as an internalized versus a social norm. *Personality and Social Psychology Bulletin,* **23,** 1300–1311. (p. 523)

Kerr, N. L., Harmon, D. L., & Graves, J. K. (1982). Independence of multiple verdicts by jurors and juries. *Journal of Applied Social Psychology,* **12,** 12–29. (pp. 187, 619)

Kerr, N. L., & Kaufman-Gilliland, C. M. (1994). Communication, commitment, and cooperation in social dilemmas. *Journal of Personality and Social Psychology,* **66,** 513–529. (p. 523)

Kerr, N. L., & Kaufman-Gilliland, C. M. (1997). ". . and besides, I probably couldn't have made a difference anyway": Justification of social dilemma defection via perceived self-inefficacy. *Journal of Experimental Social Psychology,* **33,** 211–230. (p. 522)

Kerr, N. L., & MacCoun, R. J. (1985). The effects of jury size and polling method on the process and product of jury deliberation. *Journal of Personality and Social Psychology,* **48,** 349–363. (p. 236)

Kerwin, J., & Shaffer, D. R. (1994). Mock jurors versus mock juries: The role of deliberations in reactions to inadmissible testimony. *Personality and Social Psychology Bulletin,* **20,** 153–162. (p. 627)

Kidd, J. B., & Morgan, J. R. (1969). A predictive information system for management. *Operational Research Quarterly,* **20,** 149–170. (p. 68)

Kiecolt-Glaser, J. K., Malarkey, W. B., Chee, M., Newton, T., Cacioppo, J. T., Mao, H-Y., & Glaser, R. (1993). Negative behavior during marital conflict is associated with immunological down-regulation. *Psychosomatic Medicine,* **55,** 395–409. (p. 583)

Kiesler, C. A. (1971). *The psychology of commitment: Experiments linking behavior to belief.* New York: Academic Press. (p. 284)

Kiesler, C. A., & Kiesler, S. B. (1969). *Conformity.* Reading, Mass.: Addison-Wesley. (p. 210)

Kihlstrom, J. F. (1994). The social construction of memory. Address to the American Psychological Society convention. (p. 100)

Kihlstrom, J. F., & Cantor, N. (1984). Mental representations of the self. In L. Berkowitz (Ed.), *Advances in experimental social psychology,* vol. 17. New York: Academic Press. (p. 39)

Kimball, M. M. (1989). A new perspective on women's math achievement. *Psychological Bulletin,* **105,** 198-214. (p. 337)

Kimmel, M. J., Pruitt, D. G., Magenau, J. M., Konar-Goldband, E., & Carnevale, P. J. D. (1980). Effects of trust, aspiration, and gender on negotiation tactics. *Journal of Personality and Social Psychology,* **38,** 9–22. (p. 548)

Kinder, D. R., & Sears, D. O. (1985). Public opinion and political action. In G. Lindzey & E. Aronson (Eds.), *The handbook of social psychology,* 3rd ed. New York: Random House. (p. 95)

Kingdon, J. W. (1967). Politicans' beliefs about voters. *The American Political Science Review,* **61,** 137–145. (p. 57)

Kinnier, R. T., & Metha, A. T. (1989). Regrets and priorities at three stages of life. *Counseling and Values,* **33,** 182–193. (p. 113)

Kirmeyer, S. L. (1978). Urban density and pathology: A review of research. *Environment and Behavior,* **10,** 257–269. (p. 403)

Kitayama, S. (1996). The mutual constitution of culture and the self: Implications for emotion. Paper presented to the American Psychological Society convention. (p. 42)

Kitayama, S., & Karasawa, M. (1997). Implicit self-esteem in Japan: Name letters and birthday numbers. *Personality and Social Psychology Bulletin,* **23,** 736–742. (p. 431)

Kitayama, S., & Markus, H. R. (1995). Culture and self: Implications for internationalizing psychology. In N. R. Godlberger & J. B. Veroff (eds.), *The culture and psychology reader.* New York: New York University Press. (p. 43)

Kitayama, S., & Markus, H. R. (in press). Construal of the self as cultural frame: Implications for internationalizing psychology. In J. D'Arms, R. G. Hastie, S. E. Hoelscher, & H. K. Jacobson (Eds.), *Becoming more international and global: Challenges for American higher education.* Ann Arbor: University of Michigan Press. (p. 528)

Klaas, E. T. (1978). Psychological effects of immoral actions: The experimental evidence. *Psychological Bulletin,* **85,** 756–771. (p. 142)

Klasen, S. (1994). "Missing women" reconsidered. *World Development,* **22,** 1061–1071. (p. 347)

Klayman, J., & Ha, Y-W. (1987). Confirmation, disconfirmation, and information in hypothesis testing. *Psychological Review,* **94,** 211–228. (p. 108)

Kleck, R. E., & Strenta, A. (1980). Perceptions of the impact of negatively valued physical characteristics on social interaction. *Journal of Personality and Social Psychology,* **39,** 861–873. (p. 368)

Klein, J. G. (1991). Negative effects in impression formation: A test in the political arena. *Personality and Social Psychology Bulletin,* **17,** 412–418. (p. 447)

Klein, W. M. (1997). Objective standards are not not enough: Affective, self-evaluative, and behavioral responses to social comparison information. *Journal of Personality and Social Psychology,* **72,** 763–774. (p. 394)

Klein, W. M., & Kunda, Z. (1992). Motivated person perception: Constructing justifications for desired beliefs. *Journal of Experimental Social Psychology,* **28,** 145–168. (p. 430)

Klein, W. M., & Kunda, Z. (1993). Maintaining self-serving social comparisons: Biased reconstruction of one's past behaviors. *Personality and Social Psychology Bulletin,* **19,** 732–739. (p. 102)

Kleinke, C. L. (1977). Compliance to requests made by gazing and touching experimenters in field settings. *Journal of Experimental Social Psychology,* **13,** 218–223. (p. 221)

Klentz, B., Beaman, A. L., Mapelli, S. D., & Ullrich, J. R. (1987). Perceived physical attractiveness of supporters and nonsupporters of the women's movement: An attitude-similarity-mediated error (AS-ME). *Personality and Social Psychology Bulletin,* **13,** 513–523. (p. 442)

Knight, G. P., Fabes, R. A., & Higgins, D. A. (1996). Concerns about drawing causal inferences from meta-analyses: An example in the study of gender differences in aggression. *Psychological Bulletin, 119*, 410–421. (p. 189)

Knight, G. P., Johnson, L. G., Carlo, G., & Eisenberg, N. (1994). A multiplicative model of the dispositional antecedents of a prosocial behavior: Predicting more of the people more of the time. *Journal of Personality and Social Psychology, 66*, 178–183. (p. 478)

Knight, J. A., & Vallacher, R. R. (1981). Interpersonal engagement in social perception: The consequences of getting into the action. *Journal of Personality and Social Psychology, 40*, 990–999. (p. 430)

Knight, P. A., & Weiss, H. M. (1980). Benefits of suffering: Communicator suffering, benefitting, and influence. Paper presented at the American Psychological Association convention. (p. 258)

Knowles, E. S. (1983). Social physics and the effects of others: Tests of the effects of audience size and distance on social judgment and behavior. *Journal of Personality and Social Psychology, 45*, 1263–1279. (p. 295)

Knox, R. E., & Inkster, J. A. (1968). Postdecision dissonance at post-time. *Journal of Personality and Social Psychology, 8*, 319–323. (p. 156)

Knudson, R. M., Sommers, A. A., & Golding, S. L. (1980). Interpersonal perception and mode of resolution in marital conflict. *Journal of Personality and Social Psychology, 38*, 751–763. (p. 548)

Koehler, D. J. (1991). Explanation, imagination, and confidence in judgment. *Psychological Bulletin, 110*, 499–519. (p. 109)

Koestner, R. F. (1993). False consensus effects for the 1992 Canadian referendum. Paper presented at the American Psychological Association. (p. 61)

Koestner, R., & Wheeler, L. (1988). Self-presentation in personal advertisements: The influence of implicit notions of attraction and role expectations. *Journal of Social and Personal Relationships, 5*, 149–160. (p. 435)

Kolaric, G. C., & Galambos, N. L. (1995). Face-to-face interactions in unacquainted female/male adolescent dyads: How do girls and boys behave? *Journal of Early Adolescence, 15*, 363-382. (p. 185)

Kolominsky, Y. (1991). Soviet psychology today. Invited address by Vice-President, Soviet Psychological Society, Hope College. (p. 14)

Komorita, S. S., & Barth, J. M. (1985). Components of reward in social dilemmas. *Journal of Personality and Social Psychology, 48*, 364–373. (p. 523)

Komorita, S. S., Parks, C. D., & Hulbert, L. G. (1992). Reciprocity and the induction of cooperation in social dilemmas. *Journal of Personality and Social Psychology, 62*, 607–617. (p. 554)

Koomen, W., & Bahler, M. (1996). National stereotypes: Common representations and ingroup favouritism. *European Journal of Social Psychology, 26*, 325–331. (p. 337)

Koomen, W., & Dijker, A. J. (1997). Ingroup and outgroup stereotypes and selective processing. *European Journal of Social Psychology, 27*, 589–601. (p. 176)

Koop, C. E. (1987). Report of the Surgeon General's workshop on pornography and public health. *American Psychologist, 42*, 944–945. (pp. 406, 407)

Koop, C. E. (1997, June 22). Quoted by J. Fisher and J. Schwartz, Trying to snuff out the tobacco culture. *Washington Post*, pp. A1, A3. (p. 130)

Koriat, A., Lichtenstein, S., & Fischhoff, B. (1980). Reasons for confidence. *Journal of Experimental Social Psychology: Human Learning and Memory, 6*, 107–118. (p. 109)

Korn, J. H., & Nicks, S. D. (1993). The rise and decline of deception in social psychology. Poster presented at the American Psychological Society convention. (p. 30)

Koss, M. P. (1990, August 29). Rape incidence: A review and assessment of the data. Testimony on behalf of the American Psychological Association before the U.S. Senate Judiciary Committee. (p. 408)

Koss, M. P. (1993). Rape: Scope, impact, interventions, and public policy responses. *American Psychologist, 48*, 1062–1069. (p. 408)

Koss, M. P., Dinero, T. E., Seibel, C. A., & Cox, S. L. (1988). Stranger and acquaintance rape. *Psychology of Women, 12*, 1–24. (p. 408)

Koss, M. P., Heise, L., & Russo, N. F. (1994). The global health burden of rape. *Psychology of Women Quarterly, 18*, 509–537. (p. 409)

Kozol, J. (1995). *Amazing grace: The lives of children and the conscience of a nation.* New York: Crown. (p. 92)

Krackow, A., & Blass, T. (1995). When nurses obey or defy inappropriate physician orders: Attributional differences. *Journal of Social Behavior and Personality, 10*, 585–594. (p. 222)

Kramer, G. P., Kerr, N. L., & Carroll, J. S. (1990). Pretrial publicity, judicial remedies, and jury bias. *Law and Human Behavior, 14*, 409–438. (p. 618)

Kraus, S. J. (1995). Attitudes and the prediction of behavior: A meta-analysis of the empirical literature. *Personality and Social Psychology Bulletin, 21*, 58–75. (pp. 133, 137)

Kraut, R. E. (1973). Effects of social labeling on giving to charity. *Journal of Experimental Social Psychology, 9*, 551–562. (p. 508)

Kraut, R. E., & Poe, D. (1980). Behavioral roots of person perception: The deception judgments of customs inspectors and laymen. *Journal of Personality and Social Psychology, 39*, 784–798. (p. 364)

Kravitz, D. A., & Martin, B. (1986). Ringelmann rediscovered: The original article. *Journal of Personality and Social Psychology, 50*, 936–941. (p. 300)

Krebs, D. (1970). Altruism—An examination of the concept and a review of the literature. *Psychological Bulletin, 73*, 258–302. (p. 475)

Krebs, D. (1975). Empathy and altruism. *Journal of Personality and Social Psychology, 32*, 1134–1146. (p. 475)

Krebs, D., & Adinolfi, A. A. (1975). Physical attractiveness, social relations, and personality style. *Journal of Personality and Social Psychology, 31*, 245–253. (p. 434)

Kressel, K., & Pruitt, D. G. (1985). Themes in the mediation of social conflict. *Journal of Social Issues, 41*, 179–198. (p. 552)

Kristof, N. (1993, July 22). China faces huge surplus of males as scans hold key to missing girls. *The Guardian* (England), p. 22. (p. 347)

Kroger, R. O., & Wood, L. A. (1992). Are the rules of address universal? IV: Comparison of Chinese, Korean, Greek, and German usage. *Journal of Cross-Cultural Psychology, 23*, 148–162. (p. 178)

Krosnick, J. A., & Alwin, D. F. (1989). Aging and susceptibility to attitude change. *Journal of Personality and Social Psychology, 57*, 416–425. (p. 273)

Krosnick, J. A., Li, F., & Lehman, D. R. (1990). Conversational conventions, order of information acquisition, and the effect of base rates and individuating information on social judgments. *Journal of Personality and Social Psychology, 59*, 1140–1152. (p. 110)

Krosnick, J. A., & Schuman, H. (1988). Attitude intensity, importance, and certainty and susceptibility to response effects. *Journal of Personality and Social Psychology, 54*, 940–952. (p. 26)

Krueger, J. (1996). Personal beliefs and cultural stereotypes about racial characteristics. *Journal of Personality and Social Psychology, 71*, 536–548. (p. 61)

Krueger, J. (1997). On the perception of social consensus. *Advances in Experimental Social Psychology*, in press. (p. 62)

Krueger, J., & Clement, R. W. (1994). Memory-based judgments about multiple categories: A revision and extension of Tajfel's accentuation theory. *Journal of Personality and Social Psychology, 67*, 35–47. (pp. 61, 365)

Krueger, J., & Clement, R. W. (1994). The truly false consensus effect: An ineradicable and egocentric bias in social perception. *Journal of Personality and Social Psychology, 67*, 596–610. (p. 61)

Krueger, J., & Clement, R. W. (1997). Estimates of social consensus by majorities and minorities: The case for social projection. *Personality and Social Psychology Review*, **1**, 299–313. (p. 62)

Kruglanski, A. W., & Ajzen, I. (1983). Bias and error in human judgment. *European Journal of Social Psychology*, **13**, 1–44. (p. 125)

Kruglanski, A. W., & Webster, D. M. (1991). Group members' reactions to opinion deviates and conformists at varying degrees of proximity to decision deadline and of environmental noise. *Journal of Personality and Social Psychology*, **61**, 212–225. (p. 326)

Kruglanski, A. W., Webster, D. M., & Klem, A. (1993). Motivated resistance and openness to persuasion in the presence or absence of prior information. *Journal of Personality and Social Psychology*, **65**, 861–876. (p. 276)

Kubany, E. S., Bauer, G. B., Pangilinan, M. E., Muroka, M. Y., & Enriquez, V. G. (1995). Impact of labeled anger and blame in intimate relationships. *Journal of Cross-Cultural Psychology*, **26**, 65–83. (p. 422)

Kuhn, D., & Lao, J. (1996). Effects of evidence on attitudes: Is polarization the norm? *Psychological Science*, **7**, 115–120. (p. 95)

Kuiper, N. A., & Higgins, E. T. (1985). Social cognition and depression: A general integrative perspective. *Social Cognition*, **3**, 1–15. (p. 572)

Kuiper, N. A., & Rogers, T. B. (1979). Encoding of personal information: Self-other differences. *Journal of Personality and Social Psychology*, **37**, 499–514. (p. 39)

Kunda, Z. (1990). The case for motivated reasoning. *Psychological Bulletin*, **108**, 480–498. (p. 65)

Kunda, Z., Fong, G. T., Sanitioso, R., & Reber, E. (1993). Directional questions direct self-conceptions. *Journal of Experimental Social Psychology*, **29**, 63–86. (p. 565)

Kunda, Z., & Oleson, K. C. (1995). Maintaining stereotypes in the face of disconfirmation: Constructing grounds for subtyping deviants. *Journal of Personality and Social Psychology*, **68**, 565–579. (p. 376)

Kunda, Z., & Oleson, K. C. (1997). When exceptions prove the rule: How extremity of deviance determines the impact of deviant examples on stereotypes. *Journal of Personality and Social Psychology*, **72**, 965–979. (p. 376)

Kunda, Z., & Sherman-Williams, B. (1993). Stereotypes and the construal of individuating information. *Personality and Social Psychology Bulletin*, **19**, 90–99. (p. 375)

Kunda, Z., & Sinclair, L. (1999). Motivated reasoning with stereotypes: Activation, application, and inhibition. *Psychological Inquiry*, **10**, 12-22. (p. 342)

Kunst-Wilson, W. R., & Zajonc, R. B. (1980). Affective discrimination of stimuli that cannot be recognized. *Science*, **207**, 557–558. (p. 431)

Kwan, V. S. Y., Bond, M. H., & Singelis, T. M. (1997). *Journal of Personality and Social Psychology*, **73**, 1038–1051. (p. 44)

Lackie, L., & deMan, A. F. (1997). Correlates of sexual aggression among male university students. *Sex Roles*, **37**, 451-457. (p. 408)

LaFrance, M. (1985). Does your smile reveal your status? *Social Science News Letter*, **70** (Spring), 15–18. (p. 185)

LaFromboise, T., Coleman, H. L. K., & Gerton, J. (1993). Psychological impact of biculturalism: Evidence and theory. *Psychological Bulletin*, **114**, 395–412. (p. 546)

Lagerspetz, K. (1979). Modification of aggressiveness in mice. In S. Feshbach & A. Fraczek (Eds.), *Aggression and behavior change*. New York: Praeger. (p. 386)

Lagerspetz, K. M. J., Bjorkqvist, K., Berts, M., & King, E. (1982). Group aggression among school children in three schools. *Scandinavian Journal of Psychology*, **23**, 45–52. (p. 419)

Laird, J. D. (1974). Self-attribution of emotion: The effects of expressive behavior on the quality of emotional experience. *Journal of Personality and Social Psychology*, **29**, 475–486. (p. 157)

Laird, J. D. (1984). The real role of facial response in the experience of emotion: A reply to Tourangeau and Ellsworth, and others. *Journal of Personality and Social Psychology*, **47**, 909–917. (p. 157)

Lalancette, M-F., & Standing, L. (1990). Asch fails again. *Social Behavior and Personality*, **18**, 7–12. (p. 242)

Lalonde, R. N. (1992). The dynamics of group differentiation in the face of defeat. *Personality and Social Psychology Bulletin*, **18**, 336–342. (p. 55)

Lamal, P. A. (1979). College student common beliefs about psychology. *Teaching of Psychology*, **6**, 155–158. (p. 99)

Landers, A. (1969, April 8). Syndicated newspaper column. April 8, 1969. Cited by L. Berkowitz in, The case for bottling up rage. *Psychology Today*, September, 1973, pp. 24–31. (p. 421)

Landers, S. (1988, July). Sex, drugs 'n' rock: Relation not causal. *APA Monitor*, p. 40. (p. 22)

Lane, R. E. (1998). Searching for lost companions in the groves of the market. In D. Kahneman, E. Diener, & N. Schwarz (eds.), *Understanding well-being: Scientific perspectives on enjoyment and suffering*. New York: Russell Sage Foundation, in press. (p. 593)

Langer, E. J. (1977). The psychology of chance. *Journal for the Theory of Social Behavior*, **7**, 185–208. (p. 115)

Langer, E. J., & Benevento, A. (1978). Self-induced dependence. *Journal of Personality and Social Psychology*, **36**, 886–893. (p. 181)

Langer, E. J., & Imber, L. (1980). The role of mindlessness in the perception of deviance. *Journal of Personality and Social Psychology*, **39**, 360–367. (p. 368)

Langer, E. J., Janis, I. L., & Wofer, J. A. (1975). Reduction of psychological stress in surgical patients. *Journal of Experimental Social Psychology*, **11**, 155–165. (p. 53)

Langer, E. J., & Rodin, J. (1976). The effects of choice and enhanced personal responsibility for the aged: A field experiment in an institutional setting. *Journal of Personality and Social Psychology*, **334**, 191–198. (p. 53)

Langer, E. J., & Roth, J. (1975). Heads I win, tails it's chance: The illusion of control as a function of the sequence of outcomes in a purely chance task. *Journal of Personality and Social Psychology*, **32**, 951–955. (p. 266)

Langlois, J., Kalakanis, L., Rubenstein, A., Larson, A., Hallam, M., & Smoot, M. (1996). Maxims and myths of beauty: A meta-analytic and theoretical review. Paper presented to the American Psychological Society convention. (pp. 437, 439)

Langlois, J. H., & Roggman, L. A. (1990). Attractive faces are only average. *Psychological Science*, **1**, 115–121. (p. 438)

Langlois, J. H., Roggman, L. A., Casey, R. J., Ritter, J. M., Rieser-Danner, L. A., & Jenkins, V. Y. (1987). Infant preferences for attractive faces: Rudiments of a stereotype? *Developmental Psychology*, **23**, 363–369. (p. 436)

Langlois, J. H., Roggman, L. A., & Musselman, L. (1994). What is average and what is not average about attractive faces? *Psychological Science*, **5**, 214–220. (p. 438)

Langlois, J. H., & Stephan, C. W. (1981). Beauty and the beast: The role of physical attractiveness in the development of peer relations and social behavior. In S. S. Brehm, S. M. Kassin, & F. X. Gibbons (Eds.), *Developmental social psychology*. New York: Oxford University Press. (p. 436)

Lanzetta, J. T. (1955). Group behavior under stress. *Human Relations*, **8**, 29–53. (p. 538)

LaPiere, R. T. (1934). Attitudes versus actions. *Social Forces*, **13**, 230–237. (p. 132)

Larsen, K. (1974). Conformity in the Asch experiment. *Journal of Social Psychology*, **94**, 303–304. (p. 242)

Larsen, K. S. (1990). The Asch conformity experiment: Replication and transhistorical comparisons. *Journal of Social Behavior and Personality*, **5**(4), 163–168. (p. 242)

Larsen, R. J., Csikszentmihalyi, N., & Graef, R. (1982). Time alone in daily experience: Loneliness or renewal? In L. A. Peplau & D. Perlman (Eds.), *Loneliness: A sourcebook of current theory, research and therapy.* New York: Wiley. (p. 575)

Larsen, R. J., & Diener, E. (1987). Affect intensity as an individual difference characteristic: A review. *Journal of Research in Personality, 21,* 1–39. (p. 387)

Larson, J. R., Jr., Foster-Fishman, P. G., & Keys, C. B. (1994). Discussion of shared and unshared information in decision-making groups. *Journal of Personality and Social Psychology, 67,* 446–461. (p. 313)

Larsson, K. (1956). *Conditioning and sexual behavior in the male albino rat.* Stockholm: Almqvist & Wiksell. (p. 293)

Larwood, L. (1978). Swine flu: A field study of self-serving biases. *Journal of Applied Social Psychology, 18,* 283–289. (p. 58)

Larwood, L., & Whittaker, W. (1977). Managerial myopia: Self-serving biases in organizational planning. *Journal of Applied Psychology, 62,* 194–198. (p. 68)

Lassiter, G. D., & Dudley, K. A. (1991). The *a priori* value of basic research: The case of videotaped confessions. *Journal of Social Behavior and Personality, 6,* 7–16. (p. 88)

Lassiter, G. D., & Irvine, A. A. (1986). Videotaped confessions: The impact of camera point of view on judgments of coercion. *Journal of Applied Social Psychology, 16,* 268–276. (p. 88)

Latané, B. (1981). The psychology of social impact. *American Psychologist, 36,* 343–356. (p. 231)

Latané, B., & Dabbs, J. M., Jr. (1975). Sex, group size and helping in three cities. *Sociometry, 38,* 180–194. (p. 487)

Latané, B., & Darley, J. M. (1968). Group inhibition of bystander intervention in emergencies. *Journal of Personality and Social Psychology, 10,* 215–221. (pp. 484, 489)

Latané, B., & Darley, J. M. (1970). *The unresponsive bystander: Why doesn't he help?* New York: Appleton-Century-Crofts. (pp. 486, 499)

Latané, B., & Nida, S. (1981). Ten years of research on group size and helping. *Psychological Bulletin, 89,* 308–324. (p. 487)

Latané, B., & Rodin, J. (1969). A lady in distress: Inhibiting effects of friends and strangers on bystander intervention. *Journal of Experimental Social Psychology, 5,* 189–202. (p. 489)

Latané, B., Williams, K., & Harkins. S. (1979). Many hands make light the work: The causes and consequences of social loafing. *Journal of Personality and Social Psychology, 37,* 822–832. (p. 300)

Laughlin, P. R. (1996). Group decision making and collective induction. In E. H. Witte & J. H. Davis (eds.), *Understanding group behavior: Consensual action by small groups.* Mahwah, NJ: Erlbaum. (p. 324)

Laughlin, P. R., & Adamopoulos, J. (1980). Social combination processes and individual learning for six-person cooperative groups on an intellective task. *Journal of Personality and Social Psychology, 38,* 941–947. (p. 324)

Laumann, E. O., Gagnon, J. H., Michael, R. T., & Michaels, S. (1994). *The social organization of sexuality: Sexual practices in the United States.* Chicago: University of Chicago Press. (pp. 80, 189, 408, 417)

Lawrance, K., Taylor, D., & Byers, E. S. (1996). Differences in men's and women's global, sexual, and ideal-sexual expressiveness and instrumentality. *Sex Roles, 34,* 337-357. (p. 190)

Layden, M. A. (1982). Attributional therapy. In C. Antaki & C. Brewin (Eds.), *Attributions and psychological change: Applications of attributional theories to clinical and educational practice.* London: Academic Press. (p. 588)

Lazarsfeld, P. F. (1949). *The American soldier—an expository review. Public Opinion Quarterly, 13,* 377–404. (p. 16)

Leary, M. (1994). *Self-presentation: Impression management and interpersonal behavior.* Pacific Grove, CA: Brooks/Cole. (p. 151)

Leary, M. R., & Downs, D. L. (1995). Interpersonal functions of the self-esteem motive: The self-esteem system as a sociometer. In M. Kernis (ed.), *Efficacy, agency, and self-esteem.* New York: Plenum. (p. 65)

Leary, M. R., & Kowalski, R. M. (1995). *Social anxiety.* New York: Guilford. (p. 577)

Leary, M. R., Nezlek, J. B., Radford-Davenport, D., Martin, J., & McMullen, A. (1994). Self-presentation in everyday interactions: Effects of target familiarity and gender composition. *Journal of Personality and Social Psychology, 67,* 664–673. (p. 72)

Leary, M. R., Schreindorfer, L. S., & Haupt, A. L. (1995). The role of low self-esteem in emotional and behavioral problems: Why is low self-esteem dysfunctional. *Journal of Social and Clinical Psychology, 14,* 297–314. (p. 42)

Leary, M. R., Tambor, E. S., Terdal, S. K., & Downs, D. L. (1995). Self-esteem as an interpersonal monitor: The sociometer hypothesis. *Journal of Personality and Social Psychology, 68,* 518–530. (pp. 42, 65)

Leary, M. R., Tchvidjian, L. R., & Kraxberger, B. E. (1994). Self-presentation can be hazardous to your health: Impression management and health risk. *Health Psychology, 13,* 461–470. (p. 72)

Lebow, R. N., & Stein, J. G. (1987). Beyond deterrence. *Journal of Social Issues, 43*(4), 5–71. (pp. 518, 554)

LeDoux, J. (1994, June). Emotion, memory and the brain. *Scientific American,* pp. 50–57. (p. 104)

LeDoux, J. (1996). *The emotional brain: The mysterious underpinnings of emotionsl life.* New York: Simon & Schuster. (p. 104)

Lee, F., Hallahan, M., & Herzog, T. (1996). Explaining real-life events: How culture and domain shape attributions. *Personality and Social Psychology Bulletin, 22,* 732–741. (p. 90)

Lee, J. A. (1988). Love-styles. In R. J. Sternberg & M. L. Barnes (Eds.), *The psychology of love.* New Haven: Yale University Press. (p. 452)

Lee, R. Y-P., & Bond, M. H. (1996). How friendship develops out of personality and values: A study of interpersonal attraction in Chinese culture. Unpublished manuscript, Chinese University of Hong Kong. (p. 443)

Lee, Y-T., & Seligman, M. E. P. (1997). Are Americans more optimistic than the Chinese? *Personality and Social Psychology Bulletin, 23,* 32–40. (p. 73)

Lefcourt, H. M. (1982). *Locus of control: Current trends in theory and research.* Hillsdale, N.J.: Erlbaum. (p. 52)

Lefebvre, L. M. (1979). Causal attributions for basketball outcomes by players and coaches. *Psychological Belgica, 19,* 109–115. (p. 73)

Leffingwell, A. (1892). *Illegitimacy and the influences of the seasons upon conduct.* New York: Scribners. (p. 402)

Lehman, D. R., Krosnick, J. A., West, R. L., & Fan, L. (1992). The focus of judgment effect: A question wording effect due to hypothesis confirmation bias. *Personality and Social Psychology Bulletin, 18,* 690-699. (p. 26)

Lehman, D. R., Lempert, R. O., & Nisbett, R. E. (1988). The effects of graduate training on reasoning: Formal discipline and thinking about everyday-life events. *American Psychologist, 43,* 431–442. (p. 125)

Leippe, M. R. (1985). The influence of eyewitness nonidentification on mock-jurors. *Journal of Applied Social Psychology, 15,* 656–672. (p. 602)

Leippe, M. R. (1994). The appraisal of eyewitness testimony. In D. F. Ross, J. D. Read, & M. P. Toglia (Eds.), *Adult eyewitness testimony: Current trends and developments.* New York: Cambridge. (p. 603)

Leippe, M. R., & Eisenstadt, D. (1994). Generalization of dissonance reduction: Decreasing prejudice through induced compliance. *Journal of Personality and Social Psychology, 67,* 395–413. (p. 153)

Leippe, M. R., & Elkin, R. A. (1987). Dissonance reduction strategies and accountability to self and others: Ruminations and some initial research. Presentation to the Fifth International Conference on Affect, Motivation, and Cognition, Nags Head Conference Center. (pp. 154, 275)

Lemyre, L., & Smith, P. M. (1985). Intergroup discrimination and self-esteem in the minimal group paradigm. *Journal of Personality and Social Psychology*, **49**, 660–670. (p. 360)

Lenihan, K. J. (1965). Perceived climates as a barrier to housing desegregation. Unpublished manuscript, Bureau of Applied Social Research, Columbia University. (p. 58)

Leon, D. (1969). *The Kibbutz: A new way of life*. London: Pergamon Press. Cited by B. Latané, K. Williams, & S. Harkins (1979), Many hands make light the work: The causes and consequences of social loafing. *Journal of Personality and Social Psychology*, 1979, **37**, 822–832. (p. 303)

Lepper, M. R., & Greene, D. (Eds.) (1979). *The hidden costs of reward*. Hillsdale, N.J.: Erlbaum. (p. 159)

Lerner, M. J. (1980). *The belief in a just world: A fundamental delusion*. New York: Plenum. (pp. 372, 373)

Lerner, M. J., & Miller, D. T. (1978). Just world research and the attribution process: Looking back and ahead. *Psychological Bulletin*, **85**, 1030–1051. (p. 372)

Lerner, M. J., & Simmons, C. H. (1966). Observer's reaction to the "innocent victim": Compassion or rejection? *Journal of Personality and Social Psychology*, **4**, 203–210. (p. 372)

Lerner, M. J., Somers, D. G., Reid, D., Chiriboga, D., & Tierney, M. (1991). Adult children as caregivers: Egocentric biases in judgments of sibling contributions. *The Gerontologist*, **31**, 746–755. (p. 58)

Lerner, R. M., & Frank, P. (1974). Relation of race and sex to supermarket helping behavior. *Journal of Social Psychology*, **94**, 201–203. (p. 504)

Leung, K., & Bond, M. H. (1984). The impact of cultural collectivism on reward allocation. *Journal of Personality and Social Psychology*, **47**, 793–804. (p. 528)

Leventhal, H. (1970). Findings and theory in the study of fear communications. In L. Berkowitz (Ed.), *Advances in experimental social psychology* (Vol. 5). New York: Academic Press. (pp. 262, 263)

Lever, J. (1978). Sex differences in the complexity of children's play and games. *American Sociological Review*, **43**, 471–483. (p. 184)

Levine, G. M., Halberstadt, J. B., & Goldstone, R. L. (1996). Reasoning and the weighting of attributes in attitude judgments. *Journal of Personality and Social Psychology*, **70**, 230–240. (p. 49)

Levine, J. M. (1989). Reaction to opinion deviance in small groups. In P. Paulus (Ed.), *Psychology of group influence: New perspectives*. Hillsdale, N.J.: Erlbaum. (pp. 326, 327)

Levine, J. M., & Moreland, R. L. (1985). Innovation and socialization in small groups. In S. Moscovici, G. Mugny, & E. Van Avermaet (Eds.), *Perspectives on minority influence*. Cambridge: Cambridge University Press. (p. 327)

Levine, J. M., & Russo, E. M. (1987). Majority and minority influence. In C. Hendrick (Ed.) *Group processes: Review of personality and social psychology*, Vol. 8. Newbury Park, Ca.: Sage. (p. 326)

Levine, R., Sato, S., Hashimoto, T., & Verma, J. (1995). Love and marriage in eleven cultures. *Journal of Cross-Cultural Psychology*, **26**, 554–571. (p. 455)

Levine, R., & Uleman, J. S. (1979). Perceived locus of control, chronic self-esteem, and attributions to success and failure. *Journal of Personality and Social Psychology*, **5**, 69–72. (p. 66)

LeVine, R. V., Martinez, T. S., Brase, G., & Sorenson, K. (1994). Helping in 36 U.S. cities. *Journal of Personality and Social Psychology*, **67**, 69–82. (p. 492)

Levinger, G. (1987). The limits of deterrence: An introduction. *Journal of Social Issues*, **43**(4), 1–4. (p. 518)

Levy, B. (1996). Improving memory in old age through implicit self-stereotyping. *Journal of Personality and Social Psychology*, **71**, 1092–1107. (p. 51)

Levy, S., Lee, J., Bagley, C., & Lippman, M. (1988). Survival hazards analysis in first recurrent breast cancer patients: Seven-year follow-up. *Psychosomatic Medicine*, **50**, 520–528. (p. 584)

Levy-Leboyer, C. (1988). Success and failure in applying psychology. *American Psychologist*, **43**, 779–785. (p. 263)

Lewicki, P. (1983). Self-image bias in person perception. *Journal of Personality and Social Psychology*, **45**, 384–393. (p. 62)

Lewicki, P. (1985). Nonconscious biasing effects of single instances on subsequent judgments. *Journal of Personality and Social Psychology*, **48**, 563–574. (p. 450)

Lewin, K. (1936). *A dynamic theory of personality*. New York: McGraw-Hill. (p. 241)

Lewinsohn, P. M., Hoberman, H., Teri, L., & Hautziner, M. (1985). An integrative theory of depression. In S. Reiss & R. Bootzin (Eds.), *Theoretical issues in behavior therapy*. New York: Academic Press. (p. 574)

Lewinsohn, P. M., Mischel, W., Chapline, W., & Barton, R. (1980). Social competence and depression: The role of illusionary self-perceptions. *Journal of Abnormal Psychology*, **89**, 203–212. (p. 66)

Lewinsohn, P. M., & Rosenbaum, M. (1987). Recall of parental behavior by acute depressives, remitted depressives, and nondepressives. *Journal of Personality and Social Psychology*, **52**, 611–619. (p. 572)

Lewis, C. S. (1949). Membership. In *The Weight of Glory and Other Addresses*. New York: Macmillan. (pp. 592–593)

Lewis, C. S. (1960). *Mere Christianity*. New York: Macmillan. (p. 46)

Lewis, C. S. (1974). *The horse and his boy*. New York: Collier Books. (p. 155)

Leyens, J. P., Camino, L., Parke, R. D., & Berkowitz, L. (1975). Effects of movie violence on aggression in a field setting as a function of group dominance and cohesion. *Journal of Personality and Social Psychology*, **32**, 346–360. (p. 414)

Leyens, J-P., Dardenne, B., & Fiske, S. T. (in press). Why and under what circumstances is a hypothesis-consistent testing strategy preferred in interviews? *British Journal of Social Psychology*, in press. (p. 565)

Liberman, A., & Chaiken, S. (1992). Defensive processing of personally relevant health messages. *Personality and Social Psychology Bulletin*, **18**, 669–679. (p. 264)

Lichtenstein, S., & Fischhoff, B. (1980). Training for calibration. *Organizational Behavior and Human Performance*, **26**, 149–171. (p. 109)

Liebert, R. M., & Baron, R. A. (1972). Some immediate effects of televised violence on children's behavior. *Developmental Psychology*, **6**, 469–475. (p. 28)

Liebrand, W. B. G., Messick, D. M., & Wolters, F. J. M. (1986). Why we are fairer than others: A cross-cultural replication and extension. *Journal of Experimental Social Psychology*, **22**, 590–604. (p. 73)

Lind, E. A., Erickson, B. E., Friedland, N., & Dickenberger, M. (1978). Reactions to procedural models for adjudicative conflict resolution. *Journal of Conflict Resolution*, **22**, 318–341.(p. 601)

Lind, E. A., Thibaut, J., & Walker, L. (1976). A cross-cultural comparison of the effect of adversary and inquisitorial processes on bias in legal decision making. *Virginia Law Review*, **62**, 271–283. (p. 601)

Lindeman, M. (1997). Ingroup bias, self-enhancement and group identification. *European Journal of Social Psychology*, **27**, 337–355. (p. 355)

Lindsay, R. C., Lea, J. A., Nosworthy, G. J., & Fulford, J. A. (1991). Biased lineups: Sequential presentation reduces the problem. *Journal of Applied Psychology*, **76**, 796–802. (p. 610)

Lindsay, R. C., Lea, J. A., & Fulford, J. A. (1991). Sequential lineup presentation: Technique matters. *Journal of Applied Psychology*, **76**, 741–745. (p. 610)

Lindsay, R. C. L., & Wells, G. L. (1985). Improving eyewitness identifications from lineups: Simultaneous versus sequential lineup presentation. *Journal of Applied Psychology*, **70**, 556–564. (p. 610)

Lindsay, R. C. L., Wells, G. L., & Rumpel, C. H. (1981). Can people detect eyewitness-identification accuracy within and across situations? *Journal of Applied Psychology*, **66**, 79–89. (p. 602)

Lindskold, S. (1978). Trust development, the GRIT proposal, and the effects of conciliatory acts on conflict and cooperation. *Psychological Bulletin*, **85**, 772–793. (p. 554)

Lindskold, S. (1979). Conciliation with simultaneous or sequential interaction: Variations in trustworthiness and vulnerability in the prisoner's dilemma. *Journal of Conflict Resolution*, **27**, 704–714. (p. 554)

Lindskold, S. (1979). Managing conflict through announced conciliatory initiatives backed with retaliatory capability. In W. G. Austin and S. Worchel (Eds.), *The social psychology of intergroup relations*. Monterey, Calif.: Brooks/Cole. (p. 554)

Lindskold, S. (1981). The laboratory evaluation of GRIT: Trust, cooperation, aversion to using conciliation. Paper presented at the American Association for the Advancement of Science convention. (p. 554)

Lindskold, S. (1983). Cooperators, competitors, and response to GRIT. *Journal of Conflict Resolution*, **27**, 521–532. (p. 554)

Lindskold, S., & Aronoff, J. R. (1980). Conciliatory strategies and relative power. *Journal of Experimental Social Psychology*, **16**, 187–198. (p. 554)

Lindskold, S., Bennett, R., & Wayner, M. (1976). Retaliation level as a foundation for subsequent conciliation. *Behavioral Science*, **21**, 13–18. (p. 554)

Lindskold, S., Betz, B., & Walters, P. S. (1986). Transforming competitive or cooperative climate. *Journal of Conflict Resolution*, **30**, 99–114. (p. 554)

Lindskold, S., & Collins, M. G. (1978). Inducing cooperation by groups and individuals. *Journal of Conflict Resolution*, **22**, 679–690. (p. 554)

Lindskold, S., & Finch, M. L. (1981). Styles of announcing conciliation. *Journal of Conflict Resolution*, **25**, 145–155. (p. 554)

Lindskold, S., & Han, G. (1988). GRIT as a foundation for integrative bargaining. *Personality and Social Psychology Bulletin*, **14**, 335–345. (p. 554)

Lindskold, S., Han, G., & Betz, B. (1986). Repeated persuasion in interpersonal conflict. *Journal of Personality and Social Psychology*, **51**, 1183–1188. *(b)* (p. 554)

Lindskold, S., Han, G., & Betz, B. (1986). The essential elements of communication in the GRIT strategy. *Personality and Social Psychology Bulletin*, **12**, 179–186. *(a)* (p. 554)

Lindskold, S., Walters, P. S., Koutsourais, H., & Shayo, R. (1981). Cooperators, competitors, and response to GRIT. Unpublished manuscript, Ohio University. (p. 554)

Lineham, M. M. (1997). Self-verification and drug abusers: Implications for treatment. *Psychological Science*, **8**, 181–184. (p. 572)

Linssen, H., & Hagendoorn, L. (1994). Social and geographical factors in the explanation of the content of European nationality stereotypes. *British Journal of Social Psychology*, **33**, 165–182. (p. 337)

Linville, P. W., Gischer, W. G., & Salovey, P. (1989). Perceived distributions of the characteristics of in-group and out-group members: Empirical evidence and a computer simulation. *Journal of Personality and Social Psychology*, **57**, 165–188. (p. 366)

Linz, D. G., Donnerstein, E., & Adams, S. M. (1989). Physiological desensitization and judgments about female victims of violence. *Human Communication Research*, **15**, 509–522. (p. 406)

Linz, D. G., Donnerstein, E., & Penrod, S. (1988). Effects of long term exposure to violent and sexually degrading depictions of women. *Journal of Personality and Social Psychology*, **55**, 758–768. (p. 406)

Lipsitz, A., Kallmeyer, K., Ferguson, M., & Abas, A.(1989). Counting on blood donors: Increasing the impact of reminder calls. *Journal of Applied Social Psychology*, **19**, 1057–1067. (p. 144)

Locke, E. A., & Latham, G. P. (1990). Work motivation and satisfaction: Light at the end of the tunnel. *Psychological Science*, **1**, 240–246. (p. 328)

Locke, K. D., & Horowitz, L. M. (1990). Satisfaction in interpersonal interactions as a function of similarity in level of dysphoria. *Journal of Personality and Social Psychology*, **58**, 823–831. (p. 446)

Locksley, A., Borgida, E., Brekke, N., & Hepburn, C. (1980). Sex stereotypes and social judgment. *Journal of Personality and Social Psychology*, **39**, 821–831. (p. 376)

Locksley, A., Hepburn, C., & Ortiz, V. (1982). Social stereotypes and judgments of individuals: An instance of the base-rate fallacy. *Journal of Experimental Social Psychology*, **18**, 23–42. (p. 376)

Locksley, A., Ortiz, V., & Hepburn, C. (1980). Social categorization and discriminatory behavior: Extinguishing the minimal intergroup discrimination effect. *Journal of Personality and Social Psychology*, **39**, 773–783. (p. 354)

Lockwood, P., & Kunda, Z. (1997). Superstars and me: Predicting the impact of role models on the self. *Journal of Personality and Social Psychology*, **73**, 91–103. (p. 40)

Loewenstein, G., & Schkade, D. (1998). Wouldn't it be nice? Predicting future feelings. In D. Kahneman, E. Diener, & N. Schwarz (eds.), *Understanding well-being: Scientific perspectives on enjoyment and suffering*. New York: Russell Sage Foundation, in press. (p. 47)

Lofland, J., & Stark, R. (1965). Becoming a worldsaver: A theory of conversion to a deviant perspective. *American Sociological Review*, **30**, 862–864. (p. 282)

Loftin, C., McDowall, D., Wiersema, B., & Cottey, T. J. (1991). Effects of restrictive licensing of handguns on homicide and suicide in the District of Columbia. *New England Journal of Medicine*, **325**, 1615–1620. (p. 391)

Loftus, E., & Ketcham, K. (1994). *The myth of repressed memory*. New York: St. Martin's Press. (p. 566)

Loftus, E. F. (1974, December). Reconstructing memory: The incredible eyewitness. *Psychology Today*, pp. 117–119. (p. 602)

Loftus, E. F. (1979). *Eyewitness testimony*. Cambridge, Mass.: Harvard University Press. *(a)* (pp. 602, 604, 605)

Loftus, E. F. (1979). The malleability of human memory. *American Scientist*, **67**, 312–320. *(b)* (pp. 602, 605)

Loftus, E. F. (1993). The reality of repressed memory. *American Psychologist*, **48**, 518–537. (p. 102)

Loftus, E. F., & Klinger, M. R. (1992). Is the unconscious smart or dumb? *American Psychologist*, **47**, 761–765. (p. 106)

Loftus, E. F., Miller, D. G., & Burns, H. J. (1978). Semantic integration of verbal information into a visual memory. *Journal of Experimental Social Psychology: Human Learning and Memory*, **4**, 19–31. (pp. 604, 606)

Loftus, E. F., & Palmer, J. C. (1974). Reconstruction of automobile destruction: An example of the interaction between language and memory. *Journal of Verbal Learning and Verbal Behavior*, **13**, 585–589. (p. 102)

Loftus, E. F., & Pickrell, J. (1995). The formation of false memories. *Psychiatric Annals*, **25**, 720–725. (p. 100)

Loftus, E. F., & Zanni, G. (1975). Eyewitness testimony: The influence of the wording in a question. *Bulletin of the Psychonomic Society*, **5**, 86–88. (p. 610)

Lombardo, J. P., Weiss, R. F., & Buchanan, W. (1972). Reinforcing and attracting functions of yielding. *Journal of Personality and Social Psychology*, **21**, 359–368. (p. 451)

Lombroso, C. (1899/1911). *Crime: Its causes and remedies*. Boston: Little, Brown, (p. 402)

London, P. (1970). The rescuers: Motivational hypotheses about Christians who saved Jews from the Nazis. In J. Macaulay & L. Berkowitz (Eds.), *Altruism and helping behavior*. New York: Academic Press. (p. 509)

Long, B. C., Sangster, J. I. (1993). Dispositional optimism/pessimism and coping strategies: Predictors of psychological adjustment of rheumatoid and osteoarthritis patients. *Journal of Applied Social Psychology*, **23**, 1069–1091. (p. 584)

Lonner, W. J. (1980). The search for psychological universals. In H. C. Triandis & W. W. Lambert (Eds.), *Handbook of cross-*

cultural psychology (vol. 1). Boston: Allyn and Bacon. (p. 177)

Lonner, W. J. (1989). The introductory psychology text and cross-cultural psychology: Beyond Ekman, Whorf, and biased I.Q. tests. In D. Keats, D. R. Munro & L. Mann (Eds.), *Heterogeneity in cross-cultural psychology.* (p. 181)

Lord, C. G., Desforges, D. M., Ramsey, S. L., Trezza, G. R., & Lepper, M. R. (1991). Typicality effects in attitude-behavior consistency: Effects of category discrimination and category knowledge. *Journal of Experimental Social Psychology, 27,* 550–575. (p. 377)

Lord, C. G., Lepper, M. R., & Preston, E. (1984). Considering the opposite: A corrective strategy for social judgment. *Journal of Personality and Social Psychology, 47,* 1231–1243. (p. 98)

Lord, C. G., Ross, L., & Lepper, M. (1979). Biased assimilation and attitude polarization: The effects of prior theories on subsequently considered evidence. *Journal of Personality and Social Psychology, 37,* 2098–2109. (p. 94)

Lord, C. G., & Saenz, D. S. (1985). Memory deficits and memory surfeits: Differential cognitive consequences of tokenism for tokens and observers. *Journal of Personality and Social Psychology, 49,* 918–926. (p. 369)

Lord, W. (1955). *A Night to Remember.* New York: Holt. (p. 318)

Lorenz, K. (1976). *On aggression.* New York: Bantam Books. (p. 385)

Lortie-Lussier, M., Lemieux, S., Godbout, L. (1989). Reports of a public manifestation: Their impact according to minority influence theory. *Journal of Social Psychology, 129,* 285-295. (p. 329)

Lott, A. J., & Lott, B. E. (1974). The role of reward in the formation of positive interpersonal attitudes. In T. Huston (ed.), *Foundations of interpersonal attraction.* New York: Academic Press. (p. 651)

Lott, A. J., & Lott, B. E. (1961). Group cohesiveness, communication level, and conformity. *Journal of Abnormal and Social Psychology, 62,* 408–412. (p. 232)

Lovdal, L. T. (1989). Sex role messages in television commercials: An update. *Sex Roles, 21,* 715–724. (p. 359)

Lovett, F. (1997). Thinking about values (report of December 13, 1996 *Wall Street Journal* national survey). *The Responsive Community, 7*(2), 87. (p. 57)

Lowe, R. H., & Wittig, M. A. (1989). Comparable worth: Individual, interpersonal, and structural considerations. *Journal of Social Issues, 45,* 223–246. (p. 528)

Lowenthal, M. F., Thurnher, M., Chiriboga, D., Beefon, D., Gigy, L., Lurie, E., Pierce, R., Spence, D., & Weiss, L. (1975). *Four stages of life.* San Francisco: Jossey-Bass. (p. 195)

Loy, J. W., & Andrews, D. S. (1981). They also saw a game: A replication of a case study. *Replications in Social Psychology, 1*(2), 45–59. (p. 11)

Lueptow, L. B., Garovich, L., & Lueptow, M. B. (1995). The persistence of gender stereotypes in the face of changing sex roles: Evidence contrary to the sociocultural model. *Ethology and Sociobiology, 16,* 509–530. (p. 345)

Luginbuhl, J. (1992). Comprehension of judges' instructions in the penalty phase of a capital trial: Focus on mitigating circumstances. *Law and Human Behavior, 16,* 203–218. (p. 621)

Luginbuhl, J., & Middendorf, K. (1988). Death penalty beliefs and jurors' responses to aggravating and mitigating circumstances in capital trials. *Law and Human Behavior, 12,* 263–281. (p. 624)

Lumsdaine, A. A., & Janis, I. L. (1953). Resistance to "counter-propaganda" produced by one-sided and two-sided "propaganda" presentations. *Public Opinion Quarterly, 17,* 311–318. (p. 266)

Lumsden, A., Zanna, M. P., & Darley, J. M. (1980). When a newscaster presents counter-additional information: Education or propaganda? Paper presented to the Canadian Psychological Association annual convention. (p. 253)

Lüüs, C. A. E., & Wells, G. L. (1994). Eyewitness identification confidence. In D. F. Ross, J. D. Read, & M. P. Toglia (eds.), *Adult eyewitness testimony: Current trends and developments.* Cambridge, England: Cambridge University Press. (pp. 603, 608)

Lydon, J., & Dunkel-Schetter, C. (1994). Seeing is committing: A longitudinal study of bolstering commitment in amniocenesis patients. *Personality and Social Psychology Bulletin, 20,* 218–227. (p. 221)

Lydon, J. E., Meana, M., Sepinwall, D., Richards, N., & Mayman, S. (1999). The commitment calibration hypothesis: When do people devalue attractive alternatives? *Personality and Social Psychology Bulletin, 25,* 152-161. (p. 442)

Lykken, D. T., & Tellegen, A. (1993). Is human mating adventitious or the result of lawful choice? A twin study of mate selection. *Journal of Personality and Social Psychology, 65,* 56–68. (p. 430)

Lynch, B. S., & Bonnie, R. J. (1994). Toward a youth-centered prevention policy. In B. S. Lynch and R. J. Bonnie (eds.), *Growing up tobacco free: Preventing nicotine addiction in children and youths.* Washington, DC: National Academy Press. (p. 48)

Lynn, M., & Oldenquist, A. (1986). Egoistic and nonegoistic motives in social dilemmas. *American Psychologist, 41,* 529–534. (p. 525)

Ma, V., & Schoeneman, T. J. (1997). Individualism versus collectivism: A comparison of Kenyan and American

self-concepts. *Basic and Applied Social Psychology, 19,* 261–273. (p. 43)

Maass, A., Ceccarelli, R., & Rudin, S. (1996). Linguistic intergroup bias: Evidence for in-group-protective motivation. *Journal of Personality and Social Psychology, 71,* 512–526. (p. 372)

Maass, A., & Clark, R. D., III (1984). Hidden impact of minorities: Fifteen years of minority influence research. *Psychological Bulletin, 95,* 428–450. (p. 327)

Maass, A., & Clark, R. D., III (1986). Conversion theory and simultaneous majority/minority influence: Can reactance offer an alternative explanation? *European Journal of Social Psychology, 16,* 305–309. (p. 327)

Maass, A., Milesi, A., Zabbini, S., & Stahlberg, D. (1995). Linguistic intergroup bias: Differential expectancies or in-group protection? *Journal of Personality and Social Psychology, 68,* 116–126. (p. 372)

Maass, A., Volparo, C., & Mucchi-Faina, A. (1996). Social influence and the verifiability of the issue under discussion: Attitudinal versus objective items. *British Journal of Social Psychology, 35,* 15–26. (p. 327)

Maccoby, N. (1980). Promoting positive health behaviors in adults. In L. A. Bond & J. C. Rosen (Eds.), *Competence and coping during adulthood.* Hanover, N.H.: University Press of New England. (pp. 270, 271)

Maccoby, N., & Alexander, J. (1980). Use of media in lifestyle programs. In P. O. Davidson & S. M. Davidson (Eds.). *Behavioral medicine: Changing health lifestyles.* New York: Brunner/Mazel. (p. 270)

MacCoun, R. J., & Kerr, N. L. (1988). Asymmetric influence in mock jury deliberation: Jurors' bias for leniency. *Journal of Personality and Social Psychology, 54,* 21–33. (p. 626)

MacDonald, T. K., & Ross, M. (1997). Assessing the accuracy of predictions about dating relationships: How and why do lovers' predictions differ from those made by observers? Unpublished manuscript, University of Lethbridge. (p. 47)

MacDonald, T. K., & Zanna, M. P. (1998). Cross-dimension ambivalence toward feminists: Can cross-dimension ambivalence affect hiring decisions? *Personality and Social Psychology Bulletin,* in press. (p. 345)

MacDonald, T. K., & Zanna, M. P., & Fong, G. T. (1995). Decision making in altered states: Effects of alcohol on attitudes toward drinking and driving. *Journal of Personality and Social Psychology, 68,* 973–985. (p. 578)

Mack, D., & Rainey, D. (1990). Female applicants' grooming and personnel selection. *Journal of Social Behavior and Personality, 5,* 399–407. (p. 437)

MacKay, J. L. (1980). Selfhood: Comment on Brewster Smith. *American Psychologist*, **35**, 106–107. (p. 53)

Mackie, D. M. (1987). Systematic and nonsystematic processing of majority and minority persuasive communications. *Journal of Personality and Social Psychology*, **53**, 41–52. (p. 326)

Mackie, D. M., Queller, S., Stroessner, S. J., & Hamilton, D. L. (1996). Making stereotypes better or worse: Multiple roles for positive affect in group impressions. In R. Sorrentino & E. T. Higgins (eds.), *Handbook of motivation and cognition: The interpersonal content*, vol. 3. New York: Guilford. (p. 365)

MacLachlan, J. (1979, November). What people really think of fast talkers. *Psychology Today*, pp. 113–117. (p. 258)

MacLachlan, J., & Siegel, M. H. (1980). Reducing the costs of TV commercials by use of time compressions. *Journal of Marketing Research*, **17**, 52–57. (p. 258)

MacLeod, C., & Campbell, L. (1992). Memory accessibility and probability judgments: An experimental evaluation of the availability heuristic. *Journal of Personality and Social Psychology*, **63**, 890–902. (p. 112)

Macrae, C. N., Bodenhausen, G. V., Milne, A. B., & Jetten, J. (1994). Out of mind but back in sight: Stereotypes on the rebound. *Journal of Personality and Social Psychology*, **67**, 808–817. (p. 342)

Macrae, C. N., Bodenhausen, G. V., & Milne, A. B. (1998). Saying no to un-wanted thoughts: Self-focus and the reg-ulation of mental life. *Journal of Personality and Social Psychology*, in press. (p. 343)

Macrae, C. N., Stangor, C., & Milne, A. B. (1994). Activating social stereotypes: A functional analysis. *Journal of Experimental Social Psychology*, **30**, 370–389. (p. 364)

Maddux, J. E. (1993). The mythology of psychopathology: A social cognitive view of deviance, difference, and disorder. *The General Psychologist*, **29**(2), 34–45. (pp. 562, 568)

Maddux, J. E. (in press). Personal efficacy. In V. Derlega, B. Winstead, & W. Jones (eds.), *Personality: Contemporary theory and research*, 2nd ed. New York: Nelson-Hall. (p. 51)

Maddux, J. E., & Rogers, R. W. (1983). Protection motivation and self-efficacy: A revised theory of fear appeals and attitude change. *Journal of Experimental Social Psychology*, **19**, 469–479. (p. 263)

Madon, S., Jussim, L., & Eccles, J. (1997). In search of the powerful self-fulfilling prophecy. *Journal of Personality and Social Psychology*, **72**, 791–809. (p. 121)

Magnuson, E. (1986, March 10). "A serious deficiency": The Rogers Commission faults NASA's "flawed" decision-making process. *Time*, pp. 40–42, international ed. (p. 321)

Maio, G. R., & Esses, V. M. (1998). The social consequences of affirmative action: Deleterious effects on perceptions of groups. *Personality and Social Psychology Bulletin*, **24**, 65-74. (p. 338)

Maio, G. R., & Olson, J. M. (1995).Involvement and persuasion: Evidence for different types of involvement. *Canadian Journal of Behavioural Science*, **27**, 64-78. (p. 275)

Maio, G. R., Bell, D., & Esses, V. M. (1996). Ambivalence in persuasion: The processing of messages about immigrant groups. *Journal of Experimental Social Psychology*, **32**, 513-536. (p. 265)

Major, B. (1989). Gender differences in comparisons and entitlement: Impli-cations for comparable worth. *Journal of Social Issues*, **45**, 99–116. (p. 528)

Major, B. (1993). Gender, entitlement, and the distribution of family labor. *Journal of Social Issues*, **49**, 141–159. (p. 528)

Major, B., Schmidlin, A. M., & Williams, L. (1990). Gender patterns in social touch: The impact of setting and age. *Journal of Personality and Social Psychology*, **58**, 634–643. (p. 188)

Malamuth, N. M. (1996). The confluence model of sexual aggression. In D. M. Buss & N. M. Malamuth (eds.), *Sex, power, conflict: Evolutionary and feminist perspectives*. New York: Oxford University Press. (p. 409)

Malamuth, N. M., & Brown, L. M. (1994). Sexually aggressive men's perceptions of women's communications: Testing three explanations. *Journal of Personality and Social Psychology*, **67**, 699–712. (p. 80)

Malamuth, N. M., & Check, J. V. P. (1981). The effects of media exposure on acceptance of violence against women: A field experiment. *Journal of Research in Personality*, **15**, 436–446. (p. 405)

Malamuth, N. M., & Check, J. V. P. (1984). Debriefing effectiveness following exposure to pornographic rape depictions. *Journal of Sex Research*, **20**, 1–13. (p. 407)

Malamuth, N. M., Linz, D., Heavey, C. L., Barnes, G., & Acker, M. (1995). Using the confluence model of sexual aggression to predict men's conflict with women: A 10-year follow-up study. *Journal of Personality and Social Psychology*, **69**, 353–369. (p. 408)

Malkiel, B. G. (1985). *A random walk down Wall Street*, 4th ed. New York: W. W. Norton. (p. 107)

Malkiel, B. G. (1995, June). Returns from investing in equity mutual funds 1971 to 1991. *Journal of Finance*, pp. 549–572. (p. 107)

Malpaas, R. S., & Devine, P. G. (1984). Research on suggestion in lineups and photo-spreads. In G. L. Wells & E. F. Loftus (Eds.), *Eyewitness identification: Psychological perspectives*. New York: Cambridge University Press. (p. 610)

Mandel, D. R., & Lehman, D. R. (1996). Counterfactual thinking and ascriptions of cause and preventability. *Journal of Personality and Social Psychology*, **71**, 450-463. (p. 113)

Manis, M., Cornell, S. D., & Moore, J. C. (1974). Transmission of attitude-relevant information through a communication chain. *Journal of Personality and Social Psychology*, **30**, 81–94. (p. 141)

Manis, M., Nelson, T. E., & Shedler, J. (1988). Stereotypes and social judgment: Extremity, assimilation, and contrast. *Journal of Personality and Social Psychology*, **55**, 28–36. (p. 379)

Mann, L. (1981). The baiting crowd in episodes of threatened suicide. *Journal of Personality and Social Psychology*, **41**, 703–709. (p. 305)

Manning, F. J., & Fullerton, T. D. (1988). Health and well-being in highly cohesive units of the U.S. Army. *Journal of Applied Social Psychology*, **18**, 503–519. (p. 592)

Mansur, J. W. (1987, August). No greater love. *Reader's Digest*, pp. 49–51. (p. 480)

Mantell, D. M. (1971). The potential for violence in Germany. *Journal of Social Issues*, **27**(4), 101–112. (p. 242)

Marcus, A. C., & Siegel, J. M. (1982). Sex differences in the use of physician services: A preliminary test of the fixed role hypothesis. *Journal of Health and Social Behavior*, **23**, 186–197. (p. 581)

Marcus, S. (1974). Review of *Obedience to authority*. New York Times Book Review, January 13, pp. 1–2. (p. 219)

Markman, H. J., Floyd, F. J., Stanley, S. M., & Storaasli, R. D. (1988). Prevention of marital distress: A longitudinal inves-tigation. *Journal of Consulting and Clinical Psychology*, **56**, 210–217. (p. 469)

Marks, G., & Miller, N. (1987). Ten years of research on the false-consensus effect: An empirical and theoretical review. *Psychological Bulletin*, **102**, 72–90. (p. 61)

Marks, G., Miller, N., & Maruyama, G. (1981). Effect of targets' physical attractiveness on assumptions of similarity. *Journal of Personality and Social Psychology*, **41**, 198–206. (p. 63)

Markus, G. B. (1986). Stability and change in political attitudes: Observe, recall, and "explain." *Political Behavior*, **8**, 21–44. (p. 101)

Markus, H., & Kitayama, S. (1991). Culture and the self: Implications for cognition, emotion, and motivation. *Psychological Review*, **98**, 224–253. (pp. 43, 73)

Markus, H., & Nurius, P. (1986). Possible selves. *American Psychologist*, **41**, 954–969. (p. 39)

Markus, H. R., & Kitayama, S. (1994). A collective fear of the collective: Implications for selves and theories of selves. *Personality and Social Psychology Bulletin*, **20**, 568–579. (p. 210)

Markus, H., & Wurf, E. (1987). The dynamic self-concept: A social psychological perspective. *Annual Review of Psychology, 38,* 299–337. (p. 39)

Marsh, H. W., & Parker, J. W. (1984). Determinants of student self-concept: Is it better to be a relatively large fish in a small pond even if you don't learn to swim as well? *Journal of Personality and Social Psychology, 47,* 213–231. (p. 41)

Marshall, L. (Ed.) 1912. *Sinking of the Titanic and Great Sea Disasters.* Philadelphia, PA: Universal Book and Bible House. (p. 318)

Marshall, R. (1997). Variances in levels of individualism across two cultures and three social classes. *Journal of Cross-Cultural Psychology, 28,* 490–495. (p. 43)

Marshall, W. L. (1989). Pornography and sex offenders. In D. Zillmann & J. Bryant (Eds.), *Pornography: Research advances and policy considerations.* Hillsdale, NJ: Erlbaum. (p. 406)

Martin, C. L. (1987). A ratio measure of sex stereotyping. *Journal of Personality and Social Psychology, 52,* 489–499. (p. 345)

Martin, R. (1996). Minority influence and argument generation. *British Journal of Social Psychology, 35,* 91–103. (p. 327)

Marty, M. (1988, December 1). Graceful prose: Your good deed for the day. *Context,* p. 2. (p. 33)

Maruyama, G., Rubin, R. A., & Kingbury, G. (1981). Self-esteem and educational achievement: Independent constructs with a common cause? *Journal of Personality and Social Psychology, 40,* 962-975.

Marvelle, K., & Green, S. (1980). Physical attractiveness and sex bias in hiring decisions for two types of jobs. *Journal of the National Association of Women Deans, Administrators, and Counselors, 44*(1), 3–6. (p. 437)

Marx, G. (1960). *Groucho and me.* New York: Dell. (p. 55)

Maslow, A. H., & Mintz, N. L. (1956). Effects of esthetic surroundings: I. Initial effects of three esthetic conditions upon perceiving "energy" and "well-being" in faces. *Journal of Psychology, 41,* 247–254. (p. 451)

Mastekaasa, A. (1995). Age variations in the suicide rates and self-reported subjective well-being of married and never married persons. *Journal of Community & Applied Social Psychology, 5,* 21–39. (p. 594)

Matthews, K. A. (1988). CHD and Type A behaviors: Update on and alternative to the Booth-Kewley and Friedman quantitative review. *Psychological Bulletin, 104,* 373–380. (p. 581)

Maurer, K. L., Park, B., & Judd, C. M. (1996). Stereotypes, prejudice, and judgments of group members: The mediating role of public policy decisions.

Journal of Experimental Social Psychology, 32, 411–436. (p. 341)

Mauro, C. F., & Best, D. L. (1996). The effects of playing video games on children's aggressive behavior. Paper presented to the Biennial Meeting of the Conference on Human Development, Birmingham, AL. (p. 416)

Maxwell, G. M. (1985). Behaviour of lovers: Measuring the closeness of relationships. *Journal of Personality and Social Psychology, 2,* 215–238. (p. 460)

Mayer, J. D., & Salovey, P. (1987). Personality moderates the interaction of mood and cognition. In K. Fiedler & J. Forgas (Eds.), *Affect, cognition, and social behavior.* Toronto: Hogrefe. (pp. 117, 572)

Mayton, D. M., II, Diessner, R., & Granby, C. D. (1996). Nonviolence and human values: Empirical support for theoretical relations. *Peace and Conflict: Journal of Peace Psychology, 2,* 245-253. (p. 546)

Mazzella, R., & Feingold, A. (1994). The effects of physical attractiveness, race, socioeconomic status, and gender of defendants and victims on judgments of mock jurors: A meta-analysis. *Journal of Applied Social Psychology, 24,* 1315–1344. (pp. 613, 614)

McAlister, A., Perry, C., Killen, J., Slinkard, L. A., & Maccoby, N. (1980). Pilot study of smoking, alcohol and drug abuse prevention. *American Journal of Public Health, 70,* 719–721. (pp. 285, 286)

McAndrew, F. T. (1981). Pattern of performance and attributions of ability and gender. *Journal of Personality and Social Psychology, 7,* 583–587. (p. 266)

McAneny, L. (1994, June). Alcohol in America: Number of drinkers holding steady, but drinking less. *Gallup Poll Monthly,* pp. 14–19. (p. 405)

McCann, C. D., & Hancock, R. D. (1983). Self-monitoring in communicative interactions: Social cognitive consequences of goal-directed message modification. *Journal of Experimental Social Psychology, 19,* 109–121. (pp. 72, 151)

McCarrey, M., Edwards, H. P., & Rozario, W. (1982). Ego-relevant feedback, affect, and self-serving attributional bias. *Personality and Social Psychology Bulletin, 8,* 189–194. (p. 66)

McCarthy, J. D., & Hoge, D. R. (1984). The dynamics of self-esteem and delinquency. *American Journal of Sociology, 90,* 396–410. (p. 23)

McCarthy, J. F., & Kelly, B. R. (1978). Aggression, performance variables, and anger self-report in ice hockey players. *Journal of Psychology, 99,* 97–101. (b) (p. 396)

McCarthy, J. F., & Kelly, B. R. (1978). Aggressive behavior and its effect on performance over time in ice hockey athletes: An archival study. *International Journal of Sport Psychology, 9,* 90–96. (a) (p. 396)

McCaul, K. D., Ployhart, R. E., Hinsz, V. B., & McCaul, H. S. (1995). Appraisals of a consistent versus a similar politician: Voter preferences and intuitive judgments. *Journal of Personality and Social Psychology, 68,* 292–299. (p. 444)

McCauley, C. (1989). The nature of social influence in groupthink: Compliance and internalization. *Journal of Personality and Social Psychology, 57,* 250–260. (p. 320)

McCauley, C. (1998). Group dynamics in Janis/s theory of groupthink: Backward and forward. *Orgnaizational Behavior and Human Decision Processes,* in press. (p. 320)

McCauley, C. R., & Segal, M. E. (1987). Social psychology of terrorist groups. In C. Hendrick (Ed.), *Group processes and intergroup relations: Review of personality and social psychology,* Vol. 9. Newbury Park, Ca.: Sage. (p. 313)

McCullough, J. L., & Ostrom, T. M. (1974). Repetition of highly similar messages and attitude change. *Journal of Applied Psychology, 59,* 395–397. (p. 433)

McDougal, D. (1994, August 13–19). Baywatch! *TV Guide,* pp. 12–17. (p. 411)

McFarland, C., & Ross, M. (1985). The relation between current impressions and memories of self and dating partners. Unpublished manuscript, University of Waterloo. (p. 101)

McFarland, C., Ross, M., & DeCourville, N. (1989). Women's theories of menstruation and biases in recall of menstrual symptoms. *Journal of Personality and Social Psychology, 57,* 522-531. (p. 581)

McFarland, S. G., Ageyev, V. S., & Abalakina-Paap, M. A. (1992). Authoritarianism in the former Soviet Union. *Journal of Personality and Social Psychology, 63,* 1004–1010. (p. 363)

McFarland, S. G., Ageyev, V. S., & Djintcharadze, N. (1996). Russian authoritarianism two years after communism. *Personality and Social Psychology Bulletin, 22,* 210–217. (p. 363)

McGillicuddy, N. B., Welton, G. L., & Pruitt, D. G. (1987). Third-party intervention: A field experiment comparing three different models. *Journal of Personality and Social Psychology, 53,* 104–112. (p. 552)

McGillis, D. (1979). Biases and jury decision making. In I. H. Frieze, D. Bar-Tal, & J. S. Carroll, *New approaches to social problems.* San Francisco: Jossey-Bass. (p. 613)

McGlynn, R. P., Tubbs, D. D., & Holzhausen, K. G. (1995). Hypothesis generation in groups constrained by evidence. *Journal of Experimental Social Psychology, 31,* 64–81. (p. 324)

McGrath, J. E. (1984). *Groups: Interaction and performance.* Englewood Cliffs, N.J.: Prentice-Hall. (p. 292)

McGregor, I., Newby-Clark, I. R., & Zanna, M. P. (1998). Epistemic discomfort is moderated by simultaneous accessibility of inconsistent elements. In E. Harmon-Jones and J. Mills (eds.), *Cognitive dissonance theory 40 years later: A revival with revisions and controversies.* Washington, DC: American Psychological Association. (p. 166)

McGuire, W. J. (1978). An information processing model of advertising effectiveness. In H. L. Davis & A. J. Silk (Eds.), *Behavioral and management sciences in marketing.* New York: Ronald Press. (p. 269)

McGuire, W. J. (1986). The myth of massive media impact: Savagings and salvagings. In G. Comstock (Ed.), *Public communication and behavior*, Vol. 1. Orlando, Fl.: Academic Press. (pp. 269, 415)

McGuire, W. J., & McGuire, C. V. (1986). Differences in conceptualizing self versus conceptualizing other people as manifested in contrasting verb types used in natural speech. *Journal of Personality and Social Psychology*, **51**, 1135–1143. (p. 85)

McGuire, W. J., McGuire, C. V., Child, P., & Fujioka, T. (1978). Salience of ethnicity in the spontaneous self-concept as a function of one's ethnic distinctiveness in the social environment. *Journal of Personality and Social Psychology*, **36**, 511–520. (p. 246)

McGuire, W. J., McGuire, C. V., & Winton, W. (1979). Effects of household sex composition on the salience of one's gender in the spontaneous self-concept. *Journal of Experimental Social Psychology*, **15**, 77–90. (p. 246)

McGuire, W. J., & Padawer-Singer, A. (1978). Trait salience in the spontaneous self-concept. *Journal of Personality and Social Psychology*, **33**, 743–754. (p. 246)

McKelvie, S. J. (1995). Bias in the estimated frequency of names. *Perceptual and Motor Skills*, **81**, 1331–1338. (p. 112)

McKelvie, S. J. (1997). The availability heuristic: Effects of fame and gender on the estimated frequency of male and female names. *Journal of Social Psychology*, **137**, 63–78. (p. 112)

McKenna, F. P., & Myers, L. B. (1997). Illusory self-assessments—Can they be reduced? *British Journal of Psychology*, **88**, 39–51. (p. 58)

McKenzie-Mohr, D., & Zanna, M. P. (1990). Treating women as sexual objects: Look to the (gender schematic) male who has viewed pornography. *Personality and Social Psychology Bulletin*, **16**, 296–308. (p. 421)

McLean, R. (1997). Selected attitudinal factors related to students' success in high school. *Alberta Journal of Educational Research*, **43**, 165-168. (p. 52)

McMillen, D. L., & Austin, J. B. (1971). Effect of positive feedback on compliance following transgression. *Psychonomic Science*, **24**, 59–61. (p. 495)

McMillen, D. L., Sanders, D. Y., & Solomon, G. S. (1977). Self-esteem, attentiveness, and helping behavior. *Journal of Personality and Social Psychology*, **3**, 257–261. (p. 497)

McNeel, S. P. (1980). Tripling up: Perceptions and effects of dormitory crowding. Paper presented at the American Psychological Association convention. (p. 403)

McNeill, B. W., & Stoltenberg, C. D. (1988). A test of the elaboration likelihood model for therapy. *Cognitive Therapy and Research*, **12**, 69–79. (p. 589)

Mead, G. H. (1934). *Mind, self, and society.* Chicago: University of Chicago Press. (p. 42)

Medalia, N. Z., & Larsen, O. N. (1958). Diffusion and belief in collective delusion: The Seattle windshield pitting epidemic. *American Sociological Review*, **23**, 180–186. (p. 213)

Medvec, V. H., Madey, S. F., & Gilovich, T. (1995). When less is more: Counterfactual thinking and satisfaction among Olympic medalists. *Journal of Personality and Social Psychology*, **69**, 603–610. (p. 113)

Medvec, V. H., & Savitsky, K. (1997). When doing better means feeling worse: The effects of categorical cutoff points on counterfactual thinking and satisfaction. *Journal of Personality and Social Psychology*, **72**, 1284–1296. (p. 113)

Meech, P., & Kilborn, R. (1992). Media and identity in a stateless nation: The case of Scotland. *Media, Culture and Society*, **14**, 245–259. (p. 41)

Meehl, P. E. (1954). *Clinical vs. statistical prediction: A theoretical analysis and a review of evidence.* Minneapolis: University of Minnesota Press. (p. 566)

Meehl, P. E. (1986). Causes and effects of my disturbing little book. *Journal of Personality Assessment*, **50**, 370–375. (p. 566)

Meertens, R. W., & Pettigrew, T. F. (1997). Is subtle prejudice really prejudice? *Public Opinion Quarterly*, **61**, 54–71. (p. 341)

Meeus, W. H. J., & Raaijmakers, Q. A. W. (1986). Administrative obedience: Carrying out orders to use psychological-administrative violence. *European Journal of Social Psychology*, **16**, 311–324. (p. 242)

Mehlman, P. T. & 7 others (1994). Low CSF 5-HIAA concentrations and severe aggression and impaired impulse control in nonhuman primates. *American Journal of Psychiatry*, **151**, 1485–1491. (p. 388)

Meindl, J. R., & Lerner, M. J. (1984). Exacerbation of extreme responses to an out-group. *Journal of Personality and Social Psychology*, **47**, 71–84. (p. 361)

Meleshko, K. G. A., & Alden, L. E. (1993). Anxiety and self-disclosure: Toward a motivational model. *Journal of Personality and Social Psychology*, **64**, 1000–1009. (p. 578)

Mendonca, P. J., & Brehm, S. S. (1983). Effects of choice on behavioral treatment of overweight children. *Journal of Social and Clinical Psychology*, **1**, 343–358. (p. 586)

Merton, R. K. (1938; reprinted 1970). *Science, technology and society in seventeenth-century England.* New York: Fertig. (p. 127)

Merton, R. K., & Kitt, A. S. (1950). Contributions to the theory of reference group behavior. In R. K. Merton & P. F. Lazarsfeld (Eds.), *Continuities in social research: Studies in the scope and method of the American soldier.* Glencoe, Ill.: Free Press. (p. 395)

Messé, L. A., Kerr, N. L., & Sattler, D. N. (1992). "But some animals are more equal than others": The supervisor as a privileged status in group contexts. In S. Worchel, W. Wood, & J. Simpson (Eds.) *Group process and productivity.* Newbury Park, CA: Sage. (p. 181)

Messé, L. A., & Sivacek, J. M. (1979). Predictions of others' responses in a mixed-motive game: Self-justification or false consensus? *Journal of Personality and Social Psychology*, **37**, 602–607. (p. 523)

Messick, D. M., Bloom, S., Boldizar, J. P., & Samuelson, C. D. (1985). Why we are fairer than others. *Journal of Experimental Social Psychology*, **21**, 480–500. (p. 58)

Messick, D. M., & Sentis, K. P. (1979). Fairness and preference. *Journal of Experimental Social Psychology*, **15**, 418–434. (p. 527)

Messick, D. M., Wilke, H., Brewer, M. B., Kramer, R. M., Zemke, P. E., & Lui, L. (1983). Individual adaptations and structural change as solutions to social dilemmas. *Journal of Personality and Social Psychology*, **44**, 294–309. (p. 522)

Metalsky, G. I., Joiner, T. E., Jr., Hardin, T. S., & Abramson, L. Y. (1993). Depressive reactions to failure in a naturalistic setting: A test of the hopelessness and self-esteem theories of depression. *Journal of Abnormal Psychology*, **102**, 101–109. (p. 574)

Meyers, S. A., & Berscheid, E. (1997). The language of love: The difference a preposition makes. *Personality and Social Psychology Bulletin*, **23**, 347–362. (p. 453)

Michael, R. P., & Zumpe, D. (1986). An annual rhythm in the battering of women. *American Journal of Psychiatry*, **143**, 637-640. (p. 402)

Michaels, J. W., Blommel, J. M., Brocato, R. M., Linkous, R. A., & Rowe, J. S. (1982). Social facilitation and inhibition in a natural setting. *Replications in Social Psychology*, **2**, 21–24. (p. 285)

Michaelson, R. (1993, August). Behavior gets big billing in medical schools today. *The Monitor*, p. 56. (p. 579)

Mickelson, K. D., Kessler, R. C., & Shaver, P. R. (1997). Adult attachment in a nationally representative sample. *Journal* of Personality and Social Psychology, **73**, 1092–1106. (p. 461)

Mikolic, J. M., Parker, J. C., & Pruitt, D. G. (1997). Escalation in response to persistent annoyance: Groups versus individuals and gender effects. *Journal of Personality and Social Psychology*, **72**, 151–163. (p. 419)

Mikula, G. (1984). Justice and fairness in interpersonal relations: Thoughts and suggestions. In H. Taijfel (Ed.), *The social dimension: European developments in social psychology*, Vol. 1, Cambridge: Cambridge University Press. (p. 527)

Miles, D. R., & Carey, G. (1997). Genetic and environmental architecture for human aggression. *Journal of Personality and Social Psychology*, **72**, 207–217. (p. 387)

Milgram, S. (1961, December). Nationality and conformity. *Scientific American*, December, pp. 45–51. (p. 242)

Milgram, S. (1963). Behavioral study of obedience. *Journal of Abnormal and Social Psychology*, **67**, 371–378. (p. 218)

Milgram, S. (1965). Some conditions of obedience and disobedience to authority. *Human Relations*, **18**, 57–76. (pp. 216, 219)

Milgram, S. (1974). *Obedience to authority*. New York: Harper and Row. (pp. 216, 218, 226, 229, 234, 240, 247)

Milgram, S., Bickman, L., & Berkowitz, L. (1969). Note on the drawing power of crowds of different size. *Journal of Personality and Social Psychology*, **13**, 79–82. (p. 230)

Milgram, S., & Sabini, J. (1983). On maintaining social norms: A field experiment in the subway. In H. H. Blumberg, A. P. Hare, V. Kent, and M. Davies (Eds.), *Small groups and social interaction*, Vol. 1. London: Wiley. (p. 227)

Millar, M. G., & Millar, K. U. (1996). Effects of message anxiety on disease detection and health promotion behaviors. *Basic and Applied Social Psychology*, **18**, 61–74. (p. 263)

Millar, M. G., & Millar, K. U. (1996). The effects of direct and indirect experience on affective and cognitive responses and the attitude-behavior relation. *Journal of Experimental Social Psychology*, **32**, 561–579. (p. 136)

Millar, M. G., & Tesser, A. (1992). The role of beliefs and feelings in guiding behavior: The mismatch model. In L. Martin & A. Tesser (Eds.), *The construction of social judgment*. Hillsdale NJ: Erlbaum. (p. 49)

Miller, A. G. (1986). *The obedience experiments: A case study of controversy in social science*. New York: Praeger. (p. 219)

Miller, A. G., Ashton, W., & Mishal, M. (1990). Beliefs concerning the features of constrained behavior: A basis for the fundamental attribution error. *Journal of Personality and Social Psychology*, **59**, 635–650. (p. 84)

Miller, A. G., Gillen, G., Schenker, C., & Radlove, S. (1973). Perception of obedience to authority. *Proceedings of the 81st annual convention of the American Psychological Association*, **8**, 127–128. (p. 229)

Miller, C. E., & Anderson, P. D. (1979). Group decision rules and the rejection of deviates. *Social Psychology Quarterly*, **42**, 354–363. (p. 237)

Miller, C. T., & Felicio, D. M. (1990). Person-positivity bias: Are individuals liked better than groups? *Journal of Experimental Social Psychology*, **26**, 408–420. (p. 376)

Miller, D. T., Downs, J. S., & Prentice, D. A. (in press). Minimal conditions for the creation of a unit relationship: The social bond between birthdaymates. *European Journal of Social Psychology*. (p. 353)

Miller, D. T., & McFarland, C. (1987). Pluralistic ignorance: When similarity is interpreted as dissimilarity. *Journal of Personality and Social Psychology*, **53**, 298–305. (p. 315)

Miller, D. T., Taylor, B., & Buck, M. L. (1991). Gender gaps: Who needs to be explained? *Journal of Personality and Social Psychology*, **61**, 5–12. (p. 183)

Miller, G. R., & Fontes, N. E. (1979). *Videotape on trial: A view from the jury box*. Beverly Hills, Calif.: Sage Publications. (p. 618)

Miller, J. B. (1986). *Toward a new psychology of women*, 2nd ed. Boston, MA: Beacon Press. (p. 184)

Miller, J. G. (1984). Culture and the development of everyday social explanation. *Journal of Personality and Social Psychology*, **46**, 961–978. (p. 90)

Miller, J. G., Bersoff, D. M., & Harwood, R. L. (1990). Perceptions of social responsibility in India and in the United States: Moral imperatives or personal decisions? *Journal of Personality and Social Psychology*, **58**, 33–47. (p. 482)

Miller, K. I., & Monge, P. R. (1986). Participation, satisfaction, and productivity: A meta-analytic review. *Academy of Management Journal*, **29**, 727–753. (p. 53)

Miller, L. C. (1990). Intimacy and liking: Mutual influence and the role of unique relationships. *Journal of Personality and Social Psychology*, **59**, 50–60. (p. 464)

Miller, L. C., Berg, J. H., & Archer, R. L. (1983). Openers: Individuals who elicit intimate self-disclosure. *Journal of Personality and Social Psychology*, **44**, 1234–1244. (p. 464)

Miller, L. C., Berg, J. H., & Rugs, D. (1989). Selectivity and sharing: Needs and norms in developing friendships. Unpublished manuscript, Scripps College. (p. 462)

Miller, L. E., & Grush, J. E. (1986). Individual differences in attitudinal versus normative determination of

behavior. *Journal of Experimental Social Psychology*, **22**, 190–202. (p. 136)

Miller, N., & Campbell, D. T. (1959). Recency and primacy in persuasion as a function of the timing of speeches and measurements. *Journal of Abnormal and Social Psychology*, **59**, 1–9. (p. 267)

Miller, N., & Marks, G. (1982). Assumed similarity between self and other: Effect of expectation of future interaction with that other. *Social Psychology Quarterly*, **45**, 100–105. (p. 430)

Miller, N. E. (1941). The frustration-aggression hypothesis. *Psychological Review*, **48**, 337–342. (p. 390)

Miller, N. E., & Bugelski, R. (1948). Minor studies of aggression: II. The influence of frustrations imposed by the in-group on attitudes expressed toward out-groups. *Journal of Psychology*, **25**, 437–442. (p. 359)

Miller, N., Maruyama, G., Beaber, R. J., & Valone, K. (1976). Speed of speech and persuasion. *Journal of Personality and Social Psychology*, **34**, 615–624. (p. 258)

Miller, P. A., & Eisenberg, N. (1988). The relation of empathy to aggressive and externalizing/antisocial behavior. *Psychological Bulletin*, **103**, 324–344. (p. 478)

Miller, P. C., Lefcourt, H. M., Holmes, J. G., Ware, E. E., & Saley, W. E. (1986). Marital locus of control and marital problem solving. *Journal of Personality and Social Psychology*, **51**, 161–169. (p. 52)

Miller, R. L., Brickman, P., & Bolen, D. (1975). Attribution versus persuasion as a means for modifying behavior. *Journal of Personality and Social Psychology*, **31**, 430–441. (p. 122)

Miller, R. S. (1997). Inattentive and contented: Relationship commitment and attention to alternatives. *Journal of Personality and Social Psychology*, **73**, 758–766. (p. 466)

Miller, R. S., & Schlenker, B. R. (1985). Egotism in group members: Public and private attributions of responsibility for group performance. *Social Psychology Quarterly*, **48**, 85–89. (p. 73)

Millett, K. (1975). The shame is over. *Ms.*, January, pp. 26–29. (p. 465)

Mims, P. R., Hartnett, J. J., & Nay, W. R. (1975). Interpersonal attraction and help volunteering as a function of physical attractiveness. *Journal of Psychology*, **89**, 125–131. (p. 503)

Minard, R. D. (1952). Race relationships in the Pocohontas coal field. *Journal of Social Issues*, **8**(1), 29–44. (p. 356)

Mio, J. S., Thompson, S. C., & Givens, G. H. (1993). The commons dilemma as a metaphor: Memory, influence, and implications for environmental conservation. *Metaphor and Symbolic Activity*, **8**, 23–42. (p. 525)

Mirels, H. L., & McPeek, R. W. (1977). Self-advocacy and self-esteem. *Journal of*

Consulting and Clinical Psychology, **45,** 1132–1138. (p. 586)

Mischel, W. (1968). *Personality and assessment.* New York: Wiley. (pp. 132, 240)

Mita, T. H., Dermer, M., & Knight, J. (1977). Reversed facial images and the mere-exposure hypothesis. *Journal of Personality and Social Psychology,* **35,** 597–601. (p. 432)

Mitchell, G., Tetlock, P. E., Mellers, B. A., & Ordonez, L. D. (1993). Judgments of social justice: Compromises between equality and efficiency. *Journal of Personality and Social Psychology,* **65,** 629–639. (p. 528)

Mitchell, T. R., & Thompson, L. (1994). A theory of temporal adjustments of the evaluation of events: Rosy prospection and rosy retrospection. In C. Stubbart, J. Porac, & J. Meindl (Eds.), *Advances in managerial cognition and organizational information processing.* Greenwich, CT: JAI Press. (p. 101)

Mitchell, T. R., Thompson, L., Peterson, E., & Cronk, R. (1997). Temporal adjustments in the evaluation of events: The "rosy view." *Journal of Experimental Social Psychology,* **33,** 421–448. (p. 101)

Moghaddam, F. M. (1987). Psychology in the three worlds: As reflected by the crisis in social psychology and the move toward indigenous third-world psychology. *American Psychologist,* **42,** 912–920. (p. 14)

Moghaddam, F. M. (1990). Modulative and generative orientations in psychology: Implications for psychology in the three worlds. *Journal of Social Issues,* **46,** 21–41. (p. 14)

Moghaddam, F. M., Stolkin, A. J., & Hutcheson, L. S. (1997). A generalized personal/group discrepancy: Testing the domain specificity of a perceived higher effect of events on one's group than on oneself. *Personality and Social Psychology Bulletin,* **23,** 743–750. (p. 347)

Monson, T. C., Hesley, J. W., & Chernick, L. (1982). Specifying when personality traits can and cannot predict behavior: An alternative to abandoning the attempt to predict single-act criteria. *Journal of Personality and Social Psychology,* **43,** 385–399. (p. 241)

Monson, T. C., & Snyder, M. (1977). Actors, observers, and the attribution process: Toward a reconceptualization. *Journal of Experimental Social Psychology,* **13,** 89–111. (p. 90)

Monteith, M. J. (1993). Self-regulation of prejudiced responses: Implications for progress in prejudice-reduction efforts. *Journal of Personality and Social Psychology,* **65,** 469–485. (p. 343)

Moody, K. (1980). *Growing up on television: The TV effect.* New York: Times Books. (p. 287)

Moore, B. S., Underwood, B., & Rosenhan, D. L. (1973). Affect and altruism. *Developmental Psychology,* **8,** 99–104. (p. 496)

Moore, D. L., & Baron, R. S. (1983). Social facilitation: A physiological analysis. In J. T. Cacioppo & R. Petty (Eds.), *Social psychophysiology.* New York: Guilford Press. (p. 295)

Moran, G., & Comfort, J. C. (1982). Scientific juror selection: Sex as a moderator of demographic and personality predictors of impaneled felony juror behavior. *Journal of Personality and Social Psychology,* **43,** 1052–1063. (p. 624)

Moran, G., & Comfort, J. C. (1986). Neither "tentative" nor "fragmentary": Verdict preference of impaneled felony jurors as a function of attitude toward capital punishment. *Journal of Applied Psychology,* **71,** 146–155. (p. 624)

Moran, G., & Cutler, B. L. (1991). The prejudicial impact of pretrial publicity. *Journal of Applied Social Psychology,* **21,** 345–367. (p. 618)

Moran, G., Cutler, B. L., & Loftus, E. F. (1990). Jury selection in major controlled substance trials: The need for extended voir dire. *Forensic Reports,* **3,** 331–348. (p. 623)

Moreland, R. L., & Zajonc, R. B. (1977). Is stimulus recognition a necessary condition for the occurrence of exposure effects? *Journal of Personality and Social Psychology,* **35,** 191–199. (p. 431)

Morier, D., & Seroy, C. (1994). The effect of interpersonal expectancies on men's self-presentation of gender role attitudes to women. *Sex Roles,* **31,** 493–504. (p. 198)

Morris, W. N., & Miller, R. S. (1975). The effects of consensus-breaking and consensus-preempting partners on reduction of conformity. *Journal of Experimental Social Psychology,* **11,** 215–223. (p. 231)

Morrison, D. M. (1989). Predicting contraceptive efficacy: A discriminant analysis of three groups of adolescent women. *Journal of Applied Social Psychology,* **19,** 1431–1452. (p. 134)

Morrow, L. (1983, August 1). All the hazards and threats of success. *Time,* pp. 20–25. (p. 210)

Morse, S. J., & Gruzen, J. (1976). The eye of the beholder: A neglected variable in the study of physical attractiveness. *Journal of Psychology,* **44,** 209–225. (p. 438)

Moscovici, S. (1985). Social influence and conformity. In G. Lindzey & E. Aronson (Eds.), *The handbook of social psychology,* 3rd ed. Hillsdale, N.J.: Erlbaum. (p. 326)

Moscovici, S. (1988). Notes towards a description of social representations. *European Journal of Social Psychology,* **18,** 211–250. (p. 11)

Moscovici, S., Lage, S., & Naffrechoux, M. (1969). Influence of a consistent minority on the responses of a majority in a color perception task. *Sociometry,* **32,** 365–380. (p. 326)

Moscovici, S., & Zavalloni, M. (1969). The group as a polarizer of attitudes. *Journal of Personality and Social Psychology,* **12,** 124–135. (p. 311)

Moskowitz, D. S., Suh, E. J., & Desaulniers, J. (1994). Situational influences on gender differences in agency and communion. *Journal of Personality and Social Psychology,* **66,** 753–761. (p. 204)

Moyer, K. E. (1976). *The psychobiology of aggression.* New York: Harper & Row. (p. 386)

Moyer, K. E. (1983). The physiology of motivation: Aggression as a model. In C. J. Scheier & A. M. Rogers (Eds.), *G. Stanley Hall Lecture Series* (Vol. 3). Washington, DC: American Psychological Association. (p. 386)

Moynihan, D. P. (1979). Social science and the courts. *Public Interest,* **54,** 12–31. (p. 10)

Mucchi-Faina, A., Maass, A., & Volpato, C. (1991). Social influence: The role of originality. *European Journal of Social Psychology,* **21,** 183–197. (p. 327)

Muehlenhard, C. L. (1988). Misinterpreted dating behaviors and the risk of date rape. *Journal of Social and Clinical Psychology,* **6,** 20–37. (p. 79)

Mueller, C. W., Donnerstein, E., & Hallam, J. (1983). Violent films and prosocial behavior. *Personality and Social Psychology Bulletin,* **9,** 83–89. (p. 416)

Mullen, B. (1991). Group composition, salience, and cognitive representations: The phenomenology of being in a group. *Journal of Experimental Social psychology,* **27,** 297–323. (p. 356)

Mullen, B. (1986). Atrocity as a function of lynch mob composition: A self-attention perspective. *Personality and Social Psychology Bulletin,* **12,** 187–197. *(a)* (p. 419)

Mullen, B. (1986). Stuttering, audience size, and the other-total ratio: A self-attention perspective. *Journal of Applied Social Psychology,* **16,** 139–149. *(b)* (pp. 296, 305)

Mullen, B., Anthony, T., Salas, E., & Driskell, J. E. (1994). Group cohesiveness and quality of decision making: An integration of tests of the groupthink hypothesis. *Small Group Research,* **25,** 189–204. (p. 320)

Mullen, B., & Baumeister, R. F. (1987). Group effects on self-attention and performance: Social loafing, social facilitation, and social impairment. In C. Hendrick (Ed.), *Group processes and intergroup relations: Review of personality and social psychology,* Vol. 9. Newbury Park, Ca.: Sage. (pp. 297, 301)

Mullen, B., Brown, R., & Smith, C. (1992). Ingroup bias as a function of salience, relevance, and status: An integration. *European Journal of Social Psychology,* **22,** 103–122. (p. 354)

Mullen, B., Bryant, B., & Driskell, J. E. (1997). Presence of others and arousal: An integration. *Group Dynamics: Theory, Research, and Practice,* **1**, 52–64. (p. 294)

Mullen, B., & Copper, C. (1994). The relation between group cohesiveness and performance: An integration. *Psychological Bulletin,* **115**, 210–227. (p. 317)

Mullen, B., Copper, C., & Driskell, J. E. (1990). Jaywalking as a function of model behavior. *Personality and Social Psychology Bulletin,* **16**, 320–330. (p. 233)

Mullen, B., & Goethals, G. R. (1990). Social projection, actual consensus and valence. *British Journal of Social Psychology,* **29**, 279–282. (p. 61)

Mullen, B., & Hu, L. (1989). Perceptions of ingroup and outgroup variability: A meta-analytic integration. *Basic and Applied Social Psychology,* **10**, 233–252. (p. 366)

Mullen, B., & Riordan, C. A. (1988). Self-serving attributions for performance in naturalistic settings: A meta-analytic review. *Journal of Applied Social Psychology,* **18**, 3–22. (p. 55)

Mullen, B., Salas, E., & Driskell, J. E. (1989). Salience, motivation, and artifact as contributions to the relation between participation rate and leadership. *Journal of Experimental Social Psychology,* **25**, 545–559. (p. 327)

Muller, S., & Johnson, B. T. (1990). Fear and persuasion: A linear relationship? Paper presented to the Eastern Psychological Association convention. (p. 262)

Mullin, C. R., & Linz, D. (1995). Desensitization and resensitization to violence against women: Effects of exposure to sexually violent films on judgments of domestic violence victims. *Journal of Personality and Social Psychology,* **69**, 449–459. (p. 406)

Munro, G. D., & Ditto, P. H. (1997). Biased assimilation, attitude polarization, and affect in reactions to stereotype-relevant scientific information. *Personality and Social Psychology Bulletin,* **23**, 636–653. (p. 95)

Munro, G. D., Ditto, P. H., Lockhart, L. K., Fagerlin, A., Gready, M., & Peterson, E. (1997). Biased assimilation of sociopolitcal arguments: Evaluating the 1996 U.S. Presidential debate. Unpublished manuscript, Hope College. (p. 95)

Muraven, M., Tice, D. M., & Baumeister, R. F. (1998). Self-control as a limited resource: Regulatory depletion patterns. *Journal of Personality and Social Psychology,* in press. (p. 50)

Murphy, C. (1990, June). New findings: Hold on to your hat. *The Atlantic,* pp. 22–23. (pp. 15, 18)

Murphy, C. M., & O'Farrell, T. J. (1996). Marital violence among alcoholics. *Current Directions in Psychological Science,* **5**, 183–187. (p. 387)

Murphy-Berman, V., Berman, J. J., Singh, P., Pachauri, A., & Kumar, P. (1984). Factors affecting allocation to needy and meritorious recipients: A cross-cultural comparison. *Journal of Personality and Social Psychology,* **46**, 1267–1272. (p. 528)

Murphy-Berman, V., & Sharma, R. (1986). Testing the assumptions of attribution theory in India. *Journal of Social Psychology,* **126**, 607–616. (p. 73)

Murray, J. P., & Kippax, S. (1979). From the early window to the late night show: International trends in the study of television's impact on children and adults. In L. Berkowitz (Ed.), *Advances in experimental social psychology,* vol. 12. New York: Academic Press. (p. 411)

Murray, J. P., & Lonnborg, B. (1989). Using TV sensibly. Cooperative Extension Service, Kansas State University. (p. 415)

Murray, S. L., & Holmes, J. G. (1997). A leap of faith? Positive illusions in romantic relationships. *Personality and Social Psychology Bulletin,* **23**, 586-604. (p. 449)

Murray, S. L., Holmes, J. G., & Griffin, D. W. (1996). The self-fulfilling nature of positive illusions in romantic relationships: Love is not blind, but prescient. *Journal of Personality and Social Psychology,* **71**, 1155–1180. (p. 121)

Murray, S. L., Holmes, J. G., & Griffin, D. W. (1996). The benefits of positive illusions: Idealization and the construction of satisfaction in close relationships. *Journal of Personality and Social Psychology,* **70**, 79–98. (p. 449)

Murstein, B. L. (1986). *Paths to marriage.* Newbury Park, Ca.: Sage. (p. 435)

Muson, G. (1978). Teenage violence and the telly. *Psychology Today,* March, pp. 50–54. (p. 413)

Musser, L. M., & Graziano, W. F. (1991). Behavioral confirmation in children's interaction with peers. *Basic and Applied Social Psychology,* **12**, 441–456. (p. 181)

Myers, D. G. (1978). Polarizing effects of social comparison. *Journal of Experimental Social Psychology,* **14**, 554–563. (p. 316)

Myers, D. G. (1993). *The pursuit of happiness.* New York: Avon. (pp. 117, 392, 594)

Myers, D. G. (1996). *Society in the balance: America's social recession and renewal.* Unpublished manuscript, Hope College. (p. 468)

Myers, D. G. (1998). *Psychology,* 5th edition. New York: Worth. (p. 102)

Myers, D. G., & Bishop, G. D. (1970). Discussion effects on racial attitudes. *Science,* **169**, 778–789. (p. 312)

Nadler, A. (1991). Help-seeking behavior: Psychological costs and instrumental benefits. In M. S. Clark (Ed.), *Prosocial behavior.* Newbury Park, CA: Sage. (p. 503)

Nadler, A., & Fisher, J. D. (1986). The role of threat to self-esteem and perceived control in recipient reaction to help: Theory development and empirical validation.

In L. Berkowitz (Ed.), *Advances in Experimental Social Psychology,* vol. 19. Orlando, FL: Academic Press. (p. 481)

Nadler, A., Goldberg, M., & Jaffe, Y. (1982). Effect of self-differentiation and anonymity in group on deindividuation. *Journal of Personality and Social Psychology,* **42**, 1127–1136. (p. 308)

Nagar, D., & Pandey, J. (1987). Affect and performance on cognitive task as a function of crowding and noise. *Journal of Applied Social Psychology,* **17**, 147–157. (p. 297)

Nail, P. R., & Van Leeuwen, M. D. (1993). An analysis and restructuring of the diamond model of social response. *Personality and Social Psychology Bulletin,* **19**, 106–116. (p. 243)

Napolitan, D. A., & Goethals, G. R. (1979). The attribution of friendliness. *Journal of Experimental Social Psychology,* **15**, 105–113. (p. 85)

National Council for Research on Women (1994). Women and philanthropy fact sheet. *Issues Quarterly,* **1**(2), 9. (p. 184)

National Opinion Research Center (1997). General happiness by marital status, 1972 to 1994. Data gleaned from General Social Survey data archives at http://www.icpsr.umich.edu. (p. 470)

National Research Council (1993). *Understanding and preventing violence.* Washington, DC: National Academy Press. (p. 425)

National Safety Council (1991). *Accident facts.* Chicago: Author. (p. 112)

National Television Violence Study (1997). Thousand Oaks, CA: Sage. (p. 412)

Naylor, T. H. (1990). Redefining corporate motivation, Swedish style. *Christian Century,* **107**, 566–570. (p. 329)

NCTV (1988). TV and film alcohol research. *NCTV News,* **9**(3–4), 4. (p. 417)

Needles, D. J., & Abramson, L. Y. (1990). Positive life events, attributional style, and hopefulness: Testing a model of recovery from depression. *Journal of Abnormal Psychology,* **99**, 156–165. (p. 574)

Neimeyer, G. J., MacNair, R., Metzler, A. E., & Courchaine, K. (1991). Changing personal beliefs: Effects of forewarning, argument quality, prior bias, and personal exploration. *Journal of Social and Clinical Psychology,* **10**, 1–20. (p. 589)

Nelson, L. J., & Miller, D. T. (1997). The distinctiveness effect in social categorization: You are what makes you unusual. *Psychological Science,* in press. (p. 367)

Nelson, T. E., Acker, M., & Manis, M. (1996). Irrepressible stereotypes. *Journal of Experimental Social Psychology,* **32**, 13–38. (p. 378)

Nelson, T. E., Biernat, M. R., & Manis, M. (1990). Everyday base rates (sex stereotypes): Potent and resilient. *Journal of Personality and Social Psychology,* **59**, 664–675. (p. 377)

Nemeth, C. (1979). The role of an active minority in intergroup relations. In W. G. Austin and S. Worchel (Eds.), *The social psychology of intergroup relations.* Monterey, Calif.: Brooks/Cole. (p. 326)

Nemeth, C., (1977). Interactions between jurors as a function of majority vs. Unanimity decision rules. *Journal of Applied Social Psychology, 7,* 38-56. (p. 628)

Nemeth, C., & Chiles, C. (1988). Modelling courage: The role of dissent in fostering independence. *European Journal of Social Psychology, 18,* 275–280. (p. 232)

Nemeth, C. J., & Staw, B. M. (1989). The tradeoffs of social control and innovation in groups and organizations. *Advances in Experimental Social Psychology, 22,* 175–210. (p. 324)

Nemeth, C., & Wachtler, J. (1974). Creating the perceptions of consistency and confidence: A necessary condition for minority influence. *Sociometry, 37,* 529–540. (p. 327)

Newman, H. M., & Langer, E. J. (1981). Post-divorce adaptation and the attribution of responsibility. *Sex Roles, 7,* 223–231. (p. 67)

Newman, L. S. (1993). How individualists interpret behavior: Idiocentrism and spontaneous trait inference. *Social Cognition, 11,* 243–269. (p. 90)

Newman, L. S., Duff, K., Schnopp-Wyatt, N., Brock, B., & Hoffman, Y. (1997). Reactions to the O. J. Simpson verdict: "Mindless tribalism" or motivated inference processes? *Journal of Social Issues, 53,* 547–562. (p. 615)

Nias, D. K. B. (1979). Marital choice: Matching or complementation? In M. Cook and G. Wilson (Eds.), *Love and attraction.* Oxford: Pergamon. (p. 446)

Nicholson, N., Cole, S. G., & Rocklin, T. (1985). Conformity in the Asch situation: A comparison between contemporary British and U. S. university students. *British Journal of Social Psychology, 24,* 59–63. (p. 242)

Nielsen Media Research (1990). *Report on television.* Summarized in *American Enterprise,* July/August, 1990, p. 98. (p. 411)

Niemi, R. G., Mueller, J., & Smith, T. W. (1989). *Trends in public opinion: A compendium of survey data.* New York: Greenwood Press. (pp. 199, 346, 393, 421)

Nigro, G. N., Hill, D. E., Gelbein, M. E., & Clark, C. L. (1988). Changes in the facial prominence of women and men over the last decade. *Psychology of Women Quarterly, 12,* 225–235. (p. 358)

Nisbett, R. (1988, Fall). The Vincennes incident: Congress hears psychologists. *Science Agenda* (American Psychological Association) p. 4. (p. 94)

Nisbett, R. E. (1990). Evolutionary psychology, biology, and cultural evolution. *Motivation and emotion, 14,* 255–263. (p. 398)

Nisbett, R. E. (1993). Violence and U.S. regional culture. *American Psychologist, 48,* 441–449. (p. 398)

Nisbett, R. E., Borgida, E., Crandall, R., & Reed, H. (1976). Popular induction: Information is not necessarily informative. In J. S. Carroll and J. W. Payne (Eds.), *Cognition and social behavior.* Hillsdale, N.J.: Erlbaum. (p. 110)

Nisbett, R. E., & Cohen, D. (1996). *Culture of honor: The psychology of violence in the South.* Boulder, CO: Westview Press. (p. 398)

Nisbett, R. E., Fong, G. T., Lehman, D. R., & Cheng, P. W. (1987). Teaching reasoning. *Science, 238,* 625–631. (p. 125)

Nisbett, R. E., & Ross, L. (1980). *Human inference: Strategies and shortcomings of social judgment.* Englewood Cliffs, N.J.: Prentice-Hall. (pp. 124, 125)

Nisbett, R. E., & Ross, L. (1991). *The person and the situation.* New York: McGraw-Hill. (p. 329)

Nisbett, R. E., & Schachter, S. (1966). Cognitive manipulation of pain. *Journal of Experimental Social Psychology, 2,* 227–236. (p. 46)

Nisbett, R. E., & Wilson, T. D. (1977). Telling more than we can know: Verbal reports on mental processes. *Psychological Review, 84,* 231–259. (p. 46)

Nix, G., Watson, C., Pyszczynski, T., & Greenberg, J. (1995). Reducing depressive affect through external focus of attention. *Journal of Social and Clinical Psychology, 14,* 36–52. (p. 574)

Noel, J. G., Forsyth, D. R., & Kelley, K. N. (1987). Improving the performance of failing students by overcoming their self-serving attributional biases. *Basic and Applied Social Psychology, 8,* 151–162. (p. 52)

Nolen-Hoeksema, S., Girgus, J. S., & Seligman, M. E. P. (1986). Learned helplessness in children: A longitudinal study of depression, achievement, and explanatory style. *Journal of Personality and Social Psychology, 51,* 435–442. (p. 573)

Noller, P. (1996). What is this thing called love? Defining the love that supports marriage and family. *Personal Relationships, 3,* 97–115. (p. 470)

Noller, P., & Fitzpatrick, M. A. (1990). Marital communication in the eighties. *Journal of Marriage and the Family, 52,* 832–843. (p. 469)

Noon, E., & Hollin, C. R. (1987). Lay knowledge of eyewitness behaviour: A British survey. *Applied Cognitive Psychology, 1,* 143–153. (p. 611)

Norem, J. K., & Cantor, N. (1986). Defensive pessimism: Harnessing anxiety as motivation. *Journal of Personality and Social Psychology, 51,* 1208–1217. (p. 60)

Notarius, C., & Markman, H. J. (1993). *We can work it out.* New York: Putnam. (p. 469)

Nowak, M., & Sigmund, K. (1993). A strategy of win-stay, lose-shift that outperforms tit-for-tat in the Prisoner's Dilemma game. *Nature, 364,* 56–58. (p. 554)

Nurmi, J-E., & Salmela-Aro, K. (1997). Social strategies and loneliness: A prospective study. *Personality and Individual Differences, 23,* 205–215. (p. 576)

Nurmi, J-E., Toivonen, S., Salmela-Aro, K., & Eronen, S. (1996). Optimistic, approach-oriented, and avoidance strategies in social situations: Three studies on loneliness and peer relationships. *European Journal of Personality, 10,* 201–219. (p. 576)

Nuttin, J. M., Jr. (1987). Affective consequences of mere ownership: The name letter effect in twelve European languages. *European Journal of Social Psychology, 17,* 318–402. (p. 431)

O'Dea, T. F. (1968). Sects and cults. In D. L. Sills (Ed.), *International encyclopedia of the social sciences* (Vol. 14). New York: Macmillan. (p. 282)

O'Gorman, H. J., & Garry, S. L. (1976). Pluralistic ignorance—a replication and extension. *Public Opinion Quarterly, 40,* 449–458. (p. 58)

Ohbuchi, K., & Kambara, T. (1985). Attacker's intent and awareness of outcome, impression management, and retaliation. *Journal of Experimental Social Psychology, 21,* 321–330. (p. 403)

O'Leary, K. D., Christian, J. L., & Mendell, N. R. (1994). A closer look at the link between marital discord and depressive symptomatology. *Journal of Social and Clinical Psychology, 13,* 33–41. (p. 469)

Olfson, M., & Pincus, H. A. (1994). Outpatient therapy in the United States: II. Patterns of utilization. *American Journal of Psychiatry, 151,* 1289–1294. (p. 581)

Oliner, S. P., & Oliner, P. M. (1988). *The altruistic personality: Rescuers of Jews in Nazi Europe.* New York: The Free Press. (p. 509)

Oliver, M. B., & Hyde, J. S. (1993). Gender differences in sexuality: A meta-analysis. *Psychological Bulletin, 114,* 29–51. (p. 190)

Olson, J. M., & Cal, A. V. (1984). Source credibility, attitudes, and the recall of past behaviours. *European Journal of Social Psychology, 14,* 203–210. (p. 257)

Olson, J. M., Roese, N. J., & Zanna, M. P. (1996). Expectancies. In E. T. Higgins & A. W. Kruglanski (eds.), *Social psychology: Handbook of basic principles.* New York: Guilford Press, in press. (p. 121)

Olson, J. M., & Zanna, M. P. (1981). Promoting physical activity: A social psychological perspective. Report prepared for the Ministry of Culture and Recreation, Sports and Fitness Branch, 77 Bloor St. West, 8th Floor, Toronto, Ontario M7A 2R9, November. (p. 135)

Olson, J. M., & Zanna, M. P. (1993). Attitudes and attitude change. *Annual Review of Psychology, 44,* 117–154. (p. 130)

Olweus, D. (1979). Stability of aggressive reaction patterns in males: A review. *Psychological Bulletin, 86,* 852–875. (p. 386)

Olweus, D., Mattsson, A., Schalling, D., & Low, H. (1988). Circulating testosterone levels and aggression in adolescent males: A causal analysis. *Psychosomatic Medicine, 50,* 261–272. (p. 388)

Omoto, A. M., Snyder, M., & Berghuis, J. P. (1993). The psychology of volunteerism: A conceptual analysis and a program of action research. In J. B. Pryor & G. D. Reeder (eds.), *The social psychology of HIV infection.* Hillsdale, NJ: Erlbaum. (p. 501)

Opotow, S. (1990). Moral exclusion and injustice: An introduction. *Journal of Social Issues, 46,* 1–20. (p. 508)

Orbell, J. M., van de Kragt, A. J. C., & Dawes, R. M. (1988). Explaining discussion-induced cooperation. *Journal of Personality and Social Psychology, 54,* 811–819. (p. 522)

Orive, R. (1984). Group similarity, public self-awareness, and opinion extremity: A social projection explanation of deindividuation effects. *Journal of Personality and Social Psychology, 47,* 727–737. (p. 308)

Ornstein, R. (1991). *The evolution of consciousness: Of Darwin, Freud, and cranial fire: The origins of the way we think.* New York: Prentice-Hall. (pp. 143, 223, 280)

Osbeck, L. M., Moghaddam, F. M., & Perreault, S. (1996). Similarity and attraction among majority and minority groups in a multicultural context. *International Journal of Intercultural Relations, 20,* 1–10. (p. 444)

Osberg, T. M., & Shrauger, J. S. (1986). Self-prediction: Exploring the parameters of accuracy. *Journal of Personality and Social Psychology, 51,* 1044–1057. (p. 47)

Osberg, T. M., & Shrauger, J. S. (1990). The role of self-prediction in psychological assessment. In J. N. Butcher & C. D. Spielberger (Eds.), *Advances in Personality Assessment,* vol. 8. Hillsdale, NJ: Erlbaum. (p. 47)

Osborne, J. W. (1995). Academics, self-esteem, and race: A look at the underlying assumptions of the disidentification hypothesis. *Personality and Social Psychology Bulletin, 21,* 449–455. (p. 352)

Osgood, C. E. (1962). *An alternative to war or surrender.* Urbana, Ill.: University of Illinois Press. (p. 553)

Osgood, C. E. (1980). GRIT: A strategy for survival in mankind's nuclear age? Paper presented at the Pugwash Conference on New Directions in Disarmament, Racine, Wis. (p. 553)

Oskamp, S. (1971). Effects of programmed strategies on cooperation in the prisoner's dilemma and other mixed-motive games. *Journal of Conflict Resolution, 15,* 225–229. (p. 519)

Oskamp, S. (1991). Curbside recycling: Knowledge, attitudes, and behavior.

Paper presented at the Society for Experimental Social Psychology meeting, Columbus, Ohio. (p. 134)

Osterhouse, R. A., & Brock, T. C. (1970). Distraction increases yielding to propaganda by inhibiting counter-arguing. *Journal of Personality and Social Psychology, 15,* 344–358. (p. 274)

Ostrom, T. M., & Sedikides, C. (1992). Out-group homogeneity effects in natural and minimal groups. *Psychological Bulletin, 112,* 536–552. (p. 365)

Padgett, V. R. (1989). Predicting organizational violence: An application of 11 powerful principles of obedience. Paper presented at the American Psychological Association Convention. (p. 221)

Pak, A. W., Dion, K. L., & Dion, K. K. (1991). Social-psychological correlates of experienced discrimination: Test of the double jeopardy hypothesis. *International Journal of Intercultural Relations, 15,* 243–254. (p. 538)

Pallak, M. S., Mueller, M., Dollar, K., & Pallak, J. (1972). Effect of commitment on responsiveness to an extreme consonant communication. *Journal of Personality and Social Psychology, 23,* 429–436. (p. 265)

Pallak, S. R., Murroni, E., & Koch, J. (1983). Communicator attractiveness and expertise, emotional versus rational appeals, and persuasion: A heuristic versus systematic processing interpretation. *Social Cognition, 2,* 122–141. (p. 259)

Palmer, D. L. (1996). Determinants of Canadian attitudes toward immigration: More than just racism? *Canadian Journal of Behavioural Science, 28,* 180–192. (p. 360)

Palmer, E. L., & Dorr, A. (Eds.) (1980). *Children and the faces of television: Teaching, violence, selling.* New York: Academic Press. (p. 287)

Paloutzian, R. (1979). Pro-ecology behavior: Three field experiments on litter pickup. Paper presented at the Western Psychological Association convention. (p. 268)

Pandey, J., Sinha, Y., Prakash, A., & Tripathi, R. C. (1982). Right-left political ideologies and attribution of the causes of poverty. *European Journal of Social Psychology, 12,* 327–331. (p. 91)

Papastamou, S., & Mugny, G. (1990). Synchronic consistency and psychologization in minority influence. *European Journal of Social Psychology, 20,* 85–98. (p. 326)

Parachin, V. M. (1992, December). Four brave chaplains. *Retired Officer Magazine,* pp. 24–26. (p. 500)

Park, B., & Rothbart, M. (1982). Perception of out-group homogeneity and levels of social categorization: Memory for the subordinate attributes of in-group and out-group members. *Journal of Personality and Social Psychology, 42,* 1051–1068. (p. 36)

Parke, R. D., Berkowitz, L., Leyens, J. P., West, S. G., & Sebastian, J. (1977). Some effects of violent and nonviolent movies on the behavior of juvenile delinquents. In L. Berkowitz (Ed.), *Advances in experimental social psychology* (Vol. 10). New York: Academic Press. (p. 414)

Parker, K. D., Ortega, S. T., & VanLaningham, J. (1995). Life satisfaction, self-esteem, and personal happiness among Mexican and African Americans. *Sociological Spectrum, 15,* 131–145. (p. 593)

Pascarella, E. T., & Terenzini, P. T. (1991). *How collects affects students: Findings and insights from twenty years of research.* San Francisco: Jossey-Bass. (p. 312)

Patterson, G. R., Chamberlain, P., & Reid, J. B. (1982). A comparative evaluation of parent training procedures. *Behavior Therapy, 13,* 638–650. (p. 397)

Patterson, G. R., Littman, R. A., & Bricker, W. (1967). Assertive behavior in children: A step toward a theory of aggression. *Monographs of the Society of Research in Child Development* (Serial No. 113), *32,* 5. (p. 396)

Patterson, T. E. (1980). The role of the mass media in presidential campaigns: The lessons of the 1976 election. *Items, 34,* 25–30. Social Science Research Council, 605 Third Avenue, New York, N.Y. 10016. (p. 433)

Paulhus, D. (1982). Individual differences, self-presentation, and cognitive dissonance: Their concurrent operation in forced compliance. *Journal of Personality and Social Psychology, 43,* 838–852. (p. 152)

Paulhus, D. L., & Lim, D. T. K. (1994). Arousal and evaluative extremity in social judgments: A dynamic complexity model. *European Journal of Social Psychology, 24,* 89–99. (p. 118)

Paulhus, D. L., & Morgan, K. L. (1997). Perceptions of intelligence in leaderless groups: The dynamic effects of shyness and acquaintance. *Journal of Personality and Social Psychology, 72,* 581–591. (p. 578)

Pauling, L. (1962). Quoted by Etzioni, A. *the hard way to peace: A new strategy.* New York: Collier. (p. 527)

Paulus, P. B. (1998). Developing consensus about groupthink after all these years. *Organizational Behavior and Human Decision Processes,* in press. (p. 320)

Paulus, P. B. Brown, V., & Ortega, A. H. (1997). Group creativity. In R. E. Purser and A. Montuori (eds.), *Social creativity,* vol. 2. Cresskill, NJ: Hampton Press. (p. 324)

Paulus, P. B., Larey, T. S., & Dzindolet, M. T. (1998). Creativity in groups and teams. In M. Turner (ed.), *Groups at work: Advances in theory and research.* Hillsdale, NJ: Erlbaum. (p. 324)

Paulus, P. B., Larey, T. S., & Ortega, A. H. (1995). Performance and perceptions of brainstormers in an organizational setting. *Basic and Applied Social Psychology*, **17**, 249–265. (p. 324)

Pedersen, A., & Walker, I. (1997). Prejudice against Australian Aborigines: Old-fashioned and modern forms. *European Journal of Social Psychology*, **27**, 561–587. (p. 341)

Pegalis, L. J., Shaffer, D. R., Bazzini, D. G., & Greenier, K. (1994). On the ability to elicit self-disclosure: Are there gender-based and contextual limitations on the opener effect? *Personality and Social Psychology Bulletin*, **20**, 412–420. (p. 464)

Peng, Y., Zebrowitz, L. A., & Lee, H. K. (1993). The impact of cultural background and cross-cultural experience on impressions of American and Korean male speakers. *Journal of Cross-Cultural Psychology*, **24**, 203–220. (p. 259)

Pennebaker, J. (1990). *Opening up: The healing power of confiding in others*. New York: William Morrow. (p. 591)

Pennebaker, J. W. (1982). *The psychology of physical symptoms*. New York: Springer-Verlag. (p. 579)

Pennebaker, J. W., & O'Heeron, R. C. (1984). Confiding in others and illness rate among spouses of suicide and accidental death victims. *Journal of Abnormal Psychology*, **93**, 473–476. (p. 591)

Pennebaker, J. W., Rimé, B., & Sproul, G. (1996). Stereotypes of emotional expressiveness of northerners and southerners: A cross-cultural test of Montesquieu's hypotheses. *Journal of Personality and Social Psychology*, **70**, 372–380. (p. 337)

Penner, L. A., Dertke, M. C., & Achenbach, C. J. (1973). The "flash" system: A field study of altruism. *Journal of Applied Social Psychology*, **3**, 362–370. (p. 503)

Pennington, N., & Hastie, R. (1993). The story model for juror decision making. In R. Hastie (ed.), *Inside the juror: The psychology of juror decision making*. New York: Cambridge University Press. (p. 620)

Penrod, S., & Cutler, B. L. (1987). Assessing the competence of juries. In I. B. Weiner & A. K. Hess (Eds.), *Handbook of forensic psychology*. New York: Wiley. (p. 623)

Peplau, L. A., & Gordon, S. L. (1985). Women and men in love: Gender differences in close heterosexual relationships. In V. E. O'Leary, R. K. Unger, & B. S. Wallston (Eds.), *Women, gender, and social psychology*. Hillsdale, N.J.: Erlbaum. (p. 456)

Perkins, H. W. (1991). Religious commitment, Yuppie values, and well-being in post-collegiate life. *Review of Religious Research*, **32**, 244–251. (p. 592)

Perlman, D., & Rook, K. S. (1987). Social support, social deficits, and the family: Toward the enhancement of well-being. In S. Oskamp (Ed.), *Family processes and problems: Social psychological aspects*. Newbury Park, CA: Sage. (p. 592)

Perloff, L. S. (1987). Social comparison and illusions of invulnerability. In C. R. Snyder & C. R. Ford (Eds.), *Coping with negative life events: Clinical and social psychological perspectives*. New York: Plenum. (p. 60)

Perls, F. S. (1972). Gestalt therapy [interview]. In A. Bry (Ed.), *Inside psychotherapy*. New York: Basic Books. (p. 247)

Perls, F. S. (1973). *Ego, hunger and aggression: The beginning of Gestalt therapy*. Random House, 1969. Cited by Berkowitz in The case for bottling up rage. *Psychology Today*, July, pp. 24–30. (p. 421)

Perrett, D. I., May, K. A., & Yoshikawa, S. (1994). Facial shape and judgements of female attractiveness. *Nature*, **368**, 239–242. (p. 439)

Perrin, S., & Spencer, C. (1981). Independence or conformity in the Asch experiment as a reflection of cultural or situational factors. *British Journal of Social Psychology*, **20**, 205–209. (p. 242)

Perry, L. C., Perry, D. G., & Weiss, R. J. (1986). Age differences in children's beliefs about whether altruism makes the actor feel good. *Social Cognition*, **4**, 263–269. (p. 496)

Pessin, J. (1933). The comparative effects of social and mechanical stimulation on memorizing. *American Journal of Psychology*, **45**, 263–270. (p. 293)

Pessin, J., & Husband, R. W. (1933). Effects of social stimulation on human maze learning. *Journal of Abnormal and Social Psychology*, **28**, 148–154. (p. 293)

Peterson, B. E., Doty, R. M., & Winter, D. G. (1993). Authoritarianism and attitudes toward contemporary social issues. *Personality and Social Psychology Bulletin*, **19**, 174–184. (p. 363)

Peterson, C., & Barrett, L. C. (1987). Explanatory style and academic performance among university freshmen. *Journal of Personality and Social Psychology*, **53**, 603–607. (p. 52)

Peterson, C., Schwartz, S. M., & Seligman, M. E. P. (1981). Self-blame and depression symptoms. *Journal of Personality and Social Psychology*, **41**, 253–259. (p. 67)

Peterson, C., & Seligman, M. E. P. (1987). Explanatory style and illness. *Journal of Personality*, **55**, 237–265. (p. 583)

Peterson, C., Seligman, M. E. P., & Vaillant, G. E. (1988). Pessimistic explanatory style is a risk factor for physical illness: A thirty-five-year longitudinal study. *Journal of Personality and Social Psychology*, **55**, 23–27. (p. 584)

Peterson, E. (1992). *Under the unpredictable plant*. Grand Rapids, MI: Eerdmans. (p. 33)

Peterson, J. L., & Zill, N. (1981). Television viewing in the United States and children's intellectual, social, and emotional development. *Television and Children*, **2**(2), 21–28. (p. 418)

Peterson, R. S., & Nemeth, C. J. (1996). Focus versus flexibility: Majority and minority influence can both improve performance. *Personality and Social Psychology Bulletin*, **22**, 14–23. (p. 327)

Peto, R., Lopez, A. D., Boreham, J., Thun, M., & Heath, C., Jr. (1992). Mortality from tobacco in developed countries: Indirect estimation from national vital statistics. *Lancet*, **339**, 1268–1278. (p. 129)

Pettifor, J. (1996). Ethics: Virtue and politics in the science and practice of psychology. *Canadian Psychology*, **37**, 1-12. (p. 11)

Pettigrew, T. F. (1958). Personality and socio-cultural factors in intergroup attitudes: A cross-national comparison. *Journal of Conflict Resolution*, **2**, 29–42. (p. 356)

Pettigrew, T. F. (1978). Three issues in ethnicity: Boundaries, deprivations, and perceptions. In J. M. Yinger & S. J. Cutler (Eds.), *Major social issues: A multidisciplinary view*. New York: Free Press. (p. 360)

Pettigrew, T. F. (1979). The ultimate attribution error: Extending Allport's cognitive analysis of prejudice. *Personality and Social Psychology Bulletin*, **55**, 461–476. (p. 371)

Pettigrew, T. F. (1980). Prejudice. In S. Thernstrom et al. (Eds.), *Harvard encyclopedia of American ethnic groups*. Cambridge, Mass.: Harvard University Press. (p. 371)

Pettigrew, T. F. (1986). The intergroup contact hypothesis reconsidered. In M. Hewstone & R. Brown (Eds.), *Contact and conflict in intergroup encounters*. Oxford: Basil Blackwell. (p. 536)

Pettigrew, T. F. (1987, May 12). "Useful" modes of thought contribute to prejudice. *The New York Times*, pp. 17–20. (p. 342)

Pettigrew, T. F. (1988). Advancing racial justice: Past lessons for future use. Paper for the University of Alabama Conference: "Opening Doors: An Appraisal of Race Relations in America." (p. 537)

Pettigrew, T. F. (1997). Generalized intergroup contact effects on prejudice. *Personality and Social Psychology Bulletin*, **23**, 173–185. (p. 536)

Pettigrew, T. F. (1998). Intergroup contact theory. *Annual Review of Psychology*, in press. (pp. 536, 544)

Pettigrew, T. F. (1999, October). Intergroup contact effects on ingroup reappraisal: Meta-analytic findings. Presentation at the Society of Experimental Social Psychology Convention.

Pettigrew, T. F., Jackson, J. S., Brika, J. B., Lemaine, G., Meertens, R. W., Wagner, U., & Zick, A. (1997). Outgroup prejudice in western Europe. *European Review of Social Psychology*, in press. (p. 360)

Pettigrew, T. F., & Meertens, R. W. (1995). Subtle and blatant prejudice in western Europe. *European Journal of Social Psychology, 25,* 57–76. (p. 360)

Pettingale, K. W., Morris, T., Greer, S., & Haybittle, J. L. (1985, March 30). Mental attitudes to cancer: An additional prognostic factor. *Lancet,* p. 750. (p. 584)

Petty, R. E., & Cacioppo, J. T. (1977). Forewarning cognitive responding, and resistance to persuasion. *Journal of Personality and Social Psychology, 35,* 645–655. (p. 274)

Petty, R. E., & Cacioppo, J. T. (1979). Effects of forewarning of persuasive intent and involvement on cognitive response and persuasion. *Personality and Social Psychology Bulletin, 5,* 173–176. *(a)* (pp. 265, 274)

Petty, R. E., & Cacioppo, J. T. (1986). *Communication and persuasion: Central and peripheral routes to attitude change.* New York: Springer-Verlag. (p. 254)

Petty, R. E., Cacioppo, J. T., & Goldman, R. (1981). Personal involvement as a determinant of argument-based persuasion. *Journal of Personality and Social Psychology, 41,* 847–855. (pp. 167, 261, 275)

Petty, R. E., Haugtvedt, C. P., & Smith, S. M. (1995). Elaboration as a determinant of attitude strength: Creating attitudes that are persistent, resistant, and predictive of behavior. In R. E. Petty & J. A. Krosnick (Eds.), *Attitude strength: Antecedents and consequences.* Hillsdale, NJ: Erlbaum. (p. 254)

Petty, R. E., & Krosnick, J. A. (Eds.). (1995). *Attitude strength: Antecedents and consequences.* Hillsdale, NJ: Erlbaum. (pp. 253–254)

Petty, R. E., Schumann, D. W., Richman, S. A., & Strathman, A. J. (1993). Positive mood and persuasion: Different roles for affect under high and low elaboration conditions. *Journal of Personality and Social Psychology, 64,* 5–20. (p. 261)

Petty, R. E., & Wegener, D. T. (1998). Attitude change: Multiple roles for persuasion variables. In D. Gilbert, S. Fiske, & G. Lindzey (eds), *Handbook of Social Psychology,* 4th edition. New York: McGraw-Hill. (pp. 254, 266)

Petty, R. E., Wegener, D. T., & Fabrigar, L. R. (1997). Attitudes and attitude change. *Annual Review of Psychology, 48,* 609–647. (p. 166)

Phillips, D. P. (1982). The impact of fictional television stories on U.S. adult fatalities: New evidence on the effect of the mass media on violence. *American Journal of Sociology, 87,* 1340–1359. (p. 214)

Phillips, D. P. (1985). Natural experiments on the effects of mass media violence on fatal aggression: Strengths and weaknesses of a new approach. In L. Berkowitz (Ed.), *Advances in experimental social psychology,* Vol. 19. Orlando, Fla.: Academic Press. (p. 214)

Phillips, D. P., Carstensen, L. L., & Paight, D. J. (1989). Effects of mass media news stories on suicide, with new evidence on the role of story content. In D. R. Pfeffer (Ed.), *Suicide among youth: Perspectives on risk and prevention.* Washington, DC: American Psychiatric Press. (p. 214)

Phillips, S. T., & Ziller, R. C. (1997). Toward a theory and measure of the nature of nonprejudice. *Journal of Personality and Social Psychology, 72,* 420–434. (p. 363)

Phinney, J. S. (1990). Ethnic identity in adolescents and adults: Review of research. *Psychological Bulletin, 108,* 499–514. (pp. 545, 546)

Pierce, J. P., & Gilpin, E. A. (1995). A historical analysis of tobacco marketing and the uptake of smoking by youth in the United States: 1890–1977. *Health Psychology, 14,* 500–508. (p. 269)

Pierce, J. P., Lee, L., & Gilpin, E. A. (1994). Smoking initiation by adolescent girls, 1944 through 1988. *Journal of the American Medical Association, 27,* 608–611. (p. 269)

Piliavin, I. M., Rodin, J., & Piliavin, J. A. (1969). Good Samaritanism: An underground phenomenon. *Journal of Personality and Social Psychology, 13,* 289–299. (p. 491)

Piliavin, J. A., Evans, D. E., & Callero, P. (1982). Learning to "Give to unnamed strangers": The process of commitment to regular blood donation. In E. Staub, D. Bar-Tal, J. Karylowski, & J. Reykawski (Eds.), *The development and maintenance of prosocial behavior: International perspectives.* New York: Plenum. (pp. 475, 510)

Piliavin, J. A., & Piliavin, I. M. (1973). The Good Samaritan: Why *does* he help? Unpublished manuscript, University of Wisconsin. (p. 475)

Platz, S. J., & Hosch, H. M. (1988). Cross-racial/ethnic eyewitness identification: A field study. *Journal of Applied Social Psychology, 18,* 972–984. (p. 366)

Pleck, J. H., Sonenstein, F. L., & Ku, L. C. (1993). Masculinity ideology: Its impact on adolescent males' heterosexual relationships. *Journal of Social Issues, 49,* 11–29. (p. 190)

Pliner, P., Hart, H., Kohl, J., & Saari, D. (1974). Compliance without pressure: Some further data on the foot-in-the-door technique. *Journal of Experimental Social Psychology, 10,* 17–22. (p. 143)

Plomin, R., & Daniels, D. (1987). Why are children in the same family so different from one another? *Behavioral and Brain Sciences, 10,* 1–60. (p. 200)

Plous, S. (1985). Perceptual illusions and military realities: A social-psychological analysis of the nuclear arms race. *Journal of Conflict Resolution, 29,* 363–389. (p. 530)

Plous, S. (1993). The nuclear arms race: Prisoner's dilemma or perceptual dilemma? *Journal of Peace Research, 30,* 163–179. (p. 530)

Pomazal, R. J., & Clore, G. L. (1973). Helping on the highway: The effects of dependency and sex. *Journal of Applied Social Psychology, 3,* 150–164. (p. 503)

Pomerleau, O. F., & Rodin, J. (1986). Behavioral medicine and health psychology. In S. L. Garfield & A. E. Bergin (Eds.), *Handbook of psychotherapy and behavior change,* 3rd ed. New York: Wiley. (p. 53)

Poole, D. A., Lindsay, D. S., Memon, A., & Bull, R. (1995). Psychotherapy and the recovery of memories of childhood sexual abuse: U.S. and British practitioners' opinions, practices, and experiences. *Journal of Consulting and Clinical Psychology, 63,* 426–437. (p. 566)

Porter, N., Geis, F. L., & Jennings (Walstedt), J. (1983). Are women invisible as leaders? *Sex Roles, 9,* 1035–1049. (p. 344)

Powell, J. (1989). *Happiness is an inside job.* Valencia, CA: Tabor. (p. 55)

Pozo, C., Carver, C. S., Wellens, A. R., & Scheier, M. F. (1991). Social anxiety and social perception: Construing others' reactions to the self. *Personality and Social Psychology Builletin, 17,* 355–362. (p. 578)

Prager, I. G., & Cutler, B. L. (1990). Attributing traits to oneself and to others: The role of acquaintance level. *Personality and Social Psychology Bulletin, 16,* 309–319. (p. 89)

Pratkanis, A. R., Greenwald, A. G., Leippe, M. R., & Baumgardner, M. H. (1988). In search of reliable persuasion effects: III. The sleeper effect is dead. Long live the sleeper effect. *Journal of Personality and Social Psychology, 54,* 203–218. (p. 256)

Pratkanis, A. R., & Turner, M. E. (1994a). The year cool Papa Bell lost the batting title: Mr. Branch Rickey and Mr. Jackie Robinson's plea for affirmative action. *Nine: A Journal of Baseball History and Social Policy Perspectives, 2,* 260–276. (p. 542)

Pratkanis, A. R., & Turner, M. E. (1994b). Nine principles of successful affirmative action: Mr. Branch Rickey, Mr. Jackie Robinson, and the integration of baseball. *Nine: A Journal of Baseball History and Social Policy Perspectives, 3,* 36–65. (p. 542)

Pratkanis, A. R., & Turner, M. E. (1996). The procative removal of discriminatory barriers: Affirmative action as effective help. *Journal of Social Issues, 52,* 111–132. (p. 481)

Pratt, M. W., Pancer, M., Hunsberger, B., & Manchester, J. (1990). Reasoning about the self and relationships in maturity: An integrative complexity analysis of individual differences. *Journal of Personality and Social Psychology, 59,* 575–581. (p. 195)

Pratto, F. (1996). Sexual politics: The gender gap in the bedroom, the cupboard, and the cabinet. In D. M. Buss & N. M. Malamuth (eds.), *Sex, power, conflict: Evolutionary and feminist perspectives*. New York: Oxford University Press. (p. 187)

Pratto, F., Sidanius, J., Stallworth, L. M., & Malle, B. F. (1994). Social dominance orientation: A personality variable predicting social and political attitudes. *Journal of Personality and Social Psychology*, **67**, 741–763. (p. 363)

Pratto, F., Stallworth, L. M., & Sidanius, J. (1997). The gender gap: Differences in political attitudes and social dominance orientation. *British Journal of Social Psychology*, **36**, 49–68. (p. 187)

Pratto, F., Stallworth, L. M., Sidanius, J., & Siers, B. (1997). The gender gap in occupational role attainment: A social dominance approach. *Journal of Personality and Social Psychology*, **72**, 37–53. (p. 184)

Prentice-Dunn, S., & Rogers, R. W. (1980). Effects of deindividuating situational cues and aggressive models on subjective deindividuation and aggression. *Journal of Personality and Social Psychology*, **39**, 104–113. (p. 308)

Prentice-Dunn, S., & Rogers, R. W. (1989). Deindividuation and the self-regulation of behavior. In P. B. Paulus (Ed.), *Psychology of group influence*, 2nd ed. Hillsdale, N.J.: Erlbaum. (p. 308)

Presson, P. K., & Benassi, V. A. (1996). Illusion of control: A meta-analytic review. *Journal of Social Behavior and Personality*, **11**, 493–510. (p. 115)

Price, G. H., Dabbs, J. M., Jr., Clower, B. J., & Resin, R. P. (1974). At first glance —Or, is physical attractiveness more than skin deep? Paper presented at the Eastern Psychological Association convention. Cited by K. L. Dion & K. K. Dion (1979). Personality and behavioral correlates of romantic love. In M. Cook & G. Wilson (Eds.), *Love and attraction*. Oxford: Pergamon. (p. 442)

Priester, J. R., Cacioppo, J. T., & Petty, R. E. (1996). The influence of motor processes on attitudes toward novel versus familiar semantic stimuli. *Personality and Social Psychology Bulletin*, **22**, 442–447. (p. 159)

Prislin, R., & Pool, G. J. (1996). Behavior, consequences, and the self: Is all well that ends well? *Personality and Social Psychology Bulletin*, **22**, 933–948. (p. 166)

Prohaska, V. (1994). "I know I'll get an A": Confident overestimation of final course grades. *Teaching of Psychology*, **21**, 141–143. (p. 60)

Prothrow-Stith, D. (with M. Wiessman) (1991). *Deadly consequences*. New York: HarperCollins. (p. 549)

Pruitt, D. G. (1981). Kissinger as a traditional mediator with power. In J. Z. Rubin (Ed.), *Dynamics of third party intervention: Kissinger in the Middle East*. New York: Praeger. *(a)* (p. 551)

Pruitt, D. G. (1981). *Negotiation behavior*. New York: Academic Press. *(b)* (p. 551)

Pruitt, D. G. (1986, July). Trends in the scientific study of negotiation. *Negotiation Journal*, pp. 237–244. (pp. 548, 552)

Pruitt, D. G. (1986). Achieving integrative agreements in negotiation. In R. K. White (Ed.), *Psychology and the prevention of nuclear war*. New York: New York University Press. (p. 548)

Pruitt, D. G. (1998). Social conflict. In D. Gilbert, S. T. Fiske, & G. Lindzey (eds.), *Handbook of social psychology*, 4th ed. New York: McGraw-Hill. (pp. 523, 547)

Pruitt, D. G., & Kimmel, M. J. (1977). Twenty years of experimental gaming: Critique, synthesis, and suggestions for the future. *Annual Review of Psychology*, **28**, 363–392. (p. 523)

Pruitt, D. G., & Lewis, S. A. (1975). Development of integrative solutions in bilateral negotiation. *Journal of Personality and Social Psychology*, **31**, 621–633. (p. 548)

Pruitt, D. G., & Lewis, S. A. (1977). The psychology of integrative bargaining. In D. Druckman (Ed.), *Negotiations: A social-psychological analysis*. New York: Halsted. (p. 548)

Pruitt, D. G., & Rubin, J. Z. (1986). *Social conflict*. San Francisco: Random House. (p. 523)

Pryor, J. B. (1987). Sexual harassment proclivities in men. *Sex Roles*, **17**, 269–290. (p. 408)

Pryor, J. B., DeSouza, E. R., Fitness, J., Hutz, C., Kumpf, M., Lubbert, K., Pesonen, O., & Erber, M. W. (1997). Gender differences in the interpretation of social-sexual behavior: A cross-cultural perspective on sexual harassment. *Journal of Cross-Cultural Psychology*, **28**, 509–534. (p. 79)

Public Opinion (1984, August/September). Vanity fare, p. 22. (pp. 58, 59)

Purvis, J. A., Dabbs, J. M., Jr., & Hopper, C. H. (1984). The "opener": Skilled user of facial expression and speech pattern. *Personality and Social Psychology Bulletin*, **10**, 61–66. (p. 464)

Pyszczynski, T., & Greenberg, J. (1987). Self-regulatory perseveration and the depressive self-focusing style: A self-awareness theory of reactive depression. *Psychological Bulletin*, **102**, 122–138. (p. 72)

Pyszczynski, T., Greenberg, J., & Holt, K. (1985). Maintaining consistency between self-serving beliefs and available data: A bias in information evaluation. *Personality and Social Psychology Bulletin*, **11**, 179–190. (p. 63)

Pyszczynski, T., Hamilton, J. C., Greenberg, J., & Becker, S. E. (1991). Self-awareness and psychological dysfunction. In C. R. Snyder & D. O. Forsyth (Eds.), *Handbook of social and clinical psychology: The health perspective*. New York: Pergamon. (pp. 573–574)

Quattrone, G. A. (1982). Behavioral consequences of attributional bias. *Social Cognition*, **1**, 358–378. (p. 90)

Quattrone, G. A., & Jones, E. E. (1980). The perception of variability within in-groups and out-groups: Implications for the law of small numbers. *Journal of Personality and Social Psychology*, **38**, 141–152. (p. 370)

Rachlinski, J. (1990). Prospect theory and civil negotiation. Working paper No. 17. Stanford Center on Conflict and Negotiation, Stanford University. (p. 601)

Raine, A. (1993). *The psychopathology of crime: Criminal behavior as a clinical disorder*. San Diego, CA: Academic Press. (p. 387)

Rajecki, D. W., Bledsoe, S. B., & Rasmussen, J. L. (1991). Successful personal ads: Gender differences and similarities in offers, stipulations, and outcomes. *Basic and Applied Social Psychology*, **12**, 457–469. (p. 435)

Rank, S. G., & Jacobson, C. K. (1977). Hospital nurses' compliance with medication overdose orders: A failure to replicate. *Journal of Health and Social Behavior*, **18**, 188–193. (p. 223)

Rapoport, A. (1960). *Fights, games, and debates*. Ann Arbor: University of Michigan Press. (p. 517)

Rappoport, L., & Kren, G. (1993). Amoral rescuers: The ambiguities of altruism. *Creativity Research Journal*, **6**, 129–136. (p. 511)

Rawls, J. (1971). *A theory of justice*. Cambridge, MA: Belknap Press of Harvard University Press. (p. 528)

RCAgenda (1979). November-December p. 11. 475 Riverside Drive, New York, N.Y. 10027. (p. 336)

Rector, N. A., & Bagby, R. M. (1995). Criminal sentence recommendations in a simulated rape trial: Examining juror prejudice in Canada. *Behavioral Sciences and the Law*, **13**, 113-121. (p. 614)

Reed, D. (1989, November 25). Video collection documents Christian resistance to Hitler. Associated Press release in *Grand Rapids Press*, pp. B4, B5. (p. 350)

Reeder, G. D., McCormick, C. B., & Esselman, E. D. (1987). Self-reference processing and recall of prose. *Journal of Educational Psychology*, **79**, 243-248. (p. 91)

Regan, D. T., & Cheng, J. B. (1973). Distraction and attitude change: A resolution. *Journal of Experimental Social Psychology*, **9**, 138–147. (p. 274)

Regan, D. T., & Fazio, R. (1977). On the consistency between attitudes and behavior: Look to the method of attitude formation. *Journal of Experimental Social Psychology*, **13**, 28–45. (p. 136)

Regan, D. T., Williams, M., & Sparling, S. (1972). Voluntary expiation of guilt: A field experiment. *Journal of Personality and Social Psychology*, **24**, 42–45. (p. 495)

Reid, P., & Finchilescu, G. (1995). The disempowering effects of media violence against women on college women. *Psychology of Women Quarterly, 19,* 397–411. (p. 418)

Reifman, A. S., Larrick, R. P., & Fein, S. (1991). Temper and temperature on the diamond: The heat-aggression relationship in major league baseball. *Personality and Social Psychology Bulletin, 17,* 580–585. (p. 402)

Reis, H. T., Nezlek, J., & Wheeler, L. (1980). Physical attractiveness in social interaction. *Journal of Personality and Social Psychology, 38,* 604–617. (p. 434)

Reis, H. T., & Shaver, P. (1988). Intimacy as an interpersonal process. In S. Duck (Ed.), *Handbook of personal relationships: Theory, relationships and interventions.* Chichester, England: Wiley. (p. 464)

Reis, H. T., Wheeler, L., Spiegel, N., Kernis, M. H., Nezlek, J., & Perri, M. (1982). Physical attractiveness in social interaction: II. Why does appearance affect social experience? *Journal of Personality and Social Psychology, 43,* 979–996. (p. 434)

Reis, T. J., Gerrard, M., & Gibbons, F. X. (1993). Social comparison and the pill: Reactions to upward and downward comparison of contraceptive behavior. *Personality and Social Psychology Bulletin, 19,* 13–20. (p. 395)

Reisenzein, R. (1983). The Schachter theory of emotion: Two decades later. *Psychological Bulletin, 94,* 239–264. (p. 404)

Reitzes, D. C. (1953). The role of organizational structures: Union versus neighborhood in a tension situation. *Journal of Social Issues, 9*(1), 37–44. (p. 356)

Remley, A. (1988, October). From obedience to independence. *Psychology Today,* pp. 56–59. (p. 556)

Renaud, C. A., & Byers, E. S. (1999). Exploring the frequency, diversity and content of university students' positive and negative sexual cognitions. *Canadian Journal of Human Sexuality, 8,* 17–30. (p. 189)

Renaud, H., & Estess, F. (1961). Life history interviews with one hundred normal American males: "Pathogenecity" of childhood. *American Journal of Orthopsychiatry, 31,* 786–802. (p. 565)

Ressler, R. K., Burgess, A. W., & Douglas, J. E. (1988). *Sexual homicide patterns.* Boston: Lexington Books. (p. 406)

Reychler, L. (1979). The effectiveness of a pacifist strategy in conflict resolution. *Journal of Conflict Resolution, 23,* 228–260. (p. 519)

Rhine, R. J., & Severance, L. J. (1970). Ego-involvement, discrepancy, source credibility, and attitude change. *Journal of Personality and Social Psychology, 16,* 175–190. (p. 265)

Rhodes, N., & Wood, W. (1992). Self-esteem and intelligence affect influenceability: The mediating role of message reception. *Psychological Bulletin, 111,* 156–171. (p. 273)

Rhodewalt, F. (1987). Is self-handicapping an effective self-protective attributional strategy? Paper presented at the American Psychological Association convention. (p. 71)

Rhodewalt, F., & Agustsdottir, S. (1986). Effects of self-presentation on the phenomenal self. *Journal of Personality and Social Psychology, 50,* 47–55. (p. 586)

Rhodewalt, F., Saltzman, A. T., & Wittmer J. (1984). Self-handicapping among competitive athletes: The role of practice in self-esteem protection. *Basic and Applied Social Psychology, 5,* 197–209. (p. 71)

Rholes, W. S., Newman, L. S., & Ruble, D. N. (1990). Understanding self and other: Developmental and motivational aspects of perceiving persons in terms of invariant dispositions. In E. T. Higgins & R. M. Sorrentino (Eds.), *Handbook of motivation and cognition: Foundations of social behavior,* Vol. 2. New York: Guilford. (p. 90)

Rice, B. (1985, September). Performance review: The job nobody likes. *Psychology Today,* pp. 30–36. (p. 57)

Rice, M. E., & Grusec, J. E. (1975). Saying and doing: Effects on observer performance. *Journal of Personality and Social Psychology, 32,* 584–593. (p. 494)

Richardson, J. T. E. (1990). Questionnaire studies of paramenstrual symptoms. *Psychology of Women Quarterly, 14,* 15–42. (p. 580)

Richardson, L. F. (1960). Generalized foreign policy. *British Journal of Psychology Monographs Supplements, 23.* Cited by A. Rapoport in *Fights, games, and debates.* Ann Arbor: University of Michigan Press, 1960, p. 15. (p. 515)

Riess, M., Rosenfeld, P., Melburg, V., & Tedeschi, J. T. (1981). Self-serving attributions: Biased private perceptions and distorted public descriptions. *Journal of Personality and Social Psychology, 41,* 224–231. (p. 72)

Riggs, J. M. (1992). Self-handicapping and achievement. In A. K. Boggiano & T. S. Pittman (Eds.), *Achievement and motivation: A social-developmental perspective.* New York: Cambridge University Press. (p. 72)

Riordan, C. A. (1980). Effects of admission of influence on attributions and attraction. Paper presented at the American Psychological Association convention. (p. 451)

Robberson, M. R., & Rogers, R. W. (1988). Beyond fear appeals: Negative and positive persuasive appeals to health and self-esteem. *Journal of Applied Social Psychology, 18,* 277–287. (p. 262)

Robertson, I. (1987). *Sociology.* New York: Worth Publishers. (p. 174)

Robins, L., & Regier, D. (eds.). (1991). *Psychiatric disorders in America.* New York: Free Press. (p. 593)

Robins, R. W., Spranca, M. D., & Mendelsohn, G. A. (1996). The actor-observer effect revisited: Effects of individual differences and repeated social interactions on actor and observer attributions. *Journal of Personality and Social Psychology, 71,* 375–389. (p. 90)

Robinson, R. J., Keltner, D., Ward, A., & Ross, L. (1995). Actual versus assumed differences in construal: "Naive realism" in intergroup perception and conflict. *Journal of Personality and Social Psychology, 68,* 404–417. (p. 533)

Rochat, F. (1993). How did they resist authority? Protecting refugees in Le Chambon during World War II. Paper presented at the American Psychological Association convention. (p. 226)

Rochat, F., & Modigliani, A. (1995). The ordinary quality of resistance: From Milgram's laboratory to the village of Le Chambon. *Journal of Social Issues, 51,* 195–210. (p. 226)

Rodgers, K. (1994, Autumn). Wife assault in Canada (report of a survey by Statistics Canada). *Canadian Social Trends,* pp. 2–8. (p. 383)

Rodin, M. (1992). The social construction of premenstrual syndrome. *Social Science and Medicine, 35,* 49–56. (p. 580)

Roese, N. J. (1994). The functional basis of counterfactual thinking. *Journal of Personality and Social Psychology, 66,* 805–818. (p. 113)

Roese, N. J. (1997). Counterfactual thinking. *Psychological Bulletin, 121,* 133–148. (p. 113)

Roese, N. J., & Olson, J. M. (1993). The structure of counterfactual thought. *Personality and Social Psychology Bulletin, 19,* 312-319. (p. 113)

Roese, N. L., & Olson, J. M. (1994). Attitude importance as a function of repeated attitude expression. *Journal of Experimental Social Psychology, 66,* 805–818. (p. 166)

Roger, L. H., Cortes, D. E., & Malgady, R. B. (1991). Acculturation and mental health status among Hispanics: Convergence and new directions for research. *American Psychologist, 46,* 585–597. (p. 545)

Rogers, C. R. (1958). Reinhold Niebuhr's *The self and the dramas of history*: A criticism. *Pastoral Psychology, 9,* 15–17. (p. 55)

Rogers, C. R. (1980). *A way of being.* Boston: Houghton Mifflin. (p. 464)

Rogers, C. R. (1985, February). Quoted by Michael A. Wallach and Lise Wallach, "How Psychology Sanctions the Cult of the Self." *Washington Monthly,* pp. 46–56. (p. 248)

Rogers, R. W., & Mewborn, C. R. (1976). Fear appeals and attitude change: Effects of a threat's noxiousness, probability of occurrence, and the efficacy of coping responses. *Journal of Personality and Social Psychology, 34,* 54–61. (p. 263)

Rogers, R. W., & Prentice-Dunn, S. (1981). Deindividuation and anger-mediated interracial aggression: Unmasking regressive racism. *Journal of Personality and Social Psychology, 41*, 63–73. (p. 341)

Rohrer, J. H., Baron, S. H., Hoffman, E. L., & Swander, D. V. (1954). The stability of autokinetic judgments. *Journal of Abnormal and Social Psychology, 49*, 595–597. (p. 213)

Rokeach, M. (1968). *Beliefs, attitudes, and values.* San Francisco: Jossey-Bass. (p. 444)

Rokeach, M., & Mezei, L. (1966). Race and shared beliefs as factors in social choice. *Science, 151*, 167–172. (p. 365)

Romer, D., Gruder, D. L., & Lizzadro, T. (1986). A person-situation approach to altruistic behavior. *Journal of Personality and Social Psychology, 51*, 1001–1012. (p. 499)

Rook, K. S. (1984). Promoting social bonding: Strategies for helping the lonely and socially isolated. *American Psychologist, 39*, 1389–1407. (p. 576)

Rook, K. S. (1987). Social support versus companionship: Effects on life stress, loneliness, and evaluations by others. *Journal of Personality and Social Psychology, 52*, 1132–1147. (p. 591)

Rosenbaum, M. E., & Holtz, R. (1985). The minimal intergroup discrimination effect: Out-group derogation, not in-group favorability. Paper presented at the American Psychological Association convention. (p. 356)

Rosenberg, L. A. (1961). Group size, prior experience and conformity. *Journal of Abnormal and Social Psychology, 63*, 436–437. (p. 230)

Rosenberg, R. (1984). Leta Hollingworth: Toward a sexless intelligence. In M. Lewin (Ed.), *In the shadow of the past: Psychology portrays the sexes.* New York: Columbia University Press. (p. 580)

Rosenblatt, A., & Greenberg, J. (1988). Depression and interpersonal attraction: The role of perceived similarity. *Journal of Personality and Social Psychology, 55*, 112–119. (p. 446)

Rosenblatt, R. (1993, December 21). The 11th commandment. *Family Circle*, pp. 30–32, 45. (p. 62)

Rosenblatt, R. (1994, April 24). The buck stops somewhere else. *Detroit Free Press Magazine*, pp. 6–13. (p. 130)

Rosenfeld, D. (1979). The relationship between self-esteem and egotism in males and females. Unpublished manuscript, Southern Methodist University. (p. 66)

Rosenfeld, D., Folger, R., & Adelman, H. F. (1980). When rewards reflect competence: A qualification of the overjustification effect. *Journal of Personality and Social Psychology, 39*, 368–376. (p. 161)

Rosenhan, D. L. (1970). The natural socialization of altruistic autonomy. In J. Macaulay & L. Berkowitz (Eds.) *Altruism and helping behavior.* New York: Academic Press. (p. 509)

Rosenhan, D. L. (1973). On being sane in insane places. *Science, 179*, 250–258. (p. 563)

Rosenthal, D. A., & Feldman, S. S. (1992). The nature and stability of ethnic identity in Chinese youth: Effects of length of residence in two cultural contexts. *Journal of Cross-Cultural Psychology, 23*, 214–227. (p. 545)

Rosenthal, R. (1985). From unconscious experimenter bias to teacher expectancy effects. In J. B. Dusek, V. C. Hall, & W. J. Meyer (Eds.), *Teacher expectancies.* Hillsdale, N.J.: Erlbaum. (p. 119)

Rosenthal, R. (1991). Teacher expectancy effects: A brief update 25 years after the Pygmalion experiment. *Journal of Research in Education, 1*, 3–12. (p. 121)

Rosenthal, R., & Jacobson, L. (1968). *Pygmalion in the classroom: Teacher expectation and pupils' intellectual development.* New York: Holt, Rinehart & Winston. (p. 120)

Rosenzweig, M. R. (1972). Cognitive dissonance. *American Psychologist, 27*, 769. (p. 148)

Ross, C. (1979, February 12). Rejected. *New West*, pp. 39–43. (p. 107)

Ross, L. (1977). The intuitive psychologist and his shortcomings: Distortions in the attribution process. In L. Berkowitz (Ed.), *Advances in experimental social psychology* (Vol. 10). New York: Academic Press. (p. 83)

Ross, L. (1981). The "intuitive scientist" formulation and its developmental implications. In J. H. Havell & L. Ross (Eds.), *Social cognitive development: Frontiers and possible futures.* Cambridge, England: Cambridge University Press. (pp. 38, 90)

Ross, L. (1988). Situationist perspectives on the obedience experiments. Review of A. G. Miller's *The obedience experiments. Contemporary Psychology, 33*, 101–104. (p. 217)

Ross, L., Amabile, T. M., & Steinmetz, J. L. (1977). Social roles, social control, and biases in social-perception processes. *Journal of Personality and Social Psychology, 35*, 485–494. (pp. 85, 86)

Ross, L., & Anderson, C. A. (1982). Shortcomings in the attribution process: On the origins and maintenance of erroneous social assessments. In D. Kahneman, P. Slovic, & A. Tversky (Eds.), *Judgment under uncertainty: Heuristics and biases.* New York: Cambridge University Press. (p. 95)

Ross, L., & Lepper, M. R. (1980). The perseverance of beliefs: Empirical and normative considerations. In R. A. Shweder (Ed.), *New directions for methodology of behavioral science: Fallible judgment in behavioral research.* San Francisco: Jossey-Bass. (p. 98)

Ross, L., & Ward, A. (1995). Psychological barriers to dispute resolution. In M. P. Zanna (ed.), *Advances in experimental social psychology*, vol. 27. San Diego: Academic Press. (pp. 549, 550)

Ross, L., & Ward, A. (1996). Naive realism in everyday life: Implications for social conflict and misunderstanding. In T. Brown, E. Reed, & E. Turiel (eds.), *Values and knowledge.* Hillsdale, NJ: Erlbaum. (p. 524)

Ross, M., & Buehler, R. (1994). Creative remembering. In U. Neisser & R. Fivush (eds.), *The remembering self.* New York: Cambridge University Press. (p. 100)

Ross, M., & Fletcher, G. J. O. (1985). Attribution and social perception. In G. Lindzey & E. Aronson (Eds.), *The Handbook of Social Psychology*, 3rd ed. New York: Random House. (p. 117)

Ross, M., McFarland, C., & Fletcher, G. J. O. (1981). The effect of attitude on the recall of personal histories. *Journal of Personality and Social Psychology, 40*, 627–634. (p. 101)

Ross, M., & Sicoly, F. (1979). Egocentric biases in availability and attribution. *Journal of Personality and Social Psychology, 37*, 322–336. (pp. 57, 64)

Ross, M., Thibaut, J., & Evenbeck, S. (1971). Some determinants of the intensity of social protest. *Journal of Experimental Social Psychology, 7*, 401–418. (p. 527)

Rossi, A. S., & Rossi, P. H. (1990). *Of human bonding: Parent-child relations across the life course.* Hawthorne, NY: Aldine de Gruyter. (p. 184)

Roszell, P., Kennedy, D., & Grabb, E. (1990). Physical attractiveness and income attainment among Canadians. *Journal of Psychology, 123*, 547–559. (p. 437)

Rotenber, K. J. (1997). Loneliness and the perception of the exchange of disclosures. *Journal of Social and Clinical Psychology, 16*, 259–276. (p. 576)

Rothbart, M., & Birrell, P. (1977). Attitude and perception of faces. *Journal of Research Personality, 11*, 209–215. (p. 95)

Rothbart, M., Fulero, S., Jensen, C., Howard, J., & Birrell, P. (1978). From individual to group impressions: Availability heuristics in stereotype formation. *Journal of Experimental Social Psychology, 14*, 237–255. (p. 370)

Rothbart, M., & John, O. P. (1985). Social categorization and behavioral episodes: A cognitive analysis of the effects of intergroup contact. *Journal of Social Issues, 41*(3), 81–104. (p. 376)

Rothbart, M., & Lewis, S. (1988). Infering category attributes from exemplar attributes: Geometric shapes and social categories. *Journal of Personality and Social Psychology, 55*, 861-872. (p. 376)

Rothbart, M., & Park, B. (1986). On the confirmability and disconfirmability of trait concepts. *Journal of Personality and Social Psychology*, **50**, 131–142. (p. 376)

Rothbart, M., & Taylor, M. (1992). Social categories and social reality. In G. R. Semin & K. Fielder (eds.), *Language, interaction and social cognition*. London: Sage. (p. 246)

Rothman, A. J., & Salovey, P. (1997). Shaping perceptions to motivate healthy behavior: The role of message framing. *Psychological Bulletin*, **121**, 3–19. (p. 581)

Rotter, J. (1973). Internal-external locus of control scale. In J. P. Robinson & R. P. Shaver (Eds.), *Measures of social psychological attitudes*. Ann Arbor: Institute for Social Research. (p. 52)

Rowe, D. (1994). *The limits of family influence: Genes, experience, and behavior*. New York: Guilford Press. (p. 202)

Rowe, D. C., Vazsonyi, A. T., & Flannery, D. J. (1994). No more than skin deep: Ethnic and racial similarity in developmental process. *Psychological Review*, **101**, 396–413. (p. 32)

Ruback, R. B., Carr, T. S., & Hoper, C. H. (1986). Perceived control in prison: Its relation to reported crowding, stress, and symptoms. *Journal of Applied Social Psychology*, **16**, 375–386. (p. 53)

Rubin, J. Z. (1986). Can we negotiate with terrorists: Some answers from psychology. Paper presented at the American Psychological Association convention. (p. 397)

Rubin, J. Z. (1989). Some wise and mistaken assumptions about conflict and negotiation. *Journal of Social Issues*, **45**, 195–209. (p. 551)

Rubin, J. Z. (Ed.) (1981). *Third party intervention in conflict: Kissinger in the Middle East*. New York: Praeger. (p. 554)

Rubin, L. B. (1985). *Just friends: The role of friendship in our lives*. New York: Harper & Row. (p. 185)

Rubin, Z. (1970). Measurement of romantic love. *Journal of Personality and Social Psychology*, **16**, 265–273. (p. 453)

Rubin, Z. (1973). *Liking and loving: An invitation to social psychology*. New York: Holt, Rinehart and Winston. (pp. 453, 469)

Ruehlman, L. S., & Wolchik, S. A. (1988). Personal goals and interpersonal support and hindrance as factors in psychological distress and well-being. *Journal of Personality and Social Psychology*, **55**, 293–301. (p. 592)

Ruggiero, K. M., & Taylor, D. M. (1997). Why minority group members perceive or do not perceive the discrimination that confronts them: The role of self-esteem and perceived control. *Journal of Personality and Social Psychology*, **72**, 373–389. (p. 347)

Rule, B. G., Taylor, B. R., & Dobbs, A. R. (1987). Priming ffects of heat on aggressive thoughts. *Social Cognition*, **5**, 131–143. (p. 401)

Rusbult, C. E. (1980). Commitment and satisfaction in romantic associations: A test of the investment model. *Journal of Experimental Social Psychology*, **16**, 172–186. (p. 449)

Rusbult, C. E., Johnson, D. J., & Morrow, G. D. (1986). Impact of couple patterns of problem solving on distress and nondistress in dating relationships. *Journal of Personality and Social Psychology*, **50**, 744–753. (p. 469)

Rusbult, C. E., Morrow, G. D., & Johnson, D. J. (1987). Self-esteem and problem-solving behaviour in close relationships. *British Journal of Social Psychology*, **26**, 293–303. (p. 469)

Rushton, J. P. (1975). Generosity in children: Immediate and long-term effects of modeling, preaching, and moral judgment. *Journal of Personality and Social Psychology*, **31**, 459–466. (p. 494)

Rushton, J. P. (1976). Socialization and the altruistic behavior of children. *Psychological Bulletin*, **83**, 898–913. (p. 497)

Rushton, J. P. (1991). Is altruism innate? *Psychological Inquiry*, **2**, 141–143. (p. 484)

Rushton, J. P., Brainerd, C. J., & Pressley, M. (1983). Behavioral development and construct validity: The principle of aggregation. *Psychological Bulletin*, **94**, 18–38. (p. 246)

Rushton, J. P., & Campbell, A. C. (1977). Modeling, vicarious reinforcement and extraversion on blood donating in adults: Immediate and long-term effects. *European Journal of Social Psychology*, **7**, 297–306. (p. 494)

Rushton, J. P., Chrisjohn, R. D., & Fekken, G. C. (1981). The altruistic personality and the self-report altruism scale. *Personality and Individual Differences*, **2**, 293–302. (p. 499)

Rushton, J. P., Fulker, D. W., Neale, M. C., Nias, D. K. B., & Eysenck, H. J. (1986). Altruism and aggression: The heritability of individual differences. *Journal of Personality and Social Psychology*, **50**, 1192–1198. (p. 387)

Rushton, J. P., Russell, R. J. H., & Wells, P. A. (1984). Genetic similarity theory: Beyond kin selection. *Behavior Genetics*, **14**, 179–193. (p. 483)

Russell, B. (1930/1980). *The conquest of happiness*. London: Unwin Paperbacks. (p. 434)

Russell, G. W. (1983). Psychological issues in sports aggression. In J. H. Goldstein (Ed.), *Sports violence*. New York: Springer-Verlag. (p. 421)

Rutkowski, G. K., Gruder, C. L., & Romer, D. (1983). Group cohesiveness, social norms, and bystander intervention. *Journal of Personality and Social Psychology*, **44**, 545–552. (p. 493)

Ruvolo, A., & Markus, H. (1992). Possible selves and performance: The power of

self-relevant imagery. *Social Cognition*, **9**, 95–124. (p. 50)

Ruzzene, M., & Noller, P. (1986). Feedback motivation and reactions to personality interpretations that differ in favorability and accuracy. *Journal of Personality and Social Psychology*, **51**, 1293–1299. (p. 73)

Ryan, C. S. (1996). Accuracy of Black and White college students' in-group and out-group stereotypes. *Personality and Social psychology Bulletin*, **22**, 1114–1127. (p. 366)

Ryckman, R. M., Robbins, M. A., Kaczor, L. M., & Gold, J. A. (1989). Male and female raters' stereotyping of male and female physiques. *Personality and Social Psychology Bulletin*, **15**, 244–251. (p. 27)

Saad, L., & McAneny, L. (1994, April). Most Americans think religion losing clout in the 1990's. *Gallup Poll Monthly*, pp. 2–4. (p. 417)

Saal, F. E., Johnson, C. B., & Weber, N. (1989). Friendly or sexy? It may depend on whom you ask. *Psychology of Women Quarterly*, **13**, 263–276. (p. 79)

Sabini, J., & Silver, M. (1982). *Moralities of everyday life*. New York: Oxford University Press. (p. 228)

Sacco, W. P., & Dunn, V. K. (1990). Effect of actor depression on observer attributions: Existence and impact of negative attributions toward the depressed. *Journal of Personality and Social Psychology*, **59**, 517–524. (p. 572)

Sacks, C. H., & Bugental, D. P. (1987). Attributions as moderators of affective and behavioral responses to social failure. *Journal of Personality and Social Psychology*, **53**, 939–947. (p. 573)

Sadalla, E. K., Kenrick, D. T., & Vershure, B. (1987). Dominance and heterosexual attraction. *Journal of Personality and Social Psychology*, **52**, 730–738. (p. 438)

Saks, M. J. (1977). *Jury verdicts*. Lexington, Mass: Health. (p. 628)

Saks, M. J. (1974). Ignorance of science is no excuse. *Trial*, **10**(6), 18–20. (p. 628)

Saks, M. J., & Hastie, R. (1978). *Social psychology in court*. New York: Van Nostrand Reinhold. (pp. 601, 613, 623)

Sakurai, M. M. (1975). Small group cohesiveness and detrimental conformity. *Sociometry*, **38**, 340–357. (p. 232)

Sales, S. M. (1972). Economic threat as a determinant of conversion rates in authoritarian and nonauthoritarian churches. *Journal of Personality and Social Psychology*, **23**, 420–428. (p. 282)

Salovey, P., Mayer, J. D., & Rosenhan, D. L. (1991). Mood and healing: Mood as a motivator of helping and helping as a regulator of mood. In M. S. Clark (Ed.), *Prosocial behavior*. Newbury Park, CA: Sage. (p. 498)

Saltzstein, H. D., & Sandberg, L. (1979). Indirect social influence: Change in judgmental processor anticipatory conformity. *Journal of Experimental Social Psychology*, **15**, 209–216. (p. 235)

Sampson, E. E. (1975). On justice as equality. *Journal of Social Issues*, **31**(3), 45–64. (p. 528)

Samuelson, C. D., Messick, D. M., Rutte, C. G., & Wilke, H. (1984). Individual and structural solutions to resource dilemmas in two cultures. *Journal of Personality and Social Psychology*, **47**, 94–104. (p. 522)

Sanbonmatsu, D. M., Akimoto, S. A., & Biggs, E. (1993). Overestimating causality: Attributional effects of confirmatory processing. *Journal of Personality and Social Psychology*, **65**, 892–903. (p. 108)

Sanbonmatsu, D. M., Akimoto, S. A., & Gibson, B. D. (1994). Stereotype-based blocking in social explanation. *Personality and Social Psychology Bulletin*, **20**, 71–81. (p. 375)

Sanbonmatsu, D. M., & Fazio, R. H. (1990). The role of attitudes in memory-based decision making. *Journal of Personality and Social Psychology*, **59**, 614–622. (p. 130)

Sancton, T. 1997, October 13). The dossier on Diana's crash. *Time*, pp. 50–56. (p. 491)

Sandberg, G. G., Jackson, T. L., & Petretic-Jackson, P. (1985). Sexual aggression and courtship violence in dating relationships. Paper presented at the Midwestern Psychological Association convention. (p. 408)

Sande, G. N., Goethals, G. R., & Radloff, C. E. (1988). Perceiving one's own traits and others': The multifaceted self. *Journal of Personality and Social Psychology*, **54**, 13–20. (p. 89)

Sanders, G. S. (1981). Driven by distraction: An integrative review of social facilitation and theory and research. *Journal of Experimental Social Psychology*, **17**, 227–251. *(a)* (p. 298)

Sanders, G. S. (1981). Toward a comprehensive account of social facilitation: Distraction/conflict does not mean theoretical conflict. *Journal of Experimental Social Psychology*, **17**, 262–265. *(b)* (p. 298)

Sanders, G. S., & Baron, R. S. (1977). Is social comparison irrelevant for producing choice shifts? *Journal of Experimental Social Psychology*, **13**, 303–314. (p. 315)

Sanders, G. S., Baron, R. S., & Moore, D. L. (1978). Distraction and social comparison as mediators of social facilitation effects. *Journal of Experimental Social Psychology*, **14**, 291–303. (p. 298)

Sanislow, C. A., III, Perkins, D. V., & Balogh, D. W. (1989). Mood induction, interpersonal perceptions, and rejection in the roommates of depressed, nondepressed-disturbed, and normal college students. *Journal of Social and Clinical Psychology*, **8**, 345–358. (p. 572)

Sanitioso, R., Kunda, Z., & Fong, G. T. (1990). Motivated recruitment of autobiographical memories. *Journal of Personality and Social Psychology*, **59**, 229–241. (p. 64)

Sansone, C. (1986). A question of competence: The effects of competence and task feedback on intrinsic interest. *Journal of Personality and Social Psychology*, **51**, 918–931. (p. 161)

Sapadin, L. A. (1988). Friendship and gender: Perspectives of professional men and women. *Journal of Social and Personal Relationships*, **5**, 387–403. (p. 185)

Sarason, I. G., Sarason, B. R., Pierce, G. R., Shearin, E. N., & Sayers, M. H. (1991). A social learning approach to increasing blood donations. *Journal of Applied Social Psychology*, **21**, 896–918. (p. 509)

Sarnoff, I., & Sarnoff, S. (1989). *Love-centered marriage in a self-centered world.* New York: Hemisphere. (p. 470)

Sartre, J-P. (1946/1948). *Anti-Semite and Jew.* New York: Shocken Books. (p. 4)

Sato, K. (1987). Distribution of the cost of maintaining common resources. *Journal of Experimental Social Psychology*, **23**, 19–31. (p. 520)

Satterfield, A. T., & Muehlenhard, C. L. (1997). Shaken confidence: The effects of an authority figure's flirtatiousness on women's and men's self-rated creativity. *Psychology of Women Quarterly*, **21**, 395–416. (p. 437)

Savitsky, K., Medvec, V. H., & Gilovich, T. (1997). Remembering and regretting: The Zeigarnik effect and the cognitive availability of regrettable actions and inactions. *Personality and Social Psychology Bulletin*, **23**, 248–257. (p. 113)

Sax, L. J., Astin, A. W., Korn, W. S., & Mahoney, K. M. (1996). *The American freshman: National norms for Fall 1996.* Los Angeles: Higher Education Research Institute, UCLA. (pp. 184, 189, 200, 252, 345, 392)

Scarr, S. (1988). Race and gender as psychological variables: Social and ethical issues. *American Psychologist*, **43**, 56–59. (p. 184)

Schachter, S. (1951). Deviation, rejection and communication. *Journal of Abnormal and Social Psychology*, **46**, 190–207. (pp. 237, 327)

Schachter, S., & Singer, J. E. (1962). Cognitive, social and physiological determinants of emotional state. *Psychological Review*, **69**, 379–399. (p. 403)

Schackelford, T. K., & Larsen, R. J. (1997). Facial asymmetry as an indicator of psychological, emotional, and physiological distress. *Journal of Personality and Social Psychology*, **72**, 456-466. (p. 439)

Schacter, D., Kaszniak, A., & Kihlstrom, J. (1991). Models of memory and the understanding of memory disorders. In T. Yanagihara & R. Petersen (eds.), *Memory disorders: Research and clinical practice.* New York: Marcel Dekker. (p. 51)

Schafer, R. B., & Keith, P. M. (1980). Equity and depression among married couples. *Social Psychology Quarterly*, **43**, 430–435. (p. 463)

Schaffner, P. E. (1985). Specious learning about reward and punishment. *Journal of Personality and Social Psychology*, **48**, 1377–1386. (p. 116)

Schaffner, P. E., Wandersman, A., & Stang D. (1981). Candidate name exposure and voting: Two field studies. *Basic and Applied Social Psychology*, **2**, 195–203. (p. 433)

Schaller, M., & Cialdini, R. B. (1988). The economics of empathic helping: Support for a mood management motive. *Journal of Experimental Social Psychology*, **24**, 163–181. (p. 479)

Schaller, M., & Cialdini, R. B. (1990). Happiness, sadness, and helping: A motivational integration. In E. T. Higgins, & R. M. Sorrentino (Eds.). *Handbook of Motivation and Cognition: Foundations of Social Behavior.* Vol. 2. (pp. 265-296). New York, NY, USA: The Guilford Press. (p. 498)

Scheier, M. F., & Carver, C. S. (1992). Effects of optimism on psychological and physical well-being: Theoretical overview and empirical update. *Cognitive Therapy and Research*, **16**, 201–228. (pp. 51, 584)

Schein, E. H. (1956). The Chinese in-doctrination program for prisoners of war: A study of attempted brainwashing. *Psychiatry*, **19**, 149–172. (p. 149)

Schiffenbauer, A., & Schiavo, R. S. (1976). Physical distance and attraction: An intensification effect. *Journal of Experimental Social Psychology*, **12**, 274–282. (p. 297)

Schittekatte, M. (1996). Facilitating information exchange in small decision-making groups. *European Journal of Social Psychology*, **26**, 537–556. (p. 324)

Schlenker, B. R. (1976). Egocentric perceptions in cooperative groups: A conceptualization and research review. Final Report, Office of Naval Research Grant NR 170–797. (p. 67)

Schlenker, B. R., Britt, T. W., & Pennington, J. (1996). Impression regulation and management: A theory of self-identification. In R. M. Sorrentino & E. T. Higgins (eds.), *Handbook of motivation and cognition: The interpersonal context*, vol. 3. New York: Guilford. (p. 152)

Schlenker, B. R., Dlugolecki, D. W., & Doherty, K. (1994). The impact of self-presentations on self-appraisals and behavior: The power of public commitment. *Personality and Social Psychology Bulletin*, **20**, 20–33. (p. 158)

Schlenker, B. R., & Leary, M. R. (1982). Audiences' reactions to self-enhancing, self-denigrating, and accurate self-presentations. *Journal of Experimental Social Psychology*, **18**, 89–104. (a) (p. 73)

Schlenker, B. R., & Leary, M. R. (1982). Social anxiety and self-presentation: A conceptualization and model. *Psychological Bulletin*, **92**, 641–669. (b) (p. 577)

Schlenker, B. R., & Leary, M. R. (1985). Social anxiety and communication about the self. *Journal of Language and Social Psychology*, **4**, 171–192. (p. 577)

Schlenker, B. R., & Miller, R. S. (1977). Egocentrism in groups: Self-serving biases or logical information processing? *Journal of Personality and Social Psychology*, **35**, 755–764. (b) (p. 67)

Schlenker, B. R., & Miller, R. S. (1977). Group cohesiveness as a determinant of egocentric perceptions in cooperative groups. *Human Relations*, **30**, 1039–1055. (a) (p. 67)

Schlenker, B. R., Phillips, S. T., Boniecki, K. A., & Schlenker, D. R. (1995). Championship pressures: Choking or triumphing in one's own territory? *Journal of Personality and Social Psychology*, **68**, 632–643. (p. 296)

Schlenker, B. R., & Weigold, M. F. (1992). Interpersonal processes involving impression regulation and management. *Annual Review of Psychology*, **43**, 133–168. (p. 72)

Schlenker, B. R., Weigold, M. F., & Hallam, J. R. (1990). Self-serving attributions in social context: Effects of self-esteem and social pressure. *Journal of Personality and Social Psychology*, **58**, 855–863. (p. 66)

Schlesinger, A., Jr. (1949). The statistical soldier. *Partisan Review*, **16**, 852–856. (p. 15)

Schlesinger, A., Jr. (1991, July 8). The cult of ethnicity, good and bad. *Time*, p. 21. (pp. 172, 556)

Schmitt, D. P., & Buss, D. M. (1996). Strategic self-promotion and competitor derogation: Sex and context effects on the perceived effectiveness of mate attraction tactics. *Journal of Personality and Social Psychology*, **70**, 1185–1204. (p. 441)

Schneider, M. E., Major, B., Luhtanen, R., & Crocker, J. (1996). Social stigma and the potential costs of assumptive help. *Personality and Social Psychology Bulletin*, **22**, 201–209. (p. 481)

Schoeneman, T. J. (1994). Individualism. In V. S. Ramachandran (Ed.), *Encyclopedia of Human Behavior*. San Diego: Academic Press. (p. 43)

Schooler, J. W., Gerhard, D., & Loftus, E. F. (1986). Qualities of the unreal. *Journal of Experimental Psychology: Learning, Memory, and Cognition*, **12**, 171–181. (p. 103)

Schroeder, D. A., Dovidio, J. F., Sibicky, M. E., Matthews, L. L., & Allen, J. L. (1988). Empathic concern and helping behavior: Egoism or altruism: *Journal of Experimental Social Psychology*, **24**, 333–353. (p. 480)

Schulz, J. W., & Pruitt, D. G. (1978). The effects of mutual concern on joint welfare. *Journal of Experimental Social Psychology*, **14**, 480–492. (p. 550)

Schulz, R., & Decker, S. (1985). Long-term adjustment to physical disability: The role of social support, perceived control, and self-blame. *Journal of Personality and Social Psychology*, **48**, 1162–1172. (p. 395)

Schuman, H., & Kalton, G. (1985). Survey methods. In G. Lindzey & E. Aronson (Eds.), *Handbook of Social Psychology*, Vol. 1. Hillsdale, N.J.: Erlbaum. (p. 26)

Schuman, H., & Ludwig, J. (1983). The norm of even-handedness in surveys as in life. *American Sociological Review*, **48**, 112–120. (p. 25)

Schuman, H., & Scott, J. (1987). Problems in the use of survey questions to measure public opinion. *Science*, **236**, 957–959. (p. 26)

Schuman, H., & Scott, J. (1989). Generations and collective memories. *American Sociological Review*, **54**, 359–381. (p. 273)

Schuman, H., Steeh, C., Bobo, L., & Krysan, M. (1998). *Racial attitudes in America: Trends and interpretations*. Cambridge, MA: Harvard University Press. (p. 339)

Schwartz, S. H. (1975). The justice of need and the activation of humanitarian norms. *Journal of Social Issues*, **31**(3), 111–136. (p. 482)

Schwartz, S. H., & Gottlieb, A. (1981). Participants' post-experimental reactions and the ethics of bystander research. *Journal of Experimental Social Psychology*, **17**, 396–407. (p. 493)

Schwarz, N. (1994). Judgment in a social context: Biases, shortcomings, and the logic of conversation. In M. Zanna (ed.), *Advances in experimental social psychology*, vol 26. San Diego, CA: Academic Press. (p. 110)

Schwarz, N., Bless, H., & Bohner, G. (1991). Mood and persuasion: Affective states influence the processing of persuasive communications. In M. Zanna (Ed.), *Advances in experimental social psychology*, vol. 24. New York: Academic Press. (p. 261)

Schwarz, N., & Kurz, E. (1989). What's in a picture? The impact of face-ism on trait attribution. *European Journal of Social Psychology*, **19**, 311–316. (p. 358)

Schwarz, N., Strack, F., Kommer, D., & Wagner, D. (1987). Soccer, rooms, and the quality of your life: Mood effects on judgments of satisfaction with life in general and with specific domains. *Journal of Applied Social Psychology*, **17**, 69–79. (p. 117)

Schwarzwald, J., Bizman, A., & Raz, M. (1983). The foot-in-the-door paradigm: Effects of second request size on donation probability and donor generosity. *Personality and Social Psychology Bulletin*, **9**, 443–450. (p. 143)

Schweitzer, K., Zillmann, D., Weaver, J. B., & Luttrell, E. S. (1992, Spring). Perception of threatening events in the emotional aftermath of a televised college football game. *Journal of Broadcasting and Electronic Media*, pp. 75–82. (p. 117)

Scott, J. P., & Marston, M. V. (1953). Nonadaptive behavior resulting from a series of defeats in fighting mice. *Journal of Abnormal and Social Psychology*, **48**, 417–428. (p. 396)

Sears, D. O. (1979). Life stage effects upon attitude change, especially among the elderly. Manuscript prepared for Workshop on the Elderly of the Future, Committee on Aging, National Research Council, Annapolis, Md., May 3–5. (p. 273)

Sears, D. O. (1986). College sophomores in the laboratory: Influences of a narrow data base on social psychology's view of human nature. *Journal of Personality and Social Psychology*, **51**, 515–530. (p. 273)

Sedikides, C. (1993). Assessment, enhancement, and verification determinants of the self-evaluation process. *Journal of Personality and Social Psychology*, **65**, 317–338. (p. 64)

Sedikides, C., & Anderson, C. A. (1992). Causal explanations of defection: A knowledge structure approach. *Personality and Social Psychology Bulletin*, 18, 420–429. (p. 81)

Segal, H. A. (1954). Initial psychiatric findings of recently repatriated prisoners of war. *American Journal of Psychiatry*, **61**, 358–363. (p. 149)

Segal, N. L. (1984). Cooperation, competition, and altruism within twin sets: A reappraisal. *Ethology and Sociobiology*, **5**, 163–177. (p. 483)

Segall, M. H., Dasen, P. R., Berry, J. W., & Poortinga, Y. H. (1990). *Human behavior in global perspective: An introduction to cross-cultural psychology*. New York: Pergamon. (pp. 190, 199)

Segerstrom, S. C., McCarthy, W. J., Caskey, N. H., Gross, T. M., & Jarvik, M. E. (1993). Optimistic bias among cigarette smokers. *Journal of Applied Social Psychology*, **23**, 1606–1618. (p. 584)

Selby, J. W., Calhoun, L. G., & Brock, T. A. (1977). Sex differences in the social perception of rape victims. *Personality and Social Psychology Bulletin*, **3**, 412–415. (p. 614)

Seligman, C., Fazio, R. H., & Zanna, M. P. (1980). Effects of salience of extrinsic rewards on liking and loving. *Journal of Personality and Social Psychology*, **38**, 453–460. (p. 447)

Seligman, M. E. P. (1975). *Helplessness: On depression, development and death*. San Francisco: W. H. Freeman. (p. 52)

Seligman, M. E. P. (1991). *Learned optimism*. New York: Knopf. (pp. 52, 574)

Seligman, M. E. P. (1992). Power and powerlessness: Comments on "Cognates of personal control." *Applied & Preventive Psychology*, **1**, 119–120. (p. 574)

Seligman, M. E. P., Nolen-Hoeksema, S., Thornton, N., & Thornton, K. M. (1990). Explanatory style as a mechanism of disappointing athletic performance. *Psychological Science, 1,* 143–146. (p. 52)

Seligman, M. E. P., & Schulman, P. (1986). Explanatory style as a predictor of productivity and quitting among life insurance sales agents. *Journal of Personality and Social Psychology, 50,* 832–838. (p. 52)

Semin, G. R., & De Poot, C. J. (1997). Bringing partiality to light: Question wording and choice as indicators of bias. *Social Cognition, 15,* 91–106. (p. 565)

Sentyrz, S. M., & Bushman, B. J. (1997). Mirror, mirror on the wall, who's the thinnest one of all? Effects of self-awareness on consumption of fatty, reduced-fat, and fat-free products. Unpublished manuscript, Iowa State University. (p. 308)

Seta, C. E., & Seta, J. J. (1992). Increments and decrements in mean arterial pressure levels as a function of audience composition: An averaging and summation analysis. *Personality and Social Psychology Bulletin, 18,* 173–181. (p. 297)

Seta, J. J. (1982). The impact of comparison processes on coactors' task performance. *Journal of Personality and Social Psychology, 42,* 281–291. (p. 297)

Seto, M. C., & Barbaree, H. E. (1995). The role of alcohol in sexual aggression. *Clinical Psychology Review, 15,* 545–566. (p. 387)

Shackelford, T. K., & Larsen, R. J. (1997). Facial asymmetry as an indicator of psychological, emotional, and physiological distress. *Journal of Personality and Social Psychology, 72,* 456–466. (p. 439)

Shaffer, D. R., Pegalis, L. J., & Bazzini, D. G. (1996). When boy meets girls (revisited): Gender, gender-role orientation, and prospect of future interaction as determinants of self-disclosure among same- and opposite-sex acquaintances. *Personality and Social Psychology Bulletin, 22,* 495–506. (p. 464)

Shaheen, J. G. (1990, August 19). Our cultural demon—the "ugly Arab." *Washington Post,* Outlook Section. (p. 359)

Sharan, S., & Sharan, Y. (1976). *Small group teaching.* Englewood Cliffs, N.J.: Educational Technology. (p. 542)

Sharma, N. (1981). Some aspect of attitude and behaviour of mothers. *Indian Psychological Review, 20,* 35–42. (p. 340)

Sharpe, D., Adair, J. G., & Roese, N. J. (1992). Twenty years of deception research: A decline in subjects' trust? *Personality and Social Psychology Bulletin, 18,* 585–590. (p. 31)

Shaver, P., Hazan, C., & Bradshaw, D. (1988). Love as attachment: The integration of three behavioral systems. In R. J. Sternberg & M. L. Barnes (Eds.), *The psychology of love.* New Haven: Yale University Press. (p. 461)

Shaver, P. R., & Hazan, C. (1993). Adult romantic attachment: Theory and evidence. In D. Perlman & W. Jones (Eds.), *Advances in personal relationships,* vol. 4. Greenwich, CT: JAI. (p. 461)

Shaver, P. R., & Hazan, C. (1994). Attachment. In A. L. Weber & J. H. Harvey (eds.), *Perspectives on close relationships.* Boston: Allyn & Bacon. (p. 461)

Shaw, J. S., III (1996). Increases in eyewitness confidence resulting from postevent questioning. *Journal of Experimental Psychology: Applied, 2,* 126–146. (p. 608)

Shaw, M. E. (1981). *Group dynamics: The psychology of small group behavior.* New York: McGraw-Hill. (p. 292)

Sheldon, U. (1979). The effects of effort and stigma on helping. *Journal of Social Psychology, 107,* 23-28. (p. 504)

Shell, R. M., & Eisenberg, N. (1992). A developmental model of recipients' reactions to aid. *Psychological Bulletin, 111,* 413–433. (p. 481)

Sheppard, B. H., & Vidmar, N. (1980). Adversary pretrial procedures and testimonial evidence: Effects of lawyer's role and machiavelian-ism. *Journal of Personality and Social Psychology, 39,* 320–322. (p. 608)

Shepperd, J. A. (1993). Student derogation of the Scholastic Aptitude Test: Biases in perceptions and presentations of College Board Scores. *Basic and Applied Social Psychology, 14,* 455–473. (p. 63)

Shepperd, J. A., & Arkin, R. M. (1991). Behavioral other-enhancement: Strategically obscuring the link between performance and evaluation. *Journal of Personality and Social Psychology, 60,* 79–88. (p. 71)

Shepperd, J. A., Arkin, R. M., & Slaughter, J. (1995). Constraints on excuse making: The deterring effects of shyness and anticipated retest. *Personality and Social Psychology Bulletin, 21,* 1061–1072. (p. 578)

Shepperd, J. A., Oullette, J. A., & Fernandez, J. K. (1996). Abandoning unrealistic optimism: Performance estimate sand the temporal proximity of self-relevant feedback. *Journal of Personality and Social Psychology, 70,* 844–855. (p. 60)

Shepperd, J. A., & Wright, R. A. (1989). Individual contributions to a collective effort: An incentive analysis. *Personality and Social Psychology Bulletin, 15,* 141–149. (p. 303)

Sherif, M. (1935). A study of some social factors in perception. *Archives of Psychology,* No. 187. (p. 211)

Sherif, M. (1937). An experimental approach to the study of attitudes. *Sociometry, 1,* 90–98. (p. 21)

Sherif, M. (1966). *In common predicament: Social psychology of intergroup conflict and cooperation.* Boston: Houghton Mifflin. (pp. 525, 527, 539)

Sherif, M., & Sherif, C. W. (1969). *Social psychology.* New York: Harper & Row. (p. 213)

Sherman, J. W. (1996). Development and mental representation of stereotypes. *Journal of Personality and Social Psychology, 70,* 1126–1141. (p. 369)

Sherman, S., Beike, D., & Ryalls, K. (in press). Dual-processing accounts of inconsistencies in response to general versus specific cases. In S. Chaiken & Y. Trope, *Dual process theories in social psychology.* New York: Guilford. (p. 263)

Sherman, S. J. (1980). On the self-erasing nature of errors of prediction. *Journal of Personality and Social Psychology, 39,* 211–221. (p. 123)

Sherman, S. J., Cialdini, R. B., Schwartzman, D. F., & Reynolds, K. D. (1985). Imagining can heighten or lower the perceived likelihood of contracting a disease: The mediating effect of ease of imagery. *Personality and Social Psychology Bulletin, 11,* 118–127. (pp. 112, 263)

Sherman, S. J., Presson, C. C., Chassin, L., Bensenberg, M., Corty, E., & Olshavsky, R. (1983). Smoking intentions in adolescents: Direct experience and predictability. *Personality and Social Psychology Bulletin, 8,* 376–383. (p. 136)

Short, J. F., Jr. (Ed.) (1969). *Gang delinquency and delinquent subcultures.* New York: Harper & Row. (p. 398)

Shostak, M. (1981). *Nisa: The life and words of a !Kung woman.* Cambridge, MA: Harvard University Press. (p. 457)

Shotland, R. L. (1989). A model of the causes of date rape in developing and close relationships. In C. Hendrick (Ed.), *Review of Personality and Social Psychology,* Vol. 10. Beverly Hills: Sage. (p. 79)

Shotland, R. L., & Stebbins, C. A. (1983). Emergency and cost as determinants of helping behavior and the slow accumulation of social psychological knowledge. *Social Psychology Quarterly, 46,* 36–46. (p. 482)

Shotland, R. L., & Straw, M. K. (1976). Bystander response to an assault: When a man attacks a woman. *Journal of Personality and Social Psychology, 34,* 990–999. (p. 489)

Showers, C., & Ruben, C. (1987). Distinguishing pessimism from depression: Negative expectations and positive coping mechanisms. Paper presented at the American Psychological Association convention. (p. 60)

Shrauger, J. S. (1975). Responses to evaluation as a function of initial self-perceptions. *Psychological Bulletin, 82,* 581–596. (p. 447)

Shrauger, J. S. (1983). The accuracy of self-prediction: How good are we and why? Paper presented at the Midwestern

Psychological Association convention. (p. 47)

Shrauger, J. S., Ram, D., Greninger, S. A., & Mariano, E. (1996). Accuracy of self-predictions versus judgments by knowledgeable others. *Personality and Social Psychology Bulletin, 22*, 1229–1243. (p. 47)

Shure, G. H., Meeker, R. J., & Hansford, E. A. (1965). The effectiveness of pacifist strategies in bargaining games. *Journal of Conflict Resolution, 9*(1), 106–117. (p. 519)

Sidanius, J., Pratto, F., & Bobo, L. (1994). Social dominance orientation and the political psychology of gender: A case of invariance? *Journal of Personality and Social Psychology, 67*, 998–1011. (p. 187)

Sidanius, J., Pratto, F., & Bobo, L. (1996). Racism, conservatism, affirmative action, and intellectual sophistication: A matter of principled conservatism or group dominance? *Journal of Personality and Social Psychology, 70*, 476–490. (p. 363)

Sigall, H. (1970). Effects of competence and consensual validation on a communicator's liking for the audience. *Journal of Personality and Social Psychology, 16*, 252–258. (p. 451)

Sigall, H., & Page, R. (1971). Current stereotypes: A little fading, a little faking. *Journal of Personality and Social Psychology, 18*, 247–255. (p. 133)

Silver, M., & Geller, D. (1978). On the irrelevance of evil: The organization and individual action. *Journal of Social Issues, 34*, 125–136. (p. 228)

Simon, H. A. (1957). *Models of man: Social and rational.* New York: Wiley. (p. 125)

Simon, P. (1996, April 17). American provincials. *Christian Century*, pp. 421–422. (p. 26)

Simons, E. L. (1989). Human origins. *Science, 245*, 1343–1350. (p. 173)

Simonton, D. K. (1994). *Greatness: Who makes history and why.* New York: Guilford. (p. 330)

Simpson, J. A. (1987). The dissolution of romantic relationships: Factors involved in relationship stability and emotional distress. *Journal of Personality and Social Psychology, 53*, 683–692. (p. 469)

Simpson, J. A., Campbell, B., & Berscheid, E. (1986). The association between romantic love and marriage: Kephart (1967) twice revisited. *Personality and Social Psychology Bulletin, 12*, 363–372. (pp. 455, 458)

Simpson, J. A., Gangestad, S. W., & Lerma, M. (1990). Perception of physical attractiveness: Mechanisms involved in the maintenance of romantic relationships. *Journal of Personality and Social Psychology, 59*, 1192–1201. (p. 442)

Simpson, J. A., Rholes, W. S., & Nelligan, J. S. (1992). Support seeking and support giving within couples in an anxiety-provoking situation: The role of attachment styles. *Journal of Personality and Social Psychology, 62*, 434–446. (p. 461)

Simpson, J. A., Rholes, W. S., & Phillips, D. (1996). Conflict in close relationships: An attachment perspective. *Journal of Personality and Social Psychology, 71*, 899–914. (p. 461)

Sinclair & Kunda (in press). Motivated stereotyping of women: She's fine if she praised me but incompetent if she criticized me. *Personality and Social Psychology Bulletin.* (p. 379)

Sinclair, L., & Kunda, Z. (1999). Reactions to a Black professional: Motivated inhibition and activation of conflicting stereotypes. *Journal of Personality and Social Psychology, 77*, 885-904. (p. 342)

Singer, J. L., & Singer, D. G. (1988). Some hazards of growing up in a television environment: Children's aggression and restlessness. In S. Oskamp (Ed.), *Television as a social issue: Applied Social Psychology Annual*, Vol. 8. Newbury Park, Ca.: Sage. (p. 418)

Singer, M. (1979, July-August). Interviewed by M. Freeman. Of cults and communication: A conversation with Margaret Singer. *APA Monitor*, pp. 6–7. *(b)* (pp. 281, 282)

Singer, M. (1979). Cults and cult members. Address to the American Psychological Association convention. *(a)* (p. 281, 282)

Singh, D. (1993). Adaptive significance of female physical attractiveness: Role of waist-to-hip ratio. *Journal of Personality and Social Psychology, 65*, 293–307. (p. 440)

Singh, D. (1995a). Female health, attractiveness, and desirability for relationships: Role of breast asymmetry and waist-to-hip ratio. *Ethology and Sociobiology, 16*, 465–481. (p. 440)

Singh, D. (1995b). Female judgment of male attractiveness and desirability for relationships: Role of waist-to-hip ratio and financial status. *Journal of Personality and Social Psychology, 69*, 1089–1101. (p. 440)

Singh, D., & Young, R. K. (1995). Body weight, waist-to-hip ratio, breasts, and hips: Role in judgments of female attractiveness and desirability for relationships. *Ethology and Sociobiology, 16*, 483–507. (p. 440)

Sissons, M. (1981). Race, sex, and helping behavior. *British Journal of Social Psychology, 20*, 285–292. (p. 504)

Sittser, G. L. (1994, April). Long night's journey into light. *Second Opinion*, pp. 10–15. (p. 113)

Sivard, R. L. (1991). *World military and social expenditures.* Washington, DC: World Priorities. (pp. 385, 518)

Sivard, R. L. (1995). *Women. . . a world survey*, 2nd ed. Washington, DC: World Priorities. (p. 187)

Sivard, R. L. (1996). *World military and social expenditures 1996*, 16th edition. Washington, DC: World Priorities. (pp. 384, 515)

Six, B., & Eckes, T. (1996). Metaanalysen in der Einstellungs-Verhaltens-Forschung. *Zeitschrift fur Sozialpsychologie*, pp. 7–17. (p. 134)

Six, B., & Krahe, B. (1984). Implicit psychologists' estimates of attitude-behavior consistencies. *European Journal of Social Psychology, 14*, 79–86. (p. 137)

Skaalvik, E. M., & Hagtvet, K. A. (1990). Academic achievement and self-concept: An analysis of causal predominance in a developmental perpsective. *Journal of Personality and Social Psychology, 58*, 292–307. (p. 23)

Skill, T., Robinson, J. D., Lyons, J. S., & Larson, D. (1994). The portrayal of religion and spirituality on fictional network television. *Review of Religious Research, 35*, 251–267. (p. 417)

Skinner, B. F. (1971). *Beyond freedom and dignity.* New York: Knopf. (p. 476)

Skitka, L. J., & Tetlock, P. E. (1993). Providing public assistance: Cognitive and motivational processes underlying liberal and conservative policy preferences. *Journal of Personality and Social Psychology, 65*, 1205–1223. (p. 482)

Skov, R. B., & Sherman, S. J. (1986). Information-gathering processes: Diagnosticity, hypothesis-confirmatory strategies, and perceived hypothesis confirmation. *Journal of Experimental Social Psychology, 22*, 93–121. (p. 108)

Slavin, R. E. (1980). Cooperative learning and desegregation. Paper presented at the American Psychological Association convention. (p. 542)

Slavin, R. E. (1990, December/January). Research on cooperative learning: Consensus and controversy. *Educational Leadership*, pp. 52–54. (p. 543)

Slavin, R. E., & Madden, N. A. (1979). School practices that improve race relations. *Journal of Social Issues, 16*, 169–180. (p. 540)

Sloan, J. H., Kellerman, A. L., Reay, D. T., Ferris, J. A., Koepsell, T., Rivara, F. P., Rice, C., Gray, L., & LoGerfo, J. (1988). Handgun regulations, crime, assaults, and homicide: A tale of two cities. *New England Journal of Medicine, 319*, 1256–1261. (p. 391)

Slovic, P. (1972). From Shakespeare to Simon: Speculations—and some evidence—about man's ability to process information. *Oregon Research Institute Research Bulletin, 12*(2).(p. 124)

Slovic, P. (1985, January 30). Only new laws will spur seat-belt use. *Wall Street Journal.* (p. 252)

Slovic, P., & Fischhoff, B. (1977). On the psychology of experimental surprises. *Journal of Experimental Psychology: Human Perception and Performance, 3*, 455–551. (p. 16)

Small, G. W., Propper, M. W., Randolph, E. T., & Eth, S. (1991). Mass hysteria among student performers: Social relationship as a symptom predictor. *American Journal of Psychiatry*, **148**, 1200–1205. (p. 580)

Smith, A. (1976). *The wealth of nations*. Book 1. Chicago: University of Chicago Press. (Originally published, 1776.) (p. 521)

Smith, D. E., Gier, J. A., & Willis, F. N. (1982). Interpersonal touch and compliance with a marketing request. *Basic and Applied Social Psychology*, **3**, 35–38. (p. 221)

Smith, H. (1976) *The Russians*. New York: Balantine Books. Cited by B. Latané, K. Williams, and S. Harkins in, Many hands make light the work. *Journal of Personality and Social Psychology*, 1979, **37**, 822–832. (p. 302)

Smith, H. J., & Tyler, T. R. (1997). Choosing the right pond: The impact of group membership on self-esteem and group-oriented behavior. *Journal of Experimental Social psychology*, **33**, 146–170. (p. 353)

Smith, H. W. (1981). Territorial spacing on a beach revisited: A cross-national exploration. *Social Psychology Quarterly*, **44**, 132–137. (p. 177)

Smith, J. L., Berry, N. J., & Whiteley, P. (1997). The effect of interviewer guise upon gender self-report responses as a function of interviewee's self-monitoring position. *European Journal of Social Psychology*, **27**, 237–243. (p. 72)

Smith, M. B. (1978). Psychology and values. *Journal of Social Issues*, **34**, 181–199. (p. 12)

Smith, P. B., & Tayeb, M. (1989). Organizational structure and processes. In M. Bond (Ed.), *The cross-cultural challenge to social psychology*. Newbury Park, Ca.: Sage. (p. 329)

Smith, R. H., Turner, T. J., Garonzik, R., Leach, C. W., Urch-Druskat, V., & Weston, C. M. (1996). Envy and Schadenfreude. *Personality and Social Psychology Bulletin*, **22**, 158–168. (p. 394)

Smith, S. M., & Petty, R. E. (1995). Personality moderators of mood congruency effects on cognition: The role of self-esteem and negative mood regulation. *Journal of Personality and Social Psychology*, **68**, 1092–1107. (p. 40)

Smith, S. M., & Shaffer, D. R. (1991). Celerity and cajolery: Rapid speech may promote or inhibit persuasion through its impact on message elaboration. *Personality and Social Psychology Bulletin*, **17**, 663–669. (p. 259)

Smith, T. W. (1997). Personal correspondence. Data from the General Social Survey, National Opinion Research Center, University of Chicago. (pp. 346, 393)

Smith, V. L. (1991). Impact of pretrial instruction on jurors' information processing and decision making. *Journal of Applied Psychology*, **76**, 220–228. (p. 618)

Smith, V. L. (1991). Prototypes in the courtroom: Lay representations of legal concepts. *Journal of Personality and Social Psychology*, **61**, 857–872. (p. 621)

Smith, V. L., & Ellsworth, P. C. (1987). The social psychology of eyewitness accuracy: Misleading questions and communicator expertise. *Journal of Applied Psychology*, **72**, 294–300. (p. 605)

Smith, W. P. (1987). Conflict and negotiation: Trends and emerging issues. *Journal of Applied Social Psychology*, **17**, 641–677. (p. 554)

Snodgrass, M. A. (1987). The relationships of differential loneliness, intimacy, and characterological attributional style to duration of loneliness. *Journal of Social Behavior and Personality*, **2**, 173–186. (p. 576)

Snodgrass, S. E., Higgins, J. G., & Todisco, L. (1986). The effects of walking behavior on mood. Paper presented at the American Psychological Association convention. (p. 158)

Snyder, C. R. (1978). The "illusion" of uniqueness. *Journal of Humanistic Psychology*, **18**, 33–41. (p. 58)

Snyder, C. R. (1980). The uniqueness mystique. *Psychology Today*, March, pp. 86–90. (p. 246)

Snyder, C. R., & Fromkin, H. L. (1980). *Uniqueness; The human pursuit of difference*. New York: Plenum. (p. 245)

Snyder, C. R., & Higgins, R. L. (1988). Excuses: Their effectie role in the negotiation of reality. *Psychological Bulletin*, **104**, 23-35. (p. 66)

Snyder, M. (1981). Seek, and ye shall find: Testing hypotheses about other people. In E. T. Higgins, C. P. Herman, & M. P. Zanna (Eds.), *Social cognition: The Ontario symposium on personality and social psychology*. Hillsdale, N.J.: Erlbaum. *(a)* (p. 565)

Snyder, M. (1983). The influence of individuals on situations: Implications for understanding the links between personality and social behavior. *Journal of Personality*, **51**, 497–516. (p. 205)

Snyder, M. (1984). When belief creates reality. In L. Berkowitz (Ed.), *Advances in Experimental Social Psychology*, Vol. 18. New York: Academic Press. (pp. 121, 564)

Snyder, M. (1987). *Public appearances/ private realities: The psychology of self-monitoring*. New York: Freeman. (pp. 72, 151)

Snyder, M. (1988). Experiencing prejudice first hand: The "discrimination day" experiments. *Contemporary Psychology*, **33**, 664–665. (p. 111)

Snyder, M. (1989). Selling images versus selling products: Motivational foundations of behavioral confirmation. *Advances in Experimental Social Psychology*, **26**, 206–311. (p. 274)

Snyder, M., Berscheid, E., & Glick, P. (1985). Focusing on the exterior and

the interior: Two investigations of the initiation of personal relationships. *Journal of Personality and Social Psychology*, **48**, 1427–1439. (p. 456)

Snyder, M., Berscheid, E., & Matwychuk, A. (1988). Orientations toward personnel selection: Differential reliance on appearance and personality. *Journal of Personality and Social Psychology*, **54**, 972–979. (p. 456)

Snyder, M., Campbell, B., & Preston, E. (1982). Testing hypotheses about human nature: Assessing the accuracy of social stereotypes. *Social Cognition*, **1**, 256–272. (p. 565)

Snyder, M., & Copeland, J. (1989). Self-monitoring processes in organizational settings. In R. A. Giacalone & P. Rosenfeld (Eds.), *Impression management in the organization*. Hillsdale, N.J.: Erlbaum. (pp. 72, 151)

Snyder, M., & DeBono, K. G. (1987). A functional approach to attitudes and persuasion. In M. P. Zanna, J. M. Olson, & C. P. Herman (Eds.), *Social influence: The Ontario symposium*, Vol. 5. Hillsdale, N.J.: Erlbaum. (p. 276)

Snyder, M., & DeBono, K. G. (1989). Understanding the functions of attitudes: Lessons from personality and social behavior. In A. R. Pratkanis, S. J., Breckler, & A. G. Greenwald (Eds.), *Attitude structure and function*. Hillsdale, N.J.: Erlbaum. (pp. 72, 151)

Snyder, M., Grether, J., & Keller, K. (1974). Staring and compliance: A field experiment on hitch-hiking. *Journal of Applied Social Psychology*, **4**, 165–170. (pp. 503, 506)

Snyder, M., & Haugen, J. A. (1994). Why does behavioral confirmation occur? A functional perspective on the role of the perceiver. *Journal of Experimental Social Psychology*, **30**, 218–246. (p. 27)

Snyder, M., & Haugen, J. A. (1995). Why does behavioral confirmation occur? A functional perspective on the role of the target. *Personality and Social Psychology Bulletin*, **21**, 963–974. (p. 27)

Snyder, M., & Ickes, W. (1985). Personality and social behavior. In G. Lindzey & E. Aronson (Eds.), *Handbook of social psychology* (3rd ed.). New York: Random House. (pp. 205, 240, 363)

Snyder, M., & Simpson, J. (1985). Orientations toward romantic relationships. In S. Duckk & D. Perlman (Eds.), *Understanding personal relationships*. Beverly Hills, Ca.: Sage. (p. 456)

Snyder, M., & Swann, W. B., Jr. (1976). When actions reflect attitudes: The politics of impression management. *Journal of Personality and Social Psychology*, **34**, 1034–1042. (p. 135)

Snyder, M., Tanke, E. D., & Berscheid, E. (1977). Social perception and interpersonal behavior: On the self-fulfilling nature of social stereotypes.

Journal of Personality and Social Psychology, **35**, 656–666. *(b)* (p. 121)

Snyder, M., & Thomsen, C. J. (1988). Interactions between therapists and clients: Hypothesis testing and behavioral confirmation. In D. C. Turk & P. Salovey (Eds.), *Reasoning, inference, and judgment in clinical psychology.* New York: Free Press. (p. 565)

Sokoll, G. R., & Mynatt, C. R. (1984).- Arousal and free throw shooting. Paper presented at the Midwestern Psychological Association convention, Chicago. (p. 296)

Solano, C. H. Batten, P. G., & Parish, E. A. (1982). Loneliness and patterns of self-disclosure. *Journal of Personality and Social Psychology,* **43**, 524–531. (p. 463)

Solomon, H., & Solomon, L. Z. (1978). Effects of anonymity on helping in emergency situations. Paper presented at the Eastern Psychological Association convention. (p. 506)

Solomon, H., Solomon, L. Z., Arnone, M. M., Maur, B. J., Reda, R. M., & Rother, E. O. (1981). Anonymity and helping. *Journal Social Psychology,* **113**, 37–43. (p. 506)

Solomon, L. Z., Solomon, H., & Stone, R. (1978). Helping as a function of number of bystanders and ambiguity of emergency. *Personality and Social Psychology Bulletin,* **4**, 318–321. (p. 491)

Sommer, B. (1992). Cognitive performance and the menstrual cycle. In J. T. Richardson (Ed.), *Cognition and the menstrual cycle: Research, theory, and culture.* New York: Springer-Verlag. (p. 580)

Sommer, R. (1969). *Personal space.* Englewood Cliffs, N.J.: Prentice-Hall. (p. 177)

Sommers-Flanagan, R., Sommers-Flanagan, J., & Davis, B. (1993). What's happening on music television? A gender role content analysis. *Sex Roles,* **28**, 745–753. (p. 359)

Sonne, J., & Janoff, D. (1979). The effect of treatment attributions on the maintenance of weight reduction: A replication and extension. *Cognitive Therapy and Research,* **3**, 389–397. (p. 588)

Sorenson, S. B., Stein, J. A., Siegel, J. M., Golding, J. M., & Burnam, M. A. (1987). Prevalence of adult sexual assault: The Los Angeles Epidemiologic Catchment Area Study. *American Journal of Epidemiology,* **126**, 1154–1164. (p. 410)

Sorrentino, R. M., Bobocel, D. R., Gitta, M. Z., Olsen, J. M., & Hewitt, E. C. (1988). Uncertainty orientation and persuasion: Individual differences in the effects of personal relevance on social judgments. *Journal of Personality and Social Psychology,* **55**, 357–371. (p. 276)

Sparrell, J. A., & Shrauger, J. S. (1984). Self-confidence and optimism in self-prediction. Paper presented at the American Psychological Association convention. (p. 60)

Spector, P. E. (1986). Perceived control by employees: A meta-analysis of studies concerning autonomy and participation at work. *Human Relations,* **39**, 1005–1016. (p. 329)

Speer, A. (1971). *Inside the Third Reich: Memoirs.* (P. Winston & C. Winston. trans.). New York: Avon Books. (p. 319)

Spencer, S. J., & Fein, S., & Wolfe, C. T., & Fong, C., & Dunn, M. A. (1998). Automatic activation of stereotypes: The role of self-image threat. *Personality and Social Psychology Bulletin,* **24**, 1139-1152. (p. 342)

Spencer, S. J., Steele, C. M., & Quinn, D. M. (1999). Stereotype threat and women's math performance. *Journal of Experimental Social Psychology,* **35**, 4-28. (p. 352)

Spiegel, D., Bloom, J. R., Kraemer, H. C., & Gottheil, E. (1989, October 14). Effect of psychosocial treatment on survival of patients with metastatic breast cancer. *The Lancet,* 888–891. (p. 584)

Spiegel, H. W. (1971). *The growth of economic thought.* Durham, N.C.: Duke University Press. (p. 69)

Spitzberg, B. H., & Hurt, H. T. (1987). The relationship of interpersonal competence and skills to reported loneliness across time. *Journal of Social Behavior and Personality,* **2**, 157–172. (p. 576)

Spivak, J. (1979, June 6). *Wall Street Journal.* (p. 302)

Spivey, C. B., & Prentice-Dunn, S. (1990). Assessing the directionality of deindividuated behavior: Effects of deindividuation, modeling, and private self-consciousness on aggressive and prosocial responses. *Basic and Applied Social Psychology,* **11**, 387–403. (p. 307)

Sporer, S. L., Penrod, S., Read, D., & Cutler, B. (1995). Choosing, confidence, and accuracy: A meta-analysis of the confidence-accuracy relation in eyewitness identification studies. *Psychological Bulletin,* **118**, 315–327. (p. 603)

Sprecher, S. (1987). The effects of self-disclosure given and received on affection for an intimate partner and stability of the relationship. *Journal of Personality and Social Psychology,* **4**, 115–127. (p. 465)

Sprecher, S., Aron, A., Hatfield, E., Cortese, A., Potapova, E., & Levitskaya, A. (1994). Love: American style, Russian style, and Japanese style. *Personal Relationships,* **1**, 349–369. (p. 458)

Sprecher, S., & Duck, S. (1994). Sweet talk: The importance of perceived communication for romantic and friendship attraction experienced during a get-acquainted date. *Personality and Social Psychology Bulletin,* **20**, 391–400. (p. 443)

Sprecher, S., & Sedikides, C. (1993). Gender differences in perceptions of emotionality: The case of close

heterosexual relationships. *Sex Roles,* **28**, 511–530. (p. 186)

Sprecher, S., Sullivan, Q., & Hatfield, E. (1994). Mate selection preferences: Gender differences examined in a national sample. *Journal of Personality and Social Psychology,* **66**, 1074–1080. (p. 435)

Stack, S. (1992). Marriage, family, religion, and suicide. In R. Maris, A. Berman, J. Maltsberg, and R. Yufits (eds.), *Assessment and prediction of suicide.* New York: Guilford. (p. 593)

Stam, H., Lubeck, I., Radtke, H. L. (1998). Repopulating social psychology texts: Disembodied "subjects" and embodied subjectivety. In Bayer, B. M., Shotter, J., (Eds.) *Reconstructing the psychological subject: Bodies, practices and technologies. Inquiries in social construction.* (pp. 153-186). London, England UK: Sage Publications, Inc. (p. 219)

Stangor, C., Lynch, L., Duan, C., & Glass, B. (1992). Categorization of individuals on the basis of multiple social features. *Journal of Personality and Social Psychology,* **62**, 207–218. (p. 375)

Stangor, C., & McMillan, D. (1992). Memory for expectancy-congruent and expectancy-incongruent information: A review of the social and social developmental literatures. *Psychological Bulletin,* **111**, 42–61. (p. 375)

Stangor, C., Sullivan, L. A., & Ford, T. E. (1991). Affective and cognitive determinants of prejudice. *Social Cognition,* **9**, 359–380. (p. 337)

Stark, R., & Bainbridge, W. S. (1980). Networks of faith: Interpersonal bonds and recruitment of cults and sects *American Journal of Sociology,* **85**, 1376–1395. (pp. 281, 282)

Stasser, G. (1991). Pooling of unshared information during group discussion. In S. Worchel, W. Wood, & J. Simpson (Eds.), *Group process and productivity.* Beverly Hills, CA: Sage. (p. 313)

Stasser, G. (1992). Pooling of unshared information during group discussion. In S. Worchel, W. Wood, and J. A. Simpson (eds.), *Group process and productivity.* Newbury Park, CA: Sage. (p. 324)

Stasser, G., Kerr, N. L., & Bray, R. M. (1981). The social psychology of jury deliberations: Structure, process, and product. In N. L. Kerr & R. M. Bray (Eds.), *The psychology of the courtroom.* New York: Academic Press.(p. 626)

Statistics Canada (1998). *General Social Survey: Overview of the Time Use of Canadians in 1998.* Ottawa: Statistics Canada. (p. 200)

Statistics Canada (1996). Depression. *Health Reports,* **7**, 11-22. (p. 593)

Statistics Canada (1997). *Earnings of Men and Women.* Ottawa: Statistics Canada. (p. 200)

Staub, E. (1978). *Positive social behavior and morality: Social and personal influences*, vol. 1. Hillsdale, NJ: Erlbaum. (p. 476)

Staub, E. (1989). *The roots of evil: The origins of genocide and other group violence.* Cambridge: Cambridge University Press. (pp. 224, 226, 509)

Staub, E. (1990). Moral exclusion: Personal goal theory, and extreme destructiveness. *Journal of Social Issues, 46*, 47–64. (p. 508)

Staub, E. (1991). Altruistic and moral motivations for helping and their translation into action. *Psychological Inquiry, 2*, 150–153. (pp. 480, 509)

Staub, E. (1991). Psychological and cultural origins of extreme destructiveness and extreme altruism. In W. Kurtines & J. Gewirtz (Eds.), *The handbook of moral behavior and development.* Hillsdale, NJ: Erlbaum. (p. 509)

Staub, E. (1992). The origins of caring, helping and nonaggression: Parental socialization, the family system, schools, and cultural influence. In S. Oliner & P. Oliner (Eds.), *Embracing the other: Philosophical, psychological, and theological perspectives on altruism.* New York: New York University Press. (p. 509)

Staub, E. (1993). The psychology of by-standers, perpetrators, and heroic helpers. *International Journal of Inter-cultural Relations, 17*, 315–341. (p. 511)

Staub, E. (1996). Altruism and aggression in children and youth: Origins and cures. In R. Feldman (ed.), *The psychology of adversity.* Amherst, MA: University of Massachusetts Press. (pp. 398, 419)

Staub, E. (1997). Blind versus constructive patriotism: Moving from embeddedness in the group to critical loyalty and action. In D. Bar-Tal and E. Staub (eds.), *Patriotism in the lives of individuals and nations.* Chicago: Nelson-Hall. (p. 353)

Staub, E. (1997). Halting and preventing collective violence: The role of bystanders. Background paper for symposium organized by the Friends of Raoul Wallenberg, Stockholm, June 13–16. (p. 492)

Steblay, N. M. (1987). Helping behavior in rural and urban environments: A meta-analysis. *Psychological Bulletin, 102*, 346–356. (p. 484)

Steele, C. M. (1988). The psychology of self-affirmation: Sustaining the integrity of the self. In L. Berkowitz (Ed.), *Advances in experimental social psychology,* Vol. 21. Orlando, Fl.: Academic Press. (p. 163)

Steele, C. M. (1997). A threat in the air: How stereotypes shape intellectual identity and performance. *American Psychologist, 52*, 613–629. (pp. 42, 352)

Steele, C. M., & Aronson, J. (1995). Stereotype threat and the intellectual test performance of African Americans. *Journal of Personality and Social Psychology, 69*, 797–811.(p. 352)

Steele, C. M., & Josephs, R. A. (1990). Alcohol myopia: Its prized and dangerous effects. *American Psychologist, 45*, 921-933. (p. 578)

Steele, C. M., & Southwick, L. (1985). Alcohol and social behavior I: The psychology of drunken excess. *Journal of Personality and Social Psychology, 48*, 18–34. (p. 387)

Steele, C. M., Southwick, L. L., & Critchlow, B. (1981). Dissonance and alcohol: Drinking your troubles away. *Journal of Personality and Social Psychology, 41*, 831–846. (p. 165)

Steele, C. M., Spencer, S. J., & Lynch, M. (1993). Self-image resilience and dissonance: The role of affirmational resources. *Journal of Personality and Social Psychology, 64*, 885–896. (p. 164)

Stein, A. H., & Friedrich, L. K. (1972). Television content and young children's behavior. In J. P. Murray, E. A. Rubinstein, & G. A. Comstock (Eds.), *Television and social learning.* Washington, D.C.: Government Printing Office. (p. 509)

Stein, D. D., Hardyck, J. A., & Smith, M. B. (1965). Race and belief: An open and shut case. *Journal of Personality and Social Psychology, 1*, 281–289. (p. 365)

Steinem, G. (1988). Six great ideas that television is missing. In S. Oskamp. (Ed.), *Television as a social issue: Applied Social Psychology Annual,* Vol. 8. Newbury Park, Ca.: Sage. (p. 409)

Steiner, I. D. (1982). Heuristic models of groupthink. In M. Brandstatter, J. H. Davis, & G. Stocker-Kreichgauer (Eds.), *Group decision making.* New York: Academic Press, pp. 503–524. (p. 324)

Stephan, C. W., & Stephan, W. G. (1986). Habla Ingles? The effects of language translation on simulated juror decisions. *Journal of Applied Social Psychology, 16*, 577–589. (p. 614)

Stephan, W. G. (1986). The effects of school desegregation: An evaluation 30 years after *Brown.* In R. Kidd, L. Saxe, & M. Saks (Eds.), *Advances in applied social psychology.* New York: Erlbaum. (p. 536)

Stephan, W. G. (1987). The contact hypothesis in intergroup relations. In C. Hendrick (Ed.), *Group processes and intergroup relations.* Newbury Park, Ca.: Sage. (p. 537)

Stephan, W. G., Berscheid, E., & Walster, E. (1971). Sexual arousal and heterosexual perception. *Journal of Personality and Social Psychology, 20*, 93–101. (p. 454)

Sternberg, R. J. (1988). Triangulating love. In R. J. Sternberg & M. L. Barnes (Eds.), *The psychology of love.* New Haven: Yale University Press. (pp. 452, 470)

Sternberg, R. J., & Grajek, S. (1984). The nature of love. *Journal of Personality and Social Psychology, 47*, 312–329. (p. 460)

Stiles, W. B., Shuster, P. L., & Harrigan, J. A. (1992). Disclosure and anxiety: A test of

the fever model. *Journal of Personality and Social Psychology, 63*, 980–988. (p. 464)

Stille, R. G., Malamuth, N., & Schallow, J. R. (1987). Prediction of rape proclivity by rape myth attitudes and hostility toward women. Paper presented at the American Psychological Association convention. (p. 408)

Stinson, V., Devenport, J. L., Cutler, B. L., & Kravitz, D. A. (1997). How effective is the motion-to-suppress safeguard? Judges' perceptions of the suggestiveness and fairness of biased lineup procedures. *Journal of Personality and Social Psychology, 82*, 211–220. (p. 612)

Stinson, V., Devenport, J. L., Cutler, B. L., & Kravitz, D. A. (1996). How effective is the presence-of-counsel safeguard? Attorney perceptions of suggestiveness, fairness, and correctability of biased lineup procedures. *Journal of Applied Psychology, 81*, 64–75. (p. 612)

Stockdale, J. E. (1978). Crowding: Determinants and effects. In L. Berkowitz (Ed.), *Advances in experimental social psychology* (Vol. 11). New York: Academic Press. (p. 177)

Stokes, J., & Levin, I. (1986). Gender differences in predicting loneliness from social network characteristics. *Journal of Personality and Social Psychology, 51*, 1069–1074. (p. 575)

Stone, A. A., Hedges, S. M., Neale, J. M., & Satin, M. S. (1985). Prospective and cross-sectional mood reports offer no evidence of a "blue Monday" phenomenon. *Journal of Personality and Social Psychology, 49*, 129–134. (p. 46)

Stone, A. L., & Glass, C. R. (1986). Cognitive distortion of social feedback in depression. *Journal of Social and Clinical Psychology, 4*, 179–188. (p. 117)

Stone, J., Wiegand, A. W., Cooper, J., & Aronson, E. (in press). When exemplification fails: Hypocrisy and the motive for self-integrity. *Journal of Personality and Social Psychology.* (p. 166)

Stone, L. (1977). *The family, sex and marriage in England, 1500–1800.* New York: Harper & Row. (p. 468)

Stoner, J. A. F. (1962). A comparison of individual and group decisions involving risk. Unpublished master's thesis, Massachusetts Institute of Technology, 1961. Cited by D. G. Marquis in, Individual responsibility and group decisions involving risk. *Industrial Management Review, 3*, 8–23. (p. 309)

Stoppard, J. M., & Gruchy, C. D. G. (1993). Gender, context, and expression of positive emotion. *Personality and Social Psychology Bulletin, 19*, 143–150. (p. 186)

Storms, M. D. (1973). Videotape and the attribution process: Reversing actors' and observers' points of view. *Journal of Personality and Social Psychology*, **27**, 165–175. (p. 87)

Storms, M. D., & Thomas, G. C. (1977). Reactions to physical closeness. *Journal of Personality and Social Psychology*, **35**, 412–418. (p. 296)

Stouffer, S. A., Suchman, E. A., DeVinney, L. C., Star, S. A., & Williams, R. M., Jr. (1949). *The American soldier: Adjustment during army life* (Vol. 1.). Princeton, N.J.: Princeton University Press. (p. 395, 535)

Strack, F., Martin, L. L., & Stepper, S. (1988). Inhibiting and facilitating conditions of the human smile: A nonobstrusive test of the facial feedback hypothesis. *Journal of Personality and Social Psychology*, **54**, 768–777. (p. 158)

Strack, S., & Coyne, J. C. (1983). Social confirmation of dysphoria: Shared and private reactions to depression. *Journal of Personality and Social Psychology*, **44**, 798–806. (p. 572)

Straus, M. A., & Gelles, R. J. (1980). *Behind closed doors: Violence in the American family.* New York: Anchor/Doubleday. (p. 397)

Strenta, A., & DeJong, W. (1981). The effect of a prosocial label on helping behavior. *Social Psychology Quarterly*, **44**, 142–147. (p. 508)

Stringer, C. B. (1990, December). The emergence of modern humans. *Scientific American*, pp. 98–104. (p. 173)

Stroebe, W., & Diehl, M. (1994). Productivity loss in idea-generating groups. In W. Stroebe & M. Hewstone (Eds.), *European review of social psychology*, vol. 5. Chichester: Wiley. (p. 324)

Stroebe, W., Insko, C. A., Thompson, V. D., & Layton, B. D. (1971). Effects of physical attractiveness, attitude similarity, and sex on various aspects of interpersonal attraction. *Journal of Personality and Social Psychology*, **18**, 79–91. (p. 435)

Stroebe, W., Lenkert, A., & Jonas, K. (1988). Familiarity may breed contempt: The impact of student exchange on national stereotypes and attitudes. In W. Stroebe & A. W. Kruglanski (Eds.), *The social psychology of intergroup conflict.* New York: Springer-Verlag. (p. 536)

Stroebe, W., Stroebe, M., Abakoumkin, G., & Schut, H. (1996). The role of loneliness and social support in adjustment to loss: A test of attachment versus stress theory. *Journal of Personality and Social Psychology*, **70**, 1241–1249. (p. 576)

Stroessner, S. J., Hamilton, D. L., & Lepore, L. (1990). Intergroup categorization and intragroup differentiation: Ingroup-outgroup differences. Paper presented at the American Psychological Association convention. (p. 364)

Stroessner, S. J., & Mackie, D. M. (1993). Affect and perceived group variability:

Implications for stereotyping and prejudice. In D. M. Mackie & D. L. Hamilton (eds.), *Affect, cognition, and stereotyping: Interactive processes in group perception.* San Diego, CA: Academic Press. (p. 364)

Strong, S. R. (1968). Counseling: An interpersonal influence process. *Journal of Counseling Psychology*, **17**, 81–87. (p. 589)

Strong, S. R. (1978). Social psychological approach to psychotherapy research. In S. L. Garfield & A. E. Bergin (Eds.), *Handbook of psychotherapy and behavior change*, 2nd ed. New York: Wiley. (p. 283)

Strong, S. R. (1991). Social influence and change in therapeutic relationships. In C. R. Snyder & D. R. Forsyth (Eds.), *Handbook of social and clinical psychology.* New York: Pergamon Press. (p. 589)

Strong, S. R., Welsh, J. A., Corcoran, J. L., & Hoyt, W. T. (1992). Social psychology and counseling psychology: The history, products, and promise of an interface. *Journal of Personality and Social Psychology*, **39**, 139–157. (p. 585)

Stroufe, B., Chaikin, A., Cook, R., & Freeman, V. (1977). The effects of physical attractiveness on honesty: A socially desirable response. *Personality and Social Psychology*, **3**, 59–62. (p. 503)

Sue, S., Smith, R. E., & Caldwell, C. (1973). Effects of inadmissible evidence on the decisions of simulated jurors: A moral dilemma. *Journal of Applied Social Psychology*, **3**, 345–353. (p. 617)

Suls, J., & Tesch, F. (1978). Students' preferences for information about their test performance: A social comparison study, *Journal of Applied Social Psychology*, **8**, 189–197. (p. 394)

Suls, J., Wan, C. K., & Sanders, G. S. (1988). False consensus and false uniqueness in estimating the prevalence of health-protective behaviors. *Journal of Applied Social Psychology*, **18**, 66–79. (p. 61)

Summers, G., & Feldman, N. S. (1984). Blaming the victim versus blaming the perpetrator: An attributional analysis of spouse abuse. *Journal of Social and Clinical Psychology*, **2**, 339–347. (p. 374)

Sundstrom, E., De Meuse, K. P., & Futrell, D. (1990). Work teams: Applications and effectiveness. *American Psychologist*, **45**, 120–133. (p. 329)

Svenson, O. (1981). Are we all less risky and more skillful than our fellow drivers? *Acta Psychologica*, **47**, 143–148. (p. 58)

Swann, W. B., Jr. (1984). Quest for accuracy in person perception: A matter of pragmatics. *Psychological Review*, **91**, 457–475. (p. 125)

Swann, W. B., Jr. (1987). Identity negotiation: Where two roads meet. *Journal of Personality and Social Psychology*, **53**, 1038-1051. (p. 123)

Swann, W. B., Jr. (1996). *Self-traps: The elusive quest for higher self-esteem.* New York: Freeman. (p. 54)

Swann, W. B., Jr. (1997). The trouble with change: Self-verification and allegiance to the self. *Psychological Science*, **8**, 177–180. (p. 64)

Swann, W. B., Jr., & Ely, R. J. (1984). A battle of wills: Self-verification versus behavioral confirmation. *Journal of Personality and Social Psychology*, **46**, 1287–1302. (p. 123)

Swann, W. B., Jr., & Gill, M. J. (1997). Confidence and accuracy in person perception: Do we know what we think we know about our relationship partners? *Journal of Personality and Social Psychology*, **73**, 747–757. (p. 107)

Swann, W. B., Jr., & Giuliano, T. (1987). Confirmatory search strategies in social interaction: How, when, why, and with what consequences. *Journal of Social and Clinical Psychology*, **5**, 511–524. (p. 565)

Swann, W. B., Jr., Giuliano, T., & Wegner, D. M. (1982). Where leading questions can lead: The power of conjecture in social interaction. *Journal of Personality and Social Psychology*, **42**, 1025–1035. (p. 274)

Swann, W. B., Jr., & Predmore, S. C. (1985). Intimates as agents of social support: Sources of consolation or despair? *Journal of Personality and Social Psychology*, **49**, 1609–1617. (p. 465)

Swann, W. B., Jr., & Read, S. J. (1981). Acquiring self-knowledge: The search for feedback that fits. *Journal of Personality and Social Psychology*, **41**, 1119–1128. (p. 108)

Swann, W. B., Jr., & Schroeder, D. G. (1994). The search for beauty and truth: A framework for understanding reactions to evaluations. *Personality and Social Psychology Bulletin*, in press. (p. 108)

Swann, W. B., Jr., Stein-Seroussi, A., & Giesler, R. B. (1992). Why people self-verify. *Journal of Personality and Social Psychology*, **62**, 392–401. (p. 108)

Swann, W. B., Jr., Stein-Seroussi, A., & McNulty, S. E. (1992). Outcasts in a white lie society. The enigmatic worlds of people with negative self-conceptions. *Journal of Personality and Social Psychology*, **62**, 618–624. (p. 108)

Swann, W. B., Jr., Wenzlaff, R. M., Krull, D. S., & Pelham, B. W. (1991). Seeking truth, reaping despair: Depression, self-verification and selection of relationship partners. *Journal of Abnormal Psychology*, **101**, 293–306. (pp. 108, 449, 572)

Swap, W. C. (1977). Interpersonal attraction and repeated exposure to rewarders and punishers. *Personality and Social Psychology Bulletin*, **3**, 248–251. (p. 432)

Swedish Information Service (1980). *Social change in Sweden*, September, No. 19, p. 5. (Published by the Swedish Consulate General, 825 Third Avenue, New York, N.Y. 10022.) (p. 424)

Sweeney, J. (1973). An experimental investigation of the free rider problem. *Social Science Research*, **2**, 277–292. (p. 301)

Sweeney, L. T., & Haney, C. (1992). The influence of race on sentencing: A meta-analytic review of experimental studies. *Behavioral Sciences and the Law,* **10**, 179–195. (p. 614)

Sweeney, P. D., Anderson, K., & Bailey, S. (1986). Attributional style in depression: A meta-analytic review. *Journal of Personality and Social Psychology,* **50**, 947–991. (p. 571)

Swim, J., Borgida, E., Maruyama, G., & Myers, D. G. (1989). Joan McKay vs. John McKay: Do gender stereotypes bias evaluations? *Psychological Bulletin,* **105**, 409–429. (p. 346)

Swim, J. K. (1994). Perceived versus meta-analytic effect sizes: An assessment of the accuracy of gender stereotypes. *Journal of Personality and Social Psychology,* **66**, 21–36. (pp. 184, 345)

Swim, J. K., Aikin, K. J., Hall, W. S., & Hunter, B. A. (1995). Sexism and racism: Old-fashioned and modern prejudices. *Journal of Personality and Social Psychology,* **68**, 199–214. (p. 347)

Swim, J. K., & Cohen, L. L. (1997). Overt, covert, and subtle sexism. *Psychology of Women Quarterly,* **21**, 103–118. (p. 347)

Swim, J. K., Cohen, L. L., & Hyers, L. L. (1998). Experiencing everyday prejudice and discrimination. In J. K. Swim & C. Stangor (eds.), *Prejudice: The target's perspective.* San Diego: Academic Press. (p. 368)

Swim, J. K., Ferguson, M. J., & Hyers, L. L. (1998). Avoiding stigma by association: Subtle prejudice against lesbians in the form of social distancing. *Basic and Applied Social Psychology,* in press. (p. 233)

Swim, J. K., & Hyers, L. L. (1998). Excuse me—What did you just say?!: Women's public and private reactions to sexist remarks. *Journal of Experimental Social Psychology,* in press. (p. 227)

Swim, J. K., & Stangor, C. (eds.) (1998). *Prejudice: The target's perspective.* San Diego: Academic Press. (p. 352)

Symons, C. S., & Johnson, B. T. (1997). The self-reference effect in memory: A meta-analysis. *Psychological Bulletin,* **121**, 371–394. (p. 39)

Symons, D. (interviewed by S. Keen). (1981, February). Eros and alley cop. *Psychology Today,* p. 54. (p. 438)

Tajfel, H. (1970, November). Experiments in intergroup discrimination. *Scientific American,* pp. 96–102. (p. 353)

Tajfel, H. (1981). *Human groups and social categories: Studies in social psychology.* London: Cambridge University Press. (p. 353)

Tajfel, H. (1982). Social psychology of intergroup relations. *Annual Review of Psychology,* **33**, 1–39. (p. 353)

Tajfel, H., & Billig, M. (1974). Familiarity and categorization in intergroup behavior. *Journal of Experimental Social Psychology,* **10**, 159–170. (p. 353)

Takooshian, H., & Bodinger, H. (1982). By stander indifference to street crime. In L. Savitz & N. Johnston (Eds.), *Contemporary criminology.* New York: Wiley. (p. 489)

Talbert, B. (1997, February 2). Bob Talbert's quote bag. *Detroit Free Press,* p. 5E, quoting *Allure* magazine. (p. 62)

Tang, S-H., & Hall, V. C. (1994). The overjustification effect: A meta-analysis. *Applied Cognitive Psychology,* in press. (p. 160)

Tanke, E. D., & Tanke, T. J. (1979). Getting off a slippery slope: Social science in the judicial processes. *American Psychologist,* **34**, 1130–1138. (p. 628)

Tannen, D. (1990). *You just don't understand: Women and men in conversation.* New York: Morrow. (p. 184)

Tapp, J. L. (1980). Psychological and policy perspectives on the law: Reflections on a decade. *Journal of Social Issues,* **36**(2), 165–192. (p. 628)

Tate, E., Hawrish, E., & Clark, S. (1974). Communication variables in jury selection. *Journal of Communication,* **24**, 130-139. (p. 623)

Taubes, G. (1992). Violence epidemiologists tests of hazards of gun ownership. *Science,* **258**, 213–215. (p. 425)

Tavris, C. (1988). Beyond cartoon killings: Comments on two overlooked effects of television. In S. Oskamp (ed.), *Television as a social issue.* Newbury Park, CA: Sage. (p. 421)

Taylor, D. A., Gould, R. J., & Brounstein, P. J. (1981). Effects of personalistic self-disclosure. *Personality and Social Psychology Bulletin,* **7**, 487–492. (p. 463)

Taylor, D. G., Sheatsley, P. B., & Greeley, A. M. (1978). Attitudes toward racial integration. *Scientific American,* **238**(6), 42–49. (p. 147)

Taylor, D. M., & Doria, J. R. (1981). Self-serving and group-serving bias in attribution. *Journal of Social Psychology,* **113**, 201–211. (p. 68)

Taylor, D. M., Wright, S. C., Moghaddam, F. M., & Lalonde, R. N. (1990). The personal/group discrimination discrepancy: Perceiving my group, but not myself, to be a target for discrimination. *Personality and Social Psychology Bulletin,* **16**, 254–262. (p. 347)

Taylor, S. E. (1979). Remarks at symposium on social psychology and medicine, American Psychological Association convention. (p. 53)

Taylor, S. E. (1981). A categorization approach to stereotyping. In D. L. Hamilton (Ed.), *Cognitive processes in stereotyping and intergroup be-havior.* Hillsdale, N.J.: Erlbaum. (pp. 365, 376)

Taylor, S. E. (1989). *Positive illusions: Creative self-deception and the healthy mind.* New York: Basic Books. (pp. 395, 570)

Taylor, S. E., Crocker, J., Fiske, S. T., Sprinzen, M., & Winkler, J. D. (1979). The generalizability of salience effects. *Journal of Personality and Social Psychology,* **37**, 357–368. (p. 367)

Taylor, S. E., & Fiske, S. T. (1978). Salience, attention, and attribution: Top of the head phenomena. In L. Berkowitz (Ed.), *Advances in experimental social psychology* (Vol. 11). New York: Academic Press. (p. 367)

Taylor, S. E., Repetti, R. L., & Seeman, T. (1997). Health psychology: What is an unhealthy environment and how does it get under the skin? *Annual Review of Psychology,* **48**, 411–447. (p. 591)

Taylor, S. P., & Chermack, S. T. (1993). Alcohol, drugs and human physical aggression. *Journal of Studies on Alcohol,* Supplement No. **11**, 78–88. (p. 387)

Taylor, S. P., & Pisano, R. (1971). Physical aggression as a function of frustration and physical attack. *Journal of Social Psychology,* **84**, 261–267. (p. 403)

Tedeschi, J. T., Nesler, M., & Taylor, E. (1987). Misattribution and the bogus pipeline: A test of dissonance and impression management theories. Paper presented at the American Psychological Association convention. (p. 152)

Teger, A. I. (1980). *Too much invested to quit.* New York: Pergamon Press. (p. 520)

Teigen, K. H. (1986). Old truths or fresh insights? A study of students' evaluations of proverbs. *British Journal of Social Psychology,* **25**, 43–50. (p. 17)

Telch, M. J., Killen, J. D., McAlister, A. L., Perry, C. L., & Maccoby, N. (1981). Long-term follow-up of a pilot project on smoking prevention with adolescents. Paper presented at the American Psychological Association convention. (p. 286)

Tennen, H., & Affleck, G. (1987). The costs and benefits of optimistic explanations and dispositional optimism. *Journal of Personality,* **55**, 377–393. (p. 584)

Tennov, D. (1979). *Love and limerence: The experience of being in love.* New York: Stein and Day, p. 22. (p. 498)

Tepperman & Curtis (1995). A life satisfaction scale. *Social Indicators Research,* **35**, 255-270. (p. 593)

Tesser, A. (1988). Toward a self-evaluation maintenance model of social behavior. In L. Berkowitz (Ed.), *Advances in experimental social psychology,* Vol. 21. San Diego, Ca.: Academic Press. (p. 65)

Tesser, A., Martin, L., & Mendolia, M. (1995). The impact of thought on attitude extremity and attitude-behavior consistency. In R. E. Petty and J. A Krosnick (Eds.), *Attitude strength: Antecedents and consequences.* Hillsdale, NJ: Erlbaum. (p. 314)

Tesser, A., Millar, M., & Moore, J. (1988). Some affective consequences of social comparison and reflection processes: The pain and pleasure of being close. *Journal of Personality and Social Psychology,* **54**, 49–61. (p. 356)

Tesser, A., Rosen, S., & Conlee, M. C. (1972). News valence and available recipient as determinants of news transmission. *Sociometry*, 35, 619–628. (p. 141)

Tetlock, P. E. (1981). Pre- to post-election shifts in presidential rhetoric: Impression management or cognitive adjustment. *Journal of Personality and Social Psychology*, 41, 207–212. (p. 141)

Tetlock, P. E. (1983). Accountability and complexity of thought. *Journal of Personality and Social Psychology*, 45, 74–83. (p. 141)

Tetlock, P. E. (1985). Integrative complexity of American and Soviet foreign policy rhetoric: A time-series analysis. *Journal of Personality and Social Psychology*, 49, 1565–1585. (p. 550)

Tetlock, P. E. (1988). Monitoring the integrative complexity of American and Soviet policy rhetoric: What can be learned? *Journal of Social Issues*, 44, 101–131. (p. 531)

Tetlock, P. E., Peterson, R. S., McGuire, C., Chang, S., & Feld, P. (1992). Assessing political group dynamics: A test of the groupthink model. *Journal of Personality and Social Psychology*, 63, 403–425. (p. 320)

t'Hart, P. (1998). Prevening groupthink revisited: Evaluating and reforming groups in government. *Organizational Behavior and Human Decision Processes*, in press. (p. 320)

Thibodeau, R. (1989). From racism to tokenism: The changing face of blacks in *New Yorker* cartoons. *Public Opinion Quarterly*, 53, 482–494. (p. 358)

Thomas, G. C., & Batson, C. D. (1981). Effect of helping under normative pressure on self-perceived altruism. *Social Psychology Quarterly*, 44, 127–131. (p. 510)

Thomas, G. C., Batson, C. D., & Coke, J. S. (1981). Do Good Samaritans discourage helpfulness? Self-perceived altruism after exposure to highly helpful others. *Journal of Personality and Social Psychology*, 40, 194–200. (p. 510)

Thomas, K. W., & Pondy, L. R. (1977). Toward an "intent" model of conflict management among principal parties. *Human Relations*, 30, 1089–1102. (p. 532)

Thomas, L. (1978). Hubris in science? *Science*, 200, 1459–1462. (p. 568)

Thomas, L. (1981). Quoted by J. L. Powell. Testimony before the Senate Subcommittee on Science, Technology and Space, April 22. (p. 385)

Thompson, L. (1990a). An examination of naive and experienced negotiators. *Journal of Personality and Social Psychology*, 59, 82–90. (p. 548)

Thompson, L. (1990b). The influence of experience on negotiation performance. *Journal of Experimental Social Psychology*, 26, 528–544. (p. 548)

Thompson, L. (1998). *The mind and heart of the negotiator*. Upper Saddle River, NJ: Prentice-Hall. (p. 548)

Thompson, L., & Hrebec, D. (1996). Lose-lose agreements in interdependent decision making. *Psychological Bulletin*, 120, 396–409. (p. 547)

Thompson, L., Valley, K. L., & Kramer, R. M. (1995). The bittersweet feeling of success: An examination of social perception in negotiation. *Journal of Experimental Social Psychology*, 31, 467–492. (p. 548)

Thompson, L. L., & Crocker, J. (1985). Prejudice following threat to the self-concept. Effects of performance expectations and attributions. Unpublished manuscript, Northwestern University. (p. 361)

Thompson, W. C., Cowan, C. L., & Rosenhan, D. L. (1980). Focus of attention mediates the impact of negative affect on altruism. *Journal of Personality and Social Psychology*, 38, 291–300. (p. 497)

Thompson, W. C., Fong, G. T., & Rosenhan, D. L. (1981). Inadmissible evidence and juror verdicts. *Journal of Personality and Social Psychology*, 40, 453–463. (p. 629)

Thompson, W. C., & Schumann, E. L. (1987). Interpretation of statistical evidence in criminal trials. *Law and Human Behavior*, 11, 167–187. (p. 621)

Thorndike, R. L. (1968). Review of *Pygmalion in the classroom*. *American Educational Research Journal*, 5, 707–711. (p. 121)

Thornton, B., & Moore, S. (1993). Physical attractiveness contrast effect: Implications for self-esteem and evaluations of the social self. *Personality and Social Psychology Bulletin*, 19, 474–480. (p. 441)

Tice, D. M. (1992). Self-concept change and self-presentation: The looking glass self is also a magnifying glass. *Journal of Personality and Social Psychology*, 63, 435–451. (p. 158)

Tice, D. M., & Baumeister, R. F. (1985). Masculinity inhibits helping in emergencies: Personality does predict the bystander effect. *Journal of Personality and Social Psychology*, 49, 420–428. (p. 499)

Tice, D. M., & Baumeister, R. F. (1997). Longitudinal study of procrastination, performance, stress, and health: The costs and benefits of dawdling. *Psychological Science*, 8, 454–458. (p. 583)

Tice, D. M., Butler, J. L., Muraven, M. B., & Stillwell, A. M. (1995). When modesty prevails: Differential favorability of self-presentation to friends and strangers. *Journal of Personality and Social Psychology*, 69, 1120–1138. (p. 72)

Time (1992, March 30). The not so merry wife of Windsor. Pp. 38–39. (p. 467)

Timko, C., & Moos, R. H. (1989). Choice, control, and adaptation among elderly residents of sheltered care settings. *Journal of Applied Social Psychology*, 19, 636–655. (p. 53)

Tindale, R. S., Davis, J. H., Vollrath, D. A., Nagao, D. H., & Hinsz, V. B. (1990). Asymmetrical social infuence in freely interacting groups: A test of three models. *Journal of Personality and Social Psychology*, 58, 438–449. (p. 626)

Tobin, R. J., & Eagles, M. (1992). U.S. and Canadian attitudes toward international interactions: A cross-national test of the double-standard hypothesis. *Basic and Applied Social Psychology*, 13, 447–459. (p. 530)

Toronto News (1977, July 26). (p. 56)

Towson, S. M. J., & Zanna, M. P. (1983). Retaliation against sexual assault: Self-defense or public duty? *Psychology of Women Quarterly*, 8, 89–99. (p. 614)

Travis, L. E. (1925). The effect of a small audience upon eye-hand coordination. *Journal of Abnormal and Social Psychology*, 20, 142–146. (p. 293)

Triandis, H. C. (1981). Some dimensions of intercultural variation and their implications for interpersonal behavior. Paper presented at the American Psychological Association convention. (p. 176)

Triandis, H. C. (1982). Incongruence between intentions and behavior: A review. Paper presented at the American Psychological Association convention. (p. 133)

Triandis, H. C. (1994). *Culture and social behavior*. New York: McGraw-Hill. (pp. 43, 110, 199, 398, 468, 546)

Triandis, H. C., Bontempo, R., Villareal, M. J., Asai, M., & Lucca, N. (1988). Individualism and collectivism: Cross-cultural perspectives on self-ingroup relationships. *Journal of Personality and Social Psychology*, 54, 323–338. (pp. 242, 458)

Triandis, H. C., McCusker, C., Betancourt, H., Iwao, S., Leung, K., Salazar, J. M., Setiadi, B., Sinha, J. B. P., Touzard, H., & Zaleski, Z. (1993). An etic-emic analysis of individualism and collectivism. *Journal of Cross-Cultural Psychology*, 24, 366–383. (p. 45)

Trimble, D. E. (1993). Meta-analysis of altruism and intrinsic and extrinsic religiousness. Paper presented at the Eastern Psychological Association convention. (p. 501)

Trimble, J. E. (1988). Stereotypical images, American Indians, and prejudice. In P. A. Katz & D. A. Taylor (Eds.), *Eliminating racism: Profiles in controversy*. New York: Plenum. (p. 359)

Triplett, N. (1898). The dynamogenic factors in pacemaking and competition. *American Journal of Psychology*, 9, 507–533. (p. 293)

Trolier, T. K., & Hamilton, D. L. (1986). Variables influencing judgments of correlational relations. *Journal of Personality and Social Psychology*, 50, 879–888. (p. 114)

Trost, M. R., Maass, A., & Kenrick, D. T. (1992). Minority influence: Personal relevance biases cognitive processes and reverses private acceptance. *Journal of Experimental Social Psychology, 28*, 234–254. (p. 326)

Tumin, M. M. (1958). Readiness and resistance to desegregation: A social portrait of the hard core. *Social Forces, 36*, 256–273. (p. 360)

Turner, C. W., Hesse, B. W., & Peterson-Lewis, S. (1986). Naturalistic studies of the long-term effects of television violence. *Journal of Social Issues, 42*(3), 51–74. (p. 412)

Turner, E. A., & Pratkanis, A. R. (1994). An experimental investigation of gender discrimination in childcare employment. Western Psychological Association convention. (p. 335)

Turner, J. C. (1981). The experimental social psychology of intergroup behaviour. In J. Turner & H. Giles (eds.), *Intergroup behavior*. Oxford, England: Blackwell. (p. 353)

Turner, J. C. (1984). Social identification and psychological group formation. In H. Tajfel (Ed.), *The social dimensions: European developments in social psychology*, vol. 2. London: Cambridge University Press. (p. 353)

Turner, J. C. (1987). *Rediscovering the social group: A self-categorization theory*. New York: Basil Blackwell. (pp. 292, 353)

Turner, J. C. (1991). *Social influence*. Milton Keynes, England: Open University Press. (p. 353)

Turner, M. E., & Pratkanis, A. R. (1993). Effects of preferential and meritorious selection on performance: An examination of intuitive and self-handicapping perspectives. *Personality and Social Psychology Bulletin, 19*, 47–58. (p. 72)

Turner, M. E., & Pratkanis, A. R. (1994). Affirmative action as help: A review of recipient reactions to preferential selection and affirmative action. *Basic and Applied Social Psychology, 15*, 43–69. (p. 335)

Turner, M. E., & Pratkanis, A. R. (1994). Social identity maintenance prescriptions for preventing groupthink: Reducing identity protection and enhancing intellectual conflict. *International Journal of Conflict Management, 5*, 254–270. (p. 318)

Turner, M. E., & Pratkanis, A. R. (1997). Mitigating groupthink by stimulating constructive conflict. In C. K. W. De Dreu & E. Van de Vliert (eds.), *Using conflict in organizations*. London: Sage. (p. 320)

Turner, M. E., Pratkanis, A. R., Probasco, P., & Leve, C. (1992). Threat cohesion, and group effectiveness: Testing a social identity maintenance perspective on groupthink. *Journal of Personality and Social Psychology, 63*, 781–796. (p. 318)

TV Guide (1977, January 26), pp. 5–10. (p. 412)

Tversky, A. (1985, June). Quoted by Kevin McKean, Decisions, decisions. *Discover*, pp. 22–31. (p. 124)

Tversky, A., & Kahneman, D. (1973). Availability: A neuristic for judging frequency and probability. *Cognitive Psychology, 5*, 207–302. (p. 112)

Tverksy, A., & Kahneman, D. (1974). Judgment under uncertainty: Heuristics and biases. *Science, 185*, 1123–1131. (pp. 113, 115)

Tversky, A., & Kahneman, D. (1983). Extensional versus intuitive reasoning: The conjunction fallacy in probability judgment. *Psychological Review, 90*, 293–315. (p. 110)

Tyler, T. R. (1988). What is procedural justice? Criteria used by citizens to assess the fairness of legal procedures. *Law and Society Review, 22*, 103–135.(p. 600)

Tyler, T. R. (1989). The psychology of procedural justice: A test of the group-value model. *Journal of Personality and Social Psychology, 57*, 830–838. (p. 600)

Tyler, T. R., & Cook, F. L. (1984). The mass media and judgments of risk: Distinguishing impact on personal and societal level judgments. *Journal of Personality and Social Psychology, 47*, 693–708. (p. 418)

Tyler, T. R., & Lind, E. A. (1990). Intrinsic versus community-based justice models: When does group membership matter? *Journal of Social Issues, 46*, 83–94. (p. 508)

Tzeng, M. (1992). The effects of socioeconomic heterogamy and changes on marital dissolution for first marriages. *Journal of Marriage and the Family, 54*, 609–619. (p. 468)

U.S. Department of Justice. (1980). *Sourcebook of criminal justice statistics.* Washington, D.C.: Government Printing Office. (p. 601)

Uchino, B. N., Cacioppo, J. T., & Kiecolt-Glaser, J. K. (1996). The relationship between social support and physiological processes: A review with emphasis on underlying mechanisms and implications for health. *Psychological Bulletin, 119*, 488–531. (p. 591)

Ugwuegbu, C. E. (1979). Racial and evidential factors in juror attribution of legal responsibility. *Journal of Experimental Social Psychology, 15*, 133–146. (p. 614)

Uleman, J. S. (1989). A framework for thinking intentionally about unintended thoughts. In J. S. Uleman & J. A. Bargh (Eds.), *Unintended thought: The limits of awareness, intention, and control*. New York: Guilford. (p. 81)

Umberson, D., & Hughes, M. (1987). The impact of physical attractiveness on achievement and psychological well-being. *Social Psychology Quarterly, 50*, 227–236. (p. 437)

Underwood, B., & Moore, B. (1982). Perspective-taking and altruism. *Psychological Bulletin, 91*, 143–173. (p. 497)

Unger, R. K. (1979). Whom does helping help? Paper presented at the Eastern Psychological Association convention, April. (p. 475)

Unger, R. K. (1985). Epistomological consistency and its scientific implications. *American Psychologist, 40*, 1413–1414. (p. 11)

United Nations (1991). *The world's women 1970–1990: Trends and statistics.* New York: United Nations. (pp. 198, 347)

UPI. (1970/1967). September 23, 1967. Cited by P. G. Zimbardo, in The human choice: Individuation, reason, and order versus deindividuation, impulse, and chaos. In W. J. Arnold & D. Levine (Eds.), *Nebraska symposium on motivation, 1969*. Lincoln: University of Nebraska Press. (p. 304)

Usher, J. M. (1992). Research and theory related to female reproduction: Implications for clinical psychology. *British Journal of Clinical Psychology, 31*, 129–151. (p. 580)

Vaillant, G. E. (1977). *Adaptation to life.* Boston: Little, Brown. (p. 101)

Valliant, G. E. (1997). Report on distress and longevity. Paper presented to the American Psychiatric Association convention. (p. 582)

Vallone, R. P., Griffin, D. W., Lin, S., & Ross, L. (1990). Overconfident prediction of future actions and outcomes by self and others. *Journal of Personality and Social Psychology, 58*, 582–592. (p. 107)

Vallone, R. P., Ross, L., & Lepper, M. R. (1985). The hostile media phenomenon: Biased perception and perceptions of media bias in coverage of the "Beirut Massacre." *Journal of Personality and Social Psychology, 49*, 577–585. (p. 94, 95)

Vancouver, J. B., Rubin, B., & Kerr, N. L. (1991). Sex composition of groups and member motivation III: Motivational losses at a feminine task. *Basic and Applied Social Psychology, 12*, 133–144. (p. 303)

Van der Plight, J., Eiser, J. R., & Spears, R. (1987). Comparative judgments and preferences: The influence of the number of response alternatives. *British Journal of Social Psychology, 26*, 269–280. (p. 25)

Vanderslice, V. J., Rice, R. W., & Julian, J. W. (1987). The effects of participation in decision-making on worker satisfaction and productivity: An organizational simulation. *Journal of Applied Social Psychology, 17*, 158–170. (p. 329)

Van Knippenberg, D., & Wilke, H. (1992). Prototypicality of arguments and conformity to ingroup norms. *European Journal of Social Psychology, 22*, 141–155. (p. 260)

Van Lange, P. A. M. (1991). Being better but not smarter than others: The Muhammad Ali effect at work in interpersonal situations. *Personality and Social Psychology Bulletin, 17*, 689–693. (p. 59)

Van Lange, P. A. M., Taris, T. W., & Vonk, R. (1997). Dilemmas of academic practice: perceptions of superiority among social psychologists. *European Journal of Social Psychology, 27*, 675–685. (p. 59)

Van Leeuwen, M. S. (1978). A cross-cultural examination of psychological differentiation in males and females. *International Journal of Psychology, 13*, 87–122. (p. 199)

Vanman, E. J., Paul, B. Y., Kaplan, D. L., & Miller, N. (1990). Facial electro-myography differentiates racial bias in imagined cooperative settings. *Psychophysiology, 27*, 563. (p. 343)

Van Vugt, M., Van Lange, P. A. M., & Meertens, R. M. (1996). Commuting by car or public transportation? A social dilemma analysis of travel mode judgements. *European Journal of Social Psychology, 26*, 373–395. (p. 525)

Van Yperen, N. W., & Buunk, B. P. (1990). A longitudinal study of equity and satisfaction in intimate relationships. *European Journal of Social Psychology, 20*, 287–309. (p. 463)

Vaughan, K. B., & Lanzetta, J. T. (1981). The effect of modification of expressive displays on vicarious emotional arousal. *Journal of Experimental Social Psychology, 17*, 16–30. (p. 158)

Vaux, A. (1988). Social and personal factors in loneliness. *Journal of Social and Clinical Psychology, 6*, 462–471. (p. 576)

Verplanken, B. (1991). Persuasive communication of risk information: A test of cue versus message processing effects in a field experiment. *Personality and Social Psychology Bulletin, 17*, 188–193. (p. 254)

Vidmar, N. (1974). Retributive and utilitarian motives and other correlates of Canadian attitudes toward the death penalty. *Canadian Psychologist, 15*, 337-356. (p. 623)

Vidmar, N. (1979). The other issues in jury simulation research. *Law and Human Behavior, 3*, 95–106. (p. 628)

Vidmar, N., & Laird, N. M. (1983). Adversary social roles: Their effects on witnesses' communication of evidence and the assessments of adjudicators. *Journal of Personality and Social Psychology, 44*, 888–898. (p. 608)

Visher, C. A. (1987). Juror decision making: The importance of evidence. *Law and Human Behavior, 11*, 1–17. (pp. 602, 613)

Visintainer, M. A., & Seligman, M. E. (1983, July/August). The hope factor. *American Health*, pp. 59–61. (p. 582)

Vitelli, R. (1988). The crisis issue assessed: An empirical analysis. *Basic and Applied Social Psychology, 9*, 301–309. (p. 30)

Vivian, J. E., & Berkowitz, N. H. (1993). Anticipated outgroup evaluations and intergroup bias. *European Journal of Social Psychology, 23*, 513–524. (p. 356)

Vivian, J., Hewstone, M., & Brown, R. (1997). Intergroup contact: Theoretical and empirical developments. In R. Ben-Ari & Y. Rich (eds.), *Enhancing education*

in heterogeneous schools: Theory and application*. Ramat-Gan: Bar-Ilan University Press. (p. 544)

Vollrath, D. A., Sheppard, B. H., Hinsz, V. B., & Davis, J. H. (1989). Memory performance by decision-making groups and individuals. *Organizational Behavior and Human Decision Processes, 43*, 289–300. (p. 627)

Vonk, R. (1993). The negativity effect in trait ratings and in open-ended descriptions of persons. *Personality and Social Psychology Bulletin, 19*, 269–278. (p. 83)

Vorauer, J. D., & Miller, D. T. (1997). Failure to recognize the effect of implicit social influence on the presentation of self. *Journal of Personality and Social Psychology, 73*, 281–295. (p. 37)

Vorauer, J. D., & Ratner, R. K. (1996). Who's going to make the first move? Pluralistic ignorance as an impediment to relationsip formation. *Journal of Social and Personal Relationships, 13*, 483–506. (p. 315)

Wachtler, J., & Counselman, E. (1981). When increasing liking for a communicator decreases opinion change: An attribution analysis of attractiveness. *Journal of Experimental Social Psychology, 17*, 386–395. (p. 258)

Wagner, U., Hewstone, M., & Machleit, U. (1989). Contact and prejudice between Germans and Turks: A correlational study. *Human Relations, 42*, 561-574. (p. 535)

Wagstaff, G. (1982). Attitudes to rape: The "just world" strikes again? *Bulletin of the British Psychological Society, 35*, 277–279. (p. 374)

Wagstaff, G. F. (1983). Attitudes to poverty, the Protestant ethic, and political affiliation: A preliminary investigation. *Social Behavior and Personality, 11*, 45–47. (p. 91)

Walker, M., Harriman, S., & Costello, S. (1980). The influence of appearance on compliance with a request. *Journal of Social Psychology, 112*, 159–160. (p. 233)

Walker, W. D., Rowe, R. C., & Quinsey, V. L. (1993). Authoritarianism and sexual aggression. *Journal of Personality and Social Psychology, 65*, 1036-1045. (p. 408)

Wallace, D. S., Lord, C. G., & Bond, C. F., Jr. (1996). Which behaviors do attitudes predict: Review and meta-analysis of 60 years' research. Unpublished manuscript, Ohio University. (p. 134)

Wallace, M. *New York Times*, November 25, 1969. (p. 224)

Wallach, M. A., & Wallach, L. (1983). *Psychology's sanction for selfishness: The error of egoism in theory and therapy*. San Francisco: Freeman. (p. 480)

Wallbott, H. G. (1988). In and out of context: Influences of facial expression and context information on emotion attributions. *British Journal of Social Psychology, 27*, 357–369. (p. 95)

Walster (Hatfield), E. (1965). The effect of self-esteem on romantic liking. *Journal of*

Experimental Social Psychology, 1*, 184–197. (p. 448)

Walster (Hatfield), E., Aronson, V., Abrahams, D., & Rottman, L. (1966). Importance of physical attractiveness in dating behavior. *Journal of Personality and Social Psychology, 4*, 508–516. (p. 434)

Walster (Hatfield), E., & Festinger, L. (1962). The effectiveness of "overheard" persuasive communications. *Journal of Abnormal and Social Psychology, 65*, 395–402. (p. 258)

Walster (Hatfield), E., Walster, G. W., & Berscheid, E. (1978). *Equity: Theory and research*. Boston: Allyn and Bacon. (p. 527)

Ward, W. C., & Jenkins, H. M. (1965). The display of information and the judgment of contingency. *Canadian Journal of Psychology, 19*, 231–241. (p. 113)

Warnick, D. H., & Sanders, G. S. (1980). The effects of group discussion on eyewitness accuracy. *Journal of Applied Social Psychology, 10*, 249–259. (p. 324)

Warr, P., & Payne, R. (1982). Experiences of strain and pleasure among British adults. *Social Science and Medicine, 16*, 1691–1697. (p. 590)

Wason, P. C. (1960). On the failure to eliminate hypotheses in a conceptual task. *Quarterly Journal of Experimental Psychology, 12*, 129–140. (p. 108)

Watson, R. I., Jr. (1973). Investigation into deindividuation using a cross-cultural survey technique. *Journal of Personality and Social Psychology, 25*, 342–345. (p. 306)

Watts, W. A. (1967). Relative persistence of opinion change induced by active compared to passive participation. *Journal of Personality and Social Psychology, 5*, 4–15. (p. 136)

Weary, G., & Edwards, J. A. (1994). Social cognition and clinical psychology: Anxiety, depression, and the processing of social information. In R. Wyer & T. Srull (eds.), *Handbook of social cognition*, vol. 2. Hillsdale, NJ: Erlbaum. (p. 117)

Weary, G., Harvey, J. H., Schwieger, P., Olson, C. T., Perloff, R., & Pritchard, S. (1982). Self-presentation and the moderation of self-serving biases. *Social Cognition, 1*, 140–159. (p. 72)

Webster, D. M. (1993). Motivated augmentation and reduction of the overattribution bias. *Journal of Personality and Social Psychology, 65*, 261–271. (p. 91)

Wegner, D. M., & Erber, R. (1992). The hyperaccessibility of suppressed thoughts. *Journal of Personality and Social Psychology, 63*, 903–912. (p. 342)

Wehr, P. (1979). *Conflict regulation*. Boulder, Colo.: Westview Press. (p. 551)

Weiner, B. (1980). A cognitive (attribution)-emotion-action model of motivated behavior: An analysis of judgments of help-giving. *Journal of Personality and Social Psychology, 39*, 186–200. (p. 482)

Weiner, B. (1981). The emotional consequences of causal ascriptions. Unpublished manuscript, UCLA. (p. 390)

Weiner, B. (1985). "Spontaneous" causal thinking. *Psychological Bulletin*, **97**, 74–84. (p. 78)

Weiner, B. (1995). Judgments of responsibility: A foundation for a theory of social conduct. New York: Guilford. (p. 79)

Weinstein, N. D. (1980). Unrealistic optimism about future life events. *Journal of Personality and Social Psychology*, **39**, 806–820. (p. 59)

Weinstein, N. D. (1982). Unrealistic optimism about susceptibility to health problems. *Journal of Behavioral Medicine*, **5**, 441–460. (p. 59)

Weiss, J., & Brown, P. (1976). Self-insight error in the explanation of mood. Unpublished manuscript, Harvard University. (p. 46)

Wells, G. L. (1984). The psychology of lineup identifications. *Journal of Applied Social Psychology*, **14**, 89–103. (p. 610)

Wells, G. L. (1992). Naked statistical evidence of liability: Is subjective probability enough? *Journal of Personality and Social Psychology*, **62**, 739–752. (p. 622)

Wells, G. L. (1993). What do we know about eyewitness identification? *American Psychologist*, **48**, 553–571. (p. 610)

Wells, G. L., & Bradfield, A. L. (1998). "Good, you identified the suspect": Feedback to eyewitnesses distorts their reports of the witnessing experience. *Journal of Applied Psychology*, in press. (pp. 608, 609)

Wells, G. L., Ferguson, T. J., & Lindsay, R. C. L. (1981). The tractability of eyewitness confidence and its implications for triers of fact. *Journal of Applied Psychology*, **66**, 688–696. (pp. 607, 608)

Wells, G. L., & Leippe, M. R. (1981). How do triers of fact enter the accuracy of eyewitness identification? Memory for peripheral detail can be misleading. *Journal of Applied Psychology*, **66**, 682–687. (p. 602)

Wells, G. L., Lindsay, R. C. L., & Ferguson, T. (1979). Accuracy, confidence, and juror perceptions in eyewitness identification. *Journal of Applied Psychology*, **64**, 440–448. (p. 602)

Wells, G. L., Lindsay, R. C. L., & Tousignant, J. P. (1980). Effects of expert psychological advice on human performance in judging the validity of eyewitness testimony. *Law and Human Behavior*, **4**, 275–285. (p. 602)

Wells, G. L., & Luus, C. A. E. (1990). Police lineups as experiments: Social methodology as a framework for properly conducted lineups. *Personality and Social Psychology Bulletin*, **16**, 106–117. (p. 611)

Wells, G. L., & Murray, D. M. (1983). What can psychology say about the *Neil v.*

Biggers criteria for judging eyewitness accuracy? *Journal of Applied Psychology*, **68**, 347–362. (p. 603)

Wells, G. L., & Petty, R. E. (1980). The effects of overt head movements on persuasion: Compatibility and incompatibility of responses. *Basic and Applied Social Psychology*, **1**, 219–230. (p. 158)

Wells, G. L., & Turtle, J. W. (1987). Eyewitness testimony research: Current knowledge and emergent controversies. *Canadian Journal of Behavioral Science*, **19**, 363–388. (p. 611)

Wells, G. L., Wrightsman, L. S., & Miene, P. K. (1985). The timing of the defense opening statement: Don't wait until the evidence is in. *Journal of Applied Social Psychology*, **15**, 758–772. (p. 267)

Wener, R., Frazier, W., & Farbstein, J. (1987, June). Building better jails. *Psychology Today*, pp. 40–49. (p. 53)

Wenzlaff, R. M., & Prohaska, M. L. (1989). When misery prefers company: Depression, attributions, and responses to others' moods. *Journal of Experimental Social Psychology*, **25**, 220–233. (p. 446)

Werner, C. M., Kagehiro, D. K., & Strube, M. J. (1982). Conviction proneness and the authoritarian juror: Inability to disregard information or attitudinal bias? *Journal of Applied Psychology*, **67**, 629–636. (p. 624)

West, S. G., & Brown, T. J. (1975). Physical attractiveness, the severity of the emergency and helping: A field experiment and interpersonal simulation. *Journal of Experimental Social Psychology*, **11**, 531–538. (p. 503)

West, S. G., Whitney, G., & Schnedler, R. (1975). Helping a motorist in distress: The effects of sex, race, and neighborhood. *Journal of Personality and Social Psychology*, **31**, 691–698. (p. 503)

Westera, D. A., & Bennett, L. R. (1994). Population-focused research: A broad-based survey of teens' attitudes, beliefs, and behaviours. *International Journal of Nursing Studies*, **31**, 521–531. (p. 189)

Weyant, J. M. (1984). Applying social psychology to induce charitable donations. *Journal of Applied Social Psychology*, **14**, 441–447. (p. 507)

Weyant, J. M., & Smith, S. L. (1987). Getting more by asking for less: The effects of request size on donations of charity. *Journal of Applied Social Psychology*, **17**, 392–400. (p. 508)

Wheeler, L., & Kim, Y. (1997). What is beautiful is culturally good: The physical attractiveness stereotype has different content in collectivistic cultures. *Personality and Social Psychology Bulletin*, **23**, 795–800. (p. 436)

Wheeler, L., Koestner, R., & Driver, R. E. (1982). Related attributes in the choice of comparison others: It's there, but it isn't all there is. *Journal of Experimental Social Psychology*, **18**, 489–500. (p. 394)

White, G. L. (1980). Physical attractiveness and courtship progress. *Journal of Personality and Social Psychology*, **39**, 660–668. (p. 435)

White, G. L., & Kight, T. D. (1984). Misattribution of arousal and attraction: Effects of salience of explanations for arousal. *Journal of Experimental Social Psychology*, **20**, 55–64. (p. 455)

White, H. R., Brick, J., & Hansell, S. (1993). A longitudinal investigation of alcohol use and aggression in adolescence. *Journal of Studies on Alcohol*, Supplement No. 11, 62–77. (p. 387)

White, J. A., & Plous, S. (1995). Self-enhancement and social responsibility: On caring more, but doing less, than others. *Journal of Applied Social Psychology*, **25**, 1297–1318. (p. 59)

White, J. W., & Kowalski, R. M. (1994). Deconstructing the myth of the nonaggressive woman. *Psychology of Women Quarterly*, **18**, 487–508. (p. 189)

White, M. J., & Gerstein, L. H. (1987). Helping: The influence of anticipated social sanctions and self-monitoring. *Journal of Personality*, **55**, 41–54. (p. 499)

White, P. A. (1991). Ambiguity in the internal/external distinction in causal attribution. *Journal of Experimental Social Psychology*, **27**, 259–270. (p. 80)

White, P. A., & Younger, D. P. (1988). Differences in the ascription of transient internal states to self and other. *Journal of Experimental Social Psychology*, **24**, 292–309. (p. 85)

White, R. K. (1971, November). Selective inattention. *Psychology Today*, pp. 47–50, 78–84. (p. 145)

White, R. K. (1977). Misperception in the Arab-Israeli conflict. *Journal of Social Issues*, **33**(1), 190–221. (p. 532)

White, R. K. (1996). Why the Serbs fought: Motives and misperceptions. *Peace and Conflict: Journal of Peace Psychology*, **2**, 109–128. (p. 533)

Whitley, B. E., Jr. (1987). The effects of discredited eyewitness testimony: A meta-analysis. *Journal of Social Psychology*, **127**, 209–214. (p. 602)

Whitley, B. E., Jr., & Frieze, I. H. (1985). Children's causal attributions for success and failure in achievement settings: A meta-analysis. *Journal of Educational Psychology*, **77**, 608–616. (p. 55)

Whitley, B. E., Jr., & Lee, S. E. (1997). The relationship of authoritarianism and related constructs to attitudes toward homosexuality. Unpublished manuscript, Ball State University. (p. 363)

Whitman, D. (1996, December 16). I'm OK, you're not. *U.S. News and World Report*, p. 24. (p. 68)

Whitman, R. M., Kramer, M., & Baldridge, B. (1963). Which dream does the patient tell? *Archives of General Psychology*, **8**, 277–282. (p. 565)

Whittaker, J. O., & Meade, R. D. (1967). Social pressure in the modification and distortion of judgment: A cross-cultural study. *International Journal of Psychology*, **2**, 109–113. (p. 242)

Whyte, G. (1993). Escalating commitment in individual and group decision making: A prospect theory approach. *Organizational Behavior and Human Decision Processes*, **54**, 430–455. (p. 311)

Wicker, A. W. (1969). Attitudes versus actions: The relationship of verbal and overt behavioral responses to attitude objects. *Journal of Social Issues*, **25**, 41–78. (p. 132)

Wicker, A. W. (1971). An examination of the "other variables" explanation of attitude-behavior inconsistency. *Journal of Personality and Social Psychology*, **19**, 18–30. (p. 132)

Wicklund, R. A. (1979). The influence self-awareness on human behavior. *American Scientist*, **67**, 187–193. (p. 88)

Wicklund, R. A. (1982). Self-focused attention and the validity of self-reports. In M. P. Zanna, E. T. Higgins, & C. P. Herman (Eds.), *Consistency in social behavior: The Ontario symposium*, Vol. 2. Hillsdale, N.J.: Erlbaum. (p. 88)

Widom, C. S. (1989). Does violence beget violence? A critical examination of the literature. *Psychological Bulletin*, **106**, 3–28. (p. 397)

Wiegman, O. (1985). Two politicians in a realistic experiment: Attraction, discrepancy, intensity of delivery, and attitude change. *Journal of Applied Social Psychology*, **15**, 673–686. (p. 256)

Wiesel, E. (1985, April 6). The brave Christians who saved Jews from the Nazis. *TV Guide*, pp. 4–6. (p. 474)

Wilder, D. A. (1977). Perception of groups, size of opposition, and social influence. *Journal of Experimental Social Psychology*, **13**, 253–268. (p. 231)

Wilder, D. A. (1978). Perceiving persons as a group: Effect on attributions of causality and beliefs. *Social Psychology*, **41**, 13–23. (p. 365)

Wilder, D. A. (1981). Perceiving persons as a group: Categorization and intergroup relations. In D. L. Hamilton (Ed.). *Cognitive processes in stereotyping and intergroup behavior*. Hillsdale, N.J.: Lawrence Erlbaum. (p. 354)

Wilder, D. A. (1990). Some determinants of the persuasive power of in-groups and out-groups: Organization of information and attribution of independence. *Journal of Personality and Social Psychology*, **59**, 1202–1213. (p. 260)

Wilder, D. A., & Shapiro, P. (1991). Facilitation of outgroup stereotypes by enhanced ingroup identity. *Journal of Experimental Social Psychology*, **27**, 431–452. (p. 356)

Wilder, D. A., & Shapiro, P. N. (1984). Role of out-group cues in determining social identity. *Journal of Personality and Social Psychology*, **47**, 342–348. (p. 538)

Wilder, D. A., & Shapiro, P. N. (1989). Role of competition-induced anxiety in limiting the beneficial impact of positive behavior by out-group members. *Journal of Personality and Social Psychology*, **56**, 60–69. (p. 375)

Wilder, D. A., Simon, A. F., & Faith, M. (1996). Enhancing the impact of counter-stereotypic information: Dispositional attributions for deviance. *Journal of Personality and Social Psychology*, **71**, 276–287. (p. 377)

Wilkes, J. (1987, June). Murder in mind. *Psychology Today*, pp. 27–32. (p. 384)

Wilkinson, G. S. (1990, February). Food sharing in vampire bats. *Scientific American*, **262**, 76–82. (p. 484)

Williams, D. K., Bourgeois, M. J., & Croyle, R. T. (1993). The effects of stealing thunder in criminal and civil trials. *Law and Human Behavior*, **17**, 597–609. (p. 266)

Williams, J. E. (1993). Young adults' views of aging: A nineteen nation study. In M. I. Winkler (ed.), *Documentos: Conferencia del XXIV Congreso Interamericano de Psicologia*. (pp. 101–123) Santiago, Chile: Sociedad Interamericana de Psicologia. (p. 336)

Williams, J. E., & Best, D. L. (1990a). *Measuring sex stereotypes: A multination study*. Newbury Park, CA: Sage. (p. 187)

Williams, J. E., & Best, D. L. (1990b). *Sex and psyche: Gender and self viewed cross-culturally*. Newbury Park, CA: Sage. (pp. 198, 346)

Williams, K. D., Harkins, S., & Latané, B. (1981). Identifiability as a deterrent to social loafing: Two cheering experiments. *Journal of Personality and Social Psychology*, **40**, 303–311. (p. 302)

Williams, K. D., Jackson, J. M., & Karau, S. J. (1992). Collective hedonism: A social loafing analysis of social dilemmas. In D. A. Schroeder (Ed.), *Social dilemmas: Social psychological perspectives*. New York: Praeger. (p. 301)

Williams, K. D., & Karau, S. J. (1991). Social loafing and social compensation: The effects of expectations of coworker performance. *Journal of Personality and Social Psychology*, **61**, 570–581. (p. 303)

Williams, K. D., Nida, S. A., Baca, L. D., & Latané, B. (1989). Social loafing and swimming: Effects of identifiability on individual and relay performance of intercollegiate swimmers. *Basic and Applied Social Psychology*, **10**, 73–81. (p. 302)

Williams, R. (1993). *Anger kills*. New York: Times Books. (p. 581)

Williams, T. M. (Ed.) (1986). *The impact of television: A natural experiment in three communities*. Orlando, Fl.: Academic Press. (p. 414)

Williams, T. M., Zabrack, M. L., Joy, L. A. (1982). The portrayal of aggression on North American television. *Journal of Applied Social Psychology*, **12**, 360-380. (p. 412)

Williamson, G. M., & Clark, M. S. (1989). Providing help and desired relationship type as determinants of changes in moods and self-evaluations. *Journal of Personality and Social Psychology*, **56**, 722–734. (p. 496)

Willis, F. N., & Hamm, H. K. (1980). The use of interpersonal touch in securing compliance. *Journal of Nonverbal Behavior*, **5**, 49–55. (p. 221)

Wills, T. A. (1981). Downward comparison principles in social psychology. *Psychological Bulletin*, **90**, 245–271. (p. 66)

Wilson, D. K., Kaplan, R. M., & Schneiderman, L. J. (1987). Framing of decisions and selections of alternatives in health care. *Social Behaviour*, **2**, 51–59. (pp. 262, 581)

Wilson, D. K., Purdon, S. E., & Wallston, K. A. (1988). Compliance to health recommendations: A theoretical overview of message framing. *Health Education Research*, **3**, 161–171. (p. 262)

Wilson, D. W., & Donnerstein, E. (1979). Anonymity and interracial helping. Paper presented at the Southwestern Psychological Association convention. (p. 504)

Wilson, E. O. (1978). *On human nature*. Cambridge, Mass.: Harvard University Press. (p. 484)

Wilson, G. (1994, March 25). Equal, but different. *The Times Higher Education Supplement, Times of London*. (p. 194)

Wilson, J. P., & Petruska, R. (1984). Motivation, model attributes, and prosocial behavior. *Journal of Personality and Social Psychology*, **46**, 458–468. (p. 499)

Wilson, R. C., Gaft, J. G., Dienst, E. R., Wood, L., & Bavry, J. L. (1975). *College professors and their impact on students*. New York: Wiley. (pp. 270, 313)

Wilson, R. S., & Matheny, A. P., Jr. (1986). Behavior-genetics research in infant temperament: The Louisville twin study. In R. Plomin & J. Dunn (Eds.), *The study of temperament: Changes, continuities, and challenges*. Hillsdale, N.J.: Erlbaum. (p. 387)

Wilson, T. D. (1985). Strangers to ourselves: The origins and accuracy of beliefs about one's own mental states. In J. H. Harvey & G. Weary (Eds.), *Attribution in contemporary psychology*. New York: Academic Press. (p. 48)

Wilson, T. D., Dunn, D. S., Kraft, D., & Lisle, D. J. (1989). Introspection, attitude change, and attitude-behavior consistency: The disruptive effects of explaining why we feel the way we do. In L. Berkowitz (Eds.), *Advances in experimental social psychology*, Vol. 22. San Diego, Ca.: Academic Press. (p. 48)

Wilson, T. D., Laser, P. S., & Stone, J. I. (1982). Judging the predictors of one's mood: Accuracy and the use of shared theories. *Journal of Experimental Social Psychology, 18,* 537–556. (p. 46)

Wilson, T. D., Lisle, D. J., Schooler, J. W., Hodges, S. D., Klaaren, K. J., & LaFleur, S. J. (1993). Introspecting about reasons can reduce post-choice satisfaction. *Personality and Social Psychology Bulletin, 19,* 331–339. (p. 48)

Wilson, W. R. (1979). Feeling more than we can know: Exposure effects without learning. *Journal of Personality and Social Psychology, 37,* 811–821. (p. 431)

Winch, R. F. (1958). *Mate selection: A study of complementary needs.* New York: Harper & Row. (p. 445)

Wing, R. R., & Jeffery, R. W. (1979). Outpatient treatments of obesity: A comparison of methodology and clinical results. *International Journal of Obesity, 3,* 261–279. (p. 588)

Winter, F. W. (1973). A laboratory experiment of individual attitude response to advertising exposure. *Journal of Marketing Research, 10,* 130–140. (p. 433)

Wispe, L. G., & Freshley, H. B. (1971). Race, sex, and sympathetic helping behavior: The broken bag caper. *Journal of Personality and Social Psychology, 17,* 59–65. (p. 504)

Wittenberg, M. T., & Reis, H. T. (1986). Loneliness, social skills, and social perception. *Personality and Social Psychology Bulletin, 12,* 121–130. (p. 576)

Wittenbrink, B., Judd, C. M., & Park, B. (1997). Evidence for racial prejudice at the implicit level and its relationship with questionnaire measures. *Journal of Personality and Social Psychology, 72 ,* 262–274. (p. 342)

Wixon, D. R., & Laird, J. D. (1976). Awareness and attitude change in the forced-compliance paradigm: The importance of when. *Journal of Personality and Social Psychology, 34,* 376–384. (p. 101)

Wolf, S. (1987). Majority and minority influence: A social impact analysis. In M. P. Zanna, J. M. Olson, & C. P. Herman (Eds.), *Social influence: The Ontario symposium on personality and social psychology,* Vol. 5. Hillsdale, N.J.: Erlbaum. (p. 327)

Wolf, S., & Latané, B. (1985). Conformity, innovation and the psycho-social law. In S. Moscovici, G. Mugny, & E. Van Avermaet (Eds.), *Perspectives on minority influence.* Cambridge: Cambridge University Press. (p. 327)

Wolf, S., & Montgomery, D. A. (1977). Effects of inadmissible evidence and level of judicial admonishment to disregard on the judgments of mock jurors. *Journal of Applied Social Psychology, 7,* 205–219. (p. 617)

Women on Words and Images (1972). *Dick and Jane as victims: Sex stereotyping in children's readers.* Princeton: Women on Words and Images. Cited by C. Tavris & C. Offir (1977) in *The longest war: Sex differences in perspective.* New York: Harcourt Brace Jovanovich, p. 177. (p. 357)

Wood, J. V. (1989). Theory and research concerning social comparisons of personal attributes. *Psychological Bulletin, 106,* 231–248. (p. 394)

Wood, J. V., Saltzberg, J. A., & Goldsamt, L. A. (1990). Does affect induce self-focused attention? *Journal of Personality and Social Psychology, 58,* 899–908. (pp. 497, 573, 574)

Wood, J. V., Saltzberg, J. A., Neale, J. M., Stone, A. A., & Rachmiel, T. B. (1990). Self-focused attention, coping responses, and distressed mood in everyday life. *Journal of Personality and Social Psychology, 58,* 1027–1036. (pp. 573, 574)

Wood, W., & Eagly, A. H. (1981). Stages in the analysis of persuasive messages: The role of causal attributions and message comprehension. *Journal of Personality and Social Psychology, 40,* 246–259. (p. 258)

Wood, W., Lundgren, S., Ouellette, J. A., Busceme, S., & Blackstone, T. (1994). Minority influence: A meta-analytic review of social influence processes. *Psychological Bulletin, 115,* 323–345. (p. 326)

Wood, W., Pool, G. J., Leck, K., & Purvis, D. (1996). Self-definition, defensive processing, and influence: The normative impact of majority and minority groups. *Journal of Personality and Social Psychology, 71,* 1181–1193. (p. 326)

Wood, W., & Rhodes, N. (1991). Sex differences in interaction style in task groups. In C. Ridgeway (Ed.), *Gender and interaction: The role of microstructures in inequality.* New York: Springer-Verlag. (p. 187)

Wood, W., Rhodes, N., & Whelan, M. (1989). Sex differences in positive well-being: A consideration of emotional style and marital status. *Psychological Bulletin, 106,* 249–264. (pp. 593–594)

Wood, W., Wong, F. Y., & Chachere, J. G. (1991). Effects of media violence on viewers' aggression in unconstrained social interaction. *Psychological Bulletin, 109,* 371–383. (p. 415)

Worchel, S., Andreoli, V. A., & Folger, R. (1977). Intergroup cooperation and intergroup attraction: The effect of previous interaction and outcome of combined effort. *Journal of Experimental Social Psychology, 13,* 131–140. (p. 540)

Worchel, S., Axsom, D., Ferris, F., Samah, G., & Schweitzer, S. (1978). Deterrents of the effect of intergroup cooperation on intergroup attraction. *Journal of Conflict Resolution, 22,* 429–439. (p. 540)

Worchel, S., & Brown, E. H. (1984). The role of plausibility in influencing environmental attributions. *Journal of Experimental Social Psychology, 20,* 86–96. (p. 296)

Worchel, S., & Norvell, N. (1980). Effect of perceived environmental conditions during cooperation on intergroup attraction. *Journal of Personality and Social Psychology, 38,* 764–772. (p. 540)

Word, C. O., Zanna, M. P., & Cooper, J. (1974). The nonverbal mediation of self-fulfilling prophecies in interracial interaction. *Journal of Experimental Social Psychology, 10,* 109–120. (p. 351)

Workman, E. A., & Williams, R. L. (1980). Effects of extrinsic rewards on intrinsic motivation in the classroom. *Journal of School Psychology, 18,* 141–147. (p. 161)

Worringham, C. J., & Messick, D. M. (1983). Social facilitation of running: An unobtrusive study. *Journal of Social Psychology, 121,* 23–29. (p. 297)

Wright, E. F., Lüüs, C. A., & Christie, S. D. (1990). Does group discussion facilitate the use of consensus information in making causal attributions? *Journal of Personality and Social Psychology, 59,* 261–269. (p. 324)

Wright, P., & Rip, P. D. (1981). Retrospective reports on the causes of decisions. *Journal of Personality and Social Psychology, 40,* 601–614. (p. 48)

Wright, R. (1995, March 13). The biology of violence. *New Yorker,* pp. 69–77. (p. 388)

Wright, S. C., Aron, A., McLaughlin-Volpe, T., & Ropp, S. A. (1997). The extended contact effect: Knowledge of cross-group friendships and prejudice. *Journal of Personality and Social Psychology, 73,* 73–90. (p. 544)

Wright, S. C., & Van Der Zande, C. C. (1999, October). Bicultural friends: When cross-group friendships cause improved intergroup attitudes. Presentation at the Society of Experimental Social Psychology Convention. (p. 536)

Wrightsman, L. (1978). The American trial jury on trial: Empirical evidence and procedural modifications. *Journal of Social Issues, 34,* 137–164. (p. 623)

Wu, C., & Shaffer, D. R. (1987). Susceptibility to persuasive appeals as a function of source credibility and prior experience with the attitude object. *Journal of Personality and Social Psychology, 52,* 677–688. (p. 136)

Wu, D. Y. H., & Tseng, W. S. (1985). Introduction: the characteristics of chinese culture. In D. Y. H. Wu and W. S. Tseng (Eds.), *Chinese culture and mental health.* San Diego, Ca.: Academic Press. (p. 73)

Wuthnow, R. (1994). *God and mammon in America.* New York: Free Press. (pp. 501, 512)

Wylie, R. C. (1979). *The self-concept (Vol. 2): Theory and research on selected topics.* Lincoln, Neb.: University of Nebraska Press. (p. 58)

Xu, X., & Whyte, M. (1990). Love matches and arranged marriages: A Chinese replication. *Journal of Marriage and the Family*, *52*, 709–722. (p. 457)

Yarmey, A. D., Yarmey, M. J., & Yarmey, A. L. (1996). Accuracy of eyewitness identification in showups and lineups. *Law and Human Behavior*, *20*, 459, 477. (p. 603)

Yelsma, P., & Athappily, K. (1988). Marital satisfaction and communication practices: Comparisons among Indian and American couples. *Journal of Comparative Family Studies*, *19*, 37–54. (p. 457)

Yinon, Y., Sharon, I., Gonen, Y., & Adam, R. (1982). Escape from responsibility and help in emergencies among persons alone or within groups. *European Journal of Social Psychology*, *12*, 301–305. (p. 493)

Young, W. R. (1977, February). There's a girl on the tracks! *Reader's Digest*, pp. 91–95. (p. 473)

Younger, J. C., Walker, L., & Arrowood, J. A. (1977). Postdecision dissonance at the fair. *Personality and Social Psychology Bulletin*, *3*, 284–287. (p. 156)

Yousif, Y., & Korte, C. (1995). Urbanization, culture, and helpfulness. *Journal of Cross-Cultural Psychology*, *26*, 474–489. (p. 492)

Yovetich, N. A., & Rusbult, C. E. (1994). Accommodative behavior in close relationships: Exploring transformation of motivation. *Journal of Experimental Social Psychology*, *30*, 138–164. (p. 469)

Yuchtman (Yaar), E. (1976). Effects of social-psychological factors on subjective economic welfare. In B. Strumpel (Ed.), *Economic means for human needs*. Ann Arbor: Institute for Social Research, University of Michigan. (p. 394)

Yuille, J. C., & Cutshall, J. L. (1986). A case study of eyewitness memory of a crime. *Journal of Applied Psychology*, *71*, 291–301. (p. 602)

Yukl, G. (1974). Effects of the opponent's initial offer, concession magnitude, and concession frequency on bargaining behavior. *Journal of Personality and Social Psychology*, *30*, 323–335. (p. 547)

Yzerbyt, V., Rocher, S., & Schadron, G. (1997). Stereotypes as explanations: A subjective essentialistic view of group perception. In R. Spears, P. J. Oakes, N. Ellemers, & S. A. Haslam (eds.), *The social psychology of stereotyping and group life*. Oxford: Blackwell. (p. 349)

Yzerbyt, V. Y., & Leyens, J-P. (1991). Requesting information to form an impression: The influence of valence and confirmatory status. *Journal of Experimental Social Psychology*, *27*, 337–356. (p. 447)

Zajonc, R. B. (1965). Social facilitation. *Science*, *149*, 269–274. (p. 294)

Zajonc, R. B. (1968). Attitudinal effects of mere exposure. *Journal of Personality and Social Psychology*, *9*, Monograph Suppl. No. 2, part 2. (pp. 431, 432)

Zajonc, R. B. (1970, February). Brainwash: Familiarity breeds comfort. *Psychology Today*, pp. 32–35, 60–62. (p. 431)

Zajonc, R. B. (1980). Feeling and thinking: Preferences need no inferences. *American Psychologist*, *35*, 151–175. (p. 432)

Zajonc, R. B. (1998). Emotions. In D. Gilbert, S. T. Fiske, & G. Lindzey (eds.), *Handbook of social psychology*, 4th ed. New York: McGraw-Hill. (p. 432)

Zajonc, R. B., & Sales, S. M. (1966). Social facilitation of dominant and subordinate responses. *Journal of Experimental Social Psychology*, *2*, 160–168. (p. 295)

Zanna, M. P. (1993). Message receptivity: A new look at the old problem of open- vs. closed-mindedness. In A. Mitchell (Ed.), *Advertising: Exposure, memory and choice*. Hillsdale, NJ: Erlbaum. (p. 264)

Zanna, M. P., & Cooper, J. (1974). Dissonance and the pill: An attributional approach to studying the arousal properties of dissonance. *Journal of Personality and Social Psychology*, *29*, 703–709. (p. 163)

Zanna, M. P., Crosby, F., & Loewenstein, G. (1987). Male reference groups and discontent among female professionals. In B. A. Gutek & L. Larwood (Eds.), *Women's career development*. Newbury Park, Ca.: Sage. (p. 394)

Zanna, M. P., & Olson, J. M. (1982). Individual differences in attitudinal relations. In M. P. Zanna, E. T. Higgins, & C. P. Herman, *Consistency in social behavior: The Ontario symposium*, Vol. 2. Hillsdale, N.J.: Erlbaum. (p. 151)

Zanna, M. P., Olson, J. M., & Fazio, R. H. (1981). Self-perception and attitude-behavior consistency. *Personality and Social Psychology Bulletin*, *7*, 252–256. (p. 136)

Zanna, M. P., & Pack, S. J. (1975). On the self-fulfilling nature of apparent sex differences in behavior. *Journal of Experimental Social Psychology*, *11*, 583–591. (p. 198)

Zaragoza, M. S., & Mitchell, K. J. (1996). Repeated exposure to suggestion and the creation of false memories. *Psychological Science*, *7*, 294–300. (p. 605)

Zebrowitz, L. A., Olson, K., & Hoffman, K. (1993). Stability of babyfaceness and attractiveness across the life span. *Journal of Personality and Social Psychology*, *64*, 453–466. (p. 441)

Zebrowitz-McArthur, L. (1988). Person perception in cross-cultural perspective. In M. H. Bond (Ed.), *The cross-cultural challenge to social psychology*. Newbury Park, Ca.: Sage. (p. 90)

Zill, N. (1988). Behavior, Achievement, and Health Problems Among Children in Stepfamilies: Findings From a National Survey of Child Health. In E. Mavis Hetherington and Josephine D. Arasteh (Eds.), *Impact of Divorce, Single Parenting,*

and Stepparenting on Children. Hillsdale, NJ: Erlbaum. (p. 398)

Zillmann, D. (1988). Cognition-excitation interdependencies in aggressive behavior. *Aggressive Behavior*, *14*, 51–64. (p. 404)

Zillmann, D. (1989). Aggression and sex: Independent and joint operations. In H. L. Wagner & A. S. R. Manstead (Eds.), *Handbook of psychophysiology: Emotion and social behavior*. Chichester: John Wiley. (pp. 404, 416, 441)

Zillmann, D. (1989). Effects of prolonged consumption of pornography. In D. Zillmann & J. Bryant (Eds.), *Pornography: Research advances and policy considerations*. Hillsdale, NJ: Erlbaum. (p. 405)

Zillmann, D., & Paulus, P. B. (1993). Spectators: Reactions to sports events and effects on athletic performance. In R. N. Singer, N. Murphey, & L. K. Tennant (Eds.), *Handbook of research on sport psychology*. New York: Macmillan. (p. 295)

Zimbardo, P. G. (1970). The human choice: Individuation, reason, and order versus deindividuation, impulse, and chaos. In W. J. Arnold & D. Levine (Eds.), *Nebraska symposium on motivation, 1969*. Lincoln: University of Nebraska Press. (p. 305)

Zimbardo, P. G. (1971). *The psychological power and pathology of imprisonment*. A statement prepared for the U.S. House of Representatives Committee on the Judiciary, Subcommittee No. 3: Hearings on Prison Reform, San Francisco, Calif., October 25. (p. 138)

Zimbardo, P. G. (1972). The Stanford prison experiment. A slide/tape presentation produced by Philip G. Zimbardo, Inc., P. O. Box 4395, Stanford, Calif. 94305. (p. 139)

Zimbardo, P. G. (1993). Personal communication of research findings on attributions and shyness. Department of Psychology, Stanford University. (p. 73)

Zimbardo, P. G., Ebbesen, E. B., & Maslach, C. (1977). *Influencing attitudes and changing behavior*. Reading, Mass.: Addison-Wesley. (p. 307)

Zucker, G. S., & Weiner, B. (1993). Conservatism and perceptions of poverty: An attributional analysis. *Journal of Applied Social Psychology*, *23*, 925–943. (p. 91)

Zuwerink, J. R., & Devine, P. G. (1996). Attitude importance and resistance to persuasion: It's not just the thought that counts. *Journal of Personality and Social Psychology*, *70*, 931–940. (p. 285)

Zuwerink, J. R., Monteith, M. J., Devine, P. G., & Cook, D. A. (1996). Prejudice toward blacks: With and without compunction? *Basic and Applied Social Psychology*, *18*, 131–150. (p. 343)

acknowledgements

Chapter 1

Cartoon, p. 8: © 1998 by Sidney Harris. Reprinted by permission.
Cartoon, p. 17: © 1998 by Sidney Harris. Reprinted by permission.
Cartoon, p. 18: By permission of Leigh Rubin and Creators Syndicate, Inc.
Figure 1-3, p. 22: From D. Carroll, G. Davey Smith, and P. Bennett, "Health and socioeconomic status," *The Psychologist*, March 1994, pp. 122-125. Reprinted by permission of the British Psychological Society.
Cartoon, p. 26: *Doonesbury* © 1990 G. B. Trudeau. Reprinted with permission of Universal Press Syndicate. All rights reserved.
Cartoon, p. 31: *The Far Side* © 1993 Farworks, Inc. Used by permission of Universal Press Syndicate. All rights reserved.

Chapter 2

Figure 2-1, p. 40: Adapted from P. Lockwood, and Z. Kunda, "Superstars and me: Predicting the impact of role models on the self," *Journal of Personality and Social Psychology*, 73, 1997, pp. 91-103. Copyright © 1997 by the American Psychological Association. Adapted with permission.
Figure 2-2, p. 43: From H. Markus and S. Kitayama, "Culture and the self: Implications for cognition, emotion, and motivation," *Psychological Review, 98,* 1991, pp. 224-253. Copyright © 1991 by the American Psychological Association. Reprinted with permission.
Cartoon, p. 54: Edward Koren © 1983 from The New Yorker Collection. All Rights Reserved.
Cartoon, p. 56 (top): *Frank & Earnest* reprinted by permission of Newspaper Enterprise Association, Inc.
Cartoon, p. 56 (middle): © 1975. Reprinted with permission of *Better Homes and Gardens* Magazine and Henry R. Martin.
Cartoon, p. 58: Drawing by Sempe; © 1984 The New Yorker Magazine, Inc.
Cartoon, p. 59: Robert Mankoff © 1997 from The New Yorker Collection. All Rights Reserved.
Focus box, p. 60: Reprinted with the permission of Simon & Schuster from *Waiting for the Lord: 33 Meditations on God and Man* by Gordon W. Allport, edited by Peter A. Bertocci. Copyright © 1978 by Peter A. Bertocci.
Table 2-2, p. 62: From *Family Circle*, December 21, 1993, p. 30. Reprinted

with permission of *Family Circle*. © 1993 Gruner & Jahr USA Publishing.
Cartoon, p. 63: William W. Haefeli, *The Saturday Review*, January 20, 1979.
Cartoon, p. 66: Mike Twohy © 1996 from The New Yorker Collection. All Rights Reserved.
Cartoon, p. 68: Dana Fradon © 1983 from The New Yorker Collection. All Rights Reserved.

Chapter 3

Cartoon, p. 81: Frank Model © 1976 from The New Yorker Collection. All Rights Reserved.
Cartoon, p. 91: By permission of Jeff Shesol and Creators Syndicate, Inc.
Cartoon, p. 94: *Peanuts* reprinted by permission of United Feature Syndicate, Inc.
Figure 3-7. p. 105: Adapted from M. W. Baldwin, S.E. Carrell, and D.F. Lopez, "Priming relationship schemas: My advisor and the Pope are watching me from the back of my head," *Journal of Experimental Social Psychology, 26,* 1989, pp. 435-454. Reprinted by permission of Academic Press.
Cartoon, p. 114: Reprinted with permission of Peter Steiner.
Figure 3-8, p. 118: From J. P. Forgas, G. H. Bower, and S. E. Krantz, "The influence of mood on perceptions of social interactions," *Journal of Experimental Social Psychology, 20,* 1984, pp. 497-513. Reprinted by permission of Academic Press.

Chapter 4

Cartoon, p. 141: Joseph Farris © 1984 from The New Yorker Collection. All Rights Reserved.
Cartoon, p. 143: *Blondie* cartoon by Drake reprinted with special permission of King Features Syndicate.
Cartoon, p. 144: *The Born Loser* reprinted by permission of Newspaper Enterprise Association, Inc.
Cartoon, p. 150: Robert Weber © 1987 from The New Yorker Collection. All Rights Reserved.
Cartoon, p. 151: © 1991 Mike Marland.
Cartoon, p. 159: *Bizarro* © 1997 Dan Piraro. Reprinted with permission of Universal Press Syndicate. All rights reserved.
Cartoon, p. 160: Ed Frascino © 1991 from The New Yorker Collection. All Rights Reserved.
Cartoon, p. 163: *Sally Forth* cartoon by Howard reprinted with special permission of King Features Syndicate.

Figure 4-5, p. 164: M.P. Zanna, and J. Cooper, "Dissonance and the pill: An attributional approach to studying the arousal properties of dissonance," *Journal of Personality and Social Psychology, 29,* 1974, pp. 703-709. Copyright © 1974 by the American Psychological Association. Adapted with permission.
Cartoon, p. 165: Charles Barsotti © 1988 from The New Yorker Collection. All Rights Reserved.

Chapter 5

Cartoon, p. 172: Robert Mankoff © 1991 from The New Yorker Collection. All Rights Reserved.
Cartoon, p. 175: J. B. Handelsman © 1979 from The New Yorker Collection. All Rights Reserved.
Cartoon, p. 176: Robert Mankoff © 1988 from The New Yorker Collection. All Rights Reserved.
Cartoon, p. 178: Peter Steiner © 1980 from The New Yorker Collection. All Rights Reserved.
Cartoon, p. 185 (top): *Sally Forth* cartoon by Howard, reprinted with special permission of King Features Syndicate.
Cartoon, p. 185 (middle): *The Norm* cartoon by Michael Jentze, reprinted with special permission of King Features Syndicate.
Cartoon, p. 187: Drawing by W. Steig; © 1989 The New Yorker Magazine, Inc.
Cartoon, p. 188: J. B. Handelsman © 1995 from The New Yorker Collection. All Rights Reserved.
Cartoon, p. 189: Donald Reilly © 1995 from The New Yorker Collection. All Rights Reserved.
Margin Note, p. 189: Yankelovich poll in *Time*, November 7, 1994, p. 21. © 1994 Time, Inc. Reprinted by permission.
Cartoon, p. 191: Ed Frascino © 1991 from The New Yorker Collection. All Rights Reserved.
Figure 5-1, p. 193, & Figure 5-2, p. 196: From D. M. Buss, "The strategies of human mating," *American Scientist, 82,* 1994, pp. 238-249. Reprinted by permission of Sigma XI.
Cartoon, p. 201: *Doonesbury* © 1981 G.B. Trudeau. Reprinted with permission of Universal Press Syndicate. All rights reserved.
Figure 5-4, p. 201: Data from *Report on Business Magazine*, September, 1992. Reprinted by permission of The Globe & Mail.

Figure 5-5, p. 205: From A. H. Eagly and W. Wood, "Explaining sex differences in social behavior: A meta-analytic perspective," *Personality and Social Psychology Bulletin, 17,* 1991, pp. 306-315, copyright © 1991 by Sage Publications, Inc. Reprinted by permission of Sage Publications, Inc.

Chapter 6

Cartoon, p. 211: Jack Ziegler © 1996 from The New Yorker Collection. All Rights Reserved.

Cartoon, p. 212: Drawing by Booth; © 1977 The New Yorker Magazine, Inc.

Focus Box, p. 218: Excerpt from *Obedience to Authority* by Stanley Milgram. Copyright © 1974 by Stanley Milgram. Reprinted by permission of HarperCollins Publishers, Inc. and Pinter & Martin Ltd.

Figure 6-4, p. 219: From figure on page 73 of S. Milgram, "Some Conditions of Obedience and Disobedience to Authority," *Human Relations, 18,* 1, Plenum Press, 1965, pp. 57-76. Copyright renewal 1993 Alexandra Milgram.

Figure 6-4, p. 219: From Stanley Milgram, 1977. Reprinted with permission of Alexandra Milgram.

Focus Box, p. 221: From Roger Fisher, "Preventing Nuclear War," *Bulletin of Atomic Scientist,* March 1981, pp. 11-17. Reprinted by permission of *The Bulletin of the Atomic Scientists,* copyright © 1981 by the Educational Foundation for Nuclear Science, 6042 South Kimbark Avenue, Chicago, Illinois 60637, USA. A one-year subscription is $36.

Cartoon, p. 236: Robert Mankoff © 1980 from The New Yorker Collection. All Rights Reserved.

Figure 6-7, p. 238: Adapted from D. Griffin, D, and R. Buehler, R, "Role of construal process in conformity and dissent," *Journal of Personality and Social Psychology, 65,* 1993, pp. 657-669. Copyright © 1993 by the American Psychological Association. Adapted with permission.

Cartoon, p. 240: *The Far Side* © 1982 Farworks, Inc. Used by permission of Universal Press Syndicate. All rights reserved.

Cartoon, p. 243: *Calvin and Hobbes* © 1985 Watterson. Distributed by Universal Press Syndicate. Reprinted with permission. All rights reserved.

Chapter 7

Cartoon, p. 257: Charles Barsotti © 1987 from The New Yorker Collection. All Rights Reserved.

Cartoon, p. 262: Frank Cotham © 1997 from The New Yorker Collection. All Rights Reserved.

Figure 7-6, p. 269: From W. J. McGuire, "An information-processing model of advertising effectiveness," in *Behavioral and Management Sciences in Marketing,* edited by H. L. Davis and A. J. Silk, 1978. Copyright © 1978. Reprinted by permission of John Wiley & Sons, Inc.

Figure 7-9, p. 275: Adapted from L.R. Fabrigar, J.R. Priester, R.E. Petty, and D.T. Wegener, "The impact of attitude accessibility on elaboration of persuasive messages," *Personality and Social Psychology Bulletin, 24,* 1998, pp. 339-352. Reprinted by permission of Sage Publications.

Cartoon, p. 280: Drawing by Chas. Addams; © 1982 The New Yorker Magazine, Inc.

Cartoon, p. 281: *The Far Side* © 1987 Farworks, Inc. Used by permission of Universal Press Syndicate. All rights reserved.

Chapter 8

Figure 8-4, p. 301: From Williams, K. D., J. M. Jackson, and S. J. Karu, "Collective hedonism: A social loafing analysis of social dilemmas," *Social Dilemmas: Social Psychological Perspectives,* edited by D. A. Schroeder, 1992. Praeger Publishers, an imprint of Greenwood Publishing Group, Inc., Westport, CT. Reprinted with permission.

Cartoon, p. 319: Henry Martin © 1979 from The New Yorker Collection. All Rights Reserved.

Chapter 9

Figure 9-1, p. 339: Adapted from V.M. Esses, and M.P. Zanna, "Mood and the expression of ethnic stereotypes," *Journal of Personality and Social Psychology, 69,* 1995, pp. 1052-1068. Copyright © 1995 by the American Psychological Association. Adapted with permission.

Cartoon, p. 342: Mick Stevens © 1996 from The New Yorker Collection. All Rights Reserved.

Figure 9-4, p. 348: Adapted from D.M. Taylor, S.C. Wright, F.M. Moghaddam, and R.N. Lalonde, "The personal/ group discrimination discrepancy: Perceiving my group, but not myself, to be a target for discrimination," *Personality and Social Psychology Bulletin, 16,* 1990, pp. 254-262. Reprinted by permission of Sage Publications.

Cartoon, p. 349: Dean Vietor © 1981 from The New Yorker Collection. All Rights Reserved.

Cartoon, p. 355: Ed Fisher © 1987 from The New Yorker Collection. All Rights Reserved.

Cartoon, p. 360: Michael Maslin © 1985 from The New Yorker Collection. All Rights Reserved.

Cartoon, p. 362: *Doonesbury* © 1994 G.B. Trudeau. Reprinted with permission of Universal Press Syndicate. All rights reserved.

Figure 9-7, p. 367: From P. G. Devine and R. S. Malpass, "Orienting strategies in differential face recognition, " *Personality and Social Psychology Bulletin, 11,* 1985, pp. 33-40, copyright © 1985 by Sage Publications, Inc. Reprinted by permission of Sage Publications, Inc.

Cartoon, p. 369: Don Wright © Tribune Media Services, Inc. All Rights Reserved. Reprinted with permission.

Cartoon, p. 373: Robert Mankoff © 1981 from The New Yorker Collection. All Rights Reserved.

Figure 9-8, p. 377: Adapted from D. A. Wilder, A. F. Simon, and M. Faith, "Enhancing the impact of counterstereotypic information: Dispositional attributions for deviance," *Journal of Personality and Social Psychology, 71*(2), 1996, p. 277. Copyright © 1996 by the American Psychological Association. Adapted by permission.

Figure 9-9, p. 378: Adapted from Z. Kunda, and L. Sinclair, "Motivated reasoning with stereotypes: Activation, application, and inhibition," *Psychological Inquiry, 10,* 1999, pp. 12-22. Copyright © 1999 by the American Psychological Association. Adapted with permission.

Chapter 10

Cartoon, p. 387: John Ruge, *The Saturday Review.*

Figure 10-2, p. 391: Statistics Canada Uniform Crime Report, 1996. Reprinted by permission.

Cartoon, p. 393: *Peanuts* reprinted by permission of United Feature Syndicate.

Figure 10-4, p. 404: From C. A. Anderson, W. E. Deuser, and K. M. DeNeve, "Hot temperatures, hostile affect, hostile cognition, and arousal; Tests of a general model of affective aggression," *Personality and Social Psychology Bulletin.* Copyright © 1995 by Sage Publications, Inc. Reprinted by permission of Sage Publications, Inc.

Figure 10-7, p. 411: Statistics Canada Uniform Crime Report. Reprinted by permission.

Cartoon, p. 413: Mayers, *Funny Times,* February 1994. Reprinted by permission.

Cartoon, p. 418: © 1990 Tom Tomorrow. Reprinted by permission.

Focus box, p. 422: From Martin E. P. Seligman, *What You Can Change and What You Can't: The Complete Guide to Successful Self-improvement,* by Martin E. P. Seligman, pp. 238-239. © 1994. Reprinted by permission of Alfred A. Knopf, Inc.

Chapter 11

Figure 11-1, p. 432: From R. B. Zajonc, "Attitudinal effects of mere exposure," *Journal of Personality and Social Psychology*, 9, Monograph Suppl. No. 2, part 2, 1968. Copyright © 1968 by the American Psychological Association. Reprinted with permission.

Figure 11-2, p. 439: From R. J. Sternberg, "Triangulating love," in *The Psychology of Love*, edited by R. J. Sternberg and M. L. Barnes. © 1988. Reprinted by permission of Yale University Press.

Cartoon, p. 441: © 1998 by Sidney Harris. Reprinted by permission.

Figure 11-4, p. 443: Adapted from J.E. Lydon, M. Meana, D. Sepinwall, N. Richards, N., and S. Mayman, "The commitment calibration hypothesis: When do people devalue attractive alternatives?" *Personality and Social Psychology Bulletin*, 25, 1999, pp. 152-161. Reprinted by permission of Sage Publications.

Cartoon, p. 444: Warren Miller © 1992 from The New Yorker Collection. All Rights Reserved.

Cartoon, p. 447: Robert Mankoff © 1994 from The New Yorker Collection. All Rights Reserved.

Cartoon, p. 450: By permission of Mell Lazarus and Creators Syndicate, Inc.

Cartoon, p. 454: Peter Kohlsaat copyright, 1988, Los Angeles Times Syndicate. Reprinted by permission.

Cartoon, p. 464: Robert Weber © 1989 from The New Yorker Collection. All Rights Reserved.

Figure 11-8, p. 465: From A. Aron and A. N. Aron, "Love," in *Perspective on Close Relationships*, edited by A. L. Weber and J. H. Harvey. Copyright © 1994 by Allyn and Bacon. Reprinted by permission.

Cartoon, p. 467: Mick Stevens © 1993 from The New Yorker Collection. All Rights Reserved.

Cartoon, p. 468: Mike Twohy © 1997 from The New Yorker Collection. All Rights Reserved.

Chapter 12

Cartoon, p. 477: Barney Tobey © 1972 from The New Yorker Collection. All Rights Reserved.

Figure 12-1, p. 478: From C. D. Batson, J. Fultz, and P. A. Schoenrade, "Distress and empathy: Two qualitatively distinct vicarious emotions with different motivational consequences," *Journal of Personality*, 55:1 (Spring 1987), fig. 14:1, p. 14. Copyright © 1987. Reprinted with permission of Blackwell Publishers.

Figure 12-2, p. 489: From J. M. Darley and B. Latane, "Bystander intervention in emergencies: Diffusion of responsibility," *Journal of Personality and Social Psychology*, 8, 1968, pp. 377-383. Copyright © 1968 by the American Psychological Association. Reprinted with permission.

Cartoon, p. 507: *Hi & Lois* cartoon reprinted with special permission of King Features Syndicate.

Chapter 13

Cartoon, p. 521: Steve Benson reprinted by permission of United Features Syndicate, Inc.

Table 13-2, p. 530: Reprinted by permission of Sage Publications Ltd from S. Plous, "The nuclear arms race: Prisoner's dilemma or perceptual dilemma?" *Journal of Peace Research*, 30, 1993, pp. 163-179, copyright 1993.

Figure 13-4, p. 531 From P. E. Tetlock, "Monitoring the integrative complexity of American and Soviet policy rhetoric: What can be learned?" *Journal of Social Issues*, Vol. 44, No. 2, 1988, pp. 101-131. Reprinted by permission of Blackwell Publishers.

Cartoon, p. 553: Baloo from *The Wall Street Journal*. Permission, Cartoon Features Syndicate.

Module A

Figure A-3, p. 576: From Jody Dill and Craig Anderson, "Loneliness, shyness, and depression: The etiology and interrelationships of everyday problems in living," in *Recent Advances in Interpersonal Approaches to Depression* edited by T. Joiner and J. C. Coyne. Copyright © 1998 by the American Psychological Association. Reprinted with permission.

Figure A-4, p. 577: Adapted from T.K. MacDonald, M.P. Zanna, M. P., and G.T. Fong, "Decision making in altered states: Effects of alcohol on attitudes toward drinking and driving," *Journal of Personality and Social Psychology*, 68, 1995, pp. 973-985. Copyright © 1995 by the American Psychological Association. Adapted with permission.

Figure A-7, p. 593: Statistics Canada 1996. Reprinted by permission.

Module B

Cartoon, p. 600: Danny Shanahan © 1996 from The New Yorker Collection. All Rights Reserved.

Cartoon, p. 603: Joseph Mirachi © 1984 from The New Yorker Collection. All Rights Reserved.

Figure B-1, p. 604: Allport, G. W. and L. Postman (1947, 1975). Figure from *The Psychology of Rumor* by Gordon W. Allport and Leo Postman, copyright © 1947 and renewed 1975 by Holt, Rinehart and Winston, reproduced by permission of the publisher.

Figure B-2, p. 604: From G. H. Fisher, "Ambiguity of Form: Old and New, *Perception and Psychophysics*, 4, 1968, pp. 189-192. Reprinted by permission of Psychonomic Society, Inc.

Table B-1, p. 612: From S. M. Kassin, P. C. Ellsworth, and V. L. Smith, "The 'general acceptance' of psychological research on eyewitness testimony: A survey of the experts," *American Psychologist*, 44, 1989, pp. 1089-1098. Copyright © 1989 by the American Psychological Association. Reprinted with permission.

Cartoon, p. 614: *The Far Side* © 1985 Farworks, Inc. Used by permission of Universal Press Syndicate. All rights reserved.

Cartoon, p. 614: *The Far Side* © 1980 Farworks, Inc. Used by permission of Universal Press Syndicate. All rights reserved.

Cartoon, p. 616: Charles Barsotti © 1988 from The New Yorker Collection. All Rights Reserved.

Cartoon, p. 618: Lee Lorenz © 1977 from The New Yorker Collection. All Rights Reserved.

Photo Credits

PO1 © Rogers/Monkmeyer, CO1 © Zane Williams/Tony Stone Images, 04 Dan Loh/Associated Press, 06 AP/Wide World Photos, 10 Ronald C. James, 12 © David Young-Wolff/PhotoEdit, 21 Courtesy Fathali M. Moghaddam, 25 Courtesy University of Michigan Institute for Social Research Survey Research Center, Ann Arbor, 28 © Renie Benali/Gamma Liaison, 32 PhotoNews/Gamma Liaison

CO2 © N. Phillippe/The Image Bank Chicago, 44 Courtesy Shinobu Kitayama, Kyoto University, 45 © Haruyoshi Yamaguchi/Sygma, 48 © Rick Blumberg/Stock, Boston, 49 © Michael Grecco/Stock, Boston, 54 © Marc Deville/Gamma Liaison, 61 © L.D. Gordon/The Image Bank, 64 © Barbara Rios/Photo Researchers, 67 Courtesy Barry Schlenker, University of Florida, 69 © David H. Wells/The Image Works, 73 © Chitose Suzuki/The Picture Cube

CO3 Peter Turnley/CORBIS, 79 Andrew Vaughan/Canadian Press, 80 © Grant LeDuc/Monkmeyer, 82 © Michael Newman/PhotoEdit, 85 © Arnaldo Magnani/Gamma Liaision, 89 Courtesy Daniel M. Wegner, 90 © James Schnepf/Gamma Liasion, 96 Dan Janisse/Canadian Press, 97 Myron Rothbart, 98 © Timothy Carlson/Stock, Boston, 100 © Willie Hill Jr./The Image Works, 111 Shlomi Benami/Associated Press, 112 © Robert Nichols/Black Star, 115 Harvard University, 116 © Frank Pedrick/The Image Works, 118 Courtesy Joseph Forgas, University of New South Wales, Sydney, Australia, 122 © Gary Olsen

CO4 Wolfgang Kaehler/CORBIS, 130 Tom Hanson/Canadian Press, 135

© Prettyman/PhotoEdit, 139T Roy Antal/Associated Press, 139B © Phillip Zimbardo, 143 © Wyman/Monkmeyer, 145 Courtesy Robert B. Cialdini, Arizona State University, 146 © Paul Henry Versele/Gamma Liaison, 148 Wayne Hiebert/The Ottawa Citizen, 149 © Denis Drever/Canada in Stock, Inc., 152 Courtesy Leon Festinger, 155 Photo Works/Monkmeyer, 156 © Amy C. Etra/PhotoEdit, 158 Courtesy of Fritz Strack, 162 Bemieri, F., Davis, J., Rosenthal, R. & Knee, C. (1991). Interactional synchrony and the social affordance of rapport: A validation study. Unpublished manuscript, Oregon State University, Corvallis, 165 Courtesy Claude Steele, Stanford University

PO2 © Bob Daemmrich/Stock, Boston, CO5 © Wolfgang Kaehler, 177 © Charles Gupton/Stock,Boston, 179L Ralph Bower/Vancouver Sun, 179R Canadian Press, 183L © Gottlieb/Monkmeyer, 183R © Bob Daemmrich/The Image Works, 186 © Brian A. Potts, 193L Al Staff/Canadian Press, 193C John Major/Canadian Press, 193R Alex Urosevic/Canadian Press, 194 Courtesy David Buss, 197 © David Barritt/Gamma Liaison, 198 Courtesy Mark Zanna, University of Waterloo, 199L © Willie Hill, Jr./The Image Works, 199R © Bob Daemmrich/The Image Works, 202 © Bill Bachman/Tony Stone Images, 204 © Evelyn Scolney/Monkmeyer Press

CO 6© George Rose/Gamma Liaison, 216T William Vendivert, 216B William Vendivert, 220 Stanley Milgram, 1965, from the film Obedience, distributed by the Pennsylvania State University, PCR, 222 © James Pickerall/Black Star, 224 © Benny Gool/Capetown Independent Newspaper, 225 Courtesy Stanley Milgram, City University of New York, 227 University Photographic Services, University of Massachusetts at Amherst, 228 Marc Gallant/Canadian Press, 233 Photofest, 234 © Jim Cummins/FPG International, 235 AP/Wide World Photos, 239 Courtesy Alice Eagly, Purdue University, 241 © Michael Grecco/Stock, Boston, 244 © Mark Peterson/SABA, 245 ©Chromosohm Media/The Image Works

CO7 © Will & Deni McIntyre/Tony Stone Images, 252 Courtesy of the Children's Defense Fund, 253 Fred Chartrand/Canadian Press, 256 Courtesy Playtex Products, Inc., 259 Ryan Remiorz/Canadian Press, 269 Peter Stackpole/LIFE Magazine © Time, Inc., 272 Courtesy Shelly

Chaiken, New York University, 276 Courtesy Richard Petty, Ohio State University, 276 Courtesy John Cacioppo, Ohio State University, 278 AP/Wide World Photos, 283 © Cindy Karp/Black Star, 286 Courtesy William McGuire, Yale University, 287 © Kathy McLaughlin/The Image Works

CO8 © Josef Beck/FPG International, 293 © Rob Crandall/Stock, Boston, 296 Canadian Press, 299 James Terkfurst/Herman Miller, Inc., 300 Alan G. Ingham, 303 Kevin Frayer/Canadian Press, 304 Courtesy of the Department of National Defence, 306 Courtesy of Philip Zimbardo, 308 © S. Franklin/Sygma, 314 © Doug Burrows/Gamma Liaison, 322 NASA, 323 Andrew Vaughan/Canadian Press, 325 Courtesy of Irving Janis, 328 Courtesy Charlan Jeanne Nemeth, University of California, Berkeley, 329 © Liane Enkelis/Stock, Boston

PO3 © Richard Laird/FPG International, CO9 Susan Henry/The Toronto Sun, 340 © Frank White/Gamma Liaison, 343 Courtesy Patricia Devine, 344 Porter and Geis, 1981, 350 Canadian Press, 354 © Scott Peterson/Gamma Liaison, 357 Courtesy Thomas Pettigrew, University of California, Santa Cruz, 358 © Jon Levy/Gamma Liaison, 361 © Susan Greenwood/Gamma Liaison, 365 James Blascovich, 368 © Eastcott/Momatiuk/The Image Works, 375 © Bob Daemmrich/Stock, Boston, 379 Courtesy Susan T. Fiske, University of Massachusetts

CO10 © Les Stone/Sygma, 386 The Granger Collection, 388 © Jeff Share/Black Star, 389 Tom Hanson/Canadian Press, 396 Photo Works, 400 both Dr. Nathan Azrin, 401 Chuck Stoody/Canadian Press, 402 Ryan Remiorz/Canadian Press, 405 © Bob Daemmrich/The Image Works, 407 Jack Chang/Canadian Press, 415 Photofest, 416 Courtesy Jacques-Philippe Leyens

CO11 © Esbin-Anderson/The Image Works, 428 © Frank Siteman/The Picture Cube, 429 © Frank Siteman/The Picture Cube, 433L Corbis Bettmann, 433R Corbis Bettmann, 434 © Dagmar Fabricius/Stock, Boston, 438 Courtesy Ellen Berscheid, University of Minnesota, 439 L&R Langlois, J., Kalakanis, L., Rubenstein, A., Larson, A., Hallam, M., and Smoot, M. (1996). Maxims and myths of beauty: A metaanalytic and theoretical review., 440 Nature, 1994 Vol.368, pp. 239-242. D.I. Perrett, K.A. May, S. Yoshikawa,

442L © Rick Smolan/Stock,Boston, 442ML © Paul Lau/Gamma Liaison, 442MR © Catherine Karnow/Woodfin Camp & Associates, 442R © David R. Frazier/Folio, Inc., 445 Courtesy James Jones, University of Delaware, 446 © Susan May Tell/SABA, 450 Dr. Pawel Lewicki, University of Tulsa, Oklahoma, 452 © Joe Palillio/Gamma Liaison, 455 Courtesy Elaine Hatfield, University of Hawaii, 457 © Rob Nelson/Black Star, 462 © Kagan/Monkmeyer

CO12 © Bob Daemmrich/Stock Boston, 476 Courtesy Dennis Krebs, Simon Fraser University, 479 Tom Hanson/Canadian Press, 480 Courtesy C. Daniel Batson, University of Kansas, 482 Frank Gunn/Canadian Press, 488 Courtesy John M. Darley, Princeton University, 490 © Mark Zemnick, 491 Gamma Liaison, 492 © Stephen Ferry/Gamma Liaison, 496 © Ellis Herwig/Stock,Boston, 500 Bikas Das/Associated Press, 503 Twentieth Century Fox/Shooting Star, 509 © Charles Hines/Gamma Liaison, 511 Page Collection/Gamma Liaison

CO 13 © Alix William/Gamma Liaison, 516 Tom Hanson/Canadian Press, 519 Courtesy Morton Deutsch, Columbia University, 523 Laura Tester/Canadian Press, 524 © Mark Richards/PhotoEdit, 526 Muzafer Sherif, 532 © Chris Morris/Black Star, 534 Tom Hanson/Canadian Press, 538L Robert Galbraith/Canadian Press, 538R Beth A. Keiser/Associated Press, 540 © Ian Shaw/Tony Stone Images, 541 © Mary Kate Denny/Tony Stone Images, 542 FPG International, 544 Corbis-Bettmann, 546 Sygma, 550 © Mark Antman/The Image Works, 552 Martin Mejia/Associated Press

559 © PhotoDisc, 563 AP/Wide World Photos, 567 Felicity Don/Canadian Press, 568 © Frank Siteman/Monkmeyer, 571 © LeDuc/Monkmeyer, 573 Courtesy Shelley Taylor, 577 © Frank Siteman/The Picture Cube, 584 © Jacques Chenet/Gamma Liaison, 587 © Ellis Herwig/Stock,Boston, 598 Paul Couvrette Photography

601 Detroit Free Press, 605 Courtesy Gary L. Wells, Iowa State University, 606 Courtesy Elizabeth Loftus, 606 Courtesy Elizabeth Loftus, 607 Dale A. Dunaway/Cincinnati Post, 617 Gerard Kwiatkowski/Canadian Press/Macleans, 619 Courtesy Norbert Kerr, Michigan State University, 621 © John Giordano/SABA, 629 © Alexander Jason/Gamma Liaison

name index

H

X

Y

Z

subject index